ORGANIZATIONAL BEHAVIOUR

ORGANIZATIONAL BEHAVIOUR

– A NEW LOOK
Concept, Theory & Cases

Dr. NIRAJ KUMAR

M.Com.(Bus. Admin.), Ph.D., L.L.B., A.M.S.P.I., F.M.S., P.I., F.A.I.M.C.

GOLD MEDALIST, National Awardee & Paul Harris Fellow
Advisor: Columbia Holistic University, California, U.S.A.

Former Head & Director,
Department of Business Administration,
University of Lucknow.

Himalaya Publishing House

MUMBAI • NEW DELHI • NAGPUR • BENGALURU • HYDERABAD • CHENNAI • PUNE • LUCKNOW • AHMEDABAD • ERNAKULAM • BHUBANESWAR • INDORE • KOLKATA • GUWAHATI

First Edition : 2009
Reprint : 2012

Published by	:	Mrs. Meena Pandey for **Himalaya Publishing House Pvt. Ltd.,** "Ramdoot", Dr. Bhalerao Marg, Girgaon, **Mumbai - 400 004.** Phone: 022-23860170/23863863, Fax: 022-23877178 **E-mail: himpub@vsnl.com; Website: www.himpub.com**
Branch Offices	:	
New Delhi	:	"Pooja Apartments", 4-B, Murari Lal Street, Ansari Road, Darya Ganj, New Delhi - 110 002. Phone: 011-23270392, 23278631; Fax: 011-23256286
Nagpur	:	Kundanlal Chandak Industrial Estate, Ghat Road, Nagpur - 440 018. Phone: 0712-2738731, 3296733; Telefax: 0712-2721215
Bengaluru	:	No. 16/1 (Old 12/1), 1st Floor, Next to Hotel Highlands, Madhava Nagar, Race Course Road, Bengaluru - 560 001. Phone: 080-32919385; Telefax: 080-22286611
Hyderabad	:	No. 3-4-184, Lingampally, Besides Raghavendra Swamy Matham, Kachiguda, Hyderabad - 500 027. Phone: 040-27560041, 27550139; Mobile: 09390905282
Chennai	:	No. 8/2, Modley 2nd Street, Ground Floor, T. Nagar, Chennai - 600 017. Phone: 044-28144004/28144005; Mobile: 09345345051
Pune	:	First Floor, "Laksha" Apartment, No. 527, Mehunpura, Shaniwarpeth (Near Prabhat Theatre), Pune - 411 030. Phone: 020-24496323/24496333; Mobile: 09370579333
Lucknow	:	Jai Baba Bhavan, Church Road, Near Manas Complex and Dr. Awasthi Clinic, Aliganj, Lucknow - 226 024 (U.P.). Phone: 0522-2339329, 4068914; Mobile: 09307501550
Ahmedabad	:	114, "SHAIL", 1st Floor, Opp. Madhu Sudan House, C.G. Road, Navrang Pura, Ahmedabad - 380 009. Phone: 079-26560126; Mobile: 09377088847
Ernakulam	:	39/104 A, Lakshmi Apartment, Karikkamuri Cross Rd., Ernakulam, Cochin - 622011, Kerala. Phone: 0484-2378012, 2378016; Mobile: 09344199799
Bhubaneswar	:	5 Station Square, Bhubaneswar - 751 001 (Odisha). Phone: 0674-2532129, Mobile: 09338746007
Indore	:	Kesardeep Avenue Extension, 73, Narayan Bagh, Flat No. 302, IIIrd Floor, Near Humpty Dumpty School, Indore - 452 007 (M.P.). Mobile: 09301386468
Kolkata	:	108/4, Beliaghata Main Road, Near ID Hospital, Opp. SBI Bank, Kolkata - 700 010. Phone: 033-32449649, Mobile: 09910440956
Guwahati	:	House No. 15, Behind Pragjyotish College, Near Sharma Printing Press, P.O. Bharalumukh, Guwahati - 781009, (Assam) Mobile: 09883055590, 09883055536
DTP by	:	Panacea Computer, Lucknow
	:	Shri Krishna offset Press Delhi-93

OM ASATOMA SATGAMAYA
TAMASOMA JYOTIRGAMAYA
MRITYORMA AMRITAM GAMAYA

LET US LEAD FROM UNTRUTH TO TRUTH
FROM DARKNESS TO LIGHT
FROM MORTALITY TO IMMORTALITY.

(1-3-28, BRIHADARANYAKA UPANISHAD)

GAYATRI MANTRA

OM BHUR, BHUVAH, SUVAH
TAT SAVITUR VERENAYAM
BHARGO DEVASYA DHIMAHI
DHIYO YO NAA PRACHODAYAT

(YAJURVEDA 36-3)

OM, WHO IS DEARER THAN OUR BREATH
IS SELF SUBSISTENT.
ALL KNOWLEDGE AND ALL BLESS.
WE MEDITATE UPON THAT ADORABLE EFFULGENCE OF THE
RESPLEDENT VIVIFIER OF THE MARCROCOSM, SAVITA,
MAY HE ILLUMINE OUR INTELLECTS UNTO THE RIGHT PATH.

सर्म्पण

ऊँ

शिरडी के साईं बाबा

के पावन, पवित्र चरणों में

जिनकी प्रेरणा एवं आर्शिवाद के बिना,

लेखक का यह

प्रयास असम्भव था

उन्ही को आभार सहित

सादर एवं सविनिय

यह प्रस्तुति समर्पित है।

(डॉ. नीरज कुमार सी–4/8, रिवर बैंक कालोनी लखनऊ –226018)

PREFACE

The typical problem the management has to face is primarily concerned with human beings, not technical in nature. Organizational behaviour is about people's behaviour, thoughts, emotions and allied related aspects. If this aspect is understood in its real perspective, it will positively contribute to improve our understanding and management of people, including ourselves at work.

Unfortunately, in the past the human aspect in an organization was not given its due importance in comparison to technical aspect. However, the behavioural aspect to management was characterised by simple assumptions on human relations and the solutions thereupon. This approach failed to give adequate results. Today, it is a high time to think again, time to look beyond the human relations approach; a traditional one. This shift is definitely towards a behavioural science approach in principle and organizational approach in practice based on the principles of behaviour science. This shift in emphasis is duly accomplished by an understanding rather than an evaluating approach to human behaviour in an organization, based on behavioural science approach.

Unfortunately, quite frequently organizations have sophisticated systems for evaluating and assessing the cost and benefits of almost everything, except their management of people. In a large number of organizations employees are looked as necessary evils to be tolerated as good-humouredly as possible. This results in the thinking as to how the employees are managed – careless or simplistic. Organizational behaviour seeks to counter such tendency by carefully organised and scientific study, how people can best be assessed, motivated, led, trained and developed at work for the overall success of an organization.

The present book provides a conceptual framework for the study and understanding of organizational behaviour. The author has endeavoured his best to present a palatable blend of management and behavioural science concepts, techniques and research. It is rather impracticable to sacrifice management and behavioural science at the expense or sacrifice of the other. It is expected a blend of both will positively contribute towards a better understanding of the various variables and complexities involved for a more effective management of human beings in an organization.

This book is basically intended for students in business and management and psychology, as well as those studying for professional qualifications with bodies such as the Institute of Personnel Management (IPM). The author has tried to make it suitable both for people encountering the subject for the first time and for those who already have some familiarity with it. He aims to give a clear and straight forward– but not simplistic – account of many key areas of contemporary organizational behaviour concepts. More specifically, he has tried to achieve several objectives in order to make this book as useful as possible to its readers.

First, he seeks to blend theory and practice. Both are important. Without good theory practice is blind. Without good practice, theory is not being properly used. The author, therefore, describes key theories and evaluates them where appropriate. He also discusses how the concepts described can find practical application.

Secondly, he tries to pitch the material at a level which the reader should find intellectually stimulating, but not too difficult. It is all too easy to use a slick, glossy presentation at the expense of good content. There is always the temptation to descend to over-simple "recipes for success" which insult the reader's intelligence. On the other hand, it is equally easy to lose the reader in unnecessarily complex debates. The author hopes to avoid both these fates.

Thirdly, the chosen topics are such that tend to be the most useful to potential readers of this book. Some usually appear in organizational behaviour texts, whereas others are generally found in books of a more specifically psychological orientation.

Fourthly, preceding the discussion of the organization and the human beings is a historical, behavioural science, and conceptual foundation for the study of organizational behaviour. The chapters in this initial part are concerned with changing role of practising managers; the historical development of the behavioural approach; an overview of the behavioural science disciplines of anthropology, sociology, and psychology; a discussion of scientific methodology; and a conceptual model for organizational behaviour.

Fifthly, the author has tried providing up-to-date coverage of our material.

There are currently exciting advances in many areas of organizational behaviour and the author had tried to reflect these. At the same time, where the old stuff is best, he had included it. There is nothing to be gained by discussing recent work purely because it is recent.

As said earlier this book is written for those who wish to take a modern behavioural approach to management. It does not assume the reader's prior knowledge of either management or the behavioural sciences. Thus, the book can be used effectively in the first for only management course. It may also be used in the behavioural follow-up course to the more traditional principles of management course. Moreover, the book should be useful to practising executives whose knowledge of the up-to-date aspects of organizational behaviour can increase the effectiveness of his organization, his employees, and himself.

Last but not the least, the author had made an humble attempt to avoid being too reliant on material from U.S. or U.K. Many foreign texts virtually ignore the work conducted in other parts of the world more especially in India. No doubt, the author has his own blinkers, but he has tried to include perspectives from Indian work. None the less, the West provides much valuable material. The author therefore, has made substantial use of research and theory originating from western countries. The best judges of whether the author is able to meet his objectives will be those who read this humble presentation. Comments and suggestions are welcomed and should be directed to Dr. Niraj Kumar, C-4/8, River Bank Colony, Lucknow-226018, India or e-mailed to: kumarniraj1000@rediffmail.com or nirajklko@yahoo.com.

Every author owes a deep sense of gratitude to others and I am no exception to it. Firstly, I wish to acknowledge with gratitude the help of my colleagues at department of Business Administration, University of Lucknow, in preparing this book. My academic colleagues have been stimulating and knowledge sparring partners whose perspective contributed significantly to this work. I shall be failing in my duty to acknowledge the intellectual guidance and support, I have received throughout my academic career from late Dr. K.S. Chaudhari, my research guide. My special thanks to Prof. B.K. Tandon and Prof. Ajai Prakash both of I.C.C.M.R.T., Lucknow, and Mr. Amitabh Singh.

I am deeply grateful to the authors and publishers of the various works from which consciously or unconsciously material has been drawn to prepare the present volume. However, every attempt has been made to acknowledge the debt as and where required. If any acknowledgement has been left, the author with due respect apologises for the same.

Finally, I shall be failing in my duty if I do not acknowledge my heartful thanks to my wife Poonam, daughter Charu and son Nitin, besides my publishers who kept me going with a well balanced mixture of encouragement and pressure.

C - 4/8, River Bank Colony,
LUCKNOW - 226 018

Dr. Niraj Kumar

CONTENTS

PREFACE

1.	An Overview of O.B.	1
2.	Development of O.B.	17
3.	O.B. & Related Discipline	29
4.	Management a Behaviour Aspect	45
5.	Models for Behaviour	65
6.	Individual Behaviour	83
7.	Perception	97
8.	Morale	121
9.	Motivation	137
10.	Communication	187
11.	Transactional Analysis	201
12.	Learning	227
13.	Personality	247
14.	Leadership	263
15.	Team & Team Work	285
16.	Group Behaviour	307
17.	Group at Work	331
18.	Conflict	359
19.	Change Management	385
20.	Counselling	417
21.	Stress Management	451
22.	Time Management	511
23.	Industrial Psychology	535
24.	Better Decision Making	555
25.	The Case Method	563

CASE STUDIES

A.	**NATURE OF O.B.**	**579**
1.	A Case of Betrayal	579
2.	Organic Culture of C.M.C.	579
3.	Absentee Information Sheet	0
4.	Mc Donald's Fast Food	581
5.	American Flies High	582
6.	What went wrong at G.M.	583
B.	**PERSONALITY**	**585**
1.	Nature and Nurture	585
2.,	Uma Nair – Rathan Singh	586
3.	Govindan	587

C. MOTIVATION 589
1. Fool's Paradise 589
2. Beyond Salary 589
3. The Superior Floor Covering Company 589
4. The Loyal Employee 590
5. Behaviour Modification Programme 591
6. Maid in a Hotel 591
7. Pay as Motivator 592
8. Capable But Hesitant Employee 592
9. Nilgiriside Departmental Store 592
10. The Resentful Employee 592
11. A Change in Work 594
12. Dhawan Inspires Love and Fear 594
13. Motivation at Sand Mack 595
14. The Volvo Experiment: Where Happy Workers Aren't Productive Corkers 596
15. Need Satisfaction 597
16. Motivating a Group of Winners 598
17. Motivation at The Bareilly Clothing Company 599

D. PERCEPTION 600
1. Bombay Printers 600
2. Space Shortage 600
3. Case of a Supervisor in Soup 601
4. Differing Perceptions at Hindaltex Industries 602
5. The Campbell Soup Image 603

E. LEARNING 605
1. Classical Conditioning Eve Teasing Episode 605
2. Social Learning
3. Learning – Operant Conditioning 'Indiscipline' Episode 606

F. GROUP BEHAVIOUR 608
1. Old Buddies Turned Foes 608
2. It Was Show All The Way 608
3. A Tricky Problem 609
4. The Sales Girls 610
5. The Student Worker 611
6. Major Spectacles Corporation 612
7. Betty Randall 612
8. Developing Verifiable Goals 614

G. LEADERSHIP 615
1. The Case of Overheard Conversation 615
2. Choice of a Leader 615
3. Leadership Style 616
4. Nasa and The Quest for Leadership 616
5. Who are the Effective Leaders? 618
6. Leadership at Lufthansa 618
7. The Puppet 619
8. Presidential Leadership 619
9. Leadership Style in The Quality Control Lab 620

H. POWER **623**
1. Chawla – Jitendra 623
2. Rise and Fall 623
3. Apple Computers Versus Apple Computers 624

I. COMMUNICATION **626**
1. A Case of Misunderstood Message 626
2. The Vice President, the Product Manager and the Misunderstanding 626
3. An Appointment Request in Reverse 627
4. The Credibility Gap 628
5. Image and Rumours at Proctor and Gamble 629
6. Malhotra Fashion Stores Incorporated 630
7. Castrophe in Space: A Result of Poor Managerial Communication 631
8. A Failure to Communicate 632

J. CONFLICT MANAGEMENT **634**
1. Aditya Financial Services Limited 634
2. It's the Same Story Everywhere 634
3. Student Novelist 635
4. Smart Beginning 636
5. Demanding Wife and Spoilt Children 636
6. Problem of Job Rotation 637
7. Komal Food's Products Company 637
8. The New Principal 639

K. ORGANIZATIONAL CHANGE **641**
1. Saagar Travels 641
2. Quality Control Equipment 641
3. Introduction of Computer 641
4. Industrial Engineer 642
5. Merger and Heart Burns 642
6. Scandinavian Airlines System 643
7. Agricultural Fertiliser Division of the Northern Corporation 644
8. Siemens the Sleeping Giant 645
9. Reorganising at G.M. 646
10. Home Radio and Television Company 647
11. Developing Leaders at The Sahni Group 648

L. ATTITUDE, VALUE, JOBS SATISFACTION **649**
1. Case of Velu 649
2. Employee Grievances 650
3. Executive's Tantrums 651
4. Mixed Culture 651

M. CONTROL **652**
1. Bharat Fabrication Ltd. 652
2. Patel Mills 652

N. ORGANIZATIONAL CLIMATE **654**
1. Budgets and Human Problems 654
2. The Modi Textile Mills 654
3. Self Assumed Promotion 655

4. Teaching Technologies Inc. 656
5. Three Managerial Decisions 656
O. ORGANIZATIONAL DEVELOPMENT **658**
1. Max Photo Film Manufacturing Company 658
2. Culture Shock 658
3. Restructuring At Korea's Daewoo 659
P. WORK STRESS **661**
1. A Case of Burnout 661

DETAILED CONTENTS

CHAPTER - 1 AN OVERVIEW OF O.B. **1-16**

Functions of Managers, Management Skills, Concepts, OB Applies the Scientific Method to Practical Managerial Problems, OB Defined Some of the Definitions given by the Various Authors are as follows, Characteristics of OB, OB a Working Definition, OB Focuses on Three Levels of Analysis Individual Groups and Organizations, Nature and Scope of OB, Key Elements in OB, Goals of Organizational behaviour, Dimensions and Themes of OB, OB Seeks the Betterment of Human Resources, OB Recognises the Dynamic Nature of Organizations. OB Assumes there is "NO ONE BEST" Approach, OB Confronts the Challenges of Work Force Diversity, OB Takes a Global Perspective, A Model for Understanding OB, The Dependent Variables, The Independent Variables.

CHAPTER - 2 DEVELOPMENT OF O.B. **17-27**

Scientific Management, The Early Approach, the Human Relations Movement, Elton Mayo and The Hawthorne Studies, Classical Organizational theory, Organizational Behaviour in the Modern Era, Some Milestones in the History of Organizational Behaviour, Features of Modern OB, Limitations of OB.

CHAPTER - 3 O.B. AND RELATED DISCIPLINES **29-44**

Man– The Critical Factor, The Macro and Micro Issues, Inter Discipline Relationship, Contributing Disciplines to OB, Anthropology Sociology, Psychology, Political Science, Philosophy, Logic, Ethics, Social Work, Economics, History, Jurisprudence, Education, Biology, Physiology, Synoptic View of Contributions by other Disciplines to Human Relations Approach (Organization Theory), Psychiatry Radio Technology.

CHAPTER - 4 MANAGEMENT: A BEHAVIOURAL ASPECT **45-64**

Nature of Organization, Importance of Structure Causes and Effects of Poor Organization, Objective Thinking is Required, Management Tools that Supplement a Sound Structure, Improving the Organization, The Ten Commandments of Sound Organization, The Test of Organization and Staffing, Organizations and Staffing, Direction and Leadership, On-The-Job Coaching, Management Planning Instructions, Ten Tests of Direction and Leadership, Our Performance.

CHAPTER - 5 MODELS FOR BEHAVIOUR **65-82**

Freudian Psychoanalytic Model, The Freudian Model, In Perspective Existentialistic Model, The Impact of the Existential Model, Cognitive Model, Behaviouristic Model, Rational and Emotional Models, Humanistic Model, Economic and Self-Actualising Models, Theory X and Theory Y Models, Man as a System, An Electric Model for Organizational Behaviour, The Goals of the Organizational Behaviour Model, A Causal Model For Human Behaviour, The S-O-B Model, Basic Elements of the Model, The Nature of Behaviour, Examples of Behavioural Analysis, Complexities of Behavioural Analysis, The SO-B-C Model, The Variables in the Model, The Person Variable, The Interactive Connections and Feedback loops, A Conceptual Framework for the Study of Organizational Behaviour, The Formal Organization, Organizational Participants, Organizational Consequences,

CHAPTER - 6 INDIVIDUAL BEHAVIOUR **83-95**

Motives of Behaviour, Genesis of Behaviour, Role of Material Values, How Behaviour Transforms, behaviour Vis-a-Vis Organization, Nature of Man, Individual Differences, A Whole Person, Caused Behaviour g(Motivated), Models of Man, Rational-Economic Man, Social Man, Organizational Man, Complex Man, Administration Man, Mobicentric Man, Self-actualising Man, Phenomenologic Views of People, Theory X and Theory Y Model of Man, The Manager's Job, Managerial Functions, Managerial Roles, The Human Context of Management.

CHAPTER - 7 PERCEPTION **97-119**

Process of Perception, Basic Factors Affecting Perception Special Factors Affecting Perception, Motivation, Organization of Perception, Figure and Ground, Grouping Proximity, Similarity, Continuity, Closure, Good Figure, Illusion, Causes of Illusion, Hallucination, Causes of Hallucinations, Difference Between Illusion and Hallucination, The Role of Attribution, Managerial Implications of Perception, Perception and Motivation, Perception and Hiring, Perception and Performance Evaluation.

CHAPTER - 8 MORALE **121-136**

Approaches, Classical Approach, Psychological Approach, Social Approach Nature of Morale, Significance/ Importance of Morale, Process of Morale Building, Physical Factors for High Morale, Conditions of Work, Position of Promotion, Increase in Salary, Method of Distributing Salaries, Opportunity to Share Profit, Psychological Factors, Knowledge of Success, Fulfilment of Collective Needs, Forbearance and Good Behaviour of Authorities, Freedom of Workers, Sense of Unity, Identity and Equality, Others Factors, Factors Contributing to High Morale Confidence of the Individual Members, Confidence in Leadership, Confidence in Fellow Workers, Organizational Efficiency, Definiteness of Responsibility Adequate and Effective Communication, Working Conditions and Allied Factors Fair Wages, Security and Opportunity to Rise, Work Environment, Seven Commandments to Morale, Sound Personnel Administration, Effective Communication, Worthwhile Goals, Human Relations Approach, Sound Organization Structure, Trusted Supervision, Why should Manager be concerned with Morale Administrative Measure to Promote Morale, Sound Wage structure, Security of Job Delegation of Authority, Grievance Procedure, Suggestion Scheme, Joint Consultation, Sound Promotion Policy, Employee Counselling, Recognition, Keeping the Workers Well Informed, Inspiring Credos and Mottos Workers, Measurement of Morale, Method of Measurement, Direct Method, Observation Technique, Interview Technique, Attitude Survey technique, Projectile Techniques Common Worker's Opinion Analysis, Sociological Methods, Company Records and Reports, Indirect Method, Morale and Productivity, High Morale, High Productivity Low Morale, Low Productivity, High Morale, Low Productivity, Low Morale and High Productivity.

CHAPTER - 9 MOTIVATION **137-185**

What Moves one to Excellence? Motive, Motivating, Motivation, Theories of Motivation, Scientific Management, Human Relations Model, Content Theories, Maslow's Need Hierarchy Theory, Evaluation of Maslow's Theory, Herzberg's Two-Factor Theory, Analysis of the Theory, Comparison of Maslow's and Herzberg's Theories, Alderfer's ERG Theory, Analysis of ERG Theory, Content Three Theories at a Glance, Mc Gregors Theory X and Theory Y, Theory X, Assumptions of Theory X, Theory X: A Pessimistic View, Relevance of Theory X in Modern Times, Theory Y, Assumption of theory 'V', Theory Y : An Optimistic View, Support for Theory Y, Applicability to Theory Y in India, Some Puzzling Questions, Which Theory is Right, Is it Possible for a Theory X Person to Become a Theory Y Person? Will a Theory Y Person be a Good Manager?, Beyond Theory Y : A Contingency Model, Theory Z, A Concept of Japanese Management Practice (Theory Z), Japanese Theory Z, Another View, B Theory Z Concept – Indian Context, C. Lyndal, F. Urwick's Theory Z, Prepositions, Assessment of Urwick's Theory Z, General Assessment of Theory Z, Process Theories Vroom's Expectancy Theory, Valency, Expectancy, Instrumentality, Adam's Equity Theory, Inequity can Exist under two Circumstances, Inequity Resolution Strategy, Porter's Performance Model reinforcement, Theory, Positive Reinforcement, Negative Reinforcement, Extinction, Reinforcement Schedules, Motivation: East vs West, Motivating Indian Managers, Motivating Indian Workers, The Indian Scene–Basic Differences,

CHAPTER - 10 COMMUNICATION **187-200**

The Process of Communication, Communication Vs Information, Communication: A Factor in Organization Climate, Significance of Communication, Communication, Network in Organization, A

Human Communication Model, Cost of Miscommunication, Barriers to Communication, How to Overcome Communication Barriers.

CHAPTER - 11 TRANSACTIONAL ANALYSIS **201-225**

Ego States, The Child "C", The Parent "P", The Adult "A", Our Three Forces, Types of Transactions, Ulterior Transaction, Where are you coming from? The four Life Positions, I'm Not OK–You're OK, I'm Not OK – You're Not OK, I'm Not OK-You're Not OK, I'm OK– You're OK, Work is Not the only Thing that occurs at work, Trading Stamps, Games and Prizes, Getting Unhooked from the Past and Living in the present Exercises, Your OK Child, Avoid The Parent of Others, Look for OK Child in Other, Feel Your Own OK Child, Keep Contacts with others, Observing P-A-C at Work, Cashing in Trading Stamps on the Job, Work Games, and Other Emotional Exercises, Healthy Work Climate Vs Pollution, If We Only had a Few More Creative People Around Here, Improving Efforts to Improve, Conclusion, Lessons From T.A., Key to Developing Effective Skills, Structure for Success, Make Contracts and Keep them, Confrontation is not a Dirty word, Everyone Wants to Feel–Important, Can I Go Over Someone's Head.

CHAPTER - 12 LEARNING **227-245**

What is Learning, Definition of Learning, Factors of Learning, Learning Curves, Acquisition-Learning Curves Relearning, Form of Learning, Thordinke's Principles of Learning, Classical Conditioning, Operant Conditioning, Difference Between Classical conditioning and Operant Conditioning, Insight Learning, Imitation Learning, Observational Learning, Cognitive Learning, Types of Reinforcement, Positive Reinforcement, Avoidance, Extinction, Punishment, Schedules of Reinforcement, Continuous Reinforcement, Fixed Interval Reinforcement, Variable Interval Reinforcement, Fixed Ratio Reinforcement, Variable Ratio Reinforcement, Related Aspects of Learning, Stimulus Generalisation, Stimulus Discrimination, Vicarious Learning, Punishment, Other Managerial Implications of Learning Motivation, Performance Evaluation and Rewards, Training.

CHAPTER - 13 PERSONALITY **247-262**

What is Personality? Definition, What is not meant by Personality, What is meant by Personality, Traits of Personality, Determinants of Personality, Biological Factors, Heredity, Brain, Body Chemistry, Environmental Factors, Social and Family Factors, Stratification, Situational Factors, Jung's Personality Typing, Sensation and Intuition, Feeling and Thinking, Problem Solving Profiles, Scoring Key, Classifying scores, Analysis of Personality Types, Possible Weakness, Occupational Choices and Personality Types.

CHAPTER - 14 LEADERSHIP **263-284**

Leadership – Meaning and Definitions, The Nature of Leadership, Leadership Qualities, Traits of a Leader, Are Traits Common to All Leaders, Management and Leadership, Importance of Leadership, Directing Group Activities Better Utilisation of Manpower, Source of Motivation, Developing Good Human Relations, Promoting the Spirit of Coordination, Fulfilling Social Responsibilities, Functions of Leadership, Integration. Communication, Production Emphasis, Representation, Fraternity, Organization, Evaluation of Performance, Initiation, Domination, Different Approaches of Theories of Leadership, Weaknesses of Traitists theory, The List of traits is not Exhaustive, No Common or Universal Traits, No Room for Developing Future Leaders, No Consideration for Situational Factors, Different Roles Require Different Traits, The Approach Ignores Other Variables of Leadership, Traits of an Individual cannot be known, Behavioural Approach or Theory, Situationalist Approach or Theory, It Over Emphasises the Situational Aspect, It Completely Overlooks the Traits and Behaviour, Followers Theory or Acceptance Theory, System Theory, Different Leadership Styles, Motivational Styles - Positive and Negative Leadership, Positive Approach or Leadership, Negative Approach or Leadership, Power Styles - Autocratic, Democratic and Free - Rein Leaders, Advantages of Autocratic Leadership, Disadvantages of Autocratic Leadership, Participative or Democratic Leadership, Advantages, Disadvantages, Free Rein Leadership. Orientation Style of Supervisory Style, Employee Oriented Leadership, Production or Task Oriented

Leadership, Which One is Better, Suitability of the Different Styles, Fiedler's Contingency Model of Leadership, Leader Member Relations, Task - Structure, Leader Position Power, Favourableness of the Leadership Situation, The Leadership Style , Evaluation of Fiedler's Work, Criticism, Path Goal Theory of Robert House, Instrumental Behaviour, Supportive Behaviour, Participative Behaviour, Achievement Oriented Behaviour, Situational Factors, Characteristics of the Subordinates, Ability, Personalities, Needs and Motives, Characteristics of the Work Environment, Subordinates Tasks, Work Group, Organizational Factors of Formal Authority System of Organization, Evaluation of Path - Goal - Theory of Leadership, Complicated Approach, Measurement Problem, Little Research Support, Leadership and Followership, Leadership is a Mutual Influence Process, Leader's Influence of Followers, Follower's Influence of Leader, Leadership Style and Leadership Personality, Johari Window, Public, Blind, Private, Unknown.

CHAPTER - 15 TEAM & TEAM WORK **285-305**

Teams defined, Difference between Team & Group, Historical Perspective, Types of Teams, Process of Team Development, A General Typology of Work Teams, How Successful are Teams? A Look at the Evidence, Work Team Effectiveness: An Ecological Model, Team Work Through Co - operation, Trust and Cohesiveness, Co-Operation, Co-Operation Versus Competition, Research Support for Cooperation, A Cognitive Leap, How to Build Trust, Cohesiveness, Cohesiveness, Socio-Emotional and Instrumental Cohesiveness, Lessons from Group Cohesiveness Research, Putting Cohesiveness to Work Team in Organizational Context, Managers Guidelines for Crating Teams, Improving Team Effectiveness, Potential Obstacles to Success, Team Building and OD.

CHAPTER - 16 GROUP BEHAVIOUR AND DYNAMICS **307-330**

Groups Defined, A Group in Terms of Perception, A Group in Terms of Organization, A Group in terms of Motivation, A Group in Terms of Interaction, Group Dynamics, Group Formation, Reasons for Group Formation, The Satisfaction of Needs, Security, Social, Preinquity, Shared Activities and Interaction, Esteem, Proximity and Attraction, Group Goal, Balance Theory, Exchange Theory, Economics and Social Reasons, Esteem, Power, Identity, Rewards, Accomplishment, Stages in the Development of Groups, Individual Characteristics and Group Behaviour, (1) Physical Characteristics Such as Age, Sex and Physical characteristics, (2) Abilities and Intelligence, (3) Personality Traits, (4) Expectations, Inter-and-Inter Group Relations, What Happens within the Group, What Happens Between Competing Groups, Solution to the Problems, Approaches to Inter-Group Relationship 1. Pooled Interdependence, 2. Sequential Interdependence, 3. Reciprocal Interdependence, Theories of Group Formation, 1. Theory of Propinquity 2. Homans Theory, Activity, 3. Balance Theory, 4. Exchanger Theory, Group-A System View, Group Inputs, Personal Characteristics, Situational Variables, Group Structure, Group Process, Group Task Activities, Group Building Activities, Self-Serving Activities, Group Output, Equilibrium Problems, Schachter's 'Pitch Form' Productivity Curves, Individual and the Group, Social Facilitation, Weighting, Brainstorming, Risk shift, Groupness, Group Decision Making, The Danger of Group Decisions, Techniques for Improving Group Decisions, Group Problem Solving, Problem solving Techniques, Assets and Liabilities of Group Problem Solving and Decision Making, Decision Making Liabilities, Improved Problem Solving, Reference,

CHAPTER - 17 GROUPS AT WORK **331-357**

How Work-Groups are Formed? Types of Groups, Formal Groups, Different Types of Formal Groups, Informal Groups, Different Types of Informal Groups, Distinction Between Formal and Informal Groups, Other Types of Groups, Open and Closed Groups, Changing Groups Membership, Flame of Reference, Time Perspective, Equilibrium, Primary or Small Groups, Management of Highly Cohesive groups, Disbanking the Group, Reference Groups, Sayles Classification of Groups, Functions of a Group, Task Functions, Maintenance Functions, Committee – A Formally Designed Group, The Nature and Functions of Committees, Positive Attributes of Committees, Negative Attributes of Committees, Group Think – A Problem with Committee Action, Consequences of Group Think, the Remedy for Group Think, Small Group Behaviour, Dynamics of Informal Groups, The Grapevine-Informal Communication, Structural

Dimensions or Components of Groups, Group Composition, Group Size, Group Norms, Characteristic of Norms, Norms Conformity Factors, Enforcement of Norms, Implications for Managers, How Norms Develop, Roles, Multiple Roles and Role Sets, Role Perception, Characteristics of Roles, Role Relationships or Role Activities, Real Problems, Role Ambiguity, Role Conflict, Person-Role Conflict, Intra Role Conflict, Inter Role Conflict, The Results of Role Conflict, Status Systems, How Status Structures Influence Group Behaviour, Managerial Implications, Leadership in Groups, Emergence of Informal Leaders, Successful Leadership Behaviours, Cohesiveness, Characteristics, Outside Pressure, Status of the Group, Success, Other Reasons, Effects of Group Cohesion.

CHAPTER - 18 CONFLICT 359-384

Conflict Defined, Nature of Conflicts, Changing Views of Conflict, Conflict A Modern View, The Process of Conflict, The Effects of Conflicts: Positive and Negative, Functional Conflicts(Positive) Consequences, Dysfunctional Conflict (Negative) Consequence, Levels of Conflict, Goal Conflict, Role Conflict, Interpersonal Conflict, Causes of Conflicts at Individual Level, Intergroup or Organizational Conflict, Sources or Causes of Group Conflicts, Conflicts at the Organizational Level,Stimulating Functional Conflict, Resolution of Conflict, (a) Preliminary Step, (b) Diagnosing the Issue, (c) Conflict Handling Modes, Integration and Distribution: Two Basic Dimensions of Conflict, Resolving Inter Personal Conflict, Alternative Styles for Handling Dysfunctional Conflict, Integrating (Problem-Solving), Obliging (Smoothing), Dominating (Forcing), Avoiding, Compromising, Escalative Interventions: Intensifying Conflicts to Resolve Them, Conflict Management: A Contingency Approach, Should Conflict Be Necessarily Eliminated.

CHAPTER - 19 CHANGE MANAGEMENT 385-416

Nature of Change, Organizational Change, Response to Change, Technological Change, Knowledge Explosion, Product and Service Obsolescence, Market Conditions, Social Trends, Value Gap, Why Individuals Resist Change, Causes of Resistance to Change by Employees, Disturbance in Existing Equilibrium, Imbalance in Need Satisfaction, Insecurity to Jobs, Fear of Economic Loss, Change Affects Emotions and Sentiments, Disturbance of Social Relationship, Obsolescence of Skills Lack of Classification, Opposition only for the Sake of Opposition, Habit, Failure to Recognise need for Change, Ego Defensiveness, Status Quo, Fear of Unknown Social Displacement, Peer Pressure, Cause of Resistance to Change by Employers and Management, Increase in Responsibility, Change Proposed by Government and Labour Union, Change on Experimental Basis, Structural Inertia, Work Group Inertia, Threats to Existing Balance of Power, Previously Unsuccessful Change Efforts, Organizational Structure, Resource Constraints, Organizational Culture, Examples of Organization Change, Levels if Organizational Change, Individual Level, Group Level, Organizational Level, The Dilemma of Change, Stability Versus Change, Evolutionary, Revolutionary and Planned Changes, Evolutionary Changes, Revolutionary Changes, Planned Changes, Proactive Versus Reactive Change, Approaches to Managing Organizational Change, Kurt Lewin's Change Model, Unfreezing, Changing or Moving, Identification, Internalisation, Force of Compliance, Refreezing, Lewin's Model: Another Example An Indian Experience, Additional Real Life Situations, Action Research Model, Diagnosis, Analysis, Feedback, Action, Evaluation, Response and Reactions to Change, Steps involved in Organization Wide Change, Group level of Change, The Group as a Medium of Change, The Group as a Target of Change, Implementation of Change, Plan the Change, Steps in Planning Change, Structure - Focused Change Efforts`Changing Organization by Redesigning Tasks, Changing Organization by Changing Technology, Changing Organization by Changing People, Use of Group Forces, Guidelines to Institute Change, Change of Change Agent, Shares Rewards, Co-operation of Unions, Concern for Employees, Inform, Minimise Damage, Timing, Participation, Shape Political Dynamics, Educate the Work Force, Involve Employees in the Change Efforts, Follow up on the Change, Role of the change agent, Use of Group Forces, Leadership for Change, Shared Rewards, Employee Security, Working with Unions, Working with the Total System, Desirable Consequences of Resistance to Change, Cost-benefits Comparison, Types of Opposition, Even Emotional Resistance to Change can have Desirable Consequences, Technical Specialists and Change

CHAPTER - 20 COUNSELLING **417-449**

What Counselling is ? What Counselling is not? Counselling Situations: Situation - I, Situation - II, Guidance and Counselling, Meaning of Employee Counselling, Functions of Counselling, Role of Counselling, Formal and Informal Counselling, Different Types of Counselling, Distinction between Directive and Non-Directive Counselling, Mentoring/Coaching, Difference between Coaching and Counselling, Who May Be a Counsellor, Counselling a Management Task, Stress, Illness, Absenteeism, Low Motivation, Poor Work, High Staff Turnover, What is Costs? A Response to a Crisis, Counselling Role of Manager, Discipline and Disciplinary Action, Discipline, Role of Management in Maintaining Discipline, Disciplinary Action, Disciplinary Action Policy or Reinforcement, The Counselling Approach to Disciplinary Action, Policies, Attitudes and Views Towards Counselling, Counselling An Appraisal, Group Counselling, Phases of Activities, The Process, Personal Guidance, Purpose, Emotional Characteristics of Adolescents, Hostility, Fear, Anxiety, Jealousy, Energy Resources, Types of Emotional Problems, Frustration, Anxiety, Nervousness, Stress, Neurosis, Strategies, Cooperative Counselling, Stress Reduction Model, The Skills of Counselling Relationship Skills, Listening Skills, Asking Appropriate Questions, The Kind of Questions that you will find are most useful are, The Questions you should avoid are those that are, Open questions, Closed Questions, Mirror or Reflecting Questions, Probing questions, Leading Questions, Qualified Questions, Multiple Questions, Diagnostic Skills, Confidentiality, Contract Setting, Refraining Skills, Intervention Skills, Self awareness, Empathy, Objectivity, Referral Skills.

CHAPTER - 21 STRESS MANAGEMENT **451-509**

Pressure and Stress, What is Stress? Elements of Stress, Stress: What it is not, Dynamics of Stress, Definition of Stress, Psychological Mechanism and Phases of Stress, Pathological Chemistry of Stress, A Stress Model, Types of Stress, The Nature of Stress, A Model of Organizational Stress, a Model of Occupational Stress, Stressors Environmental Factors that Produce Stress, Stress and work:
A Model, Types of Stressors, Burnout, A Model of Burnout, Burnout: Stress and Psychological Adjustment, Burnout; Some Major Causes, Burnout: Its Major Effects, Burnout; Can it be Reversed Stress Consequences, Symptoms & Diagnosis of Stress, Rating Occupation, what Causes Stress, Belief in Locus of Control, Hostility, Community, Cultural, National, International, Universal, Environmental Factors, Environmental Causes, Organization Causes, Personal Causes, Type A and Type B Personality, Type A Behaviour pattern, Type a Behaviour Defined, Cost of Stress, Physical and Mental Health, Managing Stress, Balance and Methods, Ways to Deal with Stress, Other Methods to Reduce Stress, Relaxation, Learn to Pause, The 10 Second pause, the Five minute pause, Deep relaxation, Remember Using Emotional Energy to Manage Stress, Emotional Skills Exercise, Humour, Biofeedback, Biofeedback Imaging, Meditation, Transcendental Mediation (TM), Is TM The Same As Biofeedback? Yoga, Time Management, Social Support, Organizational Strategies to Manage Stress, Job Redesign, Selection and Placement, Changes in the Nature of Jobs, Role Analysis and Clarification, Company Wide Programs, Clinical Programs, Organizational Programs, Stress Management Programs, Employee Assistance as an Approach, Role of Different Systems in Treating Stress, Managing Stress Unconventionally, Hypnosis, Panic healing, Gem Therapy, Acupuncture, Accupressure, Massage, Types of Massage, Aroma Therapy, Situation Specific Therapies, Ailment Anti-Thesis and Possible Cure Activity.

CHAPTER - 22 TIME MANAGEMENT **511-534**

What is Time Management? Managing the Basic Resource, Self-instructions, Why Time Planning is Worth More of Your Time: 1. Time Planning Prevents Future Problems, 2. Time Planning Banishes Guilt, 3. Time Planning Enhances Your Personal Time, 4. Time Planning Creates Self Discipline, Television, Not Doing it Right the First Time, Not Being Organised, Procrastination, Negative Thinking, How Time Management Works, Organising Your Time, Invert Time to Save Time, Set Priorities, Keep a Clear Focus, Avoid Works, Use of Diary, Organise Your Work, The Three Minute Rule, Do's of Time Management, Working Together, Timing, The Best person for The Job, The Worst-First Rule, Take a Break, The Expending Workload, Be Positive, Working Together, Management of Information, Thus if we Want to allocate the time it can be Stated Below as following, Whereas Potato is an Abbreviation for the, Read and

Write Effectively, Written Communication as an Effective Tool for Time Management, Time Styles of Leadership, Task and Achievements Orientation, Leadership, Dominance and Decision Orientation, Impulsive and Physically Energetic Orientation, Theoretical Detail and Structure Orientation Change New Experiences and Feeling Expression Orientation Fellowship Orientation and Defensive Aggressive Orientation, Executive Time Inventories, Allocate Time, Set Daily Goals, Keep Record on Time, Summarise for a Week or More, Estimate Daily Effectiveness, Evaluate, Procrastinating the Greatest Hindrance to Time Management, Time Demands, Work Analysis, Whereas We Will be Fruitful in TEM Through, Time Management Through Communication, Principles of Effective Listening, Don't of Time Management.

CHAPTER - 23 INDUSTRIAL PSYCHOLOGY **535-553**

Definitions of Industrial Psychology, Blum's Definition, Harrell's Opinion, Smith's Definition, Scope of Industrial Psychology, Economic Social and Psychological Aspects of Industry, Study of the Physical Aspect of Work Environment, Principles of Human Relationships, Study of Aptitudes and Motives, Study of Principles of Mental Health, Study of Human Relations, What Industrial Psychology, Selection of the Right Man for Right Job, Training for Works, Morale in Industry, Human Relations in Industry, Fatigue and Boredom, Industrial Accidents, Responses Towards Physical Environment, Problems of Production, Problems of Selling, Prevention and Solution of Industrial Conflicts, Problem of Personnel Conduct, Objectives of Industrial Psychology, Personal Selection, Care of Worker's Health, Protection of Worker's Economic Interest, Search of Proper Methods of Work, Removing Maladjustment, Reform of Working Conditions, Reform in Machines, Reform in Human Relationships Humanistic Approach in Industry, Solution of Labour Problems, Prevention of Accidents, Study of Aptitudes, Maintaining Morale, Creating Proper Leadership, Measurement of Individual Differences, Study of Efficiency, Use of Psychological Tests, Motion and Times Studies, Aid in Industrial Training, Suggestion Concerning Motives, Studies of Fatigue and Monotony, Vocation Guidance, Advertisement and Selling, Physical Conditions of Work, Intensity, Location, Distribution and Colour of Light, Temperature, Ventilation, Noise, Hours of Work, Rest Pauses, Music, Other Physical Conditions, Psychological Conditions of Work, Behaviour of Those in Authority, Mutual Relations of Workers, Security in Profession, Satisfaction of Life's Needs, Incentive in Industry, Types of Fatigue, Physical Fatigue, Mental Fatigue Difference Between Physical and Mental Fatigue, Causes of Fatigue, Long Hours of Work, Absence of Rest Periods, Incorrect Temperature, Absence of Proper Ventilation, Improper Illumination, Design of the Machinery, Absence of Adequate Seat, Excessive Noise, Unhealthy Conditions, Absence of Proper Training, Lack of Sleep, Low Morale, Defects of the Social Environment, Meaning of Reducing Fatigue, Reducing the Hours of Work, Provision of Rest Periods, Arrangements for Maintaining the Correct Temperature, Proper Ventilation, Arrangement for Proper Lighting, Improvements in the Design of Seating, Control Over the Noise, Healthy Working Conditions, Arrangements for Industrial or Professional Training, Proper Arrangements for Sleep, High Morale, Proper Social Atmosphere, Special Means of Reducing Fatigue, Criteria of Fatigue, Feeling of Exhaustion, Muscular Condition, Chemical Changes, Nervous Slackness, Change in the Blood Chemistry, Change in the Mental Condition, Increase in the Number of Accident, Fall in Production, Monotony, Measures to Remove monotony, Job Enlargement, Job Enrichment Job Rotation, Provision of Music, Employee Counselling.

CHAPTER - 24 BETTER DECISION MAKING **555-562**

From Confusion to Clarity, What are Better Decisions, What not to do to Make a Better Decision, Making a Better Decision, A Private Five-Minute Inventory, A Reliable System, the Real Need, Informed Options, But How Can People Become Aware of the Options Available?, When is one Supposed to Feel More Discouraged or When One Feels One Has the Options or When One Doesn't?, How does One Know that One Has Enough Information to Make a Decision?, How does One Discover which is Ones Best Option?, Thinking it through, The other Half-Why do People No Ask Questions More Often to Come to a Decision?, What is Difference Between Effective and Ineffective Decisions?, My Invitation, My Insight, Points to Ponder, What is my Better Decision?

CHAPTER - 25 THE CASE METHOD **563-576**

What is a Case?, Objectives of a Case Study, Association of Case Method, Utilisation of Case Method by Trainers and Training Instructions, Characteristics of the Case Method, Effective use of Case Study Method in Management Study, Development Stages of Cases, Distinction between Case Study Method and Lecture Method of Study, Benefits and Disadvantages of Case Method, How to Analyse a Case, Study, Analyse, Decide, Some More Approaches to Case Analysis, Methodical Approaches to Cases, A-Identification, B-Preparation for Solution, C-The Solution, D-Implementation, E-Followup, Common Errors in Case Analysis, 1. Unrecognised or Inappropriate Assumptions, 2. Generalisations, 3. Cliches, 4. Overemphasising One Aspect, 5. Miracle Cures, 6. Placing Blame, 7. Being Unrealistic, 8. Seeing Things as "either-or" 9. Mistaking Opinions and Assumptions for Facts, 10. Hedging, Approach to Case Discussion, Role of Case Study Method in Business, Using the Analysis of Evidence, A Support from Evidence Other than Quantitative, 1.Adequacy, 2. Balance, 3. Validity, 4. Reasonableness of Interpretations, 5. Objectivity, 6. Thoroughness of Reasoning, B-Support from Quantitative Evidence, 1. Adequacy, 2. Accurate Usage.

CASE STUDIES **577-661**

CHAPTER

1

An Overview of O.B.

David Buchanan and Huczynski remarked, "The ultimate limitation on human goals is not human intelligence or technology, but our ability to work together effectively in organizations. If we eventually destroy this planet, the main cause will not be nuclear weapons. We will have destroyed it with ineffective forms of organization." This recognizes that the human beings are a vital part of any organization and the study of human behaviour in organizations has become an important discipline in its own right.

Understanding the behaviour of people within an organizational setting has become increasingly important as managers cannot afford to ignore the personalities, perceptions, attitudes, ideologies, aspirations and satisfactions of the employees. To be effective, managers must view each employee. To be effective, managers must view each employee as a unique embodiment of beliefs, motives, philosophies, skills, perspectives, learning and perceptual capabilities. Today, organizations are much more than the processors of raw materials. In fact, they are social systems, human groupings, and behavioural units. The success of any organization is influenced by its people and their behaviour.

Management is, as is too well-known, the art of getting things done through others. Stated differently, management is social and technical process that utilises resources, influences human action and facilitates changes in order to accomplish an organization's goals.

Probably what is not too well-known is the fact that management is a vital factor in the life of an organization. Success or failure of the organization largely depends on the quality of management. Competent management will contribute to the success of the organization, whatever the constraints. Inefficient management will sure bankrupt the organization, abundance of other resources not with standing. This is true whether the organization is a profit-oriented business unit or a unit whose mission is mere service to society.

Managers are the individuals who practise the art of management. In other words, it is these people who muster the needed resources of the organization; put them to proper use and strive to reach the organization's goals. In a typical business enterprise, managers, general managers, and high-level, middle-level, and low-level managers. These managers are also called the executives. Administrators is another term generally used in this context, but its usage is more in government departments and not in profit organizations.

Functions of Managers

What are the functions of a typical manager? Going back to the early part of this century, a French industrialist by the name of Henry Fayol wrote that all managers perform five management functions, viz., planning, organizing, commanding, coordinating and controlling. How prophetic the French industrialist was! Though nine decades have passed by since the beginning of the century, functions of managers continue to be the same even today. Today's manager plan, organize, command, coordinate and control activities of others so as to realise organization's goals.

The job of a manager is indeed highly demanding and challenging. Today's manager is expected to do in a single day what his/her forerunner might have done in a whole week. More important than the volume of work is its bewildering nature. Decisions may have to be made, taking into account the policies of the

Central and State Governments, the maze of legislations on the subject, the money available, the sensitivity of trade unions and above all the sentiments of the consumers and the public.

The present-day management is a complex function. Social, economic and technological developments are rapidly changing the business environment; the increasing size of the business unit is introducing new problems; national boundaries are fast disappearing, and companies are facing competition in their domestic markets; and governments, because the national economy is so closely linked with industrial performance, are pressing for greater productivity and the expansion of export sales. Management, in its role of entrepreneur, producer and employer of labour, is the economic spearhead of society, and hence its task is to co-ordinate the factors of production efficiently, with particular regard to labour relations which probably present the greatest challenge.

Henry Mintzberg, a graduate student at MIT, in the late 1960s undertook a careful study of five executives to determine what they did on their jobs. Based on his observations of these executives, Mintzberg concluded that managers perform ten different, interrelated jobs, or sets of behaviours attributed to their jobs. As shown in Table 1, these ten roles can be grouped as being primarily concerned with interpersonal relationships, transfer of information, and decision-making.

Management Skills

Manager needs certain skills if he/she were to be successful in his/her tasks. Three essential management skills have been identified in this context. They are technical, human, and conceptual.

A technical skill is an ability to use a special proficiency or expertise relating to a method, process, or procedure. Accountants, engineers, and attorneys, for example, possess technical skills acquired through formal education. Most jobs have technical skill components. Some require formal education (e.g., engineer), while others allow skills to be acquired through appropriate training and job experience (e.g., a sales person).

Human skill is the ability to work well in co-operation with other persons. It emerges as a spirit of trust, enthusiasm, and genuine involvement in interpersonal relationships. A person with good human skills will have a high degree of self-awareness and a capacity to understand or empathise with the feelings of others. Since managers get things done through others, they must have good human skills to communicate, motivate and delegate.

Table 1. Mintzberg's Managerial Roles

Interpersonal	Informational	Decisional
Figurehead: The manager performs certain functions such as receiving important visitors and signing documents. **Leader:** The manager motivates and encourages subordinates. **Liaison:** The manager establishes and maintains a network of relationships with outside persons to bring information and favours to the organization.	**Nerve centre:** Much of the non-routine information coming into the organization is received by the manager. **Disseminator:** The manager must transmit much of the information received to subordinates. **Spokesperson:** Information about the organization must be transmitted to outsiders.	**Entrepreneur:** The manager acts as a initiator and designer of the controlled change in the organization. **Disturbance handler:** Non-routine problems must be dealt with. Resource allocator: The manager allocates the monetary and non - monetary resources of the organization. **Negotiation:** The manager frequently must negotiate with outsiders in matters affecting the organization.

Table 2 outlines number of skills that educators feel should be taught to future managers. These skills cut across the three skills just discussed. They are all well covered in the chapters that follow.

Table 2. Some "Teachable" Managerial Skills

Interpersonal Relations	- Ability to enter into and maintain effective interpersonal relationships with others in the work setting.
Leadership	- Ability to influence and direct the behaviour of others and to motivate, help, and train subordinates.
Conflict Resolution	- Ability to mediate between conflicting parties, resolve disturbances and negotiate differences with others.
Information Processing	- Ability to collect information, organising information for decision-making purposes, and disseminate information.
Decision - Making	- Ability to know when a decision is needed, diagnose a situation, search for alternative solutions, evaluate potential consequences and select an alternative.
Resource Allocation	- Ability to distribute physical and human resources among competing demands.
Entrepreneurism	- Ability to recognise problems, implement solutions, and take advantage of opportunities for constructive change.
Introspection	- Ability to understand one's job and self and to learn through self-study and awareness.

All good managers ultimately have the ability to view the organization or situation as a whole and solve problems to the benefit of all concerned. This is a **conceptual skill** that draws heavily on one's mental capacities to identify problems and opportunities, gather and interpret relevant information and make good problem-solving decisions that serve the organization's purpose.

Although all three skills are essential at each managerial level, their relative importance tends to vary across levels. Technical skills are relatively more important at lower management levels where supervisors are dealing with concrete problems. Broader, more ambiguous, and longer term decisions dominate the manager's concers at higher levels, where conceptual skills gain in relative importance. Human skills remain fairly consistent in their importance across the managerial levels.

Organization is the place where managers practise the art of management. Organization signifies an institution or some sub-units of an institution. Thus, business units, universities, and departments within these institutions are organizations. When we talk about organizations, we refer mainly to **formal organizations**. In any institution there will be informal organizations also. An informal organization denotes the relationships and interactions that occur among members but are not formally sanctioned by the formal organization. Surprisingly, informal organizations have considerable influence on behaviour of employees in any institution.

Organizations are social inventions for accomplishing goals through group effort. They combine structure and relationship–technology and human beings. Human behaviour is a vital part of any organization and human problems continue to be the major challenge facing managers today. Human behaviour in organizations is rather complex and unpredictable. It can be understood only in the framework of behavioural science. Since a manager's job is inherently one of working with and through other people, "people skills" have become a valuable asset to him.

CONCEPT

Human organizations are all around–military organizations, social clubs, hospitals, political parties, business just to name a few. Each organization has its own set of objectives, and in order to function effectively, each organization sub-divides its overall task into various jobs. As jobs differ in their requirements, likewise, people differ in aptitude, abilities and interest, and along many dimensions. Faced with such variability in people and jobs, programmes for the more human use of our human resources are essential.

The manager of tomorrow needs to develop better understanding and insight of the social reality, and the organizational dynamics, simultaneously acquiring greater competence to manage himself, thereby reinforcing himself with the relevant skills of understanding and working with people, the vital aspect of organizational life. This is where organizational behaviour comes into picture.

OB scientists and practitioners study and attempt to solve organizational problems by using knowledge derived from research in the **behavioural science**, such as psychology and sociology. In other words, the field of OB is firmly rooted in science. It relies on research to derive valuable information about organizations and the complex processes operating within them. Such knowledge is used as the basis for helping to solve a wide range of organizational problems. OB specialists have sought to learn about a large variety of issues involving people in organizations. In fact, over the past few decades OB has developed into a field so diverse that its researchers have examined just about every conceivable aspect of behaviour in organization.

The study of people at work is generally referred to as the study of organizational behaviour. It refers to the attitudes and behaviours of individuals and groups in organizations. It is concerned with the understanding, prediction and control of human behaviour in organizational context.

Organizational behaviour is the study and application of knowledge about how people act within organizations. It is a human tool for human benefit. It applies broadly to the behaviour of people in all types of organizations, such as business, government, schools, and service organizations. Wherever organizations are, there is a need to understand organizational behaviour

OB APPLIES THE SCIENTIFIC METHOD TO PRACTICAL MANAGERIAL PROBLEMS

OB refers to seeking knowledge and to studying behavioural processes. This should not be surprising since, as we noted earlier, OB knowledge is based on the behavioural sciences. Although neither as sophisticated as the study of physics or chemistry (nor as mature as these fields), the orientation of the field of OB is still scientific in nature. Thus, like other scientific fields, OB seeks to develop a base of knowledge by using an empirical, research-oriented approach. That is, it is based on systematic observation and measurement of the phenomena of interest. As we will describe later in this chapter – and as you will see for yourself as you read this book-organizational research is neither easy nor foolproof. Yet, it is widely agreed that the scientific method is the best way to learn about behaviour in organizations. For this reason, the scientific orientation should be acknowledged as a hallmark of the field of OB.

Why is it so important to learn about behaviour in organizational settings? The answer depends on whom you ask. To social scientists, learning about human behaviour on the job - "what makes people tick" in organizations – is valuable for its own sake. After all, scientists are interested in the generation of knowledge – in this case, insight into the effects of organizations on people, and the effects of people on organizations. This is not to say, however, that such knowledge has no value outside of scientific circles. Far from it! OB specialists also work hard at applying knowledge from scientific studies, putting it to good practical use. As they seek to improve organizational functioning and the quality of life of people working in organizations, they rely heavily on knowledge derived from OB research. Thus, there are both scientific and applied facets of the field of OB-aspects that not only coexist but also complement each other. Indeed, just as knowledge about physics can be put to use by engineers, and engineering data can be used to test theories of basic physics, so too are knowledge and practical applications closely inter-twined in the field of OB.

OB specialists use their knowledge about behaviour in organizations not only to help suggest ways of improving organizational problems in general, but also to conduct research designed specifically to solve problems in a particular organization. In other words, OB specialists use the scientific method to derive both general knowledge about behaviour in organizations (referred to as normal science research) and specific knowledge used to solve problems in a particular organization (referred to as action research). Although the underlying reasons for conducting the research may be different, both approaches share something in common their reliance on the scientific method. Regardless of one's goals for learning about behaviour in organizations – deriving theoretical or practical knowledge of organizational behaviour in general or insight into a specific organization – the scientific approach is a central defining characteristic of modern OB.

O.B. Defined

Organizational behaviour has emerged as an exciting and distinct discipline though it is a relatively young field of inquiry that borrows many concepts and methods from the behavioural and social sciences. It is a science of mental and behavioural life. It is concerned with the interactions between the individual, group and the organizational environment. OB has become a multidisciplinary endeavour and a way of thinking. A manager today is required to have greater sensitivity towards his "human resource", and is expected to form relationships in many directions. "People skill" runs through the various roles and activities of a manager. People in developed countries depend primarily on behavioural scientists and organizational psychologists for their progress and not on farmers, traders or landlords.

Some of the definitions given by the various authors are as follows :

1. "Organizational behaviour is the study and application of knowledge about how people act within organizations. It is a human tool for human benefit. It applies broadly to the behaviour of people in all types of organization such as business, government, schools and service organizations."
2. "Organizational behaviour is directly concerned with the understanding, prediction, and control of human behaviour in organization".
3. "It is a field of study that investigates the impact that individuals, groups, and structure have on behaviour within organizations for the purpose of applying such knowledge towards improving an organization's effectiveness."
4. "Organizational behaviour is the study of organizational components, and their impact on human behaviour and organizational performances. Such study can benefit from various behavioural and social sciences."
5. "Organizational behaviour means the study of the behaviour of individuals and groups in organizations and organizations themselves, as they act and interact to attain desired outcomes."
6. "Organizational behaviour is the systematic study of the nature of organizations : how they begin, grow, and develop, and their effect on individual members, constituent groups, other organizations, and larger institutions."
7. "Organizational behaviour is an academic discipline concerned with understanding and describing human behaviour in an organizational environment. It seeks to shed light on the whole complex human factor in organizations by identifying causes and effects of that behaviour."

Characteristics of OB

The field of organizational behaviour contains a number of features. They are the following:

1. It focuses primarily on people. It is a systematic study of the actions and attitudes that people exhibit within organizations.
2. It emphasizes the interactions and relations between the organization and individual behaviour.
3. OB is specifically concerned with work-related behaviour and job satisfaction.
4. A key activity in OB is developing an environment in which people are motivated.
5. OB takes in and goes beyond psychology, group dynamics, organizational psychology, and industrial sociology.
6. It seeks to fulfill both employee needs and organizational objectives.
7. Larry L. Cummings emphasized that organizational behaviour is a way of thinking – a way of conceiving problems and arculating research and action solutions.

An analysis of these definitions reveals that almost all of them emphasise:

1. Organizational behaviour is the study of human behaviour.
2. Organizational behaviour is about behaviour in organizations.
3. Understanding of human behaviour is important in improving organizational effectiveness.

O.B. : A Working Definition

Organizational behaviour is the field that seeks knowledge of behaviour in organizational settings by systematically studying individual, group, and organizational processes. This knowledge is sought as an end in itself by scientists who are interested in basic human behaviour, and by practitioners interested in enhancing organizational effectiveness and individual well-being in organizations. Before beginning our examination of this field, it would be useful to further describe some of the key aspects referred to in our definition.

OB FOCUSES ON THREE LEVELS OF ANALYSIS

INDIVIDUALS, GROUPS, AND ORGANIZATIONS

To best appreciate behaviour in organizations, OB specialists cannot focus exclusively on individuals acting alone. After all, in organizational settings people frequently work together in groups. Furthermore, people - alone and in groups - both influence and are influenced by their work environments. Considering this, it should not be surprising to learn that the field of OB focuses on three distinct levels of analysis – individuals, groups, and organizations.

Nature and Scope of OB

1. **A Field of Study and not a Discipline:** Organizational behaviour is regarded as an emerging field of knowledge and not a discipline. OB is not a complete and accepted science. It has just begun to synthesize borrowed concepts, and processes in the field of enquiry. Its principles are difficult to define in scientific terms and its boundaries are not clear.
2. **Interdisciplinary Approach:** OB has its roots in such well-established fields as psychology, sociology, and anthropology. It also takes relevant concepts from economics, political science, and law. It integrates the relevant knowledge drawn for these disciplines.
3. **An Applied Science:** As the applied study of human behaviour in organizations, OB is oriented towards understanding the forces that affect behaviour so that their effects may be predicted and guided towards effective functioning of organization.
4. **Behavioural Approach to Management:** OB is directly concerned with the human side of management, but it is not the whole of management. In other words, OB does not intend to replace the whole of management theory. As against the technical dimensions, OB is related with the conceptual and human dimensions of management.
5. **Concern with Environment:** Larry Cummings suggests – "The field has a distinctly humanistic tone, reflected in the concern for self-development, personal growth, and self-actualization. However, there is another side that exphasizes operant learning models and behaviour modification, which reflects a concern with environmental determinism rather than with self - actualization."
6. **Scientific Method Foundation:** OB follows the scientific method and makes use of logic theory in its investigations and in answering the research questions. The field is greatly influenced by norms of skepticism, caution, replication, and public exposure of knowledge based on facts.
7. **Contingency Orientation:** OB concepts reflect situational or contingency conditions. This approach is directed towards developing managerial actions that are most appropriate for a specific situation. The effectiveness of a particular action is contingent upon the situation in which it is utilized. To solve a particular organizational problem, the OB manager follows the "it-all-depends" proposition.
8. **Levels of Performance Analysis:** The field of OB embraces three levels of performance analysis : (i) the individual, (ii) the group, and (iii) the formal organization. These are not mutually exclusive and should be treated with equal importance. Together all three provide the proper insight about organizational behaviour.
9. **Few Absolutes:** There are only few universal principles that explain organizational behaviour. There are laws in the physical sciences that apply in a wide range of situations. But human beings are very complex and are not alike, which limits the OB manager to make simple and accurate generalizations about human behaviour.

10. A Systems Approach: OB is a systemic vision as it takes into account all the variables affecting organizational functioning. It analyses the behaviour in view of psychological, social and cultural factors. It carefully links the variables together.

11. Other Features

(i) OB is a normative and value centered science.

(ii) It is at once empirical, interpretive, critical and creative science too.

(iii) It utilizes two kinds of logic – linear and non–linear. Linear logic is concerned with systematic analysis of activities, whereas non–linear logic is related with metaphors.

(iv) It is characterized by the acceptance of a human resource model.

Luthans, conceptualised a model for organizational behaviour, reproduced in Fig. 1, below. Developing this model, Luthans very aptly conceptualised formal organizations interacting with human beings and emphasising that all behaviour is preceded and caused by this inter-action. Thus, 'represents' the integrating theme for the new behaviour approach to management.

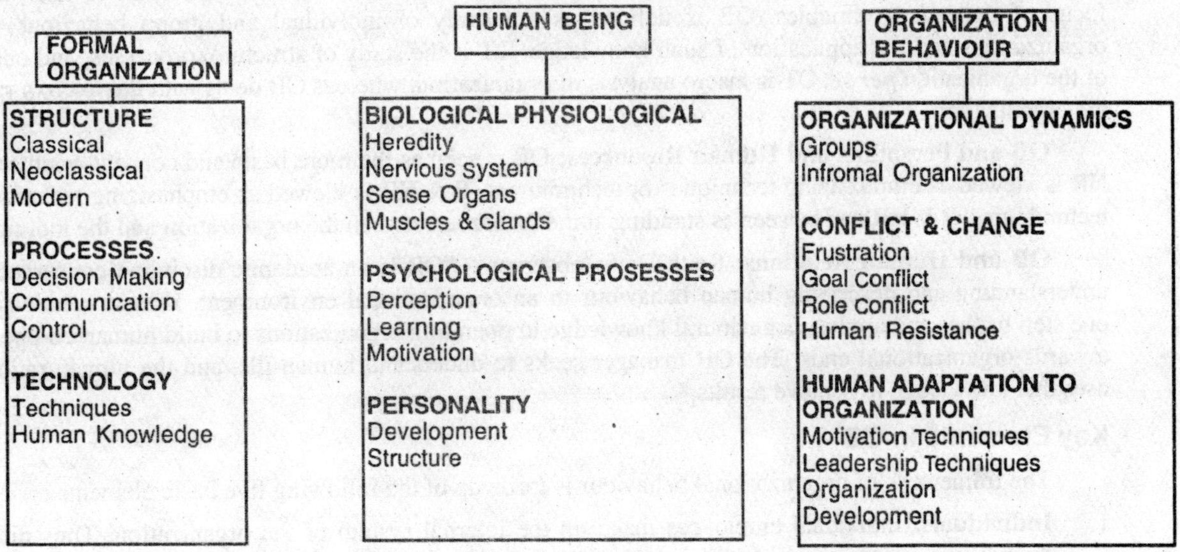

Fig.1. The Conceptual Model for Organizational Behaviour

From the standpoint of behaviour science the process of organizational behaviour is represented in Fig. 2.

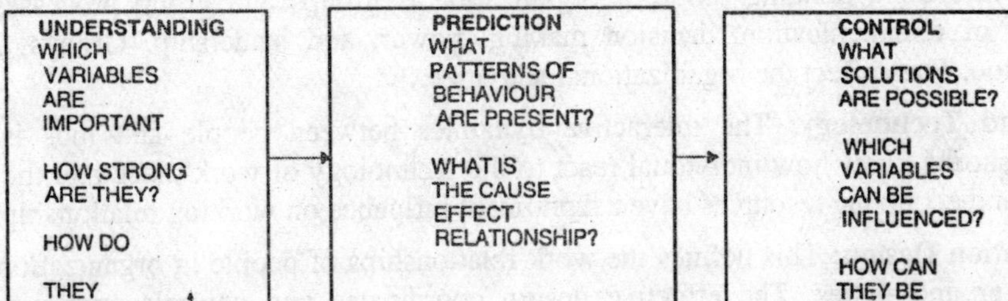

Fig. 2. Process of Organizational Behaviour

Synoptically, Organizational Behaviour is a systematic attempt to understand the behaviour of people in organizations to which they are an integral part. Kelly views it as a discipline that is concerned with the study of the behaviours and attitudes of man in an organizational setting: an organization's effect on his perceptions, feelings, and actions and his behaviour affects the achievement of the organization's purposes. Individuals, small groups, and total organization comprise the units of observations for organizational behaviour. Organizational Behaviour like organizational theory, for this purpose, draws upon various other disciplines like psychology, sociology, anthropology, political science, economics, etc., integrates the knowledge so drawn, and advances it further through the development of its own concepts, tools and techniques. Its importance as a discipline is ever increasing as it helps in-depth understanding of organizations and the people in them, behavioural science as a backbone for such a study.

Organizational behaviour has now become the widely accepted academic discipline. However, it is referred to by different names, organizational behaviour, behavioural science, human relations, or organizational theory. Though each of them studies human behaviour in organization, they differ in their approaches and emphasis. In the following paragraphs, a distinction between OB and other closely related disciplines is presented :

OB and Organizational Psychology: Both fields focus upon explaining human behaviour within organization. But their difference lies in the fact that OP restricts its explanatory constructs to those at the psychological level. OB draws constructs from multiple disciplines. However, as the domain of OP continues to expand, the difference between OB and OP is diminishing.

OB and Organization Theory: The distinction is based on two differences: unit of analysis and focus of dependent variables. OB is defined as the study of individual and group behaviour within organizations and the application of such knowledge. OT is the study of structure, processes, and outcome of the organization *per se*. OT is macro analysis of organization, whereas OB deals with the micro aspect of the organization.

OB and Personnel and Human Resources: OB is seen as the more basic and concept-oriented, P & HR is viewed as emphasizing techniques or technologies. P & HR is viewed as emphasizing techniques or technologies. P & HR can be seen as standing at the interface between the organization and the individual.

OB and Human Relations: Keith Davis observes – "OB is an academic discipline concerned with understanding and describing human behaviour in an organizational environment. Human relations goes one step further and applies behavioural knowledge in operating organizations to build human co-operation towards organizational ends. The OB manager seeks to understand human ills, and the human rationalist uses that knowledge to achieve results."

Key Elements in OB

The framework of organizational behaviour is made up of the following five basic elements :

1. **Individuals:** Individual employees make up the internal system of the organization. They differ in their skills, perception, motivation, learning abilities, and so forth. Thus, their behaviour and performance is greatly affected. People are the living, thinking, feeling beings who create the organization.
2. **Groups:** A second building block of organization is groups and group processes. These involve processes of communication, decision making, power, and leadership. Groups are dynamic and informal too. They affect the organizational activities.
3. **Tasks and Technology:** The interactive dynamics between people and jobs is important. The manager should know how individual react to the technology of work place and the work itself. The physical and economic resources have a significant influence on working relationships.
4. **Organization Design:** This defines the work relationships of people in organization. It is concerned with power and duties. The effective design coordinates and controls employee behaviour and facilitates performance.
5. **Environment:** Organizations do not exist in a vacuum but they continuously interact with their external environment. They are a part of a larger economic and social system. Environment influences the attitudes and working styles of people. Hence, it must be considered in the study of human behaviour in organizations.

These key elements and their interaction is shown in Fig. 3.

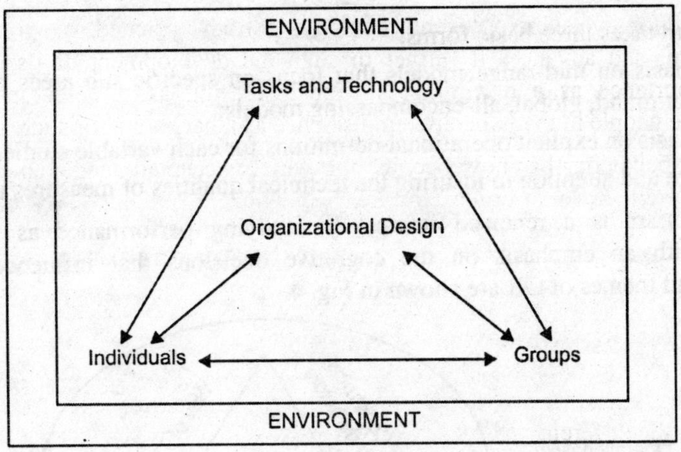

Fig. 3

Source : Adapted from David A. Nadler, J. Richard Hackman, and Edward E. Lawler III, *Managing Organizational Behaviour*, 1979.

Goals of Organizational Behaviour

The basic goal of the study of organizational behaviour is to improve the processes by which the organization functions. It helps managers and employees to understand the complex dynamics of the various components which may enhance or detract the organization from achieving its goals.

Organizational behaviour is vitally concerned with understanding, predicting and controlling human behaviour for improved performance. As Nadler and Tushman write: "Ultimately the organization's work gets done through people, individually or collectively, on their own or in collaboration with technology. Therefore, the management of organizational behaviour is central to the management task – a task that involves the capacity to understand the behaviour patterns of individuals, groups, and organizations, to predict what behavioural responses will be elicited by various managerial actions, and finally to use this understanding and these predictions to achieve control."

Dimensions and Themes of OB

Organizational behaviour is generally considered to comprise three major dimensions – technical, conceptual, and behavioural. In the past, managers either ignored the human and behavioural dimensions of their job or they made some very simplistic assumptions about them. Cummings has summarized the dimensions and themes of organizational behaviour in following way. According to him, three characteristics define organizational behaviour:

1. A body of constructs, models, and facts drawn from observations about individuals, groups, and organizations and attempting to predict and explain performance.
2. A way of thinking that emphasizes the following:
   (a) an independent variable-dependent variable orientation;
   (b) change as a desirable outcome for organizations;
   (c) a humanistic tone with concern for the interests of organization members; and
   (d) a focus on performance effectiveness.
3. A system of technology : Out of basic research in the field, a set of specific tools has emerged for practitioners including training and development techniques, job-design techniques, methods for designing organizations and personnel management techniques.

These three dimensions of organizational behaviour are not static. On the contrary, they are constantly being altered and developed under the influence of three major themes that characterize the thinking of theorists and practitioners in the field :

1. Existentialism is a recognition that the phenomena studied in organizational behaviour are very complex, and that there are few if any absolute laws that can be used to understand the phenomena.

2. Operationalism takes three basic forms:
   (a) an emphasis on mid-range models that focus on specific sub areas of the field rather than an attempt at grand, global, all-encompassing models;
   (b) an emphasis on explicit operational definitions for each variable studied;
   (c) great care and attention in insuring the technical qualities of measures used in research.
3. Neo-Behaviourism is a renewed interest in studying performance as a function of motivated behaviour, with an emphasis on the cognitive decisions that influenced the behaviour. These dimensions and themes of OB are shown in Fig. 4.

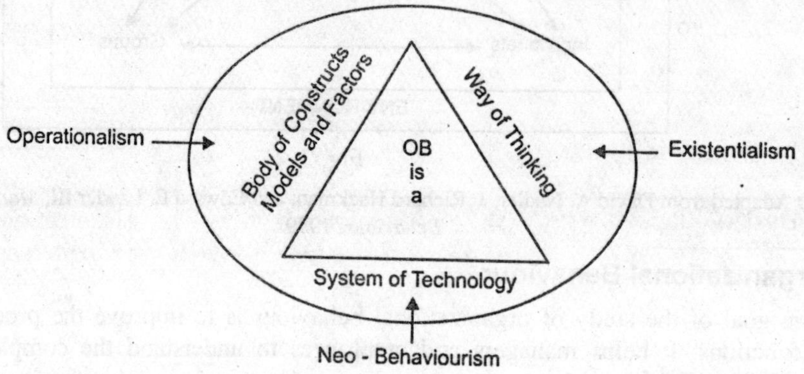

Fig. 4

Source : Adapted from Andrew D. Szilagyi, Jr. & Marc J. Wallace, Jr., *Organizational Behaviour and Performance* (1980), p.11.

OB SEEKS THE BETTERMENT OF HUMAN RESOURCES

In the early part of the twentieth century, as rail roads opened up the western portion of the United States and the nation's population rapidly grew (if doubled from 1880 to 1920), the demand for manufactured products was great. New manufacturing plants were built, attracting waves of new immigrants in search of a living wage and labourers lured off farms by the employment prospects that factory work offered. These early factories were gigantic, noisy, hot, and highly regimented in short, brutal places in which to work. Bosses demanded more and more of their employees, and treated them like disposable machines, replacing those who quit or who died from accidents with others who waited outside the factory gates. Obviously, the managers of one hundred years ago held very negative views of employees. They assumed that people were basically lazy and irresponsible and treated them with disrespect. This very negativistic approach, which has been with us for many years, reflects the traditional view of management – what Douglas McGregor called **Theory X.** This philosophy of management assumes that people are basically lazy, dislike work, need direction, and will only work hard when they are goaded into performing (that is, because there is a carrot at the end of the stick).

Today, however, if you asked a diverse group of corporate officials to describe their basic views of human nature, you'd probably find some more optimistic thoughts. Although some of today's managers still believe that people are basically lazy, many others would disagree, arguing that it's not that simple. They would claim that most individuals are at least as capable of working hard as they are of "goofing off." If employees are recognized for their efforts (such as by being appropriately paid) and are given an opportunity to succeed (such as by being well trained), they may be expected to work very hard without being pushed. Thus, employees may put forth a great deal of effort simply because they want Management's job, then, to create those conditions that make people want to perform as desired. The approach that assumes that people are not intrinsically lazy, but are willing to work hard when the right conditions prevail is known as the **Theory Y** orientation. This philosophy assumes that people have a psychological need to work and seek achievement and responsibility. In contrast to the Theory X philosophy of management, which essentially demonstrates distrust for people on the job, the Theory Y approach is strongly associated with promoting the betterment of human resources (for a summary of the differences, see Fig. 5).

As you might suspect, the Theory Y perspective currently prevails among those interested in organizational behaviour. Recognizing that people are capable of performing desirable behaviours under the right working conditions does not reflect a Pollyanna - like belief that people always will act responsibly. Rather, it assumes that people are highly responsive to their work environments; how they are treated will influence how they act.

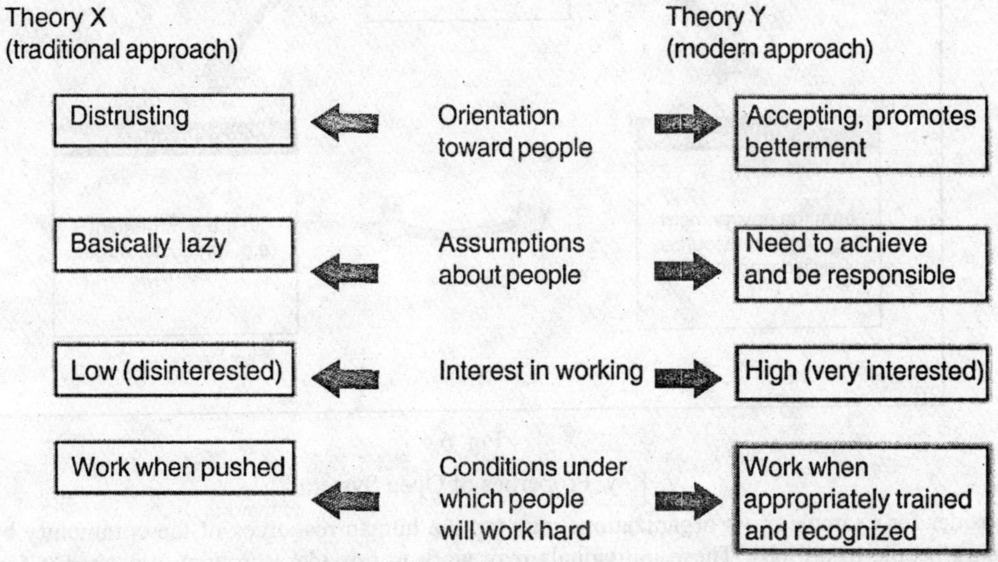

Fig. 5 Theory X Versus Theory Y – A Summary

In fact, OB scientists are very interested in learning exactly what conditions will lead people to behave in the most positive ways. The conditions in which employees are treated favourably will help them become more committed to their organizations and to go above and beyond the call of duty. In contrast, employees who are exploited will act more negatively – slacking off, behaving antisocially (e.g., stealing), or eventually quitting. In short, modern OB assumes that there are no intrinsic reasons why work settings cannot be made both pleasant and productive.

OB RECOGNIZES THE DYNAMIC NATURE OF ORGANIZATIONS

Thus far, our characterization of the field of OB has focused more on individual behaviour than on organizations as a whole. Nonetheless, it is important to point out that both OB scientists and practitioners do pay a great deal of attention to the nature of organizations themselves. Under what conditions will organizations change? How are organizations structured? How do organizations interact with their environments? Questions such as these are of major interest to specialists in OB. But before we can consider them – we must first clarify exactly what we mean by an organization. Although you probably have a very good idea of what an organization is, and would know one if you saw it, you would probably find it difficult to define an organization exactly. Thus, we offer the following definition. An **organization** is a structured social system consisting of groups and individuals working together to meet some agree - on objectives. In other words, organizations consist of structured social units, such as individuals and/or work groups, who strive to attain a common goal, such as to produce and sell a product at a profit.

In studying organizations, OB scientists recognize that organizations are not static, but dynamic and ever-changing entities. In other words, they recognize that organizations are **open system,** that is, self-sustaining systems that use energy to transform resources from the environment (such as raw materials) into some form of output (for example, a finished product). Fig. 6 summarizes some of the key properties of open system. As this diagram makes clear, organizations receive input from their environments and continuously transform it into output. This output gets transformed back to input, and the cyclical operation continues.

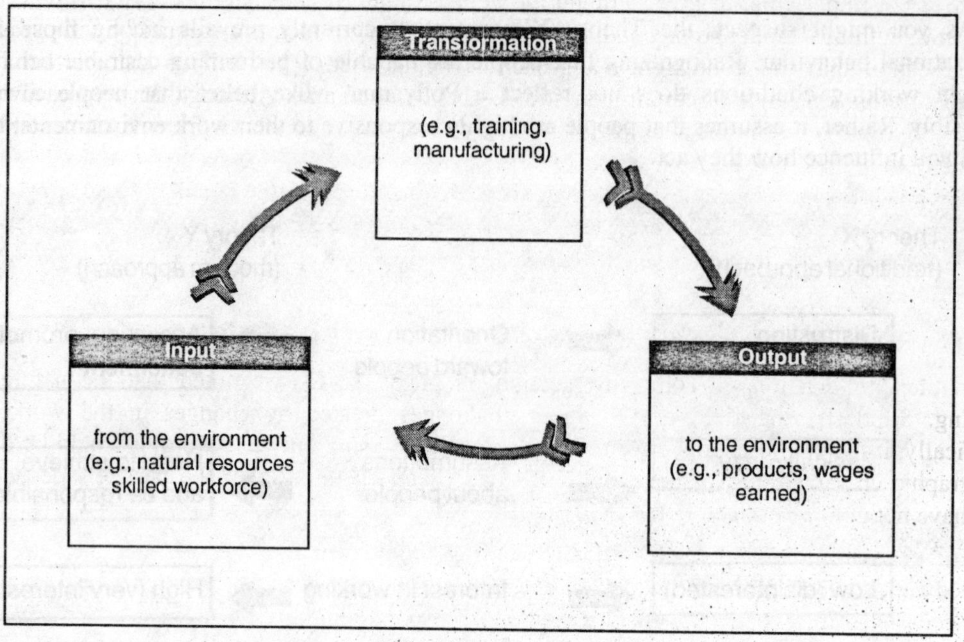

Fig. 6

Key Properties of Open System.

Consider for example, how organizations may tap the human resources of the community by hiring and training people to do jobs. These individuals may work to provide a product in exchange for wages. They then spend these wages, putting money back into the community, allowing more people to afford the company's products. This, in turn creates the need for still more employees, and so on. If you think about it this way, it's easy to realize that organizations are dynamic and constantly changing. In this way, they are like the operations of the human body. As people breathe, they take in oxygen and transform it into carbon dioxide. This, in turn, sustains the life of green plants, which in turn emit oxygen for people to breathe. The continuous flow of the open system characterizes not only human life but also organizations. The dynamic nature of organizations is particularly apparent when one considers all the changes in organizations that are likely to occur in the future.

OB ASSUMES THERE IS NO "ONE BEST" APPROACH

What's the most effective way to motivate people? What style of leadership works best? Should groups or individuals be used to make important organizational decisions? Although questions such as these appear to be quite reasonable, there is a basic problem with all of them. Namely, they all assume that there is a simple, unitary answer.

That is, they suggest that there is one best approach: one best way to motivate, to lead, and to make decisions.

Specialists in the filed of OB today agree that there is no one best approach when it comes to such complex phenomena. To assume otherwise is not only overlay simplistic and naive, but, as you will see, grossly inaccurate. When it comes to studying human behaviour in organizations, there are no simple answers. The processes involved are too complex to permit such a luxury. Instead, OB scholars recognize that behaviour in work settings is the complex result of many interacting forces. This fact is recognized in what is known as the **contingency approach,** an orientation that is a hallmark of modern OB. Consider, for example, how an individual's personal characteristics (e.g., personal attitudes and beliefs) may work in conjunction with situational factors (e.g., an organization's climate or relations between co-workers) which may all work together when it comes to influencing how a particular individual is likely to behave on the job.

When we teach OB to our students, we often find ourselves answering their questions by saying, "It depends." As our knowledge of behaviour on the job becomes more and more complex, it becomes difficult, if not impossible, to give "straight answers." Rather, it is usually necessary to report that people will do certain things "under some conditions" or "when all other factors are equal." Such phrases provide a clear indication that the contingency approach is being used. They tell us that certain behaviour is contingent on the existence of certain conditions – hence, the name. Although this approach may frustrate and disappoint some because it makes it impossible to use simple cookbook formulas to predict and explain behaviour, we believe that such a complaint is unjustified. After all, it is accuracy, and not simplicity, that is the ultimate goal of our studies of behaviour in organizations. In the chapters that follow, you will see how this approach prevails with respect to various aspects of the field. In presenting this material to you, we will attempt to walk the fine line between being so complex as to be incomprehensible and so simplistic as to be misleading.

OB CONFRONTS THE CHALLENGES OF WORK FORCE DIVERSITY

In the Organization of Tomorrow section on pages 12-13, we noted that the nature of work is changing. Similarly, the field of OB faces challenges created by changes in the work force itself. Specifically, if we had to characterize today's labour force using only one word, it would be diversity. The demographic characteristics of the work force have been changing over the past few decades, and such shifts have not gone unnoticed in the field of OB.

For example, there are more women working today than ever before, and they are more highly educated and better trained for a wider variety of positions. However, many women still find that they are victimized by stereotypes and male dominated corporate cultures that keep them from advancing Furthermore, because women tend to shoulder a disproportionate share of the responsibility for family care in U.S. society, they frequently face conflicts between their careers and their families. As you will see throughout this book, these and other issues related to gender diversity are of considerable interest to OB scientists and practitioners.

In addition to gender diversity, racial and cultural diversity is another potent demographic trend in the work force. The relative proportion of white Americans in the work force has been steadily shrinking as growing numbers of African-Americans, Hispanic-Americans, Asian-Americans, and foreign nationals enter the work force. If you consider that within these cultures there are various subcultures, it is clear that the current level of racial and ethnic diversity encountered in the work force is considerable. The matter of how this trend affects organizations is of great interest in the field of OB. Some accommodations to cultural diversity may involve simple decisions, such as offering a broader variety of ethnic dishes in the company cafeteria. But it's not always that simple. When people with different habits, values, and world views come together, the potential for misunderstanding and conflict rises.

The challenge for the field of OB is easier stated than accomplished: How can organizations tap the rich pool of resources offered by culturally diverse employees in a manner that minimizes interpersonal conflict among them? Although OB provides no easy answers to this question, it does provide some critical insight. As you will see, research on stereotyping, mentoring, communication, and conflict has contributed to our understanding of ways to work effectively in a multi-cultural environment.

OB TAKES A GLOBAL PERSPECTIVE

If you've ever travelled abroad, then you know how different from you people from various cultures can seem. Not only do they dress and speak in a different fashion, but they also may seem to behave and think quite differently. Whether these discrepancies strike you as quaint or curious, there can be little doubt that real differences exist among people of different nations. The idea that culture is an important determinant of people's actions and values is clearly an understatement – and a conclusion that has important implications for the study of organizational behaviour.

When the study of behaviour in organizations first emerged, the United States was the world's dominant economic power. As a result, much of what was learned about organizations came from a uniquely American middle class perspective. Today, however, it is clear that the economy is much more global in scope and orientation. There exist strong economic forces all over the world, and organizations operate within many different cultures. Even formerly communist nations, such as Russia, are rapidly developing into strong economic powers with growing organizations of their own. Moreover, many organizations have operations in several different countries.

Considering these trends, it would be seriously limiting – not to mention very misleading - to ignore the possibility that behaviour in organizations is affected by cultural differences. Indeed, there are clear signs that the field of OB is rapidly becoming increasingly international in its approach to the study of organizations.

Theorists have noted that the international perspective on OB is characterized by its comparative nature - that is, its tendency to examine OB concepts across different nations and cultures. Among the most popular questions asked by scientists in this area are : (1) How similar or different are people of various cultures with respect to different types of organizational behaviour? and (2) To what extent do OB theories and practices apply across different cultures?

Although it is usually very difficult to isolate the unique effects of culture (relative to other variables that might make a difference) when researching comparative cultural questions, many researchers have attempted to do so. Such efforts have proven worthwhile because they have revealed that theories of OB that the "Made in the U.S.A." may have limited value when it comes to applying them to other cultures. This is not to say that all such theories are useless. They are, in fact, far from it! Our point is that simply assuming a uni-cultural perspective can be very misleading, and that incorporating cultural differences into OB research is an effective way of learning about the cultural influences on OB.

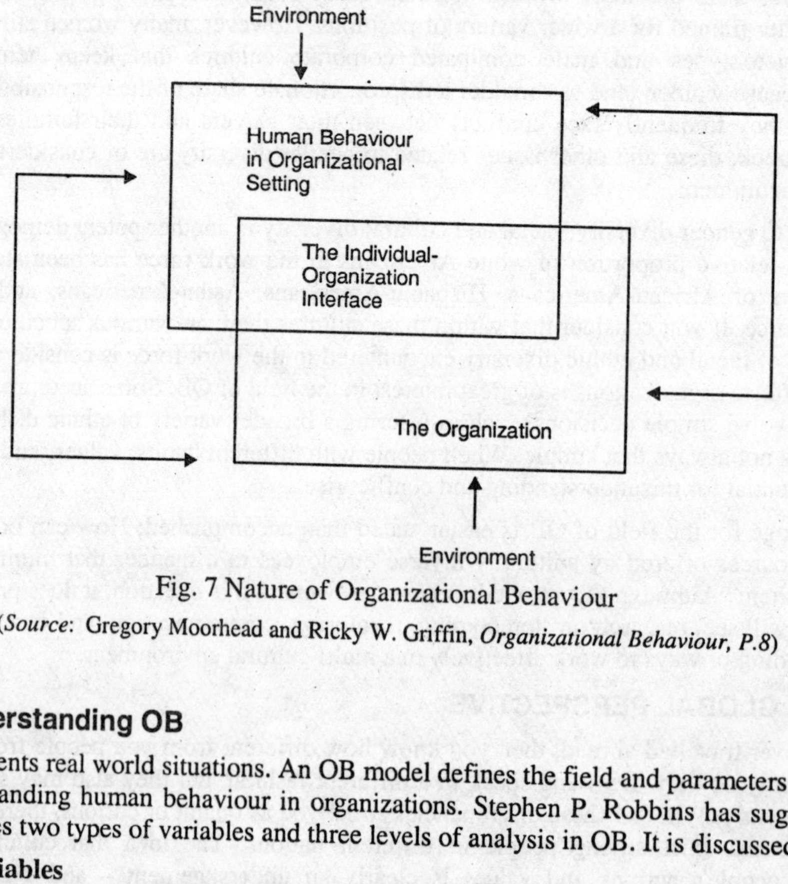

Fig. 7 Nature of Organizational Behaviour

(*Source*: Gregory Moorhead and Ricky W. Griffin, *Organizational Behaviour, P.8*)

A Model for Understanding OB

A model represents real world situations. An OB model defines the field and parameters and identifies variables for understanding human behaviour in organizations. Stephen P. Robbins has suggested an OB model which proposes two types of variables and three levels of analysis in OB. It is discussed below:

The Dependent Variables

A dependent variable is a response that is affected by an independent variable. Dependent variables are the critical determinants of an organization's human resources effectiveness. They include the following:

(a) Productivity: One of OB's major concerns is productivity. It is a performance measure and includes both efficiency and effectiveness. An OB manager must know what factors will influence the productivity of people, of groups, and of the overall organization.

(b) Absenteeism: It is a failure to report to work. absenteeism may disrupt the work flow and can result in a drastic reduction in quality of output.

(c) Turnover: A high rate of turnover increases recruiting, selection and training costs and hinders the efficient running of an organization. It is a loss of people, skills and ideas.

(d) Job satisfaction: It represents an attitude rather than a behaviour towards job. Although the belief that satisfied employees are more productive than dissatisfied employees still remains questionable, OB researchers consider it an important dependent variable.

Job stress, individual dissent, and innovation may be the new dependent variables in years to come.

The Independent Variables

Independent variables cause some change in the dependent variables. They are determinant factors. There are three levels of analysis in this OB model and each level is constructed upon the previous level:

(i) Individual level variables: People have different personality characteristics, values and attitudes and ability levels that influence their behaviour at work. In addition to these, they have different patterns of perception, decision making, learning, and motivation. Most of these factors cannot be altered by managers.

(ii) Group level variables: Robbins says that the behaviour of people in groups is more than the sum total of each individual acting in his own way. Hence, the OB manager should understand how communication patterns, group decision making processes, leadership styles, power and politics, inter-group relations, and levels of conflict affect dynamics of group behaviour.

(iii) Organization system level variables : Organizations also have the greater impact than the sum of their individual members. The formal structural pattern of the organization, its human resource policies, levels of work stress, and internal culture all influence the productivity and satisfaction of employees.

These three levels of analysis are not mutually exclusive. The field of organizational behaviour embraces them as being complementary. The OB manager should attempt to integrate these three levels of analysis.

REFERENCES

Andrew D. Szilagyi Jr. and Marc. J. Wallance Jr. *Organizational Behaviour and Performance*, Scott, Foreman and Company, Glenview, Illions, 1980, pp. 11-12.

D. Katz and R. Kahn, The Social Psychology of Organizations, Wiley, New York, 1978.

D. McGregor, *The Human Side of Enterprise*, McGraw Hill, New York, 1960.

D.A. Ricks, B. Toyne and Z. Martinez, *Recent Developments in International Management Research, Journal of Management*, Vol. 16, 1990, pp. 219-253.

Ernesto Imbassahy de Mello, *To Dignify the Human Being*, The Rotarian, July 1975, p.16.

Fred Luthans, '*Organizational Behaviour*', New York, McGraw Hill, 1989, p.6.

H. Randolph Bobbitt Jr *et al*, '*Organizational Behaviour*', New Jersey, Prentice Hall, 1978, p.6.

J. Case, A Company, of Business People, Inc. April, 1993, pp. 79-94.

J. Fierman, Why Women Still Don't Hit the Top, *Fortune*, July 30, 1990, pp. 40-46, 50-56, 57, 59-60.

J. Kelly, *Organizational Behaviour*, Richard D. Irwin Inc., Homewood, Illions, 1974.

J.M. Pennings, *Structural Contingency Theory*: A Reappraisal, in B.M. Staw and L.L. Cummings, Eds., Research in Organizational Behaviour, Greenwich. C.T., Jai Press, Vol. 14, 1992, pp. 267 - 310.

J.P. Fernandez and M. Barr, *The Diversity Advantage*, Lexington Books, New York, 1993.

Joe Kelly, *Organizational Behaviour*, Surjet Publications, Delhi, 1987, p.5.

John R. Schermerhorn, Jr. *et al*. Managing Organizational Behaviour, John Wiley & Sons, 1985, p. 26.

Kae H. Chung and Leon C. Megginson, '*Organizational Behaviour* – Development Managerial Skills', New York: Harper and Row, 1981, p.43.

Keith Davis and J.W. Newstrom, 'Human Behaviour at Work', *Organizational Behaviour*, New York, McGraw Hill, 1985, p.5.

Keith Davis, *Human Behaviour at Work*, Tata McGraw Hill Publishing Co. Ltd., New Delhi, 1981, pp. 517-522.

L.L. Cummings, *Towards Organizational Behaviour*, The Academy of Management Review, January, 1978, pp. 93-94, Quoted in Fred Luthans, *Organizational Behaviour*, McGraw Hill International Book Co. London, 1981, p.6.

M. Eldon & R.F. Chisholm, Emerging Varieties of Action Research, Introduction to Special Issue, *Human Relations*, 1993, Vol. 46, pp.121-142.

M. Maruyama, *Changing Dimensions in International Business*, Academy of Management Executives, Vol. 6. 1992, pp. 88-96.

Perrin Towers and Hudson Institute, *Workforce 2000 : Competing in a Seller's Market*, Towers Perrin, Valhalla, New York, 1990.

Quoted in *Organizational Behaviour*, Stephen P. Robins, Prentice Hall, p.5.

Richard M. Streers, *Introduction to Organizational Behaviour*, Scott, Foreman and Company, London, 1988, p.17.

Robert Albanese, Management Towards Accountability and Performance, Homewood, Richard D. Irwin. Inc. 1975, p.5.

S.E. Jackson and E.B. Aluerez, *Working Through Diversity as a Strategic Imperative*, in S.E. Jackson, Ed. Diversity in the Workplace, Guilford Press, New York, 1992, pp. 13-29.

Stephen, P. Robbins, *'Organizational Behaviour Concepts, Controversies and Applications'*, New Delhi: Prentice Hall of India 1989, p. 6.

V. Pucik, N.M. Tichy, and C.K. Barnett, *Globalizing Management*, Wiley, New York, 1993.

CHAPTER

2

Development of O.B.

Although today we take for granted the importance of understanding the functioning of organizations and the behaviour of people at work, this was not always the case. In fact, it was not until the early part of the twentieth century that the idea first developed, and only during the last few decades that it gained widespread acceptance.

New fields of study do not begin in a dramatic fashion but they have a long way of development. OB is an old concept because every civilization has taken interest in behaviour within organizations. Although, human relationships have existed since the beginning of time, the art and science of trying to deal with them in complex organizations is relatively new.

Like any other discipline, it is rather difficult, if not impossible to trace the date that represents the start of that activity. Concern for the welfare of workers has been in existence since the ages. As early as 4th century B.C. Kautilya's Arthshastra states that there existed a sound base for systematic management of human resources. The government provided systematic procedures for regulating employer-employee relationship. Even elsewhere, humans in organizations received management's attention much earlier. As early as 1800 B.C. itself 'minimum wage rate' and incentive wage plan were included in the Babylonian code of Hammurabi.

Robert Owen, a young Welsh factory owner, some time in the year 1800, was one of the first to emphasise the human factor in organization. He refused to give employment to children. He taught his workers the importance of working conditions and cleanliness. Even in his own factory Owen devoted as much attention to 'vital machines' as to 'inanimate machines.' His methods entitled him to be called the father of Personnel Management.

In 1835 Andrew Ure published his famous book 'The Philosophy of Manufactures' in which he vigorously emphasised the human factor as one of the crucial factors of production. He himself deeply believed in the importance of human factor and provided snacks, medical treatment and sickness benefits to workers.

Even in India around 1840, J.N. Tata took special interest in the welfare of his workers recognising the dignity of labour. He improved the working conditions at his factories. In 1886 he instituted pension plans and in 1895 accident compensation scheme. The Empress Mill experiment amply brings out the fact that to Jamshedji Tata, the human aspect of workers was of paramount concern to him.

The human aspect of workers which was recognised by Owen, Ure and Tata was not given due recognition and faded out with time, and even social scientists forget to mention them while tracing the history of behavioural sciences. Even, during the Second World War the importance of human being was recognised and the term was used. It will be no exaggeration if we say **Behavioural Science** is a very new science of a very ancient subject.

But experts of human behaviour have tried to chronicle the growth of the subject only from the beginning of the 19th century. The early part of 19th century is significant because it was during this period that the Industrial Revolution took place that resulted in the total transformation of the then industrial environment.

Platitudes about minimum wage rate, incentive wage plan and sound base for systematic management of human resources apart, there is no gainsaying the fact that life for an average employee, prior to the 19th century, was miserable to say the least. Working conditions in factories were brutal and back breaking.

People worked from dawn until dusk under intolerable conditions of disease, filth, danger and scarcity of resources. They had to work this way to survive, so that they had little time to improve job satisfaction.

SCIENTIFIC MANAGEMENT: THE EARLY APPROACH

The earliest attempts to study behaviour in organizations came out of a desire by industrial efficiency experts to improve worker productivity. Their central question was straightforward: What could be done to get people to do more work in less time? Attempts to answer this question were made at the turn of the century – a period of rapid industrialization and technological change in the United States. As engineers attempted to make machines more efficient, it was a natural extension of their efforts to work on the human side of the equation – making people more productive too. Given this history, it should not be too surprising that the earliest people we now credit for their contributions to OB were actually industrial engineers.

Frederick Winslow Taylor worked most of his life in steel mills, starting as a labourer and working his way up to the position of chief engineer. In the 1880s, while a foreman at Philadelphia's Midvale Steel Company, Taylor became aware of some of the inefficient practices of the employees. Noticing for example, that laborers wasted movements when shifting pig iron, Taylor studied the individual components of this task, and established what he believed was the best way – motion by motion – to perform it. A few years later, while a consulting engineer at Pittsburgh's Bethlehem Steel, Taylor similarly redesigned the job of loading and unloading rail cars so they too could be done as efficiently as possible. On the heels of these experiences, Taylor published his groundbreaking book, *Scientific Management*. In this work, Taylor argued that the objective of management is "to secure the maximum prosperity for the employer, coupled with the maximum prosperity of each employee."

Beyond identifying ways in which manual labour jobs can be performed more efficiently, Taylor's **scientific management** approach was unique in its focus on the role of employees as individuals. Taylor advocated two ideas that hardly seem special today, but were quite new eighty - five years ago. First, he recommended that employees be carefully selected and trained to perform their jobs – helping them become, in his own words, "first class" at some task. Second, he believed that increasing workers' wages would raise their motivation and make them more productive. Although this idea is unsophisticated by today's standards – and not completely accurate – Taylor may be credited with recognizing the important role of motivation in job performance. It was contributions like these that stimulated further study of behaviour in organizations and created an intellectual climate that eventually paved the way for the development of the field of OB. Acknowledging these contributions, management theorist Peter Drucker has described Taylor as "the first man in history who did not take work for granted, but who looked at it and studied it."

The publication of Scientific Management stimulated several other scientists to pick up and expand Taylor's ideas. for example, psychologist Hugo Munsterberg worked to **"humanize"** the jobs of people by explaining how the concepts of learning and motivation are relevant to the behaviour of people at work. Similarly, management writer Mary Parker Follet claimed that organizations could benefit by attempting to recognize the needs of employees.

The scientists who were closely influenced by Taylor were the industrial psychologists Frank and Lillian Gilbreth. This husband-and-wife team pioneered an approach known as **time-and-motion study,** a type of applied research designed to classify and streamline the individual movements needed to perform jobs with the intent of finding "the one best way" to perform them. Although this approach appears to be highly mechanical and dehumanizing, the Gilbreths, parents of twelve children, practiced Taylorism with a human face in their personal lives. In fact, you may even recall the story of how the Gilbreths applied the principles of scientific management to the operation of their household, as told in their classic film, Cheaper by the Dozen. The Gilbreths worked diligently applied their craft to an extremely humane goal outside their family – improving the welfare of people with physical handicaps.

THE HUMAN RELATIONS MOVEMENT: ELTON MAYO AND THE HAWTHORNE STUDIES

Despite the important contributions of scientific management, this approach did not go far enough in directing our attention to the wide variety of factors that might influence behaviour in work settings. The efficient performance of jobs and monetary incentives are very important, to be sure, although emphasizing these factors makes people feel like cogs in a machine. In fact, many employees and theorists alike rejected Taylorism, favouring instead an approach that focused on employees' own views and emphasized respect for individuals. At the forefront of this orientation was Elton W. Mayo, an organizational scientist and consultant widely regarded as the founder of what is called the **human relations movement.** This brand of management philosophy rejects the primarily economic orientation of scientific management, and focuses, instead, on non-economic, social factors operating in the workplace. Mayo and other proponents of the human relations movement were concerned with task performance, but realized that it was greatly influenced by the social conditions that existed in organizations – the way employees were treated by management, and the relationships they had with each other.

Failure of Scientific Management gave birth to the human relations movement which is characterised by heavy emphasis on employee cooperation and morale. Under this, people were to be treated as human beings and not as machines, listening to their needs and problems and involving them in decision-making in matters relating to working conditions. There are varied and complex reasons for this human relations position. Historically three of the most important contributing factors would be the Great Depression, the labour movement, the results of the now famous Hawthorne studies.

The stock exchange crash of 1929 in America marked the beginning of the Great Depression. The consequences of the Depression were wide-spread unemployment, decline of purchasing power, collapse of markets, and lowering of the standard of living of people. This phenomenon was world wide and not confined to America alone.

One positive outcome of the Depression was that management began to realise that production alone could not be its major function. Marketing, finance, and personnel were also required in order for a business to survive and grow. The Depression's aftermath of unemployment and insecurity bought to the surface human problems that managers were now forced to recognise and cope with. Personnel departments were either created or given more emphasis, and most managers now began to develop a new, awakened view of the human aspects of work. Human relations took an increased significance as an indirect, and in some cases direct, result of the Depression.

Mere creation or strengthening of personnel departments did not improve the plight of workers. Production still preceded people in order of importance in organizations. Decent hours of work, fair wages, and adequate working conditions were sacrificed for more production. There were people like Taylor, Ford, and Sloan who sincerely believed in giving labour due share. Such noble hearted souls were few and far between. In general, exploitation of labour continued.

Continued exploitation made workers realise that their protection lay in their own hands. They formed strong unions and this had the desired effect on management. Management began to place primary emphasis on employee relations, and secondary attention was given to wages, hours of work, and conditions of employment.

Unfortunately the human relations role also often came about for wrong reasons. In too many cases, it was forced on managers by labour threatening them with consequences of non-compliance. Ideally, it would have been better had human relations developed because of intrinsic motivation of practising managers to better understand and provide for the welfare of their employees.

Although the Depression and the labour movement were at least important indirect causes of the practice of human relations, the Hawthorne studies dominate the academic discussion on historical development. The studies gave academic status of the study of organizational behaviour.

In 1927 a series of studies were begun at the **Western Electric's Hawthorne Works** near Chicago. Inspired by scientific management, the researchers were interested in determining, among other things, the effects of illumination on work productivity. How brightly or dimly lit should the work environment be for people to produce at their maximum level? Two groups of female employees took part in the study. One group, the control room condition, did their jobs without any changes in lighting; the other group, the test room condition, worked while the lighting was systematically varied, sometimes getting brighter, and sometimes getting dimmer. The results were baffling: productivity increased in both locations. Just as surprising, there was no clear connection between illumination and performance. In fact, output in the test room remained high even when the level of illumination was so low that workers could barely see what they were doing!

In response to these puzzling findings Western Electric officials called in a team of experts headed by Elton Mayo. Attempting to replicate these results, Mayo and his colleagues examined the effects of a wide variety of different variables on productivity. Among these were the length of rest pauses, the duration of the workday and workweek, and the presence or absence of a free mid-morning lunch. How would these factors influence the amount of work performed? To answer this question, Mayo and his colleagues studied female employees working in the company's **Relay Room**. The results were once again quite surprising: Productivity improved following almost every change in working conditions. In fact, performance remained extremely high even when conditions were returned to normal, the way they were before the study began.

Not all of Mayo's studies showed that **Hawthorne** employees were highly productive, however. In fact, in another study conducted at the company's bank Wiring Room, male members of various work groups were observed during regular working conditions, and were interviewed at length after work. In this investigation, no attempts were made to alter the work environment. What Mayo found here also was surprising. Namely, instead of improving their performance, employees deliberately restricted their output. Not only did the researchers actually see the men stopping work long before quitting time, but in interviews the men admitted that they easily could do more if they desired.

Why did this occur, especially in view of the increased performance noted in the **Relay Room** studies? Eventually, Mayo and his associates recognized that the answer resided in the fact that organizations are social system. How effectively people worked depended, in great part, not only on the physical aspects of the working conditions experienced, but also the social conditions encountered. In the Relay Room studies, Mayo noted, productivity rose simply because people responded favourably to the special attention they received. Knowing they were being studied made them feel special and motivated them to do their best. Hence, it was these social factors more than the physical factors, that had such profound effects on job performance. The same explanation applied in the **Bank Wiring Room** study as well. Here, the employees feared that because they were being studied, the company was eventually going to raise the amount of work they were expected to do each day. To guard against the imposition of unreasonable standards (and, thus, to keep their jobs!), the men agreed among themselves to keep output low. In other words, informal rules (known as norms) were established about what constituted acceptable levels of job performance. These social forces at work in this setting proved to be much more potent determinants of job performance than the physical factors studied.

This conclusion, based on the surprising findings of the Hawthorne studies, is important because it ushered in a whole new way of thinking about behaviour at work. It suggests that to understand behaviour on the job, we must fully appreciate people's attitudes and the processes by which they communicate with each other. This way of thinking, so fundamental to modern OB, may be traced back to Elton Mayo's pioneering Hawthorne studies. In contrast with the scientific management views that prevailed at the time, this perspective was quite novel.

This is not to say, however, that the Hawthorne studies were, by any means, perfect. Indeed, by modern standards, the research was seriously flawed. The research violated several important rules. For example, no effort was made to assure that the rooms used in the study were identical in every way except for the variables studied (the level of illumination, the scheduling and duration of the rest pauses), making it possible for factors other than those being studied to influence the results. Interestingly, research on the topic of illumination is still being conducted today, although it is far more carefully conducted and sophisticated. Furthermore, because no attempt was made to assure that the employees chosen for study were representative of all those in their factory (or all manufacturing personnel generally), it is difficult to generalize the results of the study beyond those individuals studied.

The Hawthorne studies have been severely criticised particularly by Australian and English researchers as being inadequately controlled and interpreted. Despite some obvious methodological limitations, there are some interesting insights from the experiments that contribute to the better understanding of human behaviour in organizations. In particular, the experiments showed that the worker is not a simple tool but a complex personality interacting in a group situation that often is difficult to understand. The study revealed the importance of the social factor – the degree to which work performance depended not on the individual alone, but on the network of social relationships within which he operated. As more studies on organizations were carried out, it became evident that the informal associations to be found in almost every organization profoundly affect an individual's motivation to work, level of output and quality of performance.

Clearly, although the Hawthorne studies are imperfect, their impact on the field of OB is considerable. This contribution lies not with respect to what the research tells us about the effects of illumination, but what it revealed indirectly about the importance of human needs, attitudes, motives, and relationships in the workplace. In this respect, the work established a close link between the newly emerging field of OB, and the Behavioural Sciences of psychology and sociology - a connection that persists today. Although the human relations approach was gradually replaced by more sophisticated views, several of its ideas and concepts contributed greatly to the development of the field of OB. Little could those workers in that long-vanished plant outside of Chicago have guessed that their contribution to the social science of organizational behaviour would be so enduring!

CLASSICAL ORGANIZATIONAL THEORY

During the same time that proponents of scientific management got people to begin thinking about the interrelationships between people and their jobs, another approach to managing people emerged. This perspective, known as **classical organizational theory,** focused on the efficient structuring of overall organizations. This is in contrast, of course, to scientific management, which sought to effectively organize the work of individuals.

Several different theorists are identified with classical organizational theory. Among the first was Henri Fayol, a French industrialist who attribute his managerial success to various principles he developed. Among these are the following :

- A division of labour should be used because it allows people to specialize, doing only what they do best.
- Managers should have authority over their subordinates, the right to order them to do what's necessary for the organization.
- Lines of authority should be uninterrupted; that is, a scalar chain should exist that connects the top management to the lower level employees.
- There should exist a clearly defined unity of command, such that employees receive directions from only one other person, to avoid confusion.
- Subordinates should be given initiative to formulate and implement their plans.

Although many of these principles are still well accepted today, it is widely recognized that they should not always be applied in exactly the same way. For example, whereas some organizations thrive on being structured according to a unity of command, still others require that some employees take directions from several different superiors. For now, suffice it to say that current organizational theorists owe a debt of gratitude to Fayol for his pioneering and far-reaching ideas.

Probably the best-known classical organizational theorist is the German sociologist Max Weber. Among other things, Weber is well known for proposing a form of organizational structure well-known today – the bureaucracy. A **bureaucracy** is an organizational design that attempts to make organizations operate more efficiently by having a clear hierarchy of authority in which people are required to perform well-defined jobs. Weber's idea was that the bureaucracy is the one best way to efficiently organize work in all organizations (much as proponents of scientific management searched for the ideal way to perform a job). The elements of an ideal bureaucracy are summarized in Table1.

When you think about bureaucracies, negative images probably come to mind of lots of inflexible people getting bogged down in lots of red tape. (By the way, the phrase **"red tape"** is said to have become popular during **World War I**, when red tape was used on documents from the British government.

Characteristics of an Ideal Bureaucracy

According to Max Weber, bureaucracies must possess certain characteristics.

Here is a summary of the major defining characteristics of bureaucratic organizations.

Table 1

Formal rules and regulations	Written guidelines are used to control all employees' behaviours.
Impersonal treatment	Favouritism is to be avoided, and all work relationships are to be based on objective standards.
Division of labour	All duties are divided into specialized tasks and are performed by individuals with the appropriate skills.
Hierarchical structure	Positions are ranked by authority level in clear fashion from lower-level to upper-level ones.
Authority structure	The making of decisions is determined by one's position in the hierarchy; people have authority over those in lower-ranking positions.
Lifelong career commitment	Employment is viewed as a permanent, lifelong obligation on the part of the organization and its employees.
Rationality	The organization is committed to achieving its ends (e.g., profitability) in the most efficient manner possible.

Given the tendency for national governments to be bureaucratic in structure, it is not surprising that the term red tape came to refer to bureaucratic processes of all types. Weber's **"universal"** view of bureaucratic structure lies in contrast to the more modern approaches to organizational design in which it is recognized that different forms of organizational structure may be more or less appropriate under different situations. Although the bureaucracy may not have proven to be a perfect structure for organizing all work, organizational theorists owe a great deal to Weber, many of whose ideas are still considered viable today.

ORGANIZATIONAL BEHAVIOUR IN THE MODERN ERA

Based on the pioneering contributions noted thus far, the realization that behaviour in work settings is shaped by a wide range of individual, group and organizational factors set the stage for the emergence of the science of organizational behaviour. By the 1940s, clear signs appeared that an independent field had emerged.

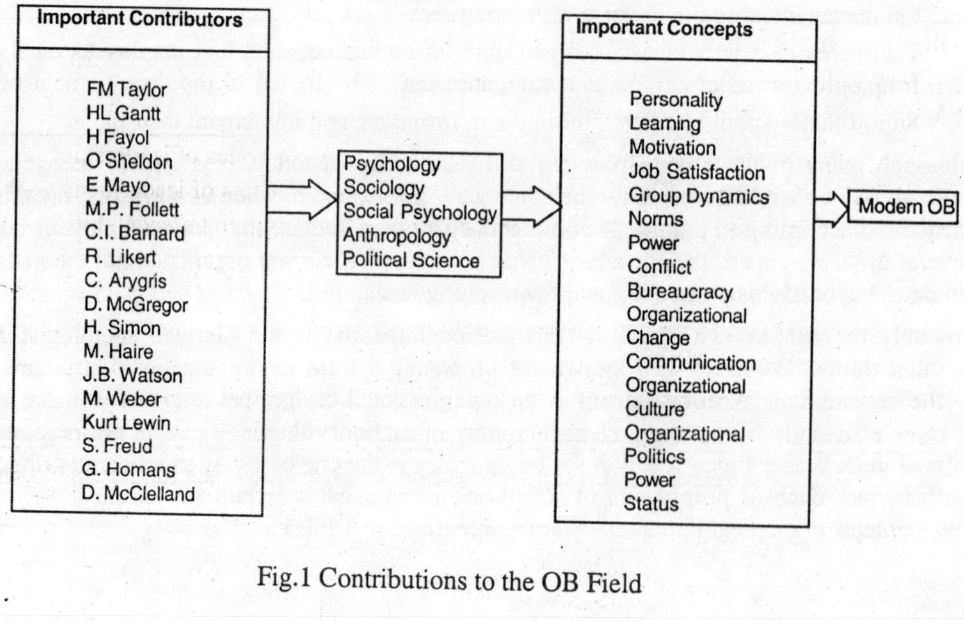

Fig.1 Contributions to the OB Field

For example, in 1941 the first doctoral degree in OB was granted (to George Lombard at the Harvard Business School). Only four years later the first textbook in this field appeared. By the late 1950s and early 1960s, OB was clearly a going concern. By that time, active programs of research were going on – research into such key processes as motivation and leadership, and the impact of organizational structure. For a summary of some of the major milestones in the development of the field of OB during the modern era, refer to Table 2.

Unfortunately – but not unexpectedly, for a new field - the development of scientific investigation into managerial and organizational issues was uneven and unsystematic in the 1940s and 1950s. In response to this state of affairs, the Ford Foundation sponsored a project by economists R.A. Gordon and J.E. Howell in which they carefully analysed the nature of business education in the United State. They published their findings in 1959, in what became a very influential work known as the Gordon and Howell report. This work recommended that the study of management pay greater attention to basic academic disciplines, especially the social sciences. This advice had an enormous influence on business school curricula during the 1960s and promoted the development of the field of organizational behaviour.

Observing the effects of these changes in business curricula in the decades following the Gordon and Howell report, Lyman Porter and Lawrence McKibbin conducted another influential study on management education. The Porter and McKibbin report, as it has come to be known, published in 1988, recognized advances made by incorporating social science notions into business curricula but pushed for further advances in several areas. These include paying greater attention to the effects of the external environment (e.g., society, government, and international developments), intensifying consideration of the international aspects of business, noting the ethical implications of business practices, and increasing attention to the growing service and information sectors of business (in contrast to the traditional manufacturing orientation). Although these recommendations (and other aspects of their report) are considered controversial, it is clearly the case that OB scientists and practitioners are taking many of these suggestions to heart. Indeed, as you continue reading this book, you will see attention paid to topics such as international differences, ethics, the business environment, and the service sector. These clearly represent areas of growing interest in the field of OB - topics that will complement the array of well-established topic areas considered in the field in the years to come.

On the basis of above discussion, synoptically we can conclude that the modern OB has the following specific features:

1. Modern OB is characterized by the acceptance of a human resource model. It takes a more positive view of human beings. People are accepted as they are and not prejudged using stereotypes.

Table 2

Some Milestones in the History of Organizational Behaviour

Summarized here are some of the major events that have contributed to the development of the field of organizational behaviour in the modern era.

1943	Lwein's studies of group climate distinguished among various styles of leadership.
1951	Ohio State leadership studies distinguished among key dimensions of leader behaviour.
1958	Fiedler's leadership theory contributed to the contingency approach to leadership.
1960	McGregor stated the Theory X and Theory Y approaches to managing people in organizations.
1964	Vroom developed the expectancy theory of motivation as it applied to people in organizations.
1967	Lawrence and Lorsch's research examined the relationship between the external environment and organizational structure.
1979	Pfeffer and Salancik established the resource - dependency perspective of power.
1987	Schein advanced the conceptual basis for organizational culture.

Source: Based on suggestions by Lawrence, 1987; see Reference No. 19.

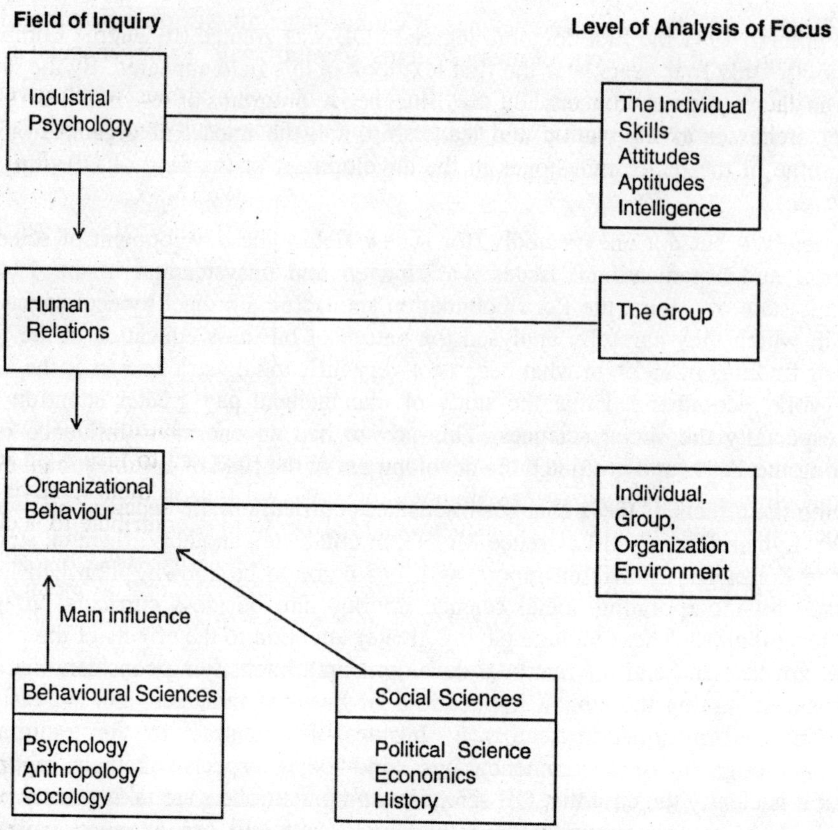

Fig. 2. The Evolution of Organizational Behaviour

Source: Adapted from Andrew D. Szilagyl, Jr. & Marc J. Wallace, Jr., *Organizational Behaviour and Performance* (1980), p.4.

2. Modern OB is a sophisticated **behavioural science**. Many of its core concepts are borrowed from other fields and disciplines like psychology, sociology, anthropology etc. Moreover, scientific methods in place of old fashioned arm chair speculation, are employed increasingly in producing OB knowledge these days.
3. Modern OB is, at once, empirical, interpretative and critical. It is an interpretative science in the pursuit of knowledge and meaning; the basic purpose is to make meaningful the facts of organizational life. Modern OB is an optic, a perspective, a process for looking at events, a way of life. It has empirical facts, interested and interesting interpretations and powerful paradigms. This is illustrated in Fig. 3.

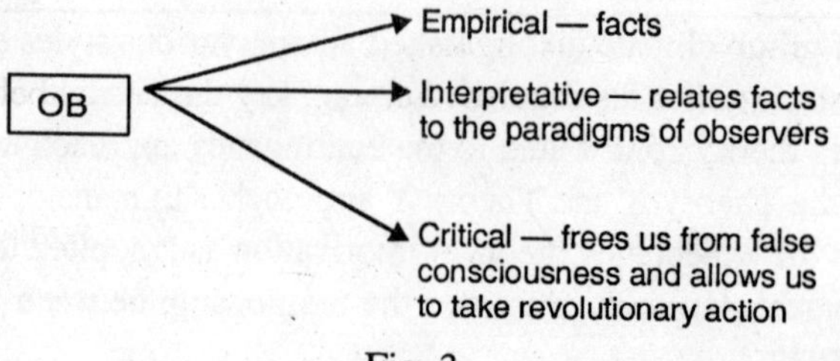

Fig. 3

Although organizational behaviour has become a widely accepted approach and an academic discipline, it does have some limitations. Keith Davis has described the following limitations.

1. OB will not abolish conflict and frustration; it can only reduce them. It is a way to improve, not an absolute answer to problems.
2. Improved organizational behaviour will not solve the problem of unemployment.

3. It will not make up for our own deficiencies. It cannot substitute for poor planning, inept organizing, or shoddy controls. It is only one of many systems operating within a larger social system.
4. People who lack system understanding may develop a behavioural bias which gives them a narrow view point. Behavioural bias can be so misapplied that it harms employees as well as the organization.
5. Overemphasis on an organizational behaviour practice may produce negative results, as indicated by the law of diminishing returns. It is a limiting factor in OB the same way that it is in economics.
6. Employee autonomy is a higher-order need that is frequently emphasized. When autonomy declines below an appropriate level, the organization fails to develop and use the talents of employees.
7. A significant concern about organizational behaviour is that its knowledge and techniques can be used to manipulate people as well as to help them develop their potential. Without ethical leadership, the new knowledge that is learned about people becomes a dangerous instrument for possible misuse.

In spite of above limitations, OB has tremendous potential to contribute to the advancement of civilization. But the major problem that organizational behaviour has had to face is an identity crisis. By building a better climate for people, organizational behaviour will release their creative potential to help solve major social problems. In this way, organizational behaviour may contribute to social improvements that stretch far beyond the confines of any one organization. A better climate may help some persons make a major breakthrough in solar energy, health, or education. The shortcomings of organizational behaviour, however, should not detract the reader from the greatest contribution of the discipline to human life - understanding human behaviour. Life in and outside organizations would not be what it is if we fail to understand ourselves and our fellow beings better.

Happily the field is ever growing. This is evident from the fact that the subject of organizational behaviour is compulsorily taught to students of humanities, particularly commerce and management courses at all levels.

Specialised institutions have been set-up to promote the study and application of the various concepts of organizational behaviour. The Indian Society of Organizational Behaviour (ISOB) is one such. ISOB is an all India organization with headquarters at Bangalore and regional centres in Kolkata, New Delhi, and Vadodara. ISOB was formally inaugurated on Feb. 11, 1987 at Bangalore. The objectives of ISOB are:

1. To organise into an association of all persons engaged in teaching and/or research and consultancy in the field of organizational behaviour.
2. To disseminate knowledge of organizational behaviour through lectures, symposia, discussions, debates and such other means as are appropriate for its objectives.
3. To publish brochures, books, journals, pamphlets to promote the study of organizational behaviour.
4. To promote and safeguard the status and the professional interests of organizational specialists.
5. To coordinate with other professional agencies, associations and other organizations so as to share experiences, information, publications and resources towards professional development of organizational behaviour specialists.
6. To elevated and establish a standard of competence for organizational behaviour specialists.
7. To develop and promote short and long-term training programmes for individuals interested in organizational behaviour.
8. To confer fellowships in organizational behaviour on those who have done or are doing noteworthy service in the field of organizational behaviour.

Similarly there is the Transactional Analysis Society of India with headquarters in Mumbai and having more or less identical objectives as that of ISOB.

Then there is the Indian Society for Applied Behavioural Science (ISABS), Secunderabad, which came into being in 1972. ISABS is a non-profit organization of behavioural scientists engaged in applying their knowledge to the well-being of persons and organizations. Its members work as independent consultants, trainers, counsellors, academicians, personnel managers, and as community change agents.

Features of Modern O.B.

By the 1950s the behavioural sciences provided a necessary foundation for the study of organizational behaviour. As a result, OB moved in the direction of becoming a truly interdisciplinary field of study. In contrast to human relations which assumes that happy workers are productive workers, the behavioural scientists consider the understanding of human behaviour to be the major means to organizational goal. As Figure 2 illustrates, OB today has become an interdisciplinary conglomerate. It can be viewed as an interdisciplinary application of behavioural science knowledge.

According to Robert A. Baron, modern OB is characterized by four major features.

(i) It has adopted a somewhat more positive view of human beings in work settings than prevailed in the past.

(ii) It has by drawing on several related fields, attained a high degree of sophistication about human behaviour.

(iii) It has adopted a contingency approach to behaviour in organization – an approach that begins with the assumption that there are no simple answers.

(iv) It is integrative in nature. That is, it seeks to comprehend behaviour in organizations by combining information from several different levels of analysis.

Limitations of O.B.

The shortcomings of the field of organizational behaviour should not be lost sight of. To start with though the subject helps an individual understand human behaviour better, he may be a failure on the domestic front. People who have a thorough grounding of behaviour disciplines have proved to be total wrecks in their own family lives.

The subject of organizational behaviour has also not contributed to improved industrial relations. Lectures, discussions and orientation programmes on various aspects of organizational behaviour organised in factories for the benefit of managers and worker representatives have not stopped workers declaring strikes and managements retaliating with lockouts. Critics are not wrong when they say that the field of organizational behaviour is only descriptive but not prescriptive. In other words, it can describe a behaviour that has taken place but cannot prevent its recurrence.

The subject of organizational behaviour has almost become a fad with managers in most organizations. Common uniforms, open offices, and shared canteens have, for example, been practised in several industrial establishments in the name of improving inter-personal relations. But wearing identical clothes has not changed the attitude of the boss towards his subordinates. Seldom is the subordinate treated as an equal, and rarely are his views respected and accepted. Removal of physical palisades in the office has not abolished the mental barriers between the manager and the managed. The boss and the subordinates may eat the same food in the same canteen. Still the former expects his subordinates to serve him the food and treat him differently.

The dual personalities of managers are often bewildering. Outwardly they talk about participative management, equality of opportunities, and open door policies. Behind the veneer of all this pep talk is the harsh reality. Most of these bosses are feudal lords. They expect the subordinates to be slaves. Any deviation from this makes the boss feel insecure. The smart subordinate is feared, hounded and finally made to quit.

Organizational behaviour is selfish and exploitative. It serves only the interest of management. It is the product of capitalistic societies. With high emphasis on motivation, efficiency, and productivity, the subject breeds a competitive spirit among employees. They are not allowed to function and live in harmony with one another.

REFERENCES

A. Bedian, Finding the Best Oneway; An Appreciation of Frank B.Gilbreth, The Father of Motion Study, *Conference Board Record*, June, 1976, pp. 37-39.

B. Gardnev and G. Moore, *Human Relations in Industry*, Irwin, Homewood, Illions, 1945.

Elton Mayo, *The Human Problems of an Industrial Civilization*, Macmillan, London, 1993.

F.J. Roethlisberger and W.J. Dickson, Management and the Worker, Hardward University Press, Cambridge. M.A., 1939.

F.W. Taylor, *Scientific Management*, Harper and Row, New York, 1947.

Fred Luthans, *Organizational Behaviour*, McGraw Hill, New York, 1989, p.13.

H. Mescalf and L.F. Urwick Eds., *Dyanamic Administration: The Cultural Papers of Marry Paper Follet*, Harper and Row, New York, 1942.

H. Ministerbergh, Psychology and Industrial Efficiency, Houghton Miffin, New York, 1913.

Henri Fayol, *General and Industrial Management*, Pitman, London, 1949.

J. Kelly, *Organizational Behaviour*, Homewood III. Irwin, 1974, p.30.

Keith Davis and Newstrom, *Human Behaviour at Work: Organizational Behaviour*, McGraw Hill Publishing Co. Ltd. New York, 1989, p.11.

Keith Davis, *Human Behaviour at Work*, Tata McGraw Hill Publishing Co. Ltd., New Delhi, 1981, p.6.

L.W. Porter and L.L. McKibbin, *Management Education and Development: A Drift or Thrust into the 21st Century*, McGraw Hill, New York, 1988.

M. Blood, The Role of Organizational Behaviour in the Business School Curriculum in J. Greenberg Ed. *Organizational Behaviour : The State of Science*, Lawrence Erlbarum Associates, Hillsdale, N.J. 1994, pp. 207 - 220.

Max Weber, *Theory of Social and Economic Organization* (A.M. Henderson and T. Parsons. Trans.), Oxford University Press, 1921.

P.R. Lowrence, Historical Development of Organizational Behaviour, in J.W. Lorsch, Ed. *Handbook of Organizational Behaviour*, Prentice Hall, Engle Wood Cliffs.,N.J. 1987, pp.1 - 9.

Peter F. Drucker, *Management: Tools, Responsibilities, Practices*, Harper & Row, New York, 1974.

R.A. Baron, M.S. Rea and S.G. Daniels, *Lighting as a Source of Environmentally Generated Positive Affect in Work Settings : Impact on Cognative Tasks and Interpersonal Behaviour, Motivation and Emotion*, Vol. 15, 1992, pp. 1-34.

R.A. Gordon and H.E. Howell, *Higher Education for Business*, Columbia University Press, 1959.

Robert A. Baron, Behaviour in Organizations, Allyn and Bacon Inc. Boston, 1983, p.17.

S.B. Flexner, I Hear American Talking, Van Nostrand Reinhold, New York, 1976.

CHAPTER

3

O.B. & Related Disciplines

Organisational behaviour, as mentioned earlier, is the study of human behaviour in organizations. The subject encompasses the study of individual behaviour, inter-individual behaviour, and the behaviour of organizations themselves.

Intra-personal behaviour covers such aspects as personality, attitude, perception, learning, opinion, motivation, and job satisfaction.

Inter-personal behaviour includes group dynamics, inter-group conflict, leadership, communication, transactional analysis, and the like.

About organizations, the study covers such aspects as their formation, structures, and formal and informal organizations.

These three levels of analysis are not necessarily mutually exclusive. The field of organizational behaviour embraces them as being complementary. In the past, the three levels were pursued with little coordination by behavioural scientists. Now, however, a major contribution of those interested in the organizational behaviour field is the attempt to integrate these three levels of analyses, although this will require much more effort. The individual focus is no more important or valuable to the manager within an organization than is the group or formal organizational focus. There is no need to choose one level of analysis and exclude the others. The managers in business, health care, education, government, and religious organizations have problems in common that require an interdisciplinary approach. This can be provided by organizational behaviour because it emphasises all these levels of analysis – the individual, the group, and the formal organization.

Man – The Critical Factor

In order to comprehend the human element in management in a wider perspective we should take the help of some fundamental formula. First of all, the important aspect is the ability of the worker. It is a well accepted fact that ability is the sum of knowledge and skill.

Ability = Knowledge + Skill

As far as motivation is concerned, it depends upon the product of situation and attitude.

Motivation = Situation x Ability

Integrating the two factors Ability and Motivation – the outcome is the performance of a worker.

Human Performance = Ability x Motivation

But for a business performance, besides the human performance various other physical factors such as Machinery, Equipment, Power, Raw material etc. are also important.

Business Performance = Human Performance x Physical Factors

Thus, it is evident that for the ultimate result (outcome) of a business, the human element is a critical factor:

Management as popularly defined is getting things done through and with people. Management itself consists of ten alphabets. Without entering into any metaphysical or spiritual interpretation, the prime objective of management is to achieve perfection by removing deficiencies in human beings (man or worker) and his environment.

The first three alphabets of management are: **MAN** – the focal point of management.

The **remaining seven alphabets** stand for:

A - Authority

G - Government

E - Environment

M - Material

E - Ethics

N - Nation or Society

T - Technology

All these seven factors are the satellites of the epicentre – Man. They derive power from the epicentre by revolving round it and emanate radiation in the process of influencing the centre.

Man is the nerve centre of the organization and society. Principles, practices and techniques of management help man to be as perfect as possible by making up deficiencies so as to reduce the incidence of wastage in human and material resources in realising his object.

Man is a social animal. To achieve his objective he requires authority to guide and direct the action of others and to structure relationship in such a manner that each one accomplishes his object without infringing on others rights and privileges, besides making motivational dynamics operant and meaningful. Authority is the source of both ambivalence and conflict. Equity in distribution forges unity but the reversal thereof causes conflict in organization and society.

Man and government are interdependent; the behaviour of government is determined by the will of its people and people's conduct is regulated by the writ of the government. If man's behaviour and conduct are less deviant, government's plans and policies will be more human and dynamic. The government's regulatory and developmental role should reflect the thinking of its people; there should exist a harmony between policy formulation by the government and policy implementation by the people.

Behaviour is the function of man and environment:

$$B = f(M, E).$$

His attitude, value system and perception, duly insulated with social beliefs and customs are reflected in his personality composition and behaviour. Social ethos and components of culture in the form of social beliefs, customs, value etc., should not be perceived as barriers but pay-offs for better behaviour.

Man's behaviour also depends on the quantity and quality of material he gets for consumption and production. In case he does not get proper quality and quantity of material in the form of consumption of goods, he may, after some stage, snatch from those who have in abundance and thus portray an abnormal behaviour. Similarly, he needs material for keeping the wheels of production in motion.

Ethics provides sanction to various roles played by man in society. It is a two-way traffic which establishes durability in relations between man and society. Similarly, technology and man's behaviour are interconnected.

Social institutions influence man as man influences society. It is a two-way traffic which establishes durability in relations between man and society. Similarly, technology and man's behaviour are interconnected.

Though most business activities are alike, except as to people. Buildings, machineries and markets are largely common instrumentalities available. But in respect of people, there are basic differences, the single most important asset of any organization is the 'people who make up the organization.'

In addition, the following major macro and micro issues create serious problems to management:

The Macro and Micro Issues

(1) Capacity utilization – machine as well as human.

(2) Combating inflation and holding the price line.

(3) Population control.

(4) Motivation, involvement and consultation.

(5) Meeting basic physiological and other needs.

(6) Reducing absenteeism, accidents, loss and damages.

(7) Generating employment opportunities, almost to the level of full employment.

(8) Generating executive leadership.

(9) Human assets accounting, profits and growth.

(10) Eliminating strikes, lockouts through voluntary arbitration.

(11) Job redesigning, enlargement, enrichment.

(12) Promoting health, self – renewal and creativity.

(13) Promoting exports and economic growth.

(14) Conservation of resources – renewable and non-renewable.

(15) Increasing the productivity of finance.

(16) Waste and cost reduction.

(17) Promoting arts, culture, religion, sports, and leisure activities.

(18) Adoption of village and communities.

(19) Promoting entrepreneurship, barefoot entrepreneurs and managers.

(20) Eliminating the discrimination of all types.

(21) Promoting a sense of national identity, awareness and contribution.

(22) Promoting industrial and national security.

(23) Eliminating poverty completely.

(24) Improving the quality of working life.

(25) Improving the quality of life.

If one goes deep into these macro and micro issues, again he finds people and human factor at the centre of all issues, whether they are economic, social, psychological, cultural or any other.

Thus it is abundantly evident from the foregoing analysis that 'Man' is a common denominator in all the issues. The study of human behaviour will obviously complement the efforts of the manager to get the job done from his people. The human factor is the critical factor in the management of any organization where the achievement of objectives and results is dependent upon human behaviour, action, motivation and behaviour.

A manager's job is to achieve organizational goals through co-ordination of the activities of the employees and other people. Since this job so heavily depends on the action of other people, it can easily be realized that the knowledge of the mechanics of human behaviour is not only of immense help but is also crucial for the completion of managerial tasks.

Motivation, learning, perception, communication and various other basic facts of individual behaviour are extensively at work in a business organization. Since most of the tasks require the integral participation of people at the same time, concepts of social behaviour cannot be ignored by a manager.

Inter Discipline Relationship

All the branches of human knowledge are inter-related to one another in some way or the other. They have certain common problems, difficulties and conclusions which make for certain similarities among them. Nevertheless they are very much different and independent with regard to their nature, scope and methods.

Whenever a discussion on the behaviour of human beings starts, we find a large number of individuals willing to discourse on what people are alike and what they do. It is not at all surprising to find that this is the case. Why not? After all, have they not had the advantage of their grey hairs? The experience acquired by them could not easily make them expect to know of others. Why not? Common sense should give them the right answer to most of the questions concerning human behaviour, if not all of the problems. It is, however, quite possible that some may have a better grasp and understanding of human behaviour than others. Why shouldn't you yourself comparatively use your own common sense in determining human behaviour. Try the short test in Table: 1.

All the answers to these questions in Table 1 are **false** even then now will you consider the common sense to be a sufficient guide to understanding human behaviour. Common sense is probably not as common as many people believe. For being not to be speculative or using other unsystematic approaches, a formal organised approach must be followed through a specific knowledge gained through scientific study of behaviour. This is the **province of behavioural science.**

Organizational behaviour is an applied behavioural science. Therefore the various disciplines on which behavioural science bases its foundation, naturally becomes the contributing disciplines to organizational behaviour too.

Table – 1 : Twenty questions on Behaviour

Sl. No.	Indicate whether the Statement is True or False
1.	Geniuses are usually queerer than the people with an average intelligence.
2.	Only human beings, not animals, have the capacity to think.
3.	Much of human behaviour is instinctive.
4.	Slow learners remember what they learn better than fast learners.
5.	Intelligent people form most of their opinions by logical reasoning.
6.	A psychologist is a person who is trained to psychoanalyze people.
7.	You can size up a person quite well in an interview.
8.	When one is working for several hours, it is better to take a few long rests than several short ones.
9.	The study of mathematics trains the mind in a manner that a person an think more logically in other subjects.
10.	Grades in colleges have little to do with success in business careers.
11.	Alcohol, in small amounts, is a stimulant.
12.	There is a clear distinction between a normal person and one who is mentally ill.
13.	Prejudices are mainly due to lack of information.
14.	Competition among people is characteristic of most human societies.
15.	The feature of a job that is most important to employees is the pay they get for their work.
16.	It is possible to classify people fairly well into introverts and extroverts.
17.	Punishment is an effective way of eliminating undesirable behaviour in children.
18.	By closely watching a person's expression, you can tell the emotion he is experiencing.
19.	The higher one sets his goals in life, the more he is likely to accomplish and the happier he will be.
20.	If a person is honest with you, he can usually tell you what his motives are.

Source : C. Morgan, 'Introduction to Psychology', McGraw Hill, New York, 1961.

Contributing Disciplines to O.B.

The academicians have done a remarkable work by putting together the scattered pieces of literature on organizations and behaviour and present them in a well-organized systematic form of organization behaviour.

The attempts to codify organizational behaviour as a separate and distinctive field of study are relatively recent. It has been only during the twentieth century that efforts have been made to develop a general theory. The contributors to this development consist of a heterogeneous group of practitioners, psychologists, academic generalists and specialists. According to Fred Luthans : "As a widely recognized and respected field of study, Organizational Behaviour has arrived. It has replaced the study of human relations as being most representative of the behavioural approach to management."

ANTHROPOLOGY

The term anthropology is derived from the Greek term 'anthropo' meaning man and the noun ending 'logy' meaning science. Thus anthropology is literally defined as the science of man, and is an extensive discipline in itself. The anthropology is basically divided into four major parts:

(1) **Physical Anthropology:** This aspect studies the biological or physical characteristics of man and traces the evolutionary pattern, leading to a knowledge of the origin of man and the human races.

(2) **Social Anthropology:** This part of anthropology focuses on the forms of culture of technology and the impact they have on individuals and groups. The Committee of the Royal Anthropological Institute of Great Britain and Ireland states, 'Social Anthropology deals with the behaviour of man in social situation.'

(3) **Archaeology:** This studies the remains of past civilizations. It usually analyzes the culture and other elements related to pre-historic civilizations.

(4) **Linguistics:** This refers to the study of speech and relationships among languages.

All the above-mentioned four areas of anthropology are related to behavioural science but the nearest to it is social or cultural anthropology. Social anthropology has developed several theories to explain the impact of culture on human behaviour. The three most important theories can be summarised by the descriptive **"isms"** of evolutionism, historicalism and functionalism. The discoveries made by social anthropology had tremendous influence upon behavioural science, more specifically the famous anthropologists, Ralph Linton and A. Kardiner influenced the behavioural science to a considerable extent. Their discoveries helped to explain the behaviour of individuals in different cultures. They concluded that in every society there is a fundamental personality type which prevents the individual from being influenced by culture in his infancy. Thus fundamental personality type differs as the cultural elements change. Putting forward the concept of functional approach in the study of culture and society, Malinowski, famous British anthropologist has helped to clarify for behavioural science as to what culture does to an individual. The findings of Franz and Otto Klineberg into physiological traits have brought to light the fact that psysiological characteristics have no relation with mental or intellectual superiority. They have also stated that differences are to be explained by differences in the social environment. Thus, social anthropology has immensely helped the behavioural science.

SOCIOLOGY

Sociology is traditionally the science of society. Sociology can be defined as a discipline that uses the scientific method in accumulating knowledge regarding man's social behaviour. The prime attention of sociology is on the social behaviour, of man in societies, institutions and groups. Thus sociology studies the patterned, shared human behaviour-the way in which people act toward one another. More specifically sociology studies, social groups, social behaviour, society, institutions, social class, customs, social mobility, status and prestige.

Durkheim's best known works, Suicide, On the Division of Labour, Rules of Sociological Method, and The Elementary Forms of Religious Life illustrate a far-reaching thinking. His concept of anomie explains certain sociological phenomena. Anomie is defined as a state of isolation or normlessness in which social rules or norms no longer have an effect on individual behaviour. Max Weber contributed significantly with the concept of bureaucracy. The major thrust common to all the areas of sociology is towards the goal of understanding independent social behaviour. The research findings of sociology have led to insights and solutions to many problems concerning the individual behaviour in modern society. Undoubtedly, sociology has made significant contribution to a better understanding of human social behaviour in general and individual behaviour in particular. To behavioural science sociology has significantly contributed in the field of bureaucracy, role structures, social system theory, group dynamics, effect of industrialisation on social behaviour, inter-personal dynamics, leadership styles, etc.

PSYCHOLOGY

The term 'psychology' is again derived from the Greek work 'psyche' meaning soul or spirit. Though traditional psychology has been defined as **'study of mind'** modern psychology is universally defined as **'science of behaviour.'** This definition of psychology is almost similar to that of behavioural science. Although psychology is one of the three disciplines which initially contributed to the knowledge of behavioural science, it is probably the most closely related with an over-all study of behavioural science than anthropology and sociology. The aims of psychology, as Thoughtless point it is to obtain rules by which we may be able to understand and predict the behaviour and thought of human beings. Thus it is evident that the interest of psychology and behavioural science are very close to each other. Both of them are positive sciences, they are factual and use scientific methods.

Psychology normally considers animal as well as human behaviour, though human beings are being classified as social animals. The inclusion of animals' behaviour in psychology is not without criticism. In a large number of cases experiments have been conducted on various animals such as rats, monkeys, cats and dogs, because of the high degree of control that can be exercised over them. The difficulty arises from trying to generalise the results drawn from the experiments conducted on animals for the applications to that on human beings. However, the researches have proved that the behavioural patterns of these animals are compatible to that of human behaviour. The understanding, prediction and control of human behaviour are the ultimate objectives of modern psychology.

One of the most important fields of psychology is social psychology. Again, here one notices a deep relationship between behavioural science and psychology. While defining social psychology, Krech and Crutchfield clarified as 'Social Psychology may therefore be broadly defined as the science of the behaviour of the individual in society.' Social psychology is so much close and similar to behavioural science that admittedly, there cannot be any difference between the two. Actually, social psychology serves as a link between behavioural science and psychology. It can be said that social psychology is to behavioural science and psychology what bio-chemistry is to biology and chemistry.

Another branch of psychology is industrial psychology. This field deals with the application of psychological facts and principles to the problem concerning human relations aspect in organizations.

The various branches of psychology study individual behaviour under various conditions – may be – normal, abnormal, social, childhood, adolescence, old age, industrial, legal and the like. Behavioural Science also studies process of human behaviour, such as learning, relearning, thinking, core cognitive process, human memory, emotion, feeling personality etc. From this point of view, the contribution of psychology to behavioural science is significant.

As we clarified in the very beginning, every one from an illiterate person to a highly qualified one is deeply involved as a student of human behaviour. Even one has his preconceived notions about human nature, which are basically based on his own experience and these beliefs are staunchly defended. This result in many misconceptions and sometimes biases towards an academic discipline that tries to attempt to tell him some thing positive about human behaviour.

We gave you a test as Table 1 to test your knowledge of human behaviour. Here we give you another test as Table 2 to put your knowledge on human behaviour to test.

Almost all the answers to the questions in test have been verified and proved by scientific investigations. Even then, as the people are deeply involved with their own and more specifically towards other's behaviour, they answer and continue arguing from their own experiences which is so limited in fact and completely ignore the scientifically verifiable facts.

The common sense has no scientific value to human behaviour. The major difference between the two may be as follows:

Table 2. True-False Test of Human Behaviour

1. Common sense is vague and scientific knowledge is precise.
2. Frequent inconsistencies normally appear in common sense, whereas the logical consistency is the characteristic of science.
3. Common sense does not explain the events systematically and ignores the need for explanation, whereas science systematically explains the event with which it deals.
4. The scientific method deliberately exposes claims to the critical evaluation of experimental analysis; the informal methods of common sense fail in testing conclusions in any systematic fashion.

Some of the more common misconceptions have been further clarified as follows:

1. Psychologist cannot "read your mind" simply by looking at you.

1. People probably never learn anything while they are soundly asleep.
2. Genius and insanity have little or no relationship to each other.
3. Better college students make less money after graduation than average students.
4. A person who learns rapidly remembers longer than a person who learns slowly.
5. All people in America are born equal in capacity for achievement.
6. Teaching a child to roller skate very early in life will give him a permanent advantage in the skill.
7. People are definitely either introverted or extroverted.
8. After you learn something you forget more of it in the next few hours than in the next several days.
9. Famous men tend to be born of poor but hard - working parents.
10. Lessons learned just before going to sleep are remembered better than those learned early in the morning.
11. On the average, men of forty-five are more intelligent than those of twenty.
12. The tendency to imitate is probably learned.
13. There is a law of compensation in nature, e.g., blind persons are born with a highly developed sense of touch.
14. An especially favourable environment can probably raise the IQ by a few points.
5. If a person born blind were to have his sight restored as an adult, he would perceive the world as we see it almost immediately.

Source: Gregory A. Kimble and Norman Garmezy, *General Psychology*, 2d ed., 1963, The Ronald Press Company, New York, p.4.

NOTE: Answers to test in Table 2 : (1) T;(2) T;(3) F;(4) T;(5) F;(6) F;(7) F;(8) T;(9) F;(10) T;(11) F;(12) T;(13) F;(14) T;(15) F;

2. Psychologists have no peculiar interest in psycho-analyzing you.
3. Psychologists are not fortune tellers.

4. Neither a psychologist nor anyone else can tell anything about a person from the bumps on his head (phrenology).

5. Neither psychologists nor anyone else can tell anything about you by the numbers of letters in your name (numerology) or by the lines in your hand (palmistry).

6. By and large, psychologists are not interested in mystical phenomena such as telepathy or clarivoyance.

POLITICAL SCIENCE

Political science is a science that studies the behaviour of individuals and groups within a political setting. It studies the laws that guide the government of a nation. It further, analyses those laws formulated by the government which are applicable to the mass of humanity which is an integral part within the jurisdiction of state. It also attempts to make an analysis of the actual behaviour of the members of political organizations. These aspects are purely behavioural in nature. Behavioural science studies the individual behaviour as an individual behaviour in society. Thus it is obvious and need no clarification, that there is a considerable **concurrence** between behavioural science and political science.

The role of government can be understood only when the individual's social behaviour is analyzed in the right perspective. Even the formulation of proper and adequate laws demand not only fundamental but also a thorough understanding and acquaintance with the behaviour and psychology of the people. The success of democracy both as form of government and as ideology mainly depends on the success in training, educating and moulding public opinion, attitudes and beliefs. This is where behavioural science serves as an essential guide. In the area of international politics, the behavioural science plays a dominant role, science in present day world political isolation mean cultural annihilations. Nations have to create and maintain international good will and proper understanding for themselves in other countries and groups. In the conditions of crisis it becomes much more important to maintain the moral of the people. Such functions can be executed effectively only when the government and its administrators are well equipped with the knowledge of behaviour science. Political institutions exert their great influence upon the social behaviour of the individual and to this extent behavioural science too requires the assistance of political science.

A behaviourally oriented political scientist abstains himself from mere philosophy, rather he looks for the empirical bases of behaviour in politics, political partie administration, voting, legislative behaviour, public opinion, pressure groups, comparative systems, international relations, legislative decisions and the like. A comprehensive scope can be seen in the work *'Political Behaviour': A Reader in Theory and Research'* edited by Eulau, Eldersveld and Janawitz, first published in 1956. In this work the theory of behavioural approach is greatly stressed upon. It is not a speculation but a theory in true sense.

In the past the term 'politics' was considered to be a dirty word. Not any more. Oganisations are becoming political entities (Read Box 1.1) and better understanding about them cannot be obtained without lending political perspective.

An Indian social scientist, Madhukar Shukla has very aptly identified various factors as detailed below which compels one to consider why are organizations have political systems.

* Organizational members enjoy power from various sources (e.g., due to position, expertise, group support, seniority, etc.) which help them in influencing each other. This creates complexity and contradictions in relationships, for instance, when a senior executive faces a trade union leader. Both have power, but sources are different.

* The decision-maker has to contend with and balance diverse and often contradictory demands arising from different constituencies (subordinates, bosses, peers, etc.). Since satisfying each group is vital for effective implementation of the decisions, the decision-making cannot remain a mere rational and objective exercise.

* By virtue of their role, certain people departments are more important for achieving organizational goals as compared to others. Thus, while on paper, all sections are equal, some are actually more important than others.

* In any organization, people differ widely in terms of their need for power and control. It would be natural for those with high need for power to interpret and respond to situations in ways that maximise their power.
* Most organizations work on the principle of resource optimisation. Thus, for an organization to function like a clock-work mechanism, the demands and resources have to be suitably matched. This is easier said than done, and so, lobbying for resources becomes a practical necessity for any well-meaning executive.
* Lastly, any viable decision needs to satisfy three kinds of goals: corporate, departmental and individual. These three, in most situations, are not congruent with each other, and therefore, call for political skills from the decision-maker.

The Fig. 1 diagramatically depicts the relationship of basic behavioural disciplines and the organizational areas to which they have significantly contributed.

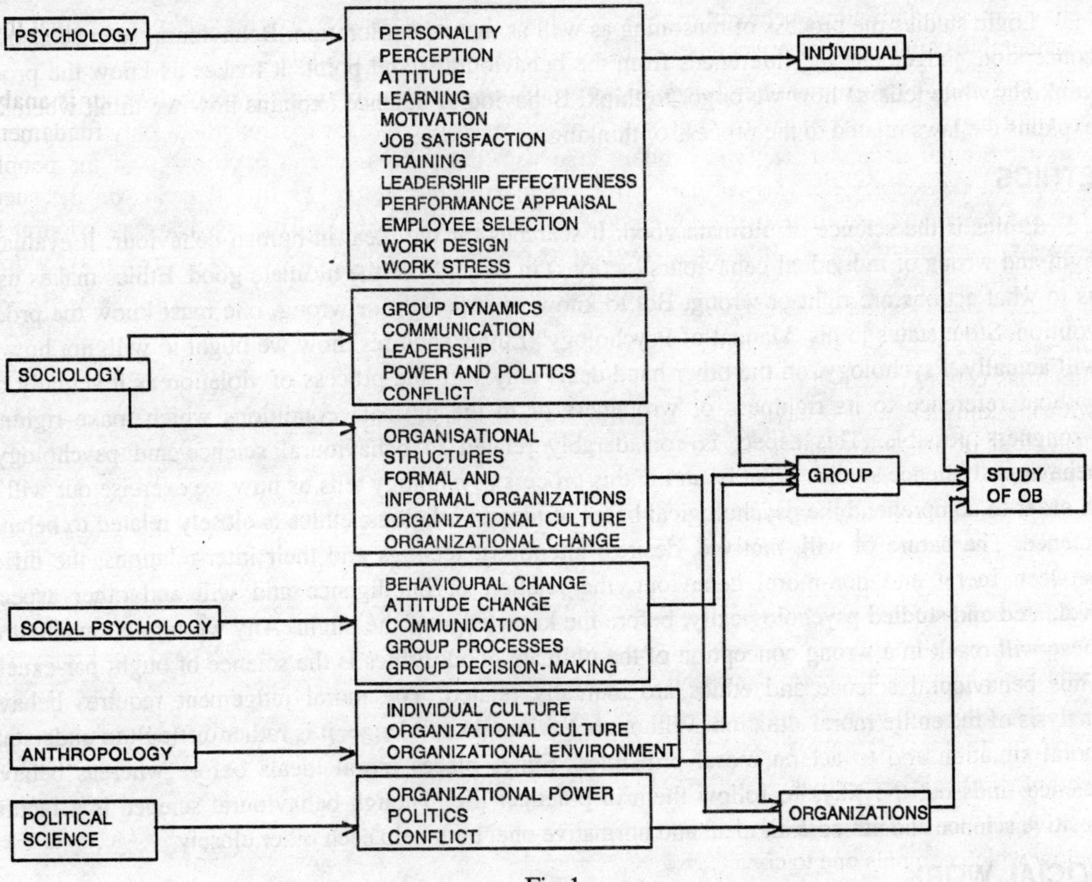

Fig.1

Major Disciplines and their Contribution to OB

Besides the above discussed four basic social science disciplines which have contributed to the development of O.B. there are many more social and pure science disciplines that have their significant contribution towards the development of O.B. The author has made an attempt to consolidate few of them as under :

PHILOSOPHY

To look at things as a whole is a philosophical attitude. Philosophy looks at facts and values in a systematic whole. In it everything is seen in the context of the whole universe. Originally, psychology and philosophy were subsumed in each other. Philosophical truths are based on psychological facts. In philosophy epistomology is based on behavioural pattern. What is the origin of knowledge? How is it realised? What is its validity? All such questions need a behavioural explanation. Metaphysics is also an important branch of philosophy. Psychology has positively contributed in meta-physics. Philosophers have held elaborate discussions on mental and physical processes such as deep sleep etc. and based their metaphysical conclusions on them. Thus Psychology has its early beginnings in philosophy, but in modern times, philosophy and psychology are independent sciences with their own respective methods and outlook.

LOGIC

Luther Burbank very aptly said, 'The greatest torture in the world for most people is to think.' Logic is the science of thinking, a higher branch of learning. It is connected with concepts, judgements and inferences. Logic has exact rules and any deviation from the rules can prove to be disastrous. There is no place of guess or common sense in Logic. Logic is actually verbal mathematics. It is also termed reasoning or mental ability.

Logic studies the process of reasoning as well as mental exploration. Behavioural science also studies conception, judgement and inferences from the behavioural stand point. It makes us know the process of thinking, while tells us how we ought to think. Behavioural Science explains how we think whereas logic explains the laws related to the process of thinking.

ETHICS

Ethics is the science of ultimate good. It searches for the ideal in human behaviour. It evaluates the right and wrong of individual behaviours (actions) in the light of the ultimate good. Ethics makes us know as to what actions are right or wrong. But to know what is right or wrong, one must know the process of volition. Stout states in his 'Manual of Psychology', Ethics enquires, how we ought to will, not how we do will actually. Psychology, on the other hand deals only with the process of violation as it actually occurs, without reference to its rightness or wrongness or to the ultimate conditions which make rightness or wrongness possible. This aspect is considerably related to behavioural science and psychology. The behavioural science studies 'what is' and in this process psychology tells us how we exercise our will. Thus, in order to comprehend the psychological bases of moral violations, ethics is closely related to behavioural science. The nature of will, motives, desires, intentions, feelings and their inter-relations, the difference between moral and non-moral behaviour, the relation of intelligence and will and other aspects are evaluated and studied psychologically, before the knowledge of the ought. Any wrong notion about any of these will result in a wrong conception of the ultimate good. Ethics is the science of ought par-excellence. Thus behavioural science and ethics are mutually related. The moral judgement requires behavioural analysis of the entire moral situation. Without behavioural knowledge, it is rather difficult to understand the moral situation and to act on moral principles. Ethics places moral ideals before whereas behavioural science finds out the ways to follow them in practical life. Though behavioural science is a factual and positive science and ethics is an ideal and normative one, both help each other closely.

SOCIAL WORK

Social work is a profession having its own philosophy, methods, techniques and skills applied for the solution of the problems of individual, group and community in order to bring mutual adjustment. In this discipline the help is rendered to the client keeping in view that he will be able to help himself. Social work is basically concerned with acts which are directed to help the helpless to help themselves. The goal of social work is to make a person as self-reliant as he can be made in an adverse situation in which he is caught. Thus, social work is related to human beings in all the stages of life as well as in rendering help to human beings suffering from physical and mental disorders.

These disorders people suffer from may be of various types. Persons could be physically, mentally, emotionally or socially handicapped. Social work in all such situations renders promotive and creative assistance and helps the individual to overcome his disability to the extent that he can lead a life of dignity and usefulness. Therefore, such matters as industrial democracy, ethical conformity and cultural desiderata and a wide gamut of theoretical positions are found among the personnel and in the formulated polices of social work organizations. Hence social work implies the possibility of rational processes of the application of the inductive principle to social study of quantitative research.

Later, social work developed in such specialised disciplines, such as industrial relation, labour welfare and personnel management, child and family welfare, community organization and tribal welfare, criminology and corrective administration and social (work) research. These developments are basically in the field of behavioural science, which provide insights into human conduct in multi-various contexts. Thus behavioural science teach social work coping and growth promoting modalities which could be adopted by it for the benefit of persons in stressful situations in the family, school, community, and in industries.

Thus, the basic knowledge of behavioural science is crucial to a social worker in meaningfully handling problems arising from absenteeism, discipline strike, lockouts, accidents, incentives, motivation, promotions, retirement and myriads of such things as constantly pose challenges to human beings.

ECONOMICS

Economics is basically a study of man's activities devoted to obtaining the material means for the satisfaction of his wants. Marshal, a famous economist, opined, "Economics is a study of mankind in the ordinary business life. It studies that part of individual and social action which is most closely connected with the attainment and with the use of the material requisites of well being." Thus, economics, on the one hand, is a study of wealth while on the other, what is more important, it studies man. Consequently, behavioural science and economics are inter-related. Both study human behaviour although they differ from each other in respect of their approach and methodology.

The theory of demand and supply, law of equi-marginal utility, theory of diminishing returns and theory of population, the foundations of economics, are closely related to behavioural pattern of human beings, the subject of interest of behavioural science. The behaviour of different classes of people and economic conditions shows distinct differences. Social interactions greatly influence economic conditions.

To a great extent the economic problems owe much to the contribution of behavioural science. Behavioural aspect plays a dominant role in economic problems. The basic understanding of behavioural science cannot be ignored wherever economic problems, such as strikes, lock outs, gross national productivity, inflation and the like are to be tackled effectively. Thus, though both the disciplines are independent, they are in practice supplementary disciplines. In order to be of practical application of economic principles, they are based upon the facts of behavioural science. To comprehend the economic laws in a better perspective, the fundamental knowledge of behavioural science is essential.

HISTORY

History could be defined and explained as a study of things and phenomena in the process of their becoming and development, in connection with the conditions determining them.

The subject matter of history comprises Ethnographic-history, Culture-history, Social-history, Intellectual-history, Economic-history and Business-history.

Thus it, (that is history), which implies an approach to Ethnographic, Cultural, Social, Intellectual, Economic and Business, phenomena and things – that consider how they arose and developed and how they will look in the future.

Traditionally history has been used to refer to attempts to provide a comprehensive explanation or interpretation of the entire historical process. It studies the questions which arise from reflection upon historical thinking and reasoning and are primarily of an epistomological or conceptual character. Here, the primary purpose is to determine what happened in the past and why.

However, conversely viewed, as a definite method of theoretical research (behavioural stimuli and reactions) history could be said to be a fixation not of any and every (even qualitative) change, but only of that which reflects the formation of specific properties and connections of things, determining their essense and specifics.

In fact, history presupposes recognition of the irreversible and successive nature of changes of things – The moment historical facts are regarded as instances of general laws, history is dismissed.

The historian reconstructs 'from within' the reasons, purposes and emotions that motivated the persons with whom he is so concerned and that found outward expression in their deeds. In fact, the study of history is affected not only by the psyche of the historian but also of the person or thing whom or which the historian studies.

This nature of history has resulted in its being a major contributor to the study of principles of sciences, such as the Behavioural Science, enabling O.B. to give an objective picture of nature and human behaviour and discover the laws governing its development.

Social scientists, such as historians and Behavioural Scientists are by no means always distinct individuals any more than are the natural historians or the natural scientists. In fact, each individual is more one than the other, thus, for example, a behavioural scientist while describing a historical character/personality incorporates a considerable amount of descriptive and narrative history of the conventional kind just as historian would express.

It could thus be said that history is viewed/seen as one's viewpoint. The viewpoint or point of view of a person is in turn moulded by the material and social conditions he or she is brought up on. In this context it is interesting and pertinent to take note of the Marxist philosophy which holds that "it is not the consciousness of men that determines their existence but their social existence that determines their consciousness."

Thus from the behaviouralists' point of view:

History is a natural objective process and is made by men themselves.

Men make history not in accordance with their arbitrary desires, but on the basis of the material conditions that take shape in the society at each stage in its development.

It is the material conditions which account for the stimuli and the result-out reactions of human behaviour.

JURISPUDENCE

The approach to law is based upon a theoretical base rather than upon practice of the profession. This is what is known a jurispudence. The term 'Jurimetrics' have been coined which is basically based on law as behavioural science. It deals with the scientific investigations of legal problems. Pound identified this development as a move to a functional concern with problems and termed with social sciences more specifically in a study of values, expectations and individual precepts.

As in the case of many social sciences discussed, the philosophical flavour of discipline is gradually decreasing and paving way to empirical support. In the area of law, too, this tendency has significantly contributed and in judicial decisions more behavioural approach is evident in recent time, the world over, rather than being limited to theoretical studies. The problem areas, such as social dynamics in a jury, criminal responsibility, efficacy of legal methods, judicial decision making process, surveys of attitudes towards law, need for new law, change in the existing law and other number of related areas have shown considerable interest in the behavioural aspect of human beings. The fact that death sentences are now rarely awarded and the benefit of doubt is invariably given to the accused is ample evidence of the role of behavioural science in law.

In this context Pound concept on society is of **Social Engineering** which means that the laws should be framed which fulfilled the needs of the individual in the society. While framing the laws, the legislation must have a survey of the society and the behaviour of the persons living in the society.

Precedents which are also one of the factors serve as sources of law. This source is considered one of the strong basis while deciding a subsequent case in a court of law.

Sometimes it is also seen that people living in a particular society or locality who are of a criminal nature commit a similar type of crime because their behaviour is similar with each other. Therefore, jurisprudential science can make their behaviour change and make them fit to live in modern society. The learned jurists are of the view that behavioural science must be studied with jurisprudential approach.

EDUCATION

The basic interest and activities in the science of teaching are primarily based upon many fields of behavioural science. An understanding of social dynamics of the individual, group and community is proving to be an important requirement for any one in today's educational system. Principles of learning and retention, growth and development, assimilation of ideas, aptitude analysis along with numerous bits of information, forms an integral part of the reservoir of knowledge in, and administration of, the educational system.

BIOLOGY

Behavioural science is a positive science. The term 'behaviour' includes both external activities and internal processes. Biology studies the activities of all living beings, including the origin and biological development of human being, describing his racial and individual characteristics and the principles of his adjustment to the environment. Darwin's theory of evolution is an example of biological theories. Contributions made by the researches in DNA factor determining the heredity and personality is also no less important. The important role of response menchanism and core-cognative process also cannot be overlooked in an understanding of human behaviour. Thus, behaviour cannot be fully explained without the knowledge of basic biological principles.

Because of such an intimate relation between biology and psychology, some psychologists forget their differences. Watson, the founder of behaviourism, whose ideas have significantly influenced behavioural science emphasized animal psychology and attempted to explain human behaviour in terms of stimulus - response. No doubt, biologists have made their own place in behavioural science for studies on animal as well as human behaviour and for inquiry into the genetic basis and bio-chemical determinants of human behaviour.

Hence, behavioural science and biology, though closely related, are independent sciences that mutually help each other.

PHYSIOLOGY

Physiology is a positive science of behaviour. It is rather based upon the close connection of mental life with organic life in general. It studies the physical activities and structure in relation with mental processes. Physiology studies, sense organs, nervous system, organism, brain, muscles, blood circulation; respiration etc. These all organs influence the behaviour in some way or other. It is said, 'healthy mind is a healthy body.' There exists a positive correlation between mental states and physical conditions. Neuroses and psychosis have close relationship and the appearance of one normally leads to the other. It has been proved scientifically that mental process have a far reaching effect on physical activities and vice versa. The role of insulin and thyroids are ample proof in themselves as to how they change the body chemistry and effect the physical as well as mental activities and in turn, ultimately the behavioural pattern of an individual.

On the basis of such close relations of the mental behaviour and physical states, sometimes it is argued that mind is only a function of brain, though it has been proved that it is not so. The study of physical processes does help in the understanding of mental behaviour, but this should not lead to the identification of both.

Synoptic View of Contributions by other disciplines to Human Relations

Approach (Organization Theory)

Anthropology
- Cultural Dynamics
- Organization Theory
- Status Symbols
- Ethnic Relations

Biology
- Organiztion Theory
- Viability
- Homeostasis

Ecology and Geography
- Location Theory
- Nucleation
- Environmental Adaptation
- Dispersion Processes
- Spatial Forces

Mathematics
- Information Theory
- Stochastic Processes
- Set Theory
- Descriptive and Inductive Statistics
- Theory of Games
- Decision-Making
- Probability Theory
- Linear Programming

Physics
- Gravitation Theory

*** Economists**
- Firm
- Markets
- Pricing

Political Science
- Administrative Law
- Administrative Theory
- Trade Regulations and Practices
- Authoritarianism
- Organization Theory
- Bureaucracy

Psychology
- Aptitude Analysis
- Personality Analysis
- Scaling Techniques
- Senses and Sensations
- Learning Theory
- Motivational Analysis
- Perception and Sensation
- Projective Techniques
- Rationality

Sociology
- Interpersonal relations
- Morale
- Role and Status
- Class Behavioural Pattern
- Class Stimuli
- Innovation and Change
- Organization Theory
- Primary Group Behaviour
- Small Group Activity
- Environmental Influences
- Public Opinion
- Sociometry
- Formal Organization
- Social Change
- Group Surveys and Testing
- Social Stratification and Values
- Social Institutions

Source : David L. Huff and Joseph W. McGuire : "The Interdisciplinary Approach to the Study of Business", University of Washington Business Review, June 1960.

* Huff and McGuire's study does not include the contribution by the economists. It has been added by the Author.

The field of behavioural science and physiology lies in physical activities while that of behavioural science lies in both the physical and the mental activities and their relation to behaviour. Though physiology studies the various physical activities in isolation, behavioural science studies the reaction of the whole organism towards the external stimuli.

Psycho-physics is a special branch of physiology. It studies the various physical activities in quantitative terms. Psycho-physics has proved through intensive experiments on the stimuli of different sense organs how much difference there should be between two stimuli so that the difference can be either perceived or observed. The well-known law – Weber-Fechner Law brings out the quantity of the least noticeable differences in the stimuli of different sense organs. Thus, it is evident that though behavioural science and physiology are independent sciences, yet they have a close relationship.

PSYCHIATRY

Psychiatry deals with the diagnosis and treatment of nervous and mental disorders. Its prime concern is with the behavioural pattern of human beings both as an individual and in groups. It analyses the right and wrong, normal and abnormal human behaviours in the light of accepted social norms, ethics and values. The psychiatrist, though a medical doctor by profession has to spend a considerable time in learning the fundamental bases of human behaviour in order that he is able to treat his patients. He gathers and applies as much behavioural science knowledge as he can, but being a clinical practitioner, his direct involvement in basic behavioural research is considerably reduced. In order to have complete and comprehensive details of his patients' behaviour the psychiatrist basically depends on introspection, observation, survey and case history, techniques frequently employed in behavioural science.

RADIO TECHNOLOGY

In the present times the radio and television plays a significant role in influencing public opinion and is effectively used as a means of mass communication. Any information or message broadcasted over radio or telecasted is heard by millions of people, thousand of miles away and are greatly influenced by it. This influence is apparent in society in the form of culture, behaviour fashion, tendencies, likes and dislikes, literature, art and everything else. Radio and Television have contributed much to the development of individual and nation. The fact that something heard or seen have greater impact, impression and conviction than something read cannot be denied and has been scientifically proved by behavioural scientists.

Behavioural science is a scientific study of behaviour both as an individual and in society. Therefore, it also studies those **interactions** that take place between the members of the group. In course of such study behavioural science makes a detailed scientific study of public opinion, propaganda, rumour etc. and discovers the behaviours facts at the root of such perceptions. After a systematic and empirical study of mental tendencies, motives, sympathy and imitation, prejudices and the like it puts forth suggestions, for improvements and success. It defines principles for transforming group behaviour in the desired manner after making a behavioural analysis. Hence, it is for behavioural science to define type and style and method of mass communication, which should be employed in moulding public opinion.

A number of systematic investigations have been conducted by various social scientists to find out the factors that can increase the effectiveness of radio and its influence upon the public. An interesting research has revealed the following factors :

1. In broadcasting, the speech of trained and practised speakers is desirable.
2. Female voice should be more frequently employed as their voice is preferred to public in comparison to male voice.
3. Emphasis should be given on clear and distinct pronunciation.
4. On any subject, a general description should be followed by a specific commentary.
5. Change is desirable as it is effective, but should not exceed a limit.
6. Sentences can be either lengthier or shorter, depending upon the subject. However, common and short sentences are preferred, but if the subject is interesting, lengthier sentences would also suffice.
7. The speed of speaking should not be too fast, it should be between 115 and 160 words per minute.

8. The pitch of the tone should be moderately average and special emphasis should be placed on pauses between the sentences.
9. On an average the programme should not be of a longer duration than 25 minutes.

No doubt, these vital facts can be brought to light by none other than a behavioural scientist.

REFERENCES

Cantrill and Allport, *Psychology of Radio.*

D. Krech and R.S. Crutch Field, *Theory and Problems of Social Psychology*, McGraw Hill Book Co., New York,1948, p.7.

Fred Luthans, *Contemporary Readings in Organizational Behaviour*, McGraw Hill Book Co., New York, 1972, p.2.

G.F. Stout, *A Manual of Psychology*, Clive, 1919, p.6.

Gregory A. Kimball and Norman Gramezy, General Psychology, The Ronald Press, Co., New York, 1963, p. 3.

Howard H. Kendler, *Basic Psychology*, 2nd. ed. Appletion Century Crafts, New York, 1968, p.14.

Karl Marx, *A Contribution to the Critique of Political Economy*, Progress Publishers, Moscow, 1977, p.21.

Madhukar Shukla, *Understanding Organizations*, Prentice Hall of India, New Delhi, 1996, p.12.

N.S. Gupta, *Organization : Theory and Behaviour*, Himalaya Publishing House, Mumbai, 1988, pp.102-103.

R. Pound, *Law Findings Through Experience and Reason*, University of Georgia Press, Athens, 1960, p.32.

R.H. Thouless, *General and Social Psychology*, University Tutorial Press, London, 1944, p.1.

CHAPTER 4

Management: A Behavioural Aspect

At an international management Congress, a report on professional management was presented. This report and its recommendations were accepted and recommendations asked to promote the development and acceptance of Standards of Managerial Competence and Behaviour vis-a-vis. to nominate regional and national Working Committees for these purposes. The Dutch working committee on Managerial Competence took as starting point the following questions:

1. What are the substantial changes in the function of the general manager in these days?
2. What is to be understood by the notion "general manager"?
3. Which competence consisting of knowledge, skills and attitude must the general manager possess as a consequence of the development of his function?

The working committee first formulated some of the recent substantial changes in the field of operation of the general manager. Financial/economic, technological changes and economic and socio-cultural changes were listed as having an internal or external impact on management.

Further the working committee described the position of the general manager in his organization. The working committee emphasized the necessity of steering qualities more than the need for an absolute leader. The definition of the managerial task which resulted from the foregoing is as follows. It belongs to the task of the general manager :

- to clarify in a continuous process the objectives of his organization, to put them up for discussion and to see that they are laid down;
- to promote that the objectives of the organization are realised by managing the organization leaning on an effective way of decision-making, which is controlled by him; and
- to harmonize the interests of all the groups involved in the functioning of the organization.

The Dutch working committee in principal agreed with the conclusions of the Report on Professional Management provided that it is accepted that the primary aim of any organization is to fulfil a social need. The Dutch committee was of the opinion that the so called internal aim of any organization namely to assure its own survival is derived from its fulfillment of a social need.

The Dutch report ends with a chapter in which the Standards of Competence are formulated. The working committee remarks that knowledges can be acquired that skills need some natural aptitude but can be trained and that attitude depends on the behavioural qualities and inclinations of the manager which in a way can be developed but not acquired. The Dutch working committee on Managerial Behaviour has based its study on the British "Code of best practice incorporating the Code of Conduct with supporting Guides to good management practice." According to the Dutch concept for a code, the general manager:

- shall not abuse his authority or position;
- shall act according to the laws – and in the spirit of the laws-applicable to his organization;
- shall act in his function according to this code and the guides to good managing practice, belonging to it.

The guides refer to general management as such, and its relation to the organization, the collaborators, the suppliers, the consumers and the environment. The working committee remarks that the draft code represents an effort to lay down rules and norms to be accepted by the majority of the general managers in the Netherlands.

The working committee refers in its introduction to the draft code to the problem of the sanction on infringement. How to bind general manager? Is this possible on a voluntary basis? Comparisons are made with other groups of professionals with a code. On the one hand the membership of such professional groups implies acceptance of the code and on the other hand the membership can be a guarantee for certain standards of quality.

The international working committee has made an attempt to combine national results of studies on both items : managerial competence and managerial behaviour. However, only a few countries have followed the recommendations of the report to form national committees. Therefore the working committee has used a questionnaire to collect information from individual general managers on certain aspects of management. to integrate the answers received was already quite a task. The answers confirmed the statement of conclusions and recommendations prepared for the congress: The function of the manager is accepted as part of the social system. Further professional training has been qualified as one of the most important means to improve the public understanding of the managerial function, task and responsibility. The acceptance of a Standard of Competence is therefore considered of great importance.

Here again the requirements for a Code of Competence are specified:

1. Knowledge which can be acquired in a learning process: Economic, legal, social, political, cultural and technological facts and developments.
2. Skills : Think and speak in a clear and purposeful way, recognize and select main facts from unimportant information, arrive at logical conclusions, lead, motivate, absorb the impact of failures etc.
3. Attitude : Conduct morale way of thinking. In the Swiss report the element "attitude" refers to perseverance, charisma, capacity to carry stress, fairness, adaptability, creativity, courage to take decisions willingness to accept responsibility, confidence in oneself, and determination for continuous training. It is the least accessible for a learning process, but by the same token it is considered to be of increasing importance thus deserving full attention of those engaged in the field of training of managers.

In the context of attitude and skills the China Productivity Center speaks of intuition, wisdom, coherency, which can hardly be learned through training.

One of the conclusions is that the way of approaching these problems by different people does not differ too much. The philosophy however which underlies the formulation of norms and values may differ greatly according to the diverse cultural backgrounds of the different people.

Therefore the question before us is: If we want to elaborate rules or standards of competence and behaviour, should we not limit this work to smaller territories, for instance territories with the same cultural background? Or should we aim at standards on a worldwide scale with such a built-in flexibility that each culture can insert its own norms and values?

The next question is : What could be the use of worldwide standards with a built-in flexibility? If you agree that we have to limit our work to territories with the same cultural background, is it nevertheless possible to draw up a general framework, in which each cultural territory can fill in its own standards based on its own norms and values? If we believe in the procession "manager", because management is a key function in this world, it seems necessary to demonstrate that it is a profession which implies that there must be some basic universal criteria. Like for other professions the profession of manager should be made recognizable not only for managers themselves but also and specifically for the public at large. This implies that those basic universal criteria should be determined.

It is stated in the report that any code of conduct needs to undergo continuous adaptation to new circumstances and changing values.

Static codes of conduct would even appear dangerous in our fast changing times where demands from suppliers of goods and services, suppliers of capital, labour, consumers and environments alter even faster. Manager cannot be bound by exact rules. Man himself has an innate sense of freedom. But on the other hand, it is clear that it is not the purpose of a code of conduct to completely tie down management. As long as a code of conduct for managers reflects the real intentions, it will be a help to improve the image of the manager which is often vague and ambiguous and rather uncertain.

However, many codes of conduct we develop, many image promoting techniques we develop, unless our action is starting from a positive attitude, for which "personality" and "maturity" are important, we are building an outer shell.

For many decades How, we have been studying "professional management" on a worldwide basis. The report recommends to continue our study on a regional basis. It is strongly recommended to consider whether those studies should be carried out on even smaller scales. At the end we can then try to compare the criteria laid down in smaller scale studies and try to compare denominators for universal use. Code of competence and codes of conduct can assist us but they can never replace the inner richness from which all our actions should flow.

NATURE OF ORGANIZATION

A sound organization structure is imperative in order to make possible a most effective management job, because it creates the pattern that determines the accountability, the relationships, and the performance of all members of management.

Importance of Structure

Lack of a sound organization structure causes many of the perplexing problems of management. Harold V. Coes, formerly Vice President of the American Management Association, and retired V.P., Ford, Bacon, and Davis, has stated : Seventy-five to eighty per cent of the problems brought to Consulting Engineers are found to arise from defects in organization structure. R.E. Gilmore, formerly V.P. Sperry Corporation, stated at a conference of the Society for the Advancement of Management: More than forty years of practical experience and observation in both government and industry have convinced me that the most shocking wastes of human spirit and capabilities occur through poor organization, ... most defects in organization arise from the disregard of a few fundamental laws.

Causes and Effects of Poor Organization

Without a clear-cut statement of the organization's basic objectives, it is very difficult to (a) design sound structure; (b) develop adequate criteria for measuring the attainment of end results desired; and (c) evaluate the effectiveness of management performance.

A study of many companies reveals the fact that their organizations have through the years, like Topsy, "jes growed." Departments have developed around strong individuals, rather than around the performance of distinct functions. Most of the fundamental operating problems of some organizations can be traced in part at least to an inadequate or faulty organization structure. A common weakness is the failure to observe the simple fundamental principle that a single executive should be solely accountable for the attainment of the organization's overall objectives (with commensurate authority). and secondly, that each executive reporting directly to the president (or whatever the title of the chief executive may be) is, in turn, solely accountable to the president for the successful attainment of a major segment of the organization's over-all objectives and end results. It is obvious that adequate delegation of responsibility and authority must be made in conformity with the organization's structure. This point will be discussed in subsequent Sessions of this Manual.

A management study conducted for the Swedish Government and reported at the Eighth International Management Congress, Stockholm several years ago reveals that defects in organization structure result in:

1. Highly-paid staff members spending time doing jobs which do not require their specialised training and experience;
2. Responsibilities, authorities and accountability are incorrectly balanced; there is uneconomical division and/or duplication of work;

3. Departments and sections do work which should be central to service groups; unnecessarily complicated routines are involved in the accomplishment of simple and less important jobs;
4. Unnecessary reports, statistics, records, etc., are maintained; and
5. Auditing and management controls are not maintained effectively.

Objective Thinking is Required

As soon as the top management of an organization recognises, and agrees, that the structure should be improved, the question is then asked: "Reorganization along what lines?" Usually, the answer is obvious: "A revised structure well-designed to accomplish most effectively the over - all objectives of the organization and the end result desired."

Whenever the careers and the status of the top managers in a company are in jeopardy of being affected by an organizational study it is likely that the fundamental principles governing the development of a sound structure will be obscured by self-interest, unless the chief executive and/or the Board of Directors have the will and the courage to be completely objective in their thinking. Whenever a company undertakes a reorganization programme it takes courage to let the chips fall where they may. On the other hand, experience indicates that no improvement is ever made so long as more consideration is given to the personal status of a few individuals who may be affected by reorganization than there is to the over-all welfare of the organization as a whole.

A sound organization structure in and of itself is not, of course, a cure all. If any of the top managers are weak, no amount of tinkering with the organization structure is going to solve that problem. The imperative need for imaginative and capable managers does not end with the adoption of an organization structure.

Executive Salary Programme: After a revised plan or organization is established, the next step is the development and adoption of a sound executive salary programme to fit the structure. This includes the design and installation of a position classification plan for evaluating and grading all management positions, the establishment of equitable salary ranges for each grade; the allocation of all positions affected from the first line supervisors to and including the president.

Executive Performance Appraisal Programme: Another important phase of the plan of organization is the development, adoption, and maintenance of a systematic programme for appraising executive performance periodically for conformity with established standards that have been related to each position and the salary programme. Wherever practicable this should also be coordinated with a well - designed financial incentive plan.

Management Controls: Concurrently with the adoption of a revised plan of organization, top management also needs to establish controls, rations (criteria for measuring performance), and reports as required to reflect adherence to the new structure and the effectiveness of the structure. This also applies to the organization as a whole; home office and field offices, and all organizational components thereof, wherever applicable.

Management Tools that Supplement a Sound Structure

Some of the most effective management tools that supplement a sound structure and enhance its usefulness are as follows:

1. An Organization Manual which contains appropriate organization and functional charts; statements of the objectives, functions, and responsibilities of each organizational division, department, section, and unit; criteria for measuring performance, and written position descriptions (and man specifications) covering all management jobs and subordinate sub-divisions thereof.
2. A Policy Manual which contains current releases of all approved policies that are needed for guiding management in the determination of day-to-day decisions that are required in the normal operation of the enterprise; guideposts that facilitate decision-making.
3. The President's Summary Report to the Board of Directors which summarises monthly, quarterly, and annually the company's accomplishments in terms of over-all results attained in conformity with broad approvals of the Board with respect to objectives, policies and budgets.

4. Periodic Operating Reports, by major departments or divisions which reveal currently the basic information needed to direct and co-ordinate the major departmental activities of the organization; to assist adherence to established plans, programmes, schedules and standards to identify trends, and to effect remedial action wherever indicated before problems become critical.
5. A Chart of Accounts, and functional accounting in conformity with the organization structure and major functional operations, so that all accounting reports and related data can be immediately identified with the appropriate organizational department and key personnel affected.

Improving the Organization

Significant improvements in its organization structure can be made by almost any company, to the extent that its management will analyse any weaknesses in its present structure and then direct remedial action in line with the principles and techniques outlined in the following pages under the headings of:

A. Designing the organization structure;

B. Putting organizational changes into effect;

C. Delegating functions and responsibilities to the major levels of management;

D. Clarifying line and staff relationships.

A. Designing the Organization Structure

The following outline summarises the essential steps in designing a sound organization structure:

Step 1. Clarify, in writing, the over all objectives and end results desired for the organization as a whole: the summary results of total resources and personnel utilised by the organization. Why was the organization established? What is it trying to accomplish? What are its total resources and annual volume of business expected to be?

Step 2. Determine what major activities are necessary in order to achieve desired objectives and results.

Step 3. Group these activities into closely-related major functions (manufacturing, distribution, finance, etc.), in conformity with the specialised abilities, interests, and skills of "functional teams of personnel" whose efforts are most closely related in accomplishing a major segment of the organization's over all objectives.

This grouping must be simple; tailor-made for each organization, accepted by those who will be affected, and contribute to the:

(a) Optimum effectiveness and economy of operations for the organization as a whole;

(b) Ease of direction, co-ordination, control and accountability, and appraisal of performance;

(c) Most effective utilization and harmonious relationships of the total work force;

(d) Future growth and development of the organization, with minimum changes in the basic structure required as the organization expands.

Step 4. Systematically unite the major functions (for which a single executive can be held solely accountable in achieving a major segment of the organization's over all objectives) into a sound, simple framework which constitutes the skeleton of the organization structure as a whole and each part thereof should be designed so as to facilitate the accomplishment of definitely established objectives and also encourage :

(a) Direct, clear-cut lines of authority, accountability, and responsibility;

(b) Smooth continuity of work flow and natural integration of all administrative activities;

(c) Optimum performance by each of the functional groups, with clean cut - off lines of accountability insofar as practicable-avoid overlaps and gaps of responsibility;

(d) Ease of co-ordination and communications – up and down and across all levels of the organization;

(e) The completion of periodic performance appraisals of the work of each functional group, in conformity with criteria that can be established on a sound functional basis that is harmonious with the organizational pattern;

(f) High morale and job satisfaction on the part of every person in the organization.

Step 5. Complete the basic organization structure and secure necessary approvals, in principle, before attempting to complete any detail breakdowns by departments, sections, and units.

Then complete each of the departmental structures in conformity with the principles outlined in steps 1-4 above.

Step 6. Observe the following techniques before attempting to put any organization structure into effect:

(a) Develop an "ideal structure," observing the principles indicated in steps 1-5; what is the best structure that can be designed for this organization?

(b) Identify the differences between the "ideal structure" and the "current structure"; why is the "ideal structure" better suited to the practical needs of the organization, and how will it facilitate improved performance?

(c) Review the potential utilization of the present staff in the proposed structure; in priority of importance, what steps would need to be taken in order to fit the present staff into the proposed "ideal structure?"

(d) Ascertain what personnel problems are involved with respect to viewpoints, vested interests, and objections to the change that may be required by the proposed structure; what are the solutions to these problems? How can adjustments be worked out insofar as practicable?

(e) Develop a revised chart which can be recommended for approval and a tentative schedule of changes that are recommended in order to bring about needed improvements that are agreed upon what is the sequence of changes to be made? When will these changes be made? Who will do what?

(f) Move the revised organization plan, as approved, forward in conformity with a well-designed schedule as rapidly as changes can be made consistent with the optimum results that must be accomplished, with the least possible disturbance of money and productivity, and the best interests of the over all organization. Determine who is accountable for following through the phases of the plan as approved.

B. Putting Organizational Changes into Effect

The effecting of changes in a large organization is a composite process. Time is the central consideration. Considerable time usually elapses before top management becomes aware that the basic causes of many major operating difficulties may be due to weaknesses in their organization's structure.

It takes time to develop a sound plan of organization. Its success, however, is dependent upon changes in the behaviour patterns of many groups and individuals in the organization. The acquisition of new attitudes and skills by the members of the management team affected by organizational changes is the crux of the problem.

It takes time, considerable time, for adults to change their habits of working. Most adults resist any changes in their environment, responsibilities, and authority.

Some of the steps that time in effecting organizational changes are:

1. Recognition of organizational defects;
2. Determination to take corrective action;
3. Making a thorough study and an accurate analysis of the total organizational situation;
4. Development of the proposed plan of organization; securing understanding through participation;
5. Securing necessary clearances, recommendations and approval of the proposed plan;
6. Announcement of the new Plan of Organization;

7. Detailing revised assignments of new functions, responsibilities, authority, and accountability;
8. Realignment of various operating procedures, relationships, and incentives in conformity with the revised plan;
9. The revision and/or preparation of necessary directives and manuals, and the instruction of key personnel in conformity with the revised plan and effective follow through to assure adequate changes in behaviour patterns;
10. Monitoring the plan and effecting remedial action wherever indicated, without delay;
11. Adjusting and revising the plan in the light of experience; and
12. Establishing effective management controls; establishing criteria for measuring management performance; conducting periodic performance appraisals as required, and maintaining minimum management reports.

The problem of how to alter changes in human behaviour is much more complex than the problem of designing a sound organization plan.

Successful performance lies not in the soundness of the plan alone but finally in the ability of the top executives and their subordinates to alter their management behaviour in accordance with the objectives which the revised plan of organization seeks to accomplish. People, however, including adults, can and will adjust to changes - if circumstances are created which influence (cause) them to do so. This is the crux of the problem in effecting changes (improvements) in a large organization.

Finally, the revised plan of organization, and the performance of the management team affected, should be measured by its effectiveness in: (1) penetrating an increased "share of the market"; (2) improving its "net earnings on invested capital"; and (3) other criteria as agreed upon prior to the approval of the plan.

C. The Major Levels of Management

The chart below, and the detailed explanations that follow, contain, in the main, the generally accepted designations of management and the primary functions that should be assigned to each level. The chart illustrates the principal departmental segments of management for which a single executive should be solely accountable to the president.

The relationships of Levels I and II usually over lap to a certain degree; also there is often an over - lapping of Levels II and III, as there is with Level III and non-supervisory personnel. There should neither be over - lapping however between the functions of Level I and Level III; nor between Level II and non-supervisor personnel. Some exception to this principle must occur, of course, in small organizations where a few management positions must cover all functions. The larger the organization the more the specialisation of each of the levels tend to be in conformity with the outlines that follow. The over-lapping indicated may be illustrated by this chart:

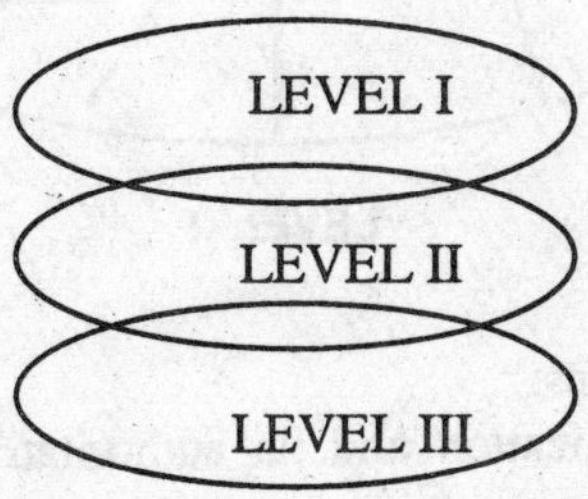

Improving the performance of management is one of the specific problems of the Board of Directors and the chief executive of the organization. A sound organization structure (plus a common understanding of the major functions and responsibilities of each of the levels of management, and their respective roles), provides the framework necessary for the development and maintenance of a smooth running organization.

Level	Designation	Accountable for
I.	Administrative Officials	- Directing Major Functions
II.	Executive Officers	- Directing Supervision of Activities
III.	Supervisors and Foremen	- Supervising Performance of Operations
IV.	Non-supervisory personnel perform specific tasks as directed	

Chart for illustrative purposes only; every structure must be designed to fit the needs of the individual enterprise which is affected.

MAJOR LEVELS OF MANAGEMENT

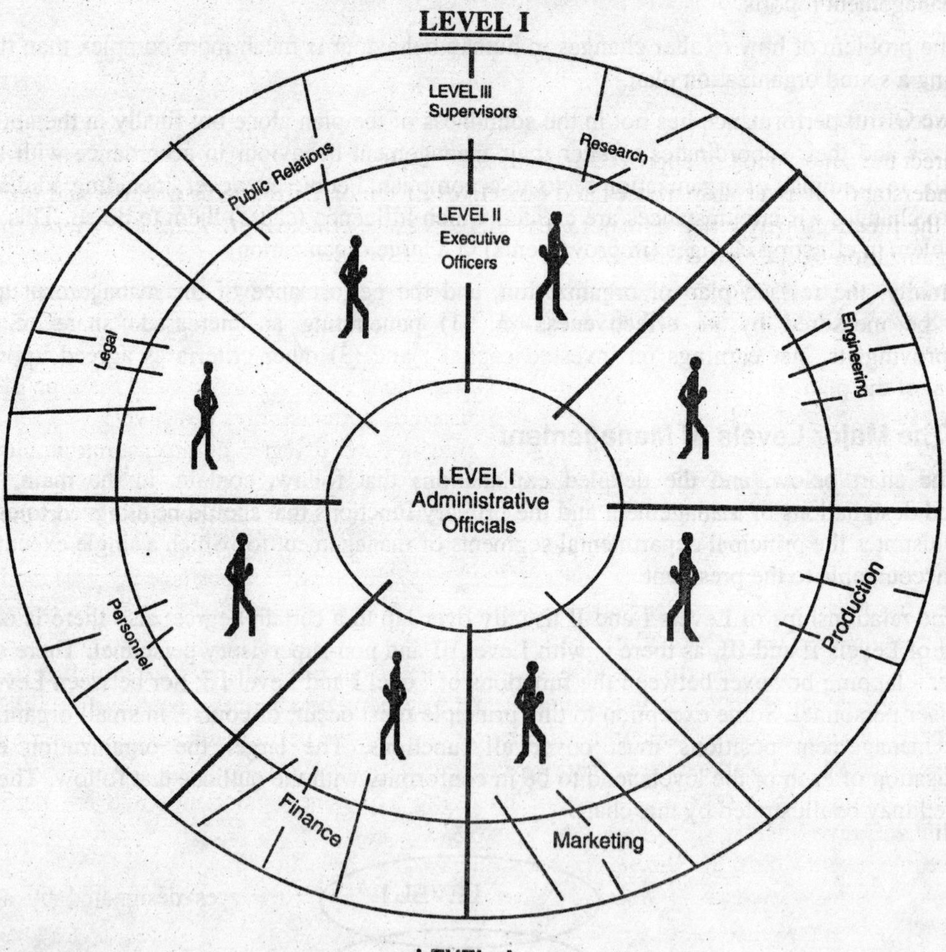

Administrative Officials

Direct the execution of major functions:

1. Interpret the purposes of the organization and its authoritative fields of action; sense the major problems and causes involved.
2. Establish objectives; determine end results desired; approve major policies, and develop an organization of persons which can accomplish those activities for which top management is held responsible.
3. Approve the organizational structure and the major plans of action for achieving established objectives. (This assumes that organization and functional charts are used to help everyone in the organization, regardless of position, to know what his job is, to whom he is responsible, and the proper channels of communication).

4. Select the chief executive(s); assign responsibilities, and delegate commensurate authority, through administrative directives, for accomplishing results through others.
5. Determine resources needed to accomplish objectives and provide adequate funds as required.
6. Co-ordinate all major staff activities and operating functions.
7. Approve the over all personnel programme of the organization including its plan of selection, promotion and compensation of all persons who perform services for it.
8. Provide for and require essential administrative controls, including adequate reports, audits and inspection, appraisal of the organization's over all operating effectiveness, and effect remedial action in consultation with executives concerned.
9. Keep aware of trends and developments affecting objectives and policies and take initiative in making needed adjustments in time.
10. Assume final responsibility for the effects of their decisions.
11. Submit to source of authority summary reports of operating results.

LEVEL II

Executive Officers

Direct the supervision of approved activities:

1. Understand the over all purposes and objectives of the organization as a whole and the relationships of the functions performed in major areas thereof, sense principal problems and causes involved in the organization of which he is executive.
2. Understand responsibilities and scope of authority as delegated; determine what operations are necessary to attain end results assigned, and recommend policies pertinent to their successful achievement.
3. Recommend major plans of actions including functions to be performed, and the type of organization best suited to accomplish the objectives designated by administrative directives.
4. Select supervisory personnel; prescribe assignments and delegate commensurate authority; approve operating procedures; enlist teamwork co-operation and loyalty.
5. Prepare and secure approval of necessary budgets and accept responsibility for the expenditure thereof.
6. Plan assignments, so far as practicable, so that the work of each subordinate is on a functional basis.
7. Approve, subject to personnel policies, the appointment of qualified persons to perform approved functions within the organization units affected.
8. Review the effectiveness of the operations of the organizational units for which responsibility has been delegated; effect remedial action through appropriate channels; ascertain facilities needed by supervisors and authorise procurement thereof; appraise the performance of supervisory personnel and develop improved performance wherever needed.
9. Keep administrative officials aware of operating experience and trends that are pertinent to their administrative functions.
10. Assume responsibility for the acts of subordinates.
11. Make summary reports in line with the end results and objectives designated by administrative directives.

LEVEL III

Supervisors and Foremen

Direct the performance of specific operations:

1. Understand the end results desired from the organizational unit supervised and the relationships of other functions affecting the operations of the unit.
2. Understand responsibilities and scope of authority as delegated, as well as policies, rules and regulations affecting the unit, and recommend procedures pertinent to the unit's most successful operations.
3. Plan and distribute the work load of the unit on the basis of the most effective operation; taking into consideration such factors as : available personnel and facilities, volume and quality of production, and unit cost.

4. Select the persons who can best perform the operations of the unit.

   Determine who does what; instruct workers correctly with regard to each specific task to which they are assigned; provide each worker with a clear statement of his work assignments, including an appropriate interpretation of the purpose of the work performed.

5. See that the workers are provided with adequate supplies and material, without waste; that working conditions within the unit are safe; that the flow of work is streamlined; that the work place is (a) properly layed out, (b) provided with adequate equipment, and (c) that it is maintained in the best possible working order.

6. Organize the work of the unit so that a satisfactory production schedule is maintained most efficiently.

7. Initiate actions affecting personnel under supervision.

8. Determine, in co-operation with workers affected, definite standards of performance which are expected for each operation as to : quality of end-results; volume of output in work units; maintenance of production and operating schedules.

Appraise periodically the effectiveness of each worker's performance on the job as compared to approved standards; his stage of progress; the over-all results of his work; his principal limitations and the utilization of his highest skills; his promotional possibilities and see to it that the training needed to improve his effectiveness is made available.

Maintain discipline, regular attendance, the observance of all regulations affecting workers, and foster the maintenance of high morale within the group.

9. Keep aware of changes in policies, regulations and procedures and take initiative in recommending needed changes at appropriate time.

10. Assume responsibility for the performance of all workers supervised; encourage and assist individual workers by giving them adequate recognition. encourage them to make suggestions and give full credit to their ideas; counsel with them on their personal problems and adjust to grievances promptly and fairly; promote teamwork and appropriate relationships between members of the group.

11. Keep higher levels of supervision informed regarding the unit's progress, operating problems; possible improvement; morale questions; and make periodic reports regarding the achievement of the objectives assigned to the unit.

    Carry out these general responsibilities:

    To superiors:

    (a) Understand superiors' objectives and policies;
    (b) Keep superiors advised and informed of activities; and
    (c) Abide by and support decisions of superiors.

    To associates on same level of authority:

    (a) Understand purposes and relationships;
    (b) Take interest in coordinating work with other units; and
    (c) Co-operate fully with all associates.

    To workers under immediate supervision:

    (a) Know each worker's record;
    (b) Develop and improve each worker's performance; and
    (c) Give full and adequate recognition for results.

LEVEL IV

Non-supervisory Personnel

Perform specific duties under general or immediate supervision:

1. Understand the end results desired from work performed.
2. Maintain self-discipline on the job, including regular attendance and the observance of all general rules and regulations affecting workers.
3. Co-operate with supervisory personnel and fellow workers in getting out maximum production from each day's effort on the job.

4. Perform specific tasks as assigned.
5. Keep work place, including equipment and supplies, orderly, clean, arranged most effectively and maintained in good working condition.
6. Organize daily work so that production standards are maintained.
7. Be dependable, loyal to the immediate group, the organization as a whole, and observe the obligations of the position.
8. Develop work habits which will eliminate any discrepancies between actual and expected performance; complete any training needed.
9. Keep aware of improved methods and new development in present occupational fields and initiate suggestions to immediate supervisor.
10. Take an interest in coordinating work with associates; maintain teamwork and appropriate relationships with fellow workers.
11. Keep supervisor advised regarding work progress and any problems affecting operations.

D. Clarifying Line and Staff Relationships

The Board of Directors

The Board is accountable to the Policyholders for the welfare and progress of the Companies.* The Board upon recommendation of the President, approves the over - all objectives, policies, annual budget, and other basic controls governing the administration of the Companies and delegates to the President final responsibility for the attainment of desired results.

The President

The President delegates to designated Line Officers responsibility and authority** for the attainment of specific results and effecting remedial action wherever necessary; and to designated Staff Officers accountability for planning, developing, and recommending patterns of action (objectives, policies, programmes, and criteria for appraising performance) and recommending any action required to assure the accomplishment of results delegated to the President by the Board.

STAFF	LINE
Create and recommend patterns of action	Carry out approved programmes of action
"The Architects"	"The Contractors"
In each functional area : 1. Conduct research and analyse needs.	In each respective echelon : 1. Attain approved objectives, about policies and programmes and accept responsibility and accountability for specific results as delegated.

* Nationwide Insurance Companies, Columbus, Ohio.

** Wherever applicable, delegations are also made by each operating President to designated Line and Staff Officers reporting directly to him.

2. Plan, develop, review, and recommend. (a) Objectives; (b) Basic policies; (c) Programmes Manuals and instructions; (d) Criteria for (standards) measuring results;	2. Plan, direct, and co - ordinate approved activities and the utilisation of personnel and resources required in order to secure desired results.
3. Conduct and report periodic appraisals of performance for conformity with approved objectives, policies, and programmes.	3. Maintain current appraisals of activities in conformity with approved schedules, standard, objectives, policies and programmes, and effect administrative action as needed.
4. Counsel and/or recommend appropriate remedial action wherever and wherever indicated.	4. Submit periodic and specific progress reports as required.

1. THE TEN COMMANDMENTS OF SOUND ORGANIZATION

There are two kinds of efficiency: One kind is only apparent and is produced in organizations through the exercise of mere discipline. This is but a simulation of the second, or true, efficiency which springs, as Woodrow Wilson said, from the spontaneous co-operation of a free people. If is your job, in the final analysis, to create and develop this voluntary cooperation among the people whom you supervise. For, no matter how powerful a combination of money, machines and materials a company may have, this is a dead and sterile thing without a team of willing thinking, and articulate people to guide it.

1. Definite and clear-cut responsibilities should be assigned to each executive.
2. Responsibility should always be coupled with corresponding authority.
3. No change should be made in the scope or responsibilities of a position without a definite understanding to that effect on the part of all persons concerned.
4. No executive or employee, occupying a single position in the organization, should be subject to definite orders from more than one source.
5. Orders should never be given to subordinates over the head of a responsible executive. Rather than do this, the officer in question should be supplanted.
6. Criticisms of subordinates should whenever possible be made privately, and in no case-should a subordinate be criticised in the presence of executives or employees of equal or lower rank.
7. No dispute or difference between executives or employees as to authority or responsibilities should be considered too trivial for prompt and careful adjudication.
8. Promotions, wage changes, and disciplinary action should always be approved by the executive immediately superior to the one directly responsible.
9. No executive or employee should ever be required, or expected, to be at the same time an assistant to, and critic of , another.
10. Any executive whose work is subject to regular inspection should, whenever practicable, be given the assistance and facilities necessary to enable him to maintain an independent check of the quality of his work.

II. TEN TESTS OF ORGANIZATION AND STAFFING

Sound organization creates the pattern – the framework, no less – that vitally affects the performance and effectiveness of all members of management. Most defects in organization arise from disregard of a few fundamental principles. The function of organization includes both structure and staffing.

How satisfactorily, in your opinion, are the principles of sound organization and staffing carried out in our organization?

Place a check mark in those spaces which indicate your true appraisal of our present attainment in each of the areas listed below:

Our Performance

1. Excellent, no changes needed now;
2. Adequate, little improvement needed;
3. Fairly satisfactory, some improvement needed;
4. Weak, considerable improvement needed;
5. Lacking, much improvement needed.

		5	4	3	2	1
1.	Accountability: Is each department organized around the achievement of a major company objective for which a single executive is held finally responsible and accountable in conformity with definite standards?					
2.	Authority: Is there a clear line of formal authority running from the top to the bottom of the organization? Does everyone know exactly to whom he reports, what he is accountable for, and what standards he is required to meet?					
3.	Progression: Do all positions within each department, and the company as a whole, provide a natural ladder of progression and increasing scope so related in sequence of difficulty that at all times employees are in training for advancements as vacancies occur?					
4.	Relationships: Have all functional responsibilities, relationships, and authorities been clarified? Are lines of command, sources of advice, and channels of communication definite and clear-cut?					
5.	Effectiveness: Does the Organization Structure (pattern) create a climate that encourages maximum executive performance, effectiveness, and accountability?					
6.	Duties and Responsibilities: Are the objectives of each organizational unit and the duties and responsibilities of every position within the organization prescribed in writing?					
7.	Qualification Requirements: Have qualifications standards for each position been prescribed in terms of specific knowledge, skills, and personal qualities required? How effectively are they being used for the selection and promotion of qualified employees?					
8.	Compensation: Have compensation standards been prescribed in terms of position classifications, grades, and adequate pay ranges applicable to every position in the organization? How effectively are they being administered?					
9.	Utilization: Is each executive and supervisor held finally responsible for the selection, compensation, development, productivity, and morale of all persons who report to him? For the maximum utilization of the highest abilities, skills, and interests of each employee within his jurisdiction?					
10.	Performance Appraisals: Is a systematic programme of periodic appraisals of executive performance at all levels carried out					

	effectively? Does Top Management require and use adequate analyses of the results of such appraisals?				

Organization and Staffing

Discussion Outline

Questions for Discussion

1. What are some of the clues that indicate whether or not a Company (or a Department) has a sound organization structure?
2. What are the most effective steps that should be observed in developing an effective organization chart?
3. What is the result likely to be if an organization structure is designed around the personal qualifications of the present staff?
4. What is the difference between an organization chart and a functional chart? Which should be developed first?
5. What are the relationships between an organization chart and position descriptions?
6. What are the most important factor headings that should be included in position descriptions? Qualification specifications?
7. Why is it important that organizations distinguish clearly the responsibilities, relationships, authorities, and accountability of :

   (a) various levels of management; (b) line and staff positions?
8. How do you identify whether unsatisfactory results are due to lack of personnel performance or faulty organization structure?
9. What are the most time consuming steps that are usually required in effecting improvements in an organization structure?
10. What is likely to be one of the greatest values in using management consultants for the purpose of reviewing a company's organization structure and recommending possible improvements?

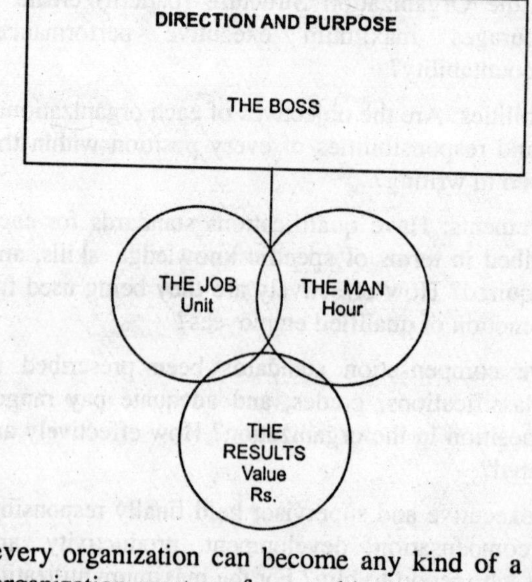

The Chief Executive of every organization can become any kind of a Manager that he wants to become! Everyone else in the organization must conform to his direction and leadership; to the king of management climate that he creates and maintains. His managerial strengths and weaknesses affect the performance of the entire organization.

Direction and Leadership

The Boss, at every level of management is an organization, can improve or retard the performance and productivity of everyone who reports directly to him, because:

The Boss can

1. Clarify or confuse: (a) the objective of the job; (b) assignments and results expected; (c) criteria for measuring performance;
2. Stimulate or inhibit optimum performance on the job;
3. Encourage or retard the utilization of employees' highest abilities, skills, and interest;
4. Provide or withhold incentives for growth and development;
5. Advance or restrict opportunities for promotion; and
6. Enhance or deter job satisfaction and morale.

The Job, where every employee spends most of his productive time thought, and effort, is the environment that is most likely to dominate his growth and development, because:

The JOB can

1. Be a continuous day-to-day challenge to improve;
2. Provide accurate measurements of improvement;
3. Motivate highest abilities, skills, and interests;
4. Inspire outstanding achievement and productivity;
5. Lead to progressively enlarged opportunities; and
6. Bring into realization the rewards and satisfactions that come out only from the joy of achievement and the thrill of creative effort.

On the negative side, the Job can also:

1. Be a dull daily routine;
2. Provide no measurement of progress;
3. Discourage growth and development;
4. Be filled with monotony;
5. Lead to a rut; and
6. Bring only frustrations.

On-The-Job Coaching

Research and observation to date indicate that high productivity and high morale, and optimum growth and development on the part of employees come principally from the on-the-job coaching and the influence that is exercised by each man's immediate boss.

Most of us are conditioned to want to do the things that please the Boss; to try to do what he expects from us, in the order and in the manner that is of greatest significance to him.

It is the policy of many organizations that the chief executive, and in turn every manager, supervisor, and foreman in the organization to be held finally accountable for the selection, performance, training, morale, job-satisfaction, and the growth and development of all persons who report directly to him. He is also accountable for seeing that all managers, supervisors, and foremen in subsequent echelons of his command likewise carry out this phase of their management responsibility with respect to the people who report to them. Staff personnel may advise and assist them in carrying out this responsibility but there is no substitute for the influence of the chain of command.

To carry out his management responsibilities of direction and leadership.

The **Boss** needs:

1. Awareness, and sensitivity, and an understanding of human relations problems;
2. Skill in modern diagnostic techniques, ascertaining the courses of problems;
3. Skill in on-the-job coaching, "telling alone is not enough"; and

4. A mastery of the art of changing the behaviour of others.

Productivity is dependent upon a variety of conditions. It involves the product, plant design, flow of work, facilities and equipment, production know-how, methods, procedures, and many other engineering actors. And in addition to engineering know-how, productivity is also dependent upon morale, a willingness to work, and job satisfaction on the part of all employees.

Top management must accept final responsibility for the productivity and the morale of its total work force, and for the utilization (or taste) of the highest abilities, skills, and interests of individual employees under its direction. Management must also accept final responsibility for attaining optimum productivity with a minimum of stress, strain, and friction; and for the teamwork, loyalty, and job satisfaction in the total work force.

Managers should be able: (a) to recognise why people do or do not produce effectively; (b) to provide adequate incentives that will motive optimum productivity within their respective operations; and (c) to create and maintain circumstances which encourage supervisors, foremen, and employees to want to excel in the performance of their jobs, and want to maintain high productivity. It is not uncommon to hear managers complain about employees not wanting to work today, without recognizing or accepting the fact that in their position of leadership they must assume accountability for creating or not creating the circumstances which cause people to want to work, or not want to work.

Morale is an attitude of mind. It is the unconscious fragile spirit that permeates the entire organization. It may take a long time to develop. It is fluid and unstable. It is never permanently established, and it must not be taken for granted.

The principal factors within an organization that affect employee's morale are:

1. Ideals – Leadership;
2. Objectives and policies;
3. Compensation.
4. Incentives;
5. Facilities;
6. Environment;
7. Organization structure;
8. Procedures and controls.

Incentives that assist managers to maintain high employee morale include:

1. Recognition of individual abilities and interests;
2. Opportunity proportionate to performance and potential ability insofar as practicable;
3. Awareness of pride in a job well done;
4. Rewards commensurate with performance: non-financial, financial, such as promotion, bonus salary, extra vacation, etc.

The highest morale to be found in any group of persons is probably within an amateur athletic team that is "on the move" to victory. It is significant that their morale is not dependent upon:

Compensation (money)	Bargaining power
Short hours	Safety
Security	Seniority

or any of the fringe benefits that are so often identified as "builders morale."

Management Controls: In order to maintain high morale and productivity, it is essential that adequate management controls be established and maintained which will assist the Board of Directors, the President, and his executive staff to:

1. Project desired results accurately in conformity with plan;
2. Identify and forecast major trends and problems;
3. Determine needs for change in advance of any emergency;

4. Detect problems in time to take corrective action before becoming critical.

Circumstances : What can top management do to create circumstances which will encourage high morale and productivity? Five important steps that managers can take are:

1. Develop, publish, and interpret the company's over all objectives and policies.

   This takes courage and skill, but whenever men place greater emphasis upon security or the status quo then they do upon opportunity, initiative and morale are likely to wither and decay.

2. Create harmonious relationships and conditions. All executives and supervisors should be proud of their organization; proud of their own jobs, and proud of the accomplishments of their subordinates. Experience proves that the performance of the total work force is directly related to the quality and the performance of management.

3. Secure acceptance. Build up in the minds of first and second lines of supervision, as well as all top executives, an understanding and acceptance of what the company as a whole is endeavouring to accomplish; a deep conviction about the importance of the organization's purposes and objectives.

4. Conduct well-planned and effective informational meetings at least (wherever practicable):
   (a) Once a year for all employees;
   (b) Three or four times a year for all supervisory employees, including foremen;
   (c) Once a month for all key management personnel, and
   (d) Weekly conferences for top management, as required. It's what happens in the executive sessions of top management when the doors are closed and the chips are down that makes for real "morale" (or lack of it) in the organization.

5. Issue well-designed and interesting publications:
   (a) Company paper: periodically, weekly or monthly;
   (b) Management reports to employees: annually or quarterly;
   (c) Reports to owners, stockholders, members, other major interests: annually;
   (d) Periodicals and special reports as required;
   (e) Handbooks, standard practice instructions;
   (f) Policy manuals, at appropriate levels;
   (g) Training materials, as required, continuously.

Leadership: Herbert H. Casson in his splendid little book, *Tips on Leadership* (B.C. Forbes Pub. Co. N.Y.) says: "Leadership is a thing by itself. It calls for more than ability. It has a technique of its own. In other words, it can be acquired to a large extent. It can be learned, as any other art. And it is the art that stands highest of all." He gives the following suggestions to the man who would acquire the techniques and the art of leadership:

1. Make decision quickly;
2. Be independent;
3. Act and stand firmly;
4. Always have a fight on;
5. Learn to make 'no's;
6. Consider defeats as lessons;
7. Form alliances with other leaders;
8. Walk towards danger;
9. Create a staff;
10. Represent your followers;
11. Reward loyalty;
12. Have a great, worthy purpose.

MANAGEMENT PLANNING

In order to maintain effective performance within any organizational unit, it is necessary that the manager of that unit :

First, understand clearly the end results he is expected to attain, and the criteria for measuring his performance;

Second, identify the essential activities and schedules his unit must carry out in order to accomplish the end results for which he is accountable, and

Third, distribute his work load and delegate responsibilities so as to maintain the optimum utilization of his total work force, consistent with the desired satisfactions of all concerned.

This Worksheet is designed to facilitate continuous improvement in these three important functions of management.

Instructions

Step 1. In the blank space in the upper left hand corner, write a brief over all statement of the objectives or end results for which your organizational unit is accountable.

Step 2. Determine and clarify, in sequence of importance, the activities that must be performed in order to secure the desired end results indicated above.*

Step 3. In the No. 1 space at the top of the page, write your name as head of the organizational unit; in the next space, the employee or officer of next highest rank; thence, the names of other members of the department in order of importance, grade, or salary.

Step 4. In appropriate squares, check the activities which are assigned to each person listed above, including yourself.

Step 5. Review the performance of each person affected and indicate with the symbol "T" all instances where additional training is needed, and, from this check list, prepare a subsequent training schedule.

Note: It is suggested that a brief description of each activity performed within the organizational unit be written on a single sheet of paper or a 3x5 card. After these have been completed, sort the items in sequence of importance, eliminate nonessential items, and then rearrange or simplify all remaining separate statements until a final pattern has been complete. Thence, copy the items on the work sheet as indicated.

III. TEN TESTS OF DIRECTION AND LEADERSHIP

Management is responsible for the morale and productivity of its total work force – for employee attitudes, willingness to produce; for attaining maximum production with a minimum of stress, strain and friction; and for teamwork, loyalty and satisfaction.

How satisfactorily, in your opinion, are the principles of effective direction and leadership carried out in our organization?

Place a check mark in those spaces which indicate your true appraisal of our present attainment in each of the areas listed below.

Our Performance

1. Excellent
   No changes needed now.
2. Adequate
   Little improvement needed.
3. Fairly Satisfactory
   Some improvement needed.
4. Weak
   Considerable improvement needed.

5. Lacking
   Much improvement needed.

	5	4	3	2	1
1. **Circumstances:** Has Management created conditions and circumstances which encourage employees to maintain high productivity on their own volition?					
2. **Morale:** Does Management recognise that the universal desire of every normal person is "to be somebody"; are work assignments, recognition awards, and opportunities for advancement planned accordingly?					
3. **Conference Leadership:** Are all members of Management skilled in conducting problem-solving conferences and group meetings?					
4. **Participation:** Does Top Management encourage as many members of the Management group as practicable to participate in the determination of over all objectives, policies, and schedules that affect their respective departments?					
5. **Development:** Is a sound programme of Management Development currently in effect which is in conformity with individual needs and designed to improve the performance of all key personnel?					
6. **Utilization:** Do executives and supervisors recognize and utilize the highest abilities and interests of their subordinates insofar as practicable?					
7. **Advancement:** Do executives and supervisors make certain that all advancements of subordinates are always made upon the basis of merit, performance, and predetermined standards?					
8. **Understanding:** Does Management make certain that every person within the organization clearly understands what he and his group and the organization as a whole are trying to accomplish?					
9. **Motivation:** Does Management appraise currently the need for improvement in performance throughout the organization and effect remedial action wherever required?					
10. **Job Satisfaction:** Do employees realise job satisfaction and appropriate recognition for work well done?					

CHAPTER

5

Models for Behaviour

Since Behaviour Science is concerned with understanding and predicting human behaviour, philosophers, theorlogians, politicians, scientists, managers, and the person on the street have been and still are preoccupied with the idea of developing techniques to find what is the real nature of human being? Are people good or bad, rational or irrational, free or biased? A number of studies have been made in this area. However, the true nature of human behaviour is largely most unfounded and still open for discussion and research.

Scholar or lay person, everyone has had abundant experience in living and dealing with, reading about, and observing fellow human beings. A normal outgrowth of this lifetime of experience is that everyone has a definite opinion about human behaviour. Unfortunately, when common sense approaches to human behaviour are put to the test of science, they are often proved wrong. Yet, it is through the applications of science that human behaviour can best be understood.

The behavioural scientist analyses human behaviour on the basis of scientific methodology. The major goal of behavioural science is to understand behaviour. On the other hand, philosophers, theologians, and managers are interested primarily in evaluating behaviour. The emphasis, on understanding versus evaluation is the major difference between the behavioural sciences and the other approaches used in analysing human behaviour.

The objective of any science is to discover truth and develop understanding. Scientists always attempt to divorce their own value judgments from this quest. The following models take an understanding, not an evaluating approach to the overall nature of human behaviour. These models serve as important background information for developing a specific model for organizational behaviour.

Freudian Psychoanalytic Model

The Freudian approach relies on a psychoanalytic or conflict model of humans. At least in Western culture, the conception of people being in constant inner conflict is one of the oldest explanations. The conflict model portrayed primitive humans constant inner struggle between good and evil. Good (angels) and evil (devils) were believed to be competing for the domination of the body and soul. Common sayings, such as "He is possessed by the devil" or "She is a little angel", reflect this view. Under this model, individuals are merely innocent bystanders and the situation completely overwhelms them. This primitive vie of conflict still exists in many parts of the world, even within subcultures of highly developed countries. Obviously, the primitive good-evil conflict model cannot be substantiated by scientific methodology. It is based on magic and the supernatural, which are outside the realm of science.

A more meaningful, comprehensive, and systematically based conflict model stems from the theories of Sigmund Freud. These theories can be summarized into what can be called the psychoanalytic model. Although Freud is most closely associated with the model, others, such as Carl Jung, Alfred Adler, Karen Horney, and Eric From, who all broke away from Freud, made additional contributions and extended the model.

Clinical techniques were used primarily to develop the psychoanalytic model. Through the clinical techniques of free association and psychotherapy, Freud noted that his patient's behaviour could not always be consciously explained. This clinical finding led him to conclude that major motivating force in humans is unconscious in nature. The personality structure can be explained within the unconscious framework.

Freud believed, by three interrelated, but often conflicting, psychoanalytic concepts: the id, the ego, and the superego.

(i) The Id: The id is the core of the unconscious. It is the unleashed, raw, primitive, instinctual drive of the freudian model. The id constantly struggling for gratification and pleasure is manifested mainly through the libido (sexual urges) or aggression. The libido strives for sexual relations and pleasure, but also for warmth, food, and comfort. Aggressive impulses of the id are destructive and include the urges to fight, dominate, and generally destroy. In a conflict sense, the id incorporates life instincts that compete with its death instincts. As individuals develop and mature, they learn to control the id. But even then it remains a driving force throughout life and an important source of thinking and behaving.

(ii) The Ego: Whereas the id represents the unconscious, the ego is the conscious. The superego provides the norms that enable the ego to determine what is right or wrong. The superego conscience should not be confused with the conscious aspects of the ego. In fact according to Freud, the superego is mostly unconscious.

The person is not aware of the workings of the superego. The conscience is developed by absorption of the cultural values and morals of a society. Accordingly, the parents have the most influence on the development of the superego. After resolving the Oedipus or Electra complex (love of parent), the child will unconsciously identify with the parents' values and morals.

The superego aids the person by assisting the ego to combat the impulses of the id. However, in some situations the superego can also be in conflict with the ego. An example is the situation where the reality-seeking ego violates the conscience. The conflict between ego and conscience provokes the wrath and vengeance of the largely unconscious superego. The inevitable struggle between the id, ego, and superego makes this to be called as a conflict model of behaviour.

The Freudian Model in Perspective

Freud's model is characterized by the conflicting personality constructs (id, ego, and superego) and unconscious motivation. Psychological adjustment occurs only when the ego properly develops to resolve the conflicts stemming from the id and superego.

The ego concept implies that humans are rational, but the id, the superego, and unconscious motivation give the impression that humans are very irrational. In the Freudian model, behaviour is based on emotion. If the ego cannot control the id, the person is an aggressive, pleasure-seeking menace to society. If the id is too severely checked by the ego, the person is equally maladjusted. Moreover, if the superego is very strong, the result may be acute anxiety and guilt.

Freud has had a great impact in many areas of twentieth - century thought. He had a great influence on treatment techniques for the mentally ill, and he did make some contribution to the understanding of human behaviour. His ideas have proved to be very far-reaching and long-lasting. Yet, today he is criticized as much as he is praised. Most of the criticism centres on the overemphasis given to sexual motivation.

From a behavioural science viewpoint, however, the most valid criticism of the Freudian model is that it is not based on empirically verifiable factors. The psychoanalytic elements are largely hypothetical constructs and not measurable, observable items for scientific analysis and verification. The id, ego, and superego are primarily a "black box" explanation of humans. This is why most modern behavioural scientists reject the psychoanalytic model as the total explanation of human personality and behaviour. Nevertheless, important insights into personality structure and the ideas of unconscious motivation are significant contributions and they serve as important tool for understanding specific behaviours of human being.

Existentialistic Model

Existentialism, broadly defined as the search for meaning, is based on the analysis of existence and being. The existentialistic model is not a behavioural science model. Its roots lie more in the realm of philosophy and literature and are not scientifically based.

Existentialism is European in origin and can be traced to the writings of the philosophers Kierkegaard, Nietzsche, and Schopenhauer. Among the philosophers with an existentialist orientation are Martin Heidegger, Martin Buber, and Jean-Paul Sartre. The best-known American spokesman has been Rollo May. May and Sartre, in particular, have been critical of the usual scientific approaches that are employed to gain an understanding of humans. They are afraid that a scientific behavioural analysis may destroy or lose sight of the person's true nature or "being."

Existentialists see a breakdown of traditional norms and the ties that individuals have traditionally with society. For example, Rollo May view people as suffering from unconstructive anxiety. He defines "unconstructive" or "neurotic" anxiety as the "Shrinking of consciousness, the blocking off of awareness; and when it is prolonged it leads to a feeling of depersonalization and apathy" which is "the state, to a greater or lesser degree, of those who have lost, or never achieved, the experience of their own identity in the world." This feeling of **"depersonalization and apathy"** is what Durkheim referred to a asnomie.

In modern times the individual is faced with a very large, urbanised environment. The existentialists believe that the depersonalizing effects of this environment force individuals to determine their own destiny. People shape their own identity and make their "existence" meaningful and worthwhile to themselves. This process is accomplished through the individual's experience of being. Coleman views this being as "a matter of commitment to increased self - awareness and self - direction, to true communication with others, to concern with values and evaluation and to acceptance of the responsibility for making choices and directing his own destiny."

The emphasis attached to self - awareness and action in the existential scheme is different from that in the psychoanalytic model. Existentially, people seek self - awareness, direction, and control. What they make of this existence is entirely up to them. The existentialist approach maintains that people have free will to chart their existence and being.

The Impact of the Existential Model

The existentialist approach becomes very relevant in a society suffering from environmental and moral decay. In a world that is overpopulated, undernourished, polluted, ravaged by war and crime, with racial injustice and poverty rampant amidst affluence and material excess, it is extremely difficult for an individual to carve out a meaningful existence. The problem is compounded if the old, tradition-bound values of the past linger on as nommas for the present although they are irrelevant and incapable of practical application under current conditions or in the foreseeable future.

Certainly some aspects of the modern Indian scene seem directly relevant to an existentialist approach. Similarly, on a micro level, human behaviour in organizations seems appropriate for existentialist study and analysis. Determining a meaningful occupational existence may be a severe challenge for an individual faced with the characteristics of the modern formal organization. Although not scientifically based and not conceptually integrated into this book, existentialism provides some very useful insights. It can be effectively used to set a tone and to supplement more scientifically based discussions of human behaviour.

Cognitive Model

The psychoanalytic and existentialistic models are on the fringe of the study of human behaviour. Two more scientifically based models can also be used to explain human behaviour. Although other names are sometimes applied and there are many other distinct models contained within each, these two important models of human behaviour are the cognitive and the behaviouristic.

The cognitive model of human behaviour has many sources of input. The gestalt and phenomenological schools of thought in psychology provide a historical base for the cognitive approach. In general, the cognitive model came about as a reaction to the other models of human behaviour. In particular, pioneering Psychologists such as Edward Tolman became disenchanted with the psychoanalytic and early behaviouristic models. They felt that the Freudian conception placed too much emphasis on negative, irrational, and sexually motivated behaviour and that the behaviouristic model was too deterministic and mechanistic. The alternative that was proposed gave humans much more 'credit' than the other models. The **cognitive model** emphasizes the positive and free will aspects of human being and utilizes concepts such as expectancy demand, and incentive.

The work of Tolman, in particular, can best demonstrate the cognitive approach. He felt that behaviour is always purposive, it is directed towards a goal. In his laboratory experiments, he found that animals learned to expect that certain events will follow one another. For example, rats learned to behave as if they expected food when a certain cue appeared. Thus, to Tolman learning consisted of the expectancy that particular event will lead to a particular consequence. This expectancy concept, of course, implies mentalistic phenomena. In other words, the cognitive explanation implies that the organism is thinking about or is conscious or aware of the goal. Behaviour is based on these cognitions.

Contemporary psychologists, such as Robert Bolles, carefully point out that a cognitive concept such as expectancy "does not reflect a guess about what is going on in the animal's mind: it is a term that describes the animal's behaviour." For example, even though Tolman used concepts such as expectancy, he considered himself a behaviourist. In other words, the cognitive and behaviouristic models are not as opposite as they appear on the surface and sometimes are made out to be. Yet despite some conceptual similarities, there has been a controversy through the years in the behavioural sciences on the relative contributions of the cognitive versus the behaviouristic model. Although the sequence is revised (only recently have behaviouristic models been proposed in organizational behaviour because of the dissatisfaction with the cognitive approach the controversy has carried over into the field of organizational behaviour. Before discussing the input that the cognitive model can make to organizational behaviour, it is necessary to understand fully the behaviouristic model.

Behaviouristic Model

Like Freudian model is the outcome of psychoanalytical school of thought in psychology, behaviouristic model represents the behaviouristic school of thought.

Its roots can be traced to the work of Pavlov and Watson. These pioneering behaviourists stressed the importance of dealing with observable behaviours instead of the elusive mind that had preoccupied the earlier structuralists and functionalists. They used **classical conditioning** experiments to formulae the stimulus-response (S.R.) explanation of human behaviour. Both Pavlov and Watson felt that behaviour could be best understood in terms of S-R. A stimulus elicits a response. They concentrated mainly on the impact of the stimulus and felt that learning occurred when the **S-R** Connection was made.

Modern behaviourism marks its beginning with the work of B.F. Skinner. Skinner is generally recognized as the most influential living psychologist. He felt that the early behaviourists helped to explain respondent behaviours but not the more complex operant behaviours. In other words, the S-R approach helped to explain physical reflexes [e.g., when stuck by a pin (S), the person will extend the lower leg (R)] and certain emotional reactions [e.g., a loud noise (S) will lead the person to cry out (R)]. On the other hand, Skinner found through his operant conditioning experiments that the consequences of a response could better explain most behaviours than could eliciting stimuli. He emphasized the importance of the **R-S** relationship. The organism has to operate on the environment in order to receive the desirable consequence. The preceding stimulus does not cause the behaviour in operant conditioning; it serves as a cue to emit the behaviour. For Skinner, behaviour is a function of its consequences.

The Role of Learning: The foundation for the modern view of behaviouristic man is learning. His behaviour is analysed according to the development and application of the process of learning. The starting point in the learning analysis of behaviour is with classical and instrumental conditioning.

Classical conditioning deals with the stimulus side of the S-R formulation, and instrumental or operant conditioning is concerned with the response side of the S-R model. There is less interest in the stimulus that activates the response and more interest in the reinforcement that follows the response. Obviously, this latter approach attempts to explain and create more complex behaviour, and its potential application is almost unlimited. Whereas the strictly mechanistic **S-R** approach is limited to physiological-emotional considerations, operant conditioning opens up the behavioural possibilities of learned drives, e.g., power, achievement, and alleviations.

Besides classical and instrumental conditioning, other learning concepts play an important role in behaviouristic man. Generalization, discrimination, and higher-order conditioning are examples. All these learning concepts are given major attention. At this point it is enough to say that the learning concepts are used to explain behaviouristic man's overt behaviour. Man's behaviour is a product of his prior learning and his present situation. In other words, behaviouristic man presents a somewhat deterministic view of behaviour.

However, it is important to understand that the behaviouristic model is environmentally based. It implies that cognitive processes such as thinking, expectancies, and perception do not play a role in behaviour. However, as in the case of the cognitive having behaviouristic concepts, some psychologists feel that there is room for cognitive variables in the behaviouristic model. Nevertheless, the cognitive model has been accused of being deterministic. Cognitive theorists argue that the S-R model, and to a lesser degree the R-S model, are much too mechanistic an explanation of human behaviour. A strict S-R interpretation of behaviour seems justifiably open to the criticism of being too mechanistic, but because of the scientific approach that has been meticulously employed by behaviourists, the operant model in particular has made a tremendous contribution to the study of human behaviour.

Rational and Emotional Models

In the rational model an individual is perceived to be a highly rational entity having computer like characteristics. Whenever faced with a problem, the individual is supposed to collect all relevant information, analyse the data and then arrive at a solution. Human beings are, thus, deliberative, serious, and computational.

In the emotional model, human beings are understood to be guided by emotions, many of which are unconscious responses. Scholars of the Freudian persuasion rely on this model. Freudians perceive human beings as irrational because of the constant conflicts among the Id, the Ego and the Superego. These inner conflicts, according to Freudians cause individuals to be subject to their emotions.

Humanistic Model

Some scholars believe that the individual can be described solely in terms of behaviour. These theorists are interested only in observable behaviour, as contrasted with thoughts or feelings. In its most radical form, the behaviouristic model holds that all behaviour is environmentally determined.

In the humanistic model, scholars believe that an individual is more philosophical than scientific. Humanists see the individual as capable of surmounting irrational impulses through conscious reasoning. In that view, people control their own destiny to a great degree, and their potential cannot be underestimated.

In recent years, a humanistic view of man has emerged. This approach gives man himself much more "credit" than the other approaches do Psychologists such as Gordon Allport, Abraham Maslow, and Carl Rogers became disenchanted with the psychoanalytic and behaviouristic models of man. They felt that the Freudian conception placed too much emphasis on negative, irrational, and sexually motivated behaviour and that behaviouristic man is too deterministic. To counter these more firmly established models, the humanistic psychologists developed a model that emphasizes the positive and free will aspects of man.

The humanistic approach does not completely negate the basic precepts of the Freudian and behaviouristic models. The humanists agree that man is characterized by unconscious motivation, irrationality, and deterministic conditioning. However, the humanistic psychologists feel they have enough clinical and experimental evidence to show that man is capable of overcoming these negative characteristics. They place more faith in man's intellectual capabilities for conscious reasoning and feeling. **Humanistic man** can reason, plan, and evaluate; he has a purpose and can control and influence his future. These qualities may be summarized by saying that humanistic man has self-awareness. This self-concept unifies the humanistic approach.

In essence, the **humanistic model** is at **opposite extreme** from the **behaviouristic model**. Humanism stresses man's intellectual reasoning abilities and efforts for self-actualization at the expense of conditioning and immediate stimulation. In other words, while behaviouristic man is deterministic, humanistic man has free will. But, although the humanistic model has many backers and a certain appeal to those with missionary zeal who are trying to improve man's image, to date the model lacks any meaningful research back-up.

On the whole, the humanistic model is more philosophical than scientific. The old human relations approach to management finds much comfort in this model. The newer, organizational behaviour approach, which this book is taking, is more influenced by the behaviouristic model. Nevertheless, the humanists have certainly tempered the strict S-R approach and emphasized that the human himself must be recognized when analysing behaviour.

Economic and Self-Actualising Models

The economic model of the human being conceptualises the individual as totally economic in orientation. The concept has been derived from the scientific management philosophy of the late 1880s. At the heart of the scientific management was a concern for standardising jobs, specialising work functions, and providing economic incentives to those whose performance was near or in excess of standard performance.

Contrast to the economic model is the self-actualising model which postulates that an individual is motivated by the opportunity to grow, mature, and become all he or she is capable of becoming. The model underlines' that the individual cannot be adequately described by economic or physiological considerations alone. People strive for loftier goals, like self-fulfillment and self-actualisation. Adherents of this model see the individual as craving personal growth, job competence, and self-fulfillment. Although individuals may be temporarily sidetracked in this quest, they eventually will return to it. The challenge of organization, therefore, is to provide the proper conditions for self-actualisation.

Theory X and Theory Y Models

Theory X assumes the individual to be lazy, uncreative, and in need of constant prodding. Theory Y views the individual as having tremendous potential, which effective management can channelise towards organizational goals. Obviously, depending on the individual manager's philosophy of human behaviour, there may be a divergence of managerial practices in the same organization.

Man as a System

Once again the systems concept seems directly applicable. It can be used to develop a model of man. Kolasa observes that "To conceive of the organism and the contiguous variables as a system may seem strange at first, but a description of behaviour in terms of a systems model can foster a better appraisal of the processes involved".

Boulding classification of the various levels of systems application was given major emphasis. The human level ranked very high in complexity on the hierarchy of potential application. Boulding lamented the lack of any appropriate theoretical system to handle this human level, saying, "We can hardly conceive ourselves constructing a system which would be in any recognizable sense 'aware', much less self-conscious." Even when these limitations are recognized, much can probably still be gained from the general systems approach if it is properly applied to the study of man. As was emphasized in the earlier discussion, systems is a concept, a point of view, and a goal-not a specific technique or area of content.

Similar to the other models of man presented thus far, the development of a systems model is deeply indebted to history. Gestalt theory, in general, and Kurl Lewin's **field theory**, in particular emphasize the importance of understanding the interacting and interdependent relationship of elements to the whole. Besides the direct contributions from particular theories, conceptual and analytical tools from the behavioural sciences are directly applicable. Homeostasis and holism are two examples. In total, there is a great deal of historical precedent for applying systems to the study of human behaviour.

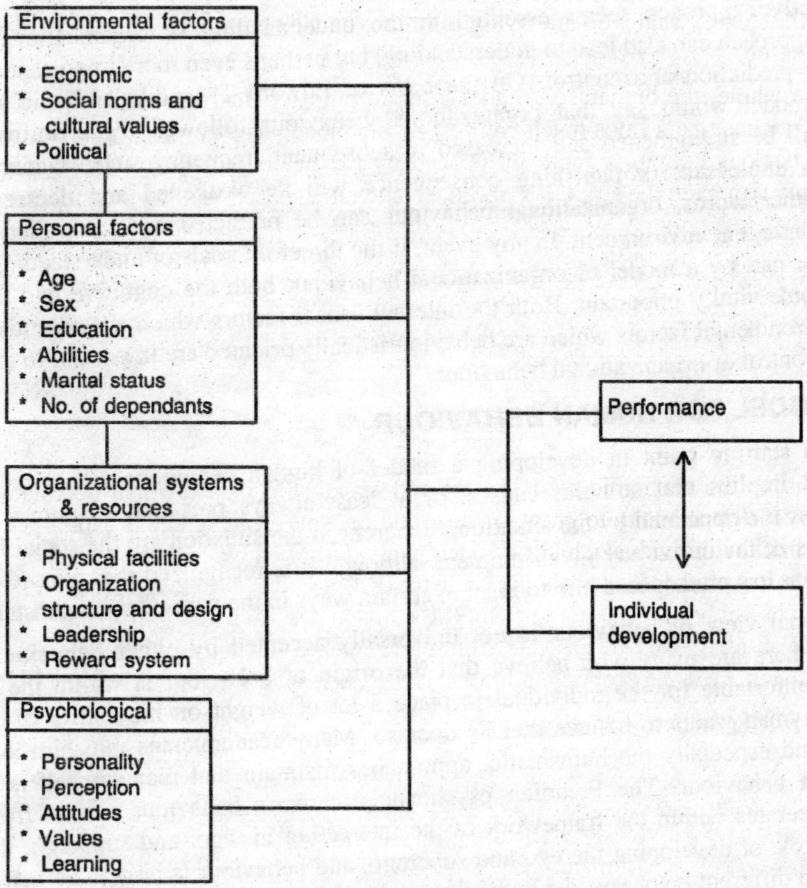

Fig. 1 Foundations of Behaviour

An Eclectic Model for Organizational Behaviour

Organizational behaviour has the advantage of being a relatively young and growing field of study. It can legitimately borrow, in an eclectic manner, the best from the various established models of human behaviour. At one point in its early development, the field of organizational orientation. Over the past three decades, most writers in organizational behaviour have taken a humanistic, cognitive approach. For example, Douglas McGregor and Rensis Likert depended mainly on a cognitive approach in their writings on organizational behaviour. In the last couple of years, the behaviouristic model has begun to be utilized in the theorizing and research on organizational behaviour. In many ways, what the field of organizational behaviour has been going through in recent years is a replay of the behaviouristic-versus-cognitive controversy that has been and, in many respects, still is going on in psychology. Now, in organizational behaviour, the time seems to have come to recognize the contributions of both models and to begin to synthesize and integrate both approaches into a meaningful model of organizational behaviour.

The Goals of the Organizational Behaviour Model

As stated earlier, the goal of the models presented so far is to better understand, not evaluate, the complex phenomena called human behaviour. Understanding human behaviour in organizations is also a vital goal for a model of organizational behaviour. In addition, however, because organizational behaviour is more of an applied field than is psychology, other desirable goals besides understanding are prediction and control. The study of organizational behaviour serves as the basis for modern human resource management. Predicting and controlling human resources are critical to the goals of modern management. Thus, the goals of a model of organizational behaviour are to understand, predict, and control human behaviour in organizations.

The cognitive approach seems essential to the understanding of organizational behaviour. The behaviouristic approach can also lead to understanding, but perhaps even more important is the contribution it can make to prediction and control. On the basis of Edward Thorndike's classic law of effect, the behaviouristic model would say that organizational behaviour followed by a positive or reinforcing consequence will be strengthened and increased in subsequent frequency, and organizational behaviour followed by an unpleasant or punishing consequence will be weakened and decrease in subsequent frequency. In other words, organizational behaviour can be predicted and controlled on the basis of managing the contingent environment. In any event, if the threefold goals of understanding, prediction, and control are to be met by a model of organizational behaviour, both the cognitive and the behaviouristic approaches become vitally important. Both the internal causal factors which are cognitively oriented and the external environmental factors which are behaviouristically oriented are important to the understanding, prediction, and control of organizational behaviour.

A CAUSAL MODEL FOR HUMAN BEHAVIOUR

The logical starting point in developing a model of human behaviour would be the classic S-R formulation. S-R implies that stimulus causes, or at least always precedes, response. Very simply, a person's behaviour is determined by the situation. "Inherent in the situation are the social forces that shape and determine his behaviour at any given moment, although it is recognized that his previous experience with such situations has predisposed him to react in certain ways in the particular circumstances."

The situational view of behaviour is not universally accepted by either behavioural scientists or laymen. In fact, there are many who believe that the origin of behaviour is within the person, not the situation. It is comfortable for the individual to place a lot of weight on his ability to control his own behaviour. The layman wants to believe that he does so. Many academicians join him in this view. The psychoanalytic, and especially the humanistic, approaches maintain that man himself is the source and cause of his own behaviour. The Freudian psychoanalytic man's behaviour results from unconscious motivation that operates within the framework of the interacting id, ego, and superego; the environment plays the limited role of developing the ego and superego, and behaviour is largely an **intraperson** event. Although it gives a different emphasis, the humanistic approach also relies on an intraperson explanation of behaviour. The humanists use the self-concept to interpret behaviour. Under this view, man has free will from within and his behaviour is not deterministic from the stimulus situation. The humanistic man's self-concept, which includes self-identity, self-evaluation, and self-ideal, will largely determine his behaviour.

The two extremes, the classic S-R and the behaviouristic view that behaviour is a product of the stimulus situation and the psychoanalytic, humanistic view that behaviour comes from within the individual, may seem to be in direct contradiction. Yet, both are founded on a sound theoretical base and, at least in the case of the behaviouristic approach, backed by research. The dilemma is solved if both, in combination, are recognized as contributing to the understanding of human behaviour. Taking an eclectic approach would incorporate the stimulus situation and the human being and would relate the two by interaction. As pointed out earlier, the situation interacting with the human being precedes and causes behaviour.

In the interaction approach, sometimes called the interpersonal approach, the situational and human variables are all-encompassing and very complex. The situation embraces not only immediate stimulation but also the physical and sociocultural environment. The human variable includes the physiological and psychological beings. The details of these situational and human variables in behaviour were discussed in the preceding sections. Now a model is needed to help clarify the relationships and provide a conceptual framework for analysing the causes of behaviour.

The S ---------- O ------------ B Model

The S -------- O ----------- B (SOB) model presented here is closely related to the widely known SOR model of psychology. Contemporary psychologists, who are influenced by both behaviourism and humanism, have recognized that the human organism plays an active mediating or intervening role between stimulus and response. They have inserted an O (for human organism) into the classic S -------R model, thus producing the S ------O ----R version. This O is not passive and immobile, as is assumed in S-R.

Instead, in S---------O---------R the O is viewed as a mediating, maintenance, and adjustment function between stimulus (S) and response (R). Floyd Ruch states that the O is "constantly active, scanning its surroundings, monitoring its own action, seeking certain conditions and avoiding others." As a maintenance function, the organs of the O are responsible for its health and growth. The three primary categories of maintenance organs are the receptors, connectors, and effectors. The adjustment function of the O monitors the person's activities in the environment so that he can overcome obstacles and thus satisfy his needs.

Even though the insertion of O in the S-R model gives some recognition to the importance of the human variable and the complexity of behaviour, it still remains a relatively mechanistic and simplistic approach. The S ------- O ------B model in Figure 2 modifies and extends the S--------O---------R model. The S and O in the S-------O-------B model encompass a much more comprehensive and broad perspective than they do in S------O------R. The second major difference is that the interactive aspects of the S and O are stressed in the S------O-------B model.

Basic Elements of the Model

S--------O---------B represents a causal sequence. S stand for the situation and incorporates all aspects of the environment, i.e., immediate stimulus, physical environment, and sociocultural environment. In short, this

SITUATION ◄──►	HUMAN ORGANISM ──►	BEHAVIOUR
Stimulus	Physiological Being	Overt Response
Energy	Heredity	Movement
Heat	Nervous system	Talking
Light	Sense organs	
Sound	Muscles and glands	
Physical Environment	Psychological Being	Covert Response
Climate	Perception	Thinking
Terrain	Learning	Listening
Resources	Motivation	
Population	Personality	
Ecosystems		
Sociocultural Environment		
Culture		
Groups		
Institutions		
Organizations		
Society		

Fig. 2. The S ---------- O ----------- B Model for Behaviour

conception of S covers everything from a loud noise to growing up in a complex, modern society. As explained earlier, when studying organizational behaviour, the formal organization is the most important aspect of the environmental situation.

The O in the model plays a very central and complex role in the causal sequence. It incorporates not only the physiological being, as in the S ---------- O ----------- R formulation, but also the psychological being. As shown in Figure 2, the physiological being includes heredity, the nervous system, the sense organs, and the muscles and glands, and the psychological being consists of the psychological processes and the personality. This conception of the human organism assumes phenomenal complexity.

The doubleheaded arrow between S and O represents interaction, a vitally important role in the causal sequence. An interactive process must occur between the situation and the human organism before behaviour results. Merely placing the S and O together is not enough. The interaction usually takes the form of the O's interpreting the immediate S. This type of interaction can be thought of as perception. However, this is only one simple form of interaction. In the S ----------- O ------- B model the perceptual process is part of the O, along with the other psychological processes of learning and motivation. When the influence of the physiological being and personality and the greatly expanded conception of S are added, the complexity of the interaction between the S and O is more realistically portrayed. Yet, despite the complexity, since all behaviour is preceded by S ------- O, it can easily be concluded that this interaction causes behaviour.

The Nature of Behaviour

Perhaps the best way to describe behaviour is to state what it is and what it is not. As noted earlier behaviour is anything that the human organism does; it is not something that is done to the organism. The nature of behaviour can be clarified by analysing two sets of examples of behaviour. In the first set are five possible behaviours of an assembly-line worker in a widget factory:

1. He started the machine.
2. He produced many widgets.
3. He did not produce many widgets.
4. He came to work late.
5. He came to work on time.

In these five instances, the worker did something. Thus, according to the simple definition, these examples are forms of behaviour. However, before jumping to this conclusion, a refinement is necessary. Each of the five examples implies a consequence of the worker's behaviour rather than the actual overt (outward) or covert (inward) behaviour. In behavioural analysis, it is extremely important to separate the actual behavioural events from the accomplishments of these events. The same five examples can be translated into more precise behavioural events in the following manager:

1. He pushed the button.
2. He moved his arms and hands very fast.
3. He moved his arms and hands very slow.
4. He walked very slowly from the parking lot.
5. He walked very fast from the parking lot.

This second set of examples describes specific, overt behaviour, not consequences of the behaviour.

Specific behavioural events are the subject for any kind of meaningful behavioural analysis. There may be many reasons for the consequences of behaviour. In the first set of examples, there are a multitude of possible reasons why the machine started, why productivity was high or low, and why the man did or did not get to work on time. Because of these many possibilities, plus the chance factor, it is extremely difficult to make an analysis of the consequences of behaviour. On the other hand, specific, overt behavioural events provide more useful data to analyse in order to determine cause and predict and control consequence. In brief, the crucial step in effective behavioural analysis is to concentrate on actual behavioural events and not on the accomplishments of those events.

The emphasis on **overt behaviour** does not imply that consequences are of no importance in the study and analysis of behaviour. In fact, some scholars include accomplishment as a vital element in the causal sequence of behaviour. Norman Maier explains that "the accomplishment may alter the stimulating conditions and thereby influence the subsequent behaviour, or it may initiate new behaviours by creating new situations for the organism. Thus, although accomplishment is an outcome of behaviour, when it is positively or negatively reinforcing it will also affect future behaviour. It is in this latter role that consequences become a very important aspect of behavioural analysis.

Examples of Behavioural Analysis

A simple example may point out the value of using the S------O-------B model to analyse the causes of behaviour. Take the common event of a person's touching a hot stove and jerking his hand away to escape the pain. In this example, the jerking of the hand is the overt behavioural event. Why does this hand-jerking behaviour occur? Many obvious answers come quickly to mind: to escape the pain; because the person wants to; or because the person has been hurt. Yet, although the reason is supposedly obvious, from the viewpoint of behavioural analysis none of these answers is a satisfactory explanation for the cause of the hand-jerking behaviour. The most obvious answer, to escape the pain, is the consequence, not the cause, of the behaviour. It is true that the person has undoubtedly learned that if he pulls his hand away from hot surfaces, the pain and skin damage will decrease. In this sense, the consequence affects the behaviour. However, another consequence of the jerking behaviour may increase instead of reduce pain. For example, jerking the hand away may literally be going from the frying pan into the fire. The other two answers, because the person wants to and because he has been hurt, are not consequences but recognize only the person, not the situation, as being the cause of the behaviour.

Using the S-----O-----B model to analyse the cause of the hand-jerking behaviour produces the following explanation:

The hot surface (S) interacting with the person (O) is interpreted (perception) by the senses (receptors) and a message (connectors) is sent to the brain (central nervous system) that "this is hot and it hurts." The person's previous experience (learning) has taught him that jerking the hand away may prevent the pain, and this message (connectors) is sent to the appropriate muscles (effectors) and the hand jerks.

Although this example is extremely simple and involves largely an autonomic (non-voluntary) response, it still can be said that the cause of the behaviour is the S interacting with the O. This interaction process is the best answer for explaining why the hand is jerked.

More complex behaviour can be subjected to the same kind of analysis as the hand-jerking example. Assume that the starting time for the secretarial staff of a business office is 8:00 A.M. At exactly 8 o'clock a secretary with her cost on is observed running down the hall toward the office. The overt behaviour in this case is the running. Why is the secretary running? One answer is to avoid being late, but this is a consequence, not a cause, of running. Another answer is that the secretary is a conscientious person and wants to be at work on time. The conscientious reason recognizes only the person (O). According to S ------- O -------- B analysis, the best explanation for the running behaviour is that somewhere the secretary has glanced either at a watch or a similar stimulus that she associates with time. (She heard a familiar radio program that starts at 8 o'clock, saw the 8 o'clock bus, or recognized some other time clue). This stimulus was interpreted (perception) by the secretary (O) that she is late (learning), and because she is conscientious (motivation), she is running. There are many possible consequences of this running behaviour. The most probable is that she will get to her desk on time and not be late for work. However, another possibility is that she will slip and fall and never be able to work again.

Complexities of Behavioural Analysis

The jerking-hand running-secretary examples demonstrate that most analyses of behaviour concentrate on the consequences or the person, while relatively little attention is devoted to the situation. Attempting to explain causes by consequences may not be completely sufficient. However, as pointed out earlier, an examination of consequences is vitally important to behavioural analysis to the extent that they affect behaviour via the learning concept of reinforcement. Similarly, using solely the person to explain behaviour is not sufficient. The psychoanalytic and humanistic approaches attempt to explain a cause by analysing the person, but they often ignore the situation. To be sure, the person (O) plays an extremely important, but not exclusive, role in behaviour. Except for the classic behaviouristic approach, the situation is generally either overlooked or deemphasized. The S--------O-------B model suggests that the situation in interaction with the human being can explain the cause of behaviour.

The S-------O--------B model is not intended to portray a simple, one, two, three analysis of behaviour. In fact, all the model does is present a relationship that shows that all behaviour is preceded and caused by the S interacting with the O. The model does not pretend to determine accurately what the cause of behaviour is, nor is it a method of prediction and control of behaviour. Both the S and O were shown earlier to be all-encompassing and extremely complex. Furthermore, just as the same behaviour may have different consequences, it may have many different situational causes (see Figure 3). Also, the same situation may lead to many different kinds of behaviour. There is an astronomical number of different combinations of the S and O that lead to behaviour. These are the reasons why it is extremely difficult, except in very simple or highly controlled situations, to determine the exact cause and then to predict and control human behaviour on the basis of this information. The purpose of the S ----- O ------ B model is to show the causal process of behaviour and to point out the variables that should be considered when analysing behaviour.

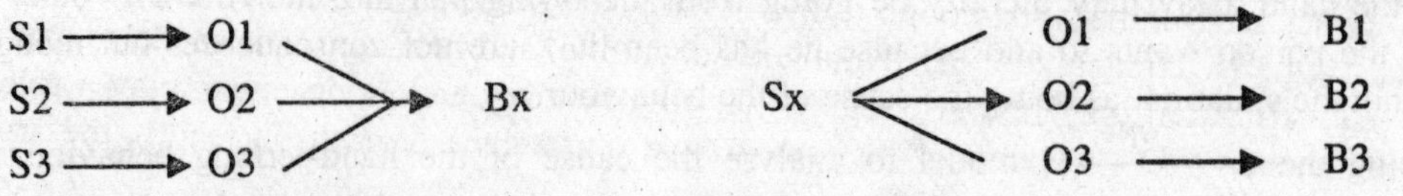

Fig. 3. Variations for Behaviour Causation.

SOURCE: Norman R.F. Maier, *Psychology in Industry*, 3rd ed., Houghton Mifflin Company, Boston, 1965, pp. 38-39.

The S - O - B - C Model

An S - O - B - C model can be formulated to incorporate both cognitive and behaviouristic approaches. The S - O - S portion is largely an extension of the widely recognized S - O - R model of psychology. The addition of the consequence (C) is given recognition by the industrial psychologist Norman Mair in his S - O - B - A model. The S - O - R model incorporates both cognitive and behaviouristic thinking. The human organism (O) plays an active mediating or intervening role between stimulus and response. The O is inserted into the classic behaviouristic S - R model, thus producing the S - O - R version. This O is not passive and immobile, as is assumed in S - R. Instead, in S - O - R the O is viewed as a mediating, maintenance, and adjustment function between stimulus (S) and response (R). Floyd Ruch states that the O is "constantly active, scanning its own actions, seeking certain conditions and avoiding other."

As a maintenance function, the organs of the O are responsible for its health and growth. The three primary categories of maintenance organs are the receptors, connectors and effectors, which are shown in Figure 4. As shown in the diagram, the nervous system plays a central role. Behaviour is mediated by neutral activity. The nervous system serves as connectors for the receptors of stimuli (sense organs) and the effectors of behaviour (muscles and glands). Significant breakthroughs have already occurred, and many scholar students of behaviour lies in this mediating structure of the human being. The adjustment function of the O monitors people's activities in the environment so that they can overcome obstacles and thus satisfy their needs.

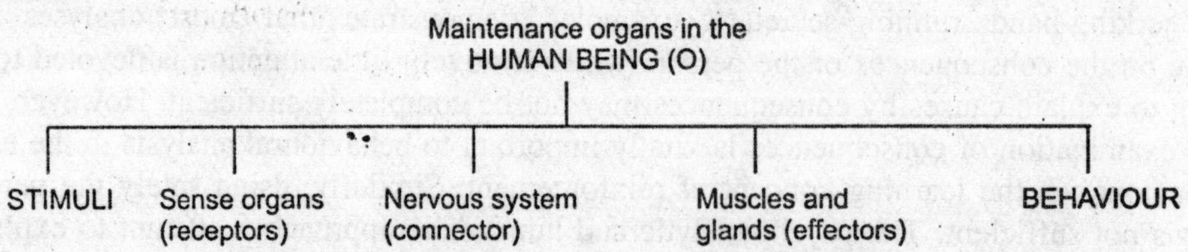

Fig. 4. The Maintenance Organs which intervene between Stimulus and Response.

Even though the insertion of O in the S - R model gives some recognition to the importance of congitive variables and the complexity of behaviour, it still does not give recognition to the important role that consequences play in behaviour. This is why the O is added to the model presented here. Figure 5 shows the S - O - B - C model, which is an expanded and modified version of the S - O - R and Maier's S - O - B - A models. The vital elements of the S - O - B - C model are the interactive effect between the situation and the human organism, the important role of consequences, and the feedback of the consequences to the situation and the human organism. In addition, of course, the S - O - B - C model has variables that are much more comprehensive than the classic S - O - R and S - O - B - A models.

The Variables in the Model

An underlying theme throughout the various models of human behaviour is the relative importance of heredity versus environment. Although different terms are sometimes used and there are differing degrees of emphasis, the psychoanalytic, existentialistic, cognitive, and behaviouristic models have all entered the controversy. Almost all psychologists agree that both heredity and environment play a role in behaviour, but a disagreement revolves around the comparative importance of each. In reality, the argument is self-defeating. It is impossible to separate heredity completely from environment for scientific analysis. From the moment of conception, the environment begins to interact with the generatically determined physical human being.

S	O	B	C
Stimuli and the physical, sociocultural, and technological environment	Physiological mediators and the psychological processes	Overt and covert responses and patterns of behaviours	Positive and negative contingent consequences and environmental dynamics and applications

Fig. 5. S - O - B - C Model

Because of the impact that the behaviouristic model has had, most contemporary psychologists favour the greater importance of the environment over heredity in analysing behaviour. However the modern viewpoint in general can perhaps best be summarized by Kurt Lewing's celebrated formula for behaviour:

B = f (P.E.)

Translated into words, the formula says that behaviour (B) is a function (f) of persons (P) and environment (E). Leo Meltzer states that "few would deny that to understand a person's behaviour at a given point of time, it is necessary to have knowledge both of the person and of his environment at that time."

The Person Variable

The S - O - B - C model incorporates both the person (O) and the environment (S and C); it follows the Lewing formula. The O variable in the model in Figure 5 incorporates both the physiological and psychological (or cognitive) mediators, which are vital to human behaviour. As explained by Dewey and Humber:

> *Man acts like man because he cannot do otherwise. Any member of a given biological order is restricted in the things that it can do and cannot do, in what it wants to do and does not want to do, and in the way it can and does feel about life, by the very nature of its biological structure.*

In other words, human being's generically determined physical and biological structure makes them behave differently from animals. Yet, humans are much more complex than merely a coglomeration of organs, senses, glands, nerves, bones, muscles, and brains. These mechanisms are essential to their maintenance and adjustment but cannot be equated with their behaviour.

Human behaviour is more a function of the psychological process than of the physiological ones. From the moment of birth, learning, perception, and motivation are an integral part of the person. Naturally, these processes do not operate as isolated, separate entities any more than do the physiological mechanisms of the body. The human being functions as a whole, not as series of parts. The psychological processes, taken as a whole, are included in the concept of personality. The latter concept plays a very major role in understanding behaviour.

The recognition of the psychological processes and personality as essential parts of the human being marks a major departure from a strict hereditary or physiological interpretation. For the purpose of developing a model of organizational behaviour, the person is considered to be made up of both the physiological and psychological processes. Both are important variables of human behaviour, although the psychological variables are considered here to have relatively much more influence on organizational behaviour.

The Environment Variable

The environment is the other variable mentioned in the Lewin's equation for behaviour. In the most basic and narrow sense, the environment consists of a stimulus. Common stimuli include lights, sounds, odours, pinpricks, and persons. In a strict S - R behaviouristic interpretation, such stimuli (S) play the crucial role in eliciting behaviour. Stimuli guides humans into action, interrupt what they are doing, and direct their choices. In this classical behaviouristic view, the immediate stimulus is the primary causal factor in behaviour. In the more modern operant view, the stimulus serves as the antecedent cue which emits (not causes) the behaviour. However, it must also be remembered that the contingent consequence is also a stimulus (R - S), and in the operant approach behaviour is a function of its consequences.

The immediate stimulus is a basic element in the S - O - B - C model, but it is not equated with the total environment. The more comprehensive environment is represented in the S - O - B - C model in both the S and the C. The S includes the immediate stimulus but also the broader physical, sociocultural, and technological environment. The C in the model is also an environmental variable. As in the operant behaviouristic model, the person must operate on the environment in order to obtain certain consequence. This is the contigent-consequence emphasis from modern behaviourism, but the C also includes broader-based dynamics (e.g., conflict) and applications (e.g., appraisal) as part of the environmental consequences of organizational behaviour.

The Behaviour Variable

Perhaps the best way to describe the behaviour variable is to state what it is and what it is not. Behaviour is anything that the human does : it is not something that is done to the person. The nature of behaviour can be clarified by analysing two sets of examples of behaviour. In the first set are five possible behaviours of an assembly-line worker in a widget factory:

1. The worker started the machine.
2. The worker produced many widgets.
3. The worker did not produce many widgets.
4. The worker came to work late.
5. The worker came to work on time.

In these five instances the worker did something. Thus, according to the simple definition, the examples are forms of behaviour. However, before jumping to this conclusion, a refinement is necessary. Each of the five examples implies an outcome to the worker's behaviour rather than the actual overt (outward) or covert (inward) behaviour. In understanding the behavioural variable, it is extremely important to separate the actual behavioural events from the outcomes of these events. The same five examples can be translated into more precise behavioural events in the following manner:

1. The worker pushed the button.
2. The worker moved his or her arms and hands very fast.
3. The worker moved his or her arms and hands very slowly.
4. The worker walked very slowly from the parking lot.
5. The worker walked very fast from the parking lot.

This second set of examples describes the specific, overt behaviour, not outcomes of the behaviour.

Specific behavioural events and the patterns of these specific behaviours are what included in the S - O - B - C model. There may be many reasons for the outcomes of behaviour. In the first set of examples, there are a number of possible reasons why the machine started, why productivity was high or low and why the worker did or did not get to work on time?

Because of these many possibilities, plus the chance factor, it is extremely difficult to make an analysis of the outcomes of behaviour. On the other hand, specific, observable behavioural events and their patterns provide useful data in order to analyse the S - O interaction which precedes the behaviour and the consequences that follow the behaviour. Such an analysis of the S - O antecedent and the consequences is crucial to the understanding, prediction, and control of the behaviour.

The Interactive Connections and Feedback Loops

The final explanation of the S - O - B - C model lies in the directionality of the connections and feedback loops shown in Figure 5. First the interactive connection between S and O. This interactive process must occur between the situation and the person before behaviour results. Merely placing the S and O together is not enough. The interaction usually takes the form of the O's cognitive interpretation of the immediate S. This type of interaction can be thought of as the process of perception. However, this is only one simple form of interaction. In the S - O - B - C model the perceptual process is part of the O, along with the other psychological processes of learning and motivation. When the influence of the physiological being and personality and the greatly expanded conception of S are added, the complexity of the interaction between the S and O becomes clear. Yet, in abstract, simplistic terms, the S - O can be thought of as the antecedent of behaviour. This S - O interaction should not be thought of as causing the behaviours in the S - R sense. Instead, S - O should be thought of as preceding the behaviour, with the S serving as an emitting cue for the behaviour, the O as the mediating physiological and cognitive processes, and the - as the complex interactive effect between the S and O that leads to (not causes) the behaviour.

The second important connection in the S - O - B - C model is the B - C relationship. This is an outgrowth of the R - S relationship of the operant model in behaviouristic psychology. One key to the connection between behaviour and its consequence is the contingency concept. A contingent relationship, is an "if - then" relationship. As used here, this simply means that the persons behaviour is affected by its contingent consequences. If the person behaves in a certain way, then a particular consequence will follow. Such contingent consequences can be used to predict and control behaviour.

The feedback loops from the consequence to the person and the situation are also important to the model. These feedback loops, shown as the dashed lines in Figure 5, show that the consequences affect the person's cognitions and the situational cues. In the simplest sense, these feedback loops can be thought of as learning. Based on the consequences of behaviour, the person's (O) perceptions and motives will be affected and situational cues (S) will become associated with or even change on the basis of certain consequences. However, just as the interaction between S and O involves more than perception, the feedback loops from C to O and S involve more than learning. Furthermore, just as perception is placed in the O portion of the model, so is learning. The S - O - B - C model is much more comprehensive than and not as rigorous as the behaviouristic and cognitive models upon which it is based.

A Conceptual Framework for the Study of Organizational Behaviour

The S - O - B - C model can serve as the conceptual framework for the study of organizational behaviour. The model attempts to synthesize the cognitive and behaviouristic explanations of human behaviour. In a very simplified summary, the S - O represents the causal, mainly cognitive factors in behaviour, and the B - C represents the modern behaviouristic emphasis on the role that consequences play in behaviour. The addition of the S in the antecedent to the behaviour and the feedback loops from the C to the O and the S represent the attempt to integrate both cognitive and behaviouristic variables. The S - O portion of the model primarily contributes to the goal of understanding organizational behaviour, and the B - C primarily contributes to the goals of prediction and control of organizational behaviour.

Obviously, the S - O - B - C model briefly summarized above is only a "barebones" sketch of the complexities of human behaviour. The purpose of the model, as with any model, is to identify the important variables and show how they relate to one another. Particularly with the field of organizational behaviour, which is still developing and searching for a theoretical base, such a model is extremely important for structuring study and further development. Figure 6 places the major variables of organizational behaviour (human behaviour in organizations) into the S - O - B - C model.

The Formal Organization

The framework shown in figure 6 plugs the formal organization into S. The formal organization, of course, is the most important situational environment for the study of organizational behaviour. Viewing the organization as a system, there are three subsystems that are especially important to the study of organizational behaviour. The first, the structure, serves as the skeleton for the formal organizational system. Structure allows the other subsystems, management processes and technology to operate. The bureaucratic model best represents the classical organization structure. Extensions and modifications of the bureaucratic model, such as centralization-decentralization, horizontal-vertical, departmentation, and line - staff, also have an important role in classical organization structures. The modern structures of organization are based on behavioural, systems, and contingency theories and are designed to meet the challenges of growth, complexity, conflict, and change. Project, matrix, and free-form designs are examples of modern structural forms.

Interacting and interdependent with the organization structure are the management processes, e.g., organizing, commanding, coordinating, and controlling, on the other hand the dynamic process are more pertinent and meaningful, which includes decision making, communication, and control. These management processes are an integral subsystem of the formal organization system.

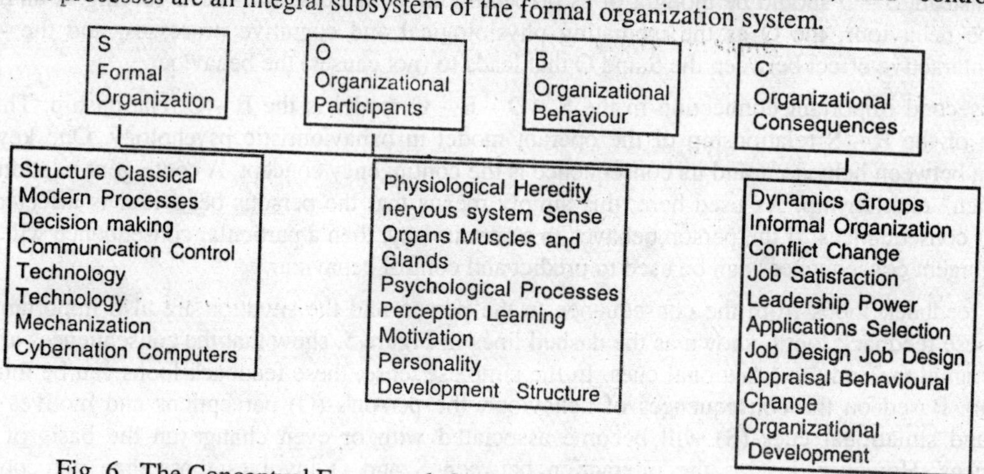

Fig. 6. The Conceptual Framework for the Study of Organizational Behaviour.

Although presented as part of the external environment, technology is also a vital subsystem of the formal organizational system. Used in this organizational context, "technology" means the internal technological environment that is used to attain the objectives of an organization. It includes productive operations, technologies such as mechanization and cybernation and, of course, computers. The technological subsystem affects and is affected by the organization structure and management processes.

Organizational Participants

Organizational participants or employees are plugged into the O portion of the model. Analogous to the formal organization, these participants can be conceptualized as a system, consisting of three primary subsystems : physiological structure, psychological process, and personality. For discussion purposes, these subsystems can be made analogous to the three subsystems of the formal organization. For instance, the physiological structure relates to and serves the human as the structure relates to and serves the formal organization. The physiological structure consists of basic units of heredity and includes the nervous system, sense organs muscles, and glands.

Analogous to the management processes of the formal organization are the participant's psychological processes of perception, learning, and motivation. These processes are at the very heart of the study of organizational behaviour. They are probably more vital than any other single part of the overall framework to the understanding of organizational behaviour. However, just as separating the processes from the formal organization is largely artificial, so is abstracting the psychological processes from the total human being.

Organizational participants behave as a whole, not as a collection of separate parts or processes. When the individual is viewed as this whole, the study of behaviour becomes involved with personality. Personality is to the organizational participant as technology is to the formal organization. Both personality and technology pervade their respective entities and are vitally responsible for the outputs. The study of the development and structure of personality is therefore very important to the understanding of organizational behaviour.

Just as the systems concept was shown to be relevant to the formal organization, the same concept seems applicable in relating the parts of the human being. The biological-physiological structure, psychological processes, and personality are related to one another and, analogously, to the formal organization subsystems in the manner shown in Figure 7. As the triangular presentation shows, the primary base for the organizational participant (formal organization) is the personality (technology). Interaction with and supporting the personality (technology) are the psychological processes (management processes). It must be realized that the triangular model represents only a very highly simplified abstraction, but it does serve as a starting point for the elementary understanding of the very complex organizational and human variables that make an input into understanding organizational behaviour.

Organizational
participant
(formal organization)

Personality
(technology)

Physiological
structure
(organization structure)

Psychological
processes
(management processes)

Fig. 7. Foundation for the Human and Organizational Systems.

Organizational Consequences

The study of the formal organization and the organizational participant lead to the better understanding of organizational behaviour. The study of the organizational consequences, on the other hand, can help better predict and control organizational behaviour. Again the reader should be reminded that this is a highly simplified generalization. Cognitive theorists are beginning to provide ways to predict and control behaviour, and behaviouristically oriented theorists are certainly contributing to the better understanding of behaviour. Nevertheless, the emphasis in the S - O is for understanding and in the B - C is for prediction and control.

Figure 6 indicates that certain dynamics and human resource management applications are especially relevant environmental consequences. The dynamics of groups, informal organization, conflict, change, job satisfaction, leadership, and power are particularly important consequences in the study of organizational behaviour. The application of managerial techniques in the areas of selection, job design, appraisal, applied behavioural analysis, and organization development can be fedback and change the formal organizational situation and, through learning, the organizational participant. In other words, these managerial applications can lead to the goals of prediction and control of organizational behaviour.

References

Blair J. Kolusa, *Introduction of Behavioural Science for Business*, John Wiley & Sons, Inc., New York, 1969, p. 207.

Donald Meichenbaum, *Cognitive Behaviour Modification, in University Programmes Modular Studies*, General Learning Press, Morristown, N.J., 1974.

Floyd L. Ruch, *Psychology and Life*, Scott, Foresman and company, Chicago, 1963, p.14.

Fred Luthans and Robert Kreitner, *Organizational Behaviour Modification*, Scott, Foresman and Company, Gleenview, Ill. 1975. for a summary of the literature on the operant model in organizational behaviour.

Fred Luthans and Robert Ottomann, *Motivation Versus Learning: Approaches to Organizational Behaviour, Business Horizons*, December 1973, pp.55-62.

Fred Luthans, Organizational Behaviour, McGraw Hill Book Company, New York, 1973, pp. 309-333 (adapted).

James C. Coleman, *Psychology and Effective Behaviour*, Scott Foresman and Company, Gleenview, III. 1969, p.33.
Kenneth E. Boulding, *General System Theory - The Skelton of Science, Management Science*, April 1956, p. 207.
Leo Meltzer, *The Need for a Dual Orientation in Social Psychology, Journal of Social Psychology*, October 1961, p.43.
Norman R.F. Maier, *Psychology in Industry*, Houghton Miffin Company, Boston, 1965.
Paul F. Second and Carl W. Backman, *Social Psychology*, McGraw Hill Book Company, New York, 1964, p.577.
Richard Dewey and W.J. Humber, An Introduction to Social Psychology, The Macmillan Company, New York, 1966, p.29.
Richard M. Hodgetts, *Organizational Behaviour Theory and Practice*, Mac Millan, 1991, p.54.
Robert C. Balles, *Learning Theory*, Holt, Rinchart and Winston Inc. New York, 1975, p.84.
Rollo May, *Psychology and The Human Dillemma*, D.Van Nostrand Company Inc., Princeton, N.J., 1967, p.41.

CHAPTER

6

Individual Behaviour

Man who is the creator of all material and spiritual values can truly be said to be the architect of this world.

Through scientific and technical achievements, man has learned to make and operate sophisticated automatic machines, to fabricate materials whose properties surpass those of natural substances, and to harness the powerful energy of water, wind, sun and even atomic nuclei for making electricity – man's loyal ally. Boundless are the potentialities of man's labour, the flights of his imagination and the commands of his purposeful will.

But despite having learned to master nature and to comprehend its laws, men are as yet unable consciously to regulate their own history. Many natural phenomena keep repeating themselves in accordance with definite laws: seasons change, night follows day just as day follows night, etc., while social life is not marked by such relentless recurrence : it is not so easy to notice the change of historical epochs, for each generation arrives on the historical scene to find a social set up shaped by earlier generations. People acting in the society have a consciousness and a will of their own, and it is not always easy to discuss the motives out of which they act.

Some believe that historical processes are governed by individuals (wise or foolish, good or evil, rules or their aides), by the nature and direction of their activity. Ideas rule the world – such is the simple conclusion to be drawn from that view. But it does not provide an answer to the questions which inevitably arise in their context : how do the ideas themselves originate?

The colonialists conquered the entire continents and enslaved their peoples not only because they were led by blood - thirsty military leaders, but also because they had definite aims and were guided by the grasping hand of those who longed for wealth. That is why the essence of colonial plunder does not change even when the plunderers claim to perform a **"civilising mission"** and allege that their sole purpose is to raise people to the heights of modern culture. Thus, it can be seen that the colonialists were compelled and propelled in their acts by material considerations. And to say, that ideas rule the world is tantamount to admitting man's impotence in the face of supernatural forces.

Motives of Behaviour

If one is to explain the true motives of human behaviour, views and actions, one should go to the roots from which the whole stream of social life springs.

That was done for the first time by Karl Marx and Fredrick Engels. Almost one and a half centuries ago, they formulated a doctrine which has come to be known as 'Historical Materialism' or the 'Materialist Understanding of history.'

The main points of the materialist understanding of history are:

- history is a natural objective process and is made by men themselves, without the interference of any supernatural forces;
- men make history not in accordance with their arbitrary desires, but on the basis of the material conditions that take shape in the society at each stage in its development;
- these material conditions are pivotal to the whole structure of the society.

Marx clearly expressed that in his well-known formula: "it is not the consciousness of men that determines their existence, but their social existence that determines their consciousness."

Genesis of Behaviour

From the behavioural sciences point of view, the formula expounded by Marx, marks an important step in the understanding of the genesis and mechanics of human behaviour. Marx has laid bare in very practical terms the motivations and propulsions that formulate and are in turn affected by the, behaviour of man.

Thus, in order to live, men should have food, clothes, housing, and other material values. But these are not to be found ready-made in nature, and have to be produced by men themselves, by their labour. At the early stages of social development were already engaged in producing various products: they hunted wild animals and roasted their, meat, caught fish, made primitive tools, built dwellings etc. Motivated by their requirements, they expanded the sphere of their labour activity and perfected their tools and the production process itself. From hunting they advanced to domestication of animals, and then on to cropping. Later on, they began to engage in the handicrafts: weaving, pottery, metal-working, etc. A subsequent stage of development saw the emergence of factories, based on handicraft techniques and manual work, which eventually developed into large-scale machine production.

Production can be defined as a process taking place between man and nature in the course of which man transforms natural substances into a product necessary for human life. Without production, the human society can neither exist nor develop. Economic and political conditions may change, and one social system may give way to another in the course of history, but production will always remain the basis of society's life.

Role of Material Values

The production of material values include three basic elements : human labour (or work), objects of labour and instruments of labour.

Human labour can be described as a process of conscious and purposeful human activity with the help of which people change natural objects. Labour could be said to be a crucial condition of human life. While animals too, often perform fairly complicated operations, but they do that by instinct, whereas man, before getting down to his work, sets himself a definite goal and aims at attaining certain results. Marx wrote: "..... what distinguishes the worst architect from the best of bees is this, that the architect raises his structure in imagination before he erects it in reality."

The point to be noted is that not every kind of work belongs to the sphere of material production. Thus, the work of doctors, teachers, artists etc. does not produce any material values.

In the process of labour, people expend their mental, nervous and muscular energy or, in other words, their Labour power. The latter is the totality of an individual's physical, mental and other capacities for work.

For the labour process (or human process) to go on, there should be a correspondingly developed human labour power. In effect, the degree of its development is a criterion for assessing the level of material production. Thus, in the production of material values, the human personality is itself developed, human labour skills are perfected, and new knowledge is gained. As the first and basic condition of the whole of human life, labour has in a sense created man himself.

As people act upon nature in the process of labour, they create and use 'instruments of labour.' The instruments of labour include: First, implements of labour or tools (machinery, equipment, tools, engines etc.); second, industrial premises.

Third, transport and communication facilities; and Fourth, reservoirs and tanks for storing objects of labour (bunkers, cisterns, cylinders, gas-holders, etc.), that is, the whole production apparatus of the economy.

The crucial role among the instruments of labour belongs to the implements of labour, whose mechanical, physical, chemical, biological, and other properties are used by people in the production of material values.

How Behaviour Transforms?

In using the instruments of labour to act upon the surrounding nature people themselves tend to change, accumulate experience and knowledge, and that creates new possibilities for developing and perfecting the instruments of labour, production technology, and for raising labour productivity. In developing his instruments of labour, man has travelled a long way from the use of a primitive stick or stone-axe to a modern robot.

It derives thus, that human behaviour is based not only inherited and learned factors but very substantially on the also social environment too. Here, to pin-point that human behaviour shapes the social environment or *vice versa* will not be entirely right but instead this could be likened to the situation where the question is as to what came first the 'Egg or the Hen.' Therefore, we can justifiably say in the most judicious sense that either way whether the human behaviour first shaped the social environment or the other way round, in the continuous social process the social environment and the social pressures prevail upon individual human behaviour and shape and move it accordingly.

Any science, studying a particular sphere of nature and the society, aims at a congnition of laws of their movement.

The society's development is made up of actions by human beings, each of whom seems to be motivated by his own interest. That invites the conclusion that all social events are accidental and arbitrary, and that nothing can be foreseen in advance.

But such a conclusion is deeply erroneous. History is indeed made by man, but this does not mean that their true goals and motives cannot be discovered. In seemingly accidental historical events and phenomena one can discern definite uniformities.

To understand the motives of human activity, one should understand the essence of what motivates human or economic phenomena.

All social phenomena, far from being isolated from each other, are interconnected and interdependant.

Economic laws are the laws of the development of production relations, and govern production, distribution, exchange and productions. They, like the laws of nature, operate independently of human will and consciousness, i.e. they are objective. They arise and operate on the basis of the concrete relations of production of a particular economic system. Men cannot arbitrarily enact, amend or abrogate economic laws. That does not mean, however, that they cannot influence these laws in some way.

Such nature of the economic laws is today reflected in the modern and dynamic disciplines such as Management, Administration, Marketing Management, Human Relations, Industrial Relations, Human Resource Management, Industrial Psychology, Human Engineering and Organizational Behaviour.

The binding factor which is also the underlying constant in all disciplines is the Behaviour of man and its study which simply stated is the Behavioural Science. It is easily discernable now that it is the Behavioural Science which forms the basis of the study of the fundamental propulsions of economic laws and laws governing other disciplines.

Thus all the functions related to a business activity become more centrally oriented towards man and his behaviour.

Behaviour Vis-a-Vis Organization

Individuals tend to behave either in group or individually. When individuals begin work for an organization they bring many personality differences to the job. They think, perceive and behave differently. The study of individual behaviour is an essential part of organizational behaviour. Understanding and working with changing individual behaviour has become one of the most significant functions of modern manager. He must make decisions about the fit between individuals, job tasks, and effectiveness. The differences in individual behaviour may be due to such human factors as ability, perception, learning, needs, values, motives, attitudes and personality of an individual. All these factors affect employee behaviour at work.

Human behaviour is an important element in the functioning of an organization. Behaviour is anything that an employee does. Completing a job, reporting to work, handling a machine, or anything that can be observed is considered behaviour. It is the observable response of subordinates. Some important assumptions about and characteristics of individual behaviour are as follows:

1. Behaviour is caused.
2. Behaviour is goal - directed.
3. Behaviour is motivated.
4. Behaviour towards goals can be disrupted by frustration, conflict, and anxiety.
5. It is an observable and measurable activity of human beings.
6. Behaviour is a cause and effect relationship and should not be taken in philosophical terms.
7. Behaviour is a complex result of our intentions, our perception of the immediate situation, and our assumptions or beliefs about the situation and the people in it.
8. The predictability of human behaviour is at best a relative matter because it is affected by large number of variables.
9. Behaviour may be orderly or arbitrary; systematic or random.

The process of behaviour can be understood by a simple model of behaviour which is presented in Fig.1. This model shows that:

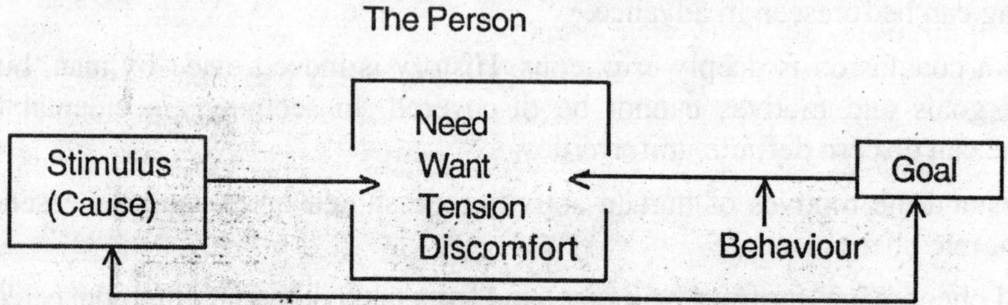

Fig. 1. A Basic Model of Behaviour

(a) the behaviour process is similar for all people;

(b) actual behaviour can differ because of physiological, environmental, and psychological variables, and such factors as frustration, conflict, and anxiety; and

(c) many of the variables influencing behaviour have been shaped before the person enters the work organization.

Nature of Man

There are four basic assumptions about the nature of man: They are (1) individual differences, (2) the whole person, (3) caused behaviour through motivation, and (4) human dignity.

Individual Differences

The idea of individual differences comes originally from psychology. From the day of birth, each person is unique, and individual experiences after birth tend to make people even more different. Individual differences mean that management can get the greatest motivation among employees by treating them differently. If it were not for individual differences, some standard, across-the-board way of dealing with employees could be adopted, and minimum judgement would be required thereafter. Individual differences require that justice and rightness with employees shall be individual, not statistical. This belief that each person is different from all others is typically called the Law of Individual Differences.

People have many things in common. People generally feel and behave alike in the movement of joy and sorrow; they have the same feeling of affection towards their sons and daughters and they are perhaps alike in the moments of anger and anguish, with varying degrees, of course. In spite of these facts people are different to each other in behaviour perhaps due to their perception, role and environment.

On the planet Earth are billions of complex people who are likewise all different (and we expect that all who follow will be different)! Each one is different from all others, probably in millions of ways, just as each of their fingerprints is different, as far as we know. And these differences are usually substantial rather than meaningless. Think, for example, of a person's billion brain cells and the billions of possible combinations of connections and bits of experience that could be stored therein. All people are different. This is a fact supported by science.

While channelising organizational behaviour towards proper direction it becomes imperative to systematise behaviour of individuals. The behaviour of individual in turn is influenced to a great extent by the programmes and policies adopted by the organization. For a manager it is essential to know individual differences so that he could take such steps and implement such policies and programmes that suit the psychology of different persons working in the organizations. In other words, "individual differences require that justice and rightness with employee shall be individual not statistical." As a result of individual differences the centre nerve of organizational behaviour is the individual. It is the individual who should feel satisfied with the role assigned to him or the efforts made in regard to human relations by management. In other words, all programmes and policies designed to improve the work environment by the management should satisfy the individual operating in the organization because the policy of general improvement may be rejected by some individuals as it may prove detrimental to their roles and perceptions.

A Whole Person

The concept of a whole person is more of a semantic nature. Whenever we think of a man or individual we think of his skill and brain together. It is not possible that the employer while employing an individual for skill may exclude his brain because both are inseparable. Hence in spite of difference in individual's traits, his skill is bound to be influenced by his background or knowledge. In other words, his skill carries with it the influence of environments in which he has been placed. Similarly, his private life is bound to be influenced by his work place in as much the same manner as his emotions and aspirations are conditioned by the physical environment around him. Therefore, people function as total human beings.

For example, consider a situation when the boss wanted his accountant to work overtime on Saturday evening to prepare the important financial statement. The accountant only had the required information, knowledge and skill for the assignment. He was also in need of an overtime allowance as he was economically pressed. However, from the accountant's point of view a social obligation compelled him not to work that day after normal working hours. The reason being, the date was his first marriage anniversary and he had long before arranged a party with a few friends at his house. This anniversary was more important for the accountant, so his boss had to consider his needs as a whole person, not just a worker.

When management practices organizational behaviour, it is trying to develop a better employee, but also it wants to develop a better person in terms of growth and fulfillment. Research suggests that jobs do shape people somewhat as they perform them, so management needs to be concerned about its effect on the whole person. Employees belong to many organizations other than their employer, and they play many roles outside the firm. If into the larger society in which each employee lives.

Caused Behaviour (Motivated)

Psychologists contend that a person's need structure causes all normal human behaviour. Hence it becomes imperative that the person's behaviour may be influenced by motivating him to fulfill his need structure as he sees it. The lever of motivation lies with management because it has the control over means through which the person may fulfill his need structure - economic, social or psychological. Management may motivate the person in two ways: one, by ensuring that the desired action will increase his need fulfilment and two, by convincing the individual that the desired action will avoid the decreased need fulfilment. For instance, a bus has come to the stand at the right time. The passengers have bought the tickets. They have boarded the bus. the bus will not start on its own. Someone, i.e., the driver, will put in the power (petrol/diesel) and only then it will run. Similarly, organizational motivation is a condition precedent to keep the organization going.

Motivation is essential to the operation of organizations. No matter how much machinery and equipment an organization has, these things cannot be put to use until they are released and guided by people who have been motivated.

Value of the person (human dignity): This concept is of a different order from the other three because it is more an ethical philosophy than a scientific conclusion. It confirms that people are to be treated differently from other factors of production because they are of a **higher order** in the universe. It recognizes that because people are of a higher order, they want to be treated with respect and dignity – and should be treated this way. Every job, however simple, entitles the people who do it to proper respect and recognition of their unique aspirations and abilities. The concept of human dignity rejects the old idea of using employees as economic tools.

Man is a very sensitive social animal. He is different from machine. He has the mind to think and heart to feel. He has emotions, aspirations and sentiments which have to be respected under every circumstance. He has to be treated with dignity and respect and not like log of wood which has no sensitivity at all. If a person is not treated in a dignified manner he will not remain psychologically fit and emotionally perfect to devote his mind and heart into the work. No work, howsoever simple may it be, cannot be fulfilled with efficiency unless the person puts his mind and heart into the work which in turn depends on the respect and recognition which he gets for his aspirations and abilities.

Ethical philosophy is reflected in the conscience of humankind confirmed by the experience of people in all ages. It has to do with the consequences of our acts to ourselves and to others. It recognizes that life has an overall purpose and accepts the inner integrity of each individual. Since organizational behaviour always involves people, ethical philosophy is involved in one way or another in each action. Human decisions cannot, and should not, be made apart from values.

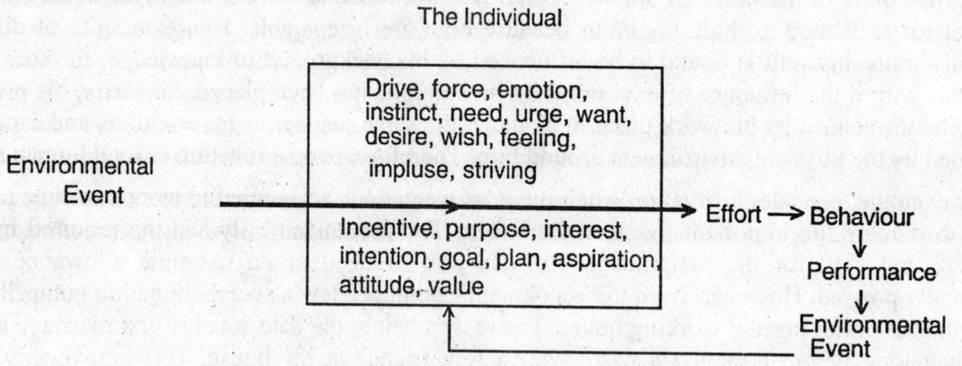

Fig. 2. Motivational Determinants of Behaviour

Source: Adapted from Szilagyi and Wallace, *Organizational Behaviour and Performance* (1980), p. 46.

Models of Man

Numerous models of man exist to help explain various behaviours of individuals at work place, at home and elsewhere. An understanding of different models of man is vital before one proceeds to study how people behave in organizations. Members of an organization are more than contributors to its activities. They are also affected by organizations – with its system and *modus operandi*. Of course, to a certain extent an individual is expected to adapt himself to organization. Individuals are similar, yet they are different. That is why different models have been developed to explain the behaviour of individuals.

These models are the "philosophies of human nature" and have been used to aid in the prediction of behaviour. These represent some major sets of assumptions that influence the thinking of manager. These explain differences in individuals. Edger Schein has identified four such models – rational economic man, social man, self-actualizing man, and complex man. In addition, we will discuss a few more advanced models by management researchers.

Rational-Economic Man

This is perhaps the oldest model. According to this, the rational-economic man strives to maximize his interests. There is a high degree of rationality in his decisions as he takes into account the costs associated with his effort and also weighs the benefits he will be getting from his work and efforts. A rational-economic man is characterized by "hedonism" and is motivated by economic incentives. Since man's feelings will constantly interfere with his rationality, according to this model, the organization can be so designed to control his feelings and consequently avoid any unpredictability in his behaviour. An economic man is largely passive, self-centered, and McGregor's assumptions of **Theory X** reflects the behaviour of this man.

The economic theory of Adam Smith also says that the marketplace should remain unregulated because the self-interest would result in a self-balancing system. Classical management theorists such as F.W. Taylor have considered employees primarily in economic terms. They viewed the worker's primary goal as economic gain.

In terms of employee behaviour, this model has the following assumptions:

1. Employees have a calculative mind. They calculate the cost of their efforts for getting any inducement. Similarly, they also calculate the value of the inducement which they receive from their efforts.
2. Employees are also to evaluate as well as know all the alternatives available.
3. Employees are primarily motivated by economic incentives and will do whatever affords them the greatest economic gain.
4. The feelings of people are essentially irrational and hence must be controlled in order to avoid interference with their rationality and self-interest.
5. Since economic incentives are under the control of the organization, the employee is essentially a passive agent to be manipulated, motivated, and controlled by the organization.
6. Organizations can and must be designed in such a way as to neutralize and control people's feelings and, therefore, their unpredictable traits.

The essence of this model is that people can be induced to produce more just by providing monetary and economic incentives. This model is essentially based on classical organization theory (see Chapters 4 and 5). Economic incentives like piece-rate system, monetary incentives for additional production and high quality work, can work as long as man is not reasonably satisfied with his money. Though rational economic man model is realistically descriptive of the behaviour of an individual in the organization, this is inadequate because it ignored the contingent and environmental factors. Joseph W. McGuire, a famous critique points out "economic man is an automation, stripped bare of any of human characteristics that all men possess."

Social Man

Social man is the outcome of behavioural science research and human relations movement. Management, unlike in the previous case of rational man, cannot afford to rely on carrot and stick policies, rather should be democratic and consultative. Better it would be if the management acts as a facilitator and supporter of the employees considering their social needs.

Social-man model shifts the emphasis from individuals to "groups" and "society" in which he functions. Actually this model lies at other opposite extreme of rational model which is discussed above. According to social man model, man is motivated by his social needs and he tries his level best to maintain relationship with group members in society. He is also responsive to group pressures and he is receptive to group problems, and sanctions. Social man also obeys all the management orders as long as they are not incongruent with group goals or his social needs.

The following assumptions can be made about social man:

1. Social needs are the prime motivator of human behaviour, and interpersonal relationships, the prime shaper of a sense of identity.
2. As a result of the mechanization, work has lost much of its intrinsic meaning, which now must be sought in social relationships on the job.
3. Employees are more responsive to the social forces of the peer group than to the incentives and controls of management.

4. Employees are responsive to management to the extent that a supervisor can meet a subordinate's needs for belonging, for acceptance, and for a sense of identity.

These assumptions have important implications for management strategy:

(i) First, the manager should not concentrate only on production, but should also give more attention to the needs of the people.

(ii) Second, instead of being concerned with directing and controlling people, the manager should be concerned with thier feelings and psychological well-being.

(iii) Third, the manager should recognize work groups and provide for group incentives rather than individual incentives.

(iv) Fourth, instead of being planner and controller of work, the manager should act as intermediary between employees and higher management, respecting the feelings of subordinates. He should be a true sympathetic supporter of employees' claims.

(v) Fifth, the source for motivation shifts from management to the worker and the manager becomes the facilitator of work.

(vi) Sixth, the manager acknowledges the existence of needs other than purely economic ones, and recognizes the total social situation in which the subordinates work.

Organization Man

William H. Whyte, a renowned editor of the Fortune magazine, has advanced a new model of man known as **"organization man."** The organization man is exactly the direct opposite of the old protestant ethic. Organization man is one who sacrifices his individuality for the sake of the group and organization. Whyte contends that the guiding credo of individual salvation through competitive struggle and hard work is effectively replaced by "social ethic" which guides "organization man." At the base of his theory, Whyte makes the following propositions:

1. The group is the source of creativity. The individual by himself is isolated and meaningless; only when he collaborates with others does he create. The individual helps to produce a whole that is greater than the sum of its parts.
2. Belongingness is the ultimate need of the individual. There should be no conflicts between man and society because what is normally considered conflict is merely misunderstanding and breakdown in communication.
3. The application of science achieves the goal of belongingness. By applying the methods of science, the obstacles to consensus can be eliminated and an equilibrium can be created where society's needs and the needs of the individual are one and the same.16

This model also proposes that the organization will take care of individual interest and hence there is no conflict between organization and individual. However, if any conflict arises, then it can be overcome by sacrificing the individual interest in favour of organization. In fact, people do not see their interests different from those of organization due to their loyalty and belongingness.

Complex Man

Man is a complex mixture of various motives, needs, goals, aspirations, perceptions, and attitudes. Hence, his behaviour remains unpredictable. Today various researches highlight human complexity and human differences. Studies show that (a) there are many complex and unpredictable variables which influence human behaviour; and (b) there are no set behavioural patterns due to individual differences. Thus, this model shows that simplistic assumptions about people and their behaviour hold no truth. It is not possible to predict human behaviour completely and accurately. There is no direct cause-and-effect relationship between needs and behaviour.

Therefore there is no one universal strategy to deal with him. This gives rise to the development of contingency models of motivation, leadership and management. The basic theme of contingency theory is that there is no one way of managing people. It depends and varies with the situation. The essense of this model is that the human behaviour is complex and is influenced by a baffling diversity of factors and need different methods of control and direction from the viewpoint of management. Following assumptions can be made about **complex man**:

1. Human needs and motives fall into many categories and vary according to stage of development and total life situation. There are many overlapping needs too; hence need hierarchy cannot be universal.
2. Since needs and motives interact and combine into complex motive patterns, it becomes difficult to understand human motivation. For example, money can be a basis for satisfying many different needs.

Similarly, some needs can be met in different ways at different stages.

3. Man is capable of learning many motives through organizational experiences. Thus, his total need pattern will be the result of complex interactions between initial needs and organizational contacts.
4. People display different patterns of needs and behaviours in different organizations or at different levels of the same organization.
5. There is no direct cause-effect relationship between need and behaviour. Hence human behaviour cannot be predicted through knowledge of human needs.
6. People can become productively involved with organizations on the basis of many different kinds of motives. Ultimate satisfaction for the individual and ultimate effectiveness for the organization depend only in part on the nature of such motivation.
7. Employees can respond to many different kinds of managerial strategies, depending on their own motives and abilities and the nature of the task. Thus, there is no single correct managerial strategy that will work for all people at all times.

Thus, complex man model depicts the real picture of human nature and behaviour. If managers hold above assumptions, their strategic actions should be in two ways: First, they must realize that there is no set action which can be taken in all situations. They should have the sensitivity and diagnostic ability to understand individual behaviour. They must adopt a contingency approach in their actions. Second, managers should learn to value differences in human nature and should have the interpersonal skills necessary to appreciate the complexity of human element in their own and employees' behaviour.

Administration Man

He is the man specially designed by Herbert Simon who states that he is an individual who is interested in satisfying, not maximizing the satisfaction. This model recognizes the limitations of maximizing behaviour (such as time and cost constraints, objectives are dynamic than static, the effect of environmental factors cannot be ignored etc.). Of all the models of man, administrative man seems most descriptive of realistic individual behaviour. According to Cyert and March "even if individuals maximize pleasure or expected utility it does not necessarily follow that organization maximizes profits. Likewise, even if individuals do not maximize, it does not necessarily follow that organizations do not." The essense of administrative man model is the satisfying behaviour.

Mobicentric Man

Another dynamic man as pointed out by Jennins is "mobicentric man," who is more descriptive of all successful individuals. Jennings developed this model from the study of over 1500 practising executives and 230 presidents from 500 large industrial enterprises. According to Jennings, mobicentric man has a different set of values from those of economic and organization man. He has noticed mobility of the successful managers and finds that these managers are characterized by following traits:

(i) High degree of mobility and action.
(ii) Having faith in themselves, not in institutions.
(iii) The fact that they measure success by their movement more than by position, title, salary or performance.

The trouble with mobicentric manager is that they never expect to complete a particular assignment or work. They start preparing themselves for departure as soon as they are in. Therefore, this behaviour may be rational from their point of view, but not fruitful from the organization's point of view.

Self - actualizing Man

Self-actualizing man is innovative in nature and is always interested in creating new things. He is characterized by high degree of dynamism and individuality. His primary concentration is on innovation and invention of the new techniques of production, marketing, motivation, leadership etc. Thus, there is a conflict between self-actualizing man and the formal organization because formal organistions does not allow him to satisfy his self-actualizing needs.

Self-actualizing man concept is an antithesis of economic person concept and a further extension of social man and organization man models. Some thinkers like McGregor (1960), Argyris (1957, 1964), and Maslow (1954) argued that many jobs in modern industry have become so fragmented and specialized that they do not permit workers to use their capacities and skills in a nature and productive way. The work has become meaningless to them. Psychologists such as McClelland, Herzberg and Maslow assume that many people are motivated by the opportunity to self-actulize-that is "to grow and mature."

Maslow summarizes the notion of self-actualization in the following manner:

"Even if all these (lower-level) needs are satisfied we still may often (if not always) expect that a new discontent and restlessness will soon develop, unless the individual is doing what he fitted for. What a man can be, he must be. It refers to the desire for self-fulfillment, namely, to the tendency for one to become actualized in what one is potentially. It is the desire to become more and more what one is, to become everything that one is cpable of becoming."

The assumptions about self-actualizing man, that normally managers make in formal organizations are basically based on McGregor's Theory Y.

They are:

(i) Human needs can be arranged in hierarchy logically. For instance, according to Maslow, needs can be arranged in a hierarchy – physiological, safety, belongingness, esteem, and self-actualizing. Self-actualization is, thus, the final goal of an individual.

(ii) Man moves from a state of immaturity to a state of maturity to satisfy this particular need.

(iii) Man is essentially self-motivated and needs no direction.

(iv) Conflict between self-actualizing man and the form of organization structure is inevitable because the formal structure is based on the assumption of "immaturity of individuals."

People in work organizations will generally appreciate more incentives, based on intrinsic factors and more autonomy and also are interested in participation.

These assumptions have drastically different implications for managerial actions:

(i) Managers will think more about how to make work intrinsically more challenging and meaningful. They will have to create meaning in work which gives employees a sense of pride and self-esteem.

(ii) Manager will act as a catalyst and facilitator rather than a motivator, director, or controller.

(iii) They will delegate more responsibility to their subordinates.

(iv) The basis of motivation shifts from being extrinsic to being intrinsic. It will be linked with organizational goals.

(v) Management systems will be designed to elicit from employees responsible adult behaviour.

Phenomenologic Views of People

There are some theorists who assume that people can be analyzed and understood in terms of consciousness and uniconsciousness. Man is viewed as rational in terms of behaviour, attitudes, and personality. According to this model, the manager must somehow get "inside" the mind of an employee to understand his behaviour because what a manager perceives is only a partial observation of the person.

Theory X and Theory Y Model of Man

Douglas McGregor has propounded one of the most influential models of man which offers two contradictory set of views about human nature, motivation and behaviour in work situations. It is termed Theory X and Theory Y. According to Theory X:

(a) The average person has an inherent dislike of work and will try to avoid it when possible.

(b) The average person lacks ambition, dislikes job responsibilities, and prefers to be closely directed.

(c) The average person is by nature self-centered and indifferent to overall organizational goal achievement.

(d) The average person is resistant to change.

(e) The average person desires job security and economic rewards above all else.

In contrast Theory Y assumes:

(a) The average person is not by nature passive or resistant to the organization's needs.

(b) Economic benefits and job security are only two of the possible rewards desired by he average person. In fact, the average person is committed to goals that will enable him to self-actualize.

(c) The average person learns, under rewarding conditions, to seek and accept job responsibilities.

(d) The average person wants to exercise autonomy and creativity to aid in his own growth and the accomplishment of organizational goals.

These two opposing sets of assumptions about man can obviously result in different managerial practices and actions.

The Manager's Job

The job of a manager is, most often described in terms of management functions and management roles. Four managerial functions and ten managerial roles are commonly defined, as illustrated in Fig. 1.

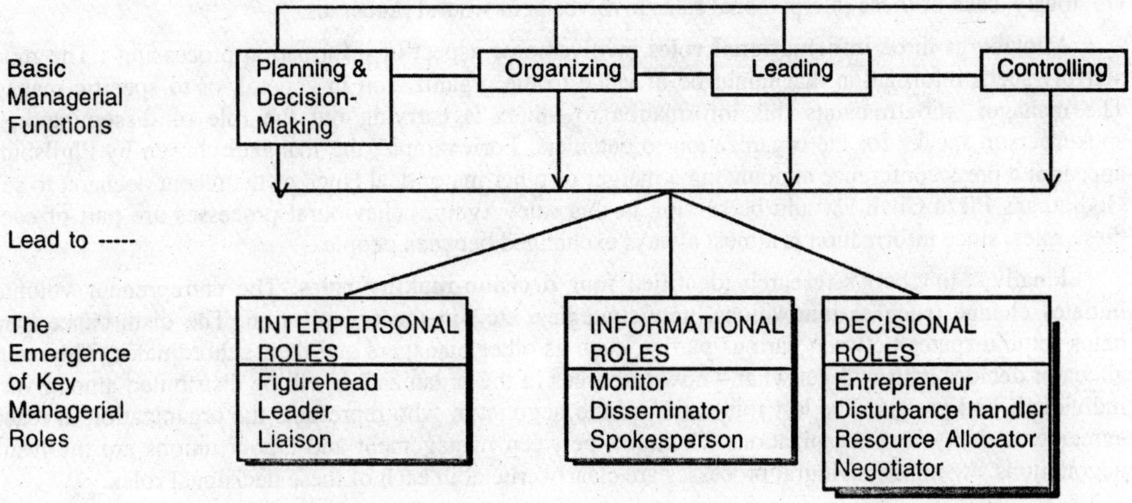

Fig. 1. The Manager's Job

MANAGERIAL FUNCTIONS

The four basic managerial functions are planning and decision-making, organizing, leading, and controlling. **Planning** is the process of determining the organization's desired future position and deciding how best to get there. The planning process at Sears, Roebuck, for example, includes scanning the environment, deciding on appropriate goals, outlining strategies for achieving those goals, and developing tactics to assist in executing the strategies. Behavioural processes and characteristics pervade each of these activities. Perception, for instance, plays a major role in environmental scanning; and creativity and motivation influence how managers set goals, strategies, and tactics.

Organizing is the process of designing jobs, grouping jobs into manageable units, and establishing patterns of authority among jobs and groups of jobs. This process designs the basic structure of the organization, and for large organizations like Sears, that structure can be extensive and complicated. As noted earlier, the processes and characteristics of the organization itself are a major theme of organizational behaviour.

Leading is the process of getting members of the organization to work together toward the organization's goals. Major components of leading include motivating employees, managing group dynamics, and leadership *per se*, all of which are closely related to major areas of organizational behaviour.

The fourth managerial function, **controlling,** is the process of monitoring and correcting the actions of the organization and its people so as to keep them headed towards their goals. Again, behavioural processes and characteristics are a key part of this function. Performance evaluation, reward systems, and motivation, for example, all enter into control.

MANAGERIAL ROLES

In an organization, as in a play or a movie, a role is the part of person plays in a given situation. Much of our knowledge about managerial roles comes from the work of Henry Mintzberg. Mintzberg identified the ten basic managerial roles in three general categories that are shown in Fig. 1.

Interpersonal roles are primarily social in nature, that is, they are roles in which the manager's main task is to relate to other people in certain ways. The manager may sometimes serve as a figurehead for the organization. Taking visitors to dinner and attending ribbon cutting ceremonies are part of the figurehead role. In the role of leader, the manager works to hire, train, and motivate employees. Finally, the liaison role consists of relating to others outside the group or organization. For example, a manager at Inter might be responsible for handling all price negotiations with a key supplier of electronic circuit boards. Obviously, each of these interpersonal roles involves behavioural processes.

Mintzbergs three **informational roles** involve some aspect of information processing : The monitor actively seeks information that might be of value to the organization in general, or to specific managers. The manager who transmits this information to others is carrying out the role of disseminator. The spokesperson speaks for the organization to outsiders. For example, the manager chosen by Phillsbury to appear at a press conference announcing a merger or other major deal (such as the recent decision to sell its Godfather's Pizza Chain) would be serving in this role. Again, behavioural processes are part of each of these roles, since information is almost always exchanged between people.

Finally, Mintzberg's research identified four **decision-making roles.** The entrepreneur voluntarily initiates change (such as innovations, new strategies, etc.) in the organization. The disturbance handler helps settle disputes between various parties, such as other managers and their subordinates. The resource allocator decides who will get what – how resources in the organization will be distributed among various individuals and groups. The last role is that of the negotiator, who represents the organization in reaching agreements with other organizations. Contracts between management and labour unions are the result of negotiations. Again, behavioural processes are clearly crucial in each of these decisional roles.

Mintzberg's research also provided quite a lot of insight into how managers allocate their time in performing these roles, especially senior managers at the top of an organization.

The Human Context of Management

In addition to understanding the on – going behavioural processes involved in their own jobs, managers must understand the basic human element of their work. Organizational behaviour offers three major ways of understanding this context; people as organizations, people as resources, and people as people.

Above all, organizations are people; and, without people there would be no organizations. A neighborhood grocery store owned and operated by a husband and wife team; Exxon, one of the world's largest industrial corporations, the Smithsonian Institution in Washington; a neighborhood street gang; the Mayo Clinic, one of this country's finest health care facilities; your college or university – all are organizations; and, although they differ dramatically in size, purpose, and structure, they have one thing in common people. Thus, if managers are to understand the organizations in which they work, they must first understand the people who make up the organizations.

As resources, people are one of an organization's most valuable assets. People create the organization, guide and direct its course, and vitalize and revitalize it. People make its decisions, solve its problems, and answer its questions. In recent years, many Americans have been alarmed by the way productivity growth in the United States has slowed in relation to that of other industrial countries, including Japan, West Germany, and France. People are at the core of many of the factors cited as possibly causing this trend. To reverse declining productivity, many organizations have taken steps to boost the contribution from their human resources. Some companies have taken steps to encourage management and labour to cooperate better, and others have increased employee participation in decision-making and problem-solving. At Westinghouse, for example, groups of employees meet regularly to study major problems faced by the company and to recommend solutions. As managers increasingly recognize the value of potential contributions by their employees, it will become more and more important for managers and employees to grasp the complexities of organizational behaviour.

Finally, there is people as people – an argument derived from the simple notion of humanistic management. People spend a large part of their lives in organizational settings, mostly as employees. They have a right to expect something in return beyond wages and employee benefits. Employees seek satisfaction, and many want the opportunity to grow an develop and to learn new skills. An understanding of organizational behaviour can help the manager better appreciate this variety of individual needs and expectations.

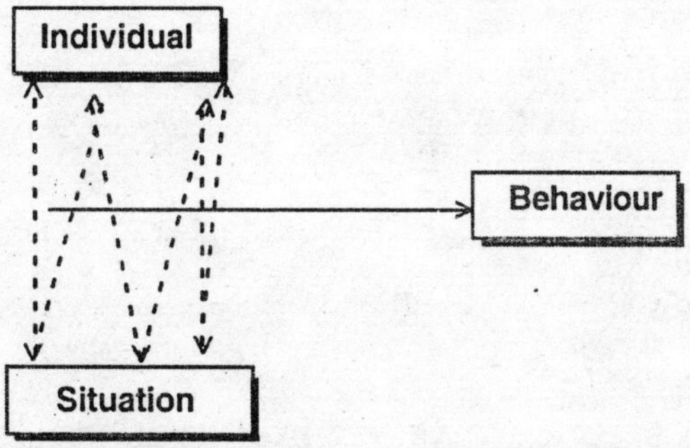

Fig. 2. The Interactional View of Behaviour

Of course, human life in organizations can have a negative side also. People who are unhappy with their jobs are more likely to be frequently absent to look for work elsewhere than people who are happy. Recent years have seen increasing attention to the causes and consequences of employee stress at work. Knowledge of organizational behaviour can help managers recognize the problems of the workplace and improve the quality of individual work experiences.

CHAPTER

7

Perception

Perception is not just what we see with our eyes. It is a basic cognitive process with many variable aspects to object behaviour. Perception is essentially a complex psychological process through which an individual selectively absorbs or assimilates the stimuli in the environment, cognitively organises the perceived information in a specific fashion according to his own interpretation in order to make an assessment about what is going on in one's environment. Hence we may say that perception is the process whereby an individual selects, filters, organizes, interprets sensory stimulations into meaningful information to the events happening in the environment. It is an internal condition 'representing external things.'

There can be no behaviour without perception and perception lies at the core of every individual behaviour. Signals and stimuli bombard our senses from every individual behaviour. Signals and stimuli bombard our senses from every direction. It is perception which narrows and focuses these stimuli into individual words of communication reality. Perception screens out that which an individual does not find relevant and involves not only the reception of physical stimuli but also the interpretation that we give to the sensation that we receive.

Therefore, the crucial question regarding a study of perception is "Why do two individuals not respond to the same stimuli identically?" "Why is the same world looked upon differently by different people?"

Obviously, the answer is perception. The subjectively perceived reality in a particular environment may be different for different people. A few definitions of perception may clarify this aspect.

(1) "Perception is the process of becoming aware of situations, of adding meaningful associations to sensations."

(2) "Perception can be defined as the process of receiving, selecting, organizing, interpreting, checking, and reacting to sensory stimuli or data."

(3) "Perception can be defined as a process by which individuals organize and interpret their sensory impression in order to give meaning to their environments."

(4) "Perception includes all those processes by which an individual receives information about his environment – seeing, hearing, feeling, tasting, and smelling. The study of these perceptional processes shows that their functioning is affected by the three classes of variables – the objects or events being perceived, the environment in which perception occurs, and the individual doing the perceiving."

An analysis of these definitions reveals that:

1. Perception is the interpretation of the meanings of sensation.
2. Sensations are the constituents as raw materials of perception.
3. Whereas sensation is the first or at least the first conscious response born out of the stimuli, perception is the second response of the stimuli after sensation.
4. Perception refers to what is immediately experienced by an individual and it is a way in which the stimuli are interpreted.

5. Perception is a mental activity which acquaints us with situations by giving us direct knowledge of it.
6. Perception screens out that which an individual does not find relevant and involves not only the reception of physical stimuli but also the interpretation that an individual gives to the sensation he receives.
7. Perception is the direct response to the sensation and only an indirect response to the physical stimulus.
8. Individual's actions, emotions, thoughts, feelings and ultimately his behaviour are set off in motion by a perception of his surroundings.

All individuals do not view the world in the same perspective. People see things differently and there are radical differences in which people think and react. For example, consider Fig. 1. How many squares are there?

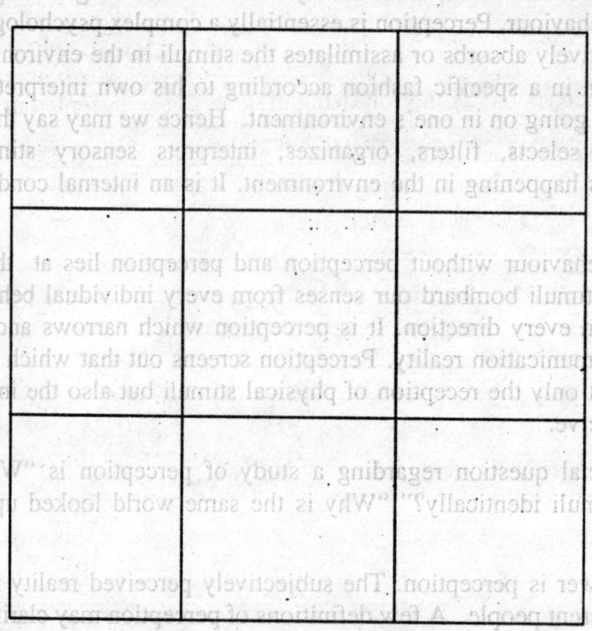

Fig. 1. Count these Squares

The immediate answer by an individual who rushes it quickly will most probably say nine squares. Another person may visualize it having fourteen squares. It is a known fact that persons look at the same thing, yet they perceive it much differently. The surprising point is that most of the people do not see reality. Most of our acts and behaviours are based on our perception.

Differences in perceptions should not, however, lead to the misleading conception that the perceived world is a chaotic one. It is rather an orderly world in which perceiver draws on interpretative meaning from the perceived object. It may be true that the same object may look clear and meaningless to one person, but it may be more meaningful, genuine or real to the one who perceives it to be so. Perception is thus formed in some orderly manner and can be studied systematically by the manager.

Process of Perception

According to our discussion, perception essentially consists of five processes, viz., receiving, filtering, assigning, interpreting and finally reacting to the stimuli. These all processes are greatly influenced by the perceiver and environment. Fig. 2 illustrates the process of perception.

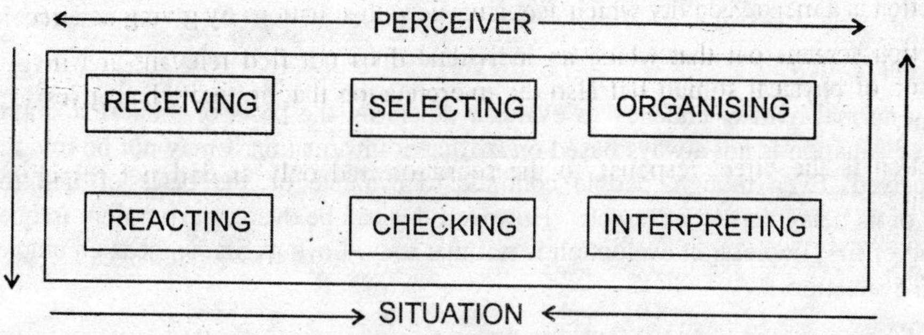

Fig. 2. Process of Perception

It is a well-known fact beyond doubt that outputs are a function of inputs. So it is true in the case of perception. Stimuli (perceptual inputs) are first received, then processed by the perceiver through his perception screen and the resultant output becomes the basis of his behaviour. A simplified model of the perceptual process can be represented by the following diagrams as represented in Fig. 3.

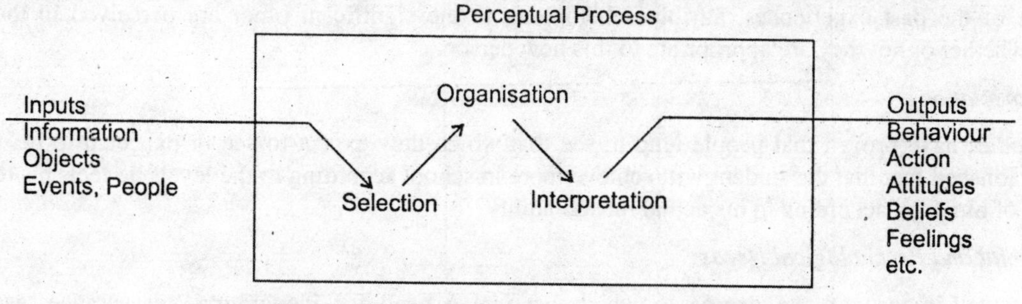

Fig. 3. The Simplified Model of Perceptual Process.

The above model consists of four variables:

1. *Inputs*: Perceived inputs are the stimuli such as information, events, objects, etc., that are received by the perceiver.
2. *Process:* The received stimuli (inputs) are processed through the selection, organization and interpretation.
3. *Outputs*: The output is obtained through the processing mechanism. These outputs may be in the form of feelings, emotions, attitude, love, hatred, action, etc.
4. *Behaviour*: The perceived outputs are reflected in terms of behaviour of an individual. The perceivers' behaviour, in turn generates responses from the perceived and these again give rise to a new set of inputs. Thereby the outputs become inputs and the process continues.

Basic Factors Affecting Perception

Perception and the resultant behaviour are greatly influenced by a considerable number of factors. They affect how we interpret and assign meanings to the stimuli which we encounter and which are bombarded on our senses. These factors include such influences as:

1. *Our Mental Set*

Mental set refers to the tendency of each individual to have a conditioned pattern reaction in a certain way to a given stimulus. Most of our mental set comes through a wide variety of past experiences and prejudices develop them. An individual (perceiver) in appraising other people, have an inherent tendency to respond either favourably or unfavourably. Thus, mental set plays an integral role in perceptual selectivity. People own characteristics and predispositions (mental sets) greatly influence the characteristics which they are likely to see in others. They select only those aspects to which they find match with their characteristics.

2. *First Impression*

It is a normal human tendency to evaluate others on the basis of their first impression. Since first impression evaluation is not always based on sufficient information it may not be true reflection of people being perceived. Even though, people continue to evaluate on the basis of first impression, though possibility of its being correct as remote. However, this can be overcome by more frequent interaction, but the erasing of first impression evaluation is not that easy. Love at first sight is an ample proof of the first impression evaluation.

3. *Past Experiences*

Previous experiences condition most of us in relation to any given situation. We only need to think a minute of the many times we have wished and we could do something over. Next time when we encounter a similar situation, our past experiences and reactions to it influence our course of action which we take in the new situation. For example, if the previous boss is friendly, generous and fair to his subordinates, the subordinates are most likely to assume that his new boss will also be friendly, generous and fair to them. Because of the past experiences, attributes belonging to the significant other are perceived in the new person whether or not they are appropriate to this new person.

4. *Expectations*

Studies have proved that people tend to see that which they expect to see or expected to be. It is a well-established fact that the student will achieve more in school according to the levels he feels his teacher expects of him than according to his actual mental ability.

5. *Social and Psychological Needs*

Our self-image and the degree to which we feel a need for recognition, reassurance, security, achievements and social acceptance affect the way we perceive something and the way we react.

A person may feel compelled to laugh at a joke that does not seem funny to him if his boss is telling it and he is expecting for a raise. The way we talk, dress and act indicates a great deal about us.

6. *Status and Group Factors*

This is to a large extent interrelated with the preceding factors.

People's social class and background cause them to see a situation differently, and an individual tends to be influenced by the shared feelings of the group to which he belongs or to which he wants to belong.

7. *Interest*

The degree to which something interests us or is important to us will sharp our perception of it and influence a positive or negative reaction.

A rock group recording of a current hit may result in positive concentration, discussion of the merits of a number of musical groups and shared enjoying among a group of teenagers but a quite different reaction from someone thirty years older with no interest in identifying the qualities of a given group.

8. *Mood*

This is simply the way we wake up feelings on any given day or time. It is the part of a dominant personality pattern that affects the way we perceive any situation or set of stimuli.

Special Factors Affecting Perception

Besides the basic factors which affect the process of perception there are certain special factors too, which influence this selectivity. These factors can broadly be classified under two major heads:

A. *External Factors*

Perception is a selective process. As we cannot assimilate all of the information coming in, we select a certain amount of information from the total outside information. Some of the main external factors influencing perception are nature, location, intensity, size, contrast, repetition, motion and familiarity and novelty.

Nature: Nature refers to any object which is either visual or auditory. If it is visual whether it entangles pictures, people or animals, it is beyond any doubt that any picture depicting human beings attracts much greater attention than a picture of inanimate objects alone, and that a rhyming auditory passage attracts attention more readily than the same passage presented as a narrative.

Location: The stimulus which is so located that it is placed directly in front of the eyes is the best location for any visual stimulus to attract maximum perception. Studies have revealed that when such a location is not possible, a position that is at the upper portion of a page is more desirable than one at lower portions and the left hand side receives more attention than the right hand side.

Intensity: Intensity of the stimulus accentuates and functions to increase the possibility of selection. If the messages are bright and loud, they immediately attract people. Similarly, underlining or highlighting a sentence attracts more attention; so authors or journalists pay more attention to italics in their works. The greater the intensity of a stimulus, the more likely it will be noticed. A loud noise, strong odour or bright light is comparatively more noticed than a soft sound, weak odour or dim light. Advertisers often employ this aspect to gain customers' attention.

Size: Size of the stimulus also influences the selectivity process. The bigger the size of the perceived object, the higher is the probability of its having been perceived. Size establishes dominance and overrides other things thereby enhancing the perceptual selection. Large posters, bold letters, a giant machine all are capable of attracting individual's attention more. In advertising, a large spread message gets more attention than a few lines in the classified section or in some corner of a newspaper or periodical.

Contrast: Stimuli that contrast with the surrounding environment are more likely to be selected for attention that the stimuli that blend in. For example, look at the Fig. 4 which illustrates the perceptual principle.

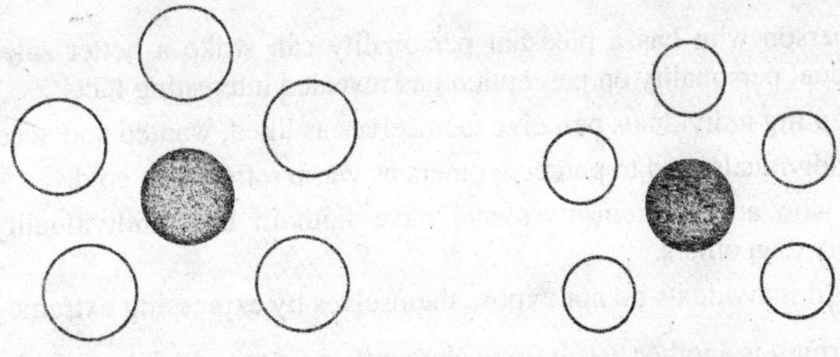

Fig. 4 A Fig. 4 B

The Contrast Principal of Perception

The black circle on the right (Fig. 4B) appears bigger than the one on the left, though both of them (in Fig. 4 A and 4 B) are of the same size, because it is contrasted with other circles.

A contrasting effect can be created by colour, size or any other factor, that is, unusual that distinguishes one stimulus from others. The contrast principle essentially states that external stimuli that stand our against the background or which are not what we are expecting will receive greater attention. One must have noticed plant safety signs have black letter on a yellow background or white letters on a red background because these contrasts more attention draw. Similarly, the contrast effect also explains why a child stands out in a group of females. There is nothing unusual about the child, but when surrounded by females, stands out and establishes his identity.

Movement: A moving object receives greater attention than an object that is standing still. Advertisers affectively use the principle of movement by displaying an object which incorporates moving parts.

Repetition: Repetition of stimuli increases sensitivity and alertness to the object. A stimulus that is repeated has a better chance of catching us during one of the periods when our attention to task is waning.

Advertisers most frequently use repetition principle by flashing the same advertisement again and again on a regular basis to catch the attention of prospective customers. This principle is also referred to as the principle of frequency.

Familiarity and Novelty: This principle states that if a stimulus is to one that is either familiar or novel to the perceiver, it can serve as a better attention getter. New objects in a familiar situation or setting or familiar objects in a new (novelty) setting are bound to draw more attention to the perceiver. In management, managers effectively employ job rotation, based on the principle of familiarity and novelty. Changing worker's job from time to time will tend to increase the attention they give to the task. Similarly, if the supervisor communicates in local dialects (familiarity) it can serve as a better method to get positive response from the worker.

B. *Internal Factors*

Besides external factors, there are numerous internal factors too, which have a significant bearing on perception. These internal factors are basically related to the psychological make-up of an individual and include personality, learning and motivation.

Personality: The personality of an individual is an internal factor which greatly influences the perceived behaviour. Optimistic people perceive things in favourable terms while pessimistic people perceive in negative terms.

Maslow argues that between these two extremes there exists a category of people who can see things more objectively and accurately. Leavitt reported on a senior executive whose biggest problem with young managers was their tendency to avoid making unpleasant decisions. The young managers paid no heed to disciplining people, to digging through boring and repetitive records, or to writing unpleasant letters.Obviously, the reason was that these unpleasant activities were not compatible with the personalities of those young managers, rather than those older executives because of their personality make-up had made them accustomed, over the years.

Similarly, a person who has a pleasant personality can strike a better sales deal. Research on the effects of an individual personality on perception has revealed interesting facts.

(a) Self-accepting individuals perceive themselves as liked, wanted and accepted by others.

(b) Secure individuals tend to perceive others as warm rather than cold.

(c) Persons who accept themselves and have faith in their individuality perceive things more favourably than others.

(d) Thoughtful individuals do not expose themselves by expressing extreme judgements of others.

Learning: Learning is another psychological cognitive factor which have its bearing on perception and probably plays the biggest role in developing perceptual set. Psychologists have used a number of illustrations to demonstrate the effect of learning on perception.

For example, read the phrases in the triangles below in Figs. 5A and 5B.

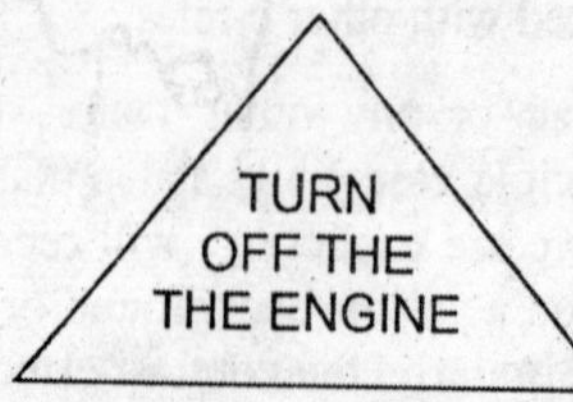

Fig. 5 A

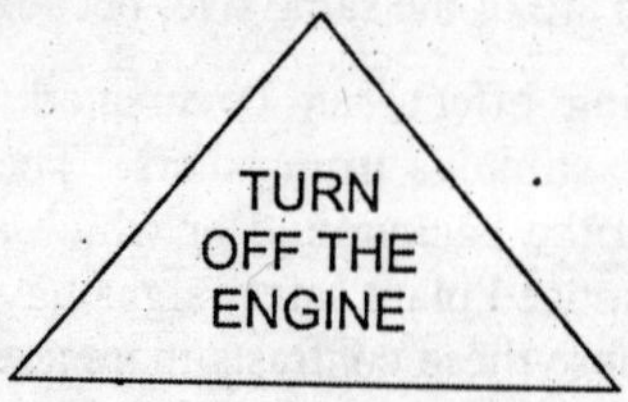

Fig. 5 B

It may take you a few seconds to notice that there is something wrong in both the phrases. This is just because of the fact that prior learning creates an expectancy and makes him see what he wants to see. Similarly, try to read the following words slowly :

M—A—C—T—A—V—I—S—H

M—A—C—D—O—N—A—L—D

M—A—C—B—E—T—H

M—A—C—H—I—N—E—R—Y

There is a very high degree of possibility that an individual is most likely to read the last word and pronounce it as 'Mac-Hinery' instead of the real pronunciation 'Machinery.' This is because due to learning the reader is caught in a 'verbal response set.'

There are many other numerous illustrations that are commonly employed to demonstrate the effect of learning on perceptual set development. See the picture in Figs. 6A-6B. What do you perceive in this picture? There is a great possibility that most of the people will perceive it as a picture of wealthy young beautiful lady wearing a fur coat.

Fig. 6 A

Fig. 6 B

Ambiguous picture of a young woman and an old woman

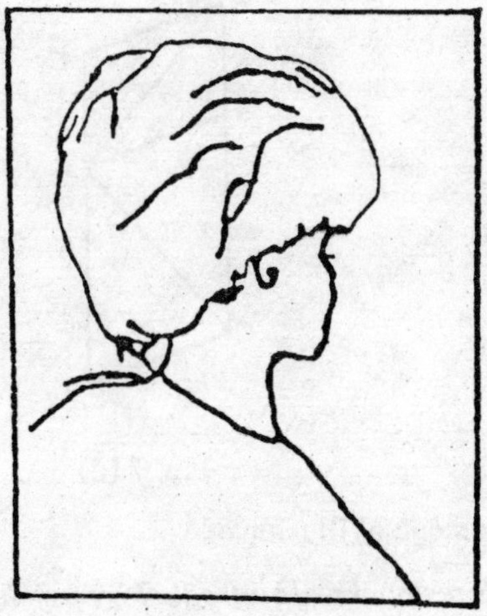

Fig. 6 C

Clear Sketch of a young woman

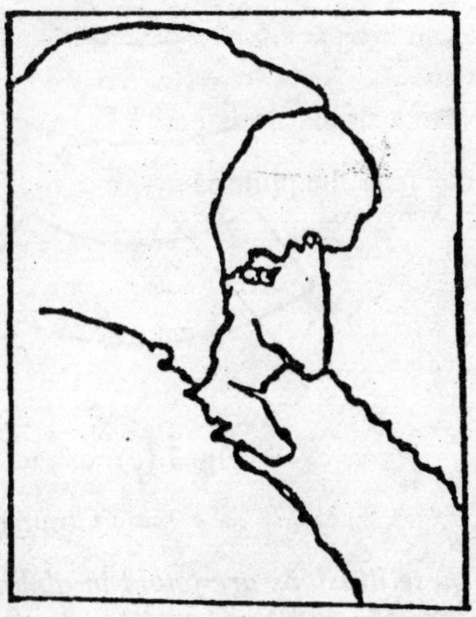

Fig. 6 D

Clear Sketch of an old woman

Source: *Edwin G. Boring, "A New Ambiguous Figure", American Journal of Psychology, July, 1930, p.444. Also see Robert Leeper, "A Study of a Neglected Portion of the field of Learning – The Development of Sensory Organization," Journal of Genetic Psychology, March, 1935, p. 62, Originally drawn by cartoonist, W.E. Hill and published in Puck, November 6, 1915.*

But after the Figs. 6A-6B if the people are shown the picture as in Fig. 6C, the sketch of a young woman, it is almost certain that people will confirm of perceiving a young lady as in Figs. 6A-6B. But on the other hand, if instead of Fig. 6C people are shown the Fig. 6D, the sketch of an ugly old woman, people will perceive the same old woman in Figs. 6A-6B. This illustration further confirms that perception is greatly influenced by a simple learned experience.

Besides this old lady-young lady illustration, there are a number of frequently used illustrations which effectively bring out the impact of learning on perception. In Fig. 7 (a) the length of the nose, from the tip of the mark 'X' is exactly equal to the vertical length of the face. Similarly, in Fig. 7(b) the height of the hat is exactly equal to the width of the brim. In Fig. 7(c) both shapes are exactly equal in size and in Fig.7(d); the lines AE, CE, CB, and DE are equal in length. This is another excellent example of perceptual illusion.

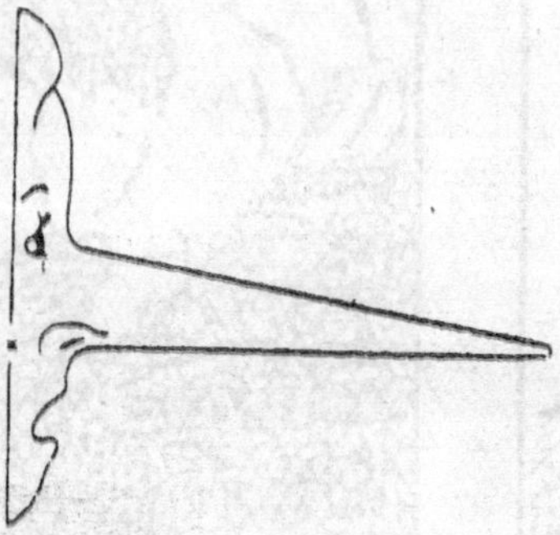

Fig. 7 (a)

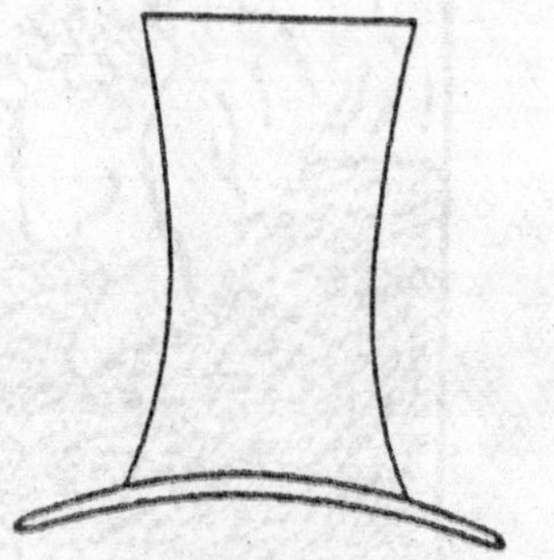

Fig. 7 (b)

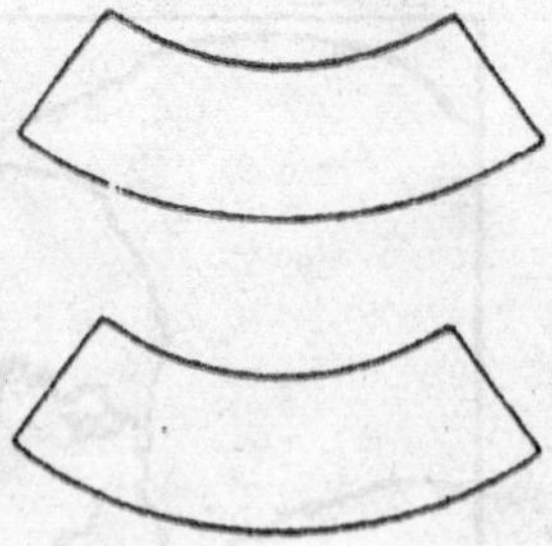

Fig. 7 (c)

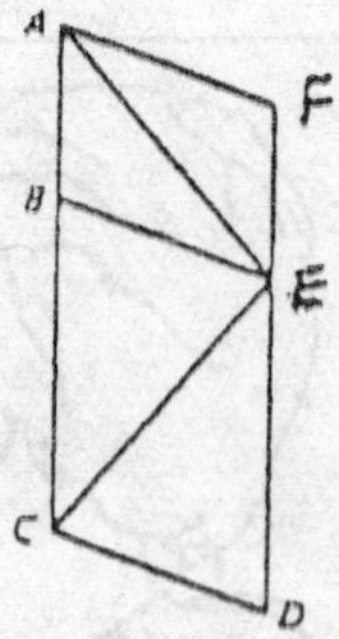

Fig. 7 (d)

Common Perceptual Illusions

Source : *These illusions are found in almost all textbooks of introductory psychology. For example, see Gregory A. Kimble and Norman Garriezy, General Psychology. The Ronald Press, New York, 1963, pp. 324-325. The face is from N.L. Munn and E.P. Johnson, Student's Manual to Accompany Psychology, 2nd Ed. Houghtom Miffin Company, Boston, 1951.*

Motivation

Physiologically needs play a significant role in perceptual selectivity. Sex and hunger are examples of primary motives which greatly affect internal perceptual selectivity. In traditional Indian society, the sex drive is largely suppressed, with the result being an unfulfilled need for sex. Therefore, any mention of sex or a visual stimulus dealing with sex is spontaneous attention getting to an average Indian. The picture of a scantily clad or naked female immediately attracts the perceptuality of the Indian male, in comparison to the males belonging to that culture where the female breasts are always exposed. This is why, nudity is increasingly taking a common place in magazines, television spots, motion pictures and advertisements. Similarly, unreal things often look real because of deprived needs. A thirsty person in the desert gets the illusion of water while seeing sand from a distance. In an experiment people who were deprived of food and kept hungry for a period of time. When they were shown pictures and were asked to describe as to what did they see in the picture, most of them reported more food items in such perceptions.

It may be noted that frequently all of a person's psychic energies are expanded in trying to satisfy the basic psychological needs for love, esteem, and adequacy. Unconsciously he may interact only with those sectors of another's personality through which he can gratify these needs. Under such conditions he can scarcely perceive the other as a whole person; only when his basic psychological needs are satisfied can he appreciate the full worth of the other.

Another example is the role of motivation in the perception of the members of an executive committee. One committee member may be self-oriented and perceive the problem being discussed as personally threatening. Another member may be interaction-oriented and perceive the same problem in terms of whether it is discussed in a relaxed, friendly way; the content is not important. A third member of the committee may be task-oriented and solely concerned with the content of the problem and bringing it to an immediate solution.

Organization of Perception

The Perceptual selection relating to internal and external factors helped in gaining the perceiver's attention to the stimuli. The information received by an individual from the environment is organized so as to assign same meaning to them. The process of organizing the bits of information into meaningful wholes is known as organization of perception.

The principles of organization were initially developed and stressed by Gestalt psychologists (Gestalt is a German word which means pattern .or configuration), can be best demonstrated by visual representations, but they equally apply to other senses as well. There are three aspects of organization of perception, viz., (a) Figure and Ground (b) Grouping and (c) Closure.

Figure and Ground

Figure and ground is supposed to be the most basic form in organization of perception. It is a distinction of a central object from the surroundings, i.e., the ability of an individual to distinguish an object from its general background, which is basic to "Form perception." Therefore, according to this concept perceived objects stand out as separable from their general background. The figure seems to be well defined, at a definite location, solid, and in front of the ground. In contrast, the ground seems to be indefinite, shapeless and continuous behind the figure. The common outline of the figure and the Ground appears to belong to the figure rather than to the ground. These distinctions are not inherent in the stimulus as is demonstrated by Fig. 8.

(a)

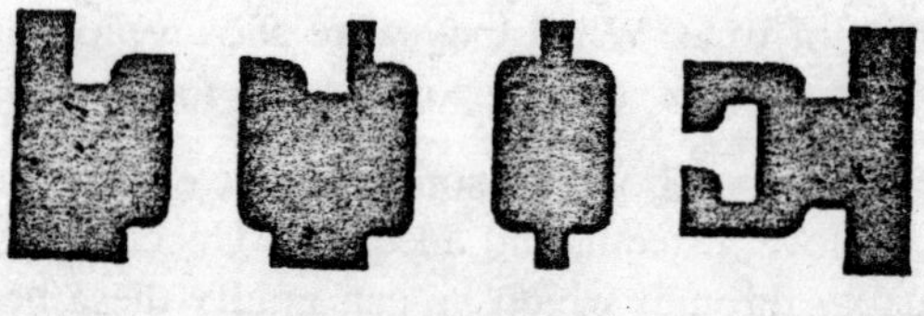

(b)

Fig. 8. Illustration of Figure — Ground

Sources : *(a) Warner Brown and Howard Gilhouse, College Psychology, Prentice-Hall, Inc., Englewood Cliffs, N.J., 1949,p.330(b) Jerome Kagan and Ernest Havemann, Psychology: An Introduction, Harcourt, Brace & World, Inc., New York, 1968, p. 166.*

At a first glance there is every possibility that a person perceives some black irregular shaped figures against a white background. When the white and black ground are interchanged or one looks at the Fig. 8 very carefully, the words 'FLY' and 'TIE' can be noticed by him. This is because the viewer is set to perceive black in relation to white. However, in the above figure reverse is true. Black is the background and white is the figure.

Another interesting Figure-Ground illustration is the famous Peter-Paul Goblet as shown in Fig. 9.

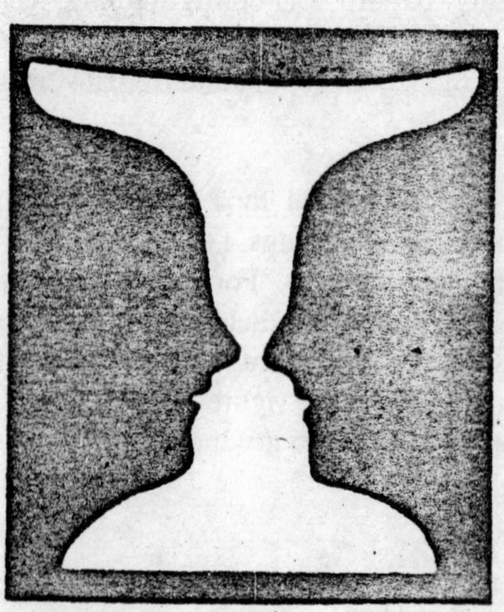

Fig. 9. Peter-Paul Goblet

What do you see? The goblet, a stylish ice-cream cup or the famous twins? However whichever you see at the first instance, try to find out the other. Now, when you have found out the other, try to turn the perception back to what it first was. Surprised! sometimes, probably at first sight, you may perceive it as a white vase or a stylish ice-cream cup and then as two faces opposing each other and on a closer look as two identical twins opposing each other.

In all these figures the same stimuli act alternately as figure and ground, changing their perceptual qualities as they change, maintaining the basic relationship between the figure and the ground.

Though learning has a bearing on what will be perceived as Figure and what as ground, the tendency to organize their perceptions into Figure and ground is inborn, natural and inherent in people. Senden in 1932 demonstrated his truth by conducting an experiment on a person who was born blind. On gaining sight after an operation, congenitally blind person exhibited Figure-ground organization before many other visual abilities.

The perception of Figure-ground relationship can also be perceived through our various sense organs beside vision. To substantiate this, Hilgard postulates that we may hear the song of a bird against a background of outdoor noises or the melody played by the violin against the harmonies of the rest of the orchestra.

Grouping

Gestalt psychology postulates that the whole is different from the sum of its parts. In a situation presenting a set of Figures, an individual is not content with the mass of unrecognised figures. He devises and perceives a fine form only, leaving the rest. In other words, when several objects are present in visual field, we tend to perceive a fine form only, leaving the rest. In other words, when several objects are present in the visual field, we tend to perceive them as organized into patterns or grouping, according to proximity, similarity and continuity.

Proximity

The principle of proximity also referred to as the principle of nearness suggests that the objects which are nearer to each other are grouped together. Just, for example, consider Fig. 10.

        *   *   *   *   *
      *   *   *   *   *
    *   *   *   *   *

Fig. 10.

In this figure you notice a row of small slanted dots grouped from lower left to upper right.

If we mark these dots as follows, you see:

        c   f   i   i
      c   f   i   i
    c   f   i   i

the form abc / def / ghi .... and so on.

The opposite organization

    *
      *
        *

ceg / fhj ....etc. is not seen.

In an organization several group of employees are identified as a single group because of the principle of proximity. Similarly, people sitting in one room of coming from the same place or working on a same machine are perceived to be belonging to the same and one group. Taking the clue of this principle the Japanese management style insists on wearing the same type of clothes, same layout and furniture in the office and having meals together at the work place for all levels of employees, so that the whole organization is perceived as on single entity and the sense of belongingness in the workers is enhanced.

Consider Fig 11, which further explains the principle of nearness. The pair of eight circles are perceived as pairs of two or four depending upon their nearness to one another.

Similarity

The principle of similarity or familiarity clarifies that the greater the similarity of the stimuli, the greater is the possibility of being perceived as a common group or whole. Any two objects similar in any way, e.g., figure, shape, size or colour, etc., have the tendency of being perceived as a group. Similarity is conceptually related to proximity but generally similarity predominates proximity. In Fig. 12 when we focus our attention on asterisks rather than circles, we perceive an organized frame of three horizontal and six perpendicular lines. Similarly, if we focus our attention or circles, we perceive two horizontal lines.

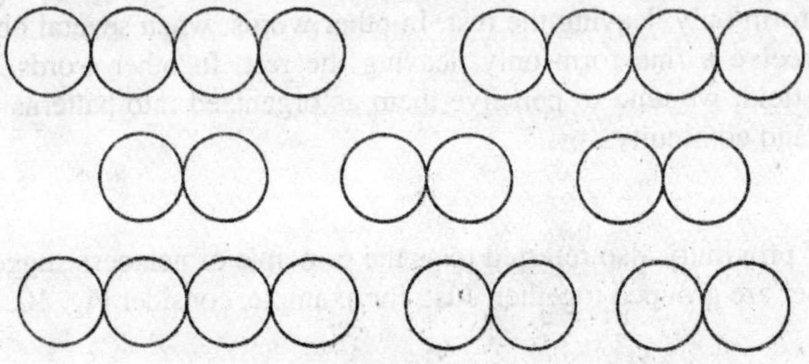

Fig. 11.

```
X   X   X   X   X   X
O   O   O   O   O   O
X   X   X   X   X   X
O   O   O   O   O   O
X   X   X   X   X   X
```

Fig. 12.

Consider another illustration as in Fig. 13. The signs in the figure are perceived as five rows (three rows of (<197>) negative sign and two rows of (+) positive sign rather seven columns, whereas the distances between the rows and columns are equal.

```
—   —   —   —   —
+   +   +   +   +
—   —   —   —   —
+   +   +   +   +
—   —   —   —   —
```

Fig. 13.

In an organization all the employees at the lower level in the hierarchy are perceived in the same category by the executives and executives are perceived in the one category by the workers.

Continuity

The Principle of continuity states that the one will tend to perceive continuous lines of patterns because an individual sees only obvious lines and fails to have some creative thinking.

Consider the illustrations in Fig.14 when perceiving the four cross in Fig. 14(A) the tendency is to perceive them not as four crosses but as a square and likewise triangle in Fig. 14 (B), circle in Fig. 14 (C) and 'B or 13' in Fig. 14 (D). The reason for such a perception is that the entire configuration is perceived as a whole and gaps in between are overlooked because of the tendency of seeing things in a complete form rather than in parts.

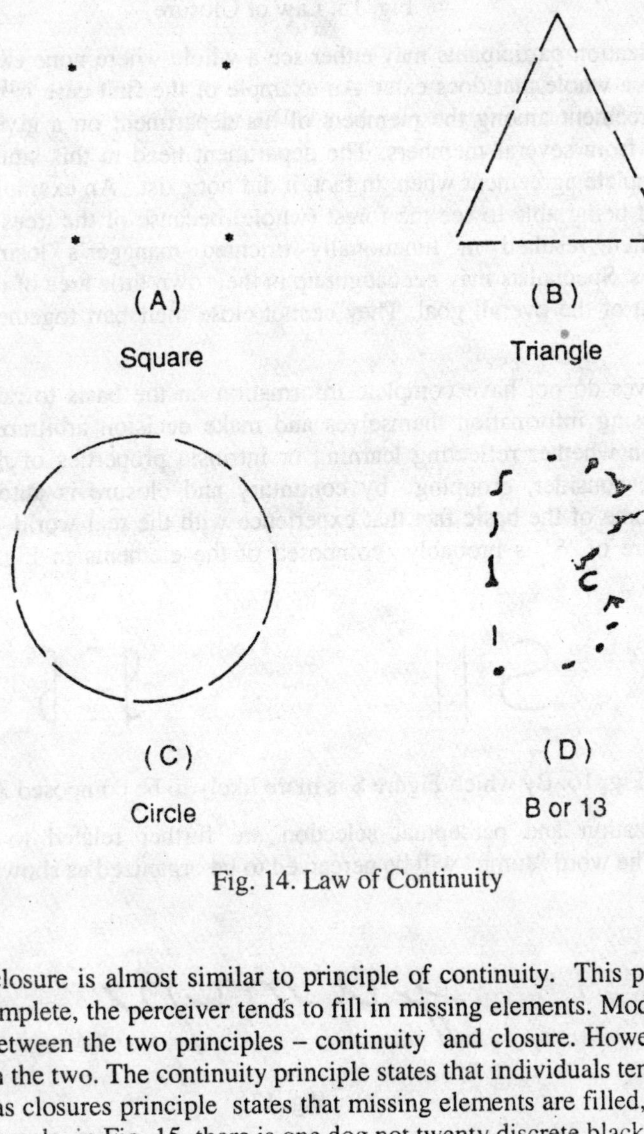

Fig. 14. Law of Continuity

Closure

The principle of closure is almost similar to principle of continuity. This principle states that if the stimulus pattern is incomplete, the perceiver tends to fill in missing elements. Modern psychologist do not make any distinction between the two principles – continuity and closure. However, there seems to be a fine distinction between the two. The continuity principle states that individuals tend to perceive continuous lines or patterns whereas closures principle states that missing elements are filled, i.e., closure supplies the missing stimuli. For example, in Fig. 15, there is one dog not twenty discrete black blotches.

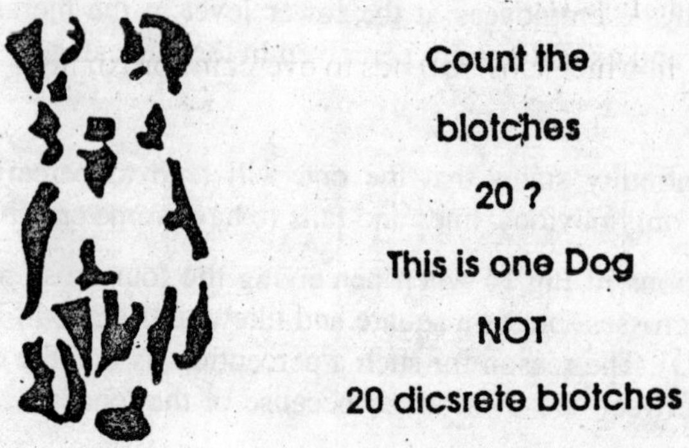

Fig. 15. Law of Closure

In a formal organization participants may either see a whole where none exists or not be able to put the pieces together into a whole that does exist. An example of the first case is the department head who perceived complete agreement among the members of his department on a given project when, in fact, there was a opposition from several members. The department head in this situation closed the existing gaps and perceived complete agreement when, in fact, it did not exist. An example of the other side of the coin is the adage of not being able to see the forest (whole) because of the trees (parts). High degrees of specialization have often resulted in functionally oriented manager's losing sight of the whole organization's objectives. Specialists may get caught up in their own little area of interest and responsibility that they may lose sight of the overall goal. They cannot close their part together with the other parts to perceive the whole.

Similarly, executives do not have complete information on the basis to rate an employee. In such cases, they fill the missing information themselves and make decision arbitrarily. These organizational tendencies of perception whether reflecting learning or intrinsic properties of the perceptual process is arguable. For example, consider, grouping by continuity and closure is automatic, spontaneous and inherent or is the outcome of the basic fact that experience with the real world and its environment has taught us that the Figure of '$' is probably composed of the elements in Fig. 16 (A) rather than the elements in Fig. 16 (B).

Fig. 16. By which Figure $ is more likely to be composed A or B

Perceptual organization and perceptual selection are further related to expectations based on individual experience. The word "Jump" will be perceived to be organized as shown in Fig. 17.

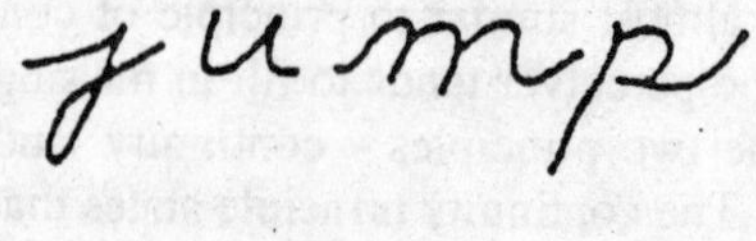

Fig. 17

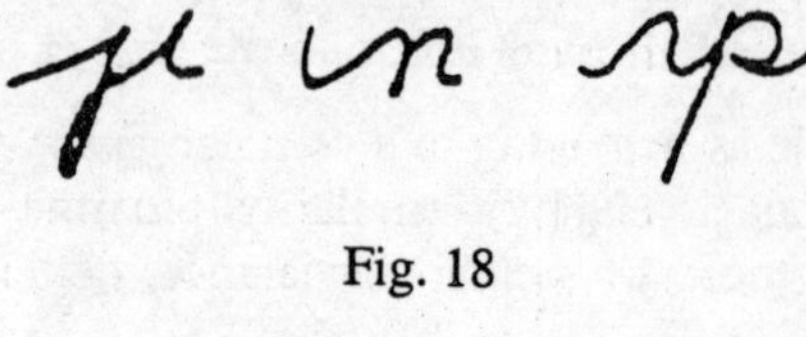

Fig. 18

But not like as shown in Fig. 18.

And examine Fig. 19, in which closure tends to overcome proximity

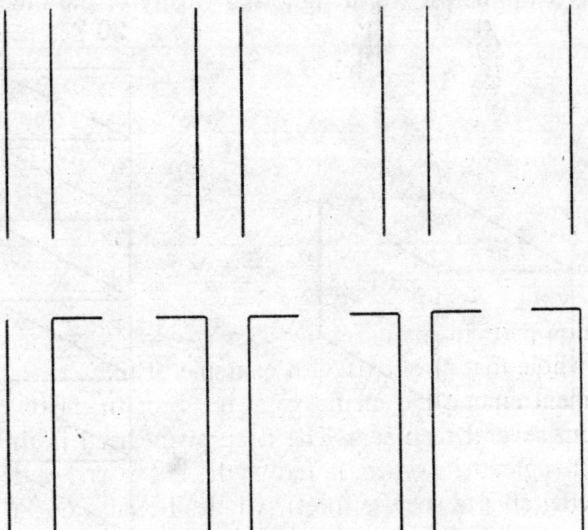

Fig. 19.

An example of the completion between grouping by proximity and grouping by closure. The seven lines above tend to fall "naturally" into three pairs and one isolate, by virtue of proximity relation. But the same lines below, with the addition of the short horizontal lines, tend to be grouped by closure with the more distant partner, overriding the influence of proximity.

Good Figure

The law of good figure states that whenever a stimuli can be organized in a number of ways the 'best' one tends to win out perceptually 'best' in terms of similarity, proximity, continuity, closure, symmetry etc. For example, can you easily identify the Fig. of 20 (A) in 20 (B) or 20 (C) or 20 (D).

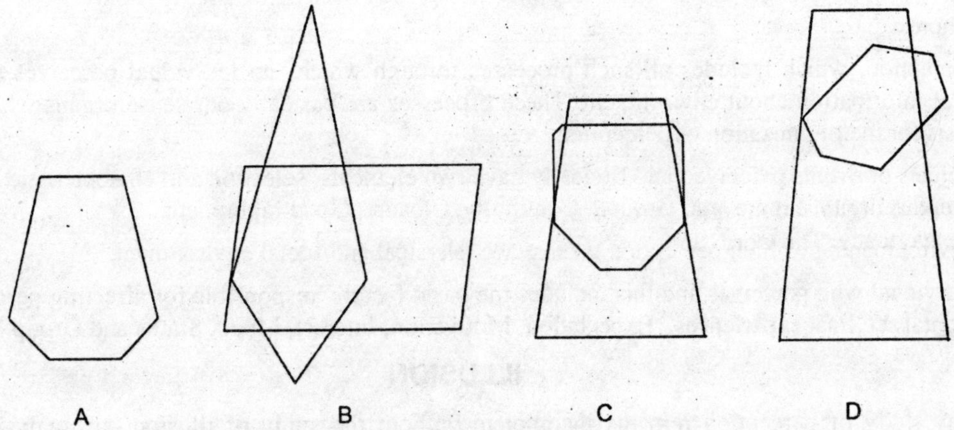

Fig. 20. Good Figure

This principle of perceiving the 'best' is used in artful concealments of military objects from enemy attacks. The real figure or information is destroyed, perceptually, by incorporating it into a complex better one, as you can yourself note as to how difficult it is to locate Fig. 21 (A) in Fig. 21 (B).

The perception of individuals as belonging to a common group is achieved according to some of the principles made familiar by Gestalt psychology: similarity, proximity, good figure, continuation, closure, etc. That is, we group together those of similar appearance, clothing, or mannerisms, assuming more congeniality, perhaps, than the similarity assures we tend to see those who live near to together or who associate together as sharing common values of beliefs (including guilt by association). We structure the social environment when a figure appears, the boundaries are sharpened and the distinction between what belong to the figure and what belong to the ground becomes clear : we may thus structure the world into the 'Free world' and the 'Communist world' ignoring many of the other difference between nation and governments.

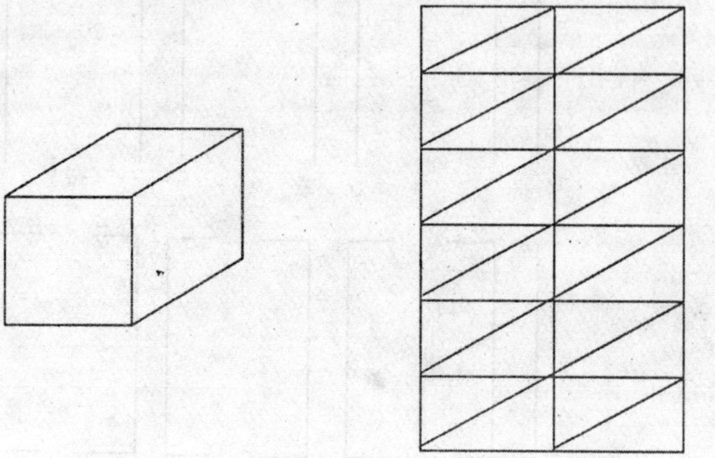

(A) (B)

Fig. 21. Camouflage Figure

Finally, these organizational demonstrations are perhaps the simplest instances of a highly general proposition applicable almost everywhere in human behaviour: people respond neither to discrete elements one at a time nor to the sum total of discrete elements : they respond to the relationships between them. And this serves as an introduction to perceptual interpretation, where this proposition is further documented.

Therefore a synoptic view of the process of the organization of perception can be represented as:

P = f (O, E, I.)

Where

P = Perception, which includes all such processes through which an individual perceives and receives total information about environment. These processes are basically our sense organs which from the basis for the organization of perception.

O = Objects or events perceived and basically have two elements selection and characteristic organization like, Similarity, Figure and Ground, Continuity, Closure, Good Figure, etc.

E = Environments in which perception takes place, physical and social environment.

I = Individual who perceives and this includes the basic factors responsible for affecting perception, like, Mental set, Past experiences, Expectation, Motivation, Interest, Mood, Status and Group Factors.

ILLUSION

Any study of perception remains incomplete without the study of illusion, an analysis of mental events which do not at first blush seem to be identical with physical events. The final perception which does not agree with other perception or reality can be known as illusion. An illusion is nothing else but misinterpretation of the real meaning of the perception. In this mental activity we misinterpret an object presented before us. It is very normal mental activity because it is experienced by all people but it is different from a normal perception. In illusion, the object which is wrongly or falsely perceived is present and imagination normally does not play any role. In other words, we may say that illusion is neither a dream, because the perceived object is present, not it is an imagination, because the object of perception is not a creation of the mind of an individual. The best example of illusion is to illustrate a stick when held partly under water appears crooked. There is a perception of course, but not in keeping with the real form of the perceived object (stick) as it is falsified due to refraction of light. If we come out of a darkroom into sun we all interpret that the light is very bright. This is also due to illusion.

Another example of illusion due to optical or visual sensation is when we perceive a stationary object as a moving one. The reality is that the object is stationary and movement is actually taking place in the field of perception. Motion-picture films present an excellent example of the same. The reality is that the pictures are still and the movement is provided by our illusions. Similarly, while we are travelling in a train we normally come across and experience that while we are sitting in a train and another train is in motion, we interpret our own train is in motion and is moving as forward.

Kinds of Illusion

A comprehensive classification of illusion can be made under four heads :

(i) Individualistic
(ii) Universal
(iii) Momentary
(iv) Eternal.

(i) **Individualistic**: Individualistic Illusions are such illusions which may occur to one individual but not to others. For example, an individual suffering from jaundice, perceives everything as yellow, whereas others do not. Thus individualistic illusions can also be termed as personal illusions and differ from individual to individual.

(ii) **Universal**: Universal illusions are those which are similar in case of every person. For example, if you peep out in a running train, every individual will notice that trees are running in opposite direction. Similarly, if you stand in between railway tracks, they seems to meet at a point.

(iii) **Momentary**: Momentary illusions occur for a short period of time and disappear as soon as the real knowledge of the object is secured. For example, in dark some people mistakenly consider a piece of rope as a snake.

(iv) **Eternal**: Eternal illusions are permanent and normally they persist. A famous example of such illusion, referred as Muller-Lyer illusion is illustrated in Fig. 22. The straight line is divided into two equal halves at the apex of the middle angle but left part appears to be longer in length.

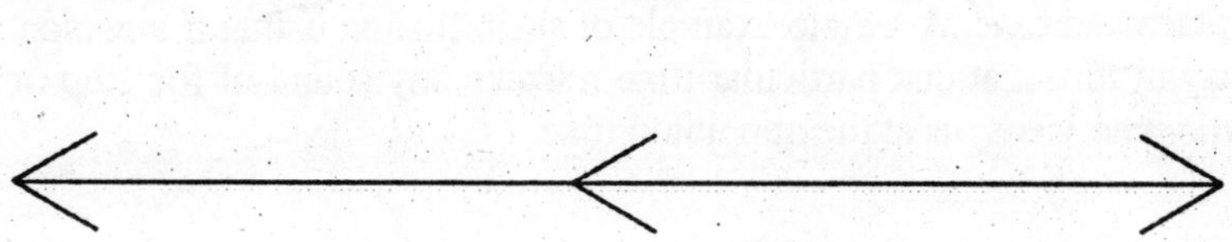

Fig. 22. Muller-Lyer Illusion

Causes of Illusion

There can be numerous reasons for illusion. However, certain factors, enumerated below, may be responsible for illusion in general and hold good to all individuals :

(a) *Eye Movement*

The movement of eyes are greatly responsible for creating optical illusion. If vision at a particular object (stimuli) requires too much of strain, an illusion may occur. Muller-Lyer illusion, Fig. 23 is an example of such illusion.

Fig. 23. Illusion Due to Eye Movement

On the basis of this experiment an attempt has been made to prove that though the lines are equal in length they look unequal when seen after straining the eyes. Line AB in the above Fig. 23 is feather headed while line CD is arrow headed. Comparatively there is more eye movement in perceiving the line AB than in perceiving the line CD. In such illusions, actual eye movement is not necessary because even an equivalent tendency to it is sufficient to cause an illusion.

(b) *Confusion*

Another major factor responsible for geometrical illusion is confusion. When impurity or inaccuracy of perception of the various parts of the object takes place we have confusion and the result is illusion. For example, it is commonly noticed that while looking at a picture or painting the person becomes so involved that he does not notice the parts in the picture and gets confused and engrossed in it.

(c) *Tendency to See as a Whole*

This aspect has already been discussed while dealing with Gestalt psychology; we have a tendency to perceive an object as a whole rather than in parts. The example cited earlier in 'Good Figure' often leads to the perception of material actually absent in the picture.

(d) *Perspective*

When we perceive an object or a figure in the context of perspective an illusion is likely to take place. It is an account of perspective that we have a three-dimensional vision.

(e) *Preconception*

When we are under the influence of a preconception or an idea we feel the happening of that thought at the appointed place and time. A simple example of such illusion is that if a person visits us at a particular hour daily, we may at times, at that particular time mistake any sound of footstep or knock at the door, for those of that person who visits us at the appointed time.

(f) *Habits*

If a person is habitual of looking a thing in a particular manner he is bound to commit a mistake in that very manner even if it is slightly different. That is why mistakes in printed pages are easily overlooked and proof readers commit mistakes in the spelling of the words. Another simple example of habit is, while we pronounce the word 'education.' The actual pronunciation is '- e-du-cation', while we pronounce it as 'e-gu-cation', and one frequently writes 'g' instead of letter 'd.'

(g) *Emotion*

When an individual is under the influence of emotion, there are all possibilities of his perception getting influenced and causing illusion. That is why when we are under the influence of fear, rope is seen as snake and the sound caused by rats turns into cracking sound made by thieves.

(h) *Imperfect Isolation*

Imperfect isolation of an object is another factor which causes illusion. Size-weight illusions are common because of imperfect isolation. If two boxes of different sizes but having equal weights are lifted by a person, the box of the smaller size will appear to him lighter than that of the bigger size box.

(i) *Contrast of Stimuli*

This is another cause of illusion when we look something good in the midst of something which is comparatively bad, the better things look far better. For example, if we look fair face among fair faces nothing unusual is perceived, but if the same fair face is viewed next to a dark face, it appear to be more fair due to sharp contrast of stimuli.

(j) *Distance*

An object placed at a near distance always looks big rather than the same object placed at a distance. That is why from an aircraft flying high in the sky, people on the ground see it as a small object and people sitting inside the aircraft perceive people on the ground as ants.

(k) *Defect in Sense Organs*

Due to defect in sense organs sometimes one may have illusion. For example, if a person has a coated tongue he may not be able to have taste of sugar correctly as sweet rather he may have the illusion of sugar being tasteless.

HALLUCINATION

Hallucination is in itself a kind of error in perception but different from illusion. Our brain has a typical characteristic which can lie about what comes to us through our senses. Our mind can play with us. Many of us have hallucinations almost daily, but we do not remember them. This is so because they generally appear in the twilight zone between sleeping and working and last only for a very short moment as we are drifting off.

A false sensation leading to perception without the presence of actual stimulus is hallucination. When we see, hear or smell things that are not present is hallucination–the stimulus is false. Therefore, sensory experiences in the absence of stimulation of receptors are referred to as hallucination, having no foundation in actual happenings, and manifested by characteristic disturbances of thinking, mood and behaviour. Because of disturbances in thinking it is marked by alternations of concept formation and ultimately lead to misinterpretation or reality-hallucinations.

Some interesting examples of hallucination are that of mirage of vision of an oasis in a desert, seeing a ghost or appartions etc., in dark lonely places, strange incidents like a beautiful woman dressed in a white robe came at midnight and sat beside him, etc. A phenomenon known as hypnagogic imagery is very usual for producing both visual as well as auditory hallucination.

Peculiar examples of hypnagogic imagery hallucination relate to sounds of familiar voices, laughter of children or a pet's bark, eye catching beautiful landscapes, water pouring down from waterfalls, ringing of telephones, etc.

Causes of Hallucinations

There can be a number of causes responsible for hallucination, including behavioural disorders due to lack of sleep, illness, mental disorders, drugs, stress, alcohol, fatigue, hypnotism, etc. In hypnosis, in response to a command from hypnotist, an individual may perceive some object which is actually not present there. Similarly, a person under tremendous disordered state of mind due to alcoholic drinks may see double figures or may feel whimsical creatures in front of him or flies crawling over his body.

Stress and fatigue are other factors which can cause a very special type of fascinating hallucination, though not very common, known as 'doppelganer.' In this an individual, when he sees his image in the mirror, normally facing him from about three to four feet away, perceives the image to be transparent, like a slide or movie projected on glass. Such hallucinations normally takes place early in the morning or late at nights and do not last long-only momentary – to normal minds under stress and fatigue. Sometimes, a person may perceive a double standing in the room or a ghost standing behind their own image in the mirror.

It is also possible to induce hallucination in a person by means of sensory deprivation. In a famous series of experiments conducted by John C. Lilly in 1950, subjects were immersed naked in a dark, silent water tank having water at body temperature. All external stimuli were deprived to the participants in order to study the concept that if stimulations are denied, it is the tendency of the mind to fill in the blanks by creating its own stimulation. After some time the participants of this experiment experienced a variety of hallucinations, mostly visual in nature. The hallucinations were remarkably graphic and most of the participants were not in a position to describe them with vivid clarity and were confused whether they were sleeping and dreaming or were awake.

Difference between Illusion and Hallucination

Illusion and hallucination in any case cannot be taken as the same. The following distinction will further clarify the point:

1. Illusion is a wrong perception whereas hallucination is a false perception.
2. In illusion there is distinct explicit and external stimulus but in hallucination generally the external stimulus is not present. The example of oasis or vision of ghost makes this point clear.
3. Illusion generally occurs to people when they are in a normal state of mind but it is not true in the case of hallucination. Hallucinations generally occurs when the subject is either mentally afflicted, tired of under the influence of some drug or alcohol.
4. In case of illusion the stimulation easily takes place from outside, i.e., stimulation is external. In hallucination the stimulation takes place in the person himself, i.e., stimulation is internal. That is why hallucination is known as 'subjective perception.'
5. Illusion is universal while hallucination is personal in nature. Illusion takes place with all people in the same manner. It is a primitive organization and the perception of the same situation is identical of all. The stick in the water appears bent to all. In hallucination, in a particular condition and same stimulation, it greatly differs from people to people.
6. In case of illusion some stimulus is present and because of our mental state we misinterpret it and make a wrong assessment of the subject. This is not the case with hallucination. In hallucination we project our mental condition without the presence of any external stimulation. Therefore, hallucination is a projection of our mental state.

THE ROLE OF ATTRIBUTION

Attribution theory, a relatively new addition to the field of organizational behaviour, has links to perception, motivation, and leadership. Here we discuss only its implications for perception.

Fritz Heider and H.H. Kelley are the best known of the scholars who have contributed to what we call attribution theory which suggests, essentially, that we observe behaviour and then attribute causes to it. That is, we attempt to explain why people behave as they do. The process of attribution is based on perceptions of reality, and these perceptions may vary widely from individual to individual.

Fig. 24 illustrates the basic attribution theory framework. To start the process, we observe behaviour, our own or someone else's. We then evaluate the behaviour in terms of its degree of consensus, consistency, and distinctiveness. Consensus is the extent to which the same person behaves in the same way. Consistency is the extent to which the same person behave in the same way at different times. Distinctiveness is the extent to which the same person behaves in the same way in other situations. As a result of various combinations of consensus, consistency, and distinctiveness, we form impressions or attributions as to the causes of behaviour. We may believe that the behaviour is caused internally (by forces within the person), or externally (by forces in the person's environment).

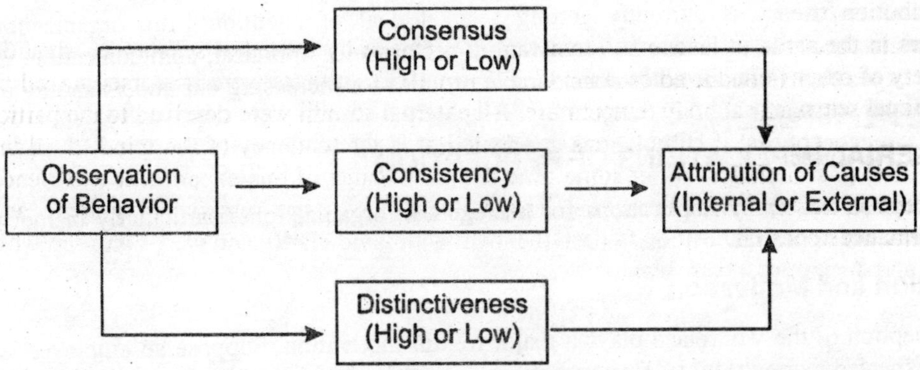

Fig. 24. The Attribution Process

For example, you might observe that one of your subordinates is being rowdy, disrupting the work of others and generally making a nuisance of herself. If you can understand the causes of this behaviour, you may be able to change it. If the employee is the only one engaging in the disruptive behaviour (low consensus), and if she behaves like this several times each week (high consistency), and if you have seen her behave like this in other settings (low distinctiveness), a logical conclusion you could reach would be that internal factors are causing her behaviour.

You might, however observe a different pattern. Perhaps everyone in the person's work group is rowdy (high consensus), and although the particular employee is often rowdy at work (high consistency), you have never seen her behave this way in other settings (high distinctiveness). This pattern indicates that something in the situation is causing the behaviour, that is, that the causes of the employee's behaviour are external.

Attributions of behaviour have important implications for managers. If we attribute poor performance to internal factors such as ability or motivation, we will develop certain strategies to improve these factors. On the other hand, if we attribute poor performance to external factors, such as resource constraints or a poorly designed job, we will take different steps to enhance performance. Examples of different alternatives are shown in Table 1.

We also make attributions regarding ourselves. If we attribute a pay raise to our hard work, we may continue to work hard. On the other hand, if we think we were given the raise because the boss liked us, we may put more effort into commenting the friendship.

Table 1 : Attributions

Attributions about success

Internal attribution	:	"Nitin is successful because he works hard and has lots of ability."
Possible response	:	Give Nitin positive reinforcement, promote him, hold him up as an example to others.
External attribution	:	Nitin is successful because he has an easy job and a strong work group.
Possible response	:	Give Nitin more work to do, promote some of his work group.

Attributions about failure

Internal attributions	:	"Poonam is doing a poor job because she lacks ability and motivation."
Possible response	:	Send Poonam to a training program or change the incentive structure.
External attribution	:	"Poonam is doing a poor job because she lacks the proper resources and has a weak work group.
Possible response	:	Increase her resources and strengthen her work group.

Attribution theory is currently getting a great deal of attention from organizational behaviour researchers in the areas of leadership, motivation, performance appraisal, communication, reward system, and variety of other fields. It holds considerable promise for increasing our understanding of behaviour in organizational settings.

MANAGERIAL IMPLICATIONS OF PERCEPTION

Perception has many implications for managers in organizations, particularly in motivation, hiring, and performance appraisal.

Perception and Motivation

Perception of the workplace plays a major role in motivation. Suppose an employee is experiencing some unexpected money trouble. Because of her disposition (she is worried) and the salience of money (it is unusually important to her at the moment), she will be especially sensitive to issues of compensation. Through projection, she may assume that everyone in the organization also cares mainly about money. A large pay raise given to another employee will seem frustrating and will intensify her efforts to get a pay raise of her own, focusing even more attention on her own pay, the pay of others, and how they compare to one another.

Obviously, attribution is also relevant to motivation, as suggested earlier. A person who believes her pay raise is attributable to effort (internal), rather than to her being the boss's niece (external), will choose to continue to work hard.

Perception and Hiring

Hiring new employees can be affected by perception in many ways. Contrast or novelty in the job applicant can affect his or her chances of getting the job. The person doing the hiring may stereotype applicants on the basis of race or sex, or may allow the halo effect to colour an overall perception of an applicant.

An interviewer's disposition during an interview or attitudes toward certain of the applicants' attributes can also affect the interviewer's perceptions of an applicant. For example, a manager. How does the toothache affect the manager's perception? Who believes that people should dress professionally for a job interview, is likely to be unimpressed by an applicant who shows up wearing sunglasses and a flowered sports coat.

Perception and Performance Evaluation

Performance evaluation is the assessment of an employee's performance to correct shortcomings, identify strengths, and provide a basis for giving rewards. Several areas of performance evaluation are especially susceptible to perceptual distortion. The contrast between two employees can affect the evaluation. Suppose, for instance, that a manager prepares several performance evaluations of her subordinates in one afternoon, one right after the other. The first two employees receive extremely good evaluations. The next person, however, is only a marginal performer. If the manger is influenced by the high evaluations given to the first two people, the third employee may suffer in comparison. That is, his evaluation may be lower than it would have been if the first two employees had been unsatisfactory may be lower than it would have been if the first two employees had been unsatisfactory workers.

Selection also may affect performance evaluation. When we have a particularly favourable impression of an employee, we may ignore instances of poor performance. The halo effect and stereotyping, too, come into play as do the evaluator's characteristics, such as salience, disposition, and attitudes. In this way, a manager who emphasizes punctuality may weigh it heavily as a standard of performance. Another manager may consider punctuality relatively unimportant and may barely mention it in a performance evaluation.

REFERENCES

A.H. Maslow, *The Farther Reaches of Human Nature*, Viking Press, New York, pp. 41-53.

Adapted from Kae M. Chund and Leon C. Megginson, *Organizational Behavior : Developing Managerial Skills*, Harper & Row, New York, 1981.

Based on Joseph H. Reitz, *Behavior in Organization*, Richard D. Irwin Inc., Homewood, Illions. 1977.

Bemard M. Bass and George D. Dunteman, *Behaviour in Groups as a Function of Self, Interaction, and Task Orientation, Journal of Abnormal and Social Psychology*, May, 1963, pp. 419-428.

Bernard Berelson and Gary A. Steiner, *Human Behavior: An Inventory of Scientific Findings*, Harcourt Brace & World, Inc., New York, 1964, pp. 111-112.

Clifford T. Morgan, and King, Richard A., *Introduction to Psychology*, McGraw Hill Book Co., New York, 1966, p. 343.

David Kretch, and Richard S. Crtitchfield, *Elements of Psychology*, Knoff 1958, p. 95.

E.R. Hilgard, *et al.*, *Introduction to Psychology*, Oxford, IBH Publishing Co., 1975, p. 136.

For a more detailed list of factors affecting perception see, George A. Field, John Douglas and Lawrence X, Tarpey, *Marketing, Management: A Behavioral Systems Approach*, Charles E. Merrill Publishing Co., Columbus, Ohio, 1966, pp. 62-84.

Fred Luthans, *Organizational Behavior: A Modern Behavioral Approach to Management*, McGraw Hill Book Co., New York, 1973, pp. 341-342.

Gilner, B. Von Halter, *Psychology*, Harper & Row, New York, 1970, p. 170.

H. Joseph Ritz, *Behaviorism in Organizations*, Richard D. Irwin Illions, 1977, p. 129.

Harold J. Leavitt, *Managerial Psychology*, The University of Chicago Press, Phoenix Books, Chicago, 1958, p. 31.

Joseph Stein, *Effective Personality: A Humanistic Approach*, Books Cole Publishing Co., California, 1972. p. 46.

Marius Sender, Raum- and Gestalt-auffasung bei operierten Blindgeborenenvor and nach der operation (*Space and Sight: The Perception of Space and Shape in the Congenitally Blind Before and After Operation*). Translated by Peter Heath, Methuen, 1960. Barth, 1932, p. 106.

Michel Wertheimer, *Principles of Perceptual Organization*, in David C. Beardsless and Michel Wertheimer, eds., Readings in Perception, Van Nostrand, 1958, pp. 115-135.

N.L. Munn, *et al.*, *Introduction to Psychology*, Oxford and IBH Publishing Co., New Delhi, 1972, p. 168.

Roy F. Street, *A Gestalt Completion Test: Teachers College*, Columbia, 1931, p. 41.

Stephen, P. Robins, *Organizational Behaviour*, Prentice Hall of India, New Delhi, 1989, p. 83.

T.W. Costello, and S.S. Zalking, *Psychology in Administration*, Prentice Hall, N.J., pp. 45-46 and D.E. Hamached, Encounters with the Self, Holt, Rinehart and Winston, New York, 1971.

Udai Pareekh, *et al. Behavioural Process in Organizations*, Oxford & IBH Publishing Co., New Delhi, 1981, p. 27.

Wilis D. Ellis, *A Source Book of Gestalt Psychology*, Harcourt, Brace & World, New York, 1938, p. 118.

CHAPTER

8

Morale

A good management is always interested in having and maintaining a better work force which is loyal to the organization and its objectives. A group whether in an industry or in any other sphere of life, is always wedded to the objectives of the group and its members keep an eye over their attainment. But mere organization of a group in the sense of assignment of duties and functions to its members will not, for obvious reasons, lead to the attainment of the goals set for it. It is obvious that a man can work effectively and efficiently only when he puts his heart into the work assigned to him. Payment of wages for the services rendered by workmen is quite insufficient to inspire them. It is obvious that a man can work effectively and efficiently only when he puts his heart into the work assigned to him. Payment of wages for the services rendered by workmen is quite insufficient to inspire them. It is possible only when, they feel inspired by the organization, its objectives and the people. They may work what might appear as virtual miracle. It on the other hand, members are cold or indifferent, if not altogether hostile towards the work and the organization, it will not prosper notwithstanding the fact that organization possesses all the resources. It is, therefore, absolutely essential that the group as a whole should be charged with enthusiasm so that the members of the group can work towards the objectives without any hurdle. Such zeal or enthusiasm is usually referred to as morale. It is the subjective feeling of the employees. It may be regarded as an attitude of satisfaction with desire to continue in and willingness to strive for, for the good of a particular group or organization. A management which is really interested in motivating its employee must try to understand the impact of its policies and practices on the attitude of workers about the work to improve their morale by removing the causes of dissatisfaction away from the workers. It is a continuous process that should be processed throughout the life of the organization.

The term morale refers to the overall attitudes of individuals and groups in an organization towards their work environment, the enterprise and the management. It is the by-product of motivation. Generally, term morale is used to describe an overall tone or climate prevailing among members of group, society and association. It is a collection of employee's feelings, sentiments and attitudes towards their jobs, superiors and the company. It reflects a state of mind of people arising out of their working and living environment. If the employees appears to feel good, happy optimistic and friendly, there may said to exist good or high morale. If they are quarrelsome, irritated, critical and restless, the condition is called poor or low morale. Thus, low morale is related to unrest. High morale is associated with superior motivation and accomplishment and low morale with frustration, discouragement and the lack of drive.

Good employee morale is the mental attitude of individual or of the group, which enables the employee to realize that the maximum satisfaction of his drives coincides with the fulfilment of the objective of the concern.

The satisfaction or dissatisfaction from the job gives to the psychological problem of morale. Morale is an individual, group feeling of competence and confidence reinforced by job satisfaction and need fulfilment. It may precede or follow performance and productivity. Morale is a total attitude towards one's work and one's colleagues. In work situations, it is a product of need satisfaction and job satisfaction level.

Morale is closely connected with motivation and willingness to work. Job satisfaction is the measuring rod for morale. If an employee is satisfied with his job, his morale is said to be high and in case he is dissatisfied, his morale is low. Motivation induces the people to work to their satisfaction in a manner most beneficial to the organization. Good motivation leads to high morale. According to Mrityunjay

Banerjee, **"Motivation is intimately connected with the morale. Good motivation leads to high morale. Poor morale is the manifestation of a weak or defective motivation process."** Thus morale is a state of mental health which is closely related to motivation.

Let us consider few more definitions of morale:

1. *"Morale means the cooperative attitude or mental health of number of people who are related to each other on some basis. " — William R. Spriegel*
2. *"Morale may be described as a readiness to cooperate warmly in the task and purposes of a given group organization" — E.F.L. Brech*
3. *"Morale is a condition as affected by or dependent upon, such mental factors as zeal, spirit, hope, confidence etc."*
4. *"Morale is a mental condition as affected by or dependent upon, such mental factors as zeal, spirit, hope, confidence etc. " — Webster*
5. *"Morale is a mental condition or attitude of individual's and groups which determines their willingness to cooperate. Good morale as defined by management is evidenced by employee enthusiasm, voluntary conformance with regulations and orders and a willingness to co-operate others in accomplishment of organizational objectives. Poor morale is evidenced by surliness, cases of insubordination discouragement, dislike of job, company and associates."*
   — E.B. Flippo
6. *"Morale is the combination or structure of employee's attitudes– towords the principal elements in the situations in which they work." — Dale Yoder*
7. "Morale is an attitude of satisfaction with desire to continue in willingness to strive for the goals of a particular goal or a particular group or organization." — Viteless
8. "The extent to which individual needs are satisfied and the extent to which the individual perceives that satisfaction, stemming from, has total job-satisfaction in morale." — Robert M. Guion

In general, it can be said, that the morale is the employee's attitude towards his firm. It is the sum of satisfaction experienced by an employee on account of his job and as member of a work team. It emphasizes the feeling of the team as a whole. It is sometimes described as a group attitude such as persistence, determination and cohesiveness. It reflects the general acceptance of group goals by group members and their agreement on the necessity for continuing the drive toward these goals.

Approaches: For organization, it is group behaviour and group satisfaction which is important and morale has been defined in this sense. There are three main approaches to the problem of morale. These are:

(i) Classical approach,
(ii) Psychological approach, and
(iii) Social approach.

(i) Classical Approach: This approach emphasizes on the satisfaction of basic needs of the employees. If the basic needs of the 13mployees are satisfied, their morale will be high or in other words, if the basic needs of the employees remain unsatisfied, their morale will be low and they will not take much interest in their work.

According to Robert M. Guron, the main follower of this theory has defined the term in these words: **"The extent to which individual needs are satisfied and the extent to which the individual perceives that satisfaction stemming from, has total job-satisfaction is morale."**

(ii) Psychological Approach: This approach supports that not only the basic needs of the people but psychological needs also influence the morale of the people. Psychological needs are main motives of morale. The following definitions may be given in support of this approach:

1. "Morale is a state of mind and emotions affecting willingness to work which in turn affects individual and organizational objectives." — *Jucious and Slender*

2. "Morale is a mental condition or attitude of individual and groups which determines their willingness to cooperate." — *Edwin B. Flippo*

This approach is related to the state of mind of the individual and the group that affects the willingness to work.

(iii) Social Approach: Followers of this approach, take the morale as a social phenomenon which pulls the men to live in society or groups in pursuit of a common goal. The following are some of the definitions supporting the view:

"Morale is the capacity of a group of people to pull together persistently and consistently in pursuit of a common goal." — *Alexander Leighton*

"Morale is the feeling of togetherness. There is a sense of identification with an interest in the elements of one's job, working conditions, fellow workers, supervisor, employer and the company".

— *Black manship*

From the analysis of the different approaches we can conclude that the morale indeed is 'willingness to work.' Though there are different approaches, yet their theme is the same. **Keith Davis** has summed up the views in the following words: **"Morale can be defined as the attitudes of individuals and groups towards their work environment and towards voluntary cooperation to the full extent of their ability in the best interest of the organization."**

However, the following point must be remembered in this context:

(a) Morale is related to the state of mental health which is closely related to loyalty, egoism, enthusiasm, etc.

(b) Morale is an identification of group interest and that of the interest of the enterprise, fellow workers and the requirements of the job.

(c) Morale is the subjective feeling of the employee. If group shows an attitude of satisfaction, its morale will be high.

Thus we see that on one hand, morale is a personal matter, while on the other hand, it is a group problem. As a matter of fact, it is an inner impulse explaining the "attitude of member employee towards his work, working conditions, fellow workers, management, job satisfaction and total organization etc. It may be low or high. The high morale is reflected in zest, active cooperation, satisfaction, and appreciation, etc. While the indicators of low morale are passive co-operation, feeling job unimportant, work – a burden, hostility and apathy. According to 1. Harell, "High morale is spirit of wholehearted co-operation in a common effort."

Nature of Morale

1. Morale is a by-product of group relationship. Morale reflects the degree of enthusiasm and willingness with which the members of a group set up to perform the allotted tasks.
2. Morale is a composite and not a single feeling. It is a collection of feelings, sentiments and attitudes.
3. Morale is a intangible factor and a relative term.
4. Morale indicates prevailing mood and spirit of group of people. It is an indicator of their mental health. It is manifest by the continuing state of mind composed of attitudes towards the accomplishment of work rather than emotions displayed during work.
5. Morale is basically a group phenomenon. It is a concept that describes the level of favourable or unfavourable attitudes of the employees collectively to all aspects of their work-the job, the company– their tasks, working conditions, superiors, fellow workers etc.

Significance/Importance of Morale : The importance of morale cannot be overemphasized. High morale is important for the successful functioning of an organization as good health for a person. What physical health is to a physical organism, morale is to a cooperative system. Positive morale definitely influences the productivity of a group and reduces the amount of supervision necessary for the desired output. High morale is reflected in the willingness to work, the will to excel, enthusiasm, etc. It exists when the employee attitudes are favourable and they willingly strive towards the attainment of organizational goals. High morale generates enthusiasm, for better performance, commitment to the organization and mutual cooperation. It reduces labour turnover, waste and labour strike. Grievances are at a minimum when the morale is high. Morale is widely regarded as of a great importance because it is assumed to be clearly related to group motivation. It is a manifestation of self-confidence, job pride, dependability and devotion among employees. According to R.C. Davis, high morale produces the following effects:

1. Willing cooperation toward organization objectives.
2. Loyalty to the organization and its leadership.
3. Good discipline or voluntary conformance to rules, regulations and orders.
4. Strong organizational stamina or the ability of the organization to take it during times of difficulty.
5. A high degree of employee interest in the job and the organization.
6. Pride in the organization.

The importance of morale can be illustrated with the statement of I. Harel who says that 'high morale' is a confident spirit of wholehearted co-operation in a common effort. The statement of Dale Yoder also throws some light on the importance of morale in the following words:

"High morale is associated with the best motivation and success while low morale is the indicator of disappointment, enthusiasmlessness and loss of objectivity."

Keith Davis has compared morale to a lady when he writes:

"Never underestimate the power of a *woman. Simultaneously, do not underestimate the power of morale."*

On the other hand, W.R. Spriegel states that low morale reflects mental unrest and frustration among employees, such mental tension inhibits the willingness to work and productivity. Low morale leads to the following consequences:

1. Reduced productivity
2. Excessive tardiness and absenteeism
3. Antagonism towards rules and regulations
4. Excessive complaints and grievances
5. High employee turnover
6. Friction among employees
7. Alcoholism
8. High accident rate
9. Lack of cooperation among employees
10. Antagonism towards the organization and its management.

According to M.S. Viteles, high employee morale is important because plant productivity & efficiency of operations depend upon employee cooperation in attaining necessary output standard.

High morale is the hallmark of sound human relations and the lubricant that keeps the wheels of business moving. It leads to good discipline and effective direction. Subordinates whose morale is high will work with vigour, confident in their ability and cooperation with their fellows to achieve given objectives as a team. Therefore, management must take steps to create and maintain high morale among employees.

Process of Morale Building

There are various factors which contribute to high morale among workers of an industrial organization. The management of the various enterprises use these factors in building the morale of their workers. Morale building is a continuous activity which means improving and maintaining the high level of morale of employees. It is a perpetual task and needs continuity. C. E. Gregory has named it as the producer of climbing a moving ladder. Just as a moving ladder has no end of steps so also the process of morale building does not end. It implies that morale building is a continuous and complex process.

The steps of morale building can be divided into two groups – individual and group efforts. In this context, the group efforts are more practical, economical and effective. Hence, the managements generally try group efforts. Another way of classifying morale building efforts is to divide them as physical and psychological factors. Their detailed description is as follows:

A. Physical Factors for High Morale

1. **Conditions of Work:** The conditions of work have an important influence upon it. If the conditions of work favour the workers and create interest in the work, morale is likely to be high. On the contrary if the conditions of work are not favourable and serve to distract the interest of the worker, morale is likely to fall. 'Conditions of work' being a comprehensive term, it includes both physical and mental or psychological conditions. Various researches have led the belief that physical conditions of work have an important influence upon morale of the workers. As Tindall and Cair have proved on the basis of their experimentation, good conditions of work help to maintain a high morale. In this connection, Cair has pointed out the influence of music on the mental conditions of workers Culier's experiments, seems to indicate that in bad conditions of work morale tends to fall because the worker evinces signs of worry, distaste, irritability, anxiety, sleeplessness, laziness, lethargy, etc.

2. **Position of Promotion:** Studying the morale of various individuals in various positions of different companies Arbrock came to the conclusion that the attitude of foremen is better than that of clerks while that of clerks is more favourable than is the case with other classes of workers. This study repeals that the morale of individuals is also susceptible to such influences as the post that he is holding. The main psychological fact at the root of this phenomenon is that if the individual in questions does not get a position that concurs with his psychological bent of mind, his enthusiasm being to wane and he loses confidence in those who are in authority above him. Hence if morale is to be kept high in any and every industry, it is essential that posts be allotted in accordance with the ability and labour of the individuals, and that these posts be improved from time to time.

3. **Increase in Salary:** It is a psychological fact that workers are primarily concerned with their salary or wages. Shepard had stressed the fact that if the workers' wages are reassessed from time to time and appropriate changes are made, the morale tends to occupy a high level. On the contrary, if the wages remain stationary for a long time, and there is no achievement, the workers' enthusiasm is dampered, and they tend to heap blame on their officers. Increase in pay should be made dependent upon hard work or other qualities. If increase in pay depends upon the personal idiosyncrasy of the individual in power, most people become cynical as they do not like to cringe before such a person. Secondly, even the ingratiating types who win increases in pay and promotions through subservience rarely have a high morale. Hence, for pay increase to have a favourable influence upon morale it is essential that the basis of increase be proper, and the same for everyone.

4. **Method of Distributing Salaries:** Morale is also influenced by the method of distribution and salary no less than by increase in it. All studies to date on the subject have not led to any conclusive idea as to which method is definitely the best. Some methods are, of course, better than certain others. Various methods will be examined briefly here.

(a) Share of Profits: Under this method, the workers in companies and factories are given bonus and share of profit from time to time. The following facts need to be mentioned in connection with this method.

   (i) This method engenders dissatisfaction in the better and efficient and skilful than themselves are driving the same benefits without actually deserving them.

   (ii) In this method, the worker is never sure of his actual income in the near future because neither the quantity of profit is shared nor the time of its distribution is certain.

Despite the above clear difficulties and drawbacks, this method have been found to meet with the approval of approximately one-third workers. Besides, this method is also rather simple, as a consequence of which it is one of the most widely used today.

(b) Remuneration According to Work: In this method, the worker is reimbursed according to the quantity. of material he produces. The research made by Mathewson on this subject has made it abundantly clear that the rate of payment will not fall, because he usually expect that if he works more he will earn more but also thereby create a reason for the company reducing rate of payment. Fear of this kind guides them to reduce their rate of working.

It is evident that if the worker can be conceived of the stability of payment rates, the piece wages method is superior to the bonus method, but it requires that the following facts be kept in mind:

(i) Attention should be concentrated not only on quantity but also on quality.

(ii) In paying the worker, it should be made abundantly clear to him that he is being paid according to a certain definite rate of a specific kind of work so that no doubt lingers in his mind and compels him to work slower.

(iii) In connection with remuneration the rate should be constant and there should be no fear of the rate of payment being reduced.

If these above facts are kept in mind and the appropriate arrangements made, the morale of the worker can be kept high through the piece wages method, because it is by this method that the worker is constantly inspired to work more and to produce better results. It is also very good from the point of view of creating good incentives.

5. Opportunity to Share Profit: Among the physical requirements, another is the possibility and opportunity of progress in any concern. If the workers in a company are being paid dividends out of its profits, then it should be equally distributed. In other words, all workers should be given the opportunity to progress and earn high wages, without any discrimination. If this is not done, most of them tend to turn against the authorities in their company while at the same time a feeling of jealousy for those who have progressed is engendered in the unfortunate ones. This destroys not only collective organization and administrative efficiency, but also the faith and belief in the authorities. Hence, the rules governing promotion and increases in salary should be equally applicable to all, and they should be clearly understood by all of them. No one should be given a chance to complain on these grounds.

(B) Psychological Factors

1. **Praise:** It is a matter of general psychological knowledge that praise of good work and effort helps to infuse further enthusiasm and energy in the worker.

Studies conducted by such eminent psychologist as Thorndike and Harlock, evinced that praise of a worker's effort helps to increase his motivation. In fact, the influence of the reward and punishment scheme of work is fairly evident and widely known. Any work that derives punishment for the perpetrator is shunned by him in future, while he desires to repeat any work that results in reward.

Praise a psychological reward. Praise by individuals for whom we have respect and in whose judgement we have faith matters a lot to us. If the authorities in the factory or office praise all good efforts, then morale becomes high among the workers. On the other hand, if good work and hard labour goes unpraised or unnoticed, enthusiasm was in the worker, as he feels that he is not being valued according to his merits. This fact is one of the important reasons why work in an impersonal psychological organization like government office is rarely of a high order of efficiency. Direct praise or blame is rarely forthcoming, except from very conscientious individual in authority.

2. **Knowledge of Success:** Some other experiments have brought to light the fact that if the worker is of the degree of success he is achieving in his work, his interest and enthusiasm in it are maintained, and so is the high level of morale. In very big factories where the individual work does no more than make only a very small cog in a very big wheel, and is not aware of the effect of his own effort towards the completed wheel, boredom, and disinterest is likely to set in very early. What is here implied is not the knowledge of the mere result. Result of work can be bad as well as good. Knowledge and failure can only serve to lower the morale, but if the worker is again encouraged to think in terms of success, morale can be regained. As a general rule, success ensures a high morale. Success is the reward of effort. And reward is a favourable element in the creation and maintenance of morale.

3. **Fulfilment of Collective Needs:** Man works not only to meet the needs of his body, such needs as food and clothing, but also to satisfy certain other collective psychological requirements. He is also desirous of feelings and emotions, thoughts and beliefs, exhibiting himself, knowing himself, and winning social prestige and recognition. Any kind of work that affords all these advantages to the worker is almost certain to create a very high morale in him, but if all these things are not made available to him, morale is likely to fall, if it was ever high. Hence, in maintaining the morale of their workers the organizers and authorities should keep in mind the fact that the workers' collective needs be also fulfilled and satisfied.

4. **Forbearance and Good Behaviour of Authorities:** Workers attach much importance to the behaviour of inspectors, managers and others in authority towards them. If conduct towards them is not all that can be desired, general morale is likely to suffer. If the worker is constantly interrupted and scolded over his work, he loses all respect for the officer. Actually, the only course of keeping workers contented that is open to the officer and authorities is that of good and considerate behaviour towards them. In such circumstances, the workers are inclined to pay little attention to other conditions around them, and are enthusiastic enough to do anything that is likely to benefit their factory or organization.

5. **Freedom of Workers:** In which company or factory a worker loses his identity to the extent of heing reduced to the level of a small cog in the huge wheel, he is dissatisfied with his work because it appears heavy and insipid to him. Hence, in order to maintain the worker's morale at a high level it is essential that he be given the maximum degree of freedom that this function and position allows. He should also not be prevented from meeting other fellow workers, in particular those individuals who are in authority. It helps in creating a more intimate and knowledgeable atmosphere, in which he can tell his troubles to the proverbial dady. But given freedom does not imply that discipline should be done away with. Independence within the framework of laws is the most desirable state of affairs.

6. **Sense of Unity, Identity and Equality:** It has been pointed out earlier that collective or group organization is indicative of high morale. Hence, it is essential that a sense of organization and unity should circulate freely among the workers. Psychologist, among them May and Wright, concluded from their examinations and study that in order to maintain a high morale among workers in industries it is essential that the workers have in themselves a feeling of being organized united or equal. The worker should be able to identify themselves with their factory or office or organization and think of its interests as if they were their own. If this is achieved, even the most difficult times can be successfully seen through by making a collective effort. Increase in the feeling of unity and identity can be vacillated by many things such as a definite name of the company or organization, a definite dress and a common badge. Besides these, certain group objectives can be set up, the achievement of which involves organised and collective effort on the part of the workers. Exerting oneself among with many others, straining for the same objective serves to lessen tension, increase mutual good will and organization. Workers should be made to realise that they are an important and responsible part of the industry. They should also be equipped with knowledge of the various aspect of the industry, so that they come to look upon it as their own industry.

7. **Other Factors:** A part of the above-mentioned physical and psychological determinants of morale, there are some other factors that influence it. For example, through his experiments and research. Super has established a relationship between age morale. Similarly, the research of Arbork has shown that the level of morale is higher in the case of women workers than in the case of male workers. Actually maintaining a very high level of morale requires careful attention to be paid to all aspects of the worker's personality and to all aspects of his work. Handling grievances at proper stage and in time, employee counselling, delegation of authority and introducing suggestion scheme are other factors which can be instrumental in improving the morale of employees.

FACTORS CONTRIBUTING TO HIGH MORALE

Morale is basically a matter of human behaviour. It is an expression of the attitudes which the members of an organization develop and adapt towards the organization, its members, its purposes and its leaders. Hawthorne Experiments made a valuable study of impulses and forces that govern the human behaviour on the basis of these researches, **Alexander Leighton** enumerates five major determinants of morale. These are:

1. Confidence of individual members in the purpose of the group.
2. Confidence of members of the group in the leadership.
3. Confidence of individual members in their fellow workers.
4. Organizational Efficiency.
5. Conditions in the group and working conditions.

We shall now discuss these five factors of morale:

1. **Confidence of the Individual Members:** In the purpose of the group. It is a matter of common sense that an individual works whole-heartedly only when he feels inspired by the purposes of group for which he is required to make the efforts along with the other members of the group. It is, therefore, imperative to impress upon the work people, the importance of the product they produce. For, once they begin to state their endeavour to the communal or national beings they will work with a crusading spirit and this is precisely what we mean by good or high morale. The workers feel that they are doing something worthwhile for the nation or community.
2. **Confidence in Leadership:** Confidence in leadership is the main essence for the building up of high morale. If leadership is of right type, it is natural that the leader will win the confidence of his subordinates or followers and it will definitely contribute towards raising their morale. In order to win the confidence, a leader should be fair to all, helpful, friendly, honest, industrious, leader should be fair to all, helpful, friendly, honest, industrious, capable, and have the full knowledge of the job and only then, he can lead the followers in the right perspective. A leader who can inspire the workers for united actions, realise them their responsibilities, and also have sympathies for their problems, is a real leader and workers have their confidence in him. To sum up, morale of the workers will be high if their leader is capable, fair minded and impartial in dealing with the cases relating to promotions, penalties, rewards, etc. and is sympathetic towards them. If he has no such quality, workers' confidence in him will be loosened and their morale will be low. So high or low morale is the result of capability of the leader in handling the affairs amicably.
3. **Confidence in Fellow Workers:** Confidence in fellow workers is another factor responsible for the high morale. Every worker wants full cooperation and guidance from his fellow workers at the time when a problem crops up in the group. Everyone in the group must be confident of getting such type of cooperation from other members of the group. They should feel secure in expressing their point of view and grievances. He must have faith in the loyalty of their workers.
4. **Organizational Efficiency:** Organizational efficiency leads to the high morale. It requires:
   (i) Definiteness of Responsibility: The line of authority and responsibility should be distinctly and firmly made clear so that there will be no confusion in the mind of workers as to whom they are responsible for their work and whose order they are to follow. The lack of clarity will disgruntle the workers and it will have an adverse effect on their morale.
   (ii) Adequate and Effective Communication: An effective and adequate communication channel between workers and the management will lead to high morale of the workers. If they think that the management listens to them, consults in matters concerning job and organization informs to them as and when their interests are affected and makes them feel that they are the real participants in the organization, their morale will be climbed at the top. A system of joint consultation should be evolved to consider the matters of mutual interest in the organization. The suggestion scheme may also be introduced in the organization to heighten the morale.
5. **Working Conditions and Allied Factors:** Morale is an index of job satisfaction. A worker can be happy and contented at his job if the organization shows a good measure of care for him and takes all possible steps to make the work place congenial for work. The following factors relating to work conditions help in raising the morale:

(i) **Fair Wages:** Workers may feel content if they have the satisfaction of having an equitable compensation for their labour and skills put in, in their respective job, if they are low paid or their wages are inequitable, their morale will naturally be low because they are not in a position to meet even their lower needs satisfactorily and on the other hand, if they are allowed a better wage and incentives to work, they will be free from worries and may devote themselves to the organization and to the work which in turn will enhance the productivity. Fair wage, therefore, is imperative to build up their morale.

(ii) **Security and Opportunity to rise:** Job security is an essential factor in raising the morale. If the organization provides security to its workers, they will get their hearts into the work and will not think to leave the organization unless it becomes necessary. Likewise, availability of promotional avenues will raise the morale of the workers because they will work with renewed zeal and vigour if they know that there are ample opportunities to get arise.

(iii) **Work Environment:** The work environment has serious impact on the morale of the workers. The building and its appearance, conditions of work and work place, machine and the location of the factory, safety measures, medical care etc. are some of the determinants of the work environment which are directly related to workers' morale.

Thus the above factors determine the high or low morale of the workers and the group.

Seven Commandments to Morale

Since morale building is a continuous and difficult process, Management must keep itself informed of current state of employee morale through attitude surveys and personal observation. The following steps can be taken to build high morale among the members of an organization.

(a) Sound personnel administration
(b) Participation
(c) Effective communication
(d) Worthwhile goals
(e) Human Relations approach
(f) Sound organization structure
(g) Trusted supervision

(a) Sound Personnel Administration: Sound personnel policies and practices are very helpful in building morale. A fair and equitable wage and salary structure developed on the basis of job evaluation, job security, scientific selection and training, good working conditions, sound promotion and appraisal systems and employee counselling are essential for high morale.

(b) The participation of employees in decision making process creates a sense of belonging. Joint councils of managers and workers provide employees an opportunity to express their feelings and ideas. Joint consultation, suggestion system, collective bargaining and other forms of participation help to create job satisfaction, sense of belonging and team work among the employees. Counselling and guidance of employees helps to solve their problems and are helpful in morale building.

(c) Effective Communication: A two-way communication system helps, helps management in developing positive attitude among employees. Employees can be kept fully informed of all matters affecting their interests. A formal grievance procedure is required for quick and proper redressal of employees' grievances.

(d) Worthwhile Goals: The objectives of the organization should be such that employees feel proud of their job and the enterprise. The members of the group must feel that the common goals are challenging as well as attainable. Meaningful and unambiguous goals should be laid down for the employees.

(e) Human Relations Approach: Each individual in the organization should be treated as a responsible human beings. Human relation approach helps to develop inter personnel competence, intergroup cooperation and mutual trust among employees. The morale has a multiplier effect on subordinates.

(f) **Sound Organization Structure:** Organization design influences the quality of employee relations. There should be clear-cut division of work, proper delegation of authority and *effective* co-ordination. Generally flat and decentralised structures tend to improve employee morale by providing scope for close inter-personnel relations and self-actualization. Job enrichment and job enlargement help to raise morale by overcoming monetary, fatigue and boredom. Morale is likely to be high when the work group is homogeneous and the task is challenging and interesting.

(g) **Trusted Supervision:** Supervisors should be fair, sympathetic and honest in their dealings with employees. They should be competent enough to inspire confidence among workers. They should be responsive to the needs and feelings of workers. They should provide an opportunity for employees to play their preferred roles.

WHY SHOULD MANAGERS BE CONCERNED WITH MORALE

Morale is the primary concern of the management because higher production and productivity of workers are the direct result of high morale. The management is really interested in higher production and productivity in order to achieve the desired goal.

The management is always keen in knowing the impact of its policies, and practices on the attitude of the workers about work and should always be ready in promoting the good feelings about the work, policies, practices and organization among the workers. They should be stimulated in accomplishing the predetermined *objectives* willingly. Highly productivity is an index of favourable attitudes of workers about the work and the organization and results in better quality production at lower cost. It is a case of high morale. **If workers** appear to **feel enthusiastic, optimistic about the group activities and mission, and friendly to each other they are described as having good or high morale. If they seem dissatisfied, irritate quickly, critical, restless and pessimistic, these reactions are described as evidence of poor or low morale.** So, management always assigns the topmost priority to the problem of morale of the workers. It persistently and consistently makes efforts to stimulate the feeling of togetherness among workers, a sense of identification with the elements of one's job, working conditions, fellow workers, supervisors and the company which is conducive to the achievement of organizational goal. It is mainly the responsibility of the management to maintain the high morale in the organization.

The military authority has rightly recognised the morale as one of the most important factors in winning or losing the war. India won the 1971 war with Pakistan only because the morale of its military was high in spite of the fact that Pakistani forces had all sophisticated weapons but morale. The case is not much different in industrial undertakings. The success or failure of an industrial organization depends on the morale of its work-force. **Keith Davis** has rightly compared the morale with a woman. He remarked, **'Never underestimate the power of a woman, and the same certainly must be said about morale, never underestimate the power of morale.'**

High morale assists the management to overcome the several labour problems such as labour turnover, absenteeism, indiscipline, grievances, etc. It also seeks cooperation of the workers in running the organization and thus getting the higher production at minimum possible cost by reducing the wastage of man, machines, materials, and time. It may serve as an index of good industrial relations.

It has been proved by the various researches that improving morale has showed a remarkable progress in industrial production. Its importance has been recognised by the governments of almost all the countries and introduced several labour welfare and social security measures to improve the morale of the labour. The management is also continuous to improve the morale of the workers and has realised the long-range damaging effects of low morale.

ADMINISTRATIVE MEASURE TO PROMOTE MORALE

We have discussed in the preceding pages, various factors, which contribute in promoting the high morale of the employees in an organization. In analysing those factors, we may understand that it is the responsibility of the management to take various steps to raise the morale of its employees to achieve the organizational *objectives*. The following measures can be suggested as being conducive to the process of morale building:

1. **Sound Wage Structure:** In order to meet their primary and derived needs, workers expect a just and fair wage corresponding to their qualifications and efficiency which provides–for the workers and their families a reasonable level of subsistence including entertainment and medium of savings. A sound wage structure based upon sound and fair incentive plans coupled with bonus earnings is conducive to high morale. A wage structure that provides a systematic procedure for the fixing up of just and fair wage rates for different categories of employees, taking into consideration the job contents, may be an ideal wage structure and it may help boosting up the morale and will encourage greater productivity,
2. **Security of Job:** The management should consistently follow a personnel policy ensuring the security of job to the competent employees so that they can devote their time fully with their heart and soul. A person under a constant fear of losing the job cannot work with devotion. His efficiency will also be adversity affected and his morale will be low. So, security of job leads to high morale.
3. **Delegation of Authority:** In order to boost the morale of the employees, delegation of authority to subordinates at different levels will be desirable. It will be advantageous to employees as well as to the organization. They will feel a sense of importance and realise the responsibility. It will naturally improve the quality of work and efficiency of the workers on the job.
4. **Grievance Procedure:** The management must establish a sound grievance procedure to ensure the employees of the impartiality and fairness of the various decisions taken by it and concerning them. It will help to create confidence in leadership among the workers and promote a sense of loyalty to the organization. This confidence in leadership will raise the morale of the workers.
5. **Suggestion Scheme:** The management should invite suggestions from the workers for the improvement in the job contents, leadership behaviour and the general environment of the organization. It will promote a sense of participation in workers. If any suggestion is considered advantageous to the organization, it should be properly rewarded and recognised. It will certainly improve the morale of the employees.
6. **Joint Consultation:** Joint consultation in matters relating to employees at large will be of great importance to the organization. The management should establish joint consultation committees in the organization consisting of the representative of workers and the management in an agreed number to consider the matters affecting their participation in management and other matters incidental thereto. It will help improve industrial relations and reduce the labour unrest. A peaceful work environment and improved industrial relations raise the morale of the workers.
7. **Sound Promotion Policy:** A sound promotion policy ensures the workers their promotion to the superior position without any hue and cry. It may be based on seniority or merit or both. The prospects to advance to the higher position according to a consistent policy heightens the morale of the workers.
8. **Employee Counselling:** The executives in the organization should make it a point to sit together with the workers, discuss and exchange views on the burning problems of the organization and the industry. They should also listen to at the grievances and complaints of the workers. Regular meetings may be arranged for this purpose with the workers and should invite or give suggestion on the problems generally faced by the employees at their work and guide them wherever required. It will develop a sense of togetherness and increase morale.
9. **Recognition:** Every worker desires that his achievements in the organization should be recognised by the superiors or in other words, he expects credit for his work. A mere word from the boss will suffice to boost his morale.
10. **Keeping the Workers Well Informed:** The management should maintain a sound communication system with the employees so that any information concerning them may be passed on to them. Some progressive management publish regular bulletins containing the latest news, views and developments about the working and the workers of the organization and circulate them among the employees. It satisfies their ego and help maintaining high morale.

11. **Inspiring Credos and Mottos of Workers:** They are the positive steps in boosting the morale of the workers to inspire the employees through Credos and Mottos which give them a sense of importance. Some organizations for this purpose organize exhibitions etc. to give the workers a feeling of importance and credit for having taken part in the production of quality products.

One should be here clear that the above mentioned administrative steps are conducive to the promotion of morale and pave the way to higher morale. It is a continuous but very slow process and management or anybody else should not expect a change overnight. The management should take various favourable measures which reduce the tension in order to develop the morale of the employees.

Measurement of Morale

We have discussed the importance of employee morale in an organization but now the question arises how to know whether there is a high or low morale in the organization. Actually, here is a problem of its measurement or appraisal. Usually, we use morale measurement and morale appraisal synonymously but it is not so. There is a slight difference in these two terms. **Measurement** is generally referred to the collection of data, analysis and assigning mathematical value to them while appraisal serves the qualitative aspect and can be understood well in the perspective of all the organizational environmental factors. We, in this sense cannot measure the morale and can only appraise it. So, we have used these two terms synonymously.

However, the measurement of morale is a very difficult task because it is basically a psychological question and it is made up of several individual tendencies. Hence, in order to measure the level of morale in a worker, the management must observe characteristics of low morale in the behaviour of a particular employee. The following are the general features of low morale:

1. Antagonistic attitude towards these in authority,
2. Lack of obedience of forced obedience,
3. Feelings of hatred, jealousy, doubt, disrespect, lack of confidence towards those in authority,
4. Disappointment, unenthusiastic insipidity,
5. Lack of collective administration and unity, belief in low effort,
6. Mental turmoil and unhappiness,
7. Lack of system and productivity in work,
8. Tendency to circulate all kind of rumours,
9. Poisoning mind of others towards authorities behind the back,
10. Lack of application to work,
11. Mutual conflicts and non co-operation.

Method of Measurement

John M. Pfiffner has suggested two ways of measuring morale:

1. Direct method, and
2. Indirect method.

1. **Direct Method:** Under this method persons at work are contacted to express their feelings. Morale is measured in terms of the extent of results achieved. The extent of increase or decrease in the profitability, productivity and other direct benefits to the organization is the indicator of high or low morale. If profitability, productivity, etc. are increasing, it is an index of high morale or if they are decreasing, it is sign of low morale. Various techniques are employed in measuring the morale under this method. They are:

   (a) **Observation Technique:** Under this technique, evaluator observes these employees on work and records their behaviour, attitude, sentiments, and feelings towards the organization, supervisor or his fellow workers. Comparing the observations of two periods, any change in the behaviour and attitude of the employees will indicate high or low morale.

(b) Interview Technique: Interview may be one of the techniques for measuring morale. Under this technique, the interviewer calls upon the employees and asks the questions. Interview may be guided or unguided.

Guided interview emahasises mainly on the question set out before hand in the form of a questionnaire in consultation with the higher management. Interviewer goes to the employees, with his printed questionnaire form, explaining them the general objects and questions with simple choice responses, included in the questionnaire which is answered orally.

Under unguided interview, the employees are encouraged to talk freely what they think about the organization and its people. There are no formal questions. Interviewer listens to and encourages them to be free with an assurance that their talks will remain secret and confidential. It may be held individually or in groups. He may ask questions of general interest.

(c) Attitude Survey Technique: Under this technique, detailed questionnaires are prepared by the organization with the help of psychologists and distributed among workers to return duly filled in forms. The surveyor then steps further to analyse them and measure the general attitude of the workers. The answers to the questions are in Yes/No or True/False items, checklists or sometimes provide space for comments.

(d) Projective Techniques: These techniques include a series of devices involving the use of written as well as verbal materials in the measurement of attitudes. The word-association, the sentence competition, the short story competition tests are some of the devices generally employed. Under this technique, the persons are allowed to express their feelings in detail with arguments. The feelings are later on analysed and projected by the analysts.

(e) Common Worker's Opinion Analysis: One very popularly used method of measuring the morale is the common worker's Opinion Analysis method in which the opinions of the average workers' are collected and analysed. For this certain scientific questionnaires are prepared that reveal the workers' opinions regarding various aspects of the industry as well as towards the authorities. The worker does not have to reveal his name in answering these questionnaires. This has the initial advantage of assuring the worker of secrecy regarding his views. When the questionnaires are received back after having been filled and duly completed by the workers, it becomes possible to see the various scores on which the workers have complained. If some particular object or subject is a matter of complaint in a large majority of cases, efforts can be made to rectify it. Success in this method depends upon the degree to which the questionnaire is scientific, and upon the degree of truth in the workers' responses.

(f) Sociological Methods: Nowadays, particularly in the case of group studies, the sociological methods are very prevalent. Moreover, a method for measuring the morale can be used to discover characteristics of the workers' group organization whereby the level of morale can be discovered. In the Jenken's experiment described earlier, only one aspect of the group organization is included. Accordingly, the worker is given a questionnaire containing certain questions intended to throw light on the characteristic of group organization. For example, the workers are asked to name and enumerate the individuals with whom they would like to work, or under who they would prefer to work, or in which sort of company do they prefer to spend their time or have anything to do with. If the answers of many individuals to this question seem to speak favourably of anyone individuals, and the answers seem to show respect, love and confidence for the individual, it is fairly evident that he is capable of becoming a good administrator. If he is already in the administrative cadre, then it evidences a high level of morale in the workers, for respect and confidence in authority is a sign of high morale. But is he not so situated, then the answer seem to show lack of confidence in the existing administration, a lack of confidence that can be rectified by promoting the desired individual into the administrative block, or otherwise by advising the existing administrative group to mend its ways and adopt others more calculated to win the confidence and respect of their subordinates. In this manner, its evident that Moreno method can help in realising the condition of morale in any unit and in discovering the means of improving existing morale.

(g) **Company Records and Reports:** The records and reports of the company prepared for other reasons and purposes, can be used to measure the morale of employees. These records can be analysed in the following manners: Change of labour ratio, man-hour lost, absence and slackness, number of grievances reported by workers and resolved by the management, number and value of accidents occurred in the factory, etc. These all variables can be interpreted as an index of morale.

2. **Indirect Method:** Under indirect method of measuring employee morale, the men at work are not directly approached but the in-depth study of variations in output, profitability, rate of labour turnover asbsenteeism, and accidents, number of grievances and accidents and their severity is made and analysed with the help of the records and reports maintained by the personnel department regarding each employee of the organization. The results are compared with the results of earlier study or budget targets or any other standard fixed for the purpose. The extent of increase or decrease in profitability or productivity may result in increase or decrease in the morale.

This method should be used carefully for measuring the employee morale because productivity or profitability is not always affected by the morale. There may be several other factors which affect the productivity and profitability. Output may decrease not because the morale of the employees is low but it may be low because of use of low quality materials or defective machines or methods. Similarly various factors leading to absenteeism, labour turnover, accidents, grievances, and complaints should be studied carefully and should draw the results. Unavoidable circumstances can be ignored while analysing the morale.

The above appraisal methods present only the tendencies or attitudes of the employees. Statistical measurement of morale is not possible because it relates to the inner feelings of human beings.

However, we can say that morale is increasing or decreasing but cannot measure how much it has increased or decreased.

MORALE AND PRODUCTIVITY

Since Morale refers to the total satisfaction, a person derives from his job, his work group, his boss, the organization and his general environment. It is reflected in the general feeling of well being, satisfaction and happiness of people.

One might reasonably expect that if people are happy with the company, their boss or the general environment of the organization, they will be high producers. Morale is the degree of enthusiasm and willingness to work with which the people perform their assigned work with zeal and sincerity resulting in good team work and have high morale. If they feel frustrations, disappointments, discontents, grudges, they will have low morale.

Where morale is high, naturally the output will also be high. Productivity will also increase because workers put their heart and soul to achieve the organization goal. A direct morale productivity relationship is widely assumed. High morale and high productivity are positively correlated. It contributes to the organization. Contrarily, the low morale will certainly affect the production and productivity adversely because they feel lack of identification with the company so there cannot be an integration of efforts and productivity and the result cannot be encouraging.

There is a general belief that morale and productivity go hand in hand and higher the morale, higher the productivity and *vice versa*. However, it is not true in all the cases and morale and productivity may not go together. Generally, there is some positive correlation between morale and productivity but they cannot be absolutely related. It is quite possible to increase morale with either favourable or unfavourable shifts in productivity.

While emphasising the importance of morale, we should not be over-enthusiastic. Generally, it is assumed that morale and productivity always go together. Some managers are of the view that high morale will certainly and automatically result in high productivity. But it is not always so. The recent researches show that the relationship between the two is not so direct and positive. It has been experienced that production level is lower in spite of high level of morale or reverse of the situation is also possible, i.e., higher production is possible but there is low morale. In fact morale and productivity may be related to each other in the following four possible ways:

(i) High morale, high productivity.
(ii) Low morale, low productivity.
(iii) High morale, low productivity.
(iv) Low morale, high productivity.

PRODUCTIVITY		MORALE: HIGH	MORALE: LOW
HIGH	A	High Morale High Productivity	Low Morale High Productivity
LOW	B	High Morale Low Productivity	Low Morale Low Productivity

Fig. 1. Morale Productivity Matrix

(i) High Morale, High Productivity: High morale in most of the cases results in high productivity but experienced only when the workers are motivated in the fight spirit and supervision is of right type, i.e., supervisors treat the men with consideration. There is a circular relationship between morale and productivity in this situation. High morale pushes up the productivity and high productivity in turn, pushes up morale and so on. But proper motivation is necessary.

(ii) Low Morale, Low Productivity: In the absence of proper motivation, morale and productivity both will be lower. Here also circular relationships exist between the two. Low morale will pull down the productivity and low productivity will shrink the morale of the employees.

(iii) High Morale, Low Productivity: This position is found in such circumstances where the men are not fully trained and supervisors are not fully competent in getting the work done. This position is also seen in organizations where supervisors are of the view that workers should not in any case, be unhappy, whatsoever be the effect on organizations goal. In such circumstances, morale of the workers may be high at the cost of productivity.

(iv) Low Morale and High Productivity: Low morale and high productivity may go together when the management is not cooperating the workers and avoids the feelings of the men at work or where management uses penalties and punishments and provides better machines and equipments to carry on the production. It means low morale with high productivity exists only when management is highly production-oriented. **But it must be remembered that high productivity with low morale cannot be sustained for long** because in such circumstances, a major work-group will be affected and thus industrial peace will be disturbed and it will further lower down the morale leading to lower productivity.

The above description shows that there no certain correlation exists between morale and productivity and therefore, it is not correct to say that high morale will lead to high productivity because there are so many other factors which affect morale and productivity. But it is certain, that high morale is one of the several factors of high productivity and it is the function of the management to try to maintain the high level of morale because it is directly related to the favourable attitudes of the work-force and accomplishment of organizational goal become easy. In the long-run high morale will certainly add to the productivity provided proper motivation of workers is there.

REFERENCES

A Zalesnik, C.R. Christensen & F.J. Roethlisberger: The Motivation, Productivity and Satisfaction of Workers, Graduate School of Business, Boston, Harvard University, 1958.

A.E.C. Hare, First Principles of Industrial Relations, 1958, PP.45-46.

A.H. Brayfield & WH. Crockett: Employee Attitudes and Employees Performence, Psycological Bulletin, Vol. 52, NO.5, Sep. 1955, pp.396-425.

Charles L. Hulin,: Effects of Community Characterstics on Measures of Job Satisfaction, Journal of Applied Psychological, Vol. 50, NO.2, April 1966, pp.185-188.

D. Katz, N. Maccoby & N. Morse: Productivity, Supervision and Morale in An Office Situation University of Michigan Survey Research Centre, 1950.

D. Katz, N. Maccoby, G. Gurin & L.G. Floor: Productivity and Morale Among Rail road Workers University of Michigan Survey Research Centre, 1951.

D.E. Mc Farland,: Personnel Management - Theory and Practice, Macmillan & Co., New York, 1968, p.484.

Dale Yoder, Management Policy and Manager Dissidence, Personnel Administration Vol. 31, NO.2, March - April, 1968, pp.8-18.

E.E. Lawler & L.W Porter: The Effect of Performance on Job Satisfaction, Industrial Relations, Vol. 7, No. 1, Oct. 1967; See also Dunnett, D. Marvin., J.P. Campbell & M.D. Hakel: Factors Contributing to Job Satisfaction and Job Dissatisfaction in Six Occupational Grops, Organizational Behaviour and Human Performance, Vol. 2, NO.2, Mar 1967, pp.143-174: Also, J.M. Shepard: Functional Specialisation and Work Attitudes, Industrial Relations, Vol. 8, NO.2, Feb. 1969. pp. 185-194.

E.R. Bremblett, Maintenance of Discipline, in Management Personnel, Quarterly, Vol. 1, NO.1, 1961, p.1 0.

F.R. Wickert, Turnover and Employees Feelings of Ego - Involvement in the Day-to-Day Operations of a Company', Personnel Psycology, VolA, 1951, pp.185-198.

F.W. Roethlisberger & W.J. Dickson, Management and the Worker, Harvard University Press, 1939.

H.C. Triandis,: A Critique and An Experimental Design for the Study of Relationship Between Productivity and Job Satisfaction, Psycological Buletin, Vol. 56, 1959. pp.309-312.

Hiamann Theo: Professional Management, Eurasia Publishing House, Delhi, 1975, p.453.

J.C. Worthy, Organization Structure and Employee Morale, American Sociological Review, Vol. 15, NO.1, April 1950, pp.169-179; See also thus, Factors Influencing Employee Morale, Harvard Business Review,

J.D. Mooney, Principles of Organization, Harper & Row, New York, 1947, p.177.

M.J. Jucius: Personnel Management, Indian Reprint, D.B. Taraporewala Sons & Co., Bombay, 1978, p.430.

M.L. Blum, & J.C. Naylor, Industrial Psycology, - Its Theoretical and Social Foundations, Harper & Row, New York, 1958, pp. 364-365.

Manu, C. Floyd, & H. Baumgartel: Absences and Employee Attitudes in An Electric Power Company, Survey Research Centre, University of Michigan, Dec. 1952.

R. Likert & S.E. Seashore, Employee Attitudes and Output Monthly Labour Review, Vol. 77, NO.6, June 1954, pp.641-649.

R.A.H. Rosen & Rosen Hjalmar: A Suggested Modification of Job Satisfaction, Personnel Psycology, Vol. 8. NO.3, 1955, pp.308-314.

R.L. Kahn & Danial Katz: Leadership Practice in Relation to Productivity and Morale in D. Cartwright, & A. Zander (eds.) Group Dynamics, Row Peterson and Co., 1953, p.616.

R.M. Guion: Industrial Morale: The Problem of Terminology, Personnel Psychology, Vol. II, NO.1, 1958, pp.59-61.

Raphael Winifred, A Study of Some Stresses and Strains within the Working Group, Occupational Psycology, Vol. 21, 1947, pp.92-101.

Ross Stagner, Motivational Aspects of Industrial Morale, Personnel Psycology, Vol. **II**, NO.1, 1958, pp.64- 70.

V.H. Vroom: Employee Attitudes in Fisk, George !ed.): The frontiers of Management Psycology, Harper & Row, New York, 1964, pp.127 -143.

Vol. 28, NO.1, Jan. 1950, pp.61-73.· -

W.A. Kerr, G.J. Koppelmeir, & J.J. Sullivan: Absenteeism, Turnover and Morale in a Metrals Fabrication Factory, Occupational Psychology, Vol. 25, 1951, pp.50-55.

West, J. Leonard: Fatigue and Performance Variability Among Typists, Journal of Applied Psycology, Vol. 53, NO.1, Feb. 1969, p.80-86.

WW Finlay, A.Q. Sartain, & WM. Tatc: Human Behaviour in Industry, McGraw Hill Co., New York, 1955,pp.223233.

CHAPTER

9

Motivation

Motivation, perhaps, more than any other behavioural concept, is a subject-matter or great importance and interest to executives in organizations, whether in India or abroad. Wherever the human element is involved, the complex human behaviour can never be explained in terms of specific responses to stimuli. When man is at work, he cannot be forced to work like a machine. Ask any manager, what is the most complicated problem he faces and the answer one will get is "I wish I had a group of motivated people working with me."

What Moves One to Excellence?

How can one be encouraged to put up his best? How will one work for me? Charles Gafield aptly said, "Today the emerging wisdom of peak performing organization is that it all boils down to people."

Motivation is an important factor in an individual's response to a stimulus. The famous old saying 'you can lead a horse to water but you can't make him drink' is applicable to all situations where the human element is involved.

Before we dwelve any further into the topic, it becomes inevitable to discuss the term 'motivation' along with its peripherals.

As the three terms–motive, motivation and motivating– are all derived from the Latin word moyere meaning to move, it is better to comprehend them first, in order to understand what is motivation, which are important concepts and have distinct connotations.

Motive

Motive is the kingpin of motivation and behaviour. The motivation of people depends upon motives. Motives give directions to human behaviour. They are generally goal directed, which may be conscious or unconscious.

Formally, a motive is an inner state that energizes, activates or moves and directs or channels behaviour towards goal. In short, a motive results in and hence can be inferred from, purpose, means- ends behaviour.

In a less formal way, motive has been described as follows:

A motive is restlessness, a lack, a yen, a force. Once in the grip of a motive, the organism does something. It most generally does something to reduce the restlessness, to remedy the lack, to alleviate the yen, to mitigate the force.

Motive is different from stimulus, because it is present there even before the stimulus. In the absence of motives there can be no response, however, intense the external stimulus may be. Though motives depend upon the changing physical condition and past experiences. For example, a burnt child dreads the fire because the memory of burning is always present in his mind.

There can be different motives behind different actions and different motives behind the same action. You often see a man throwing a coin towards a beggar. There can be two different motives behind this action–the man might have thrown the coin towards the bagger, either as a token of disgust as gesture of pity.

Thus we see people differ not only in their ability to do but also in their "will to do" or motivation. Therefore, motives are the "why" of behaviour. They arouse and maintain activity, and determine the general direction of the behaviour of an individual, and the mainspring of action.

Though some authors have differentiated between motives and needs, but one can conceptualise motives as certain critical needs in human beings that have varying degrees of potency or strength. The strong motives or needs make the individual restless and in a state of disequilibrium until the need is fulfilled or satisfied. In order to minimise this restlessness or inner disequilibrium and to keep it under control, the individual is propelled into action. Therefore, we can easily conclude that motives induce individuals to channel their behaviour towards such types of action as would reduce their state of restlessness and give inner disequilibrium. We may also say motives are the drives that energise people into action and the result of such action (behaviour) is motivation.

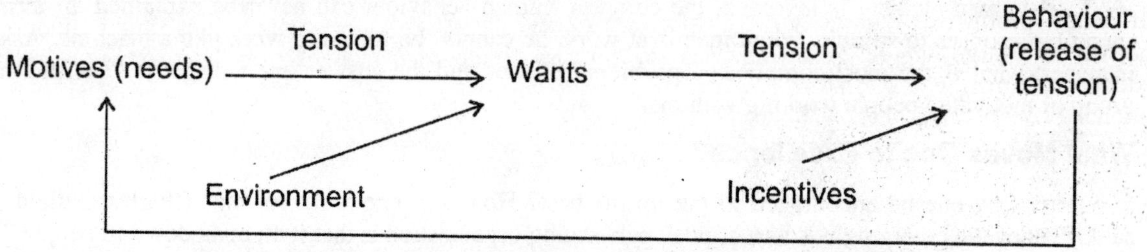

Fig. 1. Need Cause Behaviour

Although some authors have made a distinction between motives and need, but in our discussion we shall use these two terms–motives and needs – interchangeably. We can conceptualize motives as certain critical needs in human beings that have varying degrees of potency or strengths. Thus, hunger, the desire to possess a car, the wish to fly in an aeroplane, the quest for power and the like – all are motives.

Here we can draw a fine line of demarcation between needs and wants. Needs are more comprehensive in nature and include both the physiological and the psychological factors. Wants are expression in a narrow perspective and include only those desires for which a person has money and also the desires to spend money for the satisfaction and fulfilment of wants. To be more elaborate, there exists many psychological needs such as status, ego and self-esteem which do not fall under the category of needs.

In order to understand the individual in a better perspective it is necessary to understand the drives/motives/needs which motivate him.

These motives are basically divided into two groups. One group relates to the physical needs or motives or drives and includes such factors as the need for food, clothing, shelter and other physical necessities. Psychological motives form the second group. These include such motives as a desire to excel and be in some way outstanding, a desire to be loved, a desire to be aroused and desire to be financially secure. However, there are certain negative motives also, which revolve around various fears. These fears may include among others losing one's job or one's ability to earn money or even losing one's money, wages or salary, or they may be physical fears such as fears of being attacked and possibly getting injured or killed. Table I summarizes this type of motives.

Table 1: Motives

Primary or Physical Motives

Food, clothing, shelter, sex, physical security from bodily harm.

Psychological and Primary Motives

Affection, being accepted as one of a group, excellence, acquisition (collecting things), economic and cultural security, affection (both from friends and the opposite sex), respect of others :

Rational Motives

Those which can be supported by such things as utility, profitability, economic factors. Often attributed to business decisions because of need for efficiency for profits. Not altogether true, as some businessman are somewhat emotional, but tends to be true.

Emotional Motives

Those which are primarily psychological in nature and which cannot be defended from strict utility, efficiency, profit, or economic utility. Most consumers choose even basic necessities utilize emotional motives to a large degree. When luxuries are purchased emotional motives tend to govern to a greater extent, consumer may attempt to rationalize or kind himself that he is really completely interested in rational economic motives when not true.

Note : It is dangerous to generalize about motives as basic causes. Today it is felt that people may buy not from one but several motives some of which may be rational and others emotional. Many present day writers have discarded lists of motives and substituted discussion of psychological choices.

Motivating

Motivating is a term that implies that one person induces another to engage in action or work behaviour by ensuring that a channel to direct the motive of the individual becomes available and accessible to the individual. In a simpler way motivating is that activity on the part of an individual which helps in channeling the strong motives in a direction that is satisfying to an individual.

Motivation

Generally speaking we can say that motivation is psychological in nature and relates to those forces operating within an individual and which impel him to act or not to act in certain ways. However, various authors have tried to define motivation. We quote some important definitions on motivation.

1. Motivation is a result of processes, internal or external to the individual, that arouse enthusiasm and persistence to purpose a certain course of action.
2. Motivation is a process that starts with a physiological or psychological deficiency or need that activates behaviour or a drive that is aimed at a goal or incentive.
3. Motivation refers to a process governing choices made by persons of lower organisms among alternative forms of voluntary activity.
4. Motivation answers what we have considered to be the fundamental question in the area of human behaviour, the question 'why' or 'what' – it is that makes people do things. It refers to something dynamic that arises on an internal basis.

Integrating all the above definitions of motivation, we can say that every behaviour is caused, motivated and goal directed and can be represented as in Fig. 2.

And the relationships among the three basic concepts–Motive, Motivating and Motivation, discussed so far can be represented as in Fig. 3.

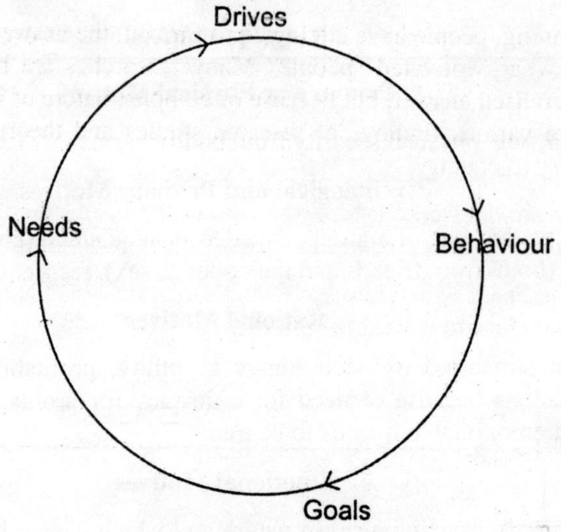

Fig. 2. Process of Behaviour

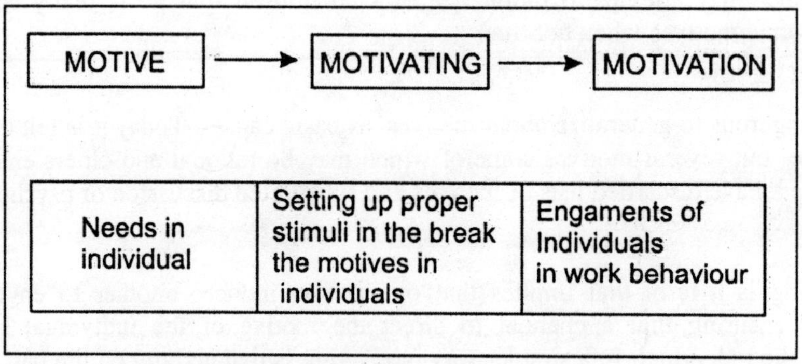

Fig. 3. Relationships among Motive, Motivating and Motivation

Motivation Process

Motivation is a process having its origin in needs when a need is satisfied it ceases to be a motivation of behaviour. Motivation is a result of sheer reaction of needs as depicted in Fig. 4.

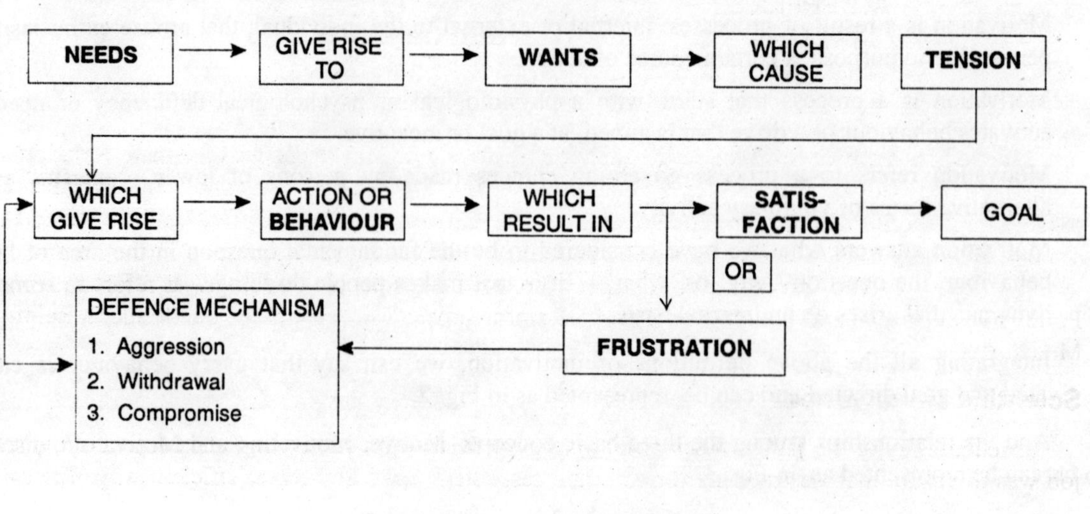

Fig. 4. Needs - Satisfaction Chain

Theories of Motivation

Since the very beginning, people have attempted to find out the answer of why or how people engage in work behaviour, i.e., what Motivated people? Many researches are being carried our constantly on motivation to find a generalised answer, but because of complex nature of human beings no generalisation is yet possible. There are various findings of research studies and theories which are affected by time, circumstances and country to country.

In a variety of way scholars who have tried to answer the complex question of motivation and tried to answer it through different approaches, resulting into a number of theories of motivation.

All these theories can be classified into two broad categories: (a) Early theories and (b) Contemporary theories, and can be further classified as shown in Fig. 5.

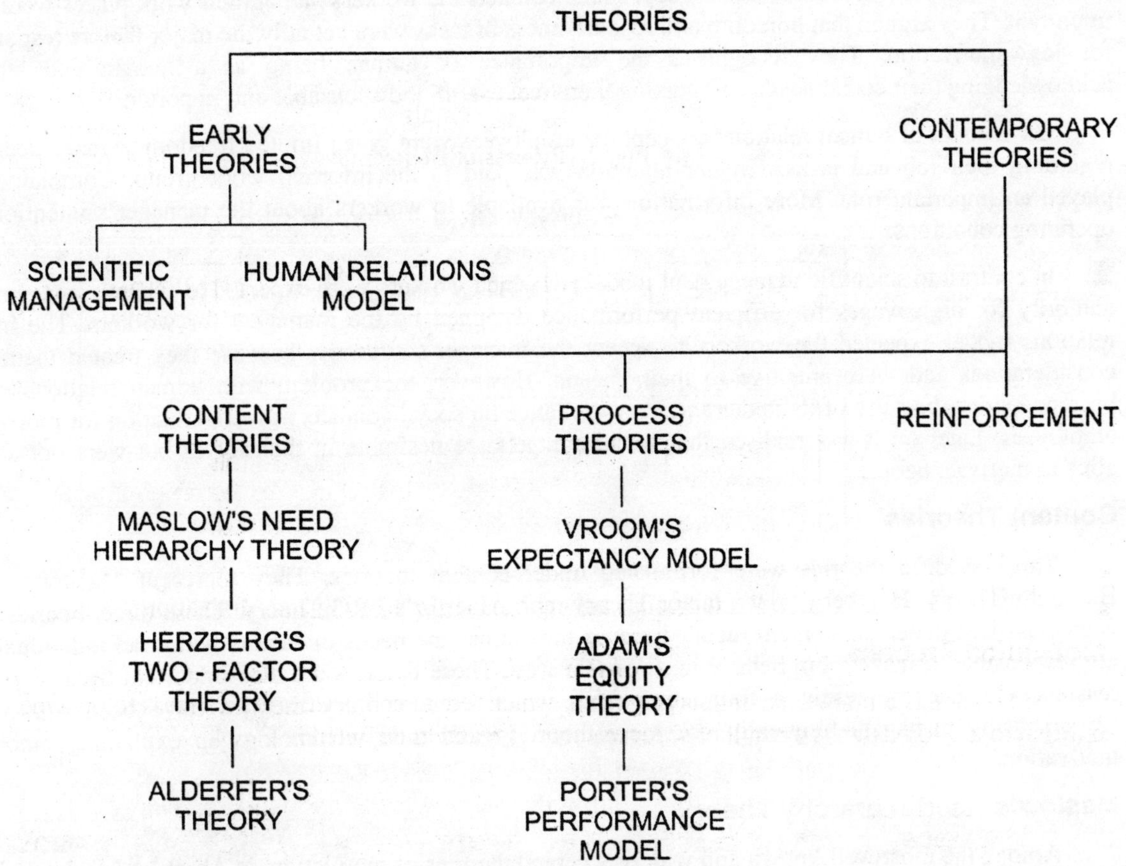

Fig. 5. Motivation Theories

The early theories of motivation include scientific management and Human Relations Model. Contemporary theories can further be classified under three broad categories: (a) Content Theories, (b) Process Theories and (c) Reinforcement Theories. Content theories include Maslow's Need Hierarchy Theory, Herzberg's Two-factor Theory and Alderfer's ERG Theory, McGregor's Theory X and Theory Y besides Theory Z. The process theories cover Vroom's Expectancy Model, Adam's Equity Theory and Porter's Performance and Satisfaction Theory. Reinforcement Theory is based on Skinner's Reinforcement Model.

Scientific Management

Frederic Taylor the father of scientific management, thought that an important aspect of the manager's job was to ensure that workers performed their respective tasks in the best efficient way. The motivation theory emphasized man as an Economic Man and stressed that it is managers who determine, what a worker should do and use a wage incentive system to motivate the workers. This theory laid emphasis on, the more a worker produces, the more he earns.

This concept took it for granted that workers were basically lazy, not interested in their work and the managers understood the workers' job better than the workers did. To make the workers perform better, i.e., if financial rewards are given the result would be better performance and have a little consideration for the labour of the workers. Initially this concept worked well and the efficiency improved considerably. Fewer workers were needed to perform the same task. But with the passage of time, lay-off became a common practice and the workers opted for job security instead of financial incentives.

Human Relations Model

The philosophy that workers were basically motivated by money alone proved to be inadequate. Elton Mayo and others found that besides money, social contacts the workers had at their work places were more important. They argued that boredom and repetitiveness of tasks were actually the major factors responsible for low motivation. They recognised the importance of human being as a human and stressed acknowledging their social needs and making them feel useful, indispensable and important.

On account of human relations concept the employees were given limited freedom to make decisions regarding their job and tasks. Greater attention was paid to the informal work group. Communication played an important role. More information was available to workers about the manager's intention and operating conditions.

In contrast to scientific management models in which workers were expected to accept management's authority for high wages for efficient performance designed by the managers for workers. The human relations model expected the workers to accept the manager's authority because they treated them with considerations and were attentive to their needs. However, the problem with human relations model became evident because of its under and heavy reliance on social contacts at work situation for motivating employees. Later on it was realised that social contacts are desirable in themselves but were not always able to motivate people.

Content Theories

Three specific theories were formulated under content theories. They represent Maslow's Need Hierarchy Theory, Herzberg's Two factor Theory and Alderfor's ERG Theory. These three theories have been classified under the content theory because they stress the needs or factors within an individual that are responsible to make them behave in a certain way. These theories are also important because of two reasons: (1) They represent a foundation from which contemporary theories have been drawn and (2) practising managers frequently use these theories and their terminology in explaining employee motivation.

Maslow's Need Hierarchy Theory

Among the most well-known and widely accepted theories of motivation is Abraham Maslow's Need hierarchy, in which he has stressed that people have five basic need levels which they tend to satisfy in a hierarchical pyramid, represented in Fig. 6.

1. Physiological needs or primary needs, are those basic bodily needs that individuals tend to satisfy. These needs include hunger, thirst, shelter, sex and other bodily needs. So long as these needs remain unsatisfied, they motivate. The famous saying 'Man can live on bread alone if there is no bread' suggests that human beings first try to acquire necessities for their survival. When these primary needs are satisfied, then only people tend to move to the second level of needs in the hierarchy. Put in another way, the person who fails to satisfy this basic need just won't be around enough to attempt satisfaction of higher need levels.

Physiological needs play a pivotal role in human behaviour. One example to substantiate this view is enough to explain the behavioural effects brought about by food deprivation. In 1970 a Peruvian airliner crashed deep into the jungles of South America. Trapped with a dwindling supply of food, the survivors who also included a Catholic priest, resorted to eating the victims of the crash. This incident clearly illustrates social and moral taboos, how deeply rooted they may be, succumb to basic biological needs under stressful conditions. No doubt, physiological needs dominate human desires, forcing themselves on one's attention before higher order goals can be pursued.

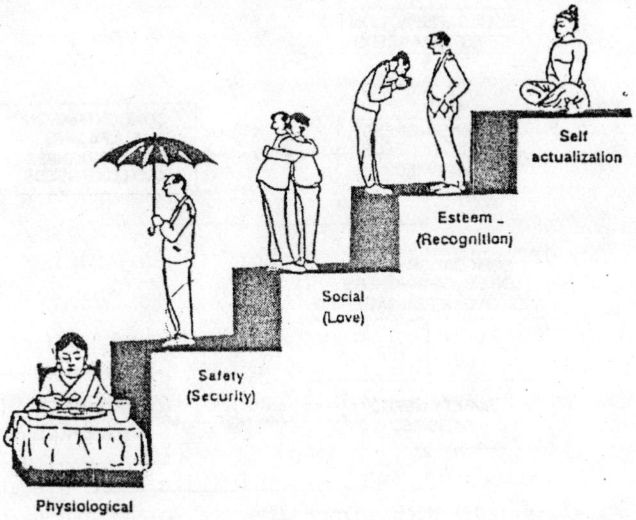

Fig. 6. Maslow's Hierarchy of Needs

2. Safety needs include security and protection from physical and emotional harm. Once physiological needs are satisfied to a considerable extent, people feel the urge to satisfy their safety and security needs that is, need for being free of physical danger or for self-preservation. Thus, people seek protection. In the organizational context, safety needs are primarily satisfied through economic behaviour - such as job security, pension schemes, insurance plans, etc.

3. Social needs constitute the third level in the hierarchy and include the need for affection, belongingness, acceptance and friendship. These needs are also referred to as love needs by some authors. After the first two needs are satisfied, the social needs third in the hierarchy arise. Man is a social being and he wants to be dominant, to belong, to associate, to gain acceptance, to give and receive friendship and affection.

Freud equated love with sex, but Maslow suggested that love involves a healthy loving relationship between two people and includes trust, admiration and mutual respect. Not being loved leads to the feeling of emptiness futility and ultimately to hostility. These needs represent a clear cut step up from the next two needs, i.e., Esteem needs and Self-actualization, the plainly physical level of the physiological needs and the quasi-physical of the safety needs. Where belongingness and love needs and the quasi-physical of the safety needs. Where belongingness and love needs are not met, severe maladjustment is probable; where the hunger for companionship is assuaged, the mental health of the organism is once again on a better base.

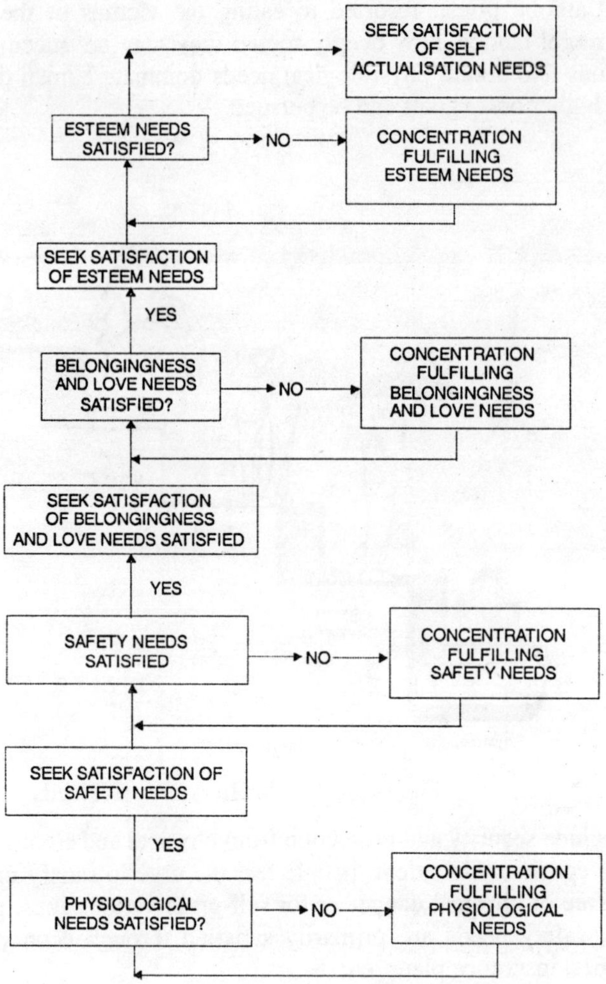

Fig. 7. Flow Diagram of Needs Satisfaction

Source: Thedore T. Herbert, *Dimensions of Organizational Behaviour*, p. 223.

4. Esteem needs include internal esteem factors such as self-respect, autonomy and achievement. These needs also include external esteem factors such as status, recognition and attention. Satisfaction of these needs generates feelings and attitudes of self-confidence, prestige, power, control. capability, strength and of being useful and necessary in the world. In contrast, according to Maslow, the thwarting of these needs creates feelings and attitudes of ineptness, helplessness and inferiority complexes.

5. Self-actualization is the need to maximise one's potential, whatever it may be. This need is normally represented by the drive to become what one is capable of becoming. Self-actualization needs include growth, achieving one's potential and self-fulfilment. If we put it in other words, self-actualization is to become the total kind of person that one wants to become to reach at the back of one's potential.

Only the gifted people are able to fulfil this need. Maslow himself estimated that less than one per cent of the people fulfil the needs for self-actualization because of three reasons: (1) People are invariably bline towards their own potential; (2) The social environment creates stumbling blocks for development towards self-fulfilment ; and (3) The strong negative influence exercise by the safety needs. For growth it is of great importance to take risks, make mistakes and break old habits. This requires courage, but one's fear and anxiety increase his tendency to revert back towards safety and security needs. Therefore, self-fulfilling people are rare individuals who come close to living up to their full potential for being realistic, accomplishing things, enjoying life and generally exemplifying classic human virtues.

As each of these needs becomes substantially satisfied, the next need in the hierarchy becomes dominant and the individuals tend to go further up, as represented in Fig. 7. If unsatisfied, the needs will hold the individual's concentration until and unless they are satisfied to a considerable extent.

Evaluation of Maslow's Theory

Maslow's need hierarchy theory has received universal appreciation and application, particularly among practising managers. It is true that man is a never wanting being and no need is everfully gratified. However, a substantially satisfied need no longer motivate. Unfortunately, however, research findings do not collaborate with the theory. Maslow provided no empirical substantiation, and several studies that sought to validate the theory found no support.

Though Maslow's hierarchy model represents a typical pattern that seems to operate most of the time. An analysis reveals the levels are not dependent, rather they are interdependent and over-lapping. However, Maslow separated the five needs into higher and lower level needs. Social or love, esteem and self-actualization were classified as higher order needs, as represented in Fig. 8.

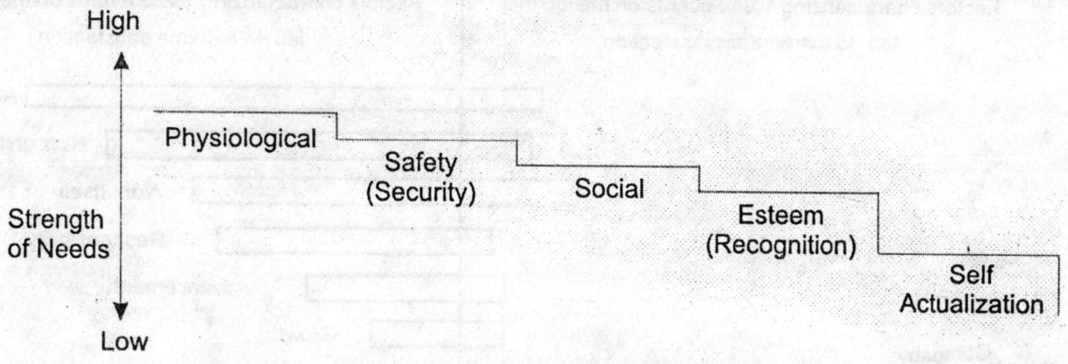

Fig. 8. Maslow's Need Hierarchy

The basis of differentiation between these two orders of need was that higher needs are satisfied internally to the person. The lower order needs are basically satisfied by external factors, such as money, wages, tenure, etc. The statement, 'If one need is satisfied, then another emerges' gives a hazy demarcation of boundaries. There are people who are deprived of lower order needs but try for the highest needs in the hierarchy, i.e., self-actualization. The example of Mahatma Gandhi is worth mentioning in this context and needs no explanation. Besides this, there are many poets, artists, musicians, etc., all over the world who have tried to self-actualize themselves.

By their immortal work without ever having satisfied their lower order needs. Most of such people have lived their entire life in poverty and without any protection during their lifetime, i.e., throughout their whole life their lower order needs were never met. These people strived to transcend themselves in their work and were constantly in the process of becoming all that they could possibly become, without ever satisfying the Maslow's Hierarchy of Needs pyramid. Hence it is possible for one if not for all, not to go step by step in the hierarchy for the satisfaction of needs. Maslow himself later agreed that there are exceptions to the hierarchical fulfilment of needs.

Korman and others reviewed the evidence and concluded that "although of great societal popularity, need hierarchy as a theory continues to receive little empirical support." He further stated that the, "available research should certainly generate a reluctance to accept unconditionally the implications of Maslow's hierarchy." Another research finding also collaborate Korman's finding and comes to the same conclusion.

In the light of the above discussion, it is most desirable to view Maslow's model of need hierarchy as a general description of the common and average individual at a specific point in time. It should be viewed as a general theoretical statement, a hypothetical construct rather than as abstraction from field research. Still in twenty-first century, Maslow's model is of significant importance in underdeveloped and developing countries. Needs, no matter how they are classified, are of basic importance for understanding the complex human behaviour. A survey of 200 workers in India concluded that workers still give top priority to lower needs.

Herzberg's Two-factor Theory

During 1959 Frederic Herzberg and his associates identified that there are two sets of factors in the work place that considerably influence the employee job attitudes. He provided an interesting extension of Maslow's need hierarchy and developed a specific content theory of motivation. This theory is also known as – Dual Factor Theory and the Motivation – Hygiene Theory.

Herzberg and his associates initially conducted a survey of 200 engineers and accountants in nine different companies in pittsburg, USA. He used 'critical incident' technique in his research and asked respondents to identify specific events, situations or incidents when (a) they felt most satisfied and (b) they were most dissatisfied. Later he expanded his analysis and collected responses from over 1600 workers in various types of jobs in 12 different studies.

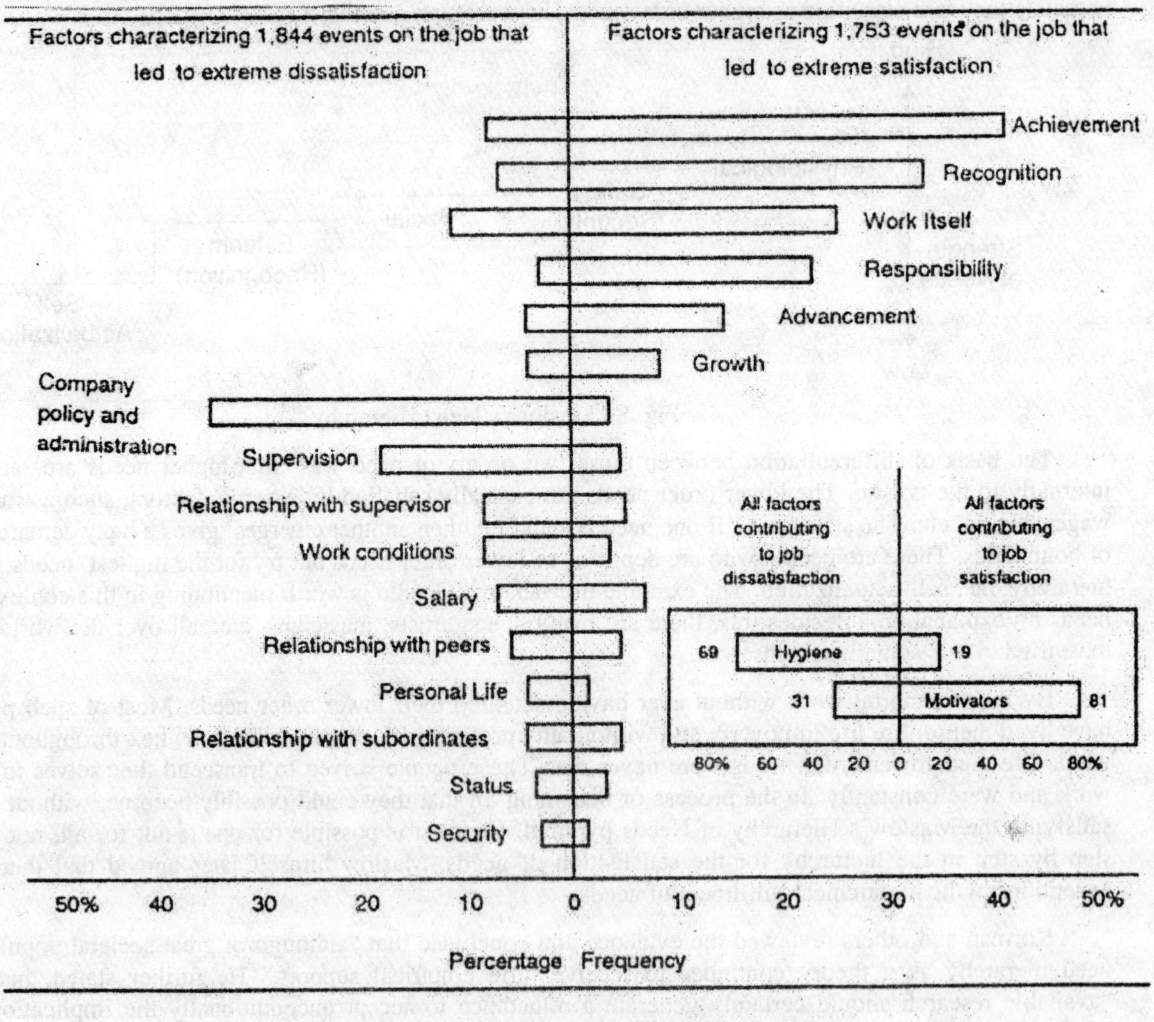

Fig. 9. Comparision of Satisfiers and Dissatisfiers

Source : Federick Herzberg, *One More Time: How do you Motivate Employees? Havard Business Review*, Jan. Feb., p. 57.

Responses obtained from these studies were interesting. Herzberg concluded that the replies people gave when they felt good about their jobs were remarkably different from the replies given when they felt bad. As seen in Fig. 9, certain characteristics tend to be consistently related to job-satisfaction (factors on the right side of the figure) and to job-dissatisfaction (the left side of the figure). He called the first set of factors 'motivator' or satisfiers and the second set of factors 'hygiene' factors or dissatisfies. Herzberg stressed that satisfaction and dissatisfaction are two different factors (hence the name Dual Factor Theory). He clarified, that the opposite of dissatisfaction is not satisfaction. In other words, a person can be dissatisfied with working conditions, but at the same time, be satisfied with the work (Fig. 10.).

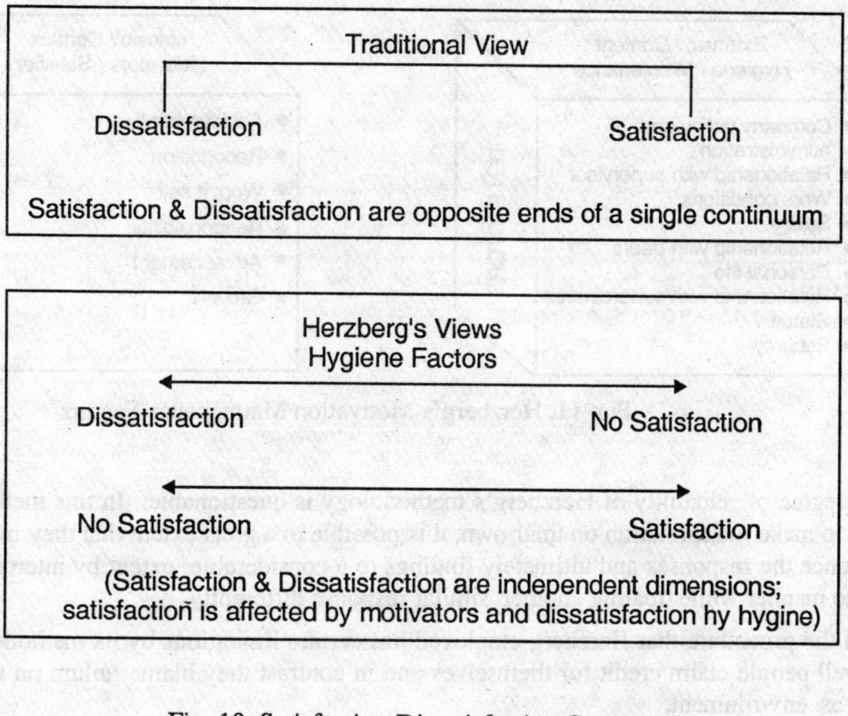

Fig. 10. Satisfaction-Dissatisfaction Compared

Herzberg's findings also confirmed that satisfaction and dissatisfaction appear to be independent of each other. They cannot be viewed as symmetrical items on a single scale, rather they can be viewed as attributes of different scales. Satisfaction is affected by motivations, 6 factors in all and dissatisfaction by hygiene factors, 10 in all, as shown in Fig. 11. He also clarified that hygiene factors serve as maintenance factor in motivation.

Analysis of the Theory

Herzberg's findings and recommendations founded the job design theory and have been subsequently developed more completely by Heckman and his associates. His theory has been applied in industry and has significantly contributed to give new insights, especially in the field of job enrichment. The idea behind job enrichment to keep maintenance factors constant or higher while increasing motivational factors in present days is due to Herzberg's theory. Nationwide polls conducted by the National Opinion Research Centre, USA confirmed that "more than half of the white male workforce in the United States believes that the most important characteristic of a job is that it involves work that is important and provides a sense of accomplishment."

Like the Maslow's Theory, Herzberg Theory has been the subject of criticism, on the following grounds:

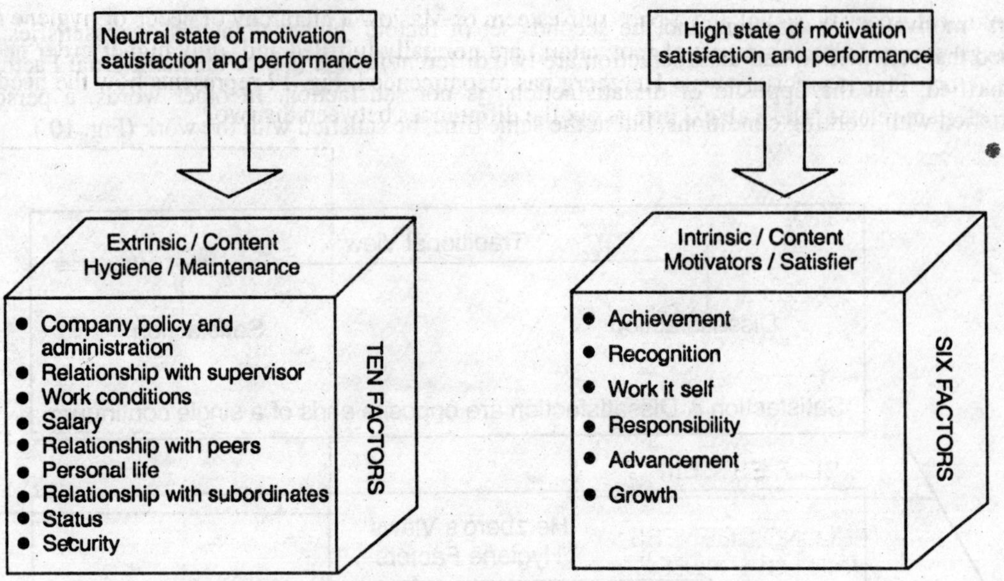

Fig. 11. Herzberg's Motivation Maintenance Factors

1. The degree of reliability of Herzberg's methodology is questionable. In this method since the raters have to make interpretation on their own, it is possible to a great extent that they may contaminate and influence the responses and ultimately findings to a considerable extent by interpreting one response in one manner while treating another similar response differently.
2. Even the procedure that Herzberg employed has certain limitations by its methodology. When things go well people claim credit for themselves and in contrast they blame failure on the extrinsic factors such as environment.
3. The theory does not collaborate with the results of previous research and the findings are inconsistent. The Herzberg Dual Factor Theory completely ignores situational variables.
4. The theory, to the degree that it is valid, provides an explanation of job satisfaction only and it is not really a theory of motivation.
5. In Herzberg model no overall measure of satisfaction was utilized. For example, a person may dislike part of his job, yet still think the job is acceptable.
6. While working on the hypothesis, Herzberg assumes that there is a direct relationship between satisfaction and productivity. But the research methodology he employed looked and evaluated only satisfaction, not productivity and their intense relationship. To make such research relevant, one must assume a high relationship between satisfaction and productivity.
7. The two factors distinguished by Herzberg are actually not distinct. Both motivators and hygiene factors contribute significantly to both satisfaction and dissatisfaction.
8. Herzberg placed tremendous emphasis on motivators. The importance of hygiene factors, which themselves serve as motivators, specially in underdeveloped countries have been totally ignored.

Comparison of Maslow's and Herzberg's Theories

Both Maslow's and Herzberg's theories are compatible to each other to the extent that both tend to simplify the motivational process, same set of relationship and basically deals with the same problem, i.e., what motivates an individual and attempts to explain the 'why' of complex human behaviour. Maslow has tried to answer in terms of five needs in a hierarchical fashion and suggested how people try for comparatively higher level needs. Herzberg recommended the use of hygiene factors to help people to attain their lower level needs and motivators for high order needs. Both writers assume that specific needs energise behaviour.

However, in socially and economically advanced countries, most of the lower order needs (physiological, security, social and a part self-esteem of Maslow's hierarchy of needs or hygiene factors in Herzbergs theory including a part of motivators) are normally fulfilled and only higher order needs serve as motivators. This is precisely what Herzberg has recommended. Fig. 12 represents how the needs in both the theories are related, and Table 2 brings out the differences between the two.

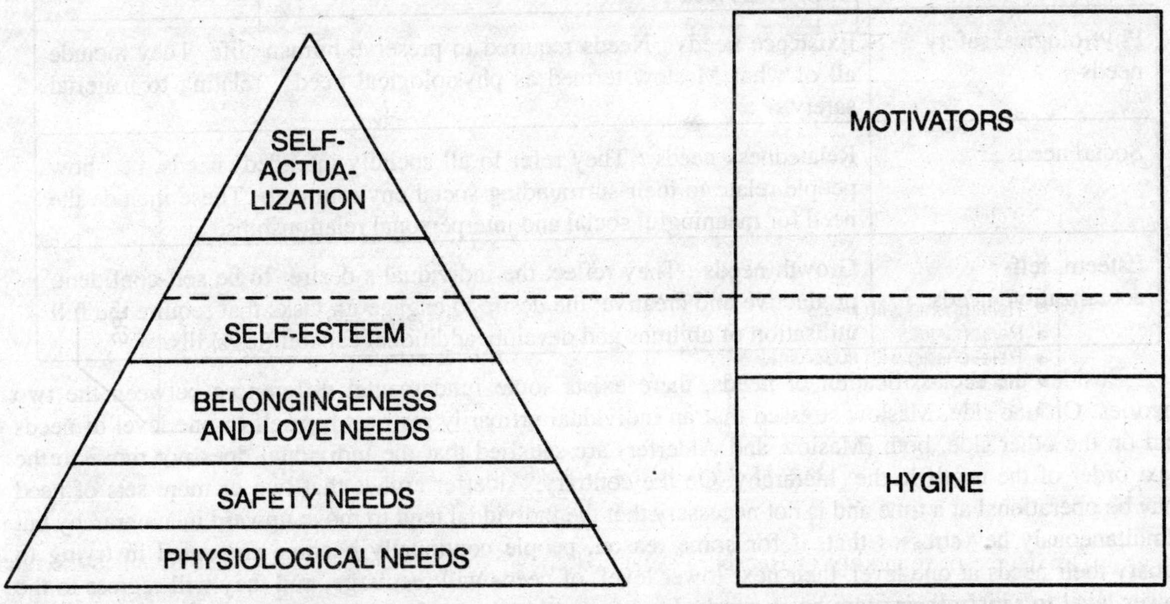

Fig. 12: Comparison of Maslow's and Herzberg's Need Factors

Alderfer's ERG Theory

In 1969 and 1972, Clayton Alderfer attempted to reformulate Maslow's Needs Hierarchy theory. Instead of Maslow's five level needs he suggested three levels and renamed them as needs for Existence, Relatedness, and Growth. The name ERG is derived from the first three letters of each of these three needs. The relationship between Maslow's and Alderfer's needs classification is represented in Table 3.

Table 2. Difference between Maslow's and Herzberg's Theories

Issue	*Maslow's Theory*	*Herzberg's Theory*
Nature of theory	Descriptive	Prescriptive
Needs Order	Hierarchical arrangement of needs	No such arnagement of needs.
Satisfaction performance relationship	Unsatisfied needs energize behaviour and this behaviour causes performance	Fratified needs cause performance
Effect of need satisfaction	A satisfied need no longer remains a motivator except self-actualization need	Satisfied need is a motivator except hygiene factors which are not motivators.
Motivator	Any need is a motivators, specially when it is relatively unsatisfied	Only higher order needs are motivators.
Applicability view of motivation	Takes a general view. Macro view deals with all aspect of existence.	Takes a micro view Micro view basically deals with work related motivational problems.
Universality	Relevant for all categories of workers at all time and place, probably more relevant to developed countries.	More relevant to white collar and professionals

Table 3. Needs – Reclassified by Alderfer

Maslow's Need	*Alderfer's Need*
Physiological safety needs	Existence needs : Needs required to preserve human life. They include all of what Maslow termed as physiological needs relating to material safety.
Social needs	Relatedness needs : They refer to all socially intended needs, i.e., how people relate to their surrounding social environment. These include the need for meaningful social and interpersonal relationships.
Esteem, self-actualization needs	Growth needs : They reflect the individual's desire to be self-confident, productive and creative; the desire to engage in tasks that require the full utilisation of abilities and develop additional capabilities/skills.

Besides the reclassification of needs, there exists some fundamental differences between the two theories. On one side, Maslow stressed that an individual primarily restricts himself to one level of needs and on the other side, both (Maslow and Alderfer) are satisfied that the individual does not move to the next order of the needs in the hierarchy. On the contrary, Alderfer argues that two or more sets of need may be operational at a time and is not necessary that the individual tend to move upward in a hierarchy but simultaneously he stresses that, if for some reason, people continually become frustrated in trying to satisfy their needs at one level, their next lower level of needs will reemerge, and they will regress to the lower level to satisfy their more basic needs. Explaining this he put forth that if relatedness needs are not satisfied and an individual continuously experiences frustration in not being able to meet those needs, his existence needs will reemerge and he will redirect his efforts to his level and try to get more of those needs satisfied. The ERG theory also argues for instance, inability to satisfy a need for social interaction have all possibilities to increase the desire for more money or better working conditions. Therefore, Alderfer's ERG Model contains a Frustration-Regression dimension, concluding that frustration at a higher level may lead to regression to a lower need level.

Table 4 shows the basic similarities and differences between Maslow's theory and Alderfer's theory.

Analysis of ERG Theory

Alderfer's theory, being more recent than the other two content theories–Maslow's and Herzberg's theories, has not yet attracted much attention and research testing where one can be certain about its accuracy and usefulness. However, the ERG theory seems to be more rational and consistent with our knowledge of individual differences among people, variables such as environment, culture, family background, education, etc. considerably effect the motivating force that a group of needs holds for an individual. There are certain evidences that confirm people in different cultures, rank the needs category differently. For example, natives of Japan and Spain place social needs before their physiological needs. People in India place love needs, before safety needs and the like. Perhaps this would be consistent with the ERG model. Because of these factors, the ERG theory represents a more valid version of the need hierarchy.

Some other studies have also supported the ERG theory but there is also evidence that it does not work in some organizations. One more study conducted by Rauschanberger and his associates in 1980 has refuted Alderfer's theory. Thus, more work is needed to test the accuracy and general applicability of Alderfer's ERG theory. However, overall, the ERG theory represents a more valid version of the need hierarchy and seems to take some strong points of the earlier content theories, but less restrictive and limiting.

Table 4. Maslow's vs. Alderfer's Theories

Similarities	The overall structure of need categories is the same, Alderfer's theory is only reconfigured need hierarchy model.
	Both the models deal with movement upward in the hierarchy. ERG theory provides a specific mechanism for downward movement in the hierarchy which Maslow does not provide. According to Alderfer, in addition to satisfaction, progression, frustration and regression can also occur if you fail to satisfy needs at a certain level.
Differences	ERG theory has a specified method, measures and theory of method for testing the theory, but Maslow did not provide for empirical substantiation.

Content Three Theories at a Glance

Maslow's, Herzberg's and Alderfer's theories are very closely related to each other in terms of need classification. Fig. 13 represents how they are related to each other.

McGregor's Theory X and Theory Y

The Hawthorne studies triggered a long series of studies. These threads were woven into a theoretical garment by McGregor. He is credited as being initiator of one of the most widely used and highly popular classification schemes for both the acceptable and unacceptable styles of today. This classification scheme was named, for want of better phraseology. Theory X and Theory Y, reflective of what he considered as two distinct perspectives of administrative action. Actually Theory X and Theory Y are attitudes or predispositions toward people. Theory X is negative, traditional and autocratic style while the Theory Y is positive, participatory and democratic. Thus, these labels described contrasting set or assumptions about human nature. For all practical purpose, these dichotomous models have become phenomenally popular pedagogical tools instructing executives to squeeze their leadership styles into a neat duality of either being autocratic or being democratic. The classification model, simple and unsophisticated, has already become a "Moralistic and normative model" of action for succeeding generations of managers throughout the world. Although McGregor never preferred one to another or never even suggested a preference either way. It is easy to recognize that McGregor `considered his Theory X to be less appropriate in general than his Theory Y.]

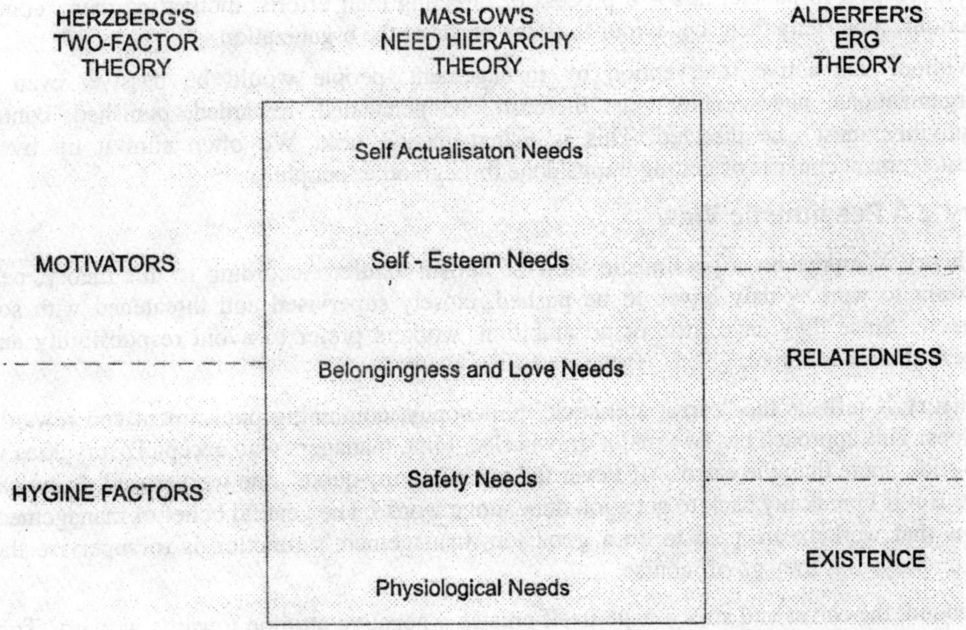

Fig. 13. Relationship among Content Theories

Theory X

Theory X is a traditional theory of management philosophy. According to this theory authority and control are centralized. The line of authority or chain of command traditionally goes direct from the top to down through various layers of organization with some delegation of authority but full and detailed accountability is up the line. People at work-level (workers) have no option except to obey the directives or orders of the authority. Power is supreme is the main theme of the theory where the people at work-level have no authority to suggest or object anything except to carry out the orders of the supervisor.

Assumptions of Theory X

The Theory 'X' is based on the following basic assumptions:

1. Most people inherently dislike work and always try to shrink their responsibility.
2. Because of this inherent character of human being, people must be coerced, controlled, directed and threatened with punishment, rebuffed or rebuked so as to get them to put forth adequate efforts towards the achievement of organizational goals.
3. The average human being prefers to be directed, wishes to avoid responsibility. He puts off the work till it is necessary.
4. Most people at work have little ambition as to the improvement of work. He does not work with interest but wait for directions and act according to it.
5. The average human being wants security and safety above all hence he tends to work slowly.
6. Most people have little capacity to contribute something towards solving the organizational problems because their importance in the management are always undermined by the authority and they are treated as an instrument of a machine. So they are indifferent towards organizational problems.
7. Working method of the people is traditional and hence there is little scope for the development and research. They do not like to adopt the change in method.
8. People can be motivated at money end. On the basis of financial greed, they can do whatever management wants.
9. Management is responsible for organizing the elements of productive enterprise–money, materials equipment, people–in the interest of economic ends.
10. With respect to people, this is a process of directing their efforts, motivating them, controlling their actions, modifying their behaviour to fit the needs of the organization.
11. Without this active intervention by management, people would be passive, even resistant to organizational needs. They must therefore, be persuaded, rewarded, punished, controlled: their activities must be directed. This is management's task. We often sum it up by saying that management consists of getting things done through other people.

Theory : A Pessimistic View

Theory X represents a pessimistic view of human nature. According to this theory, people do not really want to work – they have to be pushed, closely supervised and threatened with some type of punishment. Since they have little or no ambition, workers prefer to avoid responsibility and will seek security as their major goal.

Theory X reflects the "carrot and stick" philosophy, combining punishment and rewards to motive employees. This approach has two major drawbacks. First, managers who accept Theory X as valid tend to use the stick more than the carrot. "If I ever fall behind in my quota" one worker said, " you can bet I hear about it. But if I break my back to get a job done, not a word." The general belief of management under this theory is that workers are paid to do a good job; management's function is to supervise the work and correct employees if they go off course.

Second, the carrot and stick image itself creates a negative attitude towards workers. The supervisor or manager who views others as lazy, incompetent, reluctant to accept responsibility, and interested only in a paycheck will often treat subordinates with distrust, suspicion and little respect and will practice a form of supervision wherein fault finding, blaming and reprimands are frequent.

These negative assumptions underlie the philosophy of the assembly line and the robotization of human existence. "The organizational structure that develops from the assumptions of Theory X is the customary pyramidmulti layered, complex. It is clogged with communication blocks and distortions as orders and information limp up and down the organizational ladder." Underlying this conventional management theory are the assumptions that man is by nature indolent, lacks ambition, dislikes responsibility and prefers to be led. It is also assumed that the individual is self-centred, indifferent to organizational needs, resistive to change, gullible and not very bright. In order to accomplish objectives, therefore, management must employ coercive techniques and tight external constraints over behaviour. Accompanying this philosophy is the belief that people are motivated by money, fringe benefits and the treat of punishment. External control is clearly appropriate for dealing with unreliable, irresponsible and immature people. Employees, in turn, try to make the organization cognizant and responsive to their needs and aspirations by withholding and providing only enough to get by. If management were to adopt a "soft" line, easily giving to individual demands, employees may eat away the vitals of the organization. On the other hand, if it follows a hard line, its actions may lead to counter-action on the part of employees in the form of restricted output, militant unionism and an effective though subtle sabotage of management objectives. Thus, what is actually being observed (management's conventional beliefs) is not a consequence of man's inherent nature; it is rather, an inevitable byproduct of the structure of industrial organization. In other terms, the conventional approach of Theory X is based on a misconception of 'cause and effect.'

McGregor viewed this "Self-defeating atmosphere of a distrust and competitiveness as being not only degrading and wasteful but unnecessary." Both the hard and soft approaches fail today because they are simply irrelevant to the situation. Employees are not basically indolent, indifferent, uncooperative and unproductive but they learn these behaviours as response to the directing behaviour of managers. People behave exactly as we might predict. Thus, managers, he argued, are often caught in a web of their own making. They are often trapped into making inappropriate and ineffective decisions because of their assumptions about human behaviour. Theory X is based on a faulty conception of human behaviour and human motivation. It has as its objective the task of turning human beings into docile, glorified machine tools, of creating conditions in which they will do what they are told without resistance. It completely discounts the ideas of individual constructiveness and aggressiveness. McGregor felt that management needed practices based on a more realistic and accurate understanding of human nature and motivation. The real need was to bake an entirely new cake; managers must change to a whole new theory of working with people.

Relevance of Theory 'X' in Modern Times

A critical study of the assumptions of Theory X, one can easily conclude that the theory is quite unwarranted to the modern situation. The theory supports an authoritarian view which is unwarranted in the present day economy. One must realize that the man at work is not a machine, he is a human being and he is not only to execute the orders of the top line executives but he should also think over the order on its merits before its execution. Management can get results by coercion or through pressure tactics only is short run till people respond to pressures and controls partly out of fear of consequences of not following the orders of the top line executives. McGregor himself condemns the theory and say, "The conventional approach of Theory `X' is based on mistaken notions of what is cause and what is effect." The assumptions contained in Theory `X' do not reveal the time nature of human being. Further more the recent behavioural science research does not support the traditional view and concludes that most effective way to get better results in an organization is to work with people rather than through them.

In modern times, the governments of most of the countries have stressed that workers should be given an honourable partnership in management. In this way, this theory has now become out of date.

Theory 'Y'

Theory 'X' as we have discussed above represents the traditional view of the management philosophy which has been completely discarded by the modern management. McGregor feels that modern management grossly understands the interest and capacities of its organizational members. On the basis of the results of many psychological and social researches, he submits an opposing theory–Theory 'Y' as a more realistic assessment of the capabilities of the people.

This theory 'Y' presents an alternative management approach which does not involve abdication of managerial responsibility. Management is still responsible for achieving the organizational objectives but on different assumptions about human behaviour and motivation. The workers are fully aware of the organizational objectives which is directly related to the satisfaction of employees' needs. Thus, it pleads for a humanistic and supportive approach to managing people. Management tries to provide an atmosphere of peace and discipline within the organization but not with the oppressive measures hence people work with interest and simultaneously enjoy the benefits of congenial relationship.

Theory Y Assumes that people are not by nature, lazy and unreliable. It proposes that people can be basically self-directed and creative at work if properly motivated. Therefore, it should be an essential task of management to unleash this potential in individuals. In other words, theory Y management aims at integrating individual goals with those of the organization–at making the job the principle means through which each employee can enlarge his competence, self-control and the sense of accomplishment. It permits calculated democratisation of an enterprise wherein individual growth is encouraged and stimulated contributing to the continued growth of the enterprise as a whole. In a nut-shell, it emphasizes creating opportunities, removing obstacles, encouraging growth and providing guidance.

Assumptions of Theory 'Y'

Theory Y is based on the following assumptions:

1. The average human being does not dislike work. Work is as natural as play or rest. Depending upon the controllable conditions, work may be a source of satisfaction or punishment.
2. External control and the threat of punishment are not the only means for accomplishing the organizational objectives. Workers are committed to objective and exercise self-control and self-direction to achieve them. They are fully conscious of their job.
3. The average man born under proper conditions, not only to accept but seek responsibility. Avoidance of responsibility, lack of ambition and emphasis on security are not the inherent qualities of the man.
4. The reward for the execution of work is that his work should be properly recognised. Satisfaction of their ego and actionalization needs can be direct product of efforts directed towards organizational objectives.
5. The capacity to exercise a relatively high degree of imaginations, ingenuity and creativity in the solution of organizational problems is widely distributed in the population, i.e., labour cooperate the management in solving the problems of the organization.
6. With reference to modern industrial systems, human abilities and capabilities are not fully developed till now and management has ample scope to develop the intellectual potentialities of the average human being.
7. The theory is based on democratic principles wherein all persons are given equal chance to develop their skill.
8. The motivation, the potential for development, the capacity for assuming responsibility, the readiness to direct behaviour toward organizational goals are all present in people. Management does not put them there. It is responsibility of management to make it possible for people to recognise and develop these human characteristics for themselves.

9. The essential task of management is to arrange organizational conditions and methods of operations so that people can achieve their own goals best by directing their own efforts toward organizational objectives.

Theory Y, thus establishes cooperation between the man in authority and the man at work in achieving the objectives of the organization. The fact of interdependence in human organization is widely recognized. The theory is participative in the sense that supervisors consult their subordinates about proposed course of action before taking any decision. However, management still takes decision for the organization as a whole.

Theory Y: An Optimistic View

Theory Y reflects an optimistic view of human behaviour. According to this theory, work is an natural to people as play or rest. People's attitudes toward work depend on their previous job experiences and the conditions surrounding the work itself. If employees are able to understand and relate to an organization's goals, they will tend to be somewhat self-directed and will not need to be threatened or coerced into working. When given the proper encouragement, people will seek responsibility rather than avoid it; they will often exercise considerable imagination and creativity in carrying out their responsibilities.

Managers who accept Theory Y as valid are likely to try to understand what motivated their subordinates, and in turn become better motivated themselves. They are fulfilling their own need for self-expression and achievement as managers by discovering the needs of their employees. A healthy, two-way relationship can create a work climate in which employees want to give more. A Theory Y manager will make a continuing effort to stress how important employees' efforts are to the organization as a whole.

Support for Theory Y

One of the strongest supporters of Theory Y is Jay Hall, a social psychologist whose ideas helped trigger a dramatic turnaround at Ford Motor Company during the 1980s. In his books, The Competence Process and the Competence Connection, he drives home the point that within the great majority of workers there is a competence motive, that is, a need to demonstrate their competence. He says that workers have a personal need to perform well and that management should provide a positive work environment in which potential can blossom. Too often, he notes, we organize and manage as if workers were deficient.

Bill Moog President of Moog Inc., situated in New York, a company that manufactures electro-hydraulic control products, is someone who takes an optimistic view of his employees. When you join this company you receive an employee handbook that starts with the following statements: "Our philosophy at Moog is the simple one. We believe in the people who work for us. We believe work can be a more rewarding and satisfying experience for everyone in an atmosphere of mutual trust and confidence. This is a company without time clocks, a company that relies on each employee to report his or her performance. Moog does not have floor inspectors to check every product because employees are expected to check their own work." Theory Y seems to be alive and well at Moog Inc.

Applicability to Theory Y In India

Development of management in India is quite slow. The reason behind this is the unchanging attitude of employer and employee. Relationship of master and servant still persists between them. The development of trade unions in India is still in its infancy. So organizational behaviour in Indian industries is mainly based on the assumption of Theory X. Recently some headways have been made in this direction. Some statutory provisions regarding participative management, minimum wages, hours of work, etc. have been made by the government. In order to improve the working conditions, to bring about change in the mentality of the employers and the employees, government has provided certain facilities such as training institute for workers and managers so that they can be conversant with the modern management approaches.

Professional managers, unlike traditional managers have begun to accept the human values for the better management and repose their faith in workers' participation and profit sharing techniques. But some management still hesitate to accept the theory in full. Workers also are indifferent towards sharing the responsibility because they are inefficient and uneducated.

Thus, we can conclude that the assumptions of Theory Y have not been fully recognised by most of the management in India. We may hope that management will change its attitude towards labour and their human values which have so far been ignored.

Some Puzzling Questions

McGegor seems to have played a "very disturbing little joke", unwittingly, by drawing a sharp line of demarcation, between the two distinct perspectives of administrative action. One is equated with tradition and the other is identified with change. One is labelled as autocratic, control-centered and the other is glamorised as the epitome of democratic governance. The impression that one might get from the discussion is that managers who accept Theory X assumptions about human nature exhibit a built-in affinity for carrot and stick policies while Theory Y managers exhibit a built-in devotion to participative, behaviour-centred policies.

1. Which Theory is Right

According to Theory X man is weak, sick, and incapable of looking after himself. He is full fo fears, anxieties, neuroses, inhibitions etc. Essentially he does not want to achieve but wants to fail. He therefore, wants to be controlled. More dangerously it does not assume that people are lazy and resist work, but it assumes that the manager is healthy while everybody else is weak. It assumes that the manager knows while everybody else is ignorant. It assumes that the manager is intelligent and sincere, where everybody else is stupid and careless. These are nothing but "assumptions of foolish arrogance."

Now let us turn our attention to the so-called democratic theory based on the needs of man, addressed to his managerial brethren by McGregor in a persuasive, yet, forceful manner. Theory Y gives us an impression that everyone is mature, independent, and self-motivated. Most of the writers, no wonder, glamorised the vision of a so-called administrative democracy (simply because it is good). The rationale behind this observation, whatever is autocratic is 'bad' by definition. This may not hold good always. Sometimes, managers may have Theory Y assumptions about human nature, but they may find it necessary to behave in a very directive, controlling manner with some people in the short run to help them 'grow' up in a developmental sense, until they are truly people. One interesting question can be posed in this connection.

2. Is it Possible for a Theory X Person to become a Theory Y Person?

Probably yes, but only through "a fairly significant growth or development experiences over a period of time." Theory X places exclusive reliance on external control of human behaviour while Theory Y relies heavily on self-control and self-regulation. "This difference is the difference between treating people as children and treating them as mature adults. After generations of the former. We cannot expect to shift to the latter overnight." (McGregor)

3. Will a Theory Y Person be a Good Manager?

Theory Y person, no doubt, will have a greater potential for being a good manager, especially, at higher managerial jobs but he must have the relevant training and experience for this potential to become real. Theory X person might be more suitable in some crisis, situations, and less appropriate in more routine and formalised situation. The essential point is that Theory Y may be more desirable and productive path, reflecting 'a more reality centred view of people', to follow. It may not be the best approach for situation. The best approach, obviously, is one that is appropriate to the nature of the work done. Recognising this, MrGregor stated later that it was not his intention 'to suggest more than that these theories (Theory X and Theory Y) are examples of two among many managerial cosmologies.' For the present, let us say that under some conditions Theory X works best and under other conditions Theory Y works best. Perhaps, the optimum theory would be called Theory Z and it would take into consideration the manager's need to press into service both approaches at one time or the other.

Table 5. McGregor's Approach

	Theory X	Theory Y
	Production centered	Employee-centered
	AutocraticExternal Control	Democratic
		Internal control
A	Closer supervision	General supervision
	Initiating structure	Consideration
	Directive	Supportive
	Management's role :	
	Organizing and directing	Organizing and directing
B	Emphasis on control correction and punishment	Emphasis on growth, autonomy and reward
	view of human nature :	
C	People are lazy, lack ambition like to be led, and are motivated strictly by personal economic concerns.	People by nature enjoy work want to do well, and are motivated by self-control and self-development

Source : Adapted from T.R. Mitchell, People in Organizations : *Understanding their Behaviours*, New York, McGraw Hill, 1978, p. 158.

Beyond Theory Y: A Contingency Model

As pointed out by E.H. Schein, the problem with McGregor's theories is not that they describe no one, but they over generalise and oversimplify people as being one way or another, which seldom holds good. The framework squeezes all managerial styles and action philosophies into two extremes of conduct, appears to be quite biased and myopic. The two terms authoritative and participative are vague and can be understood only in a relative context. It would be unrealistic to think of them as being totally exclusive. Moreover, certain assumptions in Theory Y make it a stern task master. 'It has to achieve what Theory X achieved, and then do a good deal more or less, it will prove too great a burden and will make demands that human beings can't meet.' Recognizing these difficulties, Morse and Lorsch suggested a contingency theory which puts stress of organizing on a number of variables. The theory supports the idea that there is no one best way in which to organize. The design is conditional. The appropriate pattern of organization-task-fit is contingent upon 'the nature of the work to be done' and on the particular needs of the individual. There must not only be a fit between organization and task, but also between the organization and people, as well as between task and people.

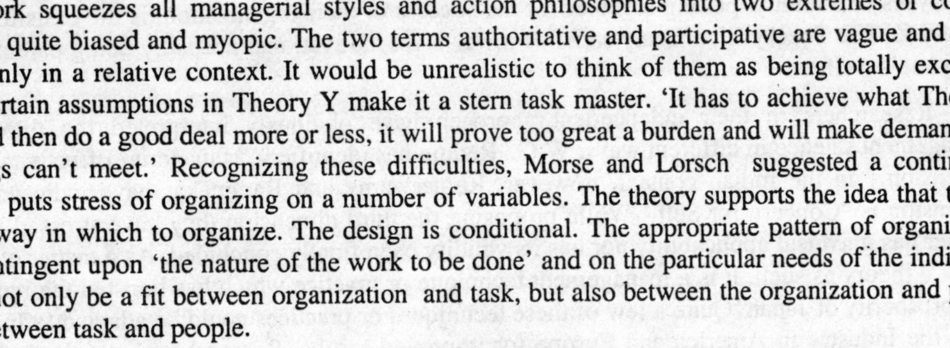

Fig. 14. Basic Contingent Relationships

A new set of assumptions are proposed supporting the contingency approach :

1) Human beings bring varying patterns of needs and motives into the organization but one central need is to achieve a sense of competence.

2) Competence motive exists in all human beings. Its fulfilment depends on how it interacts with the strengths of individuals' other needs (for power, independence, achievement, etc.)

3) Competence motivation is likely to be achieved when there is a fit between task and organization.
4) Competence motivation is a continuous feeling; once a new goal is fulfilled, a new higher one is set.

The interrelationship among task-organization-people complex but the best possibility for managerial action probably is in moulding the organization to fit the task and people.

Theory Z

In the field of management a Theory of Z has been propounded with a view to improving output of the employees of an organization. The latter 'Z' happens to be the last letter of the English alphabet.

Researchers have recommended a two-dimensional approach. One is the task-oriented approach or the aim of increasing or improving output, while the other is the employee-oriented approach, that is attaining the objective of securing the best out of workers and staff. These are the Theory 'X' and Theory 'Y' which together comprise the principles by which human behaviour can be regulated and determined. In the field of management science, it was considered that these theories are enough to explain human behaviour, but the third dimension is vital for giving management science a result-oriented potential. It is on account of this argument of logic that researchers evolved Theory 'Z.'

UCLA Management Professor William Ouchi has spent several years to studying the major corporations in Japan. He formulated Theory Z to describe characteristic common to certain successful Japanese and American companies. Organizations dedicated to this management style generally have a lifetime employment policy. Even when sales are down employees know they will not be laid off and thus have good reason to feel that their own long-term fate to be tied to the company's existence. Workers are likely to perform job tasks conscientiously and enthusiastically in order to achieve a perfect final profit. There is open communication, both vertically and horizontally, with complete trust among groups and individuals, because all employees have the same goal; for the betterment of the company. This sense of employees as a family, pulling together for the success of their organization, is the basis for the success of Theory Z. The Theory Z company satisfies lower-level motivational needs by being parental-looking after everyone's welfare.

Researchers in their independent approach have obviously interpreted the third dimension in management science in different ways. W.G. Reddin has identified "Managerial Effectiveness" as the third dimension. In the Indian context, however, Ramaswamy and Rangnekar have indicated that the third dimension is "Concern for Self.' While proposing the third dimension they have stressed that "Theory Z" neither has universal applicability nor has its validity been finally concluded. As a matter of fact. Theory Z, is not a theory as such. It is a management technique or practice which has boosted the industrial progress and prosperity of Japan. Quite a few of these techniques or practices could be adapted to Indian Industry or even the Industry in America and Europe for improved results. Researchers have, in their own way and approach, named the findings and conclusions of their study as Theory Z.

Theory Z aims at getting the best out of human nature which ranges between extreme good and extreme evil. The situation within this wide range has to be harnessed for the maximum good and once done it would help identify human behaviour which delivers the result. Man can easily be influenced or won over by reason. Social interaction is important in human behaviour and man easily responds to such conditions or objectivity of human behaviour.

It is not surprising that a number of researchers have evolved and labelled conclusions of their studies as Theory Z, but the most common amongst them happens to be that has been developed by Ouchi, based on Japanese management style.

A. Concept of Japanese Management Practice (Theory Z)

William G. Ouchi recommended several practices for Japan for adoptation in Japanese management practice in context with adaptation in the US. Ouchi first made a comparative study of American and Japanese management practices, analysed them and drew his conclusions finally which he felt would be useful for the Japanese management practice in context with America. These Practices are now being gradually introduced in Indian industry especially due to increased collaboration of several Indian

Industries with Japan like the Maruti Suzuki combine in the automobile industry and also on account of such collaborations in the Indian electronic industry.

Theory Z, also assumes that the best management involves workers at all levels. In Theory Z organizations, employees gain a psychological sense of belonging because all decisions are made in groups. In Japan, these groups may be as large as sixty to eighty people. It takes time to make final decisions with this process. Yet the advantage of this collective compromise is that once an agreement has been reached, no one in the group will try to sabotage it. Getting dozens of Indian executives to build a decision by collective compromise might tie an Indian company in knots. However, few American companies, for example, Intel Corporation has encouraged a collective approach by dividing employees into project teams; Procter & Gamble use partially self-governing work groups in some of its plants; and managers and employees at Hewlett Packard have kept worker turnover down during economic slumps by agreeing that all employees–not just those at lower levels– have to give up some working hours and privileges. Participating in decision making helps employees satisfy their higher level motivational needs may be valid to some extent but not universally true.

(i) Features of Theory Z

William Ouchi has identified five broad characteristics of Theory Z. He feels that by effectively operating these factors organizational efficiency in management could be achieved. They are: (1) Trust (2) Strong cooperation association or affiliation between the organization and its employees (3) Workers' or employees' participation or involvement in organizational matters (4) Absence of formal structure or abolition of compartmentalisation amongst employees and workers and (5) Role of leader or worker or employee groups as coordinator and faciliator of human efforts. Let us study these factors in some details:

(1) *Trust*

Ouchi is of the opinion that an atmosphere of trust and openness in an organization is the only way in which the employees can extend their cooperation. The trust in question is not a confined concept. It is a trust that cuts across status, salary structure and categories within the organization. Moreover, the trust should be mutual among workers, supervisors, work teams, groups, salaried categories, trade union, management and the government.

(2) *Strong Cooperation or Association between the Organization and Employees*

For strengthening the bonds or ties between organization and its employees, Ouchi has recommended stability in service. Stability in service would include lifetime employment, slowing down of the process of evaluation and promotion, stress on horizontal movement, reducing stagnation in service, planning for individual employees, encouragement of workers, employees and their groups and according recognition to groups' performance. Industrial management in Japan practises a traditional compensation plan formulated for age groups of employees irrespective of the nature of their work. Jobs are made interchangeable not according to salary structure but on the basis of job content and characteristics.

(3) *Workers' Participation or Employees' Involvement*

Increased workers' participation in management or the decision making process helps secure wholehearted involvement or cooperation of the employees. In this way, the employees voluntarily involve themselves in the overall activities of the organization. This involvement of the employees contributes materially towards the healthy performance of the organization. Workers' participation in management also makes them feel important. In this concept most of the decisions concerning the employees are taken jointly by the management in mutual consultation. The employees acquire confidence which makes them feel wanted and helps to reassure them that they are not being ignored in the activities of the organization. They begin to feel that they are part of the organization and help to give a positive slant to their psychology to the exclusion of their otherwise negative approach. They get inspired to contribute their best to the growth and development of the organization and work for its welfare and progress. Workers' participation in management, especially the decision-making process accords to them a sense of recognition for their contribution in the interest of the organization. It also helps to secure their commitment to the objectives of the organization and infuses in them a sense of dedication for accomplishing the best for the organization.

(4) *Absence of Formal Structure or Abolition of Compartmentalisation amongst Employees and Workers*

Under this head Theory Z stresses on group work or community culture, in which workers and employees pull together in a group rather than as individuals pulling apart. As a group, they share information and resources provided by their employment. The main objective is to help to develop a group spirit (team work) which is vital for the progress of the organization. The apparent organizational structure no longer remains visibly compartmentalised into employee groups or worker groups. Workers and employees get welded into a corporate body as a monolith and, obviously, with such a body the strength of the organization gets consolidated and becomes powerful. A rotation system of replacement governs the organization.

(5) *Role of Leader as Coordinator or Facilitator*

The leader's role under this principle is to coordinate the efforts of the work force. The leader while taking notice of the problems of the workers has to coordinate their activities towards the common welfare of the organization. For this purpose, the leader has to help workers and employees-to develop their skills, help induce a corporate culture for work and the tasks in hand promote a team spirit and to build up an atmosphere of mutual trust and confidence. The leader is not a super-worker or super-employee, but is a member or common functionary amongst the workers and employees as a group. The leader has to direct his energies and efforts for the setting up of a common canteen irrespective of status or hierarchy of personnel. The leader also induces and educates workers and employees to wear identical uniforms for work. The leader has to take all possible steps for abolition of class feelings or class distinctions or status segregation.

The manager of an organization is an important functionary. He has not merely to discharge his functions and duties but has to make concerted efforts at securing the support and cooperation of each and every section or workers and employees with whom he has a work relationship. Leadership qualities demand that he should not allow his status to act as a hindrance or as affront to his subordinates. He must be humble, tactful, farsighted, wise and inoffensive while dealing with his assistants or deputies and even workers and employees at the lowest rung of management. He must possess real leadership qualities or what is said of a Prime Minister in a ministry in a democratic set up as "he is the first amongst equals."

The Japanese system of management has demarcated the role of the management leader function wise as follows:

(1) Planning: In order to make long-term, meaningful and effective planning, the involvement of employees and workers in the decision making becomes joint decision making in actual practice. Moreover, participation of workers and employees in decision making helps to settle objectives, goals and course of action so as to make them acquire a mutual or common character. This ensures rapid implementation of tasks, easy accomplishment of work and sure achievement of targets of the organization.

(2) Organizational Function: The joint and collective character of organizational functioning, especially inducing collective accountability, helps the organization to shed its formal structure of compartments and sections. The management system under this practice becomes informal and excludes a common concern for all section of employees. This helps to develop a common work culture unifying all sections of workers and employees promoted an uniform philosophy and generated a healthy competition amongst various enterprises of an organization.

(3) Staffing Pattern: Under this principle staff is selected through campus interview or campus selection. Personnel policies under this head include slow promotion through ranks, employment is continued on long-term basis, long-term group performance is duly regarded, increments produce small differences or those given do not create disparities giving rise to hostility or animosity, besides providing the employees in service training for improving their skills and providing scope for development of their capabilities.

(4) Direction by Leader: The leader of the work force does not function as a super worker or a boss. He remains a part of the work force and an ordinary functionary discharging the responsibilities assigned to him. He is a part of the work team or a constituent of the employees as a corporate body. In other words, as in a democratic set-up, in the corporate body of a Prime Minister and his ministers, the Prime Minister is the first amongst equals, giving a direction to his ministerial team in the discharge of their duties and fulfilment of their responsibilities, while doing his own work with devotion. The members of the ministerial team are required to refer to the Prime Minister, whenever they need guidance or direction. The basic principle is open and effective communication which is an attribute to his leadership. We can say, the members of the work force under him do not hesitate nor feel diffident in consulting him in tackling problems. In fact, the two-way communication between the leader and team members is free and easy.

(5) Control System: Under Theory Z, as the stress is on group performance or coordinated group effort there is an inbuilt control mechanism. Communication being free and easy that are no secrets between the leader and his work team. Openness being the hallmark of the system, it is kept in order or controlled by peers in the set-up of the organization.

Criticism of Theory Z : Japanese management functions effectively and efficiently under Theory Z, but some experts feel that it is not applicable or feasible in Indian context.

In the Indian context, therefore, we can consider the following points:

(1) In the Indian context, lifetime employment is neither being practised nor is it considered as a feasible principle. The aspirations of the Indian workers and employees are on a different pattern. Association of affiliation of the workers or employees is not on the lifetime pattern. There is the rule of superannuation, that is the employee or the worker retires from service on attaining an assigned age. His relations with the organization end on retirement.

(2) Common culture or a unifying psychology is neither possible nor attainable because workers and employees are divided on the basis of caste, social taboos, customs and belief etc. They even differ in their food habits, dress, language, life pattern, social observances, religious faith, etc.

(3) Indian shareholders and investors may not be inclined to accept low returns on their money contributed in the purchase of shares or invested in the organization. They may not also decline to shoulder the burden of losses on their money during industrial strikes or on account of lay-off periods.

(4) In the Indian context, workers' or employees' participation in management has not yet acquired the status of industrial philosophy or industrial temper. The concept of involving employees or workers in the decision making process is somehow not yet welcome to the managerial hierarchy or the ownership apex of industrial organizations.

The Japanese system of industrial management is discussed above, it seems, is not suited to Indian conditions. The deep rooted Indian methods of solving industrial disputed or problems still lies gripped by traditional methods like wage-cuts, absenteeism deductions in pay-packets, disciplinary action for curbing trade union action, suspension, termination and removal from service. The labour law practices still recognize and perpetuate these methods through the process of conciliation, arbitration, bipartite and tripartite intervention and disposal of labour disputed in special courts, as the methods by which labour problems are being tackled in India.

Japanese Theory Z: Another View

Theory Z has received the maximum attention amidst all the contemporary motivation theories in organizational management literature. We have discussed certain aspects of this theory earlier, but we may once again examine it in a different context. In simple words, Theory Z is based on the concept that man's basic nature has both strength and weaknesses, likes and dislikes, preferences and aversions and a host of other elements that could be judiciously used, encouraged, exploited and motivated for producing the desired results. Theory Z, having a Japanese origin, comprises the modern and most useful management philosophy. This theory informs, educates and enlightens business managers how to maximise the use of human resources for the benefit of the organizations they head. Human resources in business enterprises and industrial organizations do deliver the goods for which they are paid salary or wages. But, the crucial aspect of Theory Z is how to improve the utility of the human resources in order to maximise the result quantum. Theory Z has acquired attention especially because Japan using it in industrial management has achieved notable success on many fronts. Organizational scientists using this theory have achieved phenomenal success. Scientists using this theory have achieved phenomenal success. On a comparative basis, Japan's productivity has been two to three times that of the USA during the past three decades or so. Workers and employees absenteeism in Japan has been significantly low with that in identical industrial and business units in America. In yet another parameter, the sense of organizational commitment in Japan is much more intense and high as the prevailing in America. Similarly, the turnover rate in Japan is two time higher than that in America.

Management experts finding a high degree of efficiency in industrial units of Japan analysed its management system and the result was the evolutions of Theory Z.

The analysis has revealed that there are three major reasons for the successful organization management of Japan. The Japanese system excels in technology, culture and the management system.

Analysts found that the latest technological equipment installed and being used in Japan, did not materially differ from the level of technology being used by other advanced nations. It therefore, became clear that the success and efficiency of organizations of Japan was something more than more technological perfection. On the other hand, regarding culture of workers in Japan, they did not possess traits or qualities materially different from that of the workers of American organizations. Thus, it is proved beyond doubt that technology and culture were not responsible for the success and productivity of Japanese organizations. Moreover, Japanese workers and employees are less individualistic and simultaneously more tolerant of excessive authority than their counterparts in America.

Behavioural analysts finally found on study that the success and efficiency of Japanese organizations was due to the better management system that was being practised in these organizations. The Japanese system of management in actual practice is so designed that it effectively integrates the individual workers and employees into the existence of the organizations in order to achieve high production and efficiency.

Behavioural scientists who have studied the management systems both of Japan and America have identified the basic differences between the two systems. While studying specially the "Industrial miracle" in Japan they have, in the ultimate analysis, propounded the principles comprised under Theory Z. Among other, William Ouchi and Alfred Jaetger have, after extensive study, propounded Theory Z based on a detailed examination of the Japanese and American systems of management.

It is somewhat surprising that while the concept of workers' or employees' participation in management is a fairly old one and while it found place in Western literature as well, it was translated into practice in Japan alone. In the Western industrial world and in industrial activity of developed nations as well as in India this principle was not put in action; it remained on paper only. It was Japan alone which implemented it and progressed materially to become a leader in high productivity and efficiency.

William Ouchi and Alfred Jaeger have identified seven major differences in the managerial systems of America and Japan as depicted in the following table. It would be worthwhile to examine and study these difference between the two systems of management of industrial units and companies.

(1) Period or Length of Employment

The length of employment of a worker or employee makes or unmakes his morale. The American and Japanese systems of organizational management differ materially in the length of employment. The length of employment implies the tenure of employment or determines the duration of employment.

The American system of management practices the high rates of turnover of employees. Workers in American organizations are not permanent, but transient in their tenures. They neither do therefore, possess a long-term loyalty to their work and assignment, nor do they have any long-term loyalty to their work group or employer. In the circumstances, therefore, the management aims at minimizing interdependence between takes and assignments. On the other hand, the specialized skill or a worker or expertise of an employee enables him to move or rather be shifted from one organization to another.

Table 6. Major Differences in the American and Japanese Management Systems

Variable	Type A	Type J	Type Z
Employment Decision making Responsibility Evaluation and Promotion	Short-term Individual Individual Rapid	Life time Consensual Collective Slow	Long-term Consensual Individual Slow
Control	Explicit and Formal	Implicit and Informal,	Implicit-informal with implicit for malised measures
Career paths	Specialized	Non-specialized	Moderately specialized
Concern	Segmented	Holistic	Holistic,, including family

Source : W.G. Ouchi and A.M. Jaeger, "Type Z Organizations; Stability in the Midst of Mobility", *Academy of Management Reviews*, Vol. 3, 1978, pp. 308-311.

The A-type organizations are different with regard to employment. In Z-type organizations stress is on long-term employment, which boosts up the moral of employees. In this system of management workers and employees get familiar with co- workers and colleagues and also with the working of the organization. Workers and employees get inspire and get integrated into the organization due to the expectation of getting the benefit of a long career in a single organization. The management of the organization, on its part, get the opportunity and can afford the time for investing money for developing a talent-bank within the organizational set-up. There are very few resignations by workers and employees get reassured because they know that their tenure of service is long being hired on a long-term basis. Long-term employment is, therefore, an important factor in Theory Z. Akin to marriage in which the husband-wife relationship bond is for a lifetime the worker-employee and employer relationship is in the nature of a permanent bond with the organization.

One notable aspect is the Z-type organization is that workers and employees are not hired or fired according to fluctuations in the business cycle. In other words, the Z-type organization does not fire workers or removes them from service if there is a slump or employees additional hands when there is a business boom. The Z-type organization makes adjustments in order to stabilise the labour force. Such adjustments realistic and imaginative like workers and employees on rolls are asked to work overtime instead of hiring additional hands from outside when there is a business boom, than the demand for the product increases. In case the workload becomes too heavy, the Z-type organization prefers to split the work load, give out part of it to outside sub-contractors instead of hiring or engaging additional workers or employees.

Similarly, when there is a slump in the market or the demand for a product goes down, the Z-type organization neither does undertake any anti-worker or anti-employee measures nor does it take to any anti-labour practice. The workers or employees are neither laid off nor retrenched, but the organization shortens the work week. The organization may even reduce the work-week to a 25-hour affair, so that every worker or employee shares the effects of the slump equally, including, at times reduced wages pro rata or commensurate with the shortened work hours. In this case no worker or employee stands to lose his job.

(2) *Decision Making Process*

The basic impact of the Z-type organization is that decisions in it are participative, while in the American-type organization they are individualistic. The participative decision-making in the Japanese-type or Z-type organization is dissimilar to the participative decision-making in the American type organization. In the American type organization participative decision-making is characterized by group meetings and discussions between superiors and subordinates. In the Japanese-type or Z-type organization the manager possess the problem to all members, namely workers and employees in the organization and undertakes informal discussions on the problem to all members, namely, workers and employees in the organization and undertakes informal discussions on the problem. When the entire work force is familiar with problem or proposal, then a formal request is made for taking a decision.

Thus, in the Japanese-type or Z-type organization the final decision does not imply any kind of agreement but is in the nature of a tacit agreement, that is, unwritten and implied, which includes the decision-input from individual workers or employees or work groups, who are likely to be affected by the decision.

There is yet another a vital or significant aspect in such decisions in the Japan-type or Z-type organizations. It is regarding the punishment meted out in case the decision proves to be wrong or is counter-productive. The Japanese-type or Z-type organizations do not condone the wrong decisions or those which prove to be counter productive. Heads to roll in such situations, but in a different way. The punishment meted out is more subtle and workers or employees are likely to be demoted to less prestigious units or positions. This kind of punishment has its healthy aspects as well. An employee or worker so punished is bound to make an introspection of his approach as to where it went against the interests of the organization. This increases the commitment of the worker of employee to the welfare and good for the organization and makes him more practical and constructively oriented for applying his mind and abilities at the next occasion of decision-making whenever it arises.

(3) *Responsibilities and Duties*

In the A-type or American type organization, workers and employees are fired and hired at will of the management. They come and go frequently because the workers and employees are required to shoulder responsibilities on an individual bias. In the Japanese-type or Z-type organization, the decisions being in the nature of collective responsibility, the workers or employees do not get hired or fired, but get collective punishment like demotion or transfer to another unit of the organization, they remain committed to the organization and put in re-doubled efforts for the achievement of the objectives of the organization.

(4) *Evaluation Promotion Process*

The evaluation-promotion process or onward mobility in the A type or American-type organization is much faster as compared with the Japanese type or Z-type organization. In the A-type organization the evaluation promotion process or exercise is undertaken frequently and the results are rapid. Promotions, therefore, are much more quick. Ambitious workers and employees can move up the ladder much more faster and frequently in the American type organization. And, if they find, the evaluation-promotion is slow or it falls of their expectations or ambitions, they can easily change their employer, bargaining for a better position if the new employer is a rival in business of the old organization or simply on the basis of his proven ability and capability secure a high position in the new organization.

In the Japanese type or Z-type organization because employment being a lifetime affair, upward mobility is rather slow. The evaluation-promotion process is neither frequent nor repetitive with the result that promotions come more on the basis of seniority rather than frequent evaluations and promotions as practised in the American-type or A-type organizations. This helps to promote and develop a psychology amongst workers and employees to remain faithfully dedicated to the Z-type organization and make them fully integrated into the culture of the organization.

(5) *Control Methods*

Under the American type organization the control exercised over workers and employees is formal, while in the Japanese type it is informal. The American type organization practises a formal control which may both be explicit or implicit, while the Japanese type organization exercises informal control or indirect control. The approach and psychology of the American and Japanese organization are entirely different.

The Japanese type organization in making appraisals of performance of its workers and employees takes a number of factors into account in addition to the existing level of performance. It would consider several factors amongst other personality traits, cooperation with co-workers, dedication to the objectives of the organization, besides the existing performance. Occasional mistakes by workers and employees are interpreted as lapses in the learning process. Even managers readily commit themselves to risk jobs or undertake uncertain task or shoulder undefined responsibilities, because they do not have to produce immediate results but are to be appraised in the span of the financial year. Thus Japanese type organization exercises informal or indirect control. Control methods in the American type or A-type organization is formal, that is, appraisals are made on the basis of rules, regulations, procedure, norms and prescribed methods.

(6) *Career Graph*

Career graphs in the American type or A-type organization are vertical, while in the Japanese type or Z-type organizations, they are horizontal. In other words, workers and employees in the American type or A-type organizations having specialised skills in one area or in more than one functional areas are given opportunities to achieve job specialization. This means they ascend the career path upwards, specialise in one or more than one skill and rise up the latter in their branch of speciality or expertise.

In the Japanese type or Z-type organization, the workers and employees are not kept confined to their specific area of specialisation; instead they are moved laterally to other fields of specialities or expertise. The lateral rotation of workers and employees imparts to their career graphs a horizontal character. The workers and employees are exposed to diversity in their jobs and skills so that their knowledge rather than expertise covers all aspects of activities of their organization. In the end result, workers and employees generally pursue non-specialized career paths.

(7) Concern and Care

It is important factor how an organization takes care or shows concern for its workers and employees. This concern and care can go a long way in getting the best out of workers and employees. In the American-type or A-type organization the worker or employee is important and valued only in the duration of his work-hours or duty-hours, because the philosophy is to evaluate work hours or duty hours against output.

In the Japanese-type or Z-type organization there is a general care and concern for the workers and employees. Such organizations practise the philosophy that the organizations have concern and care for the lifetime utility of the worker or employee as they are on lifetime employment. This approach therefore is exhibited by the concern which the organizations has for the total personal life of the worker or employee.

The major strategy of the Japanese organization is to implement the process of socialisation which helps to infuse the philosophy of the organization into every worker and employee. On appointment, every worker and employee is subjected to a training programme extending from six to eight months. Against the American pattern, the Japanese employee is given training which enables him to socialize with co-workers and co-employees, with the result that the entire corporate body of workers and employees get integrated and committed to the philosophy, approach, temper and the style of functioning of the organization. The skills or expertise of the Japanese worker or employee are secondary. The primary goal is to make the workers and employees get in tune with the spirit of the organization. When workers and employees have no fear of being sacked or removed from service because of their lifetime engagement, they will be readily willing to contribute something to cater to the objectives of the organization, even if their skill or expertise becomes obsolete or outdated. The worker or the employee in the Japanese organization becomes a typical "organization man."

In brief while the Japanese type or Z-type organization retains the individualistic culture of the American type organization. Yet it includes in its style or functioning the collective approach in decision-making. In the same way, explicit or formal control through rules and regulations are retained, while the implicit methods or informal concept of social control are included. Moreover, in the Japanese type or Z-type organization career graphs or paths are moderately specialized, that is, the American pattern of imparting skills and expertise to workers and employees enabling them to climb to promotions vertically upwards are not available to the worker or employee in the Japanese pattern. It might be recalled that in the Japanese-type or Z-type organization, workers and employees are given an exposure in all sections of jobs and assignments or in all activities or the organizations, so that they pursue non-specialised career paths, or move horizontally in the organization. Finally, evaluations are slower, promotions are also slow and long-term employment, that is, lifetime employment, includes a comprehensive concern for the welfare of workers and employees, which includes the care and attention which the Japanese organizations shows for the families of the workers and the employees. The sum total of these factors or the implementation of these aspects put together provides the pattern for Theory Z philosophy and approach.

B. Theory Z Concept – Indian Context

In 1972, Ramaswamy and Rangnekar propounded a fresh Theory Z that may be applied to Indian conditions. They recommended a new co-ordinate for Indian conditions, namely, "Concern for Self", which they termed as the third dimension in order to impart to the new Indian Theory Z a solid form, Rangnekar has outlined nine different management patterns, which exist in Indian conditions. The patterns in Indian industrial management can be indicated by labels which denote the effect which they produce. These are:

(1) Sleepy
(2) Politician
(3) Crazy
(4) Foolish or Absurd
(5) Buffer
(6) Ruthless
(7) Group-Maker
(8) Jolly
(9) Indian Ideal

According to S.S. Rangnekar, his Theory Z in the last concept, namely, the "The Ideal Indian" refers to that kind of manager who secures a high level performance and output from the industrial unit's workers and employees which is in tune with the objectives of the organization but, at the same time, maintains a continual liaison and communication with the top management in order to ensure that he is not deprived of the credit by the organization's politicians. In other words, the manager all the time concentrates on the projection of himself, or a "concern for self", that is, on WHIIFM (What's in it for me) factor. This, however, represents only the managerial patterns and behaviour in the Indian backdrop and context and the industrial conditions that prevail in Indian industrial units.

C. Lyndall F. Urwick's Theory Z

There are certain contradictory assumptions in Theory Z and Theory Y as developed by MgGregor. Criticizing this phenomenon Lyndall F. Urwick has proposed another theory of human behaviour at work place which he named Theory Z. In developing the theory Urwick was of the view that the primary task of every manager is to produce and distribute goods or services at prices which the consumers are able and willing to pay. And he should direct the efforts of all those who associate with him towards this end.

Propositions

L.F. Urwick proposed Theory Z, Suggests that every manager should attempt to produce or distribute goods or services at a price which the consumer is able and willing to pay and he showed direct the efforts of all the persons towards that end. In this context, he has given several propositions along with, the model operates:

In his efforts Urwick stresses that a manager should: (i) make the workers know, the organization goals and the contribution of their efforts towards that end; (ii) assure the workers needs would be satisfied in full. The theory has the following eight specific propositions:

1. Management is responsible for organising the various elements of productive enterprise–money, materials, machines and men–in the interest of economic end.
2. Economic ends in a free society are determined by the choices of innumerable individuals known as consumers.

3. This involves a network of decisions and communications through which management postulate leadership.
4. Management groups the choices of consumers as: (a) to facilitate economic production and distribution of goods and services; and (b) to enable these people in their capacity as producers and distributors of the goods and services, to satisfy their needs.
5. In a handicrafts economy, the consumer contacts direct with the producer as shown along the dotted line Zc-Zpd in figure given below. But in modern machine economy, there are eight points at which consumer are to move. The Consumer choices may be misinterpreted in terms of producer/ distributor needs. Consumer has to move from point to point all around Z instead of direct to producer from Zc to Zpd.

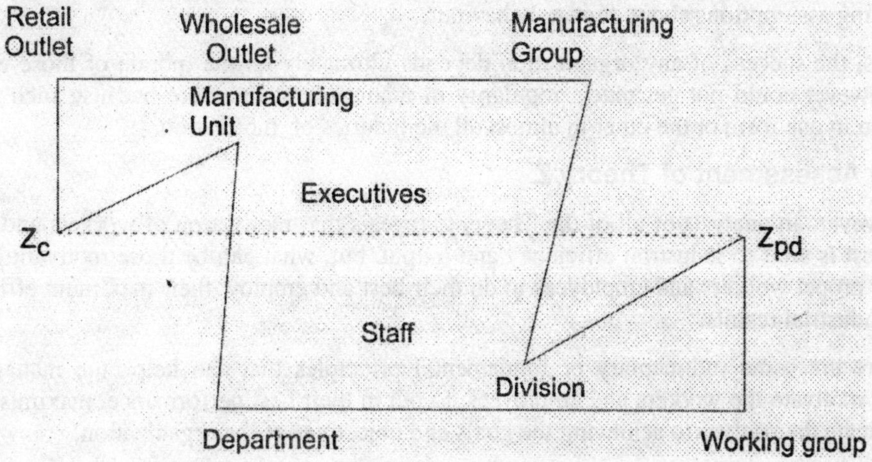

Fig. 15. Theory Z Model (Adopted from Urwick)

6. Man as a consumer insists that he requires the latest products of science and technology. So, he seeks change because there are always new developments in science and technology.
7. Man, as a producer, or distributor, is not resistant to organization needs but change threatens his human needs if he suggests :
   (a) loss of employment, his physical and safety needs are affected.
   (b) change of working patterns, his social needs will remain unsatisfied.
   (c) elimination of position to which he may have aspired, his egoistic and self-realisation needs remain unfulfilled.
8. Management can overcome these difficulties of complex communication by improving the morale of workers. This involves:
   (a) discipline, i.e., the system of communication is precise and accepted by all concerned;
   (b) confidence, i.e., each individual is confident that the organization will be benefited, so it safeguards his needs.

Assessment of Urwick's Theory Z

The following points are noteworthy in assessing this proposed Theory Z:

(i) The analysis of above propositions of Theory Z suggest that the human behaviour in economic undertakings is best expressed by the symbol Z and not by symbol X or Y. The whole economic process consists in relating the behaviour of the individual consumer at top left hand corner of the Z(Zc) to the behaviour of the same individual as a producer of distributor at the bottom right hand corner of the Z (Zpd). In between these two arms, and the diagonal of Z, representing a whole network of intermediate decisions involved in translating the behaviour Z into behaviour of the same individual as Zp or Zd.

(ii) Urwick has also indicated that the behaviour of the individual can be directed towards the achievement of organization goals under two conditions:

(a) Each individual should be aware of the organizational goal precisely and the contribution which his attempts are making towards achieving such goals.

(b) Each individual should also feel confident that the realisation of organizational goals will affect his needs positively and none of his needs will be threatened or frustrated or suppressed by accepting the membership of the organization.

(iii) Theory Z takes into account the organizational variables in shaping the behaviour of individuals. Thus a particular individual will behave differently in different organizational conditions. From this point of view, theory presents a more realistic picture of human behaviour in the organization rather than making assumptions about human behaviour.

Thus, the success of any organization depends ultimately on the morale of those engaged in it. The theory however could not get much popularity in management literature because such propositions have been given in one form or the other in almost all the theories of motivation.

General Assessment of Theory Z

However, an analysis of all of the Theory Z reveals that motivation of workers and employees to put in their best is vital to industrial efficiency and output. but, what can be those motivating factors that can inspire or propel workers and employees to do their best and employ their maximum efficiency to produce the best industrial results.

There are some rudimentary or fundamental principles that can help the manager to encourage, inspire or motivate the workers and employees to put in their best performance, maximise their efforts and help dedicate themselves to achieving the goals and objectives of the organization.

We can outline some broad principles on which a manager can motivate workers and employees to put in their best, maximise production and achieve the desired goals and objectives.

(1) *Participation Principle*: This principle is based on the concept of making the workers or employees feel important by giving them an opportunity of participating in decision-making which has direct relationship with the results they achieve. The workers and employees, according to this tenet are made to feel that they are wanted and significant in the achievement of results. Participation implies consultation with subordinates, including both workers and employees in matters related to the discharge of their duties and responsibilities connected with their jobs and assignments. It may be noted Motivation to accomplish results tends to increase as people are given opportunity to participate in the decisions affecting those results.

(2) *Recognition Principle*: Recognition for work done or for results achieved helps to further motivate workers and employees to put in their best in future tasks and assignments. According to this principle: "Motivation to accomplish results tends to increase as people are given recognition for their contribution to those results." Recognition for work, in other words, is giving his due to the achiever of results, which is a human weakness. Once recognition is given for results, the workers and employees are infused with the feeling that they have a role to play, are a class which is considered consequential in the results or simply implies that the workers and employees are given "self-importance."

(3) *The Principle of Delegated Authority*: This principle is based on the concept that the person given the authority through delegation of powers, begins to feel consequential and important in decision-making or in result achievement. According to this principle "Motivation to accomplish results tends to increase as people are given authority to make decisions affecting those results. Delegation of power or authority to workers or employees makes them feel import in the organizational set-up, in the achievement of results and in the attainment of objectives of the organization."

(4) *Principle of Communication*: Lack of Communication between the managerial setup and the workers and employees, makes the latter feel neglected or unwanted. According to this principle

"Motivation to accomplish results tends to increase as people are informed about matters affecting those results."

Process Theories

All these three above content theories stressed on the needs in the process of motivation. These scholars paid attention to the existence of these needs and held them responsible in instituting the motivational cycle. Content theories were basically based on three assumptions that : (1) all employees are alike; (2) all situations are alike and (3) there is only one best method to motivate employees, i.e., satisfying needs. Contrary to the content theory assumptions, a number of other theories have been developed after extensive study and empirical evidences. The approach has been classified under process theories, that view motivation as an individual's decision to act so as to put forth some given level of effort. Three theories, namely Vroom's Expectancy Model, Adam's Equity Theory and Porter's Performance Satisfaction Model are distinct.

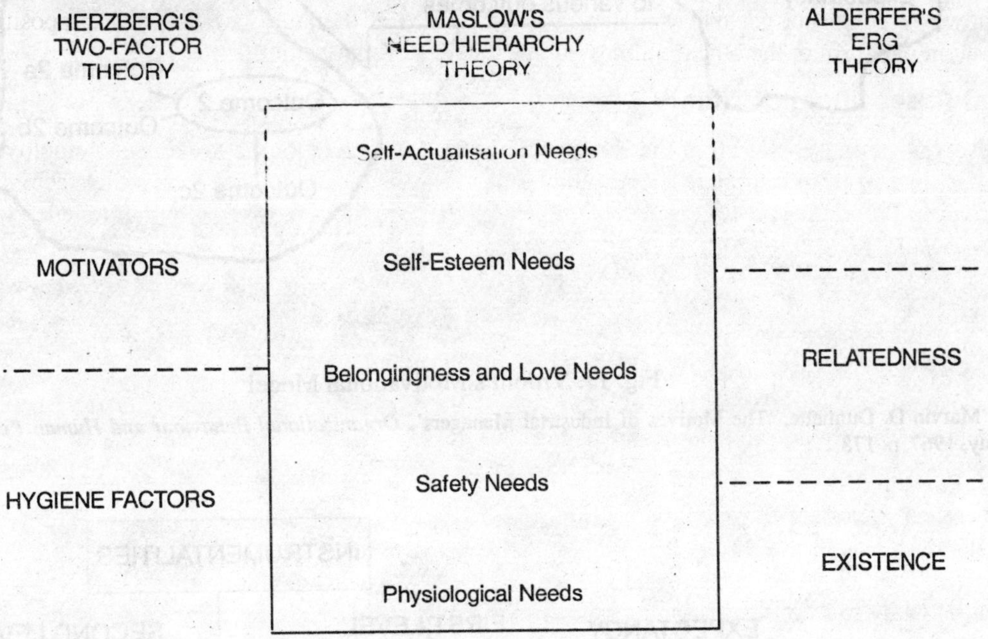

Fig. 16. Relationalship Among Content Theories

Vroom's Expectancy Theory

In 1964, Victor Vroom made a significant contribution to our understanding of motivation through his Expectancy Theory, though it has its critics, most of the research evidence supports this theory.

Vroom's expectancy theory can be classified as a process theory in contrast to the content theory primarily because it attempts to identify relationships among variable in a dynamic state as they effect individual behaviour. This systems orientation is in direct contrast to the content theories which have attempted largely to specify correlates of motivated behaviour. In the expectancy theory, it is the relationship among inputs that is the basic focal point rather than the inputs themselves.

Vroom has developed his motivation model around the concepts of value, expectancy and force. His basic assumption is "the choice made by a person among alternative course of action is lawfully related to psychological events occurring contemporaneously with the behaviour". In this theory the concept of force is equivalent to motivation and can be shown as the algebraic sum of the products of valences multiplied by expectancies. According to Vroom:

Motivation (Force) = Valency X Expectancy

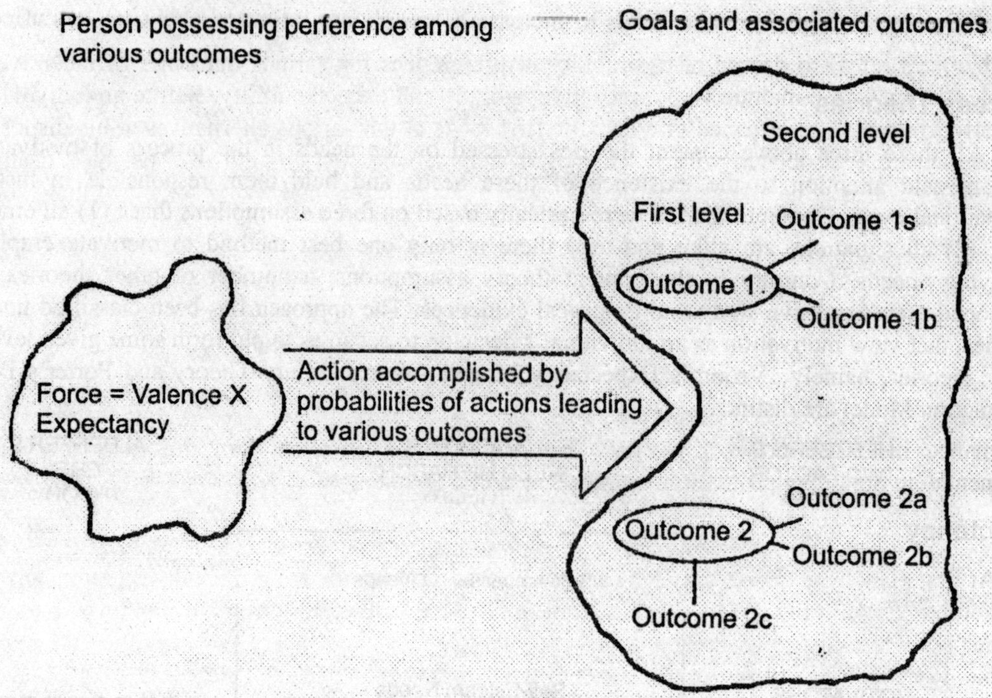

Fig. 17. Vroom's Motivational Model

Source : Marvin D. Dunnette, 'The Motives of Industrial Managers', *Organizational Behaviour and Human Performance*, May, 1967, p. 178.

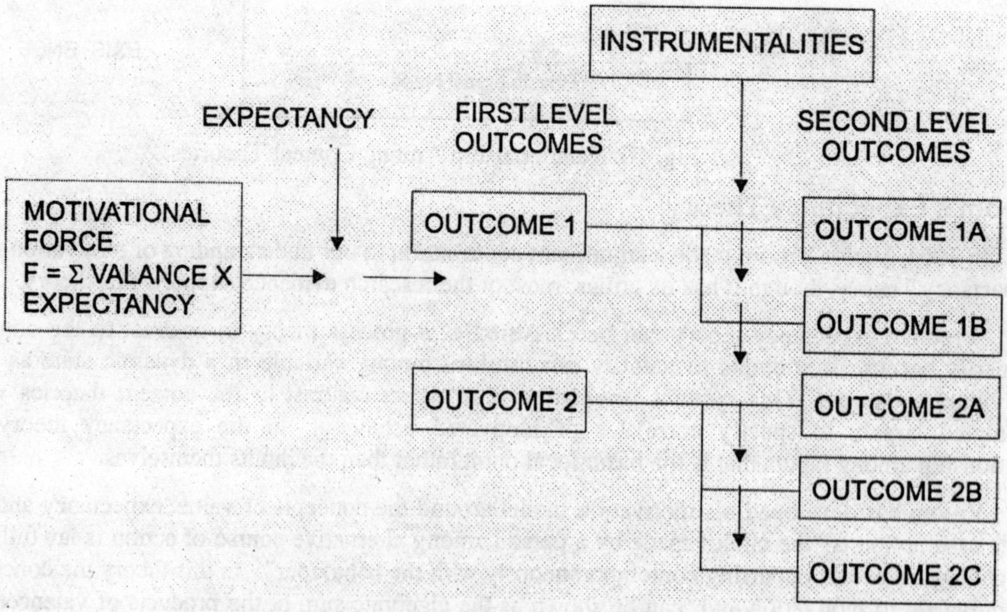

Fig. 18. Vroom's VIE Theory of Motivation

Source: Fred Luthans, *Orgarnizational Behaviour*, McGraw Hill, New York, 1989, p. 247.

The three terms referred by Vroom in his model (Fig. 18) are analysed below:

Valency

This term refers to degree of desirability or preferences for various outcomes or incentives that are available to him. These include value, incentive, attitude and expected utility. Before an individual decides to put effort into the performance of a task, he first looks at the various alternatives at his disposal and the outcome (rewards) associated with it. Hence, valency reflects the strength of a person's desires for the attraction to rewards, if he adopts a particular cause of action. Hunt and Will also opined that valency is the strength of an individual's desire for a particular outcome and it is the subjective value attached to an incentive or reward. To clarify concept they have taken the example of promotion. Assume that an individual wishes for a promotion in his organization and feels that if his performance is superior to others, it will be a positive factor for him in achieving the promotion. His first level outcomes are therefore superior, average or poor performance and his second level outcome is promotion. The individuals first level outcome, i.e., high performance acquires a positive valency by virtue of the expected relationship to the preferred second level outcome of promotion. Thus the individual would be motivated to give superior performance in order to get promoted. The superior performance, i.e., the first level outcome is instrumental in obtaining promotion, i.e., the second level outcome.

Expectancy

At first glance the expectancy may seem to be the same as the instrumentality input valence, but they are different. "Expectancy differs from instrumentality in that it relates efforts to first level outcomes where instrumentality relates second-level outcomes to each other." Since expectancy is rated as the probability of connection between effort and performance, its value ranges between O and 1. If an individual sees no chance that effort will help him to achieve the desired performance level, the expectancy is O. On the other hand, if he is confident that the task will be completed and he will achieve the desired performance level, the expectancy value assigned is 1. Thus, the expectancy of an individual will lie between these two extremes, i.e., O to 1. Hence, we can say, in order that motivation takes place, the expectancy must also be high like valence.

Expectancy = Efforts to First Level Outcomes.

(The belief that efforts lead to performance)

Instrumentality

Instrumentality refers to the outcomes (rewards) for the individual for each level of job performance (expectancy). It helps to answer such questions, 'will I be rewarded if I perform the job well?" Instrumentality is probabilities attached by an individual to each possible performance-outcome alternatives as he previously assigned probabilities to various levels of effort leading to different levels of performance. In the example given earlier, instrumentality refers to the person's perception of the relationship between high performance (first level outcome) and promotion (second level outcome). Thus perceived instrumentality is a subjective feeling, if an individual perceives that this performance is suitably rewarded the perceived instrumentality will be positive. On the other hand, if he perceives that the performance will make no difference to the rewards, the instrumentality will be low. Think of your own decision-making process on how much effort you put into studies for an examination or writing a term-paper. And you get the answer based on Vroom's model of motivation.

Vroom's theory is very popular in academic sphere and has generated considerable research because it attempts in understanding organizational behaviour in a wider perspective. This theory recognises the complexities of work motivation, but it is relatively difficult to comprehend and apply in practice. Thus Vroom's theory does not give a manager practical help in solving problems related to motivation.

Adam's Equity Theory

This theory was advocated by Stacy Adam in 1963. The concept of equity stipulates that justice and fairness should prevail. In other words, as the theory name suggests, the equity theory is based on the basic assumption that an individual can be motivated by his desire to be equitably treated in his work relationship. The process of deciding whether there is equity, involves social comparison by organizational members. Let us consider an exampl :

Mr. Prashant obtained his postgraduation in Management with specialisation in marketing management from one of the Institutes of Management located in the northern part of India. He gladly accepted the position with a multinational concern after facing a rigorous selection process. He was posted as a middle level executive with a starting salary of Rs.10,000 p.m. He was very happy that, besides the lucrative salary, he has bright prospects ahead of him. He was the highest paid recruit of the company in that year. He was also much satisfied with the challenges involved in the task assigned to him in the company. As a student, he had been rated as one of the most brilliant students. He was ambitious and articulate and this assignment came as a climax in his career.

He completed one year of his tenure in the organization and, besides earning a normal increment of Rs. 500 p.m., he was given a special increment of Rs.1,000 p.m. in recognition of his exemplary performance. However, during the last few days, it was noticed that his motivation dropped considerably. Why? Because the company had just recruited a fresh management graduate Mr. Prabhakar who obtained his MBA degree recently from a state University. Prabhakar was offered a starting salary of Rs. 12,000 p.m., Rs.500 more than what Prashant was getting at present. Now Prashant was thinking seriously of even quitting the company and getting a job elsewhere.

Prashant's situation can be explained with the help of Equity theory of motivation. An employee compares his job in posts and outcomes with those of others and then responds with a view to eliminating the inequities. Prashant got anxious and restless the moment he perceived that he was being discriminated in comparison with Prabhakar. If Prashant had perceived his ratio to be equal to that of Prabhakar with whom he compared himself, it can be said that a state of equity exists.

Thus it is evident that Adam's Equity Theory bases itself on the following two basic assumptions relating to human behaviour:

1. Individuals when make contributions (inputs), they expect certain rewards (outcomes). Inputs are in the form of experience, past training. specialized knowledge and skill, personal characteristics etc. Outcomes are in the form of recognition, prestige, pay, perks, promotion, fringe benefits, etc.
2. Individuals themselves take decisions whether or not a particular exchange is satisfactory. This is done by comparing their inputs and outcomes to those of others in the form of ratio. If an individual thinks that his input/outcome ratio of other person, with whom he has compared himself, the equity exists.

Thus, it is clear that the referent chosen by an individual is an important variable in equity theory. If the referent selected is a perceived equity or fairness, all is fine. However, if inequity is perceived, then the person feels unhappy, distressed and uncomfortable since what an individual thinks is equitable, and what has actually happened is at variance. This cognitive dissonance or uncomfortableness or restlessness and the agitation in the individual's mind propel him to take some action. This felt inequity motivates or moves people to take action. Hence flit is a motivator. In order to comprehend motivation as a function of felt inequity, the four terms are important :

1. Person : An individual for whom equity or inequity exists.
2. Inputs : Individual's characteristics, i.e., self inside, such as education, experience, skills, etc. However, these are subjectively perceived by an individual.
3. Outcomes : Salary, Promotion, Perks, etc. are also subjectively perceived.
4. Others : Any group or individual taken by an individual as a referent regarding inputs and outputs and compares himself.

Inequity can Exist Under two Circumstances

(1) When an individual feels that in comparison, he suffers a negative inequity, such as, he is being rewarded less for his efforts or performance than another.

(2) When an individual experiences a positive inequity, such as, on comparing he finds himself rewarded more than the other for a similar degree of effort or performance.

However, both the types of inequities result in cognitive dissonance or internal tension and propel an individual to action in order to reduce his cognitive dissonance.

The three situations, positive and negative inequities and equity, can be represented as in Table 5 and 6.

Table 7. Perception, Ratio Comparison, and its Reason

Perception	Ratio Comparison			Reason
Positive Inequity	$\frac{\text{Person's Outcomes}}{\text{Person's Inputs}}$	>	$\frac{\text{Other's Outcomes}}{\text{Other's Inputs}}$	Over rewarded
Negative Inequity	$\frac{\text{Person's Outcomes}}{\text{Person's Inputs}}$	<	$\frac{\text{Other's Outcomes}}{\text{Other's Inputs}}$	Under rewarded
Equity	$\frac{\text{Person's Outcomes}}{\text{Person's Inputs}}$	=	$\frac{\text{Other's Outcomes}}{\text{Other's Inputs}}$	Same reward

Table 8. Perception, Symbolic Representation and its Reasons

Perception	Symbolic Representation			Reason
Positive Inequity	$\frac{O}{I}$	>	$\frac{Oo}{Io}$	Over rewarded
Negative Inequity	$\frac{O}{I}$	<	$\frac{Oo}{Io}$	Under rewarded
Equity	$\frac{O}{I}$	=	$\frac{Oo}{Io}$	Same reward

Where : O represents — person's Outcomes
I represents — person's Inputs
Co represents — other's Outcomes
Io represents — other's Inputs

Thus, the intrinsic nature of equity theory presupposes itself on the basic question put forth by an individual before future efforts made by him in performing a task is, "Am I being fairly rewarded for my efforts in comparison to others, who are in a similar position in my organization?"

On the basis of equity theory, Adam suggested that an individual may try a number of alternatives in order to reduce the perceived inequity. He has at least the following six alternatives:

1. Change his inputs, i.e., efforts. The individual who feels that he is underpaid for his efforts does not exert as much as he is doing. And the individual who feels that he is overpaid might increase his effort (probably in order to maintain his over payment).
2. Alter his outcomes or rewards. Individuals paid on piece-rate basis might increase their production to earn more (no even if matter the quality of product deteriorates).
3. Distorting his inputs and outcomes cognitively. For example, the individual might begin to think and believe that either his inputs were not as great as should have been, or that the rewards received were moderate.

4. Try to influence the other individual, with whom he compares himself to reduce inputs. Like in office when a pen-down strike is on and one or two people do not follow the union call for pen-down strike. The informal leader of the union generally tries to influence such people to join the strike call.
5. Might quit the job or might come late or remain frequently absent.
6. Choose a different referent, i.e., might change the level of comparison. For example, he might take the situation this way, "I may not be as good as my brother, but definitely I am far better than my cousin, when he was at my age."

Inequity Resolution Strategy

Kamlesh and Alok are two computer operators in two different divisions of the same organization. Kamlesh's salary is Rs. 3000 per month and Alok is paid only 2700 per month. One day they happen to meet at their common friend's house and discover his discrimination in their salary. According to Equity theory, both Kamlesh and Alok will feel upset by this discrimination (inequity). Kamlesh will feel perturbed for being paid more than Alok. Alok will resent this underpayment and will feel frustrated. At this point of time, the basic question arises as to how to bring equity in their relationship? Now, Kamlesh can perform better or do more work than Alok and Alok can do poorer or less work in order to equalise their ratios. This method is known as 'Behavioural inequity resolution strategy.'

There can also be psychological inequity resolution strategy. Both, Kamlesh and Alok may convince themselves that Kamlesh is a real hard worker and performs better than Alok. Generally, inequitably paid employees convince themselves that they are actually not working that hard as compared to their other colleagues. Thus they try to establish equity between themselves and equitably paid employees. Therefore, in order to restore equity, the person may alter the inputs or outcomes, cognitively distorts the inputs or outcomes, change the other or leave the field.

Another technique to lower one's inputs is to remain absent from duty. Kamlesh and Alok can also make efforts to adjust their outcomes to resolve the inequity. There can be two alternatives, either Kamlesh refuses the hike in his salary or Alok demands for a raise. There also exists a possibility, that Alok may work for others against attractive salary or do overtime in an attempt to raise his outcomes. If Kamlesh lowers his outcomes and Alok raises his they are able to equalise their ratio. This ratio equalisation will help to establish a fair relationship. The other alternative may be that they decide to quit and get out of the relationship completely. Seeking a transfer, absenteeism or leaving the job are common forms for leaving the field.

Poeter's Performance Model

Lyman Porter and Edward Lawler in 1968 came up with comprehensive theory of motivation combining the various theories that have been so far discussed, but a more refinement to that of Vroom's model. This theory is largely based upon an expectancy theory of motivation. Porter and Lawler themselves explain their choice for the expectancy approach as follows:

"The emphasis in expectancy theory on rationality and expectations seems to us to describe best the kinds of cognitions that influence managerial performance. We assume that managers operate on the basis of some sort of expectancies which, although based upon previous experience, are forward-oriented in a way that does not seem to be as easily handled by the concept of habit strength.'

Elaborating further Lawler in 1971, stated that expectancy provides the theoretical foundations but, especially in more recent refinements, the model incorporates much than is found in traditional expectancy theories, and past learning still plays vital role.

The complex relationship among motivation, satisfaction and performance is shown in Fig. 19.

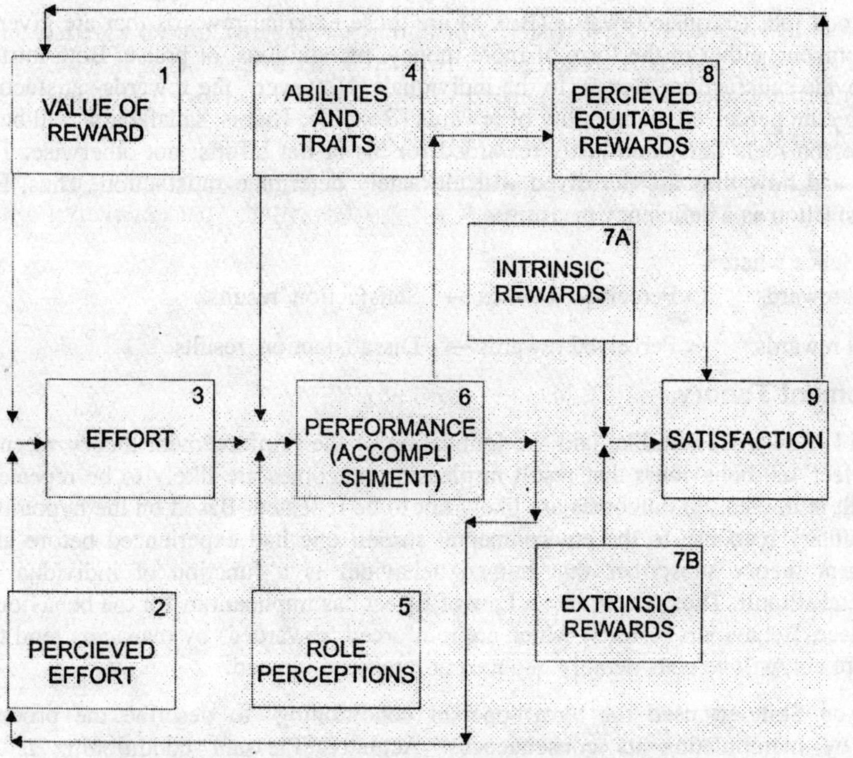

Fig. 19. The Porter and Lawler Model of Motivation

The model indicates that people first try to figure out whether the rewards that are likely to be received from doing a job will be attractive or valued to them (Box 1). For a person who is looking for more money, extra vacation time may not be an attractive reward. If the reward to be obtained is attractive or valued, the individuals will decide to put in the necessary effort, they will also try to assess the probability of certain level of effort leading to a desired level of performance, and the probability of that performance leading to certain kinds of rewards (Box 2). Based on the valence of the reward, and the effort reward-probability, people then decide to put in a certain level of work effort (Box 3). The effort put in will lead to the expected level of performance (Box 4) only if the individual has the requisite abilities and traits to perform the job (Box 5). Abilities include job knowledge, skills, and intellectual capacity to perform the job. Traits such as endurance, perseverance, and goal-directedness are also important for many jobs. If these are absent, the effort put in will not lead to the desired level of performance. Thus, abilities and traits will moderate the effort-performance relationship. In other words, only those who have the requisite abilities and traits will perform the job well when they put forth the effort; the others will not.

In addition, the individual performing the job should also have accurate role perceptions (Box 6). Role perception refers to the way in which people define their jobs. We often hear managers say that job is what the employee makes of it. Some people may take additional responsibilities and expand the scope of their job. Others may avoid some aspects of their job and hence narrow its scope. Thus people may perceive their roles (job behaviour) differently. The accuracy of role perceptions is another variable that moderates the effort-performance relationship. That is, only those who perceive their role as it is defined by the organization will be able to perform well when they put forth the requisite effort. For instance, a machinist who has recently been promoted as a supervisor will not be able to effectively get the job done through others, if he still changes on to his former role as a machinist and get the job done through them so that the production level in his department goes up. However, if he still expands all his efforts in doing the job himself, he is going to be an effective supervisor and his performance (as a supervisor) will be poor despite relationship between effort and the performance.

Performance leads to certain outcomes in the shape of intrinsic and extrinsic rewards. Intrinsic rewards (Box 7) are those feelings of joy, self-esteem, and sense of competence that individuals feel when they do a good job. Extrinsic rewards (Box 8) are those external rewards that are given by others in the work environment, either in the form of more money, recognitions, or praise. Both intrinsic and extrinsic rewards provide satisfaction (Box 9) to the individuals. However, the rewards-satisfaction relationship is moderated by the perceived equitability of rewards (Box 10). That is, satisfaction will be experienced only when the person feels fairly and justly rewarded for his or her efforts; not otherwise. Therefore, rewards that follow and how they are perceived will ultimately determine satisfaction. Thus, Porter and Lawler viewed satisfaction as a deficiency measure.

Hence where:

Actual rewards > Perceived rewards → Satisfaction results.

Actual rewards < Perceived rewards → Dissatisfaction results.

Reinforcement Theory

In 1911, Edward Thorndike laid the foundation of the reinforcement theory when he explained the 'Law of Effect' as, behaviours that result in pleasing outcomes are likely to be repeated and behaviours which result in unpleasant outcomes are likely not to be repeated. Based on the hypothesis that behaviour is an involuntary response to the environmental stimuli one had experienced before and is a cognitive. Reinforcement theory subscribes that human behaviour is a function of individual responses to the environmental stimuli. Thus, Thorndike's Law of Effect has implications for the behaviour of employees at the work place. Behaviours (efforts) which are reinforced (rewarded) by managers tend to be repeated and those that are not, will be considerably reduced or totally eliminated.

Later on Skinner, used the term 'operant conditioning' to describe the process of controlling behaviour by manipulating its consequences. Actually, Pleasant conditioning is learning through reinforcement. We have discussed all these aspects at length in the chapter on Learning.

Skinner coined the word 'Operant Conditioning' with respect to shaping the behaviour of animals. However, when the operant conditioning techniques are used to control the human behaviour, as opposed to animals, the term behaviour modification is used.

Organizational behaviour modification or OB MOD, as it is commonly referred to, is the systematic reinforcement or strengthening of desirable behaviours of employees and non-reinforce-exhibited by organizational members.

For basic techniques of reinforcement can be employed for behaviour modification. These are: Positive Reinforcement, Negative Reinforcement, Punishment, and Extinction. In addition to these, shaping, a method of introducing new desired behaviour in an individual, is also a technique based on reinforcement theory.

Positive Reinforcement

A positive reinforcer is one that strengthens association between a stimulus and a response. For instance, the manager pat on the back of an employee in recognition, who handled a tough customer tactfully. Thus, positive reinforcement involves rewarding a desired behaviour, with some type of recognition, which makes the employee happy, elevated and encourages him to repeat the same behaviour.

Negative Reinforcement

A negative reinforcer also strengthens the association between stimulus and response, but it does so by its termination rather than by its presentation. For example, a worker who was reprimanded by his supervisor for the last two days for not coming in time was not scolded the third day, when he attended to his duties in time. In this case something which was aversive or noxious to the employees was not enforced (withheld), may be to avoid unpleasantness in future. Because of this, the employee will try to exhibit the desired work behaviours. Hence negative reinforcement is closely related to punishment. The difference between negative reinforcement and punishment is that in the latter case, a noxious (harmful) consequence is applied to decrease the frequency or strength of an undesired behaviour, whereas in the former case (negative reinforcement) the harmful consequence is withheld when a desire behaviour is exhibited.

Extinction

Extinction refers to the weakening and ultimate elimination of an undesired behaviour by making it contingent on the removal of a desirable consequence for the employee. It involves three basic steps:

1. Identification of behaviour that needs to be eliminated.
2. Identification of reinforcers which encourage the behaviour to be eliminated and
3. Stopping the reinforcers.

The relationship between reinforcement and extinction is shown in Fig. 20, which confirms that if a reward no longer follows, the response rate tends to the preconditioned level (extinction).

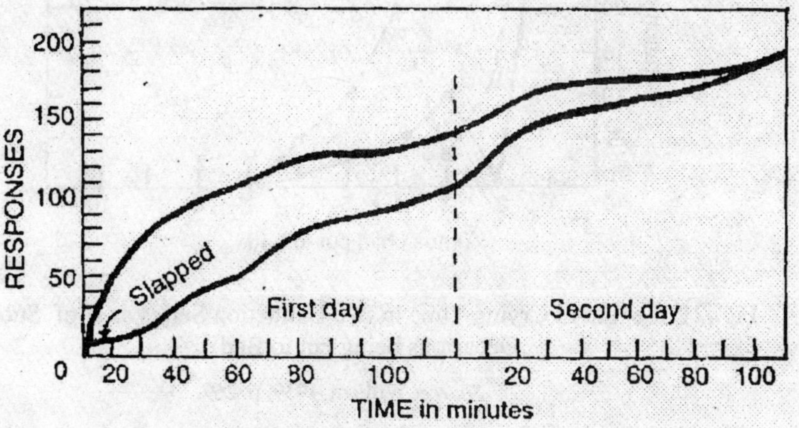

Fig. 20. Effect of Negative Reinforcement upon Extinction

Source: B.F. Skinner, *The Behaviour of Organism*, Appleton-Century-Crofts, 1988, p. 154.

In Fig. 20 the two curves are from group of four rats each, with the same experimental history. All responses made by one group during the first ten minutes of extinction were stopped. The rate is depressed for some time, but ultimately it completely recovers.

The Fig. 21 represents the course of extinction in a baby boy when reinforcement (an adult entering the room) was withdrawn from a previously reinforced response (tantrum at bedtime).

Both curves are generally similar to extinction curve obtained with subhuman subject. The second extinction series reached zero by the ninth occasion. No further tantrum at bedtime were reported during the next two years.

It should be emphasized that the treatment in this case did not involve aversive punishment. All that was done was to remove the reinforcement. Extinction of the tyrant like tantrum behaviour then occurred.

No unfortunate side or after-effects of this treatment were observed. At three and three quarters year of age, as appeared to be a friendly, expressive, outgoing child.

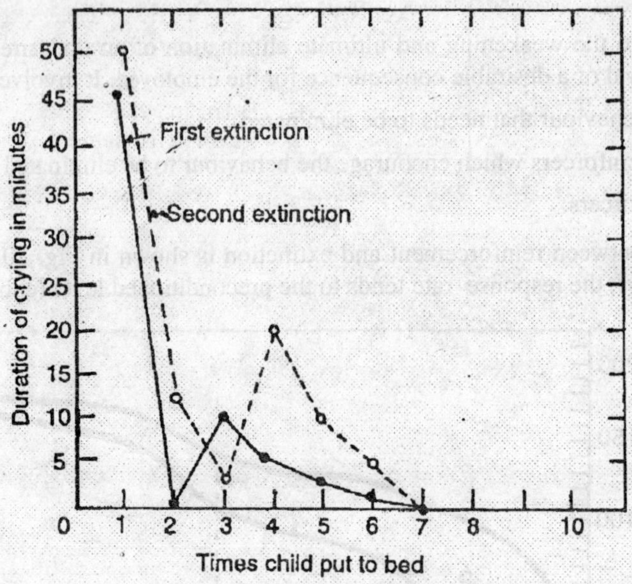

Fig. 21. Length of Crying Time in two Extinction Series as a of Successive Occasions being put to Bed

Source: William, 1959, p. 269.

Thus, depressing the frequency of response through punishment is not the same, as extinguishing the response through repeated, unreinforced trials; slapping the child for approaching the cookie jar is not equivalent to removing the cookies. In punishment, then there is active learning to avoid; the tendency to respond may persist at the same level, overcome for the moment by the tendency to avoid. This distinction is of practical significance in the control of behaviour.

Reinforcement Schedules

This theory raises a basic question, "What should be the reinforcement schedule to keep an individual motivated?" Reinforcement schedules refer to the timing or manner in which the consequences are made contingent or an individuals's behaviour. They work effectively only when they follow some schedule or pattern. Reinforcements may be administered either continuously or sporadic. There exists a definite quantitative relationship between reinforcer and response.

The relationships are as follows. In the simplest case, every correct response can be reinforced (a 100 per cent schedule). But there are several other possibilities under two general headings; ratio schedules, which reinforce every response, and internal schedules, which reinforce the first response after a given period of time, some of the most significant findings in this field deal with the effects of different schedules.

(1) A 100 per cent schedule is usually the quickest way to establish new behaviour to increase the frequency of a response; that is, learning proceeds most rapidly when every correct response is reinforced. But by the same token.

(2) Responses learned on such a schedule also extinguish most rapidly.

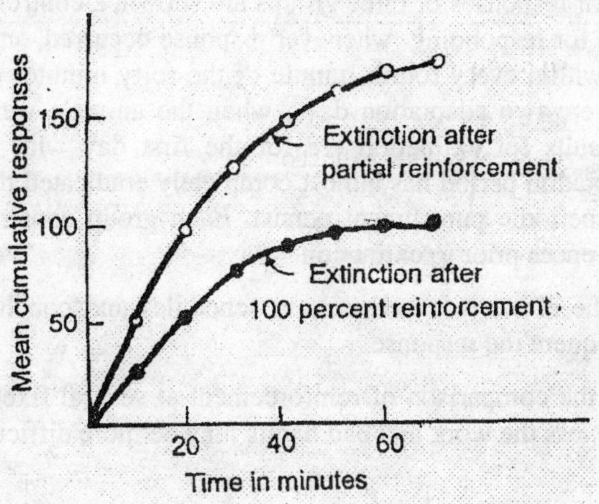

Fig. 22 Extinction Compared after 100 per cent and Partial Reinforcement

Source: Clifford T. Morgon, *Introduction to Psychology*, 2nd Ed. McGraw Hill, 1961, p. 204

A review of thirty-five such comparisons, including both human and animal subjects in a wide variety of training situations, concludes:

The most striking effects of partial reinforcement are apparent in response strength as measured by resistance to extinction. In almost every experiment, large and significant differences in extinction favouring the groups partially reinforced in conditioning over the 100 per cent ones were found. The practical implication of this principle for maintaining behaviours is obvious. Administer the reinforcing stimulus in conditioning according to a partial schedule, and the behaviour will be maintained for long period in the absence or external support from primary reward.

Punishment on a 100 per cent schedule depresses the response rate more quickly than intermittent or partial punishment, but the effects of partial punishment last longer.

In study, when punishment was discontinued, animals trained on a 100 per cent punishment schedule made for more previously punished responses than did those discouraged on an intermittent schedule.

The results of this study conducted by Hilgard, is represented in Fig. 23. It suggests that partial reinforcement is more effective in stamping behaviour either positively or negatively.

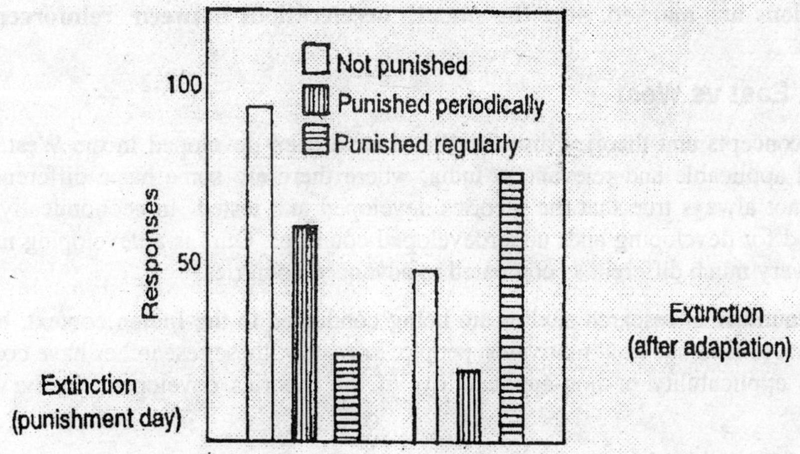

Fig. 23 Evidence that Periodic Punishment is more Effective Regular Punishment

Source: Ernest R. Hilgard, *Theories of Learning*, 2nd Ed., Appleton, Century-Crafts, 1956, p. 112.

The mean members of responses of three groups are shown, a control group extinguished in the usual manner, a group punished for responding whenever response occurred, and a group punished periodically, for responses occurring within every fourth minute of the forty minute extinction period. Following the experimental day there were two adaptation days, when the animals were placed in the boxes with the levers retracted. The results for extinction are for the first day with the exposed lever, after these adaptation days. The adaptation period has almost completely eradicated the results of regular punishment, but the consequences of periodic punishment persist. Each group consisted of 6 rats. Data from Estes (1944) corrected for differences prior to extinction.

Skinner compared the effects of various ratio schedules and concluded that the more frequent the reinforcement, the less frequent the response.

Fig. 24, respresents the comparison of reinforcement at several fixed ratios. These findings confirm that easier the pay off, the less the work and bad habits may be more difficult to break by cutting down than by quitting entirely.

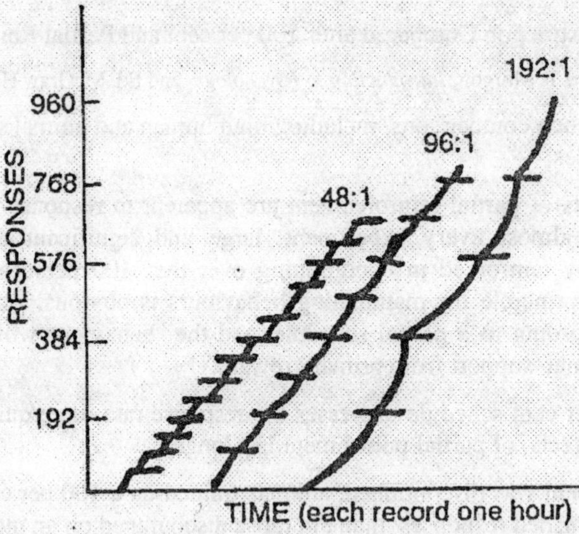

Fig. 24. Reinforcement at Several Fixed Ratio

Source: B.F. Skinner, *The Behaviour of Organism : An Experimental Analysis*, Appleton-Century Crafts, 1938, p. 288.

The rations are marked, note the smooth accelerations between reinforcement (at horizontal lines).

Motivation: East vs West

All the concepts and theories discussed here have been developed in the West. To what extent are these theories applicable and relevant to India, where there are some basic differences in the nature of people? It is not always true that the theories developed and tested in economically advanced countries may hold good for developing and underdeveloped countries. Ours is a developing nation and situational variables are very much different as compared to advanced countries.

A large number of research studies are being conducted in the Indian context, both by Western and Indian scholars, to find out what motivates people. Primarily, these researches have confined themselves to find out the applicability or non-applicability, of the theories developed in the West, in the Indian environment.

When we consider human beings in organizations for analyzing motivational pattern of Indian workers, two group of workers are identifiable – White collar and Blue collar workers. However there exists some common problems–basically in terms of their need fulfilment and satisfaction, blue collar workers identify themselves distinctly. The study suggests that this is due to the fact that white collar workers have the privilege of certain authorities in the organization to formulate plans and make decisions even to those decisions which were of vital concern for blue collar workers, while workers, were denied such an authority. Even the educational standard, family and social background, caste system, internal politics, pulls and pressures, undue influence of politicians, etc., besides competence, aspirations and growth avenues in the organization are vital factors in creating distinction between the expectations of white collar and blue collar workers in the organization.

Motivating Indian Managers

In 1967 Lahiri and Srivastava conducted a test to verify the applicability of Herzberg's Two-factor Theory in Indian Organizations. The study concluded that job, accomplishment, responsibility and domestic life were the motivational factors for middle level executives, while promotion, salary and organizational policy and administration were rather dissatisfying. A similar study was conducted in 1968 by another researcher which confirmed that most of the maintenance factors of Herzberg were satisfiers and motivators (such as working conditions, job security, organization, etc.) for Indian managers. However, on the contrary Dayal and Saiyadin found that Herzberg theory is applicable in Indian context too. Pestonjee and Basu also attempted to work on the same pattern and their results are worth considering. Motivators contributed significantly to move towards satisfaction than hygiene factors in public sector organizations. In the case of private sector motivators contributed significantly more towards the feeling of dissatisfactions than hygiene factors.

In 1971, Laxmi Narain conducted a comprehensive study of 1213 manager from 47 public sector enterprises in order to find out the relevance of Maslow's need hierarchy in Indian working conditions. His results indicate that managers rank feeling of worthwhile accomplishment, recognition for work done, authority for decision-making, opportunities for promotion and development, salary, perks and job security in that order. However there is a difference in ranking by top, middle and junior level managers, but it is of not much significance. However, a peculiar feature is that job security has been given the lowest priority. But this has a convincing explanation-in Indian context and especially in public sector where job of a worker is well secured, it does not remain a motivator any longer. Lahiri finds that importance of job factors related to various needs as perceived by different level of managers does not strictly adhere to Maslow's need hierarchy ladder. Autonomy, responsibility, promotion and personal growth, avenues are assigned higher priorities. Comparative importance of money and status among middle level managers revealed that status is more important than money factor in motivating middle manager. In another research finding, high salary alongwith self-esteem, autonomy and self- actualization were given high preference by all level of Indian managers. Middle managers ranked the five needs in a different order-security, self-actualization, self-esteemed, physiological and social. However, top managers ranked their motivational needs in this order – recognition, job contents, status and authority, salary, informal relationship with their higher ups and clearly defined responsibilities. Singh's study ranked the various factors in order advancement (promotions), self-actualization, recognition, salary (including perquisites), working conditions and security of job.

Motivating Indian Workers

Like various studies on motivating managers, several studies have also been conducted to find the answer as to what are the motivational factors for an Indian worker. Dixit attempted to review the various studies conducted in India to rank the various job factors in order of importance. The review disclosed that workers ranked the various job factors as motivational factors in this order–adequate salary, job security, personal benefits, promotional avenues, honourable and suitable work, good supervision and working conditions–in terms of importance to them. In the Indian railway workshop a study was conducted by Ganguli. This study ranked three highly motivational factors as– adequate salary, job security and promotion avenues. The magnitude of responsibility and appreciation or recognition of their work were found to be of relatively low importance.

However, Sinha found interesting work and social status as significant factors for workers' satisfaction and inadequate salary and lack of security as important factors for dissatisfaction. Bhatt, Lahiri, Singh and Baumgartell, Ganguli , Rao and others have also conducted intensive research on how to motivate Indian workers. However, the results of all such studies are at variance, and no definite line of action can be suggested.

A study was also conducted by the present author in 1993 to ascertain the factors which motivate the class I staff of UPSRTC, a state government undertaking. The results are based on the responses of 46 class I officers in the organization. The results revealed that class I officers gave greater importance to the non-financial incentives than to the financial incentives. This can be attributed to the fact that for class I officers, money is not much a problem; perhaps they get a comfortable amount as their pay packets. However, this does not mean that monetary incentives are not an important factor for motivating class I officers. They do help them to motivate to a certain extent. On the other hand, non-financial incentives seem to be a positive motivator. Quite a large number of respondents, 56 per cent considered, 'Promotion based on individual, 'performance' and sense of self-esteem at work' as the two most important factors for motivation. Even recognition for the work done, opportunity for personal growth and development ranked quite high, 52 per cent and 49 per cent respectively, as positive motivators. In contrast, in an another study conducted by the author in the same year (1993), for middle level managers the results were entirely different. 120 middle level executives who were interviewed only 22 per cent opined non-financial incentives as motivators in preference to financial incentives. However, 38 per cent considered personal family life as a major factor for work motivation.

The Indian Scene–Basic Differences

On the basis of various studies conducted by a fairly large number of social scientists on motivational pattern of Indian white collar and blue collar workers, it can be said that there exists a definite difference in the work and working environment between India and west, where most of the theories of motivation have been developed. The following differences are peculiar in the Indian context :

(1) Our social and cultural values are set norms and make it obligatory that age and experience should not only be honoured but also rewarded. Thus, promotion is generally based on seniority rather than merit.

(2) In India jobs are rather restricted, i.e., there are few jobs and more job takers. Hence the employees are not at liberty of moving from one organization to another very frequently. In other words, most of the employees stick to their jobs and do not prefer a change. This may be good or bad for both– good because organizations do not have to waste time and money on and off recruiting and training new employees and but in the sense that if they have dissatisfied work force, their productivity and quality will be low. On the other hand, it is good for employees that they need not worry for security of jobs, at least they can be tension free in this respect and can mobilise their resources towards creating organizational loyality.

(3) In spite of the work ethic as preached in Karma Yoga of Bhagwad Gita, which advocates doing one's duty to one's ability without any expectation for the fruits of labour (Your right is to work only, but never to the fruit thereof. Be not instrumental in making your action bear fruit, nor let your attachment be to inaction, Chapter II-verse 47) is conspicuously absent in average Indian workers. Lethargy and indifference still govern them. Our productivity index and man-days lost are ample example of this state of affairs.

(4) Though the concept of economic man has changed to social man in the developed countries, but in India, the concept of economic man exists. Hence the financial factors play a dominant role in motivating average Indian worker. More especially, the money and financial incentives are basic motivators for blue collar workers.

(5) Most Indian organizations do not have effective performance appraisal system. Due to the lack of this system, superior abilities and performance are rarely distinguished from mediocrity. Hence negative equity perceptions are quite prevalent and quickly fostered, resulting in, most individuals who join the organizations with great enthusiasm lose their joining the organization. Without adequate and different incentives it is rather difficult to keep the workers energised to work.

(6) Unhappy family life also serves as a major dismotivator at work place. With the changing ethos and concept of Indian culture and disintegration of joint-family concept an average Indian worker remains

tense and mentally disturbed at his workplace, ultimately affecting his work performance. To be more specific with the change of educational level of women and the laws of the nation in favour of women the male counterparts feel insecured at their home. Thus ultimately results in showing abnormal behaviour at work and lack of interest in the task assigned, as they always think of their home situation while at work. As noted earlier, the researchers have also subscribed to this view with data.

(7) Indian worker is provided very little support for his creative and innovative ideas. However, Indian workers are no less intelligent than their western counterparts. Many people of Indian origin have won Nobel Prizes. Some of the best Computer Scientists, Mathematicians, Engineers, Doctors, Physicists, Artists and other professionals in the world are Indians. Alas! They could not reach to that height until they left India. Why? They expected their ideas to be appreciated, supported, encouraged, utilized, recognized and rewarded. Unfortunately, this is what is conspicuously absent in Indian organizations.

REFERENCES

A.K. Korman, J.H. Greenhaus, and I.J. Badin, 'Personnel Attitudes and Motivation', in M.R. Rosenzwelg and L.W. Porter (Eds.) *Annual Review of Psychology*, (Palo Alto, CA : Annual Review, 1977), p. 178.

Abraham Maslow, Motivation and Personality, Harper & Row, New York, 1954.

B.F. Skinner, *The Behaviour of Organism : An Experimental Analysis*, Appleton-Century Crofts, 1938.

Berelson and Steiner, *Human Behaviour: An Inventory of Scientific Findings*, Harcour, Brace, and World, Inc., New York, 1964, p. 142.

Berelson and Stenier, *Human Behavior– An Inventory of Scientific Findings*, Marcourt, Brace and World Inc., New York, 1964, p. 240.

Blair J. Kolasa, *Introduction to Behavioural Science for Business*, Wiley Eastern, New Delhi, 1970, p. 249.

C. Alderfer, *Existence, Relatendness and Growth : Human Needs in Organizational Settings*, Free Press, New York, 1972.

C.N. Weaver, 'What Workers Want from Their Jobs', *Personnel*, May-June, 1976, p. 49.

C.P. Schneidev and C.P. Alderfer,'Three Studies of Measures of Need Satisfaction in Organizations', Administrative Science Quarterly, Dec. 1973, pp. 489-505.

Carl. D. Williams, 'Case Report: Elimination of Tantrum Behaviour by Extinction Procedures, *Journal of Abnormal Social Psychology*, 59, 1959, p. 269.

D. McGregor, The Human Side of Enterprise, New York, McGraw Hill, 1960, C.R. Holloman, What McGregor really said, Business Horizons, Dec. 1974, pp. 86-88 and N.K. Sethi, *Managerial Mirage,* New Delhi, Sterling Publishers, 1982, pp. 121-132.

D. Sinha, 'Job Satisfaction in Office and Manual Workers', *Indian Journal of Social Work,* Vol. 19, 1958.

D.K. Lahiri and S. Srivastava, Determinants of Satisfaction in Middle Management, *Applied Psychology,* No. 3, 1967.

D.K. Lahiri, 'Managerial Motivations in Public Enterprises', *Lok Udyog*, December, 1971.

D.K. Lahiri, 'Motivation of Managers: What Indian Managers want from their Job', *ASCI Journal of Management*, Sept., 1974.

D.K. Lahiri, 'Perceived Importance of Job Factors by Government and Non-Government Employees', *Indian Journal of Psychology,* 40 (1) 1965.

D.M. Pestonjee, and G. Basu, 'Study of Job Motivation of Indian Executives', *Indian Journal of Industrial Relations*, July, 1972.

D.R. Hampton, *Contemporary Management*, McGraw Hill, New York, 1981, p. 51

E.E. Lawler, *Pay and Organizational Effectiveness*: *A Psychological View*, McGraw Hill, New York, 1971, pp. 107-114.

E.H. Schein, *Organizational Psychology*, Englewood, Cliffs, N.J., Prentice Hall, 1970, W. Bennis and C. McGregor, Douglas McGregor, The Professional Manager, New York, McGraw Hill, 1967, p. 79.

F. Herzberg, Bernard Mausner and B. Synderman, *The Motivation to Work*, John Wiley, New York, 1959.

F. Luthans and R. Kreitner, Organizational Behaviour Modification and Beyond, Scott, Foresman, Glenview IL. 1985.

Fillmore H. Sanford and Lawrence S. Wrightsman Jr., Psychology, 3rd Ed., Brooks Cole Publishing Company, Belment, California, 1970, p.189.

Form 'The Hawthorne Group Studies Revisited : A Defense of Theory Y, MIT Solan School of Management Working paper, Dec, 1974 in J.R. Gordon, *Organizational Behaviour*, London, Allyn and Baum Inc. 1983, pp. 224-235.

Fred Luthans, *Organizational Behavior* McGraw Hill, New York, 1989, p. 231.

H.C. Ganguli, ' An Enquiry into Incentive of Workers in One Engineering Factory', Indian Journal of Social Work, Vol. 15, 1954.

H.C. Ganguli, 'Role of Status and Money as Motivation among Middle Management Personnel', *Indian Journal of Industrial Relations*, October, 1974.

H.G. Heneman III and D.P. Schwab, 'Evaluation of Research on Expectancy Theory Prediction of Employee Performance', *Psychological Bulletin*, July 1972, pp. 1-9, T.R. Mitchell, *Expectancy Models of Job Satisfaction. Occupations Preference and Effort : A Theoretical, Methodological and Empirical Appraisal, Psychological Bulletin* November

1974, pp. 1053-77, and L. Reinharth and M.A. Wahba, *Expectancy Theory as a Predictor of Work Motivation, Effort Expenditure, and Job Performance'*, *Academy of Management Journal*, September 1975, pp. 502-37.

H.G. Hicks and C.R. Gullete, *The Management of Organizations,* Tokyo. McGraw Hill, 1976, pp. 420-432.

Ishwar Dayal and Mirza S. Saiyadin, 'Cross Cultural Validation of Motivation Hygiene Theory', *Indian Journal of Industrial Relations,* October, 1970.

J. Rauschenbergev, N Schmidt and J.E. Hunter,'A Test of the Need Hierarchy Concept by a Markov Model of Change in Need Strength', Administrative Science Quarterly, 1980, pp. 654-670.

J.G. Hunt and J.W. Hill, ' The New Look in Motivation Theory for Organizational Research', *Human Organization,* Summer 1969, pp. 100-109.

J.J. Morse and J.W.Lorsch, *Beyond Theory* Y, HBR, May-June, 1970, p. 62.

J.L. Gray and F.A. Starks, *Organizational Behavior Concepts and Applications*, Merrill Publishing Co., Columbus, 1988, p. 104.

J.P. Wanous and A. Zwany, 'A Cross-Sectional Test of Need Hierarchy Theory', *Organizational Behaviour and Human Performance,* May 1977, pp. 78-79.

J.S. Adam, 'Toward an Understanding of Inequity', *Journal of Abnormal Social Psychology*, 1963, pp. 422-436.

J.S. Adams,'Inequity in Social Exchanges', In I. Berkowitz (Ed.), 'Advances in Experimental Social Psychology', *Academic Press*, New York, 1965, pp. 267-300.

Jay Hall, *The Competence Process*, The Woodlands, Tex : Telemeterics International, 1990, p. 36.

John Nirenberg, Constraints to effective Motivation, Supervisory Management, November, 1082, p. 27.

L. Johnson, Toward a Y System, *California Management* Review, Fall, 1974, pp. 22-29.

L.J. Bhatt, 'Incentive and Working Class', *Psychological Studies*, Vol. 7, no. 2, 1962.

L.M. Dixit, 'Employee Motivation and Behaviour: A Review', *Indian Journal of Social Work*, April, 1971.

L.M. Prasad and G.R. Gowda, 'Integrating Organizational and Individual Goals', *Indian Management*, Dec. 1977.

L.W. Porter and E.E. Lawler III, *Managerial Attitudes and Performance*, Homewood, II Richard D. Irwin 1968. D.F. Parker and L. Dyer, *'Expectancy Theory as within Person Behavioural Choice Model : An Empirical Test of Some Conceptual and Methodological Refine.*

L.W. Porter and E.E. Lawler, *Managerial Attitudes and Performance*, Richard D. Irwin, Homewod, Illions, 1968, pp. 12-13.

Larry A. Hjelle and Daniel J. Ziegier, *Personality Theories, Basic Assumptions, Research and Applications*, McGraw Hill, New York, 1976, p. 257.

M. Haire, E.E. Ghiselli and L.W. Porter,'Cultural Patterns in the Role of the Manager', *Industrial Relations*, February 1963, pp. 95-117.

M.A. Wahba and L.G. Bridwell, 'Maslow Reconsidered: A Review of Research on the Need Hierarchy Theory', *Organizational Behaviour and Human Performance*, April 1967, pp. 212-40.

M.C. Agarwal, S. Kandwala, and N. Naik, 'What Middle-Level Managers Look for in their Jobs', *ISTED Review*, May-June 1976.

M.P. Sawlapurkar, *et. al.*, 'Job Motivations of Middle Manager, *Indian Journal of Applied Psychology*, vol. 5, 1968.

Niraj Kumar, What Motivates You, Department of Business Administration, University of Lucknow, 1990, unpublished Consultancy Report, submitted to Indian Railways.

O.N. Ganguli, *'A Study of Attitude and Impact on Personnel Relation'* and *Recruitment in an Engineering Industry'*, Bombay, Central Labour Institute, 1967.

P. Hersey and K. Blanchard, *Management of Organizational Behaviour*, New Delhi, Prentice Hall, 1982, p. 49.

P. Shah, ' Need Importance and Need Fulfilment in Managerial Levels', Indian Management, May, 1976.

P. Singh, *'Occupational Value and Style of Indian Managers'*, New Delhi, Willey Eastern Limited, 1979.

P.N. Singh and R.J. Wherry Sr., 'Ranking of Job Factors by Factory Workers in India', *Personnel Psychology*, Spring 1963, pp. 29-33.

P.S. Goodman, 'An Examination of Reference Used in the Evaluation of Pay', *Organizational Behaviour and Human Performance,* October 1974, pp. 170-95; S. Roney, 'Equity Perception in Multiple Comparisons : A Field Study', Human Relations, April 1986, pp. 333-46; and R.W. Scholl, E.A. Cooper, and J.F. McKenna, "Referent Selection in Determining Equity Perception : Differential Effects on Behavioural and Attitudinal Outcomes, *Personnel Psychology*, Spring 1987, pp. 113-27.

Paul Hersey and Kenneth H. Blanchard, *Management of Organizational Behaviour*, Prentice Hall of India, New Delhi, 1978, p. 16.

Peter F. Drucker, *Management*, pp. 233-236.

R. M. Steers and L.W. Porter, *Motivation and Work Behaviour*, McGraw Hill, New York, p. 88.

R.J. House and L.A. Wigdor,'Herzberg's Dual Factor Theory of Job Satisfaction and Motivations : A Review of the Evidence and Criticism', *Personnel Psychology,* Winter, 1967, pp. 369-89, D.P. Schwab and L.L. Cummings, 'Theories of Performance and Satisfaction : A Review', Industrial Satisfaction Research, Sociological Perspective, April 1958, pp. 175-97.

Robert Levering, Milton Moskowitz and Miachael Katz, The 100 best Companies to work for in America, New York, New American Library, 1985, p. 231.

S.S. Rao, G.V. Rao and T. Ganpati, 'A Study of Factors Contributing to Satisfaction and Importance of Industrial Personnel', *Indian Journal of Industrial Relations*, October, 1973.

See, for example, E.E.Lawler III and J.L. Suttle, *A Casual Correlational Test of the Need Hierarchy Concept, Organizational Behaviour and Human Performance*, April 1972, pp. 265-87; D.T. Hall and K.E. Nougaim, *An Examination of Maslow's Need Hierarchy in an Organizational Setting, Organizational Behaviour and Human Performance*, February 1968, pp. 12-35 and J. Rauschenberger, N. Schmitt, and R.E. Hunter, *A Test of the Need Hierarchy Concept by a Markov Model of Change in Need Strength*, Administrative Science Quarterly, Dec. 1980, pp. 654-70.

Stephen P. Robbins, *Organizational Behaviour: Concepts Controversies and Applications*, Prentice Hall of India, 1990, p. 156.

T.N. Singh and H. Baumgartell, 'Background Factors in Airlines Mechanics Work Motivation : A Research Note', Journal of Applied Psychology, Vol. 50, no. 5, 1966.

Uma Shekheran, *Organizational Behaviour: Text and Cases*, Tata McGraw Hill, 1989, pp. 70-71.

V.H. Vroom, *Work and Motivation*, John Wiley, New York, 1964.

V.H. Vroom, *Work and Motivation*, Wiley Eastern, New Delhi, 1978, p. 6.

William O. Jenkins and Julian C. Stanley, Jr., 'Partial Reinforcement: A Review and Critique', *Psychological Bulletin*, 47, 1950, pp. 193-234.

CHAPTER

10

Communication

One may say in a general sense that communication means exchange of, or act of imparting thoughts, ideas, messages, experiences, wishes, emotions, moods, opinions, etc. Some social scientists have defined communication as an exchange of information. The American Management Association has defined it as 'any behaviour that results in an exchange of meaning. The special Committee on Communication in Business and Industry (National Society for the Study of Communication, U.S.A.) has tentatively defined it as: '.........a mutual exchange of facts, thoughts, opinions or emotions. This requires presentation and reception, resulting in common understanding among all parties. This does not necessarily imply agreement.' William V. Merrihue has defined communication as 'any initiated behaviour on the part of the sender which conveys the desired meaning to the receiver and causes desired response behaviour from the receiver.' By communication we mean here the broad field of human interchange of facts and opinions rather than the working of telephone, radio, television, telegraphy and the like.

The Process of Communication

Communication is, in the first instance, a process of transferring a particular information or message from an information source to a definite and particular destination. It sets employees in individual jobs, regulates their flow of work, coordinates their efforts, and secures better and higher work accomplishment. Management in action comes into existence as a direct result of communication. In other words, communication initiates human efforts and activities towards a successful execution of action plans. It is the essence of organized activity and is the basic process out of which all other functions are derived.

The Messages may be transmitted as spoken or written words, pictures or in some other form. In oral communication, the transmitter is the voice box, in telegraphy it is the key (Morese Key) which codes the message into dashes and dots. The receiver decodes the message in an understandable form to the information destination. The receiver may be the mechanism of the human ear, which converts sound waves into a form which can be recognized by the brain; a television receiver decodes the electromagnetic waves into recognisable visual representations.

Shannon and Weaver represent the communication process in a diagram (Fig.1), originally developed for physicists and mathematicians.

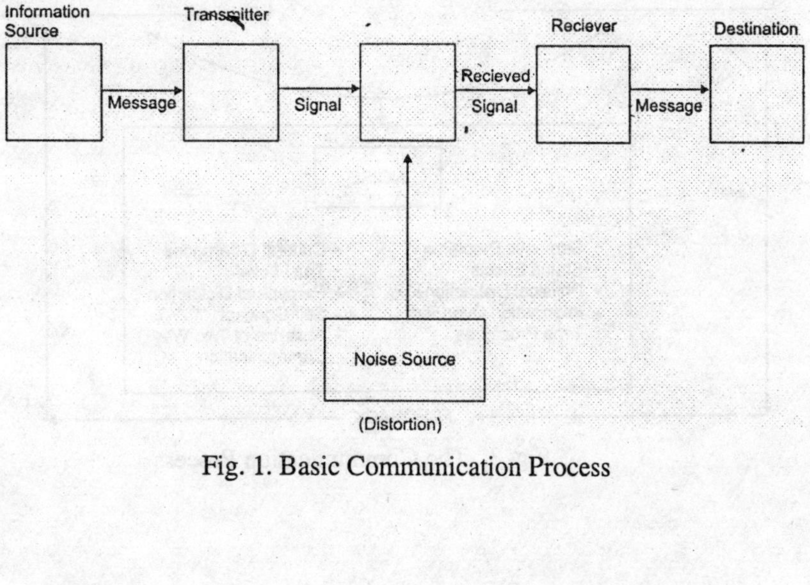

Fig. 1. Basic Communication Process

Claude Shannon, an expert in telephonic switching, and his co-author, Warren Weaver, have put forward several questions of which the two particularly concern us:

1. How accurately can the symbols of communication be transmitted ? This is an engineering problem.
2. How precisely do the transmitted symbols convey the desired meaning ? This is a problem concerned with semantics.

Shannon has propounded a very useful theory which deals with the first question. Weaver brings in the second question. Shannon's twenty-two theorems include the use of Boolean Algebra, the Stochastic Process, the Mark off Chain, Theory of Probability, etc. and finally they end in a special form of the concept of entropy.

As a social scientists, Weaver tackles the second question, following the well-known demonstration of the twenty-two theorems. He says that another box may be inserted just after the receiver box in Fig. 1, to be called 'Semantic Decoder.' This will serve to give the message a second decoding in terms of its meaning to the receiver. Also 'noise' which is always mechanical on level 1, should be expanded to cover 'Semantic Noise' or distortions of meaning not intended by the sender. It is an axiomatic truth that we shall never be able to communicate perfectly, 'noise' will always get in. But we can improve the present performance.

The diagram, after allowing for level 2, would look as in Fig. 2.

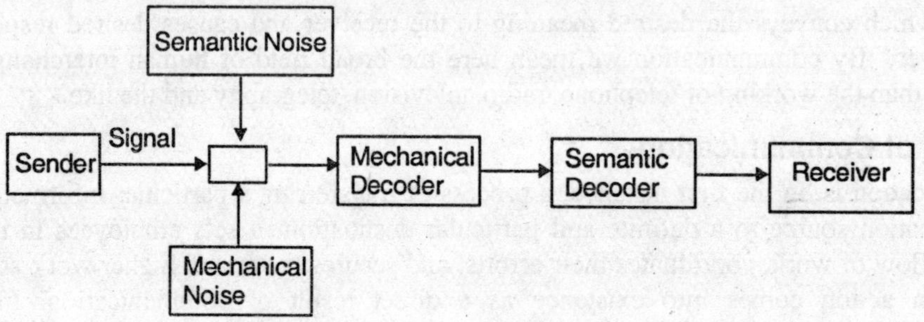

Fig. 2. Modified Communication Process

A more elaborate diagram depicting the various elements of communication would look as in Fig. 3.

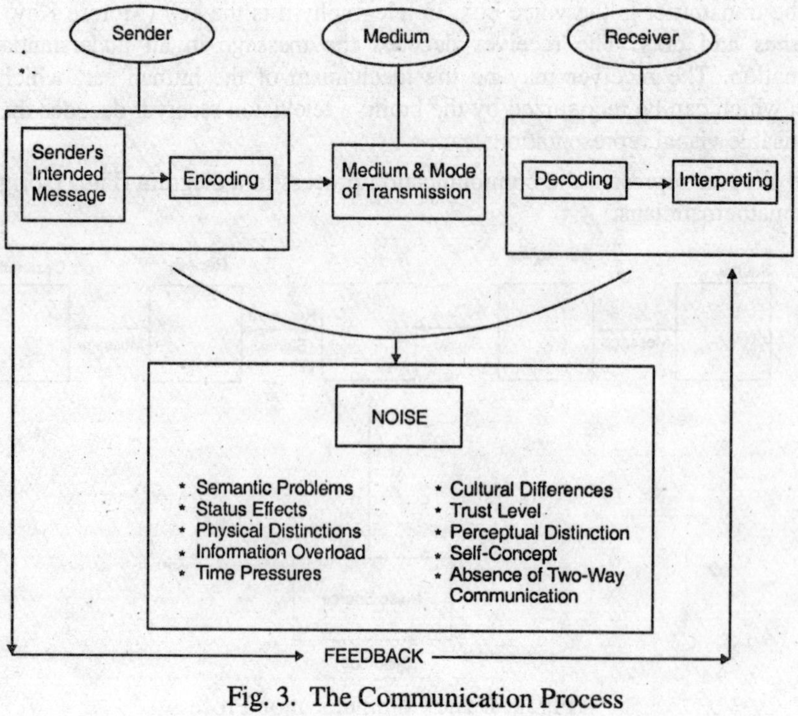

Fig. 3. The Communication Process

Communication vs. Information

Information flow in a communication network is the lifeline of a business enterprise; it is like blood flowing through the veins and the arteries of the body. It was Drucker who said:

The manager has a specific tool of information. He motivates, guides, organizes his subordinates to do their work in an effective way. Communication (verbal or non-verbal) is the only tool for a manager which helps him to do his work efficiently.

In this way, we can say that communication is very essential to the working of an enterprise, large resources of personnel and finance are devoted to the development and upkeep of communication systems.

The following is probably a useful way in which information may be defined: 'Information is a statement that describes an event or an object or a concept in a way that keeps us distinguished from others.' A garbled sequence of unintelligible signals is, therefore, not information since it cannot enhance our ability to distinguish among events, objects and concepts.

Many systems analysts differentiate between the data. 'Information' consists of data which have been measured or appraised as good or bad and say how much, relative to a standard believed compatible with the objectives and the goals of a business enterprise. 'Data' are regarded as raw materials from which information is produced, and in this sense the definition of information is again different from the one employed in information theory.

Every kind of communication is directed towards one basic objective, viz., to give and / or receive some information in one form or the other. Strictly speaking, information cannot be called 'information' unless it is given expression in some way, whether in language – spoken or written - or in some other system of signs, signals or symbols, and until there is some agency capable of receiving and interpreting that expression briefly and in an unambiguous way until it becomes an impression. Information is something which passes between two parties at least. The embryo of information generally lies dormant in the mind of the potential communicator. Here information exists only as an idea, or, sometimes, as a sequence of ideas. The difference between idea and information is that whereas idea is purely a mental activity but information is the mental activity only when it emerges into the list of day by means of a physical activity i.e., it is translated into a physical activity and thus finally becomes intelligible to another party. Of course, an idea can be translated into its appropriate symbols for the purpose of passing an information.

An idea in its most elemental form is a mental of some aspects of our experience of life, and this image may be visual, aural, tactile, guestatory, or olfactory. Hence, we can also refer to an idea as a psychical reflection of a physical sensation. The human mechanism is a subtle complex of sense organs which enables an individual to receive information and gain experience through sight, sound, touch tests, and smell– each operating either individually or in combination, and, thus, the information is received by the individual in a very specialized and particular way according to the senses being used. There are two kinds of such images: the image of things and events. Thus, we can very easily distinguish the idea and say a motor car as a static object lying on the road that of the movement of the motor car as it moves into position and starts off; and event as distinct from an object. In the general term 'referent' to cover both types of things and events which are subject to human thoughts and the begetters of mental images has been coined by Ogden and Richards. Hence, the 'referent' is thus the object or event itself as part of external reality, and the idea or thought ('reference', according to Ogden and Richards) is the mental image of that created reality by the activating mechanism of one or more of the five senses.

It must be borne in mind that although there is a necessary connection between the referent and the reference (idea, image, or thought) since the reference could not occur without the referent, and between the symbol (code, sign, or signal) and the reference, since the reference, in order to convey information, must embody itself in the symbol, there is no such necessary connection between the symbol and the referent.

Communication: A Factor in Organizational Climate

Communication is involved in all human relations. It is the 'nervous system' of any organized group, providing the information and the understanding necessary for high productivity and morale. Peter Drucker, while impressing the need for more and better employee communication as a significant factor in organizational climate, states:

To measure work against clearly defined objectives and goals of an enterprise requires a constant and uninterrupted flow of information. Management must try to convey this information – not only because the workers want it, but the best interest of the enterprise demands that he should have it. The great mass of employees may never be reached even with the best of efforts. But only by trying to convey information to every worker can management hope to reach the small group that in every plant, office or store leads public opinion and moulds common attitudes.

A number of experiments have shown that, other things remaining unchanged, the greater the amount of communication between the parties, the better is their understanding towards each other. The lack of communication leads to distrust and suspicion. Misunderstanding flourished in an atmosphere of secrecy. Any organization or business, enterprise like other institutions could progress rapidly only if it is able to march ahead in consonance with the wishes of its people. Let us take a case from the field of social psychology: anti – Negro prejudice among the Americans. It was number of times noticed that prejudice among the White sailors of America against working with the Negro sailors decreased to a considerable extent with the former sailed with the latter. Thus, we see that the greater the contact, the lesser was the anti-Negro prejudice.

During and after the World War II, management was seized of the problem of effective communication. At time, the trend of thinking went something like this:

The efficiency of our operations can be increased if we only improve the morale of our employees. We can do this improving communication with them. So let's communicate.

In the long run, one cannot get effective work done in group, corporations, armies, governments, etc., unless one can get it accomplished by individuals. It is evident, therefore, that individuals working in groups and show their best performance when each of them clearly visualizes the objective of the group of which he is a part, and understands both his work and his team work responsibilities. The tool for providing this insight and understanding is 'communication.'

Communication helps in giving job satisfaction to the employees, in attaining loyalty and cooperation from the employees while securing desired coordination of their efforts. As team work is essential for the accomplishment of jobs in many cases and appears to be of paramount importance for the purpose of coordination, managers keep the group fully informed of all the facts and situations relating to their work. Secrecy creates suspicion and separates people, and common understanding of problems unites them for showing a better record of their performance. Furthermore, mutual trust and confidence between the management and the workers can be increased by the help of a communication of what the manager expects from his subordinates and how the subordinates satisfy their boss with their works and increase the production. A clear-cut understanding provides job satisfaction to the employees, creates their confidence and loyalty towards the enterprises. Evidently, therefore, effective communication satisfies the personal and social demands of employees and stimulates their job interest and cooperation.

A study at Purdue University, which addressed a series of questions to fifty company presidents to obtain their views on implant communication, reveals the following results:

1. A definite relationship exists between communication and employee productivity.
2. Labour disputes, i.e., strike, low production, lock-out, etc., are definitely linked with breakdowns in communication.
3. A number of factors contribute to communication breakdown; but the greatest single factor is the inadequate use of communication media.

Significance of Communication

Since managing means control an organizational or business enterprise in an effective way and getting done through others, it is an obvious requirement that the manager communicates with the members of the organization. It has been estimated that a manager spend 90 per cent of his time in communicating, either sending or receiving information, because without effective verbal or non-verbal communication, the superior-subordinate relationship cannot thrive.

Barnard has given serious consideration to communication in large scale enterprises. He opines that people are linked together in an organization in order to achieve a central purpose. Group activity is impossible without proper information transfer because without it both coordination and change cannot be effected.

George R. Terry, describes the importance of communication, in this way: 'It serves as the lubricant fostering the smooth operating of the management process.' In all positive or negative action managers have to resort to communicate in their dealing with his superiors, subordinates and business clients. Personal and social interests of employees can be merged in, and harmonized with organizational interests through the permeating effect of communication.

'Evil communication corrupts good manners.' Good communication persuades superiors-subordinates to make greater efforts towards their performance.

According to S.S. Chatterjee, effective communication increases understanding of employees, gains their willing acceptance and leads them to greater efforts.

Actually, communication is the only key that unlocks the door to increased personal effectiveness, enhanced job satisfaction, and improved job performance. It is also an important tool in raising productivity, preventing conflicts and strikes, cutting costs, and contributing on the whole to the growth and profitability of any business.

Bavelas and Barrett state that it is entirely possible to view an organization as an elaborate system for gathering, evaluating, recombining, and disseminating information. It is not surprising in these terms that the effectiveness of an organization with respect to the achievement of its goals should be so closely related to its effectiveness in handling information.

Secrecy breeds mistrust and suspicion and hinders people from coming closer to each other, i.e., it prevents social cohesion and integration. Understanding of common problems unites people and enables them to give a better performance. Coordination between the members of the organization appears to be of paramount importance in securing the desired objectives and goals by the organization as a whole. Communication is a means of coordination throughout the organization.

Peter Drucker also states the impelling need for more and better employee communication, thus:

To measure work against objectives require information. Management must try to convey this information – not because the worker wants it, but because the best interest of the enterprise demands that he should have it. The great mass of employees may never be reached even with the best of efforts. But only by trying to reach the small group that in every plant, office or store leads public opinion and moulds common attitudes.

Now it is evident that today silence is not golden, it may be harmful for enterprise, misunderstanding flourishes in an atmosphere of secrecy. Business, as the other institutions in a democracy, can progress rapidly only if it is able to carry on its task in accordance with the wishes of its people; whether those people are acting in their capacities as voters, as suppliers, or as neighbours.

The following are the few specific areas where communication plays a significant role:

1. During union negotiations, to gain solid support for the company's efforts to reach an agreement without any strikes.
2. When strikes occur, to get employees back to work with a minimum of hostility towards the company and the least financial loss to themselves.

3. To maintain active participation in all employee benefit plans and gain the good will inherent in the company's contribution to these plans.
4. In elections of union representatives to give all employees full information on which to base a sound decision.
5. To increase productivity and reduce losses.
6. To develop teamwork, by accelerating the flow of information at all levels.
7. To promote health and safety and to improve safety records.
8. To help protect management's right to manage the business.
9. To gain the confidence and support or community neighbours.
10. To improve and maintain cordial employer-employee relations.
11. To maintain and improve the business climates.

The mainstream of communication at present embodies the contributions of both sociologists and psychologists and the use of these for the welfare of the enterprise. The purpose and the goals are uppermost in the minds of those who manage enterprises. To achieve these ends, they seize upon the social principles and techniques of many contributions including communication experts.

Communication Network in Organization

Communication has already been defined by us as a process of passing information and understanding from one person to another. This process of communicating is more technically defined by Cartier and Harwood as 'a process of or conducting the attention on another person for the purpose of replicating memories. For conducting this process, one person alone cannot communicate; it will always involve two persons — a sender and a receiver. In the case of an organization, these two persons are superiors and subordinates — generally the manager and the worker.

It is the communication network in an enterprise that determines the manner in which the individuals occupying different positions in the organization interact with one other in performing their tasks.

Some patterns of communication network are given in Fig. 4.

Experimental studies have shown that organizational patterns do affect accuracy, effectiveness, and speed of communication. Studies of several small work-groups have defined several organizational patterns as represented in Fig. 4. In some of them, the communication is more rapid, accurate, and effective than in others.

Several important conclusions have flowed from these studies. The most simple chain or the alternative chain, as shown in Fig.4 (see patterns 1 and 2), is a more dependable communication network having the maximum accuracy, speed, and reliability. The person in the central position 'C' tends to become a leader, but 'A' and 'B' in the extreme peripheral positions become dissatisfied and critical of the operation. Mistakes by individuals working in a circle pattern (as shown in pattern 3) were reduced to 60 per cent by removing one link and thus creating the chain. But the participants in the circle were all satisfied and enthusiastic in their participation as contrasted with the dissatisfied 'end members' in the chain. This pattern of communication is slow and inaccurate. It does not develop stability of organization and no leader appears.

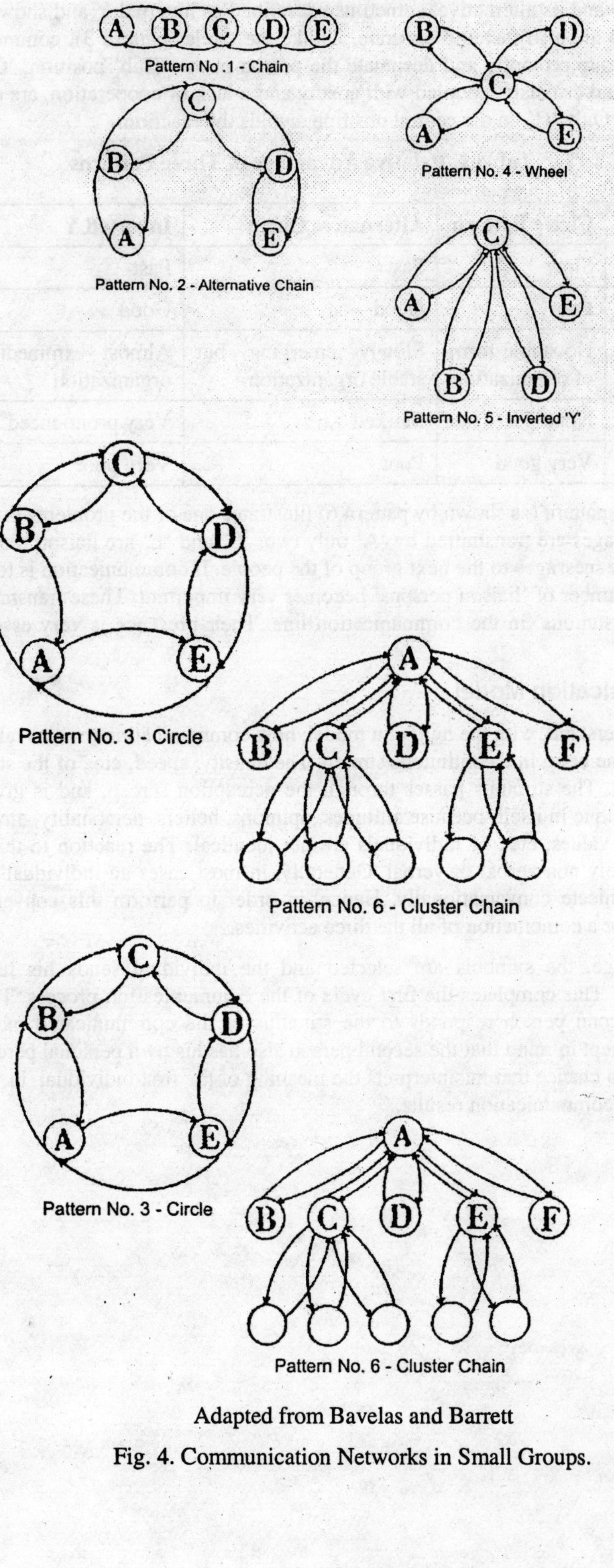

Adapted from Bavelas and Barrett

Fig. 4. Communication Networks in Small Groups.

The wheel pattern and its alternative, sometimes described as inverted Y and shown in patterns 4 and 5 respectively in Fig. 4 are also fast and accurate. Unlike the circle (pattern 3), communication networks tend to organize the group promptly and designate the person in the 'Hub' position, 'C' as leader. In the wheel, dissatisfaction and criticism, coupled with apathy and a lack of cooperation, are characteristic of all peripheral participants, Only 'C', in the central position, avoids the reaction.

Table 1. Relative Advantage of Three Patterns

	Circle Pattern	Alternative Chain	Inverted Y
Speed	Slow	Fast	Fast
Accuracy	Poor	Good	Good
Organization	No stable form of organization	Slowly emerging but stable organization	Almost immediate and stable organization
Emergence of Leader	None	Marked	Very pronounced
Morale	Very good	Poor	Very poor

The Cluster chain pattern (as shown by pattern 6) illustrates one of the problems in communication: of the five to whom messages are transmitted by 'A' only two, 'C' and 'E' are liaison transmitters; the other three do not pass on the messages to the next group of the people. If communication is to be carried beyond this single stage, the number of 'liaison persons' becomes very important. These transmitters are, in effect, amplifiers or 'booster stations' in the communication line. Their presence is very essential if the line is long.

A Human Communication Model

We may now understand, with the help of a model, how communication process takes place. The flow of a stimulus reaches the brain in a continuous stream. The density, speed, etc., of the stimulus vary as this flow reaches the brain. The stimulus passes through the perception screen, and is given meaning. Each perception screen is unique in itself, because attitudes, opinions, beliefs, personality, emotions, knowledge, thoughts, experiences, values, etc., of individuals are not identical. The reaction to this stimulus may be predominantly or entirely non-verbal or verbal. Generally, in most cases an individual's reaction to given stimulus is to communicate conversationally. Hence, in order to perform this conversation process, he selects some symbols or a combination of all the three activities.

Now, at this stage, the symbols are selected and the individual sends his response to another individual (see Fig. 5). This completes the first cycle of the communication process. The same process is repeated when the second person responds to the stimulus of the communicated messages of the first individual. It must be kept in mind that the second person also has his own personal perception screen, and, hence, there is always a chance that misinterprets the meaning of the first individual, in which case, instead of communication, miscommunication results.

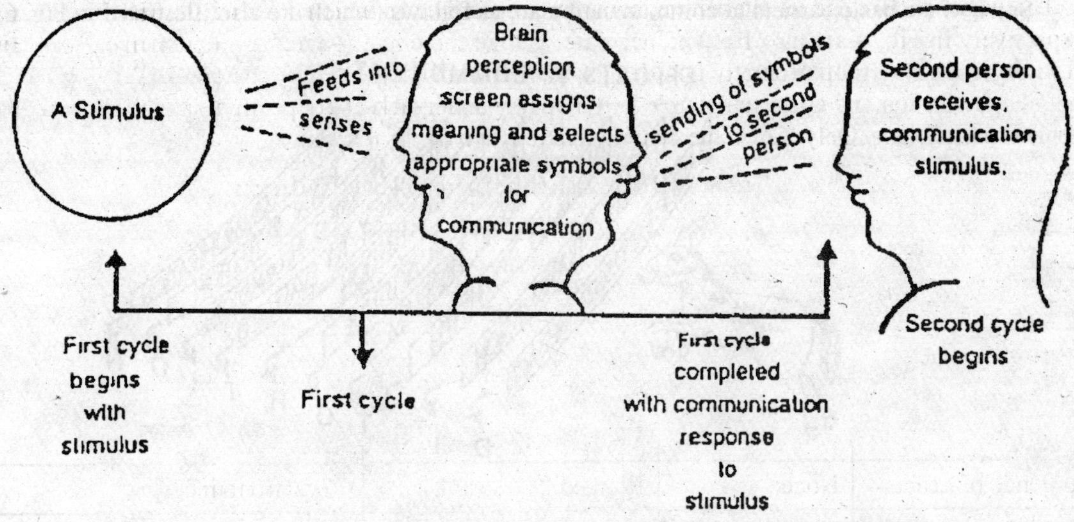

Fig. 5. A Model of Human Communication Process — First Cycle

Cost of Miscommunication

Manifold management problems arise from failure in communication or miscommunication. Disputes and frequent conflicts between management and workers have very often been described as problems of miscommunication. No doubt, the cost of miscommunication in terms of time and money involved is very high but what is more alarming is the cost arising due to misunderstanding, inefficiency, and hostility, ultimately leading to indiscipline and low morale, which might be quite prohibitive for any enterprise to bear. Someone forgets to inform the production manager that a vital material will be in short supply for the next few weeks, someone fails to notify the advertising agency that the new product will not reach the market as schedule; a promising junior executive accepts an attractive offer from another competitive company because his boss totally ignored him to give due credit for his excellent work performance; a grievance is prolonging because the foreman paid no attention to a worker's grumbling about the need for a safety guard on his machine; a departmental head's fifty — page important report goes unread because his superior wanted only a brief summary of the problem, and the like. These are a few of very common forms of mis-communication prevalent in all types of enterprises.

Barriers to Communication

There are a number of communication barriers which considerably reduce the effectiveness and perceptivity of the communication.

The basic problem in communication is that the actual message or information transmitted by the sender must be received intact by the person at the receiving end. The human sensory apparatus cannot transmit an exact duplicate of reality from the outside world into the mind of the observer. The needs and experience of human beings are related to what they see and hear in their day-to-day lives. The messages which the human beings do not want to accept are curtailed, while the others are magnified. Still others are distorted from the original form or reality. Distortion may be a matter of noise in transmission or it may result from the inadequacy of the words carrying the precise ideas of the sender. If the accountant submits a report on 'costs' to an economist distortion may result because of differences in the meanings of the word 'costs.' If the industrial engineer receives the report, he may take the ideas entirely different from those of the accountant and the economist. The financial manager may view 'costs', as outgo to funds; the production manager may think of unit costs of the manufactured product; the marketing manager may think 'costs' as a part of the total selling price; and the industrial relations manager view 'costs', as a social factor of employment. Thus, each of the specialists tend to have a different frame of rephrase within which he interprets a report.

Some of the basic barriers to communication are as follows (which are also illustrated in Fig. 6).

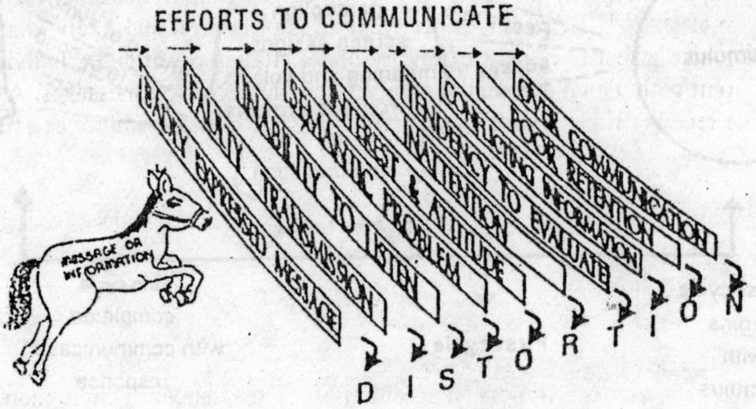

Fig. 6: Barriers to Successful Communication

1. *Badly Expressed Messages*

Irrespective of how a communication is delivered, vagueness and murkiness are too common. These faults are mostly due to poorly chosen words, careless omissions, awkward sentence structure, repetition, jargon, etc. Sometimes these barriers lead to very costly error, necessitating avoidable corrections, clarifications, and explanations.

2. *Loss in Transmission*

Successive transmission of the same message is hardly accurate; in each transmission about 20 per cent of the information transmitted is lost. Additions to the original communication and distortions are quite general, sharp specifics becoming more blurred with each handling. This barrier for effective communication operates more in oral communication than in written one.

In a number of transmissions there is always a greater probability that some of the persons in the intermediate layers may withhold, a stop, or absorb part of the message if they feel that the information, if communicated, may adversely affect their interest. In downward transmission, they may resist, absorb, or even stop messages. They may feel that by withholding the information they will be better informed than the people whom they lead. They may also stop the information flow to gain prestige or to establish identification with the upper echelons of management.

3. *Poor Retention*

Poor retention of the message communicated to human beings is also a very serious barrier to communication. Studies have confirmed that employees retain only 50 per cent of the communicated information, and supervisors about 60 per cent.

4. *Inattentive Listening*

The biggest stumbling block to personal communication is man's inability to listen intelligently, understandingly, and skillfully to the other person. This fact will be proved by an example.

A supervisor of a company one day tells an employee of his unit that the company has lost some important order. In the past whenever the company lost business, the concerned employee was thrown out of work. Therefore, he 'hears' the supervisor's version as, 'You can expect to be paid off in the near future, as the company has lost some very important order.'

Because of inattention or unwillingness to a message on the part of the receiver a chain reaction of perceptions and negative feelings is engendered within him which blocks communication. The simple failure to read bulletins, notices, reports, etc., is very common. This is sometimes evident by the common practice of arguing about an agreed matter.

5. *Interest and Attitudes*

The interest and attitude of the receiver are regarded as highly cardinal factors in communication. People listen more attentively to messages they regard as of interest and likely to affect them. Acceptance and understanding also affect to a great extent by one's attitude towards the individual message. Attitude creates the viewpoint with which a potential receiver screens incoming messages. A transmitted message is crystal clear to the receiver if he finds it interesting and regards the transmitter as a reliable source.

6. *Tendency to Evaluate*

One of the major barriers to interpersonal communication is the natural tendency of human beings to judge, evaluate, approve, or disapprove the statements of the others, which is very much heightened in those situations where feelings and emotions are deeply involved. Not only does the receiver evaluate what he hears in terms of his own background, but he also takes the sender into account: How reliable is, he as a source of information?

Often the receiver ascribes non-existence motives to the sender. This is more often seen in labour-management agreements and relations. Many union members take it as part of management propaganda to weaken the union. Similarly, management often takes it as granted that every union grievance is politically designed to win the support of employees. This type of predisposition blocks the transfer of information.

7. *Conflicting Information*

Communication sometimes miserably fails in having the desired effect because it runs counter to the other information that has already been received. For example, management may insist that the company must reduce cost if it has to complete in the market. Workers are asked to work harder and cut expenses. But some of the employees do not pay attention to this announcement, for they know that in spite of their hard labour, the goal cannot be achieved simply because other wasteful methods of manufacturing exist, and the management is not prepared to eliminate them. On account of this the communication goes unheeded. Thus, we can say that people ignore information that conflicts with what they believe.

8. *Semantic Problem*

Words mean different things to different people. A person may say one thing but the receiver may hear something different, even if the word sent and received are exactly the same. This is a matter of semantics. Language is a method of using symbols to represent facts and feeling. Strictly speaking, we cannot convey meaning. Sometimes, the same words give different meanings to different people, which are altogether different from each other. Even no words has exactly the same meaning twice.

When management says that profits are not only essential but a 'must' for the business, the management implies by the word 'profits' a means by which the company could buy new equipment, etc., and can expand. But to the employees the word 'profits' could give a picture of excess funds obtained through paying inadequate and unreasonable wages to them. Union members have little understanding of the competitive position of their employer and it is difficult for them to get the meaning of an explanation of the employer's position. Their orientation is in short different.

In order to avoid a breakdown in communication the communicator instead of using his own language should use the language of the listener. Words such as 'management prerogatives,' have acquired different symbolic meanings to management and to union representatives. The word 'efficiency' has various meanings to a union leader, a worker, a manager, or an engineer. The speaker has his own frame of reference and selects words that he hopes will convey the proper meaning. The listener, however, tends to listen and to interpret the language within his own frame of reference of experience. Therefore, we can say what a given word conveys, in short, is often dependent on local speech – patterns, individual experience, and the general social or economic position of the listener.

9. *Over Communication*

One is not sure as how much he should communicate, or when he should stop communicating. Overloading of communication channels can cause the network get jammed with irrelevant messages. More messages do not necessarily mean more information. Too much communication leaves too little time for work.

The condition of 'over communication' is actually one of the wrong kinds of information, poor timing and/or poor conditions for communication. Each of these gets a negative result which may be called over communication. It is perplexing, paradoxical and obscure. Such information always gets a negative response.

How to Overcome Communication Barriers

Researchers in communication have suggested ways and means, by the adoption of which leaders, executives, or workers can avoid pitfalls or considerably reduce the adverse effect of the above-mentioned inhibiting factors.;

We need yardstick, beyond trial and error, that can help us appraise a particular communicative act or an entire system of communication. The American Management Association has helped us by stating 'Ten Commandments of Good Communication' in this area. In our search for a practical yardstick we can easily draw on an abundance of material from the writings on communication. Certain principles can be derived from this vast material which serves as guides to good and effective communication. The following checklist presents some cardinal rules for overcoming barriers or obstacles to effective communication.

(1) *Plan and Clarify your ideas Before Communication*

A good communication fails just because of inadequate planning. Good planning must consider the goals and the attitudes of those who will receive the communicated information. Communication is a very serious matter; it requires clear-cut objectives and ideas, the premises known, the alternative weighed, and finally the message selected.

It is true, "The beginning of all communication is an idea." The idea must be clearly formulated in the mind of the communicator because there is always the likelihood of the message being misunderstood by the receiver. It is practically impossible to get a clear positive print from a blurred negative. It should always be kept in mind, "A problem well stated is half solved."

It is not only desirable but also pragmatic to seek the participation of others in planning an effective communication. The helps impart additional insight and objectivity to the message. By consulting others, before communication is planned, one is in a position.

1. to clarify and test his thinking through sharing his ideas with others;
2. to gather the ideas and suggestions of others so as to contribute to the solution of the problem, as two minds are always better than one;
3. to motivate those responsible for executing the decisions;
4. to get active and wholehearted support of those who have helped in planning the communication.

(2) *Create the Climate of Trust and Confidence*

Communication thrives best in a climate of trust and confidence. Paul Arnold, President of Arnold Bakeries, California, U.S.A., once said, "If your employee relations programme is a sound one, if your intent is true, if your people believe in that intent, and in that truth, then and only then are you successfully communicating."

(3) *Time your Messages Carefully*

Every communicator must recognize that when he is trying to tell his subordinates something, other things are also being heard simultaneously that may distort his message. One of the best ways to minimize the distortion is to communicate your information before other beliefs and attitudes aiming at distortion take hold of the listener. He should so tune his communication that the receiver has the requisite mental-set to receive and interpret his communication in the right perspective, e.g., when an athlete who hears the command, "Get Ready, Get Set." Then when he hears the command "Go", he takes off at once, without any delay.

(4) *Reinforce Words with Action*

The meanings of words are not in the words; they are in us. Words by themselves are suspect. The most persuasive kind of a communication is not only what you say but also what you do. "Action speaks louder than words." One of the best means to giving meaning to message is to act accordingly. It will help overcome barriers to communication if the verbal announcements are reinforced by action. For example, the manager's statement of `open door policy,' that is available at any time for an employee who has a problem, has no meaning to his subordinates unless his behaviour is consistent with his words. Whenever a man's actions and attitude contradict his words, people tend to discount what he has said.

(5) *Use Feedback*

Feedback ensures that the flow of information is actually having a reciprocating effect on behaviour. For this purpose, the communicator must be constantly on the look-out for clues of whether or not he is being understood. A simple way to ascertain that the communication has resulted in mutual understandings to observe the receiver and judge his response by non-verbal clues, such as expression of comprehension or bewilderment, a facial expression, such as raising of an eyebrow or a frown. This kind of feedback is possible only in face-to-face communication. The receiver may be encouraged to ask additional questions, express his opinion and comments without any fear, which will make the feedback more meaningful. Feedback is also obtained by simply observing whether the subordinate behaves in accordance with the communication, and if direct observation is not possible, the communicator must watch for reports and results. If more feedback is permitted, the speed and efficiency of communication increases.

(6) *Communication must be Directed to a Purpose and a Person*

Before communicating, think several times, 'why' you are communicating the particular information. It is of no use to start talking until you have begun thinking about the purpose of the information as it is useless to open the tap if there is nothing in the tank. It also does not serve any useful purpose to communicate without taking into account the individual or a group you are communicating with. Attitudes, feelings, experiences, and expectations of the individual or the group should be considered before you communicate.

(7) *Use Simple and Meaningful Language*

Complexities in language dilute and distort your message and lead to misinterpretation. Words which are intelligible and simple should be preferred to polysyllabic, circumlocutory or metaphorical language.

(8) *Mind the Overtones*

Whenever you communicate, your tone and pitch of voice, your expressions particularly facial expressions, your apparent receptiveness to the responses of others, your mood and way of communicating, etc., all have a tremendous effect on those you are communicating with.

These subtleties of communication often affect the listener's reaction to the message even more than its basic content.

(9) *Communication must be an Integral Part of Each Superior's Job*

Personnel specialist can advise the line and administer a programme of formal communication. Each superior is responsible for maintaining clear and consistent communication with his subordinates. This is the one responsibility that he cannot delegate.

It should be woven into the fabric of day-to-day operations at all levels with supervisors who are held directly responsible for the effectiveness of communication.

A steady application of the principle of clarity and adherence to the need for attention will gradually overcome certain barriers to communication-inattention, unclarified assumptions, loss in transmission, and poor retention. It will improve the quality of listening and reading and the communicator will most certainly feel encouraged for his efforts.

Barnard has very rightly said: "A first executive function is to develop and maintain a system of communication."

And it is also somewhat impossible to have human relations without communication and *vice versa.*

REFERENCES

A.C. Spence, *Management Communication: It's Process and Practice*, Mac Millan, London, 1969, pp. 84-85.

A.J. Ayer, What is Communication, in. A.J. Ayer and others, *Studies in Communication*, Martin Secker and Warburg, 1955, Preface.

Allex Bavelas and Dermot Barret, 'An Experimental Approach to Organizational Communication', *Personnel*, vol. 27, March 1951, p. 368.

American Journal of Communication, Vol. 4, no. 1, spring 1954.

C.K. Ogden and J.R. Richards, *The Meaning of Meaning*, 2nd. ed., Routlege, London, pp. 7-10.

Carl R. Rogers and F.J. Reothlis Berger, 'Barriers and Gate Ways to Communication', *Harvard Business Review*, vol. 30, no. 4, July-August, 1952, pp. 46-52.

Charles, E. Redfield, *Communication in Management: The Theory and Practice of Administrative Communication*, 2nd ed., University Press, Chicago, 1958, p. 12.

Chester I. Barnard, *The Functions of the Executive*, Harvard University Press, Cambridge Mass, 1938.

Claude E. Shannon and Warren Weaver, *The Mathematical Theory of Communication*, University of Illions Press, Urbana III, 1959, pp. 98-99.

D.E. Broad Bent, 'Perception and Communication', Pergamon, New York, 1966. George A. Field, Douglas, John and Lawrence X. Tarpey, Marketing Management: A Behavioural Systems Approach, Charles, E. Merrill, Columbus, Bhio, 1966, pp. 62-84, Julian E. Hochbert, 'Perception' 3rd ed., Prentice Hall, New Jersey, 1969, pp. 10-13.

Dale Yoder, *Personnel Management and Industrial Relations*, 4th. ed., Prentice Hall, New Delhi, 1973, p. 796.

F.A. Cartier and K.A. Harwood, 'On Definition of Communication', *The Journal of Communication*, November 1963, pp. 73-76.

Frank E. Fisher, ' A New Look at Management Communication', *Personnel*, vol. 31, no. 6, May 1965, pp. 487-495.

G. W. Allport and Lee Postman, *The Psychology of Rumour*, Herry Holt, New York, 1947, pp. 64-74.

George R. Terry, *Principles of Management*, Richard D. Irwin, Homewood III., 1972, p. 168.

Joseph L. Massie, *Essentials of Management*, 1973, p. 97.

Keith Davis, 'Management Communication and the Grapevine', *Harvard Business Review*, vol. 31, no. 5, Sept.-Oct. 1953, p. 42.

Niraj Kumar, Communication in Indian Industry, Milind Publication Pvt. Ltd., 1982, p. 3.

P. Ghosh, *Personnel Administration in India*, Sudha, New Delhi, 1973, p. 171.

Perrin Stryker, ' A Slight Case of Over communication in Industry', *Fortune*, March 1954, p. 116 and Paul Pigors 'Communication in Industry: A Cure of Conflict', *Industrial and Labour Relations Review*, July 1953, pp. 497-509.

Perrin, Stryker, *A Guide to Modern Management Methods*, 1960, pp. 9-13.

Peter F. Drucker, *The Practice of Management*, Harper and Bros, New York, 1957, p. 346.

R. Bellows, T.Q. Gilson and G.S. Gilson and G.S. Odiurne, *Executive Skills*, Prentice Hall, New Jersey, 1962, pp. 60-61.

S. I. Hayakawa, *Language in Thought and Action*, Allen and Unwin, London, 1946, pp. 60 and 292.

S.S. Chatterjee, *An Introduction to Management: Its Principles and Techniques*.

See Eugene Jacobson and Stanley E. Seashare, 'Communication Practices in Complex Organizations,' *Journal of Social Issues*, vol. 7, no. 3, 1951, pp. 28-40, Keith Davis, 'A Method of Studying Communication Patterns in Organizations', *Personnel Psychology*, vol. 6, no. 3, autumn, 1953, pp. 301-312 and Harriet O. Ronken, 'Communication in the Work Group', Harvard Business Review, vol. 29, no. 4, July 1951, pp. 108-114.

Willard V. Merrihue, Managing by Communication, McGraw-Hill, New York, 1960, p. 15.

William Scholz, *Communication in the Business Organization*, Prentice Hall, New-Jersey, 1963, Preface.

CHAPTER

11

Transactional Analysis

Transactional Analysis (TA) is an approach towards understanding the human behaviour. It is a technique for analysing interpersonal interaction or communications focuses on three dominant orientations. The three roles which we act out with others are parent, child and adult. Transactional Analysis focuses on the exchange the transaction and attempts to identify which of the roles; the parties are playing by analysing the words or actions each is using.

The earliest account of TA dates back to 1957, when Eric Berne contributed a paper on Transactional Analysis. Here he describes his preliminary experience with a patient during the diagnostic interview. In the course of the interview, the patient spoke sometimes as an authoritative parent a curious carefree child on the basis of his observations of mental patients, Berne sought to establish that every normal individual functions from three ego states – parent, adult and child. These three ego states are the key concepts in structural analysis the analysis of individual personality. These ego states denote the state of mind and its related pattern of behaviour.

EGO STATES

The Child "C"

The child in you is that body of data, recorded and stored in your brain when you were little. It comes from how you responded internally to what you saw and heard in the external world at that time. These recordings are feelings and conclusions about yourself based on these feelings. They include the inevitable part of the childhood. They also contain early recordings of joy, curiosity spontaneity in organization and excitement which are borne from the new discoveries also a part of the childhood. It is because of theses reasons that the child is often called the felt concept of life.

The Parent "P"

Your parent is that body of data, which is also recorded and stored in the brain that comes from your observation about the way your mother and father behaved. It is based on the events that took place in the first five or six years of life. It is a mosaic of learning which were constructed by you as a little person that is captioned. This is the way the world out there really is "Because of your smallness and dependency as a little person in a world of GIANTS your overriding assumption was that they were right. For these reasons the parent is often referred to as the "Taught Concept of Life."

The Adult "A"

The adult role is a mature personality neither the judgement "parent" nor the "dependent child." The adult has realistic knowledge of his or her capabilities and relationship to others and the environment.

The adult wants neither to judge or control others, nor to depend on others for a sense of self worth rules of conduct but accepts that any adult is entitled to personal values and rules of conduct.

Our Three Face

Since everyone has the three ego states, once you learn to identify your own P - A - C it will be easy for you to recognise the P - A - C in others.

In some ways our P - A - C's are like three different voices inside us, our parent is the voice that says things like "You must ———— You ought to ———— you should not done ever our parent tape plays back old familiar recordings as " If you want something done, idleness is the devil's playmate ——— A penny saved is penny earned ———" etc.

Any time you find yourself talking to yourself (either aloud or under your breath) and using the word you, parent is very likely addressing your child. For example, when you say yourself. That was a dump thing for you to do. "Your parent is scolding your child is the voice that says, "I want what I want I want it —— Try and make me"—— Now "Great —— Drop dead ——" etc. Any time you are experiencing feelings or emotions like happiness, sadness, fear, etc. your child is participating in the experience in some way.

Our adult operates on fact based on what's true today, it is the voice within which says thing like: What is going on here? Now I see why this happened the way it did —— what part of me came on just a few seconds ago —— my parent? Adult or child? Why did I react first the way I did? —— etc.

By listening to these different voices inside yourself though you may not always hear distinct word but you become acquainted with your own P - A - C. Sometimes you will be able to decipher massages from the feelings bubbling inside you, cannot hear the voice or directly experience the feeling occurring within our people.

By watching for the following kinds of clues you can become skilled in spotting P - A - C is other and yourself.

	Parent Ego State	Adult Ego State	Child Ego State
Voice Tones	Condescending Putting Down Accusing Nurturing Ordering	Matter of fact What is the Date? What can we estimate? Can we let each one decide?	Full of Feelings Compliance Rebellion
Words Used	Everyone knows that You should never ..... You should always .... learn understand why in the world you would ever.	How, what, when where, why, who	I am mad at you — hey, great (..... or any words that have a high feeling level connected with them)
Postures	Puffed-up super-correct very proper	Attentive, eye to eye contact, listening and looking for maximum data	Slouching, playful, best - down or burdened, self - conscious
Facial	Frowns, worried looks, chin jutted	Alter eyes paying close attention	Excitement, surprise, down cast eyes quivering lip or chin moist eyes.
Body Gestures	Hand on hips pointing finger in accusation-arms folded across chest	Leaning forward in chair towards other person, moving closer to hear and see better	Spontaneous Activity Wringing hands packing withdrawing into corner or moving away from laughter raising hands for permission.

The example in the chart are only a few of the clues.

You will become more aware of spotting these P - A - C clues in yourself once you become skilled is these P - A - C clues in other you can also get some clues from others about how you were across to them by identifying how they react to you. For example, suppose a patient reacts to something you have just said. Well I was only trying to find out where I was supposed to go for my X-ray. You might learn something about yourself by replaying what it was you said or how you said it immediately prior to the patient hurting, complaining response. Possibly the patient thought you were putting him down or scolding him in some way. It is important to stress that everyone has P - A - C ego state operating. The goal of learning TA is to strengthen the Adult in each of us. So that we cannot only ask but also answer, questions like, what part of me is coming on are these data true, appropriate and reasonable for today's reality. To put it another way, TA provides us with a means of putting our Adult in the room of today, ready to respond to the problems of daily living knock on our front door of life. This does not mean that we to be away with our parent and child. It would be dull word without them. It does mean, however, that we want to be free enough to be able to examine these two data tapes.

To the extent that our parent and child tapes are archaic and unexamined we will be dominated by the past. To that extent, however, we are able to learn the truth about how we behave, we will be free perhaps. This is one of the meanings behind the old saying know the truth and the truth will make you free.

Types of Transactions

Coming on straight, across and crooked

Scene 1

Nurse "May I see your visitor's Pass?" Visitor in angry tone "I have already shown pass to the man at the door."

Scene 2

Staff Nurse: "I would really like to get your help in solving my overtime problem."

Ward Sister: "O.K. why don't you get better organised"

Staff Nurse: "I have thought of that but I do not have sufficient help now."

Ward Sister: "Why don't you try to get more help from the students?"

Staff Nurse: "I have tried that, but they keep going for class just when I need them." etc ____

How many times have you found yourself in situations like the two scenes above? It is common for communication wires between people to get crossed in daily conversation. But why? How do these breakdowns in communication occur? And what can you do to untangle them? TA may have some ideas to help you.

In TA a transaction is an exchange of words and related behaviour between two people. For example, when you say "Good Morning Tim" and he says, " Good Morning back to you" and Tim has completed a bit of social business which we have defined as when we see each person involved in the exchange as having a parent, adult and child, we are able to draw an a accurate diagram of what happens in the transaction thus the term transactional analysis. The parent, adult or child in one person will always be answering the parent, adult, child in the other persons. The conversation is a series of transactions one exchanges after another.

Transactions can be adult to adult, adult to parent, adult to child, parent to adult, parent to child, child to parent, etc.

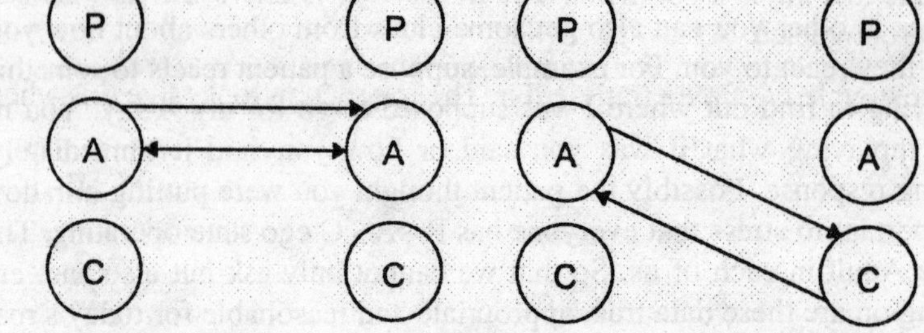

Fig. 1.

(1) If it is time to go (1) You really look tired, May I help you with your meal?

(2) I am ready let us go (2) When I am exhausted: Thanks

Example 1 and 2 are simple transactions. Who is saying what to whom is indicated by these arrows and the lines are either parallel or increased in each of these examples. The conversation can go on indefinitely as long as the lines in a transaction remain increased, with no breakdown in communication. This is the reason why they are called complementary transactions.

When we see diagram scene 1 which is an example of crossed transaction, it looks as

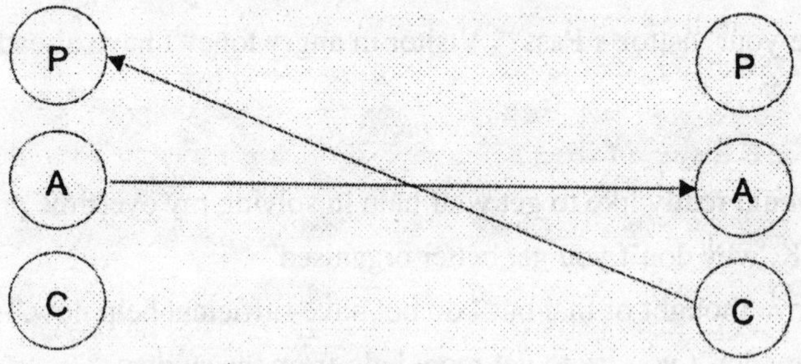

Fig. 2.

Nurse Visitor

1. May I see your visitors pass. I have already shown it to the man at the door.

The nurse is using her Adult to ask the Adult of the visitor in the example "May I see your visitors pass instead of responding with his adult with something like Yes here it is, the visitor responded angrily with his child, I have already shown pass to the man at the door. The transaction has become crossed as the visitor has reacted as if nurse has made an unreasonable demand on him from her parent when in reality she has not and as a result the communication about the visitor showing the nurse his visitor's pass has broken down.

A second rule of communication is:

Whenever the subject is abruptly directed rather than simply completed one should took for a crossed transaction.

Regarding this situation the nurse has a choice of response to this crossed transaction.

The nurse has a choice of response to this crossed transaction. She could scold the visitor with her parent for being so gruff with her or she could react with her child showing anger or hurt feelings or she could use her adult again and give more information to the adult of the visitor. Yes I am certain you did, Sir. However, the man inside gave you an admission booklet with rules and regulations written as it says the nurse will check the visitor's pass which I did like to see now. It is possible that the visitor will respond with the Adult to this last nurse's comment. The transaction is uncrossed and the business of showing the visitors' pass can be completed.

Scene 2 is an example of duplex transaction. The transaction looks like this when we diagram it

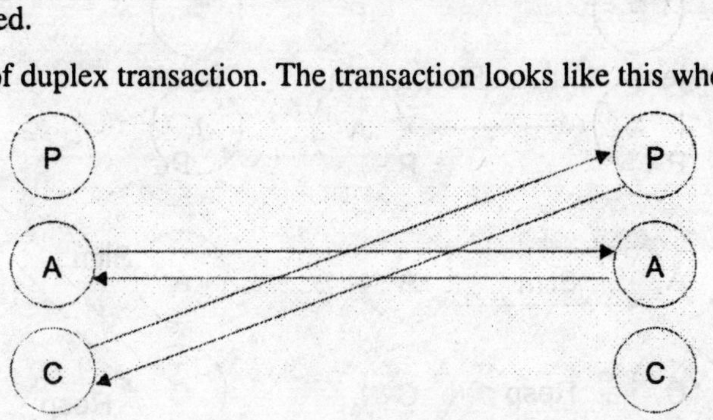

Fig. 3.

Employee	Supervisor
1. "I would really like to get your help in solving my overtime problem."	2. "OK, why don't you get better organised."
3. I have thought of that but I don't have sufficient help now.	4. Why don't you more help from the students etc.
5. I have tried that but they keep going off for class just when I need help.	

On the surface this series of transactions appears to involve as a nurse with her adult for suggestions from her ward sister. And the ward sister in turn, appear to be replying with ideas from her adult. There, is however a second, hidden, psychological level of communication occurring.

At this hidden psychological level the nurse is saying, "I am helpless to solve my own problem so I need a nice (parent) like you to solve them for me.' The ward sister, in turn, responds on the psychological level with yes I recognise my wisdom and will be happy to give you advice. But then in the 3rd and 5th parts of the transaction, the nurse rejects the advice that she appeared to be asking for.

If we look at the hidden psychological level we can begin to see that the basic purpose of the transaction was to reject advice rather than to receive it. But rejecting the ideas of the ward sister, the nurse is able, 'to prove' her superiority over the boss in the underhanded or crooked way. This type of transaction is called a duplex transaction because it involves 2 levels of communication, and social level and a hidden psychological level. Duplex transactions are commonly called games.

The transaction complementary or crossed and simple or ulterior can also be explained with the help of social action between an agent and a respondent.

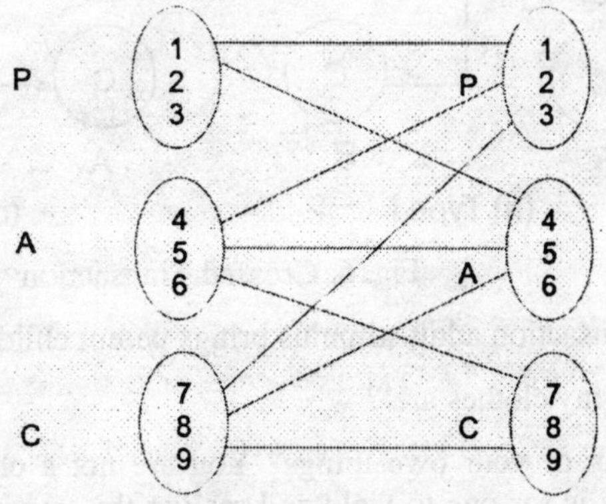

Fig. 4. Relational Diagram

Complementary transaction between psychological equals are represented by (1-1) and (1-1), (5-5) and (9-9). There are other complementary transactions (2-4) and (4-2) (3-7) and (8-6)

Complementary Transactions are shown in the diagram below. This contributes to effective relationship.

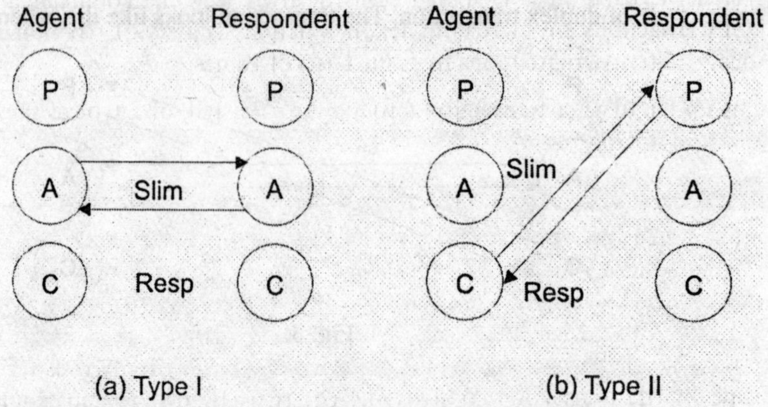

Fig. 5. Complementary Transactions

Conversely, communication is broken off when a cross transaction occurs. The most common crossed transactions causing social stresses, whether in marriage, love friendship or work is illustrated in the diagram (explained later on).

The stimulus is adult - adult.

A. 'May be, we should find out why you have been drinking more lately' ?

The appropriate response, Adult to Adult should be.

B. 'May be we should certainly like to know'? 'If however, the respondent flares up and says.'

B. 'You always blame me for everything.'

This response is typical of a child parent ego state. Here the vector cross and it becomes a cross transaction which generates ineffective relationship. In such a case, adult of A must be suspended until the vectors can be realigned. This may take time. Either A's ego state must become parental, as complement to B's adult must react as complement of A's adult ego state.

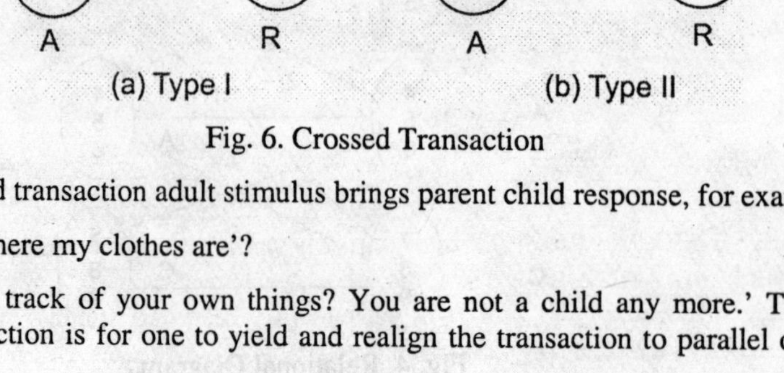

Fig. 6. Crossed Transaction

In the type II crossed transaction adult stimulus brings parent child response, for example:

A. 'Do you know where my clothes are'?

B. 'Why don't you track of your own things? You are not a child any more.' The most common solutions for cross transaction is for one to yield and realign the transaction to parallel or complementary one.

All other combinations will be known as crossed transaction and in most cases these will be as shown in the diagram later on. For instance, 3 -7 (3-7), that is, parent-child response which results in two speechless people glazing at each other if neither of them gives way, the communication is finished and they part. The ulterior transactions are more complex in which the activity of more than two ego states are involved simultaneously. Ulterior transactions form the basis of games.

Eric Berne sums up the ulterior transaction through the sales talk of a typical salesman. "This one is better, but you can't afford it.'

Housewife: 'That's the one I'll take (Berne 1961, p.33)

The adult to adult statements at the social level are 'this one is better' and 'you can't afford it.' The adult reply on the part of housewife would have been 'You are correct on both counts.' However, the psychological ulterior vector is directed by the adult ego state of the salesman to the housewife's child ego state. The correctness of two judgements is accepted by the child ego state reply of the housewife 'that the one I'll take.' At both the levels, the transaction is complementary, as her reply is taken as adult purchasing contract.The other type ulterior transaction involves four ego states (known as duplex ulterior transaction).

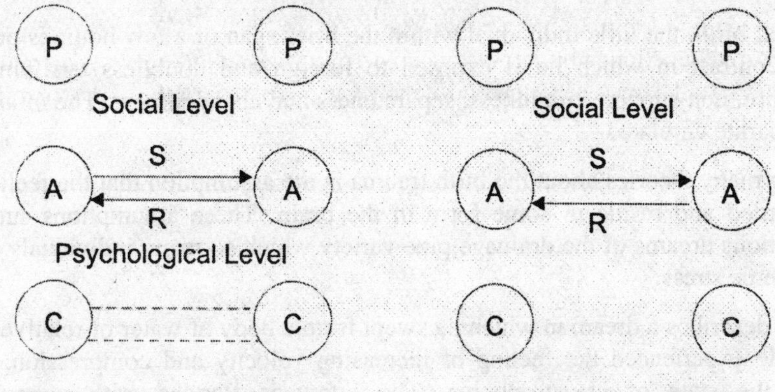

(a) An Angular Transaction (b) A Duplex Transaction

Fig. 3.

Ulterior Transaction

A: 'Come and see the river', B: 'I have loved rivers ever since I was a little girl.' The stimulus here at the social level is the adult response from the child ego state. Thus the transactions are classified as complementary or crossed, simple or ulterior.

Where are you coming from?

Your behaviour toward and reactions to other people are largely based on specific on specific assumptions you make about yourself in relation to others whether you realise it or not.

For most people, these assumptions were made very early in life by their early adult ego states. They were the result of the young persons needing to make some sense from the many hours of confusion and often contradictory data recordings in all three of his ego states but particularly in parent and child tapes.

These assumptions about yourself in relation to others are called life positions.

The Four Life Positions

Very early in life every child concludes, 'I'm not OK.' He makes a conclusion about his parents, also 'You're OK.' This is the first thing he figures out in his attempt to make sense of himself and the world around in which he lives. This position I'm Not OK – You're OK, is the most deterministic decision of his life. It is permanently recorded and will influence everything he does. Because it is a decision it can be changed by a new decision. But not until it is understood.

Hence we can note Pensfield's conclusions that the brain performs three functions:

1. Recording
2. Recalling
3. Reliving

The recall from the earliest period of life is not possible, but we can and do relieve the earliest experience in the form of returning to the feeling state of a new born infant. The reactions of infant one limited to sensations, feelings and perhaps vague, archaic fantastic because the infant cannot use words. The feelings of the infant are expressed by crying or by various body movements that indicate either distress or comfort. His sensations and fantasies, though ineffable because of his wordlessness at the time they were recorded, do replay occasionally in dreams in later life.

It is important to examine the situation of the infant to understand the implications. A line representing a span from the moment the conception to the age of five. The first block of time the nine months there occurred a beginning of life in the most perfect environment the human individual gets many experiences. This way of life is referred to as a state of symbiotic infancy.

At biological birth, the little individual within the brief span of a few hours is pushed out into a state of catastrophic contrast in which he is exposed to foreign and doubtless terrifying extremes of cold, roughness, pressure, non-support, brightness, separateness and abandonment. The infant is, for a short time, cut off, apart, separate unrelated.

Common to many theories about the birth trauma is the assumption that the feelings produced by this event were recorded and reside in some form in the brain. These assumptions supported by the great number of repetitious dreams of the drainage pipe variety which so many individuals experience following situations of extreme stress.

The patient describes a dream in which he swept from a body of water of relative calm into a sewer or drainage pipe. He experienced the feeling of increasing velocity and compression. This feeling also is experienced in the state of claustrophobia. The infant is flooded with overwhelming, unpleasant stimulations and the feelings resulting in the child are according to Freud, the model for all later anxiety.

One of the clearest statements on the development of positions is made by Kubie.

It is possible to make one certain deduction, namely, that early in life, sometimes within the earliest months and sometimes later, a central emotional position is frequently established — early in life, it becomes the affective position to which that individual will tend to return automatically for the test of his days. This in turn may constitute either the major safeguard or the major vulnerability of life infant the establishing of a central emotional position may turn out to the earliest among the universals in the emotion of the human neurotic process, since it may start even in the pre-verbal and largely pre-symbolic days of infancy —— whenever the central emotional position is painful ——— the individual may spend his whole life defending himself it, again using conscious, preconscious, devices whose air is to avoid this pain filled central position.

Transactional analysis constructs the following classification of four possible life positions help with respect to oneself and others:

1. I'm not OK – you're OK
2. I'm not OK – you're not OK
3. I'm OK – you're not OK
4. I'm OK – you're

Harris believes that a child in its first year of life makes its first tentative decision based on its experiences, I'm Not OK – You're OK. By the end of the second year it is either confirmed and settled or it gives way to position 2 or 3 I'm Not OK – You're not OK or I'm OK – You're not OK. Once finalised the child stays in his chosen position, and it governs everything he does. It stays with him rest of his life, unless he later consciously changes it to the fourth position. People do not shift back and forth. The decision as to the first three positions is based totally on stroking and non-stroking. The first three are non-verbal decisions. They are conclusions, not explanations. Yet they are more than conditioned responses. They are what Piaget calls it intellectual elaborations are the constructions of casualty. In other words 'they are a product of Adult data processing in the very little person.

I'm Not OK – You're OK

Being the infant's logical conclusion from the situation of birth and infancy this is the universal position of early childhood. There is OK-ness in this position because stroking is present. Every child is stroked is the year of life simply by the fact that he has to be picked up to be cared for. The infant would not survive without at least minimal handling and there is also Not-OK-ness. That is the conclusion about himself. The evidence points to the overwhelming accumulation of Not - OK feelings in the child, making logical his Not OK conclusion about himself.

The only guide for the infant is the reactions of others to him because the child lacks the equipment and experience necessary to form a accurate picture of himself. There is very little cause for him to question these appraisals as it is he is far too helpless to challenge them or to rebel against them. He passively accepts the judgements, which are communicated emphatically at first, and by words, gestures and deeds in this period. Thus the self-attitudes learned early in life are carried forever by the individuals, with some allowance for the influence of extraordinary environmental circumstances and modification through later experiences, I'm Not OK – You're OK. There is a kind of miserable sense in this in that the integrity of the position is maintained, but it leads to despair. The ultimate resolution of the position is giving up leading institutionalisation or suicide.

I'm Not OK - You're Not OK

If all children who service infancy initially conclude I'm Not OK – You're Not OK. what happens to produce the second position, Neither I'm nor you are OK; we both are not OK? What happened to the You're OK? What happened to the source of stroking?

Life, which in the first year had some comforts, now has one. The stroking has disappeared. If this state of abandonment and difficulty continues without relief through the second year of life, the child concludes I'm Not OK – You're Not OK. In this position the Adult stops developing since one of the primary functions greeting strokes it thwarted in that there is not source of stroking. A person in this position gives up. There is no hope. He simply get through life ultimately many end up in a mental institution in a state of extreme withdrawal, with regressive behaviour which reflects a vague, archaic longing to get back to life as it was in the first year during which he secured the only stroking he ever knew as an infant who was held and fed.

There is one condition in which I'm Not OK – You're Not OK may be the initial position, rather than secondary to the first. This is the condition of the autistic child. The autistic remains psychological unborn. Infantile autism appears to be the response of the immative organism to catastrophic stress in an external world in which there is not stroking which gets through to him. The autistic child is one who in the critical early weeks of life, did not feel himself to be rescued. It is as if he found nobody out there after his catastrophic expulsion into life.

I'm Not OK – You're Not OK

A child who is brutaliesd long enough by parents he initially felt were OK will switch position to the third or criminal positions: I'm OK–You're Not OK. There is OKness here, but where does it come from? Where is the source of stroking if You're Not OK?

Search a little person has experienced brutality, but he also has experienced survival. What has happened can happen again. I did survive I will survive. He refuses to give up. As he grows older he begins to strike back. He has seen tougher and knows how to be taught. He also has permission in his parent to be tough and to be cruel. Hatred sustains him although he may learn to conceal it with a mask of measured politeness Caryl Chessman said "There is nothing that sustain you like hate, it is better to be anything than afraid. "For this child the position of I'm OK – You're Not OK is a life saving decision. The tragedy, for himself and for society, is that he goes through life to look inward. He is unable to be objective about his own complicity is what happens to him. It is always their fault. It is all them incorrigible criminals occupy this position.

The ultimate expression of this position is homicide, fell by the killer to be justified because the person's I'm OK – You're Not OK position suffers himself from stroking deprivation.

I'm OK – You're OK

There is fourth position wherein his out hope. It is the I'm OK – You're OK position. Between the first three and the fourth position there is quantitative difference of which first three are unconscious, having been made early in life. I'm Not OK – You're Ok came first and persists for most people throughout life. For certain extremely unfortunate children this position was changed to position two and three. By the third year of life, one of these positions, one of the first functions of the infants' Adult is the attempt to make sense out of life, so that a measure of predictability may be applied to the confusion on stimuli and feelings.

The positions are arrived at on the basis of data from the parent and child. They are based on emotion or impression without the benefit of external, modifying data. The fourth position I'm OK – You're OK, because it is conscious and verbal decision. The first three positions are based on feelings. The fourth is based on thought, and faith.

I'm OK - You're OK is not a feeling but a position. The Not OK recordings in the child are eased by a decision in the present. The task at hand is how to start a collection of recordings which play OK outcomes, to transactions success in terms of correct probability estimating successes in terms of integrated actions which made sense, which are programmed by the Adult, and not by the parent or child, successes based on an ethic which an emancipated Adult has a great collection of such past experiences.

These four life positions dominate each person's life. Most people decide as small children that the only life position which seems to make sense at that time is I'm Not OK and You're OK

Taking this position helps them to explain many powerful "Not OK feelings" which they frequently experience in early life with this position dominating their lives, they spread most of their time and energy getting away from others themselves, and the daily business of taking charge of their own lives persons operating from this experience will be the getting away from type which result from the `Im Not OK - You're OK dominant position.

Living in I'm Not OK – You're OK life position is not a pleasant experience. Their very small girl or boy also discovers an antidote for the troublesome not OK feelings.

This antidote is stroking. The early rocking of the infant by a grown up who care; the holding of a refining little boy with a skinned knee the physical or verbal attentions paid to the small person with not OK feeling by a 6 foot tall OK individual.

Stroking is essential for the physical survival of infants not only an essential antidote for the destructive not OK feeling that are common to the childhood. Studies of high infant death in European orphanage revealed that is infants who were not touched and helped or stoked, soon became withdrawn and lifeless. If this process of physical deterioration was not reversed by a high quantity of stoking, the infant died.

This need for stroking, or stroke hunger, remains with us even in our grown up years. It is essential today for our psychological well being as it was for our physical survival as infants. People, however, who live is an "I'm Not OK — You're OK" position sometime become uncomfortable when others give them strokes–positive strokes in particular, make these people uncomfortable since they believe they do not deserve them. When they receive special attention or a compliment, they discount it by conducing the given must be after something or must be even more not OK than themselves on the other hand, people who are in an I'm OK – You're OK life position use their Adult ego state to obtain these essential strokes from many sources.

Work is Not the Only Thing that Occurs at Work

Many times you have heard that you are expected to put hours of work in exchange for shows or party however, it is not the only thing that occurs on the job people have different ways to spend their time.

Whether they are on the job or off makes little difference. These six times-structuring methods apply to all situations.

They include (i) withdrawal (2) rituals (3) activities or work (4) pastimes (5) games (6) authenticity of intimacy. Each of these approaches are related to the life position which you have taken.

The least risky you can fill in your time of withdrawal and one withdraws from people and situation when you are physically present by mentally putting yourself in another place or situation. As an escape from a boring or threatening present withdrawal is programmed by a child. It can also be a way of getting unimaginary strokes from unimaginary people through day dreams.

Rituals are the next way to fill your time and to get strokes. There they are fixed ways of behaving towards other people which are programmed by your patient. Rituals are closely related to good manners or the proper thing to do when you are with others; for example when you meet someone you know, usually you will say "Hello how are you today" and the other person likely say in return "Fine how are you." This is a greeting ritual in which you will give your friend several word strokes in return for several similar strokes for him. If you have good manners, you will probably be a good stroker because you can be dependent on to go through with rituals.

Another way can fill your time is through activities which is an offer called work task. Activities are aimed at getting same work done for example; taking temperature, painting a house, writing letter, fixing and serving dinner are all activities. Since work is done with or for other people it is also common way of getting or earning strokes. Play and recreation are also activities.

The fourth way you can fill your time as past time, some of which are programmed by your Adult to get more information about another person. An example of this is what kind of work do you do? Other past - time are programmed by your parent or your child to get strokes from others. Past times are usually pleasant and safe ways of exchanging strokes and getting to know people without getting too close to them.

Interpersonal games and authenticity are the fifth and the sixth way you can fill your time with other people.

Nearly all people play interpersonal games even though they really aren't much fine games are programmed by one Not OK child to help it get strokes and deal with its not OK feelings.

Authenticity is the sixth way you can fill your time with other people, it is programmed by your child and occurs when you are in the 'I'm OK – You're OK' life position. It is a means by which people really come together and is a warm straight series of transactions with another person. In authenticity you are in a most vulnerable position because you are giving more of yourself away than at any other time.

Your own experience probably tells you that all six of these for filling time occur on the job as well as off. The more time you spend with an individual, the more likely you will use all six time structuring methods. For example, the cashier or billing clerk will probably use only rituals and activities with a relative since he spends so little time with him. On the other hand, a nurse on an 8 hours shift may find that she is engaged in all six time structuring methods with her patients.

In all six time structuring ways you can use your job. Work can provide many opportunities for stroke exchanging rituals. All jobs are primarily focused on activities designed to get certain things done. It also provides you with frequent opportunities for pastimes that help you get to know other people better and exchange recognitions with them. Your job can serve as playing field for games, and your job can provide you with opportunities for authentic relationships with colleagues and sometimes even patients and relatives. Work, therefore, is not the only thing that occurs at work.

Trading Stamps, Games and Prizes

It is not easy to live with the not OK feelings which most people experience early in life and record in their child. Therefore they must learn how to handle these troublesome feelings at an early age. From the examples of important grown ups around them, they learn how to deal with bothersome not OK feelings by using trading stamps, rackets and games.

Most people learn early in life that the free expression of their feelings, both the exuberant, positive feelings as well as the negative not OK feelings often gets them into difficulty. So they learn to save their feelings for later use very much like people who save trading stamps which can be slashed in later for free prizes.

Dirty stamps and gold stamps are two kinds of trading stamps. people have these trading stamps when they save up their feelings. The former represents negative, not OK feelings such as anger, depression, guilt frustration, anxiety and fear. The latter represents positive OK feelings such as joy, affection, excitement, enthusiasm and pleasure.

Similar to the people, who collect A and H green stamps from grocery stores and service stations people save dirty stamps and gold stamps for the same reason to cash in whenever they have sufficient books for a free prize. Free in this case, means 'free of guilt.' How does this work? Let's watch Mr. Gupta, one of our visitors for a few moments. Mr. Gupta specialized in saving dirty anger stamps. He is a talented stamp collector who manages to find his brand of stamps in many places including hospitals. He particularly enjoys the free prizes, he gets for redeeming his stamp at our reception desk. We may find Mr. Gupta cashing in one book of dirty stamps for a free advertisement or two books for a free complaint letter to the dietitian or three books for a free blistering phone call to the administrator. Remember, fire prize means 'Free of guilt.' Mr. Gupta would not have to pay for his selected prize with guilt feelings since it was rightfully his. After all, anyone who had to put up with all the annoyance that Mr. Gupta has a right to get mad or to write complaint letter or to call the administrator. In this case Mr. Gupta's parent gave permission to the child to express the angry feelings he had been saving. But this permission is given only after a sufficient member of annoyances were endured to give Mr. Gupta the right to be angry. Although most people seen to save preferred brands of dirty stamps, some individuals save gold stamps. For example, Miss Kasturi is an employee who give people around her lots of strokes to she gets lot of strokes from others in return. These give her many good feelings about herself or gold stamps. She may decide to redeem a book of these gold stamps for a free new hair do on her day off or 3 books for a free week end house boat in Kashmir or 5 books for a 3-week vacation in Nainital and Simla. Again 'free' in each of these examples means guilt free. Miss Kasturi has earned the right to do these pleasant things. If you are collector of trading stamps, remember that your parent must first 'lick' the stamps before your child can paste them in her book for later use. In other words, your parents gives your child both the permission to save the stamp and the permission to cash it later on.

What are rackets and how are they related to stamp collecting? Rackets are taught by parents or by whosoever raised you. If your child has not taken and I'm OK – You're OK life position, you will find yourself in some kind of bad feeling racket.

Rackets are cooked ways that people go about collecting their favourite brand of trading stamps. One way to check out what your feelings racket might be is to think back to what happened in your home when you get tense. Did your parents respond with anger, confusion, depression, anxiety, fear or with some type of adult action? If they did not normally respond with adult action, changes are great that they taught you a feeling racket.

Games are closely related to trading stamps and rackets and few years ago was popularised by Dr. Eric Berne in the best seller, Games people play. Games are special transaction programmed by the child to help people with their Not OK feelings. These special transactions are called games because they require two or more players and always have a pay off at the end.

Games pay off, which are hidden or under the table usually come in two basic packages. One is obtaining strokes. The second is getting or giving preferred brands of dirty stamps. Because these pay off are hidden the adult apart of you does not know exactly your child or parent is upto.

This is because all games involve duplex or double meaning transactions.

There are at least six reasons why anyone play games.

1. Games help your child to 'keep up appearances' but in a dishonest way. For example, games may help you to feel that your problems are caused by others' fault instead of your own.
2. Games help you to keep from facing what you're afraid of, such a responsibility, competition, what others think of you, etc.
3. Games help you to pass the time with people you are ....close to as well as people with whom you not close to.
4. Games help you to give and get strokes.
5. Games help you to maintain your basis life position (such as I'm not OK as Other).
6. Games help you to get close to people without getting risk too close.

Why would anyone's child 'want to feel Not OK? No one would unless he was concerned from his early years that he was not as OK as others. If he was convinced of that, he will decide to 'prove.' It is others to justify his feelings that there's no use buying to change for the better.

The understanding of trading stamps, rackets and games is important because every patient and employee comes to work place as a total and complex person. Each one has his own unique P - A - C. He brings his feelings as well as his business or talents. You are also a unique person with your own P - A - C. Whether or not you are handling the friendly, concerned, I'm OK – You're OK manner, will depend on how well you can recognise and sort out feelings.

Getting Unhooked from the Past and Living in the Present

At many a time in your grown up years you can make conscious decision to throw out the old Not OK position that probably governs the course of your life and replace it with the I'm OK position. It gets us off the hook, of the past and gives us freedom of choice in the present.

Strengthening your adult is the key. First, your adult must decide after serious examination that all human lives are important and valuable. This leads you to respect your own humanity as well as humanity in others. Simply believing the slogan 'I am OK – You're OK' does not automatically turn all like into a beautiful rose garden but it does open up new possibilities.

You'll be overcome from time to time by the old Not OK feelings, but if you can use your adult to reason that I'm still not OK and so your relationships will remain open, optimistic and find, you won't pin yourself down in advance that everyone will automatically pure out rotten. Though strengthening your adult, will be more and more able to recognize you're not OK recordings from the past when they switch on. You can then have your adult turn them off and get on with the business of bring in the present. It requires hard work and sometimes ever requires the assistance of professionally trance person.

You require regular systematic exercise for strengthening your adult to maintain as I'm OK – You're OK life position.

Your adult gets these exercises through updating your old parent and child tapes. This updating involves using your adult to sort out which of the old parent and child recordings are still appropriate and valid for your good living and which are no longer appropriate or true. By sorting out these old tapes, you can produce new data about yourself which you can now store in your adult and use for living more fully in the present.

Exercises Your OK Child

Be excited, responsive, enthusiastic at every opportunity. If at first you can't make it, Your OK child may be weak from lack of exercises, and a few forced exercises in depressing OK feeling can help these feeling to become more authentic.

Avoid the Parent of Others

Be particularly alert to thing that 'hook' the parent in other, then by not arouse it. Too much playful OK child can arouse another person's parent. Similarly A not OK child response on your part can also hook another's parent.

Look for OK Child in Other

If you spot the OK child in someone else respond to it. This is the source of hidden gold in transactions with other people. Giving strokes through the use of names, smiling well turned humour and individualised attention brings out OK child in other.

Feel Your Own OK Child

To keep you alive and healthy it must be fed as well as exercise. Plans for ways for getting life sustaining strokes for many people rather than from one to two special persons. Also reserve time each day to have some fun. All work and no play makes your OK child shrivel up.

Keep Contacts with Others

You should live upto the promise if you say you'll do a certain things. By keeping contacts with others you build reliability, dependability and trust between them and yourself. Being OK is based on reliability and trust if you devalue others, you also devalue yourself.

You will be better able to see in your own way instead of the way you are taught after you become aware of your games and stamp collection. You will be free to feel as you want to feel, not as your parent tells to feel you will be rid of your bad feelings. You will have more respect for you will feel safe in letting people like you. This means you will be more willing to accept strokes from them. Once your child start feeling OK about himself you can stop listening to old Not OK rewordings stop waiting for Santa Claus and give your Adult a chance to make your decisions.

Observing P - A - C at Work

Although, men have invented new machines to speed up the processing of external data, most people have not made similar breakthroughs in processing the data of their own internal experiments. You now however, have some new TA concepts to use in processing and computing both the familiar work problems occurring around you and your own unique reaction to them.

This part will explore some of these familiar work issues using TA as road map. Assumptions about that will work us or not work or what will not happen under certain conditions are Adult assumption. These can be tested in reality. Assumption about how others are feeling or about their "OK-Ness" or Not OK-Ness" is relationship to yourself are child assumptions.

Check out which ego state you might be using when you find yourself making assumptions about another person, because your assumptions and the ego state you are using to form them can both very much influence outcomes of situations and relationships.

Often you become aware that something is not the way you would like it to be. You may also think of reversal things that you could do which might change the situation. When you develop these options for resolving the problem, you do this with your Adult. To decide which of the potential actions you thought about you are actually going to do for that you use your Adult. Sometimes it happens that you may be aware of the problem but cannot or do not decided what to do about it. In such cases, the problem will likely remain. Thus the problems can be thought of as 'Not-decisions'. Within the TA way of looking at things, there are two different kinds of problem solving.

(1) Task problem-solving involves our processing and computing data about things or non-human problems. This is what was referred to earlier as activity.

(2) Interpersonal problem solving involves getting things straightened out between yourself and someone else. This is what referred to earlier as Authenticity. But of these kinds of problem solving require to use your Adult and both lead from "Not decisions" about problems to making decisions about them withdrawal, rituals, pastimes and games are sometimes used by people attempting to solve problems. Since none of these efforts lead to decision-making, the problem (Not decision) will still remain.

Sometimes task of problem-solving is not accomplished because of interpersonal problems, which exist between two or more people who are involved in the decision-making. Authenticities between these people are necessary for the resolution of their interpersonal problems before the task problems can be resolved. Since authenticity is a for most people, they may attempt to substitute games. This will result in "Non-decisions." It means that both and the organizations will be "hung-up" until either the individuals involved are removed from the situation or they are about to apply new behaviour to their "not-decision." You should understand the Parent and Child assumptions, concentrate on the Adult assumptions since they will lead you to action options which you can check-out. Also determine if hand-up is more likely a "not-decision" involving interpersonal relationships or some portion of a task. Then check to see if you are using an approach appropriate to the type of the problem.

"Oughtmanship" is supervisory Relationships:

"Oughtmanship" is sometimes used by both supervisors and subordinates in reaction to work problem situation.

Examples are:

"If management around have to solve the absenteeism problem they ought to show more interest and concern for the employees."

"Employees around here ought to be interested in coming to work and doing their part: there is no excuse for this absenteeism."

"You employees ought to be more cost-conscious in your work: Do not you know there is a profit squeeze."

"Supervisor ought to make it easier for the employees to talk to them. We have lots of good ideas, but they will never listen to us."

Each of these statements is parent statement and these statements make a judgement or assumption about another person (or persons) being responsible for the problem or its solution. This conveniently talks the speaker off the hook by placing the total responsibility for taking action on someone else's back.

"Oughtmanship" does not lead to problem-solving since it involves the Parent rather than the Adult. This is not to say that is no room for the parent ego state in working situations and relationships. One should not forget that Adult can make decisions and solve problems. However, the Parent and Child can react to problems. An organization without a stated or implicit values system would often seem chaotic and without a compass.

"Oughtmanship" is non-effective substitute for problem-solving behaviour and should not be mistaken for problem solving.

Cashing in Trading Stamps on the Job

People often save up feeling so that they can later cash them for free prizes people collect and cash these Trading Stamps on the jobs as well elsewhere. To job situations which are dull, painful or unpleasant, individuals will often respond with various Not OK feelings. Rather than taking some kind of initiative of problem-solving of the undesirable situation, some individuals will save up their bad feelings until they have several backfill feelings. They can cash in their books for a free suit depending on the availability of other jobs. So called "legal strikes" and wildcat strikes are also major prizes for pooled books of Dirty Stamps. In either case, groups of employees will claim that they have night to talk out because of all the bad things they have had to put with.

Problem solving between the parties involved is extremely difficult unless some way can be found to ask the adult of the individuals on both sides of the dispute. Efforts of non-recognized employees to unionise the issue can be viewed as potching cashing in pooled books of employee. Dirty stamps for a free nose thumping at management as well as initiating action owned at increasing the amount latter interpretation assumes that management has either not been aware of or close to ignore the problems experienced by employees.

Work Games and Other Emotional Exercises

People play games on their jobs in the very same way as in the other places where they live out their lives and for both psychological and, monetary advances they work in organizations. Games are vital to the psychological maintenance of life since they are vital to the psychological maintenance of life since they help people to meet their stroking needs. Games can sometimes seriously interfere with an individual work group, or an organization getting, what it wants. When individuals or groups of individuals play specific games or cluster of games with such intensity that other persons are driven away as trouble is around the corner.

Several unwanted things are likely to occur since intensely played games tend to drive others away.

(1) Few "other" people are around to supply essential strokes which may result in the player or players experiencing more intensity of their games unless the cycle can be interrupted.

(2) A psychological pollution contains high levels of Not OK feelings. The social environment around the players is created when games are played intensely. This poisoned atmosphere makes it more difficult for a healthy Adult to survive. And healthy adults are essential for working on work problems (activities) and people problems (authenticity).

(3) Most individuals work in situation in which team work is important. But intensely played games usually isolate the player or players from others. Isolation creates breakdown which is an essential

communication and problem-solving between individual and groups who are important members of the team.

I. Several games are listed below which are commonly played by the people on the job.

This is usually a hierarchy game which is played by individuals or groups to blame someone else. The 'him" or "them" can represent the boss, top management, a certain tutor, headquarters, or the union.

The player himself off the hook for working on a problem and places the responsibility on someone else's back.

A. I would really do a much better job if it were not for —

B. You are probably right.

Pay Off: Person A is once again saved from trying to do something that is frightening to him.

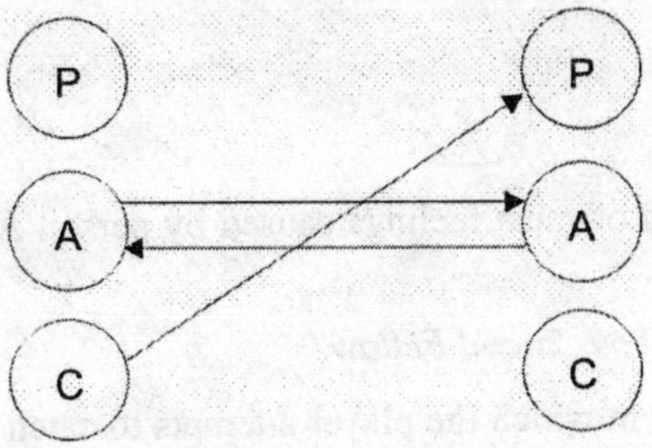

II. *Why do not you .... but*

This is also a hierarchy game. It is used by people or groups who appear to want others to "help" them to solve their problems but actually want to prove that helper are less OK than themselves. They do this by rejecting all "helpful suggestion" which are offered. Helpers commonly include bosses, staff, "experts" and outside consultants. For these reasons, this game is perhaps one of the most commonly played games between staff and the line individuals and groups.

A— And that is my problem. Any suggestion:

B— Have you ever tried ——

A. Yes, I have but —

B. Why do not you by—

C. That is A, good idea, but —

Pay off: Person A gets strokes (Attention) and give Rejections stamps at the same time.

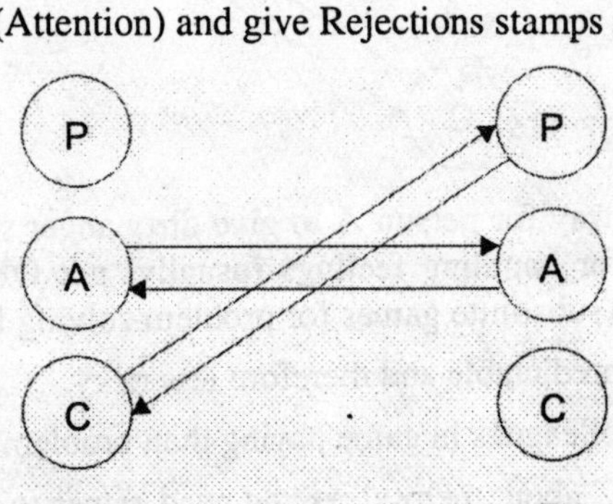

III. I am only trying to help you

This is flip-side of "why do not you — Yes but." The helpers use this game to explain their behaviour and also to justify their anger or irritation at having all of their ideas rejected. Players commonly are bosses, staff experts are consultants.

A. And that is my problem, any suggestion?

B. Why do not you —

C. That is good idea but —

D. Latter well: I was only trying to help you.

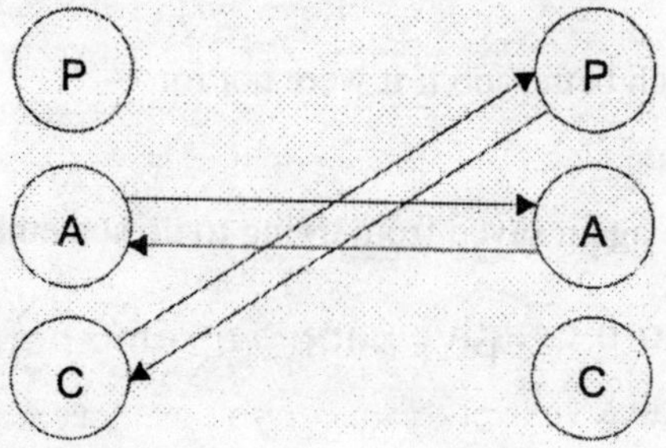

Pay off: Person B gets rid of must feelings caused by person A's rejections (That is opposite side of why do not you — Yes, but)

IV Game — Now I II Got You, Stupid Fellow.

This is a "trapping" game in which the player attempts to catch another individual or group in a good lie, moment of stupidity or some other negative situation. If the player is successfully "trapping" his prey he earns a pay off which is usually a justification for taking some negative action (fining or discipline someone cutting the managers' budget, not giving a promotion or raise, writing a critical letter, etc.). These negative actions can be taken by the player without guilt since the other individual was "caught" therefore deserved what he got." It is sometimes used as a substitute for problem solving.

A. Were you late again.

B. I am afraid, I was.

C. You have forced to take some action.

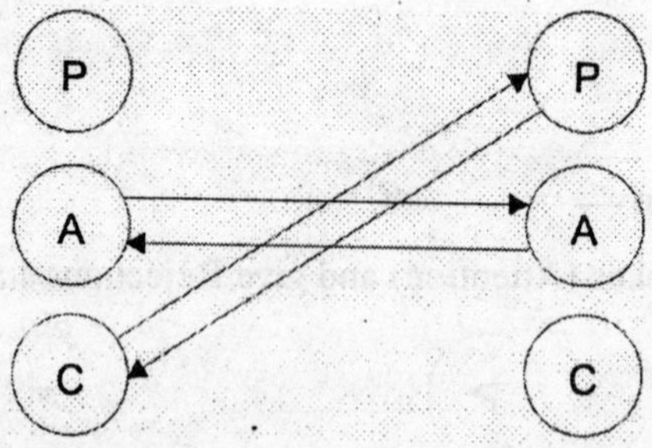

Payoff: This is a crooked way for person A to give dirty anger stamps. You should recognize games for what they are – a means for handling feelings (usually) not OK feelings and for satisfying stroke hunger. People sometimes try to substitute games for problem-solving for the following reasons:

1. Game outcomes are more predictable and therefore less risky.
2. It is often easier to enlist colleagues in game paying than problem solving.
3. Many people feel "Not OK" about themselves and need games to mask this feeling.

Healthy Work Climate versus Pollution

Work climate affects the kinds of result that individuals, groups and organizations produce. It comprises values, attitudes and underlying assumptions that determine how work gets done and problems get solved.

People need strokes to survive and spend considerable time and energy. They will get strokes one way or another. This basic hunger can be satisfied through work climate that has a lot natural and spontaneous stroking. A climate which is lack of stroking will cause people to spend more time and energy getting their needed strokes through more intense game playing, non-task related pastimes, etc.

Intense game playing caused pollution of the social environment around the individuals or groups involved. This pollution can be reduced by trying your adult to identify the games and to try problem solving difficulties which underlie the game playing oughtmanship or any other approach to work which commonly uses the parent to react to problems which will result in the lower utilization of the adult by individuals and this leads to ineffective and low effective and low efficiency problem solving. The first step is putting your adult to work more on the job is updating your own parent and child tapes. The manner in which crisis and goals are handled contributes significantly to work area characterised by game playing, or oughtmanship will help to produce less healthy climates. Reactions characterised by supportive problem solving will help produce a healthy, productive climate.

If we only had a few more creative people around here

If you are unable to solve your problems or you cannot find the solution of your problems which are disturbing you day and night, search experienced and intelligent people for 'favoured magical' solutions. One of the `magic' remedies often talked about in large organizations is creativity—" (If we only had more creative people around we could get most of these problem solved). It is not likely that you can make yourself and other more creative through magic but you can make use of some TA insight to help.

"Is it possible to foster creativity? The question is not easily answered, popular books on the subject seen to saying that the trait in questions like a muscle that profit the right place. Or they may take the line that creativity is communicable secret like a gold trip or a good receipt. But research workers believe that this trait and qualities of character temperament and intellect that contribute to it are laid down in childhood and depend to a considerable degree on relationships within the "family." (All the people are fortunate to keep their child healthy while they grow older. This probably requires a family environment that provides plenty of Adult protection for their OK kid rather than one filled with an overdose of "oughtmanship").

As the organization or society ages or grows, vitality diminishes, flexibility gives way to rigidity, creativity fades and mere is a loss of capacity to meet challenges from unexpected directions. The child who is a common resident of all new life, often gets crowded into the shadows by a demanding parent even though well intended which raises more and more concern about what is proper or appropriate. Life gets somehow turned around until it is reacting more to the demands of others (others or your own parent) than it is initiating, exploring, testing and asking why call to mind the adaptability diminishment with the year. Vigour and recklessness of some new organizations and success are our frontier settlements and reflect on how frequently these qualities are buried under the weight of tradition and history.

Similarly the infant is a model of openness to new experience respectful, curious, eager, unafraid, willing to try anything and above all not inhibited by (fixed habits and attitudes). (A beautiful definition of the child or OK kid). As the years pass, he loses these priceless qualities.

The individual of high originality having opened himself to such a varied range of experience, exhibits an extraordinary capacity to impose order on experience. And as Backmon has suggested, it may be that the creative individual could not tolerate such a wild production of ideas and experiences if he did not have profound confidence in his capacity to bring some new kind of order out of this chaos. (A person needs a strong Adult to give protection for the OK kid to do its thing). A strong Adult is also needed to give him confidence that no matter what kind of chaos his OK kid generates his Adult can figure out a way to restore order.

More significant than his receptivity to the external world is his openness with respect to his own emotions, anxieties and fantasies.

How can easily one tune on to his child without his parents censuring or blocking the experience?

"In most societies and organizations there grows up a chocking under burst of customs and precedent. There comes to be an accepted way ("Proper" as in parent) to do everything. Eccentric experimentation and radical departure from past practices are ruled out. The old hand says, "You just have to understand how we do things around her" and what he means is that how we do things "is sound, respectable and the best way" "oughtmanship stifles the creativity of the OK kid."

A Technique for stimulating creative thinking is brainstorming ground rules (which are followed by TA interpretations in parenthesis).

1. Criticism and judgement it ruled out. (Parents are kicked out. Only adults and OK kids are invited to participate).
2. Free wheeling is welcomed. The wilder the idea the better. It is easier to tame down than to pick up (The wild, impulsive OK kid gets a special engraved invitation to the part).
3. Quantity is wanted. (You are forced to give the Adult a good work out roof, the more idea you have the more options you have to choose from. This raises the probability that the solution will be an Adult decision rather than a parent "Should").
4. Combination and improvement are sought.

(The more options your OK kid has to play with and your different things which result in quadrupled originality. You can use my ideas in the exercise and *vice versa* because at least in this exercise, I am OK with you and you are OK with me).

Improving Efforts to Improve

The term improving has very high positive value attached to it in our country. People speak positively about improvement in these fields: themselves, relationships with others, specific product or service, profitability, environment etc. Through history people have been developing the ideas about improving the ways in which their affairs are managed.

Jefferson, Franklin and other had strong ideas about improving the manner in which the colonies were managed. Fredrick Taylor developed a series of ideas about improving the way, the factories of his day were managed. Today groups of people have ideas about improving the way, their schools and universities are managed. Today many people are writing and taking about how to improve the management of business and governmental orgainzations.

The terms improve implies creating some change from what is today to something different which is seen as more desirable. TA can help you to take a closer look at this process of improving through change.

Only Adult people can create improvement on purpose and they have the potentiality and capacity to change the old structure. The parent and child can only react to things, situations and others. They cannot compute and decide and therefore intentionally cause things to happen. People's parent and child ego states can and often do, however resist change.

Your parent can resist change by making reactive, non-data based judgement about the potential charge or improvement. (They are only trying to undermine our authority over our employees.) Parents resisted change or improvement is being urged on an individual or group by an outsider.

The biggest potential resister of change is probably your child change usually carries with it the element of risk and the unknown. This often causes your child to react with fear and anxieties about what will happen after the change is made. The more Not OK potential or actual charge the higher is the probability that he will resist the change. After the Not OK child of an individual will call on his parent to justify his resistance.

What can you do to minimise your own well others' resistance to charge and to improve efforts to improve? By providing or obtaining more data about the change sometimes resistance can be reduced. By involving people in some aspect of the decision-making will also help to get them unhooked from their parent or child reactions.

The method you use in trying to improve something is also extremely important. Telling people they should or must (Parent initiated "Oughtmanship") improve something will probably hook their child. For example, telling a group of employees, you must improve your customer service and also reduce costs will likely to generate only anger, guilt or fear (child reaction). Similarly telling people that they should worry (thereby looking their child) about this problem will probably not lead to improvement or change. On the other hand, the more relevant data you give employee about service and cost performance problems, the more likely you will engage their Adult in problem solving.

Script Analysis

A script is defined as a non-going life plan developed at the early childhood under the parental difference. It directs the individual behaviour in most important aspects of his life. Eric Berne has contributed the most in the understanding of the concept of script. In fact, the central theme of his book 'what do you say after you say hello's is script analysis.

To Eric Berne, script is a complete plan offering both structures, instructions, prescriptions and permission and structure which make one winner or loser in life. A winner programming is more adaptive. Usually he exercises more autonomy because he has more permission. A loser, on the other hand, has strong injunctions and inner demon. No matter how well he lays his plan, his demon comes at a critical moment and upsets all.

For longer and life script resembles the script of a drama–characters, dialogues, actions and scenes, themes and plays culminating towards a climax and ends in final curtain. This script makes a person to act out the drama though his awareness of it may be agree. Longward also uses Frederick Pearks concept of a person's two stagers for action–public stage and private stage. Eric Berne has also shown that some develop rebellious tendency against the scripts. In other words, they are just the opposite of what they are expected to do. This antiscript behaviour has been termed as identity crisis. It resembles Eric Berne's concept of identity diffusion. (Eric Berne, 1917, p. 133). Three kinds of scripts are there winners, non-winners and losers. In script languages, the loser is described as a frog, a winner as prince or princes. A winning script comes from nursing parent, a non-winning from a controlling parent and a losing script from parents of a crazy and destructive child. A winner fulfills his contract with himself and the world, a loser causes grief to himself and others. Even if a loser comes at the top, he still remains a loser because he does not know what to do either if he wins or after he wins, and ultimately loses that he has won.

In TA, for understanding the individuals' behaviour, the script is the key word. In order to make an individual effective, it is necessary that his script is understood and written if necessary. Through script analysis one can emerge as a person capable of autonomous vitality, creativity, fulfillment and satisfaction.

The roots of script analysis go back to friend who analysed the life style of Leonardo da Vinci. During the recent years Ericson analysed the life plans and life courses of distinguished leaders like Martin Luther and Mahatma Gandhi using their scripts. However, the closer approach to screen life study of script is in the work of Mc Clelland who the relationship between stones heard and read by children and their motives in living. His researches have shown that the achievers' scripts were based on the success stories while the script of the power oriented person were based on stories of risk.

Conclusion

In reviewing the literature on transactional analysis one is struck by the unchallenged influence of Eric Berne on TA Theory. There is unquestioned of the concept propounded by him. Thomas Harris, K, Tongeward and other authors in the field have built effectively of Eric Berne's contributions. It is obvious that transactional analysis has it roots in Freud but it is surprising the Eric Berne in none of his writings has acknowledged Freund's influence.

Similarly, the contributions of Gestlalt psychology in TA theory remains unrecognised by Eric Berne, though his followers such as Harris, Jongeward and others have recognised its contributions to TA theory and practice.

There has been an attempt in TA to translate the basic management theories into language TA. Gold Haber has shown that there is parallel between Mc Gregor theory and transactional analysis. In fact, he argues that theory is better understood through transactional analysis. When a manager is operating theory from the assumption of authority and control, believes apparently behaving through parent, when he is using Theory Y, the manager attempts to integrate the management of employee objectives by operating through his adult. Parent orientation and adult orientation are explained through Theory X and Theory Y, Randall translated the managerial and of Blake and Jane Mourton into TA language. He has described the various leadership styles in terms of the life possession time structuring, transaction and ego states for, e.g., 9-1 manager uses parent-child transactions, the 1-9 manager acts from child ego state and sometimes from nurturing parents state. The 1-1 manager uses transactions from not OK child stage and 9-9 manager uses his adult ego and effectively uses parent and child. The attempts to correlate transactional analysis with other theory of management is quite unique and interesting, although it appears simple. For example, 9-9 style is correlated with I am OK, You are OK position and also to the systems management though we brow that both these concepts are only remotely interested.

TA is a technology for understanding self. The frame of reference is cydyadic interaction. The setting is either individual or groups. As teams consist of individuals and individuals are building blocks of organizations, the application of TA for impressing teams effectiveness and organizational development seems practical.

The pioneers of TA believe that this technique helps the individuals to the 'winner' if the ego states and transactions follow the proper functioning. The individual knows how to be 'authentic' with others and the environment if he appropriately uses his understanding of TA. The strength of TA lies in the fact that its whole foundation is based on the simple experiences of work with individuals, groups and organizations.

Lessons From T.A.

Reviewing the whole concept of TA, in summary, one can get the following lessons; towards interpersonal communication and understanding of the human behaviour:

1. Do not expect others to be 'mind readers.' If you have to ask questions, make direct requests.
2. Always remember that it is only I, who can reject myself. No one else can reject me. It is only request that can be rejected by myself.
3. Remember not to give wild guesses of uniformed opinions.
4. Do not be like those who have answers to all questions.
5. Confront others when they renege and never make false promise. Give others an opportunity to retract.
6. Communicate directly from A to A (Adult to Adult) and see eyes to eyes. This evokes A to A transactions.
7. For healthy relations avoid cross transactions.
8. Avoid questions unless you really wish to have the information.
9. Avoid exaggerations and be factual.
10. Avoid focus on who is right or wrong, rather focus on problems.
11. Acknowledge other persons' feelings even while you disagree. You should agree to disagree.
12. Respect the individual.
13. Learn to say 'no.'
14. Do not create stroke scarce economy. Always keep in mind that you get what you give.
15. Share Natural Child (NC) feelings when Adult (A) permit.
16. If your wish to make a confrontation, confront with Nurturing Parent (NP), Natural Child (NC) or Adult (A).
17. Remember not to make an attempt to confront with Rebellious Child (RC) or Critical Parent (CP).

18. It is easy to know what is wrong with the other person, but a little harder to realise your own part in the situation.
19. It is OK to express anger, fear, sadness, and warmth when it make sense to do so (NC).
20. Live in the 'here and now', the rest of your life start from today.
21. Refuse to be involved in any activity that might victimise another.
22. Permit others to restore damaged relationships.
23. Refuse to allow small gripes to grow big.
24. Make only positive comments about those not present.
25. Do not wait for Santa Claus.
26. While talking to another person do not exaggerate your own achievements. In fact, he has no interest in them at all. You may be saying all that to put him down.
27. Talk something of the interest of the other party. (His achievement).
28. Do not raise/ask irrelevant points.
29. Be empathetic. All are prejudiced. Man is born of risen apes. Not of fallen angles. Our conflicts and crimes, our missiles and murders should cause no surprise when we remember our predatory animal origin. Some are man, and some are caricature of man.
30. Criticism will make the other person see reason.
31. Even when there is clash of interest, you can search areas of mutual interest and communicate it.
32. Accept boldly your own mistakes. Do not put blame on other.
33. Psychological games be avoided.

Thus TA can serve as a tool to bring greater effectiveness in the life of an individual by giving liberation to him. It can help him to attain autonomy in life. Eric Berne himself states that this attainment of autonomy in life is evident because of the release or recovery of the following three capacities:

(a) Awareness
(b) Spontaneity
(c) Intimacy

In the words of Eric Berne 'the aware person is alive because he knows how he feels, where he is and when it is. He knows that after he dies the trees will still be there, but he will not be there to look at them again, so he wants to see them now with as much poignancy as possible. The self-aware person learns to live here and now, and not elsewhere, the past or the future. He will not hurry because he is living in the present moment with the environment which is here: the sky and the trees as well as the feeling of motion.'

When Eric Berne refers to spontaneity, it implies the freedom to choose and express one's feelings among the various available feelings, i.e., Parent feelings, Adult feelings or Child feelings. Because of this diversity in feelings an individual gains situational sensitivity and behavioural flexibility in life. Though it is not an easy task to get liberated from the influences of one's parents in his life. These shadows are so well ingrained in the psyche and are essential for biological and social survival in the worldly world. The effect of these influences in distinctly noticeable not only in early life of an individual, but in the later stages of life too. This may vary from individual to individual and in some cases it has been noticed to effect not only during the first two or three decades of life but also beyond that. Even then, TA enables an individual in gaining intimacy in life. Though TA life becomes game free and impartial because it helps to mobilise positive feelings. Therapeutic sessions in TA help an individual increasing increased intimacy. They equip an individual with a power to struggle continuously to be able to get rid of old habits, because it is rather impossible to kick off all the parent recordings in one single stroke.

Eric Berne cautions that awareness, spontaneity, and intimacy – 'all three of these may be frightening and even perilous to the unprepared. Perhaps they are better off as they are. There is no hope for the human race, but there is hope for individual members of it.'

Key to Developing Effective Skills

Ego States Diagram

- One of the hallmarks of a healthy personality is clear, direct expression of thoughts and feelings. Sooner or later, your true thoughts and feelings do get expressed.
- Learn to express your thoughts, feelings by using personalities. Do not activate unhealthy parts of personality.
- To develop effective people skills think that every human being has intrinsic worth and dignity.
- One adopts life positions accordingly as one is parented. Decision on basic position determines the kind of life I will lead, the kind of people I will choose to relate to. These decisions are the basis of the life script.
- A - A, NP - NC, NP - NP, NC - NC, NC - NP
- Do not expect others to be mind readers. Do not assume, be appropriately assertive.
- Be empathetic, understanding, supportive.
- Give positive strokes to subordinates, peers, and supervisors. Have positive attitude about others. View all people as having inherent worth and dignity.
- Be willing to admit to not knowing the answer (some people provide answers to all the questions).
- Involve peers and subordinates in decision-making and in assumption of responsibility. To put decision into action, provide structure: who will do what, when and where.
- Be open with people. Enlarge your 'arena.' This would promote trust, cooperation, and increase managerial effectiveness. 'Feedback is the breakfast of champions.'

Structure for Success

1. People need clarity to function effectively.
2. Job description, written policies, lines of authority, decision-making policies help.
3. Inconsistent, application of above is destructive.
4. It is vital that people be held accountable for their behaviour. If this is inconsistent or non existent, organization may flounder.
5. A regular schedule for one to one supervisory sessions, is very useful because it shows that you care.
6. A key to making things happen is to define who, what, when, where, how and why (Content analysis).
7. Structure and strokes are powerful combination.

Make Contracts and Keep Them

- Contracts represent your character, keep them.
- If an agreement needs to be changed make sure you contact the person with whom you have the agreement and negotiate a different contract.
- If people break their contracts with you, confront this. If you don't, you contribute to the breakdown of future contracts with them and to the invalidation of contracts in general.
- If you do want to make an agreement, speak up in a sensitive way. If the other person is reluctant to make the contract encourage him to voice his objections.
- When making an agreement make sure that you clearly define what you want.
- Contract for 'No discounting' and set aside time to 'Level' at each session. During leveling time, share positive and negative strokes.

Confrontation is Not a Dirty Word

- When people are ineffective, inefficient, or are discounting you, somebody else, themselves or a problem, caring confrontation invites them to change their behaviours.
- If you way it straight, you are much less likely to show it crooked. Remember, that you cannot really hide strong feelings successfully.
- Confrontation is best done on a one to one basis, not in front of others.
- Confrontation should be mixed with positive strokes.
- Structure the confrontation so that the person wins by changing his behaviour. Do not be aggressive. Avoid challenging the person you are challenging.
- When people are drunk, violent, irrational, or hysterical remain self confident and take charge.
- When people won't change and you are not willing to accept this, stop transacting with them. If you do so from I am OK, you are OK position.
- You leave the door open for future discussion.

Everyone Wants to Feel Important

- Strokes are a need and it is all right to want attention.
- What you stroke is what you get. The behaviour that is paid attention to is the behaviour that will be repeated. (If you notice people it is only when they are wrong).
- Supervisors tend to give mostly negatives and employees tend not to stroke boss at all.
- People also need constructive criticism.
- Give positive strokes positively and publicly.

Can I Go Over Someone's Head

1. Handle disagreements directly, as much as it makes sense to do so.
2. Make sure you have clearly examined your own behaviour.
3. If you go to Boss's peer, for feedback, it is advisable to let him know beforehand that you are going to do this.
4. If you wish to 'go over his head' invite him to go with you so that both of you can get objective feedback.
5. Remember 'going over someone's head' is a last resort. Let him know that you are going and what you plan to say, if he chooses not to go with you.
6. The Boss must avoid taking sides. When employees come to you with problems, intervene to help them talk to each other and to resolve the conflict. If you must take a position, do so on the basis of the facts, not on the basis of whose personality you prefer.

REFERENCES

Berne, E, *Transactional Analysis: A New and Effective Method of Group Therapy, American Journal of Psychother*, 1958,12, pp. 735-43.

Freud, S. Leonardo da Vinci : *A Study in Psycho-sexuality*, New York, Vintage Books, 1955.

Erickson, E. Young Man, Luther, New York, 1958, *Gandhi's Truth*, New York,1969, both published by W.W Norton and Co.

Mc Clelland, D.C., *The Achieving Society, Princeton, D. Van Noshand Co., 1961.*

Gerald, Goldhabers, *A Content Analysis of Two Employment Manuals with Implications for Theory X, Theory Y Management Assumptions*, EPS, IIMs No. 426, April 1971.

Lyman, K. Randall, *Common Questions and Tentative Answers Regarding Organizational Development*, California Management Review, 1971, 13, 45, Lyman K. Randall, *Od Fad or Fundamental in Ptril Chase*, Ed., pp. 10 - 12, published by ASTD, July 1971.

Robert, S. Blake and Jane, S., *Managerial Grid*, Houston, Gulf Publishing, 1964, p. 12.

CHAPTER

12

Learning

You are proceeding on a road and a dog follows. You give the dog something to eat – a loaf of bread. Now whenever you happen to traverse that road, the dog follows you. A little child is taken to a doctor. The doctor examines him and prepares a syringe to give injection. The child looks on with curiosity or interest or indifferently, depending upon his nature. The doctor pricks the needle in the child's thigh and the child feels the pinch of pain. Now, when the child is taken to the doctor next time, his indifference is no longer there. As soon as the doctor picks up the syringe, the child starts screaming. Naturally, the question is why is this change in behaviour? Why did the child not react in the same manner as he did on the first occasion? The Answer is: the child learnt by experience that injections are painful. The learning caused a change in child's behaviour.

Learning is considered to be one of the fundamental basis of human behaviour. It is a most important source of information for those who wish to understand the modification mechanism. Humans and infrahumans learn in either simple or complex fashion, from the very first opportunity to react to sensory stimuli.

Learning takes place everywhere and throughout the entire existence of an individual. It is the modification of behaviour as the result of some past experience. Learning represents a broad behavioural area that encompasses training, the acquisition of skills, education, management development or any other similar change or modification process.

What is Learning?

1. *Learning is Change in Behaviour*

Learning to avoid fire, to walk, to drive a two-wheeler, to memorize lesson, to get acquainted by the implications of alternate course of action– all these activities, though varying in nature and complexity are based on the occurrence of mechanism that produce a change or an act to modify behaviour. Guilford very aptly said, "Learning is any change in behaviour, resulting from behaviour." That change may be good or bad is not a question. For example, prejudices, work restrictions, bad habits also can be learned. Typically at least learning consists in doing something new, provided this something new is retained by the individual and reappears in his later activities.

2. *Learning is an Organization of Behaviour*

The element of organization in learning is an important factor. Like when we learn to drive a car we have to organize the activities of turning the steering wheel, changing the gear, pressing and releasing the clutch and brake, etc. Similarly, when we learn to ride a bicycle we have to organize the activities of turning the pedal, balancing the handle, etc. Learning is that activity by virtue of which we organize our responses with new habits.

3. *Learning is the Reinforcement of a new Activity*

Temporary changes are not learning, they may be only reflective and fail to represent learning. Therefore, behavioural changes caused by fatigue or drugs are ruled out as learning. The change should be relatively permanent. Reinforcement helps in forming successful response and weeding out the unsuccessful ones. To quote Woodworth, "An activity may be called learning in so far as it develops the individual in any way, good or bad, and makes his environment and experiences different from what they otherwise have been."

Definition of Learning

There are two schools of thought regarding learning. One group of psychologists who stress external behaviour, consider learning to be a change of behaviour. However, the other group lay emphasis on internal changes and strongly advocates learning as change in the perception of individual.

Integrating both of these views, Murphy states, "From this point of view it would be legitimate to regard learning as a modification both of behaviour and the way of perceiving." The definition of learning propagated by Hilgrad is the essence of all the definitions. He states, "Learning is the process by which an activity originates or is changed through reacting to an encountered situation, provided that the characteristics of the change in activity cannot be explained on the basis of native response tendencies, maturity or temporary status of the organism."

Factors of Learning

There are certain vital factors without which it becomes rather impossible to say that process of learning takes place. These fundamental factors effect so greatly that no discussion on learning can be conducted without mentioning them.

1. *Motivation*

This is a basic factor because it precedes consideration of other factors in learning. Without motivation learning does not take place or at least, is not discernible. You cannot make an horse drink water unless he has a thirst *(motivation)*. A college student must have the need and drive to accomplish a task and reach a specific goal.

2. *Set or Learning to Learn*

The term 'set' implies as a predisposition or a tendency to respond. The relation to learning the concept of set goes beyond mere discussion on motivation. It has mechanical aspects which influence the course of learning. Harlow calls it 'learning to learn.' According to him, set changes the organism from one that adapts by trial and error to one that seems to develop hypothesis and insight. In an actual training situation, learning how to do similar but easier tasks in prior practice will make learning less difficult in the actual learning session. When in one training session the trainer asked trainees to describe their plan of learning ahead of time, the trainees learned faster and made fewer errors in the learning session.

3. *Knowledge of Results*

The Knowledge regarding one's own performance is an essential condition for learning. This feedback of performance enables the learner to know where he stands and to initiate corrective action if any deviation from the expected goals has taken place. In practice a trainee without information will usually try to generate his own knowledge of results that is select a goal he thinks is correct and adjust his performance accordingly.

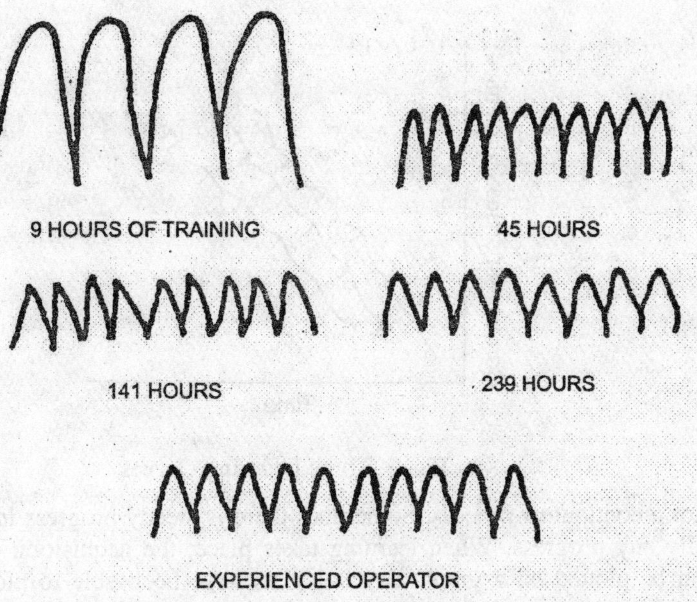

Fig. 1. Recorded Movement in Training

Lindal, as far back as 1948, demonstrated the importance of the knowledge of results in industrial training. Workers were required to hear, how to cut discs from a tungsten rod. This task required complex hand and foot coordination. Trainees were able to see their action patterns traced, on paper as they attempted to duplicate the patterns of experienced operators. Fig. 1 represents tracings indicating progress made over a period.

4. *Reinforcement*

Reinforcement in learning is a type of reward that follows the performance of activity which leads to the likelihood of the activity being performed again. Kolasa emphasises, "It has been noted reinforcement is a fundamental condition of learning. We can say without reinforcement no measurable modification of behaviour takes place. In the basic experiments on learning, the reward which accompanied or followed the behaviour was the reinforcer of that behaviour."

Learning Curves

Systematically laboratory investigations by and large have been conducted on animals and that too on rats. This practice seems to come from the Darwinian assumption that the learning process is continuous across species, i.e., basically the same wherever found.

The Fig. 2 shows three learning curves, indicating the rate of rewards hence 'correct' responses over time. The small cross marks show when rewards were administered. One of them was made by a pigeon in an experiment, by Feryter and Berelson, one was made by a rat in an experiment on anoxia by Lohr, and the third was made by a monkey in Karl Pribram's laboratory at the Hartford Institute.

Pigeon, rat, monkey which is which? It does not matter. Of course, these three species have behavioural repertoires which are as different as their anatomies. But once you have allowed for differences in the ways in which they make contact with the environment, and in the ways in which they act upon the environment, what remains of their behaviour shows astonishingly similar properties. Mice, cats, dogs, and human children could have added other curves to this figure [Skinner, 1956, pp. 230-31].

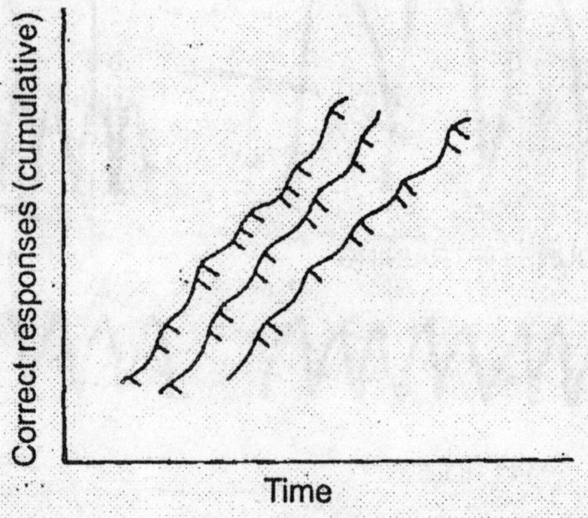

Fig. 2. Three Learning Curves

Learning is not a continuous process. Sometimes there is steady progress in learning, while at other times there is hardly any progress. When learning takes place, the acquisition of knowledge or skill is measurable and can be plotted on a graph. Psychologists have been able to plot learning curves which merely represent performance on the part of the individual or group over a time or series of trials. Frequently noticed patterns are represented as Fig. 3. In these patterns a word about regularity of lines – these have been smoothened to just show the apparent shapes of learning curves, whereas in reality it might be less regular.

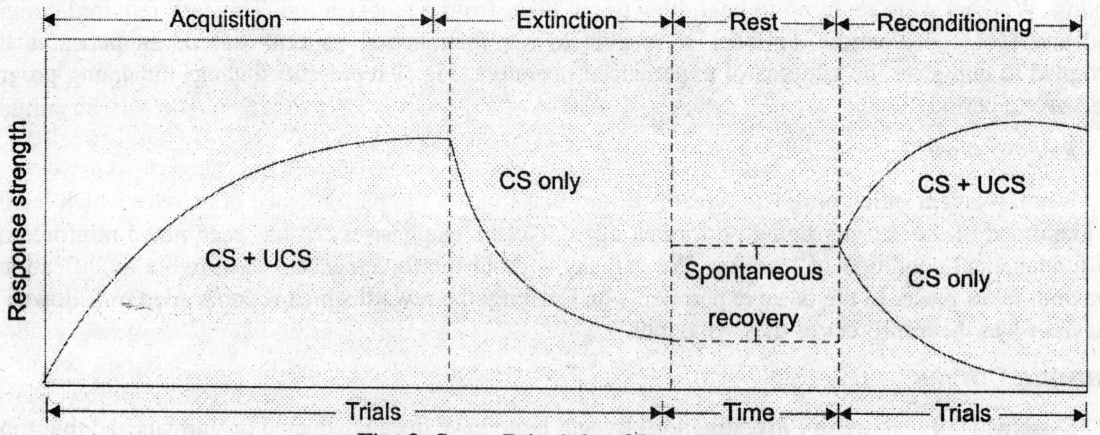

Fig. 3. Some Principle of Learning

Source: Gregory A. Kimble and Norman Garmezy, *General Psychology*, 2nd ed. 1963, The Ronald Press, New York, p. 144.

Acquisition – Learning Curves

The curve in the Fig. 3 shows principle of acquisition. There is gradually increase in strength of responses for each repeated trial. It occurs in both the classical and the instrumental conditioning. The acquisition curve can be considered as a learning curve where the vertical axis represents measured performance and the horizontal axis represents the amount of practice or experience in terms of time or number of trials. The Fig. 4 summarises the four general types of learning curves.

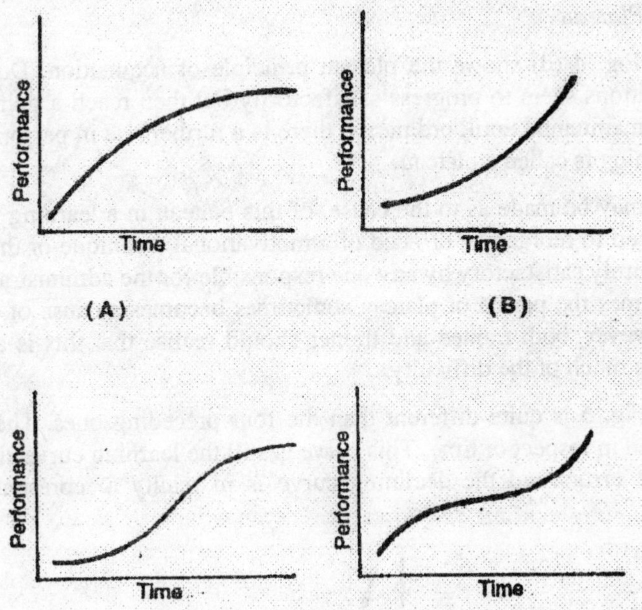

Fig. 4. Some Learning Curves

(a) Decreasing Returns Curve

The curve in the Fig. 4 (a) is negatively accelerated and is commonly referred to as the curve of decreasing returns. This curve represents the most common way where the acquisition takes place. The learning of most mental and motor tasks, show a decreasing return pattern. There is an initial spurt of learning, which then begins to slow down and finally reaches a point where there is practically no learning progress. In learning to perform most of the specialised, routine type jobs found in today's organization tend to follow negatively accelerated learning curves.

(b) Increasing Returns Curve

The curve in the Fig. 4 (b) is opposite of (a). It represents a positive acceleration that produces increasing returns. Such curve is a rarer learning curve than decreasing returns curve and generally occur only when a person is learning a completely unfamiliar mental or motor task. Such curves can be noticed in the learning process in an organization where a worker working on a very high-skilled lower level jobs. It has been found that initial learning may progress very slowly, but after a time, the learning takes giant strides.

(c) 'S' Learning Curve

The curve in the Fig. 4 (c) is commonly referred to as 'S' Shaped with learning slow at first, then picking up in rate and finally falling off in a typical way. Such curves have been observed in classical conditioning and in memorizing as well as in the development of skills. Some psychologists believe that this is the basic learning curve and the preceding negatively accelerated curve represents merely the second half of the underlying 'S' shaped curve, the first part of which was missed by the experiment because the skill being taught drew on some previous skill.

'S' learning curve is really a combination of the decreasing and increasing returns curves. For theory, all learning probably, follow and 'S'-curve if the person brings absolutely no relevant experience to the learning situation. However, in reality this is not the case. An 'S'-curve is most likely to be seen when a person attempts to learn a relatively difficult, unfamiliar work that requires insight. For example, learning, when applied to many of the highly skilled jobs in a technical industry might show the 'S'-pattern.

(d) Learning Plateau

The curve in Fig. 4 (d) shows the plateau principle of acquisition. During the process of learning many learning situations seem to progress satisfactorily but then reach a point where nothing new can be learnt. The level is maintained until, ordinarily, there is a further rise in performance to a higher level. This levelling off in learning is called a plateau.

Only guesses may be made as to the cause, of this plateau in a learning process. For instance, it may be the result of a need to reorganize or need of a motivational technique or the like. However, none of the explanations are entirely satisfactory by any one responsible for the administration of specific programmes. In training programmes the period of plateau sometimes becomes a cause of concern and discouragement for the trainer. However, both trainee and trainer should realise that this is a part of the usual course of events and alleviates much of the difficulty.

The curve in Fig. 5 is quite different than the four preceding ones. The above four performance in Fig. 4 were measured in respect of time. This curve is still the learning curve since the ordinate (the vertical axis) is in terms of errors and the declining curve is in reality a representative sketch of progress in learning.

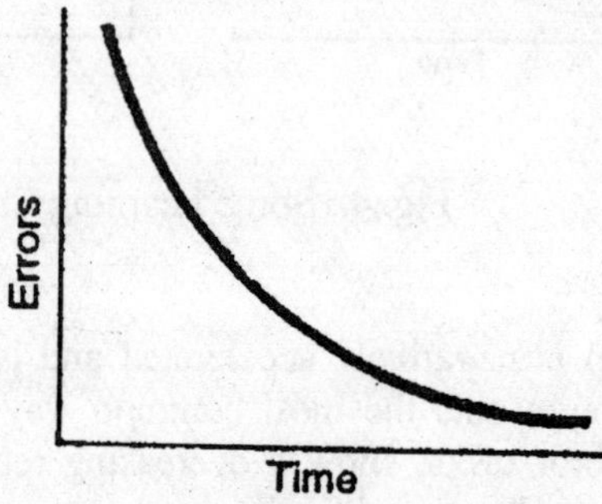

Fig. 5. Sketch of Progress in Learning

In the following Figs. 6 and 7, an attempt has been made to represent same activities (learning typewriter) in two ways. On one hand a relation is established between output and efforts and in the second diagram, amount learnt in relation to time.

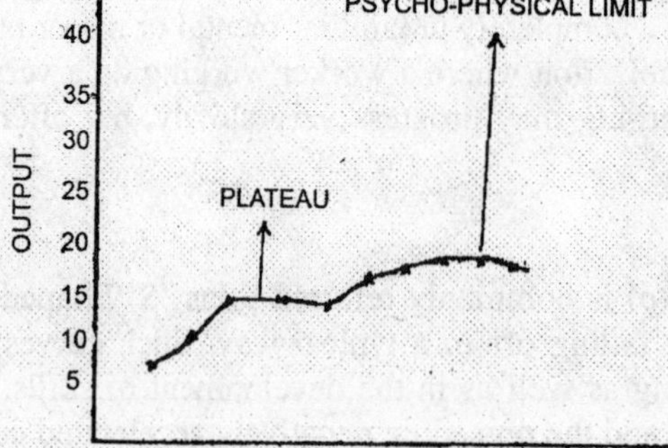

Fig. 6. Relation between Output and Efforts

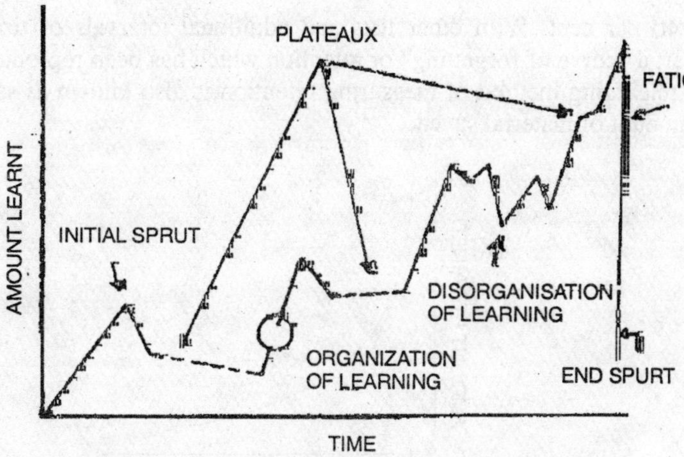

Fig. 7. Amount Learnt in Relation to Time

The result of both the learning curves confirms the following points:

(a) Initial Spurts

At the beginning of an activity there is a natural initial spurt. Normally the graph levels off at some stage, indicating that the maximum performance has been achieved. It seems at the beginning of session (learning process) the subject is highly motivated and seems to exhibit a significant urge of effort. Just for this very reason many experienced trainers exploit this initial spurt by selecting the most important item to be presented to the trainees at just start of the training session on the concept, first step is the best step.

(b) Learning Plateau

It is definite that at some point or the another in the learning process there will be a flattening off, in terms of improvement plateau.

(c) Organization of Learning

Jumping from one plateau to another plateau is known as organization of learning. This stage is achieved when the learner, discovers a new and more effective method of performing a particular task. For example, in mathematics the students learn to apply calculus to solve problems of business.

(d) Disorganization of Learning

It is an actual fall off in performance. This is more significantly evident when the subject has to choose between alternative methods of performing a task.

(e) End Spurt

The end spurt is preceded by the psycho-physical limits of an individual. Every individual has its own limitations and capacities to perform a task. After reaching its pick performance, there is evident a point at which the individual tends to decline to give higher results or learn any more, whatsoever method of reinforcement is applied. Through some training programmes it has been noticed that when the training session draws nearer to an end, and the subject realises this, there occurs resurgence of interest and effort to learn more. This revival is known as the end spurt. But in reality, it has been noticed that after the crossing of psycho-physical limits the end spurt is very rare and the efforts made by the trainer at this stage do not yield much significant results.

Relearning

The method of relearning and a definite relation between learning and forgetting was pioneered by Ebbingpaus in his studies on learning and retention. He determined the time it took him to memorise a list of no-nonsense syllables and then after a lapse of time, he noted how long it took to relearn that same list. The difference in time taken was expressed as a percentage. The learning time was 60 per cent and retention was only 40 per cent. With other lists and additional intervals of time Ebbinghuas was in a position to plot a chart a "curve of forgetting" or retention which has been reproduced below in Fig. 8. One would note that the relearning method of measuring retention is also known as savings methods since the results indicate the amount of material saved.

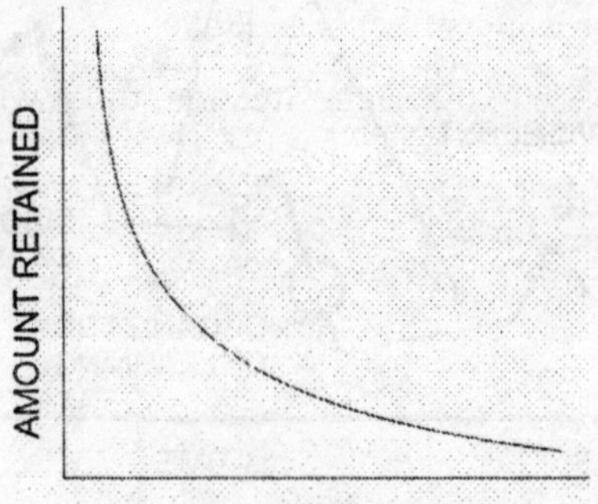

Fig. 8. The Curve of Forgetting

Form of Learning

People learn new behaviour through one of the following theories of learning:

1. Thorndike's Theory of Trial and Error.
2. Pavlov Theory of Conditioned Response.
3. Skinner's Theory of Operant Conditioning.
4. Kohlar's Theory of Learning by Insight.
5. Theory of Learning by Imitation.
6. Observational Learning.
7. Cognitive Learning.

Thorndike's Principles of Learning

This theory of learning can be better understood with the help of three major laws which are as under:

1. Law of Readiness.
2. Law of Exercise.
3. Law of Effect.

1. Law of Readiness

In Thorndike's words, the law of readiness is active in the following three conditions:

(i) When the conduction unit is prepared to go into action, its work is quite satisfactory because nothing is done to alter its working.

(ii) The inactivity of a condition unit and any reaction may arise in connection with the deficiency.

(iii) When a conduction unit is forced to act while it is not prepared to do so, its behaviour is of a nature calculated to excite anger.

From the above description, it is clear that the readiness of learning is known by the tendency for learning in the learner. It describes those situations in which the person who learns either invites the object of his learning or rejects it. Readiness includes all those preparatory adjustments which immediately precede the activity. The readiness creates a mental set for learning and turns the learner's mental attitude towards the subject to be learned.

2. Law of Exercise

This law of exercise is based on the concept of the laws of use and disuse. Any repeated application of an act, is firmly fixed in the mind whereas continuous disuse weakens the relation. Taking a cue from the universal experience, emphasize repetition of the activity in learning. Repetitive application of an activity results in the formation of habit in the muscles and the nerve fibers of the brain so that there is a facility in its execution in case of need.

3. Law of Effect

In Thorndike's own words, the effect stated thus:

Of several responses made to the same situation, those which are accompanied or closely followed by satisfaction (reinforcement) — will be more likely to reoccur; those which are accompanied or closely followed by discomfort (negative reinforcement or punishment) will be less likely to occur.

Most modern learning experts generally accept the validity of this law. Very few of us fully realise the effect of reinforcement, (reward encouragement, praise, etc.) having on learning.

It was Thorndike who for the first time declared that all learning is Trial and Error, after conducting an experiment on a cat. He placed a hungry cat inside a cage and food outside. By trial and error the cat learnt the trick to open the door of the cage and come out.

Thorndike's method of trial and error is normally used in the following circumstances:

1. It is used when the learner is completely motivated and can see the goal clearly. If the cat was not hungry, it would have never tried to come out of the cage.
2. It is used when perception done on learned activities are not sufficient. If the cat could come out of the cage by merely moving in any direction, there was hardly any need of several trial and errors.
3. When the learner fails to find the solution of the problem. If one fails to find a solution of the problem then only he proceeds blindly, tries in various directions, commits errors, eliminates them and finally arrives at a successful response.
4. It is subject to law of readiness which says unless one is mentally and physically ready to accept and implement a change it is not possible to bring about a change of lasting importance in the behaviour of the other people. Willingness to learn and change in the first essential prerequisite for attitudinal transformation.

If pressure is exercised for changing the behaviour of others, it is bound to be a futile and ineffective exercise. The ultimate message must be got physically and mentally readied to change themselves. It would be best if conditions are created in a manner that the proposal for bringing about a change comes from the change itself. The role of the changer is to act as a facilitator.

Classical Conditioning

Pavlov's classical conditions experiment with dogs (in 1900) as subjects is a pioneer study conducted in behavioural science. The association of one event with another desired event resulting in behaviour is classical conditioning.

Ivan Pavlov, the Russian Psychologist, who won the Nobel Prize for his early experiments on the subject, conducted an experiment on a dog and tried to relate the dog's salivation and the ringing of a bell.

Through a simple surgical method he was able to measure accurately the amount of saliva secreted by the dog. When he presented a piece of meat (unconditioned stimulus), Pavlov noticed a great deal of salivation (unconditioned response). On the other hand, when he just rang a bell (neutral stimulus), the dog had no salivation.

As a next step, Pavlov accompanied the meat with the ringing of the bell. After repeating it several times, Pavlov rang the bell without the meat. This time the dog salivated only to the bell alone, as the dog had become classically conditioned to salivate. (Conditioned response to the sound of the bell is Conditioned stimulus).

Therefore, the essential components of classical conditioning are:

(a) Unconditioned Stimulus (US)
(b) Unconditioned Response (UR)

(c) Conditioned Stimulus (CS)

(d) Conditioned Response (CR)

It should be noted that Pavlov first referred to the bell as neutral stimulus and later as conditioned stimulus. Neutral stimulus first acquires the capacity to elicit a certain response, which is then called a conditioned response.

The relationship among these components of classical conditioning is shown in Fig. 9.

Psychologists have now been able to classically condition everything from the flat worms to human beings in all probability; any response in an organization's behavioural repertoire can be conditioned if an unconditioned stimulus can be found that regularly produces the response and if this unconditioned stimulus can be paired in training with conditioned stimulus.

Unfortunately, as the behaviour of people in organizations is emitted rather than elicited, and it is voluntary rather than reflexive, the classical conditioning has a limited value in the study of organizational behaviour. As Skinner has pointed out, classical conditioning represents an insignificant part of total human learning. It is passive and is elicited in response to a specific, identifiable event and as such it explains simple and reflexive behaviours. In classical conditioning something happens and we react in a specific or particular fashion.

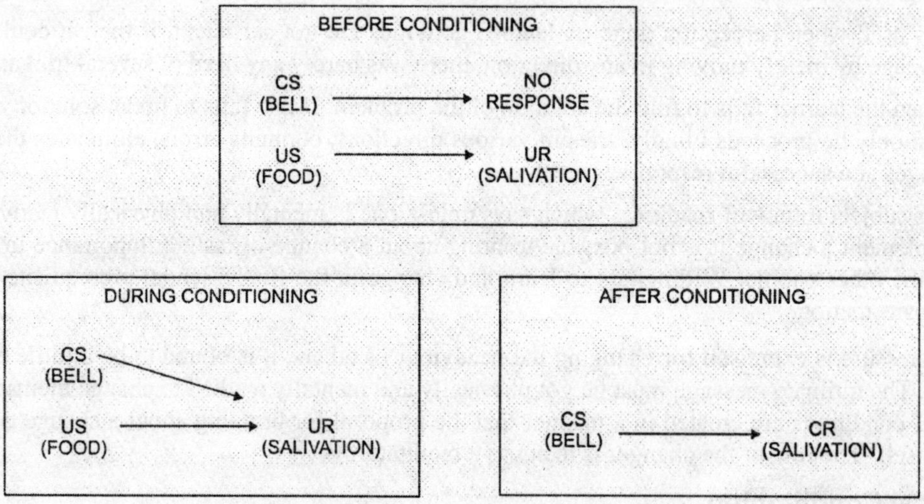

Fig. 9. A Diagram of Classical Conditioning

Even then in an organizational setting one can see classical conditioning operating. For example, at one manufacturing plant, every time the top executives from the head office would make a visit, the plant management would clean up the administrative offices and wash the windows. This went on for years. Eventually, employees would turn on their best behaviour and look prim and proper whenever the windows were cleaned even in those occasions when the cleaning was not paired with the visit from the top brass. People had learnt to associate the cleaning of the windows with the visit from the head office.

Operant Conditioning

A more complex learning form is operant or instrumental conditioning. Operant has been defined as behaviour that produces effects. What Pavlov did for classical conditioning a noted psychologist at Harvard, Skinner did for Operant Conditioning. Skinner suggests that individual emit responses that are rewarded and will not emit responses that are either not rewarded or are punished. Therefore, operant conditioning argues that behaviour is a function of its consequences. All behaviours are likely to be repeated if consequences are favourable. Behaviour is not likely to be repeated if the consequences are unfavourable. Therefore, rewards are most effective if they immediately follow the desired response. However, behaviour that is now rewarded, or if punished, is less likely to be repeated.

Operant conditioning is primarily concerned, with learning that occurs as a consequence of behaviour. The difference between classical conditioning and operant conditioning can be brought out.

Difference between Classical Conditioning and Operant Conditioning

There are two vital differences between classical conditioning and operant conditioning. The first point of difference relates to the type of response. In classical conditioning, a specific stimulus, such as food, is used to elicit a specific response. The response is elicited. In operant conditioning the response is not elicited by controlled stimulation but rather is spontaneously emitted by the subject. The precise stimuli producing the response is not elicited by controlled stimulation but rather is spontaneously emitted by the subject. The precise stimuli producing the response at the beginning of the learning period cannot be identified. Hence, it might be said that the emphasis in classical conditioning is upon involuntary responses, while the emphasis in operant conditioning is upon voluntary responses.

The second difference relates to the consequences of response. In the operant procedure, as its name implies, the subject's response operates on the environment to achieve some result, such as access to food or water, recognition by others, escape from pain or discomfort or some other desirable circumstance. In classical conditioning, the organism's behaviour is not instrumental in achieving any such result; the organism is unable to change the events of the experiment with its behaviour. Thus, food is presented or not presented in accordance with the design of the experiment– the subject's behaviour does not influence the occurrence of these events. Then there are also other less important differences.

Table 1. Some Major Differences

	Classical Conditioning		Operant Conditioning
1.	Responses are elicited from a person (reactive)	1.	Responses are emitted by a person (proactive)
2.	Responses are fixed to stimulus (no choice)	2.	Responses are variable in types and degrees (choice)
3.	Cs is a stimulus such as a sound, an object, a person.	3.	CS is a situation such as an office, a social setting, a specific set of circumstances.
4.	Reinforcement is not received by choice.	4.	Person is instrumental in securing reinforcement by "operating" on the environment.

Insight Learning

Insight learning is the best method of learning. It is an important constituent in the solution of problems, and is usually found in the higher class of animals and human beings.

A German Gestalt psychologist, Kohler, conducted a number of experiments with dogs, hens, monkeys and chimpanzees. These experiments confirmed that learning by insight has certain characteristics of its own. They are briefly as follows:

1. Insight is sudden.
2. Insight alters perception.
3. Old objects appear in new patterns and organization by virtue of insight.
4. Insight understanding is more useful than the dexterity of hands.
5. Insight is relative to the intellectual level. The higher species of human beings have more insight than the members of lower species.
6. Insight is sometimes hind sight and at others it is foresight.
7. Past experience is of great assistance in insight.
8. Maturity effects insight.

Insight method of learning is superior to that of Trial and Error method of learning in the following respects:

1. Trial and Error emphasizes the acquisition of motor skills but insight mental effort is stressed upon.
2. While Trial and Error depends upon sensory motor co-ordination, whereas insights depends upon perception.
3. In trial and error a person keeps the eyes on goal and all activity is goal-directed but in insight it is the unconscious mind which exerts the most while the conscious activities are either very few or aimless.

Imitation Learning

The Human child from the very first stage of learning learns mostly through imitation. It is quite common to notice that children imitate the behaviour, habits, manners from the ways of their parents. In imitation the learner tries to copy the behaviour of another person in totality, without understanding or thinking. Whenever this copying is observed, it is said that one has learned through imitation.

The main characteristics of learning through imitation are as follows:

1. The imitator never does it before imitation but performs the activity only after seeing it in another.
2. The imitator does not know before hand, the acting to be imitated.
3. In imitation the learner exactly copies the activity performed before him.

The process of imitation is very important in learning. The teacher makes a wide use of this fact. Education becomes easier, more understandable, interesting and perfect by demonstration. In the teaching of dramatics, dance, music, etc. demonstration is very important since imitation has an important role in them.

Observational Learning

There is a slight difference between imitation learning and observational learning. Observational learning results in as a result of watching the behaviour of another person and apprising the consequences of that behaviour. It does not require an overt response. When Mr. X observes that Y is rewarded for superior performance, X learns the positive relationship between performance and rewards without actually obtaining the rewards himself. Observational learning plays a crucial role in altering behaviour in organizations.

Cognitive Learning

Cognition refers to an individual's thoughts, knowledge interpretations, understanding or ideas about himself and his environment. The cognitive theory of learning assumes that the organism learns the meaning of various objects and events and learned responses depend upon the meaning designed to stimuli.

In the cognitive theory of learning the primary emphasis is on knowing, how events and objects are related to each other. Most of the learning that takes place in the classroom is cognitive learning. Cognitive learning is important because it increases the chance that the learner will do the right thing as first attempt, without going through a lengthy operant conditioning process.

The cognitive theory of learning differs from that of the classical conditioning and operant conditioning theories. The latter two emphasize stimulus response (S-R) associations for learning. In the S-R approach, learning is assumed to be a function of stimulus-response connections. The main criticism against the S-R approach to learning is that the contribution of the organism is minimised or ignored. In the cognitive theory the role of an organism in receiving, memorising, retrieving and interpreting stimuli, and reacting is recognised and emphasised.

Today, the cognitive theory is very much alive and relevant. Many motivation theories centre round the concept of cognition. Expectations, attributions and locus of control, and goal setting (which are in the forefront of modern work motivation) are all cognitive concepts and represent the purposefulness of organizational behaviour. Many researchers are currently concerned about the relationship or connection between cognition and organizational behaviour.

Types of Reinforcement

The consequences of behaviour are called reinforcement. A Manager may be able to use various kinds of reinforcement to affect employee behaviour. We do not mean our discussion of reinforcement to be prescriptive: we simply describe four kinds of reinforcement; how to use them depends on the situation. Fig. 10 summarizes the concepts underlying the four basic kinds of reinforcement.

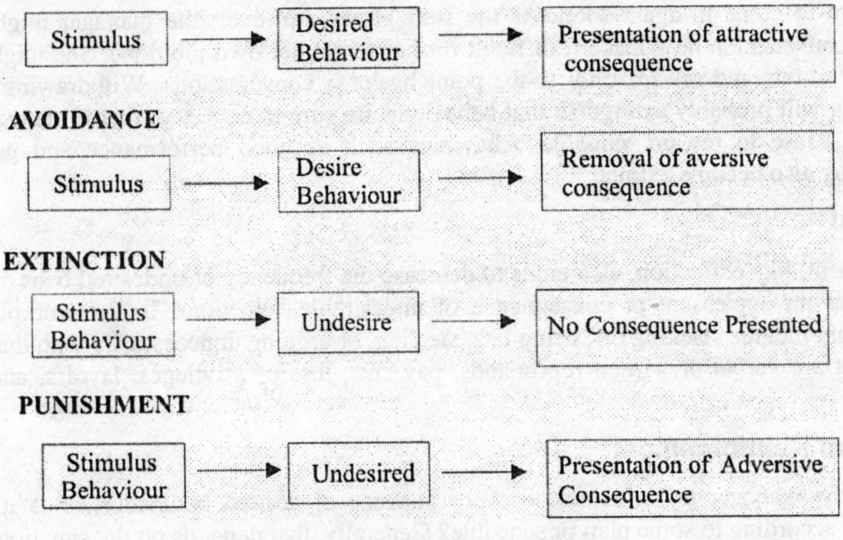

Fig. 10. Kinds of Reinforcement

Positive Reinforcement

Positive reinforcement is the concept of reinforcement theory that is perhaps most familiar to people outside the fields of psychology and organizational behaviour. Positive reinforcement is a reward that follows desirable behaviour. A compliment from the boss after completing a difficult job, and a salary increase following a period of high performance are both examples of positive reinforcement. Its effect is to maintain or increase the frequency of a desired behaviour. Managers might define desirable employee behaviour as hard work, punctuality, conscientiousness, and loyalty and commitment to the organization. When employees exhibit these behaviours, the manager may reward them with pay increases, praise, some kind of formal recognition, promotions, and the like. In terms of reinforcement theory, the rewards are intended to ensure the same type of behaviour in the future. Of course, different people work for different reasons. Therefore, to be useful as positive reinforcement, rewards should be tailored to the needs of the individual. In addition, a reward should be directly linked with the desired behaviour, and the individual should have ample opportunity to achieve the reinforcement. For example, a person who gets a raise in salary following a period of high performance should be made aware explicitly that the raise was given because of the performance. Likewise, the level of performance needed to get the raise should not be set so high as to be impossible to reach.

Avoidance

Avoidance, also known as negative reinforcement, is another means of increasing the frequency of desired behaviour. Rather than receiving a reward following a desired behaviour, the person is given the opportunity to avoid an unpleasant consequence. For example, an employee's boss may habitually criticize individuals who dress casually. To avoid criticism, the employee may routinely dress to suit the supervisor's tastes. The employee is engaging in desired behaviour (at least from the supervisor's viewpoint) to avoid an unpleasant, or aversive consequence.

Extinction

Whereas positive reinforcement and avoidance increase the frequency of desired behaviour, extinction decreases the frequency of undesired behaviour, especially behaviour that was previously rewarded. That is, if rewards are withdrawn for behaviours that were previously reinforced, the behaviours will probably become less frequent and eventually die out. For example, a manager with a small staff may encourage frequent visits from subordinates as a way of keeping to touch with what is going on. Positive reinforcement might include cordial conversation, attention to the subordinate's concerns, and encouragement to come in again soon. As the staff grows, however, the manager might find that such unstructured conversation now make it difficult for her to get her own job done. She might then brush off casual conversations and reward only to-the-point business conversations. Withdrawing the rewards for casual chatting will probably extinguish that behaviour. Be sure to note, too, that if managers, accidentally or otherwise, cease to reward valuable behaviours such as good performance and punctuality, those behaviours may also become extinct.

Punishment

Punishment, like extinction, also tends to decrease the frequency of undesired behaviour. Punishment is presented as an unpleasant or consequence of undesirable behaviour. In the workplace, undesirable behaviour might include slacking off, being late, stealing, or arguing unnecessarily with the boss. Examples of punishment are verbal or written reprimands, pay cuts, loss of privileges, layoffs, and termination of service.

Schedules of Reinforcement

Should the manager try to reinforce every instance of desired behaviour, or is it better to apply reinforcement according to some plan or schedule? Generally, that depends on the situation. Five schedules of reinforcement used effectively by psychologists and managers are summarized in Table 2.

Table 2. Schedules of Reinforcement

Continuous Reinforcement	:	Behaviour is reinforced every time it occurs.
Fixed Interval Reinforcement	:	Behaviour is reinforced according to some predetermined, constant schedule based on time.
Variable Interval Reinforcement	:	Behaviour is reinforced after periods of time, but the time span varies from one time to the next.
Fixed Ratio Reinforcement	:	Behaviour is reinforced according to the number of behaviours exhibited with the number of behaviours needed to gain reinforcement held constant.
Variable Ratio Reinforcement	:	Behaviour is reinforced according to the number of behaviours exhibited, but the number of behaviours needed to gain reinforcement varies from one time to the next.

Continuous Reinforcement

Continuous reinforcement rewards behaviour every time it occurs. Continuous reinforcement is very effective in increasing the frequency of a desired behaviour. When reinforcement is withdrawn, however, extinction sets in very quickly. The schedule poses serious practical difficulties as well: the manager must monitor every behaviour of an employee and provide effective reinforcement. This schedule, then, is seldom worth much to managers. Offering partial reinforcement according to one of the other four schedules is much more typical.

Fixed Interval Reinforcement

Fixed interval reinforcement means providing reinforcement on a predetermined, constant schedule. The Friday afternoon paycheck is a good example of fixed interval reinforcement. Unfortunately, in many situations, the fixed interval schedule is not necessarily going to maintain high levels of performance. If employees know that the boss will drop by to check on them everyday at 1:00 p.m. they are likely to be working hard at that time, hoping to gain praise and recognition, or to avoid the boss wrath. But at other times of the day, the employees probably will not work as hard because they have learned that reinforcement is unlikely except during the daily visit.

Variable Interval Reinforcement

This schedule also uses time as the basis for applying reinforcement but varies the interval between reinforcements. Although this schedule is inappropriate for paying wages, it can work well for other types of positive reinforcement such as praise and recognition, and for avoidance. Consider again the group of employees just described. Suppose that instead of coming by at exactly 1:00 everyday, the boss visits at a different time each day. Thus, he comes by at 9:30 on Monday, 2:00 on Tuesday, 11:00 on Wednesday, and so on. The following week, the times change. Since the employees do not know when to expect the boss, they will probably work fairly hard until his visit. Afterward, they may drop back to lower levels because they have learned that he will not be back until the next day.

Fixed Ratio Reinforcement

The fixed and variable ratio schedules gear reinforcement to the number of desired or undesired behaviours rather than to blocks of time. Under the fixed ratio schedule, the number of behaviours needed to obtain reinforcement is constant. Assume, for example, that a work group enters its cumulative performance total into the office computer every hour. The manager of the group uses the computer to monitor its activities. She might adopt a practice of dropping by to praise the group every time it reaches a performance level of 500 units. Thus, if the group does this three times on Monday, she stops by each time; if it reaches the mark only once on Tuesday, she stops by only once. The fixed ratio schedule can be fairly effective in maintaining desired behaviour. Employees tend to develop a feel for what it takes to be reinforced and work hard to keep up their performance.

Variable Ratio Reinforcement

Under the variable ratio schedule, the number of behaviours required for reinforcement varies over time. An employee performing under a variable ratio schedule is motivated to work hard because each successful behaviour increases the probability that the next one will result in reinforcement. With this schedule; the exact number of behaviours needed to obtain reinforcement is not crucial; what is important is that the intervals between reinforcement be not so long that the worker gets discouraged and stops trying. The supervisor, in the fixed ratio example, could reinforce her work group after it reaches performance levels of 450, 525, 325, 600 and so on. A variable ratio schedule can be quite effective but is difficult and cumbersome to use when formal organizational rewards, such as pay increases and promotions, are the reinforces. A fixed interval system is the most common way to administer these rewards.

To sum up, relying on any given schedule for all rewards is difficult or impractical. Instead, the manager should use the schedule best suited to the kind of reinforcement being used and try to link outcomes with behaviours according to the needs of the organization and its employees.

RELATED ASPECTS OF LEARNING

Several additional aspects of learning bear on individual behaviour in organizations. Among them are stimulus generalization, stimulus discrimination, vicarious learning, and the arguments for and against punishment.

Stimulus Generalization

Stimulus generalization is how people recognize the same or similar stimuli in different settings. That is, it is the process by which they can generalize a contingent reinforcement from one setting to another. Fig. 11 illustrates a simple example of the process. Following an initial stimulus-response-consequence, a person learns the behaviours likely to produce some kinds of reinforcement. Later, when presented with a similar stimulus in different surroundings, he or she knows that the same response is likely to elicit a similar consequence.

Consider, for example, the case of a plant manager with a history of effective troubleshooting. Over the years, he has been assigned to several different plants, each with a serious operating problem. After successfully dealing with the difficulties, he has always received an extended vacation, a bonus, and a boost in his base salary. He has learned the basic contingencies, or requirements of reinforcement for his job: the stimulus is the assignment, the response is correcting problems, and the consequences are several positive reinforces. When the manager gets his next assignment, he will probably generalize from his past experiences. Even though he will be in a different plant with different problems and employees, he will understand what it takes to be rewarded.

Stimulus Discrimination

Stimulus discrimination is the ability to recognize differences between stimuli. This process is also shown in Fig. 11. As in stimulus generalization, the person learns the basic stimulus — response — consequence sequence for one stimulus. When confronted with a new stimulus, however, he or she can discriminate between the two different stimuli and respond differently.

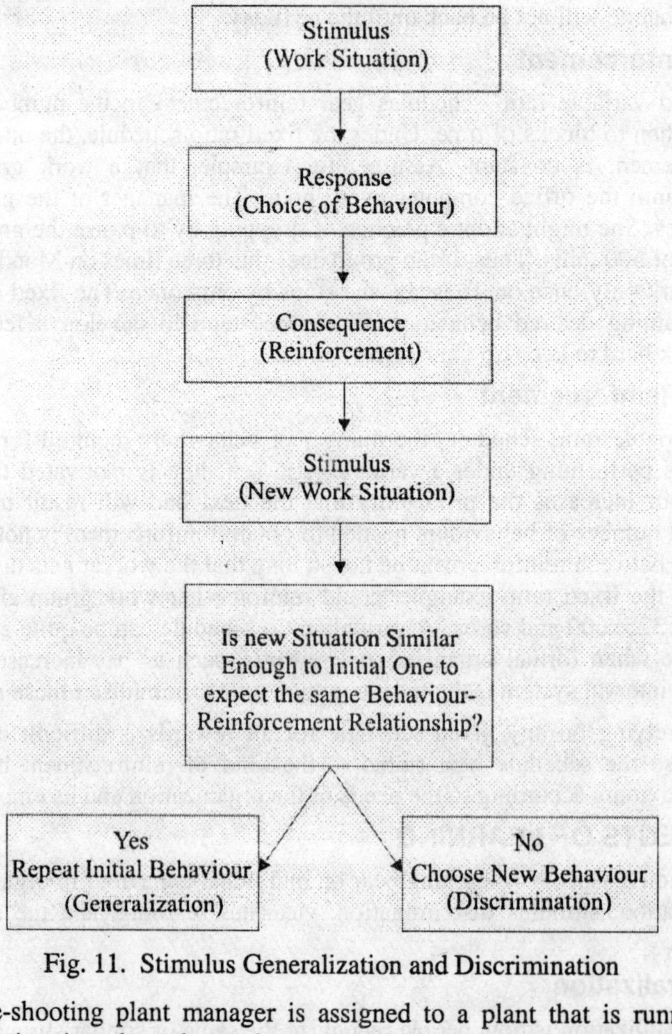

Fig. 11. Stimulus Generalization and Discrimination

Suppose the trouble-shooting plant manager is assigned to a plant that is running smoothly. His routine response to new situations has always been to identify and solve problems, but he must now discriminate between his new situation and his earlier once. He, will then, also recognize that a different set of behaviours, or responses, is needed for him to receive positive reinforcement.

Vicarious Learning

Vicarious learning or **modeling** is learning through the experiences of others. A person can learn to do a new job by observing others, for example, or by watching videotapes. And recall the earlier example where an employee learned not to be late by watching his boss chew out fellow workers.

Several conditions must be met for vicarious learning to take place. The behaviour being modeled must be relatively simple. Although we can learn by watching someone else how to push three or four buttons to set specifications on a machine, we probably cannot learn a complicated sequence of operations without also practicing the various steps ourselves.

Second, the behaviour being modeled must usually be concrete, not intellectual. We can learn by watching others how to respond to the different behaviours of a particular manager, or how to assemble a few components into a final assembly. But probably we cannot learn through simple observation how to write a computer program, or to conceptualize, or to think abstractly. Finally, to learn a job vicariously we must possess the physical ability needed to do the job. Most of us, for instance, can watch televised baseball games or tennis matches every weekend, but still will not be able to hit a curve ball like Don Mattingly or a backhand like Martina Navratilova.

In recent years, considerable attention has been devoted to a specific type of vicarious learning called social learning. Social learning theory suggests that behaviour is determined by a person's cognition and social environment. More specifically, people are presumed to learn behaviours and attitudes at least partially in response to what others expect of them.

Suppose that a new employee joins an existing work group. She already has some basis for knowing how to behave (i.e., education and previous experience). The group provides a set of very specific cues, however, that help the person see how her behaviour needs to be tailored to fit the specific situation she is in now. The group may indicate how the organization expects members to dress, how people are "supposed" to feel about the boss and so forth. Hence, the new employee learns how to behave in the new situation partially in response to what she already knows and partially in response to what others suggest and demonstrate.

Punishment

Punishment was defined earlier as the presentation of an unpleasant, or aversive consequence after an individual engages in undesirable behaviour. Thus, any unpleasant consequence that follows behaviour can be called punishment. When an attempt to punish is structured, official, and organizationally sanctioned, it is called discipline. When a boss yells at an employee who drops a bottle of solvent, punishment has taken place. If the boss formally reprimands the worker and puts a written account of the reprimand in the employee's personnel folder, this action would represent an attempt at discipline.

To be effective, discipline must be perceived as punishing, but in fact, it may not always be seen as such. For example, a subordinate, planning to quit in the near future, might find the supervisor's written reprimand amusing.

Although punishment is common in organizations, many managers and researchers question its practical value for influencing employee behaviour. They argue that punishment cannot be effective unless employee behaviour is continually observed. Punishment is likely to suppress behaviour temporarily rather than permanently extinguish it, and the side effects of punishment, such as hostility and anger, may outweigh any potential benefits. Furthermore, undesirable behaviour can often be changed through extinction or environmental engineering. For example, if two employees who must frequently interact are constantly arguing with each other, it may be possible to stop the bickering without punishing. The manager might alter their environment by having them deal with each other through a neutral third party.

Punishment may be an appropriate tool for altering behaviour in some situation, however. Many of life's events teach us what to do by means of punishment. Falling off a bike, drinking too much, or going out in the rain without an umbrella, all lead to punishing consequences (getting bruised, having a hangover, and getting wet), and we often learn to change our behaviour as a result. Furthermore, certain types of undesirable behaviour may have far-reaching negative effects if they go unpunished. For instance, an employee who sexually harasses a co-worker, a clerk who steals money from the petty cash account, and an executive who engages in illegal stock transactions should all be punished.

When punishment is needed, how is it most effectively meted out and how can its negative consequences be reduced? First, punishment should be applied before the undesired behaviour has been strongly reinforced. Thus, punishment should work better the second time an employee is late, rather than the tenth time. Second, the punishment should immediately follow the undesired behaviour to emphasize the connection between the behaviour and the consequence in the person's mind. Third, punishment should focus on the behaviour, not the person; thus, it should be impersonal, consistent across time, and impartial. Finally, the punishment should have as much information value as possible. The employee should know exactly what he or she did to warrant the punishment, the reason why punishment follows such an action, and the consequences of repeating the same behaviour.

OTHER MANAGERIAL IMPLICATIONS OF LEARNING

Beyond the day-to-day implications of learning already noted, there are others that relate to more general managerial practice. As shown in Fig. 12, these implications relate most closely to the areas of motivation, performance evaluation and rewards, and employee training.

Motivation

Motivation is related in several ways to learning. The extent to which valued rewards follow high performance, for example, will affect an employee's willingness to work hard in the future, and the cause-and-effect linkage needs to be clear. That is, employees should recognize that certain behaviours (such as hard work) cause certain outcomes (desired rewards). Similarly, if rewards do not follow performance the employee may be less inclined to work hard in the future. A lot of research on the learning process in organizations has been done recently. These studies have led to the development of a motivational perspective called organizational behaviour modification.

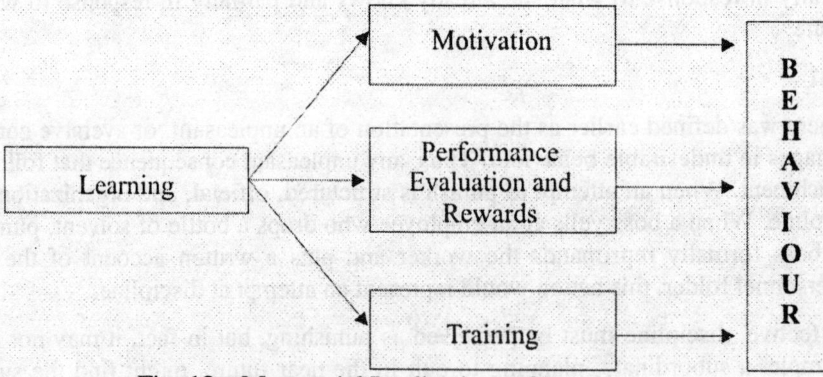

Fig. 12. Managerial Implications of Learning

PERFORMANCE EVALUATION AND REWARDS

Learning also links up with organizational practices in the performance evaluation and reward system. Performance evaluation is how managers assess the work behaviour of individuals and groups; rewards are the positive reinforcements (salary, promotion, public, recognition) that companies give for desirable behaviour.

Training

Learning is the major goal of employee training. Many organizations devote vast resources to training and development to expand the skills and abilities of their employees. Andrews Grove, president of Intel Corporation, heartily believes in the importance of employee training. Intel employee spends from 2 to 4 per cent of their time in the classrooms. Much of this training, handled by Intel's own managers, focuses on how employees can benefit the organization while enhancing their own rewards.

Besides motivation, performance evaluation and rewards, and training, there are still other implications that can be drawn from learning theory. First, learning theory can explain certain forms of managerial behaviour toward subordinates. Suppose a manager always delivers bad news to subordinates in a certain way. If the subordinates receive the news graciously and constructively, they are giving the manager positive reinforcement, so she will probably use the same mode of delivery in the future. Second aspects of the learning process underscore the manager's role as a teacher and the subordinate's role as a learner. Finally learning processes clearly influence the day-to-day interactions, both official and casual, between people in organizations. Almost everything we do in responding to others, for example, has reinforcing consequences for them.

REFERENCES

B.F. Skinner, Contingencies of Reinforcement, Appleton-Century Crofts, East Norwalk, 1971.

Berelson and Steiner, *Human Behaviour: An Inventory of Scientific Findings*, Horcourt, Brace & World Inc., New York, 1964, pp. 133-134.

Bernard M. Bass and James A. Vaughan, *Training in Industry: The Management of Learning*, Wadsworth Publishing Co., California, 1966, p. 15.

Blair J. Kolasa, *Introduction to Behavioural Science for Business*, Willey Eastern Private Ltd., New Delhi, 1970, p. 181.

E.J. Mecormick and D. Ilgen, *Industrial Psychology*, Prentice Hall of India, New Delhi, 1984, p. 230.

E.L. Thorndike, *Animal Intelligence*, The McMillan Co., New York, 1911, p. 244.

E.L. Thorndike, *The Original Nature of Man*, p. 128.

E.R. Hilgard, *Theories of Learning*, Methuen & Co. Ltd., London, 1958, p. 13.

Fred Luthans, *Organizational Behaviour*, McGraw Hill Book Co., New York, 1989, pp. 293-294.

G. Murphy, *An Introduction to Psychology*, 1951, p. 248.

H. Harlow, 'The Formation of Learning Sets', *Psychological Review*, no. 56, 1949, pp. 51-65.

H.E. Garrett, *Great Experiments in Psychology*, (Acv.ed.) Appleton-Century, New York, 1941.

J.P. Guilford, *General Psychology*, McGraw Hill Book Co., 1956, p. 343.

L. Lindhal, 'Movement Analysis as an Indsutrial Training Method', *Journal of Applied Psychology*, no. 29, 1945, pp. 420-436.

M.E. Bitterman, 'Towards a Comparative Psychology of Learning', *Psychologist*, 1960, p. 704.

N.L. Munn, *et al.*, Introduction to Psychology, Oxford and I.B.H. Publishing Co., 1972, p. 210.

R.S. Woodworth and D.G. Marquis, *Psychology*, Methuen and Co. Ltd., London, 1949, p. 491.

Stephen P. Robbins, Organizational Behaviour, Prentice Hall of India, New Delhi, 1989, p. 64.

The concept of operant conditioning can be traced back to Thorndikes' law of effect- "of several responses made to the same situation, which are accompanied or closely followed by satisfaction —— will be more likely to recur, those which are accompanied or closely followed by discomfort — will be less likely to occur", Edward Thorndike ; *Animal Intelligence*, New York, The McMillan Company, 1911, p. 244.

W. Ray, 'Verbal Compared with Manipulative Solution of an Apparatus Problem', *American Journal of Psychology*, no. 70, 1957, pp. 289-290.

CHAPTER

13

Personality

Organizations are synoptically a collection of individual human beings who have united to accomplish certain specific goals and objectives. Hence organizational behaviour is behaviour of individuals at work. The basic building blocks of an organization are individuals, who tend to behave either in a group or individually. In this chapter, we are confining to individual–describing and comparing personalities through various theories of personality.

The study of individual behaviour is an essential component of behavioural science, as the same stimuli may have different effects on different individuals. For instance, one may feel happy at a raise of just Rs. 100 per month in his salary while the other may feel otherwise and say, what will it do in the era of inflation, where the purchasing power of a rupee has reduced drastically.

This divergence in individual behaviour is basically due to differences in personality, as individuals differ from one another in their manner of responding to organizational environment. We can see how an individual behaves:

B = f (Personality, Environmental Factors)

B = f (P.E.).

In the words of D.E. James, "It is better to consider the individual aspects of person's but held together with cement." because such divergence in individual behaviour may be due to such human factors as ability, perception, learning, needs, values, motives, attitudes and personality of individuals. Personality is the fundamental and foremost determinant of individual behaviour, which seeks to integrate the physiological and psychological facets of an individual to put them into action. Personality is an organized whole without which an individual would have no meaning.

What is Personality?

The concept of personality is quite complex; even today psychologists and social scientists do not agree to any one definition. The term 'personality' is derived from the Latin word 'per sonnare' which means "to speak through." The Latin term was used to denote the masks of actors used in ancient Rome and Greece. Thus 'Personality' traditionally referred to how people influenced others through their external appearances (actions).

Emphasizing on the factual meaning of word person, Watson and Sherman had tried to define personality on the basis of external physical characteristics and physical appearances as such:

1. According to Watson, "Personality is the sum of activities that can be observed over a long enough time to give reliable information. In other words, personality is but the end product of our habit system.".
2. Sherman says "Personality is the characteristics behaviour of an individual."
3. Allport had also initially defined personality on the basis of individuals' behaviour, "Personality is the individual's characteristic reactions to social stimuli and the quality of his adaptation of the social features of his environment."

However, there are some social and behavioural scientists also, who have taken personality as an outcome of socio-cultural forces. According to them, personality of a person is the result of cultural and social forces present in the environment. Though these definitions are superior to those which considered external physical characteristics only, they are none the less comprehensive in themselves.

Personality has also been defined on the basis of all external characteristics of an individual.

Warren and Carmichael defined, "Personality is the entire mental organization of a man being at any stage of his development. It embraces every phase of human character, intellects, temperament, skill, morality and every attitude that has been built-up in course of one's life."

Woolworth considers personality as a sum total of all the traits of an individual. He defines, "Personality can be broadly defined as the total quality of an individual's, as it is revealed in his habits of thought and expression, his attitudes and interests, his manner of acting, and his personal philosophy of life.

Norman L. Munn, while defining personality, says, "Personality may be defined as the most characteristic integration of individuals, structures, modes of behaviour, interest, attitudes, capacities, abilities and aptitudes."

Personality thus traditionally referred to how people influence others through their external appearances (actions). But for an academician personality included (I) external appearance and behaviour, (ii) the inner awareness of self as a permanent organizing force and (iii) the particular organization of measurable traits, both inner and outer. Thus, a thoroughly complete definition of personality becomes a jigsaw puzzle because a human being operates as a whole not as a series of distinct parts. Though psychologists and social scientists unanimously agree to the importance of personality, they are unable to come out with a unanimous definition.

In using individual personality traits to enrich our understanding of personality, we may land in difficulties. It is because there are so many traits, and it is almost an impossible task to use them all. Allport and Odbert have found that there are three thousand to five thousand words that describe personal qualities. Gordon Allport, in fact, found more than fifty different definitions of personality and categorized these definitions into five major areas labeled as follows:

(a) *Omnibus:* These definitions view personality as the 'sum total', aggregate or constellation of properties or qualities.

(b) *Integrative and configurational:* Under this view of personality the organization of personal attributes is stressed.

(c) *Hierarchical:* These definitions specify the various levels of integration or organization of personality.

(d) *Adjustment:* This view emphasizes the adjustment, adaptation, survival, and evolution of the person to the environment.

(e) *Distinctiveness:* The definitions of this category lay stress on the uniqueness of each personality.

After considering and analyzing, historical, theological, theatrical, sociological, psychiatric, omnibus, juristic and various other definitions.

Allport has advanced an interesting and comprehensive definition of personality which is as follows:

"Personality is the dynamic organization within the individual of those psychological systems that determine his unique adjustment to his environment."

If we analyse this definition, we will obtain the following element of personality:

(1) It lays stress on individuality of each person;

(2) The inter-play of inner and outer forces; and

(3) The capacity of the system (dynamic organization within the individual) to change in response to demands from within or without.

Later writers have either accepted Allport's viewpoint (Lazarus, 1971; Maddi, 1968; Sanford, 1968) or have stressed the multiplicity of working viewpoint and the fact that significant progress in he understanding of human behaviour may be achieved even while definitional issues remain unresolved."

By now you must have noticed that personality has been defined by many people in different ways. Even within the last three decades behavioural scientists, psychologists and other social scientists have attempted to define personality. Let us focus our attention on them also.

1. "Personality is a broad, amorphous designation relating to fundamental approaches of persons to other and themselves. To the most psychologists and students of behaviour, this term refers to the study of the characteristic traits of an individual, relationships between these traits, and the ways in which a person adjusts to other people and situations."

2. "Personality is a pattern of stable states and characteristics of a person that influences his or her behaviour towards goal achievement. Each person has unique ways of protecting these states."

   In the *Dictionary of Behavioral Science* (Ed. by Benjamin B. Wolman) personality has been defined as the pattern of traits characterizing an individual person; trait here meaning any psychological characteristic of a person including dispositions to perceive different situations similarly and to react consistently despite changing stimulus conditions, values, abilities, motives defenses, and aspects of temperament, identity and personal style. Through the pattern of such characteristics is necessarily unique, "Personality comprises all of a persons' traits not merely the one that differentiates him from others ...., it may be interpreted in terms either of observable consistencies in behaviour or of informed dispositions to behave."

3. Personality is very diverse and complex psychological concept. The word 'personality' may mean something like outgoing, invigorating interpersonal abilities.

4. .... but we must also recognise and explain the fact that development results in man acquiring a distinctiveness or uniqueness which gives him identity which enables him and us to recognise him as apart from others. These distinguishing characteristics are summarized by the term 'personality'.

The definitional problem of personality becomes staggering from the point of view of its meaning. Laymen tend to equate personality with social success, or dominant style characteristics of a person, for example, height, strong, weak, etc. If we go like this, there may be thousands of words that represent personality. The descriptive adjective approach used by layman plays only an insignificant part in understanding human personality. Scholars and social psychologist operate from an altogether different angle, i.e., theoretical base.

The trait names such as honesty or aggression are nothing but shorthand fictions which enable us to describe briefly someone's characteristics and somewhat consistent patterns of responding to certain classes of situations. Therefore, people try to choose a small number of traits which they think are more important than the rest, or they choose some dimensions which are so broad in meaning that each subsumes a greater number of surface traits. Kluckhohan and Murray have beautifully concluded about this puzzling issue of 'personality' by stating that "to some extent, a person's personality is like all other people, like some other people, like no other people."

Definition

In spite of numerous definitions of personality and differences among the behavioural scientist, it would be worth focusing our attention on the following definition which is still a widely accepted one:

Personality may be defined as "the characteristic and distinctive trait of an individual, the stable and shifting pattern of relationship between these traits and the ways the traits interact to help or hinder the adjustment of a person to other people and situations."

The analysis of this definition will give the following elements of the compositions of personality:

1. Characteristic and distinctive traits.
2. Integrating and organizing agent between physiological and psychological facets of an individual.
3. It is unique in nature.
4. It becomes habitual to the person.
5. It results finally into action behaviour in relation to a person, organization or situations.

What is not meant by "Personality?"

Personality is not something that different people have more or less. One may refer to lean and thin shabby person as having no personality at all or to a handsome, tall, dominant, 'magnetic' sort of person as having 'loads of personality.' This vague term may be used by us only in our everyday conversation but not in the study of 'personality.' Both types of persons have equal amount of personality, as the term is technically used; they are simply different personalities.

Personality is not something which is good or bad, desirable or undesirable. The term 'personality' is not an evaluative one. It is true that, according to commonly accepted values, some kinds of personalities are more desirable than others.

Personality is also not something mysterious when we use the term. Many people somehow resist the notion that personality can be studied. They prefer to think of it as something too mysteriously wonderful to be described. But one should remember that personality is subject to orderly laws and principles which can be known.

What is meant by 'Personality'?

There are no settled answer, rather, there are many and varied views on personality. Indeed, no other area of psychology has such super abundance of theories and controversial views as personality. However, one should not forget as to what personality means, when merely he refers to the term "personality."

1. *Both Common and Unique Factors in Each Personality*

Personality is something which is unique to each individual. It is easy, however to exaggerate the matter of uniqueness. One should realise that uniqueness occurs only within certain limits. There are many aspects of personality which are standard in another society.

Further, there are some things which all personalities have in common, just as all mammals or all human finger prints have some thing in common. Even then, it remains true that no set of finger prints can ever be duplicated by anyone-not perfectly, even by identical twins. So each personality can never be duplicated. Personality, in all its individual complexity, is unique.

2. *Personality Refers Particularly to Persistent Qualities of the Individual*

By and large most of us are rather predictable. Personality refers to this predictable aspects of individuals' behaviour. It refers to something relatively persistent, to characteristics which tend to endure.

3. *Personality represents a Dynamic Orientation of Organism to Environment*

Personality is very closely related with motives and attitudes. It results from the things we do. It has to be acquired or learned rather than being already there at birth. We create personalities for ourselves through crossing hurdles and learning not only from our own experiences but also by noticing and responding to other people to whom we meet in our everyday routine.

4. *Personality is Integrating and Organizing Agent*

Personality exists as an integrating or organizing process in human behaviour. Stimulus is not responded into action or behaviour of an individual unless his physiology (human body) moves in accordance with the direction given by his psychology (human thinking). Physiology and psychology are integrated into action by the personality.

Implicit in the above points are certain characteristics concerning the nature of human personality. They are as:

(i) Man is unique among the species. His unique human characteristics are particularly important for the study of personality. Compared to members of other species, man is less dependent on sociological or biological factors and is more dependent on psychological factors. He is less dependent than members of other species on primary sources of motivation such as food, hunger and thirst. Man's considerable ability for conceptual thinking and language means that he can symbolise, communicate and transmit learned patterns of behaviour (culture) to a degree of being unique among the species. This ability to symbolise also means that man has a lengthened perspective of past and future time and, therefore, need not be bound by immediate stimuli. Furthermore, this ability to symbolize means that he can reflect back upon himself as a person (subject), he can consider himself as an object: that as a person he can both experience and reflect upon his self. Finally man shows a slower rate of maturation than members of other species.

(ii) Human behaviour is complex. An understanding of personality must include an appreciation of complexity of human behaviour. Often there are multiple determinants for any one piece of behaviour, and these vary from person to person. Another way of stating is that the same events may be constructed differently by individuals, and the same behaviour may have many different roots in different individuals. Complexity also exists because behaviour arises not only from personalities but in relation to situations.

(iii) Behaviour is not always what it appears to be. This means that there is no fixed relationship between a piece of behaviour and its causes. This follows from the statement above, since there may be different causes for the same behaviour manifested by two individuals at one time or the same individual at different times. In order to understand the significance or meaning of an act for the individual, we must know something about him and the situation in which the act occurred.

(iv) We are not always aware of or in control of the factors determining our behaviour. Essentially this statement follows from the notion of the unconscious, although it is not necessary to accept all aspects of the Freudian view of the unconscious to agree to it. It simply suggests that at times people cannot explain why they have acted or will act in a way that is contrary to their own expressed wishes. Whether these acts are significant or minor, frequent or infrequent, they occur and remain to be accounted for in one way or the other.

Traits of Personality

Traits form an important component of an individual's personality, though they may change in paradigm of place or situation. Some of the personality traits which reflect a person's physiology and abilities are important accompaniment of an individual and his behaviour pattern.

A trait is understood as a predisposition to respond in an equivalent manner to various kinds of stimuli. Traits, in effect, are psychological entities that render many stimuli as well as many responses equivalent. Many stimuli may evoke the same response, or many responses (perceptions, interpretations, feelings, actions), have the same functional meaning in terms of the trait. An individual in a particular set of circumstances behaves as an honest man, but in changed circumstances he behaves in a dishonest manner. Why Psychologists have opined that this is due to the traits, present in an individual. One group of psychologists (Murphy, May and Hartshone) after conducting several experiments on children, concluded that these traits do not remain stable and permanent but are dynamic in nature.

On the other hand, Allport considers that traits are general and they are responsible to bring stability in the behaviour of an individual. If any person is honest in one situation, he will remain honest in changed circumstances also because the personality characteristics condition his behaviour, sequencible and stable.

Various attempts have been made to isolate traits, but the efforts have been hindered because there are so many of them. In one study, 17,953 individual traits were identified. However, it is virtually impossible to predict behaviour when such a large number to ascertain the source or primary traits.

One researcher identified 171 surface traits but concluded that they were superficial and lacking in descriptive power. What he sought was a reduced set of traits that world identify underlying patterns. The result was the identification of sixteen personality factors, which he called source or primary traits that are the basic underlying causes of surface traits. The sixteen source traits have been presented in the following table:

These sixteen traits have been found to be generally steady and constant sources of behaviour, subject, of course to the influence of particular situations.

Earnest R. Hilgard has depicted personality as an integrated model in his book. He has shown personality as an integrated whole, which can be viewed from different directions. From one direction, we can see one kind of trait, from another we see another kind of trait.

Table 1. Sixteen Source Traits

1.	Reserved	Outgoing
2.	Less intelligent	More intelligent
3.	Affected feelings	Emotionally more stable
4.	Submissive	Dominant
5.	Serious	Happy-go-lucky
6.	Expedient	Conscientious
7.	Timid	Venturesome
8.	Tough-minded	Sensitive
9.	Trusting	Suspicious
10	Practical	Imaginative
11.	Forthright	Shrewd
12.	Self-assured	Apprehensive
13.	Conservative	Experimenting
14.	Group dependent	Self-dependent
15.	Uncontrolled	Controlled
16.	Relaxed	Tense

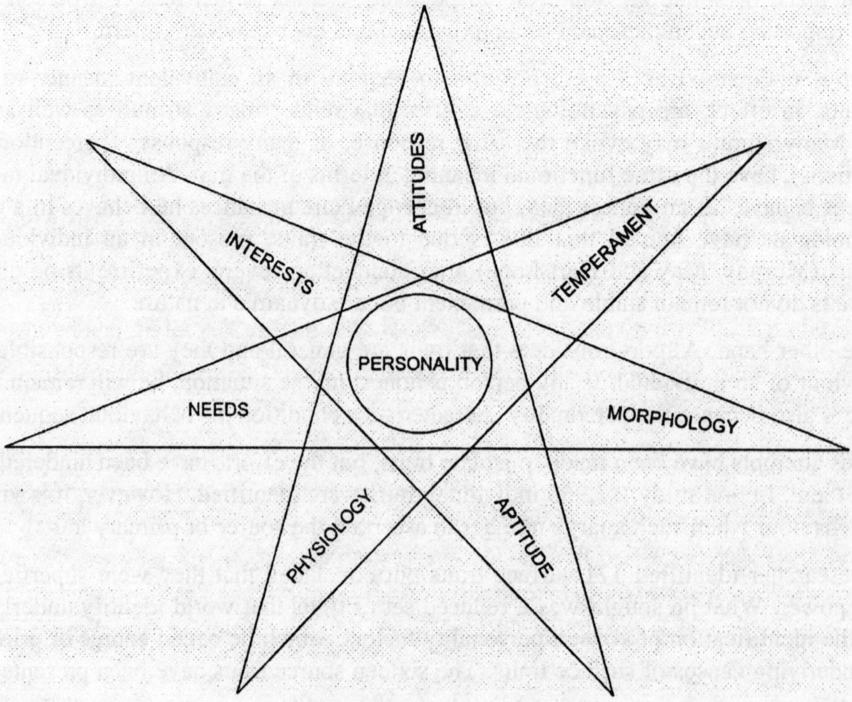

Fig. 1. Personality Traits

Source: E.R. Hilgard, *Introduction to Psychology*, Harcourt Brace, Jovanorich, New York, 1962, p. 452.

Note: In the above figure personality is shown as an integrated whole, which can be viewed from different directions. From one direction you can see one kind of trait and from another you see another kind of trait.

In a nutshell, we can say that the personality traits have the following characteristics:

1. Traits are dimensions of personality.
2. Traits are integrated patterns.
3. Traits are behaviour patterns of an individual
4. Traits are represented in individual's behaviour on the basis of continuity and equity.
5. Traits are relative.

Determinants of Personality

Often the question arises, "What are the determinants of individual personality ?" Out of the numerous questions remaining unanswered in the study of human behaviour, this question is the most difficult because people are enormously complex, their abilities and interests and attitudes are diverse. However, the major determinants of personality can be studied under four broad categories — Biological, Environmental, Social and Family and Situational.

Biological Factors

The biological factors affecting the personality can be studied under three heads — (i) Heredity, (ii) Brain or Nervous System and (iii) Body Chemistry.

Heredity

The role of heredity is unquestionable in the development of personality. This refers to those factors which were determined at conception and are known as DNA factors. This is the very determinant which remains constant. The heredity approach emphasizes that the ultimate explanation of an individual personality is the molecular structure of the genes, located in the chromosomes. At conception each parent contributes chromosomes, which contains thousand of genes. Even two children of same parents do not have identical genetic make-up. Only identical twins, which develop from the single fertilized ovum, possess the same pattern of genes.

Certain characteristics primarily physical in nature-stature, muscle composition land reflexes, biological rhythms, facial attractiveness, skin texture and colour, etc., are generally considered to be imported either completely or substantially by one's parents. Researches on animals have confirmed that both physical and psychological characteristics are transmitted through heredity. However, in case of human beings, who cannot be subjected to the necessary controls, the evidence is mush less conclusive.

Synoptically the following characteristics is said to be inherited by all human beings:

1. Physical structure (how tall or short one is, whether one has a long or short nose, large or small feet–briefly, how one is put together).
2. Reflexes (direct responses to stimuli, such as withdrawing from a pin prick, blinking when something approaches the eye).
3. Innate drives (impulses to act based on physiological tensions; but these must be linked through learning with activities which will reduce the tensions).
4. Intelligence (the capacity to learn, to modify responses).
5. Temperament (patterned and recurrent responses associated with basic emotional make-up for sample, phlegmatic, excitable, or lethargic).

Brain

Brain is another biological factor that influences personality of an individual significantly. Though to-date, psychologists have not been able to supply precise information on the contribution from this biological variable, as electrical stimulation of brain (ESB) has been conducted largely on animals, work with ESB on humans have recently started, and the research results are, in general, similar to those of animals.

Body Chemistry

The third biological factor effecting personality is body chemistry. In ancient period, the difference of temperament were supposed to be due to difference of chemical elements in different men. however, the modern psychologists do not agree with this relation of personality with the proportion of chemical elements in the body. The effect of drugs on personality are sufficient proof in itself to establish a clear relationship of body chemistry with personality. The increase or decrease of the quantity of sugar in the body has a distinct effect on both physical and mental state of the man thus affecting personality.

Environmental Factors

The environmental factors affect the personality as much as heredity factor. Environment includes culture, society, work group, and the like. At least by behavioural scientists, the culture is usually considered to make a more significant contribution to personality than the biological factors. Culture establishes norms, values and attitude that are passed along from one generation to the next. Anthropologists, to whom the subject culture belongs, have clearly demonstrated the dominant role of culture in the development of human personality. A person groomed in Western culture has a different personality from a person groomed in an Indian culture. Even a person who is biologically of the Indian descent but is brought up in an Indian culture will have an Indian type of personality and vice versa. The expressions of aggression have institutionalized penalties for deviation from these prescribed patterns. The institutionalization of some patterns of behaviour means that most members of culture will have certain personality characteristics in common. These common characteristics in people, as joint member of a culture, have led to the developments of concepts such as basic personality type, model personality and national character.

Social and Family Factors

Though culture prescribes the limit of what a person can be taught, the family and social group teach him to select, interpret and dispense the culture. Therefore, the factor too has its positive role in affecting the personality of an individual.

The role of the family and social group in combination with the culture is referred as the process of socialization. The process of socialization starts as soon as the child is born, between him and his mother. After infancy, other close relatives and even friends play influential role in shaping an individual's personality.

Stratification

Class level is generally determined by the amount of education and income, though other criteria, such as religion and family background, can be used, social class determinants emphasize the patterns of behaviour that are class related. Riesman discusses social character, that part of the personality structure is shared by members of a social group in terms of three ideal types; tradition-directed, inner-directed and other directed.

The following principles are suggested in relation to social class influences on personality.

1. Social class forces are important determinants of personality.
2. As with cultural influences, we are often unaware of the extent to which we have been shaped by class factors.
3. In terms of such pressing current social problems as mental health and education for the disadvantages, those who seek to apply their understanding of personality must pay full attention to social class factors.
4. Beyond some degree of similarity that is determined by membership in the same social class, there is considerable variation in the personality functioning of members of a class, and this variability remains to be explained on other grounds than social class.

Situational Factors

It must be recongnized that it is the immediate situation, which predominates the personality, finally. A study has confirmed that the workers who were supposed to be lazy and inefficient workers turned out to be the best workers of the organization and responsible of taking the organization to new heights, when they were shifted from their old work place and placed in new situations. This also confirms that situation factors come as the only determinant of personality which are totally variable. Knowledge, skill, language and the like are acquired by an individual through day-to-day experiences and represent important modification of behaviour. Situations as on one hand exercise control, on the other it serves as a lubricant and provide thrust on an individual. In certain cases it is not the type of person is, as the kind of situation to which he is facing, determines his actions and behavioural pattern. Milgram study demonstrated that situations have very effective impact on the behavioural expression of personality.

On the basis of above discussion, an attempt has been made to formulate a mathematical model for the measurement of personality, to quench the thirst of mathematicians as:

$$P_n \approx \int_0^n (w+x+y)dy$$

Where:

w represents	:	Biological factors, Genetic code and Childhood upbringing which remains constant in individual personality throughout the life.
x represents	:	Society, Neighbourhood, Education and training as Semi variable factor
y represents	:	Day-to-day experiences and situations as total variable factor.
p represents	:	Personality.
n represents	:	Age.

If we are able to measure the constant, semi-variable factors, in absolute terms, it is quite possible to know and predict the personality approximately at a certain age by integrating the sum of these factors, from age zero to the age at which personality is to be studied with respect to variable factor.

Jung's Personality Typing

After the appearance of Freud's The Interpretations of Dreams, C.G. Jung of Zurich, who was himself a psychoanalyst, undertook systematic investigations of unconscious dynamics by means of the association test. Jung gave sustained attention to the question of personality typing in the association test and placed heavy emphasis on topology of personality and grouping them into basic types. There were for him two fundamental types.

(1) Extrovert and (2) Introvert, who were congenitally predisposed to the outer and inner manifestations of the libido. The extrovert was primarily concerned with social relationship in which a rich fulfillment of libidinal need could be found. The introvert, preoccupied with his own inner world of fantasy and bodily activity was relatively incapable of such outgoing social participation. This conception was further elaborated by means of such division of mental operation into four fundamental activities — (1) sensing, (2) feeling, (3) thinking and (4) intuiting.

Jung's four psychological functions of grouping personality are commonly used in gathering and evaluating information. Sensing or sensation and intuition are important for gathering information and the remaining two, feeling and thinking, for evaluating or judging the situation. According to Jung, individuals are strong in either sensation or intuition while evaluating the information.

Sensation and Intuition

Individual of sensation type gather information through processing the facts and details in the environment in a methodical way whereas intuitive type through global visualizations of the depicted scene. The sensation type individual depends on a lot of information to assess the situation. They are generally pragmatic and down-to-earth, concentrating more on the present time. The intuitive type individuals, on the other hand, rely much on hunches and non-verbal cues. They simultaneously consider various alternatives, frequently and quickly discarding the non-verbal alternatives. Such intuitive type individuals are highly imaginative and have more orientation towards future. However, both sensing and intuitive type individuals have their own strengths and weaknesses.

Feeling and Thinking

The feeling type individuals evaluate and make judgements in a more personal and subjective fashion, whereas thinking type individuals in an impersonal and objective way. The feeling type individual places much reliance on human feelings and emotions. They are very sentimental, empathic and normally try to 'read between the lines' while evaluating situations. On the other hand, the thinking type individual makes a systematic inquiry. They are not emotional but highly analytical and rational in making judgements. Feeling types enjoy pleasing others, they dislike telling people unpleasant things and heavily emphasis the human aspects of dealing with organizational matters. The thinking type people feel comfortable when decisions are based on logical reasoning and analysis. Such individuals are generally not emotional and are also not very sensitive to the feelings of others. Both feeling and thinking types have their other advantages and disadvantages.

On the basis of Jung's above typology of personality, the managers could be classified into one of the following types:

1. Intuitive Feelers.
2. Sensational Feelers.
3. Intuitive Thinkers and
4. Sensational Thinkers.

1. *Intuitive Feelers*

These types of managers are quite effective especially in group settings where new ideas are to be formulated and are responsible to move the organization towards success. Such managers are trustworthy advisers, help their subordinates, personally as well as professionally. However, intuitive-feelers possess the weakness of basing certain decisions on personal likes and dislikes, rather than adopting objective criteria. They also spend considerable time in seeking approval from others.

2. *Sensational Feelers*

Managers with these predisposition are pragmatic. They deal with the confronted problems in a very systematic fashion. Such managers elicit the cooperation of the people working for them. They are well aware how to effectively use available resources rather than 'Fight the system.' Their main weakness is that they are not far-sighted and therefore unable to conceptualize a new idea or scheme and the status quo may prevail in the system.

3. *Intuitive Thinkers*

Managers with these orientations are the proactive change masters. They establish a relationship among the various goals and activities. This type of managers build new systems giving much thought to the effects of their ideas on operating effectiveness. Their major weakness is that they are not sensitive to the feelings of others and often face difficulty in handling interpersonal relations.

4. *Sensational Thinkers*

Managers who are sensational thinkers create an effective structure for their organization and insure stability. Such managers are seldom wrong with their facts and may prove dependable leaders. However their greatest weakness is that they are impatient and it results in delays and imperfections, and their ineffectiveness when quick changes are necessary as they are not able to act quickly.

In the above classification, a word of caution, it must be kept in mind that individual differences in personality predispositions have not been considered and even individual differences such as skills, educational level, training, ability, aptitude, work, gender, experience, age, family background, etc., all of which, influence to a considerable extent at work.

To help the readers to understand and evaluate their own psychological functioning style we give below a list of possible occupational situations for which each style is most likely to be best suited.

Problem-solving Profiles

Respond to the following items as required. There are no right or wrong answers.

PART I.

Circle the response that comes closest to how you usually feel or act:

1. Are you more careful about:
   (a) people's feelings.
   (b) their rights.
2. Do you usually get on better with:
   (a) imaginative people.
   (b) realistic people.
3. Which of the following two is the higher compliment:
   (a) a person has real feeling.
   (b) a person is consistently reasonable.
4. In doing something with many other people, does it appeal more to you:
   (a) to do it in the accepted way.
   (b) to invent a way of your own.
5. Do you get more annoyed at:
   (a) fancy theories.
   (b) people who don't like theories.
6. It is higher praise to call someone:
   (a) a person of vision.
   (b) a person of common sense.
7. Do you more often let:
   (a) your heart rule your head.
   (b) your head rule your heart.
8. Do you think it a worse fault:
   (a) to show too much warmth.
   (b) to be unsympathetic.
9. If you were a teacher, would you rather teach :
   (a) courses involving theory.
   (b) fact courses.

PART II.

Which work in the following pair does appeal to you more? Circle A or B.

10. (a) Compassion
    (b) Foresight
11. (a) Justice
    (b) Mercy
12. (a) Production
    (b) Design
13. (a) Gentle
    (b) Firm
14. (a) Uncritical
    (b) Critical
15. (a) Literal
    (b) Figurative
16. (a) Imaginative
    (b) Matter-of-fact

Scoring Key

This key is to be used to diagnose your responses to the questionnaire. Count one point for each response on the following four scales. Then, total the number of points recorded in each column. Instructions for classifying your scores are given below:

Sensation	Intuition	Thinking	Feeling
2b______	2a______	1b______	1a______
4a______	4b______	3b______	3a______
5a______	5b______	7b______	7a______
6b______	6a______	8a______	8b______
9b______	9a______	10a______	10a______
12a______	12b______	11a______	11b______
15a______	15b______	13b______	13a______
16b______	16a______	14b______	14a______

Classifying Scores

1. **If your intuition score is equal to or greater than sensation score — write intuition.**
2. **If your sensation score is more than intuition score — write sensation.**
3. **If your feeling score is more than thinking score — write feeling.**
4. **If your thinking score is more than feeling score — write thinking.**
5. **In case of males–write feeling if feeling equals to thinking.**
6. **In case of females–write thinking if feeling equals to thinking.**

Analysis of Personality Types

1. Sensing managers take in information through their senses and attend to the details of a problem. They like to solve problems in standard ways. They are patient with routine details and are precise in their work. They distrust creative aspirations and usually work all the way through to reach conclusions. They emphasis action, urgency, and bottom-line results.
2. Intuitive managers like solving new problems and are impatient with routine details. They perceive the problem in its totality and consider several alternatives simultaneously. They are imaginative and futuristic, enjoying mind-testing games.
3. Feeling managers heavily emphasis the human aspects in dealing with organizational problems and are more process-oriented. They enjoy pleasing people and avoid conflicts.
4. Thinking managers are logical and analytical in their problem-solving and search for additional information in a logical manner.
5. Sensational Feelers (SF) deal with concrete problems in a methodical way. They have astute powers of observation regarding the details of how an organization is run. SFs do not fight the system, but use what is available for problem solving. They are non-judgmental of their co-workers and do not look for underlying motives and meanings in people's behaviour. If organizations do not have SFs, small problems will go unattended till they become big.

Possible Weakness

SFs may be reluctant to accept new ideas and are impatient with abstract theories. They react adversely to radical changes. They have difficulty in honouring commitments and decisions made in the past since they live fully in the present moment.

6. Sensational Thinkers (ST) are decisive and excellent at decisions involving precise interpretations of facts and figures. They are persevering and precise. They are hard working and super dependable. They want the organization to run on an impersonal basis. Organizations run efficiently because of such managers.

STs cannot tolerate delays arising from complications. In periods of rapid changes they still cling to rules and procedures which is dysfunctional. When dealing with others, STs may not accurately perceive the interpersonal process. They withhold rewards unless fully deserved by others.

7. Intuitive Feelers (IF) have personal charisma and commitment to the people they lead. They communicate their caring and enthusiasm. They are comfortable in an unstructured, group-centered management system that lets employees participate in the decision-making process. Without these an organization will become cold, sterile and dull.

IFs may make decisions on the basis of personal likes and dislikes. They often try to please others all the time.

8. Intuitive Thinkers (IT) are the architects of progress and ideas. They are interested in the principles on which the organization is built and seek answers to the 'whys' of events. They have enormous drive and are creative.

If organizations do not have some ITs, change will be minimal.

ITs may not always be aware of the feelings of others, unless subordinates are intellectually competent, they may not be considered valuable. They expect a great deal from themselves and others and tend to escalate standards.

Occupational Choices and Personality Types

1. *Intuitive Feelers*
   * Aeronautical Engineers
   * Artists and Entertainers
   * Coordinators
   * Computer Specialists
   * Detectives
   * Lifeguards
   * Managers and Administrators
   * Musicians and Composers
   * Physical Scientists
   * Psychologists
   * Research Scientists
   * Therapists
   * Writers
2. *Intuitive Thinkers*
   * Chemical Engineers
   * Computer Programmers
   * Counsellors
   * Electric and Electronic Technicians
   * Doctors of Medicine
   * Managers
   * Marketing Personnel
   * Mechanical Engineers
   * Musicians and Composers
   * Protective Service Workers
   * Psychologists
   * University Professors
3. *Sensational Feelers*
   * Craftsmen
   * Computer Science Support Staff
   * Designers
   * Doctors
   * Engineering and Science Technicians
   * Healthcare Therapists
   * Journalists/Writers
   * Judges
   * Managers and Administrators
   * Media Specialists
   * Nursing Administrators
   * Pharmacists
   * Rehabilitation Counsellors
   * Restaurant Managers
   * Sales Representatives
   * Social Scientists

- * Storekeepers
- * Teachers

4. *Sensational Thinkers*
   - * Actors
   - * Certain type of Administrators
   - * Clinical Lab Technologists
   - * Counsellors in general
   - * Editors and Reporters
   - * Engineers
   - * Occupational Therapists
   - * Office Machine Operators
   - * Photographers
   - * Receptionists
   - * Teachers/Professors
   - * Speech Pathologists.

REFERENCES

Adapted from Slocum and Heuriegel, 'A Look at How Managers' Minds Work', *Business Horizons*, July-August, 1983, pp. 58-68.

Adapted from, I.B. Myers and McCaulley, *Guide to the Development and Use of the Myers-Briggs Type Indicator*, Consulting Psychologist Press, Palo Alto. C.A., 1985.

Benjamin Wolman (editor), *Dictionary of Behavioural Science*, Van Nostrand Reinhold Company, New York, 1973, p. 275.

C.G. Jung, *Psychological Types*, Routledge and Kegan Paul Ltd., London, 1923.

C.G. Jung, *The Theory of Psycho-Analysis*, Neru and Ment. Dis. Monogr, 1915, No. 19.

Cliffort T. Morgan and Richard A. King, *Introduction to Psychology*, McGraw Hill Company, New York, 1966, p. 460.

Clyde Kluckhohn and H.A. Murray, 'Personality Formulation the Determinants', in C. Kluckhohn and B.A. Murray (ed.) '*Personality*', Alfred A. Knopts, Inc., New York, 1948, p. 35.

D. Hellriegel, J.W.S. Locum and R.W. Woodman, *Organizational Behavior*, 4th ed., West Publishing Co., St. Paul M.N., 1968.

D.E. James, *Introduction to Psychology*, Constables and Company Ltd., London 1968, p. 219.

Ernest R. Hilgard, *Introduction to Psychology Brace*, Javanovich, New York, 1962, p. 452.

Floyd L. Ruch, *Psychology of Life*, 6th ed. Scott, Foresman and Co., Chicago, pp. 353-354.

Fred Luthans, *Organizational Behaviour*, McGraw Hill, New York, 1973, pp. 421-22.

G. Allport, *Personality*,.Henry Rold and Company, Inc., New York, 1937, pp. 43-47.

Garden Allport, *Personality: A Psychological Interpretation*, Holt Rinehart and Winston, New York, 1937, pp. 43-47.

Gardner Murphy, *Historical Introduction to Modern Psychology*, Routledge and Kegan Paul Ltd., London, 1964, p. 331.

Garry Dessler, *Organization and Management*, Reston Publishing Company Inc., Reston, Virgina, 1981, pp. 256-257.

Gluck, *Management*, The Dryden Press, 1977, p. 90.

H.C. Waren and Charmichael, *Human Psychology*, Houghton Miffin, 1919.

J.B. Kolasa, *Introduction to Behavioural Science for Business*, Willey Eastern Limited, New Delhi, 1978, p. 131.

J.B. Watson, *Psychology from the Stand Point of a Behaviourist*, 2nd ed. J.B. Lippin Cot, Philaphedia, 1919, pp. 426-427.

James D. Thompson and Donald Van Houten, *The Behavioural Sciences*, Ist ed., p. 81.

Jerry L. Gray and Frederick, A Starke, *Organizational Behaviour–Concepts and Applications*, McMillan, Columbus, 1980, p. 77.

Jung, 'The Association Model', *American Journal of Psychology*, vol. 21, 1910, pp. 219-169.

Louis Kaplan, *Foundations of Human Behaviour*, Harper & Row, New York, 1965, p. 24.

Mandel Sherman, *Process of Human Behaviour*, Williams & Norgate Ltd., London, 1930, p. 174.

Marvin D. Dunnette (editors), *Handbook of Industrial and Organizational Psychology*, Rand McNally College Publishing Company, Chicago, 1976, p. 573.

N.L. Munn, *Psychology*, George G. Harrap & Company, London, p. 569.

R.B. Cattell, ' Personality Pinned Down', *Psychology Today*, July, 1973, pp. 40-46.

Robert R.S. Woodworth, *Experimental Psychology*, Hol, Rinehart & Winsten, 1938, p. 194.

Stanley Milgram, 'Some Conditions of Obedience and Disobedience to Authority', *Human Relations*, February, 1965, pp. 57-76.

Stephen P. Robbins, *Organizational Behaviour Concepts, Controversies and Applications*, Prentice Hall of India, New Delhi, p. 54.

Thedore T. Herber, *Dimensions of Organizational Behaviour*, McMillan, New York, 1976, p. 136.

CHAPTER

14

Leadership

The essence of management is to get the work done by the people by directing them in the right perspective. It means subordinates should be led so as to be directed towards the common goal. Human beings are the most precious part of the civilization and this part should be developed effectively in order to make them enable to shoulder the responsibility to develop themslves and to the organization. Leadership is the quality of the behaviour of individuals whereby they guide people or their activities in organised efforts. In reality organization compete by means of their leaders than by their products. Leader gives the company the life which creates the products and innovations that it sells. Better or effective leaders develop a team of better or effective employees and the two together develop a more effective organization. According to Keith Davis,"**Leadership is the ability to persuade others to seek defined objectives enthusiastically.**"

Koontz O'Donnell in the above statement has recognised the very fact that man by nature wants to be led, and that too effectively so that his zeal to work may be maintained, his capabilities may be utilized to the maximum and his morale and confidence may be boosted. He wants an effective leadership in his own interest. Certainly he wants security, safety, income, administration, satisfaction, and authority and for that all he always looks towards his leader. Leadership is so important to group accomplishment that people have been concerned about it since the beginning of the recorded history.

In an organization, managers at all levels by whatever name called, are leaders because they all have subordinates (followers) whose efforts are to be canalised in a definite direction. As leaders, they are responsible for not only to show the way to the subordinate towards the attainment of goal but they are supposed to lead the group towards it. **Peter F. Drucker,** an original thinker on management science considers leadership as a human characteristic which lifts a man's vision to higher rights raises man's performance to higher standards and builds a man's personality beyond its normal limits.

LEADERSHIP – MEANING AND DEFINITIONS

Leadership is an important attribute for the development of an organization that set apart a successful organization from an unsuccessful organization. Without leadership, an organization is simply a mass of man, machines and materials.

Leadership is a personal quality of an individual who organises the efforts of the followers and directs their activities towards the attainment of organizational goal. Leadership is, therefore, regarded as the process of influencing the activities of an individual or a group in efforts towards goal achievement in a given situation. Leadership is a function of the leader, the follower and other situational variables. One who is in a position of influencing others (followers) whether a manager of a formal organization or an informal leader of an informal group or a head of family, may be called leader.

Leadership forms a part of management with manager as its leader who is responsible for planning and organization functions of an organization. It is undoubtedly true that a manager may be a weak leader or a leader may be a weak manager or vice versa may be equally true. So, a manager with leadership qualities is a true leader of the organization who can get the work done from the workers (followers) effectively.

Definitions

A few definitions of leadership may be helpful in clarifying the concept of leadership:

1. According to George R. Terry, 'Leadership is the activity of influencing people to strive willingly for group objectives.'
2. Tannenbaum, Weschler, and Fred Massarik define leadership as 'interpersonal influence exercised in a situation and directed, through the communication process, towards the attainment of a specialized goals.'
3. Koontz and O'Donnell state that 'Leadership is influencing people to follow in the achievement of a common goals.'
4. Invancevich, Szilagyi and Wallace define leadership as 'the relationship between two or more people in which one attempts to influence the other towards the accomplishment of some goal or goals.'
5. In the words of Keith Davis, 'Leadership is the ability to persuade others to seek defined objectives enthusiastically. It is the human factor that binds a group together and motivates it toward goals.'
6. Robbins defines leadership as the ability to influence a group toward the achievement of goals.'
7. Hodge and Johnson are of the opinion that, 'leadership is fundamentally the ability to from and mould the attitudes and behaviour of other individuals, whether informal or formal situation and that management relates to the formal task of decision and command.'Thus it is evident from the analysis of the above definitions that the **leadership is the process of influencing the behaviour, attitudes, activities and efforts of an individual or a group for achieving common goals.** It is also important that the above definitions do not mention any particular type of organization where leadership may exist. It may be anywhere and in any situation where someone tries to influence the behaviour of another individual or group, leadership is there. Following are some of the characteristics of leadership:

(i) **There must be a group of following:** Without followers, leadership cannot be imagined and leader cannot exert his authority. No matter what is the relationship between a leader and the followers in a formal or informal organization.

(ii) **Leadership is a personal quality:** of character and behaviour in a man to exert internal personal influence.

(iii) **Leadership is a reciprocal relationship:** between the leader and the led (followers). A leader influences his followers and is also influenced by his followers' behaviour.

(iv) **Leadership is the process of influencing:** the behaviour, attitudes, activities and efforts of individuals and group.

(v) **Leadership guides the individuals and group to:** the common goals of the organization and unifies and motivate the followers for this purpose.

(vi) **Leadership is related to a particular situation:** at a given point of time and under the specific set of circumstances. Its style may differ from time to time.

(vii) **Leadership is a shared function:** A leader shares credits, blames, ideas, opinions and experiences everything with his followers.

The Nature of Leadership

1. Use of influence: Leadership implies something more than mere supervisory responsibility or formal authority. It consists of influence. Leadership is the incremental influence, or additional influence, that a person has beyond his formal authority.
2. Importance of communication: Leadership is established through the communication process. Communication affects the behaviour and performance of followers. The inability to communicate is a serious deficiency in influencing people.

3. Followership: The essence of leadership is followership. It is the willingness of people to follow that makes a person a leader. Leadership always involves followers. Just as there are leaders, there must also be followers.

4. Accomplishment of goals: Leadership directs the group activities towards goal achievement. The effective leader has to deal with individual, group, and organizational goals.

5. Assumption of responsibility: The leader assumes full responsibility for all actions of his followers. He remains responsible in all situations.

6. Community of interests: This implies that the objectives of both the leader and his people are one and the same, Terry writes that "leadership is the activity of influencing people to strive willingly for mutual goals."

7. Situational variable: Leadership is behaviour as well as situational outcome. It may be the result of interaction of the leader with the members of his group in a particular environment.

8. Exemplary conduct: The leader shows the ideal behaviour for his people to follow. He sets an example before his men by his conduct.

9. Other features:
   (1) Leadership is the exercise of authority and the making of decisions.
   (2) It is the process of creating a work environment in which people can do their best work.
   (3) Leadership involves status differences as well as role differences.
   (4) Leadership may exist on both formal and informal levels. In other words, leaders can emerge from within a group as well as by formal appointment to lead a group.

LEADERSHIP QUALITIES – TRAITS OF A LEADER

What qualities, a leader has, is subject of difference of opinion among distinguished thinkers. F.M. Viscount Shim has chosen six basic qualities of a good leader. Irwin H. Paul has emphasised only on three qualities. We are giving hereunder the basic qualities of leadership as given by various thinkers in tabular form:

	Authority	Qualities
(a)	F.M. Viscount Shim	1. Courage, 2. Will Power, 3. Judgement, 4. Flexibility, 5. Knowledge, 6. Integrity.
(b)	Ordway Tead	5. Integrity, 6. Technical skill, 7. Friendliness and Affection, 8. Decisiveness, 9. Intelligence, 10. Faith.
(c)	Henry Fayol	1. Health and physical fitness, 2. Intelligence and Mutual Vigour, 3. Moral qualities, 4. Knowledge, 5. Managerial ability.
(d)	Chester I. Bernard	1. Vitality and Endurance, 2. Decisiveness, 3. Persuasiveness, 4. Stability, 5. Intellectual capacity, 6. Knowledge.

We should not be perplexed with the disagreement of various thinkers on the essential requisites of a good leader. Broadly, we may group these qualities in the following four categories:

1. Physical Qualities include:

   (a) Sound health, and (b) Vitality and Endurance

2. Psychological Qualities includes:

   (a) Personal Magnetism, (b) Enthusiasm, (c) Co-operation, (d) Ability to inspire, (e) Forcefulness, (f) Tact.

3. Intellectual Traits include:

   (a) A high degree of Intelligence, (b) An open mind, (c) A capacity for sound judgement, (d) An ability to teach, (c) A scientific Approach.

5. Qualities of Character include:

   (a) Integrity, (b) Self-discipline, (c) Fair play, (d) Willingness to accept responsibility, (e) Physical and moral courage, (f) Humanism.

ARE TRAITS COMMON TO ALL LEADERS

Personal traits though very significant in determining a successful leader but trait and leadership have no relations. The studies of past leader life indicate that certain useful traits they had that really made them leaders such as 'strength of character' or 'power' or 'dominance' but they were not the traits that made them leader, it was the environment which made the traits active. The trait approach to leadership study was especially popular during 1930-50. As traits have no direct relation with the leadership therefore common traits are hardly found in two leaders. Each leader has different traits and therefore analysis of traits in different leaders made the list of traits longer and longer but there was very little consensus over common traits among researchers.

Moreover, personal traits are only one part of whole environment. Though a number of traits exist within a person, they will come to light unless a certain group or situation calls for them.

It is also very difficult to define which and how many traits a person (leader) must have? For example, a good health is desirable in many leadership situation but history reveals that many successful leaders did not have good health. Mahatma Gandhi was very poor in health. There are so many exceptions to any general statement about leadership traits that it hardly applies.

Management and Leadership

Management and Leadership are often thought of as one and the same thing. But this is not valid. Leadership is a broader concept than management. Management is thought of as a special kind of leadership in which the achievement of organizational goals is important. Leadership occurs any time one attempts to influence the behaviour of an individual or group, regardless of the reason and direction. Leadership may not be congruent with organizational goals and may be for one's goals.

Management, managership and leadership are terms which are so closely related that the distinctions among them have become blurred. It is useful to place each of them in its right perspective.

Management is a process of planning, organising, coordinating, directing, and controlling the activities of others.

Managership is the authority to carry out these functions.

Leadership, as mentioned above, is the process of influencing for the purpose of achieving shared goals.

Both managership and leadership are management tools with which managers can influence the behaviour of employees to achieve organizational goals. The distinction between them can be made on the basis of the qualifications that managers have. Managers, by virtue of being in a managerial position, have managership, but they may not possess leadership or the ability to influence other people.

There are certain other differences between leaders and managers.

1. Leaders have followers, but managers do not have. Subordinates may obey managers out of fear but such compliance is not a response to leadership. Similarly, all leaders are not managers. Leaders have followers but do not possess authority to manage, informal leaders for example. Managership is a fundamental characteristic of a manager.
2. Leaders have emotional appeal. They are expected to be charismatic people with great visions who can alter the mood of their followers and raise their hopes and expectations. On the other hand, managers are expected to be rational decision makers and problem solvers. They are expected to use their analytical minds in the process of establishing and achieving organizational goals.

3. Leaders fulfil followers' needs. Managers and leaders try to meet organizational and employees' personal needs. But the emphasis differs. The main aim of a manager is to meet organizational goals. Similarly, the main job of a leader is to satisfy his followers' needs.

4. Peter Drucker and Warren Bennis have rightly pointed thus: 'Management is doing things right, leadership is doing right things. Management 's efficiency lies in climbing the ladder of success; leadership determines whether the ladder is leaning against the right wall.'

John Kotter also argues that leadership is different from management, but for different reasons. He states that management is about coping with complexity. Leadership, in contrast, is about coping with change. Abraham Zaleznik argues that leaders and managers differ in motivation, personal history, and how they think and act. Zaleznik says that managers prefer to work with people, and relate to people according to the role they play in a decision making process. Leaders, who are concerned with ideas, relate to people in more intuitive and empathic ways.

The distinction between management and leadership gets blurred in actual practice. In real life organizations there are no distinct leaders, there are only managers. They will be acting both in the capacity of managers as well as in the capacity of leaders. A successful manager is the one who has both the qualities and who makes use of them discretely, depending on whether he or she is required to lead or to manage.

IMPORTANCE OF LEADERSHIP

An organization, howsoever good it is, is quite inactive without effective leadership. An effective leader can only pull out the organization from darkness to light; push it to the path of development by resolving the various genuine difficulties. Without leadership, an organization is but a muddle of men, machines and materials; because all these factors of production remain idle unless they are engaged in a coordinate manner to produce more towards the accomplishment of goal of the organization.

Success or Failure of an organization depends very much on the leadership provided to it. Leadership is still an art and there is no substitute alternative to it. We can present the following points in support of its importance:

1. Directing Group Activities: Leadership in an organization is mainly concerned with the group. The main responsibility of the leadership is to get the work done effectively by fruitfully engaging them. For this purpose, he promotes the sincerity of purpose among the workers and so, directs them rightly towards the accomplishment of organizational goals. The leader by his personal conduct and behaviour infuse confidence in his subordinate and induce them, to work hard. **George R. Terry** commented – A leader shows the way by his example. He is not a pusher, he pulls rather than pushes.

Moreover a group cannot work efficiently without leadership because a leader only can consolidate the efforts of the group and divert those efforts towards the goal. But an unorganised group can never attain the goal, no matter how efficient its members are. So, directing the group activities towards a common goal is the main function of the leadership.

2. Better Utilisation of Manpower: The first management function of a leader is to make plans, policies, and programmes and to carry them out because plans, policies, and programmes cannot work themselves. He mobilises the work force, engage them to get higher performance and coordinates their efforts and it is all to utilise the available manpower effectively so as to get highest output with minimum human cost. Achieving best performance form workers is the key to success and it is possible only through effective leadership.

3. Source of Motivation: Efficient leadership is a source of motivation to the subordinates. Leadership does not mean simply the existence of leadership traits in a person but it is to utilise those traits in motivating the people at work towards the desired goal by applying a leadership style most suited to the situation. Motivation is an element of dynamic leadership and in absence of that organization success is doubtful.

4. Developing Good Human Relations: Human relations represent the relations between the leader (manager) and the subordinates (workers). An efficient leadership develops the talents of the individuals, promotes self-confidence in them, provides an opportunity to demonstrate their ability apart from the motivation towards the accomplishment of goal. Thus the leader emphasises the cooperative attitude of workers and it creates an environment of good human relations which in turn increases the productivity of the organization.

5. Promoting the spirit of Coordination: The activities of members of a group and those of different groups must be coordinated in order to achieve the desired goal. A leader promotes the spirit of coordination among workers. A dynamic leadership provides all that by following human behaviour approach.

6. Fulfilling Social Responsibilities: An effective leadership only can be able to get the work done effectively. it is a well known fact that a well satisfied workers will help serving the organization interest in his first preference under a good leadership. Good management or leadership is always concerned with the need satisfaction of its workforce which in turn, provides higher standard of living to workers, higher productivity and production to the organization, lower price to consumers, higher National Product, and increased revenue to the nation, and a fair return to the investors. Thus, organization can fulfil its social responsibilities, i.e., responsibilities towards different sections of the society, consumers, workers, investors, government, etc. only if it is guided by dynamic leadership.

FUNCTIONS OF LEADERSHIP

The main function of leadership is to explain the importance of cooperative efforts and direct those efforts towards the attainment of the goal. The following are the functions of leadership :

1. Integration: One of the main functions of leadership is to integrate the efforts of his followers and to direct them towards organization goals. The leader integrates the efforts of the group and without that, common objectives cannot be achieved and coordination is not possible. In this age of specialisation, each individual does a part of the whole work and integration of the parts of the whole is of paramount importance for a leader.

2. Communication: In order to integrate the efforts of the members of the group, communication of organizational policies, procedure and programmes is necessary. A leader communicates authority and responsibility of each individual so that he may come to know what he is to do and what not. He also comes to know the way as to how he can attain the goals and discharge his responsibilities.

3. Production Emphasis: A leader should follow the production oriented supervisory style of leadership but not at the cost of human relations and he should do all to increase the production and productivity of the organization.

4. Representation: A leader represents the organization and its objectives before those who work for it and before those who are outsiders. He represents workers before the higher management and outsiders and represents management before the workers and thus he provides link, between his leader (management) and subordinates.

5. Fraternity: Leadership should promote fraternity among the subordinates. Leadership approach and its style play an important role in developing industrial harmony. He should develop a climate of cooperation among workers in the organization to achieve the success.

6. Organization: Organizing capacity of a leader is an important trait. In organizing the activities of a group, he is to decide who will do what and how? He provides necessary inputs to get the work done effectively. If he fails in organization function, he will lose his confidence among the workers and also the organization.

7. Evaluation of Performance: A leader must evaluate the performance of his subordinates. If a worker does well he should be adequately rewarded and if he fails in discharging his responsibility, he should be punished. Both reward and punishment must aim at motivating people to improve the situation.

8. **Initiation:** A leader must lead. He should take initiative to introduce changes, wherever necessary, in the organization and the group's efforts. He should communicate the changes and reasons behind them to convince the workers about its rationality.

9. Domination: Leader dominates his followers. He holds authority and some organizational power and uses his power anyway– constructively or distructively. He can ignore his followers' wishes but he should not do that. He should be participative and must use his power in the interest of group of which he is a leader.

The above are the functions of an ideal leader but an ordinary leader cannot perform all but he should do his best in the interest of his subordinates. In the words of Stogdill, "Leadership is concerned with problems of human performance and interaction."

DIFFERENT APPROACHES OR THEORIES OF LEADERSHIP

Broadly, there are five main theories of leadership: 1. Traitists theory, 2. Situationalists theory, 3. Behavioural theory, 4. Followers theory, 5. System theory or Path-Goal Theory. We shall now explain each one of them in brief:

1. Traitists Approach or Theory: This is a classical theory. According to this theory, leadership behaviour is produced by certain Traits (qualities) inherent in a person or say, leadership behaviour is sum total of the traits. A leader behaves as his traits warrant. Studies focused the traits of past and present leaders in terms of their family background, education, career, events, character, etc. and made a list of traits or attributes which a leader should possess. The other way to identify the traits is to enquire from the leader himself how he considers himself different from others.

A number of traits have been identified by various researches to distinguish successful leaders from unsuccessful one or followers. A successful leader is supposed to have the following traits:

(i) Good personality, (ii) Tirelessness, (iii) Ability to quick decision, (iv) Courage, (v) Persuasion, (vi) Intelligence, (vii) Reliability, (viii) Imagination, (ix) Physically fit, (x) Intellectually sound, etc. The psychologists have grouped the various traits of a leader into four categories: (a) physical, (b) Psychological, (c) Intellectual, and (d) Qualities of character.

Earlier trait theories maintained that leadership qualities are inherited but later theorists conceded that many of these traits could be acquired and developed by experience and training. So, traits are not only inborn but acquired also. It has now been well established that leader is not only born but also made.

1. Weaknesses of Traitists Theory:

The theory though widely accepted for a pretty long time during 1930s-1950s suffers from the following weaknesses:

1. The List of Traits is not Exhaustive: Various thinkers have supplied different list of qualities of a successful leadership. Rarely, if ever, do two lists agree on the essential characteristics of the effective leader. None of the thinkers have listed the traits, whatever traits were presented by him, in order of importance. So, lists of traits sometimes confuse the readers.

2. No Common or Universal Traits: Neither leadership traits are common in nature nor universal. It is, therefore, very difficult to indicate what mix of traits is necessary to make an effective leader. Its measurement is problematic.

3. No Room for Developing future Leaders: The theory stresses the inborn qualities of an individual which cannot be developed or acquired but it was later accepted that such inborn traits can be developed or acquired through experience or training. Earlier it was assumed that leaders are born and therefore, it left no scope for development of future leader.

4. No Consideration for situational factors: Traitists do not consider the situational factors for leadership which influence the leaders more than their inner traits. Traits come to light only when a situation arises and they are helpful in facing a particular situation but without a situation, traits are useless.

5. Different Roles Require Different Traits: Even in the same organization. At lower managerial level, where there is direct contact between a worker and the supervisor, technical knowledge is of paramount importance. At middle management level, where policies are elaborated and interpreted, human relations skills are of prime importance. At higher management level where policies are framed, planning is undertaken, conceptual skill gains preeminent position. Leadership, in a large organization has a limited role while in a small organization it demand multiplicity of roles. So different combination of traits are required in different organization or at different organizational level.

6. The Approach Ignores other Variables of Leadership: Such as acts of leader, followers and their acts, situation, and their effects on the leader.

7. Traits of an Individual cannot be known: Unless situation arises. When an individual faces a problem, then only the presence or absence of the trait required otherwise traits remain unknown.

2. Behavioural Approach or Theory

It was apparent from the traitists theory that traits fail to explain the leadership phenomenon and the theorists diverted their attention to the study of leader behaviour. This approach was much in current during 1950s-1960s. The basis of this theory lie in how the management viewed the workers.

Under classical management approach, man or worker was regarded no more than a commodity or just an appendage to a machine. Management coerced, directed and motivated workers through the offer of economic rewards and attempted to increase efficiency or productivity by reducing wastes of times and material and no consideration was given to men as an asset. The basic assumption under this theory was taken that the people, by nature, were lazy, uncreative and irresponsible and therefore leader (manager) should be directive. However, scientific management approach in management by Taylor and Hawthorne experiments by Elton Mayo and his associates discovered that human behaviour of workers (followers) is the sole concern for the leadership.

This approach developed various leadership styles such as autocratic or democratic or supervisory style which produce different and conflicting results because behaviour of leader and followers differ in different situations.

The theory endeavoured to explain the leadership phenomenon in terms of the behaviour of the leader. What the leader does was the main concern therefore the investigators examined the style followed by the leader, i.e., authoritarian or democratic. It may be a mix of the two.

Weaknesses: The main limitation of this approach is questionnaire which has its own limitations. Scientific tests cannot be applied in studies which are likely to be affected by perceptual differences and a variety of interpretations of questions. However no measurement methodology, i.e., questionnaire, observation, or interviews has been universally accepted by behavioural researchers. This is, therefore, an unavoidable limitation.

3. Situationalist Approach or Theory

The trait approach, in effect, explained some of the desirable characteristics that a leader had or should have but it could not suggest with certainty that one who possesses particular traits shall be a leader. The behavioural approach, on the other hand explained the various practices or styles available to a leader to discharge his leadership function but this, again failed to indicate a best style of leadership which was universally appropriate. The shortcomings of these two theories – Traits and Behavioural theories – initiated further researches and it was established during 1970s that it was not the traits or behaviour of a leader that matters but it is a particular situation in which a particular trait or behaviour (style) is effective or ineffective. Both these earlier approaches ignored the situation as an important element.

The theory advocates that leadership is strongly affected by the situation in which he works. The theory believes that it is a situation that helps developing leadership and from which leaders emerge. Traits or behaviour may be supportive elements. A person may be good leader in a particular situation or set of circumstances but it may be possible that he may be quite ineffective in a different situation.

The theory further believes that there exists an interaction between a group of workers and its leader is to recognise the needs of situation and the aspirations of the followers and to act accordingly. Thus, it is a situation that produces the leadership.

Limitations: The theory suffers from the following shortcomings:

(i) **It overemphasises the situational aspect:** of leadership. Situation may affect the decision of a leader in a particular situation but it is not everything.

(ii) **It completely overlooks the traits and behaviour:** of a leader which play an important role in the emergence of a particular leader. The head and heart of a leader, definitely plays a decision role in every situation.

4. Followers' Theory or Acceptance Theory

The theory asserts that followers are important in deciding whether the a person is a leader or not. If followers accept a person as their leader he is leader irrespective of his traits or behaviour. According to this theory, followers must form groups. The theory cannot be applied without group of followers. The theory based on the assumption that groups have certain basic needs which they want to be fulfilled through their leader. A person who is successful in satisfying their basic needs, is assumed to be their leader, on the contrary, if he does not succeed in getting their needs satisfied, he can neither be said to be a good leader nor he will be allowed to function as such. Thus need of the followers is the most crucial and guiding factor in the leadership event.

The Major Weakness: of the theory is that it ignores the quality aspect of leadership. But modern managers are of the opinion that it is the followers' theory that is now playing a significant role in managing the people today. In India, following theory is playing a dominant role in the business, industrial and political leadership.

5. System Theory

Leadership is governed by a person's act rather than by his traits which influences the followers most. It followers that leadership is a sole behaviour which co-ordinates the efforts of the people and stimulates them towards the achievement of their goal in a particular situation. This approach is called system approach because it considers all the variables present at the same time, i.e., leader, followers, situation, goals, leadership traits, environments and group's nature, characteristics and needs, role, behaviour of the leader and his coordinating efforts.

This theory is recognised as the modern theory of leadership. In the modern world, this theory is rather more acceptable to followers.

DIFFERENT LEADERSHIP STYLES

The success of a business enterprise depends upon the type and style of leadership which a leader follows. Styles describe how a leader behaves with his group or how leadership is applied in practice. The following leadership styles have been developed:

1. Motivational Styles,

2. Power Styles, and

3. Orientation Styles or Supervisory Styles.

1. MOTIVATIONAL STYLES – POSITIVE AND NEGATIVE LEADERSHIP

Motivation of followers (workers in a business enterprise) is the main function of a leader. Motivational styles cover two main approach, which are generally followed by a leader: (i) Positive approach, and (ii) Negative approach.

(i) Positive Approach or Leadership: When a leader motivates the people to work hard by offering them various rewards monetary or otherwise – the approach or leadership is said to be positive. The more is the reward, the higher is the efficiency. Positive leadership promotes industrial peace. For example, encashment of leave will certainly reduce the absenteeism in the organization because it increases workers' real wages.

(ii) Negative Approach or Leadership: Where the leader (manager) induces the followers (workers) to work hard and threatens them to penalise if work is not upto the work, it is said to be a negative approach or negative leadership. It means, in a negative leadership, emphasis is laid on penalties for the shortcomings. The stronger is the penalty, the more negative it is. For example, if manager imposes a salary cut for the absence from duty it is a negative approach to improve the absenteeism.

Negative leadership gets acceptable performance in many situations, but it has high human costs. Negative leaders act domineering and superior with people. In order to get the work done, they impose the penalties like loss of job, reprimand before others. Leave without pay, etc. They display their authority with the false belief that it frightens everyone into productivity. They are bosses more than leaders.

In negative leadership, followers (subordinates) work only to protect themselves. They always try to shrink their responsibility to others.

Which of the two? Almost every manager uses both the styles off and on but the predominant style sets the tone within the group. Which of the two styles is the best? The answer is that it depends on the situation of the case, and the organizational behaviour model. A manager in a case may follow the positive approach but he may be a supporter of negative approach next time in similar case. The reason may be change in situation. So a modern manager uses both the styles according to the circumstances of the case.

The organizational behaviour model also sets the tone. The autocratic model tends to cause a negative style; the custodial model follows somewhat positive or somewhat negative or a mix of both the styles and the supportive model is clearly positive. Positive Ieadership achieves higher productivity to the organization and higher job-satisfaction to subordinates.

2. POWER STYLES - AUTOCRATIC, DEMOCRATIC AND FREE-REIN LEADERS

How a leader uses his power, also establishes a type of style. Power styles may be of three types: (a) Autocratic Leadership, (b) Democratic or Participative Leadership, and (c) Free-rein Leadership.

(a) Autocratic or Authoritarian Leadership: Under this style, power or authority and decision making are centralised in the leaders. They create work-situations and environment for their subordinates and subordinates in turn, do whatever they are told – nothing less or nothing more.

The leaders enjoy full authority and assume full responsibility. They are always power-loving and never like to be devoid of them. Subordinates or followers are not aware of the organizational goals, they are insecure and afraid of the leader's authority. **In this way leadership is negative.**

Leadership may be positive under this style if leader uses his power in the best interest of the group and disburses rewards to motivate them. Such Autocratic leaders having positive motivational style are known a **benevolent autocrat.** The benevolent autocrat gets productivity and full satisfaction because followers are habituated to such culture of many authorities in the society such as teachers, parents, government bureaucrats, etc. They feel satisfied and secured under autocratic leader. They respond well. Such benevolent autocrat leaders are more successful than the democratic leaders.

Advantages of Autocratic Leadership: Autocratic leadership enjoys following advantages:

(i) It provides strong motivation and reward for the leader.

(ii) Quick decision-making is guaranteed because single person decides for the whole group.

(iii) Less competent sub-managers can be used only to carry out the orders of the boss. They are not involved in decision-making process.

(iv) Decision-making, planning or organizing need no initiative.

Disadvantages of Autocratic Leadership: It suffers from the following drawbacks:

(i) People dislike it especially if it is extreme and the motivational style is negative.

(ii) Frustration, low morale, and conflict develop easily in Autocratic leadership because of any motivation. They work half-heatedly.

(iii) Managers are poor motivators.

(b) Participative or Democratic Leaderships: It is just opposite to autocratic leadership. Under this style, power and authority decentralised and followers are also allowed participation in decision making process and thus decisions are not unilateral. Before taking any decision, subordinates are consulted and thus they are fully aware of the path and goal of the organization. The leader and group work together as a social unit. Participative leaders exercise control mostly by using forces within the group while autocratic leaders control through authority vested in themselves.

The leader delegates his authority to his subordinates to get the work accomplished towards goals of the organization. Generally the present trend is towards wider use of the participative practices. 'Worker' participation in management is getting popularity now-a-days.

Advantages: Under this style:

(i) Workers or subordinates are consulted or participate in the decision making process hence feel satisfied.

(ii) Workers are aware of what is happening in the organization and thus they take interest in producing more and more.

(iii) Subordinates get full opportunity to utilise their capabilities.

Disadvantages: (i) Power is not centralised in the leader. He can use it only in consultation with his subordinates.

(ii) Decision-making and implementation – are delayed as compared to autocratic leadership because under this style more than one persons are involved in decision-making process.

(iii) As authority is decentralised, less competent executives cannot be used.

(c) Free-rein Leadership: Under this style, leaders enjoy no power. The leadership is employee-centred and the group of employees is free to establish its own goals and work-out its own problems. The members of the group train themselves and provide own motivation.

The leader keeps contact with outsiders to bring the group the information and resources the group needs to fulfil its job. Free-rein leadership ignores the leader's contribution in the same way approximately that autocratic leadership ignores the group. It fails to provide to the group the benefits of leader inspired motivation. Sometimes it creates chaos.

3. ORIENTATION STYLE OR SUPERVISORY STYLE

There are two types of leadership under this style: (i) Employee oriented leadership, and (ii) Production oriented or task oriented leadership.

(i) Employee Oriented Leadership: Employee Oriented leaders are concerned about the human needs of their employees and pay highest attention to their subordinates attitudes, interests, and necessities etc. They try to get more and more production and increased productivity by improving the working conditions and environments and solving the problems, if any, faced by them during the course of their action on the job.

(ii) Production or Task Oriented Leadership: Production or task oriented leaders, on the other hand, believe that they are concerned mainly with the production and employees are not of much concern. They are of the opinion that they can attain results by planning better methods, keeping people constantly busy and using them to produce. They do not consider human aspect of the workers.

Which one is better: Employee oriented and production oriented leadership styles seem to be both related and independent. They are not opposite to each other. A manager who is more employee oriented does not necessary become against production oriented or vice versa. Each orientation is somewhat independent, so a manager may have both orientations in varying degrees. So, it is prudent that a manager must combine these two orientations. He must think in terms of higher production and not at the cost of human values. He must honour the initiatives and abilities of employees and try to satisfy their needs.

SUITABILITY OF THE DIFFERENT STYLES

We have discussed above the three main leadership styles and their types. Now the question is of choosing the most effective leadership style. It is evidently a wild goose chase. The research findings suggest a universally accepted 'best' style is very-very difficult rather impossible because of the modern complexities of modern organization. If one considers a single style of leadership to be the best for every kind of organization at every level and with any kind of subordinates, one ignores important influencing factors like subordinate characteristics, task characteristics, group cohesiveness, cultural difference, customs, traditions, level of education, standard of living and the like. As a leader's style cannot operate in vacuum and influence the other's behaviour, these situational factors cannot be ignored. It is highly unrealistic to talk of a single best or normative style of leadership.

The best answer of this question is that a leader should not be rigid to any one style of leadership and he should get the work done as the situation warrants. According to the circumstances, he may be autocratic at one time and democratic at the other. Sometimes he motivates people through positive rewards and sometimes he is forced to take negative action. So, it will be better in the present circumstances, that a leader must get results through democratic methods involving the people at large in the decision-making process, satisfy human needs not at the cost of human values by following positive motivational measures. But he cannot be abstained from attempting negative autocratic style if situation so warrants.

FIEDLER'S CONTINGENCY MODEL OF LEADERSHIP

In different leadership styles, it was observed that consideration, i.e., employees and other variables, and structure, i.e., job or organization seem to be effective under different conditions. Fiedler and his associates have classified the relationship between these two, i.e., consideration and structure, and the result is **'Contingency Model of Leadership.'** Fiedler contingency theory specifies that the effectiveness of a group is contingent upon the motivational system of a leader and the degree to which the leader has control and influence in a particular situation. The leader's effectiveness can be measured with the leader-member relations; task structure, and leader position power. If leader-member relations are good, task is structured and leader position power is strong, the situation is regarded to be highly favourable to leadership effectiveness. On the contrary, if leader-member relations are not good, task is unstructured and leader position power is weak, the situation may be regarded as highly unfavourable to the leadership effectiveness, i.e., leadership is highly ineffective. As a leader operates in a particular situation, and favourableness or unfavourablness determines the effectiveness of the leadership. So, it is an important question to decide what type of leadership style is needed in a particular type of situation. The theory suggests that a particular leadership style is effective only in particular situation or effectiveness of a leader is contingent upon the relationship among all these variables.

So, there are four main variables: (i) Leader-member relations, (ii) Task-structure, and (iii) Leader position power, (iv) Leadership Style.

(i) Leader-member relations: Leadership are determined by the manner in which the leader is accepted or rejected by the group. If, suppose, in a organization there is group-frictions, orders are generally flouted, the leader member relations are said to be poor. If, on the other hand there is cooperations between leader and members, order are carried out in the manner, leader desires, the relations may be regarded as good.

(ii) Task-Structure: It may be highly structured or highly unstructured. If task is highly specific, can be done only in one way and rules and procedures are well defined, and there is no scope for different interpretations, it is said to be **highly structured:** On the other hand, if task is completely non-routine, there are many routes to reach the goal or rules and procedures are not clear, then the task is regarded as highly unstructured. In a highly structured task, leader's ability to influence the group is restricted because the task dilutes the leader's potential influence. In case of unstructured task, the leader has more knowledge that the followers and he has great potential for influencing the group.

(iii) Leader Position Power: It indicates the power provided for the position in an organization such as power to hire and fire, status symbol provided, power to give, promotion and pay rises, punishment, rewards, etc. In most business organization, the leaders possess high position power while in social organizations leader have very low position power.

Favourableness of the Leadership Situation: The three situational factors task structure, group atmosphere (Leader-member relations) and position power determine the situation's favourableness to the leader. The relationship among favourableness, situational factors and leadership style is presented in Fig.1.

The numbers 1,2,3,4,...........8 represent combinations situational variables and are arranged in order of favourableness to the leader. The Fig.1 assume that the leader will have the most influence and control when using a task oriented style under favourable conditions (1) – that is, when he is accepted, the task is structured, and he has strong position power. At the other end of the continuum (8), it is assumed that the leader's control and influence will be minimum when the leader is not accepted, the group's task is relatively complex and unstructured, and the leader has little position power.

Cell	1	2	3	4	5	6	7	8
Leader member relations			Good				Poor	
Task structure		High		Low		High		Low
Leader position power	strong	weak	strong	weak	strong	weak	strong	weak
Situational Favourableness		Favourable		Moderate Favourable			Unfavourable	

Fig. 1. Fiedler's Contingency Model

The Leadership Style: To determine the style of leadership and to investigate the leader effectiveness Fiedler introduced a Scale/Score, called Least Preferred Co. Worker (LPC). The 20-item questionnaire assesses the level of esteem in which the leader holds his least preferred co worker. The leader is asked to describe the person with whom he has worked least well in accomplishing his task. In the following example, the scores/scale on the three items shown suggests that the manager completing this questionnaire has relatively high evaluation of his least preferred coworker:

Helpful .... Frustrating
8 7 6 5 4 3 2 1

Relaxed .... Tense
8 7 6 5 4 3 2 1

Friendly .... Unfriendly
8 7 6 5 4 3 2 1

The model exhibit that a low LPC score (unfavourable evaluation) indicates the leader is willing to reject those with whom he cannot work. Therefore, the lower the LPC score, the greater the tendency for the leader to be task oriented. On the other hand, a high LPC score (favorable evaluation) indicates a willingness to perceive even the worst coworker as having some positive attitudes. Therefore, the higher the LPC score, the greater the tendency for the leader to be employee oriented.

Fiedler has considered eight possible combinations of these three variables in addition to leader's employee-orientation ranging from a highly favourable position to a highly unfavourable situation for a leader. In the middle of these two extremes is intermediate position in favourableness for the leader.

The results seem to be quite plausible. The take oriented leader performs better in **highly favourable situation.** Low least preferred worker is motivated by task-accomplishment. In case, when task is structured and leader member relations are good even the task oriented behaviour of the leader may be considered friendly but only in **favourable situation.** The workers support him. **In an unfavourable situation,** when task is unstructured, the relations between the two are not good, the power position of the leader is poor, he is more concerned with the performance and his efforts are to remove the ambiguity and anxiety. If the leader possesses a more knowledge than his subordinates, the followers are willing to accept the task-orient structure.

A leader obtains better group performance in conditions of moderate or **intermediate favourableness** in which (i) the task is structured and leader is disliked, therefore, he demonstrates that he cares for the emotions of the subordinates, or (ii) the leader is liked and the task is unstructured and the leader depends upon the willingness and creativity of the group's members to accomplish the goals.

Thus, the contingency model of Fiedler has helped to resolve confusion about optimum conditions for a considerate, people oriented leader compared with a more structured, task oriented leader. But the model is not free from criticism. The model presents only a portion of variance in leadership effectiveness. It is not a ready solution to all matters of leadership style.

Evaluation of Fiedler's Work: The model suggested Fiedler led to a great deal of research theory. The recent studies, for example, by Strube and Garcia, have supported the theory of leadership propounded by Fiedler. Robbins remarks, "Fiedler goes significantly beyond trait and behavioural approaches by attempting to isolate situations, relating his personality measure to his situational classification, and then predicting leadership effectiveness as function of the two.

Criticism

The later research studies have attempted to test the validity of Fiedler's contingency theory. While some of them have supported the model, considerable number of studies has questioned the validity of the theory. The theory was criticised mainly on two grounds: first; lack of research support and second, on theoretical perspective. Some of the major criticisms are:

(1) The critiesare of the view that the contingency model lacks a theoretical orientation. The theory was developed from research date and not from theoretical variables. It lacks explanatory power and thus it become less than a theory and more of an empirical generalization.

(2) The favourableness of a work situation defined in terms three variables, Fiedler gave most important of leader-member relations followed by task structure and position power. But some researchers have found that the task structure is the only important situational factor.

(3) Fiedler considered only a few situational variables affecting the work situations, but the subsequent researches have pointed out a good number of other situational factors affecting the leadership style and subordinate behaviour. They include expectations of the subordinates about the behaviour of the leader, congruence of the leadership styles and the ability of the leader to influence his superior.

(4) The LPC Scale as a measuring rod of leadership style has also been criticised that it is a confusing concept. It is because that the same person may obtain different LPC scores on different days.

(5) Fiedler is also criticised on the ground that he could not explain how the situational variables effect the leadership style.

In spite of these criticisms, Fiedler's contingency model has proved to be important contribution to the study of leadership in organizations. The model will continue to be an important source of ideas, and hypotheses about the situational leadership.

Path Goal Theory of Robert House

The second situational theory of leadership was propounded by Robert J. House in 1971. This approach has been called the path-goal-theory because it is an extension of Vroom's Expectancy Theory of motivation. It is more comprehensive than Fiedler's Contingency Model. The Path-Goal-Model proposes that individuals are satisfied with their job if they believe it leads to desirable outcomes. According to Path-Goal - Theory, leaders are effective because of the influence on followers motivation ability to perform and their satisfaction. That is, if the leader can influence the subordinates perceptions and clarity may increase their expectancy probabilities, greater effort and higher satisfaction and performance will result.

According to the path-goal-theory leaders should motivate subordinates by clarifying the path to personal rewards that results from attaining work goals. The path is clarified by eliminating confusion or conflicting ideas that the subordinate may hold. The leader should provided guidance and counsel to clarify the way in which these rewards can be obtained. According to path-goal-theory leaders can perform their strategic functions (that includes clearing the paths, clarity of goals, providing support and rewards, and analysing the situation, task and employees needs), by adopting the following styles of behaviour:

(1) Instrumental Behaviour (Directive): This behaviour is the planning, organising, controlling, and coordinating the activities of subordinates by the leader. It is somewhat similar to Ohio State researchers' "initiating structure."

(2) Supportive Behaviour: This includes giving consideration to the needs of subordinates, displaying concern for their well being and treats them as his equals. This is similar to Ohio State researchers "Consideration."

(3) Participative Behaviour: It is characterized by the sharing of information with the subordinates and consulting them and soliciting their ideas and suggestions in reaching group related decisions.

(4) Achievement Oriented Behaviour: The leader adopting this style sets challenging goals, expects the subordinates to perform the highest level, continuously seeking improvement in performance.

Situational Factors

According to Robert House, two factors are considered situational variables that moderate the relationship between the leader's style and the behaviour of the subordinate: (1) characteristics of the subordinates, and (2) the characteristics of the work environment.

(1) Characteristics of the Subordinates: This refers that the style selected by the leader should be based on the three characteristics: ability, personalities, and needs and motives of the followers.

Ability: If the followers are super in their ability to accomplish a task, a supportive style would be sufficient on the other hand, if they have low ability, then a highly structured and directed style would be needed.

Personalities: Internals means internally oriented subordinates who believe that they can control their behaviours prefer leaders who have more supportive behaviour. Similarly, externals, means externally oriented subordinates who believe that they can control their own behaviours prefer the directive leadership. This way the personalities of subordinates may work.

Needs and Motives: Subordinates with dominant needs, for example: individuals with high safety and security needs may accept an instrumental leader, but those with high needs affiliation and esteem needs will be satisfied with a supportive leader. Moreover, dominant needs for autonomy and responsibility may be more influenced by a participative leader. Subordinates with a high need for achievement will prefer a task-oriented leader.

(2) Characteristics of the work environment: The environmental variables include the factors which are uncontrollable of the subordinates but are significant to satisfaction. These include three broad factor: (i) subordinates' task; (ii) the work group and (iii) organizational factors or formal authority system of organization.

(i) Subordinates tasks: Robert House asserts that if the subordinates are working on highly unstructured jobs characterized by high degree of role ambiguity, a directive or instrumental leader is required. On the other hand, if the subordinates are working on highly structured or routine and well defined tasks, supportive or participative leader style is likely to increase the subordinates' extrinsic satisfaction.

(ii) Work group: The characteristics of work group may also influence acceptance of a particular leader's style. For example, the subordinate could be motivated by the work group and attain satisfaction from co-workers acceptance for sitting through job according to group norms.

(iii) Organizational factors or formal authority system of organization: This factor in the work environment concern with matters to which rules, procedures, and policies govern an individual's work, high pressures or stressed situations, and situations of high uncertainty. In such situation, a participative leader style will be acceptable to the subordinate.

Evaluation of Path-Goal-Theory of Leadership

The path-goal-theory to leadership has made a significant contribution to situational theories because it has identified key leadership styles and situational factors and has shown the relationship between these variables in complex organizational setting. However, a number of limitations have been reported on this theory. The important among them include:

1. **Complicated approach:** Because of the methodological complexities, it become difficult to test the theory empirically. The theory inconsistently predicts the individual performance.

2. **Measurement problem:** Another important dissatisfaction is the ways leadership style is measured. (by questionnaire, observations or interviews).

3. **Little research support:** The theory has not been offered as a final answer to the question of leadership effectiveness. The theory is backed by relatively little research. Scientists like Weed, Mitchel and others, do not agree with certain findings of Robert House.

The important implication of both Fiedler's contingency model and House's path-goal theory is that the relationship between the leader and his subordinates does not exist in a vacuum.

In spite of certain limitations, House's model is appreciated on the ground that it is more comprehensive to Fiedler's model and it suggests what type of leader may be more effective in a given situation. Moreover, the path-goal theory provides a foundational guidance to the new researchers in the field of leadership theory.

Leadership and Followership

Effective team building depends upon an effective leadership and committed followership. The phenomenon of leadership in organizations has been conceptualised and studied in many different ways. Leadership research has sought for our understanding of leadership in terms of the personal traits of leaders, in terms of situations in which they lead, in terms of what they do or some combination. The leadership paradigm was developed out of the study of small groups and group dynamics. The interest in the concept was created because of the awareness that groups existed at all levels in the organizational hierarchy and such groups needed direction, which was provided by the leader, who became a follower at a higher level. The interest was thus, in who leads and who follows? What situations does leading and following take place? and What conditions facilitate an effective leadership and followership?

The earliest approach used in determining leadership effectiveness consisted of studying traits and characteristics of the leaders. Such persons were supposed to possess certain endowed traits that enabled them to be successful leaders. However, such research yielded very little in the way of concrete results. The Second approach to understanding leadership has focused on the behaviour of managers. The basic contention was that since leadership involves accomplishing goals with and through people, a leader must be concerned with both task and human relationships. After 1945, the stress was on the "employee-oriented and production-oriented leadership styles."

The importance of situational factors for explaining the leader effectiveness became apparent when the "style" theory yielded few results. According to the contingency model developed by Fred Fiedler, the effectiveness of a group depends upon the interaction between the leader and the situation. His model indicates that group performance can be improved either by changing the leader's motivational structure or by modifying the leadership situation. Most studies on leadership concentrated on styles of behaviour, discussing what leaders should do given the situation, and the types of subordinate they are dealing with.

Evolving out of these theories was the gradual realisation on the part of both, theorists and managers, that there are some characteristics which must be developed in order to become skilful in both leading and following. The conclusion is "it is fruitful to discuss leadership and followership together since their crises and opportunities are indeed interrelated". Thus, leadership has been redefined, in the words of Burns, as "leaders inducing followers to act for certain goals that represent the values and the motivations, the wans and needs, the a spirations and expectancies of both leaders and followers. And the genius of leadership lies in the manner in which leaders see and act on their own and their followers' values and motivations."

The need for a better understanding of these interrelated concepts has been clarified and discussed when Smircich and Morgan state: "Many organizations are paralysed by situations in which people appeal for direction, feeling immobilised and disorganised by the sense that they are not being led. Yet other organizations are plagued by the opposite situation characterised in organizational vernacular as one of "all chiefs, no Indians" – the situation where majority aspire to lead and few to follow. Thus, successful acts of organization are often seen to rest in the synchrony between the initiation of action and the appeal for direction between the actions of leaders and the receptivity and responsiveness of follower."

So much has been written on the leadership theory in the past but the controversy between the two opposite positions still remains unresolved. As Blake and Mouton point out situationalism or contingency and advocate and interpret leadership theory as saying that no one style is more effective than another, the style you lead by depends upon the situation. "The effective style" theorists say that there is one most effective style and it involves applying the principles of leadership behaviour that are emerging in the behavioural sciences.

The stress in leadership-followership has gained significance in the late 70s and 80s because getting persons with different background, specialities, and disciplines to work together effectively is indeed a difficult task. The question asked is, who should be put together for what and for how long? The challenge of leadership lies in the fact that the expectations of team members (followers) are increasing. They are no longer satisfied with being given instruction and told what to do. In an age of specialisation, more self-awareness about one's own abilities and competence, sub ordinates are willing to take on more responsibilities, ask for more autonomy and independence to carry out tasks and are prepared to challenge authority. In such situations, the leader becomes more of a collaborator and develops the concept of "creative compromise" so that an atmosphere of "win-win" is created which, in turn, will facilitate effective team work.

What is expected of the leader of the 90s is to recognise the follower needs and expectations, create the atmosphere where individuals can further their own personal goals, at the same time not sacrificing the corporate goals. The leader has the added responsibility of using the resources offered by the followers in terms of skills and competencies. This implies for members a readiness to be flexible in what they are asked to do and what they are challenged to do. The members must be ready to seek and respond to challenge and opportunities for re-education, for training and acquiring of new skills, for new tasks and for relating to new types of leaders.

The significance of the leadership-followership paradigm for team development arises from the fact that team functioning is dependent upon the understanding between the two and their relationship. The ability of leader is accepted and dealt with the differences among the followers (team members) and getting them to work together as a unit is balanced by the needs and expectations of the followers who require understanding and support for task accomplishment.

Leadership is a Mutual Influence Process

The discussion on the nature of leadership till now makes a reader believe that leadership is unidirectional, i.e., the leader influencing his followers. It is true that leadership refers to the influence of the leader on followers. At the same time, the characteristics of employees and their tasks do yield influence on the leader. Leadership is, therefore, a mutual influence process.

Leader's Influence on Followers: Why is leader able to influence his followers? What makes followers simply obey whatever their leader says? A leader is able to change the behaviour of his followers because he enjoys power which comes to him from at least five sources. They are. (1) reward power which refers to the leader's capacity to reward followers, (2) coercive power which is the flip side of reward power and refers to the leader's capacity to coerce or punish followerism, (3) legitimate power which refers to the power a leader possesses as a result of occupying a particular position or role in the organization, (4) expert power that refers to power that a leader possesses as a result of his knowledge and expertise regarding the tasks to be performed by subordinates; and (5) referent power which is dependent upon the extent to which subordinates identify with, look up to, and wish to emulate the leader (see Fig. 2).

Followers' Influence on Leader: The fact that the followers and situations will influence their leader is a recent discovery. Several sources of influence on the leader's behaviour are identified. The more important of them are: (1) responses or performance of subordinates; (2) characteristics of subordinates, namely, male or female, young or old, personal background, and the like; (3) the nature of the task; (4) organizational policy and climate; (5) peers and their influence on the leader; and (6) influence of superiors on the leader. (see Fig. 2).

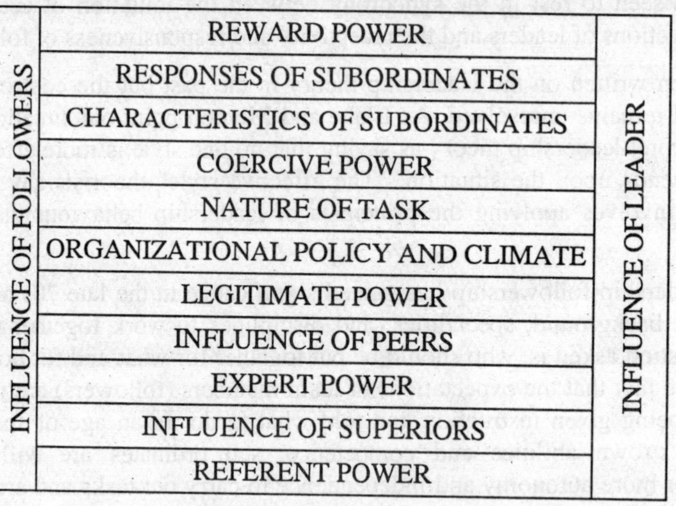

Fig. 2. Leadership is a two-way influencing process

Leadership Style and Leadership Personality

What leader possesses is the leadership personality (LP) and what influences behaviour of followers is leadership style (L.S.). Leadership personality is leader's perception of his own style plus his style as perceived by others – followers, superiors, equals, etc. Whereas leadership style is only the others perception of leadership behaviour. People respond to their perception rather than to the leader's perception of his own style. Greater the disparity between leader's and followers' perceptions greater would be the misunderstandings between the two groups. It is, therefore, better to try to bridge the gap between the two. Johari window helps us to explain how this gap could be bridged.

Johari Window

In fact the name Johari Window has absolutely no meaning. The meaning has been superposed by Joseph Luft and Harry Ingham, taking their first names to call it Johari Window. But now it has acquired a specific connotation. It is a window which enables us to see all compartments of our Leadership Personality.

This framework is shown in Fig. 3.

	Known to self	Unknown to self
Known to others	PUBLIC	BLIND
Unknown to others	PRIVATE	UNKNOWN

Fig. 3. Johari Window

The total area of Johari Window, depicting leadership personality has been divided into four quadrants, by combining areas known and unknown to self with areas of one's own personality known and unknown to others. These four arenas have been given different verbal lables, using terms from terminology in day-to-day usage. Their descriptions are.

Public

The arena of one's leadership personality which is known to self and also known to others. In the organizational context this area is extremely important. The effort should be made to increase this area. Probable effectiveness of the leader increases provided such efforts are made. The more this arena encroaches upon others the better.

Blind

This is the arena which is unknown to self but known to others. Very rarely does the leader know that while interacting with his equals and subordinates they are offended. Has anyone generally seen any authoritarian leader speaking about himself as authoriterian? Almost everyone believes that all virtues are concentrated in him. But the reality is known to others.

Private

This arena of one's personality is hidden from others, though it is known to oneself. That's why it is known as private. The leader manipulates or influences the behaviour of others. He knows it, but the followers are totally in dark about the fact that their behaviour is being manipulated. In MBO, for example, systematically efforts are made to influence the behaviour of others. But the followers are unaware of it. In prestige suggestions this happens always.

Unknown

There is a certain part of leadership personality which is known neither to self nor to others. In Freudian Psychoanalytic terminology this area may be called subconscious or unconscious about which all are unaware, however it continues to influence behaviour.

As has already been pointed out it is necessary to widen the public arena and in such efforts there is encroachment upon the Blind, the Private and the Unknown areas. But the problem is How to do?

The solution is apparently easy but rather difficult to practice. Open communication is the best way out. In simple terms open communication may be described as trying to be receptive to what others say about you and encourage them to say more and more in a frank atmosphere. In addition, without having any inhibitions or reservations express yourself freely. In the first case you get the opportunity to know more and more about the way your leadership is being perceived by others, thus resulting in a horizontal expansion of the 'Public' arena and the corresponding shrinkage of the 'Blind' arena, as shown in Fig. 4.

Feedback from others

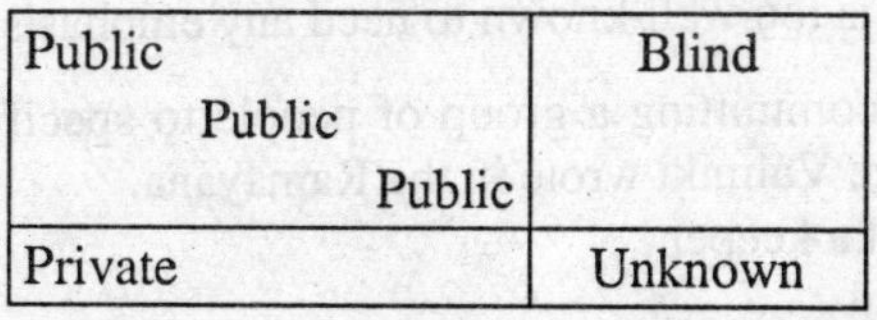

Fig. 4. Effect of feedback on Johari Window

The more you get feedback from others, larger would be the public Arena.

Along with the feedback process, process of 'disclosure' results in another kind of change in the shape of Johari Window. It leads to changes in vertical direction. The more does the leader disclose himself, the more he gives an uninhibited expression to his feelings, emotions, attitudes, tensions, etc., the more he makes them known to others, the more will be the encroachment on the private arena. His public arena will expand more and more, and to that extent the 'private' arena would shrink in size, as shown in Fig. 5.

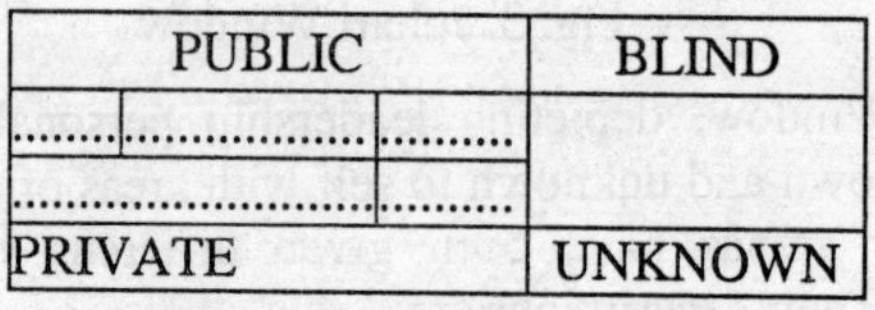

Fig. 5. Effect of Disclosure on Johari Window

Carried to its extreme if the leader is open and discloses every thing about his perception of his leadership maximally, private arena will be reduced to zero.

If two processes feedback and disclosure are considered simultaneously it may be said that two sides of Johari Window represent two directions of the communication process – vertical direction representing feedback from the leader and horizontal representing feedback from the followers. Essential requirement is that both leader and followers should be encouraged to give feedback without inhibitions and secondly both should be receptive to each other's feedback.

Greatest advantage of these two processes in that 'Unknown' arena is likely to shrink automatically if disclosure and feedback are properly taken care of. The way 'Unknown' arena is affected by these two proceses can be seen in Fig. 6.

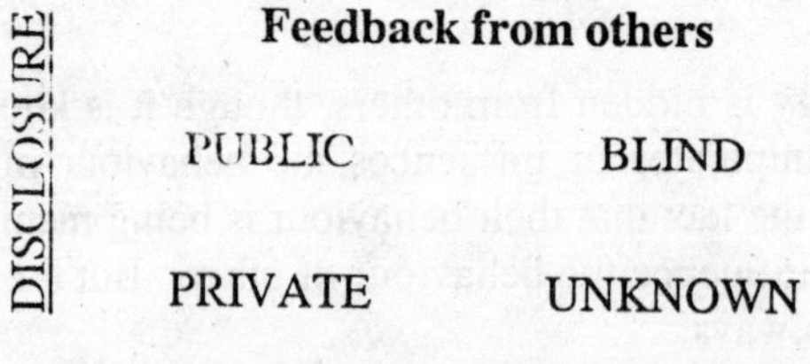

Fig. 6. Effect of Disclosure and feedback on the Johari Window

Efforts of a leader should be directed towards enlarging 'Public' arena in both vertical and horizontal directions to reap the additional benefits of reducing the 'Unknown' arena. As has already been stated previously the 'Unknown' is composed of subconscious and unconscious. They need some stimulation to enter into the conscious. This stimulation is provided by the interactions resulting at the time of feedback and disclosure. 'Why do I behave the way I do' the leader does not know. How can the followers know about it? But when environment is created in which the processes of disclosure and feedback occur simultaneously, the person himself and the counselor can pick up threads and come to understand the causes which were unknown till then. On the contrary if the process of disclosure and feedback are ignored public arena would shrink in size more and more and the Unknown would spread its antena over the entire window, the situation as it exists today in several of our organizations. Leaders usually see to it that the followers are kept in dark about several matters. In addition hardly do they pay attention to the feedback from others. Thus gradually both – leaders as well as followers are alienated from each other and continue to behave in certain ways, no one knows why.

The importance of leadership is too well-known to need any emphasis.

Leadership is the process of committing a group of people to specific goals. Without leadership, an organization would be what the sage Valmiki wrote in the Ramayana.

"Like a heard of cattle without a keeper
Like an army without a general
Like a night without moon

Like a group of cows without a bull
Such would be the country
Where the King is not seen.

A leader not only commits his followers to organizational goals, he also pools needed resources, guides, and motivates subordinates to reach the goals.

The leadership process is similar in effect to that of the secret chemical that turns the insect pupa into a butterfly with all the beauty that was the pupa's potential. Leadership, then, transforms potential into reality. This role is often seen in giant firms and tiny units. In all cases, leadership is the ultimate act that identifies, develops, and uses the potential that is in an organization and its people.

Leadership is not the mere using of people and their potential for realising an organization's goals. It has the ultimate aim of raising the level of human conduct and ethical aspiration of both the leader and the led. This aspect of leadership is what Burns calls the transforming leadership. The leader should elevate, inspire, and evangelise his followers to higher things in life.

High sounding words indeed! In reality, effect of leadership on organizational effectiveness seems to be relative because of the following possibilities:

* Poorly performing organizations find it difficult to attract best leaders.
* Not all leaders have the same abilities and experience.
* Environmental and organizational factors can override any effects the leader may have.
* Organizations continue to flourish even after the change of leadership.

REFERENCES

A. Zaleznik, *Exceprts From Managers and Leaders: Are They Different? Harvard Business Review*, May-June, 1986, p.54.

Andrew Szillagyi and Marc Wallace, Organisataional Behaviour and Performance, Scott, Foresmann and Company, Glenview, Illions, 1980, p.277.

Ashour, The Contingency Model, and C.A. Schriescheim and Setven Kerr, *Theories and Measures of Leadership, A. Critical Approach of Current and Future Directions*, Illions, 1977, pp. 9-45.

Chung and L.C. Megginson, *Organizational Behaviour – Developing Managerial Skills*, Harper and Row, New York, 1981, p. 280.

D.C. Feldman and H.J. Arnold, *Managing Individual and Group Behaviour in Organizations*, McGraw Hill, New York, 1983, p.291.

D.C. Feldman and H.J. Arnold, *Managing Individual and Group Behaviour in Organizations*, McGraw Hill, New York, 1983, p.291.

Fred E. Fiedler, *A Theory of Leadership Effectiveness*, McGraw Hill, New York, 1967.

George Garren, K. Alvares, Contingency *Model of Leadership Effectiveness: Antecedent and Evidential Results, Psychological Bulletin*, Vol. 74, 1970, p.p.285 - 296.

George R. Terry, *Principles of Management*, Richard D. Irwin Inc. Illions, 1960, p.493.

Harold Koontz and Cyril O'Donnell, *Principles of Management,* 2nd ed., McGraw Hill, New York, 1959, p.435.

Heinz Weihrich, *How to Change a Leadership Pattern, Management Review,* April, 1979, pp. 26-40.

J.C. Campbell and M.D. Dunnette, E.E. Lawler and K.E. Weick, Management Behaviour, Performance and Effectiveness, McGraw Hill, New York, 1970.

J.P. Howell, P.W. Dorfman and S. Ker, *Moderator Variables in Leadership Research, Academy of Management Review*, vol. II, No. 1, 1986, pp. 88-102.

J.P. Kotter, *A Force for Change: How Leadership Differs From Management*, Free Press, New York, 1990.

John. K. Hemphill, *Situational Factors in Leadership*, Ohio State University, Personnel Research Monograph, Columbus, 1949.

Keith Davis and J.W. Newstrom, *Human Behaviour At Work*, McGraw Hill, New York, 1989, p.204.

Keith Davis, *Human Behaviour at Work*, Tata McGraw Hill Co. Ltd., New Delhi, 1982, p.124.

Linda Smircich and G. Morgan, *Special Issues on Leadership and Followership*, JABS, vol. 18, No. 3, 1982.

Mithel et. al., The Contingency Model: Criticism and Suggestions, Personnel Psychology, Vol. 26, 1973, p.p.385 - 395.

P.C. Tripathi and P.N. Reddy, Principles of Management, Tata McGraw Hill Publishing Company Ltd., New Delhi, 1993, p.247.

Paul Merscy and K.M. Blan Chand, *Management of Organizational Behaviour*, Prentice Hall of India Pvt. Ltd., New Delhi, 5th.ed. 1988, p.5.

Peter Drucker, *Practice of Management*, Allied Publishers Pvt. Ltd., New Delhi, 1970, p.159.
R. Blake and J. Mouton, Theory and Research in Designing a Science of Leadership, JABS, vol. 18, No. 3, 1982, pp. 275-91.
R.M. Stogdill, *Personal Factors Associated with Leadership: A Survey of Literature, Journal of Psychology*, Vol. 25, 1948, pp. 25-31.
Robert Dubin, *Human Relations in Administration*, Prentice Hall, Englewood Cliffs, N.J., 1951.
Robert J. House *A Path-Goal Theory of Leadership Effectiveness, Administrative Science Quarterly Review*, Sept. 1971.
Robert Tannenbaum, Irwin Weschler and Fred Massarik, *Leaderhip and Organization. A Behavioural Science Approach*, McGraw Hill, New York, 1959.
S.P. Robbins, *Organizational Behaviour, Concepts and Controversies*, Prentice Hall, New Jersey, 1979, p. 240.
William E. Rosenbach and Robert L. Taylor, Eds., *Contemporary Issues in Leadership*, Westview Press, Mumbai, Colo, 1948, p.128.

CHAPTER

15

Team & Team Work

Teams and team work are popular terms in management circles these days. A cynic might dismiss team work as just another management fad or quick-fix gimmick. But a close look reveals that much more than catchy buzz words are involved here. The team approach to managing organizations is having diverse and substantial impacts on organizations and individuals. Teams promise to be a cornerstone of progressive management for the foreseeable future. According to management expert Peter Drucker, tomorrow's organization's will be flatter, information based, and organized around teams. This means managers will need to polish their team skills. General Electric's director of corporate management development, James Baughman, puts it this way. "The people who will excel will be those who can build a team and integrate it with other teams." Examples of the trend toward teams and team work abound.

Hospitals, for example, are installing health care teams to control runaway costs, and improve quality of care. Team policing is a growing practice in public safety departments. Commercial airline pilots are attending team-building seminars to improve cockpit communication and co-ordination skills.

Teams Defined

A team is a collection of individuals. A team may be defined as a group whose members have complementary skills and are committed to a common purpose or set of performance goals for which they hold themselves mutually accountable.

Jon R. Katzenbach and Douglas K. Smith, management consultants at McKinsey & Company, say it is a mistake to use the terms group and team interchangeably. After studying many different kinds of teams – from athletic to corporate to military – they concluded that successful teams tend to take a life of their own. Katzenbach and Smith define a team as "a small number of people with complementary skills who are committed to a common purpose, performance goals, and approach for which they hold themselves mutually accountable." Because of conflicts over power and authority and unstable interpersonal relations, many work groups never qualify as a real team. Katzenbach and Smith clarified the distinction this way: "The essence of a team is common commitment. Without it, groups perform as individuals; with it, they become a powerful unit of collective performance." (See Table 1).

When Katzenbach and Smith refer to "a small number of people" in their definition, they mean between 2 and 25 team members. They found effective teams to typically have fewer than 110 members.

Table 1. The Evolution of a Team

A work group becomes a team when
1. Leadership becomes a shared activity.
2. Accountability shifts from strictly individual to both individual and collective.
3. The group develops its own purpose or mission.
4. problem-solving becomes a way of life, not a part-time activity.
5. Effectiveness is measured by the group's collective outcomes and products.

There are a number of factors, such as pursuit of a set of common goals, task interdependency, organizational roles, which lend themselves to a cohesive group. The boundaries of group membership tend to be rather permeable, with new members joining and old ones leaving on a continuous basis. Moreover, members of one group may also be members of several additional groups, thereby dividing their time and loyalties. Because of such problems, we tend to discuss teams more in terms of specific members and their personal characteristics. Thus, one can define a team as any group of people, who share a set of norms, who generally have differentiated roles among members, who jointly pursue common goals, and who must significantly relate to each other in order to accomplish set objectives.

What is implied in the definition of team is the need for collaboration, and the team members rely on such collaborated efforts in order to experience the optimum of success and goal achievement. According to Huse, teams can be categorised as follows: groups reporting to the same hierarchical supervisor, groups involving employees with common organizational aims; temporary groups formed to do specific but short - term tasks; groups consisting of people whose work roles are interdependent; groups whose members have no formal links but whose collective purpose is to achieve tasks they cannot achieve as individuals.

Black and Mouton summarised the essence of team work as following. "The effective work team is the key to individual and organizational excellence. In any organization, every individual is member of a work team. People are bosses, subordinates, peers. They have close inter-workings, goals in common and individual goals. They share the need for co-ordination and co-operation just as each shoulders sole responsibility and effort. A work team reflects the extent to which organization members are interdependent.

Difference Between Team & Group

At this point, it is probably not entirely clear as to exactly how a team is different from an ordinary group.

This confusion probably stems in part from the fact that people often refer to their groups as teams, although they are really not teams. Yet there are several important distinctions between them. First, in groups, performance typically depends on the work of individual members. The performance of a team, however, depends on both individual contributions and collective work products-the joint outcome of team members working in concert.

A second difference has to do with where accountability for the job lies. Typically, members of groups pool their resources to attain a goal, although it is individual performance that is taken into consideration when it comes to issuing rewards. Members of groups usually do not take responsibility for any results other than their own. By contrast, teams focus on both individual and mutual accountability. That is, they work together to produce an outcome (e.g., a product, service, or decision) that represents their joint contributions, and each team member shares responsibility for that outcome. The key difference is this: in groups, the supervisor holds individual members accountable for their work, whereas in teams, members hold themselves accountable.

Third, whereas group members may share a common interest goal, team members also share a common commitment to purpose. Moreover, these purposes typically are concerned with winning in some way, such as being first or best at something. For example, a work team in a manufacturing plant of a financially troubled company may be highly committed to making the company the top one in its industry. Another, team, one in a public high school, may be committed to preparing all its graduates for the challenges of the world better than any other school in the district. Team members focusing jointly on such lofty purposes, in conjunction with specific performance goals, become heavily invested in its activities. In fact, teams are said to establish ownership of their purposes, and usually spend a great deal of time establishing its purpose. Like groups, teams use goals to monitor their progress. Teams, however, also have a broader purpose, which supplies a source of meaning and emotional energy to the activities performed.

Finally, in organizations teams differ from groups with respect to the nature of their connections to management.

Work groups are typically required to be responsive to demands regularly placed on them by management. By contrast, once management establishes the mission for a team, and sets the challenge for it to achieve, it typically gives the team enough flexibility to do its job without any further interference. In other words, work teams are usually to some degree self-managing – that is, they are free to set their own goals, timing, and the approach that they wish to take, usually without management interference. Thus, many teams are described as being autonomous or semiautonomous in nature. This is not to say that teams are completely independent of corporate management and supervision. They still must be responsive to demands from higher levels (often, higher-level teams, known as top management teams). Teams regularly report their progress to management on a regularly scheduled basis.

Pioneers of Work Teams Among Major American Companies

Although many organizations are turning to work teams today, several large companies have been using them for some time. Here is a listing of some major American companies that have been the earliest adopters of work teams.

Table 2

YEAR BEGAN	COMPANY
1962	Proctor & Gamble
1973	Cummins Engine
1975	General Motors
1982	Digital Equipment
1982	Ford Motor
1983	Company Tektronix
1985	General Electric
1985	LTV Steel
1985	Champion International

Source: Adapted from Osbum, Moran, Musselwhite, & Zenger, *Self Directed Work Teams*, Burr Ridge, Irwin II. 1990.

Historical Perspective

The initial interest in small groups working together in organizations can be traced back to the Hawthorne studies conducted in the late 1920s and early 1930s. The Hawthorne study illustrates some of the essential elements that are important in team effectiveness, for the experiment showed the possibility of taking a random collection of employees and building them into a highly productive work-team. The discussions of the Hawthorne group of researchers indicate a few critical factors contributing to team development:

The boss has a personal interest in each person's achievement. He took pride in the record of group performance, the group took pride in its achievement and had the satisfaction of outsiders showing interest in what they did, the group did not feel they were being pressured to change, the group developed a sense of confidence and candor before changes were made, the group was consulted.

Elton Mayo one of the Hawthorne researchers, stated that the study brought about an awareness that social and psychological factors influenced productivity more strongly than physical working conditions. He also indicated that social relationships not interactions, and defined or controlled by management, were the main causes for changes in productivity. The Hawthorne studies led to the development of the Human Relations School of Management brought on by the awareness that organizations are made up of people who continuously interact with each other, either formally or informally. It is these very interactions that ultimately facilitate or impede the accomplishment of organizational goals.

Following the Hawthorne studies, there was an increased research emphasis on "Group Dynamics" in the later 30s. Kurt Lewin and a group of students initiated a series of classic studies in leadership and group behaviour in the University of Iowa. The group moved to the Massachusetts Institute of Technology and formed the Centre for Group Dynamics. This was evolved out of the felt-need for a scientific approach to understand the dynamics of groups. "Dynamics" (of Greek origin) refers to forces operating in groups; the practical application of group dynamics consists of the utilisation of knowledge about these forces for the achievement of certain organizational purposes. It was only after Lewin's contribution that a school of thought emerged that viewed the group processes as the basic unit of analysis in the study of organizations.

Homans research of the "informal organization" followed, which further discussed the positive and negatives of group behaviour. He studied behaviour within small groups and indicated that people interacted with one another while performing their tasks. These interactions, in turn, result in the development of sentiments or positive or negative feelings towards one another and management. Such sentiments influence the way in which people will perform and interact in the future. Homans model thus illustrates the necessity of managing the informal organization. Group sentiments influence both behaviour and tasks and, therefore, they will indirectly influence the performance of the formal organization. Depending upon whether these interactions are favourable or not, they may result in an increase or decrease in performance, absenteeism, turnover, grievances, and other factors upon which the organizational success is contingent.

The interest in small group research continued and there were a number of studies following the Homans research.

There were over 1300 articles and books on the subject. In the sixties there were two writers in the area of management – Mc Gregor and Likert – who began to emphasise the team concept as an important part of organization theory. McGreogor indicated that, within highly effective team, their 'unity of purpose' was the main distinguishing characteristic. This was later characterised as a facilitating factor to group effectiveness, better known as "cohesiveness".

At about the same time, Likert was developing his notion of organizations as series of "interlocking groups and the manager as a linking pin." Likert believed that managers must learn to cope with a totality of people, their subordinates and not just manage individuals, on a one-to-one basis. The effective manager, according to him must view himself as a member of two groups. In one, he is the superior, and in the other he is the subordinate. It is in this context that one talks of skills of the leadership and followership functions. Through this dual membership, a member is seen as the main link between his department and the rest of the organization. He thus, becomes the communicator (upward) of subordinates needs, goals, and feelings to upper echelons and provides (downward) the channel for the flow of information on goals and objectives, procedures and policies.

Evolving out of these concepts, Likert talked of our systems of management.

System 1	:	Exploitative-authoritative
System 2	:	Benevolent-authoritative
System 3	:	Consultative
System 4	:	Participative-group

System 4 was considered "ideal" in terms of achieving results because in it he stressed three important contributory variables: (i) the manager's use of supportive relationships, (ii) the use of group decision-making and group methods of supervision, and (iii) high performance goals (which are akin to McGregor's unity of purpose"). Having defined these three key variables, he tried to measure their relationship in terms of productivity. There was strong research evidence to indicate that the manager or organization which exhibited a high degree of supportive relationships, utilised principles of group participation in decision-making, and high performance standards were set, there were much higher levels of achievement for individuals, groups, and organizations in the long run.

Very similar to system 4 was the Blake and Mouton 9.9 style of managers which they termed as "Team Management", characterised by high concern for productivity and high concern for people. The team managers believe that people and production can be integrated. They believe that situations can be created whereby people can best satisfy their needs and objectives by working towards the objectives of the organization. It is in this context, it has been suggested that the closer a manager gets to 9.9 style, the better.

TYPES OF TEAMS

Interesting fact: most major U.S. companies are now either using some form of teams or are seriously considering using them. Although there has been a great amount of recent interest in teams they have been around the workplace for some time. In fact, as shown in Table 2, many corporations have been using them for quite a few years – some, such as Proctor & Gamble, well over three decades.

In view of their widespread popularity, it should not be surprising to learn that there are many different kinds of teams. To help make sense out of these, Mohrman recently has categorized them into several different commonly found types. According to Mohrman, team vary along three major dimensions. The first has to do with their major purpose or mission. In this regard, some teams – known as work teams – are primarily concerned with the work done by the organization, such as developing and manufacturing new products, providing services for customers, and so on. Their principle focus is on using the organization's resources to effectively create its results (be they goods or services). Other teams - known as improvement teams - are primarily oriented toward the mission of increasing the effectiveness of the processes that are used by the organization. For example, Texas Instruments has relied on teams to help improve the quality of operations at its plant in Malasia.

A second dimension has to do with time. Specifically, some teams are only temporary, and are established for a specific project with a finite life. For example, a team set up to develop a new product would be considered temporary. As soon as its job is done, it disbands. However, other kinds of teams are permanent, and stay intact as long as the organization is operating. For example, teams focusing on providing effective customer service tend to be permanent parts of many organizations. The third dimension reflects the team's connection to the organization's overall authority structure - that is, the connection between various formal job responsibilities. In some organizations, teams may cross over various functional units (e.g., marketing, finance, human resources, and so on), and are said to be overlaid (i.e., their activities are superimposed over the functioning of various organizational units). For example, a quality improvement team may be expected to get involved with the activities of several different organizational units (the mission of improving quality does not belong to anyone unit working alone). As you might expect, such arrangements are often difficult because of ambiguities regarding authority. By contrast, some organizations use teams that are intact with respect to the existing structure of the organization. In fact, many organizations – such as General Motors and Ralston-Purina – are structured such that people work together on specific products all the time, and do not apply their speciality to a wide range of products. Within such organizations, teams can operate without the ambiguities created by having to cross functional lines.

It is important to note that the boundaries between all teams must be considered permeable. Indeed, people are frequently members of more than one team – a situation often required for organizations to function effectively. For example, members of an organization's manufacturing team must carefully coordinate their activities with members of its marketing team. To the extent that people are involved in several different kinds of teams, they may gain broader perspectives, and make more important contributions to their various teams.

Process of Team Development

Dyer Woodcock and Francis. and Pattern have indicated that it is possible to build teams step by step which can be classified as the methodology needed for the process of team building. The case for team building is clear. Many working groups are seen to function poorly, and fail to use the competence and ability of their individual members. Inevitably, any group would take time to become well-integrated, resourceful, and effective. However, many managers do not seem to recognise that they need to facilitate the process of team maturation to reach a level wherein they can be called effective, and function independently.

The question of "when should one initiate the process of team building" has been uppermost in the minds of managers who are trying to grapple with managerial problems. It has been suggested that team building is an appropriate strategy when the following pre-conditions exist.

The lack of effective teamwork is a serious impediment to organizational effectiveness, the culture of the organization supports a team approach to getting things done.

Teams are receptive and prepared to undertake the process, adequate resources exist internally to aid team building,

Adequate external help is available to help build teams.

The process starts by identifying teams and then assessing their present levels of competence. It is understood that each work group undergoes relatively predictable changes as it progresses from a simple collection of individuals put together to a close and effective team. Thus, team effectiveness is seen as a reflection of the state of maturity of the group which progresses from stages of immaturity to total maturity to become a well-developed team.

The stages of team maturity have been very well articulated by Woodcock and Francis:

Stage I	:	"Ritual sniffing", where the group is not really a team. Members have no clarity about objectives.
Stage II	:	"Infighting" – The team members struggle for influence and position. Competence has little relationship to team effectiveness, instead individual performance is the Key factor.
Stage III	:	"Experimentation" stage where the team has clear objectives and commitment, but individual roles and responsibilities still remain unclear.
Stage IV	:	"Effectiveness" – There is realisation that the team is interdependent, must be effective and competent in order to perform its role. The team has developed competent procedures to deal with problems.
Stage V	:	"Maturity" – Awareness that the team is inter – dependent and is collectively responsible for achieving major objectives that have a significant effect on profitability or effectiveness.

Having reached Stage V, precautions must be taken to prevent reversion to earlier stages. There is always the danger that well-developed and mature teams can become so insulated that they create further problems. Continuous emphasis and awareness about interdependence and collaboration of team efforts will help a great deal in furthering the effective functioning of teams. Team building thus becomes a continuous process which involves diagnosis, action planning and constant review. The ultimate objective is to devise strategies to remove obstacles and encourage teams to put in the maximum efforts to combine their resources to achieve common goals.

A GENERAL TYPOLOGY OF WORK TEAMS

Work teams are created for various purposes and thus face different challenges. Managers can deal more effectively with those challenges when they understand how teams differ. A helpful way of sorting things out is to consider a typology of work teams developed by Eric Sundstrom and his colleagues. Four general types of work teams listed in Table 3, are: (1) advice, (2) production, (3) project, and (4) action. Each of these labels identifies a basic purpose. For instance, advice teams generally make recommendations for managerial decisions; less commonly do they actually make final decisions. In contrast, production and action teams carry out management's decisions.

Four key variables in Table 3 deal with technical specialisation, co-ordination, work cycles, and outputs. Technical specialisation is low when the team draws upon members' general experience and problem-solving ability. It is high when team members are required to apply technical skills acquired through higher education and/ or extensive training. The degree of co-ordination with other work units is determined by the team's relative independence (low co-ordination), or interdependence (high co-ordination). Work cycles are the amount of time teams need to accomplish their missions. The various outputs listed in Table 3 are intended to illustrate real life impacts. A closer look at each type of work team is in order.

Advice Teams: As their name implies, advice teams are created to broaden the information base for managerial decisions. Quality circles, discussed later, are a prime example because they facilitate suggestions for improvement from volunteer production or service workers. Advice teams tend to have a low degree of technical specialisation. Co-ordination also is low because advice teams work pretty much on their own. Ad hoc committees (e.g., the annual picnic committee) have shorter life-cycles than standing committees (e.g., the grievance committee).

Production Teams: This second type of team is responsible for performing day-to-day operations.

Minimal training for routine tasks accounts for the low degree of technical specialisation. But co-ordination, typically, is high because work flows from one team to another. For example, railroad maintenance crews require fresh information about needed repairs from train crews.

Project Teams: Projects require creative problem-solving, often involving the application of specialised knowledge. The Boeing 777 team discussed earlier, for example, has a degree of technical specialisation. It also requires a high degree of co-ordination among organizational sub-units because it is cross-functional. A pharmaceutical research team of biochemists, on the other hand, would interact less with other work units because it is relatively self-contained.

Table 3. Four General Types of Work Teams and Their Outputs

Types & Examples	Degree of Technical Specialisation	Degree of Co-ordination with other work units	Work Cycles	Typical Outputs
Advice committees Review panels, boards Quality circles, Employee involvement groups Advisory councils	Low	Low	Work cycles can be brief or long; one cycle can be team life span	Decisions Selections Suggestions Proposals Recommendations
Production Assembly teams Manufacturing crews Mining teams Flight attendant crews Data processing groups Maintenance crews	Low	High	Work cycles typically repeated or continuous process; cycles often briefer than team life span	Food Chemicals Components Assemblies Retail Sales Customer service Equipment repairs
Project Research groups Planning teams Architect teams Engineering teams Development teams Task forces	High	Low (for traditional units) or High (for cros-functional units	High (for cross-functional units) Work cycles typically differ for each new project; one cycle can be team life span	Plans, Design Investigations Presentations Prototypes Reports Findings
Action Sports team Entertainment groups Expeditions Negotiating teams Surgery teams Cockpit crews Military platoons and squads	High	High	Brief performance events, often repeated under new conditions, requiring extended training and/or preparation	Combat Missions Epeditions Contracts, Lawsuits Concerns Surgical operations Competitive events

Action Teams: High specialisation is combined with high co-ordination. Nine highly trained athletes specialised in defensive positions. But good defensive play is not enough because effective hitting is necessary. Moreover, co-ordination between the manager, base runners, base coaches and the bull pen needs to be precise. So it is with airline cockpit crews, hospital surgery teams, mountain-climbing expeditions, rock music groups, labour contract teams, and police SWOT teams, among others. A unique challenge for action teams is to exhibit peak performance on demand.

This four-way typology of work teams is dynamic and changing, not static. Some teams *evolve* from one type to another. Other teams represent a combination of types. For example, consider the work of a team at General Foods: "About *five* years ago the company launched a line of ready-to-eat desserts by setting up a team of nine people with the freedom to operate like entrepreneurs starting their own business. The team *even* had to *oversee* construction of a factory with the technology required to manufacture their product." This particular team was a combination *advice*-project-action team. In short, the General Foods team did everything but manufacture the end product themselves (that was done by production teams).

HOW SUCCESSFUL ARE TEAMS?

A LOOK AT THE EVIDENCE

Questions regarding the effectiveness of teams in the workplace are not easy to answer. Not only are there many different kinds of teams doing different kinds of jobs operating in organizations, but their effectiveness is influenced by a wide variety of factors that go well beyond any possible benefits of teams. Such as managerial support, the economy available resources, and the like. As a result, understanding the true effectiveness of team is a tricky business at best. This difficulty has been fuelled in recent years by *cover* stories in the top business periodicals touting the success of teams. How much of this is hype stemming from the latest management fad, and how much should be accepted as valid evidence for the effectiveness of teams? Fortunately, several types of research investigations have examined this issue.

One of the most direct ways of learning about companies experiences with work teams is to survey the officials of organizations that use them. In a large-scale study, Lawler, Mohrman, and Ledford did just that. Their sample consisted of several hundred of the 1,000 largest companies in the United States. About 47 per cent used some work teams, although these were typically in place in only a few selected sites, not throughout the entire organizations. Where they were used, *however,* they were generally highly regarded. Survey results collected in 1987 and again in 1990 revealed that whereas 53 per cent characterised the teams as "successful" or *"very* successful" in 1987 , this figure grew to 60 percent only three years later. For both years, almost all the other responses fell into the "undecided" category; "unsuccessful" or *"very* unsuccessful" responses occurred in only 1 percent of the cases each year.

These optimistic results are further supported by in-depth case studies of numerous teams in many different organization. Research of this type, although difficult to quantify and to compare across organizations, provides some interesting insight into what makes teams successful and why. For example, Manz and Sims studied the work teams used in General Motors' battery plant in Fitzgerald,Georgia. The 320 employees at this facility operate in various teams, including managers working together in support teams, middle-level teams of coordinators (similar to foremen and technicians), and employee teams, natural work units of three to nineteen members performing specific tasks. Although the teams work closely together, coordinating their activities, they function almost as separate businesses. Because plant employees must perform many different tasks in their teams, they are not paid based on their positions, but for their knowledge and competence. In fact, the highest paid employees are individuals who have demonstrated their competence (usually by very demanding tests) on all the jobs performed in at least two different teams. This is GM's way of rewarding people for broadening their perspectives, appreciating the other guy's problems. By many measures, the Fitzgerald plant has been *very* effective. Its production costs are lower than comparable units in traditionally run plants Furthermore, employee turnover is also much lower than average. Employee satisfaction surveys also reveal that job satisfaction at this plant is among the highest found at any General Motors facility.

Teams also have been successful in service businesses. For example, consider IDS, the financial services subsidiary of American Express. In response to rapid growth in the mid-1980s. IDS officials realized that their operations were becoming highly inefficient, and created several teams to work on reorganizing the company's operations. As in many companies, the move to teams wasn't readily accepted by all employees. Particularly resistant were individuals who before teams had high-status jobs, with high pay to match. Naturally, they resented becoming co-equals with others when teams were formed. Still, these employees – and all others, for that matter – soon benefited from the company's improved operations. Accuracy in the processing of paperwork (e.g., orders to buy or sell stock) rose from 70 per cent before teams were created, to over 99 per cent afterward. With the help of employee teams. IDS's operations became so efficient that response time improved by 96 per cent: from several minutes to only a few seconds. During the stock market crash of October 1997, this quick response capability is credited for saving the day (not to mention lots of money), for IDS's customers.

These cases are two examples of very different companies that used teams in different ways, but with something in common – high levels of success (albeit not without some difficulties). And there are many more. Although there are far too many cases to review here (in fact, entire books have been devoted to summarizing such cases), we think you'll find it fascinating to review the summary of company experiences with teams in Table 4.

As Table 4 makes clear, many companies have reported having successful experiences with teams. Case studies paint a consistent picture of the effectiveness of teams, making the use of teams one of today's most popular management trends. The problem with such reports, of course, is that they may not be entirely objective. After all, companies may be unwilling to broadcast their failures to the world. This is not to say that case studies cannot be trusted. Indeed, when the information is gathered by outside researchers (such as those reported here), the stories they tell about how teams are used, and the results of using them can be quite revealing Still, there is a need for completely objective, empirical studies of team effectiveness.

Table 4. Team in Organizations: Some Impressive Results

COMPANY	RESULT
Federal Express Coming	Reduced errors (e.g., incorrect bills, lost packages) by 13 per cent in 1989 Defects dropped from 1,800 parts per million to only 9 parts per million in its cellular ceramics plant
Shenanadoah Life Insurance Co.	Saved $200,000 per year in reduced staffing while increasing volume of work handled by 33 percent
Xerox	Increased productivity by 30 percent
Tektronix	One team produces as many products in 3 days as an entire assembly line used to produce in 14 days
Carrier (division of United Technologies Corporation)	Reduced unit turnaround time from two weeks to 2 days
Westinghouse Furniture Systems	Productivity increased by 74 percent within three years
Sealed Air	Waste reduced by 50 percent and downtime cut from 20 percent to 5 percent
Eli Lilly	Fastest-ever rollout time for a new medical product
Citibank	Substantially improved customer satisfaction ratings in eleven key areas
Exxon	$10 million saving in six months

Case studies have reported many remarkable outcomes stemming from teams. Here is just a sampling of the impressive results. *Source*: Based on information in Wellins *et al.*, 1991, Katzenbach & Smith, 1993, and Osburn *et al.*, 1990.

Research of this type is now just beginning to be done. In one such investigation Pearson compared various aspects of work performance and attitudes of two group of employees at a railroad car repair facility in Australia: those who were assembled into teams that could freely decide how to do their jobs, and those whose work was structured in the more traditional, non-autonomous fashion. After the work teams had been in place for several months, it was found that they had significantly fewer accidents, as well as lower rates of absenteeism and turnover. Unfortunately, not all empirical studies paint such an optimistic picture of the benefits of work teams. For example, Wall, Kemp, Jackson, and Clegg examined the long-term effects of using work teams in an English manufacturing plant. Although they found that employees were more satisfied with their jobs in teams compared to those in conventional work arrangements (in which individuals take orders from a supervisor), they were individually no more productive. However, because the use of teams made it possible for the organization to eliminate several supervisory positions, the company became more profitable.

These two studies do not paint a clear and convincing case for the overall effectiveness of teams. Although teams are generally well received – that is, people enjoy working in them – it is not yet apparent that they are responsible for making individuals any more productive. From an organizational perspective, teams appear to be an effective way of eliminating layers of management: When people are highly committed toward achieving excellence, it is not surprising that their companies may enjoy the results. In fact, it is precisely these types of beneficial outcomes that are being reported by the case studies we summarized above.

In view of the fact that more and more companies are turning to teams (as many as half of us will be working in teams by the end of this decade, according to one estimate), it is important to consider some things teams can do to build performance. Based on the experiences of companies that have been successful with teams. Several recommendations can be made for ways of building effective team performance. We have summarized these in Table 5. As you will see when you review these tips, making teams effective is not an easy matter. They don't automatically work out simply because they are introduced. They need to be carefully cared for and maintained, such as in the ways listed, for them to accomplish their missions.

Table 5. Building Team Performance: Some Tips

TIP	RATIONALE
* Make the team's task urgent.	Team members are prone to rally around challenges that compel them to meet high performance standards.
* Select team members based on their skills.	When putting together a team, it is essential that members have the skills needed to succeed (or at least the potential to develop them).
* Make rules of behaviour clear.	Effective teams have clear rules about what is and is not expected (e.g., maintain confidentiality, attendance is mandatory, give constructive criticism only).
* Recognize intermediate performance goals.	To motivate and encourage team members acknowledge goals that are met prior to the major team goals (e.g., the halfway point).
* Regularly challenge the team with new facts.	Facts are needed for teams to gauge their progress toward their goals, so bringing in new data may help provide direction.
* Meet regularly.	Members will take teamwork seriously if they are frequently reminded of their obligations.
* Acknowledge and reinforce vital contributions to the team.	Making people feel good about their contributions will encourage them to make more.

Based on analyses of successful teams, it is possible to identify several things that teams can do to ensure their success. Here is a listing of some of the most important tips.

Source: Based on information in Katzenbach & Smith, 1993.

Work Team Effectiveness: An Ecological Model

The effectiveness of athletic teams is a straight forward matter of wins and losses. Things become more complicated, however, when the focus shifts to work teams in today's organizations. Fig. 1 lists two effectiveness criteria for work teams: performance and viability. According to Sundstrom and his colleagues: "performance means acceptability of output to customers within or outside the organization who receive team products, services, information, decisions, or performance events (such as presentations or competitions). While the foregoing relates to satisfying the needs and expectations of outsiders such as clients, customers, and fans, another team effectiveness criterion arises: namely, team viability, defined as team member satisfaction and continued willingness to contribute. Are the team members better or worse offer having contributed to the team effort? A work team is not truly effective if it gets the job done but self-destructs in the process.

Fig. 1 is an ecological model because it portrays work teams within their organizational environment. In keeping with the true meaning of the work ecology – the study of interactions between organisms and their environments – this model emphasizes that work teams need an organizational life – support system. Six critical organizational context variables are listed in Fig. 1. Work teams have a much greater chance of being effective if they are nurtured and facilitated by the organization. The team's purpose needs to be in concert with the organization's strategy. Similarly, team participation and autonomy require an organizational culture that values those processes. Team members also need appropriate technological tools and training. Teamwork needs to be reinforced by the organizational reward system. Such is not the case when pay and bonuses are tied solely to individual output. Philips-Van Heusen, the clothing manufacturer, is a striking example of a company that rewards teamwork. The firm's founder, Lawrence S. Philips, offered each of the top 11 executives the chance to earn a $1 million bonus over a four year period. Fortune explained the deal as follows: "The first $500,000 can be earned incrementally by meeting earnings per share goals for each year. If the company makes the combined targets in the fourth year, each of the 11 receives the second $500,000 as a kicker." Thus, each executive has a strong personal incentive to help reach collective goals.

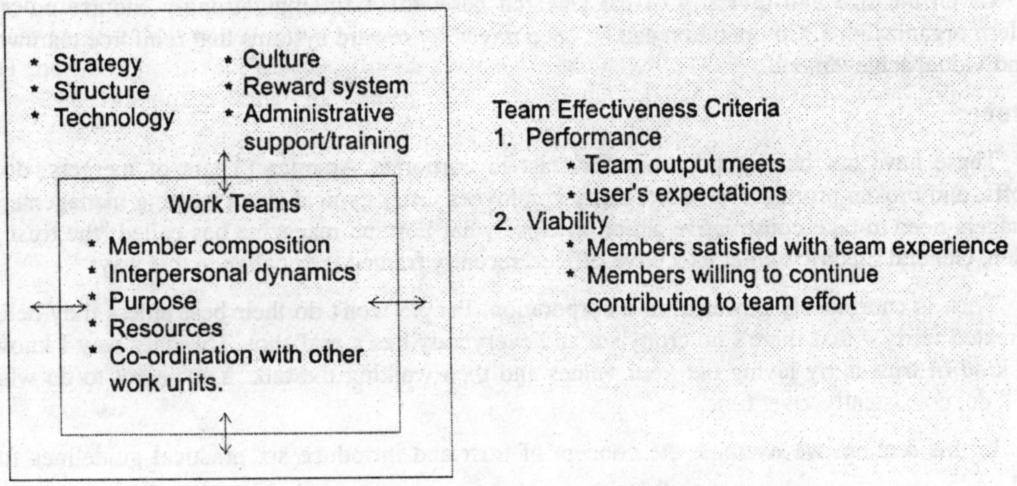

Fig.1. An Ecological Model of Work Team Effectiveness

Regarding the internal processes of work teams, five important factors are listed in Fig. 1. Additional insights lie ahead as we turn our attention to cooperation, trust, and cohesiveness.

TEAM WORK THROUGH CO-OPERATION, TRUST AND COHESIVENESS

As competitive pressures intensify, organizational success will increasingly depend on teamwork rather than individual stars. In fact, companies such as Microsoft and Xerox have gone so far as to fill the position of corporate president with a team of executives instead of an individual. According to Xerox's Chairman Paul Allaire, co-operation from top to bottom is the goal"1 would hope that we have been clear enough that one of the criteria of this new organization is working together, he says. To underscore the issue, he says future Xerox leaders will be drawn only from those who can cooperate: Anyone who is not a team player would be automatically excluded from succession", he says.

If this sort of commitment to teamwork has a familiar ring, it is because World Series baseball and Super Bowl football champions generally say they owe their success to it. Whether in the athletic arena or the world of business, three components of teamwork receiving the greatest attention are co-operation, trust, and cohesiveness. Let us explore the contributions each can make to effective teamwork.

Co-operation

Individuals are said to be co-operating when their efforts are systematically integrated to achieve a collective objective. The greater the integration, the greater the degree of co-operation.

Co-operation versus Competition: A widely held assumption among American managers is that "competition brings out the best in people." From an economic stand-point, business survival depends on staying ahead of competition. But from an interpersonal stand point, critics content, that competition has been overemphasized, primarily at the expense of co-operation.

Research Support for Co-operation: After conducting a meta-analysis of 122 studies encompassing a wide variety of subjects and settings, one team of researchers concluded:

1. Co-operation is superior to competition in promoting achievement and productivity.
2. Co-operation is superior to individualistic efforts in promoting achievement and productivity.
3. Co-operation without intergroup competition promotes higher achievement and productivity than co-operation with intergroup competition.

Given the size and diversity of the research base, these findings strongly endorse co-operation in modern organizations. Co-operation can be encouraged by reward systems that reinforce teamwork as well as individual achievement.

Trust

These have not been good times for trust in corporate America. Years of mergers, downsizings, layoffs, and broken promises have left many employees justly cynical about trusting management. Clearly, managers need to take constructive action to close what Fortune magazine has called "the trust gap". Jack Welch, General Electric's chief executive officer, recently framed the challenge this way:

Trust is enormously powerful in a corporation. People won't do their best unless they believe they'll be treated fairly – that there's no cronyism and everybody has a real shot. The only way I know to create that kind of trust is by laying out your values and then walking the talk. You've got to do what you say you'll do, consistently, over time.

In this section, we examine the concept of trust and introduce six practical guidelines for building trust.

A Cognitive Leap: Trust is defined as reciprocal faith in others intentions and behaviour. Experts on the subject explain the reciprocal (give and take) aspect of trust as follows:

When we see others acting in ways that imply that they trust us, we become more disposed to reciprocate by trusting in them more. Conversely, we come to distrust those whose actions appear to violate our, trust or to distrust us.

In short, we tend to give what we get: trust begets trust; distrust begets distrust. Trust involves "a cognitive 'leap' beyond the expectation that reason and experience alone would warrant" (see Fig. 2). For example, suppose a member of newly formed class project team works hard, based on the assumption that her team-mates also are working hard. That assumption, on which her trust is based, is a cognitive leap that goes beyond her actual experience with her team-mates. When you trust someone, you have faith in their good intentions. The act of trusting someone, however, carries with it the inherent risk of betrayal. Progressive managers believe that the benefits of interpersonal trust far outweigh any risks of betrayed trust.

How to Build Trust: Management professor/consultant Fernando Bartolome offers the following six guidelines for building and maintaining trust:

1. Communication. Keep team members and employees informed by explaining policies and decisions, and providing accurate feedback. Be candid about your own problems and limitations.
2. Support. Be available and approachable. Provide help, advice, coaching, and support for team member's ideas.

3. Respect. Delegation, in the form of real decision-making authority, is the most important expression of managerial respect. Actively listening to the ideas of others is a close second.
4. Fairness. Be quick to give credit and recognition to those who deserve it. Make sure all performance appraisals and evaluations are objective and impartial.

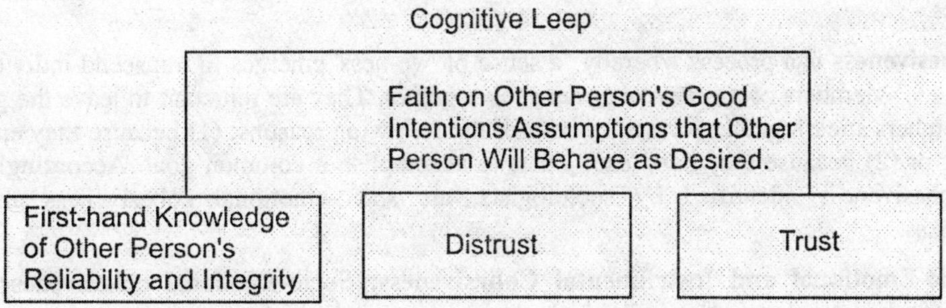

Fig. 2. Interpersonal trust involves a cognitive leap

5. Predictability. As mentioned previously, be consistent and predictable in your daily affairs. Keep both expressed and implied promises.
6. Competence. Enhance your credibility by demonstrating good business sense, technical ability, and professionalism.

Trust needs to be earned: it cannot be demanded.

Cohesiveness

One obvious determinant of any group's structure is its cohesiveness. We may define cohesiveness as the strength of group members' desires to remain part of their groups. Highly cohesive work groups are ones in which the members are attracted to each other, accept the group's goals, and help work toward meeting them. In very uncohesive groups, the members dislike each other and may *even* work at cross-purposes. In essence, cohesiveness refers to a 'we' feeling, an esprit de corps, a sense of belonging to a group.

Several important factors *have* been shown to influence the extent to which group members tend to "stick together." One such factor *involves* the severity of initiation into the group. Research has shown that the greater the difficulty people *overcome* to become a member of a group. The more cohesive the group will be.

To understand this, consider how highly cohesive certain groups may be that you *have* worked hard to join.

Was it particularly difficult to "make the cut" on your sports team? The rigorous requirements for gaining entry into elite groups, such as the most prestigious medical schools and military training schools, may well be responsible for the high degree of camaraderie found in such groups. Having ' "passed the test" tends to keep individuals together, and separates them from those who are unwilling or unable to "pay the price" of admission.

Group cohesion also tends to be strengthened under conditions of high external threat or competition. When workers face a "common enemy", they tend to draw together. Such cohesion not only makes workers feel safer and better protected, but also aids them by encouraging them to work closely together and coordinate their efforts toward the common enemy. Under such conditions, petty disagreements that may *have* caused dissension within groups tend to be put aside so that a coordinated attack on the enemy can be mobilized.

Research has also shown that the cohesiveness of groups is established by several additional factors. For one, cohesiveness generally tends to be greater the more time group members spend together.

Obviously, limited interaction cannot help but interfere with opportunities to develop bonds between group members. Similarly, cohesiveness tends to be greater in smaller groups. Generally speaking, groups that are too large make it difficult for members to interact and, therefore, for cohesiveness to reach a high level. Finally, because "nothing succeeds like success," groups with a history of success tend to be highly cohesive. It is often said that "everyone loves a winner" and the success of a group tends to help unite its members as they rally around their success. For this reason, employees tend to be loyal to successful companies.

Cohesiveness is a process whereby "a sense of 'we-ness' emerges to transcend individual differences and *motives."* Members of a *cohesive* group stick together. They are reluctant to leave the group. Cohesive group members stick together for one or both of the following reasons: (1) because they enjoy each others company, or (2) because they need each other to accomplish a common goal. Accordingly, two types of group cohesiveness, identified by sociologists, are socio-emotional cohesiveness and instrumental cohesiveness.

Socio-Emotional and Instrumental Cohesiveness: Socio-emotional cohesiveness is a sense of togetherness that develops when individuals derive emotional satisfaction from group participation. Most general discussions of group cohesiveness are limited to this type. However, from the standpoint of getting things accomplished in task groups and teams, we cannot afford to ignore instrumental cohesiveness. Instrumental cohesiveness is a sense of togetherness that develops when group members are mutually dependent on one another because they believe they could not achieve the group's goal by acting separately. A feeling of "we-ness" is instrumental in achieving the common goal. Both types of cohesiveness are essential for productive teamwork.

Lessons from Group Cohesiveness Research: After reviewing the relevant research literature, a Texas A&M University scholar concluded:

* Highly cohesive groups have greater member satisfaction than groups with low cohesiveness. High - cohesion groups are more effective than low-cohesion groups.
* Members of highly cohesive groups communicate more frequently and more positively than members of low-cohesion groups.
* In a second study of 125 groups with interaction problems, tried observers found lack of cohesiveness to be the number one problem. Leadership was the next greatest problem.

The relationship between cohesiveness and performance remains ambiguous. Studies have found a mixture of positive, negative, and neutral relationships. This unexpected trend is partially due to researchers using inconsistent measures of cohesiveness.

Although we often hear about the benefits of highly *cohesive* groups, the consequences of cohesiveness are not always positive. In fact, research has shown both positive and negative effects of cohesiveness (see Fig. 2). On the positive side, people are known to enjoy belonging to highly cohesive groups. Members of closely knit work groups participate more fully in their group's activities, more readily accept their group's goals, and are absent from their jobs less often than members of less *cohesive* groups. Not surprisingly, cohesive groups tend to work together quite well and are sometimes exceptionally productive. In fact, research has shown that high *levels* of group cohesiveness tend to be associated with low levels of voluntary turnover. People's willingness to work together quite well and to conform to the group's norms is often responsible for their success, and their willingness to stay with the group.

However, the tendency for members of highly cohesive groups to go along with their fellow members' wishes. sometimes has *negative* consequences for the ultimate group product. Consider, for example, the actions of the highly cohesive Committee to Re-elect President Nixon preceding the 1972 presidential election. The Watergate conspirators were a highly cohesive group – so cohesive that they were blinded to the possibility that they were committing illegal and unethical acts. Poor decisions resulting from too high a *level* of cohesiveness reflect a phenomenon known as groupthink. Groupthink occurs when a group is so cohesive that its members potentially lose sight of its ultimate goals for fear of disrupting the group itself, because of the negative impact of groupthink on the quality of group decision.

Group cohesion can influence productivity in many other ways. It makes sense that after a group experiences success, its members will feel more committed to each other. Similarly, we might expect a *cohesive* group to work well together and to *achieve* a high *level* of success. *However,* a work group whose members are strongly committed to each other does not necessarily perform well within an organization. For example, if a group's goals are contrary to the organization's goals, a highly cohesive group may actually do a great deal of harm to an organization, working against its interests. Highly cohesive group members who conspire to sabotage their employers are a good example. Apparently, group cohesiveness can *have* either positive or negative effects on performance.

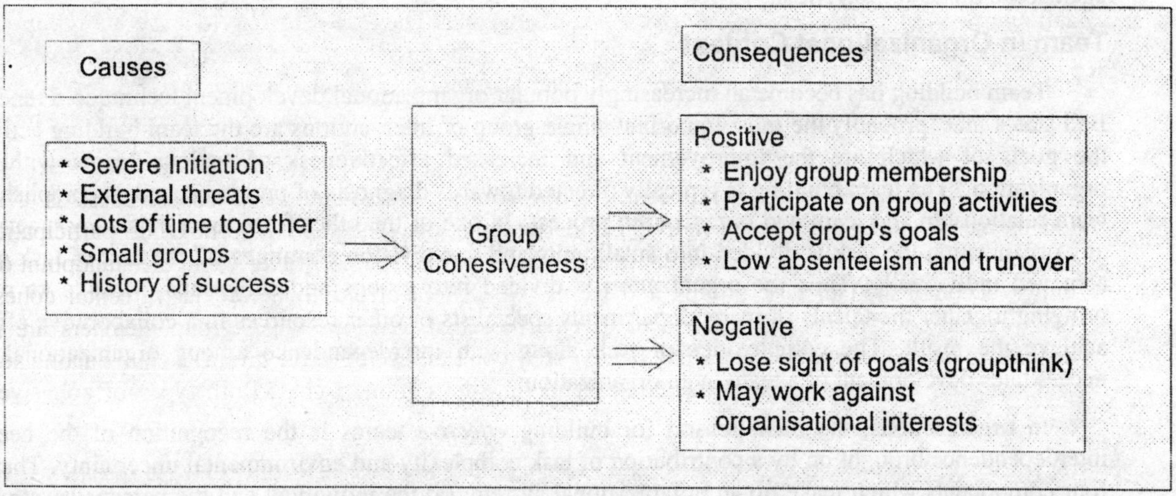

Fig. 3. Group Cohesiveness: Causes & Consequences.

Putting Cohesiveness to Work: Because cohesiveness has proved to be an important component of *effective* teamwork, managers need to take constructive steps to foster both types (see Table 6). A good example is Westinghouse's highly automated military radar electronics plant in College station, Texas. Compared with their counterparts at a traditional factory in Baltimore, each of the Texas plant's 500 employees produces eight times more, at half the per unit cost.

Table 6: Steps Managers can take to Enhance the two types of Group cohesiveness

Socio-Emotional Cohesiveness
Keep the group relatively small.
Strive for a favourable public image to increase the status and prestige of belonging.
Encourage interaction and cooperation.
Emphasize member's common characteristics and interests.
Point out environmental threats (e.g., competitors' achievement) to rally the group.
Instrumental Cohesiveness
Regularly update and clarify the group's goal (s).
Give every group members a vital "piece of the action."
Channel each group member's special talents toward the common goal(s).
Recognize and equitably reinforce every member's contributions.
Frequently remind group members they need each other to get the job done.

The key, says Westinghouse, is not the robots but the people. Employees work in teams of 8 to 12. Members devise their own solutions to problems. Teams measure daily how each person's performance compares with that of other members, and how the team's performance compares with the plants. Joseph L.

Johnson, 28, a robotics technician, says that it is a big change from a previous hourly factory job where he cared only about "picking up my pay check." Here, peer pressure "makes sure you get the job done."

Self-selected work teams (in which people pick up their own team-mates), and off-the-job social *events* can stimulate socio-emotional cohesiveness. The fostering of socio-emotional cohesiveness needs to be balanced with instrumental cohesiveness. The latter can be encouraged by making sure *everyone* in the group recognizes and appreciates each member's *vital* contribution to the group goal. While balancing the two types of cohesiveness, managers need to remember that groupthink theory and research, cautions against too much cohesiveness.

Team in Organizational Context

Team building has become an increasingly popular organizational development technique. French and Bell states that "probably the most important single group of interventions are the team building activities, the goals of which are the improvement and increased effectiveness of various teams within the organization.' The team building is typically directed towards diagnosis of problems, task accomplishment, team relationship and team and organization process. In one or the other form team exists *every*where. In any organization the task is divided into small units and this division continues till the unit of task can be achieved individually. Thus the organization is divided into groups and subgroups. Most tasks require bringing together the talents of many departments specialists or other resources in a collaborative effort to achieve the result. The complexities of task along with interdependence among organizational units necessitates development of a team in an organization.

In organizations, the main reason for building *effective* teams is the recognition of the need for interdependence brought on by a contribution of task complexity and environmental uncertainty. There are four components which make up an organizational system: (a) the individual and the personality structure, his *motives* and attitudes which condition the range of expectations, the hopes to satisfy by participating in the system; (b) the informal organization which is the intercalation pattern of arrangements that exists between the various groups within the system. The stress here is on the mutual modification of expectancies. The group has demands which it makes on members in terms of anticipated forms of behaviour and the individual has expectancies of satisfaction he hopes to derive from association with people on the job; (c) the arrangement of functions, which is the structure usually called the formal organization. Certain writers see a potential conflict arising out of the demands made by the system on the individual and the groups. This is primarily due to the fact that the organization imposes certain restrictions in terms of roles, tasks and authority relationships which may not be satisfactory to individuals and groups; (d) the organization-environment relationship which has direct implications for both team formation and team functioning. Often the uncertainty and instability of organizational environments necessitates the need for teams to deviate from their established norms of functioning and take on unprecedented tasks and responsibilities.

The interface of individual, group, organization, and environment interjected with the task-behaviour interface is what makes understanding the organizational context interesting. The problems brought about due to this interface have been summarised by Alban and Pollitt thus: "Dependent or rebelling attitudes towards authority, different feelings of equality of membership or influence in the team; feeling in or out of the group, perceptions that the financial and other rewards are inequitably administered, varied perceptions of the tasks to be performed, difficulties in inter-personal relationships, lack of clarity about work roles, lack of effective means of planning, problem solving, and decision-making, and inability to manage conflict".

Understanding the organizational context for the development of teams *evolves* out of the "structure concern" which simply means clarity about permanent roles, goals, task interdependencies, and accountability for specific results. This aspect has been emphasised because development must become a systematic process which is carried out within an overall organization structure keeping in mind the specific objectives that *have* to be accomplished. The organization environment interface takes on special significance due to the fact that it influences the formation and functioning of teams. This is more relevant in situations where the organizational environments are characterised by turbulence, uncertainty and unpredictability.

MANAGERS' GUIDELINES FOR CREATING TEAMS

As you might imagine, assembling a team is no easy task. Doing so requires not only having the right combination of skilled people, but also individuals who are willing to work together with others as a team. A model proposed by Hackman provides some useful guidance on how to effectively design work teams, suggesting that the process proceeds in four distinct stages. As we present this model, you may find it useful to refer to the summary in Table 7.

The first stage of creating an effective team is known as prework. One of the most important objectives of this phase is to determine whether a team should be created. A manager may decide to have several individuals working alone answer to him, or a team may be created if it is believed that it may develop the most creative and insightful ways to get things done. In considering this, it is important to note exactly what work needs to be done. The team's objectives must be established, and an inventory of the skills needed to do the job should be made. In addition, decisions should be made in advance about what authority the team should have. They may just be advisory to the manager, or they may be given full responsibility and authority for executing their task (i.e., self-regulating).

Building on this, stage 2 involves creating performance conditions. In this stage, organizational officials are to ensure that the team has the proper conditions under which to carry out its work. Resources necessary for the team's success should be provided. This involves both material resources (e.g., tools, equipment, and money), human resources (e.g., the appropriate blend of skilled professionals), and support from the organization (e.g., willingness to let the team do its own work as it sees fit). Unless managers help create the proper conditions for team success, they are contributing to its failure.

Table 7. Stages of Work Team Creation: A Summary

STAGE 1: DO PREWORK
• Decide what work needs to be done.
• Determine if a team is necessary to accomplish the task.
• Determine what authority the group should have.
• Decide on the team's goals.
STAGE 2: CREATE PERFORMANCE CONDITIONS
• Provide all the needed materials and equipment to do the job.
• Ensure that the team consists of all personnel necessary to do the job.
STAGE 3: FORM AND BUILD THE TEAM
• Establish boundaries – that is, who is and is not in the team.
• Arrive at an agreement regarding the tasks to be performed.
• Clarify the behaviours expected of each team member.
STAGE 4: PROVIDE ONGOING ASSISTANCE
• Intervence to eliminate team problems (e.g., members not doing their share).
• Replenish or upgrade material resources.
• Replace members who leave the team.

For teams to function effectively, they must be created properly. The four stages outlined here summarize how this may be accomplished. *Source*: Based on information in Hackman, 1987.

Stage 3 involves forming and building the team. Three things can be done to help a team get off to a good start. First, managers should form boundaries – clearly establish who is and who is not a member of the team. Some teams fail simply because, membership in it is left unclear. Reducing such ambiguity can help avoid confusion and frustration. Second, members must accept the team's overall mission and purpose. Unless they do, failure is inevitable. Third, organizational officials should clarify the team's mission and responsibilities – make perfectly clear exactly what it is expected to do (but not necessarily how to do it). Will team members be responsible for monitoring and planning their own work? If so, such expectations should be spelled out explicitly.

Finally, once a team is functioning, supervisors should provide ongoing assistance. Although once teams start operating they often guide themselves, managers may be able to help by providing opportunities for the team to eliminate problems and perform *even* better. For example, disruptive team members may be either counselled or replaced. Similarly, material resources may *have* to be replenished or upgraded. Although it may be unwise for a manager to intervene in the successful affairs of a team that has taken on its own life, it also may be unwise to neglect opportunities to help a team do *even* better.

Improving Team Effectiveness

Given the broad understanding of the organizational contexts, certain types of skills are required to promote *effective* team functioning. Efforts directed toward team building should aim at equipping managers with specific skill which would improve the team effectiveness. The following are considered to be major skill areas:

1. Strengthening inter-personal skills with peers, subordinates, organizational counterparts, and superiors. What is required is a better understanding of personality and behavioural characteristics and ability to deal with differences so that each individual contributes his best.
2. Communication skills which aim at openness and allow for exchange of information-organizational or personal. This would also involve creating better understanding of organizational expectations, goals, and clarity about individual's roles and tasks to be accomplished.
3. Problem, solving and decision-making skills to deal with the complexities that arise out of task accomplishment in a complex and uncertain organizational environment.
4. The skills of leading required to get the best from *every* member of the team. This would involve the ability to understand individual needs, creating situations where individuals can satisfy their needs while contributing to the *overall* goal accomplishment and help in the development of team members by providing support and guidance.
5. Conflict-resolution skills which would help *resolve* differences between various groups and within each group. This calls for developing the ability to create a harmonious work atmosphere where teams will realise that task interdependencies necessitate co-operation and collaboration.

POTENTIAL OBSTACLES TO SUCCESS:
WHY DO SOME TEAMS FAIL?

Although we have reported many success stories about teams, we also have hinted at several possible problems and difficulties in implementing them. After all, working in a team demands a great deal, and not everyone may be ready for them. Fortunately, we can learn from these experiences. Analyses of failed attempts at introducing teams into the workplace suggest *several* obstacles to team success, pitfalls that can be avoided if you know about them.

First, some teams fail because their members are unwilling to co-operate with each other. This is what happened recently at Dow Chemical Company's plastics group in Midland, Michigan, where a team was put into place to create a new plastic resin. Some members (those in the research field) wanted to spend *several* months developing and testing new options, while others (those on the manufacturing end) wanted to slightly alter existing products and start up production right away. Neither side budged, and the project eventually stalled. By contrast, when team members share a common vision, and are committed to attaining it, they are generally *very co-operative* with each other, leading to success.

A second reason why some teams are not *effective* is that they fail to *receive* support from management.

Consider, for example, the experience at the Lenexa, Kansas, plant of the Puritan-Bennett Corporation, a manufacturer of respiratory equipment. After *seven* years of working to develop improved software for its respirators, product development teams *have* not completed the job, despite the fact that the industry *average* for such tasks is only three years. According to Roger J. Dolida, the company's director of research and development, the problem is that management *never* made the project a priority, and refused to free up another key person needed to do the job as he put it,"if top management doesn't buy into the idea teams can go nowhere."

A third obstacle to group success, and a relatively common one, is that some managers are unwilling to relinquish control. Good supervisors work their way up from the plant floor by giving orders and having them followed. *However,* team leaders *have* to build consensus and must allow team members to make decisions together. As you might expect, letting go of control isn't always easy for some to do. This problem emerged at Bausch & Lomb's sunglasses plant in Rochester, New York. In 1989 some 1,400 employees were put into thirty-eight teams. By 1992 about half the supervisors had not adjusted to the change, despite receiving thorough training in how to work as part of a team. They argued bitterly with team members whenever their ideas were not accepted by the team, and eventually they were reassigned. An even tougher approach was taken at the Shelby Die Casting Company, a metal-casting firm in Shelby, Mississippi. When its former supervisors refused to cooperate as co-equals in their teams, the company eliminated their jobs, and let the workers run their own teams. The result: the company saved $250,000 in annual wages, productivity jumped 50 per cent, and company profits almost doubled. The message sent by both companies is clear: those who cannot adjust to teamwork are unwelcome.

Fourth, teams might fail not only because their members do not co-operate with each other, but also because they fail to co-operate with other teams. This problem occurred in General Electric's medical systems division when it assigned two teams of engineers, one in Waukesha, Wisconsin, and another in Hino, Japan, the task of creating software for two new ultrasound devices. Shortly, teams pushed features that made their products popular only in their own countries, and duplicated each other's efforts. When the teams met, language and cultural barriers separated them, further distancing the teams from each other. Without close co-operation between teams (as well as within them!), organizations are not likely to reap the benefits they hoped for when creating teams in the first place. (As you might imagine, it's a matter of not only if teams co-operate with each other, but precisely how they go about interacting with other units that will determine their effectiveness. For a description of a fascinating recent study exploring this issue.

Team Building and OD

Organization Development is a complex educational strategy intended to change the beliefs, attitudes, values, and structure of organizations so that they can better adapt to new technologies, markets and challenges, and the dizzying rate of change itself. OD is a process aimed at bringing about organizational effectiveness, and team development is one of the key elements in this process.

Bennis states that the most common goals of OD are team-oriented:

- Improvement in inter-personal competence,
- Increased understanding within and between groups so that tensions can be reduced.
- Development of more effective team management, development of improved methods of conflict resolution.

It is these very goals that indicate the relationship between team development and organization development. In fact, Pattern states that "OD through team building by definition suggests that one way management can be improved, by enabling managers to function as team, -'although there are a number of techniques available for developing organizations, team building has been considered, more useful, because it can incorporate or be used in conjunction with a wide variety of other techniques. Team building has been considered to be one of the most respected and frequently employed strategies of Organization Development. In fact, one investigation indicated that it was the dominant intervention in 40 percent of all OO programmes through 1975.

Most intervention strategies arc aimcd at the following four models of team-building.

1. The Role-Model, for examining and clarifying individual role expectations and obligations of group members.
2. The inter-personal model for increasing inter - personal relations among group members to develop a climate of mutual trust and superlativeness.
3. The goal-setting model, for directing group members to become more goals and objective-oriented.
4. The skill model, for equipping members with appropriate skills to build and sustain team effectiveness.

REFERENCES

A.P. Hare, Handbook of Small Group Research, Free Press, New York, 2nd ed. 1976.

B.T. Alban, L.L. Pollit, *Team Building*. In T.H. Patten, Ed. *OD Emerging Dimensions and Concepts*, Madison Wisconsin, American Society for Training and Development, 1973, p. 33.

C.K. Eoyang, *Organization Development - Structures, Process, or Systems*. In Cummings T.G. Ed. *Systems Theory for OD.*, John Wiley, New York, 1980 pp. 223-245.

CAL. Pearson, *Autonomous Work Groups: An Evaluation At An Industrial Site, Human Relations*, Vol. 45, 1992, pp. 905-936.

D. Cartwright, *The Nature of Group Cohesiveness*, in D. Cartwrigth and A. Zander, Eds. *Group Dynamics*.

D. McGregor, *The Human Side of Enterprise*, McGraw Hill. New York 1960.

D.L. Forsyth, *An Introduction To Group Dynamics*, Book Code, Montercy, CA 1983.

D.R. ligen, DA Major, A Holenbech and D.J. Sego, *Team Research in the 1990s,* in M.M. Chemers and Ayman Eds. *Leadership Theory and Research*, Academic Press, San Diego, 1993, pp. 245-270.

E. Aronsonand J. Mills, *The Effects of Severity of Initiation of Liking For A Group, Journal of Abnormal and Social Psychology*, Vol. 59, 1959, pp. 177-181.

E.E. Lawler 111, SA Mohrman and G.E. Ledford Jr., *Employee Involvement and Total Quality Management*, Jossey Bass, Sanfrancisco, 1992.

E.F. Huse, *OD and Change*, West Pub. New York, 1975, pp. 71-82.

Elton Mayo, *The Human Problems of an Industrial Civilisation*,-Macmillan, New York, 1983.

G. Humans, *The Human Group*, Harcourt & Brace. New York, 1950.

I.L. Janis, *Group Think. Psychological Studies of Policy Decisions and Fiascoes*, Houghton Miffin, Boston, 2nd. ed. 1982.

J. Hoerr, *The Payoff From Team Work Business Week*, July 10, 1989, pp. 58-62.

J.M. George and K. Bettenhausen, *Understanding Pro Social Behaviour, Sales Performance and Turnover, A Group Level Analysis in a Service Context, Journal of Applied Psychology*, Vol. 75, 1990, pp. 698-709.

J.R. Hackman, Ed. Group That Works and That Don't, Jossey Bass, Sanfrancisco, 190.

J.R. Hackman, *The Design of Work Teams*, in J.W Lorsch, Ed. *Handbook of Organizational Behaviour*, Prentice Hall, Englewood Cliffs, N.J., 1987, pp. 315-342.

J.R. Katzenbach and D.K. Smith, *The Discipline of Teams*, Harvard Business Review, Vol. 71, No. 2, March-April, 1993, pp. 111-120 and C.C. Manz and H.P. Sins Jr. *Business Without Bosses*, John Wiley & Sons, New York, 1993.

J.R. Katzenbach and O.K. Smith, *The Wisdom of Teams*, Harvard Business School Press, Boston, 1993.

K.P. De Meuse Jay Liebowitzs (1981) - *An Empirical Analysis of Team Building Research, Group and Organization Studies* 6 (3) p. 358.

Kurt Lewin *The Conceptual Representation and the Measurement of Psychological Forces,* Duke University Press. Durham, NC, 1938.

L. Wendell, French, H. Cecil, Bell Jr., *Organization Development – Behavioural Science Intervention for Organization Improvement*, (3rd ed.) Prentice Hallindice ~ 1989 .140.

M. Woodcock, D. Francis, p. 191.

M. Woodcock, D. Francis, *Team Building – Yea or No?* In W.W. Burke and L.D. Goodstein. Eds. *Trends and Issues in OD.* University Associates, San Diego, 1980, p.185.

M. Woodcock, D. Francis, *Team Building Yes or No?* p.187.

M.D. Maginn, Effective Teamwork Business, One Irwin, Burr Ridge il. 1994.

M.E. Shaw, *Group Dynamics: The Dynamics of Small Group Behaviour*, Mc Graw Hill, New York, 3rd ed. 1981.

P. Hare, *Handbook of Small Group Research*, The Press of Glenco. New York, 1962.

R. Blake and J. Mouton, *Corporate Excellence Through Grid OD: A Systems Approach*, Gulf Pub., Houston, 1968 pp. 101-2.

R.S. Wellins, W.C. Byham and J.M. Wilson, *Empowered Teams*, Josscy Bass, Sanfrancisco, 1991 and J.D. Osburn, L Moran, E. Musselwhite and J.H. Zenger, Self Directed Work Teams, Irwin, Burr Ridge, iI., 1990.

Research and Theory, Harper & Row New York, 3rd ed., 1968, pp. 91-109.

Resis Likert R. *The Human Organization*. McGraw Hill. New York, 1967.

Resis Likert, *New Patterns of Management*, McGraw Hill. New York, 1961.

S. Long, *Early Integration of Groups: A Group to Join and A Group to Create, Human Relations*, Vol. 37, 1984, pp. 311-332.

SA Mohrman, *Integrating Roles and Structures in the Lateral Organization* in J.R. Galbraith and E.E. Lawler, Eds. *Organising For the Future*, Jossey Bass San Francisco, 1993, pp. 109-141.

T Douglas. *Groups: Understanding People Gathered Together*, Tavistock, New York, 1983.

T. Doughlas, Understanding *People Gathered Together*, Tavistok, New York 1983.

T.D. Wall, N.J. Kemp,. R.R. Jackson, C.W. Clegg, *Outcomes of Autonomous Work Groups: A Long Term Field Experiments, Academy of Management Journal*, Vol. 29, 1986, pp. 280-304.

T.H. Patten, *Organization Development Through Team Building*, p. 1.

T.H. Pattern, *Organization Development Through Team Building*. John Wiley, New York, 1981, pp. 1-13.

W. Burke, Ed. *Current Issues and Strategies in OD, Human Science Press*. New York, 1978.

W. Dyer, *Team Building*, Reading, Addison Wesley, Mass. 1977, pp. 8-11.

WG. Bennis, Quoted in W. Burke and L.D. Goodstein Eds. *Trends and Issues in OD*, University Press, San Diego, 1980, p.5.

WG. Dyer, *Team Building* pp. 15-20.

CHAPTER

16

Group Behaviour & Dynamics

Man, since birth lives in groups and therefore, he is called a social animal. A man cannot exist without group. Group may be large or small. Sometimes an individual gets membership for more than one groups, in some of them he plays an active role while in some others, he is quite inactive.

Persons when come together and interact each other for a common purpose where all are psychologically aware of one another and if they perceive themselves to be a group, may form a group. So, if a crowd standing at the bus stop or railway platform does not necessarily constitute a group.

Imagine three people waiting in line at the cashier's stand at a supermarket. Now compare them to the board of directors of a large corporation. Which collection would you consider to be a "group"? Although in our everyday language we may refer to the people waiting in line as a group, they are not a group in the same sense as the members of the board. Obviously, a group is more than simply a collection of people. But what exactly is it that make's a group a group?

Groups Defined

No generally accepted definition of a group exists. Instead, we present a range of available views developed over many years in a variety of disciplines. From these different perspectives, we develop a comprehensive definition of a group.

A Group in Terms of Perception

Many behavioural scientists believe that for a collection of individuals to be considered a group, its members must perceive their relationships to others. For example:

A small group is defined as any number of persons engaged in interaction with one another in a single face-to-face meeting or series of such meetings, in which each member receives some impression or perception of other member distinct enough so that he can, either at the time or in later questioning, give some reaction to each of the others as an individual person, even though it may be only to recall that the other was present.

This view points out that the members of a group must perceive the existence of each member as well as the existence of the group.

A Group in Terms of Organization

Sociologists view the group primarily in terms of organizational characteristics. For example, as a sociological definition, a group is an organized system of two or more individuals who are interrelated so that the system performs some function, has a standard set of role relationships among its members, and has a set of norms that regulate the function of the group and each of its members.

This view emphasizes some of the important characteristics of groups, such as roles and norms, which are discussed later in this chapter.

A Group in Terms of Motivation

A group that fails to aid its members in satisfying their needs has difficulty remaining viable. Employees who are not satisfying their needs in a particular group will search for other groups to aid in important need satisfactions. This view defines a group as a collection of individuals whose existence as a collection is rewarding to the individuals.

As pointed out in an earlier chapter, it is difficult to ascertain clearly which facets of the work organization are rewarding to individuals. The problem of identifying individual needs is a shortcoming of defining a group solely in terms of motivation.

A Group in Terms of Interaction

Some theorists assume that interaction in the form of interdependence is the core of "groupness." A view that stresses interpersonal interactions is the following:

We mean by a group a number of persons who communicate with one another often over a span of time, and who are few enough so that each person is able to communicate with all of the others, not at second-hand, through other people, but face to face.

Social scientists have formally defined a **group** as a collection of two or more interacting individuals with a stable pattern of relationships among them who share common goals and who perceive themselves as being a group.

One of the most obvious characteristics of groups is that they are composed of two or more people in social interaction. In other words, the members of a group must have some influence on each other. The interaction between the parties may be either verbal (such as sharing strategies for a corporate takeover) or nonverbal (such as exchanging smiles in the hallway), but the parties must have some impact on each other to be considered a group.

Groups also must possess a stable structure. Although groups can change, and often do, there must be some stable relationships that keep group members together and functioning as a unit. A collection of individuals that constantly changes (e.g., the people inside an office waiting room at any given time) cannot be thought of as a group. To be a group, a greater level of stability would be required.

A third characteristic of groups is that their members share common interests or goals. For example, members of a stamp-collecting club constitute a group that is sustained by the mutual interest of members. Some groups form because members with common interests help each other achieve a mutual goal. For example, the owners and employees of a sewing shop constitute a group formed around a common interest in sewing, and the common goal of making money.

Finally, to be a group, the individuals involved must perceive themselves as a group. Groups are composed of people who recognise each other as a member of their group and can distinguish these individuals from nonmembers. The members of a corporate finance committee or a chess club, for example, know who is in their group and who is not. In contrast, shoppers in a check-out line probably don't think of each other as being members of a group. Although they stand physically close to each other and may have passing conversations, they have little in common (except, perhaps, a shared interest in reaching the end of the line) and fail to identify themselves with the others in the line.

By defining groups in terms of these four characteristics, we have identified a group as a very special collection of individuals. As we shall see, these characteristics are responsible for the very important effects groups have on organizational behaviour.

1. Are motivated to join.
2. Perceive the group as a unified unit of interacting people.
3. Contribute in various amounts to the group processes (i.e., some people contribute more time or energy to the group).
4. Reach agreements and have disagreements through various form of interactions.

Group Dynamics

The word "dynamics" has been derived from the Greek word meaning "force." "Hence group dynamics refers to the study of forces operating within a group." In other words, "The social process by which people interact face to face in small groups is called group dynamics."

Group dynamics in the paradigm of organizational behaviour is primarily concerned "with the interactions of forces between group members in a social situation". In spite of expressing different views and different things, the one expressed by Kurt Lewin has received wider acceptability. Kurt Lewin is known as the founder of group dynamics movement. His findings are based on the experiments he conducted on small groups in 1930s. The other experiments having status of historical landmarks were those which were conducted by Elton Mayo and his associates in 1920s and 1930s.

In short, group dynamics may be stated as the behaviour of individuals as members of a group in an organizational setting. Apart from Hawthorne experiments, the other notable studies in this regard were:

(i) the Lippitt and White leadership studies;

(ii) the Coach and French studies relating to mechanics to overcome resistance to change, and

(iii) Trist and Bamforth's study of two groups of carpenter and bricklayers and William H. Whyte's work on restaurant industry."

The term was popularized by Kurt Lewin in the 1930s. But through the years different meanings have been given to it as under.

(i) One view is that group dynamics describes how a group should be organized and conducted.

(ii) Another view of group dynamics is that it consists of a set of techniques such as role playing, brainstorming, buzz groups, group therapy, sensitivity training, team building, transactional analysis, etc.

(iii) According to third view group dynamics is concerned with the internal nature of groups, how they form, their structure and processes, and how they function and affect individual members, other groups, and the organizations.

This third view is more close to Lewin's original idea.

Group Formation

A man does not live in isolation. He joins one group or the other. At home he is the member of the family group, at work-place he is the member of the labour union or other formal or informal groups, in the neighbourhood he is the member of the group perhaps organised by the dwellers of the locality. In this way he is the member of one group or the other. This fact raises a few questions: Why people join the group? What makes group attractive?

Reasons for Group Formation

There may be three possible approaches to understand "people's propensity" to form and join groups. these three approaches are:

(i) Psycho-analytical which relates to the instinct of group formation inherited from the primal family;

(ii) Cognitive approach which suggests that people join the group because they have the expectation that membership will benefit them; and

(iii) Operand approach which relates to people's conviction that by joining group they will experience "positive reinforcement from social and group behavior."

Whatever be the approach, the reasons for joining the group may be as follows:

The Satisfaction of Needs

The desire for need satisfaction can be a strong motivating force leading to group formation. Specifically, the security, social, esteem, and self-actualization needs of some employees can be satisfied to a degree by their affiliation with groups.

Security: Without the group to lean on when various management demands are made, certain employees may assume that they are standing alone, facing management and the entire organization system. This "aloneness" leads to a degree of insecurity. By being a member of a group, the employee can become involved in group activities and discuss management demands with other members who hold supportive views. the interaction and communication among the group's members serve as a buffer to management demands. The need for a buffer may be especially strong in the case of a new employee, who may depend heavily on the group for aid in correctly performing the job.

Social: The gregariousness of people stimulates their need for affiliation; the desire to be a part of a group points up the intensity of social needs. The need to socialize exists not only on the job but away from the workplace, as evidenced by the vast array of social, political, civic, and fraternal organizations one can join.

Propinquity: Every individual wants to share his view regarding any objective or problem with others. The individual will naturally try to share with the person geographically closer to his. In an organization employees who work in the same area of plant or office, or executives with offices close to one another would more probably form into a group than those who are not physically located closer, this is called propinquity theory.

Shared Activities and Interaction: George Homans is of the opinion that people, who get an opportunity to interact with each other, share the activities of each other and also understand and share the sentiments of other, are likely to form a group. The more activities people shares the more numerous will be their interaction and the stronger will be their sentiments for each other. The more interaction will be between each other, the more shared will be their activities and sentiments. Thus, Homan's view is that Group is formed due to closer interaction, shared activities and sentiments. Persons in a group interact with each other not only due to proximity but also to solve problems, attain goals, facilitate coordination, reduce tension and achieve a balance.

Esteem: In a particular work environment, a certain group may be viewed by employees as having a high level of prestige for a variety of reasons (technical competence, outside activities, etc.). Consequently, membership in this group carries with it a certain status not enjoyed by non-members. For employees with high esteem needs, membership in such a group can provide much-needed satisfaction

Proximity and Attraction

Interpersonal interaction can result in group formation. Two important facets of interpersonal interaction are proximity and attraction. Proximity involves the physical distance between employees performing a job. Attraction designates the degree to which people are drawn to each other because of perceptual, attitudinal, performance, or motivational similarity.

Individuals who work in close proximity have numerous opportunities to exchange ideas, thoughts, and attitudes about various on-and off-the-job activities. These exchanges often result in some type of group formation. Proximity also makes it possible for individuals to learn about the characteristics of other people. To sustain the interaction and interest, a group is often formed.

Group Goal

A group's goals, if clearly understood, can be reasons why an individual is attracted to it. for example, an individual may join a group that meets after work to become familiar with a new personal computer system that is to be implemented in the work organization over the next two years. The person who voluntarily joins the after hours group believes that learning the new system is a necessary and important goal for employees.

Identifying group goals is not always possible. The assumption that formal organizational groups have clear goals must be tempered by the understanding that perception, attitudes, personality, and learning can distort goals. For example, a new employee may never be formally told the goals of the unit that he or she has joined. By observing the behaviour and attitudes of others, individuals may conclude what they believe the goals to be. These perceptions mayor may not be accurate. The same can be said about the goals of informal groups.

Balance Theory

People form group with persons having similar attitudes towards common objectives and goals. Once a relationship is formed it strives to maintain a symmetrical balance between the attraction and the common attitudes. If the balance is disturbed people try to restore it failing which the group dissolves.

Exchange Theory

People also form group with persons who can be helpful in getting some need satisfied. It is both ways. It expects that one may have to do something for others for getting something as reward for satisfying his need. This can be possible if individuals get opportunity of interaction and they have similar attitude. This is based on the principle of exchange.

Economic and Social Reasons

People form group for economic security, or social reasons. Economically, weaker may form a group to work on project to get more wages or may form a union to demand higher wages. For security, forming a group provides united front. Sometimes people form a group because group satisfies the most intense social need, need for affiliation.

Esteem

The esteem of an individual increases by his association with a group of high status. He automatically gets the needed recognition from outsiders. Similarly, the group provides an atmosphere of safety, encouragement and self-expression. As a group member he feels free; he may complain about his work, his loss, his pay, etc. He is sure to have favourable response because his feeling fails in line with the feeling of other members of the group.

Power

By joining the group, he gets the power. It depends on the notion that "united we stand and divided we fall". In other words, collectively members enjoy greater power than individually.

Identity

A person gets an identity by associating with the group. He understands about the self and others in the group. In fact group provides information about "oneself and about the outside world." It also serves as a basis of comparison with others. Similarly, new information from others' experience is also available.

Rewards

As a member of the group he may get the reward in the form of friendship, recognition, status and financial benefit.

Accomplishment

Many people join the group to share knowledge of others. They may even need to pool their talents, tools and contacts.

STAGES IN THE DEVELOPMENT OF GROUPS

Just as infants develop in certain ways during their first months of life, groups also show relatively stable signs of maturation and development. One popular theory identifies five distinct stages through which groups develop. As we describe these below, you may want to review our summary of the five stages shown in Figure. 8-3.

The first stage of group development is known as forming. During this stage of group development, the members get acquainted with each other. they establish the ground rules by trying to find out what behaviours are acceptable, with respect to both the job (how productive they are expected to be) and interpersonal relations (who's really in charge). During the forming stage, people tend to be a bit confused and uncertain about how to act in the group and how beneficial it will be to become a member of the group. Once the individuals come to think of themselves as members of a group, the forming stage is complete.

The second stage of group development is referred to as storming. As the name implies, this stage is characterized by a high degree of conflict within the group. Members often resist the control of the group's leaders and show hostility toward each other. If these conflicts are not resolved and group members withdraw, the group may disband. However, as conflicts are resolved and the group's leadership is accepted, the storming stage is complete.

The third stage of group development is known as norming. During this stage, the group becomes more cohesive, and identification as a member of the group becomes greater. Close relationships develop, shared feelings become common, and a keen interest in finding mutually agreeable solutions develops. Feelings of camaraderie and shared responsibility for the group's activities are heightened. The norming stage is complete when the members of the group accept a common set of expectations that constitutes an acceptable way of doing things.

The fourth stage is known as performing. During this stage, questions about group relationships and leadership have been resolved and the group is ready to work. Having fully developed, the group may now devote its energy to getting the job done – the group's good relations and acceptance of its leadership helps the group perform well.

Recognizing that not all groups last forever, the final stage is known as adjourning. Groups may cease to exist because they have met their goals and are no longer needed (such as an ad hoc group created to raise money for a charity project), in which case the end is abrupt. Other groups may adjourn gradually, as the group disintegrates, either because members leave or because the norms that have developed are no longer effective for the group.

To help illustrate these various stages, imagine that you have just jointed several of your colleagues on your company's newly created budget allocation committee. At first, you and your associates feel each other out: you watch to see who comes up with the best ideas, whose suggestions are most widely accepted, who seems to take charge, and the like (the forming stage). Then, as members struggle to gain influence over others, you may see a battle over control of the committee (the storming stage). Soon this will be resolved, and an accepted leader will emerge. At this stage, the group members will become highly cooperative, working together in harmony, and doing things together such as going out to lunch as a group (the norming stage). Now it becomes possible for committee members to work together at doing their best, giving it their all (the performing stage). Then, once the budget is created and approved, the group's task is over, and it is disbanded (the adjourning stage).

It is important to keep in mind that groups can be in anyone stage of development at any given time.

Moreover, the amount of time a group may spend in any given stage is highly variable. In fact, some groups may fail long before they have had a chance to work together. Research has revealed that the boundaries between the various stages may not be clearly distinct, and that several stages may be combined, especially as deadline pressures force groups to take actions. It is best, then to think of this five-stage model as a general framework of group formation. Although many of the stages may be followed, the dynamic nature of groups makes constant progress through the various stages in a set, predictable order unlikely.

Individual Characteristics and Group Behaviour

Individual members of group bring with them characteristics that may influence group behaviour. The study of the influence of individual characteristics on groups is important to the manager because individual characteristics can determine what the individual member is able to contribute to group activities. The individual characteristics that influence group behaviour can be divided into four major categories.

(1) Physical Characteristics Such as Age, Sex, and Physical Characteristics

Although there are no hard and fast rules regarding physical characteristics, certain tentative relationship have been found of which managers to be careful. For example, increasing age has been shown to be related to increased social interaction, an increased tendency to be a leader, but decreased conformity to group norms. Overall, the results indicate that certain physical characteristics may influence group activity.

(2) Abilities and Intelligence

Individuals have abilities that can be used by the groups to accomplish goals. In general studies have shown that the individual who has specific and crucial abilities and intelligence will be more active in the group activity and generally contribute more.

(3) Personality Traits

Personality traits are individual characteristics that may have a strong influence on how the individual will interact with other group members. Traits that have been considered include authoritarianism and dominance, acceptance of others, anxiety, extroversion or introversion, self-reliance and dependability, and sociability. The results reveal that personality traits have a significant impact on group processes and interaction, but only a minor influence on group performance.

(4) Expectations

An individual's behaviour is effected by the way he anticipates that events will occur. Three sets of expectations are generally operates in groups:

- Expectations held by individuals that they are able to do a competent job and to perform well.
- Expectations individuals have for their group, including the degree of participation by other members, interpersonal relationships, and rewards for good performance.
- Expectations the group has for individual's contributions to group activity and eventual goal accomplishment.

The first expectation concerns the individual's perception of this own ability to do a competent job. The individual's and group's expectations of one another can generally be clarified by the manager through the use of standard rules, procedures, and policies.

Inter-and-Inter Group Relations

The existence of groups leads to inter-group competition. This was studied by Sharief, Harvay, White, Hood and Sherief (1961). This whole phenomenon may be studied under two heads:

(i) what happens within the groups? and

(ii) what happens between competing groups?

What Happens within the Group

1. Each group becomes a closely-knit organization by burying their internal bickerings and differences.
2. The group climate changes; it switches over from being informal, casual and playful to task-oriented. It shifts from member's psychological needs to task accomplishment.
3. Leadership changes; the group is not prepared to tolerate even the autocratic leadership.
4. Group becomes structured and organised.
5. Group expects more loyalty and conformity from members in order to present a "solid front."

What Happens Between Competing Groups

1. Each group looks to each other as a competitor rather than interdependent part of the same organization.
2. Each group develops distortions of perceptions because of dominating competitiveness. It concentrates only on its good points and refuses to perceive its weakness; similarly it perceives only the bad points or the shortcomings of other groups; this feeling is so dominating that it is not prepared to consider the good of its competitors.
3. Inter-group hostility increases which leads to reducing inter-group interaction and communication. This leads to distortion in perception.
4. When groups are forced into interaction they will only listen to their own representatives rather than of the other. Each will try t? find faults of others.

Solution to the Problems

1. Locating a common enemy
2. Bringing leaders or subgroups of the competing groups into interaction
3. Locating subordinate goals
4. Experimental inter-group training
5. Preventing inter-group conflict

Approaches to Inter-Group Relationship

Inter-group relationship may be presented in two ways:

(i) as portrayed by Likert, and

(ii) as stated by Thompson.

According to Likert organization encompasses a series of overlapping groups. Each group is linked with the rest of the organization by persons who hold membership in more than one group. These people are called "linking pins" as they forge link between different groups. Though the success of decision-making depends on group process and interaction, occurring at different levels, but everything revolves round the "linking pins." Apart from the linking pins, the success of organization depends on:27

(i) good group process of decision-making; and

(ii) supervision

Both these elements duly insulated by "linking pins" will generate inter-group confidence and trust; it will enhance the problem-solving ability of the group which will result in better productivity level.

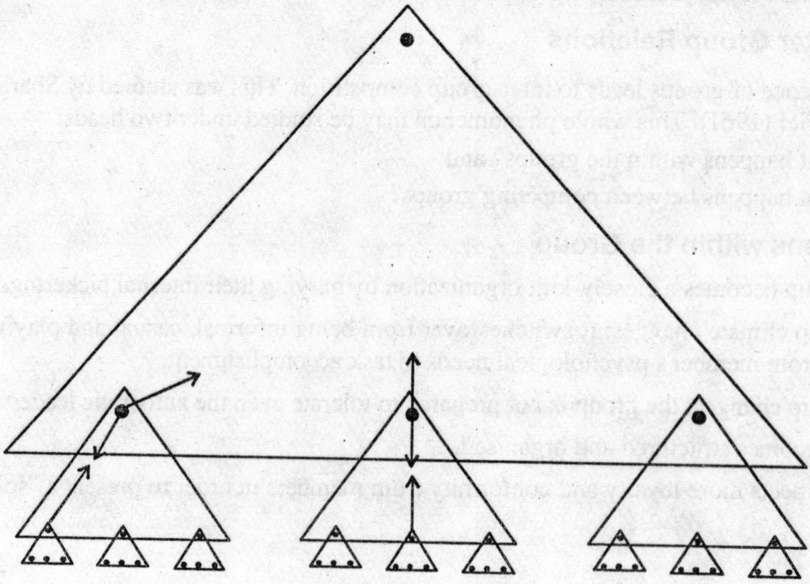

Fig. 1.

Though Likert's theory is very well accepted but it is based on the assumption that there exists equal interdependence among different groups. Thompson suggests that there are three different kinds of interdenpendence among groups. They are:

(i) pooled;
(ii) sequential; and
(iii) reciprocal.

1. **Pooled Interdependence:** It occurs when both groups do not need any interdependence. They only need through total organization which supports both of them. Suppose the employees of Bata Shoe Company working in Jammu may have no interdependence with their counterparts in Ludhiana but both are interdependent because they are part and parcel of the Bata organization. Success or failure of one may be reflected in another through the medium of the total organization system. Pooled interdependence does not need any interaction between groups; hence conflict does not arise. Coordination may, however, be forged through standardisation and the rules formulated by the parent office.

2. **Sequential Interdependence:** It means that the work of one group depends on the performance of another. For instance, the finished job, i.e., output of a group becomes the input of another group. However both groups are sustained by the organization. The interdependence is both pooled and sequential.

Sequential interdependence may be regulated by proper planning and controlling. The chances are that conflicts between the groups are higher than the pooled interdependence.

3. **Reciprocal Interdependence:** Reciprocal interdependence means each group is dependent on another. The output of one is the input of another. For example the teacher and students in the class. When the teacher comes to the class, the students are supposed to be present. So the class cannot be held without the students. Conversely, if the students and the teacher are absent, the class cannot be held. Hence both groups of teachers and students are reciprocally interdependent.

Reciprocal interdependence ought to be coordinated by mutual adjustment between the groups. It requires greater communication and understanding to avoid possible conflict. Styles identified both intergroup and intragroup dynamics, which seemed to explain the variations in group activity. According to him a work group's respective ranking among other groups in the system (in terms of the rewards it received from the organization) was an important factor in predicting its reaction to system authorities. Similarly, the way the intergroup dynamics might influence small group behaviour was observed in the Bank Wiring Room Study by Roethlisberger and Dickson, where external group membership, ethnicity, and age were the prominent variables which were ignored in the original analysis; and in the coal mining studies by Trist, Where the intergroup consequences of the breakdown of small work group boundaries were observed.

Events growing out of intergroup relations, therefore, play a significant part in determining the behaviour of small groups in organizations. Relations with other groups in its environment may determine how a group forms, the nature of its emotional climate, how roles are structured for individuals who represent group interests, the distribution of resources for group members, the reaction of the group to system authorities, and the effectiveness of the group in achieving its objectives. Thus, to understand group behaviour in organizations, a knowledge of intergroup dynamics is essential.

Theories of Group Formation

Theories of group formation may be divided under the following heads:

1. Theory of Propinquity

It means individual's affiliation with one another because of spatial of geographical proximity. For instance, students sitting with one another are likely to form the group than the students sitting opposite or at a distance.

2. Homans Theory

It is based on the elements of activities, interactions and sentiments. These elements are related to one another. Interaction or participation in the organization tends to result in a powerful group formation. Interaction between persons takes place to attain goals, facilitate coordination, reduce tension and achieve a balance.

Homan studied group by analysing the factors such as internal nature of the group, how they form, their structure and process and how they affect individual members and influence other groups and the organization. Thus, he analysed the factors which are internal to group and the factors which are external to group.

The Homan Model describes group behaviour in terms of three behavioural elements.

Activity: This refers to what an individual does like, tasks that people perform such as operating a machine, inspecting a component, walking to work, making a computation etc.

Interaction: This refers to the behaviour that occurs between people in performing an activity. It includes verbal and non-verbal communication as well as contacts that actually take place between people. Students discussing a forthcoming class examination, a quarterback calling signals in the huddle and an employee waving at an acquaintance on the other side of the office are all examples of people interacting with one another. Frequency, duration, and order of interaction give us insight into the importance of interaction and the relative status of those who are interacting.

Sentiments: They include values, attitudes and beliefs of a person. They also include positive as well as negative feelings that group members hold about each other. Because feelings are often not directly observable, they are inferred from the activities and interactions. The employee who performs below his capabilities despite the incentive of group bonus holds certain sentiments towards task group members.

The three elements are thus interrelated in the following manner and are common to both formal and informal groups:

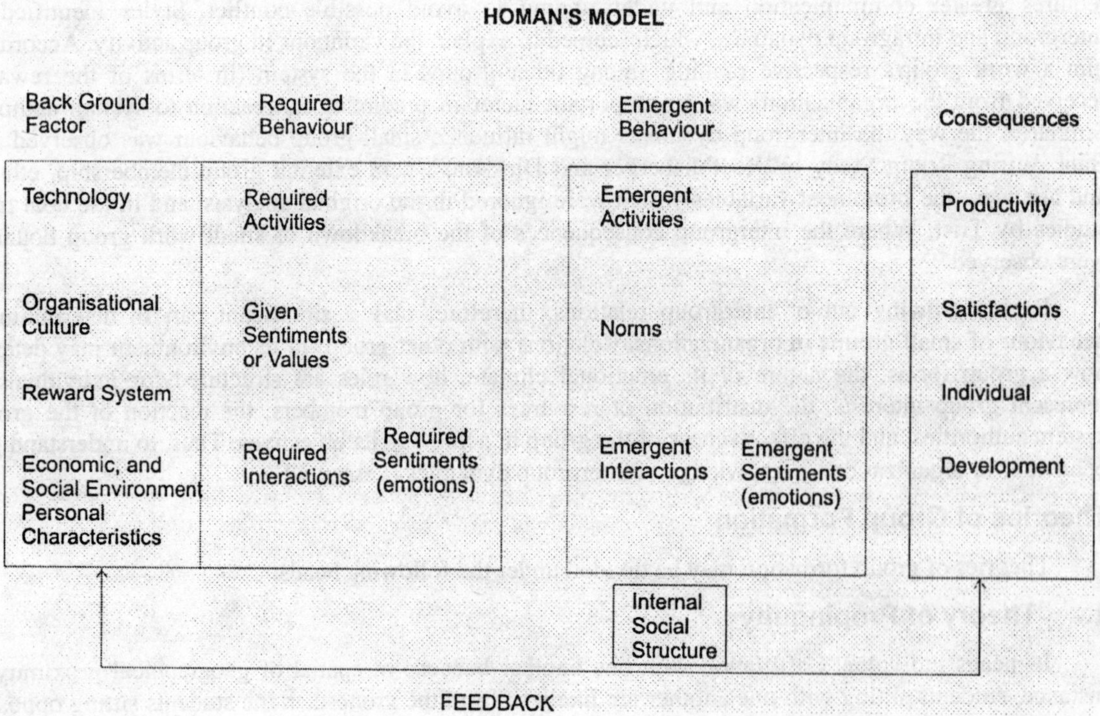

Fig. 2. Group Behaviour Model

The above model Fig. 2 on group behaviour suggests that certain background factors coupled with the required activities, interaction and sentiments within a group, along with the personal characteristics of the members create both a formal and informal internal system. This, in turn determines the group's productivity, its level of satisfaction, and its ability to develop, change and innovate.

Homan said the internal system develops out of the external system; but the two interact after the internal system is well developed. The factors which Homan has considered to be a part of the external system include the enterprise's organization structure and control system, the technology of the job and its required communication and interactions. He has described the internal system as one which consists of three interacting behavioural element of activities, interactions and sentiments. Activities are the things people undertake as a part of their jobs; interactions are the way people relate to one another; and sentiments include the feelings, values, opinions, and beliefs held by an individual or a group. The larger the number of activities persons share, the more numerous will be their interactions and the stronger will be their sentiments; the more frequent the interactions between persons, the more will be their shared activities and sentiments; and the more sentiments persons have for one other, the more will be their shared activities and interactions.

3. Balance Theory

This theory has been propounded by Theodore Necomb. It states that persons get attracted towards one another on the basis of "similar attitudes toward commonly relevant objects and goals." Once the relationship is forged, it will continue to maintain symmetrical balance between the attraction and the common attitudes. Whenever an imbalance occurs, a balance is sought to be established.

4. Exchange Theory

The exchange theory is based on reward-cost outcomes of interactions. People will attract towards one another for the formation of group when they feel that the reward is greater than the cost. Rewards seek to satisfy the needs of the members while costs involve anxiety, frustration and fatigue.

It may be stated that propinquity, interaction and common attitudes play an important role in exchange theory.

GROUP-A SYSTEM VIEW

Group may be viewed as input-process-output system. In this system's model developed by S.E. White, T.R. Mitchell there are three important components. They are:

(1) Inputs;
(2) Process; and
(3) Outputs.

Inputs are three as shown in Fig.1. They are:

(i) Personal characteristics of individuals;
(ii) Situational characteristics; and
(iii) Group structure.

Personal characteristics comprising (a) attitudes, (b) ability, (c) personality, and (d) background of the groups are apt to influence the decisions of the group. Like personal characteristics, the variable of group dynamics is situational characteristics. These characteristics have been identified as:

(a) space;
(b) nature of task;
(c) group size; and
(d) reward system.

The third variable, the group structure, consists of such elements as:

(a) influence;
(b) attraction;

(c) status; and
(d) communication.

These three enter the group process of interaction among the members of the group which has been stated as "who says what to whom and why and with what results."

The inputs after being processed in the system come out as outputs in the form of three sets of effects - the effects on individuals in the form of attitudes and knowledge, on group in the form of new norms or interaction patterns and on environment in the form of productivity.

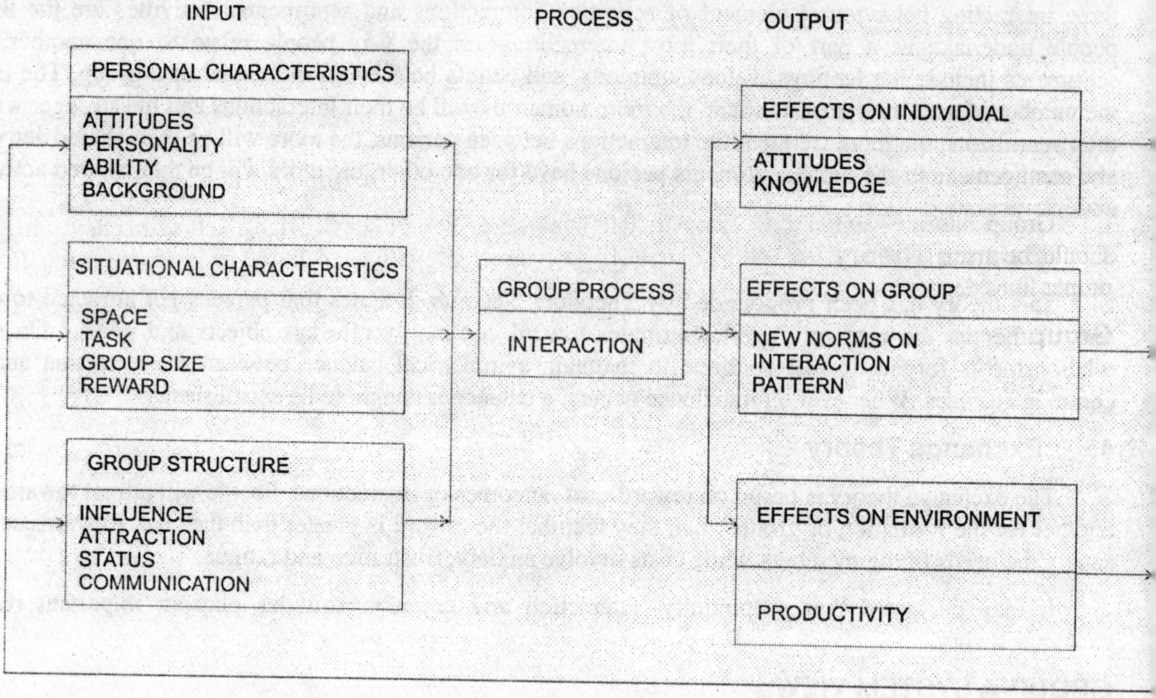

Fig. 3. Input-Process-Output Model (System View)

(Adapted from Terrance R. Mitchell, *op.cit.* 180).

GROUP INPUTS

Personal Characteristics

Group's behaviour depends to a great extent on the characteristics of the members of the group. Personality of the individual members comprising the group will determine the style and functioning of the group. More the aberrations in the personality of members of the group, more the likelihood of group facing a number of problems in the organization. Personality is cast in the mould of environments which has also been stated earlier. The ability of the members depends on the education and training and other forms of development through which they passed through.

The ability may be instrumental in reducing conflict in the group and thus ensuring stability to the organization. Attitude, the other characteristic, depends on the personality and the environment of the individuals.

Situational Variables

Situations or the conditions obtaining in the organization influence the behaviour of the group. Space, according to the authors of the model, relates to the sitting or standing arrangement of the members of the group. Efforts should be so made that the members get maximum opportunity of interaction by way of talking to each other, helping each other. The personal contact among the members will strengthen the bonds of commonality of sharing space, tools and equipment and ultimately common problems at work. One thing has to be borne in mind. The space once allotted to the employee should not be withdrawn from him. A person after having worked for a long time on a particular seat, in a room or table feels psychologically attached to such an extent that when they are withdrawn from him and given to someone else he feels emotionally upset which may tend to generate disharmony among the co-workers.

Harmony of the group also depends on the tasks designed in the organization and the assignment thereof to the members of the group. The manager ought to carve out tasks in such a manner that each member of the group gets the job of his own choice. Each one is capable of performing the task as independently as possible; there is no overlapping or duplication of tasks so that the individual could get whatever commendation or criticism available to him.

Task performance and reward system are interdependent. The management should lay down objective criterion for the evaluation of the task performance. The member who performs his task better and in instrumental in helping the group to realise its objective should be rewarded appropriately. For this purpose the management shall have to design the system of recognition and reward system.

Group harmony and group size are interconnected. For better harmony and efficiency, the group should be manageable. Each member is able to interact properly and forge inter-personal relations on proper lines depending on the size of the group. The group ought to be small to be manageable.

Group Structure

After the formation and the development of the group the structure of the group comes into existence. The structure in terms of authority relationship, task distribution, span of control depends on inter - personal attraction of group members. They feel attracted to each other on the basis of common goal, common behalf and value system and more importantly a common cultural background. Even cultural heterogeneity may be made ineffective with potential and effective communication system which forges the bonds of inter-personal relationship.

Psychologically every human being is status-conscious. Every person wants upliftment in his status. The upliftment depends on the availability of the status within the group or the organization. The management should design the structure of hierarchy in such a manner that everyone gets status due to him within a reasonable period. Like other variables, influence of members and leaders affects the structure of the group.

GROUP PROCESS

A number of approaches relating to group process have been developed by different experts. However, the one developed by Benne and Sheats has the widest acceptability.

Before we discuss the process, it will be relevant to define process. Process may be defined as the method used by the leader to convert the inputs into the output of the groups. He takes the help of participating members and the communication methods to bring about the desired results. In other words, the group process is concerned not with the task itself.

The group process relates to

(i) group task activities;
(ii) group-building activities; and
(iii) self-serving activities.

In addition, there are two basic areas of the process. They are:

(a) what to look for in the group; and
(b) criteria for effective feedback.

Let us discuss the concept of process in details.

Group Task Activities

They include "initiating, clarifying, coordinating or orienting the group to its goals, giving and seeking information and establishing contact with the outside world-help the group attain its primary goals and objectives." Group roles include orientation, information, seeking, clarifying and information-giving.

Group-Building Activities

Group building is possible through harmony, reduction in tension through humour, and encouraging people to participate and compromise. Interaction is also helpful in group - building.

Self-Serving Activities

These activities in the form of attention getting, dominating, aggression and withdrawal are helpful to group members to meet his set of needs, values and goals.

The other areas are what to look for in the group. These elements are:

(i) Participation;
(ii) Influence;
(iii) Styles of influence;
(iv) Decision-making procedures;
(v) Task functions;
(vi) Maintenance functions;
(vii) Membership;
(viii) Feelings; and
(ix) Norms.

Effective feedback has the following characteristics:

(i) Descriptive;
(ii) Specific;
(iii) Needs of both the *receiver* and the *giver* of feedback considered;
(iv) Controlled behaviour on the part of the receiver;
(v) Ought to be asked for rather than imposed;
(vi) Timing;
(vii) Clear communication; and
(viii) Giver and receiver should be able to check the accuracy of the feedback.

GROUP OUTPUT

The effects on individual have been stated in the form of attitudianl change and the acquisition of knowledge about oneself and others. In the process of interaction when each member of the group discusses individual's problems and group's problems, *every* member gets an opportunity of understanding each other. The plus and minus of oneself and others will widen the horizon of knowledge to understand each other as well as the group. This understanding may nourish conformity to group's purpose which encourages readjustment of individual attitude.

The group will encourage more cohesiveness; it will devise new norms of interaction in which individuals may get equal opportunity of contributing the best of themselves towards realisation of the group's objective.

Finally, the productivity of the group will go up through better organizational environment. In this environment, there exists harmony among members who are prepared to contribute on the basis of reciprocity and mutuality, through appropriate reward system, better structuring of tasks and better understanding of each other in the group.

Another useful insight into the dimensions of group functioning has been provided by Gahagan. according to whom working groups may be considered to occupy space within two independent dimensions. One dimension represents the extent to which a group exists solely for the attainment of some goal extrinsic to itself or exists solely for the relationship between its members. The other dimension is the nature of the goal – that is, whether it is single and highly specific or whether it is diffused and unspecific. Fig. 4 illustrates his concept.

Equilibrium Problems

Most working groups, except those at the extreme end of the 'group's activities' dimension in fig A have two basic interdependent problems: one is the problem of group members moving towards the goal in a co-ordinate fashion and the other is that of keeping the relationship sufficiently harmonious and personal outcomes sufficiently high so that the members may not desert the group. The problem of striking a balance between the demands of the task confronting the group and the demands created by the personal and interpersonal feelings of group members is the equilibrium problem. A theory as to how this equilibrium may be brought about has been formulated by Bales, according to whom this equilibrium may be brought about by the behaviour of the influential members of the group. He has studied small, initially leaderless, discussion groups by observing their behaviour and recording which people interact with each other and how they do so. These groups were brought together for the purpose of study and consisted of strangers. They were set the task of discussing a case history and reaching agreement on the right course of action to be taken by the character in the case, for which they were allowed forty minutes. Each group met several times, at intervals of one week, for the same procedure. A record was kept of period of time for which each member talked and to whom he addressed his remarks. Then his remarks were classified according to a scheme developed by Bales. Bales has reduced a list of 87 possible interactions to 12 actions both positive and negative related to task and socio-emotional interaction. These may be listed as follows:

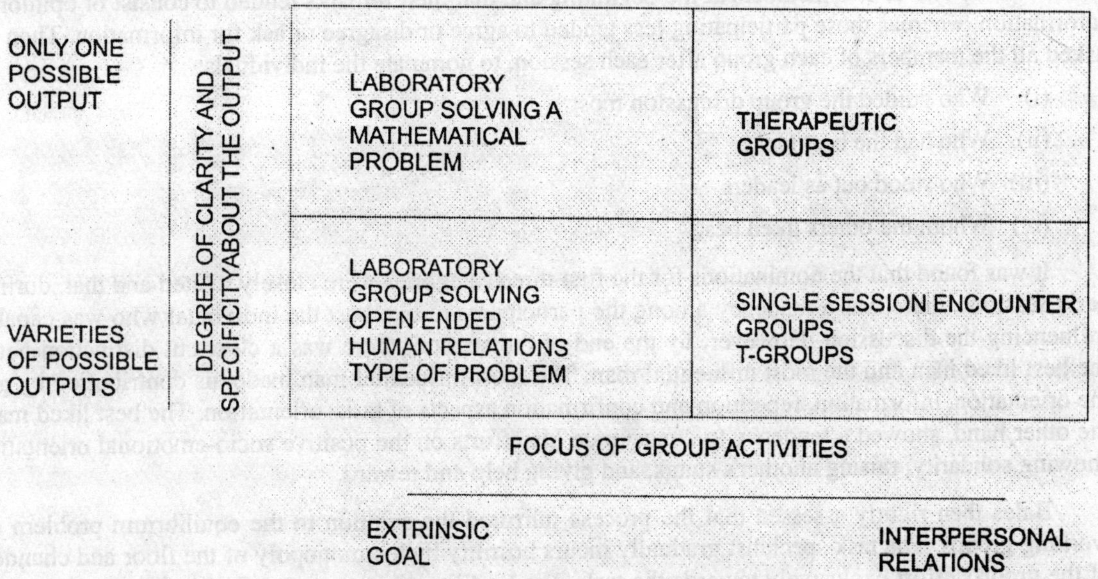

Fig. 4. Dimensions of Group Goals and Activities

I. Socio-Emotional Orientation

(a) Emotionally Positive Responses

(i) Showing solidarity, raising on other's status, giving help and reward;

(ii) Showing release of tension, joking, laughing, and showing satisfaction;

(iii) Agreeing, showing passive acceptance, understanding and complying.

(b) Emotionally Negative Responses

(i) Disagreeing, showing passive rejection, and withholding help;

(ii) Showing tension, asking for help, withdrawing from the field;

(iii) Showing antagonism, deflating another's status, defending or asserting oneself.

II. Task Orientation

(a) Problem Solving Responses: Answers

(i) Giving suggestions and directions, implying autonomy for others;

(ii) Giving opinions, evaluations, analysis, and expressing feeling and wishes;

(iii) Giving orientation, information, repetition and confirmation.

(b) Problem-Solving Responses: Questions

(i) Asking for orientation, information, repetition and confirmation;

(ii) Asking for opinions, evaluation's analyses, and expression of feelings;

(iii) Asking for suggestions, directions and possible ways of action.

In order that this procedure be useful, a number of observers watching the some group should agree with one another about who contributed what and the nature of the contribution. Bale's categories have been used by many researchers to elicit a reasonable degree or agreement among trained observers.

In his observation of the peculiar features of group interaction--Bales noted that participation was dominated by one or two members at the beginning and that their remarks tended to consist of opinions and information, whereas those participating less tended to agree or disagree or ask for information. Then Bales asked all the members of each group after each session, to nominate the individuals:

(i) Who guided the group discussion most

(ii) Who had the best ideas

(iii) Who stood out as leaders

(iv) Whom the others liked best.

It was found that the nominations for the first three categories were closely related and that, during the early sessions, there was a tendency among the participants to like best the individual who was capable of influencing the discussion. However, by the end of the session, there was a clear-cut distinction between the best liked man and the most influential man. The most influential man made his contribution by giving the orientation, information, repetition and confirmation aspects of task- orientation. The best liked man, on the other hand, showed a tendency to concentrate his efforts on the positive socio-emotional orientation of showing solidarity, raising another's status, and giving help and reward.

Bales then rightly assessed that the process mirrored the solution to the equilibrium problem of all working groups. The task specialist gradually incurs hostility by his monopoly of the floor and channelling of the group's effort exclusively towards the task. The hostility can threaten the achievement of the goal as well as the group's existence. The socio-emotional specialist, by countering and neutralizing the hostility with his contributions, keeps the group together. It should be noted, however, that not all of the many groups Bales and others have observed have shown exactly this pattern. For example, some of the groups did not show agreement among their members on who was the most influential man or who was the best liked man right from the beginning.

It has been suggested by Verba that the process is particularly marked under the conditions of a laboratory study and that, in real life functioning groups, the task leader would be someone who was already established in the role of the leaders, i.e., his leadership would be legitimate because of his holding the post by virtue of his qualifications or seniority, and his right to direct the group would behaviourally appropriate to the role, in contrast to Bales situation in which all group members would regard themselves as equal in status. 'Nevertheless, in varying degrees, according to the basis for the leader's authority, the nature of the goal, the group members' motivation to reach it and the possibility of members leaving the group, Bales' analysis is rather plausible.

Schachter's 'Pitchform' Productivity Curves

Another related study, which sheds further light on group dynamics reinforces Bales' study, is that of Stanley Schachter, who tested the effect that group cohesiveness and induction had on productivity. The independent variables in the experiment were cohesiveness and induction, and the dependent variable was productivity. The 'pitchfork' productivity curves in this study imply that highly cohesive groups have very powerful dynamics, both positive and negative, for the organization; while low conhesive groups are not so powerful. The variable of induction is of even greater importance to the organization. The direction in which the highly cohesive group goes, breaking production records or severely restricting output, depends on how it is led. However, leadership will not have a serious negative or positive effect on the low cohesive group. Although Schachter's experiment did not obtain a statistically significant difference between the high and low cohesive groups that were positively induced a follow-up study, which used a more difficult task, obtained it. We now relate Bales study with Schachter's study, whereby additional insight is gained into the process of group dynamics for the solution of the equilibrium problem.

It is obvious that, in a real life functioning group, the task leader, who is often already established in his leadership role, has the continuous task of maintaining a high cohesive group through socio-emotional orientation, so that his high participation, which may not be challenged by group members, does not lead to low cohesiveness. Schachter's study points out that while the situation of low cohesiveness is safe for the management as leadership does not have a serious negative or positive impact on the group; the management, it wishes to maximise productivity, will have to build a cohesive group through socio-emotional orientation and then give it a positive induction or leadership through task orientation. It is only Quadrant II in Fig. 5 which resolves successfully the equilibrium problem, for it is here that the balance is struck between the demands of the task confronting the group through positive induction and the demands created by personal feelings of group members through socio-emotional orientation leading to high cohesive group. in Quadrant I, productivity is low because of low cohesiveness due to low socio-emotional orientation; in Quadrant III, the problem arises because of lack of task orientation. Quadrant IV hardly implies any group phenomenon, for it lacks both socio-emotional and task orientation.

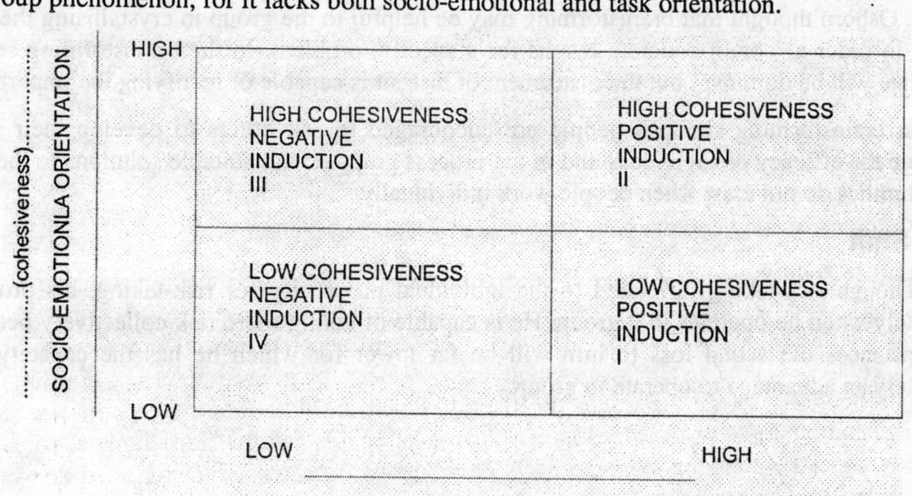

Fig. 5

INDIVIDUAL AND THE GROUP

It is generally seen that a person's behaviour is different when he is alone; even a highly articulate student with a high degree of militancy will be quite submissive and respectful to teachers and university administrators when alone but he will put up a completely different behaviour when he is in the company of his friends in a group. Similar may be the case with the worker in an organization.

This difference in individual behaviour may be on account of the following factors:

(i) Social facilitation;
(ii) Weighting;
(iii) Brainstorming;
(iv) Risk shift; and
(v) Groupness.

Social Facilitation

Social facilitation implies the effects of mere presence of people on individual behaviour. Researches have proved that the perception, judgement, attention and motivation of person change in the social context. Man's perception and judgement when in group are different because he perceives everything through social angle and expectations. In group he is more concerned about his evaluation by the group members. Any soft posture adopted by him may perhaps not be approved by the group members. "So being in the group causes arousal, and in some cases this arousal can be helpful."

Weighting

The weighting of a person individually may be different than collectively in the group. If five persons are working independently on a problem then the individual contribution may be 20 per cent. But the contribution of the same may be much more in a group if he is more articulate, bright, competent and assertive. In a group of five persons if two are assertive then their contribution may be 50 per cent. Sometimes this may cause problem to the group and sometimes it may save the group from complete collapse. In a group of five persons if some loss is sustained then the share of each member will be only 20 per cent as against 100 per cent when he is functioning individually.

Brainstorming

There is the tendency among the group members to evaluate the suggestions given by the other group. One's own idea can at best be pondered or self-introspected. In the process some minor changes may be expected. But in the group each one gets the chance of evaluating the experiences and suggestions of others. Osborn thought that brainstorming may be helpful to the group in crystallising the idea put forth by others in order to obtain concrete results for a specific problem. In the brainstorming session only a few articulate will be dominant but the instrument of dissent is capable of rectifying the imperfections.

In brainstorming sessions people are encouraged to ask others to develop their ideas, assess and evaluate the efficacy of such ideas and in the process grapple with suitable solutions to the problems. These opportunities do not exist when people work individually.

Risk Shift

Though risk-taking is related to the individual propensity for risk-taking, his propensity increases definitely when he operates in a group. He is capable of taking more risk collectively because in the worst circumstances the actual loss to him will be far lower for which he has the capacity to bear. This is definitely an advantage to operate in group.

Groupness

Person operating collectively lead to development of unity in the group. Every member considers himself as a connecting link to prepare a strong chain which may be utilised for achieving wider social purpose.

Oneness or groupness can serve better political and social interests. In a group setting many sub-groups drawn from different departments will thrash out common problems and seek solutions within the set group objective. Similarly, people will achieve their social and political purposes.

In short, the behaviour of people is different in group; it is manifested in the following forms:

(i) People are aroused in the group;

(ii) They can take more risks;

(iii) Groups provide a forum for the exchange of ideas, information and also achievement of socio-economic or political objectives; and

(iv) Finally, it is instrument in forging unity of purpose.

Group Decision Making

A decision is a choice among alternative actions, made after consideration of the likelihood of various out comes occurring as a result of the choice, and according to a decision rule that forces the decision to be made in line with the decision maker's objectives or goals.

Group decision-making is an activity that is based on the old adage that "two heads are better than one".

It permits the coming together of people with heterogeneous characteristics who can understand the problems in a better way and hence, develop creative alternatives leading to effective group performance. Most decisions in organizations, no wonder, are made in a group context only. However, group decision-making is different in process and outcome from decision-making done by individuals.

Group decision-making permits the coming together of people with heterogeneous characteristics who can understand the problems in a better way and hence, develop creative alternatives leading to effective group performance. Experts agree that group decision situations are different from individual decision situations in many ways:

1. The level of group involvement in the decision: For example, an individual leader makes decisions for the group or every group member had an equal vote in the decision making.
2. Complexity: Decision making in groups becomes more complex as the power over the decision becomes more diffused among group members and as conflict over objectives arises.
3. Effectiveness of decisions: There is still great debate among experts about the relative effectiveness of group and individual decisions. As the greater amount of time will be taken to reach a decision, a more step-by-step approach will be taken, more politicking and power brokering will occur, and groups may resort to group decision-making strategies to ultimately arrive at a manageable decision. One hears pros and cons about the relative effectiveness of group versus individual decisions:
   - Several people can gather more information than a single person can do
   - Several people will represent a broader range of values than a single person
   - People will be more committed to the decision if they have participated in several number.

The Danger of Group Decisions

Irvin Janis describes group decisions as most dangerous, a phenomenon he calls 'groupthink.' According to him groupthink is a failure to arrive at an effective decision because of pressures within the group to achieve consensus. According to Janis, pressures for consensus particularly among high level decision groups can lead to the following major symptoms:

1. **Invulnerability:** Group members develop the illusion of invulnerability, which leads them to ignore the expected dangers thus takes dangerous risks.
2. **Rationale:** Group members make extreme rationalizations to explain danger signals or opinion contrary to the consensus of the group.
3. **Morality:** Janis points out that an easy step logically following morality is for group decision makers to ignore the ethical or moral consequences of their acts. Members of the group begin to put their consensus with a mantle of holiness and divine right. Thus group members start to cast debate in absolute terms with moral overtones. Opposing views can then be cast in terms of their inherent evil.
4. **Stereotypes:** Groupthink leads group members to think in stereotyped terms of other people and groups. Opposing leaders on groups can be cast as evil types never to be trusted.
5. **Pressure:** Members under the influence of groupthink place several pressure on other members to the consensus, which has now become a norm.
6. **Self-censorship:** Members who fear that a decision is wrong, or that a better alternative decision might be tried, hold their own counsel and do not share their doubts or questions with other members.
7. **Unanimity:** Self-censorship leads to-the illusion for unanimity of opinion within the group. The illusion of unanimity leads the members to be complacent in their decision and fail to examine the consequences of the decision.
8. **Mindguards:** Many members take on self-appointed roles as protectors of the leadership and key people in the group. These mindguards make sure that key group members are protected from information that might shake the group's confidence. For example, Janis cites the instance of Attorney General Robert Kennedy warning Arthus Schlesinger not to share his doubts about the Bay of Pigs invasion plan with President John F. Kennedy because the President's mind was already made up.

Techniques for Improving Group Decisions

Scientific attempts have been made to develop techniques for improving group decisions. The major among them include the following:

1. The Nominal Group Technique and
2. Delphi Techniques

The nominal group technique is specifically designed to protect group decisions from groupthink problems.The technique demands that groups take specific step to ensure that all views are expressed independently. A nominal group meeting proceeds as follows:

- Each member silently expresses his ideas about the problem and alternative solutions with no consultation with other group members.
- At the end of a time period, say after 15 minutes, each member shares his views with the other members in a highly structured fashion.
- A Secretary then writes down the idea discussed in the meeting. All ideas on the board are then discussed according to their merits.
- The group then votes silently and secretly on the ideas and comes up with a consensus regarding the ordering or ranking of the ideas.

The Delphi technique does not require the physical presents of group members. The gathering of opinion take place through mailed questionnaire or some other form of communication. The anonymous input tends to eliminate the counter productive effects that status, intimidation, emotion, face-saving and argumentation can have in traditional interacting group decision-making procedures. The important steps involved in Delphi techniques are as follows:

1. The problem is first identified by the chairperson and accordingly carefully made questionnaires are sent out to the members of the group.
2. Each member answers the questionnaires and returned to the chairperson who gets a feedback report prepared on the basis of the suggestions received from the members.

3. A feedback report and another questionnaire (more advanced) are sent again to the members for reassessment.
4. Each member, then list out the priority ideas on the basis of carefully analysed feedback report. This process is repeated until a clear-cut solution to the problem arrived at.

This method takes much time in arriving at solution to the problems. However, many large companies adopt this technique to identify and solve complicated problems. The Nominal and Delphi techniques are valuable because they force the group to consider a number of divergent analyses of problems, alternatives, and values in a decisive situation. The structure of the techniques prevent the think symptoms detracting from the quality of the group's decision process.

Group Problem Solving

Problem solving is one of the important functions of leaders. Improved problem solving demands the knowledge of certain important points in the mind of the leader.

They include:

1. The leader must convene a meeting only when there is good reason for it.
2. Rather elaborating the answer to a decision problem, try to define it.
3. Create at atmosphere in which all group members participate freely and actively and allow them to express conflicting views.
4. Try to elicit ideas from the group members rather than supplying to them.
5. Look for best solution to a problem by discussing all the possible alternatives.
6. While resolving conflicting problems, try to find out the trouble makers and prevent blow up situations.
7. Observe the following ruleslaid down by A. Jay, in holding the meetings, such as control the garrulous; draw out the silent; protect the weak; encourage the clashes of ideas; watch out for the suggestion-squashing reflex; come to the most senior people last; close on a note of achievement.

Problem Solving Techniques

Murnighan has suggested the following techniques which are helpful to the managers in better decision making and for improved problem solving:

1. **Group interaction:** This is the general method of holding meeting in which the chairman of the meeting convenes it and explains the problem to the group members. The deliberations are somewhat unstructured and social pressures exert influence. In order to have improved decision making abilities of the group, the leader must clarify the input and try to resolve the conflicting views satisfactorily.
2. **Brainstorming:** It means to use the brain to storm a problem. It is an effective technique to improve the problem solving abilities of groups and increasingly applied by almost all the organizations. Under this technique a group is assembled, presented with the problem and encouraged to produce as many ideas and solutions to a problem. No one is allowed to criticise until the group members came out with new suggestions.
3. **The nominal group technique (NGT) :** NGT restricts verbal interaction between members during the decision-making process. The nominal group consists of a number of individuals acting independently on a paper work and their actions are added together at the end. The nominal group follows a highly structured procedure containing the following steps:
   (1) The target group members are selected and the group leader outlines the problem.
   (2) Each member records his own ideas silently without any interaction with group members and presents his best idea.
   (3) A discussion is held to clarify and evaluate the ideas and the meeting vote on priorities through a ranking or rating procedure.

The nominal group decision is the pooled outcome of the individual votes. This technique is widely used in industry, education and health, etc. in these days.

Assets and Liabilities of Group Problem-Solving and Decision-Making

Every group brings to the problem-solving task some assets and some liabilities. If the assets are utilized and the liabilities avoided, groups are better decision-making units than individuals. According to Maier, the decision-making assets of the group are:

1. **Greater knowledge and information:** A group has more information than an individual. Because many individuals are involved, more data and information can be brought to bear on the decision. The group provides specialized inputs in defining variables and suggests alternatives that the manager acting alone would be unlikely to come up with. The tremendous amount of information and knowledge so generated might help in improved decision-making.
2. **More approaches to a problem:** A group can bring to bear a wider experience, a greater variety of opinion and a more thorough probing of facts than a single individual. Members not only bring new information to the problem but also generate more alternative solutions. "Since group members do not have identical approaches, each can contribute by knocking others out of ruts of thinking."
3. **Increased acceptance:** Participation in decision-making and problem-solving increases acceptance commitment. Many studies have shown that when participation is given, people see the solution as 'their own' and acquire a psychological stake in its success.
4. **Better comprehension of the decision:** When a manager makes a decision individually he must relay it to those who carry it out. Failure to implement decision effectively can often be traced to garbled communication. When those who must execute the decision have participated in making it, the chance of communication failure is reduced. People understand the decision better because they saw and heard it develop.

Decision Making Liabilities

1. **Time consuming:** Groups are notorious time wasters. In the meetings, minutes are taken but hours are wasted. The time spend in discussion, quite often, within committee may exceed the importance of the issue itself.
2. **Pressures to conform:** Groups create pressures toward conformity. Other infirmities like group think attack work groups and prevent them from being more effective. A clubby feeling of 'we-ness' compels members to become chummy and compromise on the first satisfying decision that emerges. The final decision may be so extremely watered down or 'compromised to death' that the horse does not turn out to be a camel. The decision arrived at may not be satisfactory to anyone.
3. **Individual domination:** Group members are not as alike as peas in a pod. In many groups a dominant individual emerges and slices out more than his share of influence on the outcomes, even though his problem solving ability may be poor. Thus quite a good number of decision arrived at in group meetings are in fact product of excessive compromise, logrolling and one-person domination. Domination is counterproductive; it puts a damper on the group's best problem solvers.
4. **Conflicting alternative solutions:** When groups are confronted with a problem, the major goal is to obtain the best possible solution. But as alternative solutions are put forward, group members may begin to view and defend their own from a 'win or lose' standpoint, instead of examining objectively the merit of each. "The clash of ideas that develops in a group can breed resentment and hurt feelings."
5. **The problem of responsibility:** The group is composed of several individuals and hence, it is easy to pass the buck in decision-making. Moreover, by spreading the responsibility for a decision, groups can occasionally come up with ill-conceived or irresponsible conclusions.

Improved Problem Solving

Improved problem solving is an important function of leaders. From this standpoint, a leader has one major task: to manage discussion so that the group engages in true problem solving. According to Maier true leaders must forego the temptation to sell their own solutions through dramatic monologues during group sessions and rely on the resources of the entire group. Improved problem solving demands the observance of the following points:

1. The leader must call for a meeting only when there is a good reason to have one.
2. Establish precise times for meetings to begin and end.
3. Rather than emphasizing the answer to a decision problem, emphasize defining the problem (like the Japanese).
4. See that all group members participate actively, allow them to air conflicting views freely.
5. Try to elicit ideas from the group; do not supply them.
6. Discuss all the alternatives; look for a best solution rather than to sell a particular alternative.
7. While resolving conflicting views spot the trouble shooters promptly and prevent blow ups.
8. Observe the following rules while conducting the meetings control the garrulous; draw out the silent; protect the weak: encourage the clashes of ideas; watch out for the suggestion-squashing reflex; come to the most senior people last; close on a note of achievement.

REFERENCES

R.F. Bales, *Interaction Process Analysis: A Method for the Study of Small Groups*, Addison-Wieley Publishing, Reading, Mass, 1950, p.3.

J.W. McDavid and M. Morari, *Social Psychology: Individuals, Groups, Societies*, Harper & Row, New York, 1968, p.237.

Bernard M. Bass, *Leadership, Psychology and Organizational Behaviour*, Harper & Row, New York, 1960, p.39.

G.C. Homans, *The Human Group,* Harcourt Brace Jovanovich, 1950, p.1.

D.L. Forsyth, *An Introduction to Group Dynamics*, Brooks, Cole, Monterey C.A., 1983.

Keith Davis: "Human Behaviour at Work", Tata McGraw Hill Publishing Company Ltd., New Delhi, Sixth Edition, 1982 (Reprint), p.183.

Fred Luthans: "*Organizational Behaviour*", McGraw Hill, Kogakusha, Tokyo, International Student Edition (Second Edition), 1977, p.363.

For details refer to Joe Kelly: "Organizational Behaviour", New Edition, Richard D. lrwin Inc. and The Dorsey Press, Homewood, 111., 1974, p.366.

For details refer to Terence R. Mitchell: "People in the Organizations: Understanding the Behaviour", McGraw Hill Book Co., New York, 1978.

E.L. Trist and W. Bamforth, "Some Social and Psychological Consequences of the Longwall Method of Coal Getting", Human Relations, Vol. 4, No.1, 1951, pp.3-38.

William F. Whyte, "*Human Relations in Restaurant Industry*", McGraw Hill Book Company, 1948.

Linda N. Jewell and H. Joseph Reitz, *Group Effectiveness in Organizations*, Scott Foresman, Glenview, III. 1981.

George C. Homan, *The Human Group*, Marcourt. Brace and World Inc. New York, 1950, pp. 41-44.

William G. Scott, *Organization Theory*, Richard D. Irwin Inc. Homewood, 1967, p.83.

K.W. Mossholder. A.G. Bedeian. and A.A. Armenakis, "*Group Process – Work Outcome Relationship: A Note on the Moderating Effects of Self-Esteem*," Academy of Management Journal, September 1982, pp. 575-85.

Daniel Brass, "*Men's and Women's Networks: A Study of Interaction Patterns and Influence in an Organization*," Academy of Management Journal, September 1986, pp. 327-43; Connie Sitterly and Beth Duke, *A Woman's Place: Management* (Englewood Cliffs, N.J.: Prentice Hall, 1988).

Amsa, "*Organizational Culture and Work Group Behaviour: An Empirical Study," Journal of Management Studies*, May 1986, pp. 347-62.

See Larry Hirschhorn, *The Workplace Within: Psychodynamics of Organizational Life* (Cambridge, Mass.:p MIT Press, 1988).

M. Theodore, *New Combination: The Accquintance Process*, Holt Richart and Winston, New York, 1961.

John W. Thaibout and Harold H. Kelly, *The Social Psychology of Groups*, John Wiley & Sons, New York, 1959.

Szilagyi and Wallace, *Organizational Behaviour and Performance,* pp. 261-264.

J. Weitz, *Job Expectancy and Survival, Journal of Applied Psychology*, 1956, pp. 245-247.

M. E. Shaw, *Group Dynamics, The Psychology of Small Group Behaviour*, McGraw Hill, New York, 1971, pp. 169-180.

R. Libert, *The Human Organization: Its Management and Value*, McGraw Hill, New York, 1967.

J. Thompson, *Organization in Action*, McGraw Hill, New York, 1967.

Libert's Linking Pin Theory from New Patterns of Management by R. Libert, McGraw Hill Book Company, New York.

F.L. Trist, G.W. Higgin, H. Murray and A.B. Pullock, Organizational Choice, Tavistock, London, 1963.

C.P. Alderfer, Groups and Intergroup Relations, in J.R. Hackman and J.L. Suttle, Eds. *Improving Life at Work: Behavioural Science Approaches to Organizational Choice*, Good year Publishing Co., California, 1977, p.230.

Leon Festinger, Stanley Schachter and Kurt Black: "Social Pressures in an Informal Group: A Study of Human Factors in Housing", Standard University Press, Stanford, Calif., 1963.

George C. Homans, "The Human Group", Brace and World, Inc.,' New York, 1950, pp. 43-44.

William G. Scott: "Organization Theory", Richard D. Irwin, Inc., Homewood, 111., 1967, p.83.

Theodore Newcomb: "The Acquitance Process", Holt, Rinehart and Winston, Inc., New York, 1961.

John W. Thibant and Harold H. Kelley, "The Social Psychology of a Group", John Wiley & Sons, Inc., New York,1959.

Quoted in Terrence R. Mitchell, "*People in Organization*", McGraw Hill Book Co., New York, 1978, pp. 180-200.

Gahagan, Judy, *Interpersonal and Group Behaviour* (Ed.), Peter Herriot, London, Methuen and Co. Ltd., 1975, pp. 98-105.

Balės, R.F.K., and Salter, P.E., *Role Differencetiation in Small Decision-Making Groups*. In T. Parsons and R.F. Bales (Eds.), *Family, Socialization and Interaction Process*, New York, The Free Press, 1955.

Bales, R.F., Interaction Process Analysis: A Method for the Study of Small Groups, Reading, Massachusetts, Addison-Wesley 1950.

Verba, S., Small Groups and Political Behaviour – a Study of Leadership, N.J., Princeton University Press, 1961.

Schachter, S. Ellertson, N., McBride, D. and Gregory, Doris: 'An Experimental Study of Cohesiveness and Productivity', Human Relations, 1951, 4, pp. 222-239.

Berkowitz, Leonard, 'Group Standards, Cohesiveness and Productivity', Human Relations, 1954, 7, pp. 509-519.

Irvin Jaanis Victims of Groupthink, Boston, Houghton, Miffilin, 1972.

N. Daldey, *The Delphi Method; An Experiment Study of Group Opinions* Santa Monica, Rand Corporation, 1968.

F. Luthans and M.J. Martinka, *The Practice of Supervision and Management*, Toyko, McGraw Hill, 1979, pp. 346-350.

Jay, *How to Run a Meeting? HBR*, March-April, 1976, pp. 43-57.

J.K. Murnighan, *Group Decision Making: What Strategies Should You Use? Management Review*, Feb. 1981, pp. 55-62.

N.R.F. Major, "*Assets and Liabilities in Group Problem Solving*", *Psychological Review*, July, 1967, pp. 239-249. See also R. Tillman Jr., "Committees on Trial", *HBR*, May-June, 1960.

F. Luthans and M.J. Martinko, *The Practice of Supervision and Management*, Tokyo, McGraw Hill 1979, pp. 346-350.

CHAPTER

17

Groups At Work

What do the following have in common: a military combat unit, three couples getting together for dinner, board of directors of a large corporation, and the three-person cockpit crew of a commercial airliner? As you probably guessed, the answer is that they are all groups. But, of course, they are very different kinds of groups. People join for different reasons.

HOW WORK-GROUPS ARE FORMED?

Work-groups are small groups within the work-organization. Such groups may be formal or informal.

Formal groups are departments, sections, units, plant, etc. created by the organization while informal groups within organization are trade unions, worker-associations, etc. But now the question is how these work-groups are formed?

When a new employee joins the department of an organization he is quite innocent, does not know anybody and therefore there is no interaction between him and the other members of the department. But as soon as he comes into contact with others while at work in the department, old employees or say his colleagues talk to him about matters-though quite informal, relating to his work, work-group, supervisor, his family, etc. Soon, they all become familiar to each other. They sit, smoke, take tea or lunch together. In this way, they began to interact with each other. Gradually, the new employee is accepted as a member of the group. They teach him group-norms and culture. Soon, he feels himself as a member of the group.

Types of Groups

An organization has technical requirements that arise from its stated goals. The accomplishment of these goals requires that certain tasks be performed and that employees be assigned to perform these tasks. As a result, most employees are members of a group based on their positions in the organization. These are formal groups. In addition, whenever individuals associate on a fairly continuous basis, groups tend to form whose activities may be different from those required by the organization. These are informal groups. Both formal groups and informal groups exhibit the same general characteristics.

FORMAL GROUPS

Formal groups are deliberately structured to subserve organizational interest. They are formed to accomplish the specific functions and organizational goals. These functions and goals are related to overall organizational goal. They serve as means to formal ends. They are shown on the organizational chart. Groups are empowered with the authority by the institution. Authority is always delegated to the position and not to the person. Therefore, position is important and not the person in the formal groups. Authority in formal groups is not acquired but delegated from the above and it always flows downward and never upward.

The status of a group is determined by its position on the organizational chart or responsibilities of the job, it performs. It is developed according to the technical requirements.

All communications to formal groups are sent through chain of command. There are predetermined rules and regulations which are to be followed by every member of the group. The behaviour of members is regulated through such rules and regulations. Any violation of rules and regulations attracts penalty-financial or non-financial.

Formal groups are formed by the management of an organization, so they are controlled and can be abolished by the management at any time it likes.

Different types of Formal Groups: The formal groups may be classified as followed:

1. **Permanent and Temporary Formal Groups:** On the basis of permanent formal groups may be permanent or temporary. Permanent formal groups may be permanent or temporary. Permanent formal groups are formed by the organization on the permanent basis and more or less exist till the organization exists. Board of directors, departmental units, staff groups, standing committees are some of the examples of formal groups.

Groups formed by the organization, to carry the particular work or to perform the specific task are temporary formal groups. A committee or study groups, appointed to analyse or review the pay structure in the organization are examples of temporary formal groups. These groups come to an end as soon as the tasks assigned to them.

2. Command Groups: The authority structure forms and determines the boundaries of divisions, departments and section within the organization and these departments or sections, or divisions are known as command groups. The smallest command group consists of supervisor and his subordinates and the largest one consists of top management and the total personnel in the work force. There is so many other group in between these two extremes.

The chain of command as expressed by authority, responsibility and accountability, allocates the roles of each individuals in the command group. It also spells out the member-authority relationship which exists between them. The superior of a particular group is the leader who performs important functions for his group. He sets goals for the group, suggests ways and means to get them and settles jurisdictional issues which arise between subordinates. The superior is an effective instrument for downward communication and an initiation for upward communication.

3. Functional Groups: Functional groups are those groups whose primary task is to carry on the operations. In many cases, the functional groups may be congruent with the authority groups. Thus, a single department in the organization would probably be both command group and a functional group. The department is a command group within the authority structure but the staff working in that department engaged in a particular activity and directed and coordinated by the same superior may form a functional group such as typists, clerks, salesman, etc. Thus a command group may have several functional groups.

The functional groups can be again classified into team, task and technological groups. The distinction between these group involves the method role allocation and role fulfilment.

(a) Team Group: specifies no fixed role to its individual. The general role of the group is set and the members of the group are allocated the roles according to the needs of the goal. Thus, roles of member in a team group are interchangeable without any clash.

(b) Task Group: specifies a fixed job for each of its members and lays down the job description. Thus, roles of the members are not interchangeable and if superior does so, it is not without much personal resistance and friction between superior and the member.

(c) Technological Group: is something different. Here the roles are assigned by the management. The position of the job is fixed and the methods are laid down and the speed of work is fixed by some device. Thus, members of the group have no choice over the method and the speed of the work.

The difference between these groups is not clear and more research needs to be done in this direction for, there is reason to believe that a group can be organized in a number of ways.

4. **Status Group:** Status groups involve the member of the same status in an organization. The term is ambiguous in the sense that in includes a number of different rankings of positions which are frequently inconsistent with each other. Moreover, the formally prescribed status distinction is extremely hazy. It makes distinction on a functional basis between manager and workers, on an authoritarian basis between superiors and subordinates, and on a payment basis between salary and wages earners. In some cases status distinction is made on the basis of facilities or amenities to be enjoyed by the members. More often, the status distinction is made on wage and salary structure that leads to all sorts of status reactions amongst work groups.

(b) INFORMAL GROUPS

The members of the formal groups are asked to perform the functions which are necessary for him considering his role status in the organization. But as because men can be engaged to work as a whole and not in parts, there are number of needs which cannot be satisfied through formal groups. So, they form other groups by interacting each other, to satisfy some of their other needs which could not be satisfied by formal groups. These other groups are called informal groups. There may be innumberable informal group in a formal organization. They are generally small and serve different interests of their members.

An informal group arises voluntarily and spontaneously and they generally satisfy the social needs of the members of the group. Each informal group has its own informal leader who is elected among the members of the group not on the basis of authority he possesses in the formal group but on the basis of age, seniority, technical knowledge, respect etc. So authority is to be earned from members of the group. Authority in the informal group is given to the person and not to the position. As soon as the members lose their confidence in him, he will no more be the leader of the group.

Communication in informal groups posses through informal channel, mostly verbal or by gesture. Behaviour of members are regulated by norms, values and beliefs of the group. Violaters of norms are punished through non-financial modes such as social boycott, loss of prestige and status within the group.

Informal groups, unlike formal ones, cannot be abolished. Any attempt to destroy them may cause several

Different Types of Informal Groups: Informal groups may be of different types as follows:

1. **Friendship Kinship Group:** This kind of group involves close personalities as friends or relatives who are well-known to each other beforehand. Mostly these groups are found in pairs and are useful in spreading influence and information.
2. **Cliques:** These groups consist of colleagues and associates who normally observe certain norms and standards. They are closely intimate to each other. The number of members tends to be smaller say five or six (4). The object of this type of group is to provide recognition to each other and exchange information of mutual interest.

   Dalton has noted **three types of cliques:**

   (i) **Vertical Clique:** Such cliques consist of people working in the same department irrespective of their rank difference. Such groups develop because of earlier acquaintance of people or the dependence of superior upon his subordinates for some formal purposes.

   (ii) **Horizontal Clique:** This group consists of people of more or less same rank and working more or less in the same area. Such groups are formed cutting across organizational boundaries. Such members find some points of commonness and keeping the objectives in mind, come together. This is the most common form of informal group.

   (iii) **Random or Mixed Clique:** This group is a mix of vertical and horizontal cliques. People come from different ranks, departments and locations to form such type of clique, having some common objective in mind. The member may be residing in the same locality, travelling by the same bus or trains or may be members of the same club.
3. **Sub-Cliques:** The group consists of some members of a clique inside the organization along with some other persons outside the clique. The members of the clique in a sub-clique recognise, but

partially, members included in a sub-clique but who are not the members of the main clique because of their association with them.

4. **Isolates:** Actually it is not a group. An individual who is not the member of any group is called isolate. Such isolates do not participate in any social activity organised by the group. They avoid people and people avoid them.

If employees attainting patterns were documented, it would become readily apparent that they belong to numerous and often overlapping groups. A distinction has been made between two broad classifications of groups, formal and informal. The major difference between them is that formal command and task groups are designated by the formal organization as a means to an end. Informal interest and friendship groups are important for their own sake. They satisfy a basic human need for association.

The Close-Up on avoiding apathy illustrates clearly the importance of groups and how intelligent managers recognize their importance and try to use them productively.

(c) DISTINCTION BETWEEN FORMAL AND INFORMAL GROUPS

We have explained explicitly the meaning and nature of formal and informal groups. Now, we shall make an attempt to distinguish these two groups on the basis of their basic characteristics. These two groups differ from each other on the following grounds:

1. **Origin:** A formal group is deliberately structured and planned to subserve organizational interest. The manager decides about the activities of each individual and his interaction with others. The come together because of the interdependence of their operations or their mutual dependence on their common boss. An informal group, on the other hand emerges voluntarily and spontaneously. In fact, the formal organization itself contains the seeds for the emergence of informal groups. It allocates people in different departments, work – locations and time – schedules and while performing their tasks, the members develop their activities, interactions and sentiments towards each other which are not cared for by the formal organization.
2. **Purpose of the Group Formation:** The main purpose of formal groups is to serve the organization as means to formal ends. While the informal groups provide social satisfaction and stability to work groups.
3. **Authority:** The authority to a formal group is given by the institution according to the position on the organization chart. It is given to the position and not to the man concerned. Whosoever be in that position, will enjoy the authority. Authority in such groups is acquired through delegation from the above to the downward. Contrarily, the authority in an informal group is earned or given permissively by the members of the group. It is given to a person considering his age, seniority, competence, etc. and not to the position and so it flows horizontally or at times, even upward.
4. **Communication:** All messages – upward or downward – pass through the chain of command strictly as given on the organization chart. In an informal group, all messages are passed through informal channel because there is no such chain of command. People remain in mutual contact with each other, they learn about every person of group what is going on in the organization.
5. **Control on Behaviour:** Behaviour of the people of the formal group is regulated by the rules and regulations framed with an intention to attain rationality and efficiency. Violation of any rule attracts penalty and punishment. In an informal group, on the other hand, behaviour of the members is controlled through norms, values and beliefs of the group. The members of the informal group may compel any member of the group to disassociate himself from the group, if he is continuously violating the norms of the group after giving him proper warning.
6. **Size:** Formal groups are quite large because personal relations have no concern there while the informal groups tend to remain smaller so as to keep it within limits of personal relations.
7. **Nature of Group:** Formal groups are stable in character and continues for a longer period. Informal groups are quite unstable because they are subject to sentiments and feelings of the group members. A particular informal group ceases to exist as soon as its purpose is solved.

8. **Sanctions to Members:** Members are suitably rewarded or punished for their work done in a formal group according to the formal rules and regulations of the group. Rewards or punishments may be financial or non-financial. But in an informal group, the efforts of the person are recognised mainly through non-financial rewards or punishments generally in terms of feelings, status, and prestige.
9. **Abolition of the Group:** As formal groups are subject to management control, they can be abolished at the discretion of the proper authority while a particular informal group cannot be destroyed because any attempt to destroy it may lead to formation of several other groups because there is no management control over it. Management cannot destroy it because it has not formed that.
10. **Number of Groups:** The whole organization (formal group) is divided into several units and sub-units working for the common cause but a large number of informal groups are found in an institution and some even outside the institution. An individual may be the member of a number of informal groups for different purposes. So, there is overlapping of membership and multiple groups.

Thus formal groups can very easily be differentiated with informal groups on the basis of the above grounds.

Other Types of Groups

Open and Closed Groups

This distinction may be highlighted in relation to four important variables:

(i) Changing group membership;

(ii) Frame of reference;

(iii) Time perspective; and

(iv) Equilibrium.

Changing Group Membership

An open group is constantly adding and losing members. In a closed group, the membership is stable.

Frame of Reference

The frame of reference expands with the induction of new members with the ideas. Accordingly, the group's activity also gets expanded in an open group. In a closed group everything is stabilised.

Time Perspective

The open group brings in constantly change and instability. This results in member's perspective to orient towards the present or very near future. Conversely, the closed group maintains much longer time perspective horizon of the group.

Equilibrium

Equilibrium may be stated as a state of balance or stability. An open group must develop methods for counteracting the disequilibrium of constant change. Increasing the size of group is suggested as one method of maintaining equilibrium. Another means of increasing the state of equilibrium is association of old members of the group such as alumni organization with business.

Examples: Students' organizations are open but a Board of Directors is a closed group.

Primary or Small Groups

Primary group has been defined by Charles H. Coolay. He stated the definition in his book "Social Organization", first published in 1909: By primary groups, I mean those characterised by intimate face-to-face association and cooperation. His concept was improved further by George Homans who has described the primary group as The Human Group. He has described it as a "number of persons, who communicate with one another, often over a span of time, and who are few enough so that each person is able to communicate with all the others, not at secondhand, through other people, but face-to-face".

Analysing further, a primary group apart from being small must have a feeling of comradeship, loyalty and a commonsense of values among its members.

Thus all primary groups are small groups but all small groups are not primary groups. The small group has to fulfil only one consideration and that is smallness of the membership or size of group, e.g., family or a group of peers.

Reference Groups

A reference group is a group which is referred to by an individual as a standard for self-evaluation. It is also referred to as a source of personal value and attitude of individual to which he belongs. Analysing further, the reference group provides two functions to the individual: (i) Social comparison and (ii) Social validation.

Social comparison provides any individual the opportunity of comparing himself with other fellow members of the group and find out the possibilities of read just in one's own behaviour to conform to social behaviour in to form of behaviour pattern of other members of the group.

Social validation, in other words, is social sanction or approval of a certain act of an individual in the group.

In case there is divergence in the behaviour of an individual and other members of the group, he shall have to mend himself according to the norms of social validation.

Sayles Classification of Groups

The creation of informal groups depends very much on the physical location of people, the nature of their work, their time schedules, and so on; these groups, therefore, arise out of a particular combination of 'formal' factors and human needs. The Hawthorne Studies were the first to point out their importance for organizational effectiveness. While numerous studies have focuses on work groups, one of the most important for the managers is that of Lanyard Sayles.

Although many approaches to group behaviour do not differentiate among types of groups, he recognised the fact that some groups consistently react quite differently from other; and in one respect in which non-management work groups vary considerably in their level of protest activities of their tendencies to petition for improved working conditions.

Between 1951 and 1955, Sayles studied three hundred work groups from a hundred plants in variety of industries to determine the factors which influence the nature and frequency of protest actions taken by work groups. In reviewing the data from his sample.

Sayles made another classification of informal groups in an organization from the standpoint of pressure tactics adopted by them, emergence of clearly identifiable leadership, internal unity and their participation in union activity. The basis for this classification is their orientation towards formal organization. He pointed out four types of such informal groups as: 1. Apathetic group, 2. The erratic group, 3. The strategic group, and 4. The conservative group.

1. **The Apathetic Group:** These groups are the least likely to develop the grievances or engage in any pressure tactics. Although incidents occur on various occasions but workers are mostly disinclined to challenge the decision or attempt to gain something. Extra for themselves. There are evidences of workers' discontent but often it is not focused in terms of any specific demands or grievanes. In the group no one emerges as an acceptable leader and therefore there is lack of clearly identified leadership.

These groups do not engage in union activities and generally are jealousies and interpersonal problems within the group. Group cohesiveness is absent as a primary characteristics of the group. The members are generally low paid and from the low skilled job. Thus, there are four behaviour characteristics of these groups:

(i) Relatively few grievances or use of pressure tactics.

(ii) Lack of clearly identified or accepted leadership.

(iii) Internal disunity and frictions over petty matters.
(iv) Evidence of suppressed discontent.

2. **The Erratic Group:** Members in the erratic group are easily inflamed and easily pacified. The employees themselves are not very much serious about their problem raised and they take the grievance as minor. Sometimes they infuriate with the management without working into a major conflagration, mass demonstration or a wild-cat strike etc. They may be pacified even in no time gaining nothing from the management. Deep-rooted grievances exist within these groups over long period without any apparent reaction in terms of group behaviour.

Any active member within the group may assume the leadership. Management puts these groups in the very dangerous list because the time and the energy of management and union officials in evolving a grievance procedure are lost in solving the problems of these tension areas. There is cooperation and unity in the group. Internally these groups have autocratic leadership that keeps them in line. The groups are generally consist of members doing similar and identical work.

3. **The Strategic Group:** The strategic group refers to member's ability to prepare a strategy and not the location of the group. These groups plan have a well planned and consistent grievance activity and exercise continuous pressure. They seem to be shrewdly calculating pressure groups which never tire of objecting to unfavourable management decisions, seeking loopholes in existing policies and policies that rebound to their benefits and comparing their benefits with those of other groups in the plant. The demand constant attention for their problems and have the ability to reinforce their demands by group action. The amount and kind of pressure the strategic groups exert are carefully measured, so the degree of their behaviour is predictable and this consistency in their behaviour is seen as a virtue.

Members of such groups are generally performing technologically independent job and are well placed. They are highly united and maintain cohesiveness within their group. The leadership of these groups is consisted of highly active and influential group members each of whom specialise in such function as dealing with the management, dealing with the union, maintaining internal unity or taking the lead in voicing dissatisfaction.

4. **Conservative Group:** The conservative group consists of persons who possess critical or scarce skills. They are in the strong position in the organization and the management is also worried about them but they are least active in union politics and certainly there was little chance of using concerted action without warning. These are strong hence are most stable among informal groups. Such groups exercise restrained pressure for highly specified objectives and display internal unity and self-assurance. Thus these groups are much more conservative in their grievance activities. There are very little evidences of turmoil, trouble or concerted activity.

Functions of a Group

One reason why groups are so common is that they fulfil a wide range of functions both for their members and for the larger organization. Basically they serve two kinds of functions in organizations i.e., task and maintenance.

Task Functions

These are the group activities performed to achieve organizational goals. They include:

- Working on a complex and interdependent task which is too difficult for anyone individual to perform and which cannot be easily broken down into independent tasks.
- Generating new ideas or creative solutions to solve problems that require inputs from a number of people.
- Serving liaison or coordinating functions among several work groups whose work is to some extent interdependent.
- Facilitating the implementation of complex decisions.
- Serving as a vehicle for training new employees.

Maintenance Functions

Organization members bring with them a variety of needs, and groups can satisfy many of them. The aspects of group activity that help organizational members satisfy their needs are called maintenance functions. They include the following:

- Fulfilling members' need for social interaction, including the needs for affiliation, friendship, support and love,
- Providing sense of identity and self-esteem. People identify themselves by the groups they belong to,
- Reducing anxiety and uncertainty. By talking over and sharing their concerns with other members in the group, people can reduce their anxiety and sense of powerlessness,
- Helping group members solve their own personal problems. Group members help each other in dealing with personal problems such as sickness and boredom, and provide emotional support.

The following table summarises the functional activities of the group.

Table 1. Functional Activities of Groups

Task Functions	Maintenance Functions
1. Initiating, suggesting a new way of looking at a problem, or new activity.	1. Harmonizing, compromising, reconciling disagreements, getting others to explore differences.
2. Seeking useful information or opinions. Requesting facts, asking about feelings, asking for ideas or values.	2. Gate keeping, inviting others to talk, suggesting time limits or other procedures to permit wider participation.
3. Giving useful information or opinions Offering facts, stating a belief, making. suggestions.	3. Encouraging, being friendly, warm, responsive through works or facial expression.
4. Clarifying, providing for meaning, defining terms restating, enlarging or stating issues.	4. Following, going alongwith the group, being a good listener, showing that words are heard.
5. Summarising, reviewing, bringing related ideas together, restating suggestions of others.	5. Standard setting, testing the group attitude towards its procedures, stating values or ethics.
6. Consensus testing, checking to see if the group is ready to decide sending up a trial balloon.	

In essence, groups are important in organizations because they have the potential to satisfy both organizational and individual goals. A group can function effectively if it can perform both the task and maintenance functions.

What do groups do for Organization?

Organizational life is replete with horror stories of how groups operate a 'demolition squads' cutting down organizational work to meaningless levels. In an effort to cut down much militant groups to size managers arrogantly try to impede group relationships by making frequent transfers, by assigning people who are known to be incompatible to the same work group or by erecting physical barriers between departments considered to be vulnerable 'spots' for group pressures. Such efforts, though justifiable in extreme situations, backfire, because, as we have seen, employees have a strong need for affiliation. Lack of social interaction is likely to lead to greater turnover, absenteeism, accidents, lower quality of work etc. Managers must understand that groups are an inevitable and useful future of organizational life. Their essential job will be to manage organizational groups in such a way as to make them more productive and satisfying to their members. Groups perform three functions that are important to an enterprises success.

(a) **Socialization of new employees:** The work group teaches the new employee the work norms, that is, how to behave at work. It orients and educates the new employees into the enterprise's work rules and norms and helps him under control.

(b) **Getting the job done:** The work group teaches the employee how to cope with the job. Truly speaking, it is the organization that provides the necessary training for employees to do the job, but in practice it is the work groups within the organization, that help the employees learn how to interact with the rest of the organization and how to get the job done.

(c) **Decision making:** Well established groups that are operating effectively can contribute to organizational members by turning out better decisions. Two heads are better than one.

Committee – A Formally Designed Group

Any discussion of group within the context of organizational behaviour would not be complete without thorough analysis of the committee form of organization. The committee is the most important type of formally designated group found in today's organizations. Unfortunately these committees are often described in the following manner:

A camel is a horse designed by a committee.

The best committee is a five-man committee with four members absent.

In a committee, minutes are taken but hours are wasted.

A committee is a collection of the unfit appointed by the unwilling to perform the unnecessary.

If you want to kill an idea, form a committee for it.

Although these remarks are jokes, they represent the widespread negativism attached to the committee form of organization.

Despite the attacks, all indications are that the use and perceived value of committees in organizations is on the increase. Studies have found an increasing number of committees with enlarged responsibilities and power. Most committees seem to serve as a focal point for the exchange of different view point and information, but some are making major decisions. There is an indication that the use of committees is directly related to the size of the organization. A survey of more than a thousand Harvard Business Review subscribers found that 94 per cent of the firms with over 10,000 employees had formal committees, while only 64 per cent of the companies with fewer than 250 employees utilized committees. With today's organizations becoming increasingly large and complex. The committee form of organization undoubtedly becomes more important and more widely used in the future.

The Nature and Functions of Committees

There are many definitions of committees. Haimann and Scott say that 'a committee is a group of people who function collectively.' Koontz and O'Donnell state that "a committee is a group of persons to whom, as a group, , some matter is committed." These and most other definitions stress the idea that committees consist of groups that are formed to accomplish specific objectives. They can be conducted in either a formal or an informal manner. Most often, committees have specified duties and authority. Some committees meet on an ad hoc basis to solve some specialized problem and then disband. Committees may be referred to as teams, commissions, boards, groups, or task forces.

Committees are found in all types of organizations. There is a myriad of committees in government, educational, religious, and business organizations. For example, the board of directors is a type of committee present in all corporate forms of organization. Other prevalent types in business are the finance, executive, operations, bonus, audit, and grievance committees. Although they are more frequent at the top of the pyramid, there is usually some type of formal committee on every level of the organization.

Committees perform many different functions. They may act in a service, advisory, coordinating, information, or final decision-making capacity. In the decision-making function, a committee acts in a line capacity and is usually termed a plural executive. Many companies are moving toward the plural-executive concept rather than a single executive head. One top executive noted.

There is a tendency to include more than a single man in the role of chief executive in order to provide greater breadth. I suspect that this will become more and more popular in larger and more complex companies.

Positive Attributes of Committees

Committee action has many advantages over individual action. Perhaps the greatest attribute of the committee group is the combined and integrated judgment which it can offer. It is the adage that two heads are better than one. To speak optimistically, committee members bring with them a wide range of experience, knowledge, ability, and personality characteristics. This agglomeration lends itself to the tremendous amount of diverse knowledge that is required to solve modern organizational problems. An averaging of personalities and a source of creative ideas are also needed by today's organizations. The committee form of organization can contribute a great deal to these requirements.

Committees can be a very effective organizational device to help reduce conflict and promote coordination between departments and specialised subunits. Through committee discussion, each member can empathize with the other fellows purposes and problems. In effect committees foster horizontal communication. An example is the interdepartmental meeting where each member receives information and insights about the other departments. The production department is informed of delivery dates being promised by sales, and sales gets a first-hand look at the problems it may be creating for production scheduling and inventory. The committee is about the only formalised vehicle for horizontal communication in most traditional forms of organization structure.

From a human standpoint the biggest advantage of committees may be the increased motivation and commitment derived from participation. By being involved in the analysis and solution of committee problems individual members will more readily accept and try to implement what has been decided. A committee can also be instrumental in human development and growth. Group members, especially the young and inexperienced, can take advantage of observing and learning from other members with much experience or with different viewpoints and knowledge. A committee provides the opportunity for personal development that the individual would never receive on his own.

Negative Attributes of Committees

The last section pointed out some definite advantages of committees. Traditionally, management theorists stressed the negative aspects. The classical theorist Luther Gulick wanted to limit the use of committees to abnormal situations because he thought they were too dilatory, irresponsible, and time-consuming for normal administration. Urwick was an even harsher Eritic. He listed no less than fourteen faults of committees, the main ones being that committees are often irresponsible are apt to be bad employers and are costly. Thus, the classicists tended to emphasize the negative but the more modern view recognizes that committees have both positive and negative attributes.

One very practical disadvantage is that committees are indeed time-consuming and costly. Anyone who has participated in committee meetings can appreciate the satirical definition cited earlier that a committee takes minutes but wastes hours. The nature of a committee is that everyone has an equal chance to speak out but this takes a great deal of time and time costs money.

Most often, cost is discussed with regard to committee versus individual action. Taking another approach, it can be argued that committees are actually less expensive when compared to a series of repetitious conferences. In terms of man-hours, a committee meeting where an executive meets with five others for one hour represents six man-hours. On the other hand, if the same executive meets for one hour with each of the five men individually, the expended time turns out to be ten man-hours. However one cannot automatically condemn all committees as being excessively expensive. The nature and purpose must be considered when assessing cost. Furthermore, it is difficult, if not impossible, to quantify for cost purposes the advantages of a committee in terms of member motivation and quality of decision or problem solution.

From an organization standpoint there are some potential problems inherent in committees. The most obvious is divided responsibility. Urwick made the analogy that a committee is like a corporation with "neither a soul to be damned nor a body to be kicked." This is saying that in a committee there is group or corporate but no individual responsibility or accountability. Thus, critics argue the committee in reality turns out to have no responsibility or accountability. In fact, individuals may use the committee as a shield to avoid personal responsibility for bad decisions or mistakes. One solution to this problem is to make all committee members responsible and another is to hold the chairman responsible. Both approaches have many obvious difficulties. For example, if the entire committee is held responsible for a wrong decision, what about the individual members who voted against the majority? Holding them accountable for the committee's decision could have disastrous effects on their morale but holding only those who voted for a particular decision responsible would create an inhibiting effect that would destroy the value of committee action.

Besides being time-consuming, costly and having divided responsibility committees may reach decisions that are products of excessive compromise logrolling and one-man or minority domination. The comment that the camel is a horse designed by a committee points out this limitation. It represents the reverse of the advantages of integrated group judgment and the pooling of specialized knowledge. Where unanimity is either formally required or an informal group norm the difficulties are compounded. The final decision may be so extremely watered down or "compromised to death" that the horse actually does turn out to be a camel. The strength of committee action comes through a synthesis and integration of divergent viewpoints not through a compromise of the least common denominator. One way to avoid the problem is to limit the committee to serving as a forum for the exchange of information and ideas. Another possibility is to let the chairman have the final decision-making prerogative. Yet, these solutions are not always satisfactory because when the committee is charged with making a decision considerable social skill and a willingness to cooperate fully must exist if good, quality decisions are to evolve. Committees should be subjected to the same intensive research that has been conducted on small groups. Much can be learned from behaviour science research on the small group, but more effort needs to be directed specifically at the form organization committee as a form of group dynamics.

Groupthink – A Problem with Committee Action

A dysfunction of highly cohesive groups is called "groupthink." Iring Janis defines it as "a deterioration of mental efficiency, reality testing, and moral judgement that results from in group pressures". Groupthink is an approach to conform and reach consensus under pressures. Committees that suffer from groupthink reach consensus without realistic appraisal of alternative courses of action in decision and suppress the minority or deviant views.

Janis has described the following symptoms of groupthink tendency:

1. There is the illusion of invulnerability. There is excessive optimism and risk-taking.
2. Group members rationalize any resistance to the assumptions they have made.
3. The group ignores questionable ethical or moral issues.
4. Those who oppose the group are stereotyped.
5. There is direct pressure on any member who questions the stereotypes.
6. There is self-censorship of any deviation from the apparent group consensus.
7. There is the illusion of unanimity. Silence is interpreted as consent.
8. There are self-appointed mind guards who protect the group from adverse information.

Consequences of Group Think

Under group think conditions the following consequences maybe identified:

1. Discussion is limited to only a few alternatives.
2. Once a decision is taken, re-examination is unlikely even in the light of (valuable thought) new information.
3. Little or no time is spent trying to find ways to overcome the problems that have made rejected alternatives seem undesirable.
4. Little or no effort is made to obtain information from experts within the organization.
5. Facts are ignored unless they are supportive of the group.
6. No contingency plans are developed by which to cope with foreseeable difficulties that could endanger the success of the group's chosen course.

The Remedy for Group Think

When group think does occur, positive action must be taken if the group is to be effective in performing its task. As we have seen, concurrence-seeking will smoother objective consideration and evaluation of alternatives. The following steps are recommended by Janis to overcome group think tendencies:

1. Encourage the group members to express doubts and criticisms of proposed solutions to problems. Permit critical evaluation of group's ideas by members freely.
2. Allow key members to adopt an initial impartial stance on solutions.
3. Divide the group into subgroups to stimulate ideas. Then have the subgroups confront one another to examine why they differ.
4. Periodically intive qualified outsiders to challenge group views.
5. Allow atleast one member to playa devil's advocate role to oppose the views of other group members.
6. After arriving at a tentative decision in a particular way, allow the group to hold a second chance meeting wherein members fully describe every possible doubt they have about the solution reached.

Small Group Behaviour

According to R.F. Bales "A small group is defined as any number of persons engaged in interaction with one another in a single face to face meeting or series of such meetings, in which each member receives some impression or perception of each other member distinct enough so that he can, either at the time or in later questioning, give some reaction to each of the others as an individual person, even though it may be only to recall that the other was present."

To understand small group behaviour it is necessary to note general characteristics of small groups. These are: (a) Small groups have common mutually agreed goal; (b) They share a common socio - cultural background; (c) Members interact with one another in a simple face - to - face way; (d) Each member performs a well-defined task; and (e) Members perceive the existence of each member as well as the existence of a group .

Dynamics of Informal Groups

Informal groups play a crucial role in the dynamics of organizational behaviour. Formal and informal groups should not be treated as two separate entities, rather they are inseparable and coexist. Blaue and Scott have pointed out that "It is impossible to understand the nature of a formal organization without investigating the networks of informal relations and the unofficial norms as well as the formal hierarchy of authority and the official body of rules, since the formally instituted and the informally emerging patterns are inextricably interwined. The distinction between the formal and the informal aspects of organization life is only an analytical one and should not be verified; there is only one actual organization."

Informal groups mainly evolve from the following four status positions of the participants in the groups: (1) Group leader ,(2) Member of the primary group; (3) Fringe status; and (4) Out status. Closely related to status positions are the norms and roles in informal groups.

In modern organizations employees often assume some informal roles such as technique-oriented, rule enforcers, rule evaders, etc. Mintzberg has also suggested three classes of informal managerial roles. These are classified as: (a) interpersonal roles, (b) informational roles, and (c) decisional roles.

Informal organization has both functions and dysfunctions. Some dysfunctional aspects of informal organization may be mentioned as conflicting objectives, conformity, blocking of ambition, intertia, restriction of output, and resistance to change. On the other hand, some practical benefits of informal groups may be listed as under:

1. It blends with the formal organization to make a workable system for getting the work done.
2. It lightens the workload of the formal manager and fills in some of the gaps of his abilities.
3. It gives satisfaction and stability to work groups.
4. It is a very useful channel of communication in the organization.
5. Its presence encourages a manager to plan and act more carefully than he would otherwise.

The Grapevine: Informal Communication

The term grapevine refers to the informal communication system in an organization. It basically serves as a bypassing mechanism and becomes faster than the formal system it bypasses. The term grapevine arose during the Civil War period in U.S.A. when telegraph lines were strung loosely from tree to tree like grapevine. Since messages from the lines often were incorrect or confusing, any false information or rumour that came along was said to come from grapevine.

Negatively, grapevine is equated with rumour. Although the grapevine is often misused and has potential dangers, it has many positive aspects. It can effectively supplement the formal channels of communication. It can quickly disseminate pertinent information that assists the formal systems to attain goals. It is flexible and usually involves face-to-face communication.

Research has indicated certain predictable patterns of informal communication as under:

1. People talk most when the news is recent.
2. People talk about things that affect their work.
3. People talk about people they know.
4. People working near each other are likely to be on the same grapevine.
5. People who contact each other in the chain of procedure tend to be on the same grapevine.

Today's managers should recognize that grapevine, in most of the cases, remains accurate and fast and it carries much information that is needed to supplement the formal systems of communication. Grapevine can be instrumental in attaining the organization objectives.

Structural Dimensions or Components of Groups

Group structure is the framework or pattern of relationships among members that assists the group to achieve its goals. Within any group some form of structure for group activity develops over a period of time. To understand group behaviour it is necessary to consider various structure dimensions of groups, which include the following:

1. Group composition, 2. Group size, 3. Status system, 4. Role, 5. Norms, 6. Leadership, and 7. Cohesiveness.

Group Composition

How well a group performs largely depends on the qualities of its members. The diversity versus redundancy of members' traits and abilities is an important factor in explaining group performance.

Diversified groups tend to do better on many problem-solving tasks than do homogenous groups of highly similar individuals. Such groups tend to generate innovative solutions. Hence, attention must be paid to the relevance of the members' attributes and the mix of these attributes within the group. This is important to note that members are more socially conforming in mixed-sex groups. This suggests that members of mixed-sex groups focus more on interpersonal relations, while members of same-sex groups tend to be more concerned with accomplishment of task.

Group Size

The size of a group can have profound implications on how the group behaves internally and with regard to other groups. It is an important factor determining the number of interactions of individuals in a group. In a small group face-to-face interaction is quite easy and uncomplicated. Members can easily communicate with other group members. Research evidence confirms the fact that small groups are *effective.* On the other hand, in larger groups members *have* a better chance of finding people they like to work with. The potential for greater *variety* of talents is also greater. But the disadvantages of size more than offset its *advantages.* Larger groups offer greater opportunities for differences between and among individuals.

"The sheet volume of interactions then necessary would tend to make any concerned actions much more difficult. Larger groups tend to develop splinter groups whose goals maybe divergent with those of the larger organization. But then how to *achieve* a happy balance? What is the correct size of a group? The problem of defining the size of a small group is, particularly troublesome. Interaction is a necessary ingredient of small groups. As such, the minimum size of a group is always two people (dyad). The upper limit is usually specified by some rule of thumb. Prescriptions in this connection *vary* from situation to situation. Generally speaking the size of a group depends to a large extent on the group's situation and purpose. *However,* some studies *have* come up with definite numbers: for example, 7 is the ideal maximum for a decision making group and 14 is the maximum for a fact-finding group.

Some possible effects of size on groups are summarised below:

Table 2. Effects of Size of Groups

	2-7 members	8-12 members	13-16 members
Dimensions:			
Leadership			
1. Demand on leader	Low	Moderate	High
2. Difference between leaders and members	Low to	Moderate to	High
3. Direction to leader	Low	Low to Moderate	Moderate to High
Members			
4. Tolerance of direction from leader	Low to	Moderate	High
5. Domination of group interaction by a new members	High	to High Moderate	High
6. Inhibition in participation by ordinary members	Low	Moderate	High
Group Processes			
7. Formalization of rules and procedures	Low	Low to Moderate	Moderate to High
8. Time required for reading decisions	Low to Moderate	Moderate	Moderate to High
9. Tendency for subgroup to form	Low	Moderate to High	High

Group size has observable effects on group performance. Some important researches relating to group size can be noted:

(a) In larger groups, the potential contribution of each individual is somewhat diminished.

(b) Members appear to become more tolerant of authoritarian and directive leadership as group size increases.

(c) Larger groups are more likely to have formalized rules and set procedures for dealing with problems.

(d) Job satisfaction is lower in larger groups. This occurs because people receive less personal attention and fewer opportunities to participate.

(e) Very small groups show more tension, agreement, and asking of opinions, while larger groups show more tension release and giving of information.

Group Norms

Norms are standards or rules of behaviour that are established by group members. In other words, a norm is a rule conduct that has been established by group members to maintain consistency in behaviour. It tells an individual how to behave in a group. Norms are essential if a group is to be a viable unit. In the words of Szilagyi and Wallace, norms are standards or rules of behaviour that are established by group members to give group saw fit, the result would be increased frustration, anxiety, stress, and conflict and decreased morale and group performance.

Characteristics of Norms

According to Hackman, norms have the following characteristics:

1. Norms summarize and simplify group influence processes.
2. Norms apply only to behaviour, and not to private thoughts and feelings.
3. Norms are generally developed only for behaviours which are viewed as important by most group members.
4. Norms usually develop gradually, but the process can be shortened if members so desire.
5. Not all norms apply to everyone. High status members often enjoy more freedom to deviate from the norms than do other members.

According to Ivancevich, Szilagyi and Wallace, Norms have the following characteristics:

1. Norms may apply to every member or they may apply to only some members.
2. Norms may be accepted differently by group members.
3. Different types of norms apply to different positions in the group.

Norms Conformity Factors

1. **Personality Factors:** Research in personality suggested that more intelligent individuals are less likely to conform the group norms than are less intelligent individuals. A more authoritarian individual is less likely to conform to group norms.
2. **Situational Factors:** Situational factors are such variables as group size, communication patterns, structure of group, and the social context group interaction.
3. **Stimulus Factors:** Stimulus factors are faced by individual each day. The more ambiguous the stimulus, the greater will be the conformity to the group norms.
4. **Intergroup Relationships:** This refers to the relationships among members of the group. It includes such variables as the kind and extent of group pressure exerted, the success the group has in achieving goals, and the degree to which a member identifies with the group.

Enforcement of Norms

It is not an easy task to enforce the group norms. Litterer has suggested the following steps for enforcement of group norms:

1. **Education:** Creating a desire in group members to remain in the group by educating them that how the group's stands contribute to the achievement of goals. This can be done by increasing active participation of each member towards the group's work.
2. **Surveillance:** Following the group norms is essential to the survival of the group. This step enforce to detect deviance from the group norms so that it could be corrected the deviance in time.
3. **Warning:** A warning is given to each group member that he who does not conform to the group standards will be removed from the unit. Litterer suggested that provide a friendly and supportive contact to the deviate so as to bring him back to comply with the norms. "Should he refuse to do so, stop the educational process and allow him to have a feel of the negative consequences; razzing, argument, etc."
4. **Sanctions:** Sanctions are imposed for enforcing discipline. This is enforced as a last resort when the deviant refuses to come back to the norms. This step involves in physical violences, tampering with personal possessions, etc.

Implications for Managers

Among the manager's most important tasks are learning the norms of the different groups, finding out which are critical and which are not, and determining the degree of conformity needed and degree of non-conformity allowed. Effective managers try to change norms that challenge the accomplishment of organizational goals.

How Norms Develop:

The question of how group norms develop has been of considerable interest to organizational researchers. An insightful analysis of this process has been presented by Feldman (see summary in Table 3). First, norms develop because of precedents set over time. Whatever behaviours emerge at a first group meeting will usually set the standard for how that group is to operate. Initial group patterns of behaviour frequently become normative, such as where people sit, and how formal or informal the meeting will be. Such routines help establish a predictable, orderly interaction pattern.

Second, norms develop because of carryovers from other situations. Group members usually draw from their previous experiences to guide their behaviour in new situations. The norms governing professional behaviour apply here. For example, the norm for a physician to behave ethically and to exercise a pleasant bedside manner perceived role inaccurate. The perceived role is how the individual thinks he or she should perform to fulfil the expected role. The enacted role is the behaviour that a person actually carries out. Much of what we do is determined by these roles.

Role Problems: The role characteristics give rise two kinds of role problems: (1) Role ambiguity and (2) Role Conflict.

Role Ambiguity: Role ambiguity is the result of lack of clarity in the individual's duties, authority and responsibility. It can be caused by a number of factors:

(i) Due to lack of a clear job description for a position.

(ii) Individual's task becomes more complex coupled with lack of training, experience and clear job responsibilities, result in confusion, conflict, and poor performance.

(iii) Due to certain individual characteristics classified as "self-confident" perceive less role ambiguity.

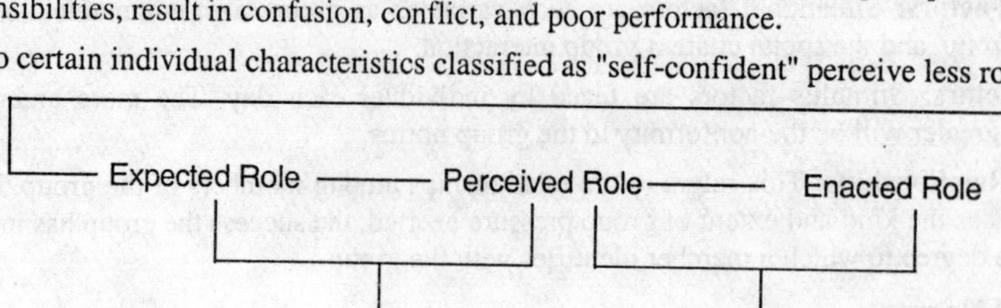

Fig. 1. Role Relationships

Role Conflict

Because of the multiplicity of roles and role sets, an individual may face a complex situation of simultaneous role requirements where the performance of one role precludes the performance of the others. When this occurs, the individual faces a situation known as role conflict. Several forms of role conflict can occur in organizations.

Person-Role Conflict

Person-role conflict occurs when role requirements violate the basic values, attitudes, and needs of the individual occupying the position. A supervisor who finds it difficult to dismiss a subordinate with a position. A supervisor who finds it difficult to dismiss a subordinate with a family and an executive who resigns rather than engage in some unethical activity are examples of individuals experiencing person-role conflict.

Intrarole Conflict

Intrarole conflict occurs when different individuals define a role according to different sets of expectations, making it impossible for the person occupying the role to satisfy all of them. This is more likely to occur when a given role has a complex role set (many different role relationships). The supervisor in an industrial situation has a rather complex role set and thus may face interarole conflict. One the one hand, top management has a set of expectations that stresses the supervisor's role in the management hierarchy. On the other hand, the supervisor may have close friendship ties with members of the command group who may be former working peers. This is why supervisors are often described as being in the middle.

Interrole Conflict

Interrole conflict can result from facing multiple roles. It occurs because individuals simultaneously perform many roles, some of which have conflicting expectations. A scientist in a chemical plant who is also a member of a management group might experience role conflict of this kind. In such a situation, the scientist may be expected to behave in accordance with the expectations of management as well as the expectations of professional chemists. A physician placed in the role of hospital administrator may also experience interrole conflict. The next chapter describes how this type of role conflict often causes conflict between groups in many organizations.

The Results of Role Conflict

Behavioural scientists agree that an individual confronted with role conflict experiences psychological stress that may result in emotional problems and indecision. Research has shown that role conflict does occur frequently and with negative effects on performance over a wide spectrum of occupations.

While managers can do little to avoid certain kinds of role conflict, many can be minimized. For example, some role conflict (especially intrarole conflict) can result from violations of the classical principles of chain of command and unity of command. The early management writers' rationale for these two principles was that violation would probably cause conflicting pressures on the individual. In other words, when individuals are faced is generalizable from one hospital to another. Such carryover norms can assist in making interaction easier in new social situations.

Table 3. Norms: How do they develop

	BASIS OF NORMS DEVELOPMENT	EXAMPLE
1.	Precedents set over time	Seating location of each group member around a table
2.	Carryovers from other situations	Professional standards of conduct
3.	Explicit statements from others	Working a certain way because you are told "that's how we do it around here"
4.	Critical events in group history	After the organization suffers a loss due to one person's divulging company secrets, a norm develops to maintain secrecy

Source: Based on Feldman, 1984; see Note 13.

This table summarizes four ways in which group norms can develop.

Third, sometimes norms also develop in response to an explicit statement by a superior or co-worker.

Newcomers to groups quickly "learn the ropes" when someone tells them. "That's the way we do it around here." This explanation is an explicit statement of the norms; it describes what one should do or avoid doing to be accepted by the group. Often the explicit statement of group norms represents the accepted desires of more powerful or experienced group members.

Fourth and finally, group norms may develop out of critical events in the group's history. If an employee releases an important organizational secret to a competitor, causing a loss to the company, a norm to maintain secrecy may develop out of this incident.

Roles

The concept of role is very important to the understanding of group behaviour. Role refers to the expected behaviour patterns attributed to a particular position in an organization. The roles of physician and patient are familiar to everyone. Those roles are culturally defined expectations associated with particular positions.

A Role may include attitudes and values as well as specific kinds of behaviour. It is what an individual must do to validate his or her occupancy of a particular position. In other words, what kind of physician or patient an individual is depends a great deal on how he or she performs the culturally defined role associated with law enforcement officers, your own perceptions of the roles associated with law enforcement officers, military officers, politicians, college professors, and business executives.

In the formal organization, every position has certain activities that are expected. These activities constitute the rule for that position from the standpoint of the organization. the organization develops job descriptions that define the activities of each particular position and how it relates to other positions in the organization. However, for both formal (task and command) and informal (interest and friendship) groups, roles may not be set forth explicitly and yet be clearly understood by group members. For example, members of the marketing department in a bank may know that only the director of marketing represents the bank at national conventions and that they have no chance of attending, even though this has never been explicitly stated. Thus, whether they are formally or informally established, status hierarchies and accompanying roles are integral parts of every organization.

Multiple Roles and Role Sets

Most of us perform **multiple roles.** We occupy many different positions in a variety of organizations-home, work, church, civic groups, and so forth; within each of these organizations, we occupy and perform certain roles. We may simultaneously be playing the role of parent, mate, supervisor, and subordinate. Each position involves different role relationships. For example, the position of college professor involves not only the role of teacher in relation to students but also numerous other roles relating the position to administrators, peers, the community, and alumni. Each group may expect different things: students may expect good classroom performance, research, and publication; the college community may expect community service; and alumni may expect help in recruiting students and athletes. This we term the **role set.** A role set refers to others' expectations for the behaviour of the individual in the particular role. The more expectations, the more complex is the rule set. For example, a college professor probably has a more complex role set than that of a forest ranger but one less complicated than that of an ambassador to Hungary.

With conflicting expectations or demands from two or more sources, the likely result is a decline in performance.

In addition, interrole conflict can be generated by conflicting expectations of formal or informal groups, with results similar to those of intrarole conflict. Thus, a highly cohesive group whose goals are not consistent with those of the formal organization can cause a great deal of interrole conflict for its members.

Status Systems

Status is defined as a social ranking within a group and is assigned to an individual on the basis of position in the group or individual characteristics. Status can be a function of the title of individual, wage or salary level, work schedule, mobility to interact with others within or outside the group or seniority.

All kinds of organizations have mainly two status structures; known as the formal system and informal system. The formal system of status is closely related to chain or command, which is called hierarchical structure of organization. In formal status structure values and norms of the group determine the status of a particular member. A person is given status because of some personal characteristics such as age, skill, sex or education. The oldest nurse in a group may enjoy higher status because of her age, tenure, and expertise on the job.

Every work group. has a status system. The various work of the group is subdivided into different prestige values. Status develops in a group because of particular individual possesses or contributes values to the organization that are highly regarded by the members. Research studies have revealed that individual can easily identify status values in groups. One's dress, titles, etc. even convey status.

The existence of status systems in organizations can have both positive and negative consequences for the manager. Because status systems can clarify the relationships between group members by providing for clear definitions of authority and responsibility. However, an over emphasis on status tends to reduce both the interaction between group members and the frequency of communications.

How Status Structures Influence Group Behaviour

It is highly important for employees to believe that the organization's formal status system is congruent.

Status congruency is said to exist when all the status attributes are ranked equally by all members of a group. Status congruency provides for more consistent and predictable behaviour. Status structures may create excessive social distance between such personnel as physicians and nurses, professors and students who could benefit from closer interaction.

Status systems can have a direct influence on group performance through status congruence which is agreement among group members on the status of individual group members. When there is full agreement on member status, the major activity of the group is directed toward goal accomplishment. However, when there is disagreement on status within the group (status incongruence), some group activity is diverted from goal accomplishment and toward resolving this conflict.

Status is the social position a person holds as compared with that of the other members of his or her group, and refers to the fact that members of a group have a differential worth to that group. Status is reflected in the differential rights of and obligations incurred by different people. In many real life groups, inequalities of status exist from the start. Many groups have fixed positions which are arranged hierarchically in terms of their status value, and positions are filled by individuals having the relevant characteristics and qualifications. However, groups may come to agree upon other characteristics which earn status but at an informal level.

Status may by sought through striving and competitive mastery of the roles linked to it, or it may be ascribed to a person on the basis of such characteristics as sex, race, age, etc. Thus, while an achieved status is attained by performing valued roles, activities and efforts, the personal qualities of the individual are the basis for the ascribed status and cannot be readily altered. When group members act as if one of them holds a status, these acts are referred to as deference behaviour. Deferential behaviour takes the form of responding to the influence of the person with a high status in satisfying that person's needs and aiding in the achievement of his or her goals. Status symbols, for example, well-decorated spacious rooms, most courteous treatment, gifts, attentiveness, praise, are acquired to communicate the existence of the status and to facilitate its recognition by others within the organization.

In this connection, Wofford, Gerloff and Cummins observe: "Status has a significant impact upon the communication process in groups, and communication variables, such as 'how often', 'who', 'to whom' and 'what', are influenced by status. High status people generally communicate more frequently than do low status people. They also have greater influence and more power than low status people. Communication patterns tend to emerge along status lines. Persons of equal status tend to communicate with one another rather than with persons of different status."

According to Wofford, Gerloff and Cummins, the content of communication varies among status positions. Whereas high status people tend to give information and opinions in group discussion, low status people assume a passive role which involves such responses as agreement, disagreement and requests for information. Studies have shown that higher status workers in seniority and pay seldom ask for advice or help from those equal to or lower in status than themselves. If an individual is ranked high on status in one or two respects, he is expected to show himself as high on all related characteristics in the process of maintaining status congruence. Managers, therefore, should be aware of the barrier which their status erects against the flow of information and opinions from lower - status people. They can improve the quality of their communication by reducing the perceived status differentials between themselves and subordinates.

Goerge Homan has drawn attention to another way in which status differences affect group functioning. He says that, in working groups, people compare their investment and rewards with those of other people and expect the resulting equation to reach equal ratio.

$$\frac{\text{My investments}}{\text{His investments}} = \frac{\text{My rewards}}{\text{His rewards}}$$

This equality he referred to as distributive justice. A number of studies have shown failure to uphold distributive justice resulting in dissatisfaction and even a decline in productivity, because people then feel guilty for having a better investment reward outcome or resentful for having a worse investment reward outcome than their peers.

How Status Develops in a Group?

Every work group has a status system. The various jobs into which the work of the group is subdivided have different prestige values in the eyes for workers. Status develops in a group because a particular individual possesses or contributes values to the organization that are highly regarded by the members. A number of research studies have shown that people can quickly identify status differences within groups. There are many cues and symbols: One's air, composure, dress, titles, even such things as parking space, number of tables etc., convey status.

A peon with college education would find his job very uncomfortable in a place where illiterates are recruited for such positions. Unless able to play down the educational attributes, he is likely to be labelled as a city guy or the college kid. It will be difficult to gain full acceptance. Status incongruence creates, psychological tension and this state is unpleasant and dissatisfying. It is therefore, highly important for employees to believe that the organization's formal status system is congruent. Status congruency is said to exist when all the status attributes are ranked equally by all members of a group. In other words, there is equity between the perceived ranking of an individual and the status he is given by the organization. Status congruency provides for more consistent and predictable behaviour.

1. Status incongruence can cause uncertainty and ambiguity. Low morale, high tension and high anxiety may be the result. William F. Whyte's famous studies on human relations in restaurant industry indicated that tension and conflict often resulted in between cooks and employees who served food at the counter. A common factor in these instances of conflict was that lower status employees were giving orders regularly to higher status persons, communication patterns tend to emerge along status lines. Persons of equal status tend to communicate with one another rather than with persons of different status.

2. Status structures may create excessive social distance between such personnel as physicians and nurses, professors and students who could benefit from closer interaction.
   (i) For example studies have shown that higher status workers rarely seek advice or assistance from those equal to or lower in status than themselves. Under certain conditions, they may also restrict free and open communication between individuals.
   (ii) Behaviour is oriented toward preserving status hierarchies especially by people in high status positions.
   (iii) Behaviour is oriented toward improving one's position in the hierarchy – especially by people in lower positions.
   (iv) Any change perceived as being destructive to the status hierarchy is considered threatening - especially by people in higher positions.
   (v) Any change perceived as potentially blocking status equilibrium is perceived as threatening.

MANAGERIAL IMPLICATIONS

Status is an important kind of cement that binds an organization together. Loss of status is more than loss of its emoluments; it is more than loss of prestige. It is a serious injury to the personality. Therefore it is highly important to achieve status congruency in the organization.

To meet this objective, it is necessary to distribute the rewards according to the perceived value of the skills demanded by the task. In this way the status system is kept insistent with the reward system.

Managers must also try to demolish the barriers erected by status structures by seeking information and opinions from lower status people. In addition, the behavioural problems arising from status incongruence can be avoided by:

(i) Selecting or promoting those people whose characteristics are all congruent with the job, or

(ii) By changing the group's values about what leads to high status.

Leadership in Groups

An important responsibility in working with groups is the recognition of leadership forces. The formal leader who is appointed by the management exercises the powers and authority defined to him within the organizational framework. He can exert formal influence on the activities of the group. The leader is responsible for the direction and goal accomplishment of the group and can reward or punish individual members when they do not comply with the directions, orders or rules of the group. Because the organization supports the leader's influence, he has the power to make the group members comply with directives.

In informal group, leaders generally are individuals who are respected by other group members and who have acquired special status. The informal group leader generally:

(1) Aids the group in directing its activities towards goal accomplishment

(2) Embodies the values of the group

(3) Acts for the group in presenting their viewpoint when interacting with management or other groups.

(4) Facilitates the activities of the group by initiating group actions and assisting in resolving group conflict.

The informal group leadership role can and often change from one person to another, depending on the particular circumstances exist.

The relationship between internal group cohesion and external conflict relates to the role of group leaders. In a study Hambling cleverly created conditions of crisis in a group and observed their effect on leader emergence. It was evident from his experiment that a group perceives itself to be threatened and to be unclear about what to do, produces more leadership behaviour than the one that does not. In another study of the question of the emergence of informal leaders in seventy two conference groups in business, political and industrial organizations, it was found that where groups held divergent opinions about their goals, they generated informal leaders significantly more often than the groups which were in agreement. In the situations in which an external threat provokes internal cohesion, some traits have been commonly found among individuals who move to assume leadership roles. It has been found that leaders were distinguished from non-leaders by their tendency to dominate group effort, to express themselves clearly and concisely, and to push the group to stay on the work agenda. The rise of intergroup conflict changes the status of young man, who may be considered a bully, to that of a hero. Another group deposed a leader who, in the minds of his followers, did not take a sufficiently belligerent stance in relation to other groups. It is evident, therefore, that intregroup conflict tends to set in motion forces which bring more authorharian leaders into prominence. Such leaders maintain cohesiveness.

Leaders with authoritarian styles tend to provoke external conflict as means of justifying the suppression of dissent among their followers. However, a leader acting as a negotiator for his group during a conflict faces strong pressures to concede little to the opponents; the followers reward him for being tough and for making non-negotiable demands; and indications on the part of the leader that he is open to views from the other side evoke doubt, mistrust, and other forms of punishment from his associates. Moreover, this authoritarian leadership behaviour is provoked, not only by followers and the leader's own needs, but by their adversaries as well, who question their motives and are quick to highlight the personality flaws which become noticeable under the pressure of negotiation. In one of the experiments on intergroup conflict, it was found that the leader whose group loses in competition, faces substantial reduction in his influence with the group. This may give rise to authoritarian leadership behaviour, for the leader who suffers from this loss of power within his group may argue that members should put aside their differences with him so that, together, they may fight against a common external threat. According to Deutsch, the association between internal cohesion and external conflict may, therefore, be based on the causal processes and threats may be provoked by leaders who wish to enhance their powers by increasing the cohesion of their followers.

The formal leader possesses the power to discipline and or fire members of his work group. Informal leaders, on the other hand, tend to emerge gradually as group members interact. They emerge from within the group according to the nature of the situation at hand.

Table 5

	Formal Leaders	Informal Leaders
1.	Represents the organization.	Represents the values of the group.
2.	Taks oriented, gets the job done.	Group oriented, welfare of the group.
3.	Attempts to dominate and impose.	Leadership role is based on group consensus and acceptance.
4.	Attempts to achieve goals by strict adherence to rules and regulations.	Prisoner of group values and norms, tries to achieve group goals without violating group norms.

What factors encourage other members to accept a person as leader?

Emergence of Informal Leaders

1. The member who talks and participates most actively in the group activities is the one most likely to emerge as leader.
2. The member who possesses more information enabling him to contribute more than other members to solution of the group task tends to emerge as leader.
3. The member who respects group norms and values and attempts to fulfil group's social needs by encouraging feelings of solidarity tends to emerge as leader.
4. The member of the group who possesses the greatest technical knowledge, skills, qualities necessary to achieve the purpose and accomplish the tasks of the group in a particular situation is likely to emerge as leader.

5. The member who is able to perceive the values of the group, organise them into an intelligible philosophy and sell the same successfully to other groups and non-members is likely to emerge as leader.

Successful Leadership Behaviours

The primary function of an informal group leader (formal group leader) is to facilitate the accomplishment of group goals. He aids the group in accomplishing its goals. To survive, the group must gear its efforts to achieve its primary goals. The cricket team that fails to win a single match ultimately loses its cohesiveness, its sense of togetherness and disintegrates. The informal group leader personifies the values and aspirations of group. He initiates action, provides direction and compromises differences toward the accomplishment of goals. He differs from followers in ability to initiate and sustain interaction with a wide range of personalities. "He protects the weak and under chosen, encourages participation of less capable members, is tolerant of the deviate, and accepts rather than rejects a wide range of member personalities. He constantly evaluates, directs and motivates member behaviour toward overall goals. Thus an informal group leader is an embodiment of the values of group, an initiator of group activities, a prisoner of group norms a facilitator of group conflict.

Cohesiveness

Some groups seem to have a certain atmosphere of closeness or common attitudes, behaviour and performance, that is lacking in other groups. This closeness, is known as group cohesiveness. It is generally regarded as characteristics of the group in which the factors acting on the group members to remain and participate in the group are greater than those acting on members to leave it.

Cohesiveness causes more harmonious behaviour among the group members. A cohesive group is always able to act as one body to achieve the objectives.

Characteristics

1. Cohesiveness is an important indicator of the degree of influence the group has as a whole. The greater the cohesiveness, the greater the group's influence on members.
2. Highly cohesive groups are usually characterized by good feeling among members and an absence of tension.
3. Highly cohesive groups are potentially better performers than noncohesive groups. Factors determining the Degree of Cohesiveness.
1. Factors that can increase cohesiveness:

1. Agreement on group goals

If the group agrees on the purpose and direction of its activities, this will facilitate goal accomplishment.

2. Frequency for interaction

When the group members can interact frequently with each other, the closeness increases and that will increase cohesiveness.

3. Personal attractiveness

If mutual trust and support already exist, cohesiveness is increased when members are attracted to one another. Personal attraction helps group members to overcome obstacles to goal performance.

4. Intergroup competition

Competition with other groups, within and outside the organization, brings group member closer together for attaining common goals.

5. Favourable evaluation

If a group has performed well some recognition for its outstanding performance will elevate the group members to feel proud about being members of the group. Such awards help to develop cohesiveness and to support enhanced performance.

2. Factors that decrease cohesiveness:

1. Disagreement on goals

Disagreement on goals bring conflict and infighting, thus decreasing cohesiveness.

2. Group size

When the size of the group increases, the frequency of interactions between members decreases. This will decrease the probability that cohesiveness will develop.

3. Unpleasant experiences with the group

When there is a lack of trust and confidence between members of a group, interaction may become a unpleasant experience, resulting in a lack of closeness in the group.

4. Intragroup competition

Although intergroup competition brings groups together, intragroup competition causes conflict, infighting. Such situation creates when the managers are showing favouritism to individual members of the group.

5. Domination

When one or more group members dominate the group because of some personality traits, cohesiveness cannot develop.

Outside Pressure

A favourite topic of novelists is to describe the plight of two warring individuals who, through some quirk of fate, find themselves dependent on each other for survival or gain. External threats create higher bonds between members. When the members perceive that the group is threatened by an external force, they strive together to combat the collective threat. In the face of a common enemy, members forget their common differences and become cohesive.

Status of the Group

A high status group that is successful in achieving its goals tends to have greater cohesiveness. Membership in such a group is highly rated than membership in a group widely denounced by all. It is better to be a "big fish in a little pond" or "a little fish in a big pond" than remain unnoticed as a "little fish in a little pond."

Success

There is nothing like success to increase group spirit and cohesiveness. A near universal finding is that cohesiveness generally increases with success.

Other Reasons

Other reasons like compatible goals (goals of the group and the members are essentially alike and expressed in a clear language) attractive leaders (the group has a dynamic, energetic leader) collective power (people join groups to obtain personal power) also compel members to seek membership in well-knit groups.

Effects of Group Cohesion

Researches have generally shown that a cohesive group is more productive than a less cohesive group provided the group's attitude aligns with the goals of the organization. For example, if the group norm is a high level of performance, the more cohesive group is likely to influence each member toward higher productivity. On the other hand, if cohesiveness is high but attitudes unfavourable, productivity declines. A highly cohesive group is like a 'time bomb' in the hands of management. Where the group norm is not supportive of performance, cohesive groups are less productive. Resistance to organizational changes is greater and where proper leadership is not provided, such groups can restrict output severely. "If management wishes to maximize productivity it must build a cohesive group and give it proper leadership.

Management of highly cohesive groups

Guidelines to managers: The problem for the manager is to finding how the activities of highly cohesive group directed toward organization goals. Although there is no active research support in this matter, certain guidelines are given as below:

1. Task-accomplish emphasis

One approach involves redirecting the activities of the group from interpersonal issues to emphasis on task accomplishment. If management could increase the group's commitment to goals that were more compatible with organizational goals, the level of group performance could be positively influence.

2. Participative Management

Another possible approach is to incorporate participative management in the group. Participation in establishing goals and norms creates a commitment in those participating. If the established goals and norms are challenging, the group may concentrate more on task accomplishment than on interpersonal issues.

3. Intergroup competition

If managers can get group members to compete with other groups in the organization, a team spirit can develop that result not only in higher cohesion but also in greater group commitment to the accomplishment to the task. Intergroup competition, however, can have long run negative consequences for the organization.

Disbanking the Group

One final strategy if for management to partially or totally disband selected cohesive groups by transferring members to other departments. This can allow the manager to work with a relatively new group and exert influence on the entire group formation and development process.

REFERENCES

"Committees on Trial," *Harvard Business Review*, May-June 1960, p.8.

"Committees: Their Role in Management Today". *Management Review*, October 1957 , pp 4-10, and 75-78; and *Top Management Committees: Their Function and Authority*, AMA Research Study 48, American Management Association. New York, 1961.

A.J. Lott and B.E.Lott, *Group Cohesiveness as Interpersonal Attraction: A Review of Relationship and Antecedent and Consequent Variables, Psychological Bulletin*, October 1965, pp.259-309.

Charles S. Cooley: *Social Organization*, Charles Scribner's Sons, New York, 1911, p.23.

Connie J.G. Gersick, *Marking Time Predictable Transactions in Task Groups, Academy of Management Journal*, June 1989, pp. 274-309.

D.C. Feldman, *The Development and Enforcement of Group Norms, Academy of Management Review*, No. 9. 1984, pp. 47-53.

Deborah L. Gladstein, *Group in Context: A Model of Task Group Effectiveness, Administrative Science Quarterly*, December, 1984, pp 499-517.

F Luthans, *Organizational Behaviour*, Tokyo, McGraw Hill 1977, p.369.

For an analysis of some of the organizational implications of this type of conflict, see L. Roos and F. Starke, "Roles in Organizations," in Handbook of Organizational Design, ed. W Starbuck and P. Nystrom (Oxford, England: Oxford University Press,1980).

For classic discussions of the conflict-laden position of foreman, see F.J. Roethlisberger, 'The foreman: Fred Luthoans, McGraw Hill Book Company, New York, 1973, pp 449-453 (adapted).

G.C. Hommans, *Social Behaviour – Its Elementary Forms*, Harcourt Brace, New York, 1961.

George C. Homans: "The Human Group", Harcourt.

Harold Koontz and Cyril O'Donnell, *Principles of Management*, 5th ed., McGraw-Hill Book Company, New York. 1972, p. 371.

Irvin L.Janis, *Victims of Groupthink*, Houghton Miffin, Boston 1972, p.9.

J.F. Wofford, B.A. Gerloff and R.A. Cummins, *Organizational Communications – The Key stone to Managerial Effectiveness*, McGraw Hill, New York, 1977, p. 256.

J.R Wanous, A.E. Reichers and S.D. Malik, *Organizational Socialisation and Group Development, Towards an Integrative Perspective, Academy of Management Review*, Vol. 9, 1984, pp. 670-683.

J.R. Hakamn, *Group Influence on Individuals*, Land McNally, Chicago, 1976.

Jeffrey H. Greenhaus and Nicholas J. Beutell, "Sources of Concflict between Work and Family Roles," *Academy of Management Review*, January 1985, pp. 76-88.

John M. Ivancevich and James H. Donnelly, Jr., "A Study of Role Clarity and Need for Clarity for Three Occupational Groups," *Academy of Management Journal*, March, 1974, pp. 28-36; L. Chonko, "The Relationship of Span of Control to Sales Representatives' Experienced Role Conflict and Role Ambiguity," *Academy of Management Journal*, June 1982, pp.452-56; P.J. Nicholson, Jr., and S.C. Goh, "The Relationship of Organization Structure and Interpersonal Attifudese to Role Conflict and Ambiguity in Different Work Environments," *Academy of Management Journal*, March 1983,pp.148-56.

K. Battenhausen and J.K. Murnighan, *The Emergence of Norms in Competitive Decision Making Groups, Administrative Science Quarterly*, 1985, No.30, pp. 350-372.

Keith Davis, *Communication Within Management, Personnel*, November, 1954, p. 215.

Keith Davis, *Human Behaviour At Work*, Tata McGraw Hill Book Company, 1981, p. 435.

L. Berkowitz, "Group Standards, Cohesiveness, and Productivity", *Human Relations*, Nov. 1954, pp.509-19.

L.R. Sales, *Behaviour of Industrial Work Groups*, Wiley, New York, 1958.

L.R. Sayels, *Behaviour of Industrial Work Groups, Prediciton and Control*, John Wiley & Sons, New York, 1958.

Luther Gulick, "Notes on the Theory of Organization." in Luther Gulick and L. Urwick (eds.). Papers on the Science of Administration, Institute of Public Administration, New York, 1937,p.36.

Lyndall F. Urwick, *Committees in Organization*, reprint from the British Management Review by Management Journals, Ltd., 1933, p. 14; and *The Elements of Administration*, Harper & Row, Publishers, Incorporated, New York, 1943. pp. 71-72.

M.T. Reitan and M.E. Shaw, *Group Membership, Sex-Composition of the Group and Conformity Behaviour*,

Master and Victim of Double Talk, "Harvard Business Review, September-October 1965, pp.23ff;FC. Mann and J.K. Dent, "The Supervisor: Member of Two Organizational Families."

More Room at the Top? *Dun's Review*, March 1967, p. 29.

R. Dubin, *Human Relations in Administration*, Prentice Hall, New Delhi, 1970, p.300.

R.C. Andre de la Porte, "Group Norms: Key to Building a Winning Team", *Personnel*, Sep.-Oct. 1974, pp. 60-67.

R.F. Bales, *Interaction Process Analysis: A Method for the Study of Small Groups*, Addisson Wesley, Cambridge Mass, 1950, p. 33.

R.L. Hamblin–*Leadership and Crisis, Sociometry* Vol. 21, 1958, pp.322-335.

R.L. Kahn, *Organizational Stress*, Studies in Role Conflict and Ambiguity, New York, 1964.

R.M. Steers, *An Introduction to Organizational Behaviour*, Scott Foresman, Gleenview, 1984.

R.M. Stogdill, *Handbook of Leadership: A Survey of Theory and Research*, Free Press, New York, 1974, pp.230-231.

Robert F Bales, *Interaction Process Analysis: A Model for the Study of Small Groups*, Addison-Wesley, Cambridge Mass, 1950, p. 33.

S.E. Seashore, *Group Cohesiveness in the Industrial Work Group*, Ann Arbor, *Mich: Institute for Social Research*, University of Michigan, 1954.

Susan E. Jackson, Sheldon Zedeck, and Elizabeth Summers, "Family Life Disruptions: Effects of Job Induced Structural and Emotional Interference," *Academy of Management Journal*, September 1985, pp. 574-86.

T.R. Mitchell, *People in Organizations*, McGraw Hill, New York, 1978, p.248.

Theo Haimann and William G. Scott, *Management in the Modern Organization*. Houghton Mifflin Company. Boston, 1970, p.280.

Urwick, *The Elements of Administration*, p.72.

W.J. Duncan, *Organizational Behaviour*, Boston, 1978, p. 189.

WH. Crockett., Emergent Leadership in Small Decision Making Groups", *Journal of Abnormal Social Psychology*, Vol. 51, 1955, pp. 378-383.

Zaleznik, G.R. Christensen and FJ. Roethlisberger, *The Motivation, Productivity and Satisfaction of Workers – A Prediction Study, Bureau of Business Research*, Harvard University, 1958.

CHAPTER

18

Conflict

Mention the term conflict and most people envision fights, riots, or war. In fact, on virtually everyday of every year one can find approximately two dozen armed combat situations somewhere in the world. But these extreme situations represent only the most overt and violent expressions of conflict. During the typical workday, managers encounter more subtle and non-violent types of opposition such as arguments, criticism, and disagreement. Conflict, like power and organizational politics, is an inevitable and sometimes a positive force in modern work organizations.

Words stress and conflict are several times used interchangeably which is basically wrong. They usually go together. One may experience stress even in the absence of conflict. Marketing manager wants to increase the sale of his product. In his efforts to identify the market he encounters a number of problems and difficulties. Such situation may lead to an experience of stress. But there is no conflict in this situation. Aero plane pilot my experience stress when he is on his regular commercial flight. Stress may be defined as 'a feeling of tension on the part of an individual leading to emergence of certain physiological and/or psychological symptoms resulting from any real or imaginary problem' any goal directed physical activity may lead to an experience of tension. But tension resulting from physical activity may be called strain and not stress. A person operating a lathe machine experiences strain. An executive trying to deal with a certain labour problem experiences stress and not strain.

The term 'conflict' has wide connotation. It is subject to different interpretations in different context. It is generally referred to a psychological state of mind where a person cannot decide the behaviour this way or that way. Sometimes, the term is used as a difference of opinion between two persons or groups irrespective of their status in the organization. For example, we say they have conflicting views. No less frequent is the phenomenon where people are engaged in slowdowns or showdowns, each party developing strategies to meet the challenge of the other and get polarised into two warring groups. Conflict is a powerful process having both desirable and undesirable consequences, so, it cannot be eliminated, it can be and should be managed properly and timely.

Conflict is a psychological state of mind within or outside the organization when people are in a state of dilemma, whether to do or not to do anything and seriously engage themselves in weighting pros and cons of the possible behaviour but still feel themselves unable to take a decision either way. Thus, it is a state of wavering mind. We often hear people saying, 'There is a conflict in his mind,' implying that he is not in a position to take a decision for and against a particular view. People, very often say, 'they have two persons or groups'. In advance stage of conflict, two conflicting parties engage themselves in slowdowns or showdowns and each party develops strategies to accept and meet the challenges of the other party and get polarised into two warring factions. We say 'they are in conflict.' In any case the party concerned is faced with the problem of decision making.

The history of all hitherto society has been the history of class struggles. Greame Salaman (1978) has argued that organizations are harmonious, cooperative structures where conflicts are seen to arise from misunderstandings and confusions, personality factors, or from extra organizational factors. Charles B. Handy writes, 'a world without differences is perhaps inconceivable. But one thing we should be sure: a world without differences of opinion, values, priorities, talents and personalities would be a world without sun and shadows, a bland, dull world.'

Conflict Defined

It is not possible to compress the essential ingredients of 'conflict' in a precise definition because it occurs in many different settings and may take several forms – 'an enemy to be defeated, a moral dilemma to be resolved a woman or man to be won, a contract to be signed, a production quota to be beaten etc.' Often, it is couched in such colourful expressions like controversy, strife, battle, clash and internecine warfare. But the essence of conflict appears to be disagreement, contradiction and incompatibility, More specifically, conflict is a process in which an effort is purposefully made by one person or unit to block another that results in frustrating the attainment of the other's goals or the furthering of his or her interest. Thus, it is a process in which (for example) A deliberately tries to offset the efforts of B by some form of blocking that will result in frustrating B in attaining his goals or furthering his interests. The above definition acknowledges awareness (perception), opposition, scarcity and blockage:

Stephen Robins defines conflict as "all kinds of opposition or antagonistic interaction." It is based on scarcity of power, resources or social positions and differing value systems. Research reveals that managers spend approximately 21 per cent of their time dealing with conflict, so they need to be well grounded in conflict theory. research, and practice.

Conflict has been defined by writers in different ways. James D. Thompson defines it as "that behaviour by organization members which is expended in opposition to other members." Kenneth W. Thompson has described it as the "process which begins when one party perceives that the other has frustrated or is about to frustrate, some concern of his" and Morthon Deutsch calls it as a situation whenever incompatible activities occur."

Conflict has been defined by Killmon and Thomos as the condition of objective incompatibility between values or goals achievement, and emotionally in terms of hostility.

Handy defines conflicts as harmful differences. K.W. Thomas defines conflict "as the process that results when one person or a group perceives that another person or group is frustrating, or about to frustrate, an important concern."

Chung and Megginson define conflict as "the struggle between incompatible or opposing needs, wishes ideas, interests, or people. Conflict arises when individuals or groups encounter goals that both parties cannot obtain satisfactorily," Though interpersonal conflict is not made explicit in the definition, the first sentence implies intra-individual conflict as well.

March and Simon suggested that the term 'conflict' is used in sense of breakdown in the standard mechanism of decision making. In fact, it is a psychological state of mind, when two opposite forces weigh their power and the person concerned is bound to behave or adjust his behaviour according to force which is more powerful or that overpowers the state of mind. In the context of organizational behaviour, however, the term conflict refers primarily to instances in which units or individual within an organization work against rather than with one another. More formally, according to one widely accepted definition, conflict is a process in which one party perceives that another party has taken some action that will exert negative effects on its major interests, or is about to take such action. In other words, the key elements in conflict seem to include (1) opposing interests between individuals or groups (2) recognition of such opposition, (3) the belief by each side that the other will thwart (or has already thwarted) these interests, and (4) actions that actually produce such thwarting (See Fig. 1).

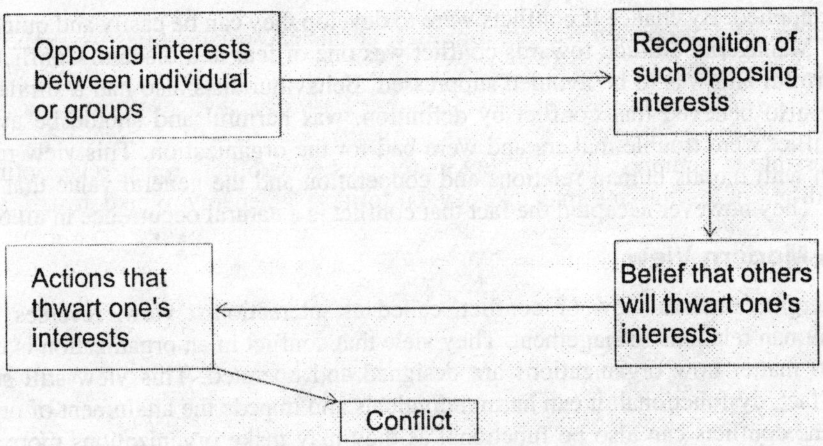

Fig.1. The Nature of Organizational Conflict

Nature of Conflicts

1. Conflict is inevitable. Stephen Robbins says that it is a purposeful activity.
2. Conflict is not necessarily good or bad, but must be evaluated in terms of its individual and organizational functions and dysfunctions.
3. Conflict occurs when two or more parties pursue mutually exclusive goals, values or event it is based on the assumption that there are two or more parties whose interests or goals appear to be incompatible.
4. Conflict must be perceived by the parties to it; whether or not conflict exists is a perception issue.
5. Conflict arises out of two perceptions. If X perceives his goals to be incompatible with those of Y and X has no opportunity to frustrate the goal attainment of Y there is no conflict.
6. Conflict involves opposition or incompatibility and some form of interaction.
7. Conflict refers to deliberate behaviour. X deliberately tries to prevent Y from attaining his (Y's) goals. If interference is accidental, there is no conflict.
8. Conflict is determined by structural factors such as the physical shape of a building the design of a career structure, or the nature of a class system.
9. Conflict is integral to the nature of change. It is a way of instituting revolutionary change.
10. A minimal level of conflict is optimal. Conflict, rather that being disruptive and dissociating, may indeed be a means of balancing and hence maintaining an organization as a going concern.
11. Conflict can exist either at the latent or overt level, but generally speaking, conflict is a term that is limited to overt acts.
12. Conflict is different from competition. In conflict one side seeks an opportunity to interfere with the other's opportunity to acquire resources or perform activities. In competition both sides try to win, but neither side actively interferes with the other. Competition exists when both mutual assistance and antagonism are low. Also, competition does not have purposeful interference. When either party does not follow the "rules of the game", antagonism develops and competition deteriorates into conflict.

Changing Views of Conflict

Over the years, three distinct philosophies that refer to different managerial attitudes toward conflict have been identified; the classical, behavioural and interactionist philosophies. The classical approach viewed conflict as an organizational abnormality, a potentially dangerous process. Conflict induces mainly negative outcomes: anger, resentment, confusion, lack of cooperation etc. It disrupts the smooth functioning of organizational processes and created chaos and disorder. Conflict is bad and must be avoided at all costs. The organization structure with its clear policies, elaborate rules and well defined specifications of authority and responsibility should not permit conflicts occur if sound management principles are applied. By chance if conflicts were to develop they can be easily and quickly resolved by the management. Managerial attitude towards conflict was one of fear and disdain. Conflict by definition was viewed as harmful and was to be avoided suppressed. Behaviouralists also had a similar jaundice view of conflict, they also believed that conflict by definition, was harmful and should be avoided. Those who generated conflict were trouble makers and were bad for the organization. This view reflected a "Popular preoccupation with morals human relations and cooperation and the general value that peace is good and conflict bad." They however accepted the fact that conflict is a natural occurrence in all organizations.

Conflict: A Modern View

The emerging modern view of conflict, called as interactionist view, reverses many of the cozy nostrums of human relations management. They view that conflict in an organization is inevitable and even necessary. No matter how organizations are designed and operated. This view still suggests that much conflict is, in fact, dysfunctional. It can harm individuals and impede the attainment of organizational goals. However, some conflicts can also be functional as they may make organizations more effective. Conflict can lead to search for solutions. Therefore, conflict is an instrument of organizational innovations and change. The interactionist view of conflict has a broader scope. They recognises that in some cases conflict may be helpful, facilitative and functional. The interactionist views can be summarised as following:

1. Conflict is not an organizational abnormality. On the other hand, it is a normal aspect of social intercourse. It is a fact of life that must be understood rather than fought.
2. Conflict is inevitable. It is an inherent structural component in all social relations.
3. Conflict is neither bad nor good for organizations. Perfect organizational health is not free from conflict.
4. Conflict is not always caused by trouble makers. It is rather determined by structural factors like the design of a career structure, the physical shape of a building etc.
5. Conflict is integral to the nature of change.
6. Conflict is not only inevitable but sometimes desirable.

A minimum level of conflict is optimal. In the words of S.P. Robbins "while the behavioural approach accepted conflict the interactionist view encourages conflict on grounds that a harmonious, peaceful, tranquil and cooperative group is prone to becoming static, apathetic, and non-responsive to needs for change and innovation."

Table 1. Traditional and Current Views of Conflict

Traditional View	Current View
Conflict is avoidable.	Conflict is inevitable.
Conflict is caused by management error in designing organizations or by trouble makers.	Conflict arises from many causes, including organizational structure, unavoidable differences in goals, differences in perceptions and values of specialised personnel, and so on.
Conflict disrupts the organization and prevents optimal performance.	Conflict contributes and detracts from organizational performance in varying degrees.
The task of management is to eliminate conflict.	The task of management is to manage the level of conflict and its resolution for optimal organizational performance.
Optimal organizational performance requires the removal of conflict.	Optimal organizational performance requires a moderate level of conflict.

(*Source*: Stoner, *Management*, p. 408).

According to Thomas, it is important to view conflict as a process – a complex series of events over time that both reflect external conditions and, in turn, affect them. More specifically, Thomas notes that conflict episodes between individuals or groups stem from preceding events and conditions, and produce results and outcomes. In other words, conflict is part of a continuing, ongoing relationship between two or more parties, not an isolated event that can be considered in and of itself. What, then, are the key elements in this continuing process?

The first is awareness of the conflict. Thomas suggests that conflicts are, to a large extent, in the eyes of the beholders - they occur only when the parties involved recognize the existence of opposing interests. This, of course, is why conflict sometimes fails to emerge when outside observers notice deep divisions between potential opponents. The parties themselves do not notice (or care to notice!) these conditions, and if they do not, conflict remains only a possibility.

Second, once aware of the conflict, both parties experience emotional reactions to it and think about it in various ways. These emotions and thoughts are crucial to the course of the developing conflict. For example, if the emotional reactions of one or both sides include anger and resentment from past wrongs or from contemplated future ones, the conflict is likely to be intense. If such reactions are absent, or if other emotions (e.g., fear over the potential costs) are dominant, it may be of lower intensity and develop quite differently. Similarly, the parties' reasoning concerning the conflict can have profound effects on its form and ultimate resolution. Here, both rational – instrumental reasoning (e.g., thoughts concerning potential costs and benefits, the conflict's bearing on major goals) and normative reasoning (e.g., concern about what is appropriate in the situation or how others would react) are important.

Third, on the basis of such thoughts and emotions, individuals formulate specific intentions – plans to adopt various strategies during the conflict. These may be quite general (e.g., plans to adopt a conciliatory, cooperative approach) or quite specific (e.g., decisions to follow specific bargaining tactics).

In the next step, such intentions are translated into actual behaviour. These actions then elicit some response from the opposite side, and the process recycles. That is, the opponent's reactions affect current thoughts and feelings about the conflict, intentions concerning further behaviour, and so on. (See Figure 2 for a summary of this process).

Thomas's model of organizational conflict is quite sophisticated and rests on a firm base of empirical research. However, there can be little doubt that it will be modified in the years ahead as additional information about conflict and its components accumulates. Perhaps its main contribution, then, is that it calls attention to the following important facts: (1) organizational conflict is an ongoing process that occurs against a backdrop of continuing relationships and events; it is definitely not a short-term, isolated occurrence; (2) such conflict involves the thoughts, perceptions, memories, and emotions of the people involved; these must be taken into account in any complete model of organizational conflict; and (3) conflict stems from a very wide range of conditions and events – one relating to individuals and one relating to the structure, norms, and functioning of the organization. It is to these factors – the major causes of conflict.

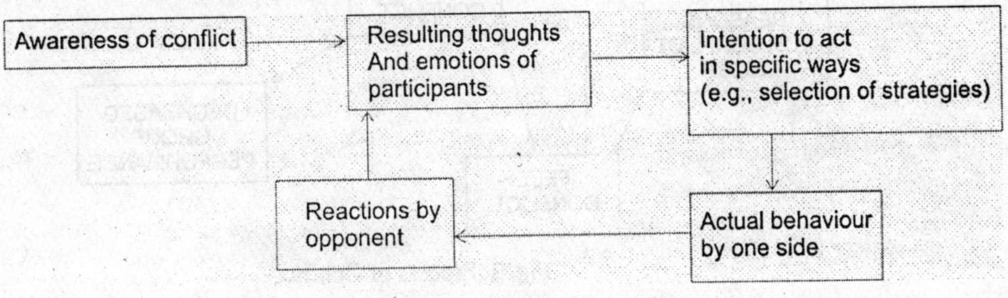

Fig. 2. Conflict: A Modern View

The Process of Conflict

The Process of conflict generally consists of four stages. The process has been diagrammatically represented in Fig. 3 and the stages have been classified as under:

Stage I

Antecedent conditions for conflict exist at the interpersonal level. One party plans to block the attempts of another party from achieving a goal. In organizations, some potential danger and harm threaten the harmonious functioning and perhaps their very existence.

Stage II

The person whose attempts are sought to be thwarted perceives the harm that might be done to him and feels or realises the potential damage. Realisation makes him emotionally involve himself. Emotional involvement makes him feel frustrated, anxious and tense all of which are symptoms of conflict. The same pattern prevails between two groups or departments in organizations.

Stage III

In the third stage of conflict a party engages in action that was planned in Stage I. In other words, he now blocks the other party's attempts in attainment of goals. The conflict is out in the open.

Stage IV

The conflict finally results in an outcome which may be functional or dysfunctional. If conflict is handled well, the result is functional conflict. If it is mismanaged the result is dysfunctional conflict.

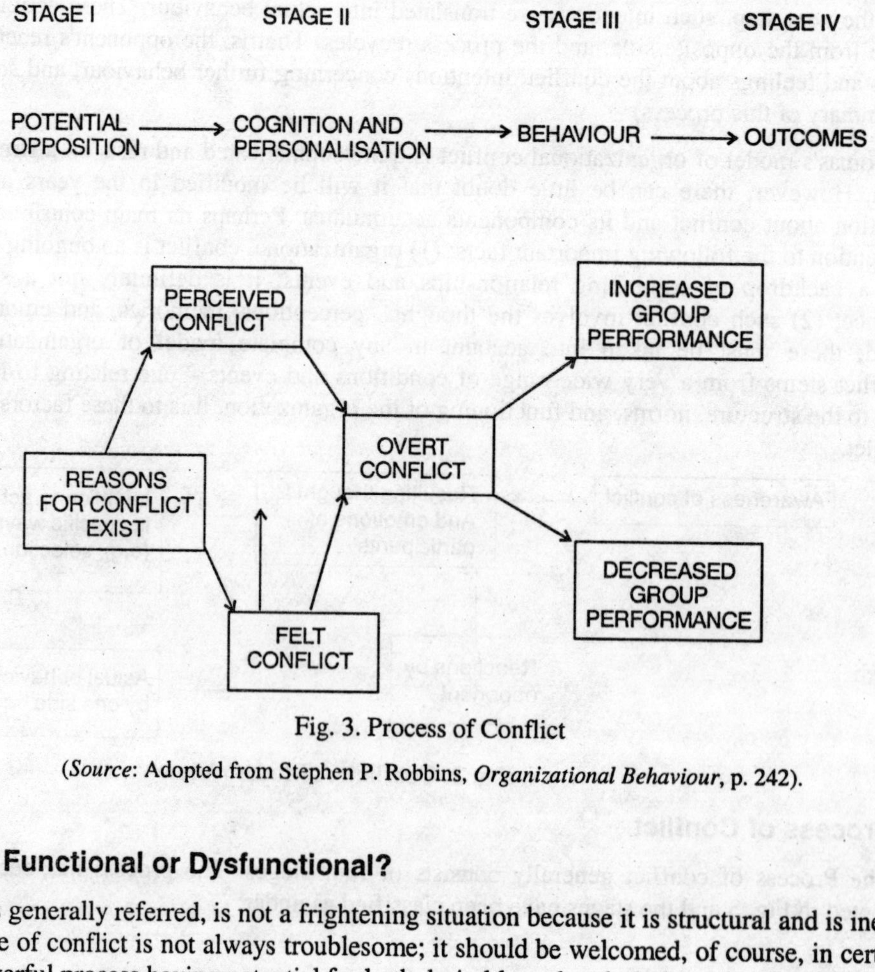

Fig. 3. Process of Conflict

(*Source*: Adopted from Stephen P. Robbins, *Organizational Behaviour*, p. 242).

Are Conflicts Functional or Dysfunctional?

Conflict, as generally referred, is not a frightening situation because it is structural and is inevitable to happen. The state of conflict is not always troublesome; it should be welcomed, of course, in certain cases. Conflict is a powerful process having potential for both desirable and undesirable consequences.

Functional conflict refers to confrontation between two ideas, goals and parties that improve employees and the organization's performance. Well managed conflict helps workers anticipate and solve problems, feel confident, strengthen their relationships, and be committed to the organization. Constructive conflict is crucial for effective functioning of organizations.

A dysfunctional conflict is any confrontation or interaction between groups that harms the organization or hinders the achievement of organizational goals. Management must seek to eliminate dysfunctional conflicts.

The Effects of Conflict: Positive and Negative

In everyday speech, the term conflict has strong negative connotations. It seems to imply anger, direct confrontations, and harsh, damaging behaviour. In fact, however, conflict in work settings actually operates like the proverbial "double-edged sword." Depending on why it occurs and how it develops, conflict can yield beneficial as well as harmful effects.

That conflict can lead to such a mixture of negative and positive outcomes that leads to ambivalence about conflict. Conflict is not necessarily bad or good, but must be evaluated in terms of its individual and organizational functions and dysfunctions.

Before taking any decision for its elimination or management, we should consider its advantages and disadvantages or its functional or positive and dysfunctional or negative consequences.

Functional Conflicts (Positive) Consequences

Conflict has its positive side too. Conflict is not necessarily dysfunctional and to be avoided. Its positive consequences may be as follows:

1. It provides an individual a chance for self introspection, to think again and having a second look on the original or existing situation, may it be procedural or relating to policies, equipment or behaviour.
2. It generates search behaviour and helps seek clarification.
3. It is very necessary for the very existence of the organization because it leads to innovation and at times to new direction.
4. It energises people especially in times of crisis. It leads to mild stimulation and one is at one's best in times of crisis. It helps them test their capacities.
5. It serves as a cementing force between members of a group and incredible unity is also witnessed in times of tension even in a heterogeneous group or groups especially when the cause is common for all the groups in the organization or when source of conflict is common for all groups.
6. For some, it is exhilarating or it is their hobby to accept challenge and meaning to their lives.
7. Conflict is an essential part of a cybernetic system and whenever any of parts of the system is disturbed, the whole system comes into fire. So, conflict draws immediate attention of the management or the person most concerned of the conflict in the organization to the malfunctioning part of the system. It is an indication that the situation calls for improvement.
8. At times, it is also used as a means to an end. The interested parties in order to maintain or strengthen their own position create confusion or set subordinates against each other so that the a attention of the person may be diverted from the main problem. It is sometimes used as a strategy by the management toward thwarting off existing problems temporarily. It may not be viewed as a positive outcome of the conflict in the strict sense of the term from the organizational point of view but still it may be viewed as an unavoidable cost of the pursuit of one's aspiration.
9. Some long-standing problems that continue to agitate people's mind but nobody dares to bring them into light, come to surface through conflicts. They are able to release their tension and unburden themselves. They display creativity in identifying solutions and thus problems are dealt with.
10. A problem can be resolved in a way that is acceptable to all parties involved.
11. The parties will be more predisposed towards cooperation in future situations.

12. Conflict can reduce the potential for "group think."
13. Conflict can help overcome the "yes man" syndrome. This will improve the quality of decision-making.
14. Sometimes, a certain moderate level of stimulation and tension can improve performance and can increase the sense of enjoyment.
15. Some studies suggest that groups in which participants have diverse interests and views, often create better solutions. Conflict can lead to creative searches for alternatives.
16. Conflict arouses discussions. It can help test the merits of arguments, assumptions, and value of ideas. Thus, it creates expanded understanding of the issues.
17. Conflict increases awareness of what problems exist, who is involved, and how to solve the problem.
18. Conflict motivates organizational members to consider problems. They are energised and psychologically focused on the problems and motivated to put plans into action.
19. Conflict promotes change. Persons are more aware of injustices, inefficiencies, and frustrations, and see the need to correct them.
20. Conflict enhances morale and cohesion. Organizational members deal with and clear up their frustrations and resentments. They conclude that their relationships are strong enough to withstand stress and to handle difficulties. They also learn about each others needs, styles, and values through conflict.
21. High quality decisions result when person express their opposing views and perspectives. They share their information to check each other's reasoning to develop new decisions.
22. Conflict stimulates interest and creativity. Being in conflict often sparks curiosity and stimulates viewing problems from several perspectives and combining the best of these positions to form a creative solution. Conflict is exciting as people learn about what makes them and others angry, frustrated, and willing to fight.
23. Conflict adds to the fun of working with others when not taken seriously. Many people find conflict enjoyable to competitive sports, games, movies, plays, books, and in teasing.

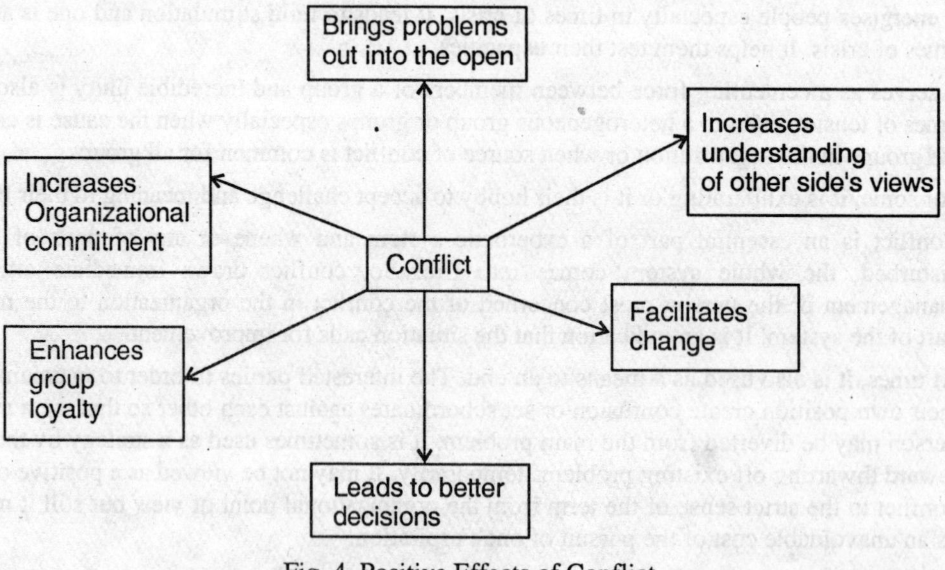

Fig. 4. Positive Effects of Conflict

Dysfunctional Conflict (Negative) Consequences

From the above positive points we are going to suggest that conflict is always functional and has only positive outcome. It is sometimes very disastrous and needs certainly elimination. In the following cases it may be viewed as disastrous:

1. As, it is not, in any way, productive and investment of time and efforts goes waste, production is reduced or held up sometimes for long. It certainly does not lead to a solution of the problem.
2. It is seriously harmful because people work against the organizational objectives. It is certainly a work for their own defeat. People fully involve themselves into conflict and they ignore their main objective to work for organization.
3. It is undesirable even because it creates distrust and suspicion in the minds of people against each other, against management or against the organization. It develops a sense of antagonism instead of a spirit of cooperation.
4. Conflict involves intensification of internalisation of sub goal, ignoring the overall organizational goals.
5. As a consequence of conflict, labour turnover increases.
6. Conflict with management may lose its objectivity and treat the disagreement as disloyalty and rebellion, an opportunity for real creativity should be deemed to have been lost: Management, then, may entangle itself in activities like penalisation, harassment, exploitation, etc., so as to weaken the movement.
7. It creates dissatisfaction, low morale, increased turnover, and decreased productivity.
8. It yields less cooperation in the future.
9. It creates more loyalty to one's own group and more unproductive competition between groups and more unproductive competition between groups within the organization.
10. The parties perceive the other as an "enemy" and experience the feeling of hurt, antagonism, and hostility.
11. It reduces interaction and communication between the conflicting parties.
12. An enormous amount of energy is drained away from the achievement of organizational objectives.
13. Information flow is distorted; low-quality decisions are made. Sometimes, "winning" the conflict becomes more important than effectively solving the real problem.
14. Conflict is a symptom of the lack of social skills. It may threaten the emotional well-being of individual persons.
15. According to March and Simon, conflict is a breakdown in the standard mechanisms of decision making.

Synoptically we can say that though conflict is often cast in the role of a villain, it has long been recognised that conflict is not inherently pathological or destructive. Its very pervasiveness indicates that it has many positive outcomes. Most experts today view conflict as a potentially useful aspect or organizations. It is said that an organization void of constructive conflict is an organization void of excitement, diversity and viability. Conflict prevents stagnation; stimulates interest and curiosity. It is the medium through which problems can be aired and solutions arrived at. It is the root of personal and social change. Conflict provides an adequate platform wherein people can 'blow of steam', that is, it permits immediate and direct expression of rival claims. Without conflict, organizations would be only apathetic and stagnant. The fact is that we cannot imagine an organization, whether small or large, which is altogether free from conflicts.

Levels of Conflict

There are basically 4 levels of conflict :

1. Intra Individual conflict
2. Inter Personal conflict
3. Inter Group conflict
4. Intra Individual conflict

This type of a conflict has also been referred as intra personal conflict by various authors. It is a conflict within individuals, therefore it is internal to the person and probably the most difficult type of conflict to analyse. Synoptically we can say such conflict arises because of frustration, numerous roles that demand equal attention but is not always possible to devote, and goals having both negative and positive aspects.

To begin with, all of us have needs. These needs form the basis for our behaviour at work, at home, at play and in every activity we pursue. Everything we do is directed at satisfying some need. Humans are, to put it in simple terms, goal directed. Need satisfaction spurs people on; non-satisfaction of needs frustrates people and leads to behaviour that negatively affects job performance. Organizations are basically formed for the purpose of meeting humanistic and economic needs of individual. However, the nature of formal organization is such that it tends to create innumerable problems for individuals working therein. The goals of organizational life are in direct conflict with the individuals goals of workers causing them to be frustrated, alienated and threatened. In the words of Davis 'organizations are systems of medieval torture which suppress and subjugate their victim– the individual. He lives in helpless conformity, stripped off his self esteem in a phony and artificial environment, there is no challenge for psychological fulfillment.' Most of the people working in organizations are like inert instruments, mere appendages in the production process there is little chance to be creative. As organizations grow, they tend to be less responsive to the needs of individuals. In addition to loss of freedom the individual is stripped off his identity also. The incongruity model developed by Chris Argyris postulates that there is a lack of congruity between the needs of healthy individuals and the demands of the organization.

The individual is caught in the web of his own making. He faces a conflict within himself. A smooth progression of the need drive goal motivational cycle does not occur. He is confronted with many puzzling questions: Whether to hang on to the present job in spite of its in built disincentives? Whether to tolerate the inhuman treatment meted out daily by the Boss? Whether to manipulate the figures to carry favour with the boss and prosper? To do or not to do? Basically interpersonal conflict can be related to two things: conflict arising due to divergent goals, or conflict arising from out of multiple roles to be played daily ultimately leading to frustration.

Frustration occurs when a motivated drive is blocked before a person reaches a desired goals. Fig. 5 illustrates the way frustration occurs.

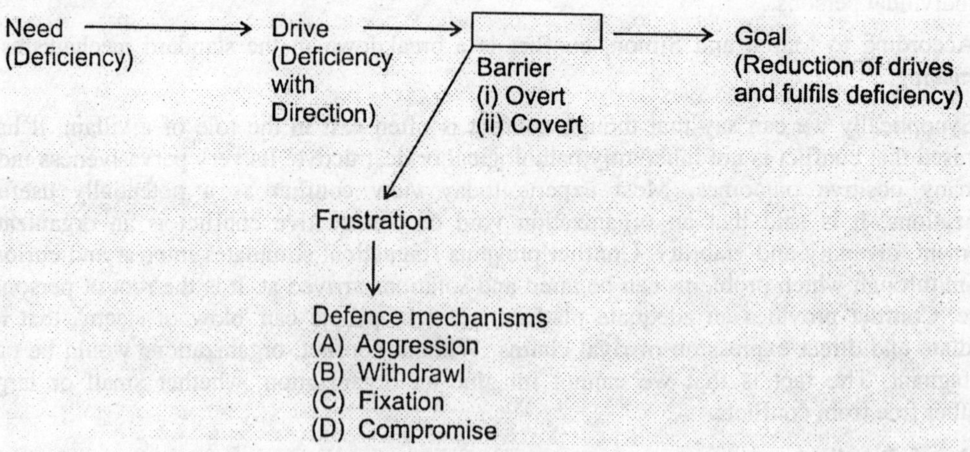

Fig. 5. Frustration Model

An individual driven by an inner state of deficiency engages himself in some action to fulfil the deficiency.

But his attempts to reach the goal are checked by barriers which may be overt (external) or covert (internal). External barriers include floods, power failure, and break down of transportation. These are non social in nature. There are external barriers which are social; they are placed by others in the way of reaching one's goals. Examples of social barriers are: parents forcing a child to sit on the toilet, making him refrain from sex play, making him stay in the room, or denying him the pleasure of watching television.

Internal barriers are: personal limitations are disabilities which thwart one's aspirations. Weakness, physical deformities, lack of skill, or low intelligence may stand in the way of achievement. Internal barriers are more lasting than external ones.

Blocked by overt or covert barriers, the individual becomes frustrated as he is unable to reach his goal.

Frustration normally triggers defence mechanisms in the person. Defence mechanisms (the term first used by Freud) refer to unconscious process that protect an individual from anxiety. They protect him from external threats or against internal anxiety arousing impulses by distorting reality in some way. Defence mechanisms do not alter the objective conditions of danger, they simply change the way the person perceives it. They all involve an element of self-deception.

The frustrated individual adopts any of the four defence mechanism: aggression, withdrawal, fixation, or compromise. Aggression refers to the attack of the barrier, physically of symbolically. Withdrawal refers to backing away from the barrier. Fixation refers to the continuation of efforts to break the barrier. Compromise refers to the search for a new goal conflict which occurs in a defence mechanism situation.

Goal Conflict

Goal conflict is more complex than conflict from frustration. Such type of a conflict normally occurs when a goal that an individual is attempting to achieve has both positive and negative features, or when two or more competing goals exist.

As the subunits of organization become specialised, they often develop dissimilar goals. A goal of a production unit may include low production costs and few defective products. A goal of the research and development unit may be innovative ideas that can be converted into commercially successful new products. These different goals can lead to different expectations among the members of each unit. Production engineers may expect close supervision, while research scientists may expect a great deal of participation in decision making. Because of the different goals, conflict can result when these two groups interact. Finally, marketing departments usually have a goal of maximum gross income; in contrast, credit departments seek to minimise credit losses. Depending on which department prevails, different customers might be selected. Here again, conflict can occur because each department has a different goal. Because of differences in goals, certain conditions foster intergroup conflict.

Therefore we can say that goal conflict normally occurs when the attainment of one goal excludes the possibility of attaining another. We can classify the goal conflicts in the following three major forms:

1. Approach-Approach Conflict
2. Approach-Avoidance Conflict
3. Avoidance-Avoidance Conflict

1. Approach-Approach Conflict

This conflict arises when the individual is caught between two or more positive but mutually exclusive goals.

Approach-approach conflict is hardly a conflict at all, because whichever choice the individual makes, he will attain a positively valued outcome. But the problem, arises when desirabilities of the choices are more or less equal. For instance, a psychological conflict occurs when a person is hungry and sleepy at the same time. In the social context, a conflict may arise when one wants to go to a political rally or a swimming party which are scheduled for the same night. The proverbial donkey is said to have starved to death because he stood half way between two piles of hay and could not decide which to choose. Actually, neither people nor donkeys starve to death merely because they are in conflict between two positive goals. Such a conflict is easily resolved by satisfying first one goal, then the other, for instance, eating first, then sleeping. Alternatively, this conflict is resolved by giving up one of the goals. Obviously, approach-approach conflict does not generate much anxiety. See Fig. 6.

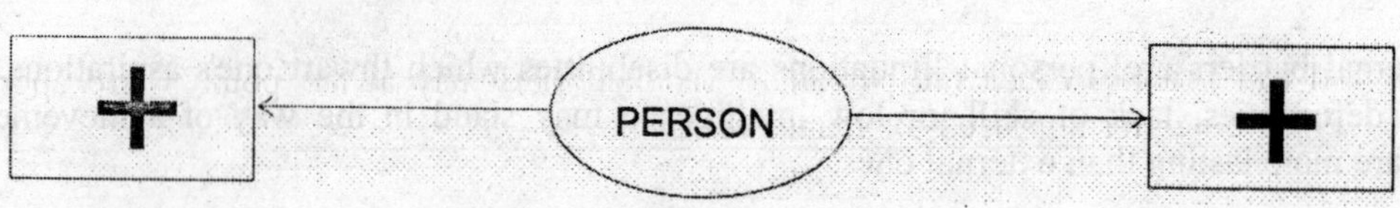

Fig. 6. Approach-Approach Conflict

2. Approach-Avoidance Conflict

This conflict occurs when an individual is simultaneously attracted to and repelled by a single goal object.

For example, a person picks up the telephone receiver and begins to dial the number of someone from whom he wants to ask a favour, but fearing he may insult the other person or be turned down, he quickly puts the receiver back on the hook.

Similarly, a young bride may have been brought up in an atmosphere where sexual activities were treated as ugly and sinful things. As a consequence, sexual matters have a negative valence for her. At the same time her normal sexual drive, as well as other social values involved in marriage, provide martial situation with a positive valence. Now as she enters marriage, she experiences anxiety because she is caught between her sexual motives and the attitudes learned in her early environment.

This type of conflict has maximum relevance in the context of organizational behaviour. In this type both positive and negative rewards are associated with the same goal. Thus if they try to seek the goal (approach) they get positive rewards, but negative rewards also being equally potent, they repel (avoidance) the person from the goal. For example – looking at the success of a manager, he gets the promotion and is given charge of a certain branch. The manager accepts promotion and takes over the charge. But when he starts functioning at his new branch he comes to realise that new position is not a bed of roses but it is associated with a number of pricking thorns also. At this position he can neither ask for the reversal to the original position as he is likely to lose the benefits of new position, nor can he continue because of unanticipated consequences.

This type of conflict is also called double approach-avoidance conflict. If he goes back to the previous position he will have to stand humiliation (negative) but at the same time he may get relief (reward). When managers are at such a stage where approach equals avoidance, they may break down, develop tension, blood pressure, ulcers and they may even become neurotics.

Generally, the approach-avoidance conflicts that are most pervasive and difficult to resolve take place in the following areas:

1. Independence Versus Dependence

In times of stress one feels like resorting to the dependency characteristic of childhood, to have someone to take care of a person and solve his problems. But he is taught to stand on his own feet which is a mark of maturity.

2. Co-operation Versus Competition

One is taught to compete with others and make a success of one's efforts. At the same time one is taught to cooperate and be helpful to others.

3. Impulsive Expression Versus Moral Standards

All societies place some degree of regulation upon impulse control. Sex and aggression are two areas in which one's impulses most frequently conflict with moral standards, and violation of these standards may generate strong feelings of guilt.

The approach-avoidance conflict is most relevant to the study of organizational behaviour. Generally, organizational goals have both positive and negative aspects for organizational participants. For example, superior performance from the job and consequent accolades from management, contrasted with sacrifice of family and outside pursuits. Naturally, the organizational goal will arouse a great deal of conflict within a person and can actually cause the person to vacillate anxiously at the point where approach equals avoidance. Fig. 7 diagrams approach-avoidance conflict.

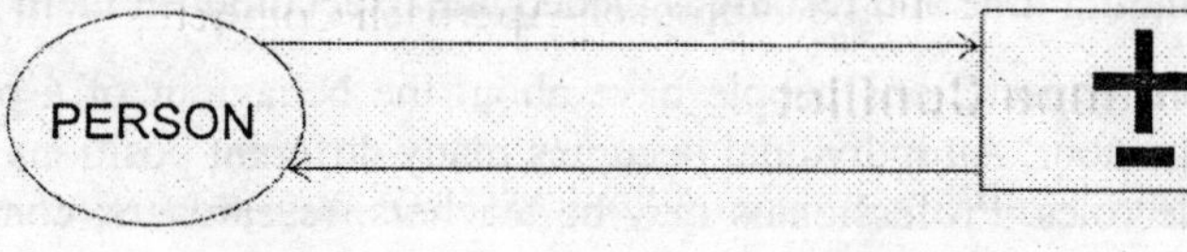

Fig. 7. Approach-Avoidance Conflict

4. Avoidance-Avoidance Conflict

This type of conflict is exactly opposite of the Approach-Approach conflict. This conflict also can be solved easily and usually does not pose any problem of organizational behaviour particularly in developed countries. In case an employee has to work under two bosses it is possible that he wants to avoid both of them. However, he cannot do it unless he leaves the situation. In India there are very few employees who are working in their respective organizations because they are happy or satisfied. Their continuation with the organization is forced upon them by circumstances. Because of non-availability of jobs outside, they have to tolerate their bosses whom they want to avoid.

Nations in which the governments are overthrown frequently and one military rule is followed by another, people may be said to be facing the avoidance-avoidance conflict. In this situation also people cannot escape. At home the child may be required to face a similar conflict if the child does not like both the disciplinarian parents. It, therefore, may be said that in developing countries where problem of unemployment is grave solving even avoidance-avoidance conflict is a difficult task.

Avoidance-avoidance conflict is shown in Fig. 8. In the context of an organization, avoidance - avoidance conflict may be exemplified by a worker who is caught in the dilemma of bearing with the supervisor whom he (worker) detests most and quitting the organization and remaining jobless.

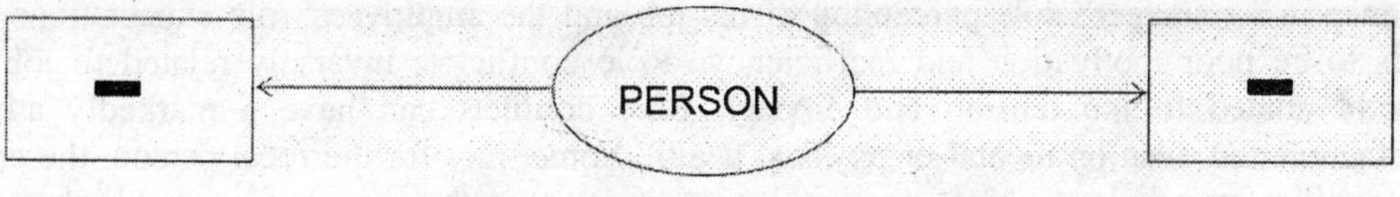

Fig. 8. Avoidance-Avoidance Conflict

Similarly, a child must do his arithmetic or get a spanking. Or, a student must spend the next couple of days studying for an examination or face the possibility of failure. A man must work at a job he dislikes most, or be prepared to lose his income. Such conflicts typify the saying "between the devil and the deep sea."

Two kinds of behaviour are likely to be conspicuous in avoidance conflicts. The first is vacillation. As is well-known the growth of a goal increases the closer a person is to the goal. As the person approaches the negative goal, he or she finds it increasingly repelling. Consequently, the person tends to withdraw. But when the person does this, he or she comes closer to the other negative goal and finds it, in turn increasing in negative valence.

A second feature of this kind of conflict is an attempt to leave the conflict situation theoretically, a person might escape avoidance conflict by running away from it altogether. In practice, however, there are additional negative goals in the periphery of the situation and these prevent us from leaving. A child who does not want either to do his arithmetic or to get a spanking may think of running away from home. This has more negative consequences, so he does not do it. The person in avoidance conflict may report to other means to get relief from anxiety aroused by the conflict. The person may resort to daydreaming instead of facing upto the problem. A student may at times instead of studying for the examination may start daydreeming. A person may even conjure up an imaginary world, or recreate in his or her mind the carefree world of childhood in which no unpleasant tasks have to be performed.

Role Conflict

Another major reason for interpersonal conflict is the need of are individual to play multiple roles simultaneously, but finding time and resources inadequate to accomplish them leads to role conflict.

A role is a set of expectations people have about the behaviour of a person in a position. It is an expected modé of behaviour. An individual occupies many different positions in a variety of organizations and performs multiple roles. Professionals may be teachers, researchers, consultants, wives or husbands, community leaders. In organizations such roles are formally prescribed and others are created by the informal activities of the organization members. When we examine the concept of role three types of roles clearly emerge: the expected role, the perceived role and the actual role. The expected role is what other people expect from an individual. For example, a college teacher is expected by his role partners (Principal, colleagues, students) to behave in a specific way. The perceived role is how the individual thinks he or she should behave to fulfil the expected role. The enacted role is the way the person actually behaves in an organization. Thus in the complex theatre of modern life, most people play not to one audience but to several, and they play multiple roles simultaneously.

Although all the roles which individual bring into the organization are relevant to their behaviour in the study of organizational behaviour, the organizational role is the most important. Roles such as assembly line worker, clerk, supervisor, sales person, engineer, systems analyst, department head, and chairman of the board often carry conflicting demands and expectations. The classic example of an organizational role in constant conflict is that of the foreman. The foreman is generally promoted from among workers. Till yesterday, the foreman was a part of workers. Today he finds himself in the cadre of management. The dilemma of the foreman becomes acute when there is a dispute between labour and management.

An individual confronted with role conflict will experience psychological stress leading to emotional problems.

The likely end result will be a decline in performance. 'Research shows that where there is wide variance in a manager's role perception of his job and the employees' role expectations of that job there tends to be poor motivation and inefficiency.' Role conflict is inversely related to job satisfaction and directly related to job tension and anxiety. Role conflicts can have a markedly adverse impact on satisfaction and even on mental or physical health. Sometimes for the focal person, the emotional costs of role conflict include low job satisfaction, low confidence in the organization and high scores on the multi item index of tension.

Organizations using participative management tend to minimise role conflict. Persuasion and group pressures can be exercised to bring subordinates' goals closer to organizational goals. Role conflict cannot be completely planned away. The management's approach towards resolving role conflicts should be to avoid situations where such conflicts arise. The important aspect will be matching situations and approaches. As pointed out by R.L. Khan, a ceremony of confrontation and joint problem solving would seem to be a useful mode of (role) conflict resolution.

Interpersonal conflict

When two individuals are in confrontation with each other, it may be said an inter individual conflict. For example, two boys fighting for one cinema ticket, two men vying for one woman, two managers competing for the same promotion, two executives maneuvering for a larger share of corporate capital – examples of conflict between individuals are legion and quite familiar. Such conflict situation are made up of at least two individual who hold polarised points of view, who are somewhat intolerant of ambiguities, who ignore delicate shades of grey, and who are quick to jump to conclusions.

Interpersonal conflict may be between two individuals of the same group. In that case, it may be called 'intragroup conflict.' If conflict is between two members of the different groups and it may simply be regarded as inter individual conflict but if it is blown up, it may develop as inter group conflict.

Causes of Conflicts at Individual Level

There are a number of causes why individual conflicts arise within an organization. We may summarise them as follows:

(i) The one of the main reasons of conflicts at individual level is mismatching of individual needs with organizational reward. A man joins the institution with a number of psychological needs which he expects to be satisfied and in turn works to achieve organization goal. He also bring certain beliefs values and perception to the organization. As the starts working, he elaborates beyond his formal behaviour and finds himself unable to translate his ideas into reality because his initial needs constantly change on the one hand, and he is bound to work under certain rules and regulations. Therefore, conflict arises with the clash of individual and organizational goals.

(ii) The second cause of conflict may be the situation of widespread uncertainty and scarcity of acceptable alternatives which are caused by the complexity of problems and lack of past experience in handling such problems. The less the complexity of decision situation and the greater the amount of past experience with a decision situation the less probable the intraindividual organizational conflict is. For example, a policy of frequent transfer from one department to another will cause uncertainty in the minds of people because they cannot accumulate experience.

(iii) Conflict may also develop if there exists a disparity between aspiration levels and achievement that causes individual dissatisfaction. The greater the disparity, the higher is the probability of individual conflict. The best solution of such disparity lies in providing better environment in the organization otherwise the gap between aspirations and achievements will continue to develop and if there is considerable time lag in the adjustment, the conflict will intensity. The disparity between these two variables develops especially in times of low organizational performance or where organizational performance and aspirations both rise, any check on the fulfilment of aspirations will cause conflict.

If the disparity between aspiration level and achievements exist persistently for a long time, it develops frustratively aggressive behaviour or the individual concerned will make an attempt to overcome an obstacle. Studies show that the relationship between frustration and aggression is not invariable one. Sometimes due to persistent frustration, the individual adjust his sights and reconciles with situation.

(iv) Sometimes intraindividual conflict is an outcome of interindividual conflict. Many a time, the organization puts two individual in a conflicting situations. For example, if the organization has reward system depending upon individual performance, but performance is not an independent factor, it is rather interdependent. Such situations open up the floodgates of interindividual and intraindividual conflict.

Intergroup or Organizational Conflict

Intergroup conflicts are also referred as organizational conflicts. Such conflicts are between two groups– department or sections in an organization. .

Intergroup conflicts over authority, jurisdiction and resources are exceedingly common. Every group is in at least partial conflict with overt other group it interacts with. Most of the departments in the organization complete for the allocation of scarce resources and power. They differ in goals, work activities, power and prestige the seeds of intergroup conflict are sown in these differences.

Conflicts at the group (formal and informal) level may also be intragroup conflicts and intergroup conflicts.

(i) Intergroup Conflicts

When conflicts develop between two individual members of the same group, it is intergroup conflict. Sometimes intragroup conflicts develop due to the following reasons:

(i) The group faces a novel problem,

(ii) New values are imported from the social environment, or

(iii) A person's extra group role gives birth to intragroup conflict.

(ii) Intragroup Conflicts

When two members of different groups come into conflict, it may be an interindividual conflict if groups are not involved in the conflict but when interindividual conflict between members of two groups involves two groups then, it assumes the proportion of an intergroup conflict. Sometimes intragroup conflict divides the members of the group into two small groups, then the intragroup conflict is also transformed into intergroup conflict.

Sources or Causes of Group Conflicts

The source of intergroup conflict lies in:

(a) Need for joint decision making; and

(b) The differentiation of goals or of perception or of both.

Both the above conditions must be satisfied for an intergroup conflict. If there is a need of joint decision making and all people agree on the proposal, there would be no conflict. Similarly, if there is differentiations of goals or perception or both but joint decision of all persons are not necessary even then, there is no conflict. But in real organizational situations, both conditions exist still numerous intergroup conflicts arise.

(a) The need for decision making arises because of the following:

(i) **There are limited resources** with every organization which have to be shared with a group. Moreover, technological considerations create interdependence and therefore, activities are to be scheduled. Need for sharing of limited resources and scheduling of activities make groups so interdependent that no one group can take decisions independently.

(ii) There may be **need for joint decision making to determine the appropriate area for joint decision making** such as authority and power relationship. Who will enjoy how much authority and what functions should be performed by whom etc. This decision making does not create any problem if the attitude of all the groups is cooperative. The problem arises only when groups and subgroups internalise their subunit goals regardless of overall organizational goals. These groups in such circumstances become competitive rather than complementary.

(iii) **The need for joint decision making increases with the increase in the organizational level** as things are coordinated at higher levels. This phenomenon is greatly found in interdependent departments. The interdependence is most important to the head of all departments rather than to heads of various departments. So, the claim and counter-claim and the conflict develops. Sometimes conflict may develop between head of all departments (superior) and heads of the various departments (subordinates).

(iv) **Lack of availability of resources in plenty poses a serious problem.** Mutual dependence on limited resources is, in fact, an organization system and that sets people in competition for acquisition of means. This problem may arise intra or inter group posing a high tension. This type of competition is disruptive of group cohesiveness. Resources may be financial or personnel or materials etc.

(b) The differentiation of goals or perceptions or both occurs because of the following:

(i) **Individuals' backgrounds such as family, education, culture, experience, etc.** differ and so their values, beliefs and norms also differ which they bring to the organization. Their own goals and professional ethics may have considerable effects upon them. The organization attempts to obtain a homogeneous set of people through recruitment procedures.

(ii) **A person may be member of different informal groups** and those groups may have different goals. At times, not only the goals of some groups of which he is member may conflict but also the roles he plays in different groups may conflict.

(iii) **The division of labour and task specialisation create groups which internalise their subunit goals regardless of overall organizational goals.** Which themselves are generally highly non-operational, imperfectly rationalised, ambiguous or vague. The obvious case is that of line and staff personnel. The former has to implement what latter proposes. The goals of the two kinds of personnel come into conflict.

(iv) Differentiation of goals in an organization increases as the interactions of people are reduced because by interaction, they develop cohesiveness.

(v) Often individuals and groups are set in competition for positions or resources which are, scarce. The situation worsens if the rewarding system is linked to a very vague criterion, capable of different interpretation for different rewarding authorities. If resources are further reduced, this will generate tensions among people and groups. Moreover, reward distribution in organization is also dependent upon the bargaining strength of the members of the group, not consistent with one's merits. Organizational environment also influences the reward system. As the reward remains undefined and ill-defined hence inconsistencies and ambiguities creep into the system which in turn cause goal differentiation.

Thus we have seen that conflicts at group level may be intragroup and intergroup conflict. **March and Simon** have illustrated that intergroup conflicts arise mostly between inter-connected departments. The closer the connections the greater will be the felt need for joint decision making and less the differential of goals the less the differentiation for perceptions. The actual degree of conflict depends upon the strength of the individual effects the interaction among them.

3. CONFLICTS AT THE ORGANIZATION LEVEL

Conflicts at organization level may also be of two types:

(i) Internationalisation and (ii) interorganizational. Intraorganizational conflicts comprise of all intraindividual, interindividual, intragroup and intergroup conflicts because they all are the parts of the same organization. They may assume organization wide proportions and turn into hierarchical conflicts, functional conflicts, professional. versus functional conflicts, management versus shop floor conflicts or union versus union conflicts. What we have discussed above, is all about intraorganizational conflicts.

The interorganizational conflicts are assumed between two organizations or between a business organization and the government.

The discussion in this chapter is restricted mainly to intraorganizational conflicts.

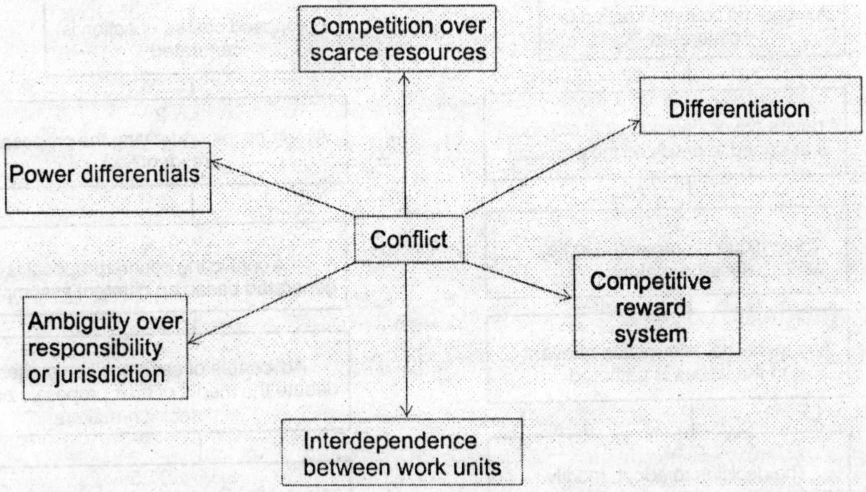

Fig. 9. The Organizational Causes of Conflict

Stimulating Functional Conflict

Sometimes, committees and decision-making groups become so bogged down in details and procedures that nothing substantive is accomplished. Carefully monitored functional conflict can help get the creative juices flowing once again. Managers basically have two options. They can fan the fires of naturally occurring conflict – but this approach can be unreliable and slow. Alternatively, managers can resort to programmed conflict. Experts in the field define programmed conflict as "conflict that raises different opinions regardless of the personal feelings of the managers." The trick is to get contributors to either defend or criticise ideas based on relevant facts rather than on the basis of personal preference or political interests. This requires disciplined role playing. Two programmed conflict techniques with proven track records are devil's advocacy and the dialectic method. Let us explore these two ways of stimulating functional conflict.

Devil's Advocacy: This technique gets its name from a traditional practice within the Roman Catholic Church. When someone's name came before the College of Cardinals for elevation to sainthood, it 'was absolutely essential to ensure that he or she had a spotless record. Consequently, one individual was assigned the role of devil's advocate to uncover and air all possible objections to the person's canonization. In accordance with this practice, devil's advocacy in today's organization involves assigning someone the role of a critic. In the left half of Fig. 10 note how devil's advocacy alters the usual decision-making process in steps 2 and 3. This approach to programmed conflict is intended to generate critical thinking and reality testing. It is a good idea to rotate the job of the devil's advocate so that no one person or group develops a strictly negative reputation. Moreover, the periodic devil's advocacy role-playing is good training for developing analytical and communicative skills.

The Dialectic Method: Like the devil's advocacy, the dialectic method is a time honored practice. This particular approach to programmed conflict traces back to the dialectic school of philosophy in ancient Greece. Plato and his followers attempted to synthesize truths by exploring opposite positions (called thesis and antithesis). Court systems in the United States and elsewhere rely on directly opposing points of view for determining guilt or innocence. Accordingly, today's dialectic method calls for managers to foster a structured debate of opposing viewpoints prior to making a decision. Steps 3 and 4 in the right half of Fig. 10 set the dialectic approach apart from the normal decision-making process.

A major drawback of the dialectic method is that "winning the debate" may overshadow the issue at hand.

Also, the dialectic method requires more skill training than does devil's advocacy.

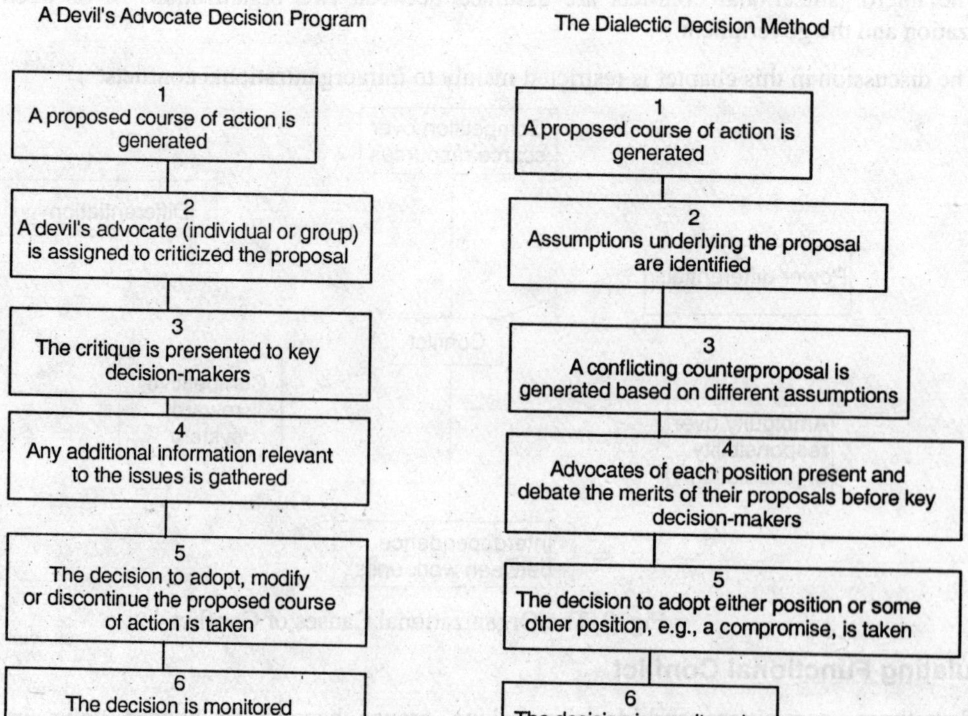

Fig. 10. Techniques for Stimulating Functional Conflict: Devil's Advocacy and the Dialectic Method

Regarding the comparative effectiveness of these two approaches to stimulating functional conflict, however, a laboratory study ended in a tie. Compared with groups that strive to reach a consensus, decision-making groups using either devil's advocacy or the dialectic method yielded equally higher quality decisions. In light of this evidence, managers have some latitude in using either the devil's advocacy or the dialectic method for pumping creative life back into stalled deliberations. Personal preferences and the role players' experience may well be the deciding factors in choosing one approach over the other. The important thing is to actively stimulate functional conflict when necessary (such as when as when the risk of blind conformity or groupthink is high).

RESOLUTION OF CONFLICT

When a conflict has arisen whether intraindividual, interindividual, intragroup or intergroup in an organization, it must be resolved as early as possible. In an organization there must be, someone to intervene before the situation goes worse and generally a superior helps improve the situation. In order to resolve the conflict effectively the superior should handle the situation carefully and take the following actions without further delay:

(a) Preliminary step – knowing the reasons of conflict.

(b) Diagnosing the issue.

(c) Applying any of the conflict handling modes.

We are discussing these steps hereunder:

(a) PRELIMINARY STEP

The first stage in resolving the conflict is to know the full details of the conflict. As soon as the conflict comes to the knowledge of the superior, he should handle the conflict skilfully.

The first thing to note is the stage of conflict because, if it is in its initial stage, it requires less efforts and much efforts will be needed at advance stage of conflict. Even the strategies used may also differ from stage to stage though there is hardly a relationship between the stage of conflict and strategies used.

Before analysing the issues involved in the conflict, it should also be considered that the person who is being entrusted the responsibility to intervene and resolve the conflict, should be objective enough in handling the problem. Though, it is very difficult to keep emotions and sentiments out of the job and attain absolute de-personalisation, yet one can be objective if he keeps an open mind. For this purpose, one should listen to views of individuals who are in conflict though they may not be fully in agreement with him provided the individual concerned does not carry rigid perception. The superior must try to keep the individuals' mind open.

(b) DIAGNOSING THE ISSUE

In diagnosing the issue, the issues involved in the conflict should be analysed and it should be understood what this conflict is about. How far it has already evolved. Thus the nature of conflict should be found out. Generally conflict may arise due to facts, goals, methods, and values. In other words, facts at the disposal of two parties may differ or their goals may differ or their methods to be used for doing a particular task may differ or their views about what is good, bad, wrong or right may differ. So, the person entrusted to handle the conflict must find out what the conflict is about.

The next thing in diagnosing the issue is to know why these differences between the two parties have arisen.

The factors responsible for promoting the differences may informational, perceptual, role factors and the like. At times, the information received by two parties may be different and therefore they may draw different conclusions. People may also have different backgrounds. Their beliefs, attitudes, values, and cultural norms may differ and therefore their perception may differ. An individual may have different roles in different groups of which he is a member and these roles may clash or the role of one individual may differ from another individual. For example a superior may have an urgency of getting a particular work done but the subordinate does not think so. It may lead two persons to clash.

Once the problem is identified and what has caused the problem becomes known, the stage at which it has already reached can be properly understood. The next important step is to develop a strategy to deal with the situation.

(c) CONFLICT HANDLING MODES

Kinds of strategies.

We can easily categorise all strategies into following five:

1. To avoid appearance of conflict.
2. Not permitting conflict to surface.
3. Mediation.
4. Letting the parties in conflict to settle their scores, and
5. Mutual problem solving.

We shall now discuss each of them one by one:

1. To Avoid Appearance of Conflict. This approach suggests that such conditions should be created in the organization in which may not arise and if it arises, it should be ignored as far as possible. This situation is possible when the organization is staffed with the like-minded people and possibly keeps a watch over their interpersonal relations. Such people whenever they interact, they should focus problem of their superior rather than to discuss their own problem. They are always submissive to their superior and never aggressive or in conflict with him. If, anyhow, there is a difference of opinion between the two, it is ignored.

Evaluation. This kind of conformity and agreement may be necessary where blind faith in the leader of the group is required. It is very common in political and religious organizations which demand total commitment of members towards the goals and ideals of the organization. But in this approach, creativity of the members is lost and they are not able to put forward their ideas for the sake of simple conformity.

2. Not Permitting Conflict to Surface. This strategy suggests that loyalty and cooperation to the group is supreme and not disagreement is tolerated and may be treated equivalent to disloyalty to group. People who are loyal and cooperative are rewarded and those, who are not, are punished. As soon the conflict is known to the superior, the parties in conflict are warned of the serious consequences and are ordered to sink their differences or the matter is referred 'upstairs' or superior insists on his own way.

Evaluation. This kind of approach of repression and forcing may work where talent difference is not so important as the pressure of the time but such suppressed differences may erupt at any time appropriate for the organization and may hit safe targets. This approach does not create a satisfying situation and if the matter is allowed to brew for long, the party concerned whose views are suppressed always looks for an opportunity embarrassing the position of authority holder.

3. Mediation. Under this approach, an attempt is made by the authority holder to sweep out the difference and to smoothen the affair to make it look like as if the problem never existed. He may exercise persuasion highlighting the merits and demerits of their cases. He may conciliate mediate, bringing home to them the commonness in their viewpoints and if necessary, even arbitrate. It is quite possible that both the parties may leave the case to the superior to give his judgement, in case of failure of finding any solution of the case, and both will accept his decision. It may also be possible that a compromise takes place or they may arrive at a mutually acceptable agreement.

Evaluation. Under this approach both parties make a shift in their stand on give and take thesis. It may be with or without the intervention of superior. This strategy is most commonly used.

4. Letting the Parties in Conflict to Settle their Scores. Parties adopt a rigid attitude and not answerable to reason or appeal, they are allowed to fight out the issues. They are given an opportunity to test their strength and capacities and to bear the consequences whatsoever. In such cases it can be possible that the party may have the realisation of each other's strength and leave their priorities, accept the ideas and interpretation of others and resort to bargaining. The parties, before using this approach should assess the cost of such conflicts – economical and social.

Evaluation. This approach has far reaching consequences. In case the opposition feels defeated, there will develop personal distance that will never be reduced. The losing party will always try to find out ways how to revenge. Besides such potentially disruptive consequences of this approach, it almost necessarily places strains on the status and power system in the organization, if acknowledge and legitimise the heterogeneity of goals. This approach is not willingly or frequently adopted.

5. **Mutual Problem Solving.** When two parties are conscious about the existence of a problem and try to resolve their difference themselves, it is called mutual problem solving or collaborating. As both parties are interested in finding a solution, the reference should always be made of the shared goals, generally the subordinate goals. The perceptions of people are not rigid.

Evaluation. This approach is better when time pressure is not serious though it is a very time consuming process to come across a commonly acceptable solution. If in the meanwhile a party loses patience, all efforts are likely to go waste. Therefore a solution should be resolved before a party loses patience.

Whatever may be the approach for handling conflicts, it is necessary to be sure that communication channels are neither blocked nor broken down. Free of flow information must be maintained otherwise lack of information or blocked communication channels cause disruptive behaviour. As a result, the gap between two parties widens and then it will be irrepairable. It may also be suggested that whatever may be the nature, stage or class of conflict, it should always be regarded as individual (and not group conflict) and analytic conflict. In short, an impression should not be created that the conflict has engulfed the whole organization. The approach should be problem solving and persistent persuasion of the parties.

INTEGRATION AND DISTRIBUTION: TWO BASIC DIMENSIONS OF CONFLICT

In your dealings with other people, to what extent do you focus on your own interests, maximizing your outcomes? And to what extent do you focus on other's interests – assuring that they are treated fairly, or that the size of the available "pie" (whatever it is) is maximized for all concerned? These questions are difficult to answer accurately because most cultures have strong norms against pure selfishness-concern purely with one's own outcomes. Yet the temptation to pursue one's own interests is strong and hard to resist in many situations. Several basic models of conflict take careful note of these facts, suggesting that conflict, as an organizational or interpersonal process, can best be understood in terms of two key dimensions: distribution, concern with one's own outcomes; and integration, concern with the outcomes of others. A large body of research evidence indicates that these dimensions are important and that they are largely independent. Thus, in a given situation, it is possible to pursue actions that are high in both distribution and integration, low in both dimensions, or high in one and low in the other. In fact, various combinations of these motives underlie five distinct styles of handling conflict with others: competing, collaborating, avoiding, accommodating and compromising.

Fig. 11 illustrates the position of each of these styles with respect to integration and distribution. Compromise, which involves splitting issues down the middle, is in the middle on both dimensions; it reflects moderate degrees of concern with one's own interests and the interests of others. In contrast, competition represents a style of conflict resolution reflecting high concern with one's own interests but low concern with the interests of others.

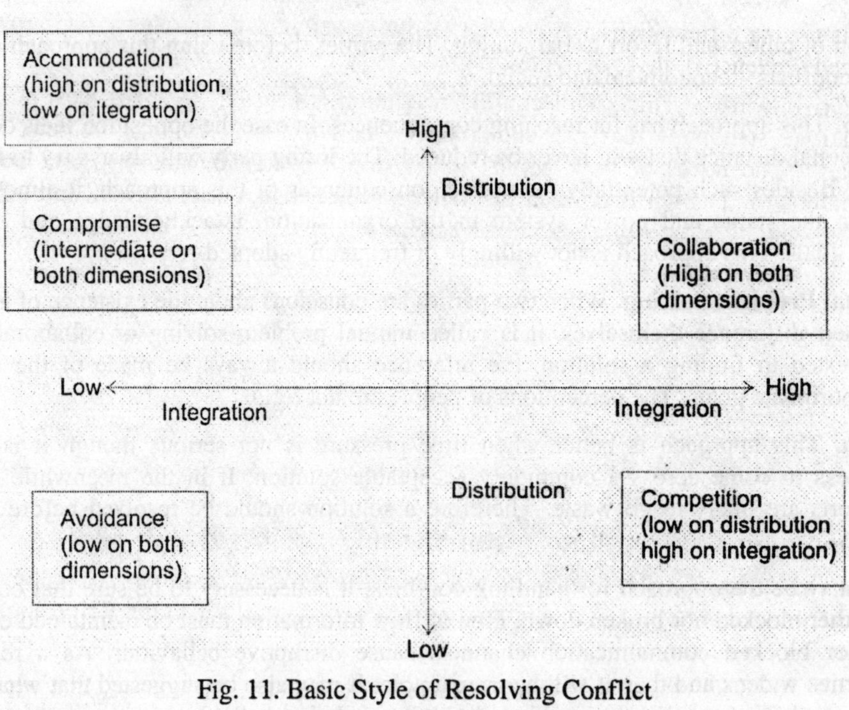

Fig. 11. Basic Style of Resolving Conflict

Avoidance reflects low standing on both dimensions, whereas collaboration-seeking maximum outcomes for both sides – is high on both dimensions. Finally, accommodation-giving others whatever they want – is low in distribution but high in integration. (Are these styles equally likely to occur throughout the world, or do people from various cultures prefer different styles of resolving conflicts? For an examination of this question, see the Global Organization section below).

Resolving Inter-Personal Conflict

The strategies suggested for reducing intra-personal conflict will be useful to resolve inter-personal conflict also. The additional approaches to resolve inter-personal conflict are: the lose-lose, win-lose and win-win strategies. Transactional Analysis, which was discussed earlier, will also be useful in overcoming the inter personal conflict. Finally, inter-personal conflict can be resolved *bV* changing behavioural inputs.

Lose-Lose: In a lose-lose approach to conflict resolution, both parties stand to lose. This approach can take several forms. One of the approaches is to take a compromise or middle ground to a dispute. A second approach is to pay-off one of the parties to a dispute. The payment may take the form of bribe. A third approach is to involve a third party as an arbitrator. The final approach is for both parties to resort to existing regulations or bureaucratic rules to resolve the conflict. Lose-lose strategy is sometimes the only one available but is less effective than the win-lose or win-win approach.

Win-Lose: In this strategy one party to the conflict tries to marshal all the resources to win, and the other party loses. Examples of win-lose strategies can be found in superior-subordinate relationships, line-staff confrontations, union-management relations, and many other conflict situations formed in contemporary organizations. Though win-lose strategy he1ps defuse conflict, it may not be a permanent solution since the loser will tend to be bitter and vindictive. A most healthier strategy is to have both parties in a conflict situation win.

The following points make win-lose strategy more clear:

1. The conflicting parties view the issue from their own points of view.
2. The emphasis is on solutions rather than on the attainment of goals, values or objectives.
3. There is a clear we-they distinction between the parties.
4. The parties direct their energies towards each other in an atmosphere of victory and defeat.
5. Conflicts are personalised and judgmental.
6. The parties take a short-run view of the issues.

7. There is neither differentiation of conflict resolving activities from other group processes, nor is there a planned sequence of those activities.

Win-Win: A win-win strategy of conflict resolution is probably the most desirable from the human and organizational standpoint. Energies and creativity are aimed at solving the problems rather than beating the other party. The needs of both parties in the conflict situation are met, and both parties receive rewarding outcomes. Though it is often difficult to accomplish a win-win outcome of an inter-personal conflict, this should be a major goal of the management of conflict.

Transactional Analysis: Inter-personal conflict can be resolved by encouraging as many complimentary transactions as possible between parties to the conflict. Of more significance for conflict management is the adult to adult transaction between the parties. Interaction between two adult ego states will improve communication. Improved communication is the sure way of resolving conflict.

Altering the Behavioural Inputs: Finally, inter-personal conflict may be resolved by focusing on the behaviour of the individuals involved. Conflict arises out of the perceptions and attitudes of people. These can be changed through training programmes. T-group or sensitivity training assumes relevance in this context.

Alternative Styles for Handling Dysfunctional Conflict

People tend to handle negative conflict in patterned ways referred to as styles. Several conflict styles have been categorized over the years. According to conflict specialist Afzalur Rahim's model, five different conflict handling styles can be plotted on a 2 x 2 grid. High to low concern for others, forms the vertical axis. Various combinations of these variables produce the five different conflict handling styles: integrating, dominating, avoiding, compromising, and obliging.

There is no single best style: each has strengths and limitations and is subject to situational constraints.

Integrating (Problem-Solving)

In this style, interested parties confront the issue and cooperatively identify the problem, generate and weigh alternative solutions, and select a solution. Integrating is appropriate for complex issues plagued by misunderstanding. However, it is inapppropriate for resolving conflicts rooted in opposing value systems. Its primary strength is longer lasting impact because it deals with the underlying problem rather than merely with symptoms. The primary weakness of this style is that it is very time consuming.

Obliging (Smoothing)

"An obliging person neglects his or her own concern to satisfy the concern of the other party." This style, often called smoothing, involves playing down differences while emphasizing commonalities. Obliging may be an appropriate conflict-conflict-handling strategy when it is possible to eventually get something in return. But it is inappropriate for complex or worsening problems. Its primary strength is that it encourages cooperation. Its main weakness is that it is a temporary fix that fails to confront the underlying problem.

Dominating (Forcing)

High concern for self and low concern for others encourages 'I win, you lose' tactics. The other party's needs are largely ignored. This style is often called forcing because it relies on formal authority to force compliance. Dominating is appropriate when an unpopular solution must be implemented: the issue is minor, or a deadline is near. It is inappropriate in an open and participative climate. Speed is its primary strength. The primary weakness of this domineering style is that it often breeds resentment.

Avoiding

This tactic may involve either passive withdrawal from the problem or active suppression of the issue.

Avoidance is appropriate for trivial issues or when the costs of confrontation outweigh the benefits of resolving the conflict. It is inappropriate for difficult and worsening problems. The main strength of this style is that it buys time in unfolding or ambiguous situations. The primary weakness is that the tactics provide a temporary fix that sidesteps the underlying problems.

Compromising

This is a give-and-take approach involving moderate concern for both self and others. "Each party is required to give up something of value. Includes external or third party interventions, negotiations and voting." Compromise is appropriate when parties have opposite goals or possess equal power (such as labour-management contract negotiations). But compromise is inappropriate when overuse would lead to inconclusive action (e.g., failure to meet production deadlines). The primary strength of this tactic is that the democratic process has no losers, but it is a temporary fix that can stifle creative problem-solving.

ESCALATIVE INTERVENTIONS: INTENSIFYING CONFLICTS TO RESOLVE THEM

Perhaps the most intriguing approach to managing organizational conflict suggested in recent years is one that seems, at first glance, to fly in the face of common sense. This approach, known as escalative intervention, seeks to intensify existing conflicts as a means of resolving them and attaining several related goals as well. The reasoning behind this strategy is as follows: increasing the intensity of a conflict brings matters to a head. The underlying causes of friction or disagreement are clarified, and the motivation to search for effective, integrative solutions is increased. Then, instead of continuing to smolder beneath the surface, conflicts emerge into the open and can be resolved to the satisfaction of those involved.

According to Van de Vliert, several tactics can be used to intensify ongoing conflicts. First, steps may be taken to add to the existing causes of conflict. For example, present channels of communication may be blocked, or the incompatibility of various goals can be emphasized. Similarly, various barriers to open conflict can be removed or lessened (e.g., direct contacts between the opposing sides can be increased; both sides may be urged to express negative feelings about one another). Second, the range of issues on which the conflict is based can be extended by calling attention to additional matters about which the disputants disagree. Third, additional parties can be added to the conflict, thus fueling its scope or intensity. In a fourth strategy, actions that serve to escalate the conflict can be encouraged (e.g., one side is urged to prove to the other that it is right, or to cause the other to lose face). Finally, the two sides may be encouraged to perceive hostile intentions in each other's actions, or to express strong disapproval of one another's proposals.

To the extent that such tactics succeed, ongoing conflict is intensified. Thus, strong pressures toward reaching a resolution are generated, and several benefits may follow. First, and most important, faced with mounting tension and a situation that is fast becoming intolerable, the two sides may increase their efforts to reach effective, integrative agreements. In addition, other benefits, such as the stimulation of major change, discouragement of avoidance behaviours, and a clearer diagnosis of underlying problems within an organization, may also result (see Fig. 12). However, these favourable outcomes are certainly not guaranteed. They follow only when the individuals managing such an intensification of conflict are skilled in this task and are able to direct the growing tensions and friction into constructive channels.

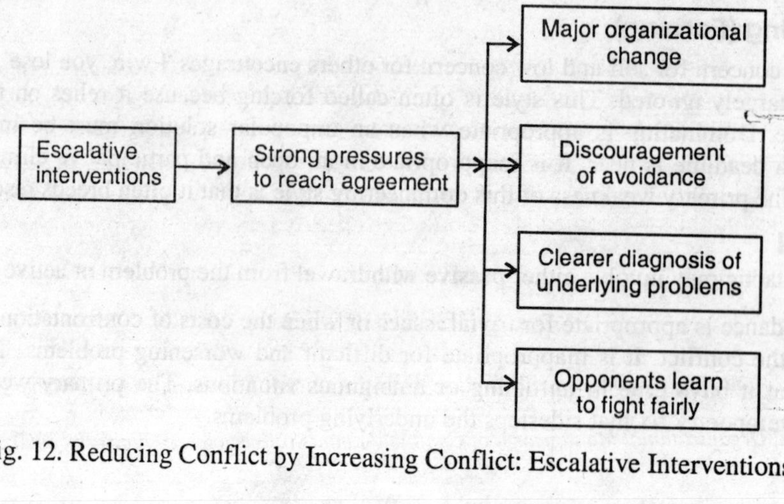

Fig. 12. Reducing Conflict by Increasing Conflict: Escalative Interventions

Is it actually possible to direct escalating conflicts in this fashion? Research evidence suggests that it is, and that escalative interventions are indeed helpful in several contexts (e.g., in marital disputes as well as organizational ones). Thus, in this context, there appears to be a favourable trace off between controlled, temporary escalation of conflict and its effective long-term management.

CONFLICT MANAGEMENT: A CONTINGENCY APPROACH

There realities dictate how organizational conflict should be managed. First, conflict is inevitable because it is triggered by a wide variety of antecedents. Second, too little conflict may be as counterproductive as too much. Third, there is no single best way of resolving conflict. Consequently, conflict specialists recommend a contingency approach to managing conflict and actual conflict need to be monitored. If signs of too little conflict such as antecedents of conflict, such as apathy or lack of creativity, appear then functional conflict needs to be stimulated. This can be done by nurturing appropriate antecedents of conflict and/or programming conflict with techniques such as the devil's advocacy and the dialectic method. On the other hand, when conflict becomes dysfunctional, the appropriate conflict - handling style needs to be enacted. Realistic training involving role playing can prepare managers to try alternative conflict styles.

Managers can keep from getting deeply embroiled in conflict by applying three lessons from recent research: (1) establish challenging and clear goals, (2) disagree in a constructive and reasonable manner, and (3) refuse to get caught in the aggression-breeds-aggression spiral.

SHOULD CONFLICT BE NECESSARILY ELIMINATED

On the whole, conflicts do present a gloomy picture of the organization and an ignorance of facts may imply that there is something frightening in the organization. This notion prevails in spite of the fact that people know that there is no organization even non-profit organization which is altogether free from conflicts. Its inevitability is recognised by an individual only when he himself is faced with a conflict situation.

The traditionalists or classicists were of the view that organizational structure should be so designed not to permit any conflict to arise. It should prepare detailed elaboration and specification regarding authority, responsibility, accountability, policies, procedures, rules, etc., leaving no chance for conflict. And if conflict still develops it should be eliminated immediately in the nip of its bud.

The non-classicist emphasised the view that management should try to understand the individual psychology, informal groups and their leadership, develop a democratic participative leadership style etc. to avoid conflicts. Management must provide satisfaction on the job to individual through power equalisation techniques.

The modern theorists are of the view quite different from that of classicists and non-classicists. According to them, presence of conflicts does not necessarily be frightening. The conflicts are structural origin inevitable and endemic to the organizational surroundings.

It is not always dysfunctional as we have seen in the above lines. It is a product of the system and is not always caused by trouble makers but is determined by structural factors and is integral to the nature of change. Where human beings congregate and interact, there are bound to be conflicts. Even an individual faced with decision problem may suffer from conflict problem. Therefore, regardless of nature and size of organization conflicts appear. When conflicts are bound to appear, then our efforts should be not to eliminate them but to direct them towards maintaining and developing a better understanding among persons. Conflicts should be welcomed and handled efficiently rather than 'swept under rug.'

REFERENCES

Stephen P Robbins, *Managing Organizational Conflict: A Nontraditional Approach*, Prentice Hall, Englewood Cliffs, N.J. 1974.

James D. Thompson, *Organizational Management of Conflict, Administrative Science Quarterly*, 1960, p.389.

Kenneth W. Thomas, *Conflict and Conflict Management*, in M.D. Dunnette ed. Handbook of McNally, Chicago, 1976, p.889.
James C March and Herbert A Simon, *Organizations*, John Wiley & Sons. New York, 1958, p.112.
R.A. Barron, *Positive Effects of Conflicts, A Cognitive Perspective, Employee Responsibilities and Rights Journal,* U.S.A., Vol. 4, 1991, pp.25-36.
R.E. Walton and R.B. McKersie, *A Behavioural Theory of Labour Negotiation: An Analysis of a Social Interaction System*, McGraw Hill, New York.
N.L. Munn *et al, Introduction to Psychology*, Oxford and IBH, 1975, p.442.
Fred Luthans, *Organizational Behaviour*, McGraw Hill, New York, 1989, pp.413.
Van de Vliert, *Conflict: Prevention and Escalation* in P.J.D. Drenth, H. Thierry, PJ. Willems and C. J. de Wolf (eds).
Van de Vliert, *Escalating Intervention in Small Group Confllicts, Journal of Applied Behavioural Sciences*, Vol. 21, 1985, pp.19-36..

CHAPTER

19

Change Management

Change is a law of nature, we live in a dynamic world where nothing remains static. Everything around us keeps on changing. We visualize change in all living creatures, social customs and traditions, political and economic environment, seasons and in perceptions, conceptions and behaviour of human beings. These changes may be slow or rapid, deliberate or spontaneous, permanent or temporary, cyclic or non-cyclic, controllable or non-controllable, desirable or undesirable. So the change is the inevitable phenomenon of life.

Management of organizations is the management of change. Familiar clichés like. "It's the same old thing," "Nothing has really changed", "You're the same as always were," are simply not true. Change is constantly occurring in all people and all things. Rather than let change occur as a natural consequence of the passage of time, knowledgeable managers work toward creating conditions that help control organizations. Failure to recognise change can be disastrous not only to a specific business but to an entire industry.

Change is a fact of organizational life. Kimberly and Miles aptly states. "Organizations are born, grow, and decline. Sometimes, they reawaken, and sometimes they disappear." Organizations exist and operate in turbulent environments.

Organizations that are not able to adjust to change face difficulty in surviving. As change is taking place too fast, Alvin Toffler predicts a massive "adaptational breakdown" in organizational life. He believes that there is a limit to the amount of change that we humans can handle. He describes the stress of change, or "the disease of change" as future shock. Toffler defines future shock as "a time phenomenon, a product of the greatly accelerated rate of change in society. It arises from the superimposition of a new culture on an old one. It is culture shock in one's own society."

Nature of Change

According to Stephen P. Robbins, change is concerned with making things different. Things must be different because they change constantly. Technological development changes the methods of producing goods and services. Jobs become increasingly complex and technologically more interdependent. People receive more education and demand more control over their work environment. Concerns over energy shortages, full employment, and the environment call for an increased role for government. In addition, there is increasing globalisation of business. Organizations today compete in world markets. All these developments make change inevitable and pervasive in organizational life.

Let us consider another definition, "When an organizational system is disturbed by some internal or external force, change frequently occurs. Change, as a process, is simply modification of the structure or process of a system. It may be good or bad, the concept is descriptive only."

Keith Davis explains the nature of work change by experimenting with an air-filled balloon. He contends "when a finger (which represents change) is pressed against the exterior of the balloon (which represents the organization), the contour visibly changes at the point of impact. The molecules of air in the balloon represent firm's employees. Repeated pressure at the point may unnecessarily weaken the balloon at the point. Pressure and motion create friction and heat. Eventually a rupture occurs, and the organization collapses." An organization is much more complex than the illustrated balloon. This comparison is merely intended to emphasize the point that just as molecular equilibrium organizations also seek equilibrium. An organization strives to achieve equilibrium of its social structure. By equilibrium we mean that people learn to expect various relationships within their working surroundings. They basically learn how to deal with others, how to perform their jobs, and what is expected. In other words, when equilibrium exists, it becomes easier for people to adjust and adapt. The essence is that change requires new adjustments and new equilibrium. The nature of work change is so complicated that the management should gain acceptance for the change, and restore the group equilibrium and personal adjustment that change upsets.

Organizational Change

Organization change refers to the alteration of structural relationships and role of the people in the organization.

It is largely structural in nature. These changes may be pressurized by internal or external forces, may affect only one or all the levels and departments or may be related to the organizational structure (hierarchy), people, technology working or social environment. When any alteration in the organizational relationship takes place, it disturbs the existing equilibrium. As a matter of fact, when an organization goes on operating for sometime, an adjustment between its people, their structural relationship and technical set up is established. People get adjusted and get used to a set of working relationships, social groups and a set pattern of organizational and individual life. So long as this equilibrium exist, it is easier for the people to adjust in organization. But when a change is introduced, the existing equilibrium of relationships is disturbed and the problem of new adjustment is created. The problem of readjustment creates various fears and apprehensions in the mind of the people and generates vivid problems and difficulties.

Successful managers must recognise the need for change in order to keep their organizations competitive in a dynamic environment. They must face 'the challenge of change.' Bennis called the new "organic" organizations required to cope with unpredictable change adaptive structures. Alvin Toffler called these new organizations adhocracies.

Jerald Hage defines organizational changes as "the alteration and transformation of the form so as to survive better in the environment's According to Ivancevich, Donnelly, and Gibson, "Organizational change is the planned attempt by management to improve the overall performance of individuals, groups, and the organization by altering structure, behaviour, and technology."

Thus, organizational change refers to the alteration of structural relationships and roles of people in organization in order to improve its adaptive capacity. It is an alteration that occurs in the work environment.

Edgar H. Schein offers the following observations about the nature of change in organization:

1. Any change process involves not only learning something new, but unlearning something that is already well integrated into the personality and social relationships of the individual.
2. No change will occur unless there is motivation to change, and if such motivation to change is not already present, the induction of that motivation is often the most difficult part of the change process.
3. Organizational changes in authority structures, processes, and systems occur only through individual change by key members of organizations.
4. Change involves altering attitudes, values, and behaviour. The unlearning of present responses can initially be painful and threatening.
5. Change is a multistage process, a cycle of behavioural modification. It is complex and requires a systematic approach.
6. Change is initiated by some kind of "disorganising pressure" or trigger arising either within or outside the organization.
7. Change rarely takes place smoothly. Instead it happens in an "untidy" way. Some parts of the organization change more rapidly than others.
8. Change is a human as well as a technical problem.

Since change occasionally results in disequilibrium in the environment conditions of the organization, the most changes disturb the equilibrium of situation and environment in which the individuals or groups exist. In order to remove this disequilibrium, and to return to a normal state of balance, people take time for adaptation and adjustment to change. Man being dynamic adjust himself according to the environmental situation. He may be prepared to adapt or introduce change as soon as he gets education and training in adapting the new techniques in the interest of the organization. The introduction of these changes (training and education) may again create disequilibrium and the problem of adjustment. Now, it is the duty of the management to facilitate adjustment, especially prior to the initiation of change so that a new state of equilibrium can be adapted quickly and chance of little or no-resistance may be restored. If, on the other hand, management ignores this fundamental fact of human behaviour, and does nothing to help the people adjust, resistance will occur and disequilibrium will exist in the environment. **Thus organizational change involves disequilibrium in the situation and environment in which the people and the group exist.**

Change may affect an individual, a group, and the whole organization. If the change is beneficial to parties affected, it may be immediately and willingly accepted. If, on the other hand, change affects no one, the people will be quite indifferent but if anyhow change is detrimental to their interest, they will resist the change to their full strength. The reaction is based upon not necessarily on facts but on their perception of the situation, i.e., how they perceive the change."

Response to change. Work change does not produce a direct adjustment but instead it operates through each employee's attitudes to produce a response conditioned by feelings towards the change.

Roethlisberger confirmed through various studies made in Hawthorn plant that there was no direct relationship between the change and the response but it was attitude of the people that disturbed the set pattern. Each change is perceived and interpreted by individuals according to their own attitude and respond accordingly.

The attitude or feeling of people towards change **is the result of several causes:**

(i) One cause of such attitudes is the **personal history** of the individual which refers to biological process of people, their backgrounds and their social experiences away from the work.

(ii) A second cause of a particular attitude is the **work-environment** itself. It reflects the fact that workers as a members of the group are influenced by its norms, codes, and patterns of the group.

(iii) The **attitude of workers** are mostly *governed* by the group interests. This effect is named as:

Hawthorn Effect which refers that people individually interpret change, they often show their attachment to the group by joining hand with it in some uniform response to change. At times, there may be some illogical responses though unintended, but people respond just to show their affinity with the group, they are to follow other members of the group. For example, walkout by a few persons from a meeting to express their dissatisfaction *over* the situation may be psychological binds for others to follow the path to affirm their cohesion to the group.

Effect of Change on Social System

The dynamic force of change affects the whole social system. All its elements, i.e., its people, formal organization, informal organization, operating environment, communication pattern, decision making and patterns of cooperation, are bound to change. There is an equilibrium, group develops responses to return to its perceived best way of life whenever any change occurs. Pressure produces counter pressure within the group which results in self-correcting mechanism by which balance is established. This self-correcting characteristic of organization is called **Homeostasis,** i.e., people act to establish a steady state of need fulfilment and to secure themselves from disturbance of that balance. Thus it is an idea of social equilibrium.

The social equilibrium implies that frictions, jokeying and trading among departments is a normal condition in the organization because its social system is in continuous motion. A social system can *never* be frictionless. Therefore, each social system develops programmes to accommodate change as it occurs.

When change is minor and is within the self-correcting mechanism, it is a routine but if change is major or unusual, more serious upsets may occur in the social system.

CAUSES OF CHANGES

Following are some of the causes of organizational changes which lead to disequilibrium and resistance:

1. Change in Tools, Machines and Equipment

Technological or mechanical changes in machines, tools and equipments may bring change in the organization.

For example, installation of an automatic machinery in place of old machinery, may result in displacement or replacement of people or loss of job to people and may create disequilibrium.

2. Change in Methods and Procedures

Man is a creature of habits. He feels irritated when change occurs in methods and procedures of work of which he is accustomed to. As it takes time to adjust to the new environment, it creates disequilibrium till the complete adjustment to the new environment.

3. Change in Business Condition

Changes in business conditions such as change in the quality of the product, change in the marketing system or practices, business cycles, change in industrial policy etc. all create disequilibrium in the work-environment and it needs adjustment accordingly.

4. Change in Managerial Personnel

Change in the managerial personnel in the organization may result in disequilibrium. A personnel may retire or change place or may be appointed afresh, this will all affect the policies, practices, procedures and programmes of the organization and the people are to adjust themselves accordingly.

5. Change in Formal Organization Structure

The formal organization structures establish a form and line of command of authority and responsibility in an organization. Along with these lines, channels of communication and interpersonal relations are established. If there is a change in this formal organizational structure, there will be a change in the formal relationship which creates disequilibrium.

6. Change in Informal Organization

Informal organization is a must in *every* formal organization and is a *very* important part of our existence because many of our *motivational* forces find satisfaction in these relationships. Consequently when management likes to introduce any change that disturbs the informal relationship established among people, there is bound to be a state of imbalance.

7. Deficiencies in Existing Organization

Organizations once established cannot be said to be good for all times. Many defects may appear with the passage of time such as extension of the plant, change in managerial functions, evolution of complex organization relationship etc. This cause imbalance and need correction. So change is necessary to *remove* such deficiencies.

8. Technological Change

Computer technology and automation have tremendously affected all aspects of industrial activities. New machines and new technological processes have revolutionized not only production techniques, but also the social conditions of work.

9. Knowledge Explosion

The explosion of knowledge is on an accelerated path. It has influenced the working styles, values and thinking in modern organizations. Knowledge-based society is emerging very fast. Thus, new occupations have been created.

10. Product and Service Obsolescence

Obsolescence of procedures, programmes and treatments in service, and health is also happening due to the changing technology and knowledge. Due to the keen competition the product life cycle is getting shorter and shorter.

11. Market Conditions

The changing nature of market conditions such as demands of customers, tastes and preferences of users, design and quality of products etc. has become a challenge for the management to adapt changes.

12. Social Trends

Many social trends such as changing lifestyles, expectations, social equality, better education, freedom of expression, democratic values etc. are emerging in human society. Managers must be "tuned in" to these pressures and movements over which they have no control but which shape fate of the firm. Governmental policies, political chess and public opinion are environmental forces for change that organizations must cope with and recognise.

13. Value Gap

The socio-cultural climate of society is also changing. People now have a different set of values from that of people in their old decades. Douglas T. Hall has pinpointed six areas of value gap that are relevant to managing change behaviour in modern organization:

(a) There is now more concern about values per se, not just different values.

(b) Action is more important. Merely talking about values is not enough. One's values must be backed by action.

(c) Values such as integrity, honesty, openness, and realness are more important.

(d) More humanistic values are emerging.

(e) There is increased concern for the ultimate social value of one's work.

(f) Authority based on expertise, personal styles, and convictions or accomplishments is more legitimate than authority based on age or position.

Thus, the above reasons emphasise change in the organization which create imbalance in the relationship between employer and employee, and between employee and employee. So, people generally resist the change.

Why Individuals Resist Change

There is a common thinking that every change in the organization is resisted either by the employees or by the management. It is because psychologically a man is not prepared to change of the situation in which he is accustomed to work. But it is not always. All changes are not resisted. Some changes are beneficial to the people and are liked and accepted. Such changes do not create any problem. Some other changes are too trival and routine, that resistance is too small to be evident. But many others which are detrimental to the interests of the party concerned are strongly opposed by them. The reasons why changes are resisted by the people may be analysed in the following lines under two heads: (a) Resistance by employees, and (b) Resistance by employer or management:

(a) CAUSES OF RESISTANCE TO CHANGE BY EMPLOYEES

Employees generally resist the change on the following grounds:

1. Disturbance in Existing Equilibrium

A basic reason of the resistance of change by the employees, whether they manifest it in the form of apathy and indifference, or in the form of opposition or hostility, is that most changes disturb the existing equilibrium in situation and environment. Workers are habitual to work in a particular situation and the change disturbs that situation of the environment in which individuals and the groups exist. The general feeling among people is that every change is resisted by the employee though it may prove beneficial to them in the long run. How serious the situation will be, is, of course, impossible to guess, because it depends upon the nature of the people and the change concerned.

2. Imbalance in Need Satisfaction

Change creates imbalance in need satisfaction. It is assumed that prior to change people existed in an environment where their need satisfaction was at a high degree of stability. With the occurrence of change, it is immediately manifested that change may prevent or decrease need satisfaction.

3. Insecurity to Jobs

A quick and violent resistance is possible where the change threatens either the status or job security to the employees. In a case when job security is at stake, i.e., if some of them are being rendered unemployed or laid off, even a minor change or revision of policies and procedure may evoke profoundly disturbing reactions. Introduction of automatic machinery or technological changes in machines and methods may threaten the security of job and workers will certainly resist the change.

4. Fear of Economic Loss

Some changes may cause economic loss to most of the people such as stoppage of overtime, reduction in wage-rates, abolition of promotional avenues etc. and therefore they will suffer economically and psychologically.

In order to recoup the financial loss, they are to learn some new skills in place of their existing skills which are proved to be worthless to the organization. In such cases, people do resist change because of economic loss or because they may have to spend time and money in learning new skills. It is still more difficult when persons reach at a certain age, to get a new employment to commensurate their existing skill or to learn new things.

5. Change affects Emotions and Sentiments

People are affected by change psychologically also. Apart from fears and apprehensions – real or imaginary about what will happen after the change, people are also emotionally and sentimentally disturbed only with the name of change. Besides, some people develop attachment towards certain things and they are psychologically disturbed when they fear detachment from them.

6. Disturbance of Social Relationship

Change is likely to disturb the social relationship. Some persons are very loyal to their group. Change may affect groups, norms, customs, etc. or even the composition itself. When a group is broken and a new group is to be formed, it is a very frustrating situation. This kind of disturbance occurs where jobs are transferable. Family life of a person becomes disturbed.

7. Obsolescence of Skills

The rate at which the knowledge is exploding is incredible. As a result, knowledge in any particular field quickly becomes obsolete. Whenever people sense that new machinery (change) poses a threat of replacing or degrading them they simply resist such a change. For instance, the subsonic rate at which computer-based technology is growing has conveniently outclassed the expertise based on experience. A twenty-years experienced account is quite likely to resist. A twenty-years experienced accountant is quite likely to resist the introduction of a computer for preparing the wage bill because he feels that might affect his position and pay. This kind of phenomenon is commonly found in those managers who possess no real marketable skills and whose knowledge is obsolete and outdated. These people strongly resist change and try their best to maintain status quo person, who is transferred to some other place of the same organization, is disturbed and he is to start afresh in a new environment.

8. Lack of Classification

Resistance can be expected if the nature of change is not made clear to persons how are they going to be influenced by the change. Different people will see different meanings and interpretations in the proposed change. Some people may realise the change as an indication of their poor performance on the job while some others may assume that their office would soon be abolished. Thus, lack of clarification regarding the nature of change invites resistance from the workers.

9. Opposition only for the Sake of Opposition

Sometimes, resistance to change is quite illogical and is only for the sake of opposition. Change may be beneficial even and some do not oppose it, but some others will oppose it only for the sake of opposition without having any reason or without understanding its pros and cons or may have initially certain reservations and apprehensions and become hostile to any change. Thus change may be resisted emotionally and sentimentally without going into the logic of it.

10. Habit

Jobs that are well learned and become habitual are easy to perform. The prospect of changing the way jobs are done challenges people to develop new job skills. Doing this is clearly more difficult than continuing to perform the job as it was originally learned.

11. Failure to Recognise Need for Change

Unless employees can recognise and fully appreciate the need for changes in organizations, any vested interests they may have in keeping things the same may overpower their willingness to accept change.

12. Ego Defensiveness

Sometimes change may be ego-deflating. An ego-defensive subordinate or manager always try to resist change. For instance a profitable suggestion made by a sales person to the marketing manager regarding the expansion of sales may be turned down because the manager perceives that his ego may be deflated by accepting the suggestion. It should, however, be noted that not all but some managers who have ego-defensiveness (or egocentred) resist such changes.

13. Status Quo

Perhaps the biggest and most sound reason for the resistance to change is the status quo. Change may pose disturbance to the existing comforts of status quo. Venturing the change may involve uncertainty and risk and may be at the cost of the convenience and happiness of the employees. Most of the people are comfortable with status quo and strongly resist change. It is because people typically develop patterns for coping with or managing the current structure and situation. Change means they will have to find new ways of managing them and their environment - the ways that might not be successful as those currently used.

14. Fear of Unknown

Change presents unknown which causes anxiety. Whenever people do not know exactly what happens they are likely to resist it. The unknown poses a constant threat and soars them. People fear any untoward and uncomfortable change and its consequences. For instance, a sales manager may wonder what might happen if he is relocated to company headquarters akin to another State. He might ask if his family would like it and if he could find friends. Uncertainty in the situation arises not from the change itself, but from the consequences surrounding change. To avoid making decision and fear of unknown, manager may refuse promotion that requires relocating. Further any gap in the information renders the mind of the employees wandering over uncertainty about the future and he thinks the better way would be to oppose change.

15. Social Displacement

Introduction of change often results in disturbance of the existing social relationships. It may also result in breaking up of work groups. Normally people in the working environment develop informal relationships. When the friendship with fellow-members is interrupted then there is a possibility for the employees to experience psychological let down. Research reveals that in combat situations soldiers often fight the tendency to make friendship among the other members of their platoon, because if one is killed or injured, the effect on the group can be disastrous. They would not be mentally prepared to execute their jobs and could be injured or commit-suicide. Thus when social relationships develop, as normally is the case, people try to maintain them and fight social displacement by resisting change.

16. Peer Pressure

Situations are not rare where individuals are prepared to accept change at their individual level, but refuse to accept it for the sake of the group. Whenever change is unwilling to the peer, they force the individual subordinate employees who are bent of accepting the change to resist it. Group, when there is perfect cohesiveness, tends to resist some changes collectively.

Thus, these are certain reasons why workers resist a change. Now we shall discuss the reasons why sometimes management or employers resist the change.

(b) CAUSE OF RESISTANCE TO CHANGE BY EMPLOYERS AND MANAGEMENT

Not only the employees, but the employers or the men in management resist the change on the following grounds:

1. Increase in Responsibility

Any change warranted by the situations are generally opposed by the employers and management because it brings out a problem of readjustment of equilibrium of situation and environment. Management is to retrain the workers according to proposed changes and responsibility of introducing change. Thus change increases responsibility of the management.

2. Change Proposed by Government and Labour Union

Sometimes changes are proposed by labour union and because the management takes it as an insulting matter to implement the change proposed by the union hence, they oppose any proposal for change. Some changes are forced by the government for the industries to implement. Such changes, though they have to implement it, are resisted by them because mentally they are not prepared to implement it.

3. Change on Experimental Basis

In few case, changes are introduced on experimental basis, viz., if it is proved beneficial, it will be extended further and be made permanent otherwise it will be abolished. In other words, it is a temporary phase. Some men in the management does not favour such temporary phase and oppose it if change does not suit them.

4. Structural Inertia

Organizations are designed to promote stability. To the extent that employees are carefully selected and trained to perform certain jobs, and rewarded for doing them well, the forces acting on individuals to perform in certain ways are very powerfully determined-that is, jobs have structural inertia. Thus, because jobs are designed to have stability, it is often difficult to overcome the resistance created by the forces that create stability.

5. Work Group Inertia

Inertia to continue performing jobs in a specified way comes not only from the jobs themselves but also from the social groups within which people work–work group inertia. Because of the development of strong social norms within groups, potent pressures exist to perform jobs in certain ways. Introducing change disrupts these established normative expectations, leading to formidable resistance.

6. Threats to Existing Balance of Power

If changes are made with respect to who's in charge, a shift in the balance of power between individuals and organizational subunits is likely to occur. Those units that now control the resources, have the expertise, and wield the power may fear losing their advantageous positions resulting from any organizational change.

7. Previously Unsuccessful Change Efforts

Anyone who has lived through a past disaster understandably may be reluctant to endure another attempt at the same thing. Similarly, groups or entire organizations that have been unsuccessful in introducing change in the past may be cautious about accepting further attempts at introducing change into the system.

8. Organizational Structure

Some organizational structures have in-built mechanism for resistance to change. For instance, consider a typically bureaucratic structure where jobs are narrowly defined, lines of authority are clearly spelled out, the flow of information is stressed from top to bottom. In such organization the channels of communication make the new idea difficult to travel and eventually it increases the probability that the new idea/innovation will be screened out because it is not suitable for the structure of the organization.

9. Resource Constraints

Organizations many a time operate under some resource constraints. If the resources with which to operate are available in abundance there will be no problem of introducing change. But the necessary financial, material and human resources may not be available to the organization to make the needed changes. So non-availability of resources inadequate resources also act as a resistance to change.

10. Organizational Culture

Culture helps an organization shape and maintain own identity. Culture also guides employee behaviour. As a rule, employees stay with an organization because the work helps them meet their life goals and because their personalities, attitudes, and beliefs fit into the organizational culture. Indeed, many employees identify with their organization and take its gains and losses personally. As a result they may feel threatened by efforts to make radical changes in the organization's culture. Hence, the resistance to change.

EXAMPLES OF ORGANIZATION CHANGE

For many years, American Telephone and Telegraph (AT&T) provided a full range of telephone services: manufacturing equipment, installation, and repairs. AT&T defined its mission as providing universal telephone services to all customers. To achieve this mission, AT&T developed a strategy of maintaining its monopoly through high-quality and low-cost telephone services. The company was organised along functional lines (manufacturing, research, and sales), but manufacturing and research dominated the decision processes at AT&T. Since it operated in a regulated environment, the sales function played a less important role. Over time the company recruited, developed, and rewarded people who could function well in a highly structured environment. In addition, AT&T created a strong corporate culture that stressed the importance of manufacturing efficiency and quality services. This combination of strategy, structure, and corporate culture worked well for one hundred years prior to the deregulation of the industry in the early 1980s.

Starting in the late 1960s and continuing through the 1970s, the regulatory environment posed serious challenges to AT&T's monopoly status. After ten years of court battles with the Federal Communication Commission (FCC), the U.S. Department of Justice, and potential competitors, AT&T decided to give up its twenty two operating companies and to focus on long distance telephone and information processing businesses in a deregulated environment. To meet this challenge, AT&T had to change its strategy to become more competitive and market oriented. As competition intensified, the task became more technologically oriented and faster paced, requiring higher degrees of cooperation, and coordination among various units of the organization. To meet this need, AT&T went through a series of reorganizations in 1974, 1978, 1980, and 1982.

AT&T's task and structure have changed in response to the external pressures, but these changes were not accompanied by the needed changes in behavioural components. The needed cooperation arid coordination between functional groups did not occur as hoped. More important the corporate culture was not fully adjusted to the new strategy and task. The manufacturing oriented, not the market-driven, culture still dominated the organization long after deregulation.

The AT&T case reveals the major issues involved in a major organizational change. First, there are external (or internal) pressures for major changes in management. Second people initially resist any changes in their organizations. Human inertia and complacent attitudes built on past success work against change and innovation. Finally, a major organizational change usually requires top management's support and involvement. When a change is planned and executed with or by top management's support, its chance to succeed increases.

Over the past decade, General Electric (GE) has been undergoing a series of widespread changes in its basic strategy, organizational structure, and relationship with employees. In this process, it experienced several of the barriers just identified. For example, GE managers had mastered a set of bureaucratic traditions that kept their habits strong and their inertia moving straight ahead. The prospect of doing things differently was scary for those who were so strongly entrenched in doing things the "GE way." In particular, the company's interest in globalizing triggered many fears of the unknown. Resistance to change at GM was also strong because it threatened to strip power from those units that traditionally possessed most of it (e.g., the power systems and lighting division). Changes also were highly disruptive to GE's "social architecture"; friendship groups were broken up and scattered throughout the company. In all, GE has been a living example of many different barriers to change all rolled into a single company.

LEVELS OF ORGANIZATIONAL CHANGE

There are two methods of analysing levels of organizational change. One method is to examine individual, group, and organizational levels, and the other is to examine the degree of change required of those affected by the change. The combination of level and degree of change products a matrix for analysing the relationships, as shown in Figure 1.

The effect upon each level in the system is partially determined by the magnitude of the change. For example, individual changes usually do not affect the total organization, but large changes at the individual level can have an effect, such as change in the chief executive. The information in Fig. 1 gives examples of the various degrees and levels of changes.

LEVEL OF CHANGE

Degree of Change	Individual	Group	Organization
Small	Promotion of individuals	Add new employee to Group	Create new Staff Department
Medium	Training Programme for Managers	Merge Group	Reduction of Workforce
Large	Change M.D.	Disband Work Group	Major Restructuring of Organization

Fig. 1. Examples of Interactions Between Levels and Degree of Change.

Individual Level

Changes at the individual level seldom have significant implications for the total organization, although there is the occasional exception. Examples of changes at the individual level are changes in a job assignment, a physical move to a different location, or the change in maturity of a person which occurs naturally over time. Any change in the system will affect other parts of the system, but the effects are often so small, they are undetectable except to the trained observer or to the individuals themselves. If a major change occurred in an individual, the ramifications would be such that changes would also occur on the group level. This, in turn might influence the wider organization.

From an applications perspective, it is useful to understand that only the smallest of changes would have an effect at the individual level only. As noted earlier, although such changes only rarely affect the total organization, a manager who wished to implement a major change at the individual level should understand that the change will likely have repercussions beyond the individual. For example, if a manager decides to transfer an employee, this may disrupt the social functioning of the work group.

Group Level

Most organizational changes have their major effects at the group level. This is because most activities in organizations are organised on a group basis. The groups could be departments, project teams, functional units within departments, or informal work groups. Changes at this level can affect work flows. Job design social organization, influence and status systems, and communication patterns. In all such cases managers must consider group factors when implementing change. Informal groups can pose a major barrier to change because of the inherent strength they contain. Formal groups can also resist change, as exemplified by the resistance shown by unions to the changes proposed by management. Because of the powerful influence that groups can have on individuals, effective implementation of change at the group level can frequently overcome resistance at the individual level.

Organizational Level

Change at the organizational level generally referred to as "Organization development." Changes at this level involve major programmes that affect both individuals and groups. Decisions regarding these changes are generally made by senior management and are seldom implemented by only a single manager. Frequently they occur over long periods of time and require considerable planning for implementation. Examples of these changes would be reorganization of the organization structure and responsibilities, revamping of company compensation systems or major shifts in an organization's objectives.

The relationship between the three levels of change is represented in Fig. 2. It suggests that changes at any level affect the other levels, with the dominant effect being from the total organizational level down to the individual level. The strength of the effect will vary with the source, for example, organizational changes will tend to have major impacts on individuals, but individuals have minimal impacts on organizations. The group, or intermediate level, tends to have moderate effects on both individuals and the organization.

EFFECT	SOURCE: Individual	Group	Organization
Individual	-----	L	L
Group	M	-----	L
Organization	S	M	-----

S = Small, M = Medium, L = Large

Fig. 2. Interaction Effects of Different Levels of Organizational Change.

The major focus in this unit will be on managing change at the individuals and group level since it is here that most managers will experience problems.

THE DILEMMA OF CHANGE

1. Stability Versus Change

Successful managers do not wait for future; they make the future by managing change. Here organizations face a dilemma. They prefer to accomplish their day-to-day activities in a predictable, routine manner. The fewer the changes that are undertaken by organization, the more predictable and efficient it becomes. But unfortunately, the external environment is changing constantly; change is inevitable and abundant. Change demands modification of the existing relationships, an alteration of the status quo. But paradoxically, in some organizations stability is so crucial that a strategy of no change at all is not only feasible but mandatory.

No Change ⟵⟶	Rapid change
Stability	Flexibility
Certainty	Uncertainty
Predictability	Unpredictability

Fig. 3.

Organizations desire change in order to remain competitive, in order to remain in harmony with the ever changing environment. Organizations also want to achieve internal stability because of the predictability and certainty it provides. As such, organizations sit on the horns of a dilemma with reference to change.

Organizations handle the stability-change dilemma depending on the amount and type of innovation required. The organic organization is, for example, suitable when frequent technological changes are required. The organic organization is always oriented towards change rather than stability. Mechanistic organizations, on the other hand, are oriented towards technological stability. Organizations, thus, resolve the stability-change dilemma by structuring in an organic way when the organization needs new ideas and frequent changes, and by structuring in a mechanistic way whenever possible to obtain efficiency. The point is that to resolve the dilemma organizational change process must be managed. To the extent change is planned, uncertainty and unpredictability is reduced.

2. Evolutionary, Revolutionary and Planned Changes

Changes can be seen in a variety of ways. This poses another major dilemma. Basically there can be three types of changes which are discussed below:

Evolutionary Changes

Some changes are evolutionary in nature and do not greatly violate the traditions and status quo expectations.

They are usually piecemeal, take place one by one. Because they are adjustments within the status quo, they seldom promote great enthusiasm, arouse deep resistance, or have dramatic results. Since they do not constitute significant departures from the past practices, they are unlikely to provoke resistance. One limitation of such changes is that they are very slow and organization may fall behind the requirements.

Revolutionary Changes

Change sometimes may be cataclysmic. The revolutionary changes result in overturning the status quo arrangement, causes violations, rejections or suppression of old expectations. The revolutionary churnings generally pose strong resistance and sometimes only an exercise of power can order the implementation of such changes. Revolutionary changes are rarely introduced except where situation becomes highly intolerable having no other acceptable options.

Planned Changes

A new and scientific way of viewing change is "the planned alteration in the existing organizational system."

According to Blake and Mouton, "it does not start with the acceptance or rejection of status quo but begins with a normative intellectual model of what should be the model that is blueprint for action." Planned changes are made by the organization with the purpose of achieving something that might otherwise be unattainable, or accomplishable with great difficulty. Through planned changes organizations reach new frontiers and progress more rapidly toward given set of goals and objectives. Edgar Williams logically lists four general reasons for designing the orderly change in organizations. They are:

(i) To improve the means for satisfying somebody's economic wants.

(ii) To increase profitability.

(iii) To promote human work for human beings.

(iv) To contribute to individual satisfaction and social well-being.

Planned organizational change, thus, is the intentional attempt by an organization to influence the status quo itself. Planned change is magic elixir to development; it is an arcanum to growth.

3. Proactive Versus Reactive Change

Proactive change takes place when some forces to change lead an organization to conclude that a particular change is desirable. Reactive change occurs when these forces to change make it necessary for change to be implemented. For instance, introduction of a new employee-benefit scheme is proactive as the management strongly believes that it enhances satisfaction and motivation to employees. The introduction of scheme would be reactive if the benefit plan as introduced because of demands made by the employees. Thus proactive change is the change initiated by an organization because it is identified as desirable (Le., it is not forced on the organization). On the other hand, reactive change is the change implemented in an organization because it is made necessary by outside forces.

There is no close agreement among the researchers about the extent to which organization change occurs.

Perrow describes change as "glacial", whereas Griener considers change as 'revolutionary', rather than 'evolutionary.' But change is 'real' and organizations must cope with it or fail to survive.

Approaches to Managing Organizational Change

Organizational change calls for a change in behaviour and attitudes of the employees. There are two popular approaches to managing change. These are - Kurt Lewin's Three Step Model and Action Research Model.

Kurt Lewin's Change Model

Kurt Lewin, a famous behavioural scientist has developed a model of change, which involves three basic phases: unfreezing, changing, and refreezing. This model is also known as Force Field Analysis.

1. Unfreezing

Unfreezing is the state in which employees would become ready to learn new behaviour. It is the process of preparing the system for change through disconfirmation of the old practices, attitudes, or behaviours. Unfreezing involves stimulating people to feel and recognize the need for changes. It is a 'thawing out' process where the forces acting on an individual are so rearranged that he sees the need for rejecting old behavioural patterns and adopting new ones. It is the breaking down of the norms, customs, and traditions of individuals to accept new alternatives.

According to Edgar H. Schein, the unfreezing process, to be successful, needs the following elements:

(a) The physical removal of the individuals being changed from the accustomed routines, sources of information, and social relationships;

(b) The undermining and destruction of all social supports;

(c) Demeaning and humiliating experience to help individuals being changed to see their old attitudes or behaviour as unworthy and thus to be motivated to change; and

(d) The consistent linking of reward with willingness to change and of punishment with unwillingness to change.

In terms of force field analysis, unfreezing could be effected in two ways – either by increasing the driving forces or by reducing the restraining forces that resist change.

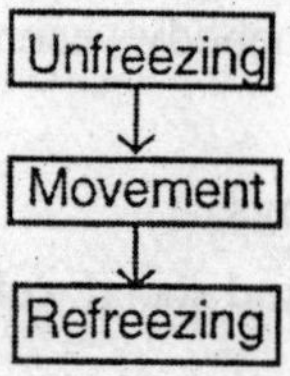

Fig. 4. Lewin's Three Step Change Model

2. Changing or Moving

It is the phase where the changes that have been planned are actually initiated and carried out. Once individuals have become motivated to change, they are opened up to new patterns of behaviour, new information and new concepts. Changes could relate to the mission, strategy, objectives, people, work roles, technology, structure, or any other aspects of organization. The process occurs through one of three mechanisms.

(a) Identification

It occurs when one or more models are provided in the environment from whom individuals can learn new behaviour patterns by identifying with them and trying to become like them.

(b) Internalization

It occurs when an individual is placed in a situation in which new behaviours are demanded of him, if he is to operate successfully in that situation.

(c) Force or Compliance

Kelman has described compliance as a third mechanism for attitude change. It occurs when an individual is forced to change by the direct manipulation of rewards and punishment by someone who has positional power. Compliance is often dropped when supervision is removed. Hence, it can be treated as a tool for unfreezing, rather than a mechanism of changing.

3. Refreezing

Refreezing occurs as the newly created patterns of behaviour become part of ongoing organizational processes and individual's personality. It means making new change permanent. It is the process of stabilizing new behaviour and integrating it into actual practice. As Schein contends, "if the new behaviour has been internalized while being learned, this has automatically facilitated refreezing because it has been fitted naturally into the individual's personality. If it has been learned through identification, it will persist only so long as the target's relationship with the original influence model persists unless new surrogate models are found or social support and reinforcement is obtained for expressions of the new attitudes."

As most individuals "try on" new behavioural changes before actually "buying", it is necessary to provide for recognition, reinforcement and training programmes to refreeze preferred behaviour.

According to the 'force-field' theory of Kurt Lewin, any behaviour is the result of an equilibrium between driven and restraining forces. The driving forces push one way, the restraining forces push the other. The performance that emerges is a reconciliation of the two sets of forces. An increase in the driving forces might increase performance, but it might also increase the restraining forces. For example, a manager may believe that he or she can get improved results by telling subordinates that there will be absolutely no time off until productivity increases. But the likely response of hostility, distrust and greater resistance may cause additional declines in productivity, even though the formal prohibition against taking time off is observed.

The natural tendency for most of us, if we want change, is to push. However, the equally natural tendency of whomever or whatever is being pushed is to push back: Driving forces activate their own restraining forces. Decreasing the restraining forces, therefore is normally a more effective way to encourage change than by increasing the driving forces.

Lewin's model (see Fig. 5) reminds us to look for multiple causes of behaviour rather than a single cause. It is applicable to our purposes because it is generalized. The forces can be of many types, and the behaviour or performance can be that of an individual, group, or entire organization. The equilibrium concept also suggests that organizations have forces that keep performance from falling too low, as well as forces that keep it from rising too high.

Present Condition Average ⇨ Desired condition Excellent grade

Driving Forces		Restraining Forces
Desire to be admitted into the MBA graduate Programme at X University	⟷	Need to work part-time to pay for tuition and expenses.
Would enhance my self-esteem	⟷	Like to date several times a week.
Parents would be pleased	⟷	Bridge games between classes very enjoyable.
Studying usually enjoyable	⟷	Haven't done very well on term papers - not thorough enough.
Mare job opportunities	⟷	Don't have typewriter at home.
Attractive marriage proposals	⟷	Hard to study at home-commotion of younger brothers and sisters.
	⟵	Like to play records on my new stereo.
	⟵	Tend to procrastinate about studying for exams.

Fig. 5. Why Is My Grade Point Average Lower Than Desired?

A Force Field Analysis

Programmes of planned change are directed toward removing or weakening the restraining forces and toward creating or strengthening the driving forces that exist in organizations. Lewin also studied the process of bringing about effective change. He noted that individuals experience two major obstacles to change. First, they are unwilling (or unable) to alter long-established attitudes and behaviour. A manager told that he or she needs to learn a new analytic technique may accept this information with little or no difficulty. But if that same manager is told that he or she is too aggressive and abrasive in dealing with others, the manager is much more likely to resent and reject the information. Suggesting the need to make a change in managerial style or attitude is perceived as a violation of one's self-image and an indication of inadequacy.

The second major obstacle noted by Lewin was that change frequently lasts only a short time. After a brief period of trying to do things differently, individuals often return to their traditional patterns of behaviour.

To overcome obstacles of this sort, Lewin developed a three-step sequential model of the change process.

The model, later elaborated by Edgar H. Schein and others, is equally applicable to individuals, groups or entire organizations. It involves "unfreezing" the present behaviour pattern, "changing" or developing a new behaviour pattern, and then "refreezing" or reinforcing the new behaviour.

1. Unfreezing involves making the need for change so obvious that the individual, group, or organization can readily see and accept it.

2. Changing requires a trained change agent to foster new values, attitudes, and behaviour through the processes of identification and internalization. Organization members identify with the change agent's values, attitudes, and behaviour, internalizing them once they perceive their effectiveness in performance.

3. Refreezing means locking the new behaviour pattern into place by means of supporting or reinforcing mechanism, so that it becomes the new norm.

Lewin's Model: Another Example – An Indian Experience

The management of a large oil company decided to recognise its marketing function in North India. The firm had three divisional offices in the North, located in Agra, Mathura, and Jaipur. The decision was made to consolidate the divisions into a single regional office to be located in New Delhi. The recognisation meant transferring over 150 employees, the elimination of some duplicate managerial positions, and the institution of a new hierarchy of command. As you might guess, a move of this magnitude was difficult to keep secret. The rumour of its occurrence preceded the announcement by several months. The decision itself was made unilaterally. It came from the executive offices in New Delhi. Those people affected had no say whatsoever in the choice. For those in Agra or Jaipur, who may have disliked the decision and its consequences - the problems inherent in transferring to another city. Pulling yougsters out of school, making new friends, having new co-workers, undergoing the reassignment of responsibilities - their only resource was to quit. This actual case of an organizational change may be used to illustrate the unfreezing, movement-refreezing model.

The status quo can be considered an equilibrium state. To move from this equilibrium-to overcome the pressures of both individual resistance and group conformity–unfreezing is necessary. It can be achieved in one of the three ways. The driving forces, which direct behaviour away from the status quo, can be increased. The restraining forces, which hinder movement from the existing equilibrium can be decreased. A third alternative is to combine the first two approaches.

Using the above recognisation example, management can expect employee resistance to the consolidation.

To deal with that resistance management can use positive incentives to encourage employees to accept the change. For instance, increases in pay can be offered to those who accept the transfer. Very liberal moving expenses can be paid by the company. Management might offer lowcost mortage funds to allow employees to buy new homes in New Delhi. Of course management might choose to unfreeze acceptance of the status quo by removing restraining forces. Employees could be counselled individually. Each employee's concerns and apprehensions could be heard and clarified specifically. Assuming that most of the fears are unjustified, the counsellor could assure the employees that there was nothing to fear and then demonstrate, through tangible evidence, that restraining forces are unwarranted. If resistance is extremely high, management may have to resort to both reducing resistance and increasing the attractiveness of the alternative if the unfreezing is to be successful.

Once unfreezing has been accomplished, the change itself can be implemented. In reality, there is no clear line separating unfreezing and moving. Many of the effort made to unfreeze the status quo may, in and of themselves, introduce movement. So the tactics for dealing with resistance that the change agent uses may work on unfreezing and/or moving.

Additional Real Life Situations

In 1971, in response to its increasing size, and nationalisation of the banking sector the State Bank of India embarked on an organization-wide restructuring exercise. Taking the help of external consultants, and through the involvement of a top management steering group, it managed to implement major changes in the organization: a shift from a functional structure to a market segment-based structure; introduction of a budgeting and performance review system; differentiation and strengthening of planning and staff functions; and, creation of more unified channels of command of branches from the local head offices.

In 1981, when Gurucharan Das took over as the President of Richardson-Hindustan Ltd. (now, Proctor & Gamble India), the company was in a bad shape. Profitability was low, return on equity had gone down from 25.2 per cent in 1977 to 11.4 per cent, industrial relations were poor, and inter departmental relations were marred by politics and rivalry. To improve the situation, Das went ahead creating a "people oriented culture" where "new ideas thrive and people develop their full potential; otherwise good people do not stay." What followed was a massive OD exercise for changing the values and attitudes of people at all levels. In 1984, RHL had gone up by almost 30 per cent.-

The Steel Authority of India (SAIL) had suffered losses of Rs. 2,760 million during 1980-84. When V. Krishnamurthy became the CEO, he met almost 25,000 employees, either individually or in groups and, based on the discussions with them prepared a list of priorities of action. Company-wide discussions on these priorities were initiated by calling meetings and mailing the list to all its 2.5 lakhs employees. As a result a great amount of decentralisation was introduced, cost savings were made on overtime payments and fuel consumption, a flatter organizational structure was introduced at plant-levels, more efforts were put in to develop human resources, and so on. In 1988-89, the company registered a profit of Rs. 3600 million.

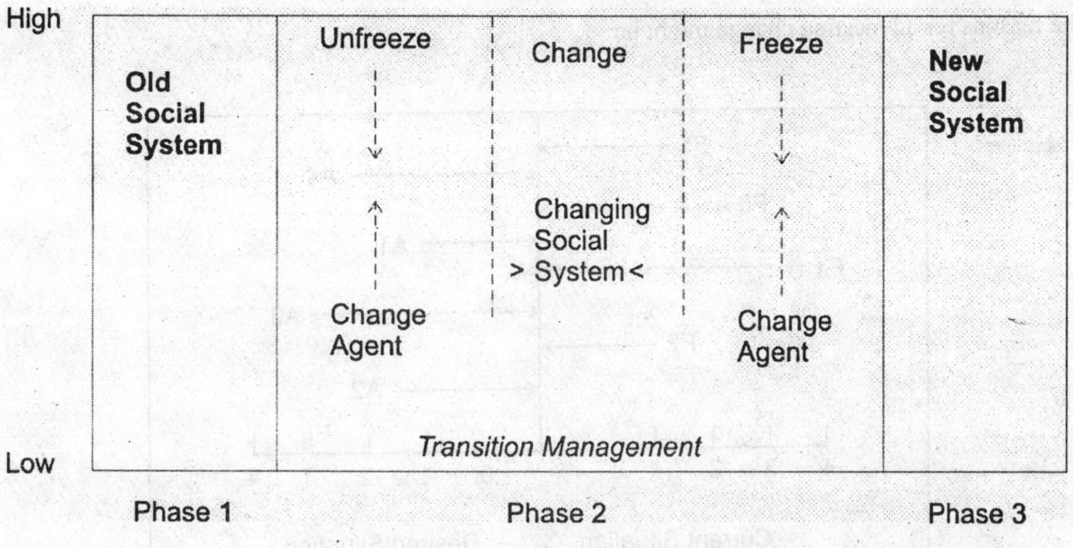

Fig. 6. Process of Organizational Change
(*Source*: Moorhead and Griffin, *Organizational Behaviour*, p. 675)

Unfreezing		Changing		Refreezing
Recognising the need for change, casting aside old values, behaviour, or organizational structures.	→	New values, behaviours and structures replace old ones. Action oriented.	→	Making change permanent. Practice what was learnt in the second stage.

Fig. 7. A Model of Change

For unfreezing, the manager must understand the causes for resistance to change. It is common knowledge that there are people who desire status quo and there are also individuals who push for change, And the two groups may be equal in their force as shown in Fig.8. The forces against change (labelled A) have strengths equal to those forces pushing for change (labelled F).

An example of four forces pushing in each direction is seen in the case of the organization that has announced the introduction of a new monthly cost report. After careful analysis, a top manager may find various reasons given by subordinates for resisting change, on the one hand, or for promoting change, on the other hand. Among the reasons given for resisting change might be:

The old report is easy to fill out because the data are readily available.

The old report takes very little time to think.

Top management has never used this report in the past for control purposes.

The new report will be very comprehensive and requires more time to fill out.

The reasons for advocating change might be:

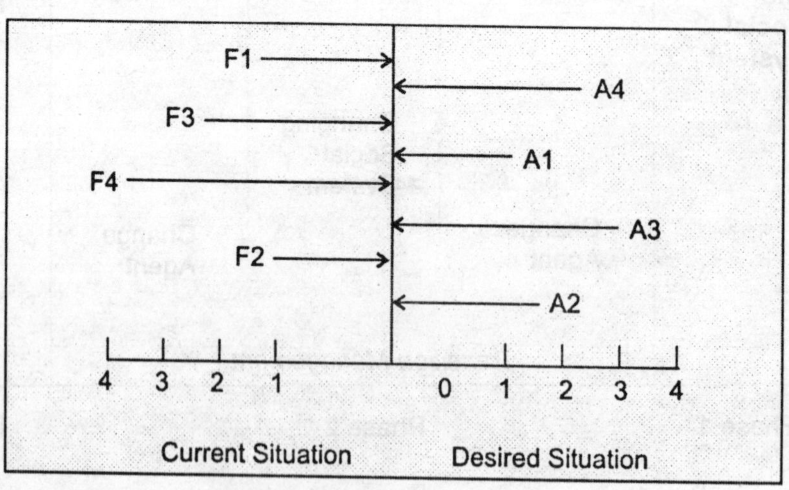

Fig. 8. Equal Forces for Change

(*Source*: Richard M. Hodgetts, *Organizational Behaviour*, MacMillan, 1991, p. 454).

1. An organizational streamlining of reporting forms is necessary.
2. Organizational control is getting out of hand.
3. If a report is going to have to be filled out, why not make it a meaningful one.
4. This new report is going to be analysed by staff personnel, and useful recommendations will be forwarded to each manager who has filled one out.

In such a situation, the manager must unfreeze the equilibrium. In doing so, three courses of action are available: (a) increase the strength of forces that push for change; (b) decrease the strength of forces that resist change; and (c) change a resisting force into one supporting the change.

Action Research Model

The concept of action research was also proposed by Kurt Lewin. It is a research on action with the goal of making that action more effective. Action research is both an approach to problem solving and a problem solving process - a series of activities and events. It is a change process based on systematic collection of data and then selection of a change action based on what the analysed data indicates. As an ongoing series of events and actions, it provides for a scientific procedure for managing planned change.

The process of action research consist of the five steps: Fig. 9.

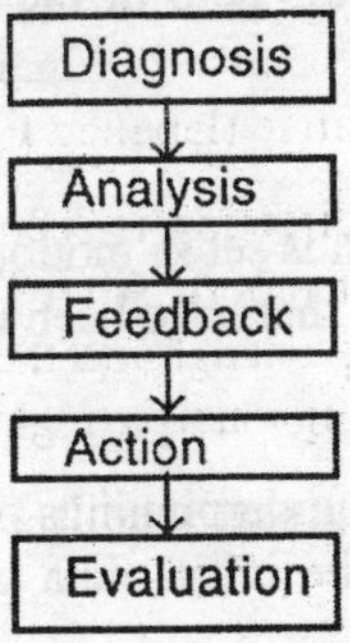

Fig. 9. Action Research Process

Diagnosis

The change agent, often an outside consultant in action research, begins by gathering information about problems, concerns and needed changes from members of the organization. This diagnosis is analogous to the physician's search to find what specifically ails a patient. In action research, the change agent asks questions, interviews employees, reviews records and listens to the concerns of employees.

The following table provides a bird's eye view of the various techniques that are used in the diagnosis, their potential benefits and disadvantages.

Table 1

Method	Major	Potential Problems
Interviews	Adaptive – allows data collection on a range of possible subjects. Source of rich data.	Expensive
	Emphatic	Interviewer can be biased (for example, he can bias the responses)
	Builds rapport	Coding/Interpretation problems. Self-report basis.
Questionnaires	Responses can be Qualified and easily summarized. Easy to use with big samples. Relatively inexpensive.	Non-emphatic. Pre-determined questions may miss some issues
		Data may be overinterpreted. Response-bias may be there.
	Can obtain large volume of data.	Interpretation problems
Observations	Collects data on behaviour rather than reports of the behavior. Real-time, not retrospective. Adaptive.	Sampling problems Observer bias Costly exercise
Secondary data Unobtrusive measures	Non-reactive, non-response bias. High face validity. Easy for quantification.	Access/retrieval possibility problems. Potential validity problems. Interpretation problems.

Source: David Nadler, "Feedback and Organization Development using Data-based methods", Reading, Addison-Wesley, 1977, p. 119.

Analysis

The information gathered during the diagnostic stage is then analysed. What problems do people key in on?

What patterns do these problems seem to take? The change synthesizes this information into primary concerns, problem areas, and possible actions.

Feedback

Action research includes extensive involvement of the change targets. That is, the people who will be involved in any change program must be actively involved in determining what the problem is and participating in creating the solution. So the third step is sharing with employees what has been found from steps one and two. The employees, with the help of the change agent develop action plans for bringing about any needed change.

Action

Now the action part of action research is set in motion. The employees and the change agent carry out the specific actions to correct the problems that have been identified.

Evaluation

Finally, consistent with the scientific underpinnings of action research, the change agent evaluates the effectiveness of the action plans. Using the initial data gathered as points of reference, any subsequent changes can be compared and evaluated.

Action Research provides at least two specific benefits for an organization.

1. It is problem focused. The change agent objectively looks for problems and the type of problem determines the type of change action. While this may seem intuitive behaviour, a lot of change activities aren't done this way. They are solution centred. The change agent has a favourite solution for example, implementing, flextime or a management by objectives program and then seeks out problems that his or her solution fits.
2. Because action research so heavily involves employees in the process, resistance to change is reduced. In fact, once employees have actively participated in the feed backstage, the change process typically takes as a momentum of its own. The employees and groups that have been involved become an internal source of sustained pressured to bring about the change.

Response and Reactions to Change

When change occurs, both managers and subordinates may react either positively or negatively. CA Carnall comments that "People experience change in all manner of ways. For some, a particular change will bring satisfaction, joy, advantage, a sense of job well done; for others, that same change may bring disadvantage, pain, sadness, even humiliation. Still others may barely perceive the change at II, experiencing it indifferently at most." Thus, change can be seen as totally destructive, threatening, natural, relatively acceptable, or as having some satisfying consequences.

Research shows some typical responses to changes as follows:

1. People may deny that change is taking place.
2. People may ignore the change.
3. People may resist the change.
4. People may accept the change and adapt to it.
5. People may also anticipate change and plan for it.
6. Change is supported, if it is directed at the real cause of the problem.

7. One's response to change may be an emotional matter.
8. "Wait and see" attitude is probably the most frequent response of employees.
9. Roethlisberger's "X" Chart illustrates that each change is interpreted by individuals according to their attitudes. The way those people feel about a change then determines how they will respond to it.
10. Hawthorn effect explains that "when people are observed, they act differently." Mere observation of a group changes it.
11. Though people individually interpret change, they often show their attachment to the group by joining with it in some uniform response to the change.
12. In a change situation, people always try to maintain equilibrium. People act to establish a steady state of need fulfilment and to protect themselves from disturbance of that balance. Organizations also have a self-correcting mechanism by which energies are called up to restore balance whenever change threatens (Homeostasis concept).

Figure 9. illustrates the factors affecting response and reactions to change.

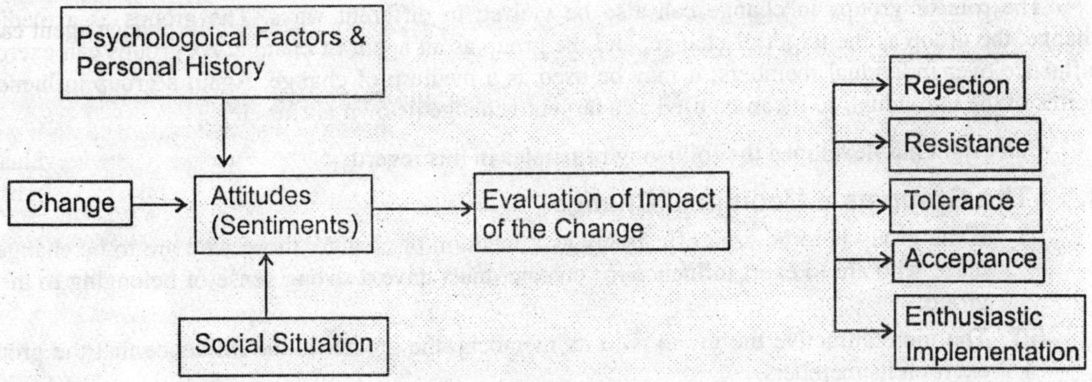

Fig.10. Response to Change

Source: Theodore 1. Herbert, *Dimensions of Organizational Behaviour*, 1981, p. 351.

STEPS INVOLVED IN ORGANIZATION WIDE CHANGE

Some changes are of such a nature that affects the whole organization and has several consequential effects. For example, a promotion at higher level affects several hierarchical levels below. If the job of an individual is being changed, it will change his role set, also his self-concept which is in part a product of his culture, his reference groups and also his education and training. All these, he will bring in line with the formal task to display a cooperative behaviour. If the formal task role and the self-concept differ and cannot be in congruent there will be adaptive response either to leave the organization or to make an attempt to change formal task role or to change the self-concept. In this way, any action has a chain reaction and causes a series of other changes, depending, naturally, upon the extent of its strength. Such changes that have a wide impact in the organization are organization wide changes.

Any change in the organization affects the people in terms of skills, status, social relationship or otherwise but organization wide change is just like a major surgical operation. If remained unsuccessful, it may endanger the very existence of the organization, and if successful, it may give a new life to the organization. Therefore, there is a need of careful planning. Allen lists the following steps in this regard:

(i) development of clear objectives;

(ii) analysis of existing organization;

(iii) preparation of an ideal plan;

(iv) trying out the plan;

(v) preparation of phase plan;

(vi) establishment of uniform nomenclature; and

(vii) overcoming resistance to change.

To be on a safe side, it should be undertaken only when it is felt necessary and only with the proper planning for that we must try to understand what we have and what we would like to have. Such organization wide change should not be very frequent and we should have a time prospective and project into the future. This will facilitate identification of gap both in terms of men or materials and for this purpose an action plan should be prepared.

In implementing organization wide change, it affects people throughout the organization, so there may be many upsets and setbacks. Status, system, titles and appellations may seriously be disturbed and designations should be immediately awarded as soon as the change is complete. Some people may be given training to reequip them for handling new jobs. As change often evokes resistance, step should be taken to overcome them. (We have already discussed the reasons of resistance to change and steps to overcome them).

GROUP LEVEL OF CHANGE

The role of groups in change can also be viewed in different ways. The groups as a medium of change, the group as the target of change, and the group as an agent of change. As groups can exercise its influence over individual members, it may be used as a medium of change. Again a group influences the norms of the individual, so it can be used as a target to change its own norms etc.

Cartwright has developed the following principles in this regard:

1. The Group as a Medium of Change

(i) If the group is to be used effectively as a medium of change, those who are to be changed and those who are to exert influence for change, must have a strong sense of belonging to the same group.

(ii) The more attractive the group is to its members, the greater is the influence that the group can exert on its members.

(iii) In attempt to change attitudes, values and behaviour, the more relevant they are to the basis of attraction to the group, the greater will be the influence on members.

(iv) The greater is the prestige of a group member in the eyes of other members, the greater the influence, he can exert.

(v) Efforts to change individuals or sub-parts of a group which if successful, would have the result of making them deviate from the norms of the group will encounter strong resistance.

2. The Group as a Target of Change

(i) Strong pressure for change in the group can be established by creating a shared perception by members of the need for change, thus making the source of pressure for change be within the group.

(ii) Information relating to the need for change, plans for change, and consequences of change must be shared by all in the group.

(iii) Changes in one part of the group produce strain in other related parts which can be reduced only by eliminating the change or bringing about readjustments in the **related parts.**

Implementation of Change

Having selected the appropriate strategy and having identified the focal points of concentration the manager's immediate job is to implement change. Here he confronts a biggest challenge through resistance by the employees. Research and experience reveal that creating change is more difficult than might seem. David Nadler is right when he says, "It is seductive to think of an organization as a large machine whose parts can be replaced at will." The task of changing behaviour of people in organizations, groups and structure have turned out to be a difficult and frustrating endeavour. Nadler and Tushman assert that any change encounters three problems in implementation – resistance, power and control.

First is the problem of resistance to change. Different reasons can be attributed to the resistance. Some of them are:

(i) Most of the people prefer stability and security. Change presents unknown which causes anxiety.

(ii) People feel that changes imposed on them reduce autonomy and self-control.

(iii) People generally develop certain patterns of managing the current behaviour. Change means that they have to find new ways of managing their tasks and environment.

(iv) People who are in the power resist change because they feel change threatens their power.

(v) People have vested interest in status quo.

(vi) For some ideological reasons also people resist change. They truly believe that the way things are done currently is better than the proposed change.

Manager in implementing change has to overcome such resistances to change (resistance to change and the methods to overcome resistance have already been elaborately discussed in this chapter).

The second problem in implementation of change programme relates to control. Change disrupts normal course of events in the organization. It disrupts and undermines the existing systems of management control. During the implementation of change the organization may easily lose control over certain issue.

The third problem is regarding the power. Any significant change poses the possibility of upsetting or modifying the balance of power among the groups in the organization. An organization is a political system made up of different individuals, groups, coalitions competing for power.

These problems, their implications and the various action steps are presented in the following table:

Table 2

Problem	Implication	Action Steps
Resistance	Need to motivate change	Surface dissatisfy the present state. Participation in change Rewards for behaviour in support of change Time and appointments to change from resistance Develop and communicate a clear image of the future
Control	Need to manage the transition	Use multiple and consistent leverage points Develop organizational arrangements for transition Build-in feedback mechanisms
Power	Need to shape the political dynamism	Assure the support of key power groups Use leader behaviour to generate energy in support of change. Use symbols and language. Build-in stability

Source: David Nadler "Concepts for Management of Organizational Change" in Hackman, Lawler, and Porter (Ed). "*Perspectives on Behaviour in Organizations*", McGraw Hill Co., 1983, p.560.

Plan the Change

Planning is perhaps the most crucial phase in the management of change. It involves answering three vital problems what, how and when to change. According to Harold Leavitf "all organizational changes can be classified as changes in structure, task, technology or people." Changing structure involves reorganization of the departments, re-specification of span of control, decentralization etc. Changing task includes job enrichment, job specification and specialization and job redefinition or any other changes concerned with the task of employees. Changing technology involves introduction of new lines of production, installing new control system, instituting new selection and recruitment etc. And finally, changing people comprises of training, meetings, development activities etc.

Steps In Planning Change

A change agent must consider the following steps before he plans the necessary change. He should:

1. Make clear the need for change or provide a climate in which group members feel free to identify such needs.
2. Permit and encourage relevant group participation in clarifying the needed changes.
3. State the objectives to be achieved by proposed changes.
4. Establish the broad guidelines for achieving the objectives.
5. Leave the details for implementing the proposed changes to the group in the organization or to the personnel who will be affected by change.
6. Indicate the benefits or rewards to the individuals or groups that are expected to accrue from the change.
7. Materialize the benefits or rewards, i.e., keep the promises made to those who made the change.
8. Selection of strategy is on essential part of planning. In solving organizational change problem, a manager pursues the strategies differently to solve a wide variety of problems.

Structure-Focused Change Efforts: These changes primarily include:

(i) Changing the number of organizational levels.
(ii) Altering the span of management.
(iii) Changing from one base of departmentation to another base.
(iv) Altering the line and staff, and functional authority relationships.

A manager's strategy here, sometimes, is reorganization. Reorganization involves entirely a redesign of the structure of the organization. It also calls for remarkable changes in the departmentation, span of control and coordination. Reorganization is proved to be effective and most widely used strategy in the case of serious problems. Alfred Chadler found empirically that after the Second World War the rapid rate of new product development rendered the centralized structure ineffective at both Washington House and General Electric, later, both firms decentralized their organizations. General Motors is another classic example of reorganization and after the change a great deal of redundant effort was eliminated and has speeded numerous new technologies into production.

Changing Organization by Redesigning Tasks

Redesigning tasks is another strategy a manager uses in change. Industrial engineering, scientific management by F.W. Taylor, improvements and creation of highly specialised jobs etc. all belong to this category of strategy. Jobs vary in scope and depth; and change efforts directed at the task (Job) are attempting to alter this scope and depth. By Job scope we mean the number of operations performed by the job holder and the frequency of the repetition of the job cycle. Whereas, relative influence of the job holder over the work environment and the degree of self-control in planning and performance of the job determines job depth. The process of upgrading, enlarging or enriching a job by increasing its depth and scope is called vertical job loading and also called job enrichment. Task-focused changes include:

(i) High internal work motivation.
(ii) High quality and work performance.
(iii) Job enrichment.
(iv) Scientific management.
(v) Industrial engineering, etc.

Changing Organization by Changing Technology

Computerization is the fashion of the day in today's organization. The increasing technology and especially computer has profound influence on the organization and its employees. For instance, it results in more mechanistic organization structure. Since departments tend to be consolidated, span gets reduced, functional departmentation replaces divisions, resulting in a centralized control. At the lower rungs it results in more routine jobs as well as more compartmentalized jobs in which worker's interaction is less and infrequent.

Computerization yet, is only one aspect of technological change. Other changes include introduction of new production technology, new employment procedures, new performance evaluation programmes etc.

Technology-focused changes comprise of:

(i) Changing problem-solving and decision-making procedures.

(ii) Introduction of computer to facilitate managerial planning and control.

(iii) Converting from unit production to mass production technology.

Changing Organization by Changing People

A change in the organization requires a corresponding change in the individual's personality. Changing personality is a challenging task because the basic personality factors are usually formed and developed in the early childhood of the employee. However difficult it might be, it is another strategy of change.

There is no dearth of techniques that can be used to change people in organizations. According to Robert House "if the development is to be successful it must be geared not only to the participant's needs and learning abilities but also to the particular requirements and practices of the organization in which he manages." House contends that the technique used must appropriately fit the situation. Harrison is of the view that 'surface' techniques interventions such as management games, lectures, conferences, seminars etc., are helpful for providing the employees with new skills to do the job and are used in mechanistic or organic structures. He further emphasizes that the developmental change requires emotional involvement of the managers in employees' problems. Motivational theories need no reiteraction here. To meet rapidly changing conditions 'in-depth' organizational development interventions (for example, sensitivity training) are appropriate.

People-focused changes can be made through the following techniques:

(i) Sensitivity training.

(ii) Transactional analysis.

(iii) Assertiveness training.

(iv) Team building workshops.

(v) Job-training programmes.

(vi) Leadership and supervisory training.

(vii) Management by objectives.

Kotter and Schlesinger have suggested six methods of introducing change (see Table 3). The change agent must understand that there is no one universal approach to overcome resistance. Depending on each . situation a different approach needs to be adopted. Change is a situational problem and a realisation of this fact is essential for bringing about a change.

Table 3 contains six approaches for introducing change together with the situations where each change intervention is most appropriate. The advantages and drawbacks of each approach are also listed in the table. Management must examine the nature of the resistance and then review the possible approaches to fit the situation.

The six approaches listed in Table 3 will help unfreeze and change the values and behaviours of people. In other words, the approaches enable the managers to introduce change successfully. The next crucial stage is to make the change stick otherwise there is the danger of people reverting to the pre-chang position.

How to make the change permanent? The methods suggested for the purpose are: use of group forces use of leadership, shared rewards, working with unions and concern for employees.

Use of Group Forces

The group exercises considerable influence on the behaviour of members. The behaviour, attitudes beliefs, and values of the individual are all firmly grounded in the groups to which he belongs. How aggressive or co-operative a person is, how much self-respect and self-confidence he has, how energetic and productive his work is, what he aspires to, what he believes to be true and good, when he loves o hates, and what beliefs and prejudices he holds all these characteristics are highly determined by the individual's group membership. Whether they resist or accept change largely depends on the groups. The change agent must make use of the groups to bring about change.

Table 3 : Methods for dealing with resistance to change

Approach	Commonly used situations	Advantages	Drawbacks
Education + Communication	Where there is a lack of information or inaccurate information and analysis	Once persuaded people will often help with the implementation of the change	Can be very time consuming lots of people are involved
Participation + involvement	Where the initiators do not have all the information they need to design the change and where others have considerable power to reist	People who participate will be committed to implementing change & any relevant information they have will be integrated into the change plan	Can be very time consuming participants design inappropriate change
Facilitation + Support	Where people are resisting because of adjustment problems	No other approach works as well with adjustment problems.	Can be time consumi expensive, and still fail
Negotiation + agreement	Where someone or some group will clearly lose out in a change and where that group has considerable power to resist	Sometimes it is a relatively easy way to avoid major resistance	Can be too expensive in ma cases if it alerts others negotiate for compliance
Manipulation + Co-optation	Where other tactics will not work or are too expensive	It can be a relatively quick and inexpensive solution to resistance problems	Can lead to future problems people feel manipulated
Explicit + implicit	Where speed is essential and the change initiators possess considerable power	It is speedy and can overcome any kind of resistance	Can be risky if it leaves peop angry at the initiators

Guidelines to Institute Change

Because organizational change is inevitable, managers should be sensitive to the barriers to change so that resistance can be overcome. This, of course, is easier said than done. However, several useful approaches have been suggested, and the key ones are summarized here .

Change of Change Agent

The change agent must himself change. It is only then that he will be able to reinforce a psychological climate of support for change. Unwillingness of the managers to give up traditional managerial practices and their unpreparedness to accept new methods are the most serious barriers to the introduction of change and to make it permanent in organizations.

Shares Rewards

Another way to build support for change is to ensure that the people affected derive benefit out of the change. Benefits include increased pay, promotion, training, recognition, and the like.

Co-operation of Unions

Taken into confidence, unions themselves can act as change agents, though they are generally considered to be anti-change. Many union leaders are accepting the installation of CNC machines, though it means displacement of the work force. This has been possible because of their participation before, during, and after the change has been introduced. A change introduced without their support may not stay for long.

Concern For Employees

A change should not be introduced for the sake of it. Change needs to be introduced only when necessary and it must be by evolution and not by revolution. Any change must ultimately benefit employees. In the short-run the needs and requirements of employees should not be affected. Any problem that has taken place because of change needs to be looke into and corrected immediately.

Inform

Communicate to those involved as far in advance as possible the reasons for the change and the associated benefits. People need to know what is going to occur and why to dispel their fears. This is sometimes difficult because it can place confidential information in the hands of competitors or inappropriately leak information (decisions that could affect stock prices). Informed people make informed judgements; rumour and uncertainty are too frequently converted into veiled threats and protectionist stances.

Plan

Plan proposed changes in detail and allow time for reflection. This should include a consideration of all repercussions including retaining, relocation, the need for a new procedures and policies, and influences on morale and the reward structure. It is important to set the stage for change.

Minimise Damage

Protect those who will potentially be damaged by the change. Reductions in pay or job classifications should not be permitted. Make transfers voluntary where possible, and handle reductions in-force through attrition.

Allow people to bid on new job openings. Provide generous allowances for retraining and make career consultation available to everyone involved. Avoid making people lose face in the change process.

Timing

Make changes as gradually as conditions will permit. People tolerate evaluation more than they do revolution.

Participation

Involve people in planning the change where possible. Those affected should be permitted to express their objections in advance. If people participate in what is happening, they will be more likely to go along. Participation is the key concept in gaining acceptance. People support what they help to create.

When the executive vice president asked the controller about his progress, he was given a negative answer.

The vice president was disturbed with this reaction and was determined to settle the problem once and for all. He called an executive meeting that included the controller and the auditor. At the meeting, the possibility of centralizing some of the operations of the branches in order to afford better administrative control was discussed. Someone suggested the possibility of buying some National Cash Register posting machines to help solves some of the operating difficulties.

After a lengthy discussion it was decided that these machines were the key to the elimination of many of the association's reporting problems. The controller admitted that they would make it easier to control operations, and the assistant vice president felt that their acquisition would add greatly to the customer service capacities of the association.

Three new machines were installed the following month. After closing hours each teller was instructed in the proper techniques of operating them. The management felt that they had made a sound investment, and their only worry was over the ability of the tellers were older women and seemed to be slow and reluctant to learn the new process.

One month after practice machines had been placed in the association; these shortcomings became so acute that immediate action had to be taken. The management realized that the morale of the teller staff was depressed and that the smoothness of operations at the time office had been completely disrupted. The personnel manager suggested that some type of formal training programme should be developed and that the management should explain to the members of the work force their personal roles in the anticipated progress of the association.

The personnel manager has neither found a method of eliminating the discontent, nor has he been able to give an adequate reason for it to the rest of the officers. Finally one officer stated in a committee meeting that he felt the work force had been "over human-relationed." He suggested that in many instances negative leadership was far superior to positive leadership. He stated in forceful language that he would inform those tellers who were complaining and failing to learn the process either to learn it quickly or be fired. Another officer felt that since some of them were employees who had been with the association for many years and whose work had always been satisfactory, some alternative must be found.

Shape Political Dynamics

We cannot underestimate the important role of organizational politics in achieving desired goals. Politics is also involved in getting organizational changes accepted. Politically, resistance to change can be overcome by winning the support of the most powerful and influential individuals. Doing so builds a critical internal mass of support for change. Demonstrating clearly that key organizational leaders endorse the change in an effective way to get others to go along with it – either because they share the leader's vision or because they fear the leader's retaliation. Either way, the political support will facilitate acceptance of change.

Educate the Workforce

Sometimes, people are reluctant to change because they fear what the future has in store for them. Fears about economic security, for example, may be put to rest by a few reassuring words from power holders. As part of educating employees about what organizational changes may mean for them, top management must show a considerable amount of emotional sensitivity. Doing so makes it possible for the people affected by change to become instrumental in making it work. Some companies have found that simply answering the question "what's in it for me?" can help allay a lot of fears. For example, sales reps at New Jersey-based Sandoz Pharmaceuticals balked at first when laptop computers were introduced as a means for compiling and transmitting sales report.

Then, once it was explained how this new technology would free them from the cumbersome job of writing weekly sales reports (a task that used to consume much of their weekend time), the computers were not only accepted, but embraced.

Involve Employees in The Change Efforts

It is well established that people who participate in making a decision tend to be more committed to the outcomes of that decision than are those who are not involved. Accordingly, employees who are involved in responding to unplanned change, or who are made part of the team charged with planning a needed organizational change, may be expected to have very little resistance to change. Organizational changes that are "sprung" on the workforce with little or no warning might be expected to encounter resistance simply as a knee-jerk reaction until employees have a chance to assess how the change affects them. In contrast, employees who are involved in the change process are better able to understand the need for change, and are therefore less likely to resist it. Says Duane Hartley, General Manager of Hewlett-Packard's microwave instruments division, "I don't think people really enjoy change, but if they can participate in it and understand it, it can become a positive [experience] for them." It is precisely these kinds of efforts at participative management that are credited with the successful change in Southwestern Bell after the breakup of AT& T.

Follow-up on The Change

Management of change is incomplete without proper follow-up. Organization must evaluate the effects of change. Objectives must be present and be compared with the performance to see the degree of success in change. End results should be operationally defined and measurements must be done both before and after the implementation of change. This enables the manager or change agent, to compare the performance after the introduction of change with the one prior to it. The manager must make sure that the change is implemented in such a fashion as to maximize the benefits to the organization by the effective changes.

Although these suggestions may be easier to state than to implement, any effort to follow them will be well rewarded. Given the many forces that make employees resistant to change, managers should keep these guidelines in mind. If organizational change is to be beneficial, all employees must work toward accepting the change rather than using it as a rallying point around which conflic~ and dissension may focus.

Role of the Change Agent

A professional process consultant may act as a change agent or insight managers may act change agent.

The change agent influences innovation decisions in a direction consider desirable by the change agency. The change agent has to fill seven roles in the change process:

1. He makes the client organization realize the need for change.
2. He identifies and diagnoses the clients problems. He anticipates certain problems.
3. He prepares the blue print for implementation of change. He solicits the support of the client system to do so.
4. He makes himself acceptable to the client organization.
5. The client is made receptive to the change which is never thrust upon the client.
6. He stabilizes the change. He sees to it that the organization does not revert to the earlier position.
7. He hands over the changed organization to the Client at opportune time, and dissociates himself, terminating his relationship with the client.

One of the buffing problems a change agent confronts in the management of changes is the resistance from the organizational participants. Often people working in organizations develop their established ways of working, Interpersonal relationships, norms and values. They try to assess the environmental impacts and predict the outcomes of their efforts and behaviour. They function, in other words, in a state of their own contrived equilibrium. Any change in the organization may disturb this equilibrium.

Since change creates tension and emotional turmoil in the minds of employees, according to Harris, some people attempt to avoid tension by creating barriers whereas some others tend to minimize tensions by a quick adjustment to change. Change thus results in resistance quite frequently, negative reactions doom the success of the change programme especially when a manager is unable to handle it properly. A manager should also note that the individuals and groups react very differently to change from passively resisting it, to aggressively trying to undermine it, to sincerely embracing it.

To overcome resistance is no mean task. Probably because of this reason Neccolo Machievalli rightly contended "……… it must be considered that there is nothing more difficult to carry out, nor more doubtful of success, nor more dangerous to handle, than to initiate a new order of things". Managers are therefore to grapple with continue uncertainty and change especially because of resistance problem.

Keith Davis has also suggested some ways to overcome resistance to change. They are as follows:

1. Use of Group Forces

Group is an important tool for bringing strong pressure on its members to change. As one's behaviour is firmly grounded in the group to which he belongs, changes in group forces will encourage changes in individual behaviour.

2. Leadership for Change

Capable leaders reinforce a climate of psychological support for change by applying appropriate leadership style. Change is more likely to be successful if the leaders introducing it have high expectations.

3. Shared Rewards

To minimize resistance it should be made sure that there are enough rewards for employees in the changed situation. Rewards give employees a sense of progress with a change.

4. Employee Security

Along with shared rewards, existing employee benefits must be protected. Security during a period of change must be ensured. Seniority rights, opportunities for advancement, and other benefits should be safeguarded when a change is made.

5. Working with Unions

Unions sometimes support management in encouraging workers to accept change. Unions may approve changes in the interest of workers. Managers in cooperation with workers' unions can easily initiate changes.

6. Working with The Total System

Resistance to change can be minimized by helping employees to recognize the need for each change, to participate in it, and to gain from it. Management's responsibility for change is four-fold:

(a) Make only useful, necessary change. Change by evolution, not revolution.

(b) Recognize the possible effects of change and introduce it with adequate attention to human needs.

(c) Share the benefits of change with employees.

(d) Diagnose the problems remaining after a change occurs and treat them.

DESIRABLE CONSEQUENCES OF RESISTANCE TO CHANGE

Change is not always opposed. Some changes are liked and sponsored or supported by the workers themselves. Some other changes are so trivial and routine that resistance, if any, is too small to be evident. Many other changes are strongly resisted by workers if it harms their interests as an individual or as a group.

Although people tend to resist change, this tendency can be offset by their desire to learn something new and for the rewards that come with change. The management should learn a lesson from this behaviour of people towards change that any change either can be successful or can be developed into a behavioural problem, depends upon how skilfully it is managed to minimise resistance.

The group affected by the change may be intelligent or otherwise. But it is not necessary that an intelligent group does better understand and accept change. Often the opposite is true. Groups advance certain more rational reasons for not affecting a change. Intelligence can be used either for or against change, depending upon how management motivates the group.

Resistance to change is neither always bad. Sometime resistance produces certain desirable consequences. We may discuss hereunder some desirable consequences of resistance of change:

1. Cost-benefits Comparison

Opposition to changes are not always an undesirable human response, nor is change always a positive good. Experience shows that many changes made by management and technical specialists are quite unwise and their opposition is quite correct. Proposals for changes inherently are not desirable. They require a close cost benefit analysis to determine its usefulness economically. If cost is higher than the benefits derived from it, there is no logic for the change and resistance in that case is quite desirable.

In making a comparison of cost with benefits, all types of costs and benefits should be thought over because in spite of net economic benefits, social and psychological costs have great influence over benefits. These social and psychological cost must be considered in decision making progress though they cannot be reduced to members. Almost, every change involves some psychological loss because of strain that it imposes on people as they try to adjust.

2. Types of Opposition

There are two types of opposition to change: (i) Rational opposition to change which is based on a reasonable analysis of cost and benefits and if cost is higher than the benefits, the opposition is said to be rational. (ii) The second is resistance to change that is not based on analysis of costs and benefits but on emotions and selfish desires which cannot be said to be reasonable hence is undesirable. So rational opposition to change is desirable but sometimes it becomes very difficult in making a distinction between these two.

Even emotional resistance to change can have desirable consequences and cannot be classed as a negative factor in organizations. One possible benefit from this resistance is that the changing agents (managers or employers) come to know the cause more explicitly for the opposition and the desirable result the members want to accomplish by negating the change. They (managers) should also examine more carefully the negative aspects and their side effects as defined by the workers. This type of examination may be desirable because it will reveal the following results which may be beneficial to the organizations to understand the behaviour of their people:

(i) Emotional resistance may be an indication of low job satisfaction and poor motivation and morale in the organization. By this analysis, the change agents may locate such areas and take necessary steps to improve it.

(ii) It can pin point the weaknesses in communication process and because of in adequate communication about change situation has become so explosive. The management may try to strengthen it.

(iii) Emotional resistance can cause management to give more attention to improved organizational behaviour because they see that it will reduce resistance to change.

3. Technical Specialists and Change

Technical specialists are mainly concerned with suggesting or making the change that affects others in the organization. In suggesting the change, they mostly ignore the human and behavioural problems of change. Though modern thinking in this respect is somewhat different and includes behavioural problems with their main job speciality but practice is quite different. Because it is their technical job hence they have no logic for the social problems they cause. Their thinking is that logically, their idea or suggestion is quite correct and only fools should oppose it. It is because they ignore psychology of the people.

In this case also, because human, social and psychological problems have been ignored while suggesting or introducing change, any resistance from the operating force may be said to be desirable. One more logic in their resistance is that specialists do not suggest any change for themselves or for their own work.

Thus these are circumstances where resistance to change is thought reasonable and management should take note of such resistance.

REFERENCES

Alvin Toffler, *Future Shock*, Bantom Books, New York, 1972, p.11.

Stephen P. Robbins, *Organizational Behaviour*, Prentice Hall of India, New Delhi, 1989, p.527.

H. Randolph Bobbit, Jr. *et al.*, *Organizational Behaviour*, Prentice Hall, New Jersey, 1978, p.34.

Keith Davis, *Human Behaviour at Work*, Tata McGraw Hill Book Co., New Delhi, 1975, pp.154-155.

Jerald Hage, *Theories of Organ is at Ions*, John Wiley, New York, p.262.

Ivancevich, Donnelly and Gibson, *Managing for Performance*, Business Publication Inc., Dallas, Texas, 1980, p. 396.

Edgar H. Schein, *Organizational Psychological*, Prentice Hall Inc., Englewood Cliffs, N.J., 1980, pp.243-244.

Douglas 1. Hall, *Potential for Career Growth Personal Administration*, May-June, 1971, pp.18-19.

D.A. Nadler, *The Effective Management of Organizational Change*, in J.W. Lorsch, Ed., *Handbook of Organizational Behaviour*, Prentice Hall, Englewood Cliffs, N.J., 1978, pp.358-369.

D. Katz and R.L. Kahn, *The Social Psychology of Organizations*, John Wiley & Sons, New York, 1978.

M.T. Hannan and J. Freeman, *Structural Inertia and Organizational Change, American Sociological Review*, No.49, 1984, pp.149-164.

N.M. Tichy, *Control Your Destine or Someone Else Will*, Doubleday Currency, New York, 1993.

N.M. Tichy, *Revolutionise Your Company, Fortune*, December 13, .1993, pp.114-115, 118.

Richard L. Daft, *Organization Theory and Design*, West Publishing Co., New York, 1983, p.288.

Larry E. Short, *Planned Organizational Change*, MSU Business Topics, Vol. 21 , No. 4, Autumn, 1973, pp. 53-61

Blake and Mouton, *Change by Design Not Default, Advanced Management Journal*, April 1970, pp.29-34.

Edgar Williams, *Changing System and Behaviour, Business Horizons*, August 1969, pp.53-58.

Charles Perrow, *Is Business Really Changing, Organizational Dynamics*, Summer, 1974, pp.30-44.

Larry E. Griener, *Patterns of Organizational Change, Harvard Business Review*, May-June, 1969, pp.119-130.

Kurt Lewin, *Field Theory in Social Science*, Harper & Row, New York, 1951.

Edgar H. Schein, *Management Development as a Process of Influence* in David R. Hampton, Behavioural Concepts in Management, Dickson Publishing, Belmont, Calief., 1968, p.11 o.

H.C. Kelman, Compliance, Identification and Internalisation: Three Process of Attitude Change, Conflict Resolution, 1958, pp.51-60.

Richard M. Hodgetts, *Organizational Behaviour*, MacMillan, 1991, pA55.

D.D. Warrick, Ed. *Contemporary Organization Development: Current Thinking and Applications*, Scott Foresman, Glenview, 11., 1985, pp. 438-448.

Megginson, Donald Mosley and Paul Pietri. Jr., *Management Concepts and Applications*, Harper and Row, London, 1983, pA23.

F.J. Roethisberger, *Management and Morale*, Harvard University Press, Cambridge Mass, 1941, p.21.

Darwin Cartwright, *Achieving Change in People, Some Applications of Group Dynamics Theory, in Human Relations Management*, ed. l.L. Hechmann Jr. and S.G. Huneryager, Spugh-Western Publishing Co., Cincinnati, 1960, ppA64-467.

David Nadler; *The Effective Management of Organizational Change in J.W. Lorch Ed., Handbook of Organizational Behaviour,* Prentice Hall, Englewood Cliffs, N.J. 1987, pp.358-389; David Nadler, *Feedback and Organization, Development, Using Data Based Methods*, Addison Wesley, Reading, Mass, 1977, pp.118-143 and M.L. Tushman, A. *Political Approach to Organizations: Review and Rationale, Academy of Management Review*, 1977, pp.202-216.

Harold J. Leavitt, New Perspective in Organization Research, John Wiley & Sons. Inc., New York, 1966.

Watson, Goodwin and Edward M. Glasser, *What We Have Learned About Planning For Change, Management Review*, American Management Association, November, 1965, pp. 34-46.

How G.M., *Turned Itself Around, Fortune*, January, 1978.

Robert J. House, *Management Development*, p.11.

John P. Kotter and L.A. Schlesinger, *Choosing Strategies for change, Harvard Business Review*, March-April, 1979, pp. 106-114.

Keith Davis and New Newstrom, *Human Behaviour at Work*, McGraw Hill, New York, 1981, p.297.

S. Farber, *When Employees Ask: What's In It For Me, Business Month*, September, 1989, p. 79.

W.A. Pasmore and M.R. Fagans, *Participation, Industrial Development and Organizational Change: A Review and Synthesis*, Journal of Management, Vol. 18, 1992, pp.375-397.

J. Huey, *Managing In The Midst of Chaos, Fortune*, April 5, 1993, pp. 38-41,44, 46-48.

Z.E. Barnes, *Change in The Bell System*, Academy of Management Executive, vol. 1.1987, ppA3-46.

O. Jeff Harris, *Managing People At Work; Concepts and Cases in Interpersonal Behaviour*, John Wiley & Sons pp 403-405.

Niccolo Machievalli, *The Difficulty of Change*, Readings 36, in Keith Davis Eds *Organizational Behaviour. A Book of Readings*, McGraw Hill Book, Co., 1977, p.245.

Kotter and Schlesinger, Power *Dependence and Effective Management, Harvard Business Review*, July-August, 1977.

D.M. Pestonjee, *Change Process and Resistance to Change*, in Udai Pareek, R.V. Rao and D. M. Pestonjee, Ed. *Behavioural Process in Organizations*, Oxford IBH, 1981, p.271.

CHAPTER

20

Counselling

First try saying what you believe counselling to be. Just write down your own definition; it will probably be helpful when you come to compare it with the issues raised in this chapter and be more helpful in comprehending the issues and the techniques of counselling in the true perspective.

There are a number of ways to define counselling. Even professional counselling organizations, like the British Association for Counselling, find it difficult to come up with one precise definition, so if you find it hard, you are not alone. All counselling agencies and professionals agree on one thing, however, except in specific circumstances counselling is not advice giving, despite the common misconception that this is precisely what it is.

So, if you have given a definition that talk about counselling primarily as giving advice, think again. Try writing down another definition that omits any mention of advice.

- There are a number of important implications if you accept this definition of counselling:
- Counselling is a process, not a technique or a once off, quick fix answer to people's problems.
- Counselling is about helping somebody else to clarify that is to make sense of what his or her problem is or he/she is facing with it.

Counselling is about getting the person with the problem to accept responsibility for it where that is appropriate. If it is not their responsibility, then it's not their problem and the counselling is aimed at helping them to recognise and accept that. What this means, is that we need to help people get to the root of what their problem is. So, for example, if the person's problem is stated as 'I cannot stand the way my boss treats me', there are two separate issues. One is that it seems as though the boss has the problem (although he or she may not see that). Second, the staff member may need to deal with the issue of personal self-esteem, or guilt at not being able to deal with the boss.

Counselling should always lead to a resolution of the problem. In this last one, always remember that a resolution is seldom to be found in the giving of any answers or advice. There is a place for advice giving; but that isn't counselling. Where the real problem is something like dealing with unwarranted guilt or low self esteem, no amount of advice will change that.

What Counselling Is

Study the above definition of counselling carefully. How does it relate to your own understanding of what counselling is? If you have significant differences of opinion, give some thought to what you have actually described. If you accept our definition as close to your own perception, what follows will help you to carry it forward.

While counselling may be seen as giving guidance, it is guidance given in a way that leads the staff member to his or her own understanding of the problem and towards taking the action that will solve it. That is why counselling is a longer term development process. If you simply told people how to solve their personal problems (in the nicest possible way), they may take your advice, but it is doubtful whether they would have learned to take responsibility for dealing with their own problems in the future.

The applications of the counselling process range from helping your staff to resolve problems of relationships or addictive behaviour to simply listening and allowing them to vent everyday frustrations.

In order to carry out the process of counselling effectively, you will have developed your mental, imaginative and emotional powers to quite a high degree. In other words, you need to be able to observe and analyse, visualise and be creative, have empathy and understand your own feelings.

What Counselling is not?

You will already have seen that counselling is neither giving advice nor solving other people's problems for them. If you are that kind of manager, you will not be in the business of assisting your staff to develop their own potential. More likely, your staff will be disgruntled because they never learn anything and you will be rushed off your feet doing other people's work for them.

In that respect, the counselling approach is similar to the skills of coaching, where you will be assisting staff to discover their own solution. The difference is that counselling is usually response to a staff member's personal problem.

You can deal with those personal problems in a number of ways. One way is to set up a disciplinary process. Counselling is often seen as something that 'somebody needs' in order to prevent them from carrying out unacceptable behaviour. Counselling is not a disciplinary interview. The outcome of such an interview may lead to the staff member realising that there is a problem and asking for some help. But please do not confuse the two by pretending to offer counselling when you really want to discipline somebody.

A general rule that will tell you whether you are in a position to be offering to counsel a staff member is to ask who is setting the agenda. If you want to be giving your (or the company's) point of view; if you want to offer your advice or information about an aspect of the person's behaviour; if you have a complaint to make, then this is your agenda and it's inappropriate for you to offer counselling. If you are open to the staff member bringing you his or her concerns and problems, are able to give sufficient time and attention to these concerns and are just prepared to listen without judgment, then it looks as though you are about to offer some counselling support.

Counselling situations

Here are two examples of potential counselling scenarios. Write down your response to them. Are they both appropriate for counselling? How would you handle them?

Situation I

Nitin approaches you in your office. He asks if you could spare a minute, and then says he would like a couple of days' leave because he has to move home. When you ask him more about it, he reveals that he and his wife are going through a divorce and he is moving out, leaving his two young children with his wife and going to a small flat on the other side of town. 'I just need a couple of days', he says, 'I will be quite all right after I've settled in. Do not worry, it would not affect my work and I will make up the time.

Situation II

Poonam stops you in the corridor. 'Look', she says, 'I wish you would do something about Renu. She keeps disappearing and wandering off. I found her in the washroom of the third time today. All she says is that she needs the time to think and that she cannot do her work without thinking. But she won't talk about it and I think she has got a problem. Anyway, she is not pulling her weight and it is not fair to the others.

In the first example, Nitin may well need the support that counselling can give him. As the manager, you could simply respond to his request for two days' leave. This may be all that Nitin requires from you to arrange his affairs. As someone prepared and able to offer counselling, you might also be the most appropriate person to help him go through a difficult personal time and one that might well disrupt his work, whatever he says at this point.

He had chosen to confide in you already. This is sufficient reason to believe that he would find it helpful to talk it through with you at greater length if you show that you are prepared to listen.

In the second example, you might take this further as a disciplinary matter and see it as nothing more. A warning to Renu. Once you have established that Poonam has been accurate in what she has said, could be sufficient to change her behaviour. But there may be much more to this. If you take a counselling approach, you are more likely to ask Renu what is bothering her and whether she would like to talk about it in confidence. If she understands what you are offering, she knows that she has the option to take up counselling. It is up to her how she responds.

Now make a note of some counselling situation from your own experience. Do not use real names, and disguise the actual events if necessary. There may be situations where you had, or could have done with, some counselling in the past, or where you offered or might have offered counselling to someone else.

Counselling is referred to the discussion of an emotional problem with an employee with an objective of reducing its intensity. No matter how well human relationships at work are maintained and handled people, will still develop emotional problem. The main reason behind this is that each individual differs in behaviour, needs and ideas. They interact each other. Individual differences may cause misunderstanding which in turn may develop emotional conflicts. Conflicts may develop between any two persons in the organization irrespective of their status in organization. Counselling involves discussion in order to release the tension. It is simply a process of adjustment or seeking a new emotional equilibrium for an employee. Frustration, conflict, and stress are the important causes of emotional problems.

Guidance and Counselling

Guidance is the assistance made available by qualified and trained persons to an individual of any age to help him to manage his own life activities, develop his own points of view, make his own decisions and carry on his own burdens.

Guidance means assisting individual to select courses of study appropriate to their needs and interests, achieve academic excellence to the best possible extent, derive maximum benefit of the institutional resources and facilities, inculcate proper study habits, satisfactorily participate in curricular and extra curricular activities.

Counselling is a process of enabling the individual to know himself and his present and possible future situations in order that he may make substantial contributions to the society and to solve his own problems through a face to face personal relationship with the counsellor.

Counselling is a learning oriented process carried on in a social environment in which the professionally competent counsellor attempts to assist the counsellee using appropriate procedures to become a happy and productive member of the society by formulating realistic and purposeful goals for total personal growth. Counselling is not just giving information, or giving advice, suggestions and recommendations, even when requested for.

Counselling is, therefore, primarily aimed at

- bringing about desired changes in the individual for self realisation
- providing assistance to solve problems through an intimate personal relationship

The objective of counselling are to enable an individual

* to achieve positive mental health
* resolve their problems
* improve personal effectiveness
* maximise individual freedom to choose and act within the conditions imposed by the environment

Employees' feelings cannot be ignored altogether or argued about. The are situational facts that need to be accepted, understood and dealt with because managers supervise the people in their totality rather than only their work. Counselling functions are advice, reassurance, communication, emotional release, clarified thinking and reorientation. These functions are performed by the management except the function of reorientation that is usually performed by the specialists or professional counsellors.

MEANING OF EMPLOYEE COUNSELLING

Organizations are social entities where employees execute their job assignment in groups. Their attitudes, their feelings and their individual needs differ from each other as each individual is different by nature. Individual differences may cause misunderstanding, resisting sometimes in emotional conflicts which is certainly not a positive sign of good employee-management relations. Conflicts may be between employee and employee or between employee and executive such as manager or supervisor or between supervisor and supervisor/manager. The best way to get rid of these misunderstandings and conflicts is counsel parties concerned. **Keith Davis** has defined the term as **"discussion of an emotional problem with an employee with the general objective of decreasing it."** The **implications** of the definition are as under:

1. **Counselling is an emotional problem.** It has no concern with other problems like technical methodological, job inconvenience, occupational guidance and legal problems which are by nature non-emotional but any emotional problem connected with these exceptions, will require counselling'. Sometimes, guidance in these areas may be called counselling.
2. **Counselling involves discussion, i.e.,** it is an act of communication. Successful counselling depends of communication skills, primarily oral by which one person's emotions can be shared with another.
3. **The main objective of couselling is to understand or decrease an employee's emotional disorder.**Simply a discussion between two persons socially on an emotional problem of one of the person, it is a social problem and not counselling because intention of counselling is not there. The main purpose of counselling must be seeking understanding or help from the counsellor and the counsellor must be ready to offer it.
4. **Counselling is in no way limited to professionally trained counsellors.** Whose services are no doubt required for some serious emotional problems, but for non-serious emotional problems, **supervisors or managers may counsel.**

FUNCTIONS OF COUNSELLING

The general objective of counselling is to help the employee in dealing with their emotional problems so that they can work well for the accomplishment of common goals in self confidence, self control, understanding and ability to work effectively. These objectives can be achieved through performance of the following counselling functions:

1. **Advice.** Generally counselling is looked upon as an advice giving activity, but in reality it is but one of the functions of counselling. Actually counselling requires some judgement about the emotional feelings of a person and to suggest the necessary course of action. It is very difficult to a counsellor to understand the other person's emotional feelings, and moreover he is quite unconcerned of them. However, advice giving is a routine counselling matter between the worker and a supervisor/manager.
2. **Re-assurance.** Reassurance is another function of counselling. Reassurance is a way of giving courage to workers to face a problem or to pose a confidence in themselves that they are following the right path. Sometimes supervisors are heard saying 'Well, you are making good progress' or 'Don't worry, go ahead', or 'You are all right', they are all reassurances. But, it should always be kept in mind that reassurances must be given at a right moment.
3. **Communication.** Counselling helps improve both upward and downward communications. **In an upward direction** it is a key for employees to make the management know their feelings at the lowest level in the organization chart. Counselling initiates an upward signal. An another part of the counsellor's job is to discover emotional problems relating to company's policies and to interpret those problems to top management. Counselling helps **downward communication** because counsellor is to interpret the company policies and procedures to employees as they discuss their emotional problems relating thereto.

4. **Release of Emotional Tension.** One of the important functions of counselling is to release the counselee's emotional tension. It is also called 'emotional catharis.' People tend to get an emotional release from their frustration and all other problems as soon as they tell them to some sympathetic listner. They feel relaxed. The release of tension does not necessarily solve their problem, but it removes mental blockade and gives courage to the counselee to face the problem boldly and think constructively over them again.
5. **Clarified Thinking.** Realistic thinking is also an important function of counselling. Counselling encourages clarified thinking because mental blocks are cleared and the counselee is forced to think rationally especially in cases where he knows that counsellor knows the facts and is not emotionally involved. Clarified thinking is normal result of emotional release. A skilled counsellor brings about clear thinking more quickly. In clarified thinking, counsellor does not advice what is right but he encourages the counselle to accept responsibility for emotional problems and to be more realistic in solving them.
5. **Reorientation.** Reorientation involves a change in the employee's psychic self through a change in basic goals and values. Mostly, it needs a revision of the workers' level of aspiration to bring it more in line with actual attainment. It is largely a job of professionals. The manager of the organization must recognise those who are in need of reorientation so that timely help of professionals can be sought before it becomes so severe.

Thus counselling through its various above-noted functions improves the organizational climate by solving the emotional problems of the workers in the organization.

ROLE OF COUNSELLING

Need of Counselling: National Association for Mental Health, America study showed that one person out of every ten is mentally disturbed or is in emotional disorder, a few of such persons are employed. This phenomenon may be of permanent character such as over sensitiveness, anger, or over enthusiasm etc. or such disorder may be temporarily due to broken love affairs, alcoholic and drug addicts, inability to face retirement etc. These all characteristics affect the productivity and performance, so the managers must not tolerate such things and they should understand the emotional feelings of their workers and help keeping their emotional balance through proper counselling.

Here, it is not implied that emotional upsets are undesirable or wrong. Sometimes, it is more disastrous to suppress an emotion such as anger than expressing it. Though such emotional upsets do not help workers any way, nor the firm. Sometimes, they leave the firm on triflings or reduce their productivity or undermine their morale. These reactions are very important for the organization because they affect the performance and increase cost. The managers always want that their workers must maintain a reasonable emotional equilibrium and channel their emotions along constructive lines so that both employer and employee can work together productively and cooperatively and with economic, social and psychological satisfaction. For this purpose, counselling is regarded the best way to pursue the employee to maintain their mental equilibrium. Feelings of both must be honoured.

Counselling programmes were given large attention during World War II for a number of reasons such as high labour turnover, lack of experience of workers etc. Supervisors who were burdened with production and inexperienced too they gladly accepted the staff counselling services but after the war, such programmes were dropped and counselling duties were returned to supervisors.

Causes of Counselling Needs. Counselling may be needed in any condition or set of conditions; both on and off the job. We have discussed some of the conditions earlier such as job dissatisfaction, resistance to change and alienation. We shall discuss hereunder some other causes as frustration, conflict and stress:

1. **Frustration.** Frustration is a result of motivation drive being blocked to prevent one from reaching a desired goal. For example, suppose a worker while on work is interrupted time and again, his goal for the day remains unfulfilled he will feel irritated and frustrated. The situation becomes more serious when it is long-run frustration such as blocked opportunity for promotion. Reaction to frustration such as irritation, uneasy feeling or some other reactions are known as **defence mechanism.**

Reactions of frustrated behaviour are aggression, apathy, withdrawal, resignation, fixation, physical disorders, substitute goals and compromise. These reactions are in no way favrourable to the individual nor to the organization, so it is desirable to reduce the frustrating conditions in the organization.

There are **different sources of frustration.** One of them is **management.** A worker may be demoted or the other may supersede him. It will all frustrate him. Another source is **fellow workers** who may be a barrier in goal attainment. Some **physical objects** may cause frustration such as faulty machines, unhealthy working conditions. A person, **himself** may be the source of frustration if his goal is much higher than his present abilities.

2. **Conflicts.** Emotional disorder may be caused by interpersonal and inter group conflicts. The conflicts are due to different backgrounds, points of view, values, needs and personality of the fellow men or due to organizational change. Thus, conflicts are inevitable in an organization, sometimes substantial.

Conficts may be advantageous. It stimulates people to search for improved approaches to yield better. It brings hidden problems such as frustrations to surface where they may be solved and understanding among people develops.

The probable disadvantages of conflicts are deterioration in cooperative and teamwork spirit. They lose their self image and motivation. It may cause emotional upsets.

3. **Stress.** Stress is a condition of strain on one's emotions thought processes and/or physical conditions that seem to threaten one's ability to cope with environment. Stress on the job may be desirable to some extent if it is a mild stress and not sustained over a long period of time. Excessive stress or stress over a long period of time may result in physical and emotional disorders and lowered effectiveness. Stress is also affected by the tolerance power of the person concerned.

Stress may be on-the-job and off-the-job. The main causes of stress on the job are job itself (work-overload, pressure of work, tension and insecurity), role conflicts and role ambiguity, conflicts with people (mainly when it is with the supervisor or any other authority) etc. causes of off - the - job stress may be family and financial problems.

Stress is a major contributor to emotional disorder to employees. It leads to physical disorder such as stomach disorder, body ache or headache and much permanent disorder may be ulcer, heart attack, kidney problem, etc.

So, counselling is necessary to disperse the emotional disorders caused by stress. It is one of the several methods employed.

Formal and Informal Counselling

Counselling may be 'informal' or 'formal.' 'Informal Counselling' occurs in the natural course of human relations among individuals who have mutual confidence and respect for each other's judgements. Quite often, the superior or his subordinate or both do not know or realise that counselling is taking place. Informal counselling essentially takes place in the work situation without any plan or schedule and is usually a recognised aspect of a manager's role. Although such counselling occurring in the informal or unplanned relationships of people at work may be helpful in preventing some employee problems or difficulties from getting worse, it should not be relied upon for removing or solving serious problems of difficulties of employees and, therefore, uses of such counselling are much limited. 'Formal Counselling' implies the direct intention of the management leadership to structure a counselling relationship between the employee and his supervisor or, sometimes, a counselling specialist with adequate professional training. It provides a well-planned programme of established organizational policies and procedures with due recognition of the useful leadership/supervisory role in the restoration of employee's effective work-performance lost by him because of his personal difficulties or anxiety. Such counselling on a systematic and planned basis may take place at three main levels, viz., (a) supervisor's counselling through day-to-day contacts with his subordinates; (b) professional counselling within the organization by staff members of the personal department; and (c) Counselling by psychiatrists or clinical psychologists inside or outside the organization. Although a counselling programme in industry may, in general, consist of the combined efforts of individuals at all the above mentioned levels, most of the employee counselling in an organization, as observed by Henry Eilbert, takes place through managers or supervisors and personnel specialists and only in a few cases, there may be counselling psychologists with a primary interest in personnel counselling in industry.

Regarding technical work or job-related employee problems, the line manager/supervisor knows well from his experience how and what changes he may suggest that help restoration of employee's effective performance. Concerning career problems or problems of vocational choice, counselling that the employee requires is known as vocational guidance and the supervisor may refer such cases to the personnel specialists within the organization who are usually best equipped to provide it whenever any employee has such a problem to resolve. Since the employee with some problems may not know what to do and may delay seeking assistance, effective manager/supervisor must know his subordinates well enough to observe or notice changes in them and should remain accessible and available for necessary help. It is important that the supervisor must be skilled enough to recognise the need for counselling because any delay may make the problem worse so as to prevent an easy or early solution. Line managers or supervisors usually find it difficult to deal with or provide adequate counselling in case of the personal, emotional or adjustment problems of the subordinates. It is important for the supervisor in case of such problems to know his limitations in resolving such problems and he must know as to whom and how to make the proper referrals without abdicating his own responsibilities. Even so, he must work closely with the personnel staff member or the counselling specialist and provide continued observation and help and participate in the plans for achieving better adjustment of the employee. He may have to make changes and correct internal difficulties as a result of which the employee's problems have been caused or intensified. Some managers/supervisors may be reluctant to recognise, accept and deal with such matters as anxiety or worry even after they are able to notice their manifestations. But those supervisors who develop a close and supportive coaching relationship with subordinate find it difficult to keep themselves aloof from helping employees in resolving their personal problems because they recognise that personal and job-related problems are largely inseparable and the employee brings his total personality to his work – a fact which the supervisor must face.

Many organizations now employ counselling specialists whose primary functions are to "(a) counsel employees which supervisors refer to the personnel department and whose problems cannot be handled by the supervisor alone; (b) counsel employees who seek assistance without first going to their supervisors; (c) work with supervisors in improving their counselling activities, and (d) advise the company on policies and procedures as they affect the satisfactory personal adjustment of employees." Counselling specialists play both a *'curative'* as well as *'preventive'* role; they not only provide for supervisors a basic technical resource in resolving their perplexing employee problems but they also provide them a source of help outside the *'subordinate-superior'* relationship they may be specially important in a situation where status and authority involve in that relationship itself is part of the employee problem. The counselling specialist must, therefore, not only demonstrate that he is not part of the hierarchical authority system controlling the employee but he must also make the aims and methods of counselling clear in order that the employee may be encouraged to make his problems know to the counsellor in confidence. The training and experience of counselling specialists varies considerably. Some of them are personnel specialists with a broad background and an interest in counselling while some are industrial psychologists trained as counsellors and still others in a few cases are full-time clinical psychologists or psychiatrists for preliminary diagnosis and treatment of the employee's mental health problems who are generally located in the safety and health section of the personnel department.

DIFFERENT TYPES OF COUNSELLING

Counselling in terms of degree of direction given by the counsellor to the counselee may be classified into following three categories:

1. Directive Counselling.
2. Non-Directive Counselling.
3. Co-operative Counselling.
4. Coaching or Mentoring.

1. **Directive Counselling.** Directive counselling is a process of directing the employees to solve their emotional problems by classified thinking. **In this process,** counsellor first listens the emotional problem of the employee patiently, and then decides with the employee what to do and then telling and motivating the employee to do it. The counsellor takes an active part in discussing every aspect of the problem and helps in devising the solution. He does not tell the solution but directs the employee towards solution and suggest the ways to get it. It is assumed in this way of counselling that the counsellor is superior to counsellee and knows what to do.

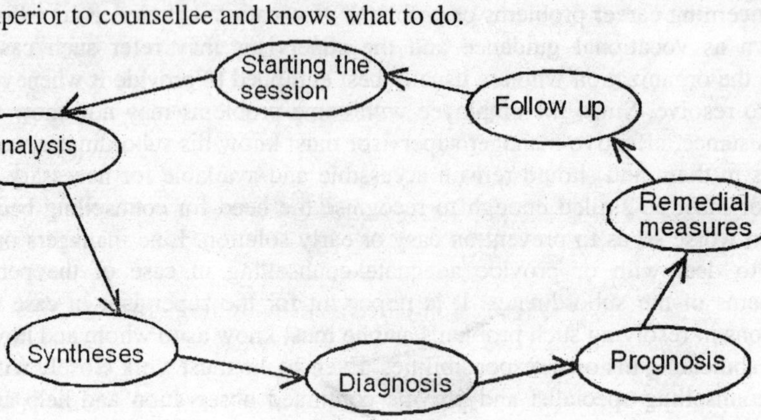

Fig. 1. Directive Counselling Process

Directive counselling mainly accomplishes the advice function of counselling but it may reassume communicate, give emotional release and to a minor extent clarify thinking. The function of reorientation is seldom achieved in directive counselling. An act of advice is not a wise step in counselling because it is very easy to advice, so it remains always questionable. But other functions of counselling are achieved by directive counselling. If directive counsellor is a good listener, then the employee will feel relaxed. Emotional release plus counsellor's ideas lead the employee to clarify thinking. Furthermore, useful communication probably takes place. Both advice and reassurance may give the employee a courage to take a workable couse of action that the employee supports.

2. **Non-Directive Counselling.** Non-directive or client-centred counselling is the process of skilfully listening and encouraging a counselee to explain bothersome emotional problems, understand them and determine the course of action. The central point in such type of counselling is 'the counselee' and not the counsellor. Counselee acts as a judge and as an adviser. This technique is mostly used by professional counsellors but managers can also practise it in their organization.

Under non-directive counselling, the role of counsellor is amply to listen to the person and try to understand his feelings and encourage to discover and follow improved course of action. He should not suggest or reassure any course of action rather he should accept his feelings without any judgement. He should also avoid blame or praise or doubts during the course of counselling otherwise the role of counsellor will change because it may be possible that the person may not come out with his true feelings and the very purpose of such counselling may be defeated. The counsellor throughout the interview should attempt to ask discerning questions, restate exists a fluid and sensitive relationship between the counsellor and counselee that requires minute attention to every detail in the overall situation.

The advice and reassurance functions of counselling are not normally used by professional non-directive counsellors but the other four functions are accomplished. **Communication** occurs but primarily upward to the management through counsellor. **Emotional release of tension** taken place, even more effectively than with directive counselling because the counsellor does not suggest anything and the counselee is free to express his feelings and **clarified thinking** tend to follow. The main advantage of this counselling is its ability to cause the employee's reorientation. It stresses on the changing of person instead of dealing with the immediate problem.

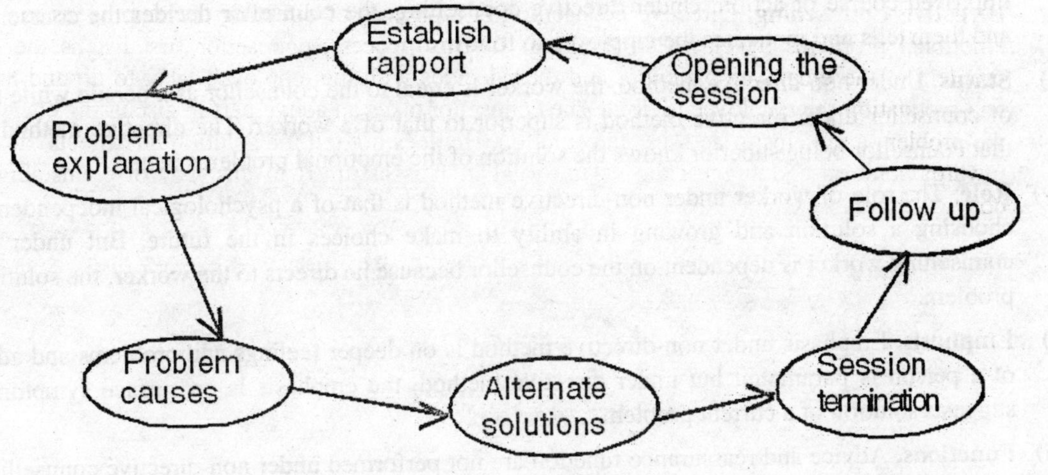

Fig. 2. Non-Directive Counselling Process

The professional counsellor treats such counselee as social and organizational equal. They follow an **iceberg model** and try to 'listen between the lines' in order to learn the full meaning of employee's feelings. They should always encourage the employee to open up and reveal deeper feelings which are painful and the employee tends to avoid talking about them. In order to encourage the employee to open up his hidden feelings, counsellor may ask appropriate questions during the course of conversation.

Limitations of Non-directive Counselling. Apart from its advantages, the non-directive counselling has the following limitations:

1. **It is more time consuming.** Just one employee with one problem takes several hours of counsellor. So, he can assist only few workers. So its utility at work is very limited.
2. **It is expensive too.** Non-directive counselling is mainly practised by the professionals and they require professional education and training. Training and education are quite expensive and times consuming hence their services for organization are also expensive.
3. **It is client-centred** and much depends upon a capable, willing employee. It assumes that worker possesses a desire for mental health, has enough social intelligence to perceive what problems need solution and sufficient emotional stability to deal with them.
4. **The non-directive counsellor needs to be cautious** not to become a crutch for emotional hypochondria is to bank on while avoiding their work responsibilities.
5. **It produces sometimes a weak situation** as it returns the workers to the same environment which causes the problem. The worker needs better environment for psychological support. In this situation the counsellor may step beyond the counselling role and give advice to the management to take corrective action.

Distinction between Directive and Non-directive Counselling

The non-directive counselling differs from the directive counselling in the following ways:

(i) **Counselling Method.** The employee mainly controls the direction of conversation and does most of the talking under non-directive counselling, while in directive counselling, the counsellor controls the situation and the direction of conversation.

(ii) **Responsibility.** The responsibility of the solution of the problem lies with the worker himself in non-directive counselling because the counsellor simply encourages the counselee to discover and follow improved course of action. Under directive counselling, the counsellor decides the course of action and them tells and motivates the employee to follow it.

(iii) **Status.** Under non-directive method, the worker is equal to the counsellor as a person while the status of counsellor under directive method is superior to that of a worker. The directive method assumes that counsellor being superior knows the solution of the emotional problems better.

(iv) **Role.** The role of worker under non-directive method is that of a psychological independent person, choosing a solution and growing in ability to make choices in the future. But under directive counselling worker is dependent on the counsellor because he directs to the worker, the solution of the problem.

(v) **Emphasis.** Emphasis under non-directive method is on deeper feelings and problems and adjustment of a person is paramount but under directive method, the emphasis is on surface symptoms and it suggests solution of a current problem.

(vi) **Functions.** Advice and reassurance function are not performed under non-directive counselling while these functions form the main basis of directive counselling. Reorientation function stressing on changing the person under non-directive technique while under directive technique, it is nowhere applicable.

3. **Cooperative Counselling.** Directive and non-directive counsellings are two extremes of the counselling problem. Keeping in mind the disadvantages of these two extremes of the string, a third type of counselling **'cooperative counselling'** has come into practice. It is best for the modern managers because it compromises between the two extremes of directive and non-directive counselling. It integrates the advantages of both the systems and throws off many of the disadvantages of both.

Cooperative counselling is neither counsellor-centred nor counselee-centred but rather both counsellor and counselee mutually cooperate to apply their different knowledge, perspective and values to the problem. Keith Davis defines the "Cooperative counselling" as 'a mutual discussion of an employee's emotional problem and a cooperative effort to set up conditions that will remedy it." It means an emotional problem is a mutual problem, and both, mutually settle it.

Cooperative counselling starts with the listening technique of non-directive counselling but as the interview progresses, the counsellor plays a much more important and positive role than he plays in non-directive technique. The counsellor initiates the discussion and discusses the problem with the employee from his broader perspective of the organization thus throwing various perspectives before the employees for comparison.

Cooperative counselling applies four functions of counselling, i.e., reassurance, communication, release of tension and clarified thinking. It has no room for advice. If reorientation is needed, the counsellor refers the employee to a professional counsellor.

If direct action is required, the manager takes the action but he does so in his capacity as a direct supervisor and not as a counsellor.

Cooperative counselling may be practiced by non-professionals but it avoids the authoritarian approach of direct counselling. It requires training and takes time to practice but no so much that managers cannot do and use it.

Cooperative counselling seems to be the most desirable type of counselling except in some special situations. The main contribution of non-directive counselling was to pull the managers away from the directive counselling towards the more non-directive approach of cooperative counselling.

4. Mentoring/Coaching

It has become increasingly clear over the years that employees who aspire to management levels in organizations need the assistance and advocacy of someone higher up in the organization. These career progressions often require having the favour of the dominant "in-group," which sets corporate goals, priorities, and standards.

When a senior employee takes an active role in guiding another individual, we refer to this activity as **mentoring or coaching.** Just as soccer coaches observe, analyze, and attempt to improve the performance of their athletes, "coaches" on the job can do the same. The effective coach, whether on the diamond or in the corporate hierarchy, gives guidance through direction, advice, criticism, and suggestion in an attempt to aid the employee's growth. These individuals offer to assist certain junior employees in terms of providing a support system. This system, in part, is likened to the passing of the proverbial baton – that is, the senior employee shares his or her experiences with the protege, providing guidance on how to make it in the organization. Accordingly, in organizations such as Motorola, Tenneco, and Prudential, that promote from within, those who aspire to succeed must have the "corporate support system" in their favor. This support system, guided by a mentor, vouches for the candidate, answers for the candidate in the highest circles within the organization, makes appropriate introductions, and advises and guides the candidate on how to effectively move through the system. In one study, this effort generated significant outcomes. For example, these researchers found that where a significant mentoring relationship existed, those proteges had more favourable and frequent promotions, were paid significantly more than those who were not mentored, had a greater level of commitment to the organization, and had greater career success. But there was a caution in this study; that is, those benefits that accrued because of mentoring generally went to white-male employees. Why this outcome? In the past, women and minorities have found it difficult to get a mentor, and therefore their upward mobility was often limited.

The technique of senior employees coaching individuals has the advantages that go with learning by doing, particularly the opportunities for high interaction and rapid feedback on performance. Unfortunately, its two strongest disadvantages are: (1) its tendencies to perpetuate the current styles and practices in the organization, and (2) its heavy reliance on the coach's ability to be a good teacher. In the same way that we recognize that all excellent goalies do not make outstanding goalie coaches, we cannot expect all excellent employees to be effective coaches. An individual can become an excellent performer without necessarily possessing the knack of creating a proper learning environment for others to do the same; thus, the effectiveness of this technique relies on the ability of the coach. Coaching of employees can occur at any level and can be most effective when the two individuals do not have any type of reporting relationship.

Difference Between Coaching & Counselling

Employee Counselling: In an attempt to assist employees in performing the job they have been assigned, it sometimes may be necessary for the manager to counsel them. In terms of employee counselling, however, a distinction needs to be made. In the discussion above, we've referred to coaching and mentoring techniques as means for helping to develop employees and to assist in their career growth. Although employee counselling is similar in its approach, there is one aspect that differentiates it from coaching. For instance, we typically use employee counselling when a performance problem arises. Thus, the focus of this discussion is more appropriately aligned with the discipline process.

Whenever an employee exhibits work behaviours that are inconsistent with the work environment (i.e., fighting, stealing, unexcused absences, and so forth) or is unable to perform his or her job satisfactorily, a manager must intervene. But before any intervention can begin, it is imperative for the manager to identify the problem. If as managers we realize that the performance problem is ability-related, our emphasis becomes one of facilitating training and development efforts. This type of intervention is then more closely aligned to coaching. However, when the performance problem is desire-related, where the unwillingness is either voluntary or involuntary, employee counselling is the next logical approach.

Table 1. Counselling : Some Fundamental Steps

1.	**Document all problem performance behaviour.** Document specific job behaviours, like absenteeism, lateness, and poor quality, in terms of dates, times, and what happened. This provides you with objective data.
2.	**Deal with the employee objectively, fairly, and equitably.** Treat each employee similarly. That means that one should not be counselled for something that another person did, and nothing was mentioned. Issues discussed should focus on performance behaviours.
3.	**Confront job performance issues only.** Your main focus is on those things that affect performance. Even though it may be a personal problem, you should not try to psychoanalyze the individual. Leave that to the trained specialists! You can, however, address how these behaviours are affecting the employee's job performance.
4.	**Offer assistance to help the employee.** Just pointing the finger at an employee serves little useful purpose. If the employee could "fix" the problem alone, he or she probably would have. Help might be needed - yours and the organizations. Offer this assistance where possible.
5.	**Expect the employee to resist the feedback and become defensive.** It is human nature to dislike constructive, or negative feedback. Expect that the individual will be uncomfortable with the discussion. Make every effort, however, to keep the meeting calm such that the message can get across. Documentation, fairness, focusing on job behaviours, and offering assistance helps to reduce this defensiveness.
6.	**Get employee to own up to the problem.** All things said, the problem is not yours, it is the employee's. The employee needs to take responsibility for his or her behaviour, and begin to look for ways to correct the problems.
7.	**Develop an action plan to correct performance.** Once the employee has taken responsibility for the problem, develop a plan of action designed to correct the problem. Be specific as to what the employee must do (e.g., what is expected and when it is expected); and what resources you are willing to commit to assist.
8.	**Identify outcomes for failing to correct problems.** You're there to help, not carry a poor performer forever. You need to inform the employee what the consequences will be if he or she does not follow the action plan.
9.	**Monitor and control progress.** Evaluate the progress the employee is making. Provide frequent feedback on what you're observing. Reinforce good efforts.

Source: Adapted from Commerce Clearing House, "The Do's and Don'ts of Confronting a Troubled Employee," *Topical Law Reports* (Chicago: Commerce Clearing House, Inc., October 1990), pp. 4359-60; Gerald D. Cook, "Employee Counselling Session," *Supervision* (August 1989), p.3; and Andrew E. Schuarts, "Counselling the Marginal Performer," *Management Solutions* (March 1988), p.30.

WHO MAY BE A COUNSELLOR

In a formal organization where employer is the representative, counselling may be done by three major groups – supervisors, specialists, and professional counsellors.

1. **Supervisors.** Supervisors are the best counsellors because they are nearest to the situation and hence are better able to tackle with minor emotional problems and for major emotional problems, he should refer the employee to the professional counsellor.

   The counselling responsibility of supervisor is three fold:

   (a) **Firstly, they should look for the poor state of employees' mental health.** They can do something unusual or against his normal behaviour such as increased errors, nervousness, antagonism, repeated absence, excessive alcohol, withdrawal and preoccupation.

   (b) **Secondly, they, thereafter, give counselling,** if they think necessary and appropriate in the given situation being a leader and boss. And

(c) **Thirdly, they should refer the more serious cases to the professional counsellor.** Sometimes, counselling by supervisor may aggravate problems rather than to resolve them because it may be possible that emotion of the supervisor while counselling may provoke the workers and in that case, the situation will become more serious. Before counselling, he should understand his own emotional nature because his emotions may affect others emotions. So, knowledge of himself is a must.

Supervisor must recognise his own limitations. He should avoid counselling when he knows that (i) a person does not like to discuss the problem with him because he has an authority over him, or (ii) he himself is one of the parties of the problem so worker does like to discuss the problem with any person other than the supervisor. In such cases, supervisor should refer them to the professionals.

2. **Specialists.** A second type of counsellor is specialist. Specialist is a person who is a technical expert in a field – such as personnel expert, social welfare expert, legal experts, doctors, behavioural scientists, etc., other than the job of counselling thus they are experts in their own field and not in counselling but they have knowledge of human behaviour relating to his main assignment or they should have counselling training to deal with such emotional problems just as supervisors do. For example, persons dealing in pension, may have to face the emotional upsets of the pensioners and they will have to satisfy them psychologically though it is not their prime duty. Because many emotional problems involve some technical aspect of the work, the counselling responsibilities of specialists are growing day by day.
3. **Professional Counsellors.** A third type of counsellor is professional counsellor. They are trained psychologists or psychiatrist and deal with emotional upsets on-the-job as well as off-the-job. They are full time counsellors and counselling is their profession. They counsel managers and employees both. Like workers managers, also have emotional breakdowns. Counselling for managers is rather more important because their emotional disorder will be spread over to other employees having interpersonal relations with them. In addition, the main responsibility of professionals is to advise the managers to pursue the proper mental health approach towards their employees.

Counselling a Management Task

Not so long ago counselling was seen as a 'soft' and marginal practice only to be found in the welfare departments of larger organizations and it is still seen that way in many unenlightened places of work. More companies began to accept counselling as a method of dealing with their own guilt when it came to large-scale redundancies, in an attempt (usually too late) to assist staff in finding new careers. Counselling cannot only deal with many staff problems; it also brings significant beneficial economic results to the organization. Just consider some of the symptoms of frustration being shown by people known to you, possibly working within your own organization. Then do some quick sums to see the effect of those symptoms on the well-being of the organization itself.

Stress

People experience stress when they have more frustration than they can handle. Often the stress is self-imposed, although it is usually attributed to external factors. Those factors may be personal; for example, bereavement, divorce or other major life changes or they may be to do with work, the fear of redundancy changes in the structure or working practices, anxiety about being able to achieve what is expected bad relationships within the workplace.

Some people thrive on pressure. That is when they seem to achieve the most. Others may find the same pressure too much, so they become paralysed or ineffective. This is when pressure turns into stress. What the manager has to be aware of is when this change occurs, the person who has always operated well under pressure may suddenly find everything too much. The busy person piles on the work until nothing can be done properly, then explodes. Another common occurrence is that this same person finds it hard to cope well when things are apparently quiet. Instead of using that time to plan ahead, he or she becomes disruptive or morose.

The person who has an apparent low threshold of pressure may have a different pattern of working that might still be very productive as long as this is recognised.

In all circumstances of stress, while there are usually external factors that you may be unable to change, counselling can help individuals to deal with how they feel and to be able to reach a constructive and positive form of action. In other words, reducing the stress, people feel more efficient and make productive use of human resources.

While stress is a symptom of a person's frustration, through some change that is difficult to cope with, there are a number of symptoms that indicate when a person is under stress. Stress has been dealt in detail in separate chapter.

Illness

A clear link has been shown between stress and illness. Backaches, stomach-aches and other internal physical problems, headaches and migraine, tiredness and depressive or other mental illnesses might all be related to each other and to the incidence of stress in a person's life.

Our bodies and our minds are constantly sending each other messages. At the simplest level, just think about a time when you experienced some stress. Perhaps you stood up to talk to a large group of people for the first time, went for an interview, had an argument, got married, gave up smoking. How did you feel? Did you have any physical symptoms? Sweaty palms, headaches, nausea, neck ache, for example? If so multiply this by a few times and you might see how easy it is for people to become quite ill from being under stress. If you did not experience any of this, you are probably unique in the history of humankind.

Absenteeism

The number of days lost through illness, much of which can be attributed to stress, is significant enough to cause an increasing number of businesses and other organizations to establish counselling programmes. The primary reason is not an overwhelming desire to be nice to people. It is to reduce the number of working days lost and increase the efficiency and productivity of personnel.

People often absent themselves from work, giving illness as an excuse, when the real reason is a temporary inability to cope with work or personal pressures, perhaps from a bad relationship with the manager. Signs of such dissatisfaction indicate, not that the staff needs counselling, but that the manager might.

Low Motivation

Change of any kind can induce stress especially when this change is outside the control of the individual. In turn this may lead to a lack of willingness to carry out work as effectively as possible.

Low motivation is a common symptom of a person experiencing some problems. It is seldom, if ever a natural part of a person's make-up. People are motivated when they are heard and feel themselves to be a valuable and respected part of a group. They usually are motivated when they feel they have some control over decisions and actions for which they are responsible. The effect of low motivation among staff is that managers are faced with extra work, disciplinary action, and constant frustration. It tends to become a vicious circle with everyone eventually reducing their motivation to perform well.

Poor Work

The results of stress, illness, absenteeism and lack of motivation are inevitable. They add up to poor work. Customers will experience the effects. Profits will fall.

Errors and inadequacies may be due to a variety of reasons. Training might be insufficient, work might be organized inappropriately, and communication may be poor. Those things need to be attended to, since they indicate management ineffectiveness, rather than individual staff being sloppy. Once again, it is the managers who might need counselling.

However, where you notice that a person whom you regard as capable in turning out uncharacteristically bad work, this may be a signal that something is going wrong in that individual's work or personal life. Getting to the root of poor work being produced and being aware of changes in people's behaviour is vital if you are to focus your attention on counselling as a tool for improving performance.

High Staff Turnover

People leave their employment for all sorts of reasons. If your organization has a higher than average staff turnover, you may need to look at the reasons behind it. Some movement of staff is a healthy part of the organization's as well as the individual's development. But people often leave because they are dissatisfied or unhappy with their work, the people around them, and the unrealistic expectations of them and, most commonly among the most able people; the lack of responsibility and opportunities for initiative they are given. The costs of any staff changes are far higher than the costs of attending to staff who would otherwise stay and continue to give added value. Listening to staff, helping them to overcome problems that they may be facing while at the same time taking account of general changes that are needed, are all potentially beneficial results of counselling.

What it Costs?

Rather than give a very general and therefore not very helpful or relevant cost benefit analysis of counselling, here is an exercise you can do to enable you and your colleagues to become clearer about the costs to your own organization.

First, decide how you can best get the statistics. You are probably better off looking at a typical segment of the organization, then multiplying by the proportionate number of people working for the organization as a whole. You might also want to look at a month, or a three-month period rather than a year, then multiply by twelve or four to get the annual figures.

Look at the numbers and the costs to the organization of absenteeism, poor work, staff turnover over the past year. You will have to decide how to make the calculations. If your business makes or sells goods, for example, poor work can be measured by returns, duplicated work, repair time, cancelled orders and so on. If you are a service organization, you may have to look at complaints, waiting time, loss of customers and so on. Calculate all the staff time (and therefore costs) as well as material wastage and loss of profits on an order. Do not forget the costs of engaging and training new staff to replace those who have left.

Symptom	Time Cost	Material Cost	Overall Cost
Absenteeism			
Poor Work			
Staff turnover			
Other			

Not all of this could have been eliminated by counselling. From your own knowledge and experience, however, give some thought to some of the circumstances that you can identify. Then make some calculation as to the proportion of savings that might have been made by listening to people properly before errors, absenteeism or resignations took place.

The argument for counselling your staff is that it is cost effective way of preventing disasters before they take place. That is as true for the organization as it is for the individual being counselled.

Counselling, especially in the workplace, is not only a way of helping people to solve their problems, it is a way of strengthening relationships between people, clarifying where staff need particular support, identifying needs for changes in the workplace and creating an atmosphere of trust and care within the organization. In other words, it is a way of acknowledging and valuing the people who work with you.

This is what improves motivation of staff and enhances their performance.

A Response to a Crisis

Individuals usually seek counselling when they are at a crisis point. This means that counselling has to be available when the person need it. The problem with this is that organizations usually offer counselling when they have initiated a crisis themselves.

While there are many professionals and agencies offering counselling, those who need it seldom have easy access to them or even know anything about them. People in work who are in crisis could find it far easier and appropriate to go to a designated person within the workplace. Organizations that offer counselling as part of the process of management will be able to respond to people going through a difficult time, when they need help.

The more common organizational response, however, is one that brings in counselling when there has been a big redundancy or redeployment programme, or a restructuring that causes significant turbulence to employees. This is not the mark of a healthy or positive approach. For counselling to work properly to the benefit of both employee and organization, it should be readily available as a normal part of what managers do.

This means that counselling is most effective when it is part of the culture of the organization. As with all cultural items this takes time. Setting up any counselling process, therefore, takes considerable patience, acceptance at all levels within the organization, and attention to detail.

The first step is to establish your case for counselling, or if there is already an accepted counselling process, to understand what the case is.

Imagine you are to present a case to the boss. Your mandate is to show why and how counselling might be an important part of the management process, in economic terms. The cost of counselling will be the time taken by managers and staff to include any training that is needed by managers. Consider your own circumstances, the issues facing the organization and the loss in profits due to such things as absenteeism, staff turnover and poor work.

COUNSELLING ROLE OF MANAGER

Managers from the lowest to the highest level in an organization may be proved a good counsellor because they interact workers in day-to-day business. Worker first contacts the manager as soon as an emotional problem starts and the manager should try to resolve it. He should never ignore or refuse to hear the emotional problem of the employee because emotions are part of the whole employee and must be considered a part of total employment situation for which the manager is responsible. So, managers at all levels in the organization need training to help them understand the emotional problems of the employee and counsel them effectively.

Almost all the problems brought to the notice of the manager have a combination of objective fact and emotional content in them. The manager should not keep busy himself in the psychological aspect of each problem and spent the whole day in understanding and solving it unless rational answer is not available. The manager needs to counsel sparingly to encourage employees to be self-sufficient and stand on their feet emotionally. Counselling should not be in mediocres hence manager should have patience of job, the wisdom, and human insight. At the same time a manager should recognise that even the most trivial incident may cause emotional dificulties with workers.

A manager can well perform all the functions of counselling except reorientation function. For reorientation problem, he can refer the employee to professional counsellor. For resolving other problems, he must have sufficient knowledge and understanding of human behaviour or he may refer the employee to the professional counsellor, if available. But availability of professional counsellor does not mean that he should transfer all the problems to them. He should refer either the orientation problems or where he fails in resolving the problem satisfactorily, to the professional counsellors.

DISCIPLINE AND DISCIPLINARY ACTION

The main function of the management is to get the work done by people in the organization for the best interest of the organization. In order to achieve the best results out of the minimum efforts, control on individuals is a must. In order to have a control on individuals to direct them in the right direction, certain rules and regulations are necessary to lead them to the right path. If individuals work according to rules and regulations framed to control them, it is called discipline, i.e., rules and regulations give the organization a standard and in order to maintain the standard, organization makes the worker to follow strictly the discipline. If discipline or the binding rules and regulations are not followed, it is called indisciplinary state of affairs and disciplinary action is warranted under such circumstances. We are discussing hereunder the problems of discipline and disciplinary action and the role of counselling.

DISCIPLINE

Discipline means following the rules and regulations and procedures by the work force of an organization in the manner and sense in which they are prepared and conveyed. Discipline reflects the quality of an organization's climate. The following definitions may clarify the meaning and concept of discipline:

1. "Discipline is the force that prompts an individual or group to observe rules, regulations, procedures that are deemed necessary to the attainment of an objective." – William R. Spriegal
2. "Discipline is employee's self-control to meet organizational standards and objectives." – Keith Davis

Thus discipline is necessary for the self-control of the employees to fulfil the standards and goals of the organization. It gives self-control that underlies all genuine team work. It prompts the workers to follow the rules, regulations, and procedures prepared to control them.

Discipline is developed by the management and by the workers – individuals and their work - groups. Employees themselves exert their pressure on others in the group to toe the line, to keep up and to get with it and if these employee pressures are guided toward attaining the standards and objectives of the organization, the group itself becomes a strong supportive force of discipline.

Discipline is not similar to morale. Discipline relates to employee conduct whereas morale relates to employee attitudes.

ROLE OF MANAGEMENT IN MAINTAINING DISCIPLINE

Management in the organization is responsible for developing and maintaining the discipline. In doing so, it must follow the following principles:

1. **It must make all the rules,** regulations, policies, programmes and standards, goals and objectives of the organization **known to its employees** along with the penal provisions in case of their defiance. If the employee does not know what standards are expected from them by the organization, their conduct is likely to be erratic or misdirected.
2. It must frame the rules, regulations, and standards **with the consent of the workers** so that they may support them willingly because they have helped them create.
3. In gaining the support of the workers, the management **must state the standard positively** rather than stating them negatively. The penal provisions in the code of conduct should be avoided as far as possible. The stress should be laid on the prevention of indisciplined acts of the workers rather than to insist on penalties.
4. The management should be fair, consistent and flexible in maintaining discipline. There should be **fair treatment to all** according to rules and regulations set out in the code and any biased view should be avoided. The rules must be followed consistently to all members. Similar act of indiscipline should attract similar treatment. The rule of natural justice should be followed and in discipline worker should be given an opportunity to be heard. The management should also be flexible enough in maintaining the discipline. There must be provisions for reviewing the decision and giving the worker a chance to improve his conduct in the desired direction.

5. In maintaining the discipline, the management should note that decision should not be delayed otherwise it loses its importance.

Thus management's role in maintaining and developing the discipline is important.

DISCIPLINARY ACTION

If a worker fails to meet the standards or to obey the rules and regulations set forth for maintaining the discipline in the organization, a penalty is invoked in order to maintain the discipline. It is disciplinary action. **The effective disciplinary** action condemns the wrongful act of the employee and not the employee as a person. **The final or ultimate disciplinary action** is the discharge of an employee from the employment. Discharge of an employee is evidenced as a failure of the management but this view is not realistic, because no one is perfect – neither manager nor worker and therefore some problems may remain unresolved. If a worker continuously fails in maintaining standard, it is better for him to seek employment somewhere else because organizations cannot bear such poor employee for long. Before taking any disciplinary action, its effect on other employees should also be considered.

The main objectives in initiating disciplinary action against a worker are as follows:

(i) The main aim of disciplinary action is to reform the offender. A penalty – monetary or otherwise – is invoked with a view not to hear any repetition of faulty actions.

(ii) The disciplinary action aims at deterring other workers from repeating the action for which the worker has been punished.

(iii) By taking disciplinary action, the organization can maintain its integrity among workers if action is unbiased.

DISCIPLINARY ACTION POLICY OR REINFORCEMENT

Before taking disciplinary action, a policy should be framed and the action should be initiated accordingly. The policy may be of two types: (a) Consistent disciplinary policy, and (b) Flexible disciplinary policy. The management while formulating the policy, has to resolve the conflict between consistency and flexibility and to take the decision in the best interest of the organization. Now we shall discuss these two policies.

(a) Consistent Disciplinary Action Policy. This follows the principle of consistency. It refers to the similar action for similar faults without any deviation. It supports equal treatment to all. Situational adjustments have no place in it. It makes no concession, and refuses to recognise extenuating circumstances.

Advantages. The consistent policy has the following advantages:

1. **Equal treatment is given to all** in similar circumstances and it does not disturb teamwork. The management can advocate for its action before the union. The policy does not make concessions and allow deviations from the set rules.

2. As principle of consistency is followed, it allows **administrative simplicity.** There is not much debate or dialogue in taking disciplinary action.

3. Labour - unions which presumably represent the best interest of their members, defend the action in order to secure **a more stable union-management relationship.** Unions, more often, insist the management to make specific rules and to follow them strictly without exception and they bring management to task if it varies its interpretations in different cases before an arbitrator or court.

Disadvantages. The consistent policy have several limitations as follows:

1. Every worker is not the same and the situations in which disciplinary action is taken may be unique, consistent action cannot be warranted. Each person is different in nature and approach and each situation cannot be similar. Moreover the effect of disciplinary action on other workers should also be visualised and only then disciplinary action should be taken. So similar action is not possible.

2. It ignores the individual in the organization. The same treatment to all workers gives passive acceptance of things beyond the employee's control. It fails to motivate people towards positive attitude. As all are treated alike in disciplinary action disregarding their uniqueness, personal relations with management become impersonal. Workers become the victims of a lifeless system and real injustice may be the outcome.

(b) Flexible Disciplinary Action Policy. It is just reverse of the consistent policy. Flexible policy is required because people and situations are unique and consistency in disciplinary action cannot be maintained. So, a flexible attitude should be taken in maintaining discipline and taking disciplinary action. **We may justify the flexible disciplinary action policy on the following grounds:**

(i) The senior workers having a long good standing in the organization often are given special consideration.

It is not prudent step to dismiss them from the organization for a very small matter, especially in the circumstances when they have a good record of service for many years. It may be possible that similar rule infraction may justify dismissal for a quite new employee who was not adjusted.

(ii) It is sometimes argued that special considerations should be given to less experienced workers with work values. They are not fully aware of the traditional social standards expected by the organizations. For example, they turn up late to the work or are careless to the organization property because they have not learnt punctuality or responsibility for property. In such circumstances, they should be given a reasonable time to learn work-habits and conduct, and only a warning may suffice. But a senior worker cannot be spared for similar reasons. A strict disciplinary action can be initiated against him.

But there is one limitation. The management should take special consideration only when it is fully justified and is supported by documents so that the action taken by the management is not interpreted by the unions, employees, arbitrator as management's standard practice for that type of rule infraction.

Which one is better? Since there are so many different interpretations of the organization to go to the other extreme and may be possible for the organization to go to the other extreme and may avoid rules and regulations and leave disciplinary action solely, to human judgement. Either of the extremes - following the rules consistently and avoiding the rules altogether – are not justifiable. The better solution will be a compromise between the two extremes and a midway should be followed.

For a compromise, a flexible interpretation should be allowed to established standards of conduct. The flexible approach seems more in accord with behavioural research and concepts. It respects human dignity and individual differences because it allows interpretation. The employer should treat the employees alike so far as they are alike and differently so far as they are different and unique in different situations. So, it is better for the management to treat the individual according to the individual situation and disciplinary action should be contingent upon the circumstances.

Following a flexible policy does not mean inconsistency with the basic aim of disciplinary action. Because disciplinary action is aimed at encouraging future conduct of the employees rather than punishment so flexibility should be there within the rules. Since different people respond differently to the same treatment, different disciplinary action may be incorporated in the policy to achieve what might be called equal results. There must be sufficient scope for personal judgement too.

THE COUNSELLING APPROACH TO DISCIPLINARY ACTION

Some organizations use counselling as a measure for disciplinary action and a few of them have developed the entire procedure of counselling. In this approach an employee is advised to correct the action rather than to penalise him progressively for the first few breaches of organizational standards. In first breach, a private discussion may be initiated with the supervisor to correct the action. Second violation may also be resulted in further discussion with a focus on correcting the behaviour. A third violation may lead the supervisor to counsel the immediate supervisor and to locate the roots of employee's malfunction. Further violations of rules may be warned of serious consequences such as suspension or termination. The more serious offences such as theft should be kept out of the procedure and immediate action should be taken.

The main purpose of counselling approach is fact finding and guiding the employee to correct his behaviour instead of invoking penalties to discourage the employee. In this way employee's self image and dignity are retained and labour relations remain cooperative and constructive.

Policies, Attitudes and Views towards Counselling

Organizational policies and managerial attitudes or view towards counselling range from '*completely negative to highly positive.*' Those who do not favour or recognise the importance of the counselling process in industry or business do not accept the view that counselling contributes to gains and, therefore, hold that the organization should not be involved in the personal problems of employees because the managers / supervisors are probably not competent enough to deal with employee problems. On the other hand, those who favour formal counselling believe that employee's personal problems cannot be separated from their work or job-related problems and they feel that all employees at one time or another face crises, difficulties or tensions requiring the attention and help from someone in authority at places of work and, therefore, the organization must establish counselling practices and procedures and identify appropriate managerial roles in this area. They also advocate that the counselling by managers or supervisors should be supplemented by the provision of professional or specialist counsellors so as to improve employee productivity and job satisfaction. The views of unions have generally been negative towards counselling as they feel that it is a device to make employees dependent, docile and willing to accept management logics without question and that counselling allows management to manipulate employees and foster anti-union sentiments.

Counselling : An Appraisal

Personnel counselling is a method of understanding and helping people who have technical, personal and emotional or adjustment problems interfering with their work-performance, Counselling must be recognised as a basic part or industrial or business psychology as long as people work with other people. However, the counselling activity, as it exists today in industry, may be said to have emerged from the founding stages of the human relations movement when the Hawthorne Plant of the Western Electric Company in Chicago installed a personnel counselling programme that utilised special rules for interviewing derived from the need of eliciting from the employees' matters of emotional significance to them. Initially, this counselling programme was remarkable in respect of the company's effort to listen to all employees with problems but over the years the programme deteriorated because of economy drives and other problems. Most counselling programmes since then have been less ambitious and smaller in scope than the early pioneering effort.

The general objective of the management leader or supervisor in counselling subordinates is to help the individual remain effective in his job and performance of his duties or responsibilities in the organization. The main purpose of counselling in industry is to help employees in overcoming their neurotic or emotionally based illness that accounts for a substantial part of employee absenteeism and turnover and their personal problems as well as emotional disturbances that may seriously affect their job performance which proves costly to the organization.Group Counselling

Group counselling is a technique where a group of persons are counselled by applying group interaction method for the purpose of arriving at a solution to the problem common to the group. All the group members are provided with an opportunity to discuss their problem together, in a free atmosphere. To the extent possible an indirect approach is followed during this type of counselling.

In group counselling, group work helps the individual, in understanding and finding out a solution to their problem. This is because dynamic interaction occurs among the group members who meet together for a commonly agreed purpose. Several important experiences like knowledge of reality, self-knowledge and self-realisation can be achieved through group interaction process. These help to modify certain faulty social learning and to relearn certain attitudes and dispositions which are essential for healthy adjustment.

Phases of Activities

In group counselling the counsellor has a very important role in the beginning, the counsellor interested in organising group counselling must have some knowledge about group interaciton processes. Several other traits like understanding the background of the group, knowledge of various psychological problems, the specific needs of each participant are needed for organizing group counselling. The following are the phases of activities followed in group counselling:

- Selection of participants
- Starting the session
- Orientation towards discussion
- Checking the unwaranted behaviour
- Assisting in self-disclosure
- Assisting in decision-making process
- Closure of the session
- Follow up

The Process

The participants for the group counselling are chosen on the basis of their common problem. They must have some similar problem. For example, the problem may be difficulty in speaking with the opposite sex, fears of public speaking, over anxiety, stress etc.

The group meets as per prior scheduled date and time the counsellor starts the session by introducing himself. He then requests each group member to introduce themselves. Now it is time to start the discussion over the problem. In most of the cases, the counsellor has to take the lead. He briefs the purpose of the meeting and invites others' participation in the discussion. Sometimes no one comes forward in discussion. In that case, counsellor can ask any individual by saying 'O.K., Mr. Nitin, what do you think about this problem?' Or he may say 'Well, Mr. Prashant, How do you feel about such type of behaviour'? Once the participants start talking, the counsellor keeps a close watch over the conversation.

When there is a natural flow of communication, the self-disclosures come from the group members. Self disclosure is the explicit communication of personal information that one does not otherwise disclose to others. In the group counselling process one takes a risk to get benefit from others. If the other group members show warm acceptance, the individual feels encouraged and the chain process goes on. Generally, group goal decides the type of self-disclosure. Counsellor should see that these self-disclosures occur gradually and according to the readiness of the group member to deal with it.

In the group counselling process, resistance may be shown by some group members. This may be in the form of negative attitude or avoidance of closeness to other members. When the group members get support and acceptance, they may withdraw their defences. In this way, a safer atmosphere eradicates resistance.

The ultimate phase of the group counselling process is decision making. The group takes such a decision which is acceptable to all. In the counselling group, through open communication, every one gives him opinion and shows respect for others' viewpoint. With mutual consent the group finally makes a decision. This decision is generally accepted by others.

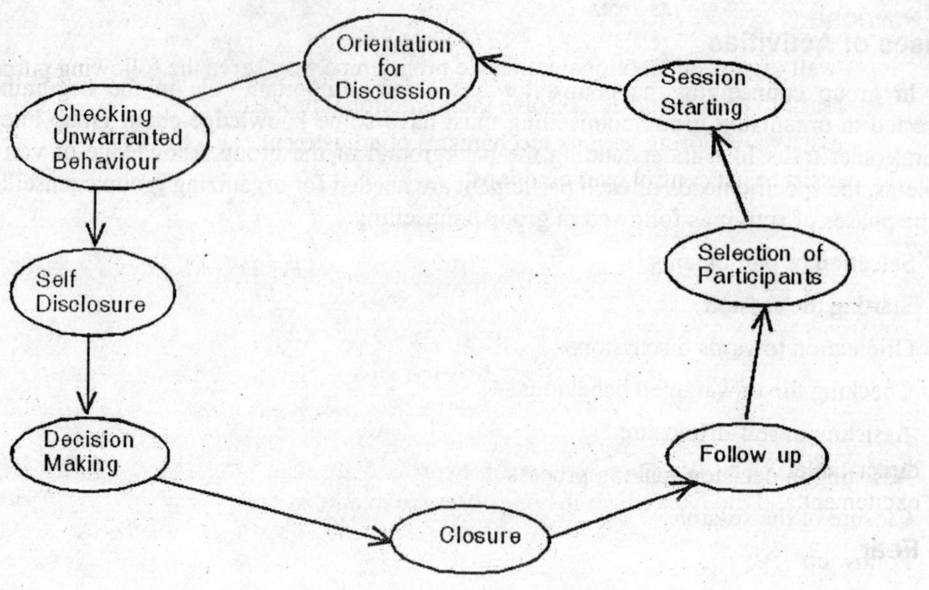

Fig. 3. Group Counselling Process

When the decision making is over, the group decides when to terminate the session. When all the members get satisfied with the outcome of that session, the counsellor comes forward to end up the sesion. The counsellor concludes the session very slowly with all the formalities like assuring further help, offering thanks for cooperation etc.

Follow up is also needed in group counselling. The counsellor should see that each member of the group who participated in the process is progressing. If he feels that some of the group members are not showing much improvement in their problem behaviour, he organizes another session to find an alternative solution and readjustment strategy for the problem.

The counsellor should have a thorough knowledge of interaction process and group work method. Otherwise he may face great difficulties in the phases like self-disclosure, checking hostility, and decision making process.

Sometimes, the size of the group may cause problems to the counsellor or to the group members. The group should not be too large or too small. A group comprising eight to ten members is ideal for the purpose.

Personal Guidance

Personal guidance is the assistance given to any individual to solve his emotional problems and to assist him to control his emotions. Controlled emotion is most significant characteristic of a mentally healthy individual. An individual having control over his emotions when threatened with conflicts and frustrations is able to maintain a mental balance by working against stress.

People who are in the adolescent period of their growth and development exhibit heightened emotionally. At times they lose their control over very trivial matters. They become extremely emotional when the situation causes intense feelings. Several factors like failure in love, unsatisfactory academic performance, maladjustment at home and with peers cause emotional problems.

Anxiety and frustration also result in emotional tension. These may be accompanied by irritability and tendency for emotional outbursts. Their heightened emotionality may be due to environmental and social factors. Students at this stage feel the urgency of breaking down old habits of thought and action. They are upset during the period of adjustment. Once they explore certain coping mechanisms of adjustment, the excessive emotionality usually disappears. Such people greatly need assistance in understanding the various coping mechanisms of adjustment.

Purpose

A well organized emotional guidance programme may serve the following purposes:

- assist to understand and resolve their emotional problems.
- assist in exploring various mechanisms of adjustment.
- assist to get control over emotions.

Emotional Characteristics of Adolescents

Several emotional patterns of special significance have been identified during adolescence.

Hostility

When the individual is confronted with a succession of frustrating situations, the immediate reaction may be one of anger or hostility. In many respects anger and hostility are difficult emotions to deal with. Both involve tension which demands discharge. But the conditions of civilised living permit only a few direct outlets. The hostile behaviour is expressed through intolerance, aggression, and impatience, over excitement and the like, which may be observed in adolescents.

Fear

Fear is one of the emotions which may be related to material objects, social relationships or to self. The things we fear are actual or potential sources of frustration. Specific dangers tend to arouse fear. Ordinarily, fear elicits a withdrawal or flight reaction. In the face of intense fear, the individual may panic or freeze and become unable to function in any organised manner.

Anxiety

Many situations give rise to anxiety. Situations causing worry is generally accompanied by anxiety. Stress situations inducing anxiety are often difficult to cope with. This is because, the nature of the threat is usually unclear to the individual adolescents quite often expressing this motion.

Jealousy

Jealousy is one of the emotions which is social in origin. In its extreme form it may take the form of violence. Jealousy and annoyance may arise together. The causes of annoyance have a broader canvas than jealousy.

Energy Resources

The emotional types discussed above generally have adverse effects on the individual. But like biological drives, emotions may arouse, sustain and direct activity and as such play an energising role in behaviour. Emotions also may serve as emergency sources of power. For example, in stress situations which habitual reaction patterns are not adequate, strong emotions make maximum energy resources available and thus help the organism for meeting such energy resources available and thus help the organism for meeting such emergencies. The emotions like, joy, pleasure, delight, affection etc., are mostly helpful in overcoming the stress situation and thus protect the self from crisis and frustration. These emotions also dominate during the adolescence period.

Types of Emotional Problems

Emotional disequilibrium produces conflict within a individual. When emotional conflicts are unresolved, he becomes emotionally problematic. Emotional conflict is a painful mental state in which opposing and contrary wishes and thoughts are ranged against each other and pull the individual in opposite directions. Conflicts arising out of emotions may vary greatly in their kind and intensity.

Frustration

Frustration is a feeling of inadequacy and tension caused by blocking of desires or pathways to a goal. This may happen consciously or unconsciously. The manifestation of an emotional problem may be observed in such behaviours as fear of meeting people, psychological withdrawal, loneliness, rejection by peers, and lack of mental abilities.

Anxiety

Anxiety is frustrated fear. Students suffering from anxiety exhibit feelings of insecurity, lack of self-confidence, fear about their ability to achieve their goals and meet difficulties of life and world.

A number of causes for emotional problems have been identified. These are favouritism by teachers, heavy load of home work, lack of concentration, threat of self due to bias, insult, contradiction, being teased, sarcastic comments etc. Emotional insecurity is also one of the major causes of anxiety reaction.

Nervousness

Nervousness means a large variety of reaction. The nervous students are restless, unable to concentrate on studies, get upset at the slightest defeat or threat. On the surface, such a student may show behaviour like biting his nails, playing with his handkerchief or buttons, moping the forehead again and again etc. These meaningless activities help him to get over from the tension.

It has been observed that students who suffer from nervousness have gone through great insecurity in their life time. This feeling of insecurity may be due to poverty, neglect, loss of parents, occasional threats and dangers. In some cases the students may acquire this insecurity from their parents.

Stress

'Psychological stress is the state of an organism where the student perceives that his well being (or integrity) is endangered and that he must devote all of his energies to its protection' (Coffer and Appley 1964). In psychological stress the integrity of the organism is involved and he cannot find a normal adjustive response. Frustration and anxiety produce tension within the individual and prolonged tension causes stress. Almost all behaviour manifesting stress are similar to anxiety. But in stress their degree of intensity may be more.

In the every changing environment every individual must change his behaviour to maintain emotional stability. Adjustment to change is a conscious process involving reasoning, imagination and learning new behaviour. Emotional conflict may arise out of a stressful situation, the degree of which depends on the individual's personality structure. Emotional conflict produces anxiety and tension within the individual and when all the coping mechanism fail to adjust the individual undergoes stress.

Neurosis

Neurosis is a milder form of mental ailment which generally originates from prolonged emotional stain and emotional conflict. It gives a lot of trouble to the individual in the form of anxiety and causes a number of adjustment problems. The neurotics are unhappy, anxious, inefficient and ineffective. They are over sensitive, lack maturity, self centred and always complain of physical ailments like tiredness, indigestion, headaches and sleeplessness.

Neurotics believe that they are the victims of misfortunes over which they don't have any control. They are highly suggestible and obstinate.

Case histories of neurotic people reveal the underlying causes such as violent emotional conflicts, distressing emotional experiences, loss and disappointment in life, violent discord in social relationships or some frightening happenings. Unfavourable early training, non congenial environment also cause neuroticism. If the life at home and institution are full of tensions, annoyances, fears and anxieties. Students are likely to develop a neurotic personality.

Strategies

Several strategies depending on the nature of the problem and the purpose can be used for emotional guidance. Strategies discussed in the chapter can be used for resolving emotional problems. Two other strategies, viz., cooperative counselling, and Stress Reduction Model are discussed here.

Cooperative Counselling

Cooperative counselling 'is a blend of the direct guidance and authority typical of directive counselling and the non-judgmental, active listening behavior, typical of non-directive techniques' (Halloran, 1978). In cooperative counselling the following phases of activities are followed:

- The data and time of counselling session is fixed by the counsellor with the consent of the counsellee.
- The counselling session is to start with self-introduction.
- The counsellor tries to stimulate client's thinking by asking questions.
- When the counsellee remains silent, the counsellor waits for the response.
- The counsellor restates the counsellee feelings and message.

The counsellor assists the counsellee to choose appropriate coping mechanism.

The counselling traits as per prefixed date and time. The counsellor introduces himself with his brief professional expertise. The student who comes for help also introduces himself.

In the begining of the session the counsellor asks a few questions to the counsellee. These questions are asked in a non-threatening manner. The purpose of asking these questions is to stimulate the clients' thinking. These questions are specific and related to counsellee's emotions and attitude. Thus, the client is encouraged to express his thoughts. When non-threatening questions work, these stimulate deep communication.

Silence and pause are also customary in cooperative counselling. When the counsellee does not speak for a few seconds, the counsellor has to wait. When the counsellee speaks, the counsellor does not interrupt. He again waits for the thought to be completed.

Sometimes emotional outbursts may result in the process of counselling. The counsellor has to keep patient, till the outburst is over.

In cooperative counselling, the counsellor restates the counsellor's own feeling and message. This is known as mirroring. This process enables the counsellee to get an insight into his problem.

When the counsellee understands his problem then both the counsellor and the counsellee start exploring the adjustment strategies. The counsellor helps the counsellee to select the appropriate strategy.

When the counsellee is satisfied with the outcome, the session is terminated slowly. The counsellee is assured of further help, when needed. Thus, cooperative counselling is very useful to find out the real cause of an emotional problem and exploring a suitable strategy to overcome the problem.

Stress Reduction Model

Emotional conflicts produce anxiety and stress within the individual. Anxiety produces increased blood pressure, rapid pulse rate and increased blood circulation to the muscles and results in tension on those muscles. Other symptoms might be rapid shallow breathing, a strong fast heart beat, and cold sweaty palms. Thus when the individual feels anxious, he or she experiences an accompanying sense of threat and physical tension. Wolf proposed the model to reduce muscle tension by systematically relaxing the primary muscles of the bodies. The primary feature of the model is the progressive and systematic relaxation of different sets of muscles from head to toe. The technique inhibits the psychological reaction to stress by introducing a competing response. The physical and mental procedures interact with each other and produce gain in energy.

The following are the phases of activities in stress reduction model:

- Find out a suitable place for relaxation
- Sit or lie down comfortably
- Begin to let your whole body relax
- Start your relaxing journey throughout your body
- Notice your breathing in mid way

– Experience the pleasant relaxed state that you are in

– Slowly awake

No special material or physical support is necessary for this model. It is helpful if the environment is a quiet one. A comfortable chair is sufficient for the individual. The individual sits down or lies down comfortably. He removes his glasses and adjusts clothing for making himself comfortable. Then he closes his eyes. He must think that everything is comfortable and relaxed. Gently, he must focus on feet and feel that muscles of that area are very calm and relaxed. Then slowly he shifts his attention to calves, hips, abdominal wall, lower, middle and upper back, and feel that muscles of those areas are gradually getting relaxed.

At this point notice how he is breathing. He must imagine each time breathing as if he breathes out a little more tension. Now, slowly he allows his attention to move to his neck muscles. Let them go and feel that they are becoming more and more relaxed. In the same process he shifts his attention slowly to other upper parts of the body such as his arms, face, forehead. Once he covers his whole body, he should allow his attention to travel from the top of his head down through his body. Feel that the left over tension is moving away then for a few minutes he enjoys the pleasant sensation of relaxation.

Now slowly he returns to breathing and feels that cool air presses in his nostrils and warm air passes out. He must be a passive observer of his breathing for few moments and slowly open his eyes. He then awakes fully and becomes aware of the room and surroundings.

The stress reduction model can be practised for physical, mental and emotional relaxation and harmony. As a side effect it reduces anxiety and tension.

Personal problems are mostly emotional in nature and hence difficult to deal with. Guiding employees and others for solving such problems mostly require the application of psycho therapeutical approaches which clinical psychologists and psychiatrist can handle. But this does not mean that managers have no role in personal guidance programmes they have to identify the individuals who have personal problems and show empathy to them. If the problem is serious in nature, the manager can refer the same to the clinical psychologists and psychiatrists for further action.

The Skills of Counselling

Counselling probably springs from two sources. The first is the normal human responses that helping people have always given to others. The second springs from the original work of Sigmund Freud and Carl Jung and their followers.

There are many schools of counselling and a plethora of approaches. They include the Gestalt approach of Fritz Perls, Transactional Analysis, developed by Eric Berne, the Psychodynamic Approach favoured by many therapists and the Person Centred Approach of Carl Rogers. If you are starting out, you would not need to learn all these approaches, although it is helpful to know that they exist. What is important and common to all approaches are the basic skills needed to carry out any counselling.

Relationship Skills

You do not need to be the life and soul of the party, in fact this would not be a helpful attribute for a counsellor; but you do need to be someone who can communicate with people at an individual level.

This means that you need to be genuinely interested in other people. The persons who is purely ego centred, or self-interested, is not likely to come across as open and trustworthy. In order to make satisfactory relationships of any kind, you must be able to give acknowledgement to the other person and to show that you value them. This means putting your own interests on the back burner for at least half of the time. In counselling, your own interests should be entirely secondary to those of the persons being counselled.

Listening Skills

This is the key skill in counselling. In fact, it is probably the key skill in almost any management or person centred activity. If you can get this one right, you have an immensely powerful and positive tool with which to succeed and to help others succeed.

However good you think you are at listening, you will certainly need to gain additional practice in order to counsel anybody.

Asking Appropriate Questions

In order to listen to what the person is really saying and to help that person towards some resolution, you will need to ask questions. The timing and the type of those questions, as well as the way you ask them, will determine how helpful you are.

Too many or too few questions, put in an inappropriate way or at the wrong time, will have the effect of putting off the other person and counteract your good listening.

There are various questions that you can ask during a counselling session. Getting those questions clear for yourself will help you, not only with your counselling, but also with your interviewing and coaching techniques and the other interpersonal skills that you need as a manager.

The kind of questions that you will find most useful are:

* Open
* Closed
* Mirror or reflecting; and
* Probing

The questions you should avoid are:

* Leading
* Qualified; and
* Multiple

Open Questions

These are questions that require more than a simple answer, demanding that the other person thinks about the response and perhaps answers at some length. The questions will often begin with how or what, such as 'How did you become involved in that?' or 'What kind of work do you enjoy doing?'

Avoid asking questions that begin with 'Why.' Such questions may appear threatening and discourage an open response from the person. 'Why did you do it that way?' Can imply (even if you don't intend it) that you disapprove, causing a defensive response.

Other open questions can start with 'Tell me about' or 'Would you like to describe what happened? or it would help if I understand more about.'

Open questions are the most appropriate in identifying the issue stage. In other words, you use these kinds of question in order to hear what someone is really saying and to identify the key issue or issues.

Closed Questions

There is nothing wrong with closed questions as long as you don't use them too often, otherwise it will become an interrogation session. Closed questions, as you probably know, are ones that require only a simple factual answer. 'Did you know that?' How long have you been here? Had you known her before? are all examples of closed questions.

You can use these in the contract setting stage and in checking things for yourself later on, particularly in the summarising stage. Always take care when using closed questions that you are not closing the person down or leading them to the easy option. Asking 'Do you feel better now?' is probably meant more for you than the other person, so that when you get a 'Yes, thanks' (what else are they going to say?) you're the one who actually feels better.

Mirror or Reflecting Questions

These are probably the most useful (and underused) types of questions. Good counsellors will use a great deal of mirroring questions, usually without the other person even being aware of it. You will use this type of question during the clarifying stage.

It is almost as though you are, literally, holding up a mirror so that the other person can see him or herself more clearly; or more accurately, playing back a tape of what they said. It is partly a brief, interim summary of what you've heard, but it is there in order that the person being counselled is constantly aware of what he or she is presenting.

Notice that we use the term 'presenting' rather than 'saying' since you may need to reflect back not just words, but also feelings that you have picked up.

A mirror type question may be something like I have understood you to say that ... is that right so far? Even more effectively, you might simply repeat the last few words of what someone has said, in the same way that they have said it. Using the same words in the same tone is a very powerful way of conveying to the other person what he or she is presenting. It takes a lot of practice to do this in a way that is helpful rather than patronising.

Probing Questions

Once you have helped the other person to identify the key issues and are in the process of clarifying things, you will have highlighted some areas that need further exploration in order to understand more fully what is going on/or to find out the present state of mind.

Probing questions take you further. They may not even be in the form of questions. When it is a question, the most common one will be to ask what something means to the person who said it, 'When you said that you don't enjoy that work, can you say what it means to you?'

Just as likely, you can probe silently. Try simply remaining quiet when someone is talking to you. Listen attentively, showing that you are listening. When the other person finishes, try nodding your head, perhaps giving little more than a grunt of approval or quizzical glance. You may be surprised at the effect as long as you don't overdo it.

Leading Questions

A leading question suggests the answer. Do not use it in counselling. It is used in order to manipulate people, and they always know when that is being attempted, just as you would. An example: 'You wouldn't do that, would you?'

Qualified Questions

Do not add to your questions by qualifying them. If you do not think that a question is clear enough, it would not help to add explanations. If the other person is taking time to answer, do not interrupt his or her train of thought by asking the question in another way.

Counselling must respect people enough to know that if something needs explaining, they will ask and if they need time, they should have it.

Multiple Questions

When you find yourself asking two or three questions at the same time, you are probably nervous. Stop, take a deep breath and start again.

If you have asked more than one question you will either confuse the other person, or you will get a response only to the one that he or she chooses to answer.

Practice and getting feedback for yourself is the best way of knowing that you asked the right questions in the right way.

Find somebody else whom you can rely on to help you in this way. Ideally, use a tape recorder so that you can listen to the session afterwards and analyse how you did.

Carry out an interview. It might be a counselling session, or it could be on anything that the two of you agree. It might be a continuation of the practice session you had from the previous task. Make a note afterwards of the type of questions you asked and the kind of responses you got. Most important of all, ask the other person how he or she reacted to specific questions and the way you asked them. Listen to the tape and the feedback and practise again the things that need to be improved upon.

Diagnostic Skills

You are not expected to make a diagnosis on the state of mental or physical health of the person you are counselling. That is definitely the province of a professionally qualified person. What you do need is an ability to analyse what is being presented to you, to make sense of it and to be able to respond accordingly.

Signals and Messages, have more to say on this aspect.

The counsellor must be a good observer and adept at making sense of what is being conveyed.

The signals you get will include the words that are spoken and the way they are said, such is the tone of voice, the emphasis given to certain words or phrases, the things that are repeated, the accompanying eye, hand and body movements, generally referred to as Kinetics.

When you consider all the signals you pick up from what someone conveys, you will recognise that the non-verbal and the body signals tell you far more than the actual words alone.

As always, practice is needed to become fully aware of the kinds of signal that people give out when they communicate with you. You probably already know what most of the signals are, but may not use them in a conscious way to make sense of what is being presented.

Next time you are with someone, whether in an informal conversation or perhaps at a meeting, do some conscious observing. Afterwards make a note of what you have picked up, using the headings given here.

Key words or phrases	Tone of voice	Non-Verbal signs

You might need to do this a few times before you really begin to pick up the essential signals. Once again, it will be helpful for you to share this exercise with somebody else and get some direct feedback.

Here is an edited transcript of what Prashant presented during a counselling session. Prashant is in his mid forties, has worked with the company for 15 years, has reached a low to middle grade level of management and is faced with the prospect of change due to a restructuring process within the company.

Prashant :I do not know where to start really. (Silence; Prashant shifts in his chair, crosses his legs).

Counsellor : Where would you like to start?

Prashant : (Clears his throat, looks down at the floor, then at the counsellor). I want to know what is going on and what is going to happen to me.

Counsellor : What do you mean, Prashant?

Prashant (Looks at counsellor with an angry glance). Well, I mean, with all the changes going on and the rumours flying about, nobody told me anything. I suppose I am just supposed to wait until my redundancy notice is handed out, or they move me to another department. You would think after all this time, they'd have the courtesy to let me know where I stand. I mean, what am I supposed to do? (His voice is raised, he folds his arms, leans back in his chair).

There are quite a few signals in this short excerpt

The signals allow you to ask some questions, of yourself at first. For example: What or who really makes Prashant angry? Why the angry glance at you? What is he saying when he asks what he is supposed to do? Who are they?

If you ask all these questions you will certainly finish up looking like an interrogator, reinforcing what Prashant probably already feels about you as an authority figure. Instead, you must both make some sense of what is going on.

The message is the sum of the signals that Prashant is giving you. In this instance, it is something like this.

Prashant appears to be angry at an anonymous authority and feels unable to control his own destiny.

Note that you can only say what appears to be the case. You have little information so far (although much more than Prashant may realise he has given you) and need to check back with him what he is presenting to you. So, having got this small amount and put together some message, it enables you to ask a key question or make a key comment that will help Prashant to clarify things.

Responding to the message

What would you say at this stage? We would suggest something like this:

'You seem to be pretty angry, Prashant. I understand that you have felt left out and are unclear about what you are supposed to do. Can you tell me who is making you so angry?'

The point is (if we are right), that Prashant needs help to pin down someone tangible if he can. It is difficult, if not impossible, for someone to deal with a problem if it is vague and unnamed.

In this case, Prashant was able to talk about his boss and the anger he felt at being overtaken in the promotion stakes. He saw his boss at distance and evasive, unprepared to discuss the future with Prashant or given him any positive opportunities for discussion.

When this became clear, Prashant saw that he had to confront his boss and discuss this with him. The outcome was a changed perception. His boss told Prashant that he had felt uncomfortable about being promoted above Prashant and was unsure whether Prashant would welcome being consulted, especially when the boss was unsure about the impact of impending changes. Between the two of them, they agreed to prepare a presentation to the senior management team, describing the effect of current uncertainties and suggesting alternative scenarios for change.

What had happened here was that Prashant, perhaps for the first time, was encouraged to take some positive action himself in his own destiny.

We do not want to pretend that this was as easy as it sounds or took place as a result of one session. In fact, the action took place after four sessions, during which Prashant explored some of the source of his feelings about authority. It transpired that he had always felt dominated by his parents, who had pushed him into his family life, where he always acted passively in any decisions relating to his children, then became angry when they took little notice of him.

What this extract shows is that, if you listen and observe, using the skills described, you are able to ask the questions that will get you, and the persons being counselled, to the nub of the problem and towards its eventual resolution.

Confidentiality

The essence of a counselling session is that it is confidential. This has to be made quite clear at the beginning of any session with the staff member being counselled. It is an issue that has caused much debate, so you will have to be certain about any departures from this rule and make them explicit to anyone whom you counsel.

Consider whether there are any instances where, in your case within the organization, you would not be bound to maintain confidentiality. If there are any circumstances, include them in this exercise. Write down a summary of what you would say to a member of staff coming to you for counselling in relation to the confidential nature of that counselling.

Contract Setting

You need to include more than just statements about confidentiality in any initial discussion about counselling. It is very likely that anyone coming for counselling for the first time will have no idea what to expect or what the rules are.

Where you are counselling staff it is even more important than usual to make it very clear what the person should expect, how you will be working, what your role is and many of the little, but crucial details. For example, how long a session might be, how many sessions and how regularly they occur, where you will meet, what you will do about interruptions and so on. There may be things that the member of staff wants to say as well, so you should give him or her a chance to ask questions or add any further rules. This is the contract between you.

Refraining Skills

Part of asking the right questions at the right time is knowing when to refrain from asking or saying anything. Remember that the most important part of counselling is to listen to the other person. For that you must suspend your own judgment or thoughts about what you might do or what your experience is.

Since counselling is not only giving advice, you might sometimes wonder what you are supposed to say when someone shares a problem with you. Whenever you are tempted to give an answer, or to talk about a similar experience that you had, or if you find your head whirling with ideas, the best thing to do is nothing.

Knowing when to hold back and being able to do so is an underused and considerable skill. Your response always needs to have the aim of helping the other person to make progress. Keeping quiet, while being attentive, can often be the catalyst to that progress. Regard the time you have with the staff member as that person's time to talk about the things that he or she really needs to share.

Intervention Skills

There are times when you will need to stop the persons from talking. This is when you recognise that the staff member is just going round in circles, repeating lengthy descriptions of similar circumstances or bemoaning his or her fate as though there is nothing that they could ever do about it.

At such points you need to be strongly, but gently assertive; bringing the person back to hear what they have been saying and repeating, several times if needed, that they continue to return to the same issues without making the connection between them or taking responsibility for changing things.

Self-Awareness

It is unlikely that you can be of any help to anyone else in counselling if you are not aware of your own strengths and weaknesses, your values and emotions, your likes and prejudices. An important part of the training for counsellors is that they have counselling for themselves as part of their own development programme. So you don't need problems to have counselling.

Empathy

This word is much used in counselling, but not generally understood. It means having the ability to understand and accept the feelings of another person. It is not the same as feeling sympathetic, although it is close to that. Once you feel sorry for someone, it becomes hard to counsel them. But it is also hard to counsel someone if you have no grasp of how they are feeling.

Carl Rogers, who founded the 'person centred' school of counselling, believed that empathy was the essential attribute needed in order to offer positive counselling support to another person.

Objectivity

You are treading a tightrope, trying to balance a whole range of skills here. While you need empathy, you also need to be objective. Once you start to get involved in other people's problems you have lost the ability to counsel them. All that you end up with are two people sharing the same problem. You might even finish up feeling worse than the person you're trying to help.

So, be with the person, but remain separate from his or her problem. Remember that it is that person's issue, not yours. Also remember that the moment you start to make judgments, or to show in any way that you disapprove of the person's actions or behaviour, you are no longer able to counsel him or her.

Referral Skills

There is much debate as to whether or not you need to know about a subject before being able to counsel somebody. For example, do you need to know about teenagers in order to counsel someone who is having a problem with a teenage child? Do you need to be an expert on AIDS to counsel someone concerned about that? Do you have to know about alcoholism to assist someone with an addictive drink problem?

Our answer is no, you do not need to be an expert in all or any of those things in order to counsel somebody. But you do need to be aware of your limitations and have access to people or agencies who can provide such specialist guidance when that is needed. Always be clear about your own role and the contract you have with the person being counselled. When someone needs and is prepared to take other support, give the information about the relevant agency, while maintaining your own support for as long as is appropriate.

REFERENCES

Black, John D.: *'Some Principles and Techniques of Employee Counselling'* (Dartnell Corporation, Chicago), 1955, pp. 2-3.

Commerce Clearing House, "Should Your Company Encourage Mentoring?" *Human Resources Management: Ideas and Trends* (July 20, 1994), p.122.

Daniel B. Turban and Thomas W. Dougherty, "Protege Personality, Mentoring, and Career Success," in Jerry L. Wall and Lawrence R. Jauch (eds.) *Academy of Management Best Papers Proceedings 1992,* Las Vegas, Nevada (August 9-12, 1992), p.419.

Dunnette, Marvin D. & Dirchner, W.K.: 'Psychology Applied to Industry' (Appletoncentury-Crofts, New York), 1965, p.84.

Eilbert, Henry: 'A Study of Current Counselling Practices in Industry', *Journal of Business,* Vol. 31, No. 1, Jan., 1958, pp. 28-37.

For a discussion of mentoring and minorities, see David A. Thomas, "The Impact of Race on Managers' Experiences of Developmental Relationships: An Intra-Organizational Study," *Journal of Organizational Behaviour,* Vol. 11, No. 6 (November 1990), pp. 479-92. For an opposing view of mentoring and women/race issues, see Belle Rose Ragins, and Terri A. Scandura, Gender and the Termination of Mentoring Relationships, *Academy of Management Best Papers Proceedings,* Dorothy P. Moore, ed., (August 14-17, 1994), pp. 361-65.

For an excellent discussion of these issues, see William Whitely, Thomas W. Dougherty, and George F. Dreher, "Relationship of Career Mentoring and Socioeconomic Origin to Managers' and Professionals' Early career Progress," *Academy of Management Journal,* Vol. 34, No. 5 (June 1991), pp. 331-51.

Goerge E. Dreher and Ronald A. Ash, "A Comparative Study of Mentoring Among Men and Women in Managerial Professional, and Technical Positions," *Journal of Applied Psychology,* Vol. 75, No. 5 (October 1990), pp. 539-46.

Gomberg, William: 'The Use of Psychology in Industry: A Trade Union Point of View', *Management Science',* Vol. 3, No. 4, July, 1957, pp. 348-370., See also *Barbash, J.:* 'The Practice of Unionism' (Harper & Bros., New York), 1957.

Landsberger, H.A.: 'Hawthorne Revisited' (Cornell University Press), 1958; See also Rogers, C.: 'Counselling and Psycholotherapy' (Houghton Miffin Co., Boston), 1942.

Levinson, Harry: *'Emotional Health in the World of Work'* (Herper & Row, New York), 1964. See also, Levinson, Harry *et al.*: *'Men, Management and Mental Health'* (Harvard University Press), 1962; Kornhauser, Arthur: *Mental Health of the Industrial Worker* (John Wiley, New York), 1965.

McFarland, D.E.: *'Personnel Management: Theory & Practice'* (Macmillan, New York), 1968, p.366.

Michelle Neely Martinez, *HR Magazine,* Vol, 36, No. 6 (June 1991), p.46.

Roethlisberger, F.J. & Dickson, W.J.: Management and The Worker' (Harvard University Press), 1939, pp. 590-604.; See also, *Dickson, W. J. & Roethlisberger, F. J.:* Counselling in an Organization: A Sequal to the Hawthorne Researches' (Division of Research, Harvard Business School), 1966.

See for example, Michael Emery, and Margaret Schubert, "A Trainer's Guide to Videoconferencing," *Training* (June 1993), pp. 59-64; and Bob Filipczak, "Distance Teamwork," *Training* (April 1994), p.71.

See Shellenbarger, "Corporate America Grooms Women Execs," *Working Woman* (October 1993), pp.13-14.
See Shellenbarger, p.13.
See, for example, "Survival Training for Employees," *ABC World News Tonight/American Agenda* (July 21, 1993).
See, for example, James A. Wilson and Nancy S. Elman, "Organizational Benefits of Mentoring," *Academy of Management Executive,* Vol. 4, No. 4 (November 1990), pp. 88-94.
Shepherd, William G.: 'Advice, Guidance and Counselling', *Personnel Journal,* Vol. 25, 1946, pp.167-170.

CHAPTER

21

Stress Management

In 1956 a machine operator James Carter had a nervous breakdown while working on the General Motors production line in Detroit in America. He sued General Motors, claiming that the stress of his job had contributed to his condition. It was an important law suit which Carter won and which established the relationship between stress and industry in the minds of executives and lawyers all over the world. Researchers have not only built up evidence of link between industrial stress and ill health but also proved that it is possible to link specific occupations with specific types of stress induced disease.

Raised blood pressure, nervousness, cold sweating, depression, constant daily headaches, loss of interest at work, a peptic ulcer and upset stomach which does not get used with time, black outs etc. These are some of the major symptoms of work related stress. Tensions related daily work are said to be a major factor in almost all of the above-mentioned physical ailments. With most of the organizations reducing staff (retrenchment) the employees who survive the axe are being expected to bear the increased work load. Meeting dead lines, enhanced ambitions at work, stiff competitions from colleagues, constant fear of being fired, increased work loads due to lack of expert manpower, deteriorating intrapersonal relationships are resulting in increased stress levels.

In Japan where 16 hours workdays are not uncommon it is estimated that about 14,000 Japanese die of sudden heart attacks triggered by overwork. In our country also more deaths and physical ailments are being identified among the urbanites, due to overwork. The work related stress has also been identified as the major cause of strained relationships at home with their spouses and children. This results in more children going astray than ever due to lack of proper parental guidance and care.

In the competitive environment of today, where everyone is trying to outclass each other and almost everyone is trying more and more hard to achieve their goals in the shortest possible time, we identify more and more physical, and psychological breakdowns. We normally call this phenomenon as work stress.

In modern age no one is immune from stress. It affects persons from all strata of life. The question arises as to why we are so susceptible to stress these days. It stands to logic that perhaps human beings were not designed for the type of complicated world in which they live today. They were designed for a world in which running and fighting were essential for survival. However, even when our environment has totally changed, our biological adaptation has not taken place. If we take back our attention to the age of 'cave man' we will realise that for him to survive was either a fight or flight. For either act, he needed additional sudden burst of energy. On sudden encounter with animals, response mechanism would involve pituitary gland activation to release adrenaline in the blood stream resulting in sudden boost of energy for the body to either fight or fly. This Flight Mechanism has following implications for human body:

a. Release of sugar, conversion of glycogen in glucose.

b. Raised pulse and blood pressure.

c. Dilated pupils.

d. Digestion stoppage.

e. Diversion of blood supply from stomach to other parts of the body.

With the advent of civilisation the life style has changed, however the body chemistry has not changed. Whenever a superior scolds a subordinate, the subordinate's body chemistry responds in similar fashion as it used to respond for cave man encountering the tiger. However, in case of modern day subordinate person neither he is fighting with his boss nor quitting the place of work. Thus additional burst of energy is not only useless but also harmful. The adrenaline is metabolised. The result is 'Executive Diseases' which are psychosomatic in nature. It need not be emphasised that the pituitary does not distinguish between anxiety caused and response mechanism of body remains the same.

Pressure and Stress

Since stress is our response to an appropriate level of pressure. There are two particularly important words in this concept – 'response' and 'inappropriate':

1. The word 'response' emphasises that stress arises as a result of how we react to pressures – and this alerts us to the fact that some stress management skills are about controlling our reactions, as well as controlling our pressures. I shall return to this point later.
2. The word 'inappropriate' emphasises that stress is not just a matter of too much pressure, but can also arise as a result of too little pressure; that is, when we are bored or under stimulated.

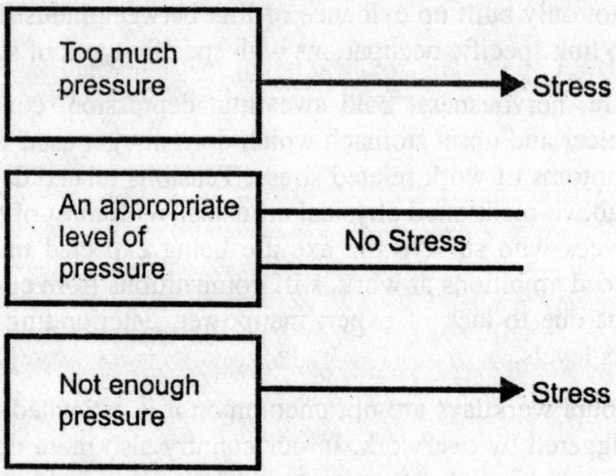

Fig. 1. Levels of Pressure

From these interrelations (see Fig.1), we can see the difference between pressure, which can be positive, a source of stimulation and motivation or negative, a source of worry and tension, depending on the circumstances, and stress which is always negative and harmful, so, we can see that:

* Stress is not the same as pressure – pressures are inevitable, but stress can be avoided;
* Stress is more likely to occur when there is too much or too little pressure;
* Stress depends on not just the level of pressure we experience, but also now we respond to those pressures.

It is important that we are clear about this distinction so, if you are not quite sure about the difference between the two, it is worth re-reading the explanation above before going on to the next section.

What is Stress

Stress is the experience of unpleasant over or under stimulation which actually or potentially leads to ill health. No human being can function without stimulation and challenge. It is part of life and provides excitement impetus and motivation, as well as distress and anxiety. As long as you feel in control, challenge can be invigorating. However, with some of the challenges you meet, the more disabling feelings and actions associated with stress can take hold. Stress is the result of a mismatch between the challenges you experience and your belief in your ability to cope. The challenges may come from external sources and may be the result of too much or too little pressure. They also come from within you, and be a product of your own value systems, needs and expectations. Everyone has powerful personal histories which affect their attitudes and actions. Therefore everyone perceives and interprets stress in different ways. However it has been identified that moderate amounts of stress is good and you can improve you performance –

efficiency and productivity. Too much stress can generate disabling emotions overwhelming anxiety and tension.

Table 1 : Consequences of Workload

Underload	***Optimal Level***	***Overload***
Bored	Highly motivated	Irritable
Overqualified for	Mentally alert	Absent
the work	Calm under pressure	Accident prone
Irritable	High level of energy	Indecisive
Absent	Exhilarated	Withdrawn
Lethargic	Excellent perception	Lack of memory
Negative attitude	Keen memory	Poor judgement

(*Source*: Richard M. Hodgetts. *op. cit.*, p. 338)

In the words of Szilagyi and Wallace, stress is an internal experience that creates a psychological or physiological imbalance within an individual and results from factors in the external environment, the organization, or the individual.

This definition indentifies three main elements of stress in organization: 1. Stimulus element, 2. Response elements and 3. An interaction element.

Elements of Stress

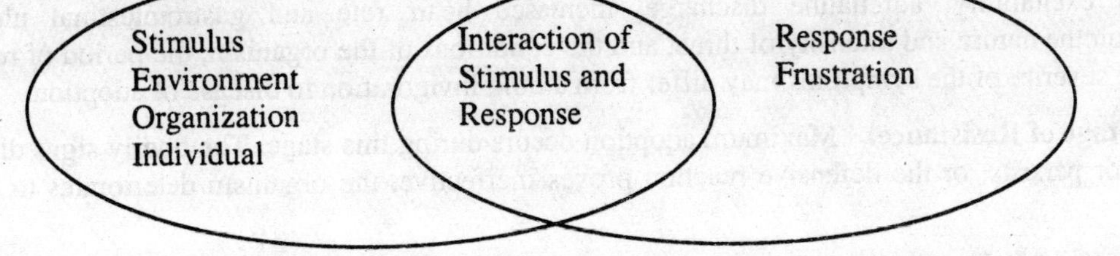

Fig. 2. Components of Stress

Source: Adrew Szilagyi and Marc Wallace, *Organizational Behaviour and Performance*, 1990, pp. 220

1. **The stimulus element or component :** This includes the initiating forces that result in a feeling of stress. Stress stimuli can originate from the environment, the organization, and the individual.

2. **The response component :** It involves physiological, psychological, or behavioural reactions to stress. Two responses to stress are most frequently indentified. One, frustration which is caused by any obstruction between a behaviour and its goal and second, the anxiety which the feeling of being unprepared to respond appropriately in some situation. Stress associated with organizational activities is called job stress.

3. **The interactive component :** The interactive component of stress is the interaction of stimulus and response stress factors. For example, for the air traffic controller, stress is a complex interaction of environmental, organizational, and personal feelings and responses.

STRESS: WHAT IT IS NOT

Because people so often misuse the term stress, we thought it would help you clearly understand this important concept if we addressed some of these common misperceptions. With this in mind, we will now consider what stress is not.

* Stress is not simply anxiety or nervous tension. Although these reactions may be seen in people suffering adverse reactions to stress, they are not the same as stress. In fact, it is possible for people suffering from stress to not exhibit any signs of anxiety or nervous tension at all.
* Stress need not necessarily be damaging. People frequently experience stress without any strain at all. Daily life activities, such as a rousing game of tennis, or a warm embrace, may be quite stressful, but not at all harmful.
* Stress is not always due to over stimulation. We usually think of the "stressed-out" individual as one who has too much to do, and cannot keep it all straight. But, as we will see later in this chapter, stress also may result from having too little to do.
* Stress cannot be avoided. It is important to realize that stress is an inevitable part of life, and that it cannot be avoided. What can be avoided, however, are the negative reactions to stress which we have described. Later in this chapter we will describe several techniques that can be used to help people cope-that is, to avoid the potentially damaging consequences of stress.

Dynamics of Stress

In 1976 Selye postulated three stages of physiological response when an organism is confronted with the threat:

(a) **Alarm Reaction:** The first stage includes an initial 'Shock phase' in which resistance is lowered, and a counter stock phase in which defensive mechanism become active. This phase is characterised by autonomous excitability, adrenaline discharge, increased heart rate and gastrointestinal ulceration. Depending on the nature and intensity of threat and the conditions of the organism, the period of resistance vary and the severity of the symptoms may differ from a mild invigoration to disease of adoption.

(b) **Stage of Resistance:** Maximum adoption occurs during this stage. The bodily signs disappear. If the stressor persists, or the defensive reaction proves ineffective, the organism deteriorates to the next stage.

(c) **State of Exhaustion:** When adoption energy gets exhausted the signs of alarm reaction resurface and resistance level begins to decline irreversibly and the organism collapses. A diagrammatic illustration of three stages is as shown.

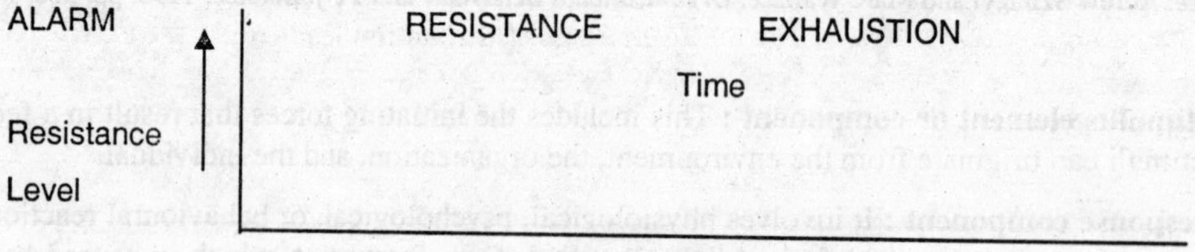

Fig. 3. Resistances-Time Relation.

Definition of Stress

Ask five people what stress is, and you are likely to hear at least five definitions. The businessperson views stress as frustration or emotional tension; the air-traffic controller sees it as a problem of alertness and concentration; the biochemist thinks of it as a purely chemical event. In an uncomplicated way, stress is best considered as something that involves the interaction of the individual with the environment. Most definitions of stress recognize the individual and the environment in terms of a stimulus interaction, a response interaction, or a stimulus-response interaction.

A *stimulus definition of stress* would be: Stress occurs when a force or stimulus acting on the individual results in a response of strain, where strain is pressure or, in a physical sense, deformation. One problem with this definition is that it fails to recognize that two people subjected to the same stress may show far different levels of strain.

A *response definition of stress* would be: Stress is the physiological or psychological response of an individual to an environmental stressor, which is a potentially harmful external event or situation. In the stimulus definition, stress is an external event; here, it is an internal response. This definition fails to enable anyone to predict the nature of the stress response or even whether there will be such a response.

An example of a *stimulus-response definition* is that stress is the consequence of the interaction between an environmental stimulus and the response of the individual. Stress is viewed as more than either a stimulus or a response; it is the result of a unique interaction between stimulus conditions in the environment and the individual's predisposition to respond in a certain way.

Stress is a dynamic condition in which an individual is confronted with an opportunity, constraint or demand related to what he or she desires and for which the outcome is perceived to be both uncertain and important.

When an individual gets an opportunity, e.g., exam or interview or sports competition, he is under stress. This stress can be used positively to excel in performance. Thus stress should not be viewed in negative sense only.

Constraints are the terms of reference or parameters defined for accomplishing a task, for example, an architect may have fabulous design of constructing a hotel but he has to restrict himself within the cost stipulated. Fixed time frame could be another constraint.

Demand relates to expectations of superior authority from a person. Suppose office timings are upto 5 P.M. only but your boss demands that you stay put till 7 P.M. daily. This will upset your complete schedule unnecessarily and will lead to stress.

Opportunities, constraints and demands give rise to stress when there is uncertainty over the outcome and the outcome is important. For example, if in a secluded place you encounter a shady person with a weapon, you will become tense since he might rob you or even kill you and this uncertainty and significance of likely event leads to instant stress.

Psychological Mechanism and Phases of Stress

The stress syndrome has three distinct phases. Each is related to heart/pulse-rate, respiration and digestion.

1. Immediate Reaction

The immediate reaction of striking or withdrawing from a stressful situation leads to:

* rise in blood pressure
* rise in blood sugar level
* indigestion because the release of Hydrochloric Acid is less
* rise in the breathing rate
* pale face
* tense/tight muscles.

2. Adamantine Reaction

This is a continuation of the first phase. With energy still left for facing the crisis there is a nature resistance reaction. In case this tense state continues for long it, can lead to a state of 'distress' or to the subsequent phase of 'nervous exhaustion.'

3. Nervous Exhaustion

This condition is called 'distress' when the individual feels completely nervous about coping with the emergent situations of stress, with a feeling of having been left with no strength and stamina.

This is a situation which is reached if stress in the earlier stages is not channelised in a creative direction.

The Physiological consequences of this situation are:

* loss of potassium because all the functions are reduced and reach the track of meeting their death.
* rise in sugar level.

This has a number of physical consequences, some of which are not so serious but others are quite so.

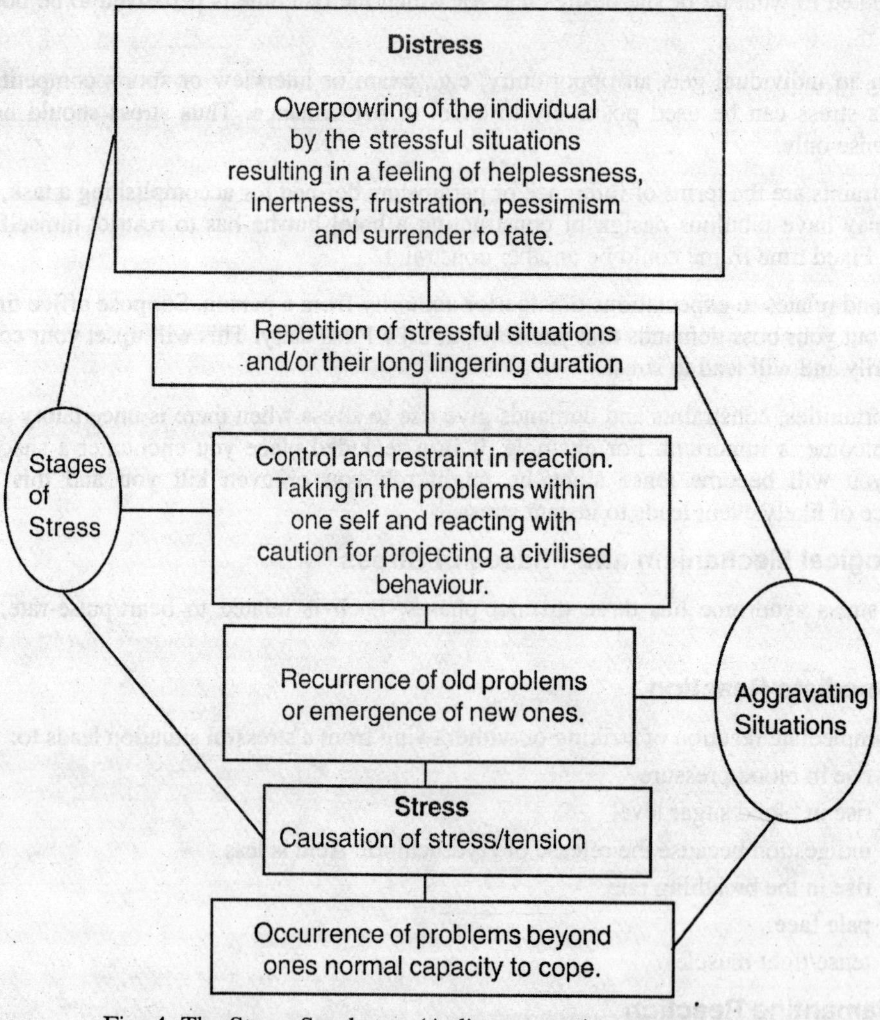

Fig. 4. The Stress Syndrome (A diagrammatic representation)

Pathological Chemistry of Stress

Stress is a PSYCHO-SOMATIC ailment ('Soma' is a Greek word meaning body and 'psychology' is the study of the mind). Stress in the context of being Psycho-somatic relates to mind and body as a unit. The term is normally referred to physical diseases having a psychological origin.

Doctors A. Venkoba Rao and S. Parwathi Devi in their article on 'Stress, Meditation and Medication' published in the Hindu on May 15, 1996 have given scientific explanations about the Chemistry of Stress in the following words:

"Stress causes an arousal response felt as distress and agitation. The Psychological component of this response is the release of chemical messengers from the hypothalamus (in the brain) which stimulates the pituitary gland to secrete ACTH (Adernocor-ticotropic hormone) into the blood. ACTH drives the adrenal glands (capping the kidneys) to produce adernaline and norepinerphrine. Consequent to this are the speeding up of body metabolism, a rise in blood pressure; hurried breathing and an acceleration of the heart rate and muscle tension. These form the so called 'fight' or 'fight' reactions enabling the organism to face the stress or beat a retreat."

With the latest research findings, it is not possible to think of the 'body' and 'mind' as two separate entitles in the Cartesium terms. They should be conceived as a single coherent unit.

Molecules called 'neuropeptides' provide a crucial connection between the mind and the body. They are biochemical units of emotion and convert emotion into bodily symptoms. Monocyte is a prime cell in our immune system. It is covered with receptors for peptide. Viruses also penetrate our body cells through the receptors. If the peptide cover of the receptor is thick the viruses find it difficult to get in, if on the other hand it is thin, it becomes easier for the viruses to enter.

A Stress Model

Fig. 5 shows a model of stress. As seen in the Figure. Stress is caused by organizational, group, individual and environmental factors. The consequences of stress range from heart problem, diabetes, ulcers, high blood pressure, depression, irritation, anxiety, fatigue, lowered self-esteem to reduced job satisfaction. Addiction to drugs and alcohol is also the result of stress. Burn out is another consequence of stress.

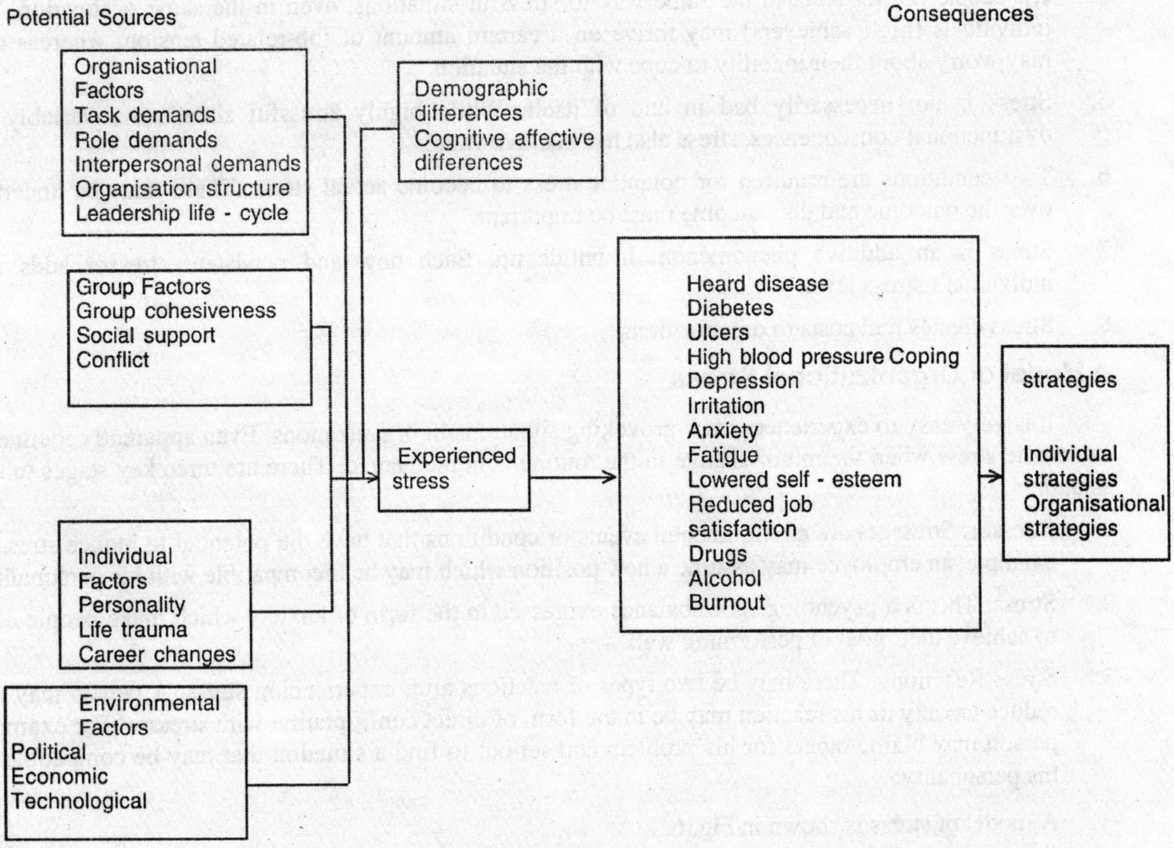

Fig. 5. A Model of Stress

But the consequences of stress are moderated by demographic as well as cognitive affective differences.

Coping strategies include individual as well as organizational schemes.

Types of Stress

According to Dr. Pestonji of I.I.M. Ahmedabad, the stress can be categorised as under:

(a) **Eustress:** It is a by-product of over excitement. It is a state of happiness which is temporary and occasional.

(b) **Hyper Stress:** Urgency to execute a particular work and eleventh hour rush results in Hyper Stress. It can be avoided by good planning.

(c) **Hypo Stress:** It is caused by lack of optimum activity. On retirement people become depressed. The effects are slow but long lasting. It gives a feeling of hollowness, neglect and diluted self-esteem.

(d) **Distress:** This type of stress has maximum adverse effects on executives. It is caused due to demands of the modern life and anxiety to cope up with them. It results in feelings of inadequacy, anxiety, nervousness etc.

The Nature of Stress

1. Stress is a natural part of human functioning. It is pervasive in the work environment. A zero stress condition is impossible.
2. It is the reaction of individuals to characteristics of the environment that pose a threat.
3. Stress is associated with constraints and demands.
4. All people do not react in the same way to stressful situations, even in the same occupation. Some individuals (high achievers) may thrive on a certain amount of job-related tension, whereas others may worry about their inability to cope with the situation.
5. Stress is not necessarily bad in and of itself. While highly stressful situations invariably have dysfunctional consequences, stress also has positive value.
6. Two conditions are required for potential stress to become actual stress. There must be uncertainty over the outcome and the outcome must be important.
7. Stress is an additive phenomenon. It builds up. Each new and persistent stressor adds to an individual's stress level.
8. Stress creates real costs to organizations.

A Model of Organizational Stress

It is very easy to experience stress-provoking situations in organizations. Even apparently routine jobs can create stress when the minor change in the routine is implemented. There are three key stages in stress as under:

1. Stressor: Stressors are environmental events or conditions that have the potential to induce stress. For example, an employee may assume a new position which may be incompatible with his personality.
2. Stress: This is a psychological imbalance expressed in the form of anxiety which make people unable to achieve their goal of performing well.
3. Stress Reactions: There may be two types of reactions after experiencing stress. A person may try to reduce anxiety or his reaction may be in the form of direct confrontation with stressor. For example, a person may blame others for his problem and set out to find a situation that may be compatible with his personality.

A model of stress is shown in Fig. 6.

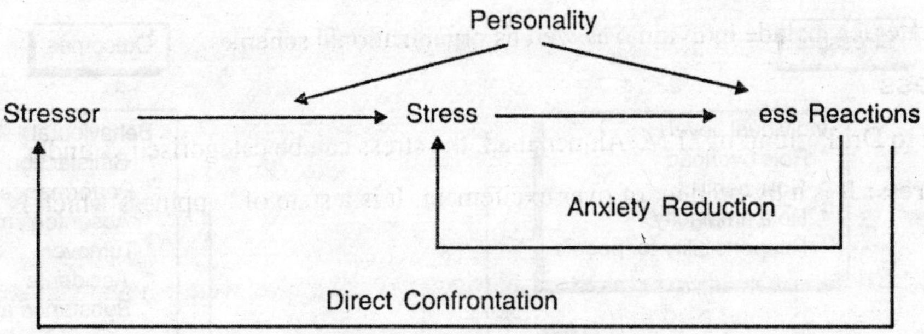

Fig. 6 A Model of Stress

Source: Gary Johns, Organizational Behaviour, 1988, p.465.

A MODEL OF OCCUPATIONAL STRESS

OB researchers Michael Matteson and John Ivancevich developed an instructive model of occupational stress. As illustrated in Fig. 7 stressors lead to stress, which in turn produces a variety of outcomes. The model also specifies several individual differences that moderate the stressor-stress-outcome relationship. A moderator is a variable that causes the relationship between two variables – such as stress and outcomes – to be stronger for some people and weaker for others.For example, a recent field study of 102 clinical staff in a hospital revealed that employees with high organizational commitment reported less stress and job displeasure than did people with low organizational commitment. Organizational commitment moderated the effects of stress. Let us consider the major components of this stress model.

STRESSORS' ENVIRONMENTAL FACTORS THAT PRODUCE STRESS

Stressors are environmental factors that produce stress, stated differently. Stressors are a prerequisite to experiencing the stress response. Fig. 7 shows the four major types of stressors: individual, group, organizational, and extra-organizational, individual-level stressors are those directly associated with a person's job duties. For example, emergency room nurses experience stress uniquely associated with treating patients who are high on drugs and alcohol. The most common examples of stressors are role overload, role conflict, and role ambiguity: these role characteristics create stress because they make people feel both overworked and uncertain about what they should be doing. Managers can reduce these stressors by providing direction and support for their employees.

Group-level stressors are caused by group dynamics and managerial behaviour. Managers create stress for employees by (1) exhibiting inconsistent behaviours, (2) failing to provide support, (3) showing lack of concern, (4) providing inadequate direction, (5) creating a high productivity environment, and (6) focusing on negatives while ignoring good performance.

Organizational stressors affect large numbers of employees. Organizational climate or culture is a prime example. For instance, a high-pressure environment that places chronic work demands on employees fuels the stress response. In contrast, research provides preliminary support for the idea that participative management can reduce organizational stress. Finally, the office design and general office environment are important organizational-level stressors. Research demonstrates that poor lighting, loud noise, improper placement of furniture, and a dirty or smelly environment create stress. Managers are advised to monitor and eliminate these stressors.

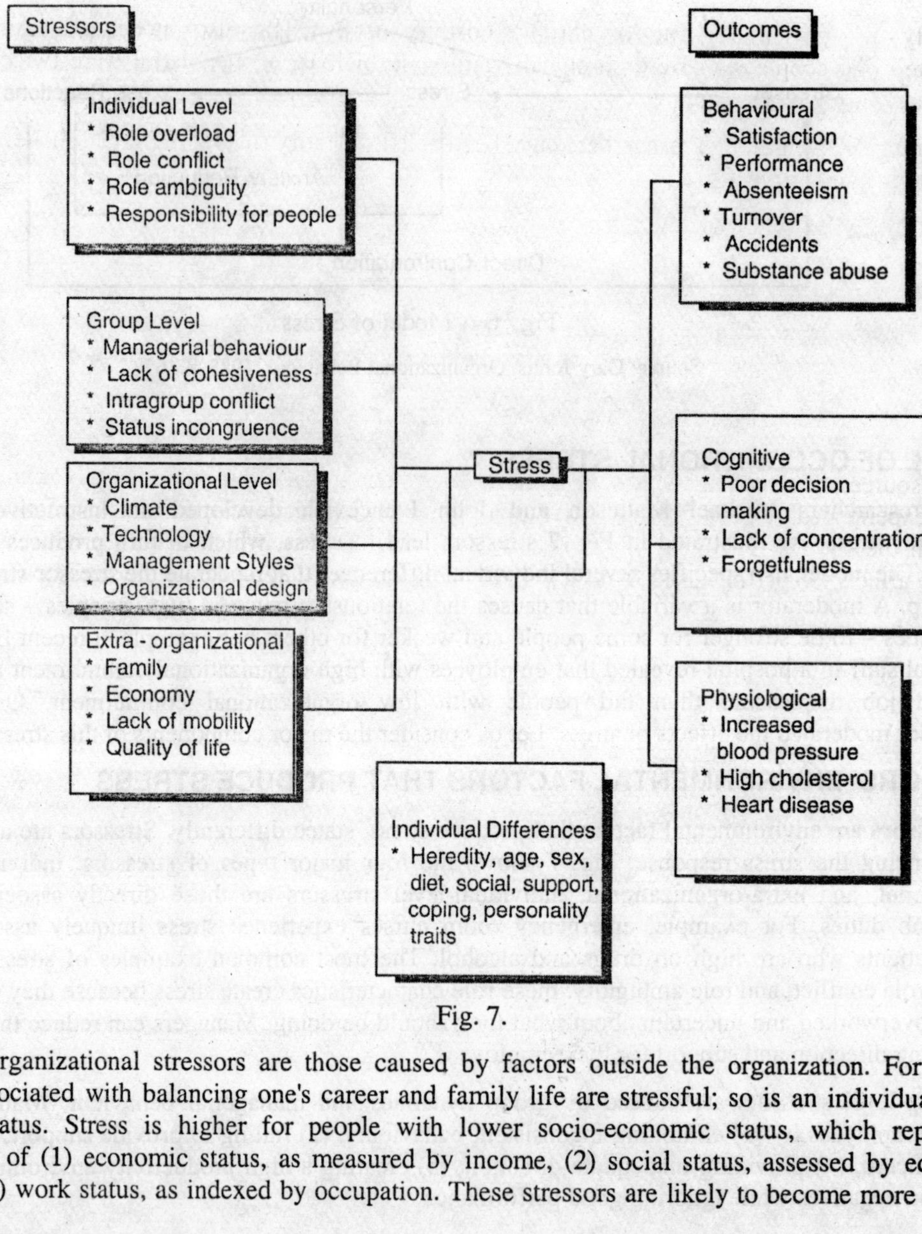

Fig. 7.

Extra-organizational stressors are those caused by factors outside the organization. For instance, conflicts associated with balancing one's career and family life are stressful; so is an individual's socio-economic status. Stress is higher for people with lower socio-economic status, which represents a combination of (1) economic status, as measured by income, (2) social status, assessed by educational level, and (3) work status, as indexed by occupation. These stressors are likely to become more important in the future.

Outcomes: Theorists contend that stress has behavioural, cognitive, and physiological consequences, or outcomes. For example, the International OB describes the manifestation of these stress outcomes in Saddam Hussein, President of Iraq, just prior to the war with the United Nations coalition forces in 1991. A large body of research supports the conclusion that stress produces harmful physiological outcomes. But researchers have only begun to examine the relationship between stress and work-related behavioural and cognitive outcomes. These studies indicate a negative relationship between stress and turnover, job satisfaction, and performance.

Individual Differences: People do not experience the same level of stress or exhibit similar outcomes for a given types of stressor. As discussed later, stressors are less apt to produce stress for people with a strong social support network and those who employ a variety of coping strategies. Perception of a stressor is another important moderator: if a stressor is perceived as threatening, an individual tends to experience greater stress and more negative outcomes. A recent study of 90 married couples further showed that men and women experienced different levels of stress when they argued. Women had higher stress than men when the interaction was nasty.

Finally, the personality trait of chronic hostility or cynicism also moderated stress. Research demonstrated that people who were chronically angry, suspicious, or mistrustful were twice as likely to have coronary artery blockages.

In summary, even though researchers have been able to identify several important moderators, a large gap still exists in identifying.

STRESS AND WORK: A MODEL

For most employed individuals, work is more than a 40 hour a week commitment. Even if the actual work time is 40 hours, most individuals spend 10 or more hours a day and work-related activities when hours for travel time, preparation for work, lunchtime, and so on, are added in.

Not only is a lot of time spent on work-related activities but many individuals find a substantial portion of their satisfaction and identity in their work. Consequently, work and non-work activities are interdependent. The distinction between stress at work and stress at home is an artificial one at best. For example, sources of stress at work spill over into a person's non-work activities. As a consequence of stressors experienced at work, the individual may come home irritable, short tempered, and fatigued and argue with the spouse. The resulting marital conflict may be a source of subsequent stress that in turn negatively affects job performance. Thus, stress at work and stress away from work are often interrelated.

This chapter's main concern, however, is with stressors at work. To better understand the link between stressors, stress, and consequences, we have developed an integrative model of stress and work. A managerial perspective is used to develop the parts of the model shown in Fig. 8. The model divides stressors at work into four categories: physical environmental, individual, group, and organizational. The model also presents five potential categories of the effects of stress. In this book, we are concerned primarily with the effects that influence job performance.

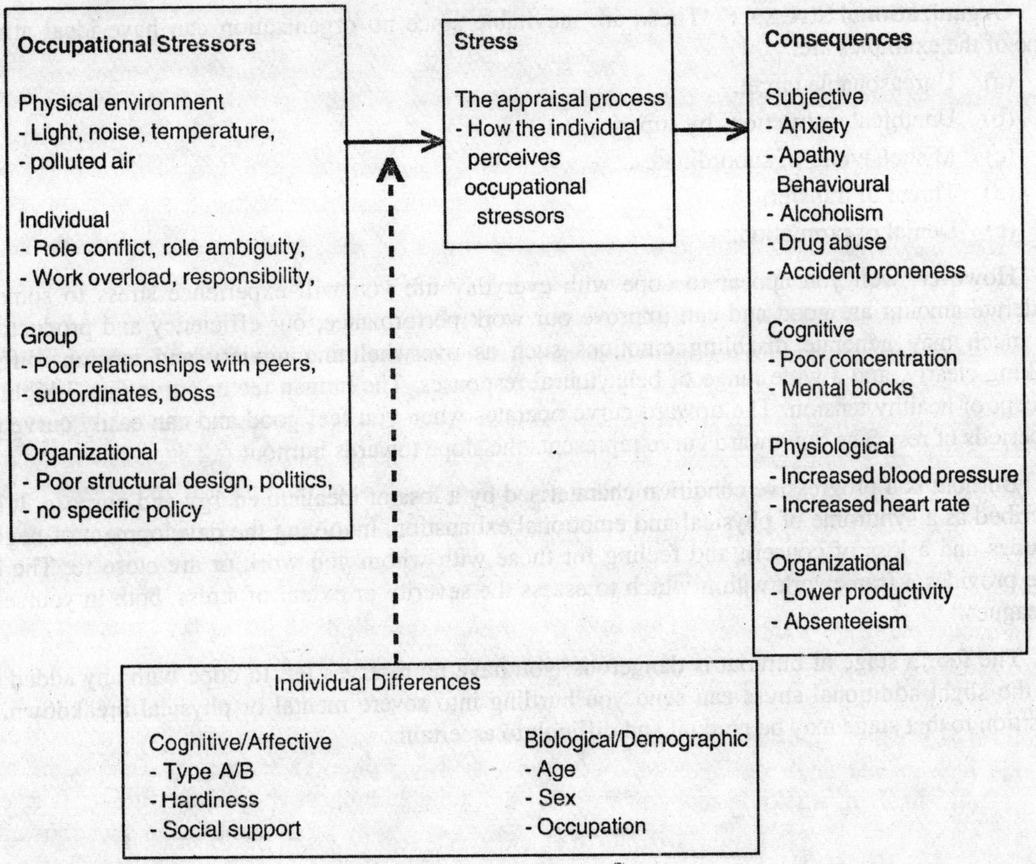

Fig. 8. Stress and Work: A Model

The model introduces "individual differences" that can affect reactions to stress. Individual differences investigated by occupational stress researchers have included age, sex, work additional, self-esteem, and community involvement. We will discuss the three that have received the most research attention:

Type A, life change events, and social support.

Types of Stressors

Stressors are the factors which create stress. These can be categorised as:

(a) Cateclysmic Phenomena.

(b) Individual Crisis.

(c) Daily Hassles.

(d) Psychological.

(e) Organizational.

Cateclysmic Phenomena: Natural disasters and those events which cause stress in the life of large segment of people are clubbed in this category.

Individual Crisis: Death of relative or own accident are examples of such stressor.

Daily Hassles: Routine problems which do not pose great adoptive difficulty yet are such as commuting to office, neighbourhood problems etc.

Psychological Stressor: Life of living creatures is a series of adoption to challenges of life and thus stress is accompanying them like a shadow. When our sentiments are hurt we carry stress for a long duration.

Organizational Stressor: These are inevitable since no organization can have ideal atmosphere; some of the examples are:

(a) Unreasonable target.

(b) Unethical instructions by superiors.

(c) Misbehaviour of subordinates.

(d) Threat of transfer.

(e) Denial of promotion.

However, well you appear to cope with everyday life you will experience stress to some degree. Moderate amount are good and can improve our work performance, our efficiency and productivity. But too much may generate disabling emotions such as overwhelming anxiety and tension, difficulty in thinking clearly, and a wide range of behavioural responses. The human factor curve Fig. 3 highlights the concept of healthy tension. The upward curve operates when you feel good and can easily curve tiredness by periods of rest. The downward curve represents the slope towards burnout.

Burnout is a progressive condition charaterised by a loss of idealism energy and purpose. It has been described as a syndrome of physical and emotional exhaustion, involving the development of negative job attitudes and a loss of concern and feeling for those with whom you work or are close to. The burn out scale provides a framework within which to assess the severity or extent of stress, both in yourself and in colleagues.

The fourth stage of burnout is dangerous; you have no reserves left to cope with any added pressure and the slight additional stress can send you hurtling into severe mental or physical breakdown. Yet the transition to that stage may be gradual and difficult to ascertain.

Fig. 9. Stages of Burn out

Majority of the stress can affect us in four different ways. These could be as:

a) Physically causing headaches or stomach upsets, heart strokes or high blood pressure.
b) Emotionally creating tensions and irritability.
c) Mentally by improving logical thinking.
d) Behaviourally, by affecting the way we act.

BURNOUT

When people are exposed to high levels of stress over prolonged periods of time, they may experience burnouts. This syndrome involves physical, mental and attitudinal exhaustion, plus feelings of low personal accomplishment.

Burnout is a stress-induced problem common among members of "helping professions such as teaching, social work, employee relations, nursing and low enforcement. It does not involve a specific feeling, attitude, or physiological outcome anchored to a specific point in time. Rather **burnout** is a condition that occurs over time and is characterized by emotional exhaustion and a combination of negative attitudes. Table 2 describes 10 attitudinal characteristics burnout. Experts say a substantial number of people suffer from this problem. For example, a recent national study of 3,718 Americans indicated that 59 per cent were burned out. This result implies that Burnout is not limited to people working in the helping professions. To promote better understanding of this important stress outcome, we turn our attention to a model of the Burnout process and highlight relevant research and techniques for its prevention.

Table 2 : Attitudinal Characteristics of Burnout

Attitude	Description
Fatalism	A feeling that you lack control over your work.
Boredom	A lack of interest in doing your job.
Discontent	A sense of being unhappy with your job.
Cynicism	A tendency to undervalue the content of your job and the rewards received.
Inadequacy	A feeling of not being able to meet your objectives.
Failure	A tendency to discredit your performance and conclude that you are ineffective.
Overwork	A feeling of having too much to do and not enough time to complete it.
Nastiness	A tendency to be rude or unpleasant to your co-workers.
Dissatisfaction	A feeling that you are not being justly rewarded for your efforts.
Escape	A desire to give up and get away from it all.

A Model of Burnout

A model of Burnout is presented in Fig. 10. The fundamental premise underlying the model is that Burnout develops in phases. The three key phases are emotional exhaustion, depersonalization, and feeling a lack of personal accomplishment. As shown in Fig. 9.1, emotional exhaustion is due to a combination of personal stressors, and job and organizational stressors. People who expect a lot from themselves and the organizations in which they work tend to create more internal stress which, in turn, leads to emotional exhaustion. Similarly, emotional exhaustion is fuelled by having too much work to do, by role conflict, and by and type of interpersonal interactions encountered at work. Frequent, intense face-to-face interactions that are emotionally charged are associated with higher levels of emotional exhaustion. Over time, emotional exhaustion leads to depersonalization, which is a state of psychologically withdrawing from one's job. This ultimately results in a feeling of being unappreciated, ineffective, or inadequate. The additive effect of these three phases is a host of negative attitudinal and behavioural outcomes.

Research Findings and Prevention: Burnout develops in phases. It is also significantly associated with personal stressors, job and organizational stressors, a lack of feedback, low job satisfaction, turnover, absenteeism, impairment of interpersonal relationships with family and friends, insomnia and quality and quantity of performance. This research underscores the organizational need to reduce the stress-induced problem of Burnout.

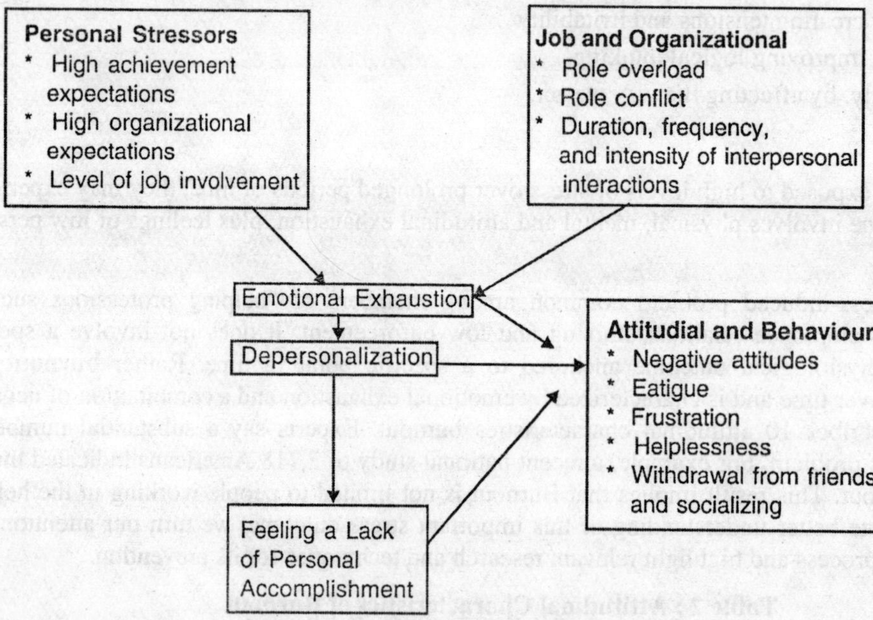

Fig. 10. A Model of Burnout

Removing personal stressors and job and organizational stressors is the most straightforward way to prevent Burnout. Managers also can reduce Burnout by buffering its effects. Buffers are resources or administrative changes that alleviate the symptoms of Burnout. Potential buffers include extra staff or equipment at peak work periods, support from top management, increased freedom to make decisions, recognition for accomplishments, time off for personal development or rest, and equitable rewards. Decreasing the quantity and increasing the quality of communications is another possible buffer. Finally, managers can change the content of an individual's job by adding or eliminating responsibilities, increasing the amount of participation in decision-making, altering the pattern of interpersonal contacts, or assigning the person to a new position.

There are also two long-term strategies for reducing Burnout that are increasingly being used by companies. Apple, Computer, American Express, IBM, McDonald's Corporation, and Intel, for instance, use sabbaticals to replenish employees' energy and desire for work. These programs allow employees to take a designated amount of time off from work after being employed a certain number of years. McDonald's grants paid sabbaticals after 10 years of employment; for Intel, it is eight weeks off with pay after seven years for every full-time employee. An employee retreat is the second long-term strategy. Retreats entail sending employees to an outside location for 3 to 5 days. While there, everyone can relax, reflect, or engage in team and relationship building activities. Hallmark Cards uses retreats to help in the fight against Burnout.

BURNOUT: STRESS AND PSYCHOLOGICAL ADJUSTMENT

Most jobs involve some degree of stress. Yet, somehow, the people performing them manage to cope; they continue to function despite their daily encounter with various stressors. Some individuals, though, are not so fortunate. Over time, they seem to be worn down by repeated exposure to stress. Such people are often described as suffering from burnout, and they demonstrate several distinct characteristics.

First, victims of burnout suffer from physical exhaustion. They have low energy and feel tired most of the time. In addition, they report many symptoms of physical strain such as frequent headaches, nausea, poor slep, and change in eating habits (e.g. loss of appetite). Second, they experience emotional exhaustion. Depression, feelings of being trapped in one's job are all part of the practice. Third, people suffering from burnout often demonstrate a pattern of attitudinal exhaustion (often known as depersonalisation). They become cynical about others, tend to treat them as objects rather than as people, and hold negative attitudes toward them. In addition, they tend to derogate themselves, their jobs, their organizations, and even life in general. To put it simply, they come to view the world around them through dark grey rather than rose-coloured glasses. Finally, they often report feeling of low personal accomplishment. People suffering from burnout conclude that they have not been able to accomplish much in the past, and assume that they probably would not succeed in the future, either. In sum, burnout can be defined as a syndrome of emotional, physical, and mental exhaustion coupled with feelings of low self-esteem or low self-efficacy, resulting from prolonged exposure to intense stress. See Figure 7 for a summary of the major components of the burnout syndrome.

BURNOUT: SOME MAJOR CAUSES

What are the causes of burnout? As we have already noted, the primary factor appears to be prolonged exposure to stress. However, other variables also play a role. In particular, a number of conditions within an organization plus several personal characteristics seem to determine whether, and to what degree, individuals experience burnout. For example, job conditions suggesting that one's efforts are useless, ineffective, or unappreciated seem to contribute to burnout. Under such conditions, individuals develop the feelings of low personal accomplishment that are an important part of burnout. Similarly, poor opportunities for promotion and the presence of inflexible rules and procedures lead employees to feel that they are trapped in an unfair system and contribute to the development of negative view about their jobs. Another important factor contributing to burnout is the leadership style used by employees' supervisors. In particular, research has shown that the lower the amount of consideration demonstrated by their supervisors (i.e., the less they are concerned with employees' welfare or with maintaining friendly relations with them), the higher employees' reported levels of burnout.

One of the most important factors contributing to burnout is the coping styles people use. Whereas some individuals are proactive and invest a great deal of energy in taking change over events in their lives (control coping), others tend to simply react, let things happen to them, and try to avoid the consequences (escape coping). Research has found that these different styles are related to burnout. For example, Leiter studied this issue by administering a questionnaire to a group of employees of a mental hospital. Among other things, it measured their various coping behaviours, and the degree of burnout they experienced. The relationship between these measures are quite interesting. Mental health workers who used control strategies to address their difficulties at work were generally less exhausted and had more positive assessments of their personal accomplishments (two key components of burnout) than those who did not. By contrast, those who used escapist coping strategies were more prone to be exhausted emotionally and attitudinally (depersonalisation). These finds make a convincing case that the way people respond to stressors in their lives can have an important effect on the likelihood of becoming a victim of burnout

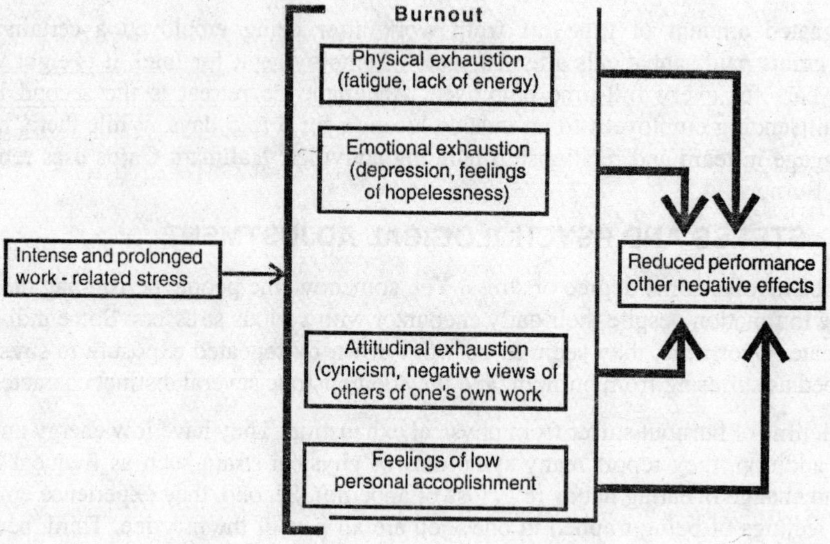

Fig. 11. Major Components of Burnout

BURNOUT: ITS MAJOR EFFECTS

Whatever the precise causes of burnout, once it develops it has important individual consequences. Burnout also has important consequences for the directions people take in their career. Specifically, it may lead individuals to seek new jobs or careers. In one study concerned with the impact of burnout, Jackson, Schwab, and Schuler asked several hundred teachers to complete a questionnaire designed to measure burnout and to report on the extent to which they would prefer to be in another job or career. As expected, the greater the teachers' degree of burnout, the more likely they were to prefer another job and to be actively considering a change of occupation. Second, people suffering from burnout may seek administrative roles where they can hide, from jobs they have grown to hate, behind huge piles of forms. Although this pattern certainly occurs, it appears to be relatively rare. More victims of burnout seem either to change jobs or to withdraw psychologically and mark time until retirement.

BURNOUT: CAN IT BE REVERSED?

Before concluding, we should comment briefly on one final question: can burnout be reversed? Fortunately, growing evidence suggests that it can. With appropriate help, victims of burnout can recover from their physical and psychological exhaustion. If ongoing stress is reduced, if burnout victims gain added support from friends and co-workers, and if they cultivate hobbies and other outside interests, at least some people, it appears, can return to positive attitudes and renewed productivity. Such results can be attained, however, only through active efforts designed to overcome burnout and to change the conditions from which it develops. The major signs that burnout is having fall into three categories: physical condition, behavioural changes, and work performance which is summarised in Table 3 given below.

Table 3. Symptoms of Burnout

Physical Condition	Behavioural Changes	Work Performance
* Headaches	* Increased irritability	* Reduced efficiency (more time spent working, but with less productivity)
* Sleeplessness * Weight loss * Frustration	* Changing moods * Reduced tolerance	* Dampened initiative
* Gastrointestinal disturbances	* Increased suspiciousness	* Diminished interest in working
* Exhaustion and fatigue	* Greater willingness to take risk	* Reduced capacity to perform effectively under stress
	* Attempts at self medication * (use of alcohol and tranquillisers)	* Increased rigidity of thought (closed thinking, inflexible)

Source: Based on material reported by Moss, 1981; *Management Stress Reading*.

Table 4. Stress Vs Burnout

Stress		Burnout
The person feels fatigued	→	The individual encounters chronic exhaustion.
The person is anxious	→	The individual is hypersensitive.
The person is dissatisfied with his or her job	→	The individual is bored and cynical about the work.
The person's job commitment has dropped off from the organization.	→	The individual's job commitment is virtually nil; he or she is mentally detached.
The person feels moody irritable, and unwilling to talk to others.	→	The individual feels impatient.
The person feels guilty depressed.	→	The individual encounters mental fatigue.
The person is having difficulty concentrating; he or she tends to forget things	→	The individual does not seem to know where he or she is; forgetfulness is becoming more and more frequent.
The person undergoes physiological changes such as psychosomatic complaints, increased blood pressure and heart beat	→	The individual begins to voice.

(*Source*: Richard M. Hodgetts, *Organizational Behaviour*, p. 345).

STRESS CONSEQUENCES

Mobilization of the body's defence mechanism is not the only potential consequence of contact with stressors. The effects of stress are many and varied. Some, of course, are positive, such as self-motivation, stimulation to work harder, and increased inspiration to live a better life. However, many are disruptive and potentially dangerous. Cox has identified five categories of potential effects of stress.

Subjective : anxiety, aggression, apathy, boredom, depression, fatigue, frustration, loss of temper, low self-esteem, nervousness, loneliness.

Behavioural : accident proneness, alcoholism, drug abuse, emotional out bursts, excessive eating or smoking, impulsive behaviour, nervous laughter.

Cognitive : inability to make sound decisions, poor concentration, short attention span, hypersensitivity to criticism, mental blocks.

Physiological : increased blood glucose levels, increased heart rate and blood pressure, dryness of the mouth, sweating, dilation of pupils, hot and cold flashes.

Organizational : absenteeism, turnover, low productivity, alienation from co-workers, job dissatisfaction, reduced organizational commitment and loyalty.

These are neither all-inclusive nor are they limited to effects for which there are universal agreement and clear scientific evidence. They merely represent some of the potential effects frequently associated with stress. It should not be inferred, however, that stress always causes the effects listed above.

Stress can have serious consequences for both our health and our work performance. In terms of health, the current belief among many medical practitioners is that 50 to 70 per cent of all physical illnesses are related to stress. The link between stress and heart disease is well-known. High levels of stress are also associated with diabetes, ulcers, high blood pressure, and arteriosclerosis. Stress can cause depression, irritation, anxiety, fatigue, lowered self-esteem, and reduced job satisfaction. Sustained over a long period, stress can lead to attempts to escape through the use of drugs or alcohol. It may also lead to burnout which has been defined as a state of mind resulting from prolonged exposure to intense emotional stress and involving physical, emotional and mental exhaustion.

Table 4 provides a contrast of stress and burnout. As the table reveals the two differ vastly.

The most serious consequence of stress relates to performance. It is said that moderate levels of stress stimulate the body and increase its ability to react. Individuals then perform better. But too much stress places unattainable demands or constraints on a person, which results in lower performance.

Symptoms & Diagnosis of Stress

Symptoms of stress take a variety of forms. Some of these come to be known to the sufferer himself, while in other cases are observed and yet in some others they need to be diagnosed by the healer.

The symptoms of stress could be related to the mind, the emotions, the nervous system, the physical health or the endocrine glands of an individual.

a) Related to the Mind

Poor memory, lack of concentration, lack of sleep, inability to make choices in taking decisions confusion and poor judgment.

b) Related to Emotions

Feelings of restlessness, helplessness, frustration, desperation, anger, irritation, guilt, depression, and lack of self-confidence.

c) Related to the Nervous System

Shortness of breath, high heart beat, high blood pressure, headaches, cold hands and feet, nausea.

d) Related to Physical Health

Heart burn/acidity, constipation/diarrhoea, problems with urination, faster aging, easy fatiguability, backaches, hair loss, fragile nails, obesity, rings under eyes, lumber pains, food allergies, impotencey.

e) Related to Endocrine Glands

Arthritis, diabetes, pain in joints, fast fatigue, menstrual difficulties, change in skin colour, skin rashes, colitis, stomach ulcers.

f) Related to Beauty/Handsomeness

Stress and beauty/handsomeness are not good allies. Stress attacks beauty in a number of ways like; fast hair loss, premature greying of hair, wrinkles, acne, light face.

This is likely to be a cause of great to the women folk because, beauty is not perpetual.

Symptoms of stress are the basis of diagnosis of the kind and degree of ailment for the prescription of treatments.

Apart from the above-mentioned symptoms there are some other approaches and signs for diagnosing stress. Some of these are briefly mentioned below:

Irodology (diagnosis through the iris)

According to this approach the nervous system surfaces in the eyes, with the iris of the left eye registering changes in the left side of the body and the iris of the right eye of those of the right side of the body.

Dr. Ignatz Von Peczely of Hungary in the 19th century conducted research on mapping different parts of iris related to different parts of the body and the state of health of that part.

Kampo

This is a Chinese system which deals with six graded stages of illness from 'health' to 'disease.' These stages are progressional with the next one more acute than the former.

The first stage is known as 'Yang' and the last one as 'Yin.' The first stage is the stage of normal health and the last one indicates that stage of the disease, which if untreated could lead to death.

As each individual is different from the other, the stage of illness is first diagnosed as also the peculiar features of the individual health for the commencement of the treatment.

The process is known as 'SHO' which when translated means 'the assessment of the patient.' In this system there are four facts of the process of identifying the ailment:

Visual: The diseases of the liver lungs and intestines are possible to be detected through this.

Auditory: Sounds give powerful indications about the diseases of the heart and lungs.

Physical Examination: Symptoms of some other diseases are amendable to detection through physical examination of the patient.

Questioning: Questions from the patients also yield good dues about the ailments.

While Kampo basically suggests a system of diagnosis for physical diseases infecting an individual, they have great relevance in the sphere of 'stress' as a number of physical ailments emanate from and result in stressful situations.

Further Effects of Stress

Role Conflict

Stress affects the behaviour of a person. A person under stress experiences organizational role conflicts described below:

(a) Role Stagnation

Conflicting expectations from different roles.

(b) Role Stagnation

Affected person feels that his career is not growing.

(c) Role Erosion

Suppose a person who was sole evaluator is told that half of his responsibility and authority is assigned to a new evaluator, he will feel cut off.

(d) Role Expectation

When a person experiences conflicting expectations from other members of the organization.

(e) Role Overload

It is self-explanatory.

(f) Role Isolation

When a person feels that others are not willing to assist or are not at all connected with his role.

(g) Personal Inadequacy

Feeling of lack of expertise.

(h) Role Ambiguity

When a person feels that he does not have adequate resources to carry on his duties.

Boss

It is abbreviation of Burnout Stress Syndrome. It is a psychological condition brought about by unrelieved work stress. It has four stages:

(a) Honeymoon.

(b) Fuel Shortage Chronic Symptoms.

(c) Crisis.

(d) Hitting the wall.

It is important for you to calculate, where are you on the burnout scale. Burnout is a progressive degenerative process which if not checked leads to ill health. Burn out scale has been divided four stages.

Stage 1 Suggests that you have lots of energy and enthusiasm, you are over conscientious and over worked. You start generating doubts about your ability to cope with work pressure feeling of uncertainty creeps in you.

Your warning signs are that you are too busy to take holiday, you are reluctant to take days' off, you start bringing work at home, you start giving too little time with your family, you start getting frustrated with the results, you're unable to refuse more work.

Stage 2 Starts with short lived bouts of irritation. Tiredness and anxiety creeps in. Feeling of stagnation at work. People in this stage start blaming others for their failures.

The warning signs are that your start complaining about the quality of other people's work. You find yourself incapable to cope with work pressure and work commitments. You start working for long hours. Your time management gets jeopardised.

Stage 3 identifies increasing anger, resentment, and lowering of self-esteem. General discontent and guilt grows in this stage. You start showing low emotional commitment at work and at home general apathy sets in.

Warning signs are lack of enjoyment of life, extreme exhaustion with much work, reduced commitment to work and reduced commitment at home.

Stage 4 is described as the most dangerous stage and if precautions and proper care is not taken it is also called the point of no return. This stage is marked with signs of withdrawal, some illness sets in, feelings of failure and extreme personal distress are identified.

Danger signs are to be immediately treated. These are identified as increasing absenteeism, avoiding colleagues, reluctance to communicate; you start loving isolation, physical ailments sets in like peptic ulcer or blood pressure or even diabetes. Alcohol and drug abuse may be very high.

Rating Occupation

It has also been identified that different occupations also are the cause of stress in many individuals. Researches have divided occupations in four broad categories:

(a) Active Jobs

(b) Low Strain Jobs

(c) Passive Jobs

(d) High Strain Jobs

Active jobs have heavy pressure to perform but allow leeway for problem solving. The working hours tend to be long out are partly at the worker's discretion. Doctors, engineers, farmers, executives etc., hold active jobs.

Low Strain jobs put low demands on people and give them a high degree of decision-making latitude. Professors, carpenters, repair people and successful artists hold low strain jobs.

Passive jobs combine low demands on skills and mental processes with little leeway for learning or decision making. There are no scope for innovation. Billing clerks, night watchmen, dispatchers fall in this category.

High Strain jobs have heavy pressure to perform and little leeway for decision making. These jobs tend to have long hours, require adherence to rigid procedures and allows very little latitude for taking breaks/time off for personal needs. Assembly line workers, waiters and telephone operators hold high strain jobs.

What Causes Stress

Is never the result of one single cause. Instead it is created by a number of interrelated factors such as pressure at work, too many social commitments, an uncomfortable living or working environment, or inability to organize and manage your time effectively.

In order to decide on the most appropriate strategies for dealing with the stress in your life, you first need to establish the main contributing factors.

Stress is caused by the following reasons.

Individual

This is caused by your own beliefs emotions, ways of thinking and acting. Most of the times unrealistic expectations of ones' self also causes stress. Other individual causes are inability to manage time efficiently. Lack of organization, feelings of inadequacy, under or over estimating abilities the basic need to control everything, inability to delegate work, financial concerns and inability to set limits, for example by saying no.

Interpersonal

These are related to specific people with whom you have contacts. Most of the problems start with you being required to fulfil others' expectations, demands for perfection from family or superiors. Lack of autonomy at work is identified as a major stress. Dealing with aggressive or manipulative people, being taken for granted, not being involved in decision making are some of the problems causing stress.

Organizational

These are specific to the particular organization in which you work. They may include: poor communication system, extremes of management style, working with an inexperienced staff, lack of clarify and agreement about the values and goals of the organization, lack consideration for the individual within the organization, lack of positive and / or critical feedback to employees. Some more problems causing stress can be inadequate staffing levels for the job at hand, lack of team and organizational identities, highly competitive structures. Numerous factors within the organization cause stress.

(a) Task Demands

These factors include nature of individual's job, working conditions and the physical work layout. Working in an over crowded room can cause more stress.

(b) Role Demands

The performance expected from an individual may be hard to reconcile or satisfy. Limited time and role overload can cause stress.

(c) Interpersonal Demands

These are pressure created by other employees. Lack of social support from colleagues can cause considerable stress.

(d) Organization Structure

It relates to level of differentiation. Excessive restrictions and lack of participation in decisions affects the employees.

(e) Organization Leadership

The managerial style of top leaders can also be a cause of stress. Some top executives create a culture characterised by tension, fear and anxiety. They establish unattainable targets, impose unnecessary restrictions and behave in rude manner with subordinates.

Belief in Locus of Control

Locus of control is the degree to which people believe they are masters of their own fate. Those who believe that they are masters of their own fate are called internals. Those who feel they are powers of fate are labelled externals. Evidence indicates that the internals perceive their jobs to be less stressful than do externals.

Hostility

Behaviour of executives can be broadly categorised as type A and Type B. The type A individual is aggressively involved in a chronic, incessant struggle to achieve more and more in less and less time. They feel impatient with the rate at which most events take place. The opposite of type A is type B. Type B never suffer from a sense of time urgency. Research has proved that only the hostility and anger associated with type A behaviour is actually related to heart disease. The chronically angry, suspicious and mistrustful person is at risk. However, just because a person is workoholic and impatient does not mean that he is unduly susceptible to heart disease or other negative effects of stress.

Community

These are specific to the locality in which you live or work. These include noise pollution, traffic congestion, lack of space, lack of sense of community, high crime rate etc.

Cultural

They arise from commonly accepted values, ways of living or expectations of people in particular roles. Racial, religious and sexual prejudice and discrimination, rigid expectations of certain types of behaviours from people according to their gender, class or status irrespective of their individuality, are some of the reasons for stress.

National

They are applicable to the country in which you line. More problems which cause stress can be government policies affecting defence, the economy, unemployment, public services, taxation and rates, civil unrest, national disasters, war and the threat of war.

International

These are the issues in which world problems affect you. Difficulties in understanding different values, politics, cultures, migration, war was and disasters in other countries, environmental damage affecting large parts of the entire planet.

Universal

Stress that apply to every single human being - these may include the experience of being vulnerable, accepting the frailty of the human body, having to sacrifice some individuality of function in a group, partnership or team. The transitions that must be made as you grow older, spiritual ambiguities, the comparative insignificance of the individual human to them, the universe, the inevitability of death.

Environmental Factors

Environmental uncertainty influences stress levels among employees in that organization. There are three types of environmental uncertainties:

(a) Economic Uncertainty

This is created by changes in the business cycle. Downward swings in the economy are often accompanied by permanent reductions in the work force, temporary lay-offs, reduced pay, shorter workers etc. These cause stress amongst employees.

(b) Political Uncertainty

If a country does not have stable political system then political threats do cause stress.

(c) Technological Uncertainty

New innovations can make an employee's skills and experience obsolete in a very short period of time. Computers, robotics, automation and other forms of technological innovation are a threat to many people and cause stress.

Synoptically we can classify the causes of stress under three broad categories as: (A) Environmental causes, (B) Organizational causes and (C) Personal causes.

(A) Environmental Causes

The environment, which include the state of the economy and predicted trends, has multiple and complex effects on stress. Environmental causes may include the following:

1. Economic uncertainties: Changes in the business cycle create economic uncertainties that increase anxieties for people about job security.

2. Political uncertainties: Unstable political system, political threats and changes can be stress-inducing.

3. New innovations: Computers, robotics, automation, and other forms of technological innovation may cause stress for employees. These innovations can make an employee's skills and knowledge obsolete in a very short period of time.

(B) Organizational Causes

These include the following factors:

1. Role overload: It occurs when too many tasks must be performed in too short a time period. This usually causes anxiety, frustration, a sense of hopelessness and loss of reward.

2. Heavy responsibility: The work load of the employee may not be heavy but it can have extremely important consequences for the organization and its members. These "make - or - break" responsibilities may confront employees with severe stress.

3. Role conflict: It result when a worker is given contradictory tasks or it also results from informal group forms being at odds with the formal organizational requirements.

4. Role ambiguity: It results when a worker has unclear expectations regarding what he should do or how he is going to be evaluated.

5. Job boredom: People with less challenging jobs have more depression and tension.

6. Interpersonal demands: Lack of social support and poor interpersonal relations can cause considerable stress.

7. Organization structure: Excessive rules, lack of participation in decisions, rigid controls might be the potential sources of stress.

8. Organizational leadership: It denotes the managerial style. Some managers believe in work culture of tension, fear and anxiety.

9. Organization's life state: Organizations grow, become mature, and at last decline. These life stages create different problems and pressures for employees.

In addition to these factors, poor physical conditions, inadequate authority, responsibility relationships, poor channels of communication, underutilization, poor job design can also induce stress.

(C) Personal Causes

1. Type A personality: Some people are more stress-prone than others. Type A persons are often susceptible. They tend to be impatient, competitive and they constantly remain under time pressure.

2. Changes in one's life: Changes can have a strong impact on a person's health. Some life changes such as getting fired or the death of a spouse are especially stressful.

3. Locus of control: Locus of control can influence experienced stress by affecting perceived ability to cope with stressful environment. Internals (persons who feel that surrounding events are largely under their own control) are more likely to be upset by threats to the control of surrounding events.

4. Cognitive appraisal: This means that stress occurs only to the degree that the persons involved in a situation perceive it to be harmful, threatening, or challenging. Stress is largely where we perceive it.

Health-Related Consequences of Stress

Just about any maladies you can think of have been linked to stress. The major health-related consequences fall into three categories: medical, behaviour, and psychological.

Table 5. Health-Related Consequences of Stress

MEDICAL CONSEQUENCES	BEHAVIOURAL CONSEQUENCES	PSYCHOLOGICAL CONSEQUENCES
* Heart disease and stroke	* Smoking	* Family conflict
* Backache and arthritis	* Drug and alcohol abuse	* Sleep disturbances
* Ulcers	* Accident proneness	* Sexual dysfunction
* Cancer	* Violence	* Depression
* Diabetes	* Appetite disorders	
* Cirrhosis of the liver		
* Lung disease		

Source: Based on J.C. Quick and J.D. Quick, *Organizational Stress and Preventive Management*, McGraw Hill, New York, 1984.

TYPE A AND TYPE B PERSONALITY

One dimension of personality which is getting attention both from organizational as well as medical researchers is the Type A and Type B behaviour profiles. A person exhibiting Type A behaviour is generally restless, impatient with a desire for quick achievement and perfectionism. Type B is much more easy going, relaxed about time pressure, less competitive, and more philosophical in nature. Some of the characteristics of Type A personality are given below:

* Is restless, so that he always moves, walks, and eats rapidly.
* Is impatient with the pace of things, dislikes waiting, and is impatient with those who are not impatient.
* Does several things at once.
* Tries to schedule more and more in less and less time, irrespective of whether everything is done or not.
* Usually does not complete one thing before starting on another.
* Does not have time to relax and enjoy life.

Type B behaviour is just the opposite and is more relaxed, sociable and has a balanced outlook on life.

Type A behaviour profile tends to be obsessive and managers with such behaviour, are hard-driving, detail-oriented people with high performance standards. Such managers have difficulties in developing cordial interpersonal relationships and they create a lot of stress for themselves and other people. They feel specially pressurized if they have to complete a task within a given deadline. The B persons, on the other hand, do put in extra effort in order to meet a deadline but do not feel pressurized.

Those persons who are classified as Type A have a strong desire and tendency to control all aspects of the situation and, if they are unable to control a situation, they react with anger and frustration. Because of their obsession with perfection, they are more apt to fear failure and, even if their work is good, they tend to underestimate the quality of their work. In the case of negative outcomes, they blame themselves more than external factors. A comprehensive identification of Type A personality is given by Karen A. Mathews as follows:

"The Type A pattern can be observed in any person who is aggressively involved in a chronic, incessant struggle to achieve more and more in less and less time and if required to do so against the opposing efforts of other things or other persons. The over manifestations of this struggle include explosive accelerated speech; a heightened pace of living; impatience with slowness concentrating on more than one activity at a time; self-preoccupation; dissatisfaction with life.

Research has indicated that such patterns of behaviour, as exhibited by Type A personality lead to health problems, and specially heart related illness. In contrast, Type B persons may be hard working but feel no pressing conflict with people or time and hence, are not prone to stress and coronary problems.

Type A Behaviour Pattern

Cardiovascular disease is the leading cause of death among adults in Western industrialized countries. Because Type A Behaviour was linked to cardiovascular disease, researchers made a significant effort in identifying Type A characteristics and situations that elicit this behaviour pattern.

Type A Behaviour Defined

According to Meyer Friedman and Ray Rosemen (the cardiologists who isolated the Type A syndrome in the 1950s):

Type A behaviour pattern is an action-emotion complex that can be observed in any person who is aggressively involved in a chronic, incessant struggle to achieve more and more in less and less time and if required to do so against the opposing efforts of other things or persons. It is not psychosis or a complex of worries or fears or phobias or obsessions but a socially acceptable – indeed often praised – form of conflict. Persons possessing this pattern are also quite prone to exhibit a free-floating but extra ordinarily well - rationalized hostility. As might be expected there are degrees in the intensity of this behaviour pattern.[23]

Type A Characteristics: While labelling Type A behaviour as "hurry sickness" Friedman and Rosenmen noted that Type A individuals frequently tend to exhibit most of the behaviours listed in Table 6. In high-pressure, achievement-oriented schools and work environments, Type A behaviour is unwittingly cultivated and even admired.

TYPE A RESEARCH AND MANAGEMENT IMPLICATIONS

OB research has demonstrated that Type A employees tend to be more productive than their Type B co-workers. For instance, Type A behaviour yielded a significant and positive correlation with 920 students' grade point average, the quantity and quality of 278 university professors' performance, and the sales performance of 222 life insurance brokers. On the other hand, Type A behaviour is associated with some negative consequences.

A recent meta-analysis of 99 studies revealed that Type A individuals had higher heart rates, diastolic blood pressure, and systolic blood pressure than Type B people. Type A people also showed greater cardiovascular activity when they encountered the following situations:

Unfortunately for Type A individuals, these situations are frequently experienced at work. A second meta-analysis of 83 studies further demonstrated that the hard-driving and competitive aspects of Type A are related to coronary heart disease, but the speed and impatience and job involvement aspects are not. This meta-analysis also showed that feelings of anger, hostility, and aggression were more strongly related to heart disease than to Type A behaviour.

Do these results signal the need for Type A individuals to quit working so hard? Not necessarily. First the research indicated that feelings of anger, hostility, and aggression were more detrimental to our health than being Type A. We should all attempt to reduce these negative emotions. Second, researchers have developed stress reduction techniques to help Type A people pace themselves more realistically and achieve better balance in their lives; they are discussed in the next section of this chapter. Management can help Type A people, however, by not overloading them with work despite their apparent eagerness to take an ever-increasing workload. Managers need to actively help, rather than unthinkingly exploit, Type A individuals because the premature disability or death of valued employees erodes long-run organizational effectiveness.

Table 6. Type A Characteristics

1.	Hurried speech: explosive accentuation of key words.
2.	Tendency to walk, move, and eat rapidly.
3.	Constant impatience with the rate at which most events take place (e.g., irritation with slow-moving traffic, and slow-talking and slow to act people).
4.	Strong preference for thinking of, or doing two or more things at once (e.g., reading this text and doing something else at the same time).
5.	Tendency to turn conversations around to personally meaningful subjects or themes.
6.	Tendency to interrupt, while others are speaking, to make your point or to complete their trains of thought in your own words.
7.	Guilt feelings during periods of relaxation or leisure time.
8.	Tendency to be oblivious to surroundings during daily activities.
9.	Greater concern for things worth having than with things worth being.
10.	Tendency to schedule more and more in less and less time; a chronic sense of time urgency.
11.	Feelings of competition rather than compassion when faced with another Type A person.
12.	Development of nervous tics or characteristic gestures.
13.	A firm belief that success is due to the ability to get things done faster than the other guy.
14.	A tendency to view and evaluate personal activities and the activities of other people in terms of "numbers" (e.g., number of meetings attended, telephone calls made, visitors received).

Type B Behavioural Pattern

The person with Type A behavioural pattern (TABP):

– Chronically struggles to get as many things done as possible in the shortest time period.

– Is aggressive, ambitious, competitive, and forceful.

– Speaks explosively, rushes others to finish what they are saying.

– Is impatient, hates to wait, considers waiting a waste of precious time.

– Is preoccupied with deadlines and is work oriented.

– Is always in a struggle – with people, things, events.

Conversely, the individual with a **Type B behaviour pattern** generally feels no pressing conflict with either time or persons. The Type B may have considerable drive, wants to accomplish things, and works hard, but a confident style allows him or her to work at a steady pace and not to race against the clock. The Type A has been likened to a racehorse, the Type B to a turtle.

Type B behavioural pattern is a name given to a person who is relaxed, patient, steady and even-tempered. He is opposite of Type A.

As cardiologists, Friedman and Rosenman observed numerous coronary patients, most of whom were Type A's. They described one incident that highlighted what individuals with TABP were like. An upholsterer, called to fix the seats of chairs in their reception room, told them that he noticed a peculiar thing about the wear and tear on the officer furniture: only the front edge of each seat was worn out. Friendman and Rosenman, after a significant period of time and being puzzled by their data, interpreted the upholstery phenomenon to indicate the impatience of their patients sitting on the edge of their seats to see the doctor. Type A's waiting impatiently in an office would tend to do such things.

Table 7. Typical A Type and B Type Personality Characteristics

	Type A People	Type B People
I.	Do things rapidly (walk, talk, eat, move very rapidly).	May be ambitious but may work steadily.
II.	Impatient with the speed.	May not always be impatient.
III.	Try to do more than one thing at a time (may think about one thing and talk about different things).	Plan and execute things which they feel are within their capacity.
IV.	Are tense during leisure time or rest hours and may even feel guilty of wasting away their time.	May truly enjoy leisure, forgetting their involvement in work or goals.
V.	Unable to appreciate things of beauty or nature that may relax mind.	Appreciate things of art and beauty.
VI.	May undertake more things than they can cope with.	May undertake manageable tasks.
VII.	May make nervous gestures such as tics, clenched fist.	May only show tensions occasionally, or signs of stress.
VIII.	Constantly evaluate their own and others worth in terms of number of things achieved and mostly neglect qualitative aspects of achievement.	May be more concerned with the quality of their work than quantity.

Cost of Stress

From a managerial perspective, each of the five categories of stress effects are important. However, withdrawal and non productive behaviours such as absenteeism, turnover, alcoholism, and drug abuse are especially troublesome in terms of lost productivity and costs.

Withdrawal. Being absent and quitting are two forms of withdrawal behaviour that can temporarily reduce job stress in some cases. Researches indicates a relationship between job stress and absenteeism and turnover. For example, one study indicated that over a 15-year period, absenteeism attributed to physical health problems increased 22 per cent while absenteeism associated with psychological health problems increased 152 per cent for men and 302 per cent for women.

A study for 175 hospital employees examined stress as a predictor of turnover. Organizational commitment, job satisfaction, and working conditions were unable to predict turnover. However, high levels of stress were a significant predictor of intentions to leave the hospital. The researchers concluded that employees with low stress levels had expectations of longer tenure at the hospital.

Alcoholism. Alcoholism is a disease characterized by repeated excessive drinking that interferes with an individual's health and work behaviour. The negative effects from drug and alcohol abuse are estimated to cost the United States $ 116 billion annually. Absenteeism, lower productivity, and accidents related to alcoholism are part of the cost to organizations. Experts estimate that approximately 9 per cent of males and 5 per cent of females in the U.S. population are at risk for alcoholism or serious drinking. Thus, an estimated 10.5 million Americans are alcoholics. Probably no one factor can cause alcoholism, which is a complex entity. Rockwell International Corporation, with 100,000 employees, placed the cost of alcoholism to its operations at $250 million. The Illinois Bell Telephone Company set wage replacements due to alcoholism at $ 418,500. To curb this cost, an increasing number of employers have been establishing alcohol control programs. Over 12,000 such programs are now being operated in organizations.

No correlations have been established between specific types of work stress and the use of alcohol as a response to stress. However, researchers have found that alcoholics have a high need for emotional support, make aggressive demands, show impulsivity with easy decision making, and engage in efforts at control by repression and suppression. Surprisingly, alcoholism is not always accompanied by deteriorating job performance in the early stages of the disease. But as the disease progresses, both quantity and quality of job performance eventually suffer.

Early identification of alcoholism is important because the prognosis for successful treatment is more favourable if treatment is initiated at the early stages of the disease. Managers can look for these signs of alcoholism:

1. Excessive absenteeism patterns: Mondays, Fridays, and days before and after holidays.
2. Unexcused and frequent absences.
3. Tardiness and early departures.
4. Poor judgment and bad decisions.
5. Sloppy personal appearance.
6. Marked increase in nervousness and occasional hand tremors.
7. Marked increase in hospital-medical-surgical claims.

These signs signal problems to alert managers, who must understand that job stress can contribute to a person's need for and use of alcohol. They should also realize that professional help needs to be applied early if the individual is to be successfully treated. Furthermore, although the use of alcohol develops in response to stress and serves to alleviate it, drinking can itself become a source of stress as the pattern of use progresses into alcoholism.

Drug abuse. As long as a significant portion of the American population takes drugs, people will continue to bring their drugs with them to work. Some firms, admitting that drug abuse occurs at work, use a variety of means to combat the problem. Drug-sniffing dogs search work areas at Mobay Chemical Corporation in Baytown, Texas; Humphrey & Associates, an electrical firm in Dallas, gives blood tests to anyone who has an accident on the job; and Sunkist Products Group of Ontario, California, requires employees who behave strangely on the job to take a urine test.These drug detection programs have their critics and raise serous legal questions. However, more and more organizations have been getting on the antidrug bandwagon, both for humanitarian reasons and because drug and alcohol abuse has an estimated cost of over $ 116 billion annually.

According to most experts, cocaine, crack, and ice use is growing faster than other forms of drug abuse. At least three widespread myths have contributed to cocaine's increasing popularity. Myth 1 is that cocaine is harmless. In fact, it can cause respiratory collapse or heart failure. Myth 2 is that primitive people have used it for years to ward off cold and exhaustion. In reality, the coca leaves chewed by Bolivian Indians are not comparable in potency to the power snorted by employees. Myth 3 is that cocaine is non-addictive. In fact, cocaine is the most addictive of any drug that employees abuse. Cocaine changes people who had no intention of being changed.

One of the causes of drug abuse is stress stemming from the job. Stimulants and hallucinogens (e.g., marijuana and cocaine), narcotics (e.g., heroin and Demerol), and sedative-hypnotics (e.g., barbiturates and Valium) are taken by employees across all job categories to relieve job boredom, excessive stress, and related work problems. To combat drug abuse, management has to first recognize that work-related stress can lead or contribute to drug abuse. Next, it is in management's interest to combat drug abuse with a humane and effective program.

Combating drugs requires managers to focus primarily on the effects of drug use on job performance. Other suggestions based on the experiences of companies fighting drug abuse are:

1. *Establish and communicate a clear policy on drug use.* Management must inform employees about the health and safety risks caused by drugs and the danger posed in the workplace by drug abuse. Management must also communicate that it is determined to obey the law.

2. *Reinforce the drug abuse policy.* High-level management must back supervisors who enforce the firm's drug policy.

3. *Anticipate the problem, and do not be surprised by it.* Management must be aware of the magnitude of the drug abuse problem in society, articulate its drug policy, and enforce that policy consistently.

4. *Maintain good relationships with law enforcement agencies.* In some cases, the police are needed to take action. They should be viewed as a part of the team fighting drug abuse in the workplace.

5. *Don't attempt to deal with the problem on your own; seek professional advice.* Most organizations lack the investigative capability and skills needed to investigate and assemble evidence on drug abuse.

Organizations that have developed and implemented antidrug programs have accepted the role of helping employees with drug problems who are willing to seek assistance. As well as being good employee relations, such a policy is also good from an economic standpoint. Retraining, hiring, and arbitration costs are avoided, and a favourable public image results from a well-run antidrug program.

Physical and Mental Health

Of the potential consequences of stress, those classified as physiological are perhaps the most controversial and organizationally dysfunctional. To hypothesize a link between stress and physical health problems is, in effect, to suggest that an emotional response is responsible for producing a physical change in an individual. In fact, most medical textbooks attribute between 50 and 75 per cent of illness to stress-related origins.

Perhaps the most significant of the potential stress-physical illness relationship is that of coronary heart disease. Although virtually unknown in the industrialized world 60 years ago, CHD now accounts for half of all deaths in the United States. The disease is so pervasive that American males who are now between the ages of 45 and 55 have one chance in four of dying from a heart attack in the next 10 years.

Traditional risk factors such as obesity, smoking, heredity, high cholesterol, and high blood pressure can account for only about 25 percent of the incidences of coronary heart disease. There is growing medical opinion that job and life stress may be a major contributor in the remaining 75 per cent.

Even this brief overview of the health consequences of stress would be incomplete without some mention of mental health effects. Arthur Kornhauser extensively studied the mental health of industrial workers. He did not find a relationship between mental health and such factors as salary, job security, and working conditions. Instead, clear associations between mental health and job satisfaction emerged. Poor mental health was associated with frustration growing out of not having a satisfying job.

In addition to frustration, the anxiety and depression experienced by individuals under a great deal of stress may be manifested in the form of alcoholism, drug dependency, hospitalization, and, in extreme cases, suicide. Even the relatively minor mental disruptions produced by stress, such as the inability to concentrate or reduced problem-solving capabilities, may prove very costly to an organization.

Managing Stress

Analysing the causes of stress can sometimes leave you feeling helpless. Since the problems you face can appear so unsurmountable. However, it is possible to reduce the stress in your life. First learn to make realistic action plans. Action the stressor ever which you can have the most influence. It is is your home or workplace that is affecting you make the necessary changes and improvements. You do not need to do anything at once; take it in small steps. Even with the most extensive stressor, you can do something. If national or international events or situations cause you to become stressed. You can raise manager contribute to a charitable organization which attempts to deal with the problem. This takes very little time and effort on your part but helps to reduce your feelings of helplessness and thus your stress. You do not have to do everything alone. Just talking to a friend, writing a memo or a letter to someone in power is one small step that also reduces helplessness. This will help to lighten your load and reduce the stress that is associated with coping alone.

When learning to cope with stress, you must balance the methods that you use. First, you must assess the resources you already have that can be used to manage stress:

Avoid the exclusive use of any one of the particular method. An over reliance on and overuse of any one means of coping can cause more problems than it solves. For example, sleeping pills or alcohol to help you relax can be valuable on an occasional basis, but daily use leads to sluggishness and addiction.

By the time you reach adulthood you will probably have developed your own individual stress toolkit, which is your set of coping strategies that work for you. You may find however, that organizational and social change, as well as your individual process of getting older, can render your will established coping mechanisms ineffective and this may happen before you realise it.

Balance the Methods

You need to have a wide variety of coping strategies in order to be able to manage each stressful situation appropriately. It is important that you aim to achieve a balance between various means you use. In the same way that specific methods can be over used, over reliance on certain types of methods can in turn, lead you to further stress.

For example, a person who relies too much on tackling problems head on but does not allow himself to express his feelings can become exhausted and emotionally distant even from the people he is supposed to be closest. Someone who is unable to nurture himself, but is expect outdistracting himself by helping other people with their problems, will find that he becomes drained and over whelmed by endless demands.

There are four most used categories of methods used in dealing with stress. These categories need to be balanced for you to effectively manage stress. Some of the methods listed can be used before, during or after a specific stressful event, and some are means of dealing with stress of life in general. Others can perform both functions.

Following are the basic categories to deal with the stress:

(a) Tackling a problem
(b) Active distraction
(c) Self nurturing
(d) Emotional expression

Use the categories to determine which type of stress control you are already practising and which areas you are weak and in need to develop further.

You may find that you are terrific at active distraction but rarely ever practice self nurturing. You may also find that you rely too heavily one of the areas and ignore the others. The secret of managing stress is to balance all of the methods using every type that is available.

Remember that once you have learned to balance the different categories of stress control you will find that the new skills enable you to:

(a) Raise your energy levels
(b) Develop your potential to take on more responsibility
(c) Use talents you may not be aware of
(d) Improve your relationships to work and home
(e) Initiate change which helps you to develop as a person

Ways to Deal with Stress

(i) **Tackling Problems:** There may be three ways to tackle a problem :

(a) Thinking

This involves analysing the problem, brain storming solutions, deciding priorities and goals, planning, obtaining information on resources.

(b) Utilizing Other People

This way involve you in asking for help or advice. It also calls for asserting your wants and needs. Challenging some one causing the stress can also lower stress.

(c) The Organization System

This way is effective to manage stress because it involves you to talk to people in power and making them aware of your views. You can also help services make a case for change, joining a political group can also be beneficial.

(ii) Active Distraction

It has been proved that if mind can be distracted into some other activity to a great deal stress is brought under control. Their are two most used ways to actively distract yourself.

(a) People

There are excellent mediums for active distraction. Converting topics not related to the source of stress and helping someone can be beneficial.

(b) Hobbies

These are potential distracters as they are activities that keep us physically and mentally busy. Physical exercise is also an excellent means of active distraction.

(iii) Self-nurturing

Self nurturing is the way you treat your body. Most of us in the stressed urban environment forget the importance of Self Nurturing which is so important for our physical relaxation and mental rejuvenation.

(a) Rest

Taking proper breaks, relaxation, exercises, getting away from the stressful conditions and situations, spending holidays and weekends with family and friends.

(b) Diet

Most of us feel that this body is a garbage dump and we can feed it with anything and everything. Eating proper meals, eating nourishing food.

(c) Luxuriating

Window shopping, going for movies, buying something special, picnics, spending time with friend, hosting parties & lunches are some of the way to luxuriate. A hot bath, a good Sauna, and having a good massage are also various forms of luxuriating.

d. Emotional Expression

a. Expressing Your Feelings Verbally

In stress it is very important to unburden your feelings to a friend, colleague or counsellor. Writing down your uncensored feelings, then tearing up the paper, joining a support group are helpful.

b. Catharsis

Having a good cry, letting steam off you without abusing anyone, screaming or snorting into pillow will help a lot.

c. Creative Emotional Expression

Writing poetry painting, playing a musical instrument, surging and dancing are excellent ways to keep stress at its lowest ebb.

Other Methods to Reduce Stress

Beside the above narrated techniques there are several other techniques which are helpful in reducing stress. Some of them are being discussed here.

RELAXATION

Just as stress is an adaptive response of the body, so is the adaptive anti stress response, relaxation. Herbert Benson reports that in this response muscle tension decreases, heart rate and blood pressure decrease, and breathing slows. The stimuli necessary to produce relaxation include: (a) a quiet environment, (b) closed eyes, (c) a comfortable position, and (d) a repetitive mental device.

The research evidence on relaxation is limited. Self-report assessments, the lack of comparable control groups, and short time periods of study are found to be problems in most studies. Until better research designs are used, skeptical managers will probably not pay significant attention to relaxation methods.

If you take the time to learn some simple relaxation exercises you will find that you will be able to combat the fatigue and lack of concentration that accompany stress. The physical tension that comes with stress is a waste of effort and energy. It dulls your minds and makes you tire more quickly.

Tension reduces the blood supply to your muscles, causing a build up of waste products and a variety of aches and pains. The circulatory system has to work harder to get the blood around your body and result in high blood pressure.

You may find that if you are constantly under stress and tension you begin to accept the reactions they evoke, and may find it difficult to notice their presence or effects.

Learn to Pause

The art of relaxation not only includes relaxing at the end of the day, at the weekend or on holiday, but also involves being able to pause frequently throughout the day. Busy people can get into the habit of over-reacting to stimuli, or it may be that you find yourself on the go all the time unable to slowdown when there is a lull or a break. "This is the road to burn out."

If you practice pausing you can prevent yourself being caught in this trap. Pausing can clear your mind, reduce some of your habitual tensions and help you make more efficient use of your time and energy.

Pauses can be taken anywhere, and need last a few minutes at the very most. You can use the 10 second pause at the beginning and the end of each task or a section of that task.

The five minute pause gives your mind and body the chance to rest and recharge; use it while travelling when someone keeps you waiting, during tea breaks, or at home after work.

Try to fit at least three five minute pauses into the most active part of your day. You will find it easier to summon the energy for the next phase of work and your life outside work, and easier to get to sleep at night. The last of these might seem, surprising, but short relaxation pauses during the day prevents the overstimulation of your systems that can lead to insomnia.

The 10 Second Pause

This can be done anytime, and anywhere. Make a conscious effort to have plenty of these pauses throughout the day.

1. Breath in slowly and deeply to the count of five expanding your abdomen as you do so.
2. Put both feet flat on the floor and your hands in your lap.
3. Breath out slowly to the count of five, maintaining the spinal stretch that happened as you breath in.
4. Let your breathing become normal, and then you can get on with the next task at hand.

The Five Minute Pause

Before you begin, try to ensure that you will not be interrupted for five minutes. Sit with your feet flat on the floor and your knees comfortably apart. Place your hands in your lap. Keep the base of your spine at the back of the chair, with your back upright and your head balanced, close your eyes.

(1) Take a slow deep breath in, expanding your abdomen, then slowly breath out.

(2) Focus in turn on earth part of your body paying particular attention to your head and habits. Imagine that each part is becoming warm and relaxed keep your spinal upright.

(3) Start with the back the back of your head, working behind the cars. Then relax the top of your head, forehead, eyelids, eyes, and face. Keep your slightly open and your tongue from touching the top of your mouth.

(4) Work down your throat, neck and shoulders, concentrate on your arms, starting with the right. Work around the hand, from the palm through each of your fingers and up the arm to your shoulder. Feel each part of your arm relaxing as you do so.

(5) Relax your shoulders, then work down your left arm and hand in the same order as you did your right.

(6) Now relax your back, abdomen, pelvis, buttock, legs and feet.

(7) Take one more slow deep breath in and out.

(8) Stretch your hands and feet and open your eyes.

Deep Relaxation

This takes considerably longer time than pausing, but should be performed at least once a day when you are under stress. It takes about 20 to 30 minutes and you need to be sitting or lying down with the whole of your body supported, preferably on a flat hard surface.

With practice you will learn deep relaxation of your body and mind. This will significantly enhance your mental and physical energy. It will also result in more restful sleep at night and even save time by reducing the amount of sleep you need.

There are a variety of methods for deep relaxation. They help you to focus your attention on various parts of the body and to instruct the muscles in that area to relax at a deeper and deeper level. Individuals develop different preferences, one method may help you to relax more than others.

Initially using tapes can be a useful way of learning the skill. Eventually you will be able to do it without the tape. Ensure that any commercially produced tape has voice and background music that you find soothing. Alternatively, you can make your own relaxation tape.

To do this expand and write down the five minute pause exercise as if it were a script. Tell yourself what to do step by step. Have the entire sequence repeated three times. Ask someone whose voice you find relaxing to tape record your script, reading it more and more slowly as he progresses. Arrange for your favourite relaxing music to be recorded in the background.

Remember

Practice your relaxation techniques and gradually build up the time you spend using them. Like most other methods of dealing with stress relaxation needs to be practised to achieve a level of skill. At first use the techniques during periods when you are not feeling particularly stressed. People who are very stressed often complain that they have no time to practice relaxation. However, relaxation exercises can save your time, you will be more energetic and efficient as a result.

Using Emotional Energy to Manage Stress

All forms of stress have an emotional element, but the emotional energy created by stress can be used to your advantage. Emotions are resources which when used with understanding and skill, will have a positive effect.

First of all it is important to distinguish between thought, intuition, sensations and emotions. You will find that the word feeling is often used to apply to these four distinct aspects of human functioning.

When you intention is to communicate emotions, but you end up talking about thought, intuition or sensation. You will probably cross message with the person you are addressing.

Emotional skills

Emotional skills can be learned and developed. There is a common misconception that once a person reaches a state of 'maturity' they have learned all they can about emotions. However, just as you can develop new technical or intellectual skills you can go on building your emotional skills. These skills include:

(A) Control

Emotional control is an essential skill. There are many occasions when you need to hold back rather than hurt someone or control your emotions during times of stress:

1) Learn beathing, relaxing and meditating techniques so that when you are under stress you can easily use them to control your emotions and responses.
2) Remove yourself from the stressful situation to collect yourself.
3) Focus on the positive aspects of what is going on, even if they are minor problems.

(B) Awareness

This includes being aware of your own emotions and the extent to which they can influence behaviour. Awareness is essential so that you can selectively control emotions rather than part of blanket repression on all of them or express them too freely. This leaves room for choice about expressing emotions and using them as a resource:

(1) Accept that you are allowed to have emotions.

(2) Notice the areas of tension in your body. They will often help you realise how you are really feeling.

(3) Realise that you can feel more than one emotion at a time and that these emotions may be contradictory.

(4) Notice how particular emotion affects your actions.

(C) Communications

Self disclosure helps to build trust in relationship. It includes taking the risk of sharing positive feelings, revealing your emotional vulnerability, and giving constructive criticism.

(1) Practice finding works that describe what and how you are feeling.

(2) Start lightly preparing your ordinary conversation with words which describe pleasant feelings and mildy difficult ones.

(3) Share some of your warm emotions with other people.

(4) When you feel vulnerable, ask some one just to listen while you get a problem off your chest. Explain that you do not expect them to find a solution or say anything in particular.

(5) When your feel uncomfortable with someone, tell them how you feel.

(6) Take an interest in how other people feel but do not probe farther than the level corresponding to your own willingness to make parallel revealations about yourself. Do not give advice unless you are asked for it. Listen, do not criticise when someone is talking about his/her feelings.

(D) Catharsis

As a skill, this is a controlled process of letting go. You are aware of what you are doing and choosing to do it safely at the appropriate time and place. It is also called emotional release or letting off steam.

(1) Pick an appropriate time and place to let off your steam cathartically.

(2) If you are not used to catharsis, carry out very short periods at first, using control techniques to get yourself out of it each time.

(3) Go through the motion of some of the cathartic techniques even if they do not feel spontaneous. Being in control of letting go is a skill which needs practice.

(4) Scream and shout into a pillow, or shout loud if you will not be overheard, when you are feeling most pent up.

(5) Come up with cracked crockery in an easily accessible place. Get it out and smash it mostly, when you feel pent up.

(E) Transformation

This is the transformation of the energy of emotions into constructive thought or action. It is often called transmutation– a name that comes from the days of Alchemy the attempt to turn base metal into gold.

(1) Move around physically to unblock your energy, then proceed to do something constructive. For example, if worrying about a report, go for a brisk walk, then start it immediately.

(2) Pour out your feelings into something creative.

(3) Gradually elevate your body fitness, you can then use vigorous exercise to do something useful when under stress.

(4) Learn deep meditation skills in which you can change the feelings into creative ideas.

Exercise

Epidemiological studies indicate that physically inactive individuals have a higher incident of heart attacks and death than do active individuals. Sachs and Buffone have compiled a bibliography of over 1,000 references pertaining to the psychology of exercise. Most of the studies claim that exercise reduces depression, anxiety, and phobias. In general, evidence that exercise buffers the negative impact of stress comes from three sources; anecdotal reports, negative impact of stress comes from three sources; anecdotal reports, controlled laboratory studies, and a limited number of cross-sectional studies.

Researchers have concluded that exercisers are loss stressed and tense, more self - confident, and more optimistic. Folkins conducted a randomised study of exercise in which he assigned subjects to an exercise or a control group, paying careful attention in both groups to issues of compliance. Both groups met three times weekly for 12 weeks. The exercise group showed a significant decease in levels of stress and depression. The emphasis on compliance may have been a crucial ingredient in this study's findings. One of the problems found in many exercise studies is that control subjects frequently drop in to exercise centres and exercise even though they were assigned a different activity. This makes measurement of treatment effects more difficult.

Although it seems reasonable to assume that exercisers are less stressed and depressed and have higher morale than non-exercisers caution in necessary. In available studies on exercise, subjects have rarely been randomly assigned to the various treatment groups. Also, exercise is usually administered or initiated with a great deal of enthusiasm and high expectations. Is it the exercise or the enthusiasm and expectations that contribute to improvements?

Humour

Is laughter the best response to stress? Some research indicates that humour is used by children to handle stressful home life, that professional comedians come from family backgrounds filled with uncertainty and tension, and that laughter may be a good therapy for combating some illness.

A longitudinal study examined the development of humour in children. The children who laughed the most were those who had been exposed to tension and tough situations. In contrast, children who had been "babied" and protected from conflict had a less developed sense of humour.

Research also indicates that most professional comedians tended to be funny as children and continued this style of relating to people in adulthood. Carol Burnett, for example, had alcoholic parents who fought frequently. She describes using humour as a way of gaining strength rather than "buckling under" in her tension-filled home. Humour created a playful state of mind, helping her divert her attention away from the tension.

Norman Cousins used humour to help himself - recover from a serious illness. He was hospitalised for a rare, crippling disease of the connective tissue, from which he was told he would not recover. Working with a cooperative physician, he checked out of the hospital and into a hotel room. For several months, he consumed vitamin C and for hours every day watched old "Candid Camera" films and other belly-laugh-filled movies. He recovered from the incurable disease.

Humour therapy surpasses all others of its kind in the management of stress. Those who laugh a lot even at themselves are less prone to getting subjugated to stress. It could, therefore, be safely suggested that people should find some time to be with peers and friends, with whom they can interact freely without any constraints. These are people whose legs you can pull and who can pull your legs without being offended or misunderstood. This would be a circle beyond the circumscribed boundaries. Some joint picnics with families, some social activity, or any other similar pursuit is always useful.

A joke book or a book of amusing statements as a constant companion, is a very effective medicine. Some of these you may even remember and quote. Some such examples are as under:

"A hospital is a place where a nurse wakes you up, to give you a sleeping pill."

"Marriage is not even a lottery .... In a lottery, you at least have a chance."

"Love is like a football game, you don't score a goal always, but you do often get kicks."

"If someone calls you a donkey ignore him, if two call you a donkey, check your hoof-prints and if three call you a donkey get a saddle."

"The young girl made a lasting impression on me. The doctors say, the scars will never disappear."

Jokes transport your mind from a state of stress to a state of ecstasy. You forget your problems and even though the phenomenon is momentary it exerts, a lasting influence on your nerves at the sub - conscious level, which provides great relief to a troubled mind.

Humour as a therapy acts in following manner:

(a) it enables you to forget your worries

(b) it provides a fly-over for crossing the road of stress

(c) it unconsciously soothes the nerves

(d) it cures stress at the sub-conscious level

(e) it elevates you to a sublume state, much above the mundane one of worry, tension, stress.

Is it then not worth trying this simple, inexpensive, and unprescribed, self-administered therapy?

Biofeedback

While a great deal of public interest in biofeedback has been triggered in recent years, very few people actually use biofeedback devices at home or in the office. In reality, there is nothing new about biofeedback – it has been around as long as humans have. Every time you take your pulse, check your breathing rate, or place your hand on your forehead to see if you have a fever, you are using biofeedback. What is relatively new is the instrumentation, the machines that monitor bodily processes and give us information about them.

Research suggests that biofeedback may have an important role in stress management for at least two reasons. First, it helps demonstrate to the user that physiological responses can actually be voluntarily controlled and that stress does, in fact, elicit physiological responses. Second, it provides reinforcement for the user regarding progress made over time.

The potential role of biofeedback as an individual stress management technique can be seen from the bodily functions that can, to some degree, be brought under voluntary control; brain waves, heart rate, muscle tension, body temperature, stomach acidity, and blood pressure. Most, if not all, of these processes are affected by stress. The potential of biofeedback, then, is its ability to help induce a state of relaxation and restore bodily functions to a non-stressed state. One advantage of biofeedback over non-feedback techniques is that it gives precise data about body functions. By interpreting the feedback, individuals know how high their blood pressure is, for example, and through practice discover means of lowering it. When they are successful, the feedback provides instantaneous information to that effect.

As an individual stress management strategy, biofeedback not only offers some advantages but also has some disadvantages. On the positive side, a growing body of research points to its effectiveness in a wide variety of applications. Biofeedback training has been useful in reducing anxiety, lowering stomach acidity and thus reducing the likelihood ulcer formation, controlling both tension and migraine headaches, reducing stress-related hypertension, modifying Type A behaviour, and in general reducing negative physiological manifestations of dysfunctional stress. James Manuso reported on organizational applications of biofeedback at the Equitable Life Assurance Company. Employees suffering from chronic tension headaches and anxiety due to stress overload were given nine weeks of biofeedback training in the company's facility. Among the positive outcomes reported by Manuso were a 50 percent reduction in headaches, a decrease (from 18 per cent to 14 per cent) in daily time lost due to stress symptoms, and an 80 per cent reduction in visits to the health centre for stress-related problems during a year.

On the negative side, however, biofeedback requires the purchase of equipment, which comes in great variety - much of it of questionable accuracy and reliability. Further complicating matter is the wide variation in equipment price, with little apparent association between price and quality at least at the lower end of the price scale. While feedback trainers can be purchased at prices ranging from $ 400 is severely lacking in sensitivity and accuracy. (One company sells a "biofeedback trainer" for $ 2.95; it is nothing more than a plastic mood ring.) Individuals interested in biofeedback should proceed carefully in the selection of instrumentation.

Bio feed-back Imaging

The technique has been developed by Ms. Thrity Engineer, a Surrey psychologist whose public lectures were reported in 'The Hindustan Times' on January 6, 1996.

She has attempted to further the ancient Indian philosophy and subsequently developed a therapy based on the '*Chakras*' or nodal points in human body which she calls 'the wheels of light.' It may however be stated that what has now been scientifically substantiated and proved was in fact known to Indians in ancient times. In her work she has taken into cognisance the researches done by *Nicola Tesla* (1891) *Seymon and Valentina* in 1930s with Kirlian Photography and more recently by *Dr. Valorie Hunt* at UCLA. These researches have proved the existence of energy radiations from different centres in the human body which cannot be seen with the naked eye.

The interpretation of colours in the energy field is also based on Chakras. Each colour is related to and connected with an energy centre. Each Chakra effects the physical, mental, emotional and spiritual aspects of a person in a different way because each person is a different personality.

She (Ms. Engineer) calls herself a teacher of life enhancement. She believes that self-understanding is the key for understanding the world around. For example, *anger is not important but the causes leading to it are and they need introspection because the real help lies within.* One has, therefore, to discover how one handles emotions and how one uses his potentials to coordinate and balance the good and the evil.

According to the approach of Bio-feedback Imaging, it enables the ego to get straight to the truth.

A specially devised polaroid camera-attached sensor is used. The patient puts the hand on the sensor, which picks up bio-feedback parameters. The computer then processes the information and sends it to the camera, which produces an instant photograph giving visual evidence of a unique energy field. This yields valuable diagnostic clues to proceed ahead with tackling the disease.

Meditation

When you think of successful executives at work, what picture comes to mind? Most of us would probably conjure up an image of someone on three phones at once, surrounded by important papers, or something similar. Probably the farthest thing from your mind would be the image of someone resting calmly in a serene setting. Yet for a growing number of today's employees, this picture is quite common. At Symmetrix (the Lexington, Massachusetts, software developer), for example, many of the company's 125 employees spend as long as 20 minutes a day behind closed office doors quietly meditating. Rather than something that the company merely tolerates (after all, employees are paid to work, not rest), relaxing is a practice that it actively encourages - and has even paid consultants to teach employees to do! Moreover, this company is not unusual; others, such as Mariott, Polaroid, and The Boston Co. (an investment firm), have done the same.

What's going on in these companies is designed to help people become more productive, not in the traditional stress – inducing way, but by helping them cope more effectively with stress. One technique used in this regard is **meditation,** the process of learning to clear one's mind of external thoughts, often by repeating a single syllable (known as a mantra) over and over again (see Figure 7-12). Essentially, meditation requires sitting quietly in a comfortable position, closing your eyes, relaxing your muscles, and breathing slowly. The trick is to not break your concentration by letting other thoughts enter your mind (if you do, experts say, you should just shrug them off and return to your mantra). Doing this once or twice a day for 10-20 minutes per session, is believed to be an effective way of enhancing one's capacity to work and to enjoy life in general.

Meditation evokes the auto-immune systems within the body, where the organs of the body are not only treated but also defended from other outside disturbing elements.

Meditation in a nut-shell reduces the degree of stress with which we may have been inflicted, neutralises the negative effects of this condition and finally restricts it from growing further.

Meditation imparts the ability to silence your mind and to isolate it from the external environment for getting in touch with your inner self. In this state, mind becomes quiet and body peaceful. This readies the mind and body for repairing itself.

The effects of meditation are similar to those of biofeedback techniques, without expensive gadgetry.

In a state of meditation there is an increased secretion of melatonin from the pineal glands. (These glands are often referred to as tranquillising organs of the body). Their level is also high in this state, as compared to low levels during the state of stress, distress, depression and suicidal ideation.

Melatonin is a 'peace-related' hormone as against 'Cortisol' which is 'stress-related.'

Meditation is ideally done

- ❑ by closing the eyes and thus blocking the passage of external visual interference
- ❑ by sitting in a cross legged posture
- ❑ by keeping the body and the mind free
- ❑ by intracting with oneself in solitude of mental thought and mental activity.

Only the investment of 20 minutes every morning and evening make all the difference between stress as a fact of life and stress as a way of life.

Transcendental Meditation (TM)

Executives function constantly under stress producing conditions, and that stress is costly. It takes its toll on health, productivity, creativity, and personal growth. It reduces mental clarity, energy and stamina, ability to deal effectively with people or to derive satisfaction from work.

As pressure mounts, dependency on alcohol, tranquillisers, sleeping pills, and anti-depressants mounts right along with it. Resistance to stress induced illness is lowered, and blood pressure tends to skyrocket. In short, stress is one of the most serious problems facing the corporate world today, and one which obviously demands a solution.

What one thing could bring you increased efficiency in your work, better relations with others, decreased tension and anxiety, increased intelligence and improved learning ability, faster reaction time, improved health, and perhaps a better tennis game? A miracle drug? No, but maybe twenty minutes of the Transcendental Meditation technique morning and evening.

Transcendental meditation may be like some ancient religious practice and indeed, it is an Indian technique that predates Hinduism. But a growing number of executives are finding it an effective way to reduce stress. And experts acknowledge its value. Unlike other stress relievers – pills, alcohol, sauna, exercise, or hobbies – TM can be practised anywhere, anytime, with no ill side-effects. There is nothing mystical about TM. "It has nothing to do with theology or philosophy."

Transcendental Meditation was introduced in this country by Maharishi Mahesh Yogi, a Hindu monk with a degree in physics. Since beginning a series of teacher-training sessions in 1966, the Maharishi has prepared some 4,000 TM teaches and established branches of the International Meditation Society (IMS) in every state.

What is Transcendental Meditation? As described by IMS's parent organization, American Foundation for the Science of Creative Intelligence (AFSCI), Los Angeles, it is "a process of establishing a physiological state of deep rest; it is practised twice daily for about 20 minutes, morning and evening, by sitting comfortably with closed eyes."

"TM works by providing the mind with the opportunity to temporarily cease the activity of the waking state, while cultivating a high degree of awareness and alertness," AFSCI continues. During this time, "the body carries out repairs and adjustments which are not possible during activity and not accomplished during deep sleep."

The transcendent state is one of deep rest with heightened mental alertness. The technique itself is simple and effortless. Twice a day, for 20 minutes each time, you simply assume a comfortable sitting position, close your eyes, and think of your "Mantra." The Mantra is not a thing, but an unspoken, one or two-syllable sound on which the mind focuses. Everyone's Mantra is different. "The Mantra is pleasing to the nervous system and leads the mind within," explains Earnest Robson, international vice-president of the American Foundation for the Science of Creative intelligence (AFSCI).

After a minute or two of focusing on your Mantra, your mind drifts and your body relaxes as if you were in a deep sleep. But you do not go into a trance; you are fully awake and can come out of the transcendent state at will.

A meditative technique originated in India which most managers might be expected to dismiss as nonsense – is gradually gaining acceptance in the business community.

The reason? Transcendental Meditation (TM) is becoming known more for its favourable track record as a problem-solver than for its off-beat origin.

And the claimed benefits of TM may literally be just what the manager's doctor ordered, in both his professional and personal life.

TM's proponents say the technique acts as a natural tranquilliser, reducing stress, stimulating the mind, and leaving the body free of potentially harmful drugs. The result can often be improved relations with co-workers and family, greater self-assurance, and the reduction of such stress symptoms as spastic colitis and high blood pressure.

Research conducted at Boston City Hospital by Dr. Herbert Benson and Dr. R. Keith Wallace, both of the Harvard Medical School, demonstrated a correlation between the practice of TM and reductions in several physiological traits associated with anxiety.

It also indicated a high correlation between the practice of TM and reduced drug abuse.

And the director of the M.B.A. (Master of Business Administration) program at a small Midwestern college contends that when people in the business community become mediators their productivity goes up. He says this effect is significant at the production-line level and "phenomenal" at the managerial level.

Our days are structured in cycles with a period of rest (night's sleep) and a period of activity (the day and evening). TM adds two additional periods of revitalising rest-making the entire structure of activity more flexible and more enjoyable.

Rest is the basis of all our activity. How well we perform depends on how rested we are. When we have a good night's sleep, the activity of the day is effective and almost effortless. When we have a poor night's sleep, activity is ineffective and very difficult. When we have no rest at all, activity is all but impossible.

So we see that rest is the basis of successful activity. Successful activity leads to fulfilment, and the automatic result of fulfilment is happiness. Thus, basically, our happiness depends upon the quality of our rest. TM provides the deepest state of rest yet measured, deeper even than sleep.

"The transcendental Meditation technique is a skill," Says Peter Muldavin, director of the New York AFSCI office. It's a skill of effortlessly minimising mental activity so the body settles into a state of rest deeper than deep sleep while the mind becomes clear and alert.

"The unique state of deep rest, which has been measured by researchers at Harvard to be twice as deep as deep sleep, allows the body to carry out repairs and adjustments that are not possible during activity and not accomplished during sleep."

"By gaining this uniquely revitalising state of deep rest twice daily, an individual enjoys enrichment of everything he does because he gains access to inner reserves of energy and intelligence that had not been previously available to him."

Synoptically we can say TM is simple, natural, easy, effortless, effective and fun, method of reducing stress. T.M. is not a religion, a diet, a life style, concentration and contemplation. It is not a difficult way to reduce stress.

IS TM THE SAME AS BIO-FEEDBACK?

No. Bio-feedback is process whereby a person learns to control some aspect of the body's functioning which is usually not under conscious control – for example, the heart rate, circulation, or brain activity. This is done by connecting some light or sound with what is being controlled so that the subject can see or hear what his body is doing, and learn to change the light or tone by changing the physiology.

There are two major differences between TM and biofeedback. First, TM is completely effortless. Everything that happens, happens spontaneously, unlike biofeedback, which requires conscious control and effort to produce some specific change. The changes in the body and mind during TM come without our willing them or learning to do them.

Second, and even more important, TM produces far more than one specific change such as more alpha wages. TM produces a spontaneous state of deep rest and alertness for the body and the mind. This shows up as an integrated physiological response that includes whole pattern of brain wave activity. The brain waves found in TM (including alpha) reflect the unique restful alertness that improves the functioning of every aspect of the mind, the body, and the emotions. It produces these changes simultaneously, in a completely balanced way.

Alpha waves are a specific frequency of brain waves, or the electrical activity of the brain, measured on the electroencephalograph (EEG) machine. Since some research several years ago connected alpha waves, of 8-12 cycles per second, with meditation, tranquillity, and subjective good feelings, biofeedback has been used to train people to produce more alpha activity. Although restfulness does produce alpha, alpha does not produce much restfulness. It does not really work both ways.

Yoga

Yoga is probably the most effective remedy for stress. Yoga has been used in our countries for centuries. Its usefulness has not been realised with greater enthusiasm in our country and abroad. The two fundamental principles of Yoga are:

(a) Satya (reality)
(b) Parinama (outcome/change)

Whatever we see, feel and experience is true and this is always changing. The mind, its activities and its purpose are central to Yoga. The techniques of Yoga are aimed at refining the mind which gives rise to many physical and mental problems, when it gets disturbed. Yoga is seen as a means of purification of the mind. This happens in four stages:

(a) Knowing the mind
(b) Refining the mind
(c) Directing the mind
(d) Moving beyond the mind

Yoga accomplishes these four steps for linking through 'Asanas' and 'Pranayam' which are its basic techniques.

(a) the body
(b) the breath and
(c) the mind

No doubt physical exercise and Yoga are remedies for many maladies. In regard to stress, they have a great preventive role to play. They keep stress under control by:

(a) improving the respiratory and cardiac functions and thereby increasing the power of resistance both by the mind and the body.
(b) engineering a better intake of Oxygen into our body, thereby providing the needed nourishment to our cells.
(c) channelising pent up energy to gainful purposes, thereby reducing the levels of stress.
(d) augmenting physical and mental capabilities thereby improving self confidence.

The other incidental outcomes of these pursuits are:

* greater self-esteem
* good humour
* better mental disposition

In spite of the above similarities, Yoga moves beyond physical exercises in many ways. It has the capacity of even stepping into the unconscious in its curative role. What is called 'Raj Yoga' is a sublime pursuit of being one with God. This discipline of Yoga among other things attempts the conquest of the 'Chakras' one by one to gain salvation. An incidental gain of this concentration on various 'Chakras' is the accumulation of energy to fight the externally inflicted maladies. Yoga practices are several but the following are said to be useful to cope with the stress:

Annamaya Kosha Kriyas: Traditional voluntary internal cleansing techniques, Yogasanas and Shavasana.

Praanamaa Kosha-Praanamaa: Five types of systematic regulated slow deep respiration with or without breath holding.

Manomaya Kosha: Meditation and devotional session.

Vijnanamaya Kosha: Practising joy under all circumstances.

Studies have revealed that Yoga has cured several stress-related diseases. Datey *et al.* (1973) and Patel (1973) showed that the practice of Shavasana effectively reduced the blood pressure. Yoga therapy has been found to be effective in controlling Asthma (Bhole, 1967; Anadananda and Varandani, 1975;

Melkote, 1973; Varandani *et al.*, 1973), and neuroticism (Kochan and Pratap, 1971 and Fochar, 1971). Yoga, however, needs to be tried under expert supervision.

Time Management

Most of us are poor in time management. The result is feeling of work overload, skipped schedules and attendant tension. The truth is if one can manage time effectively, he or she can accomplish twice as much as the person who is poorly organised. Some basic principles in time management are:

(i) preparing daily a list of activities to be attended to;

(ii) prioritising activities by importance and urgency,

(iii) scheduling activities according to the priorities set; and

(iv) handling the most demanding parts of a job when one is alert and productive.

One of the major causes of stress for managers comes from time pressures. No matter how fast some managers' work and how much time they put in, they are still unable to get all their work done. One of the most effective ways of dealing with this problem is the use of time management techniques. Today many organizations are training their managers how to get more work in less time. Some of the most helpful guidelines for effective time management are as following:

1. Make out a 'to do' list that identifies everything that must be done during the day. This helps keep track of work progress.
2. Delegate as much minor work as possible to subordinates.
3. Determine when you do the best work morning or afternoon and schedule the most difficult assignments for this time period.
4. Set time aside, preferably at least one hour, during the day when visitors or other interruptions are not permitted.
5. Have the secretary screen all incoming calls in order to turn away those that are minor or do not require your personal attention.
6. Eat lunch in the office one or two days a week in order to save time and give yourself the opportunity to catch up on paperwork.
7. Discourage drop in visitors by turning your desk so that you do not have to contact with the door or hallway.
8. Read standing up. The average person reads faster and more accurately when in a slightly comfortable position.
9. Make telephone calls between 4.30 and 5.00 p.m. People tend to keep these conversations brief so that they can go home.
10. Do not feel guilty about those things that have not been accomplished today. Put them on the top of the 'to do' list for tomorrow.

No doubt without any hesitation one may claim that effective time management have a definite and positive effect on the following:

(a) Reduction in blood pressure

(b) Clarity in thinking

(c) Steep decrease in the consumption of tranquillisers

(d) Relaxed feeling in action

(e) Reducing tension

(f) Overcoming stress

Social Support: It is truism that people need and benefit from social support. Applied as a strategy to reduce job stress, this would entail forming close associations (also called net works) with trusted, empathetic co-workers and colleagues who are good listeners and confidence builders. These friends are there when needed and provide support to get the person through stressful situations.

Some research indicates that **social support** reduces or buffers the adverse psychological impacts of exposure to stress and stressful. Interaction with another person or a group is sure to involve social support if it is perceived by the recipient as esteem enhancing or if it involves stress-related interpersonal aid. The term perceived support refers to a generalized appraisal individuals make in various situations that they are cared for and valued, that significant others are available to them in times of need, and that they are satisfied with the relationships they have.

The major social hypothesis is that it buffers the impact of stressors on an individual. However, findings have been somewhat inconsistent. Several studies report evidence of the buffering effect. LaRocco, House, and French reported that social support moderated the effects of stressors on health outcomes such as depression and somatic complaints, but they found no evidence of that effect on job dissatisfaction and boredom. Kobasa and Puccetti reported that support from the boss buffered the effect of critical life events on illness symptoms but that support from the family did not. Terry Beehr noted that work group support tended to increase the impact of role ambiguity on job dissatisfaction.

The inconsistency in results may be due to various methodological shortcomings. Much of the available research on social support has used a limited number of stress measures (e.g., role ambiguity and role conflict); certainly, other organizational stressors may be related to outcomes. Also, the size of samples used in most social support studies has been relatively small. Thus, obtaining statistical power sufficient to tease out interactions of typically small effect size has not been possible. Larger samples need to be studied. There is also the problem of accurately assessing who is providing the social support: supervisors, co-workers, friends, families, or strangers.

The best evidence to date on the importance of social support derives from the literature on rehabilitation, recovery, and adaptation to illness. For example, better outcomes have been found in alcohol treatment programs when the alcoholic's family was supportive and cohesive. Managerial use of social support research in reducing stress will be expanded as more organizationally based research is conducted.

Organizational Strategies to Manage Stress

Although people may be able to increase their own resistance to stress, they cannot by themselves eliminate many of its causes from their work environments. In other words, while they may be able to help minimize its effects, they may not be able to prevent stress in the first place (see Figures 7-13). For this reason, organizations can play a key role in stress management. In particular, they can adopt changes in their internal structure and procedures, or alter the nature of jobs, to reduce stress among employees. Although such actions will certainly not eliminate stress altogether, they can go a long way toward eliminating many sources of stress in the workplace.

An astute manager never ignores a turnover or absenteeism problem, workplace drug abuse, a decline in performance, reduced product quality, or any other sign that the organization's performance goals are not being met. The effective manager, in fact, views these occurrences as symptoms and looks beyond them to identify and correct the underlying causes. Most managers today are still likely to search for traditional causes such as poor training, defective equipment, or inadequate instructions; in all likelihood, stress is not on the list of possible problems.

The very first step in any program to manage stress so that it remains within tolerable limits is recognition that it exists. Any intervention program must first determine whether stress exists and what is contributing to its existence.

Job Redesign

Job redesign involves enriching jobs either by improving job content factors (such as responsibility, recognition and opportunities for achievement, advancement, growth etc.) or by improving core job characteristics (such as skill variety, task identity, autonomy, and feedback). Enriched tasks will eliminate the stress found in more routine and structured jobs.

Selection and Placement

Certain jobs are more stressful than others. Individuals too differ in their response to stress situations. Individuals with little experience or an external locus of control, tend to be more stress-prone. Selection and placement decisions should take these facts into consideration. Obviously, while management should not restrict hiring to only experienced individuals with an internal locus, such individuals may adapt better to high stress jobs and perform those jobs more effectively.

CHANGES IN THE NATURE OF JOBS

Careful attention to the nature of specific jobs can also reduce stress. For example, the stress resulting from boring, repetitive tasks can be lessened through job enlargement – efforts to broaden the scope of required job activities. At the very least, supervisors can try to put some variety into tasks that are by nature dull and repetitive, and to give employees opportunities to socialize with one another.

This is precisely the approach taken by Maids International, a franchised house-cleaning service operating in the United States. The company cannot afford the high turnover rates traditional in this industry, so they have attempted to improve conditions - and reduce stress - for employees in many different ways. As Dan Bishop, CEO of Maids International, comments, we focused the whole concept of the company on the labour. Fatigue and boredom are what burn people out. We tried to eliminate them." To accomplish this task, the company tries to train employees in efficient ways of doing various cleaning jobs so that the amount of effort required is reduced. And time for socializing is built into the schedule during the drives between customers' houses. The result: employees stay on the job for an average of nine months, twice the industry average of under five months.

Role Analysis and Clarification Employees must have a clear understanding of the job; they must know what the company expects and be confident that can fulfil these expectations. Stress occurs when employees are confused about their work roles or fear they cannot do their jobs. When excessive stress exists in a role, management can initiate adaptive responses such as these: redefine the person's role, reduce role overload by redistributing the work, and implement procedures for reducing stress when it occurs (e.g., allow the employee to have a meeting with those who are causing problems so that a solution can be worked out).

Each of these methods attempts to improve the fit between the person in a particular role and the job or organizational environment. This same logic is used in job enrichment programs. Job enrichment involves redefining and restructuring a job to make it more meaningful, challenging, and intrinsically rewarding. In the context of job stress, the objective of job enrichment is to make the job more stimulating and challenging. Assigning tasks that are intrinsically rewarding improves the fit between the jobholder and the job.

Company wide Programs

Stress management programs can be offered on a companywide basis. Some indicate a specific focus: alcohol or drug abuse, job relocation, career counselling, and so forth. Others are more general: the Emotional Health Program of Equitable Life, AT & T's Total Life Concept, the Employee Assistance Centre at B.F. Goodrich, the Illinois Bell Health Evaluation Program, and the Caterpillar Tractor Special Health Services. According to the National Survey of Worksite Health Promotion Activities, greater than 50 per cent of the general programs were in place for fewer than five years.

Originally, labels such as mental health were used. However, to get away from the connotation of serious psychiatric disease, companies have changed the names of their programs. Today, a popular label is stress management. Two prototypes of stress management programs – clinical and organizational - are in use. The former is initiated by the firm and focuses on individual problems; the latter deals with units or groups in the work force and focuses on problems of the group or the total organization.

Clinical Programs

These programs are based on the traditional medical approach to treatment. Some of the elements in the programs include:

Diagnosis. Person with a problem asks for help. Personnel in the employee health unit attempt to diagnose the problem.

Treatment. Counselling or supportive therapy is provided. If staff within the company cannot help, employee is referred to professionals in the community.

Screening. Periodic examination of individuals in highly stressful jobs detects early indications of problems.

Prevention. Education and persuasion are used to convince employees at high risk that something must be done to help them cope with stress.

Clinical programs must be staffed by competent personnel if they are to provide benefits. The trust and respect of users must be earned. This is possible if a qualified staff exists to provide diagnosis, treatment, screening, and prevention.

Organizational Programs

These programs are aimed more broadly, at an entire employee population. They are sometimes extensions of the clinical program. Often, organizational programs are stimulated by problems identified in a group or a unit or by some impending change such as the relocation or closing of a plant or the installation of new equipment. Such programs are found in IBM, Dow Chemical, Control Data, and Equitable Life.

A variety of programs can be used to manage work stress. Included in a list of such organizational programs would be management by objectives, organizational development programs, job enrichment, redesigning the structure of the organization, establishing autonomous work groups, establishing variable work schedules, and providing employee health facilities. For example, such companies as Xerox, Rockwell International, Weyerhaeuser, and Pepsi-Cola are spending thousands of dollars for gyms equipped with tread-mills, exercise bicycles, jogging tracks, and full-time physical education and health care staffs. One of the more impressive programs is found at Kimberly-Clark, where $ 2.5 million has been invested in a 7,000-square-foot health testing facility and a 32,000-square-foot physical fitness facility staffed by 15 full-time health care personnel.

STRESS MANAGEMENT PROGRAMS

Because it is not always feasible to redesign entire organizations or individual jobs so as to prevent stress, companies are faced with having to concentrate on methods of reducing stress once it occurs. One of the most popular approaches calls for directly training employees to minimize the harmful effects of stress. Systematic efforts by organizations designed to help employees reduce and/or prevent stress, known as **stress management programs,** have been widely used in organizations.

Some of these programs have involved extensive in-house training concentrating on many of the techniques we described earlier (e.g., meditation, relaxation, lifestyle management) as well as others. For example, the Equitable Life Insurance Company's "Emotional Health Program" offers a program in stress management to its employees that relies mostly on the physiological techniques described above. Company officials estimate that each $33 it spends on employees helps relieve symptoms that would have cost the company $ 100 in lost productivity. Similarly, B.F. Goodrich Tire's Group Learning Centre has prepared a nine-hour training program designed to help its employees learn how to identify the stressors in their own lives and to assume responsibility for changing their responses. Other companies, such as Liz Claiborne Fashions offer much more modest, forty-five-minute sessions during lunchtime (including one entitled "Wellness and Your Funny Bone"). Finally, because many companies cannot afford to create their own stress management programs, they often rely on pre-packaged programs by outside consultants, or using widely available off-the-shelf audiovisual programs on video cassettes (even the actress Morgan Fairchild has her own: Morgan Fairchild's Stress Management).

Companies that do not use stress management programs have other systematic ways of helping their employees. Many rely on help from their **employee assistance programs (EAPs)** – plans that provide employees with assistance in meeting various problems (e.g., substance abuse, career planning, financial, and legal problems). The Metropolitan Life Insurance Company (MetLife) is one company whose EAP has been actively involved in helping its employees reduce stress. It reaches out to its 42,000 U.S. employees by providing toll - free telephone consultation for those in need of help, as well as access to on-site and external medical and psychological professiohals. Although EAPs are as extensive as MetLife's, the cont-effective nature of such programs is making them an increasingly common form of worker benefit in today's organizations.

As we have shown, companies rely on many different methods for dealing with the problem of stress. The mere fact that so many organizations have been so resourceful in dealing with employee stress provides a good indication of just how critical such problems can be. (As you might imagine, such efforts are particularly important in the case of organizations whose employees are subject to high levels of stress on a regular basis).

Employee Assistance Programmes

Employee assistance programmes (EAPs) began appearing in organizations around 1950, when alcohol abuse was first addressed as a major problem. The initial EAPs used "constructive confrontation" as the method of addressing the problem. Today EAPs have a broader, more comprehensive approach. Counselling, confidentiality, and referral services are used for a wide range of problems – mental, marital, drug abuse, alcohol abuse, stress related.

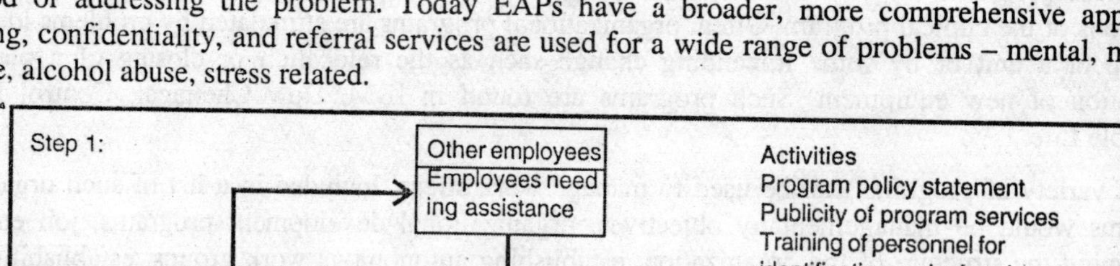

Fig. 12. EAP Model

Source: Steven H. Appelbaum and Barbara T. Shapiro, "The ABCs of EAPs" *Personnel*, July 1989, pp.39-46.

General Motors may have the largest EAP, its programme, endorsed by top management and union executives assists more than 500,000 employees in North America. Full-Time union representatives, physicians, and social workers develop joint union-management committees. Each year about 100,000 employees use the EAP for alcohol and drug abuse problems.

The EAP three-phase model presented Fig. shows the identification referral, and treatment phases of assistance. Note that referral can occur when a manager identifies a work performance problem or when as employee admits himself or herself to the programme.

An important aspect of EAPs is the confidentiality of information. In devising an EAP, planners need to specify who will have access to what information and under what conditions. Unless personal data is confidential and the guidelines are followed, employees with problems are likely to stay away from EAPs.

Hardiness

A characteristic that seems to distinguish stress-resistant people from those who are more susceptible to its harmful effects is known as **hardiness.** Actually, this term refers to a cluster of characteristics rather than just one. Hardy people seem to differ from others in three respects. They show higher levels of commitment, deeper involvement in their jobs and other life activities; control, the belief that they can, in fact, influence important events in their lives and the outcomes they experience; and challenge – they perceive change as a challenge and an opportunity to grow rather than as a threat to their security. Together, these characteristics tend to arm hardy people with high resistance to stress.

Some researchers propose that to improve the predictability of illness or poor job performance as a consequence of stress, one needs to separate individuals into categories: those who are and are not susceptible to illness under conditions of stress. The basis of this categorization is that (a) stress cannot be conceived in terms of an external event independent of the individual's appraisal of the event and (b) some individuals are more likely than others to appraise events in such a way as to evoke a stress response.

Following the logic of the categorization, Kolasa has advanced the notion of **hardiness.** She interprets hardiness as a personality style that expresses commitment, control, and challenge. Commitment is the ability to believe in the truth, importance, and interest value of who one is and what one is doing; control refers to the tendency to believe and act as if one can influence the course of events; and challenge is based on the belief that change, rather than routine and stability, is what people seek.

In a study illustrating this point, Oullette-Kolasa and Pucetti asked executives at a large public utility to complete questionnaires designed to measure their level of hardiness, the number of stressful life events they had recently experienced, and their current health. Results indicated that people classified as high in hardiness did indeed report better health than those low in hardiness, even when they had recently encountered major stressful life changes. Similar results have been reported in several other studies with people from different occupations (e.g., nurses, lawyers, police officers). Together, such findings suggest that hardiness is a useful concept for understanding the impact of stress.

The theme of the hardiness approach is that among people facing significant stressors (e.g., a nagging loss, a time deadline, a negative personal life event), those high in hardiness will be significantly less likely to fall ill, either mentally or physically, than those who lack hardiness or who display alienation and powerlessness in the face of change. Hardiness facilitates a form of coping that includes:

1. Keeping specific stressors in perspective. Everything is not a life - or - death struggle.

2. Knowing that one has the creativity and resources needed to deal with stressors.

3. Seeing stressors as opportunities instead of always as threats.

The most cited study of hardiness was the initial research of Kolasa conducted at the Illinois Bell Telephone Company through the use of a questionnaire, 100 Bell executives reported high levels of stressful life events and high levels of general physical symptoms and illnesses, while 100 other executives with comparably high stressful life events experiences were not showing the same high illness patterns.

In order to study the executives more closely, a personality survey was designed to assess all three hardiness components. The high-stress/low-illness executives did differ from high-illness counterparts on the three hardiness components. To examine the Bell executives over time, a prospective test was designed, and 259 executives from whom personality, stress, and health data had been completed earlier were studied for the next two years. Even when prior illness was controlled for, stressful life events (work and non work) led to an increase in debilitation, and hardiness predicted a decrease. The researchers concluded that a significant stress and hardiness interaction was an indication that being hardy is especially important for health when one is undergoing an intensely stressful time.

It is premature to conclude that hardiness is a unitary phenomenon. Critics have found that commitment and control have been related to health outcomes; the challenge subcomponent has not held up in a number of studies. Perhaps, we need to examine more closely the measurement properties of the three subcomponents. Until measurement and empirical issues are clarified and problems resolved, it is too early to recommend to managers that they maintain and enhance the hardiness of employees in various ways. We still cannot say with confidence that by addressing hardiness managers will be taking a step toward improving the quality of work life.

STRESS AND MEDICAL HELP

Medical help is absolutely essential to treat stress. A doctor or a healer is a must in each case. All treatments have but to be under expert guidance.

The formal systems of medicine or those called as naturopathic approaches both treat the outcomes of stress, as displayed through dispersant behavioural systems, as also those discovered through modern diagnostic devices. Their approach lousiest of tackling the after effects of stress.

However, getting to the root cause of stress and the treatment of those cases could provide a more comprehensive and permanent cure. This can be done only by an experienced healers through long sessions of head-to head dialogues with the sufferer, which calls for both time and patience.

Allopathy as an approach

Among all the systems of medicine 'Allopathy' is sometimes mistaken to be the only system and other systems are not upto mark.

The treatments in all the systems are based on research and empirical evidences of trial and error experiments.

Allopathy, however, has been the beneficiary of scientific research through latest tools and technologically advanced techniques. It has therefore, gained an edge over others in some sectors like:

* Precision of diagnosis
* Effectiveness in surgery
* Fire fighting approaches of treatment in emergencies
* The use of technological gadgets in treatment

In fact in the world of today, Allopathy has come to occupy the 'supreme' position in treatment of ailments among humans, animals, as also in the vegetable kingdom. The availability of technological gadgets have enabled it to acquire greater exactness in diagnosis and speed in the curing process. The discoveries based on experiments and inventions of modern times, based on scientific advances, have imparted continuous support to this system to further strengthen its base.

The other systems of medicine did not have that advantage and they are now increasingly using allopathic diagnostic approaches for prescribing medicines.

By way of comparison, it may also be said that in all systems of medicine, products of nature (herbs, minerals, etc.) are the main ingredients of medicines. Allopathy has even started the use of synthetic man-made cures for treating diseases and a host of other medicines of other unconventional systems of medicine.

Other established approaches to deal with stress

1. Homoeopathy
2. Ayurvedya
3. Unani
4. Chinese system
5. Tibetan system
6. Siddha system

Though much is known about allopathy, certain basic elements of other systems and the approaches of the heals are not widely known. Here are some of the salient features by way of a synthesis for their appropriate appreciation and a better understanding.

All these systems

(a) have a strong philosophical tradition

(b) couch the concepts of body and mind and their functions in terms of nature and its elements

(c) believe that health is not confined to the body alone but is also linked to the spirit and socio-cultural background

(d) pressure a 'person-oriented' approach rather than a 'problem-oriented' one. They take disease or sickness as not something related only to the organs of the body but also to the conditions of the mind and the spirit

(e) deem treatment as an art, based on the experience of the healers.

The healers in these systems too, have a concept of their own and it is also worthwhile to know about this.

(a) The health care professionals of these systems do not call themselves as 'doctors' but as 'healers' and have a great faith and a strong belief in the traditions they practice.

(b) They believe that they can provide a complete solution in sickness management.

(c) They are not very keen to look for external validity for their work.

(d) They believe that the healing systems should not only be confined to healing the sick but also be extensively used for transforming the environment, which exerts a powerful influence on health.

Role of Different Systems in Treating Stress

The treatment of stress cannot follow the same approach or logic as the one in the treatment of bronchitis or jaundice. The roots of stress do not lie in the body alone. The environmental situations play a more prominent role in precipitating the symptoms that overtake an individual and lead him to stressful conditions.

Stress does not need the treatment of only the outcomes of the ailment like insomnia but requires an in-depth probe into the causes. It is more the treatment of causes which automatically takes care of the effects.

In regard to ailment like stress the direction and the approach which the treatment has to follow is from 'causes of effects' and not from 'effects to causes', though some aggrieved effects may have to be treated first in emergency situations.

The holistic approach adopted by the naturopathic systems of medicine is proving to be highly efficacious in treating many diseases. They are also gaining ground in the west. The strong side effects, the symptom suppressing approach and the subsequent recurrence of the one treated diseases are coming to be the main source of disillusionment of people with the new and so called scientifically produced medicines. Even allopathic doctors are now suggesting to their patients to try the remedies of other systems.

Managing Stress Unconventionally

Some of the age old unconventional approaches for treating the disease are quite effective. Some of these are also dubbed as folk medical approach or spiritual modes of treatment and cure. In modern times people are increasingly turning to them.

One may accurately measure the blood pressure or determine the presence of a cancerous growth in a part of human body or the nature of bone fractures in an accident, but to diagnose the nature and degree of stress with that degree of confidence and perfection is really not possible. The tools and techniques incorporating the most scientifically advanced technologies can also often fall short of this desired purpose. It may therefore be necessary in this realm to deliberate on the other not so scientific approaches. These are no doubt available and ought therefore to be tried, with the help of experts in their respective fields. Some of these are being touched upon her as an "awareness" exercise and no more to enable the choice of the therapy which can best suit an individual need.

Magnetic Therapy has also been successfully tried in a number of symptoms related to Stress.

1. Insomnia:

The north pole of a round magnet when placed between the eye-brows of an individual lying in a resting position for 10 minutes on alternate days, before going off to sleep, helps good sleep after four sittings.

2. Hysteria:

The North Pole of this magnet when placed above the uterus and the South Pole on the back side of the body for 154 minutes, in twice a week sittings, has shown very encouraging results in four weeks time.

3. Lower Back ache:

The patient lies in a belly-on-bed position. The north pole of a round magnet is placed for ten minutes first in the middle of the back and then for five minutes each on either side of the spine in weekly sittings. This has shown good results in six weeks.

4. Arthritis:

Use of two bar magnets alternately with the north pole on two sides of the ailing part (say a knee), first from top and bottom for 10 minutes and them from right and left for another 10 minutes has succeeded first in providing relief in pain and subsequently in facilitating movement of the knee joint.

The above and some more ailments are amendable to the treatment of physical ailments which often have roots in the mind and cause or are caused by stress.

In the common cases of lack of concentration, confusion, and inability in taking decisions, magnets can be placed on different pats of the head between 5 to 10 minutes each time, once a week for four weeks for outstanding outcomes.

HYPNOSIS

It can be safely stated that eighty per cent of our problems are stress related and that hypnosis has been successfully used for effectively treating a number of extreme cases in this field.

Hypnotic suggestion enables one to buckle on the armour of determination and resolve to overcome ones problems. No one needs to fail who wishes to succeed.

Hypnosis attempts to remove the barriers between 'conscious' and the 'sub-conscious' thereby enabling the sub-conscious to make greater achievements.

In a hypnotic state, the body and the mind are in a stage of complete relaxation. Such a state is a state of great receptivity to constructive suggestions and these suggestions can help improve his performance.

Hypnotism is a therapeutic approach accepted by the British and American Medical Associations, as also by the Vatican and is being extensively used now.

In a hypnotic state an individual continues to be the master of his thoughts and it is wrong to say that he succumbs to the will of the person hypnotising him.

There are two basic conditions for the success of hypnotism as a tool for treatment: (a) thoroughness and (b) a determined refusal to allow any deterrent to the realisation of ones desire.

It is only practice that can make the hypnotic healer gain the power of easy coordination of the functioning abilities.

The talisman for the success of the healer depends on the development of the power of control over his potential for convincingly channelising the will of others.

Hypnotism becomes successful through five essential.

(a) the fixation of the gaze of the operator

(b) the execution of certain passes, which is necessary for the operator to know

(c) the delivery of a command or a suggestion in a tone of voice, filled with authoritative conviction

(d) the ability of the operator to concentrate on the suggestion, which he wants to impart

(e) the ability of the subject to assume a passive state, with concentration on the suggestion given and willingness to accept it.

For achieving success, the hypnotiser ought to divide the complicated whole of hypnotism into simplest parts and master each part successfully.

To produce a positive effect, attention must be focused on the desire to exercise the influence. This necessitates concentration which is closely connected with the optic nerves. This concentration can be created either with eyes closed or with a gaze fixed on something.

The common man's suspicious about hypnotism as a process of getting enslaved to the will of the hypnotiser is not based on logic. Hypnotism has been used for ages and can be used even now with great effectiveness in dispelling fears and in helping an individual to rise from pessimism to optimism, from helplessness to self-confidence, from inertness to activity and so on.

However, it needs expertise which is acquired through experience. It may be mentioned that it is not always necessary to go to somebody to get hypnotised. Auto suggestion is also a type of treatment which serves well.

Pranic Healing

The Indian Rishis, the Chinese Taoists and the Tibetan Monks have been using 'Prana' as an energy for healing. It was however taught and practised secretly for fear of misuse.

The World Pranic Foundation setup in Manila by Master Choa Kok Sui has evolved a 'no-touch-no medicine' healing system popularly known as 'Pranic Healing.' Details about this were available from the public lectures of Master Kok Sui which was put on paper by R. Nair in 'The Hindustan Times.'

Master Chao Kok Sui in his book 'Ancient Science and Art of Pranic Healing' published in 1987 has suggested a simple healing technique which can be practiced by one and all. The system believes that vital energy or 'life force' in the form of an 'aura' embalms the physical body. This aura is invisible to the naked eye but now stands fully documented by the high frequency Kirlian photography.

According to this approach, the energy rests in 'Chakras' (vital organs of the human body) and the 'Nadis' (blood vessels). In a state of perfect health, the Chakras stay balanced and Nadis (Ida, Sushmana, Pingala) free flowing. Any imbalance caused by (a) under activation or (b) over activation or (c) depletion or (d) congestion of Chakras or (e) blocks in the Nadis causes indisposition.

The Pranic healer scans the aura (Some can sense it while others can even see it) to check the condition of the Chakras and Nadis. In this process – the energy leaks from the Chakras and detected and sealed, besides cleaning the Chakras and Nadis by removing the diseased energy and replacing it with fresh vital energy. This energy for healing is obtained from three known vital elements – air, sun, earth and the fourth elements is the divine 'Prana.'

If your knee is aching with pain exposc it to Sunlight through a red coloured cellophane paper for 20 minutes a day for a week and you get relieved of pain.

In case of depression, red light is used for stepping up metabolism. A person is kept in a closed room with red light for 15 minutes a day for 10 days.

A hyperactive person should be subjected to a combination of blue and white light.

Heliotherapy takes 10 days to show results. Gems take longer.

Quarts crystals are also used to balance the aura around a person.

The medicinal uses of colours stand accepted by both allopaths and nature curers. When a new born develops jaundice it is put under white light. The white light penetrates the skin and destroys the excess 'Billirubin' which is causing Jaundice.

It is also said that wearing rich colours each day keeps one in harmony with nature. Pursuing this theory the astrologers suggest the following:

Monday	⟷	White
Tuesday	⟷	Red
Wednesday	⟷	Green
Thursday	⟷	Yellow or Brown
Friday	⟷	White
Saturday	⟷	Black or Blue
Sunday	⟷	Red

The colours do exert a powerful influence on body metabolism. Their use constitutes an important aspect of naturo-therapy.

Gem Therapy

Wearing gems too is considered to be a valuable way of healing, though that is a slow process.

Gem therapy has an ancient origin and gems have been used quite successfully to ward off the evil influences of the stars. They are normally prescribed by astrologers.

Taking a cue from the beneficial influences of the gems, some naturopaths are also now using them, for the treatment of poor health conditions or for improving health further.

Of course, an expert will surely have to be consulted and an astrologer too for a second opinion in the wearing of gems.

One specific condition in the use of gems which is commonly prescribed is that the stone concerned should come directly in contact with the body to show results. Furthermore, some gems are recommended to be worn on different parts of the body. The rainbow symbolising colours of the stones also stand clustered and classified for producing a certain effects some examples of which are given in Table 8.

Acupuncture

This is an established system offering treating treatment of diseases through the nerve centres in the body related to them.

On the basis of the diagnosed symptoms, a conclusion about the ailment is reached. The related nerve center is then identified for treatment.

At these identified spots, sterlised needles are pricked. They are allowed to remain pricked for sometime and they are then lifted back. Sometimes they are pricked again in the same sitting after changing their positions.

Table 8. The Rainbow 'Vibgyor' Of Stones

The Rainbow 'Vibgyor' Of Stones		
Colour of Gems	**Names of Some Prominent Gems**	**Therapeutic Qualities**
Violet Stones	Amethyst Fluorite	Induce sleep and produce mental peace
Indigo Stones	Sapphire Azurite	Help treat mental ailments and disorders
Blue Stones	Sapphire Turquoise Lapis lazuli Acquamarine	Produce calm and sound sleep
Green Stones	Emerald Jade Malachite Peridot Aventurine	Generate good health and creativity and bring about a harmonious soothing influence
Yellow Stones	Topas Citrine Amber Golden Topas	Keep the balance of the nervous system
Orange Stones	Carnelian Orange Coral Orange Jasper Orange Jasper	Favourably influence digestion and circulation of blood
Red Stones	Ruby Coral Garnet Red lesner	Cure anaemia nutrition deficiencies depression and lethargy

This needle pricking therapy has a Chinese origin and is known for yielding very valuable results in curing a number of ailments.

Even soft placing of needles on certain parts of the body has been found to be effective. The placement of the round end of an allpin on the temple of a destructive child while sleeping for 10 minutes has been found to be effective in toning him down within a week.

Acupuncture has been practised in China for over 5000 years. Medical interest in this form of treatment has been continuously growing. The World Health Organization (WHO) too has recommended Acupuncture as a treatment for over 40 chronic ailments including arthritis and asthma. It is also reported that acupuncture is being used, as a supplementary therapy besides drugs by over 1000 doctors in the USA, 30,000 doctors in France and 5000 physicians in Germany. Thus, the therapy now stands as an established one and needles are pricked to augment the healing chemistry of the body.

Acupressure

This line of treatment follows a philosophy, similar to that of acupuncture with the difference that instead of needles, pressure is applied at different identified spots for curing the ailment.

Massage

The encyclopedia describes massage as "a systematic and scientific manipulation of body tissues, performed with the hands for therapeutic effect on the nervous and muscular system and on systematic circulation."

In India massage has a long history. References are available in the works of Charak and Sushruta. Description in ancient Indian lore also exists about specially designed wooden beds, carved to match the body contours for purposes of a massage. Details of herbal medicines for preparing oil for massages have also been indicated.

In oil massage which is still common in many parts of the world, oil is applied on the head, temples, ears, shoulders, chest, back hands and feet. These oils usually have herbal ingredients possessing aromatic odours. Massage then continues until the oil gets evaporated/absorbed by the skin pores. There is also a custom of an oil bath preceding the bath with water and an old saying is that if oil can give a new life to dead skin (leather) you can imagine about its effect on live skin.

Types of Massage

Scientifically performed massage assumes three basic forms:

- ❑ Palm and finger strokes. The pressure applied by the fingers and the palm and the direction of the movement of pressure gives relief. These pressures are bearably (hard or light) and they help in increasing the flow of blood to the heart.
- ❑ Compressing is the second type of massage. It consists of kneading and squeezing. It stretches tissues, muscles and tendons and helps improve movement by removing stiffness of joints and muscles. Fingers play the main role in this type of massage. Movements are often swift but not hard.
- ❑ Percussion is the third form of massage. In this, the sides of the hand, on the side the small finger and also sometimes the wrist come into play. The strokes are bearably hard. The strokes are provided to bring the stained muscles to a stage of rest and peace.

Beneficial Outcomes of Massage

Massage is first of all very comforting and it proves helpful in several ways like:

- ❑ Easing of mental and physical fatigue
- ❑ Ensuring good and sound sleep
- ❑ Removing the stiffness of muscles and joints
- ❑ Soothing aches and pain of the head and the body
- ❑ Speeding up the healing process following strain and sprain injuries
- ❑ Toning up the muscle fibres for peak performance
- ❑ Rejuvenating the body

Curative Effects of Massage

Massage possesses proven therapeutic qualities. By making the body to perspire, it helps the release of wastes and toxins for relaxing the body. Massage creates situations for body peace, which automatically helps in the cure of ailments like:

Rheumatism
Diabetes
Joint Pains

Massage also creates a glow in the skin which gives others a feeling of an individual being in good health and to the individual himself a satisfaction of being physically fit.

An improvement in eyesight has also been reported as an outcome of massage.

Role of Massage in Stress and Depression

The easing of blood pressure naturally makes massage a contemporary of Hypnosis and Meditation in managing tension, stress and other psychosomatic disorders.

Massage has been found to be very effective in treating stress when combined with aromatherapy (incense, perfume etc.)

Massage has both a preventive curative and a rehabilitative role in stress management. It is certainly better than steroids.

Reiki

This is a technique of transferring the energy existing in the air, sun, water and earth into our body.

'REI' means 'universal' and 'KI' means 'life.'

Buddhas Lotus Sutras were passed on by him to 22 of his disciples. These disciples were then known as masters of REIKI.

The process consists of concentrating attention on the seven chakras in quietude. It has been found to be helpful not just in treating diseases but also in arresting the tendencies related to compulsive habits, the non-satisfaction of which causes stress.

The approach is quite akin to that of Raja Yoga.

Soft Music

Soft music has been established as a therapeutic aid by the Heart Foundation of India.

Their study has conclusively demonstrated that soft music ensures quicker recovery after heart attacks and shortens the stay of the patients in the intensive care units.

Stress healers too have found from experience that soft music, both vocal and instrumental, acts

- ❑ as both a prevention and a cure for stress
- ❑ as a facilitator in dispersing the concentration of stress
- ❑ as an agent for increasing the body capacity for combating diseases by stimulating flow of beneficial body enzymes.

Music is more effective if it approximates the natural rhythm of the heart beats and is not jarring or loud.

A recent research study at the Louisiana University by Subhash Kak provides valuable insights about the functioning of the brain in a soft music atmosphere.

Aromatherapy

Kiran Manral has attempted an exhaustive treatment of the subject and many of the facts presented here are based on her contributions.

Though with an ancient origin "Aromatherapy" had receded to the background in the immediate past. It is however, picking up again.

It is said that Cleopatra's ship sails were dipped in rose perfume and evoked the desired mood and response.

Gatte Fosse has written a book on the subject. He claims that blood vessels could be reached through aromas to produce the desired results. Dr. Marcia Angel, Executive Editor of New England Journal of Medicine and the recent researches conducted at the Milan University as also at the Indian Council of Ayurvedic Research also confirm the therapeutic uses of Aromatherapy.

Research on the subject is also currently on. Dr. George Dodd (who lectured in Chemistry at the University of Warwick and who is called the father of the psychology of perfumery), has chemically identified all the human 'Pheromones.' He has concluded that the sexually compatible enjoy each others odour and that there is an odour conversation between them.

A group of experts have also devised an electronic nose with 12 electronic sensors which has the potential of coming up with an olfactory finger print of human pheromone samples.

Dr. Dodd has developed a synthetic human pheromone booster. He has also identified some families of human pheromones which correspond to the aroma of some food items. Some odours like that of Rose tone the capillaries soothe the nerves, normalise blood pressure levels and improve blood circulation on the surface of the skin to refresh a person's looks.

The essential oils of the perfumes used to have their origins in vegetative products. Now of course odours have also been invented and are even being produced synthetically. Those that are extracted from flowers are: lavender, jasmine, peppermint, rosemary, violet and yiang. Among the perfumes extracted from leaves are geranium petitgrain, patchouli.

Some fruits also yield perfumes like juniper from berries, myrrh incense and strax from resin and vetivery from roots.

Essences are basically composed of three notes – top, middle and base. The top notes include lemon, thyme and bergamot. As they evaporate quickly they uplift the mind and the body. The middle notes like camomile, juniper and lavender are moderately volatile affecting digestion, metabolism and menstruation. The base notes are those of marigold, camphor and rose which act as sedatives.

As these perfumes are highly concentrated they ought to be used after being diluted.

Situation Specific Therapies

It is always possible for an individual to get at least some inklings about his suffering from Stress much before it is formally diagnosed. The signs of Stress of stress become known to the patient as soon as they start the process of germination. These should not be allowed to grow into plants and trees to finally become difficult to up root. As has been repeatedly stated earlier the patient should not patiently wait for the severe symptoms to emerge to start treating them. Stress is acquired accidentally through otherwise insignificant situations but is cured through laboriously drawn long-term plans and so it has too be 'shot at sight.'

Consulting a therapist, may become necessary in some cases though it is not always imperative. There are certain therapies which are possible to be self-administered and no expert is necessary to be consulted in regard to them. However, if you start late and the disease has grown significantly, you should not depend solely on these and immediately start your leg work to reach the healer.

Such therapies which are possible to be self-administered on the basis of your personal discovery of some symptoms at the elementary stage, could certainly be tried with the confidence of gaining success.

These are briefly listed below. The symptomatic ailment is first given along with its antithesis. The antithesis describes the corresponding state of normal health in regard to the observed symptom of ailment which ought to be reached. This is followed by a suggested activity as a prescription.

Table 9: Ailment, Anti-thesis and Possible Cure Activity

Ailment	Anti-thesis	Possible Cure Activity
Disturbed mind	Peace	Soft music
Helplessness	Self confidence	Helpful social work
Pressure of restrictions	Freedom	Painting landscapes
Distraction	Concentration	Star-gazing
Unhappiness	Happiness	Do things that give happiness
Over-work	Leisure	Read joke books or watch a comedy
Monotony	Variety	Take on a creative hobby
Annoyance	Cordiality	Socialise
Lethargy	Activity	Play with children
Wavering thoughts	Firmness	Play chess

Ailment, Anti-thesis and Possible Cure Activity

Stress in the modern world is like synthetic products. It is created easily but takes a long time to be destroyed. It needs only the determination on the part of the sufferer to get over their disturbances. The determination yields perseverance and perseverance yields cure. After initial training some of these cures can also be practised by the patients themselves.

Pray do not drum-beat your fears, apprehensions, and/or disabilities. You could and rather should confide only in the confidants who you are sure will not relay and broadcast the news.

As your body movements betray you, adopt outward postures of hope, confidence and determination. Allan Pease, the New York Behavioural Expert and the author of 'How to Use Body Language for Success and Love' suggests some very useful behaviour patterns for boosting ones image.

1. The hand on hips stance though it may give an aggressive stance could easily convey to others that you are confident and ready for picking up the challenge. A lean forward with hands on your knees while sitting, also conveys the same idea.
2. Yet another signal of dominance and superiority could be displayed by showing your thumbs be they over the pockets, belts or jackets.
3. Always be the first to extend your hand to greet others. Such a use of "palm power" successfully conveys the impression of being in control.
4. Move away from your regular seat and lean on something that belongs to the other person, an almirah or a chair. (Do not lean on other persons' table as these are bad manners).
5. Keep off from displaying any signs of anxiety, diffidence or fear in the course of a conversation, by frequently touching your nose, rubbing your ears and eyes, scratching your neck etc. These convey signals of impatience and reduce your confidence in yourself.
6. Fiddling with a watch or a bracelet or hand bag or with anything else also reveals lack of confidence. Another powerful negative signal of lack of confidence is offered by the stance of crossing arms.

These postures could successfully neutralise your anxiety or diffidence and earn for you the confidence of the others in you, while restoring your own confidence in yourself.

REFERENCES

A.M. Pines, E. Aronson and D. Kufru, *Burnout: From Tedium to Personal Growth*, W.H. Freeman, New York, 1981.

Andrew D. Szilagyi and Marc Wallace, Organizational Behaviour and Performance, Scott Foresman and Company, Glenview, Illions, 1980, pp. 219-220.

B. Brown, New Mind, New Body (New York: Harper & Row, 1974).

B.H. Gottlieb, *Social Support Strategies,* Sage Publications, Beverly Hills, Calif. 1983.

C. Folkins, "Effects of Physical Training on Mood," *Journal of Clinical Psychology*, April 1976, pp. 385-90.

C. Maslach, Burnout: *The Cost of Caring*, Prentice Hall, Englewood Clipps, N.J., 1982.

D.C. Ganster, M.R. Fusiler, and B.T. Mazis, "Role of Social Support in the Experience of Stress at Work," *Journal of Applied Psychology*, February 1986, pp. 102-10.

Delores A. Rumpel, "Motivating Alcoholic Workers to Seek Help," *Management Review*, July 1989, pp. 37-39.

French and Caplan, *Organizational Stress and Individual Strain.*

G. E. Schwartz, "Stress Management in Occupational Settings," in *Managing Health Promotion in the Workplace*, ed. R.S. Parkinson *et al.* (Palo Alto, Calif.: Mayfield Publishing, 1982), p.74.

Gregg D. Jacob and Joel F. Lubar, Spectral Analysis of the Central Nervous System Effects of the Relaxation Response Elected by Autogenic Training, *Behavioural Medicine*, Fall, 1989, pp.125 132.

Gregory Strayhorn, "Expectations – Versus Reality, Social Support, and the-Well-Being of Medical Students," *Behavioural Medicine*, Fall 1989, pp. 133-139.

H. Selye, *Stress in Health and Disease*, Butter worths, Boston, 1976.

Herbert Benson and R.L. Allen, How Much Stress is too much, *Harvard Business Review*, Sept., Oct., 1980, p. 88.

Herbert Benson, *The Relaxation Response* (New York: William Morrow, 1975).

Hull *et al.*, "Hardiness and Health."

J. Gaines and J.M. Jermeier, *Emotional Exhaustion in High Stress Organizations, Academy of Management Journal*, Vol,. 31, 1983, pp. 567-586.

J. Stelzer and R.E. Numerof, *Supervisory Leadership and Subordinate Burnout, Academy of Management Journal*, 31, 1986, pp. 439-446.

J.C. Finney, D.F. Smith, D.E. Skeeters, and C. Aurvenshine, "MMPI and Alcoholic Scales," *Quarterly Journal of Studies on Alcohol*, November 1971, pp.1055-60.

J.C. Latach, Coping with Job Stress: Measures and Future Direction For Scale Development, Journal of Applied Psychology, Vol. 71, 1986, pp.377 - 385.

J.C. Quick and J.D. Quick, *Organizational Stress and Preventive Management*, McGraw Hill, New York, 1984,

J.C. Quick and J.D. Quick, *Orgnisational Stress and Preventive Management*, McGraw Hill, New York, 1984

J.D. Kearns, Stress in Industry Priory Press, London, 1973.

J.E. Dimsdale, B.S. Alpert, and N. Schneiderman, "Exercise as a Modulator of Cardiovasculr Reactivity," in Handbook of Stress, Reactivity, and Cardiovascular Disease, ed. K.A. Matthews *et al.* (New York: Jon Wiley & Sons, 1986), pp. 365-84.

J.F. Kc Kenna, P.L. Oritt, and H.K. Wolf, "Occupation Stress as a Predictor in the Turnover Decision", *Journal of Human Stress*, December 1981, pp. 12-17.

J.J. House, *Work Stress and Social Support*,: Addison-Wesley Publishing, Reading, Mass. 1981.

J.M. LaRocco, James S. House, and John R.P. French, Jr., "Social Support, Occupational Stress, and Health," *Journal of Health and Social Behaviour*, June 1980, pp. 202-218.

Jack Stoltzfus, "A Soviet-American Dialogue on Alcoholism," *EAP Digest*, November, December 1988, pp. 26-32.

James S. Manuso, "Executive Stress Management," *Personnel Administrator* 24 (1979), p.23-26.

Jay. G. Hull, R. Ronald, Van Treuren and Suzanne Virnelli, Hardiness *and Health: A Critique and Alternative Approach, Journal of Personality and Social Psychology*, September 1987, pp. 518-530.

John M. Ivancevich and Michael T. Matteson, *Stress and Work*; A Managerial Perspective, Scott Foresman, Glenview, Ill, 1980, p. 215.

Johnathan D. Brown and Judith M. Siegel, "Exercise as a Buffer of Life Stress: A Prospective Study of Adolescent Health," Health Psychology, Winter 1988, pp. 341-53.

K. Albrecht, *Stress and the Manager*, Prentice Hall, Englewood Clipps, N.J., 1979, pp.33-34.

K. Helker, R.W. Swindle Jr. and L. Dusenbury, Component Social Support Process; Comments and Integration, *Journal of Consulting and Clinical Psychology*, 1986, pp. 466-470.

Karen A. Mathews, *Psychological Perspectives on the Type A Behaviour Pattern, Psychological Bulletin*, March 1982, pp. 293-323.

L. Moss, *Management Stress*, Reading, Addison Wesley, M.A., 1981.

Leonard Moss, "Partners for a Drug-Free Workplace," Across the Board, December 1989, pp. 22-31.

M.B. Sobel and L.C. Sobell, "Functional Analysis of Alcohol Problems", in *Medical Psychology; Contributions to Behavioural Medicine*, ed. C.K. Prokop and I.A. Bradley, *Academic Press*, New York, 1981, pp. 81-90.

M.H. Brenner, "The Stressful Price of Prosperity, "*Science News*, March 18, 1978, p.166.

M.P. Leiter, *Coping Patterns as Predictors of Burnout: The Function of Control and Escapist Coping Patterns, Journal of Organizational Behaviour*, vol. 12, 1991, pp.123-144.

Marjory Roberts and T. George Haris, Wellness At Work, *Psychology Today*, May 1989, pp.56 - 58.

Meyer Friedman and Diane Ulmer, *Testing Type A Behaviour and Your Heart*, Alfred. A. Knopf, 1984, pp. 3-4.

Meyer Friedman and Ray H. Rosenman, *Type A Behaviour and Your Heart,* Alfred A. Knopf, New York, 1974.

Michael D. Newcomb and P.M. Bentler, "Cocaine Use among Adolescents: Addictive Behaviours," 1986, pp. 263-73; Steven Flax, "The Executive Addict," *Fortune*, June 24, 1985, pp. 24-31.

Michael L. Sachs and Gary W. Buffone, "Bibliography: Psychological. Considerations in Exercise, including Exercise as Psychotherapy, Exercise Dependence (Exercise Addiction), and the Psychology of Running," 1983.

Michael T. Matteson and John M. Ivancevich, *The Coronary-Prone Behaviour Pattern, A Review and Appraisal, Social Science and Medicine*, July 1980, pp. 337-351.

Michail T. Matteson and John M. Ivancevich, *Controlling Stress in the Workplace: An Organizational Guide,* Jossey - Bass, San Fransisco, 1987.

Norman Cousins, *The Anatomy of an Illnes as Perceived by a Patient: Reflections on Healing and Rejuvenation* (New York: W.W. Norton, 1979).

Oullette, S.C. Kolasa and M.C. Pucetti, *Personality and Social Resources in Stress Resistance, Journal of Personality and Social Psychology*, vol. 45, 1983, pp. 839-850.

P. Astrand and K. Rodahl, *Textbook of Work Physiology*, McGraw - Hill, New York, 1970.

P.A. Thoits, Social Support Is Coping Assistance, *Journal of Consulting and Clinical Psychology*, 1986, pp. 416-423.

P.B. Bensinger, "Drugs in the Workplace," *Harvard Business Review*, November-December 1982, pp. 48-60.

P.E. McGhec, *Humor: Its Origin and Development* (San Francisco: W.H. Freeman, 1979).

P.M. Roman, and T.C. Blum, *Alcohol Problem Intervention in the Workplace: Data on Present Status and Future mplications. Alcohol Health and Research World*, Vol. 13, 1989, pp. 375-380.

R. S. Schuler, *Definition and Conceptualisation of Stress in Organizations, Organizational Behaviour and Human Performance*, April, 1980, p.189.

R.E. Mitchel, A.G. Billings, and R.M. Moos, "Social Support and Well-Being: Implications for Prevention Programs," *Journal of Primary Prevention*, February 1982, pp. 77-98.

R.T. Golombiewski, R.F. ninzenrider and J.G. Stevenson, *Stress in Organizations: Towards a Phase Model of Burnout*, Praeger, New York, 1986.

Rahul CAttano, "Public Opinions about Alcoholism and its Treatment," *Journal of Studies of Alcohol*, March 1987, pp. 153-60.

Robert F. Pritchard and Gregory C. Potter, Fitness Inc. Dow Jones, Irwin, *Homewood*, III; 1990, p.91.

Robert R. Holt, *Occupational Stress*, in Handbook of Stress, Leo. Goldberger and Shlomo Breznitz, Eds. *Free Press*, New York, 1982, pp.419-444.

S. Reynolds and D.A. Shapiro, Stress Reduction in Transition: *Conceptual Problems in the Design, Implementation, and Evaluation of Worksite Stress Management Interventions. Human Relations*, Vol. 44, 1991, pp.717 - 733.

S.B. Philips and M.H. Mushinshki, *Configuring An Employee Assistance Programmee to Fit the Corporation's Structure: One Company's Design* In J.C. Quick, L.R. Murphy, & J.J. Hurell, Jr. Stress and Well-being at Work, American Psychological Association. Washington, DC, 1992, pp. 317 - 328.

S.E. Jackson, R.L. Schwab and R.S. Schuler, *Towards an Understanding of the Burnout Phenomenon, Journal of Applied Psychology*, No. 71, 1986, pp. 630-640.

S.H. Applebaum, "A Human Resources Counselling Model: The Alcoholic Employee," *Personnel Administrator*, August 1982, p.35.

Salvatore R. Maddi and Suzanne C. Kibasa, *The Hardy Executive: Health under Stress* (Homewood, III: Dow Jones-Irwin, 1984).

Stephen K. Robbins, *Organizational Behaviour*, Prentice Hall of India, New Delhi, 1991, p. 617, Stephen P. Robbins, *Organizational Behaviour*, MacMillan, 1991, p.617.

Stephen P. Robbins, *Organizational Behaviour*, Prentice Hall of India Pvt. Ltd., New Delhi, 1993, p.642.

Suzanne C. Cobasa and M.C. Puccetti, "Personality and Social Resources in Stress Resistance," *Journal of Personality and Social Psychology*, October 1983, pp. 839-850.

Suzanne C. Kobasa, "Stressful Life Events, Personality, and Health: An Inquiring into Hardiness," *Journal of Personality and Social Psychology*, 1979, pp. 1-11.

Suzanne C. Kobasa, Salvatore R. Maddi, and S. Kahn, "Hardiness and Health: Prospective Study," *Journal of Personality and Social Psychology*, 1982, pp. 168-77.

Suzzanne C. Kolasa, *Conceptualisation and Measurement of Personality, in Job Stress Research in Occupational Stress: ssues and Development in Research*, Joseph J. Hurrell Jr. Lawrence R. Murphy, L. Steven, and Cary L. Cooper, Taylor and Francis, New York, 1988, pp. 100-109.

T. Cox, Stress, *University Park Press*, Baltimore, 1978, p.92.

T.A. Beehr, "Perceived Situational Moderators of the Relationship between Subjective Role Ambiguity and Role Strain," Journal of Applied Psychology, February 1976, pp. 35-40.

T.A. Stewart, *Do You Push Your People Too Hard, Fortune*, October 22, 1990, pp.121, 124, 128.

Timothy L. Baker, "Preventing Drug Abuse at Work," *Personnel Administrator*, July 1989, pp. 56-59.

V.L. Rich and A.R. Rich, *Personality, Hardiness and Burnout in Female Stuff Nurses*, Paper presented at the annual meeting of the American Psychological Association, Los Angeles, August, 1985.

William F. Fry, Jr., and Melanie Allen, Make 'em Laugh (Palo Alto, Calif.: *Science & Behaviour Books*, 1975).

William J. Judge and David Evans, "Drug-Testing Decisions: Implications for EAPs," EAP Digest, September-October 1989, pp. 25-32.

CHAPTER

22

Time Management

Keeping in view the consideration of changing concept of management such as globalisation of market, changed facets of human relation approach, hybrid technology, recognisation of optimum utilisation of resources, privatisation of public sectors, etc. the prime importance of utilisation of resources has changed dramatically.

In this changed environment man can cope up with everything by the avenues available to him, but it is quite difficult for a human being, a group or an Industry to balance his all changed activities within the purview of his working environment. Under these conditions the basic aspect which is very much needed or wanted is Time. Once it has gone, can never be recouped or regenerated. It has got a fleeing nature. No body nor even a machine can generate or give rebirth to time. Once it has gone it has gone for ever. So one has to conserve it.

While distributing the fate, wealth, happiness, health and vigour etc. God has discriminately distributed the same unevenly. However, it is the time which has been evenly distributed to all; whether you are a Monarch of a country or a common citizen, everybody has got a day of twenty four hours. Whether you are on the top level or a labourer in your day there will be twenty four hours only. Thus to plan, to arrange, to disburse or to allocate time for your work the most urgent is time. And that it can finish within a stipulated limit with desired success.

The meaning of time have been defined by people and academicians in numerous ways. According to some, time is money. It is very precious. It is valuable. Therefore they price it and tailor the programmes, policies and plans to use it to the maximum level. However, others consider it complementary and free as air and therefore their approach is to treat it as cheap. Some of the managers and administrators without giving importance waste this precious resource. There is a proverb – 'the essence of a genius lies in knowing what to ignore, therefore, they are associated and creatively engaged in a variety of time wasters.' However there is no doubt that one of the most vital and irreplaceable asset is time.

Time management is normally a topic associated with high-flying managers and executives, and so its importance for all people workers is often not fully appreciated. Indeed, time management is associated with a number of misunderstandings and misconceptions concerning what is is, how it works, why it is important, and so on. A central aim of this chapter, therefore, is to clear up some of the confusions by presenting a clear and user-friendly introduction to time management.

What is Time Management?

A significant distinction commonly made is that between 'effectiveness' (doing the right things) and 'efficiency' (doing things right). While effectiveness is clearly a central concern, time management is primarily concerned with efficiency. Time is a scarce resource and therefore needs to be used to maximum effect, and certainly not wasted or channelled into efforts that get us nowhere.

In the business world, the saying 'time is money' is well-known and very influential. In working with people, time can be our most precious resource. In the caring professions it is commonly recognised that our time is often the best thing we can give people – all the more reason, then, that time should not be wasted or misdirected.

However, time management is not simply about organising our time and avoiding wasting it. An important – in fact, essential – aspect of good time management is the ability to manage energy levels, to keep motivation and commitment at optimal levels. That is, time management is concerned not only with the quantity of time, but also its quality.

The question of energy, motivation and commitment is a particularly important and relevant one for people workers. The types of problems and situations we encounter can leave us feeling drained, demoralised and, in some cases, hurt and angry. Conversely, people work can also be tedious, unstimulating and 'unstretching', the paperwork, for example. The outcome of these two sets of factors is that motivation can be seen as a significant issue. It raises the vitally important question: What can we usefully do to maintain motivation and commitment in the extremes of people work?

This chapter, then, needs to address two fundamental areas: how time can be organized to best effect, and how energy can be maintained at optimal levels. First though, we need to consider, albeit briefly, how time management works and what the process actually entails.

Managing the Basic Resource

What is your basic resource? It is not money, not brains, not who you know. Your basic resource is time.

Unless you use your time well, you will never even get a glimpse of what your potential is. Using your time well is not easy - which is why so few people do it. We all have problems with organising our lives, setting priorities, and planning our time.

Regarding of what we do, time is money. If you get a cheque of Rs. 86,400 and are told, "From this moment you have twenty four hours to invest it. You can invest in anything you want to, with this money. What even you don't invest, I will take it back at this time tomorrow.'

What would you do during the next twenty fours hours? You'd be out there working hard and fast to invest Rs. 86,400. Would not you?

That being your attitude, why are you not busily investing as much as you can of the 86,400 seconds given to you every day? That's right - at the beginning of every day are all given 86,400 seconds. As each second ticks by, we've lost it forever unless we find a way to invest that moment in the future.

These are the seconds of your life – and that's the way you live it, one second at a time they can be invested in countless ways that will bring you a future return. Many of those ways will give you repeated returns stretching over many years. You can invest your seconds in the creation of future income in gaining knowledge and acquiring useful methods of gaining future benefits from present time are myriad. And so are the ways of wasting time. The seconds you squander vanish forever if you do not invest your daily treasure of 86,400 seconds wisely, in essence you hand them back at the end of each day, to the force that gave them to you.

Self-Instructions

"I understand that life comes down to how I spend my seconds."

"I don't squander my time, I invest it carefully and intelligently."

"I'm always on the lookout for better ways to invest my time."

"I maintain a strong defence against time wasting people."

Why time planning is worth more of your time

Most people do not set out to waste their time. They want something for it – in fact, all but a few of us want every penny we can get for our time, when we are selling it. This is as it should be. But most of us are less determined to bring all other values from our time that are there for the taking. In other words, most of us don't work as effectively as we could at the business of becoming more productive.

The way to change this is through time planning. Let us identify why it is so important.

1. Time planning prevents future problems

On some level of our minds, we know about most problems before they reach us. But usually we do not look at there until they get really severe. Why not? Because we haven't planned our time well enough to be out a head of events to where we can see clearly. Running with the pack, we cannot see a head, to the sides, or back. All we have time to think about is making our legs move fast enough to keep from being trampled by change. While we were doing that, unnoticed problems are growing. All of a sudden we're overwhelmed. Do you ever have days when there are so many things to do, that you get nothing done?

2. Time planning banishes guilt

One of the most common reasons for feeling guilty is knowing that you're not really working when you're at work. Putting your time in activities without being productive is deeply disturbing. Almost no one is comfortable with a tiny voice inside your head saying, "What you do is not worth a penny. You are a parasite. All you are doing in this world is taking up space."

In all jobs you climb out of bed and get ready in the morning, just like you were going to work effectively. You go to the office, just like you were going to work effectively. You sit down at your desk, just like you were going to work effectively. Then you can shuffle papers, talk on the phone, and confer with other people just like you were working and producing something of value. Are you really producing as much as you possibly can? If you're in any type of consulting or sales job, you can only produce when you are in front of some one who can say yes to your offer. Everything else you do is preparatory to that.

This means that in all such careers, anyone sitting in the office instead of being out meeting new people is not working.

3. Time planning enhances your personal time

There are two types of time that you can spend with your family – enhanced time and flop time. Setting demanding goals for yourself often means that there won't be as much time for the family.

Which time would you like to spend with your family, flop time or enhanced time?

Let us define our terms. Enhanced time is time that's been planned with the family so that everyone gets as much pleasure and benefit from it as possible. This means that you go one-to-one with each person in your family to ask questions, and that you then act on their answers that you truly share the decisions with your loved ones about how, that time will be spend. Flop time is the time you spend with your family when you are too tired to do anything else.

So pull your family closer together by cutting the flop time and giving them more enhanced time instead.

What most people need to make this possible is a short exercise session daily – help an hour in a lap pool, a game of badminton or a jog. Your work creates stress – what success seekers cannot avoid? Erase your mental tiredness and emotional exhaustion with a little physical activity everyday, then arrive home ready to enjoy some enhanced time with your family.

Some people take pot shots at you when they see that you're driving hard to achieve more than they have their sights set on. They go or wander away from their families. Their families may say, "Oh yes we want him to be more successful but we want him home."

On the other hand there are people who would religiously reach their homes at 5.30 and won't leave till 10.00 in the morning. Their families are heard saying, 'We wish to had get up and go to do something, desire in him. We all know that some of these men are firmly 'committed to three goals: 1. Drinking six pegs every evening 2. Never missing any programme on TV. 3. Getting home by 5.30 p.m. from work. Since they achieve these goals regularly and that makes them happy. There is a vital point here if you are making yourself happy don't let someone else make you unhappy because your goals are not like their goals.

4. Time planning creates self-discipline

It literally creates a disciplined way of living. All of us have habits that are time wasters unless we've worked hard to eliminate them. Every business has a few time wasters; every relationship has some time wasting aspects. Here are some common time wasters that are gold mines of time that you can save.

(a) Television

Television is a wonderful invention. But like Kentucky bourbon, Plum cake, rose cookies, or any other good products, TV. has to be used properly. The problem today is not only the time wasted it is also the content. The average person under seventeen years old spends more time in front of the TV than at any other single activity. Be careful about that, Watch, what you watch, in your home.

(b) Not doing it right the first time

The next time you have to do something over because you did not get it right the first time, analyse how much time went into making that job right. Include all the discussion and hassle time that was involved. Keep track and see what percentage of things you are doing over. Then figure out how much extra time you will save for productive work, by eliminating rework.

(c) Not being organized

Organize so that you can run your life. Unless you are organized, random happenings run you don't run them. People who get up in the morning with no plan for the day inevitably find that their day takes over and runs them in time wasting patterns.

(d) Pro castigations

It is easy to avoid writing down what you should do. Most people don't want to make a plan for tomorrow because they know they would not follow it. They just are not that much interested in doing what they know they should do. Every time they let there mind stray into thinking about what they should be doing, they feel guilty. So they close there minds to the simple, obvious methods that work. If they do not write down what they should do, they would not blame themselves so much for not doing it. You can play these little games with yourself if you want to but the losses are still yours to suffer. Having a time acting on a time plan instead of procrastinating plan, answers this questions. Are you out to succeed or are you not?

Look in the mirror every morning and ask yourself why you are not the person, you want to be. Stop blaming others – your friends, you company, the market, the government policies.

(e) Negative thinking

All resentment and down-talk are brutal time wasters. Fear, anger, jealousy – they all lead you away from what is best for you. When you are tuned out whether other people are pulling a head of you and what other people might be thinking, you can concentrate on the best thing that you can do with this minute. When you've reached the point where that is the main thing on your mind, you are solidly on the road to success.

How time management works

A common approach to time management is the 'time and motion' philosophy which involves looking in detail at how time is normally spent by an individual within the work environment. Detailed logs and time-diaries are not uncommon methods and have gained a lot of popularity over the years. While this approach does have benefits, particularly in terms of developing an overview of how one's time is used, it also has drawbacks. One particularly significant problem is that, if we focus too closely on how our time is used, the exercise can become time-consuming and therefore counterproductive. Also, an emphasis on the minute of time use can distract attention from the significant roles of energy and motivation.

The approach advocated here, then, is rather different. It is geared towards helping you to understand (and encouraging you to implement) the basic principles of time management, in terms of organizing your time and maintaining energy levels. From this point of view, time management involves becoming sensitive to the ways in which time and energy play such a central role in getting the job done (or not getting the job done, as the case may be). Studying the basic principles of time management is presented as a useful and important way of developing this sensitivity.

Also of importance in understanding how time management works are the following key points:

- There are no right answers. What works for you may not work for other people, and vice versa. It is important to develop an approach which is well-suited to your own personality, needs and circumstances.
- You can't fit a quart into a pint pot. No matter how well-developed your time management skills become, there is only so much work that can be achieved in a day. That is, while good time management can help to ensure that you do not become overburdened, it cannot guarantee that you will not be overworked.
- Time management can be learned. At the beginning of the book, it was emphasised that skills are often mistaken for qualities. It is often assumed that some people are 'cut out for being organised' while others are not. This is a defeatist attitude, and one which needs to be abandoned, as we all have the potential to improve our time management skills.

Organizing your time

The ability to organise one's time to best effect is an important part of working with people, as the nature of the work rarely, if ever, allows a rigid, timetabled approach. The individual worker usually has at least some degree of responsibility for deciding how to use the time available. Despite the importance of this ability, however, its significance is not often fully appreciated, and is therefore rarely given the attention it deserves. Consequently, it is not unusual to find skilled and experienced workers who struggle with the basics of time management and therefore allow their good work to be undermined and their effectiveness to be impaired. For this reason, time spent getting to grips with the principles of organising our time is, in itself, time well spent – indeed, this notion of investing time underpins the first principle to be considered.

Invest time to save time

Some people make the mistake of becoming 'too busy' to plan or organize their time. When this situation occurs the person concerned has lost control, and is likely to find it very difficult to regain it. Good time management is premised on setting aside a certain amount of time to plan how the rest of the time should be spent, so that priorities can be set, problems anticipated, opportunities recognised and so on. That is, it is necessary to invest time in planning and organising in order to save time. The person who fails to invest this time may save a little time in the short-term but is likely to waste a lot of time in the long run.

One important point to note, however, is the danger of investing too much time in planning. For some people, planning work becomes a substitute for doing the work. Consider, for example, the tendency to make lists of what needs doing, without actually finding the time to do any of them. An important skill, therefore, is to be able to find the balance between investing not enough time and investing too much. Planning is a means to an end and not an end in itself.

Set Priorities

When we are faced with a long list of things to do, it is helpful to decide which are the most important ones and which ones need to be done first. That is, we need to set priorities.

Three things can make this difficult:

- There are few, if any, clear criteria as to which items are more important than others.
- There may be so many important items on the list that not all of them can be done in the time available. That is, some hard decisions may have to be made as to which important things do not get done.
- There may be a conflict of interest. For example, you may consider a particular item on your list a high priority, while someone else who can influence you (your boss, perhaps) attaches far less significance to it.

Setting priorities, then, is not necessarily a straightforward task and can be fraught with difficulties. However, a little bit of practice in undertaking this task should help to convince you that the benefits very strongly outweigh the difficulties. One word of caution worthy of note relates to the danger of being too rigid and regimented in setting priorities. If we lose a degree of flexibility, setting priorities can become more of a hindrance than a help.

Keep a clear focus

A lot of time can be wasted when we lose track of what we are trying to achieve, when the focus of what we are doing becomes blurred and unclear. Indeed, this can become a vicious circle. Being busy can lead us to lose our focus, to become side-tracked and this, in turn, can put us under greater time pressure, which increases the tendency to become unfocused– and so the circle goes on.

In view of this, the skill of keeping a clear focus, even at times of great pressure, can be seen to be an important basis of effective time management. The notion of keeping a clear focus is closely allied to systematic practice and so this is an issue to which due importance should be given.

Avoid waste

At one level, it may seem obvious that it is important not to waste time. However, despite this being self-evident, it is surprising how often basic steps to avoid wasting time are not taken. Examples would include: personal visits being made to seek information that could have been obtained by phone; two members of a team attending a meeting at which only one team member's presence was necessary; lengthy and detailed records being kept when a brief account of the salient points would have sufficed; undertaking tasks that are better suited to others, such as clerical work; continually phoning and failing to make contact when a brief letter would allow the task to be done.

This is not to say, for example, that all home visits should be replaced by telephone calls. Clearly, that would be absurd. However, there are times when a visit is not essential and is an unnecessary waste of time. What is needed, then, is the ability to identify occasions when time is likely to be wasted and use the time more constructively. This links it with the discussion of self-awareness in so far as a higher level of sensitivity and awareness is called for. The skill of recognising opportunities to save time is one that can be developed through effort and experience – and one that repays the investment.

Use of diary

A diary is a basic tool of time management. It can be used as a means of planning, monitoring and coordinating. It is not simply a place to keep a note of appointments. For example, if an important report needs to be written, a diary can be used for allocating time to write it. In this way, the diary becomes more than a reminder for appointments; it becomes a central focus for time management.

There are skills and techniques in using a diary that can be developed, as the following example illustrates:

"a diary gives you a greater sense of control over your own time and guards against the embarrassing problem of forgetting a particular appointment or being 'double-booked.' One simple but very effective technique for putting a diary to good use is to draw a line down the centre of each page. You can then note down time commitments or appointments on the left and things that need doing on the right .... At the beginning of each day you can look at the previous day's list and cross out those that have been done or are no longer applicable. Then, those that remain are the ones that need to be 'carried over'; that is, they need to be written on the right hand side of today's page."

Organise your work

The total work in an organization can be divided as:

(i) Regular routinised work

(ii) Urgent work

(iii) Important work

(iv) Top priority work

It has been noticed that in most of the cases regarding time there is confusion in depicting activity and productivity. Busy behaviour encompasses full of activities. But the question is what is the price, if we contemplate it from the view point of contribution, vision and addition of value. The main focal point is overlooked and people try to be exhibitionists. It is not uncommon to see that many executives are engulfed or encircled in a kind of activity trap. This catching is a phenomenon which trap leads only to an emphasis of:

(1) visibility (2) publicity (3) drum beating and (4) clique culture

In fact, the staff of lower hierarchy are more conversant to attend to the same skilfully. However executives tighten their belts to do these activities at their level for becoming effective. One should develop an approach of utilising time effectively, economically and efficiently.

Now the vital question before us is, how this can be done? Complex problems always have simple solutions.

The simple answer to this problem is to plan. Planning is forecasting. Fore means future. The future is required to be shaped, moulded and casted. Therefore, it requires a critical and analytical approach. Future is not known to anyone.

Therefore, it is the process of gestimation, i.e., we go on guessing and do estimation. By combining these activities cautiously and consciously we can manage the time properly and in this regard we ought to think about the tangible and intangible aspects.

Controllable and uncontrollable factors and their impact in the course of time is another aspect to be considered.

We therefore, design an action plan. We contemplate about the alternatives. We weight them and the best solution is accepted.

Time management is neatness. Time management is well organised work. It is proportional to structural daily routine. Organising embraces three aspects in this jurisdiction. These three aspects are:

(i) management of time
(ii) management of people
(iii) management of papers

An effective manager reviews the work to be accomplished. He should prepare a list of activities. In an office, the manager's task covers reading, writing, dictating, listening, communicating, attending, meeting, taking decisions, attending to visitors, superiors, peers subordinates and so on.

The time should not be spent it should be invested. An efficient person uses tacts, facts, skills thoughts, time and imagination. Therefore the essence of time management lies in knowing the art of delegating and planning intelligently.

The enlisted works are to be prioritised in the light of every day schedule then compartmentalise the work in the following segments :

(i) priority work
(ii) important work
(iii) urgent work
(iv) regular work
(v) routine work

Using the secretarial services can be examined and explored in the proper perspective.

The secretaries should be trained and activated properly to do the job to the topmost desired satisfaction.

Secretaries can take up their duties as readymade competent people who know just what they are supposed to do their sphere of activities can cover following activities:-

(i) see the visitor
(ii) evaluate importance of their business
(iii) give the executive an assessment, compose and type letters.

However, though authority can be delegated responsibility cannot be. Hence trustworthiness of the secretaries needs to be checked properly. The only magic word for team building is "trust." Still the evaluation of loyalty, morality, integrity and trust worthiness of the personal Secretary in the light of the work activities is needed. The attitude of learning for tomorrow what you can do today is called "Procrastination."

This is a big problem in managing time. Prolonged action creates unpleasantness. Delay makes project implementation difficult, indecision makes the problem more critical thus turning the situation from bad to worse. A stitch in time saves nine. Decision making is an advanced step in time management. It precedes collection of information correct it for error freeness compare it, compile it comprehensively. Then frame the alternatives. The alternative solutions are to be measured in terms of benefits, disadvantages, limitations, past experience and practicability.

(Thompson, 1993a, pp.128 - 9)

The Three-minute Rule

In the course of a week, a number of minor, 'bitty' tasks can so easily accumulate. Each of these may be a simple or undemanding task, but when they build up into a pile, they can present quite a headache. Wading through a number of small tasks can be very tedious, and so there is a tendency to procrastinate. Once this starts to happen, of course, the 'pile' gets bigger and this, in turn, increases the aversion to tackling them - and so a vicious circle is set up.

A simple way to prevent this problem arising is the 'three-minute rule.' If you are presented with a task that can be completed in less than three minutes (signing a form, writing a brief reply to a memo, and so on), then do it straightaway. This prevents a backlog building up, and ensures that more time-consuming problems do not occur later as a result of a delay in the completion of one of these brief tasks.

Table 1

DO'S OF TIME MANAGEMENT

1. Draw out clear Key Result Areas (crunch areas), time bound objectives and detailed plans for your job.
2. Plan your day ahead. List out the most important things to be done the next day in order of importance. Have one sheet for A & B tasks and another for C class tasks.
3. Do delegate matter which you do not have to decide yourself. Insist on exercise of delegated authority.
4. Be predictable. Know your staff and let your staff know your mind.
5. Record occasionally for some stretch of time how you spend your time and analyse critically your time management.
6. Do accept that whatever your superior wants is urgent and important (till you are able to convince him that it is not really so). But as a superior decide priorities with reference to organizational needs.
7. Do set aside fixed hours in a day when your staff can meet you or you will call them, other than in an emergency.
8. Do set aside some time a week for innovative thinking and long range planning regarding your areas of responsibility. So as to anticipate problems and heighten your contribution to the organization.
9. Set aside some time preferable towards the end of the day for 'Administrative' matters.
10. Insist on completed staff work.
11. Finish the task you have taken up before getting to another.
12. Develop the habit of single-handling, i.e., making a decision or disposing of a paper at the first opportunity itself.

Working together

Collaboration and teamwork can enable sharing of tasks and/or the most appropriate allocation of tasks (capitalising on people's strengths, avoiding weaknesses), and can therefore make a significant contribution to effective time management. Note, however, the significant word 'can.' It is by no means certain that working together will produce better use of time. Attempts at collaboration can also lead to overlap, gaps, inconsistencies and a considerable amount of time wasted on fruitless debate, leading to indecision and poor use of available resources, including time. 'Working together', therefore, needs to be more than a slogan and requires an investment of time and energy to make it work. Effective collaboration requires clear parameters and role expectations to prevent confusion and conflict halting progress.

Timing

Some of us are 'morning people', and some of us are definitely not 'morning people.' That is, some people function very well first thing in the morning, whereas others lay struggle at that time but come to life later, when perhaps the early birds are starting to fade. The implication of this it pays to know our optimum time periods so that we can plan our tasks accordingly. For example, it could well be a mistake to schedule a difficult and demanding task for a time of day when we are not at our best. This, then, is an aspect of time management that links closely with the discussion in Chapter 1 of self-awareness. We can benefit from understanding not only our strong and weak points, but also our strong and weak times. Careful and informed planning can therefore help to match our energy peaks and troughs with the varied tasks we face in a way that uses that energy to maximum effect.

The best person for the job

Tasks are often allocated within a team or staff group with little or no consideration of who is the best person for the job. This can be a barrier to effective time management in so far as it misses opportunities to build on strengths. Each of us has strengths and weaknesses, as well as aspects of our job that we enjoy and aspects we do not enjoy. By focusing on what we are good at and what we enjoy, higher levels of motivation can be maintained, and more can be achieved in the time available. It is therefore worth exploring within a team or staff group what people's preferences are so that each person can, as far as possible, play to his or her strengths.

The worst – first rule

When we face tasks that we are not looking forward to, or we actively dislike doing, it pays to do them sooner rather than later. That is, by 'getting them out of the way' we can achieve a sense of satisfaction and relief – and this can have a positive effect on morale and energy. An example of this would be making a potentially difficult phone call first thing in the morning.

If, by contrast, we procrastinate and do not tackle these unpopular tasks, they can 'niggle' us, wear down our motivation and generally have a negative effect on our work performance. It therefore helps to go for the 'worst first' by identifying the tasks we are reluctant to do, and doing them first.

Take a break

The notion that 'I am too busy to take a break' is a dangerous one. It is also misinformed in so far as it does not recognise that a refreshed worker can achieve more than a tired one:

When time is tight and we have a lot to do, we can easily fall into the trap of trying to press on without taking a break. But we need to recognise that this is a false economy. For example, a person who works for an hour and a half, then takes a fifteen minute break and then works for a further hour and a quarter is likely to achieve more (and probably of a higher standard) than someone who works straight through for three hours without a break. Working on without a break will leave you feeling tired and jaded, more prone to errors and generally functioning at a less than full capacity.

(Thompson, 1993a, pp. 131-2)

The expanding workload

If we are not careful, work can expand to fill the time available. If we are not sufficiently time-conscious, tasks can take longer to complete than they need to. This is important in terms of motivation. If motivation is low, tasks can take more than their fair share of time and thus in turn, can sap motivation.

By making the effort to complete work tasks in a reasonable time, we can obtain a sense of achievement, greater control and confidence. In this way, the effort to avoid the 'expanding workload' problem can be repaid by increased motivation, rather than the drain on motivation associated with it.

Be positive

Energy levels and motivation can be maintained and enhanced by a positive attitude. A negative outlook, by contrast, contributes to low morale and less job satisfaction. This can become a vicious circle in which negativity and low morale reinforce each other and, over a period of time, make each other worse.

Being positive, on the other hand, can produce a 'virtuous circle' in which a positive outlook leads to a higher level of job satisfaction and morale, and these, in turn, contribute to a positive outlook.

Working together

Just as working together can be of benefit in terms of organising our time, so too can it be of help in terms of energy and motivation. Teamwork, collaboration and mutual support can pay dividends with regard to generating positive feelings of:

* Security and confidence (safety in numbers);
* Commitment to supporting others;
* Camaraderie, group identity and a sense of belonging;
* Enhanced pride and pleasure in joint successes.

Management of Information

Another important aspect of time management is management of information. Organizational complexity leads to unmeasurable flow of papers both incoming and outgoing. This flow is required to be controlled. In certain organizations we find neatness.

But neatness does not signify anything. The real problem is the problem of decision making. For that purpose the right quality of information in the right quantity must be available at the right time at the right location. The incoming and outgoing papers are needed to be skimmed.

In this regard certain papers have to be dealt exclusively by a manager. One can take action because one has to act on it himself. Some papers may not be needed today but these are necessary for reference. purpose is the future. So file them in record papers in the relevant corresponding files. However, care must be taken to see that those references are instantaneously made available when demanded spontaneously. Whereas certain papers are irrelevant not needed and not useful they should be thrown burnt or sold. The above said technique is called –

R – refer to
A – act
F – file
T – throw/toss it away.

Thus if we want to allocate the time it can be stated below as following:

1. Decision on immediate issues
2. Delegating time
3. Problem solving time
4. Correspondence

Time management is required for getting the best out of your time effectively. Delegation is an art. Delegation mirrors ones attitudinal image. Every task which one should not do should be delegated. You ought to understand your people their education, level of perception, skill, knowledge, attitude, aptitude value, capacity to work capability to shoulder responsibility and so on. Delegation is the most important part of planning. Merely planning is of no use. It is synonymous today in dreaming. Planning processing, evaluation and control are the sequential activities which need to be constantly and continuously persuaded. The total time required to be consumed for completing a task needs to be specified. All the concerned are required to join hands together. A 'product approach' is not desired but a process approach is worth rewarding. One of the authorities has designated this concept as - Rice & Potato. The word rice is an acronym for :

R – Respect
I – Internal
C – Customer
E – Expectation

Whereas potato is an abbreviation for the :

P – Process
O – Orientation
T – Technique
A – All
T – Through the
O – Organization

One of the time grabbers of an executive is the interruption on account of phone calls, visits of outsiders and drop its from the staff. These events and activities take noticeable time. Some of the calls relate to superfluous enquiries or courtesy calls, wishing hello. This stretches to management polities. The interruption on account of these events distracts the attention from important matter where concentration is a must. Thus as discussed above the utilisation of secretarial services and the services of the executive assistant can assist in breaking down the interruption.

The conversational factor is another aspect. The executive requires to exchange his thoughts, get the information, dissipate information and also take care of the emotional aspects of people. When we talk about people, its definition encompasses subordinates, superiors, peers, clients etc. At times they drag into unnecessary conversation. Few people seek credibility and compel to listen to the loaded version of their understanding and involvement in project assigned to them for every incumbent. There is an assembly of child ego state, parent ego state and adult ego state. A sharpened edged question asking the present status will confuse the person talking tall talks and thus you can achieve your goal. One must also learn when and how to say no for effective communication. One has to achieve four factors. These four factors are:

(i) Clarity
(ii) Understanding
(iii) Commitment
(iv) Creativity

In a nutshell an executive's time is consumed in innumerable activities. Some of these activities are enlisted below:

1. Communication – verbally
2. Meeting
3. Dictation
4. Writing
5. Studying report
6. Imparting instructions
7. Providing guidance
8. Decision making

9. Telephone calls

The list can be further extended. Hence setting the goal to manager the utilization of time effectively is indispensable.

One has to plan his time by setting goals about what he wants to do. These goals are to be compartmentalised into long-term plans and short-term plans and objectives. Determine the time you plan to *devote* to each of the goals. One goals are set prioritise them. Goals should become an integral part of life.

This can summarise the time in macro level by the following paragraph :

Let us find out how well you are managing your time. This will help in understanding where you are standing at present and determine where you want to go as well as knowing what to do to bridge the gap.

Read and Write Effectively

To make an effective network of time management we must know how to read effectively and how to write effectively. To read effectively we can understand properly through the following diagram:

1. understanding (Active apprehension)
2. discern and discriminate
3. involvement – churn
4. familiarity – churn
5. enhancing knowledge
6. skill and wisdom – churn
7. not required (delegate or reject)

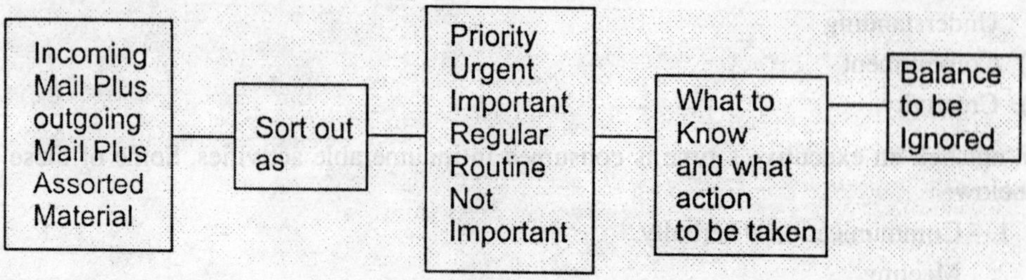

Written communication as an effective tool for time management

Written communication is one of the effective tools of expression. The writer sends the message and the other person one who receives it can preserve the same. This enables the recipient to analyse, assimilate the details at length and in depth as long as he wants. Another advantage of written communication is that simutaneously different recipients can receive the message transmitted. However, one cannot control the feedback. In case the decision is taken to resort to written communication then only we have to write. The reasons attributing to this decision can be indicated as below:

1. There is no need to have personal contact.
2. The information is required to be submitted well within the time limit.
3. The purpose of written document must be crystal clear. For example, if its a contractual document or a report, then contents are needed for reference, record, perusal in the future.
4. It is a proof of action taken on in specific problem.
5. To express views and opinions.

The possible purpose of communication can be compartmentalised as –

1. to inform
2. to convenience
3. to enlighten
4. to entertain
5. to impress
6. to excite
7. to actuate

Writing is certainly a powerful instrument of change. Hence ensure the quality in it.

Time styles of leadership

Another factor which should be taken into consideration for time management is related with the style of leadership. Leadership styles effects time management in lot of spares.

Robert Pears has studied the effect of individual leadership styles on executive skills such as planning, delegating and decision making. In particular he has evaluated a great number of profiles and developed the following typical style related to time use patterns:

1. Task and achievement orientation

The executive with a strong need to furnish task personally, typically has difficulty in delegating. The inner compulsion to finish things makes him feel worthy doing so combined with the role of the hard instance worker it leads him to pour large amounts of time and energy into doing rather than managing.

2. Leadership, dominance and decision orientation

Executives with strong impulses to play the hard hitting leader role enjoy dominating and controlling subordinates and pride themselves on quick decision making. There is a 'take-change' role and they have difficulty in delegating.

3. Impulsive and physically energetic orientation

These are fast moving, energetic action oriented men who see the executive job as that of a 'shaker and mover.' They are often frantically active, making impulsive decisions and moving back and forth from office to plant with high physical energy.

4. Theoretical detail and structure orientation

The theoretical minded executive is apt to spend much time in careful analysis of abstractions and concepts.

He is important in technological companies. He may overlook the practical or implementation part of his work with a high need to attend to detail personally; he may become a nit picker if not careful. He shows things down by his preoccupation with details and tends to spend time setting up systems and rigid organization pattern in which he feels most comfortable. He shows things down by his preoccupation with detail and tends to spend time setting up systems and rigid organization pattern in which he feels most comfortable. He may have emotional difficulty moving freely in unstructured situations.

5. Change, new experiences and feeling expression orientations

The change oriented executive becomes bore with routine. He seeks new experiences and resents work.

That requires time use in repetitive patterns. The emotionally calm executive tends to use time in ways that will insulate him from emergencies.

6. Follower ship orientation and defensive-aggressive orientation:

The executive who needs to defer to authority spends much time in seeking to please the boss. He is often regarded as 'trustworthy.' If he does not carry his follower ship to excess he may be emotionally soothing to superiors but he has difficulty in managing his own time on independent assignments where he is unable to check with his boss for assurance he is doing what most pleases him. The rules and supervision-oriented executive has difficulty in structuring his own time unless he has carefully spelled out rules and regulations to go by. He is most comfortable in bureaucratic organizational where he may carry out assignment by the book. The defensive aggressive executive carries a large chip on his shoulder and spends time arguing with others. He may feel others are out to get him. He loves a good fight and so attacks or counter attacks either in one to one business relationships or on terms or committees.

Executive Time Inventories

This is a list of stipulated time to allocate, disburse and complete the work within the lead time.

The executive time inventory is particularly developed with three distinct purposes in mind.

1. to require the planned allocation of the executive's time.
2. to require a daily listing of most important tasks to be accomplished on the following day.
3. to require to daily estimate of effectiveness, based on the number of priority tasks that were actually completed and on the proportional utilisation of time as measured against its planned allocation.

1. Allocate Time

Decide on principle categories of time expended and the percentage of your time you wish to allocate to each.

2. Set daily goals

Each evening before leaving work list the principle items to be accomplished the following day and arrange them in order of importance.

3. Keep record on time

As the day progresses record results achieved for every 15 minute period. Do not wait until the end of the day to fill in the chart.

4. Summarise for a week or more

After you have kept the inventory for at least one week add the total hours spent in each category and place the totals in the far right hand column by category. Then compute the percentage of the total time spent on each.

5. Estimate daily effectiveness

One of the basis of daily goals accomplished – how well your time actually spent compared with your planned allocation, estimate your effectiveness for each day. If it exceeds 30% you are above the estimated national 'average.'

6. Evaluate

On the basis of your own objectives for a time management programme analyse your areas of greatest effectiveness and those of least effectiveness. Plan a strategy for improvement. Implement this strategy immediately.

Procrastinating the greatest hindrance to time management

Often an unpleasant task can be avoided deliberately. Procrastination is the attitude of leaving a thing/ decision for tomorrow or for future, which one could have done today itself. It ranks high on the list of time wasters of nearly every group of managers. It is a close relative of incompetence and a handmaiden of inefficiency. Managers who habitually procrastinate become interruption prone and actually invite interruptions. The welcome matter is always out for a diversion. Thus a lot of time wasters like visitors, meetings, phone calls and the like invade the executive domain.

Countering these habits requires self-discipline and perseverance. Norman Vincent Pears describe how procrastination nearly swamped him until he faced up to it. He has given these simple guidelines to win the battle.

1. Pick one area where procrastination plagues you and conquer it.
2. Learn to set priorities and focus on one problem at a time.
3. Give yourself deadlines, set deadlines for yourself and let them be known. Ask a friend to check up on you.
4. Don't avoid the most difficult problems. That just insures the hardest part will be left when you are most tired. Get the big one done its downhill from then on.
5. Don't let perfectionism paralyse you. If you put everything off till you are sure of it, you will get nothing done.

Planning work is an important step in time management. Essentially the planning process involves:

(i) analysing the present situation (where I am now)
(ii) developing relevant assumptions (what conditions are likely to exist within the time span of plan)
(iii) establishing objective (what I want to achieve)
(iv) developing alternatives (what different ways might attain these objectives)
(v) making and implementing the decision.
(vi) establishing review and control procedures.

In this regard following suggestions should be taken:

(i) protest your time
(ii) setting objectives & goals
(iii) setting priorities
(iv) managing by exception
(v) deciding what not to do
(vi) learning to say no
(vii) getting organised

In this respect we can organize the following steps:

(i) organizing the work space
(ii) office landscaping to reduce distractions
(iii) creating more and more functional offices
(iv) desks and their proper uses
(v) to avoid the stacked-desk syndrome

Taking the following steps is the helpful method for avoiding the above syndrome.

1. Clear your desk of everything related in any way to project other than the one at hand. The one ought to be your top priority for the moment.
2. Do not permit any other items to be put on your desk until you are ready for them. This means that all projects must have place in a file or drawer and ought to be in that place.
3. Resist temptations to leave the project you are working on for other more appealing tasks, because of attractive interruptions or because you are tried of it. Be sure you have taken all possible action indicated before disposing of it.
4. Send it on its way, recheck your priorities then start on next morning most important project.
5. Have standing orders with your secretary to see that the desk is cleared before you arrive in the morning and that the material necessary for starting on the no. 1 priorities for the day is on your desk.
6. Make it a continuous responsibility for your secretary to inspect your desk and continue to keep it clear. Cooperate with her in every way possible to make this easy.

The other system that can be followed in this regard are the following:

1. the filing system
2. the pocket or desk diary
3. correspondence
4. short, fast answers
5. dictating equipment
6. memoitis
7. reading habits
8. speed reading
9. selective reading

The other relevant and important areas which should be taken into consideration in managing the time are as follows:

(a) Blocking interruptions in this regard we have to deal with the following factors:

1. coming of visitors
2. managing their visit
3. closing the open door
4. putting a strict control on socialising the office activities
5. putting a blockage over the causes of telephone slavery means a strict control over incoming calls
6. and outgoing calls
7. meetings with why, who, when and where
8. discourage time over runs
9. peoples' role played in meetings
10. starting on time
11. getting and sticking to the point
12. time limiting factors in the agenda
13. ending of the time schedule
14. summarising the meetings

(b) The next thing to be considered in time management is to Handling the decisions – sometimes it becomes quite difficult process due to following reasons:

1. fear of mistakes
2. the meaning of mistakes
3. setting deadlines
4. timing response deadlines

(c) Delegating the works

As a key activity of the manager, delegation has benefits both direct and derived – four of the most significant delegations are:

1. Extends results from what a man can do to what he can control
2. Releases time for more important work
3. Develops subordinates' initiative skills, knowledge and competence
4. Maintains decision level

In this respect following factors usually take shape in making it a successful programme:

1. the myth of decision level
2. managing versus operating
3. are you managing or doing
4. the effect of management level on time allocation
5. operating priority
6. the fallacy of omnipotence means I can do better myself
7. fear of being disliked
8. lack of confidence in subordinates
9. reverse delegation
10. chances of too much accountability for delegated responsibilities
11. rate yourself as a delegator

(d) Managing the time of subordinate sometimes,it creates numerous troubles due to following reasons:-

1. are you inviting subordinate's problems
2. communicating instructions poorly
3. keeping subordinates waiting
4. Interrupting subordinates work
5. Encourage - managing the boss

(e) Working with Secretary

The next problem arises due to non-congenial atmosphere related with secretary of a manager. These are related with the following factors:-

1. how your secretary organized you
2. seeing the boss first
3. screening calls, visitors and mail
4. attacking the paper blockade
5. creating desk organizing files
6. monitoring priorities and projects

To overcome these problems it is suggested that management must create the following conditions:

1. Job description for an executive secretary
2. Job description for a boss
3. Provide management training to staffs
4. Pay him what he is worth for

Let us now consider time management through various pros & cons of management.

The entire time management series can be illustrated through following chart schedules:

1. Time Demands

What areas can be of most troublesome in terms of demand on our time and one has to specify these demands.

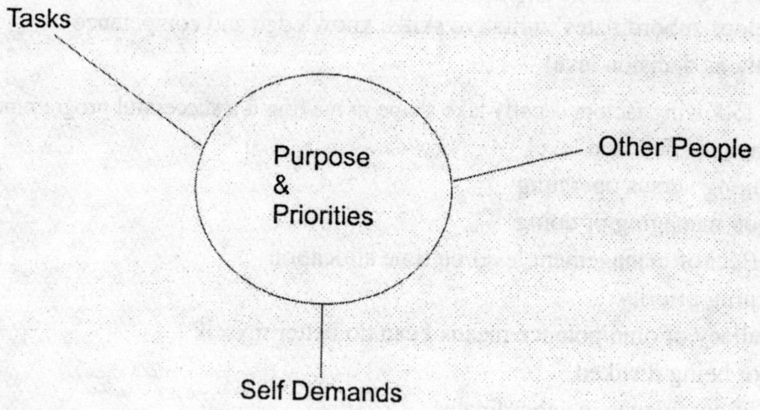

2. Work Analysis

It includes
(i) job purpose and priorities
(ii) input analysis
(iii) output analysis

Therefore, in a nutshell the time management factor we can better say that self-appraisal in the management is the time management and self management can be literally done only through with the fastest communication techniques, the world is shrinking in size. The competition is becoming sharper. To achieve competitiveness, a timely qualitative approach and attitude is needed. The comparative component of competition is quality. Quality of the end product and also quality of services. The other important factor is cost effectiveness. Effectiveness of cost can be achieved both by cost control technique and also cost reduction technique. If we want to outshine in the market, which is a buyer's market in the true sense, our persistent endeavour to maintain constant and consistently improving quality, dependability on timely delivery, error free paperwork, reliability of quality and services reasonability of prices has got tremendous importance.

Elaborate and comprehensive meaning of the word "Quality" which will embrace all parameters, angles, attributes of the meaning of the word is rather difficult. Compliance and conformance to customer's requirement is designated as quality. Consumer or customer has certain requirement expectations. His way of perception is different. Hence, the performer must translate his expectation. So that these expectations are thoroughly, satisfied and totally met. To achieve what we need –

(a) the management of change and
(b) applying TQM philosophy
(c) TEM applications and therapy to the work environment

TQM means total quality management and TEM means total efficiency management. To achieve TQM therapy we needs –

(i) quality in design
(ii) quality in raw material, components, accessories, assembles,
(iii) quality in production, manufacturing assembly,
(iv) conformance to customer's need
(v) quality in packaging
(vi) quality in after sales services

The word 'service' connotes many aspects. It ranges the activities undertaken to give a sense of pleasure and satisfaction to the customer/consumer to deal with the specific organization; the velocity of responsiveness, completeness in the approach, the endeavours/efforts to mitigate specified needs, the way of communication, the art of negotiation, trouble taken to comprehend the culture and value from customers' stand point.

To survive in a cut - throat competitive atmosphere and succeed, cost effectiveness in every sphere of activities is absolutely essential. A significant scope in maintaining consistency and ensuring noticeable reliability is available. And if personal contact is minimal, its importance is unquestionable. This is so because the chances of misperception, misinterpretation are significantly alarming. If one wants to gain high altitudes, a change in attitude should be done. Timely delivery is an essence of a contract. Therefore, credibility in honouring the schedule of delivery is of paramount importance. Undoubtedly and unquestionably, a closest possible attention to ensure strictest accuracy in documentation and complete as well as comprehensive contents are also important.

Whereas we will be fruitful in TEM through –

i. physiological study of managing people
ii. managing conflict for effective time management
iii. programme for self-improvement
iv. self-planning
v. development of people in the organization
vi. managing people at work through influence and tactics
vii. organizing perspective
viii. creating organizational effectiveness
ix. influencing employee behaviour
x. time management through change management
xi. making transactional analysis and motivation of employees through time management techniques

The latest concept known as Total Quality Management has actually undergone a spectacular revolution. From early Quality Measurement concept to Quality Control and to Quality Assurance, finally, teaching the destination of TQM.

This process of evolution of quality function is depicted below in a format to have the information at a glance.

Table 3

Phase	Scope	Action Jurisdiction	System Adopted	Function	Status Reports & Operation
Quality Measurement	Product	End of Line	Appraised	Inspection	Production Supervisor
Quality Control	Materials Products	End of Line	Appraisal Control	Inspection	Supervisor Works Manager
Quality Assurance	Material Product Product Process	On Line	Appraisal Prevention	Inspection Analysis	Manager G.M.
QM	Material Product All process	Before the Beginning	Prevention Appraisal Improve	Plan Control President Adult	G.M.IV.P. M.D.

One is required to be proactive. "Proactive" means we are neither reactive nor overactive. This focuses on initiative and responsibility. Responsibility is response ability. The thrust on TQM initiative is on following areas:

(1) Enhanced satisfaction level of customer.

(2) Improvement in the effectiveness of cost.

(3) Speedier introduction of new products.

(4) A combined result of 1, 2 and 3 above is improved competition, capability and compatibility.

This process is depicted in a diagram below.

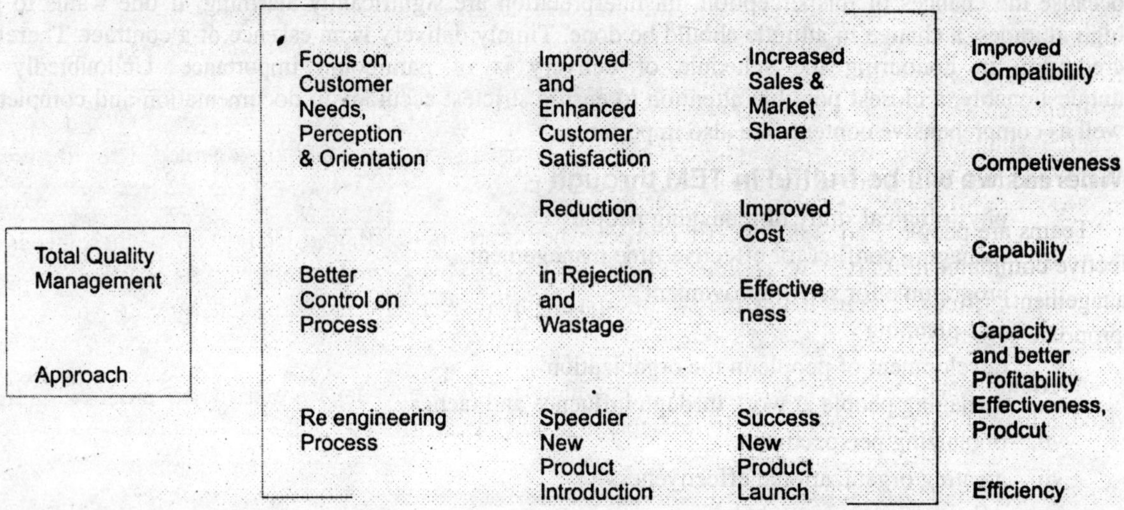

Fig.1. The TQM Process

The extent interest and enthusiasm shown by the guiding force, i.e., the leader has remarkable impact on the success. Success comes to those who have the dare and courage to act. The involvement, contribution and the vision are the inputs of a leader in the process of development.

The span of vision of the leader must be very wide. The leader does not only see but he has a vision. Vision is followed by mission. Mission leads to strategic plans which, in turn reflects objectives and goals. The goal associated with this programme must be:

Specific
Measurable
Achievable
Reasonable
Time-bound

The people associated with the task must enjoy Rice & Potato technique.

Respect
Internal
Customer
Expectation
And the other things are
Process
Orientation
Technique
All
Through the
Organization

For achieving astonishing results therefore, communication which catalyses commitment, appropriate provision of resources, initiative, cultural transformation, a total system approach and a consistent continued improvement approach is needed.

Time Management through Communication

Work at the workplace often breaks down and creates obstacles. When people communicate poorly in the workplace, they waste time and squander resources, fail to attain the goal and even the personal relationship also suffers and sometimes breaks down. As the organization grows the work activities become complex and communication also becomes difficult. In fact, the achievement of an organization is the result of the combined efforts of each individual. Team spirit is what gives so many organizations an edge over their competitors. The success of any team depends on the individuals who makes up the team. And team spirit depends upon your skill of communication. This helps to push up the team to new heights of energetic, solution-oriented and motivated group. Ineffective communication coupled with different attitudes and lack of activation can create a big hue and cry.

Teams are people. People have certain needs when working together in teams. One of these needs is effective communication. It is the essence of success of team work because it emphasises on effective time management. Effective communication is the starting point for understanding interpreting and taking appropriate action.

A communication at workplace is very conductive. Their exchange are likely to produce mutual understanding, agreement and action. In fact, this is one of the jurisdiction where continuous improvement has got significant scope. For improvement, evaluation is essential. For evaluation, the process of communication should be broken down into its components to decide, determine, distinguish and discern why problems do crop up.

The communication process is an interdependent reciprocal activity. It involves transmission and reception of messages. Communication is an active process. It has other three noticeable characteristics. Those are its continuity, reciprocity and dynamism, associated with it. Written and verbal communication are the aids for controlling. A well-knit and effective communication process is the foundation upon which the executory, administrative and managerial function depends. The main and major portion of managerial time is invested or wasted in carrying out the activity of communication. This involves three essentially important areas. These are as follows:

(i) Development of new ideas;

(ii) Flow of information

(iii) Exchange of feelings

In a company, communication serves predominantly four functions, namely, controlling, motivating expression of emotion and exchange of information. In the process of communication on the one hand, there is a sender. On the other, there is a receiver. This is an interdependent and reciprocal activity. Defective communication can originate at either of the end. The defect can also be attributed to the wrong way in which messages are sent or received.

A chart given below [Table 4] shows the communication barrier and suggests some strategies to overcome at a glance.

One has to also bear in mind Murphy's law of communication. It vindicates, 'if a message can be understood in different ways; it will be just understood in just the way that does the most harm.'

Table 4

Communication barriers	Strategies to Overcome barriers
(1) Sender's Related Behaviours	(1) Sender should pay the attention to the following areas
(i) Communication goal (ii) Communication skill (iii) Interpersonal sensitivity (iv) Differing levels of references (v) Non-verbal signals (vi) Fear (vii) Sender's credibility	(i) Objectives and aims (ii) Language (iii) Empathy (iv) Credibility (v) Feedback (vi) Face-to-face communication (vii) Redundancy (viii) Trust (ix) How he poses the picture (x) Receiver's responsibility such as
(2) Situation Related Barrier	
(i) Words used are jargon type (ii) There is an overloading of information (iii) A significant pressure on your time (iv) Climate (v) Distance (vi) Noise (vii) Mechanical failure	(a) Listening (b) Avoidance of untimely & premature Judgment (c) Responsive feedback - do-
(3) Receiver Related Behaviour	
(i) Selection and Poor listening (ii) Evaluating source (iii) Perception (iv) Lack of feedback (v) Non-verbal communication	(i) Listen carefully and patiently. (ii) Avoid premature judgment (iii) Responsive feedback

For the purpose of effective listening, one has to concentrate on certain basic principles. These are enumerated below:

(i) Non - verbal listening responses.

(ii) Paraphrase the same.

(iii) Reflect the implications.

(iv) Invite contribution.

(v) Reflect underlying action.

(vi) Confirm and affirm understanding.

In fact step (vi), i.e., confirmation of understanding is required to be persuaded after every step narrated above thereafter, the subsequent step is to be followed up.

The practical principles of the process of communication are tabulated below in Table 5. This Table 5 also gives the tested action programmes.

Table 5. Principles of Effective Listening

Sr. No.	Principle	What does the good listener do
1	Jurisdiction of interest to be explored.	(1) Endeavour to get personal is enlightenment and/or information. The potentially interesting topics are to be contemplated.
2	Errors of delivery	(2) No one is perfect in the world. Certain errors are on account of language usability. The language in India is different after every 10 to 15 kilometres. Hence attend to meaning. Pay attention to the contents. The delivery errors are to be ignored.
3	Postpone Judgment	(3) Quickest possible judgments are not backed by square thinking. Those may get crippled because of in-factually correct information.
4	Listen to ideas	(4) Creative ideas may be fruitfully effective. Identify the main point.
5	Take notes	(5) Notes help you to have all relevant points concisely.
6	Be actively responsive	(6) Responded frequently
7	Resist distraction	(7) Distraction is to be avoided
8	Challenge your mind	(8) The horizon of understanding is to be enlarged
9	Capitalise on mind speed	(9) Use listening time to summarise. Anticipate message.
10	Assist and encourage speaker	(10) Ask for clarifying information and example. Reflecting phrases are to be used. Assist to rephrase ideas.

The business of the business is its business. As the organizations grow their activities become more complex. And simultaneously coordination also becomes difficult. For making decisions the concept followed is "two heads are better than one." Therefore, committees are constituted and meetings are conducted. In the meeting one should be firm about his appointment. One should not take on more than he can cope with reasonably; rushing from meeting to meeting produces harassed personalities, grass-hopper mind, faulty assessment, hasty judgment and possibly ruined health. A quickest possible decision saves time. If decisions are delayed or not taken, the result is wastage of time. Hence ability to discern, discuss and discriminate the matter is of prime importance. One should not get stuck up to trivial matters. Go to the root cause of the problem. Hit the crux of the problem and once the decision is taken, expeditiously implement it. When you decide the action in a committee, people from various walks of life, varied experience, different logical thinking examine the pros and cons. But what is important is the sense of proportion. Prolongation creates unpleasantness and the inordinate delay further makes the project implementation more difficult. Further indecision makes the problem much more critical. Such situations turn from bad to worse. Therefore, the crux is that a stich in time saves nine.

DON'TS OF TIME MANAGEMENT

Don't succumb to the temptation to attend to the easiest tasks – the trivial many – in preference to the difficult cases the vital few.

1. Don't be lost on urgent tasks ignoring important tasks.
2. Don't spend time on subjects or with people solely because you like.
3. Don't use more time than the importance of the job merits, don't refine more than the matter or occasion demands.
4. Don't get into the habit of leisurely way of working, of extending the time available, of saying
5. 'There is always tonight.'
6. Don't procrastinate.
7. Don't allocate time for job too hopefully and unrealistically.
8. Don't be erratic and ad hoc in your decision.
9. Don't make a practice of crisis management.
10. Don't totally manage by your subordinates.
11. Don't be a cause of your subordinates' problem:
    (a) Don't keep them waiting to see you.
    (b) Don't keep them in your office unnecessarily.
    (c) Don't interrupt their work unneccessarily.
    (d) Don't decide on issues delegated to them.
    (e) Don't let them pass the issue back to you.

Being well-organized in terms of the use of time is not, as we have seen, a fixed quality. It is a set of skills that can be learned and developed through practice and experience. The suggestions given here can take you some way towards improving your time management skills. However, they can only work if you are committed to them – going through the motions as if they will help you without your believing in them will be. of little value.

The essential ingredient, then is confidence – in two senses. First, we need confidence in ourselves that we can learn, that we can develop new skills. Second, we need confidence in the techniques that we are using. If this confidence can be mustered, then the scope for improved personal effectiveness is immense.

CHAPTER

23

Industrial Psychology

Industrial psychology, as the name indicates, is that branch of psychology which studies human behaviour under industrial circumstances. Psychology is a normative science of behaviour which can be observed in the social, economic, educational and other spheres. In the modern period the different branches of psychology have developed during the study of human behaviour in these various fields. Educational psychology has been developed to study human behaviour in the field of education while social psychology is concerned with the study of human behaviour in a social environment. This is an age of industrial progress, in which each progressive. nation is expanding the scope of its industries. But industries cannot be made to function without human beings, because individuals are required in the capacity of managers, administrations and workers. And, wherever there are human beings their behaviour will be influenced by their relationship. If, in the industrial field, human relations deteriorate, then the result is strikes and lockouts which have a widespread impact upon the economy of the nation. Since the future of every nation depends upon its industrial development and progress, this particular field of human behaviour becomes extremely important. It is the aim of Industrial Psychology to study the principles governing behaviour in the industrial field and to undertake research.

Psychology is not merely a theoretical science for it not only enunciates general laws concerning human behaviour but also tries to improve human life by applying these principles. Like any other science, therefore, psychology also has two aspects – the theoretical and the practical. Industrial psychology is naturally a branch of practical psychology because it is fundamentally a study evolved for the improvement of human relations in the industrial sphere. The knowledge provided by it is used to solve the problems of people who work in industry, as well as to solve these non-human problems which emerge from time in industries. Nowadays psychologists are appointed to study the problems which arise in the field of industrial psychology. A glance at the history of Industrial psychology will show us that universities have been responsible for the research concerned with it, but even more important research has been carried on in big industries under actual conditions. It is, therefore, more appropriate to consider Industrial Psychology as a branch of practical psychology. This aspect of the subject can be even better understood by studying the following definitions:

DEFINITIONS OF INDUSTRIAL PSYCHOLOGY

Some of these main definitions of industrial psychology are the following:

1. **Blum's Definition:** According to Blum, a famous psychologist, 'Industrial Psychology is simply the application of psychological facts and principles to the problems concerning human relations in business and industry.' Blum shows in this definition that psychological facts and principles are used in human relations in the field of business and industry and this constitutes Industrial Psychology. By using them the industrial psychology tries to solve the problems that arise in the industrial sphere. As Blum says further Industrial Psychology provides practical solutions to the problems that arise in the industrial society and its economic organization.

2. **Harrell's Opinion:** Harrell has defined the subject in his book entitled *Industrial Psychology* in the following words: 'Industrial psychology is the study of people at work industry and business.' In his opinion, then the industrial psychologists makes a study of the behaviour of people working under conditions of business and industry. Harrell has further clarified that the subject matter of the industrial

psychology is always the human being because it is the human being which is the object of a psychological study. Even in a business or industrial environment this continues to be true. Just as social psychology studies the human being under social circumstances. Industrial Psychology studies the individual in a business environment. As Harrell himself has put it 'Individual Psychology is a complicated study of a number of things, but it is always primarily the study of people as individuals or in groups – in the work situations.' It need hardly be explained that the individual psychologist focuses his attention upon human beings.

3. Smith's Definition: Smith has defined industrial psychology in the manner: 'For practical purposes Industrial Psychology may be defined as the study of conduct of those who exchange the work of their hands and brains for the means to live.' Defined in this way, industrial psychology becomes concerned with the study for all people in an industry, whether they work by hand or by brain. Here it has been called the study of contract, but it would be better to substitute the word 'behaviour' for this term because conduct is more properly the concern of ethics, not of behaviour.

Thus, from the above definition it is clear that Industrial Psychology is the branch of psychology which studies human behaviour in industrial circumstances. It studies physical human behaviour in industrial circumstances. It studies physical as well as mental aspects of the work, behaviour of the people at work and the relationship of work and job satisfaction.

Scope of Industrial Psychology

Pointing out the scope of industrial psychology Harrell has laid stress on the following things:

1. Industrial psychology is concerned with the physical aspect of the environment of work, for example, the effect of life and temperature on work and safety.

2. It is primarily a study of the behaviour and principles of human relationship.

3. It is a study of the causes that lead to indifference and disinterest and the motives and attitudes that influence zeal and high morale.

4. It is a study of the methods by which neurotic people can be bought back to a level of normal health.

5. It is a study of the factors that create co-operation between labourers and the management, a study of the relation between the supervisor and his subordinates and of industrial conflicts.

It is clear from the above exposition that industrial psychology studies, apart from the physical environment, the principles of human relationships, the factors which lead to and maintain mental health and the basis of high morale. Briefly, then the scope of Industrial Psychology is the following:

1. Economic Social and Psychology Aspects of Industry: Industrial Psychology is concerned with human behaviour in the entire industrial environment. Consequently, it studies the economic, social and psychological aspects of human behaviour. In the modern age most economic factors have some psychological influence. The various factors in the communal life of workers living in an industrial environment also influence the psychology of worker. Industrial psychology studies this also.

2. Study of the Physical Aspect of Work Environment: In an industry the worker is greatly influenced by the conditions under which he works. If the conditions are to his liking the worker feels satisfied and remains healthy while on the other hand, if the conditions are not good the number of accidents goes up and workers become dissatisfied. Working conditions include a number of factors such as clean air and water, arrangement of necessary rest, less noise, clean atmosphere, sufficient light, good relations between the worker and the management. In all these, guidance by the psychologist can prove of immense value. For example, it is better to consult the psychologist about the arrangement for lightening, about the quantity of intensity of the light and the angle from which it should come. Even the colour of the walls, floors and ceiling of the factory influence the workers. It has been seen in experiments that if the colour scheme of the environment is good, there are fewer accidents and the atmosphere remains good.

And it is for the psychologist to suggest what should be the colour of the machines, roofs, floors and ceilings. It can thus be said that Industrial Psychology studies the physical working conditions.

3. Principles of Human Relationships: Irrespective of the automation introduced in any industry, the human element cannot be eliminated. Even the biggest and the most efficient machine needs an engineer to run it, and because the engineer is a human being the importance of the psychological element in the running of the factory cannot be denied. The efficiency of the man will depend very much upon the nature of his relations with the management. In the last century most industrialists behaved like autocrats and considered the workers as nothing more than tools. But in that period the level of efficiency was never very high. It has been seen that an industrialist can achieve a higher rate of production if he behaved sympathetically with his employees. In the present age, the industrialist can no longer do as he wills, because of the existence of labour unions. An industrialist who cannot maintain good and cordial relations with his workers does not succeed for long. Being the science of behaviour, industrial psychology tries to discover principles for improving human relationships in an industrial environment. At the root of most of the lockouts and strikes, with common forms of expressing discontent seen to frequently in most industries today, have only distorted and injured human relationships. Industrial psychology helps to solve these problems.

4. Study of Aptitudes and Motives: As in any other circumstance, human behaviour in the industrial environment is influenced and formed by attitudes and motives. Behaviour change with the change in stimuli. Hence it is necessary to study the rules pertaining to correct attitudes and motives. Industrial psychology pursues this kind of study. One example of a study of this kind is the study conducted by the Hawthorn Works Western Electric Company into the effect of the attitudes of workers upon production. This study is known as the Hawthorn studies.

5. Study of Principles of Mental Health: Today, intelligent people realise the importance of maintaining the proper health of workers. The worker's mental health is profoundly influenced by the conditions under which he works and by the attitude of other people towards him. Industrial psychology studies the factors influencing the mental health of industrial workers and tries to discover principles for maintaining their mental health. Industrial psychology also gives suggestions for improving the mental health of these who are suffering from mental disease or are otherwise unbalanced.

6. Study of Human Relations: Industrial psychology is the study of human behaviours in an industrial context. As has been pointed out earlier, the physical condition of work have a direct and strong influence upon human behaviour. The manner in which the supervisors or the manager behaves towards the worker has a direct influence upon the efficiency, attitudes and motives of the worker. Some employees try to spread maladjustment among industrial workers, for purely personal reasons. Even this is a problem of human relations. Being a branch of psychology, industrial psychology is particularly concerned with the observation of study of human relations about which it reaches conclusion through experiments and other study. On the basis of these conclusions it tries to discover general principle which can help in improving social relations between the worker and the management.

What Industrial Psychology Solves

In this book *Industrial Psychology and its Social Foundation* the psychologist Blum has stated, "Industrial Psychology offers a dynamic solution to the perplexing problems which confront industrial society and economic system." What are these problems concerned with industry of profession? These are the problems of psychology in nature that arise in any sphere of industry. Briefly, the problems of industrial psychology are as follows:

1. Selection of the Right Man for the Right Job: If success is to be achieved in any industry it is essential that the right man should be found and appointed to the right job. This involves first an accurate work study and also the selection of the most qualified individual from among the applicants to suit that particular job. This is basically a problem for the psychologist because the selection involves many kinds of psychological tests to discover the various abilities of the individuals. It also happens sometimes that an individual working on a particular post cannot work efficiently for personal reasons, even though he is otherwise perfectly qualified to hold that post. In such a situation the industrial psychologist is faced with the problem of giving suggestions which will once again render the individual fit for work.

2. Training for Workers: Although different individuals have varying degrees of ability to perform different kinds of functions, training can be useful in improving these abilities to such an extent that the individual becomes capable of doing work which could not have been done without training. The kind and length of training required to train a particular individual to bring him up to a certain level of efficiency can be determined by the psychologist. Hence another problem for the industrial psychologist is the training of workers.

3. Morale in Industry: Despite the best possible working conditions in an industry the highest efficiency cannot be achieved unless the workers also have a high morale. Morale can be seen on the other hand in the enthusiasm and zeal with which work is tackled and on the other hand in the mutual cooperation extended to others in group activities. How a proper morale can be maintained in industry and what steps are necessary to create it is a problem for psychology, and it is the industrial psychologist who solves it.

4. Human Relations in Industry: The problem of human relations in industry has assumed greater importance and complexity with the formation of trade unions which have channeled the power of the workers into single channel. Now no industry can run successfully and smoothly for any length of time in the absence of good relations between the management and the workers' union. If the relations deteriorate, the level of production falls, accidents increase, and lockouts and strikes are the result. The problem of human relation is primarily the concern of social psychology and the person best equipped to solve it is the industrial psychologist.

5. Fatigue and Boredom: In industry, as in any other sphere of human activity, individuals become tired and bored after a long spell of mechanical work. Their psychological fatigue increases with this. Fatigue is both physiological and psychological. Scientifically viewed, the work and the instruments used in an industry should be so designed and planned as to result in the least possible amount of fatigue and the highest possible quantity of work. Specialists of engineering psychology have designed various kinds of machines and tools with this objectivity in view. They have also given many suggestions about the improvement of methods of work. Industrial psychologists also have conducted many experiments on mental fatigue and boredom, and given many valuable suggestions on the basis of their results. It has been observed, for example that if there is arrangement for music and light entertainment in certain kinds of mechanical work the extent of fatigue and problem is greatly reduced.

6. Industrial Accidents: If we want machine to function without any accident, two things are necessary. In the first place the machine itself should be in good working order. In the second place the worker maintaining it should be using it correctly, and his mental condition must be normal. For the first factor engineering psychologists have given useful suggestions for keeping the machines functioning properly and without accidents. Regarding the second factor they have given some suggestions for the development of safety habits, proper maintenance and the maintenance of normal mental health. Hence, one important problem before Industrial Psychology is the prevention of accidents.

7. Responses Towards Physical Environment: It has already been pointed out that the physical conditions existing in an industry such as the quantity, quality and direction of light, arrangement for fresh and clean air, proper ventilation, hygiene, level of noise, the amount of humidity in the air, etc., have an important influence upon the efficiency of the worker. In order to find out the kind of conditions that should exist in a particular industry it is necessary to find out the workers response to their environment. Clearly, it is the industrial psychology who can find out and determine the quantity and the quality of these physical conditions which are desirable.

8. Problems of Production: Maximum production in any industry can only be achieved under certain circumstances. Even if the machines are the best, it is essential that the worker handling them must also be capable. How can this ability be tested? In every factory many machines are installed. How can one find the particular person best suited to operate each particular machine? And out of the many people who apply for a job in a factory how can one discover the few who may prove to be really capable? In order to achieve maximum production it is necessary that machines should be so designed as to include the minimum fatigue and the lighting so arranged to give the least possible strain to the workers. Besides, most people soon become bored with their work. How can their enthusiasm be reawakened? How should be factory work designed so as to reduce the number of accident? Psychology is needed to solve all these problems which be set every industry.

9. Problems of Selling: The work of an industry does not end with the production of things, but carries on till the produced goods are sold. If one does not get success in selling the final produce, its quality and quantity matter less than nothing. And in order to sell things, it is necessary that people should be acquainted with the product, its qualities and should develop the need to buy them. Advertisement serves the purpose, and successful advertisement is based on appeal. Hence, the value of psychology in the field of advertisement can hardly be disputed.

10. Prevention and Solution of Industrial Conflicts: No industry is free and completely out from quarrels and conflicts of a minor or major kind. At times these conflicts get out of hand and lead to strikes by the workers and lockouts by the management. There are extreme cases in which such conflicts lead to widespread arson, gheraoes, murder and wilful destruction of public and private property. Although some economic demands or political factors may be at the root of such industrial conflicts, the most important factor influencing the action of workers and management alike is the Psychological element. This is why sometimes even great issues are overlooked so that no conflict occurs while relatively insignificant incidents like the impolite words of a manager to a worker may lead to a strike and violent conflicts. It is the psychological factor which results in strikes and conflicts becoming extremely violent. If then, such conflicts are to be resolved, the mere satisfaction of economic demands is not enough. It is necessary also to remove those factors which, from the psychological stand point, are responsible for the occurrence of such conflicts. If these psychological factors are kept in view right from the beginning, it is possible to reduce the number of conflicts. And it is the task of Industrial Psychologist to study these factors.

11. Problem of Personnel Conduct: While the majority of workers are inspired to revolt and conflict because of some defect in the environment, there are a few workers in whom the root cause of misconduct and conflict is due to some defect of personality and character. In such cases, it is necessary to consult the industrial psychologist that can trace the causes of the individual's maladjustment and offer a solution.

The importance and value of the industrial psychologist's advice in big industrial complexes is evident from the above exposition of his role in solving various problems of industry. It is for this reason that in all developed countries industrial psychologists are invariably employed in all large-scale industries.

Objectives of Industrial Psychology

As a branch of applied psychology, industrial psychology has the following objectives:

1. Personal Selection: Industrial psychology tries to find out how a suitable individual can be selected to perform a particular task. If these can be done, then the work gets the correct worker where the worker himself gets the work he can do best.

2. Care of Worker's Health: If the worker does not have good mental and physical health the work of the industry cannot progress smoothly. His mental and physical health is profoundly influenced by the conditions under which he is required to work and by this relations with the management. The objectives of Industrial Psychology is to discover the ideal conditions in which the best mental and physical health of the worker can be maintained.

3. Protection of Worker's Economic Interest: Mental health cannot be maintained unless a person's economic interests are secure. Besides the worker cannot be encouraged to give of his best if he is uncertain about his economic condition. Hence Industrial Psychology evaluates the efficiency of the worker and determines an adequate salary or suggests scientific principles on the basis of which an adequate salary can be determined.

4. **Search of Proper Methods of Work:** One important reason of accidents and mishaps in factories is the improper methods of work. Improper working also promotes fatigue and boredom. Hence, another objective of Industrial Psychology to find out the proper methods of work so that accidents are prevented and fatigue and boredom reduced to the minimum.

5. **Removing Maladjustment:** Another important factor which causes industrial conflicts is the lack of adjustment between the worker and his circumstances and the conditions in which he works. This maladjustment is primarily psychological in nature. It is the task of the industrial psychologist to locate the cause of maladjustment and to suggest means of rectifying it. This is another objective of Industrial Psychology.

6. **Reform of Working Conditions:** It is the task of the industrial psychology to find out the ideal conditions in which the highest efficiency can be attained and the worker maintained at the peak of mental and physical health. The most important working conditions are – arrangement for adequate and proper lighting, proper ventilation, absence of noise, provision for periodical rest, normal conveniencies for the male and female employees, etc.

7. **Reform in Machines:** The worker and the machine are equally responsible for the number of accidents and amount of fatigue induced in the worker. Prevention of accident and reduction in fatigue can be achieved by the proper designing of machines. Industrial psychologists give useful suggestions for the improvement of machines and tools.

8. **Reform in Human Relationships:** In order to maintain a proper atmosphere and a high degree of morale among the workers in an industry it is necessary to have proper and cordial human relations between the workers and the management. One objective of the industrial psychologist is to suggest means of improving human relations.

9. **Humanistic Approach in Industry:** Psychological studies have established that human relations industry cannot do good unless a humanistic approach is adopted. Hence the relations existing between the management and the various level of workers should be improved and the barriers between them removed. Industrial psychology helps in spreading the humanistic approach in industry.

Progress in the field of industry depends not only on advances in technology but also upon the cordiality and pleasantness of human relations. In the field of industry these human relations are also the industrial relations, and are fundamentally psychological in nature. They depend upon the interest, motives, sentiments, and passions of individuals. If their nature is to understood and they are to be made more profitable, it is necessary to undertake a study of interests, motives, sentiments and passions, which is the task of psychology. for this reason, psychological study in the sphere of industry is of great value. The following facts can be pointed out about the contribution of Industrial Psychology to industry:

1. **Solution of Labour Problems:** Conflicts between management and workers is almost a normal feature of every industry and can be caused by almost any factor. Often they become so violent that it results in severe losses in terms of money and lives to both the management and the workers. At the root of all such conflicts are some psychological tensions. It is the task of psychology to study these conflicts, and for that reason psychology can help in the solution of these problems. Most of the means adopted today to improve the relations between the management and the worker are in fact evolved from psychological observation and testing under actual industrial conditions over a long period. They cannot be changed by the wish of any one individual. The truth of the matter is that a conflict can be resolved only if the various factors inherent in it are separated and analysed. Even in the sphere of industrial conflicts, only the psychologist can do this. One major cause of conflict, for example, is the individual differences between individuals which are studied by psychology. Just as a doctor is consulted in the case of bodily disease, and the sociologist consulted about social problems, the industrial psychologist should be considered a specialist on psychological problems in industry and his help should be sought..

2. **Prevention of Accidents:** Psychology has provided valuable suggestions not only in the solution of conflicts but also in the prevention of accidents. Psychologists have discovered the kinds of machines that should be designed, the manner in which they should be operated and the plan according to which they should be arranged in a factory. The purpose of this study is to find means of preventing

accidents. The psychologist finds out how much accident prone the workers are and suggests methods of getting rid of this propensity.

3. Study of Aptitudes: Irrepsective of the quality and nature of the physical conditions prevailing in a factory, it depends upon the worker's aptitude towards the work if aptitude is there, the work will get done but if his aptitude is not suitable then even the best conditions cannot persuade the worker to work. The study and measurement of aptitude is the subject of psychology and is the psychologist who can help the industrialist here.

4. Maintaining Morale: In order to maintain a certain level of production and to improve the quality of production, it is necessary in every industry and profession to maintain a high level of morale among the workers. Morale is influenced by a large number of psychological factors such as affection and freedom, the desire to make sacrifices, availability of proper leadership, etc. By studying these the psychologists can give suggestions for maintaining morale.

5. Creating Proper Leadership: The study of leadership is the responsibility of social psychology. In the field of industry the supervisor must not only be an official but also a capable leader because otherwise he cannot guide the worker properly and encourage them to work hard, Social Psychology can help in the field of industry by pointing out the qualities that are necessary for leadership and by explaining how such qualities can be developed. It can also tell the industrialist about the person who has qualities or how is capable of developing them.

6. Measurement of Individual Differences: Success in industry of a profession can be achieved only if the most capable workers are assigned jobs which they are best capable of performing. If this can be done, the worker perform their functions with interest and can thus increase production and improve its quality. And individual differences can only be discovered by a wide variety of psychological tests. Hence, the assistance of the psychologist can prove of great value in his sphere.

7. Study of Efficiency: In an industry all the workers do not have to be of same degree of efficiency. Nor is this required, because there are many different kinds of functions to be performed, for which varying levels of efficiency are needed. The psychologist finds out which person has the requisite efficiency to perform a particular job. In addition to this the psychologist can also give suggestions for improving efficiency by removing those obstacles which hinder efficient working.

8. Use of Psychological Tests: In the present day psychological test are being extensively employed to select the most qualified individuals for particular jobs in industry. The chief tests are those of intelligence, interest, aptitude and personality. Sometimes many of these tests are included in a single test battery. Some of these tests are used on individuals while others are used to study the group qualities of workers. All of these tests have their own limitations but even then they are successfully used in the recruitment of employees in the industry.

9. Motion and Times Studies: Different people take varying amount of times to complete a specific job because they work at different speed. Today times and motion studies are conducted to find out the efficiency of individuals and even of machines. These studies have also been used to find out means by which a specific work can be done better in a shorter time. Labour and time are saved by analysing motion studies so that essential movements can be isolated and concentrated upon. Time studies help in economizing upon the time spent in a particular operation. In modern factories the machines, the specific places at which particular workers sit and the positions in which they sit are so arranged as to save time and to improve efficiency. All this is done to eliminate all unnecessary movement and duplication of work.

10. Aid in Industrial Training: It is now accepted that the efficiency of a worker can be appreciably improved by the proper kinds of training and that the expense involved in training is paid off doublefold. Trained people can avoid accidents while the quality and quantity of their production is far higher than that of untrained people. Hence, different kinds of training programmes for different jobs are now called for. At the same time training programmes for workers at all level are now organized regularly. The industrialist stands to gain by all such training imparted to his employees. Such training programmes can be devised only by the psychologist who can point out the basis of such training and the methods in it.

11. Suggestion Concerning Motives: An employee must be motivated if he is to progress in his job. This motivation can be supplied through increase in wages, promotion, and praise or in many other ways. In the absence of motivation or on account of disappointment, the quality upon the quantity of the workers, output both suffer. The special study of motivation is the task of psychology. Only a psychologist can point how a worker can be motivated to improve the quality and quantity of his produce, how the workers' motives can be prevented from leading them to strike, how wages should be paid so as to constitute a permanent motive. All these suggestions tremendously help in the working of an industry.

12. Studies of Fatigue and Monotony: The most important obstacle in the way of increasing production is fatigue and monotony. Psychologists have conducted extensive studies into the cause of both and into the ways and means of eliminating them. These suggestions can be of great help in removing fatigue and monotony from industrial work.

13. Vocation Guidance: Vocation guidance involves the finding out of an individual's capabilities through psychological tests and suggesting the profession for which the individual is best suited. It is the suggestion given by a psychologist, which if acted upon by the worker, will help to exploit his own talent to the greatest extent. In most of the progressive nations an individual is given vocational guidance about the various professions he can enter profitably, even before he has completed his education. The chief benefit of this method is that the individual can then pursue a course of studies which will train him for the right profession.

14. Advertisement and Selling: In the sphere of industry the psychologist's advice is not limited only to suggesting methods of improving production but is also concerned with suggesting methods of advertisement and selling. Advertisement is based upon the psychology of appeal. Psychology studies those factors which are involved in appeal. It then gives suggestions about the subject matter and the layout of the advertisement so that it can attract the attention of the greatest possible number of people. One example of this is the use of neon signs for advertisement during the night. Apart from advertisement, modern industries try to make use of psychological ideas in selling so that they can convince the customer of the utility of the goods and persuade him to buy it. Psychologists have analysed the process of buying. They not only explain how the salesman should persuade the customer to buy his stock but also how the customer should avoid being trapped into unnecessary expenses by the salesman.

It is clear from the above explanation that psychology has great importance for industry and this importance is increasing day by day.

In different factories, offices and other professional premises, the worker is compelled to work under certain conditions. He may be required to continue his effort, of a definite kind, in some specific place. His health stands to be influenced greatly by virtue of the fact whether his place of work is adequately and properly ventilated or not. Provision of adequate lighting is an essential condition and one which justifiably occupies the worker's mind, since it will influence his eye-sight, thereby his fatigue and consequently his efficiency and the quality of his output. It is well-known that noise can be a disturbing element, and may put one off one's work. One of the conditions of work is that there be little if any noise: hence this must be taken into consideration. Temperature or the climate is another factor that influences the potential of a worker, as it is known that is certain temperatures a worker cannot work well while in more moderate or suitable temperature his work takes a turn for the better. Temperature, also must be taken into consideration when looking out for the place of work. In addition to these physical conditions, there are many other psychological conditions that also influence the worker and consequently his work. Of these, some are the behaviour of those in authority, mutual relationships among the workers, their respective family lives, incentives to work, etc.

In this manner the condition of work can be divided into two classes:

1. Physical conditions,
2. Psychological conditions,

Of the physical conditions, the main ones are:

1. Intensity, location, distribution and colour of light,

2. Temperature,
3. Ventilation,
4. Noise,
5. Working Hours,
6. Rest Pauses,
7. Music,
8. Other Physical Conditions.

Of the psychological conditions that affect work, the main are:

1. Behaviour of the Authorities,
2. Mutual Relations of the Employees,
3. Security,
4. Satisfaction of Needs,
5. Incentives.

Physical Conditions of Work:

1. Intensity, Location, Distribution and Colour of Light: The kinds and intensity of light differs with the age of the workers as well as with the occupation that they have adopted. As a normal rule, individuals over 30 require light of a greater intensity than their younger counterparts. If the objects handled are minute, then naturally, the light must be fairly bright while in work where objects handled are of a large size, and the workers are fairly young, intense light is not necessary. Light provided should never be in tense enough to cause glare, and never dim enough to cause strain in concentrating upon an object to be worked. Work that requires light of high intensity also requires the use of special protected glasses, as is the case with welding where the light of a very high intensity is produced by the welding flame. Protection from its harmful effects is achieved by the use of coloured glasses.

The source of light should be so located as to avoid falling directly upon the eyes; instead, it should fall on the instrument that is to be manipulated and then also in a manner to avoid all reflection into the eyes of the person handling it. Hence, light should be evenly distributed and for this, tube lighting has been found to be superior to bulb lamps, which are now considered obsolete.

Daylight is naturally uniform in its distribution; it is only when the work is done at night that the problem of uniform and even lighting arises, and it is a problem that requires expert handling and planning.

Besides the intensity and location of light, it is necessary to pay attention to its colour. It has been uniformly experienced in a large number of cases the light that resembles day light very nearly is the best and most beneficial. Hence, white light has been considered the most superior. And in coloured lights, the best is a light yellow but a healthy yellow and not a sickly pale yellow. All other coloured lights harm the eyes in some measure.

2. Temperature: Temperature of the working premises has considerable and direct influence on the worker's health, it having been found that working in too high or too low temperature leads to disease and accident. Proper temperature maintains good health in the workers, and reduces the number of accidents as external conditions do not divert the attention of the worker and thus reduce his efficiency. H.M. Vernon found that in the British mines in temperatures about 75 Fahrenheit there were greater number of accidents while the perception and sensibility for workers were also adversely affected. Extreme temperatures in working areas cause discomfort to the worker, so much so that the quality as well as quantity of his output is reduced. Temperature further influences the ventilation in a room, as it is essential for proper ventilation and flow of air to have only an adequate temperature.

3. Ventilation: Inflow of fresh air is essential in a place of work, as its absence tends to increase the fatigue and laziness or drowsiness of the workers. Air easily becomes contaminated in places where large number of individuals work together, such as mines, factories and offices. For this the use of exhaust fans is particularly desirable. Transport should be freely and easily available in places of work. Health is adversely affected if the percentage of Oxygen in air is varied even within very narrow limits. According to Poffenberger, when the percentage of Oxygen in air tends to fall below 14, the workers show signs of adverse effect, Ventilation also influences the body temperature of the workers, and if the body temperature varies it leads to fatigue and drowsiness. Another important factor is the presence as well as the percentage of humidity in the air. Excessive humidity in undeniable percentage of humidity influence.

4. Noise: Excessive noise normally distract attention and obstruct smooth working. It is for this reason that in every industry now attention is paid to the noise produced, and efforts are made to curb noise that distract attention. But noise of a continuous nature is often found to be more soothing than disturbing, and when it is discontinued it disturbs the attention of people used to it. The truth of the matter is that only excessive noise is harmful and has the worst effect on the authority system. Keeping in mind these observations, efforts should be made to regulate noise.

5. Hours of Work: Profession in which the hours of work are so long and unhygienically planned that the worker is completely fatigued by the time he stops working, finds himself confronted with the, problem of continuously decreasing efficiency. In addition to this, these professions become prey to all kinds of very serious problems of human relationships. When a worker is compelled to work for long hours beyond his physical endurance limits, he becomes diseased and loses his efficiency. Besides, his irritability increases significantly. For this reason in most progressive nations, the government promulgates certain orders whereby the hours of work for different occupations, for individuals of different ages and of different sexes, are determined. If need for more work arises, the employer is faced either with the alternative of including an illegal activity or remunerating the worker for this extra labour. But if he chooses to evade these laws, he incurs the displeasure of the law, and this is never to his advantage.

6. Rest Pauses: Whenever the ability and endurance of an individual, even if he be abnormal in this respect, he cannot work continuously for long period of time. After a certain period of time, he feels the need for a rest, and his need has been found to have psychological justification as it has been found that better results can be obtained by working in shifts and period than by working continuously. Increase of between ten and twenty per cent in production have been found to ocur as a result of provision of rest in between work. The length and frequency of rest that is required depends upon the nature of work, the endurance and age of the worker and the general conditions of work. Hard work requires relatively longer and greater number of rest pauses. Similarly women, young children and old require longer and greater number of rest pauses, then young men. Nowadays in practically every profession and occupation, rest of 15 minutes to an hour are provided once or more so that the worker may be able to take refreshments and restore his vitality otherwise. Rest in between hours of work not only removes fatigue, it also eliminates the element of monotony and boredom, thereby regenerating enthusiasm and vitality.

7. Music: One of the conditions of work taken into consideration is music. From their experiments W.A. Keir, and H.C. Smith concluded that music has a beneficial and desirable influence upon the mental condition of worker, and thus it helps to induce some increase in their productive capacity. And one often sees people singing at their work, a phenomenon particularly obvious in the case of Indian women working at the grinder or in the fields or even when at their domestic chores. The rhythm in music has a beneficial effect on the rate of working. Tata in India provide music in their various factories. In Western countries, particularly in the United States, the use of music in factories and other working places is steadily on the increase. Through a questionnaire H.C. Smith collected the views of one thousand workers regarding the provision of music in working places, and found that as many as 98 per cent of them are in favour of it, as they found considerable pleasure in it. The influence of music on routine work is as yet under extensive study.

8. Other Physical Conditions: In addition to these above conditions, there are other physical and material considerations which influence the worker and his works. For example, if there is good and clean provision of urinals, latrines, bathrooms, refreshment rooms, canteen, etc., the workers' time in the office becomes more pleasant, and many of his difficulties are removed. A place of work should neither be foul smelling, nor should it be dirty or dusty, as any of these conditions disgusts the worker.

Psychological Conditions of Work

1. Behaviour of Those in Authority: A worker's mind is very susceptible to the behaviour of his boss. If the behaviour of authorities is desirable and good, the worker's enthusiasm and interest in his work is maintained, but if their behaviour is bad and inconsiderate, it is potentially a dangerous state as it can lead to conflict and unnecessary tension that has the worst effect upon production. Good behaviour does not imply laxity in administration and in dealing with the workers as in such circumstances it is inevitable that the lazy and designing individuals in the organization will have a field day and do not work at all. It is essential that constant attention be paid to the worker's performance, but fact and diplomacy should be employed if it becomes necessary to point out his shortcomings. Senior officials and employers, who are in the habit of constantly haranguing and bickering with their staff, are very often faced continuous conflict and non-cooperation. Employees are not inclined to respect and work for people who are irritable, highly inflammable and ingratiating types. Working under a considerate individual not only keeps the worker happy but also inspires him to work more and work better.

2. Mutual Relations of Workers: One of the psychological conditions of working is the nature of relations that exist between the workers themselves. Where the number of workers is fairly large, and the nature of work demands their constant cooperation, better results are obtained if the workers have happy relations. If the relations are not all that can be desired, work suffers. And particularly work that requires comparative effort is a total loss as there is no co-operation.

3. Security in Profession: If the worker is confident that he is secured in his job, then his work shows definite improvements. In a profession that offers no security of employment, or in a position in which one can never be confident of remaining safe a worker cannot work with enthusiasm or with his mind on the work. Hence, a profession must offer security of future employment. After a certain predetermined period of service has been completed, the worker should be made permanent in his position, as is now done in all government jobs and many private firms. Even most government in any countries have made laws regarding such employment procedure. Besides, this minimal security of profession, other inducements are insurance, during unemployment, old age insurance, and security or insurance in the event of accidents that render the individual incapable of further work. Nowadays, in all progressive states, government and other general employers make provision for these benefits, as in their absence it is only natural for the worker to spend time in wondering about his future and making efforts to secure it that enables him for his regular work.

4. Satisfaction of Life's Needs: Every individual has some personal and other family requirements, such as adequate food and housing for his family, and purchasing power to the extent of his other reasonable needs. Besides this, there are certain needs that foster self-respect, and these, too cannot be neglected. Progress has made it necessary for employers to pay attention to these aspect of the human personality also. Consequently they have to initiate and finance certain schemes of labour welfare that involve some expenditure, but which provide many direct and indirect benefits to the worker that place him in a very favourable state of mind. Their needs being fulfilled, they are inclined to respect and obey their employers, to work for their better being, in turn. They are thus helped in leading a pleasant and contended life, and they bend their backs to their work with a will. They have confidence in their employers, and thus they are never induced to work contrary to the interests of their employers.

5. Incentive in Industry: Motives have an important place in the life of man. In the absence of a motive no individual can either work hard or do anything to better his lot in life or improve his work in any way. Inspiration of this kind is available to the individual in his trade in the forms of various kinds of incentive such as increase in wages, praise by authorities, promotion, bonus, etc. Incentives are now an important part of any geared up industry. In most progressive nations, the workers stand to benefit through bonus if the production, and thus the earning of their enterprise, goes up. In most professions, an individual is promoted to a senior position if he shows satisfactory or more than satisfactory work. If the people in authority are sensible people, they will always praise the extra efforts of their subordinates. Their wages can also be increased so as to form an extra inducement.

All the afore mentioned physical and psychological conditions have considerable importance for commerce and industry. Psychologists have now seriously drawn the attention of the industrialist to this aspect. It is necessary not only with regard to economic or fiscal gain, but also with regard to humanity that the workers should have opportunity to work in beneficial conditions, both physical and psychological. Workers being part and parcel of the fibre of the nation, the government also should take steps to have such conditions created. When such a system is in existence in industry, the conflicts are materially reduced and the production materially increased with the results that the employer, the employee and the state all benefit.

Fatigue of workers is an important problem in motivation and industrial psychology. Fatigue is a sort of negative appetite for activity. It arises due to continuous or large work. Interest in work and quantity of output both decline as fatigue increases. Of course, fatigue may be due to excessive physical or mental demands on employees or to the nature of working assignments. Whatever, the causes, it is an important motivational problem.

Types of Fatigue

Fatigue can be both mental and physical, their description is as follows:

1. **Physical Fatigue:** In physical fatigue, as is evident from the name itself, one finds physical characteristics of fatigue. Physical efficiency and capacity fall down and physical coordination becomes difficult. A poisonous fluid known as lactic acid is produced in the muscles and the nervous system, and when this increases beyond a certain level the entire body becomes lax. If it is confined to any one part of the body, then that particular part becomes tired but when exhaustion increases it is introduced into the blood stream and steadily spreads over the entire body. In addition to lactic acid, the body also produces ammonia and carbon dioxide during fatigue. Both these elements are poisonous and by their influence the energizing elements in the body steadily decrease while the poisonous matter increases. Many psychologists have examined the condition of fatigue, the most valuable work having been done by Miller, Helmholtz and Wundt. Miller confined his study to the state of the nerves in a condition of fatigue. Later on Helmholtz made a study of the function of the sensory nerves and motor nerves and discovered that in a condition of fatigue the experience of anything is conveyed to the brain in greater time while the motor nerves take a longer time to react than under normal conditions. Helmholtz invented the Myograph, an instrument used to measure the contraction of muscles. It was later used in 1858 by Wundt in his experiments. This instrument is now used to measure fatigue.

2. **Mental Fatigue:** Fatigue is not merely physical because it is sometimes manifested even when one has done no physical work. This is mental fatigue. Mental fatigue is normally apparent after excessive physical fatigue. The symptoms of mental fatigue are in absence of desire to work, emotional condition, lack of interest and concentration, lack of normal efficiency in work, desire to rest, etc. At times one's efficiency does not suffer despite some mental fatigue but this is a rare case. One example of mental fatigue is boredom in which one experiences mental fatigue because one's energy has not been properly consumed. One important cause of mental fatigue is the absence of motivation and of a proper aptitude. In such a case an individual loses interest in his work even though he is not physically exhausted. People complain of fatigue despite good working conditions if their aptitude is nct correct and is there if absence of sufficient motivation.

Difference between Physical and Mental Fatigue

Despite the differences between physical and mental fatigue mentioned above, the two should not be taken to be entirely different, for they are intimately related to each other. A person who complains of fatigue is in fact suffering both from mental as well as physical fatigue. Sometimes a person does not feel physical fatigue if a strong motivation is coupled with absence of mental fatigue. In most forms of fatigue one finds both physical and mental symptoms. According to Watson, mental fatigue is caused by the contraction of the vocal cord. It is also caused by damage to the nerve centres in the higher regions of the brain. Mental work cannot be done efficiently in a condition of physical fatigue, nor can physical work be done well in a condition of mental fatigue. For this reason it is better to define fatigue as a psychosomatic or psychophysical condition rather than a physical condition in which the individual's mental and physical efficiency is reduced. The truth of the matter is that the physical and mental aspects of fatigue can be distinguished only verbally, because in actual fact they are not independent of each other.

Causes of Fatigue

In different professions, there are different causes which lead to fatigue. Important causes can be briefly summarised as under:

1. **Long hours of work:** In some industries the hours of work are so long that the workers become exhausted while in fact these longer hours of work do not result in a proportionate increase in production. Many researches have thrown light on this fact. Muscio has mentioned the case of one lady worker who worked only six hours instead of the conventional twelve hours a day observed by the other workers and still showed a higher level of production than any other worker. In this factory the working hours were from 6 to 8 in the morning, eight-thirty to twelve-thirty-one-thirty to five-thirty and from eight-thirty to twelve-thirty. This particular lady refused to work before breakfast and late at night, explaining that by working for such a long time she could not maintain her efficiency. Over a period of one month it was seen that she worked for 150 hours as compared to the other workers who worked for 237 hours, despite which she showed more output than the others. It is evident from the research conducted in various countries on the methods of work that production is higher in shorter working week than in longer working weeks.

2. **Absence of rest periods:** If a person works for a long time continuously then he feels fatigued if he does not take rest and continues to work, then his fatigue increases even more rapidly because he is working in an exhausted condition. If he is allowed to rest as soon as he begins to feel exhausted, then he returns to his work refreshed and his fatigue does not increase. Hence it is seen that fatigue is eliminated in all working methods where the workers are allowed to rest for short periods during their working hours because during the period of rest they can regain their energy. Absence to rest period is an occupational conditions which promotes fatigue. Even if some workers steal a few minutes of rest where it is not officially provided for, they do not feel relaxed and rested because during that period their aptitude is not correct. In fact, relaxation of this kind results in greater fatigue. Gillbreath's experiments successfully established that production can be increased by providing periods of rest for the workers instead of keeping them at work continuously.

3. **Incorrect temperature:** Incorrect room temperature in another occupational condition which results in fatigue because in the cases the room is earlier too hot or too cold. In both cases the mental and physical condition of the workers deteriorate and he soon feels exhausted.

4. **Absence of proper ventilation:** If a person does not get clean air in the room in which he is working he soon gets tired. In an office or factory in which the air is polluted the incidence of fatigue will be far greater than in any other factory where there is adequate ventilation.

5. **Improper Illumination:** Fatigue also increase if the illumination in the working area is not adequate and proper because the eyes begin to feel exhausted and dry if the light is not enough or too bright. Hence, it is desirable that there should be proper arrangements for illumination in factories and offices. Proper lighting from the right direction. For example, in working, it is desirable that the light source should be placed behind and to the left of the worker. If this is not done, then the eyes suffer great strain. In working on a machine it is desirable that those instruments should be lighted up which are to be seen constantly by the operator. Hence the light provided should neither be too little nor too much, for in both these conditions the strain on the eyes leads to fatigue.

6. **Design of the Machinery:** Certain machines are so designed that they tend to exhaust and tire the operator working on them. Hence modern psychologist give suggestions even in the construction of machines so that they should be designed to minimise fatigue and increase production. This branch of industrial psychology involves the least possible amount of movement while maintaining the highest level

of production. When the workers become used to operating such machine their fatigue is reduced and their work improves.

7. Absence of Adequate Seat: It is a well-known fact that a person feels exhausted much earlier if he has to operate a machine while standing. That is why the absence of an adequate seat is one occupational condition which causes fatigue. Another important feature of the seat is that should not offer too much confront because in the case the operator feels sleepy. On the other hand it should not be so hard that the operator may discomfort. Arrangement for a proper seat can help in reducing fatigue.

8. Excessive Noise: Another occupational condition which increase fatigue is the presence of excessive noise at the place of work. An individual can work for a long time in an atmosphere which is peaceful and free of noise. Some degree of noise can be tolerated, for it has no appreciable effect on work but when noise rises above a certain level it creates fatigue. Now experiments are made to find out if the noise produced by the machinery is of a high enough pitch to induce fatigue. If this happens, then efforts are made to reduce the pitch of sound produced and so reduce the level of noise, Karnhouser conducted an experiment for our typists who worked in a noisy environment for four days. The psychologist came to the conclusion that their work went down by 3.2 per cent while the incidence of errors went up by 23 per cent. In an experiment conducted by Western worker engaged in stitching showed 7.5 per cent more production when working in peaceful surrounding than when working in a noisy environment.

9. Unhealthy Conditions: Fatigue is intimately connected with health. the occupational conditions are such that they do not promote good health then they are also conducive of fatigue. Unhealthy conditions include such factors as incorrect room temperature, improper ventilation, excessive noise, etc. In addition to these certain other occupational conditions like excessively humidity, absence of rest, presence of some disturbing smell, inadequate arrangement for medicine and medical attendance or the total lack of such facilities also have a bad influence upon the health of the workers with the result that they soon become tired.

10. Absence of Proper Training: In every profession there are certain functions which require some training before they can be properly performed. If such functions are entrusted to untrained employees then these workers become exhausted very rapidly. Hence the employees should be trained by the best methods about the easiest and least training way for handling certain instruments. They should also be guided in adjusting the hours of work and the periods of rest according to their individual differences. Hence, the absence of proper training is also an occupational condition which results in fatigue.

11. Lack of Sleep: In factories in which the workers have to work at night and cannot get adequate rest during the day, lack of sleep forms another factor which results in fatigue. To eliminate these facilities for sleep should be provided for the workers so that they can sleep during their period of rest. Absence of sleep is invariably an exhausting factor, irrespective of the condition which leads to it.

12. Low Morale: Conditions which are conducive to low morale are also conducive to fatigue. Conditions which result in low morale and harmful attitudes towards the management, hatred, suspicion and jealousy, dissatisfaction with work and absence of any hope, mental unrest and dissatisfaciton, uninteresting work, improper rules governing promotions, absence of a proper wage increase, improper methods of distribution for wages, lack of adjustment on the part of management, etc. In all such conditions fatigue also increases rapidly and leads to physical fatigue. Conditions in which high morale can be generated also leads to energetic work.

13. Defects of the Social Environment: The defects of the social environment of an occupation in which many people work also lead to fatigue. A worker cannot maintain high morale in a condition in which the relations between the employers and employees are not good or in which the atmosphere is one of hate or suspicion. The result is that in such conditions the workers feels exhausted very quickly. Since people have now understood the significance of maintaining a healthy social atmosphere in the place of work efforts are made to make the social atmosphere cooperative and refreshing or encouraging. This must be done so that the worker can work for a long time without feeling exhausted.

In fact, all occupational conditions which have an adverse influence upon the worker's mental and physical condition are conducive to fatigue because in such conditions mental and physical fatigue is very rapid. Hence all such conditions should be corrected if fatigue is to be avoided. But for this all workers and the managers and the government will have to work cooperatively.

Meaning of Reducing Fatigue

Roughly speaking the chief method of reducing fatigue is to eliminate all occupational conditions which increase it. Hence, mention will here be made of this means by which fatigue can be reduced. It should always be kept in mind that work invariably results in some degree of exhaustion and that there can be no ways of eliminating fatigue completely. One can only hope to devise means by which fatigue can be reduced or controlled before it becomes excessive. Briefly, this can be done in the following ways:

1. **Reducing the Hours of Work:** One way of reducing fatigue is to reduce the hours of work. It has been seen in many experiments that fatigue is reduced when working hours are reduced, whereas the production does not fall proportionately but in many cases actually increases. In 1928 Sheppard pointed out that for the previous thirty years workers were made to work ten hours a day for six days a week in all American industries. On the other hand, the workers are now made to work eight hours, besides which on Saturdays they are required to work only four hours, while Sunday is a day of rest. But actually production has increased as a result of this decrease in the hours of work. Many other experiments have substantiated Sheppard's conclusions. Hence, one way of reducing fatigue is to reduce the hours of work. But at the same time care should be taken to avoid reducing working hours to such an extent that the worker's energy is not fully utilized. The most appropriate method is to the have sufficient working hours in which the worker can continue to work without feeling totally exhausted. Evidently working hours will differ from industry to industry, according, to the nature of the work.

2. **Provision of Rest Periods:** Another way of reducing fatigue is to introduce appropriate properly timed periods of rest. An appropriate period of rest involves calculation of the total rest period allowed in proportion to the work expected from the worker. And a properly timed rest period implies the time at which this rest should be allowed and the frequency with which it should be allowed. Many experiments on this subject have yield a fund of valuable facts. According to Vernon, the worker should be allowed rest after every hour while according to Sheppard the worker who works for hours a eight day should be allowed to rest for 16.6 per cent of the total working time. It is evident that in providing rest periods, one must consider the total rest period in proportion to the working hours as well as the frequency and duration for which it should be given.

3. **Arrangements for Maintaining the Correct Temperature:** In order to reduce fatigue it is necessary to maintain the correct room temperature in the place of work. Arrangements should be made to raise the temperature in winters and to lower it in summers. If the temperature is adequate then the workers can work longer without experiencing fatigue. For this reason many modern factories have air-conditioned rooms or other means of reducing the heat during the summers while heaters and other contrivances are used to increase the temperature in the winter months.

4. **Proper Ventilation:** Fatigue can also be reduced by improving the ventilation so that the polluted air is eliminated and fresh air admitted into the factory. Most factories make use of exhaust fans designed to suck the polluted air out of a room or a hall.

5. **Arrangement for Proper Lighting:** Fatigue can also be reduced to some extent if proper provision is made for lighting up the area in which the workers work. For this it is necessary that the light should come from the light direction and should be of a particular intensity. The advantage in this is that the eyes do not suffer strain and hence the workers do not become tired quickly.

6. **Improvements in the Design of Seating:**

7. **Proper Seating Arrangement:** A proper seating arrangement for the worker also helps to reduce fatigue. As far as possible the workers should be allowed to work while sitting. The seat should provide normal comfort to avoid fatigue but it should not be too comfortable; for in that case it will induce sleep. But it should also not be too hard.

8. Control Over the Noise: Since excessive noise also induces fatigue, it is desirable to have some control over the amount of noise in or near the working place, if fatigue is to be avoided. This can be done in many ways. It is more difficult to reduce the noise made by the machines installed in the factories but efforts should be made to control the noise produced. If the noise in the factory or office is less, the worker's fatigue will also be less.

9. Healthy Working Conditions: If the working conditions are conducive to health then fatigue always remains at a low level because the workers health and his fatigue are directly related to each other. In order to create healthy conditions it is necessary to pay attention of the ventilation, sufficient light, absence of noise, proper room temperature, control over the humidity, medical facilities, adequate arrangement for rest and food, etc. All these things help to refresh the worker.

10. Arrangements for Industrial or Professional Training: The worker feels less fatigue in manipulating a machine for which he has been trained because he does not make any necessary movements. Hence professional training can also help to reduce fatigue.

11. Proper Arrangements for Sleep: In many kinds of work it is necessary to provide some arrangement for sleep. Even if the worker is given a chance to sleep on a comfortable bed for only half an hour out of the total working time, much of his fatigue disappears. Such an arrangement is particularly useful for the workers working in night shifts.

12. High Morale: High morale can also help to reduce fatigue among the workers. Maintenance of high morale requires an attitude favourable to the management, self-generated discipline, group administration, enthusiasm, mental satisfaction and peace, respect for and confidence in the management, etc. If these factors are present, the incidence of fatigue is much lower.

13. Proper Social Atmosphere: Even the social atmosphere plays an important role in reducing the worker's fatigue. The worker's enthusiasm can be easily maintained and fatigue kept at a low level if good relations with the management can be created and if the general atmosphere is one of cooperation.

14. Special Means of Reducing Fatigue: In addition to the factors explained above many other means are now being adopted to reduce the workers fatigue. For example, in many factories arrangements have been made to play music to the workers while they are engaged in their work because the workers feel less tired if they sing as they work. Many new experiments are being conducted on this aspect these days. Besides, change in the nature of work also helps to keep the worker's interest alive. Hence efforts are made to make the work interesting in many different ways. As industrial psychology progress many new ways of reducing fatigue will definitely be discovered.

Criteria of Fatigue

The criteria of fatigue implies the symptoms by which its presence can be diagnosed and recognised. In order to understand that it is essential to keep in mind the various aspects of fatigue. Since fatigue is a psycho-physical condition its symptoms are both mental and physical. It can be recognised by the following factors:

1. Feeling of Exhaustion: The chief symptom of fatigue is the feeling of fatigue even if the individual is not feeling physically exhausted. In a state of exhaustion the desire of work is noticeably reduced and the desire to rest is clearly heightened. Generally it also leads to a fall in the individual's production, though this is not universally true. In the state of exhaustion the individual's feeling about work changes and he evinces no desire to do any kind of work.

2. Muscular Condition: In a state of fatigue the muscles lose their power to contract and expand. Hence, psychologically, fatigue is muscular condition and the fatigue of the muscles to contract and expand is one criterion of fatigue.

3. Chemical Changes: As a person works the production of acetic acid and other poisonous chemicals in his body increases. In a healthy body the Oxygen is properly distributed through the blood stream with the result that poisonous matter is eliminated from the body. When the muscles become tired this process of elimination does not work sufficiently. This leads to a fall in the quantity of glycogen in the body along with an increase in the quantity of poisonous matter. In this manner many chemical changes occur in the body during fatigue, and it can be recognised by these chemical changes.

4. Nervous Slackness: One criterion of mental exhaustion is nervous slackness. Sometimes it is caused by muscular fatigue but it also has many other causes. In a state of nervous exhaustion the nerves lose their power to react with the result that the individual cannot work efficiently. Many experiments have established that, in a condition of exhaustion, the nerves and muscles do not have the power to react properly or to achieve the normal state of excitation. As a result of this slackness the sense organs do not react properly. The sense of smell is particularly influence while the powers of seeing, hearing and touching are also adversely influenced.

5. Change in the Blood Chemistry: Some symptoms of exhaustion can also be found in the tired persons' blood. If some of this blood is introduced in the blood of some healthy person one will find the symptoms there too. The same is true of the muscles also. On the one hand the blood stream helps to eliminate poisonous matter from the body but on the other hand it also helps to distribute the fatigue all over the body. For this reason the whole body shows signs of exhaustion even when only one part of the body is bearing all the strain. If any one part of the body is put to excessive use then that part shows signs of fatigue earliest but soon these symptoms can be seen all over the body because exhaustion is communicated by the blood.

6. Change in the Mental Condition: One criterion of fatigue is the change in the mental condition because in an exhausted condition the individual experiences deterioration of his mental powers and a loss of interest. He cannot concentrate upon anything for a long time and becomes bored with work. Because of his influence upon the mind, fatigue is considered a psycho-physical phenomenon.

7. Increase in the Number of Accident: An analysis of accidents in industry has revealed the majority of accidents occur either in the morning or late in the evening. This fact has been generally substantiated by studies in Germany, England and America. A study of fatigue has also known that it is greatest early in the morning and late in the evening. Hence one can estimate the extent of industrial fatigue from the number of accidents. For these reasons now provisions are made for introducing rest periods in the early hours and in the late evenings. This patterns of accidents can be seen in almost any industry but while the morning accidents are uniformly present, the late evening accidents follow various patterns in different industries. Accidents in the late evening take place more rapidly but the total number is not much more than that of accidents in the morning. One can see a difference in the number of accidents that take place during the morning and the night shifts. Hence, the relationship between fatigue and accidents is obvious.

It should be kept in mind that despite the clear relationship between fatigue and accidents fatigue is not the sole cause of accidents and for this reason an increase in accidents is not a criterion of increasing fatigue. Many other factors apart from fatigue often prove for more important in causing accidents. For example, women are more accidents prone than men because women tend to tire easily and more rapidly. It cannot be denied that in a state of exhaustion the individual becomes restless, he cannot control his movements properly, he may even go to sleep, he lacks concentration. Despite this, fatigue cannot be accepted cause of accidents.

8. Fall in Production: Sometimes fatigue is defined in terms of the fall in production. As has already been mentioned in connecting with accidents the early morning shift and the late evening shift result in accidents and also in a fall in production. The cause of this fall in production is believed to be fatigue because as fatigue increases the efficiency of the worker decreases. During the first hour in the morning the production rate rises steeply because this is the warning up period. The warming up can be due to numerous mental and physical causes. And the period consumed in warming up to one's work will depend as much upon the work as upon the individual differences between one worker and another. Two factors which are responsible for the rate of the worker's performance are the worker's health and the nature of the conditions under which he has to work. It is normally seen that production reaches its highest peak in the third hour after which production again begins to fall due to fatigue. It is for this reason that a rest period is provided after the third hour of work.

In addition to the above factors all other symptoms of physical and mental fatigue can be accepted as the criteria of fatigue. Fatigue can be recognised by such mental and physical conditions as change in respiration, blood circulation, blood pressure, disinterest, lack of concentration, slackness, etc. Nowadays, many scientific instruments are also used to measure fatigue.

Monotony

Monotony is also a mental condition that is reflected in labour output. Monotonous operations (or, rather, operations that appear to the individual employees as monotonous) tend to result in shifts of interest, with intervals of disinterest and day dreaming. Monotony is not characteristic of work, rather it is an impact of work and the mental condition of a worker. The major causes leading to monotony may include the routine nature of work, to repeat the same work lack of change in work, lack of variety in movements, etc. Sometimes, the purpose of the work also makes a work monotinous. If the worker does not think the work useful and positive, we will 'feel monotony and boredom in that work. Excessive division of work, mechanisation of operations, lack of human relations have also contributed the problem of monotony.

Measures to Remove Monotony

The following steps are useful to remove monotony:

1. **Job Enlargement:** Job enlargement involves a horizontal loading or expansion or the adding of more tasks of the same general nature or type. It provides the necessary change for the worker and he does not feel boredom and monotony in the work.

2. **Job Enrichment:** It is an extension of job enlargement. The difference between job enrichment and job enlargement lies on the nature of addition to the job. Job enrichment involves vertical loading, adding giving more challenge. Thus, it applies to improvement of job in such a way that it has more wide dimensions, more opportunities for achievement, recognition, responsibility, achievement and growth.

3. **Job Rotation:** Job rotation involves the change in work and work place. If possible, job rotation should also be applied in order to overcome monotony.

4. **Provision of Music:** The provision of music also makes the work interesting and pleasing. The researches have proved the utility of music in routine types of jobs.

5. **Employee Counselling:** Employee counselling is also an important method of overcoming monotony in work. The opportunity of counselling makes the workers interested in work, keeps him involved in it and change the attitude of the workers towards the work.

REFERENCES

A. Kornhauser & A.A. Sharp, *Employee Attitudes: Suggestions from a Study in a Factory, Personnel Journal*, Vol. 10, 1932, pp.393-404, See also R.N. Murry: Efficiency, Work Satisfaction and Neurotic Tendency: A Study of Bank Employees Personnel Journal, Vol. II, 1932, pp.201-210.

A. Marro, *Management by Participation*, Harper, New York, 1965.

A.K. Rice, *Productivity and Social Organization – The Ahmedabad Experiment*; Tavistock Publication Ltd., London, 1958.

Carl Rogers, *Counselling and Psychotherapy*, Boston, Houghton Mifflin, 1942, Also Carl Rogers & R.F. Dymond (ed.) *Psychotherapy and personality Change*, Chicago: University of Chicago Press, 1954.

F.W. Roethelisberger and W.J. Dickson, *Management and the Worker*, Cambridge, Mass, Harvard University Press, 1938.

H.C. Ganguli, *Industrial Productivity and Motivation – A Psychological Analysis*, Asia Publishing House, 1961.

H.C. Ganguli: *Industrial Productivity and Motivation – A Psychological Analysis*, Asia Publishing House, 1961.

H.C. Ganguly, Study of Effect of Union Membership on Industrial Morale, Indian Journal of Psychology, Vol. 29, Part I, II, 1954.

H.C. Smith, Psychology of Industrial Behaviour, McGraw Hill, New York, 1955.

H.M. Misra, *Music in Industry, Indian Journal of Social Work*, Vol. 9, No. 4, 1949, pp.275-286. Refd. Indian Psychology, Abstracts from Industrial & Organizational Psychology, Vol. 6, 1976 Item No. 592, p.166.

Ishwar Dayal, *Workers Involvement in the Organization, Industrial Relations, Journal of Indian Institute of Personnel Management* Vol. 28, No. 1, Jan.-Feb., 1976, pp.12-20.

J.Wooward, *Management & Technology*, Her Majesty's Stationery Office, London, 1958.

Keith Davis, *Human Behaviour at Work*, Tata McGraw Hill Publishing Co. Mumbai, 1977, p.40.

Kurt Lewin, *Forces Behind Food Habits and Methods of Change*, Bulletin of the National Research Council, 1943, Also Cartwright Dorwin and A. Zander (Eds.) Group Dynamics, Evanston, III, Row, Pewterson & Company, 1952, 32.

M.L. Blum & J.C. Naylor: *Industrial Psychology – Its Theoretical and Social Foundations*, Harper & Row, New York, 1968, pp. 364-365.

M.L. Blum: *Reading in Experimental Industrial Psychology*, Prentice Hall, Englewood Clifs, 1952, p.107.

N.R. Chatterje, *Industrial Psychology*, Sudha Publication (P) Ltd. New Delhi, 1969, p.335.

Rensis Likert, *The Human Organization*, McGraw-Hill, New York, 1965.

Robert Blake, and Jane Mouton, Managerial Facades, *Advanced Management Journal*, July 1966, p.31.

T.W. Harrell, *Industrial Psychology*, Holt, Rinehart & Winston, New York, Indian Edition Published by Oxford Co., 1964, p.258.

The Survey Research Centre, *Institute for Social Research*, University of Michigan, USA.

White Ralph and Ronald Leder Lippit, Behaviour and Member Reaction in Three Social Climates, in Group Dynamics, Ed. by Dorwin Cartwright and Alvin Zander, Row, Paterson & Co., New York, 1956, pp. 585-611. See also H.C. Ganguli, *Industrial Productivity and Motivation*, Asia Publishing 1961, Chapter 5.

CHAPTER

24

Better Decision Making

In this world everybody in not able to make the best decision in his work or life. Most of the people (due to lack of meaningful experience or proper guidance) make a series of poor decisions in many fields. How can we make better decisions? What is the sole of mind and heart to make better decisions? What is the difference between effective and ineffective decisions? How can we analyse or prepare ourselves to make better decisions? What is the role of intuition and insight? And so many related problems are discussed here in an effective way, which will open the new ways for the decision makers.

From Confusion to Clarity

The results of poor decisions are evident everywhere, e.g., in corporations, in small business enterprises, in educational institutions, in government agencies and too often, in personal life. This happens very often because people are usually never consciously taught how to make decision. Decisions making is often considered to be either something inherent or something which is learnt over time with experience.

Many times people want to make the best decision, but they do not know what is good enough. Perhaps for this reason one does not always need to make the best decision. For things to get better, one only needs to make better decisions, and if one continues to do so, one will eventually do well.

What Are Better Decision

A better decision is one that makes us feel better about we make it and that which gets better results. Many a time people feel that they are indecisive or that they make half decisions ones that they feel may not be good enough. One can overcome this feeling by using a reliable system of doing two things using our heads and consulting our hearts to soon arrive at a better decision. The details of this system has been discussed in the latter pages.

What not to do to Make a Better Decision

Just simply stop doing whatever you are doing. To make a better decision, first stop proceeding with a poor decision, because only they one will create a void which can be filled in with something better.

Usually people feel afraid to give up what they have in fear of not finding anything better. It takes courage to let go of what is familiar and conformable. But in reality, it is actually a safer and more reliable way to get better results. Because once what is not working for you is finally out of your way, you are able to find something better. And one usually does, quite quickly.

The ancient Chinese had an expression in this wisdom: If you want to have a hot cup of tea, must first empty your cup. Pouring hot tea into a cup full of cold tea means the hot tea cannot enter the cup but rather spills over into the saucer.

Suppose one wants to drive west and suddenly realises that he / she is going east, what would one do? The obvious answer to the above question is that one would turn around and change the direction. Similarly our better decision-making concept involves us going in a better direction. To get right direction, one should have good map of ones own on which he / she can rely, rather than rely on other's direction. It is a challenge for us to find a better way on our own and any of us can do it by using the Yes or No system. And to check whether it will work or not, one can begin by using this simple inventory.

Making a Better Decision: A Private Five-Minute Inventory

A Business or Personal Decision:

What is the problem for me – a situation at work or in my life that I wish would improve?

My Initial Decision is to: (I write in my initial decision now)

What am I going to do about it?

For now, I am going to do nothing.

I am going to do something, but I am not sure of what or when.

May be, I will do the following:

My Better Decision is to: (I write this at the end).

A Reliable System

To make any decision, it is recommended to adopt a Yes or No system. This is a two-part journey to arrive at a better decision. To get there, we look at both sides of a decision by asking ourselves two questions – a practical question and a private one and only after that we make our decision.

The system can be explained as follows:

First, we make an initial decision in our normal way by avoiding indecision and half – decision based on half truths.

Then we a reliable system to consistently make better decision: a cool head and a warm heart.

We use our heads by asking ourselves a practical question and consult our hearts by asking a private question.

Finally, after listening to ourselves and others, we make a better decision and act on it.

The key is to use this reliable system because the system produces better results consistently and even if mistakes are made sometimes and never flaws in a person, but they are in the system of thinking which the person, may be using. In the day by day changing world, we all need to make better decisions faster just to survive, let alone prosper.

After making the initial decision, one can make a better decision by using ones head or consulting one's heart in any order that one likes. Both the head and heart questions have three ideas embedded in them. One will probably find that one or two of the ideas will be most useful. These will be the few areas where you feel and need to look at in a particular situation, or during a certain phase of your own life.

Once the system has been learnt, it becomes a mental circle and can enter at any point. The entire process may take varying lengths of time depending upon how important the decision to a person and how clear one is. One can focus on one part of the question which may help one to make a better decision in just a few minutes, or one can spend more time asking all three parts of both questions and hence make an even better decision. The more often one asks the head question and heart question, the faster and easier it becomes, since it becomes more of a habit.

The Yes or No system is a written summary of the inside and the questions in the Yes or No system. It is an instrument which can be referred to briefly when one wants to reach a better decision. The beauty of the system is that it reminds one how to find one's own way.

The Real Need

There are two valuable questions that person can ask oneself to make a better decision. One can use one's head by asking the first question:

Am I meeting the real need, informing myself of options and thinking it through?

While answering the above questions, the author warns that one should remember to answer strictly in terms of Yes or No and not give answers such as sort of or may be because these indicate signs of indecision.

The first part of the question is: Are you meeting the real need?

Now if the reply to this question is No then as soon as one answers No to question, one can pay more attention to it and then arrive at a better decision.

Most of us set out to go and get what we want. Usually it is because we do not know what we need. So we go off in the wrong direction.

But how does one know what the real need is? One can begin by asking this something : I merely want or is it what I really need? A want is a wish, while a need is a necessity. A want is just as attractive distraction which we may pursue but later find unfulfilling. Even if we finally get what we wanted, it often leaves us still wanting. A need, however, is basic and nurturing. A need is what a situation requires.

Truly successful people pursue first what they need. In life, we may want a fancy house but need a lovely house. When we pursue what we often miss getting what we really need. Hence, it is only after you have done what you need to that you can do what you want to.

The key is focusing on the real need. Focusing is seeing a vision of only the results you really need and focusing on these results so clearly and in such detail, that you can already see yourself achieving them. And one can only focus on the real need by saying No to everything else, to get better results. One can focus well on things by writing down in great detail, the results that one needs and then looking at this often. Decision making people clearly know what the real need is, so they can quickly judge whether or not a specific decision would support or undermine what they need. We want a lot but we need a little when we focus the decision down to only what we need, i.e., what makes us feel really successful, it becomes a much easier decision.

One must ask oneself this question:

Do I just want this or do really need this? But then how can one tell the difference between the percentage what I want and what I need?

This is a very simple solution to this query: To see what one merely wants, one must ask oneself what do I wish and I could do? To see what one really needs, one must ask oneself what would I like to have done? But the irony of the situation is that people often discover the difference between what they want and what need only after they get what they want and realize then that it did not work out as well as they had hoped. Too many people do this in business harming not only the organization but also themselves in the process. Hence one must clearly ask oneself:

Am I meeting the real need?

Yes or No.

Informed Options

Thus we deal with the second part of the practical question – Am I meeting my real need, informing myself of options, and thinking it through?

Very often while making decisions, people don't realise that they do have options which they can consider before arriving at any decision. They are usually heard saying, " I have no other choice." But this is untrue. It is only that people are not aware of their options.

But how can People Become Aware of the Options Available?

Simply, by asking questions and gathering needed information. Needed information is only what you actually need to know to make a better decision. Anything else is extraneous information. While gathering information, one should not try and avoid what one does not want to hear, because then one will never become aware of all the real options. Hence, in order to get all the needed information, one must make ones own realistic observations. One can become more observant by talking with and listening not to accept someone else's view of reality without first validating the information yourself.

One seldom learns of ones options by just sitting and waiting for them to come to you. But very often people do just that this is because they are often immobilised by a subconscious fear and fear fogs our vision. Let me give the example of a sad father, who after the suicide of his twenty years old daughter said "Think of all the choices she did not see she had." The saddest part is that what frightens people and paralyses them is something which is usually not real. And when one does find what is real by gathering information from real world, one becomes more aware of the alternatives that one has had all along. One feels much better when one gathers a piece of realistic information, which often leads to more information and just by gathering information, one can become less native and become realistically informed. One has to see reality.

When one is supposed to feel more discouraged or When one Feels one Has the Options or When one Doesn't?

One should feel more discouraged when one does not have any options rather than when one have them. To be realistically aware of what is going on, one needs to get outside oneself and inform oneself of options from the outside world. Information is more than just a collection of facts. It is also how people feel about the facts.

How Does one Know that One has Enough Information to make a Decision ?

There are two kinds of information:

(a) Information that is nice to have.

(b) Information that one needs to have.

One may feel that one never has all the information that one wants, but it is important to first collect the information that one needs. You need information without which you cannot make a better decision.

How Does One Discover which is one's Best Option?

This can be done by asking oneself a simple question: will this option best help me to meet the real need?

Thinking it Through

It is often noticed that at work and at home, people wish to have a mentor an older person to guide them. It may be useful for people to know that everyone has an older mentor to onself: As an elder and hopefully wiser person, one can examine ones past decisions and results. By doing so, one can learn more from anyone else. One can learn what not to do from one's poor results and what to do from one's better results.

Before making the final decision, one must ask oneself the last bit of the practical question "Am I thinking it through?" Thinking involves asking oneself a lot of questions like: What would the results have to be to fill the real ? If I act on my decision, what would probably happen? Then what? result ? What would be the best result? What would I do in the worst / best case? How clearly do I foresee the most likely results? For others? Have I thought it through? Yes or No.

The Other Half

Why Do People Not Ask Questions More Often to Come to a Decision?

This happens either because one does not always know what to ask, or because one not really wants to ask or because one wants to be given the answer without taking the time to even ask the questions. The questions are like alarm clocks which wake up people to reality to what is really going on around us and within us.

What is the Difference between Effective and Ineffective Decisions?

Our ineffective decisions are based on illustration, we believe in at a time and our effective decisions are built on realities we recognise.

That is why it is useful to ask ourselves probing questions to help us distinguish illusion from reality. The questions shine light on the illusion. An illusion is a fiction we believe in because we want to. Even though it turns out to be false.

Whether one realises it or not, one often makes decisions based on what is in one's heart. Such decisions are half decisions based on half truths. The thinking half which is the head must also be consulted to consistently make better decisions. More often than one realises the best way to quickly arrive at better results is to get around the obstacle that is in one's way – this usually is one's obstructive self.

One character is a collection of personal beliefs, and how one acts on them. How to make a decision depends mostly on what one believes in. Beliefs are often forgotten choices that one made long ago, though they still remain influential through our subconscious, upon our decisions. Beliefs are private matter and hence one may not want to share them with everyone. But one may need to examine them more closely for oneself.

Personal beliefs have a lot to do with one's practical decisions. One uses only those part of ones character that one believes has real value and may affect ones decisions greatly. Practical decisions are mirrors of ones personal thoughts, feelings and beliefs on display for everyone to see. They clearly reveal the way one views the world and oneself. One can see another person's beliefs just by looking at enough of his or her decisions.

There are two questions that one has to ask oneself:

(a) A practical head question about one's situations and

(b) A private heart question about oneself, i.e., the decision maker.

The private question concerns one's personal beliefs about one's integrity, intuition and insight into ones own worth.

Looking closely at ones own character makers many of us comfortable. But the more aware one's is of one's character the more often one makes better decisions.

People who have integrity don't fool themselves about a situation. They cut through the nonsense and get to the true core of things quickly.

The quickest way to find the truth is to look for the fiction or the untruth that one wants to believe is truth because it is more convenient or more comfortable to believe in it. Truth is the opposite of fiction and reality remains to be reality regardless of one's belief in one's illusion. Believing in an illusion does not make it reality. Thus the basis of all better decisions is seeing the truth and being honest with oneself.

It is usually one's ego that holds on to an illusion one believes. Scholars have suggested three points to judge oneself. Firstly, to make more realistic decisions, one could start by first putting one's ego aside and then asking others what they saw because usually other people see our mistakes more easily than we do. Secondly, people who care about you, are the right people who might be able to help you to see your illusion. Thirdly, the sooner I see the truth, the sooner I make a better decision.

My Intuition

Here I shall deal with the second part of the private question: "Am I Trusting My Intuition?" This question can be answered by asking oneself a simple question. How do I feel about making this decision? "Do I feel calm or anxious'? Paralysed or confident? Drained or energised?"

If the way one feels about one in making a decision does not feel right to the person, one probably needs to change ones decision, one has to ask oneself whether one is relying on others' opinion or relying on one's own feelings – one's better intuition. One's intuition is one's own unconscious knowledge based on one's own personal experience. The person may feel a sense of calm or stress, a sense of effort or of ease, may feel afraid or enthusiastic.

It's important that a person realises that one has to develop his / her past decisions, i.e., try and recall about what one sensed at the time of making a specific decision and then looking at the consequences and relating the two. It is often found that when one feels poorly while making a decision, the results are usually poor. If however one asks oneself probing questions and still feels really peaceful, one may be making a decision based on truth and hence the results will be far better.

But the important question is, how can one learn to face more questions with less efforts, anxiety, or poor feelings. This can be done simply by trusting one's own intuition. One has to first realise that one's real feeling is a personal guide, a sort of an internal mentor which one listens to and trust.

Intuition means being 'in tuition.' Tuitions comes from a Latin verb *tuni* which means to watch over or to teach. Thus a person's intuition protects him / her by teaching him / her based on what has worked for the person in the past and what is most likely to work for one presently.

A distinction is drawn between a better intuition and simply intuition. A better intuition is reserved for the most important decisions – it is an intuition which gets better results. It is what one senses is right after asking ones 'better guide' for guidance. It is a source which provides an even greater wisdom than ones own experience. If tuition means teaching. intuition is what we have learned, i.e., ourselves and hence better intuition is going beyond ourselves. One has to ask for better guidance either through prayer or meditation, or by communing with nature or simply by taking a quiet walk alone. One has to ask oneself: "Am I making my decision with fear or enthusiasm"? The word enthusiasm comes from a Greek word enthuse which means the God within on the other hand all decisions based on fear simply mean feeling separated from the God. Thus if one wants to stay calm even in most frantic business / personal situations, one must use one's intuition making everyday decisions and one's better intuition for the more important decisions.

My Insight

Sometimes one can sense that one is making a poor decision, but then does not seem to care. He / she just goes ahead and makes it anyway. Thus, sometimes people do things to undermine ones own success, because they believe they do not deserve better. Sometimes, people stop at particular level of success of happiness and go on further, because one believes one does not deserve any better.

The word deserve come from the Latin word deserve which means 'to serve zealously.' But how many of us zealously serve what is really in our better interests? One may think that one deserves better but cannot believe in it or act on it. The key to consistently making better decisions is to consciously choose to believe that one really deserves better and to act on that belief.

Better than what? People may ask themselves. Better than other people ? But why should anyone deserve better than others – a caring person may want to know. But the catch here is any better than others, but better than what one is doing to oneself. Everyone deserves that. Thus anyone may be tempted to ask oneself the following questions. Before I make a decision, do I usually ask myself valuable questions? Do I focus on the real need instead of what I want? Do I get the needed information and inform myself of my options. Do I think my decision through to better results? Or do I not really believe that I deserve better and therefore sabotage myself by not telling myself the truth? Or by not telling myself the truth? Or by not trusting my own intuition? Or by believing I do not have the ability to do better, or enough education, or the right social connections?

One must remember that decisions are only effective when one acts on them in time and to see whether the decisions are effective one must repeatedly ask oneself.

Does my decision show I am honest with myself, trust my intuition and deserve better?

Yes or No?

Points to Ponder

In each of us resides 'a guide' – an internal mentor that each of us is given to show us our wisdom. Our guide is ourself.

One must learn to say 'Yes' to reality and 'No' to illusions.

Everyone must continue to use one's head to ask probing questions and heart to find better answers.

Stay focussed on the real need, personally gather or verify needed information and become more aware of options. Think each of your options through to gain better results.

Remember that one can distinguish reality from illusion by simply telling oneself the truth, trusting one's better intuition and acting on the belief that 'you deserve better.'

Don't just learn questions, but learn them regularly. Remember that the 'Yes or No' system works best only when you use it.

Whosoever will use this 'Yes or No' system to better decision making sincerely will be able to see the difference in himself in his personal life and organizational life both. The person becomes less naive and more aware of what is going on around him and within him. The person feels personally renewed and enjoys a spirit of prosperity and peacefulness.

By asking other people you make yourself aware of this 'system' – everyone in our families, organization and communities, could learn to make better decisions both at work and at home. It would benefit everyone not only by way of better decisions but would also make everyone a lot happier.

Follow the chart given below and try to answer the questions in Yes or No. This chart would help you to a considerable extent to provide an insight to arrive at a better decision.

The Guide: To A Better Decision

'Yes' or 'No'

I avoid indecision and half-decisions based on half-truths. Use both halves of a reliable system to consistently make better decisions: a cool head and a warm heart.

I Use My Head

By asking myself a practical question:

and

I Consult My Heart

By asking myself a practical question then, after I listen to myself and others, I make a decision and act on it.

To Use My Head, I Ask a Practical Question:

Am I Meeting the Real Need, Informing Myself of Options, and Thinking it Through?

Yes-or-No

Is it a mere want or a real need? What information do I need? Have I created options? If I did "X" then what would happen? Then What ?

To Consult my Heart, I Ask a Private Question:

Does my decision show
I am honest with myself,
Trust my intuition,
and deserve better?
Yes - or - No

Am I telling myself the truth? Does this feel right? What would I decide if I wasn't afraid?

What would I do if deserved better?

If 'Yes' I Proceed.

If 'No' I Rethink.

What is my Better Decision?

Thus, if one's approach to making decisions is based on behavioural science, then those who were making a series of poor decisions would be in a better position to make good decisions. If would not be difficult for anyone to know and evaluate as to where did he err and what could be done to set the things in a right perspective. This is basically because the decisions which we took earlier were not based on logic and behavioural approach, rather they were merely based on illusions or beliefs which we held at the time of taking the decisions. The realities were kept aside.

Life in itself is a great teacher. Reflecting back upon the events of the past provides an excellent basis for improving the quality of our decisions. Challenges come in life one after the other. Changes keep on taking places from childhood to adolescence stage and onwards to adulthood, we keep on facing the problems and learn to cope with these in a natural way.

Now if we face a problem arising out of 'change' in future, this knowledge of how one coped with the problem of change in the past provides then a guiding post. Involvement is a scuffle leading to legal punishment, teaches one how to avoid undesirable consequences whenever such problem arise subsequently. Our friends betray, money given is not returned, books lent do not come back – all these bitter experiences give us a lesson.

Another significant way to move towards better quality decisions is to learn from the experience of others. Women, in particular, face difficult problems of change in their lives. Moving from parents home to a new one, meeting the demands of bringing up child in the home and meeting the demand of works in the office, odd behaviour on the part of in-laws and manage to emerge victorious out of the situation. How do they succeed in their endeavour. If we evaluate the behaviour adopted by one such successful being, we can learn to cope with the problems and improve ourselves a lot.

Past can provide us a good lesson and a clear cut guideline for improving the quality of future decision, which we propose to take. One should develop the habit of reflecting upon the poor decisions made in the past with a view to move towards better qualities. The habit to learn from the past has a vast potential in it to guide towards making quality decisions.

And if more and more people make better decisions in their day-to-day lives, together they can create a much better understanding not only in their personal lives but also in making a better society in large, better families and ultimately a better business. Lastly, we should always keep in our minds that all of us are our own guide to make better decisions. By practicing this we can also help others to discover this behavioural approach to better decision-making.

REFERENCE

This chapter is based on *Yes or No*, Spencer Johnson, An imprint of Harper Collins Publishers India Pvt. Ltd., 1992.

CHAPTER

25

The Case Method

Human behaviour is dynamic. The dark and mysterious domain of the mind keeps buried in itself numerous events, big or small which result in formations of habits and behaviours which are sometimes difficult to identify. Humans from the earliest of civilisations have learned to grow by sharing and understanding each other. The experience was passed down the generations which enabled the later civilizations to adapt themselves in a better manner against natural calamities and disasters.

As man grew in his experience and technology, so grew his problems both mental and physical in nature. To cope with those he needed the help of the experienced people. The help came in the form of counselling, guidance and therapy of various forms.

To understand the problem better, the counsellor asked certain questions which explored the problem to root cause. The exploration of the sequence of events was later called the case method in inquiry.

What is a Case?

The case refers to a chronology of events involving usually problem data. The problem is very difficult to identify because it is usually buried and intermingled with numerous facts and situations. Another quality of case materials relates to their stress on action. A business case is more akin to a medical case than a law case. Like a medical case the symptoms have to be analysed, a diagnosis has to be made and action has to be taken which is to be reviewed in the light of the results. Just as the healthy and diseased cases provide material for study to medical students the management students can learn from both successful organizations and from those overwhelmed by hurdles. Thus although cases are usually problematic they can also be illustrative of effective practices as well as descriptive in nature. The cases are records of events which have actually happened. Fictitious cases offer nothing for learning and discourage the entire objective of the case method. Therefore, they should not be used in formal instructions. Only those cases should be cited which are as close as possible to the facts of human behaviour at work.

Objectives of a Case Study

Though case study has the only one objective to reach to the root of the problem but according to **Schnelle** the case method has the following objectives: (a) The description of real business situations to acquaint the students with the principles and practices obtained in work settings (b) introduction of realism into formal instruction (c) demonstration of infinite types of goals, problems, facts, conditions, conflicts and personalities obtained in organizational settings (d) development of decision making ability (e) demonstration of the significance of business research as a tool for problem solving and (f) development of independent thinking but cooperative approach to work in team situations.

The usefulness of the case method are evident from the objectives cited above. The limitations of the case method depend upon the quality of the teacher and the students. The teacher is required to be the best discussion leader whereas the student must be highly motivated to learn. The student should be mature enough to understand social relationships and possess some prior business experience to understand things properly. The case method is more suitable for some areas of subjects such as personnel management, business policy and human relations than other areas including accounting, statistics and economics.

Association of Case Method

The word case has an intimate association with the court cases and as a matter of fact in management education it has been borrowed from legal education. The case method of instruction originated in the Harvard Law School and therefrom it was transferred to the Harvard School of Business Administration by Dean Edwin F. Gay, the first Dean of the school. Since 1908 the case method has been an integral part of management education at the business school all over the world.

Normally a case is simply a written statement of an actual situation taken from a real organization. The situation may involve people at the lowest or highest levels of the organization. It may relate to one or to several operating functions or it may embrace the overall situation of an organization. It may focus on a unique situation or it may deal with broader issues. Generally a case describes a situation in which a manager has to make a decision and take action. The same information as far as possible is supplied to the student as was available to the manager.

Utilisation of Case Method by Trainers and Training Instructions

Performance of an Individual in a given role is determined by three sets of factors. These are his own abilities to do the job, his motivation to do various tasks and the support he receives from the organization. If any of these factors are low the individual performance is likely to be poor. Poor performance of an individual at lower levels can be observed easily and is limited to smaller losses in production. But poor performance in supervisory and managerial level is always not visible and may result in many invisible losses for an organization. A worker in the operating level directly influences organizational output in terms of the goods he produces. Hence performance fluctuations are noticeable. A head of the production department may demoralise his entire supervisory staff and make the work place a place of frustration and demoralisation through his work style and yet go unnoticed. It may therefore be useful to talk of performance at lower levels and effectiveness at supervisory and managerial levels. The factors influencing individual performance as mentioned above are stated in the form of a performance equation in some of the textbooks of organizational behaviour as follows:

Individual Performance = Ability x Work Effort x Organizational Support

This equation appears simplistic but when one goes deeper the complexity and inter relatedness of the factors becomes evident.

The Ability factors deals with the competencies the individual has in order to perform various tasks and functions associated with his role. These include his knowledge attitudes and skills (technical, managerial, human and conceptual). While at lower levels technical competencies play a significant role at higher level human and conceptual competencies play an important role. Organizations should make continuous efforts to understand competency requirements for each role, assess competency gaps and help employees develop their competencies. This is relatively easy as far as technical and managerial competencies are concerned. It is more difficult in relation to human and conceptual competencies. This is because identifying competency gaps in behaviour (human competency) domain requires special sensitivities and skills. Most of the line manager are not well equipped with these sensitivities. It is only in the last few years with more exposure to Behavioural Science Training Programmes that line managers are getting equipped with such competencies. One of the ways to equip them with such human process competencies is through an analysis of real life cases and simulation exercises like role plays using these real life situations. The cases are intended to serve as instruments for training executives in human processes competencies.

The second sets of factors included in the performance equation are motivational factors. Unless the individual is interested in performing the various tasks associated with his role he will not perform. Motivation to work depends on various factors again: perception that the task are a part of his role (role clarity) work habits, a sense of commitment to work and loyalty to the organization, an ability to see challenges and obtain self-fulfillment, personnel policies of the organization reward systems, sense of belongingness etc. Thus the factors that influence the motivation to work are both internal and external to the individual. Some people are workaholics and a few others have tendencies to avoid work. Some people find challenges in whatever work is assigned and others look constantly for rewards. Some jobs are intrinsically more challenging and motivating whereas other jobs may be less interesting. Support from the organization in terms of resource availability, encouragement from supervising executive's cooperation from subordinate's training opportunity, personnel policies, work conditions, etc. also influence performance.

These factors are interactive and every time a crisis occurs a conflict takes place, a decision is taken, a mistake is made, a task is accomplished or an event occurs it may be resultant combination of a variety of factors, including the individual, his abilities, motives, the nature of work, the organizational policies and support the abilities and motivation of other people involved and so on.

Thus in organizational life human processes play an important role in determining the effectiveness of an individual in a given role. The cases are illustrative of how these sets of factors lead to a conflict, a resignation, a crisis, a mistake, a wrong decision, frustration, alienation, loss of motivation, realisation of a competency gap etc. In some of the cases the role played by a good counsellor (Human Resource Manager or another line manager) and counselling skills in resolving problems is also very effectively highlighted.

A good way to learn from these cases is to analyse the case in terms of various sets of factors outlined above. The following questions may be asked:

1. What is the problem? What is that the organization or the Manager in the case should be concerned about?
2. What will happen if the organization/manager lets things go on as they are?
3. What are the events that have led upto this situation?
4. What are the competency gaps of various individuals in performing their roles?
5. What organizational policies seem to effect the individuals in this case?
6. What are the points of view adopted that have led to the present situation?
7. What can be done to solve the problem? Who should initiate action?
8. What is the role of the HR manager?
9. What things should change in the organization? What should change in different individuals involved in case in terms of their attitudes, values, perceptions, etc.?
10. What lessons can be drawn from this case for the organization? the line manager and the HR Manager?

These questions are suggestive. As the cases are varied in nature some questions may be more relevant and useful for some cases than others. The performance equation suggested in the beginning may provide a good basis for analysing some of the cases and deriving learning.

Characteristics of the Case Method

While it is relatively easy to define by description a case, the case method itself cannot be defined more precisely than: the method used by a teacher to handle a case. Every teacher of the case method adapts the case to suit himself the particular class and the topic and hence there is no really typical example of the case method in action. Keeping this in view let's explain how cases are in practice used as the central device in the somewhat distinctive educational strategy called the case method.

The student is generally confronted with a case on account of a concrete organizational situation. He is asked to examine the case independently, analyse the situation in terms of what is going on in it, why it is going on, what is likely to happen next and what should be done about it if anything happens. The student is asked to diagnose – to conclude from any symptomatic evidence available – the nature of any organizational issues or problems. In an appropriate case he may be asked to arrive at a prognosis to forecast the future course of the problem if left unchecked and to elaborate or prescribe some treatment, some plan of action for managing the situation in terms of the diagnosis.

Effective Use of Case Study Method in Management Study

Much of the theory is shared in a management programme. Sometimes it becomes important to share with the student the real life situations so that a discovery of a variety of facts can take place. It has been identified of late, more can be learned, understood and inferred from such cases.

Case studies have helped the students to arrive at conclusions never possible before. It is now understood that as medico students are exposed to live cases for better understanding of theory in practice, so is the case study method in business. Various management students have immensely benefited by case studies.

Even though the cases are mostly shared by the faculties of these courses much of the responsibility for learning, rests with the student rather than with the teacher. The case method demands active participation of the student in the following ways:

* First the student must do a great deal of preparation beyond simply reading and understanding the facts of the case. The preparation often involves evaluating material, much of which may not be factual and developing a plan of action based on this evolution.
* In the case method of learning, the teacher plays a multifaceted role, guiding discussion, asking questions, providing perspectives, summarising comments but rarely providing answers. It is the responsibility of the individual students to arrive at meaningful conclusions based on the facts of the case.
* Further, each student, not only, must analyse, the case information and develop an effective action plan but also must be able to present the plan to other group members in a forceful manner and gain their acceptance.

When the management student examines the case independently he discovers a variety of complex variable operating in the situation some or all of which he connects via some frame of reference with what happens in it and what may be done about it. Subsequently he discusses the case in a small or large students group. To his surprise he may find others putting an altogether different emphasis on points based on symptomatic evidence which he might have dismissed as arrival of insignificant. This might ultimately pave the way for alternative diagnoses of problems and action prescriptions. In the course of discussion all these perceptions, cognitions, values, assumptions and action plans and inconsistencies developed by members of the group would be explored and reviewed. Individual and group study of the case thus permits the student to compare his analysis with those of others and encourages him to go deep into the likely differences between them and learn from the experience. Case methods apparently place the ball of learning squarely in the student's court and provide support of various kinds for the student's attempt to improve his game. The teacher's task is to create and maintain an environment conducive to learning.

Development Stages of Cases

The case method usually compels the student to go through three distinct stages of development while examining the cases.

* The student would realise that the original ideas, thought processes and action plans would ultimately pave the way for more refined outcomes.

  After you have spent considerable time preparing a case and developing creative action plans it can be disconcerting that others in the group have considered to you and that they have developed what seem to be perfectly feasible action plans based on these considerations.
* He would realise that no one person has a monopoly on good analyses or creative solutions. He recognises the importance of peeping into the minds of others and sharing their thoughts on a particular issue. As time rolls by, he tries to learn from other's ideas and uses the same in improving his own analytical skills.
* Finally he would realise that even teachers do not know all the right answers and even if they might, each person in the group is welcome to present or preserve his own views.

Distinction Between Case Study Method & Lecture Method of Study

At this stage it may not be out of context to draw the distinction between the traditional lecture method of teaching and case method. In the former case the lecturer is assumed to have superior subject knowledge. Students are expected to absorb what the lecturer has to offer. The lecturer holds the centre of the stage all the time and communication, more or less, takes a one way street. Students are placed in a position of dependency in relation to the lecturer. The method is, thus, essentially hierarchical and authoritarian. Under the case method:

* Most of the burden of case analysis is placed on the student, not the lecturer.
* All members of the class as well as the lecturer are in possession of the same basic material, the case, which is the focus of attention.
* Each, has an opportunity to contribute to the analysis of the case.
* Communication takes a two way route.
* Thus, the case method is essential a more democratic group centered on at least participative educational strategy than the lecture method.
* Over a period of time, this helps the student to build up a soundly based repertoire of diagnostic schemes for the analysis of organizational situations, and skill in their use. By confronting the student with open ended, realistic organizational problems the method fosters his creative and innovative talents.

The case method of teaching has become increasingly popular over the last few decades, particularly in the field of management education. It is a method which incorporates several of the tenets of sound educational theory ; it aims to build up understanding on a framework of experience, to encourage learning by doing, and to promote interest and enthusiasm by requiring the student to solve problems in realistic situations.

Benefits and Disadvantages of Case Method

According to Roy McLennan, 'Cases may be profitably used to make knowledge usable, as a test bed to marry theory and concrete reality. They provide students with practice in exploring a range of managerial issues in a variety of organizational situations, in this way presenting a series of opportunities to practice responsible managerial analysis, diagnosis and action prescription. Cases also force the synthesis of variety of concepts in the need they activate to understand individual concrete situations.' As an educational strategy, case method offers the following benefits:

* It would bring out the knowledge and understanding of the students and nurture the qualities of expression.
* It would develop in the students the qualities of restraint and disciplined disagreement among the participants – each argument on either side being fully supported by points bearing on the students learning.
* More specially, it would provide the student the opportunity to experience many different types of organizational situations; increase the ability to predict what will happen in organizations; increase the ability to develop alternate ways of handling a situation. It requires the student to make a decision which he should be ready and able to defend in the face of criticism. It stimulates the student to study and learn.

At this stage certain criticisms and disadvantages of the case method of learning must also be noted, for example:

* A student may sit through a discussion and take no part at all or at best, merely make some comments based upon what he has heard rather than on a true study of the case. In larger classes many who may wish to speak do not find the opportunity.

* The method, even when operated well, is time consuming. A case may require several hours of private work and a full discussion to establish a principle which the teacher could have put over by lecture and illustration, in perhaps, forty or fifty minutes.
* It can breed in the student the dangerous belief that answers to case problems can be applied to the problems he meets in later employment.

How to Analyse a Case

There is no perfect way to analyse a case. Different authors advocate different approaches, each with its advantages and disadvantages.

The case can be analysed from as many angles as there are interested groups. For example, any case can be analysed from the viewpoints of labour and management groups. To analyse a case properly, the case analyst must read it thoroughly with a view to getting adequate understanding of the overall problem and its components.

Raymond provides the following questions which should be raised by the analyst while analysing a case:

(a) What are the actual problems involved in the case?

(b) What are the relevant facts?

(c) What are the crucial unknown aspects of the scene?

(d) What are the major critical questions related to each specific event?

(e) In what ways can logic and reasoning be used to determine crucial inferences, connections and relationships?

(f) In what manners contradictory facts and arguments can be weighed in making decisions?

(g) What should be the proper timing of decisions? and

(h) In what ways can those decisions be best executed?

There are three more steps to be followed for a proper analysis:

Study

- Read the case thoroughly and be sure you understand the information provided therein.

Analyse

Isolate, breakdown, synthesise, compare, evaluate, and prioritise the data.

Decide

Make a commitment. Choose one course of action and develop a plan of implementation.

Harry, R. Knudson, C. Patrick Fleenor and Robert E. Calahan have advocated the following sequential order while studying, analysing and deciding about a case:

1. Read the first few paragraphs of the case, then continue almost as fast as you can read, asking yourself, What is the case all about? What kinds of information am I being given to analyse?
2. Read the case again very carefully, underlining or noting key bits of information. Write no more than one or two short paragraphs that describe the situation and identify the salient issues. Writing forces you to be more specific.
3. Think about the case for a day or two, We realise the many demands upon a student's time, but our experience strongly suggests that if you first read a case a few days before the class discussion is scheduled you will do a much stronger analysis than if you read it just before class. The process of 'mulling over' the data seems to be very valuable and will usually results in a much more effective action plan.

4. Do some analysis. Look for the significant components of the case problems, opportunities, issues that must be considered, decisions that must be made. You should consider using some of theoretical constructs from the field of organizational behaviour in this analysis. For example, if you are trying to understand why certain individuals in the case behaved as they did, an application of need reward theory or expectancy theory or Maslow's need hierarchy or theory Z would be useful. If you are dealing with a situation involving change, you might find force field analysis useful.

5. Identify the major problems in the case. Be certain that you are dealing with the real problems rather than merely symptoms of the problems. For instance, a case might relate that a significant number of people regularly come to work late. In all probability, their tardiness is symptom of a deeper problem. It might be that the psychological rewards they get from coming to work are so meagre that they can hardly drag themselves in the door or it may be that the city transportation system can't handle all the traffic at the hour. But the important thing is to look beyond the symptoms to see whether you can discover the underlying cause.

   Remember that the description or a problem may depend greatly on the perspectives of the people describing it. A problem as seen from one point of view may not be considered a problem at all by others who have a different viewpoint.

6. Identify data from the case that confirm your description of problems. Is something a problem simply because you say it is or do you have data to support your conclusion? Students sometimes complain about the lack of data in a case when they have not used appropriately the data available.

7. List the problems in order of priority. Which are the most important, the next most important, and the least important? Don't forget that rankings of priorities will differ according to one's perspective, just as descriptions of problems will. Why did you make the rankings you did?

8. Develop two or three feasible action plans for each of the major problems. Each alternative action plan should include:
   (a) the specific actions to be taken
   (b) who should take which actions
   (c) the purpose or objective of taking the actions
   (d) a time frame specifying when the actions will be taken
   (e) any additional or different resources that might be needed to carry out the action plan and how these will be obtained
   (f) the trade offs that are being made in the proposed action plan
   (g) the predicted outcome of the plan.

9. Select from the alternative plans the one you will follow. Why did one alternative make more sense to you than the others? Upon what analysis is your choice based?

If this procedure sounds like a large order and a lot of work, it is! But it's exactly the same process that a manager goes through, or should go through, in making decisions. And your task is simpler. In the organizational world, no one presents a manager with the data nicely arranged in a case form.

Remember that the primary purpose of case analysis is to give you the opportunity to make decisions and to develop plans of action to implement the decisions. This is a demanding task, which will not be successfully accomplished without considerable effort on your part, in cooperation with your classmates and instructor.

Some More Approaches to Case Analysis

The Harvard system involves five steps in case analysis defining central issue, selecting the relevant areas of consideration, analysing the considerations and ascertaining their relative significance, surveying other possibilities, and drawing a final conclusion.

Schnelle visualises a 10 point complex problem solving model: identification of the problem, determination of the facts, ascertainment of alternative courses of action, analysis of advantages and disadvantages of alternatives, assessment of advantages and disadvantages, prediction of occurrence of advantages and disadvantages, selection of the best alternative, execution of the decision, filing the problem solution and comparing expected with the real results of the decision.

The procedure for identification of the problem includes the preparation of a list of all problems, both observed and suspected; assignment of weightage to each problem in terms of case of solution; establishment of deadlines for solving immediate problems; formation of problem hierarchies in terms of preeminence of dependency; partial analyses of few easy problems; partial analyses of few urgent problems; partial analyses of all primary problems, solution of all primary problems first; and determination as to whether solutions are in line with expected solutions to primary problems.

The procedure for determination of the facts include the use of immediately available facts to make a preliminary analysis of the solution; application of personal judgment to make a preliminary selection of the problem on the basis of this analysis; preparation of a list of additional facts required on the basis of the preliminary analysis and the preliminary definition of the problem; use of suitable research techniques to explore as many of the required facts as possible; use of the present available facts to reexamine the definition of the problem; use of the new available facts to rewrite the case; exploration of additional facts to abridge the gaps in the written case; and use of these facts to complete the analysis.

The procedure for ascertaining the alternative courses of action incorporates the choices of alternatives (not less than three and not more than seven alternatives); selection of one alternative from each of the two extremes on the alternative continuum; and the selection of another alternative from the middle of the continuum.

The analysis of the advantages and disadvantages of alternatives involves the preparation of three analysis sheets each for one alternative; the sheets indicating the specific alternative on the top; presentation of ideas as rapidly as possible; initiating with the advantages of the first alternative; employing the brainstorming (head shrinking technique) to discover as many advantages as possible; and the repetition of the same procedure for the disadvantages as soon as ideas on advantages stop flowing. The same procedure should be repeated for all the three alternatives.

The assessment of advantages and disadvantages involves the revision of lists of advantages and disadvantages for the sake of clarity and unity; elimination of duplications within lists; examination of items to ensure that entries lie on the correct sides of the sheets; determination of whether advantages under one alternative are also advantages under one or more of the other alternatives; determination of whether advantages under one alternative form disadvantages under one or more of the other alternatives; elimination of insignificant items from all lists; preparation of fresh analysis sheets; assignment of rupee values to all advantages and disadvantages; estimation of the likelihood of occurrence for each payoff; and computation of adjusted values for each advantage and disadvantage for all alternatives multiplying certainty values by probabilities of occurrence.

These procedures are rarely followed in usual classroom instructions. However, they have been described here to provide a basic understanding of case analysis technology. The complex problem solving model as presented by Schnelle incorporates many more items which have been dropped out for the sake of convenience.

Methodical Approach to cases

According to W. Allan Bay and Cameron a pattern of methodical approach to the case method consists of the following steps:

A. Identification

1. Is there a problem?
2. What information is available?
3. Is this information indicative of a situation needing corrective action? Even if the facts do not seem to be true should I investigate them and/or discover why they were reported?
4. What is to be achieved by the solution? Set up an objective.

5. What difficulties have to be overcome to achieve the objective? Define the problem.
6. What aids are to be found in the situation?
7. Does the problem appear to be mainly a technical, organizational or human one?
8. Does the problem appear to be a symptom of a deeper cause so that the solution will have to be approached in two or more stages?

B. Preparation for Solution

1. What limitations are there in the situation? For example, time, company policy, money, equipment, man power, etc.
2. Do I know enough to be able to deal with this problem?

... Enough about the situation itself?

... Enough about the background?

If not can I obtain information. Advice from other sources?

3. Have I sufficient authority to deal with the problem?

If not can I obtain the necessary authority? Alternatively should I pass the problem up to the appropriate authority level?

4. Should the problem be delegated to a subordinate?
5. Should the problem be transferred to another department?
6. If it is my problem, am I biased in regard to the situation?

If so, what steps can I take to minimise the effect of my bias?

C. The Solution

1. How do I evaluate reports on the situation?

   Reliability of sources of information?

   Confirmation or conflict between different statements or reports?
2. What inferences and judgments can be made from the factual statements?
3. From what is now known, do questions A.3, A.4, A.6 require amendment?

   Is there really a problem?
4. What obstacles have to be overcome by the solution?

   These questions should be ranked in order of importance in respect of 'must be dealt with."
5. What alternative solutions are there?
6. How do the alternatives compare in respect of

   ... Dealing with the major aspects of the problem?

   … Dealing with aspects of the problem successively ranked lower than major aspect ?

   … Estimated cost of implementing solution?

   … Estimated time for solution to become effective?

   … Flexibility?

   … Probable secondary problems created by introduction of the solution ?

   … People involved in the solution? For example: Others within the department? Others within the company ? Others outside the company?
7. Which is the best alternative?

8. Does this best alternative leave some aspect or the problem unresolved ? If so, have I estimated the risk taken in using it?
9. Will the best alternative create secondary problems? If so, can I minimise the risk of such problems by providing means of identifying the onset of the effect of secondary problems?
10. Finally, have I checked the solution against my definition of the problem (question A.3, A.4, A.5, A.6 and C.4)

D. Implementation

1. Have I selected the best person to implement the solution?
2. Have I effectively communicated to him?
3. Have I provided him with sufficient resources?
4. Have I provided him with authority?
5. Have I defined what progress reports I need?

E. Follow up

1. Has the solution been effective?
2. If the problem was in the nature of a symptom of a root cause, when should I tackle the root cause?
3. What lessons have I learned from this incident?

When handout has been issued, the tutor can make such comments as may be necessary.

Common Errors in Case Analysis

While there is no one best or correct solution to a case, some solutions are better than others. The better ones avoid the following common errors in analysing cases.

1. Unrecognised or Inappropriate Assumptions

All of us make assumptions all of the time. You will very legitimately make assumptions in analysing cases. Recognise, that action plans should be based on analysis rather than on assumptions. You should clearly identify your assumptions so that others in the group can be aware of what you are doing. Often, decisions are based on assumptions of which even the decision maker is unaware.

2. Generalisations

Such statements as all of the employees dislike, the boss or no one in the factory is very interested in increasing productivity are inappropriate. Be specific. Don't make general statements when they are not accurate.

3. Cliches

Such statements as the problem is "one of poor communications" or the problem is due to lack of motivation are not helpful.

4. Overemphasising One Aspect

Don't spend all of your time and effort looking at one small part of the solution. You may be ignoring other, perhaps more important considerations.

5. Miracle Cures

If your plan of action consists of hiring a consultant to solve the problem, your instructor will probably say. "OK, assume your are the consultant, what would you do ?

6. Placing Blame

The question "Why did this problem arise?" is useful and can help you design a creative plan of action. "Who is to blame for this situation? will probably not lead to a productive discussion.

7. Being Unrealistic

Recommending a course of action that is not appropriate to the organizations situation is not useful. If your solution requires the purchase of three new factories in a period of depression, you should not expect critical acclaim from your classmates. Similarly, if the success of your action plan depends upon the CEO voluntarily resigning, we would predict difficulty. Likewise if the working capital you need must come from winning the state lottery.

8. Seeing things as "either-or"

Don't assume that either this must happen or those consequences will result. Almost always another outcome or alternative is possible. You should continually ask yourself "What other possibilities are there in this situation.

9. Mistaking Opinions and Assumptions for Facts

You must discriminate between facts, opinions, and assumptions and treat them differently. To know for a fact that production is down should not be confused with someone's opinion that production is down. That people oppose the new policy is different from someone's assumption that people will oppose the new policy.

10. Hedging

Enumerating five or six things that a manager might do without recommending what should be done is inappropriate. Avoid the "on the other hand" syndrome. Make a specific recommendation.

Although it's unlikely that you will never make one or more of these errors, try to keep this list in mind as errors to avoid.

Approach to Case Discussion

As the case provides some problem data for analysis, the actual learning results not from the case itself but from the process which is developed from it by the participants. There are some factors in this process which the instructor must understand. Although at the surface of the discussion there appear to be some viewpoints, opinions, concepts, etc., at depth he may find significant meanings in view of the identification, projection, group structure, personal needs of the participants and their past experience. It is the skill of the instructor which contributes through the discussion process to meaningful learning and not the case itself. We find here two approaches – directive and non-directive.

The directive approach refers to an approach in which the instructor directs the group towards a certain viewpoint of decisions. The mode of interaction in such a discussion is frequently directed towards satisfaction and attitudes of employees. It is possible to measure preferences of employees objectively in respect of desirable work-group fellows. For example, 'socio metric' technique can be employed to identify work-teams whose members form a cohesive group. The cohesive group is believed to have high morale and high output.

Role of Case Study Method in Business

In the case study method learning takes place as the students try to discover, define and answer critical questions using real life situations described on paper. The end goal of case analysis is to suggest management action based upon the analysis.

How effective is this method? In the opinion of training directors in a study, the case study method was rated highly effective for the training objective of improving problem solving skills. Unfortunately the research on effectiveness of case study as a training approach is very limited. Only a few studies have been found that involved more than an attempt to obtain testimonials from course participants. Solem found that the case study method was effective for learning, how to derive solutions to complex problems. Fox found that about two-thirds of the students exposed to case study analysis improved moderately or significantly in their ability to handle cases, however the other one-third made no improvement.

Another training objective of case study analysis is knowledge acquisition. The training experts mentioned previously rated the case study method quite high for attaining this objective. Again the scientific research in this area is limited. However, in a well controlled study in which a class taught by the case method was compared to a class taught by the lecture and discussion approach, the case study section scored significantly higher on achievement tests.

In the pure case study method theories are ignored and specific knowledge acquisitions are not expected. However, the case method may include a rigorous conceptual structure or theory as a basis. Thus the conceptualisation may be linked to the described practice.

In the past, cases sometimes have not had adequate coverage of certain concepts such as the policy generating structure, budget allocations and organizational outcomes. Thus the policy analyst using these cases is somewhat limited. He must do the best he can with what he has and add to his information where possible. Sometimes current information from the library, newspapers, business magazine or the organization itself is available and proves helpful.

Cases developed in the last few years are giving greater attention to the role stakes and pressures of managers at different organization levels including specially the middle manager affected by strategy implementation. In addition more attention has been shown recently to the stages of organization development and to relating those stages to product market scope, to resource allocation processes and to various aspects of organization structure.

Using the Case Method: Some Important Aspects

1. This method of learning calls for the maximum individual participation in class discussion. One cannot learn as an observer he must be a participant.
2. In class discussion one must accept a critical atmosphere and be willing to submit his conclusions to rebuttal.
3. While learning under the case method is a group process to which one must adjust, this does not imply conformity to group opinion.
4. One must be willing to accept the risk of stating one's conclusions and overcome the fear of making and admitting a mistake.
5. Intelligent analysis calls for the recognition and identification of assumptions.
6. Effective classroom case discussion and analysis can be realised only if each participant has the facts of the case in his analysis well in hand. One does not seek to uncover facts or use his analysis during the discussion, although modifications of the facts and analysis will evolve through the insights provided by the group's efforts.
7. The teacher is a discussion leader not lecturer or major contributor of facts and analysis.
8. Decisions have to be made without all the data one would desire and this is an asset not a liability in case analysis for it reflects the condition management often faces.
9. There may be several acceptable solutions to a problem in a case. Definitive answers are rarely if ever available. The solution is not as significant as the basis from which it is derived.
10. Learning by the case method or any other educational approach is in the final analysis an individual proposition calling for a maximum of personal effort and responsibility.

No single approach to case problem solution is ideal, however the student may use the following procedure in handling the cases assigned in his course.

Situational Analysis

The first step consists of recognising the existence of a problem and determining the significant issues with which management must deal. Please remember that the firm's strategies and policies are derived from its basic purposes and objectives which in turn are influenced by the constraints of the company's internal and external environments.

An analytical study of the case facts is required to determine why and when the problem arose, who is concerned and how critical the situation is. In addition, the adequacy of company resources and the probable impact on organizational performance capability must be properly evaluated.

Use and Analysis of Evidence

A. Support from Evidence Other than Quantitative

1. Adequacy

A persuasive analysis usually provides an accumulation of evidence to support its position. A particularly dangerous weakness in this area is excessive reliance on generalisations and principles rather than cases.

2. Balance

An analysis which consistently recognised only evidence favourable to its own conclusions leaves the critic or valuator with a feeling that the analyst did not see the other side and so cannot have properly considered its merits.

3. Validity

Some of the evidence in a case is established fact. Other evidence is in the form of statements, opinions, estimates, feelings and the like. The validity of such evidence must be examined to determine its value.

4. Reasonableness of Interpretations

The analyst takes the facts before him and through a series of interpretations arrives at a judgment as to their effect on the issues. At each step he applies how own judgment supported by case evidence and or of general knowledge.

5. Objectivity

First there are the analysis which omit arguments other than those favouring their position. Second there are those in which interpretations appear to be based on prejudices or preconceptions of the analyst which blind him to other interpretations. These analyses frequently rely on strong generalisations rather than sufficient consideration of case evidence.

6. Thoroughness of Reasoning

The degree of thoroughness required for each point is determined by such questions as "How important is this point? and How deep must I go to be convincing?

B. Support from Quantitative Evidence

1. Adequacy

Though figures such as cost data and market statistics should be as conclusive and precise as possible, rough estimates and approximations should not be omitted if they are the only figures available and might give valuable evidence.

2. Accurate Usage

In a particular case several methods of calculation will usually be possible to make a given set of figures useful. You should especially beware of applying textbook techniques mechanically without establishing their value in the immediate problem.

Identification and Valuation of Action Alternatives

What can be done to solve these problems? (or expressed in another way what are the alternatives of action ?) Some alternatives are clearly infeasible these can be discarded at once. All others must be formally evaluated. This requires a determination of yardstick by which their feasibility utility and risk may be evaluated. It is not enough that a given action would reduce costs. There may be other off-setting disadvantages. Human factors are always significant and a lack of capital might prohibit certain courses of action.

Conclusions and/or Recommendations

A. Relation to Analysis

The decisions should follow directly from the analysis. If they come as a surprise either because they are inconsistent with or not related to the analysis is the effect or the discussion is weakened.

B. Detail of Development

In this respect you should be careful in the use of generalities of panaceas like "The manager should get better staff help or environmental audits should be made more effective." Indicate the specific means for carrying out your recommendations. For example "Has the manager taken the following steps.

1. .... 2. ....

3. .... 4. ....

C. The Action Decision -

Logical reasoning and evaluations will eventually narrow the several feasible alternatives to the one with the least risk and/or the greatest potential reward. This should be adopted. It must solve the problem faced tend to optimise profits and costs and be feasible in terms of people's satisfaction existing functional relationships and resources available.

D. Implementation of the Action Decision

The decision is not complete until operational plans for its implementation have been drawn up. An effective date for initiation of action must be stipulated, market factors and the business cycle must be favourable. Resources must be assembled. Finally all persons involved in the action program must be told of its timeliness and validity.

REFERENCES

K.E. Schnelle, *Case Analysis and Business Problem Solving*, New York, McGraw-Hill Book Company, 1967.

T.J. Raymond, 'Written Analysis of Cases, in M.P. Mc Nair (ed.). *The Case Method at the Harvard Business School*, New York, Mc Graw-Hill Book Company, 1954, p.141.

Abad, Ahmad, 'Introductory Note', in Indian Cases in *Business Management*, Delhi. Department of Business Management and Industrial Administration, University of Delhi, 1968.

Indian Cases in *Business Management*, Delhi, Department of Business Management and Industrial Administration, University of Delhi. 1968.

Case Studies

A. NATURE OF O.B.

A CASE OF BETRAYAL

Vijay, an M.Com. and an ICWA, joined the finance department of a Bangalore based electric company (Unit 1) which boasts of an annual turnover of Rs. 400 crores. He is smart, intelligent but conscientious. He introduced several new systems in records keeping and was responsible for cost reduction in several areas. Being a loner, Vijay developed few friends in and outside the organization. He also missed promotions four times though he richly deserved them.

GM, Finance saw to it that Vijay was shifted to Unit 2 where he was posted to purchasing. Though purchasing was not his cup of tea, Vijay went whole hog, streamlined the purchasing function and introduced new systems, particularly in vendor development. Being honest himself, Vijay ensured that nobody else made money through questionable means.

After two years in purchasing, Vijay was shifted to stores. From finance to purchasing to stores was too much for Vijay to swallow. He burst out before the Unit Head, and unable to control his anger, Vijay put in his papers too. Unit Head was aghast at this development but did nothing to console Vijay. He forwarded the papers to V.P. Finance, Unit 1.

V.P. Finance called in Vijay, heard him for a couple of hours, advised him not to lose heart, assured him that his interests would be taken care of and was requested to resume duties in purchasing in Unit 2, Vijay was also assured that no action would be taken on the papers he had put in.

Six months passed by. Now, the time to effect promotions. List of promotees was announced and to his dismay Vijay found that his name was missing. Angered, Vijay met the Unit Head who told cooly that Vijay could collect his dues and pack off to his house for good. It was great betrayal in the life of Vijay.

QUESTIONS

1. Why did the management behave as it did towards Vijay?
2. What went wrong with Vijay?
3. If you were Vijay what would you have done?
4. Role play the first interaction between V.P. Finance and Vijay.

ORGANIC CULTURE AT CMC

CMC is a relatively young enterprise of the Government of India. It was formed in the late seventies to take over the computer maintenance and support business of IBM which had decided to get out of India. CMC started with a staff of less than 200. It was headed by Dr. P.P. Gupta, a visionary technocrat. By 1990, CMC was India's largest information technology company with a staff of nearly 2000, and the company was into such other areas as environmental engineering, systems consultancy, data communication and computer networks, education and training programmes, turnkey projects, exports, and research and development. Despite being government owned, CMC avoided bureaucratic practices. In 1990, the company's policies attested to its organic culture:

* An open appraisal system, in which the boss shared his appraisal of the subordinate with the subordinate.
* No rigid job specifications. Roles were broadly defined; all staff members were expected to take initiative when they saw any gaps, and to take necessary action.
* Management by committees and task forces. A 'matrix' form of organization was in operation in which people worked not only in their areas of specialization but on inter-disciplinary, multi-functional projects.

* Policies and guidelines which responded to needs rather than to a rule book. For example, there was no sick leave and casual leave. But there was no limit to the number of days of time off a staff member could avail during a year for a genuine need such as an illness.
* An 'open door' policy. No cabins were provided. Even the Chief executive had no cabin. There was a 'speakout' scheme which allowed any staff member to write directly to the chief executive about any personal problems or suggestion. There were common cafeterias and toilets for all staff including top level executives.
* There was no overtime, since it was assumed that all staff members were dedicated and would complete their tasks on that basis.
* Aptitude, ability, achievement and potential were the main criteria for promotion. Appointments and promotions were not determined by vacancies but by inherent capability and potential of the persons.
* People rose in the organization not only through the management cadre. Technical and professional staff could rise to the highest levels without being in line management.
* The manager was seen as a role, not as a step in the pecking order. It was not uncommon for professionals reporting to a manager to draw a greater salary than the manager. Authority and power stemmed more from a person's competence and expertise than from his position in the organization.
* There was a strong emphasis on manpower development through training. All staff in CMC including the top executives, underwent a minimum of one week of training annually.
* Financial assistance was provided to staff members desirous of acquiring higher qualifications. Publications of articles etc. attracted cash awards. Purchase of books, journals, other educational materials were subsidised. A staff member could take a study leave up to a year with full pay.
* As far as possible, CMC permitted staff members to choose their own career paths within the broad outline of their respective functions.
* There was an active encouragement of social and cultural development. There was a "CMC Fest" every two years. Staff recreation clubs in each region promoted social and cultural activities. There was a 'CMC Day' on which family members were invited. There was an art gallery at the corporate headquarters.
* Aesthetics in office decor were emphasised.
* There was an active suggestions scheme.
* CMC believed that the cost of mistrust is far greater than the cost of trust. Thus there were no formal, detailed budgetary controls.

CMC's culture was rather like that of a voluntary organization of professionals. It challenged that stereotype of the slow-footed, procedure bound, controls infested, bureaucratic government-owned enterprise and demonstrated that a counter-culture could take root in the public sector, and what is more, give good results.

(Source: Pradip N. Khandwalla, *Organizational Designs For Excellence*, TMH, 1992, P. 11)

QUESTIONS

1. Do you want to work for CMC? Why or why not?
2. If Gupta's approach to managing people so effective, why do so many organizations try hard to create a serious work climate?

MCDONALD'S: FAST FOOD

Ray Kroc opened the first McDonald's restaurant in 1955. He offered a limited menu of high-quality, moderately priced food served fast in spotless surroundings. McDonald's QSC & V (quality, service, cleanliness, and value) was a hit. The chain expanded into every state in the nation. By 1983 it had over 6000 restaurants in the United States.

In 1967 McDonald's opened its first restaurant outside the United States, in Canada. By 1985 international sales represented about one-fifth of McDonald's total revenues. Yet fast food has barely touched any cultures. While 90 percent of the Japanese in Tokyo have eaten a McDonald's hamburger, few outside the cities know what a hamburger is. In Europe, McDonald's maintains a very small percentage of restaurant sales but commands a large share of the fast food market. It took the company 14 years of planning before it opened a restaurant in Moscow. But the planning paid off. People stand in line up to 2 hours for a hamburger. After waiting for such a long time, they have to pay $ 14.40 (at the official rate) for a Big Mac and French fries. Despite the high prices, McDonald's restaurant in Moscow attracts more visitors – on a average, 27,000 daily – than Lenin's mausoleum (about 9000 people), which used to be the place to see.

The taste for fast food, American-style, is growing more rapidly in countries abroad than at home. McDonald's international sales have been increasing by a large percentage every year. Every day more than 18 million people in over 40 countries eat at McDonald's.

Its traditional menu has been surprisingly successful. People with diverse dining habits have adopted burgers and fries wholeheartedly. Before McDonald's introduced the Japanese to French fries, potatoes were used in Japan only to make starch. The Germans thought hamburgers were people from the city of Hamburg. Now, McDonald's also serves chicken, sausage, and salads. One of the latest items, a very different product, is pizza. This new venture is risky and can be either a very profitable addition or a costly experiment.

The fast, family-oriented service, the cleanliness, and the value accounted for much of McDonald's success. McDonald's was one of the first restaurants in Europe to welcome families with children. Not only are children welcomed, but in many restaurants they are also entertained with crayons and paper, a play-land, or may be even Ronald McDonald, who can speak twenty languages.

McDonald's golden arches promise the same basic menu and QSC & V in every restaurant. Its products, handling and cooking procedures, and kitchen layouts are standardized and strictly controlled. McDonald's revoked the first French franchisees because the franchisees failed to meet its standards for fast service and cleanliness, even though their restaurants were highly profitable. This may have delayed its expansion in France.

The restaurants are run by local managers and crews. Owners and managers must attend the Hamburger University near Chicago to learn, how to operate a McDonald's restaurant and maintain QSC & V. The main campus library and modern electronic class-rooms (which include simultaneous translation systems) are the envy of many universities. When McDonald's opened in Moscow a one-page advertisement resulted in 30,000 inquiries about the jobs; 4000 people were interviewed and some 300 were hired. The pay is about 50 percent higher than the average Soviet salary.

McDonald's ensures consistent products by controlling every stage of distribution. Regional distributions centers purchase products and distribute them to individual restaurants. The centers will buy from local suppliers if the suppliers can meet detailed specifications. McDonald's has had to make some concessions to available products. For example, it is difficult to introduce the Idaho potato in Europe.

McDonald's uses essentially the same competitive strategy in every country. Be first in market, and establish your brand as rapidly as possible by advertising very heavily. New restaurants are opened with a bang. So many people attended the opening of one Tokyo restaurant that the police closed the street to vehicles. The strategy has helped McDonald's develop a strong share in the fast food market, even though its U.S. competitors and new local competitors quickly enter the market.

The advertising campaigns are based on local themes and reflect the different environments. In Japan, where burgers are a snack. McDonald's competes against confectioneries and new "fast sushi" restaurants. Many of the charitable causes McDonald's supports abroad have been recommended by the local restaurants.

McDonald's has been willing to relinquish the most controls to its Far Eastern operations, where many restaurants are joint ventures with local entrepreneurs, owning 50 percent or more of the restaurant.

European and South American restaurants are generally company-operated or franchised (although there are many affiliates – joint ventures – in France). Like the U.S. franchisees, restaurants abroad are allowed to experiment with their menus. In Japan, hamburgers are smaller because they are considered a snack. The Quarter Pounder didn't make much sense to people on a metric system, so it is called a Double Burger. Some of the German restaurants serve beer; some French restaurants serve wine. Some Far Eastern restaurants offer oriental noodles. But these new items must not disrupt existing operations.

Despite success, McDonald's faces tough competitors such as Burger King, Wendy's, Kentucky Fried Chicken, and now also Pizza Hut. And fast food in reheatable containers is now also sold in supermarkets, delicatessens and convenience stores, and even gas stations. McDonald's has done very well, with a great percentage of profits coming now from international operations. But can this success continue?

QUESTIONS

1. What opportunities and threats did McDonald's face? How did it handle them? What alternatives could it have chosen?
2. Before McDonald's entered the European market, few people believed that fast food could be successful in Europe. Why do you think McDonald's succeeded? What strategies did it follow? How did these differ from its strategies in Asia?
3. What is McDonald's basic philosophy? How does it enforce this philosophy and adapt to different environments?
4. Should McDonald's expand its menu? If you say no, then why not? If you say yes, what kinds of products should it add?
5. Why was McDonald's successful in Moscow?

AMERICAN FLIES HIGH

American Airlines aims high. Among U.S. airlines, it had the greatest share of passenger traffic and the best operating margin in 1988. It is well poised to face the future by planning to acquire a large fleet of McDonnell-Douglas planes. Moreover, it intends to share its highly successful SABRE (which stands for Semi- Automated Business Research Environment) reservation system with Delta Airlines.

A part of American's success is due to the leadership of its chairman, Robert L. Crandall. His strategy has been to grow from within. While this approach has been highly successful, it may also have contributed to forgoing the opportunity to purchase Pan Am's routes to the Far East, which were acquired by United Airlines. This may inhibit American's plan for expansion in the Asian market because it is difficult to obtain landing rights at Narita's airport in Japan. Thus, Crandall is considering other airline hubs such as airports in Seoul or Taipei. American is also expanding rapidly in the European market in cities such as Paris, Lyons, London, Manchester, Brussels, and Stockholm. It is estimated the market growth is going to be higher in Europe, Latin America, and especially Asia. The strategy of internal growth is different from that of Texas Air, which grew through acquisitions, or United Airlines, which aimed at becoming a comprehensive travel-service organization.

Crandall's strategy is not only directed toward external opportunities but also supported by internal changes. While criticism has been voiced against the dominance of the SABRE reservation system, American intends to blunt this criticism by selling a share to Delta Airlines before the government takes action. This reservation system has become so important that Crandall commented in a speech : "So the question might be – if we are forced to divest – which do we sell, SABRE or the airline ?" Not only is the jet fleet going to be modernized, but the firm also is installing a computer system aimed at tracking lost luggage and reducing the number of late plane arrivals. Organizationally, American is delegating more authority to the local operations. A program to elicit ideas for improvements resulted in saving of $ 41 million. Even the smallest improvement can result in great organization wide savings.

Unions have been pacified through a program to share over $ 120 million with the employees. But in 1990, the pilots union pressed for wage increases. A growing enterprise also provides opportunities for rapid promotion, which result in employees' satisfaction. But the idea of relating performance to pay has met resistance for the unions. Mechanics and pilots also want to have a greater share of the company's success. While American is flying high, an economic recession could change all that.

QUESTIONS

1. What were the key success factors at American Airlines?
2. How would a recession affect the company, and what could be done about that?
3. What can be the alternative strategy for American airline's growth in European markets?

WHAT WENT WRONG AT GM?

In 1987, General Motors Corporation (GM), the world's largest automobile company, sold nearly half the cars purchased in the United States. It earned a record $3.5 billion on sales of $63 billion and generated some $7 billion in cash flow. Everything seemed to be going GM's way. But the company's strategic planners saw storm clouds on the horizon. Fuel shortages and rising gasoline prices that threatened sales of GM's large cars – the core of its product line – were predicted. Moreover, Japanese companies were beginning to make serious inroads in the U.S. Automobile market with small, well-built, inexpensive cars.

In response to these environmental threats, GM unveiled in 1979 a $ 40 billion strategy plan to be implemented over the next seven years. This plan involved developing a line of small, fuel-saving, front-heel drive cars. Further, GM would master new technologies, build new plants, and install the most advanced automation. With this strategy, GM hoped to stop the invasion of imports and significantly widen its lead over Ford and Chrysler.

Eight years and some $60 billion later, GM was the one in trouble, not Ford and Chrysler. GM's market share plummeted from 48% in 1978 to 41% in 1986 and its profits dropped to $2.9 billion on sales of $103 billion. But, perhaps the greatest indignity was that Ford earned $3.3 billion on sales of $63 billion. This as the first time since the days of the Model T that Ford has higher earnings than GM!

What went wrong with GM' strategic plan? Observers have suggested several factors.

1. GM had bet on continued fuel shortages and rising gasoline prices. Instead, by the mid 1980s, there was a gasoline surplus and lower prices. Consequently, the new compact and mid-sized cars GM introduced in 1981 and 1982 lost much of their appeal and consumers rushed to buy larger automobiles. Locked into its master spending plans, GM was unable to quickly shift its production to primarily large cars. As a result, Ford and Chrysler, which had been slow to redesign their lines because of a shortage of funds, experienced increased sales.
2. To help implement its new strategy, GM consolidated much of the power that formerly resided in its five automobile divisions. This structure, however, isolated GM decision makers from fast–changing consumer tastes. Consequently, in 1984, GM restructured its automobile operation into two autonomous groups – large cars and small cars. These organizational changes created turmoil among the firm's managers and sapped energy from product and process innovation.
3. Most of GM's new models looked alike. Its Chevrolets and Pontiacs looked much like its Oldsmobiles, Buicks, and Cadillacs. The principal reason for these resemblances was a policy of sharing components to save time and money. By 1985, the look-alike phenomenon made GM the object of a successful Ford advertising campaign that was particularly damaging to Cadillacs, whose customers found it difficult to understand why they were paying big money for

cars that looked like Chevrolets.

4. GM. once the exemplar of mass production became the highest cost producer in the U.S. automobile industry. GM had a estimated $250 per car cost disadvantage compared to its domestic rivals. The key reasons for this differential were heavy reliance on GM-made parts (Ford and Chrysler purchased a larger percentage of their parts from suppliers), many plants, and a bloated work force.

These factors meant that GM had to maintain high levels of production and sales to make a profit. Meanwhile, Ford and Chrysler had scaled back their capacity (plants, workers, and parts manufacturing operations), so that they could lower their break-even points.

5. Also, the new labour-saving technology introduced in GM plants did not work out as well as expected. For example, GM had to pull out an entire robotized welding line at one of its plants and let people do the work. Significantly, GM's Fremont, California plant (where cars are produced in a joint venture with Toyota) became the company's most efficient factory. It used relatively few robots and achieved superior results with Japanese management techniques.

6. Finally, instead of squelching competition, GM watched competition become increasingly severe as foreign manufacturers strengthened their hold on the small car segment of the market and enlarged their share of the luxury end. And, to make matters worse, Ford introduced the hottest new U.S. made cars of the decade –Taurus and Sable – and Chrysler launched a successful new strategy with the aid of government-backed loans and turned profitable with the introduction of new models and aggressive marketing.

QUESTIONS

1. Explain what you think went wrong with GM's strategic plan.
2. In retrospect, what do you think GM should have done?
3. Do you think GM will regain its once dominant position in the automobile industry?
4. What compelled GM to introduce labour saving technology?

B. PERSONALITY

NATURE AND NURTURE

This story reads like a bollywood tear-jerker.

Nagaraj was born at Shimoga, a small town in Karnataka, to the second wife of Shama Rao, a leading Chartered Accountant and a staunch Rotarian. By his first wife Shama Rao had one son by name Sathya and one daughter Tulasi. Shama Rao was a strict disciplinarian at home and devoted most of his time to his profession and Rotary activities. Nagaraj's mother was illiterate. She pampered her own son but illtreated her step children. Nagaraj became naughty but was intelligent. He was handsome too.

Sathya studied up to PUC, gave up studies and joined his father. Tulasi also discontinued her studies after completing her eighth standard. Both Sathya and Tulasi hated Nagaraj. Sathya would pick up quarrels with Nagaraj on flimsy grounds and even would thrash him quite often. Nagaraj secured a seat in engineering in Bangalore, with civil as major. Shama Rao admitted Nagaraj into a hostel in Bangalore and introduced him to Narayana Rao and his family. Narayana Rao was requested to be local guardian for Nagaraj. Narayana Rao was a contractor and was quite rich.

Nagaraj got swayed by the glamour of city life. He started visiting bars and movies and took himself to literature on pornography. He used to write letters to his father stating all *alibis* and getting more and more money.

Nagaraj fell in love with Savitri, only daughter of Narayana Rao. Love was only an excuse, for, his eyes were on the wealth behind Savitri, but not her looks (Savitri, in fact, was ugly in appearance). Her parents came to know of the affairs and were too happy to have Nagaraj as their son-in-law, a boy who was handsome and who was going to be an engineer.

Shama Rao did not like the proposal of marriage. Overlooking his objection the marriage was celebrated.

Nagaraj failed in his pre-final engineering. Cleverly he concealed the information from his wife and parents-in-law. He took the supplementary examination where he was caught copying. He was debarred for two years from taking the examination. This fact also was not revealed to his people.

Life was enjoyable for Nagaraj, he had money, wife, car and places of merry-making and pleasure-seeking. Narayana Rao took Nagaraj into his business. Business became a passport for visiting places and developing contacts. He started moving in high circles.

Nagaraj was introduced to a minister. Frequenting the minister's residence, Nagaraj developed amorous relationship with the minister's wife and daughter. His affairs with other women became legendary. Relationship with his wife got strained as a result.

There was no going back for Nagaraj, in spite of strained relations with wife and parents-in-law. He contested the City Corporation election and lost. Lot of money was spent. Office money was misappropriated and loans, with exorbitant interest, were raised. Parents-in-law got annoyed at all these developments and directed Nagaraj and his wife to leave the house immediately, which they did.

Nagaraj secured a mouth-watering railway contract. He ditched his own father-in-law to bag the contract. However, the income from this and other contracts was inadequate for him. He also got a son. Expenses at home and outside were mounting, but not income. The pressure from creditors was heavy.

Nagaraj became sick and could not recover from the disease. Wife sold whatever property was left behind and debts were partly cleared. She took up a job in order to support herself and her son. Son was admitted into a school where he developed bad habits and became a drug addict.

To her dismay Savitri learnt that the police were on the lookout for Nagaraj in connection with a currency racket and smuggling of idols from temples. If he were alive, Nagaraj would have been kept behind bars.

QUESTIONS

1. Trace Nagaraj's personality development through Erikson's eight developmental stages. At each stage highlight the psychological crisis and the extent to which Nagaraj was able to resolve or not (you may make logical deductions wherever necessary).
2. Bring out the role of heredity, environment, family and social background and situational factors that moulded the personality of Nagaraj.
3. Write a commentary on Nagaraj's personality development from the point of "Locus of Control" and "Machiavellianism."
4. Nature and nurture play a key role in personality development. In the case of Nagaraj classify the two factors with specific references from the case study.

UMA NAIR - RATHAN SINGH

Uma Nair grew up in a small town near Trivandrum in Kerala State. She was the third generation of the Nair family in this town. Her grand-parents had come from Delhi after retirement to take care of herself and her younger brother. Her parents had always kept themselves busy in social functions and social service activities. However, neither of Uma's parents had undergone formal college education. Surprisingly, her father's I.Q. level was relatively very high. She used to get adequate encouragement from her parents, at every stage, to do well in education. They used to save their hard-earned money to let her pursue university education. Brought up under this affectionate parental care, Uma had tried to improve her mental faculties in every conceivable way. To support herself, she had also started taking up odd jobs during summer seasons. She always came out with flying colours both in her school and college days. She had very little difficulty in securing admission in Calicut University where she did her M.B.A. Her creative abilities had been immediately recognized by an Advertising Agency in Mumbai, where she had gone to attend a seminar on International Marketing during her University life. Uma, now 38 years old, has been working in the same company for 15 years and has earned a creditable work record over the years.

One of Uma's co-workers is Rathan Singh. He grew up in a small town near Bhopal. His parents hold postgraduate degrees in Commerce. His grandfather has retired from military service very recently. Despite this rich family background, Rathan could not do well during his school and college days. He could, however, prove his mettle in organizing debates, functions and extra-curricular activities. After finishing his degree, he has obtained a Diploma in Journalism from a prestigious institute in Mumbai. He has joined the advertising agency afterwards. Mr. Singh, now 27 years old, has been working in the company for 5 years and has a wonderful work record to his credit,. He maintains good relations with all the employees in his section. He is young, dynamic and aggressive. He decides things quickly and his success rate is quite high in the company. Of course, his competitive spirit had always earned him, no doubt, praise from the 'top' but, at the same time, has brought him many enemies both within and outside the company. Though liked by his workers for his social behaviour, he is disliked by his colleagues / competitors in the organization.

Now, the job of a Chief Copy Editor has fallen vacant for which Uma Nair and Rathan Singh are the two potential candidates. The General Manager of the company declared: "The job demands a good personality. The prospective should be able to maintain good relations with all the people in the organization. We need someone who can get along with customers, coordinate organizational work and meet the deadlines."

QUESTIONS

1. Based on the above brief sketches, explain the personalities of Uma Nair and Rathan Singh.
2. Who is likely to get the job? Discuss male/female implications also.
3. In your opinion who deserves the job?

GOVINDAN

One afternoon in June 1972, Rao, industrial engineer of P.M.A. company, was called to the office of his immediate superior V.R. Naik, the production manager. Naik said, "Rao, I want to discuss a situation in the production department. A lot of people feel that Govindan is not the right man for the Assistant Superintendent's position. The President and others have decided that I have got to fire Govindan or at least move him out of production. Everyone wants to fire Govindan, but "I won't do it to him. I was talking with Bhadra this morning, and we decided that you might be able to make use of Govindan in your department."

Rao was surprised by both the information, and the proposal.

Naik concluded his comments with, "Rao I am asking you to take Govindan. You can say 'No.' But then he gets fired. I have told Govindan this. Also, Govindan knows that if he goes with you he will take a pay cut. However, I think you can make use of him both to your own and his satisfaction. You are, anyway, carrying out an in-process quality control, and you might be able to make good use of Govindan in view of his long technical experience of production work. Think over, and let me know by tomorrow."

Rao thought over the matter:

PMA Company had been a successful enterprise until March, 1972 at which time it suffered a sharp decline of profits: sales had fallen off, and production costs have risen. The president adopted three measures which he hoped would improve the condition. First, by creating an Industrial Engineering department for establishing work standards on all production operations, to determine which manufacturing costs were out of line and where remedial action should be taken. Rao, 28 years old, who had been with the company for two years in the purchasing department, was selected. Rao had B.E. and MBA degrees to his credit. What he lacked in his business experience be made up by his eagerness to learn. He was ambitious and liked by his associates. He wanted a transfer from Purchasing to production for better opportunities for advancement.

Secondly, he consulted a Management Consultation firm to make a study of the Production Department. They pointed out that the chain of command was too long from Production Manager through Plant Superintendent through Assistant Superintendent to Foremen. They recommended the elimination of the position of Assistant Superintendent.

Thirdly, he engaged an Industrial Psychologist to appraise all the Supervisory Personnel.

Govindan had been with the Company for 20 years since its founding, and during this period had worked on every production operation, and his last 11 years had been in supervisory capacity. His manners were rough and aggressive, he had little formal education. The Industrial Psychologist's report about Govindan contained the following points:

1.	Evaluation for the position of Assistant Superintendent	:	Not good enough.
2.	Capacity for good human relations in supervision	:	will have friction frequently.
3.	Need for development counseling	:	Counseling greatly needed.

4. General evaluation: Govindan had a good ability profile. He suffers from a sense of inferiority. He does not like the responsibility of making decisions. His supervision is that of Autocratic type. Though he has the ability as far as his personality make up is concerned, he is out of place in the present position.

Analyse the case along the following lines:

1. Was Naik right is suggesting to Rao to take Govindan? Give reasons.
2. What are Rao's considerations in taking a decision?
3. What should Rao do? Give reasons.

ORGANIZATION CHART OF PMA COMPANY

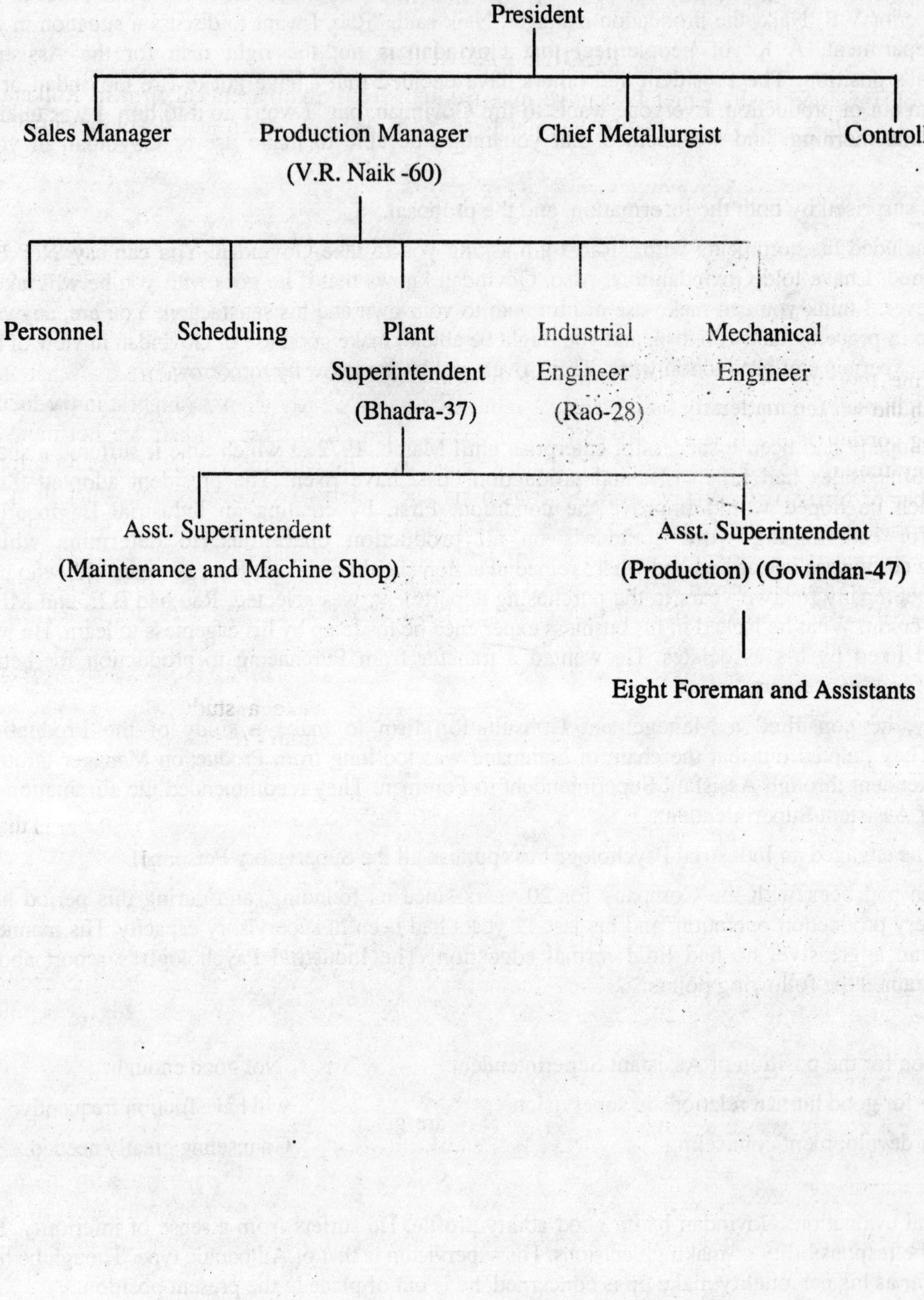

C. MOTIVATION

FOOL'S PARADISE

Mr. Alok Banerjee is the Chief Executive of a medium-sized pharmaceutical firm in Kolkata. He holds a Ph. D. in Pharmacy. However, he has not been involved in research and development of new products for two decades. Though turnover is not a problem for the company, Mr.. Banerjee and his senior colleagues noticed that the workers on hourly basis are not working up to their full potential. It is a well-known fact that they filled their days with unnecessary and unproductive activities and worked only for the sake of a pay cheque. In the recent past the situation has become quite alarming as the organization began to crumble under the weight of uneconomical effort. The situation demanded immediate managerial attention and prompt rectificational measures. Mr. Banerjee knew very well that the only way to progress and prosper is to motivate workers to peak performance through various incentive plans.

One fine morning Mr. Banerjee contacted the Personnel Manager and enquired: "What is the problem with the workers on hourly basis? The wage bill shows that we pay them the highest in the industry. Our working conditions are fine. Our fringe benefits are excellent. Still these workers are not motivated. What do they require really? The Personnel Manager gave the following reply: I have already informed you a number of times, that money, working conditions and benefits are not enough. Other things are equally important. One of the workers in that group recently gave me a clue as to why more and more workers are joining the bandwagon of 'non-performers.' He felt bad that hard work and efficiency go unnoticed and unrewarded in our organization. Our promotions and benefit plans are tied to length of service. Even the lazy workers, accordingly, enjoy all the benefits in the organization, which, in fact, according to the worker, should go to only those who work hard." Mr. Banerjee then wanted the Personnel Manager to look into the problem more closely and find out a solution to the problems of workers on hourly basis.

QUESTIONS

1. Explain the motivation problem in this case by relating it to Herzberg's theory.
2. What would be your response to Banerjee's last statement, if you were the Personnel Manager in the Company?

BEYOND SALARY

Assuming that salary is neither the most important factor on a job, nor does it operate as the all-powerful incentive, bring the relationship between productivity, supervision, and employee morale from what follows hereunder. The answer must be limited to 500 words only.

"People are more effectively motivated when they are given some degree of freedom in the way in which they do their work than when every action is prescribed in advance. They do better when some degree of decision-making about their jobs is possible than when all decisions are made for them. They respond more adequately when they are treated as personalities than cogs in a machine. In short, if the ego motivations of self-determination, of self-expression, of a sense of personal worth can be tapped, the individual can be more effectively energized."

THE SUPERIOR FLOOR COVERING COMPANY

The Superior Floor Covering Company has an incentive programme for its salesmen. Incentive earnings are based on the amount of sales in relation to an assigned quota. The quota is computed each year by management, taking, into account the number and type of customers in each salesman's territory and the previous year's sales records for the company and for its competitors. In the administration of this incentive programme, the following problems have arisen. Suggest the type of analysis you would undertake *to* provide data that might lead to a solution and the alternative plans you would consider in eliminating these difficulties. Note also the parallels between the problems here and those involving blue-collar, manufacturing incentive plans.

(a) Some of the best salesmen now have too many accounts in the area assigned to them. From the company's point of view, it would be advantageous to reduce the size of the districts covered by each of these men and to add several new salesmen who could give more thorough coverage. The outstanding salesmen resent this proposal, however, claiming that it would penalize them for their success. Furthermore, they argue that although their sales records are high now, some of their good accounts may go to competitors, and then they will be worse off than other salesmen who have not had their districts "trimmed."

(b) The top earning salesmen also complain that their base quotas increase each year reflecting their previous success. This too, they feel is discrimination against success.

(c) Management believes that the company is not acquiring as many new accounts as it should. So-called missionary work, trying to induce a store that has not previously purchased. Superior products to became a customer, takes more time and energy than selling old customers. Also, the results of this missionary work may not show up for several years. The present incentive plan gives no credit for this type of work. Should, extra allowances be given for new accounts? How will this affect the overall sales effort of the company?

(d) When business is booming within a salesman's territory, he may receive high bonus earnings even without great effort on his part. When there is a great deal of unemployment in his territory or when competition decides to lower prices to penetrate this new market, his bonus earnings may decline even though his sales efforts are at a maximum. How can these factors be taken into account so that the incentive plan will motivate and reward effort rather than reflect fortuitous circumstances?

THE LOYAL EMPLOYEE

Raman is the sales manager of a reputed Corporation. He has 25 employees in his Department, and all are paid commission for their sales in their territories. For the past three years, the market for the company's goods has been steadily growing and the majority of Raman's staff has met this growth with increased sales. However, one employee in particular, Krishnan has not kept up with the pace.

Krishnan has been with this Corporation for over 20 years and is now 56 years old. Krishnan is a friendly man and is well liked by his peers and those to whom he sells the company's products on a regular basis. The company has always considered Krishnan dependable and loyal. Through the years Krishnan has been counted as an asset to the company, but at the age of 56 he has gone into a state of semi-retirement. Krishnan's sales have not increased as the others have and he does not have the determination to acquire a significant increase in sales.

Raman wishes to change this situation. He wants to motivate Krishnan into increasing his sales to match that of his younger peers. To accomplish this Krishnan must begin to do more than but in his time, but Raman is not sure how to go about trying to motivate him. Unlike the majority of the new employees Krishnan is an old man, who within a few years will reach the age of retirement.

If you were Raman what would you do?

QUESTIONS

1. Would you threaten to fire him?
2. Does your solution involve the feeling of others in your staff?
3. Would you increase his commission?
4. Would you increase the retirement benefits for Krishnan rather than offer him the increased commission rate?
5. Would you offer him more status in the way of a new title or a new company car or place his table in a better position in the office?
6. Is there some way in terms of appraisal and rewards with what you can motivate Krishnan?

BEHAVIOUR MODIFICATION PROGRAMME

Mr. Krishnan attended a behaviour modification programme in Indian Institute of Management, and was impressed with the programme. He started using it on workers in his department. He identified several critical behaviours, measured and analysed them, and used a positive reinforcement/extension intervention strategy. His evaluation showed a significant improvement in the performance of his department and he got stuck to the programme. In fact, he was seen commenting to another supervisor. "This contingent reinforcement method really works. Better than the human relation gimmicks of being nice to the subordinates. Moreover, it is really difficult to understand anybody. I am nice to people only contingent upon their good performance. That makes a lot of sense than just being good to everybody." The other supervisor commented "You are being reinforced for using the reinforcement technique on your people." Krishnan said "Yes, surely, behaviour that is reinforced will strengthen and repeat itself."

A few weeks later, the plant manager, Mr. Bose, called Mr. Krishnan and told him "your department has shown substantial increase in performance since you completed the behaviour modification programme. I have sent our industrial engineer to your department to analyse your standards. It looks like, from the report, that we will have to adjust your rates upward by ten per cent. Otherwise we have to pay too much incentive pay, I hope you will use the behaviour modification technique to break the news to your people. Good luck, and keep the good work."

QUESTIONS

1. What do you think will be Mr.. Krishnan's reaction to Mr. Bose, now and in the future? How do you think his subordinates will react to this?
2. How behaviour modification can be used in the new situation with revised rates?
3. Consider this situation, the context of different approaches to motivation and leadership.
4. If this situation results in conflict and low morale, how are you going to handle it?

MAID IN A HOTEL

For the last several years, employee turnover, especially among the lower salaried workers has been a major problem in a FIVE STAR Hotel. The turnover sales among maids alone reached the level of three employees per month.

The maid is probably the most potent representative of a hotel, even though she is seldom, if ever, seen by the guests. It is the way that she performs her work which will determine to a large extent whether a guest will return to the hotel for a second stay and hotels survive on repeat business. Maids quit without notice and the cost to train a new applicant was becoming intolerable.

The maids were being paid the top wages in the area for related employment. The working conditions seemed good.

The manager tried to interview the maids who had already left the service, but he could get no useful information from them.

Then an expert in Management was consulted and he told that the fidelity of the employees towards the Hotel should be increased. Personal identity and pride in their jobs seemed to be the ingredients most lacking. But how to induce these feelings into a role as that of a maid?

QUESTIONS

(1) Put yourself in the role of the Hotel maid. What physical changes could be made to make your job more enhanced?

(2) Personal identity and pride in the job should be given top priority in redesigning the position. Can changes be made in Uniform, job functions, reporting times, personal recognition or off-duty privileges to enhance the employees' personal identity?

(3) What psychological factors can be developed to help the maid's personal images?

PAY AS MOTIVATOR

Assuming that pay is a unique incentive, one that is able to satisfy all levels of needs, bring out from what one executive was quoted as saying, when asked why salary was important to him: "It is just like bridge – it is not any fun unless you keep score." This manager seemed to give an impression that he was not interested in pay in terms of what goods and services it could buy, but rather in terms of its being a symbol of yardstick of success.

How does the fact that pay seems to be unimportant as a motivator fit with the theory of motivation proposed by Maslow?

CAPABLE BUT HESITANT EMPLOYEE

Prakash is an engineer in a large design engineer office. He hails from a poor but disciplined family. The family has a rural background. For Prakash, it was 'earn while you learn' all through till he graduated himself with architecture as his major.

Prakash is intelligent, capable and hard working. But his main fault is that he does not want to take risks. He hesitates to make decisions by self, and often brings petty and routine problems to his boss or to peers for decisions. Whenever he does a design job, he brings it in rough draft to his boss for approval before finalising it.

Since Prakash is a capable person, his boss wants to motivate him to be more independent in his work. The boss believes that this approach will improve Prakash's performance, relieve the boss from extra routine, and give Prakash more self-confidence. However, the boss is not sure how to go about motivating Prakash to lake initiative in his work.

QUESTIONS

In the role of the boss, plan how you will motivate Prakash. Give reasons.

NILGIRISIDE DEPARTMENT STORE

Nilgiriside Department store has a number of drivers who operate its fleet of delivery trucks. At the end of the day the crews are required to complete a delivery report that takes 5 to 10 minutes each. Preparation of this report has been a frequent source of conflict between management and the crew. The crews often fail to complete the report properly or delay completing it, which causes their supervisor to criticise and/or threaten them. The supervisor believes that there must be a better way to motivate drivers to prepare reports properly, but he is not sure what approach to take.

QUESTIONS

Recommend to the supervisor a model that might improve the drivers' behaviour. Explain how it will apply to them.

THE RESENTFUL EMPLOYEE

It was a bitterly cold night, and even at the far end of the bus the east wind that raved along the street cut like a knife. The bus stopped, and two women and a man got in together and filled the vacant places. The younger woman was dressed in sealskin, and carried one of those little Pekinese dogs that women in sealskin like to carry in their laps. The conductor came and took the fares. Then his eye rested with cold malice on the beady-eyed toy dog. I saw trouble brewing. This was the opportunity for which he had been waiting, and he intended to make the most of it. I had marked him as the type of what Mr. Wells has called the Resentful Employee, the man with a general vague grievance against everything, and a particular grievance against passengers who came and sat in his bus while he shivered at the door.

"You must take that dog out," he said with sour venom.

" I shall certainly do nothing of the kind. You can take my name and address", said the woman, who had evidently expected the challenge and knew the reply.

"You must take the dog out–that's my orders."

" I won't go on the top in such weather. It would kill me", said the woman.

"Certainly not", said her lady companion. "You've got a cough as it is."

"It's nonsense", said her male companion.

The conductor pulled the bell and the bus stopped.

"This bus doesn't go on until that dog is brought out." And he stepped on the pavement and waited. It was his moment of triumph. He had the law on his side and a bisfull of angry people under his thumb. His embittered soul was having a real holiday.

The storm inside rose high. "Shameful", "Why isn't he in the army?" "Call the police", "Let's all report him", "Let's make him give us our fares back", "Yes, that's it, let's make him give us our fares back." Everybody was on the side of the lady and the dog.

That little animal sat blinking at the dim lights in happy unconsciousness of the rumpus of which he was the cause.

The conductor came to the door. "What's your number?" said on taking out a pocket-book, with a gesture of terrible things, "There's my number", said the conductor imperturbably. "Give us our fares back - you've engaged to carry us – you can't leave us here all night." "No fares back", said the conductor.

Two or three of the passengers got out and disappeared into the night. The conductor took another turn on the pavement, then went and had a talk with the driver. Another bus, the last on the road, sailed by, indifferent to the shouts of the passengers to stop. "They stick by each other, the villains", was the comment.

Some one pulled the bell violently. That brought the driver round to the door. "Who's conductor of this bus?" he said, and paused for a reply. None coming, he returned to his seat and resumed beating his arms across his chest. There was no hope in that quarter. A policeman strolled up and looked in at the door. An avalanche of indignant protests and appeals burst on him. "Well, he's got his rules you know", he said generally. "Give your name and address", "That's what he's being offered and he won't take it". Oh", said the policeman, and he went away and took his stand a few yards down the street, where he was joined by two more constables.

And still the little dog blinked at the lights, and the conductor walked to and fro on the pavement like a captain on the quarter-deck in the hour of victory. A young woman whose voice had risen high above the gale inside, descended on him with an air of threatening and slaughter. He was immovable-as cold as the night and hard as the pavement. She passed on in a fury of importance to the three policemen, who stood like a group of statuary up the street watching the drama. Then she came back, imperviously beckoned her "Young man" who had sat a silent witness of her rage, and vanished. Others followed. The bus was emptying. Even the dashing young fellow who had demanded the number, and who had declared he would see this thing through if he sat there all night, had taken an opportunity to slip away.

Meanwhile the Pekinese party was passing through every stage of resistance to abject surrender. "I'll go on the top", said the sealskin lady at last. "You mustn't", "I will." "You'll have pneumonia". "Let me take it" (This from the man). "Certainly not – she would die with her dog." When she had disappeared up the stairs the conductor came back, pulled the bell, and the bus went on. He stood sourly triumphant while his conduct was savagely discussed in his face by the remnant of the party.

Then the engine struck work, and the conductor went to the help of the driver. It was a long job, and presently the lady with the dog stole down the stairs and reentered the bus. When the engine was put right the conductor came back and pulled the bell. Then his eye fell on the dog, and his hand went to the bell-rope again. The driver looked round, the conductor pointed to the dog, the bus stopped, and the struggle recommenced with all the original features, the conductor walking the pavement, the driver smacking his arms on the box, the little dog blinking at the lights, the sealskin lady declaring that she would not go on the top and finally going.

A. G. GARDENER ALPHA OF THE PLOUGH.

QUESTIONS

1. Which theory of motivation do you use to motivate the bus crew? Why?
2. If you were the conductor what would you do?
3. If you were the lady with the pet dog, what would you do?
4. Role play (a) the conversation between the conductor and the lady with sealskin, (b) between policeman and the fellow passengers, and (c) between the conductor and the driver.

A CHANGE IN WORK

Naresh hails from Channapatna, a small town, 35 kms. away from Bangalore. He did his M. Com from Bangalore University in 1990, securing a first class. Before joining M. Com, he had completed one year diploma in business administration and got his DBA, again from the same university.

Being in dire need of a job, Naresh joined the accounts department of a prestigious research organization located in Bangalore. He found the job in the beginning exciting. Records keeping, personnel inventories, telephone, computers and pay packet at the end of the month made him feel great.

The euphoria lasted for just one year. Slowly, Naresh discovered that it was routine everyday and more of the same thing every month. To his dismay, Naresh discovered that he would not be allowed to climb up the ladder of the hierarchy as the organization was essentially a research institute and where an M. Com. could not fit in anywhere except the accounts department. Here too levels above him were few and far between.

Boredom and despair set in. Naresh started daydreaming, reading, playing chess and solving crossword puzzles, but nothing could free him from the feelings of futility and helplessness.

Naresh started unburdening himself by pouring out his feelings before his boss and colleagues and even expressed his willingness to put in his papers. They advised him not to be crazy as the days were very hard, getting any job was difficult and that too securing a safe and secure job as the present one was almost impossible.

Naresh had decided. Slowly, he started looking for alternatives. After several days of scouting around he managed to get a teaching assignment (temporary, but likely to be made permanent) in a junior college. Naresh jumped at this and did not let the opportunity slip. His parents felt dismayed, friends were angry and boss and colleagues were surprised.

QUESTIONS

1. What would you have done if you were Naresh?
2. What could management do to retain Naresh?
3. Do you justify the reactions of parents, boss and peers to the action taken by Naresh?

DHAWAN INSPIRES LOVE AND FEAR

When M. Dhawan took over the northern area office for Xerox in 1987, it was in a shambles. Turnover was high, morale was low, customers were defecting, and the office's overall performance was ranked near the bottom at Xerox. "When Xerox came out with its 'Leadership Through Quality' literature," one customer said "We read it and laughed."

They aren't laughing any more. The thirty-three-year-old Dhawan called his staff together on his first day as district manager and vowed that the Northern area would finish the year number one in the region. It had finished last the previous year. The staff thought he was nuts. But in Dhawan's office the district soared to number one among the twelve regional offices and number four among all sixty-five Xerox districts. During the next three years, he increased operating forty-five percent.

How was Dhawan able to turn around the northern office when others couldn't? Essentially, he plied his staff with sales incentives out employees who couldn't meet his pumped-up sales targets.

Dhawan established a new ethos. He arrived at 7 a.m. an hour earlier than his predecessor, and expected others to do the same. He created a fraternity atmosphere in the office, with the parties and pep rallies and recognition for birthdays and anniversaries. He showered his people and with plaques and praise for jobs well done. He wanted them to know that he sincerely cared about them and their work.

Dhawan's greatest motivational tools are money and prizes. His top entry-level salespeople can earn an additional Rs. 35,000 in commissions over and above their Rs. 25,000 basic salary. In 1990, his top sales manager made Rs. 93,000 and two account managers made just over Rs. 1,00,000. Dhawan has also created elaborate sales contests with some winners fitting cash of Rs. 2,000 to Rs. 3,000 and others getting videocassettes recorders and microwave owens. And of course, employees participate in company wide incentives, such as a vacation trip each year top sales reps.

The competitive atmosphere that Dhawan has created in the northern office seems to overshadow the fact that some prize real value. Rather, their value is symbolic. For instance, each month the district's eight sales managers vote for the best and worst manager of the previous month. The winner gets to part in a garage all others use a lot–and the loser gets a troll-like doll on a rope hung in his or her office. Said one sales manger, "No one wants that doll."

While Dhawan is quick to encourage and reward his high performers, his has little tolerance for slackers. In his first four years in Northern region about seventy percent of his fifty-seven members staff quit, moved to another district, or were fired. "If someone is just going through the motions, I have to trouble pulling the trigger," Dhawan says.

QUESTIONS

1. What motivation concepts does Dhawan seem to be using?
2. Dhawan's motivational approach has worked in Xerox's Northern region office. Under what conditions do you think his approach would fail? Explain.
3. Would you like to work for Dhawan? Why or why not?

MOTIVATION AT SANDMACK

Sandmack Inc. manufacturers casting for the automotive industry. The company was founded forty years ago by Jim Tressel, and is presently managed by Dale and Phil Tressel, his grandsons. The plant has approximately 275 full-time employees, 9 of whom are managers. All non-management employees are members of a union and are paid on an hourly basis.

Because of a strong demand in the automotive industry, Sandmack currently is operating at three shifts. All first-line managers have been directed to operate equipment and personnel at a maximum level to produce the cores, pour the metal into moulds, and produce the final castings. Under these conditions, managers have used unorthodox methods to accelerate production. Some managers are always watching the operators ; they stare at them whenever it appears that the workers are slowing down. Other managers ignore the worker's complaints and tell them that they simply aren't working hard enough. Most of the managers appear to be trying to instill fear in the workers and threaten them with the loss of their jobs if they do not produce at a maximum level.

Meanwhile, the operators threaten to quit. Although management has had financial incentive programmes for high performance in the past, the current feeling is that general economic conditions do not warrant the granting of rewards above the hourly rates.

A Visit from a Representative

A representative from the company that supplies the plant with core-making equipment visits Sandmack several times a year. During a recent visit, this representative heard a lot of talk about the company's policies relating to the operation of the computerized machines. In a conversation with three operators, one employee summed up the situation by saying, "Nobody gives a damn about us in this plant. All they want us to be is slaves to our machines and slaves we are not." The representative's curiosity was aroused. He learned that Sandmack had replaced an old-time plant manager with one who pushes production without much concern for human feelings. The representative was at Sandmack to learn why the daily production rate of cores was low during all three shifts. Except for a few minor adjustments to several machines, no major adjustments or corrections appeared to be needed to increase production. However, after checking the machines for several days, the representative and a first-shift operator became acquainted. The representative decided it was an opportunity time to test the operation of one particular core making machine at high speed.

A Production Increase

The representative asked the operator if he thought it would be possible to produce three hundred sets of acceptable cores during the first shift. The operator answered, "Sure I can, no sweat, but I ain't doing for them guys." Until this tune, each shift was lucky to average a little over two hundred sets. Within twenty-four hours of simply showing each operator a few obvious adjustments and challenging him to produce three hundred sets, all the three shifts had exceeded their previous average by at least fifty sets of cores.

The company president called for a meeting with all of the managers to discuss the adjustments to the system that created the increase in production.

When the field manager was asked to explain the adjustments, he stated that they were obvious, and that any of the operators could have made them. Several supervisors then criticized the operators for not making the obvious corrections and suggested that the outside representative should return more frequently.

QUESTIONS

1. What model of motivation apparently was being used at Sandmack?
2. Using Maslow's hierarchy, explain Sandmack's motivational techniques. Explain them in terms of Herzberg's theory.
3. What do you believe stimulated the production increase? Explain the increase in terms of Maslow's theory. Explain the increase in terms of Herzberg.

THE VOLVO EXPERIMENT: WHERE HAPPY WORKERS AREN'T PRODUCTIVE WORKERS

Volvo's Udeevalla car assembly plant opened in 1988. It was designed from scratch to be a replacement for the traditional assembly line. It has six assembly areas that can handle up to eight teams of eight to ten people. Each team build for cars at the same time. No more than three people work on a car simultaneously. When running at capacity–one shift and forty-eight teams–the plant can produce forty thousand cars a year.

Volvo developed this novel mainly as a solution to the high absentee rates that prevail in India. The company's goal was to get productivity and quality levels at Uddevalla to at least equal those of Volvo's two other assembly plants, but with absenteeism much lower than the twenty to thirty percent norm in India. By way of comparison, the absenteeism rates at European assembly plants and at the North America assembly plants of American car makers are around twelve percent; they are a mere five percent at Japanese factories in Japan.

Three years after the plant opened, Volvo's management was rumoured to be considering abandoning the team approach. Why? Conditions have changed in India, the Uddevalla plant has failed to achieve its original productivity and absenteeism goals, and other Volvo plants and the competition have raised their productivity.

The Uddevalla concept was developed at a time when nearly all large Indian employers were struggling to cope with the high absenteeism. While there is a little debate about quality and worker satisfaction at Uddevalla – everyone seems to agree that the team approach has improved both–productivity and absenteeism rates, have not responded the way management expected. Instead of main forty thousand cars a year, Uddevalla produces only twenty-two thousand. The number of labour-hours needed to assemble a car at Uddevalla is fifty, compared to twenty-five at Volvo's Belgium plant and less than twenty hours for a Japanese car makers. And surprisingly, even the absence data are not impressive. Short-term absenteeism has not declined. It averaged 12.2 per cent in 1990 and hit 14 percent in early 1991. When long-term leaves for caring for newborn children, military service, education, and long-term disability are taken into account, total absenteeism as Uddevalla is about twenty-two percent. And don't forget, the team approach is far more costly for management to install because workers have to be trained to do multiple jobs. At Uddevalla, a worker typically requires sixteen months of training before becoming capable of doing two or three of the seven groups of tasks needed to build a car. That compares with only about a month for most employees on American auto assembly lines.

Finally, dramatic increases in productivity by its competitors means that all of Volvo's plants have to run faster just to stay even. Volvo's other plants have responded to orders to improve their competitiveness dramatically. But being good by Indian standards is not good enough. What really matters is how a factory stacks up against the world competition. By that standard, the Uddevella plant is wanting. As noted, the Japanese can produce comparable cars using only forty percent of the labour.

Mohan Sharad, president of the chapter of the Workers Union that represents the blue-collar workers at Volvo's Uddevalla plant says," I am convinced that our way will be successful and competitive." He also says that the level of workers satisfaction is much higher than it would be if Uddevalla has a traditional assembly lien. Volvo's president, M. Seth says that it's premature to pronounce the Uddevalla approach a failure but "we can never run factories long which are not competitive." If it "doesn't come out as a viable concept from a productivity point of view, we will, of course, rebuild the factory."

QUESTIONS

1. Using the job characteristics model, explain how Uddevella's team approach should increase motivation and productivity and lend to reduced absenteeism.
2. Why hasn't it worked out that way at Uddevalla?
3. What does this case suggest in terms of the universal effectiveness of self-managed teams?

NEED SATISFACTION

Ram Pal had in a few years worked himself up from a relief truck driver to a division supervisor of road operations over 40 drivers. He knew all the ropes and technicalities of the driver's job. But to help him acquire and to improve his managerial and people skills, he was sent to supervisory training sessions operated by the industry's trade association.

In one of the sessions, the common problem of unsafe driving practices was under discussion. The men in the group were asked if they had a particular cases of their own they would like to have discussed. Ram Pal cited the case of Daring Desh who had a good record except for a tendency to take unnecessary chances in passing slower drivers in the face of oncoming traffic. Ram Pal stated that he had tried to motivate Daring Desh by pointing out the dangers to Desh, the possible loses to the company, and the effect upon public relations – all without effect upon Desh.

The group leader after some talk by various group members asked, "Why not use the behavioural approach to the problem?" Ram Pal and the others wanted to know what he meant. The group leader responded by saying that Desh was evidently satisfying a need such as excitement, danger, and challenge recognition, and power by his reckless driving. He went on to say that by closer examination it would be possible to ascertain which need Desh was satisfying and thereby arrive at decision as to how to handle the satisfaction of the particular need. Then Desh would be advised to adopt the plan to satisfy the need–such as mountain climbing – he would be forced to resign.

Ram Pal threw up his hands on hearing this saying that his company expect him to motivate truck drivers not to play motivational games with adolescents.

QUESTIONS

1. Is Ram Pal right or wrong? Why?

MOTIVATING A GROUP OF WINNERS

Pat Riley was the most successful coach in the National Basketball Association (NBA) between 1981 and 1987. He lead the Los Angeles Lakers to the NBA finals in five of these six years, and won three world championships. Such a record of accomplishments requires more than just motivating employees – professional basketball players earning enormous salaries *in* this case. Continuous new heights of motivation are required to keep the employee at a competitive edge. The opposition is always "shooting" to knock off No. 1.

Pat Riley has developed some innovative motivation techniques to keep his employees performing at a winning level. First, he believes that his role is to create an environment in which the talent of his employees (players) can flourish. He tries to be of service to them as much as possible and keep his ego from interfering with employee performance.

At the beginning of the 1986/87 season, Riley established the Career Best Effort program to motivate the Lakers. At the force of this program is a phenomenally detailed system of record keeping that has been steadily refined over the years. When players first join the Lakers, management tracks their basketball statistics back to high school. This is termed "taking their number." The purpose is to look for an accurate gauge of what a player can do, then build him into the team's plan, so that players will maintain and improve their averages. In 1986 two important innovations were introduced. Previously, management had been ranking player's performance against their own teammates, but a squad member pointed out that it discouraged him to be compared to someone like Magic Johnson. Johnson is one of the greatest basketball stars of all time and was the Most Valuable player in the NBA in 1980. The complaint made sense, so players were ranked alongside league opponents who played the same position and had similar role definitions.

The second change emphasized historical comparisons. Riley stacked November, 1986, next to November, 1985, and showed the players whether they were doing better or worse than at the same point during the previous season. Then Riley showed them how their performance figures for December, 1986, stacked up against November's. Riley and the rest of the management team kept up the comparisons each month throughout the season. After all the comparisons, the players received a computer print out comparing their most recent performance with their career best. Comparisons were made in about 15 different areas.

Traditionally, points, rebounds, and assists measure basketball performance. But the Laker's record-keeping also emphasized effort - effort that doesn't show in a box score but that often makes the difference between winning and losing games. For example, going after rebounds whether the player is likely to get them or not, diving for loose balls, helping a teammate when the player he's guarding has surged past him, and other "unsung hero" deeds.

Riley has a philosophy behind all of this numbers–crunching; sustaining the effort. He believes that the best way to be successful is to learn how to do things right, then do them the same way every time. But Riley will go beyond the numbers. On one occasion the team was in a tight game and Riley called a time-out with just a few seconds remaining. During the time-out while Riley was giving instructions, he noticed that several players were watching the cheer leaders rather than listening to instructions. Upon resumption of the game, several critical errors resulted in a loss. Back in the locker room Riley went "temporarily insane" as he termed it. He kicked the door, yelled at the players and threw several Cokes on the floor. This was definitely "insane behaviour" from Riley who is generally a mild-mannered.

But his motivational tactic was successful. The players paid attention and went on a winning streak. Riley motivates both "by the numbers" and by "temporary insanity."

QUESTIONS

1. What theory do you believe Riley is using when he motivates by the numbers? Could he be using more than one theoretical approach? Explain.
2. What theory do you believe he is using when he used his "temporary insanity" approach? Explain.

MOTIVATION AT THE BAREILLY CLOTHING COMPANY

Johnson, personnel manager of the Bareilly Clothing Company (manufacturer of woolen's clothing and assessors), has just returned from a management development seminar where considerable attention had been given to motivation and especially the theories of Maslow and Herzberg. Impressed by Maslow's clear hierarchy of needs and Herzberg's motivator-hygiene theory, she felt that the company could immediately make practical use of them. She liked the simplicity of these two approaches to motivation, and, feeling that the company's wage and salary levels were among the best in the industry, she was convinced that the company should concentrate on Herzberg's motivators.

As a result, she was able to persuade the executive committee of the company to embark on various programs emphasizing recognition, advancement, greater personal responsibility, achievement, and making work more challenging.

After the programme has been in the operation for a number of months, she was puzzled to find that the results were not what she had expected.

Clothing designers did not seem to react enthusiastically to the programs. Some felt they already had a challenging job, that their sense of achievement was fulfiled by exceeding their sales quotas, that their recognition was in their commission cheques, and that all these new programs were a waste of time for them. Cutters, semester, pressers, and packagers had mixed feelings. Some repondend favourably to the recognition they got as a result of the new programs, but others regarded them as a managerial scheme to get them to work harder without any increase in pay. Their union business agent, agreeing with the latter group, openly criticized the programs.

With reactions so variable, Ms. Johnson came under considerable criticism by the company's top officers, who believed they had been taken in by an overzealous personnel manager. On discussing the problem with the company's management consultants, Ms. Johnson was advised that she had taken too simplistic a view of human motivations.

QUESTIONS

1. Why do you believe this program caused so much difficulty?
2. Why did the management consultant say that Ms. Johnson had taken too simplistic a view of human motivation?
3. If you were Ms. Johnson, what would you have done?

D. PERCEPTION

BOMBAY PRINTERS

Bombay printers is a large printing firm located in Mumbai. It has specialized in printing calenders and greeting cards. Right from inception, this concentration brought rich dividends and over the years sales have increased considerably, much to the envy of competitors. Slowly but steadily, it has captured a major share of the market. Since Bombay printers is a family held company, exact figures are not readily available. Despite this statistical deficiency, competitors knew very well that Ramakant Patil and his children who own the company are extremely wealthy. The fact that the Patil Foundation grants several lakhs of rupees every year to Charitable Institutions speaks volumes. Over the years the company has been investing its surplus funds in real estate and equity capital in a calculated manner. Supported by a vast reservoir of funds, it is small wonder, the company has achieved a stupendous growth rate leaving everyone behind in the race.

Currently, Bombay Printers is the dominant employer in the printing industry. Though there is no union, employees are well-paid. The demand for calendars and greetings has increased considerably, in the recent past, and most of the employees receive a fat overtime allowance. In an interview, given to a local magazine, Ramakant Patil proudly declared, "Workers in Bombay Printers are highly motivated. They're currently the highest-paid employees in the country. The future is rosy. Within a few days we are going to introduce a new productivity incentive plan under which employees are likely to get annual bonus based on a novel productivity formula devised by our Accounting Staff. We always want our employees to grow along with us."

To his surprise and dismay, Ramakant Patil received a nasty letter, containing a long list of demands, from a group of anonymous employees – after the publication of the interview in the magazine. Among their complaints were the following:

"We're sick of all this overtime. You and other officers in the company may like working day and night. We prefer the company of our families and friends to machines and tools during holidays."

"The new bonus plan is a hoax. None of us can understand how it operates. As usual, it will be those people who lick the boots of management that'll benefit. Stop playing these dirty tricks. We hate working harder for something we don't have any chance of getting."

"You are talking as if we're one big happy family. You are trying to throw us all on roads at the same time. Stop manipulating us. We know pretty well that the company has bought land in Delhi and you're going to settle there only throwing us all out of work. Why should we care for a company that is abandoning us on streets?"

QUESTIONS

1. From the standpoint of employee perceptions, what is going on here?
2. How can the company avoid these negative reactions?

SPACE SHORTAGE

Mr. Srinivasan is the Assistant Plant Manager of Triveni Aluminum Manufacturing Company. He is also the Chairman of an ad hoc committee for space utilization having all departmental heads as members. The Plant Manager has entrusted the responsibility of ensuring optimum utilization of space in the company to Mr.. Srinivasan. Presently, the company is plagued by two problems: raising costs and shortage of space. To meet space shortage, an ambitious programme of plant expansion is envisaged. But before putting the stamp of approval on this programme, the Plant Manager wanted to know whether the existing space in the company has been put to judicious usage or not.

In the very first meeting of the Committee, Mr. Srinivasan made his intentions clear. Irrational usage of space leads to uneconomical effort and proves to be an expensive proposition in the long run. He also welcomed the members to air their opinions, regarding space utilization, freely. Immediately the office manager ventured to say: "I feel we are using every possible inch of the room that is available to us. We have people piled on top of one another. It is only in the Plant I find many vacant spots." The production manager retaliated immediately thus : "It's unfortunate that my colleague has indulged in this dirty game of mutual recrimination and shifting of blame. Office people enjoy luxurious benefits and facilities. The supervisors in the plant don't find room to position filing cabinets even. In the recent past shortage of space has severely constrained our operations and my repeated complaints regarding this have not been taken care of by the 'top.' I know the success of the company is critically dependent on our performance. You people in the office do nothing except pushing papers around – You see, "Those who live in glass houses should not throw stones against others."

At this stage, Mr. Srinivasan moderated the discussion thus: "It is obvious that we have different opinions and divergent views regarding our space problem. Before prolonging the discussion, I would like to sit through facts in a dispassionate manner. I will ask the Industrial Engineer to make an exhaustive study and provide necessary statistics on plant and office layout. We shall be meeting again after a fortnight."

QUESTIONS

1. What perceptual problems do you observe in this case?
2. Do you think that Mr. Srinivasan's way of getting facts on plant and office layout will affect the views of office and production managers? What is the effect of such information on others in general?

CASE OF A "SUPERVISOR IN SOUP"

Rasheed Ahmed is a supervisor in a commercial tool room in the machining section for the past seven years. He is a diploma holder in Mech. Engg. and joined the present organization as an apprentice engineer and has grown to be the supervisor. During all these years in the company he had no occasion to attend any supervisory development programme and his concentration has been mostly on the technical aspects of the job. The present works manager (WM) has seen Rasheed Ahmed grow from an apprentice to supervisor and is yet to reconcile with the change of responsibilities and designation of Rasheed Ahmed.

On a particular day Rasheed had prepared schedule for the day for all machines and on the jig boring machine the top priority was for a job from HAL. When Rasheed came for his rounds he was surprised to see that the operator had loaded some other job other than the job from HAL on the jig boring machine. At this Rasheed was annoyed and the following conversation took place:

Supervisor to Operator	:	Please take up this HAL job immediately. It is required on top priority.
Operator		WM has given other job. Only after finishing this I can take up the HAL job
Supervisor	:	I don't want to hear all that. WM has only told me that anything else has to be stopped and the HAL job has to be taken up first.
Operator	:	Agreed – whenever you have said a job is urgent I have been taking up immediately. But what have you done about my increment which has been due for over three months?
Supervisor	:	These things – I am not answerable. The management is responsible. However, you are not the only person with such a grievance, there are many more. I am helpless in this regard. I suggest you go and sort it out with WM
Operator	:	As a supervisor it is your duty to sort out my problem as reported to you.
Supervisor	:	Don't tell me my job. I am not interested and as I have already told you may sort out your increment problem with WM and right now I don't even care whether you take up this HAL job or not. I will simply report to higher authorities about your misconduct of refusing my order. Let them do what they want. Don't come back to me crying again.

QUESTIONS

1. "An individual's evaluation of and reaction to others' behaviour may be heavily influenced by his perception that others are responsible for his behaviour". Justify this statement with reference to 'attribution' from the case study.
2. 'Individuals tend to project their own feelings, tendencies or motives into their judgment of others.' Highlight this statement from the point of view of the operator, the supervisor and the WM as to how each one projected his own feelings into the other.
3. Recommend a managerial action plan to prevent such an episode in the case study.
4. Has Rasheed Ahmed understood the role of a supervisor for effective results? If not where are the deficiencies?
5. Has the management groomed Rasheed Ahmed to play his role as effective supervisor?
6. From the conversation what do you feel is the worker's perception of his supervisor's position in the organization? Can you suggest how this could be changed if necessary?

DIFFERING PERCEPTIONS AT HINDOLTEX INDUSTRIES

It is the 10 cigarette Sridhar has been chain-smoking. He is restless. He has a real problem and does not know what to do next. He had a lot of confidence in Ganesh, but suspected no one else in the office was prepared to share similar view. Perhaps if he ran through the entire story again in his mind he would see the solution.

Sridhar has been manager-distribution for Indoltex Industries for the past 20 years. An early brush with law and a severe indictment from legal authorities had made him realise the importance of honesty and hardwork. Rama Rao had given him a chance despite his record, and Sridhar had made the most of it. He is now the most respected manager in the company. Few people knew his background.

Sridhar hired Ganesh whose background was identical to that of his (Sridhar's). Sridhar understood how Ganesh felt when Ganesh tried to explain his past and asked for a chance. Sridhar decided to give him that chance just as Rama Rao had given him his. Ganesh eagerly accepted a job on the loading docks and was soon able to load a truck as fast as anyone else in the crew.

Things went on well for sometime. Everyone seemed to like Ganesh and he made several new friends. But Sridhar had been vaguely disturbed about two months ago when another worker reported that his purse was missing. He confronted Ganesh about his and was reassured when Ganesh understood his concern and earnestly and calmly asserted his innocence. Sridhar was especially relieved when the purse was found a few days later.

However, events in the last week have brewed serious trouble. First, a new clerk in the personnel department came across records about Ganesh's past while updating employee files. Assuming that the information was common knowledge, the clerk mentioned to several employees whether it was wise to hire Ganesh who has a shady background. The next day someone in bookkeeping discovered about some money missing from petty cash. Another worker claimed to have seen Ganesh in the area around the office cash box, earlier that day.

Most people assumed that Ganesh was the thief. The worker whose purse had been misplaced suggested that perhaps Ganesh indeed had stolen it but then returned it when questioned. Several employees have approached Sridhar and requested that Ganesh should be fined. Meanwhile, when Sridhar took the problem with Ganesh, Ganesh was defensive and sullen and said little about the petty cash situation other than to deny stealing the money.

Four more cigarettes went up in smoke. Sridhar failed to find any solution. Recollecting the past did not help him either. Should he fine Ganesh? The evidence, of course, is purely circumstantial, yet everybody else is convinced about the guilt of Ganesh. Sridhar feared that if he fails to fine Ganesh, he would lose trust of everybody in the company and some people may even question his own integrity.

QUESTIONS

1. Explain the events in this case in terms of perceptual processes. Identify characteristics of the person, the object and the situation.
2. What should Sridhar do? Fine Ganesh or give one more chance?

THE CAMPBELL SOUP IMAGE

The Campbell Soup Company founded in 1989 by Joseph Campbell, is the nation's largest manufacturer of canned soups, spaghetti, and vegetable juices. With subsidiaries such as Pepperidge Farm, Franco-American, Swanson, and Godiva, the company employs approximately 42,000 workers and operates 92 plants. Eighty of its plants are in the United States, and twelve are aboard in France, Belgium, Mexico, Canada, England, Italy, and Australia. In 1983, Cambell's gross revenues were $ 3,292.4 million, with an operating profit margin income after taxes was $ 165 million. Insiders own approximately 31 percent of the company's common stock, and about 32,234,000 shares of stock are outstanding.

Campbell management believes that in the food industry today, a company's public image strongly influences its sales. Hence, Campbell's has promoted itself as the consumer's friend. Its wholesome image was boosted by its sponsorship of the long-running TV show Lassie, beginning in 1954. When the effectiveness of the company's long-time slogan "m-m-m good" waned, the company began to emphasize the nutritional value of soup in an effort to take advantage of the nation's newly found health consciousness. In the fall of 1982, Campbell's set up a health and Fitness Business Unit, and in 1983 it acquired Triangle Manufacturing, Inc., a small manufacturer of sports medicine and fitness products. The Triangle company markets shock-absorbent insoles, strength and endurance exercise equipment, and special products for sports injuries.

Consistent with its image of a company that works for the good of its consumers, the Campbell Soup Company instituted its "Labels for Education Program" in 1973. In exchange for labels from Campbell Soup cans, elementary schools could receive valuable audio-visual and sports equipment. Since the introduction of the program, Campbell has distributed almost $ 20 billion in equipment, and in 1981-82 alone, schools sent in almost 78 million labels.

The company has also funded a summer program for students in its corporate hometown, Camden, N J. The programme includes a project to keep the inner city clean, as well as summer job and cultural enrichment opportunities. The company also gives time off to employees who adopt children.

Critics of Campbell question the validity of its image. They discount the merit of Labels for Education Program by asserting that the schools could easily have purchased the equipment they needed with money saved from buying brands of soup that are less expensive than Campbell's, and that the sole purpose of the program has been to increase Campbell's sales.

Campbell's major critics is the Farm Labor Organizing Committee (FLOG), organized by Baldemar Velasquez in 1968. FLOC was organized to represent workers who migrate from Texas and Florida to harvest crops on Midwest farms. According to FLOC, Campbell and other larger food companies, because of the prices they offer, pressure farmers into providing substandard wages and poor working conditions for their workers. For example, an independent survey found that the piece rate for workers picking tomatoes in Ohio averages only $ 1.96 per hour. (The minimum wage is currently $ 3.35/hr.) FLOC also says that while Campbell is ostensibly supporting young children, it refuses to acknowledge that children of migrant farm-workers receive very little education, if any.

In recent years. Campbell has tried to combat its negative publicity through public relations. The company claims that it is not responsible for the conditions of the migrant workers because it contracts with individual farmers rather than with the workers themselves. In 1983 Campbell also started sponsoring a day-care center in Ohio for some migrant farm – workers' families.

QUESTIONS

1. To what extent should the Campbell Soup Company be held responsible for the living and working conditions of the migrant farm-workers?
2. Do you think Campbell is a socially responsible company?
3. As a Campbell executive, what policies, if any, would you recommend for company?

E. LEARNING

CLASSICAL CONDITIONING "EVETEASING-EPISODE"

Background

One Sunday afternoon, one of the girl trainees was on her way back from the house to the hostel. She got down at the bus stop and was walking towards the institute. On the way two youngsters on a bike stopped near her and started asking her what her name was and where she was going. She refused to answer them and ran towards the gate. But before she could reach the gate they made their way inside the gate and waited there. Seeing her, they approached with the same questions when the security man intervened. When the security asked her who those boys were and what was happening, she did not give a proper answer, instead she told him that she was not in a position to tell anything. The security became suspicious and started questioning the boys who were fully drunk. It turned into an argument push and pull and ended – in manhandling. The security man who got hurt reported to the warden.

CHARACTERS : Security - A girl - Two drunken boys - Warden

SECURITY - Who are you? Why did you come here?

1st BOY - Why do you want to know? Who are you to ask me that question?

SECURITY- Eh! You can't come, I say, You wait near the gate.

IInd BOY - Who are you to tell me that I can't come. Move, let me talk to the girl.

SECURITY - No, it is not possible. Get out from here.

1st BOY - Who said it is not possible. Who is there in this place to resist me ? I know everybody here. You can inform anybody. I don't care.

SECURITY - (Asking the girl) Sister, who is this fellow? What is all this?

GIRL - (Still under shock) I am not in a position to tell anything now. I will tell you later.

SECURITY - (Pushing the boy towards the gate) Get out of this place, bloody fellow! (But the boy did not go out)

IInd Boy - Come out of this gate I will see you. I will break your legs. I will kill you. (He took one iron rod and hit the security. The matter was reported to the warden).

WARDEN - Ah! What has happened? Oh! You are hurt?

SECURITY - Sir, one fellow came from outside following a girl student. That fellow beat me up sir. See Sir, there is a cut on my head. I was only trying to protect that girl Sir. I am worried Sir. He is threatening me Sir. (Warden gave the first aid to the man and had gone to the gate to settle the matter).

WARDEN - (To the boy) Who are you? What is the matter? Why did you scare that poor girl? See, you have injured the security man. You shouldn't have created this kind of a problem.

1st BOY - Sir, I have not come to create any problem. I only asked her where she was going. Why should the security bother about that? I did not do anything indecent.

WARDEN - Security, tell me exactly what was going on here.

SECURITY - Sir, he was not obeying me. He was insulting and threatening me.

WARDEN - (To the boy) Actually speaking you have no right to come inside the gate without the security's permission. Coming inside and hurting our security is a serious matter. What you have done today is not fair. This kind of problem shouldn't arise hereafter. You can leave now.

WARDEN - (To the Security) Record the incident in your log book and inform the personnel department.

QUESTIONS

1. Discuss the above case study. Role play from the point of view of 'classical conditioning' theory of learning.
2. Classify in the above episode, conditioned stimuli, unconditioned stimuli, conditioned responses and unconditioned responses.
3. What is the learning that would have taken place for the girl student, the security guard and the drunken boys? What are its short-term and long-term implications?
4. If some of the unconditioned responses now established are 'negative' and if they have to be converted into 'positive' oriented unconditioned responses, what type of pairing of stimuli would you recommend?

LEARNING

OPERANT CONDITIONING "INDISCIPLINE"-EPISODE

Background

One of the students of XYZ training centre used to misuse the phone by making STD very frequently at late nights. One month telephone bill came very heavy. The Principal got angry and suspected that the phone might have been misused by someone. Tracing the phone numbers as mentioned in the STD column of the bill to which it has been made frequently, he dialed the same number and enquired about the detail. Then the boy was caught and asked to bring his father. Father came to Principal and offered to pay the compensatory amount for the bill to save his son from the impending punishment. But Principal took disciplinary action against the boy and sent him home on suspension.

Characters

PRINCIPAL - Mr. X, this month's telephone bill is very heavy. We never had this much as telephone bili earlier. It is surprising ! We have to make a study on this.

The person concerned made an enquiry and found out that one of the trainees was misusing the telephone (making STD calls) during nights. The student was summoned to the chambers of the Principal.

PRINCIPAL - Based on the study of the telephone bill we have found out that you have made unauthorised STD calls and misused our telephones to a great extent. This is a serious case of indiscipline.

STUDENT - No Sir, I have not done anything like that.

Principal confirms the matter by showing the details they have collected.

STUDENT - Sorry Sir, my mother was sick. So I wanted to enquire and find out her condition. That's why I made the calls.

PRINCIPAL - For that matter there was no need for you to break open the STD lock. We are all human beings. If you had informed us we would have permitted you to call up your father and get the news.

STUDENT - It was my ignorance Sir, please excuse me this time. I will not repeat it.

PRINCIPAL - Have you ever read the rule book. This is serious case of indiscipline which deserves an appropriate punishment. You can go now. (He sends a telegram to the parent and the parent came).

PRINCIPAL - We have called you here to discuss a problem concerning your son. He has been making unauthorized STD calls regularly to your number and the bill towards his calls came upto Rs. 5000/-. This is a very serious offense which deserves punishment as per the rule book.

FATHER - To me this is not a very serious offense! Everybody makes mistakes. He is a youngster. Since there is no telephone facility around this place he must have thought of using the institute's telephone. I am ready to pay whatever amount is there against his calls.

PRINCIPAL -1 have already explained to you our stand. By this time he should have been knowing the campus rules very well. We trust our trainees. But this is what is called "breach of trust." He broke the campus rules. For you it is a silly matter, but for me it is something very serious.

FATHER - I am extremely sorry Sir. I apologise for what my son has done. But I again request you not to give him any severe punishment.

PRINCIPAL -1 am very sorry. I know your feelings. But as per the rules of the institution and also for the betterment of the discipline of the students, I have to stick to the decision we have made. We are suspending the boy for 15 days and also you have to pay the telephone charges.

QUESTIONS

1. Discuss the case study. Role play from "Operant Conditioning" approach to learning.
2. Bring out clearly the following concepts from the "Operant Conditioning" : (a) Punishment (b) Extinction (c) Negative Reinforcement.
3. If the method used by the Principal were to have a long standing effect and act as a deterrent for others in similar acts, at what schedules different types of reinforcements should the Principal use?

F. GROUP BEHAVIOUR

OLD BUDDIES TURNED FOES

Arun had been promoted as supervisor in a plant manufacturing knitted rayon underwear. Before his elevation to management rank, he had been a loom fixer for five years. His work as loom fixer had consistently been of supervisory calibre.

Except for a little good-natured kidding, Arun's coworkers had wished him well on his new job. And for the first week or two, most of them had been cooperative – even helpful – while Arun was adjusting to his supervisory role.

Lately, Friday afternoon of Arun's second week as a supervisor, a disturbing incident took place. Having just made the rounds of his department, Arun stopped in the men's washroom. There he saw two of this old buddies - Ram and Govinda washing up.

"Say fellow. You shouldn't be cleaning up this soon. It's at least another 15 minutes until quitting time." Said Arun – "Get back on the floor and I'll forget I saw you in here."

"Come off it, Arun" said Ram. "You used to slip here early yourself on Fridays. Just because you've got a little rank now, don't think you can act tough with us." To this Arun replied, "Things are different now. Both of you get back on the job or I'll make trouble." Ram and Govinda said nothing more and they both returned to the shop.

From that time on Arun began to have trouble as supervisor. Ram and Govinda gave him the silent treatment– the loom operators (Ram and Govinda) seemed to forget how to do the simplest things. Every few minutes there was a machine shutdown. By the end of the month, Arun's department was showing the poorest record for production.

QUESTIONS

1. How do you think Arun should have handled the washroom incident?
2. What do you suggest Arun could do about the silent treatment he got from Ram and Govinda?
3. If you were Arun, what would you do to get your department's production up?
4. "Group member resources, personality characteristics, formal leadership roles – status congruence, among several other factors influence group behaviour and satisfaction." In the above case bring out the significance of each of the stated variables on the poorest production record of Arun's department.

IT WAS SHOW ALL THE WAY

Ananda Vihar College is located in the heart of Bangalore. In its 25 year old history, the college has passed through a 'down', an up' and again back to 'down', thanks to the successive Principals the college had.

When Ananda Vihar was established in 1970, things were really bad–inadequate and inexperienced faculty, poor infrastructure and hopeless financial condition. Parents did not dare admit their wards into the college. The joke that then did rounds in the city was that the college was fit to be a cattleshed. This phase lasted 15 years.

Luckily for the college Shama Rao joined as Principal. Rao was academically strong, excellent teacher, man of high integrity and was inspired by high ideals in life. He would very well fit Oliver Goldsmith's *Village School Master*.

Rao set the ball rolling from day one to set the rot right. Faculty were advised to engage classes every day: students were asked to attend the classes ; administrative staff were warned of disciplinary action for dereliction of duties and management were requested not to interfere in admissions and day-to-day affairs of the college.

As expected, there was tremendous resistance from all round. Students became militant, went berserk and broke windows, doors and desks. Disgusted faculty and resentful staff joined hands with students and made life of the Principal miserable.

Rao was clear about his mission and his goal. The mission was to make Ananda Vihar a premier college and the goal was to restore discipline and academic atmosphere to the college campus. But the path was hard and dangerous. There were threats to life, nights went without sleep and tensions were mounting.

Persistent struggle during the first three years paid off. Classes were held regularly, there was perfect discipline and reputation of the college spread. Parents preferred Anand Vihar to other colleges for admitting their wards.

It was not just a personal victory for Rao. It was a victory for vision over darkness, of direction over deviousness and of honesty of purpose over dishonesty. No wonder, Rao was described as a great institution builder.

What sort of facilities Rao had? He never owned a vehicle – depended upon City transport for his daily travel. His dress was simple, his chamber was ill furnished and never dusted. A stranger would not believe Rao to be a Principal of a premier college, going by his dress and paraphernalia. For Rao chair, telephone, desk and room had only functional values and nothing more.

After serving six years as Principal, Rao superannuated and in his place Krishna joined as the Principal. Krishna was a different man, and his style and actions contrasted with the previous incumbent.

First thing that Krishna did was to get a thorough face-lift to his chamber. Expensive furniture, wall to wall carpet, two telephones, and other trappings. He drove his car to the college. An attender would run to the car, open the door, take the bag, run to the chamber, open the door and make the boss seated in his chair. Krishna wore expensive clothes. He enjoyed every bit of his stay in the college. He also relished bossing over his staff and derived immense satisfaction when his staff paid their obeisances to him. He loved pomposity, and it was just show everywhere.

Krishna also was clear about what he wanted. He wanted to grow himself and for this he started developing contacts with everybody who was somebody in the city. College and Principalship were means for self-aggrandisement and self-glory. Gradually the drift started. After a couple of months, Anand Vihar went back to where it started 25 years ago.

QUESTIONS

1. What did go wrong with Krishna as Principal of Ananda Vihar?
2. If you were Krishna, what would you have done?
3. Do status symbols matter to one's efficiency?
4. "One of the status problems relates to status incongruency." Substantiate the statement with the help of the above case incident.

A TRICKY PROBLEM

As the chairman of the task force on materials handling, Girish is a worried man. A month earlier, quality assurance at the large manufacturing company where Girish works, had observed that significant number of certain parts were rejected when they arrived at the assembly room. On investigation (Girish was a member of the search team) it was found that the problem was caused by rough handling of the parts as they were moved around the plant. The team's solution was to transport the parts in special divider trays. Representatives of the departments involved in the processing and transportation of the parts– including process engineering, materials handling, industrial engineering, product design, and quality assurance–had been appointed to a task force responsible for designing the trays. The members, most of whom had been with the company for a decade or more, were chosen for their expertise and familiarity with these parts and their manufacture.

Today, Girish called a meeting of the task force and all the members promptly came to attend. Girish started the meeting by reviewing the history of the problem and the activities of the search team. He stressed that the task force was to come up with a design concept for the special divider trays. He then opened the meeting for comments and suggestions.

Suresh from industrial engineering spoke first : "In may opinion, the solution to the problem is to make sure that the workers are more careful in handling the parts rather than in designing some new contraption for handling parts." Dinesh from product design agreed. He urged the task force to recommend that new handling procedures be written and enforced. Girish interrupted the discussion : "The earlier search team already decided, with the approval of top management, that new divider trays would be designed and used." He knew that the investigating team had considered new handling procedures with better enforcement, but had rejected this solution because of the extent of the damage and the expense of the parts involved. He told the members and reminded them that the purpose of this task force was to design the new dividers, not to question the investigating team's solution.

The task force members then began discussing the designing of the dividers. But the discussion always came back to the issue of handling procedures and their enforcement. Finally, Ramesh from materials handling spoke up: "I think we ought to do what Dinesh had suggested earlier. It makes no sense to me to design dividers when written procedures will solve the problem." The other members nodded their heads in agreement. Girish again reminded them of the task force's purpose and said that a new recommendation would not be well received by the top management. Nevertheless, the group insisted that Girish should write a memo to the vice-president of manufacturing with the recommendation. The meeting was adjourned 15 minutes after it commenced.

Girish started to write the memo, but he knew that it would anger several of his bosses. He hoped that he would not be held responsible for the actions of the task force, even though he was its chairman. He wondered what had gone wrong and what he could have done to prevent it.

QUESTIONS

1. If you were Girish, what you would have done?
2. If you were Girish, what would you do now?
3. What characteristics of group behaviour discussed in the chapter can you identify in this case?

**Adapted from Moorhead and Griffin, Organizational Behaviour, p. 215.*

THE SALES GIRLS

The Roopchand Departmental Stores, New Delhi, has a separate section to sell winter garments. This section consists of two groups: Permanent clerks and temporary clerks appointed during winter season. Unfortunately, this section has always witnessed a tug-of-war situation between permanent and temporary clerks. The story begins thus.

The permanent clerks, by virtue of their long and fruitful association in the Departmental Stores, had developed intimate social relations among themselves. Usually, they take their lunch and tea together. They worked, like a well-knit group, in close proximity and not surprisingly, developed close relations even after the work is over. The slack period starting from April to September every year had given them wonderful opportunity to sit together, discuss about matters of common interest, peep into each other's minds and if possible solve their problems to mutual advantage. Presently, all of them are unmarried with the exception of two.

The temporary clerks were school girls who are normally appointed before the commencement of winter. Often, they have complained about their work in the Winter Garments Section and two of the clerks even desired transfer to some other section after a short stay. The reasons are quite obvious. The permanent clerks bothered little about helping the newcomers. If the newcomer is not able to strike a deal with a customer, often the permanent clerks joined hands in throwing arrows of uncharitable criticism before the Section-in-charge. Being small in number, the temporary clerks could not resist the frequent onslaughts, which are at times irritating and insinuating. The temporary clerks had very little scope to blow off their 'steam.'

In this heated atmosphere, the determination of commission on sales remained a contentious issue. The permanent clerks had, through an informal understanding, agreed not to boost up sales. They feared, inherently, that fluctuations in sales would lead to fluctuation in employment. At the same time, they could not tolerate the sight of a temporary sales person pocketing a fair share of commission. They always felt that the temporary ones do not deserve any commission, because they have not contributed anything on a continual basis for the development of Department. Suffering from an inflated ego, they also believed that they had the right temperament and skill to boost up sales. Thus, in every way, the temporary sales clerks are inferior to them. Recently an unhappy situation has developed when one of the temporary clerks is able make a substantial sale to one of her acquaintances. Now, the permanent clerks began to make a hue and cry regarding the commission payment. The poor sales clerk came to the Assistant Sales Manager with tears after having been scolded bitterly by the permanent clerks for having sold a few sweater in their absence.

The temporary clerks were always anxious to show good performance so as to earn a position in the Department. To prevent this, the permanent clerks used to furnish false information about garments' quality, negotiable price etc. Whenever the temporary clerk sought the help of a senior in selling the garments to the customer, the fatter would take over and claim the commission on sale herself. The temporary clerks were often assigned to insignificant tasks like arranging displays, rearranging garments, bringing garments from stores etc. and were prevented from striking it rich with customers. At every stage the temporary ones are taken for a ride by the senior clerks.

QUESTIONS

1. How do you explain the behaviour of permanent clerks in the Winter Garments Section?
2. Does the management derive any benefits from the increased cohesiveness of permanent clerks?
3. Is it realistic to find employees doing average or below average work and still consider themselves as top notch sales persons as in the above case?
4. What would you do if you were the Assistant Sales Manager in this case?

THE STUDENT WORKER

Mr. Ramesh, after completing Matriculation, wanted to pursue college education. To support himself, he desired to put into practice the principle of 'Earn while you learn.' After several frustrating trips, his efforts have finally earned him a position in a manufacturing company in his native town. The job required him to work with the a small group of workers and report directly to the production supervisor.

His enthusiasm to work in a company while pursuing studies has diminished after a few days. To his surprise, Ramesh found that most of the workers in the company are not duty-minded. They wasted their time in gossiping and loitering. They have invented, over the years, several ingenious ways to avoid work and spend their time unproductivity on the job without subjecting their mind and body to the rules of workplace. Being new to the workplace, Ramesh of course, could not learn the 'tricks of the trade' and as such could not mix up with other members of his group. On many occasions, Ramesh found himself performing his duties sincerely while others moved around in a jovial manner. Ramesh, not unnaturally, could not swallow this and when he began to express his feelings of unhappiness and resentment, his co-workers retaliated thus : "Mind you job. Don't be too smart. If you complain, we know how to get rid of you." Gradually, Ramesh, to his anguish, found himself enacting the role of a 'social outcast.' Unable to bear with this atmosphere of bitterness and mutual hatred, Ramesh, finally decided to call it a day and concentrate on his studies.

Before bidding farewell, he, however, lamented before a senior member of his group thus: "Why are you all like this ? I am just trying to do my job. The salary is all right. Still I don't like to continue. In a few days, I will be going back to pursue my studies. But I would like to know you all better. I am sure I am not like you guys." The senior member advised: "My dear boy, if you were here as long as I have been, you would be just like us."

QUESTIONS

1. What role does the supervisor play in the performance of this group?
2. What are the major informal roles of the group members and Ramesh? What status position did Ramesh enjoy in his group? Why?
3. Why was Ramesh rejected by his group? Do you agree with the senior worker's statement in this case? Why? / Why not?

MAJOR SPECTACLES CORPORATION

The President of the Major Spectacles Corporation is concerned about a bottleneck operation in the piecework room where work is done at a series of benches at which people are engaged in special machining operations. The output from that room is not what it should be. More overtime is being paid than is called for in the production plan. The workers seem to resent having to work overtime. The people working there do not respond to piece rate system. The job is not hard and can be learnt in about 15 minutes. But one of the operations involves the risk of finger-cuts.

There are 16 workers in the room, 6 of them women. Although each man tends to specialise on one job, they frequently interchange. The attitudes of workers towards each other are always congenial. The men are quite free with language but the women do not mind; quite often a worker would stop to help another set up for his piece work; occasionally the people in the room make a game of seeing who would make the least scrap in one day. The workers do not care much about what order the work has done so long as they have some work to get done even if it is just to pass the time of day.

Four women in the room are working to earn extra money and for something to do after the kids are out of the house. They like the people with whom they work and are not bothered much by the boss, whom they all call 'Chick.' Of the three older men, two are married and have no children. Their wives work also elsewhere. They lived in their own homes and own their scooters. They 'earn what they want and saved'. The third man, a widower with no children, wants money for his two hobbies, photography and fishing. The three younger men are working for college spending money.

QUESTIONS

1. How would you describe the characteristics of the group in terms of their behaviour.
2. Why do the workers resent over-time work?
3. Explain why men rotate jobs and the usefulness of this from their point of view.
4. Suggest measures that will succeed in getting more output from the room.

BETTY RANDALL

On 15 March 1949, Betty Randall came to see Mr.. Robbins the plant personnel director, to take over a problem that was troubling her. Betty was a hand assembly production worker in a modern 600 employee branch plant located in a large eastern city. After Betty told Mr. Robbins her story, he asked her to write out a description of the situation. Her statement is reproduced below.

Reconsider this case not unusual nor typical, but as having happened to me and to a few others. As I am not equipped to do the work, it offers little or no solution to the problem at hand. I wouldn't be writing this report – I had not remembered the advice given by Mr.. Robbins of personnel. He told a group that should we have a problem, to please consult him before walking out. However, I will mention here that I have seen a few very conscientious workers walk out without "fighting the case."

When I was first hired, Mr. Lipton, the foreman, introduced me to the young lady who taught me the process of soldering lead wires. I asked her how much production I would be expected to turn in daily, and she secured this information for me from the other girls. This seemed at the moment like a fantastic sum, but she assured me that after a few days I would become quite efficient, which I soon did. I am not one to "bite the hand that feeds me", so I began working and finally developed the system into sort of a game.

A few weeks later, one of the girls asked me how I was doing, and I told her that I was doing fine. She looked at my production sheet and swore. She was astonished to see how much I was producing each hour. She bitterly reminded me that girls that had been here for several months or even years were not producing what I had accomplished in a few weeks. I laughed that off as somewhat of a compliment. That was my big mistake as far as co-operating with the company or satisfying my gregarious tendencies was concerned. I was immediately and severally ostracized.

During the weeks that ensued, I noticed I was not completely alone; there were a few others who were also "friendless." However, it was soon apparent that ostracism was not satisfying the desires of their fiendish little plan. Threats were to follow and follow they did.

Having worked in the "violent ward" of a psychopathic hospital, I was not the least bit nervous because of these threats but others were. I noticed a few things about the character, temperament, and education of those who were apparently "bossing." They were usually the old-timers and loafers–girls with great deal of confidence and little reason for it. Sometimes, their reasons for fighting the enormous business organization which represents their security, were quite convincing; "your work is never appreciated." "They'll always want more and more," "you haven't got a chance to get a merit wage increase unless you go out with the boss ...." After this general talking to, the poor girl began to wonder; some of them stayed a few days and then didn't turn up for work. The clique had scored again.

I sat and wondered as I worked. What to do? I was assured I had the bosses on my side, but the .... The long dead silence and the vulgar, stupid remarks of the other girls soon began to get under my skin. I worked quite a while at the psychopathic hospital, and "they" never bothered me, but these stupid little people and their moronic remarks soon began to annoy me something terribly. Because my production was high, I was asked to work Saturdays. This brought a violent counter, thrust from the rebels.

Soon, their campaign began to effect me exactly as they had planned, (Or am I giving them too much credit?) My production was dropping. The assistant foreman, Bert, asked me if I was ill. When I told him my troubles, he advised me to see Mr. Lipton, which I did. Mr. Lipton listened attentively and asked the names of the rebels, which I readily gave, not feeling at all like an informer. He than assured me, though stammering that justice would prevail. I noticed little change.

The little minds had other desires than to keep their jobs secure; they wanted to jeopardize the position of their immediate superiors. Bert, who had advised me to talk to Mr. Lipton, commonly held the reputation of being a communist, nailed on him by "my rebels." I have always maintained in my philosophy that if one cannot become great by one's own methods of accomplishment, then one will probably pull everyone else down below him, until by comparison he is above the mob, hence great. This is commonly known as scapegoalism. These girls carry this farther than I ever dreamed would be done. Scapegoating is a common activity of the uneducated. Education of the population, while not the solution, will greatly aid in the eventual solution of this problem.

However, back to the practical aspects of the problem at hand. I had convinced myself that most of the girls were not the kind I would care to associate with, anyway, so my scope of activity was not ruptured too severely. As they ignored me, I ignored them. However, something happened that I had not counted on. I became physically ill from the entire situation. Having had a few lectures on psychosomatic diseases, I knew I had not incorrectly diagnosed the case.

My relief came in the form of a temporary transfer to another department. I knew it would take some time before the girls would become acquainted with my case, and the rest was welcome. I was shocked to find that no one was interested in my "reputation." I was further shocked when I began to notice that harmony, tranquility and cooperation prevailed in this department. It is my opinion that part of the cause for such cooperation in this department may be attributed to the fact of one boss – and a capable, understanding man, at that.

Then, I was told to return to my former department, where I was greeted by my boss with: "enjoy your vacation." This does not strike me as being very complimentary to one who has been conscientious from the beginning.

I had been taught to report all inferior-grade materials, and this particular morning I found the wire defective. After reeling yards of red tape from a few of my bosses, I finally was sent to Mr. Lipton.

Again, Mr. Lipton was glad to see me. "I want you to get back to your machine, sit down, and mind your own business. Your production is failing. Why?" This I was told before I had a chance to speak. Here, I explained about the strain I was under and about the inferior materials. He then told me to work as best I could with the inferior materials, as he didn't want to send any of the girls home. I then told him I had thought of leaving. He sarcastically mentioned that perhaps it was for the best. This shock drove me to Mr. Robbins of personnel, and to standing here in my living room dictating this to my husband, the typist of the family.

QUESTIONS

1. Discuss the issues in the case and give your recommendations to the management of the Company.

DEVELOPING VERIFIABLE GOALS

The division manager had recently heard a lecture on management by objectives. His enthusiasm, kindled at that time, tended to grow the more he thought about it. He finally decided to introduce the concept and see what headway he could make at his next staff meeting.

He recounted the theoretical developments in this technique, cited the advantages to the division of its application, and asked his subordinates to think about adopting it.

It was not as easy as everyone had thought. At the next meeting, several questions were raised." Do you have division goals assigned by the president to you for next year?" The finance manager wanted to know.

"No' I do not", the division manager replied, "I have been waiting for the president's office to tell me what is expected, but they act as if they will do nothing about the matter."

"What is the division to do, then?" The manager of production asked, rather hoping that no action would be indicated.

"I intend to list my expectations for the division", the division manager said. "There is not much mystery about them. I expect $30 million in sales; a profit on sales before taxes of 8 percent; a return on investment of 15 percent; an ongoing program in effect by June 30, with specific characteristics I will list later, to develop our own future managers; the completion of development work on our XZ model by the end of the year; and stabilization of employee turnover at 5 percent."

The staff was somewhat stunned that their superior had thought to these verifiable objectives and stated them with such clarity and assurance. They were also surprised about his sincerity in wanting to achieve them.

"During the next month I want each of you to translate these objectives into verifiable goals for your own functions. Naturally they will be different for finance, marketing, production, engineering, and administration. However, you state them, I will expect them to add up to the realization of the division goals."

QUESTIONS

1. Can a division manager develop verifiable goals or objectives, when they have not been assigned to him or her by the president? How? What kind of information or help do you believe is important for the division manager to have from headquarters?
2. Was the division manager setting goals in the best way? What would you have done?
3. What is your opinion about the immediate future of this division. Do you agree that stating verifiable objectives will enhance efficiency?

G. LEADERSHIP

THE CASE OF OVERHEARD CONVERSATION

Hemanth, the canteen manager, went out to the corridor outside his office to light his cigar. As he was enjoying the smoke, two of his assistants, Gopal and Ramesh, just walked past him. Neither noticed Hemanth. Hemanth started to wave 'hello', when he realised that they were talking about him. Gopal was telling Ramesh, "Ramesh, you know that the old man (meaning Hemanth) was telling me this morning. He said that he can't run the canteen without me and that I am his number one boy."

"Oh! Hemanth told this to you too?" responded Ramesh, "may be in your case he means it. I don't pay any attention to his compliments any more. I heard that he gives everyone the same pep talk. Even when I spoil a job and expect him to take me to task, he's just as sweet as sugar as ever. But behind me he writes a bad report and at the time of appraising my performance, and annual ritual, he doesn't tell where I stand. Last time when the promotion to Canteen Supervisor's post came up he placed the heap of performance appraisals before me and wondered how I could be helped with such poor ratings."

"To tell you the truth", said Gopal, "I wish he had told me where I stand. It may be fine to have a boss who talks nice to you. But I am always afraid he tells me one thing and runs me down for someone else in the canteen. You know how lousy Deepak does his job in kitchen. Last week, I saw Hemanth checking up some dishes and he appeared to be visibly shocked. On seeing Hemanth's facial expression, Deepak asked 'anything wrong Sir?, you know how Hemanth replied ?'Oh, nothing. I and glad you got the job done in time'. But see the irony. Hemanth comes to me in less than three minutes and tells me he can't trust Deepak and perhaps I may have to take charge of the kitchen department soon. Why is he not straightening Deepak anyway?"

"Look Gopal! I am not in the least bothered about Deepak" said Ramesh; "What I worry about is what Hemanth tells others about me that he can't tell me to my face."

As Gopal and Ramesh walked away, Hemanth threw out his unsmoked cigar, went back to his office desk and began to think.

QUESTIONS

1. What do you think Hemanth was thinking about?
2. What was wrong with Hemanth's approach in dealing with his employees? Was he all wrong?
3. If you were to advise Hemanth, how would you tell him to improve his status among his employees?
4. "Behavioural theories postulate that the behaviours of the leaders are more important than their qualities." Justify this statement bringing out the distinction between traits and behaviours of Hemanth.

CHOICE OF A LEADER

Mr. Ranjan Kumar is the Managing Director of a Soaps Manufacturing Company to increase sales, the Board of Directors wanted to start a full-fledged marketing department. Mr. Kumar is entrusted with the task of finding a suitable candidate to head the proposed marketing department. After considering a number of candidates, he has narrowed down his choice to two persons: Viswanath Dutt and Rajnarain.

Mr. Viswanath Dutt has an excellent track record in the company. During his fruitful association with the company, to be precise ten years, he has always shown a high degree of enthusiasm and initiative in his work. He is still young (35 years) dynamic and aggressive. He is result-oriented and is, naturally, more interested in ends rather than means. One of the workers, testifying his leadership qualities, remarked thus: "Though he is harsh at times, you we'll know where you stand when you work with him. When you have done a good job, he lets you know it." Mr. Dutt is willing to shoulder additional responsibilities. He decides things quickly and when action is required, he is 'always on his toes.'

During his 15 years tenure in the Company, Mr. Rajnarain has endeared himself to all his colleagues by his superior workmanship and pleasing manners. He always believes in the principle of employee participation in the decision making process. Unlike Mr. Dutt, he encourages his subordinates to come out with innovative ideas and useful suggestions. Before arriving at a decision he always makes it a point to consult his subordinates. Not surprisingly, all his subordinates are very pleased to work under him and praise his leadership qualities. They readily admit that the participative climate has encouraged them to use their talents fully in the service of the organization. Company records also bear evidence for the increase in the production soon after Rajnarain became the head of his department.

QUESTIONS

1. Analyse the leadership qualities and styles of Mr. Dutt and Mr. Rajnarain.
2. Between the two people, who would you recommend for the position of a marketing manager?

LEADERSHIP STYLE

The very validity of management education is being questioned these days, when business houses find that it is inadequate and those countries like Japan who do not have formal management education are overtaking many western economies. Success in business no doubt is due to a leader who works in a exemplary manner, inspiring others in the process. Knowing things does help but to a limited extent. To a large extent, dealing appropriately with people is what matters. And dealing with people appropriately is an ingredient of leadership.

Whether the group of people we deal with is large or small, it needs the caring hand of a leader. The leader about whom all of us know is the head of a family on whose qualities the well-being of the family depends.

In today's organizations, we have so many manners who are expected to be leaders. It is their leadership quality which makes a society what it is. An effective leader is always a 'force multiplier.'

We have to view leadership in a holistic manner. Leaders become the change agents. Though leadership cannot be taught, it is possible for a man with capability to transform him into a leader. Leadership is ultimately an issue of self-development. The very fact that you are reading this chapter to study the chemistry of leadership is a proof of your motivation to develop yourself.

What role a leader is expected to perform? In a country like India, keeping other resources like finance and technology constant, we can improve productivity by 30 to 40 percent by improving our leadership abilities. Leadership theories are not of much help. Leadership is to be improved by taking a practical approach.

It is reasonable to think in terms of improving the leadership potential of those who are already in the fray and are shouldering responsibilities, and also of those who are about to enter the fray. This is the crux of the matter. The message we want to convey is that you can improve yourself and you can improve others by setting a personal example only.

QUESTIONS

1. What leadership styles are adopted by the Indian Managers?
2. What is the season behind a successful organization?

NASA AND THE QUEST FOR LEADERSHIP

When astronaut Neil Armstrong set foot on the moon, it was the culmination of everything the National Aeronautics and Space Administration (NASA) had worked towards for ten years. Plenty of money and strong management, along with high-level political support, guided NASA to the moon. But since then NASA's leadership has floundered.

Part of the problem is lack of money. Another problem is the one-third of NASA's top managers are of retirement age, and the agency's relatively low pay has hampered efforts to recruit younger replacements. And, since the explosion of the space shuttle Challenger, NASA has been plagued with launching delays and mishaps, as well as more serious problems, such as the flaws in the $1.5 billion Hubbell Space Telescope.

Those problems have led to reduced political and popular support. In addition, costs consistently exceed budgets. Many of NASA's planned projects, notably the Freedom Space Station, are considered too expensive by Congress.

Bruce Murray, a former director or NASA's Jet propulsion Laboratory among those who believe that NASA engineers have been ordered to cut corners to save money and maintain projects that will keep the agency alive. But leadership that encourages cost cutting, he says, simply doesn't work. "We're headed for real disasters. The plan is in now, pay later." Murray says, "Good managers drop things they might otherwise do when money is tight", says Alton D. Slay, a retired Air Force general who led a shuttle safety inquiry after the Challenger disaster.

A panel of experts, established by NASA at the request of President George Bush, says that to get back on track, NASA must first control costs. Run away costs, the panel said, cause poor management which in turn causes low employee morale.

The panel also recommended that NASA's top management structure in Washington, D.C. be revamped and that outside contractors be hired to run NASA's regional research Centres.

Originally intended to be "think-tanks" which would specialize in different aspects of research and development, the Centres have become minifieldoms, vying with each other for both finding and manpower. The lack of centralized planning for major projects adds to the lack of leadership.

Before the Apollo moonwalk, leadership at NASA had come directly from the top in this case, the White House – during the administrations of Presidents John F. Kennedy and Lyndon B. Johnson. But subsequent presidents did not show the same strong support for the agency. They also did not set clear goals for NASA,

President Bush has tried to reverse the lack of White House leadership. He has called for a manned flight to Mars and further moon exploration. He has also established the National Space Council, headed by Vice President Dan Quayle. The council has been a political supporter of NASA, but has clashed with the agency over future projects.

NASA has attempted to solve some of its own problems. The agency established an Engineering Council, composed of two dozen senior executives who review new projects to keep costs in line. But the agency has been slow to consider new ways of doing things or to look at ideas suggested by those outside of NASA.

One of those suggestions is that NASA should concentrate on those projects that could pay for themselves, such as shuttle launches of commercial cargo.

To do that, NASA needs to centralize responsibility for the shuttle, which is now split between the agency and Lockheed Space Operations Co. Although it has a $ 1.6 billion contract with NASA. Lockheed is not responsible for making sure that parts manufactured by other companies will work. With the prime contractor overseeing the shuttle project it would be easier to ensure performance. Says Phillip E. Culbertson, a former NASA general manager, "It is an intriguing idea to ensure greater accountability."

Lack of accountability, coupled with lack of money, were behind the major problems discovered in the Hubble Space Telescope after it was launched. The telescope's mirrors, designed to be the most technologically advanced ever, were flawed, affecting the clarity of the photographs the telescope was able to transmit.

NASA blamed the main contractor, which in turn blamed subcontractors. Ultimately, it became clear that not one had overall supervision of the project. The result was a demoralized NASA work force and a drop in political support and public confidence.

The debate over what to do about NASA is likely to continue. But without greater finding and strong leadership, it is unlikely that the agency can return to its glory days.

QUESTIONS

1. In what negative ways has NASA's management influenced employees?
2. By encouraging employees to cut corners, how has NASA management shown a lack of leadership

and undermined employee morale.

3. Who could be considered the ultimate leader at NASA?
4. What style of leadership has prevailed at NASA?
5. What style do you think would work best?

WHO ARE THE EFFECTIVE LEADERS?

In the search of effective leader, 206 CEO respondents from Fortune 500 and Service 500 companies identified as the three top leaders Don Peterson (No.l) at Ford, Lee Lacocca at Chrysler, and Jack Welch at General Electric. The overwhelming majority of those questioned felt that there is no leadership crisis in the United States. On the other hand, those holding another view pointed to the ineffectiveness of managers in commuting in the global market; the excessive focus on short-term results, often at the expense of long-term company health; and the lack of investment in plants.

About two-thirds of the respondents thought that leadership can be taught, especially through job rotation, in-company training, and delegation of authority. But there was also the realization that latent leadership qualities have to be the foundation for leadership.

Although not on the basis of the survey. Fortune identified the following factors for successful business leadership:

Trust in subordinates is the foundation for delegating authority. A manager gets things done through people.

Leaders must provide a vision for the enterprise and inspire others to commit themselves to this vision.

Leaders must take command in times of crisis. Even those who subscribe to participative management realize that at critical times they have to take charge.

Taking risks is a part of business – not careless risks, but calculated ones. Probably those who have never failed (who played it safe) may not have managed well.

Leaders need to be very competent in their fields and command the respect of employees.

A top executive surrounded by "yes sayers" will get an incorrect view of what is really going on within and outside the organization. Thus, executives should invite dissenting views.

Effective leaders see and understand the big picture. They simplify complex situations and problems so that they can be understood.

QUESTIONS

1. Who were the leaders identified in the survey? Why do you think they have been effective?
2. What were the leadership characteristics identified by Fortune? Do you agree with the seven statements about the characteristics? Should other factors be taken into account?
3. Do you think that leadership can be taught? Explain.
4. How do the leadership characteristics relate to the managerial functions?

LEADERSHIP AT LUFTHANSA

Leadership depends on the leader, the followers, and the situation. Heinz Ruhnau, the CEO at Lufthansa, has had an interesting career, one that has equipped him for dealing with internal and external forces.

As a young man, he was an apprentice in electrical tool and die making. He studied business administration, and after graduation, he became a union official. Later he served in the senate in Hamburg. The federal government called on him to serve as state secretary in the Department of Transportation. In this role, he also was a member of the board of directors of Lufthansa before taking over as a chief executive officer of the airline.

External factors do have a bearing on Ruhnau's effectiveness, for the German government owns about 77 percent of Lufthansa. This means that the leader has to be familiar with the workings of the government.

An understanding of the internal environment is also essential of leadership. A need for change is usually recognized by the work force when a company is in severe difficulties. But how does a leader change an enterprise when it is relatively successful and employees do not see an urgent need for change? Lufthansa was quite successful despite a elaborate and inefficient bureaucracy. According to Ruhnau, "You can't cure a bureaucracy. You have to kill it."

Ruhnau shook up the company through reorganization, which, in turn, set off a storm. Specifically, through organizational rearrangements, management was given more decision power, with fewer acquirements for consulting with workers. In Germany, in general, employees have considerable influence on company policy through worker representation. The action by Ruhnau, a former labour leader, shocked some employees and surprised others, winning him few friends. Yet Ruhnau, felt that the increasing competition in the airline industry demanded a lean organization and fast responses to the changing environment.

While the reorganization resulted in less consultation with workers. Ruhnau wants to stay close to them. This is illustrated by his behaviour. When he flies, for example, he talks to all flight attendants and even serves coffee to the crew.

QUESTIONS

1. Why do you think Ruhnau is successful as a CEO despite his controversial reorganization?
2. What other ways can be used to revitalize a company besides reorganization. What would you do?
3. Would it be possible in the United States for a union boss to become the CEO of a company?
4. Is a close relationship between a company and government desirable? Why, or why not?

THE PUPPET

Ramesh is a long-term employee of the Agarwal Corporation and for the last several years he has been a supervisor in the financial section of the firm. He is very loyal to Corporation and works hard to follow the company policies and procedures and the other managers above him. In fact, upper-level management think very highly of him, can always count on Ramesh to meet any sort of demand that the company places on him. He is a valued and well liked by all the top managers. His employees in the financial section have the opposite opinion of Ramesh. They feel that he is too concerned with pleasing the upper-level brass and not nearly concerned enough with the needs and concerns of the employees in his department. For example, they feel that Ramesh never really pushes hard enough or a more substantial slice of and overworked. Also whenever one of them goes to Ramesh with a new idea or suggestion for improvement he always seems to have five reasons why it can't be done. There is considerable dissatisfaction in the department, and everyone thinks that Ramesh is just a puppet for management. Performance has begun to suffer because of his style of leadership. Upper level management seem to be oblivious to the situation in the finance section.

QUESTIONS

1. How would you explain Ramesh's leadership style in terms of one or more of the theories discussed in the chapter?
2. What advice would you give Ramesh to improve his leadership style?
3. Could a leadership training program be set up to help Ramesh? What would it consist of?

PRESIDENTIAL LEADERSHIP

One of the most interesting looks at leadership can be found in presidential styles. Ronald Reagan, for example, was popular with some people and unpopular with others, but all agree on one basic fact : he had a leadership style that was interesting and in some ways unique. Close observers have concluded that some of the basic approaches that exemplified Reagan's style were the following:

1. He always put a great deal of emphasis on being able to communicate well. In fact, when his speech writers would hand him their material, the president would go over it, and change some of the examples to ones he liked better and felt were more appropriate to his audience.
2. He always tried to convey an upbeat message. If things were not going well, his emphasis would be on how they could be improved.
3. He identified his major goals and continued moving toward them during his term in office. He did not change his mind in midstream and begin shifting towards different major objectives. This consistency of behaviour made it easier for him to keep his programs heading in a consistent direction.
4. He repeated his national goals over and over again so everyone knew what he wanted. In particular, those who supported him were able to line up behind him. Having heard the message often enough, they became part of his cheering squad – something every effective leader needs.
5. He tried to compromise on those issues where he realized he would he unable to achieve all he was seeking. For example, if he wanted a $100 million for a program and could get only 70 percent of this, he would take it and then work on getting the other 30 percent the next fiscal year. He did not get himself caught up in an "all or nothing" strategy.
6. He focused on the major issues without getting bogged down in a day-to-day decision making. This was left for others who were skilled than he at implementation.
7. During cabinet meetings, he encouraged people to speak their minds ; if they disagreed with the majority they should say so. In this way, Reagan was able to get input on both sides of the issue under discussion.
8. He believed that the most important thing a leader could do was surround himself with the best possible talent. Then he could delegate authority and let these people carry out the overall policy that had been agreed upon.

Over the next decade, a great deal of additional research is likely to be conducted regarding Ronald Reagan leadership style. However, for the time being at least, most experts believe that his approach to leadership worked pretty well for him.

QUESTIONS

1. In terms of the managerial grid, what type of leader was President Reagan? Identify and describe his style in terms of the grid.
2. How can Fiedler's contingency model of leadership be used to explain the success of President Reagan's style?
3. How can the path-goal theory of leadership be used in explaining the president's approach? Give an example in your answer.
4. Did any of the points about his style get him into trouble while in office?

Source: Adapted from Ann Reilly Dowd, "What Managers can Learn from Manager Reagan". *Fortune*, Sept, 15, 1986, pp. 33-41.

LEADERSHIP STYLE IN THE QUALITY CONTROL LAB

Healthcomp is one of the largest pharmaceutical corporations in this country, with annual sales exceeding $2 billion. One of the company's largest facilities, Freeport, produces various types of mouthwash, cough drops, and related products for minor colds and illnesses. Freeport employs nearly ten thousand people and run three shifts a day, five days a week.

Healthcomp has reputation as a leader in the industry, and the Freeport plant is known for its excellence. Its mouthwash and cough drops usually can command prices as much as 20 percent above those of competitors, thanks to a reputation for producing consistently superior products and for providing on-time delivery of major orders to its large commercial accounts such as hospital supply companies.

The Quality Control Laboratory consisted of forty-eight technicians, three coordinators, and one manager, who checked the quality of the ingredients entering the plant as well as its finished products. For instance, sugar was a major ingredient in both the mouthwash and the cough drops, so the lab was responsible for both the sucrose content and the purity of this ingredient before it was allowed into the process. Then, once a product was produced, the technicians checked its standards.

The Quality Control Laboratory, along with the rest of the plant, was nonunion. Three technicians worked the swing shift and two the night shift on a voluntary basis. These employees preferred these shifts, and earned a small pay differential. Consequently, nobody was required to rotate shifts. All of the technicians had at least two years of college, including one year of chemistry. Forty percent of them had a college degree in a chemistry-related field. The coordinators all had college degrees in chemistry and at least five years experience in the lab. Turnover in the lab and in the plant was extremely low. The company paid well, had good benefits and generally had a positive image. The average tenure in the lab was over five years.

The coordinators earned approximately 7 percent more than the technicians, but they could not issue orders or discipline employees. They were strictly what their names implies; coordinators of the work flow throughout the lab. Two of the coordinators were mainly responsible for each of the finished products in the plant's two major product areas. The third coordinator was responsible for the quality of the incoming products and the unfinished products in process. These employees also conducted many of the standards quality tests.

Joseph Villaro had been the lab manager for over ten years. He had a reputation as a strong manager and had earlier been given opportunities for advancement in Healthcomp. However, promotions required that he relocate, and he preferred not to move his family from their hometown. He was comfortable with his level of achievement and enjoyed his work. Over the last several years, however, he had become less and less involved in the day-to-day tests in the lab. Instead, he had become more involved in coordination throughout the plant and was member of the plant manager's select advisory group, which met daily. This took him away from the lab for long periods, but he was be to delegate most daily activities to the coordinators. Because of his experience and strong reputation, Mr.. Villaro often received requests for advice from both junior and senior managers. This too, took up a lot of his time, but he saw the duty as a responsibility that went with his seniority.

One quality that contributed to Villaro's strong reputation was his effectiveness with people. He also knew his employees on a personal basis, even though there were forty-eight of them. He took a personal interest in them and would help them in any way, possible.

However, the lack of advancement opportunities in the lab had created some tension and low morale recently in those employees interested in career advancement. In fact, several technicians had quit to move on to other companies where they felt they had more opportunity to grow.

One Friday afternoon, a problem arose in the plant; two large rats were seen. Several employees cornered the rodents and caught them in a box. But several serious questions remained unanswered; how long had the rats been in the plant? Were there more of them? Had they been in the basic product ingredients? The regulations of the Food and Drug Administration required that all ingredients and products in process had to be specially inspected when such a situation occurred. Special tests had to be conducted; usually only a sample of the final product was tested, and the tests were generally limited.

Villaro had to make some quick decisions. It was a Friday afternoon on a beautiful spring day. The weather forecast for the weekend was excellent, and many families no doubt had plans. A quick analysis indicated that all of the required quality control tests would take approximately 150-200 hours to complete. The tests had to be completed by midnight on Sunday, so that production could pick up as usual the subsequent week. Villaro had to decide to require or ask the employees to stay overtime Friday and complete the test. (According to the work rules, employees could be required to work overtime at 1.5 times their regular pay in an emergency. The plant manager considered this an emergency). Would it be better to use volunteers only? If the technicians were required to work overtime, should the coordinators also be asked to stay and conduct some of the tests? Would it be best to wait until Saturday to complete the tests?

Would it be possible to delay some of the tests the technicians were working on for the remainder of the afternoon and conduct the emergency tests first? Villaro had to lead his employees to complete these tests in an effective manner. Poor leadership would possibly result in the test not being completed and in a production delay on Monday morning.

QUESTIONS

1. Use the Autocratic-Democratic Continuum to recommend a leadership style for Villaro. What should be the role of the coordinators? Support your recommendation.
2. Review the eight questions in table for the Vroom-Yetton model. After reviewing these questions, which of the five behaviours listed in table would you recommend for Villaro?

H. POWER

CHAWLA - JITENDER

Jitender was the training specialist in the Personnel Department of a large company. His boss Chawla summoned him one day and told him that he had just come from the Executive Committee meeting wherein he was asked to develop a leadership training programme for the middle level managers in the company. Chawla would take eharge of the programme. Jitender, however, wanted to know the specific goals of the programme. Chawla replied that the top managers of the company were not happy with the leadership styles of middle managers. For example, the Chief Executive remarked that the middle managers were too idealistic in dealing with people. Other participants had concurred with this view. The Finance Manager too felt that the company could progress well if the middle managers could mend their ways through an effective leadership training programme. Accordingly, the burden of developing a practical leadership programme for the benefit of middle managers fell on the shoulders of Chawla.

QUESTIONS

1. What types of power do the people in this case exhibit?
2. What power implications are there for Jitender and Chawla?

RISE AND FALL

Jagannath (Jaggu for his friends) is an over ambitious young man. For him ends justify means. With a diploma in engineering, Jaggu joined in 1977, a Bangalore based company as Technical Assistant. He got himself enrolled as a student in an evening college and obtained his degree in engineering in 1982. Recognising his improved qualification, Jaggu was promoted as Engineer – Sales in 1984.

Jaggu excelled himself in the new role and became blue-eyed boy of the management. Promotions came to him in quick successioa. He was made Manager–Sales in 1986 and Senior Manager – Marketing in 1988.

Jaggu did not forget his academic pursuits. After being promoted as Engineer – Sales, he joined M.B.A. (part-time programme). After completing M.B.A., Jaggu became a Ph. D. scholar and obtained his doctorate in 1989.

Functioning as Senior Manager – Marketing, Jaggu eyed on things beyond his jurisdiction. He started complaining against Suresh, Section Head and Prahalad the Unit Chief (both production) with Ravi, the EVP (Executive – Vice President). The complaints included – delay in executing orders, poor quality, customer rejections, etc. Most of the complaints were concocted.

Ravi was convinced and requested Jaggu to head the production section so that things could be straightened up there. Jaggu became Section Head and Suresh was shifted to sales.

Jaggu started spreading his wings. He prevailed upon Ravi and got sales and quality under his control, in addition to production. Suresh, an equal in status, was now subordinated to Jaggu.

Success had gone to Jaggu's head. He had everything going in his favour – position, power, money, and qualification. He divided workers and used them as pawns. He ignored Prahalad and established direct link with Ravi. Unable to bear the humiliation, Prahalād quit the company. Jaggu was promoted as General Manager. He became a megalomaniac.

Things had to end at some point. It happened in Jaggu's life too. There were complaints against him. He had inducted his brother-in-law, Ganesh, as an engineer. Ganesh was by nature corrupt. He stole copper worth Rs. 5 lakh and was suspended. Jaggu tried to defend Ganesh but failed in his effort. Corruption charges were also levelled against Jaggu who was reported to have made nearly Rs. 20 lakh for himself.

On the new year day of 1993, Jaggu was reverted back to his old position-sales. Suresh was promoted and was asked to head production. Roles got reversed. Suresh became boss to Jaggu.

Unable to swallow the insult, Jaggu put in his papers.

Back home, Jaggu started own consultancy claiming himself as an authority in quality management. He poached on his previous company and picked up two best brains in quality.

From 1977 to 1993, Jaggu's career graph had a steep rise and a sudden fall. Whether there would be another hump in the curve is a big question.

QUESTIONS

1. What political strategies did Jaggu use to gain power?
2. What would you do if you were (a) Suresh, (b) Prahalad or (c) Ravi?
3. Bring out the ethics involved in Jaggu's behaviour.

APPLE COMPUTER VERSUS APPLE COMPUTER

Political maneuvering. Power plays. Millions of dollars. These were the theme of Apple Computer in the mid-1980s, The result was that the chairman of the board, Steve Jobs, lost his power to the man he had hired several years earlier, John Sculley. It's ironic that a founder of a major corporation would ultimately be discharged by the company he founded; however, this is the story of Apple Computer and Steve Jobs.

Colleagues and friends agree that Steve Jobs is a charismatic, persuasive leader – in person with vision who can generate tremendous enthusiasm and commitment for a project. How then did he lose his power base?

As a co-founder of Apple in 1977, Jobs led the company to astonishing growth. By 1983, he had to hire a professional manager to run the company. John Sculley, at age forty-four, was hired from Pepsi Cola U.S.A. to become President of Apple, and Steve Jobs, age twenty eight, became Chairman of the Board. Initially Jobs and Sculley enjoyed a remarkable friendship. They spend hours in conversation and took long walks in the woods together. It was almost a father-son relationship.

Meanwhile, Jobs took over the operating responsibilities of Apple's Macintosh Division. He saw the Macintosh Computer as the next generation personal computer. As chairman, Jobs was able to allocate major resources to the development of the Mac. In addition to large budgets, Mac employees received special little "perks" such as fresh orange juice at their desks and even messages. As a result, employees of this "favoured" group were frequently resented by other divisions. After its introduction in 1984, the Mac immediately enjoyed record sales. But the computer industry was in a slump, business users were not purchasing the Mac, and sales quickly began to decline. The Mac was coming under attack on major fronts for some basic technological and design shortcomings. However, Jobs went to great efforts to defend some seemingly major weaknesses in the Mac. By late 1984, Apple experienced a reduction in sales and profits. Meanwhile,Jobs was alienating key company employees and members of the board with his exclusive attention to the Mac. Also, it appeared that he was not willing to listen to advice about the Mac's problems.

In December of 1984, key board members goaded Sculley to assert his authority over the company. Several directors began to wonder if Jobs has lost objectivity and questioned some of his moves with the Mac division. Sculley and Jobs began to disagree frequently because of their management philosophies and visions for the company. Jobs held 11.3 percent block of Apple stock, which made him a disproportionately powerful member of the company.

About this time John Sculley recommended a major company reorganization that included the assimilation of the Mac division by other divisions. Jobs was extremely unhappy! He could see that little power would remain for him. Jobs began saying that Apple was too small for both Sculley and him. Jobs called his closest company allies together to attempt a coup against Sculley, but met with little enthusiasm. Sculley got wind of the plot and quickly called a board meeting. He dearly stated he was there to exert control – the board responded by approving a reorganization that left Jobs with little to do. He has lost all power in the Mac Division, and the directors had circumvented his authority on the boards. Jobs announced he was taking an extended vacation. He was aware that he was losing power in the very company he founded and in which he owned a major block of stock.

After this extended vacation, Jobs told the board that he was leaving to start another company. The board members, including Sculley, wished him well. What Jobs did not tell them was that he was taking five key Apple employees with him. In addition, his new company would be a direct competitor to Apple. Sculley was livid and threatened to sue Jobs for taking trade secrets from Apple. To outsiders it appeared that although Jobs had lost the power struggle to control Apple, he was not giving up the battle. He was going to fight Sculley and Apple Computers, even though Jobs still owned several million dollars of Apple stock.

QUESTIONS

1. What type of power did Jobs have as the founder of Apple? What type of power did he lose as problems developed in the Mac division?
2. What type of power did Sculley have? Explain.
3. Why do you think Jobs lost his power base at Apple?

I. COMMUNICATION

A CASE OF MISUNDERSTOOD MESSAGE

Indane Biscuits is located in an industrial area. The biscuits factory employs labour on a daily basis. The management does not follow statutory regulations and are able to get away with violations by keeping the concerned inspectors in good books.

The factory has a designated room to which employees are periodically called either to hire or to fire.

As a part of National Safety Day the Industries Association, of which the Indane Biscuits is a member, decided to celebrate collectively at a central place. Each of the members was given specific tasks.

The personnel Manager, Indane Biscuits, desired to consult his supervisors and to inform everybody through them about the safety day celebrations. He sent a memo requesting them to be present in the room meant for hiring and firing. As soon as the supervisors read the memo they all got panicky thinking that now it was their turn to get fired. They started having 'hush-hush' consultations. The workers also learnt about it and since they had a lot of scores to settle with the management they extended their sympathy and support to the supervisors. As a consequence everybody struck work and the factory came to a grinding halt.

In the meantime the Personnel Manager was unaware of the developments and when he came to know of it he went immediately and tried to convince the supervisors about the purpose of inviting them and the reason why that particular room was chosen. To be fair to the Personnel Manager, he selected the room because no other room was available. But the supervisors and the workers were in no mood to listen.

The Managing Director, who rushed to the factory on hearing about the strike, also couldn't convince the workers.

The matter was referred to the labour department. The enquiry resulted in all irregularities of the factory getting exposed and imposition of heavy penalties. The Personnel Manager was sacked. The factory reopened after prolonged negotiations and settlements.

QUESTIONS

1. In the case of the Indane Biscuits bring out the importance of 'context' and 'credibility' in communication.
2. List out the direct and indirect causes for the escalation of tension at the Indane Biscuits.
3. If you were the Personnel Manager what would you do?

THE VICE PRESIDENT, THE PRODUCT MANAGER, AND THE MISUNDERSTANDING

Tom Brewster, one of the field sales managers of Major Tool Works, was promoted to his first headquarters assignment as an assistant product manager for a group of products with which he was relatively unfamiliar. Shortly after he undertook this new assignment, one of the company's vice presidents, Nick Smith, called a meeting of product manager, was unable to attend, so the director of marketing, Jeff Reynolds, invited Brewster to the meeting to help orient him to his new job.

Because of the large number of people attending, Reynolds was rather brief in introducing Brewster to Smith, who, as vice president, was presiding over the meeting. After the meeting began, Smith – a crusty veteran with a reputation for bluntness – began asking a series of probing questions that most of the product managers were able to answer in detail. Suddenly he turned to Brewster and began to question him quite closely about his group of products. Somewhat confused, Brewster confessed that he really did not know the answer.

It was immediately apparent to Reynolds that Smith had forgotten or had failed to understand that Brewster was new to his job and was attending the meeting more for his own orientation than to contribute to it. He was about to offer a discreet explanation when Smith, visibly annoyed with what he took to be

Brewster's lack of preparation, announced, "Gentlemen, you have just seen an example of sloppy staff work, and there is no excuse for it!"

Reynolds had to make a quick decision. He could interrupt Smith and point out that he had judged Brewster unfairly; but that course of action might embarrass both his superior and his subordinate. Alternatively, he could wait until after the meeting and offer an explanation in private. Inasmuch as Smith quickly became engrossed in another conversation, Reynolds decided to follow the second approach.

Glancing at Brewster, Reynolds noted that his expression was one of mixed anger and dismay. After catching Brewster's eye, Reynolds winked at him as a discreet reassurance that he understood and that the damage could be repaired.

After an hour, Smith, evidently dissatisfied with what he termed the "inadequate planning" of the marketing department in general, abruptly declared the meeting over. As he did so, he turned to Reynolds and asked him to remain behind for a moment. To Reynolds surprise; Smith himself immediately raised the question of Brewster. In fact, it turned out to have been his main reason for asking Reynolds to remain behind. "Look", he said, "I want you to tell me frankly, do you think I was too rough with that Kid?" Relieved, Reynolds said, "Yes, you were. I was going to speak to you about it."

Smith explained the fact that Brewster was new to his job and not registered adequately when they had been introduced and that it was only some time, after his own outburst that he had the nagging thought that what he had done was inappropriate and unfair. "How well do you know him ?" he asked. "Do you think I hurt him?"

For a moment, Reynolds took the measure of his superior. Then he replied evenly, "I don't know him very well yet. But, yes, I think you hurt him."

"Damn, that's unforgivable," said Smith. He then telephoned his secretary to call Brewster and ask him to report to his office immediately. A few moments later, Brewster returned, looking perplexed and uneasy. As he entered, Smith came out from behind his desk and met him in the middle of the office. Standing face to face with Brewster, who was 20 years and four organization levels his junior, he said, "Look, I've done something stupid and I want to apologize. I had no right to treat you like that. I should have remembered that you were new to your job. I'm sorry."

Brewster was somewhat flustered but muttered his thanks for the apology.

"As long as you are here, young man" Smith continued, "I want to make a few things clear to you in the presence of your boss's boss. Your job is to make sure that people like myself don't make stupid decisions. Obviously we think you are qualified for your job or we would not have brought you in here. But it takes time to learn any job. Three months from now I will expect you to know the answers to any questions about your products. Until then, "he said, thrusting out his hand for the younger man to shake, "you have my complete confidence. And thank you for letting me correct a really dumb mistake."

QUESTIONS

1. What do you think was the effect on Brewster and the other managers of Smith's outburst at the meeting?
2. Was Reynold justified in introducing Brewsler and if not what alternative approach should Reynold have taken?
3. Do you think the approach taken by Smith is justified?
4. Do you have any alternative approach?
5. If yes, do you think that this approach is complete and does not need any supplementary action.

AN APPOINTMENT REQUEST IN REVERSE

Mr. Prashant Singhal, the General Manager of M/s Surya Cable Company was desperately eager to have an audience with Mr. Krishna Chandra Agarwal, the Chief Engineer of the State Electricity Board. Mr. Prashant, for the last three months left no stone unturned to seek an appointment with Mr. Agarwal.

Mr. Agarwal was a potential customer for a large and continuous supply of cables for the state Electricity Board.

While Mr. Prashant Singhal was on a pleasure trip to Darjeeling along with his family, for ten days, a fax message arrived at Mr. Prashant Singhal's office from Mr. Krishna Chandra Agarwal. The Fax message read as – Mr. Krishna Chandra Agarwal, the Chief Engineer of the State Electricity Board would make himself available on this Thursday at 3.30 p.m. in his office. If Mr. Prashant Singhal wanted to see him.

Mr. Ravi Kumar Saxena who was Mr. Prashant Singhal's Assistant received this important message and gave it a casual treatment. However, after two days of the receipt of Mr.. Agarwal's Fax message, Mr. Ravi wrote back to Mr. Agarwal that his (Mr. Agarwal's) request for an appointment would be brought to Mr. Prashant's attention when he (Mr. Prashant) returns from his pleasure trip next Tuesday.

Request for appointment indeed, infuriated Mr. Krishna Chandra Agarwal. He gave the magnificent order worth Rs. 25 Lakhs he had intended for Mr. Prashant Singhal to his business rival Mr. Sumesh Bajpai. All because a simple communication had been not paid due attention and mishandled.

QUESTIONS

1. Why was the Communication distorted and what were the shortcomings or drawbacks in each person's Communication?
2. If you would have been Mr. Ravi Kumar Saxena, what would you have done?
3. What will you do if you were Mr. Prashant Singhal?

THE CREDIBILITY GAP

Amit was pleased to be interviewed and hired by the high-water Oil Company just prior to graduating from college. The interviewers from the company emphasized the importance of initiative, aggressiveness and innovative ideas on the part of the employees. Amit was impressed with the company and their philosophy of management and was eager to go to work.

Amit's initial assignment was as a field representative in the automotive division. He was given a territory in the Southwest to call upon 120 High-water service station. His major duties consisted of helping train dealers in marketing of new automotive products and keeping inventories up-to-date. He was also instructed during his induction period to report market conditions and customer attitudes towards the company merchandising policies and products.

Amit soon observed that customers preferred a competitor's automotive engine additive designed to release sticky valves. The competing product was much lighter and more fluid than his company's. He reasoned that customers were reluctant to put his company's sluggish product in their engines.

He reported his observations by a carefully prepared memorandum to the home office as he had been instructed. In due tune, his manager asked him to stop by his office to "chat" about a problem. The following week Amit checked in with the district manager, Mr. Wadhwan, the following conversation occurred:

"Amit, about those reports you sent to the home office – we've got a problem."
"What's the matter, didn't they like my suggestions?"

"To tell the truth, Amit they most certainly did not," replied Mr. Wadhwan. "There's something you have to learn about this company if you want to continue working here. And that's a very simple rule–only good news is sent up-the-line."

"What do you mean, only good news goes up-the-line?" asked Amit.

"It's like this," explained Mr. Wadhwan. "Top management considers reports like yours as criticism of their managerial ability. If you want to get ahead in this company, always tell them what they want to hear things couldn't be better."

"But I was told that reporting market conditions and customers' attitudes were part of my job," exclaimed Amit.

"That's perfectly true," replied Mr. Wadhwan "as long as you give them that information at the right time, under the proper circumstances and in the acceptable form, translated that means, very simple, not telling top management the truth."

After leaving Wadhwan's office, Amit wondered to himself just what type of company High-water Oil was turning out to be.

QUESTIONS

1. If management received distorted information, what effects will this have on company operations.
2. Make suggestions for improving communication in this company.
3. If you were Amit what would you do now?

IMAGE AND RUMOURS AT PROCTOR AND GAMBLE

Since, the late 1970s, Proctor and Gamble has been plagued by rumours connecting the company with Satanism and devil worship. The rumours have come in two cycles from late 1981 to the end of summer 1982, and from fall 1984 into early 1985.

Proctor and Gamble primarily manufactures and distributes household products, including Crest toothpaste and Pampers disposable diapers. The company attributes its success to the developing products based on consumers' needs and promoting these products with extensive advertising. It contacts consumers through an extensive network of toll-free telephone numbers and market research projects.

The first rumour that surfaced was that the company was owned by the church of Satan. The "proof of this relationship was Procter and Gamble's hundred-year-old trademark, a quarter moon and thirteen stars.

Proctor and Gamble was not overly concerned until late October 1981, where a second rumour began to circulate. It claimed that John Smale, the president and chief executive, had appeared on the "Phil Donahue Show" or a similar talk show where he supposedly stated that he was a member of the Church of Satan, that the company contributed money to the Church, and that "there aren't enough Christian in the world to stop it." He had never been on any such program, of course, but the rumors also urged a boycott of all Procter and Gamble products.

Calls began flooding the toll-free telephone lines asking about the legitimacy of the rumours. Most of the calls were from retailers informing the company that some customers were returning Procter and Gamble products or asking why the goods weren't off the shelves. Employees were being threatened, and some had their tires slashed. The number of calls peaked at 15,000 in one month, July 1982.

Proctor and Gamble counterattacked by sending out a fact sheet to 48,000 Southern churches. This group was targeted because the rumours were being spread by fundamentalist religious groups, mostly in the South. The company also enlisted the aid of clergymen, including the Rev. Jerry Falwell, president of the Moral Majority, and the Rev. Donald E. Woldmon, chairman of the Coaliton for better Television. The clergymen issued statements discrediting the rumors and suggesting that people continue using Procter and Gamble's products. The company also obtained statements from television talk show producers confirming that no one from Procter and Gamble had appeared on their programmes.

The public relations campaign dispelled the notions about the company's supposed link to the devil. The rumours died down and the number of called decreased to thirty or forty per month.

After the success of this counterattack, Proctor and Gamble was surprised when the number of calls jumped suddenly to a thousand in September 1984, and then tripled to three thousand in October. This time the rumours concerned the company's trademark and its supposed symbolism of devil worship and Satanism. Unlike, the first wave of calls, these calls seemed to come from across the country.

Proctor and Gamble began sending around media information kits, similar to those previously used, containing a brief history of the logo. They included letters from the producers of the television talk shows, and letters from the clergymen. The company also sent a security team to track the rumour's sources and to look for patterns in its transmission. They even threatened to sue anyone caught spreading the rumour.

However, by spring 1985, the problem had gotten out of control. The company was forced to change the logo, which was then 103 years old. Observers agreed that this was the right move, because hysterical rumours can outlast the time the logo had been changed. The company had spent several hundred thousands dollars on anti rumour public relations and on extra telephone staff to handle calls about the matter. The final result was that the company lost a historical symbol and had stood for trustworthy, reliable products to millions of consumers.

QUESTIONS

1. What category of communication is Proctor and Gamble concerned with in this case?
2. The three changes that take place in a grapevine message are leveling, sharpening, and assimilation. How does each apply to this situation?
3. What change, if any, would you have recommended for the company's initial strategy (in 1982) to stop the rumours?

MALHOTRA FASHION STORES INCORPORATED

Ravina Malhotra, just graduated from college, joined her father, Sameer Malhotra, president of Malhotra Fashion Stores, Incorporated, a chain of thirty women's apparel stores in the Northern India. The company had been founded by Mr. Malhotra's grandfather over 50 years ago. With her grandfather's and, for the past 20 years, her father's drive and knowledge of women's fashions and of how to buy and sell them, the company had developed from a single store in Haldwani (U.P.), to a fairly large and highly profitable chain of stores. Sameer Malhotra was much like his father before him. He knew what he was doing and how to do it, and he prided himself on being able to keep his hands on details in buying, advertising and store himself on being able to keep his hands on details in buying, advertising and store management. Everyone of his store managers, as well as his top vice-presidents and headquarters staff people, met with the president every 2 weeks in Delhi. Between these meetings, Mr. Malhotra spend 2 to 3 days each week visiting the stores and working with store managers.

But his major worries were communication and motivation, he felt that, at the conferences he held, all his managers and staff people listened carefully, but differing from what they did. He began to wonder whether they heard him or whether they indeed had listened carefully. He observed that many of his policies were not being strictly followed in the stores, he often had to rewrite advertising copy; in some of the stores the employees had joined the clerks' union; and he increasingly heard of things he did not like. Among them were reports that many of his employees and even some of his managers felt that they could do better if they had a chance to communicate with Mr. Malhotra and his Vice-presidents at the headquarters. He also has a strong feeling that many of his managers in headquarters and in the stores, as well as most of the store clerks, were merely doing their jobs without showing any real imagination or drive. He was also concerned that some of his best people had quit and taken positions with a competitor.

When his daughter walked into his office to take a position as his special assistant, he said, "Ravina, I am worried about how things are going. Apparently, my two problems are communication and motivation. Now I know that you took some courses in management in school. I have heard you talk of the problems, barriers, and techniques of communication. I have heard from you about some fellows – Maslow, Herzberg, Vroom, McClelland, and other-who you thought knew a great deal about motivation, while I doubt that these psychology types knew much about business and I feel that I know what motivates people–primary money, good bosses, and a good place to work–I wonder if you have learned anything that will help me to communicate better. I hope so, for that college education of yours has cost me a lot of money. What do you suggest?"

QUESTIONS

1. If you were Ms. Malhotra what would you say to your father?
2. How would you go about analyzing the communication problem, and what problems do you see already from the case?
3. How would you suggest that the motivation and communication theories you have studied might be applied to the Malhotra Fashion Stores? Is there anything else you would want to know?

CATASTROPHE IN SPACE: A RESULT OF POOR MANAGERIAL COMMUNICATION

On Tuesday, January 28, 1986, the nation was shocked as a result of the Challenger accident. All seven of the spare Shuttle's passengers went to their death in a ball of flame as the nation watched on T.V. The nation had tremendous confidence and respect in the technological capabilities of NASA. The U.S. was a leader in space technology. What happened?

Two complex systems are required to launch a space shuttle : the space shuttle and a managerial system. The Challenger failure may have been as much a managerial failure as a technical failure. It was a failure of NASA's command system, a system supposedly honed for years in the proper handling of last-minute "go/no go" choices. At virtually every NASA launch, engineers have raised last-minute technical questions. They make hundreds of last-minute decisions. The Challenger launch was delayed four times; the previous launch was delayed four times; the previous launch of Columbia was delayed seven times. But NASA failed to stop this disastrous launch on January 28.

The technical failure is easy to understand. Large synthetic rubber rings designed to seal the joints between the stacked sections of the solid-fueled booster rockets failed. Engineers at Morton-Thiokol, the designers and producers of the O-rings, had extensive evidence of O-ring erosion that would make it difficult for them to seal properly in cold temperatures. Anything below 53 degree Fahrenheit was considered a potential problem. The morning of the launch it was 18 Fahrenheit. The evidence was so strong that the Senior Engineer present at the launch site for Morton-Thiokol refused to sign off on the launch even after lengthy argument. This refusal forced the conference call in which the Marshall Space Centre managers persuaded or, depending upon one's views, pressured Thiokol executives to override the company's engineers.

The Challenger's Final Hours

The following description provides some insights to the cause of the disaster:

Monday, Jan. 27, 2 P.M. The launch suffered its fourth postponement, this time to the following morning. Four Key NASA launch decision people were at the Kennedy Space Center in Florida along with the director of the Marshall Space Flight Centre of Huntsville, Alabama. (Although the shuttle was launched from Florida it was designed, developed, and tested in Alabama). The weather forecast was for clear and cold, with an overnight low of 18 degree Fahrenheit. The team talked over the possibility of ice in the trough below the launch pad that moderates the main engine blast.

2:30 P.M. NASA asked Morton-Thiokol in Utah to have its engineers review the cold snap's possible effects. Five key engineers reported that they firmly believed the cold could make the O-rings so stiff that they could not properly seal the joints against the hot gases.

8:45 P.M. A teleconference began among 34 engineers and managers from NASA and Thiokol. The Thiokol engineers showed charts of a history of O-ring erosion and blow-by-blow for the primary seals. A chief engineer said that the cold made the rubber rings so stiff and hard that squeezing the O-rings into the gap would be like trying to shove in a brick. Thiokol's recommendation was not to launch below 53 degree.

At that, NASA's deputy director of science and engineering exclaimed that he was "appalled." He said that he thought the booster was qualified for a launch at any temperature from 40 -90 degree Fahrenheit. He was quoted as saying, "This is a hell of a time to change figures on us!" Another NASA official was quoted to have remarked: "My God, Thiokol, when do you want me to launch, next April?" Thiokol quickly asked for a five-minute caucus off the teleconference set.

10:30 P.M. The Thiokol caucus among the 14 engineers and managers at the Utah plant lasted close to 30 minutes. During a heated discussion, several key engineers argued that the O-rings were not safe. No one was listening; they went back to their seats, realizing they had done all they could do.

After that, Thiokol's top management held a final review. Several managers were still reluctant to go against the engineer's objections, but the vice-president of the Utah operations urged: "Take off your engineering hats and put on your management hats." At last all the managers agreed that the O-ring design left enough margin for error. Not one engineer or technician, however, supported a decision to launch.

11:00 P.M. Resuming the teleconference, the group in Utah reported they recommended launching. The NASA officials in Alabama asked Thiokol to send their recommendation by facsimile to the Kennedy Space Centre. In addition to the O-rings the top Thiokol representative at Kennedy would not recommend a launch for several reasons; one, thick ice over the launch pad; and two, the Atlantic Ocean was treacherous and it would be difficult to send ships out to recover the boosters.

11:30 P.M. NASA officials involved in the teleconference made their launch recommendation to the managers. Later analysts found that this recommendation did not include any report relating to Thiokol's engineers' concern about the O-rings.

Tuesday 8:30 A.M. Challenger's crew were strapped into their seats.

9:00 A.M. During the final review, no concern about the O-rings was expressed. 11:38 A.M. Flight 51-L lifted off. The ambient temperature was 36 degree Fahrenheit. Fuel apparently began to leak around the O-rings immediately.

11:39 A.M. Challenger was destroyed; all seven on the board died.

QUESTIONS

1. Identify the communication failures in this situation.
2. What do you believe were the causes of these failures?
3. What approach should have Thiokol taken to make his press release about the seriousness of the situation?

A FAILURE TO COMMUNICATE

While union membership has been on the decline in recent years, there are other pressing problems currently facing labour leaders these days. In many cases the leadership of national unions is having difficulty keeping the rank and file in line. For example, more and more union members are refusing to ratify the contracts that have been painstakingly hammered out by their union officials. Here are some examples that have occurred over the last few years :

Why are the rank and file so angry at their union leadership? One reason is that they believe their officials are buckling under to management and not fighting hard enough for better wages and working conditions. In particular, many union members are upset over the concessions that were made to management during the early 1980s when the economy was in poor shape. They want to see their lowered wages and benefits given back through vigorous bargaining. This is especially true among union members in companies such as those in the auto industry that have bounced back and are now making large profits.

Another cause of rank-and-file anger is the breakdown of pattern bargaining. For decades unions had been able to hammer out labour agreements in which companies in the same industry paid the same rates. However, because of such factors as deregulation, increased competition, and foreign imports, such pattern bargaining has been weakened. As a result, union workers in firms that compete with one another in the same industry sometimes have different pay rates. The rank and file wants everyone to be moved up to the highest rates.

Some union members have gone on strike and in spite of demands by their leadership that they return, have stayed out. Moreover, other locals around the country have begun to assist these rebellious units by sending them money and other forms of support.

The bottom line in this latest development in the labour movement is that the leadership appears to be out of step with the membership. As one individual put it, "what we have here is a failure to communicate". This communication failure appears to be mostly a result of the leadership's failure to get feedback from the members regarding the direction in which they would like to see the union move. As a result, some labour relations experts are wondering how effective unions can hope to be over the next few years if the members are moving in one direction and the leadership is moving in another.

QUESTIONS

1. Why does there appear to be a breakdown in communication between the rank and file and the leadership? After all, aren't the elected elders supposed to be representing their members?
2. Is this breakdown a result of poor upward communication or poor downward communication? Explain.
3. How can the problem discussed in this case be resolved? What steps need to be taken? Explain.

J. CONFLICT MANAGEMENT

ADITYA FINANCIAL SERVICES LIMITED

Aditya Financial Services Limited (AFS) is a medium-size finance company headquartered in Bangalore. During the last decade the company has achieved phenomenal success– partly due to the adoption of liberal policies by the Government toward financing companies and partly due to favourable customer response – and the Chairman of the Company, Bangrappa, having tasted success already, wants to carve out a niche for himself in the market in the near future. Consequently, about 5 years ago, he has established branch offices in all parts of South India and wants to peep into the Northern Region also in the next five years.

To meet the challenge, AFS decided to revitalize some of its marketing activities – through centralised advertising campaigns, offering attractive discounts to promoters of Fixed Deposits etc. Among other things, AFS wanted to enlarge the marketing area to include contact calls on potential large depositors, small investors and trading communities.

AFC hired its first marketing manager, Raja Ram, an ambitious and hard-working young man, from one of the highly successful investment companies in Andhra Pradesh. Raja Ram did an excellent job setting up a separate marketing department and getting it organised. Then after three and one-half years on the job, Raja Ram, obviously attracted by the lucrative terms, left to head the marketing division of another investment company.

AFC then hired Shyam Kumar, a thirty year old MBA of HM, Bangalore. Shyam Kumar had worked in the marketing department of another savings and investment company in Madras. He is married, has no children, and wants to build up his career quickly.

Unfortunately, the road to prosperity is not smooth. Time and again, he is confronted with puzzling questions from different quarters. It is true that he has been given the credit for having developed four major investment plans, which, when implemented according to his suggestions, would yield fruitful results. For some inexplicable reason, the branch managers have not shown any enthusiasm to translate his plans into action. Only two branch managers have cooperated. Others did not evince any interest. The Branch Managers are:

Armugum, B.	25 year old, B.Com.; Holds Diploma in Marketing, Madras University; 4 years with AFS: He refuses to cooperate.
	Raja Rao, P. 34 year-old MBA, Andhra University; 5 years with AFS. He cooperated.
	Nijalingappa, E. 46 years old, M.Sc., Bangalore University, 7 years with AFS. He cooperated.
Gopalakrishnan Nair	55 year old, B.A., Kerala University; 14 years with AFS. He agree to cooperate and then forgets.
Rajasekhar, S.	26 year old, MBA, Madras University; 4 year with AFS. He is reluctant to accept the proposals.

You work for AFS and Shyam Kumar has asked for your advice on how to increase his effectiveness with the branch managers. Please advance your suggestions briefly.

IT's THE SAME STORY EVERYWHERE

Prakash hails from a hard working, immigrant family. Right from his childhood he wanted to achieve something and acquire power for himself. Unfortunately, he could secure only a low-paid job in the assembly line in a large manufacturing firm. It is a charmless job having no promotional opportunities. Since he has to support a large family, he needed a well-paid job and all his efforts in this direction had gone waste. To blow off his steam and to relieve himself from worldly woes, he started living in "fool's paradise" and spent most of his day-dreaming. Not surprisingly, he fell a prey to drinking and other vices. After exhausting his meagre financial resources, he would get depressed and start worrying about his family.

It has been a vicious circle and he wants to come out of it. Unable to bear with this miserable situation, one fine morning, he wanted to seek advice and counsel from his supervisor. But since his relationship with his supervisor is not-too-intimate, he sought help from his union leader. The union leader has listened to Prakash's woes patiently. He told Prakash in a sympathetic tone: "There is no use working in this company. We have innumerable problems, and not a single problem is solved by management so far. The working conditions are pathetic. Our salary is too low. And let's not talk about our benefit plans. After our contract finishes, let's unite together and fight with management for better salary and working conditions."

QUESTIONS

1. Analyse the nature of role conflict experienced by Prakash in this case.
2. What type of conflict resolution strategy is the union leader suggesting in this case?
3. How do you advice Mr. Prakash?

STUDENT NOVELIST

Mr. Rama Sharma was a doctoral student in the Department of Telugu in one of the reputed Universities in Andhra Pradesh. Unlike other students, he joined the Ph.D. Programme at the age of 36 years. He was nearly 10 years older than most of the other students in the department, He did not receive any fellowship from any financial agency. However, he was rich enough to stand on his legs during the programme.

Sharma's background was quite well-known. After obtaining M.A. degree in Telugu, he joined as a lecturer in one of the colleges in Hyderabad. During his. leisure time, he used to write short-stories. At the age of 26 years, he could publish his first novel which was highly acclaimed by the public. Thousands of the copies of the book were sold. His second novel was published after two years. With this, he could establish himself in the market firmly. This novel, too, had enjoyed phenomenal popularity. His third novel was the best-seller. The copyrights of the book were sold for a hefty sum.

Mr. Sharma, however, was not happy with his achievements. He had developed an aspiration for academic excellence. He wanted to become a professor in a University and loved constant interaction with young brains so as to share his thoughts and feelings. To this end, he wanted to complete Ph.D. programme by joining the University Department as a full-time research scholar.

Life was not easy in the Department. His professors could not relish neither his ideas nor his popularity. He had to struggle a lot while collecting information for doctoral programme. He had to cross several hurdles and impediments thrown in his way by faculty members. One professor, after a heated argument with Mr. Sharma burst out: 'You don't deserve a place here, You've no talent. You may be popular as a novelist but you don't deserve the doctoral degree. I'll see that you never get it."

Sharma's frustration knew no bounds. He wondered why all faculty members are tossing brickbats against him. It is true that he is popular novelist. But that has nothing to do with academic pursuits. Like any other student, he is humble, sincere and hardworking. It is now clear to him that his success in the department is critically dependent on his relationship with professors alone.

QUESTIONS

1. What is the actual conflict Mr. Sharma was undergoing?
2. Analyse the situation in terms of inter-personal conflict.
3. How can Sharma overcome the problem to obtain his degree?

SMART BEGINNING

Miss Kalyani hails from a sophisticated family. She is twenty-two year old and will be receiving her M.A. degree from Andhra University at the end of this semester. She has spent the past summers working for a large dress-making company STYLES, designing clothes for women while the permanent employees of the organization took their vacations. Having undergone training in USA for about six months when her father was posted there, she had no problems in designing clothes for women and her designs were appreciated and readily accepted by both management and customers. It is small wonder, then that she has received and accepted an offer to join STYLES on a permanent basis upon her post graduation, as a Chief Designer in the Design Department.

Styles is a large dress-making company taking care the development of latest designs for gents, ladies and children in Andhra Pradesh. In the headquarters office alone, where Miss Kalyani will be working, they employ 800 employees. The company believes strongly in the personal development of all its employees, and takes every care to meet employee expectations.

The job Kalyani will be assuming requires her to direct the activities of 12 designers. Their job require a certain amount of training so as to develop attractive designs for women and children. The designs have to be approved by the Chief Designer before they see the light of day.

Kalyani's group is composed of all females ranging from 19 to 50 years of age, with a median of 23. For the most part they have high school education, well supported by a certificate in Dress Designing awarded by a reputed Design Institute in Andhra Pradesh. The salary range is 400-1000 per month. Miss Kalyani will be replacing a long time employee, Mrs. Vanaja, who is retiring after 37 years with Styles, the last fourteen years as Chief Designer. Since Kalyani had spent a few weeks in Styles group last summer, she was familiar with Styles work ethic and norms and also knew most of the group members. She expected no problems from any of her soon – to be employees, except possibly from Mrs. Vimal Mrs. Vimal was well into her fifties, had been a Designer for a dozen of years, and as the'grand old lady carried a lot of weight with group members. Miss Kalyani concluded that without Vimal's support her job could prove difficult.

Kalyani is determined to get her career off on the right foot. As a result, she has been working hard on how to win over Vimal and other group members.

QUESTIONS

1. What strategies do you advise Kalyani to pursue?
2. What if, Vimal revolts along with her teammates?

DEMANDING WIFE AND SPOILT CHILDREN

Reddy is a fitter in the assembling section of a public sector electronics unit located in Bangalore. He has four daughters and a son. His personal life is miserable. Wife is illiterate, arrogant, quarrelsome, alcoholic, and leads a life which Reddy can't afford. Reddy run into debts every month.

When young, Reddy dreamt of big things in life for him – a bungalow, a car, dogs and other trappings of a luxurious life.

Now Reddy finds himself cheated by fate. Not enough money even to run through all the 30 days in a month. No own house, forget about car and dogs. Demanding wife and spoilt children add to his woes. Reddy has taken to alcohol to forget his worries.

Reddy borrowed heavily in his work place and outside. Unable to face creditors in factory, Reddy started absenting himself from duties. Unauthorised absences resulted in pay-cuts which further added to Reddy's woes.

Listen to what three characters talk about Reddy:

Krishna, the schoolmate, now well settled:

"I have been advising Reddy to limit his family size. He insisted on having a son resulted in having first four daughters. I have also been advising him to live within the means, to straighten his wife and cut his borrowings. He never cared, I helped him several times, financially and otherwise. What is the use? He is beyond repair. Forget him."

Gangadhara, the supervisor:

"It is becoming too much for me. Reddy's absences, drunken behaviour are causing indiscipline in the assembling section. No use in showing mercy. Something serious needs to be done."

Subramanya, the union president:

"Reddy is a poor chap. Problem is with this damned management. Why can't they pay more? Why can't they sanction some loan to Raddy so that he can clear debts? Wait for the next settlement we will sure extract better deal for the employees."

Reddy however, continues to languish and there appears to be no hope of better future.

QUESTIONS

1. Explain Reddy's behaviour in terms of the frustration model.
2. What conflict resolution strategies do Krishna, Gangadhara and Subramanya recommend to Reddy?
3. What strategy would you recommend to resolve Reddy's conflict?
4. Explain the concept of role conflict in terms of Reddy's behaviour.

PROBLEM OF JOB ROTATION

Ramprasad is a supervisor in charge of a manufacturing operation in a medium-sized company. A recent change in company procedures made it possible for employees to engage in job rotation. In a staff meeting held to discuss the possibility, Ram Prasad became aware that two subordinates wanted to change to a job rotation schedule, when one did not. After pondering over the problem, Ramprasad determined that four alternative approaches may be followed to manage this conflict situation:

1. Simply tell three subordinates that job rotation will begin immediately.
2. Convince all the three that their interpersonal relationships are more important than any job rotation, thus getting them to agree to rotate jobs.
3. Workout an arrangement where job rotation occurs for a while, is stopped for a while, and so on, thus allowing each person to have his or her way part of the time.
4. Drop the idea of job rotation.

QUESTIONS

1. What conflict management styles are represented by each of the four alternatives suggested above?
2. Which of the four approaches should Ramprasad choose to follow in this situation? why? Or should an alternative approach be taken?
3. What special interpersonal skills should Ramprasad need to succeed in this problem situation? Defend your answer.

KOMAL FOOD PRODUCTS COMPANY

The Komal Food Products Company, which was founded in 1935 to manufacture and sell grocery and food products, had in the course of years grown into a vast enterprise having offices and branches in almost all the important cities of the country. Its annual sales amounted to Rs. 60 to 70 lakhs.

The Company's head office and factory were situated at Kolkata.

Its products were distributed through five Zonal Sales Offices which directed 25 District Sales Offices throughout the country.

The administrative responsibility of each Zonal Office was borne by a manager whose duty it was to promote sales in his Zone. He was advised and instructed by the Head Office from time to time.

Under the control of each Zonal Manager, there were four functional heads, viz., the Personnel Manager, the Accounts Manager, the Sales Manager and the Office Manager. These executives advised and assisted the Zonal Manager in all matters relating to the Zonal administration. Each functional head enjoyed sufficient freedom and independce in respect of his own work.

On matters relating to sales, the Zonal Manager received advice from the Sales Manager at the Zonal Office. The latter often formulated policies, developed plans and schedules for sales operations, suggested improvements in district sales administration, and submitted his views on all matters concerning sales to the Zonal Manager. Many times, he also issued orders and instructions to the District Sales Managers, but all these were routed through the Zonal Manager. Ordinarily all this views and advice were accepted and approved by the Zonal Manager.

The Zonal Sales Manager was assisted in his work by three product Managers, who were considered to be experts in their- respective fields. Their duty was to travel with the Sales Supervisor of the various districts and study the market for the company's products; survey the competitive position of the company's products; study dealer and consumer reactions, trends in sales etc., and advice the District Sales Manager and the Sales Supervisors from time to time regarding the steps to be taken for promoting sales in the districts. Every month each of them submitted a report on the sales activities of the company to the Zonal Sales Manager. The relationship between the Zonal Sales Managers and his Product Managers was the same as that between the Zonal Manager and himself.

Directly responsible to the Zonal Manager were five District Sales Managers in addition to the four functional heads. Each District Sales Manager was responsible for sales in his territory. In promoting the sales of the company, he was assisted by five Sales Supervisors, each in-charge of several salesmen. The duties and functions of the District Sales Manager were to:

1. select, train and supervise his sales supervisors and salesmen in consultation with the Zonal Manager.
2. make a study of the nature of consumer demand, changing markets and existing stocks and to formulate plans for sales promotion.
3. fix targets for sales to be attained in his territory from time to time.
4. formulate credit policies to be followed in consultation with the Zonal Manager.
5. develop better team-work among the sales supervisors and salesmen.
6. see that customers were satisfied with the company's service.
7. attend to such other functions and duties as might be assignee to him from time to time by the Zonal Manager.

Every month each District Sales Manager submitted a detailed report on the sales activities of the company in his district to the Zonal Manager. Ordinarily these reports were passed on the Zonal Sales Manager for suggesting necessary action to be taken with respect to each district.

On the morning of 6 June 1961, the following conversation took place over the telephone between Mr. Rajan, the Sales Manager at the South Zonal Office, and Mr. Shankar, one of the District Sales Managers in the Zone:

Shankar: I wish to bring to your notice an important matter that needs your urgent consideration. The Product Managers are interfering too much with the sales activities of my district. I receive frequent complaints from the Supervisors that they are not able to carry out my instructions due to unnecessary interference from these people. If this state of affairs continues, it will be very difficult to maintain our sales. The morale of the Supervisors would be seriously affected. I will not be responsible if sales go down this time in our area on this account. You must take some steps to see that harmonious relationship is maintained between line and staff.

Rajan: Mr. Shankar, you need not worry about it, I shall call on the Product Managers and see that they maintain proper relationship with you.

Next day Mr. Rajan called all the Product Managers and, after discussing some routine matters, said, "I was told by Mr. Shanker that his Sales Supervisors are complaining that you are interfering with their activities. Definitely you are all expected to advise them on the steps to be taken for increasing sales. But at the same time, please remember that you have to play only an advisory role. While advising these people you must also see that the line authority is respected."

The Product Managers did not say anything.

In the subsequent months Mr. Rajan did not receive any complaint from the District Office. But in the first week of October, while scrutinizing the sales progress reports of the various districts for the previous quarter, the Zonal Manager found an unusual decline in sales in the district which was under the supervision of Mr. Shankar.

The Zonal Manager called Mr. Shankar and asked him why there had been so much decline in sales in his territory while all the other districts showed very good progress.

Shankar replied, "During the past three months the Product Managers did not seem to have advised our men properly. In fact, they never cared to advise the supervisors on the recent changes and the latest trends in the market. They seem to be unwilling to cooperate with our sales force. What can we do? Even then, we have done our best to maintain sales."

When the Zonal Manager asked the Product Managers about this, one of them said, "we used to give advice to this district office also as we usually do to other district offices. On a complaint, it seems, from Mr. Shanker, we had been told by Mr. Rajan that we were exceeding our authority and unnecessarily interfering with the activities of this district. We had been asked to restrain ourselves. The District Sales Manager takes advice directly from the Sales Manager. We have nothing to do with this."

QUESTIONS

1. Discuss the issues and give your recommendations to the management of the Company.

THE NEW PRINCIPAL

For seven years the college in which I have been teaching was under the leadership of Mr. Rama Rao. As principal has was autocratic (by almost anybody's definition) but he had the personal qualities necessary to command respect, obedience and loyalty. He made and enforced all rules, regulations and policies in almost infinite detail. He was willing to accept complete responsibility not only for his own actions but those of all his teachers, as long as their actions were within the well-defined limits of his policies. Consequently, the faculty as a group was always careful to adhere strictly to his wishes. He can best be described as a paternalistic autocrat.

Mr. Rama Rao's methods left little to the individual lecturer's imagination about experimentation, freedom in teaching, the handling of students, but did provide an atmosphere hi which everybody, both teachers and students, knew exactly what was expected.

In spite of, or perhaps because of, Mr. Rama Rao's leadership philosophy, faculty morale seemed generally high and faculty turnover was quite modest during his tenure. The faculty sentiments were best described by my colleague, Rama Krishna, thus:

"I have taught here for fourteen years under four principals. There were time I wanted to strangle the old crank, but he always knew what he was talking about. I didn't mind being told what to do, when to do it, and how to do it, because I always knew where I stood. I always tried to do a good job because I knew I could trust him. I would like to teach under him again."

Attitudes could generally be termed passive, subservient, respectful, dependent, and as my colleague's comment suggests, ambivalent. I asked ten teachers if they thought his manner impaired his teaching. Only four believed that the quality of their teaching would have been better in a less restrictive atmosphere.

Practically all professional contacts between administration and faculty originated at the top. Individual lecturers rarely sought out the principal except when a special problem arose which needed his help. Mr. Rama Rao always remained somewhat aloof on the job, but frequently visited socially at the homes of faculty members.

It is not easy to get a good picture of how well a college is running, an effectiveness is often inferred from a variety of statistical evidence of conformance to rules. The measures of punctuality showed no unexcused tardiness on the part of lecturers and lecturer absences averaged only three days per college year. Scholastic achievement, measured in terms of percentage of graduates enrolled in college and the percentage of those graduating from college to date, was above average for the State.

Mr. Rama Rao died suddenly last year. In January, 1986, he was replaced by Mr. Nageswara Rao, who had several years of experience as Vice-principal in a college in another city. He had been selected from a field of many applicants. I, along with the other faculty members saw him for the first time at first staff council meeting in the second week of January 1986.

At the meeting, Mr. Nageswara Rao voice a strong belief in the principles of a demoralized administration. He said that the goals of modern education could best be reached through a cooperative effort of administration and faculty. He then pointed out several budgeting, scheduling, and other matters formerly decided by Mr. Rama Rao in which he was considering a greater role for faculty–decision making. Specifically, he indicated that the faculty, because of its intimate knowledge of class room needs, might be in the best position to allocate University grants for purchasing books and equipment, if they could get together, express their needs and preferences, and decide on some priorities. He suggested that faculty might also wish to pursue some special or innovative educational activities, such as organizing seminars, workshops and extension lectures. He offered to help with administrative arrangements for these activities if his help was needed. He also said that not only did he feel that faculty administration cooperation was desirable, but that he wanted to make genuine student participation in administration a reality. He requested faculty cooperation to achieve that end. In concluding the meeting, Mr. Nageswara Rao asked the faculty to give ahead of these matters some thought before the next meeting at which time we could discuss them.

Two weeks later, at the next meeting, Mr. Nageswara Rao asked for discussion of the issues previously mentioned, but no discussion was forthcoming. He attempted to evoke discussion by mentioning several alternatives, but still no discussion followed. He then asked for a vote on each proposal. The faculty voted almost unanimously to reject each proposal, and several teachers openly expressed the belief that Mr. Rao should handle these problems himself, as Mr. Rama Rao did. The meeting quickly broke on an unpleasant note. Mr. Nageswara Rao subsequently took action on each of the issue himself, which the faculty accepted.

After the meeting adjourned, many of the teachers regrouped informally, minus Mr. Nageswara Rao, in the faculty room. Their comments emphasized a variety of matters, but one recurrent theme was a feeling that the topics on which Mr. Rao wanted faculty cooperation, budgeting and scheduling, were not proper matters for faculty decision. They amounted to a burden the principal should bear as his predecessor had done. He shouldn't try to foist these duties off on the faculty. Morale was quite poor. One lecturer said, "when they pay me a principal's salary, I'll do a principal's work and not before."

Mr. Nageswara Rao made no specific assignments of the faculty extra curricula duties in their meeting. Instead, he anticipated that all the teacher would continue to attend assemblies and faculty meetings, be punctual etc. But the anticipated cooperation didn't materialize: Only about one-fifth of the teachers attended assemblies hardly enough to maintain good order; only one-half to two-thirds attended faculty meetings; lectures arrived at college only a few minutes before classes began, and frequently left college in the afternoon before the students had actually left the college; only three lecturers continued to patrol the grounds during 'peak' session : morning time.

QUESTIONS

1. What is happening here?
2. What should Mr. Nageswara Rao do?

K. ORGANIZATIONAL CHANGE

SAAGAR TRAVELS

Saagar Travels is a large Travel Agency with an employee population of 140 having branches in five metropolitan cities: Delhi, Mumbai, Kolkata, Chennai and Hyderabad. Each branch has separate counters for rail and air reservations. The Agency is known for its excellent service. Over the years, it has built up good reputation and has carved out a niche for itself in travel business. In recent years, the head office in Delhi is finding it increasingly difficult to monitor the information especially on air tickets received from other centres through manual operations. To avoid delay and inconvenience to customers and to improve accounting operations, the Agency is seriously thinking of introducing computers on a gradual basis. Now this move is resisted by employees working in various centres vehemently, fearing retrenchment. In spite of repeated requests from management, they are planning to go on strike.

QUESTIONS

1. How to resolve the impasse?
2. Discuss the reasons for employee resistance to change in light of the information provided above.
3. Outline an appropriate change strategy that satisfy the expectations of both management and workers.

QUALITY CONTROL EQUIPMENT

Mr. Chandrasekhar is the supervisor of 25 unskilled workers working in a grocery warehouse. To reduce the costs, the management has decided to install mechanized materials-handling equipment. Since the workers lacked training and knowledge about productivity and cost reduction effects of this equipment, the supervisor had to struggle a lot to introduce the change by involving all of them in it. Ultimately, the new equipment was installed with the active cooperation of his workers.

A few months afterwards, Mr. Chandrasekhar has been asked to install a sophisticated quality control equipment among a group of technical workers. Since this group consisted of educated employees, who are in a better position to understand the company's problems, he expected little opposition to the proposed change. Accordingly, he did not exert himself much before introducing the new equipment as he had done earlier in the case of unskilled workers. Contrary to his expectations, this group resisted tooth and nail the introduction of the new system until it was given up. However, the mistake proved to be very costly to Mr. Chandraskhar. He lost his job!

QUESTIONS

1. How do you explain the behaviour of the two groups in accepting or rejecting the change contemplated by the management?
2. What should have been done by the supervisor to avoid resistance by the technical group of workers to the proposed change?

INTRODUCTION OF COMPUTER

Mr. Rajender Prasad is the head of the accounting section in a fast growing manufacturing company. In the section, he has 30 employees under his control. The company has three hundred employees mostly drawn from nearby areas. The recent changes in science and technology have prompted management to introduce mechanization in the accounting section. Mr. Prasad is asked to explain the importance of having a computer in the accounts department to his employees. The introduction of computer, undoubtedly, affects the lives of all those who are working in the section. Some fifteen employees will have to restructure their job responsibilities; ten employees require training in the use of computer and the remaining five employees may have to knock the doors of other companies for jobs. Of course, all these chances though painful, take place gradually.

This situation is quite similar to another situation witnessed by Mr. Prasad some time back. Eight months ago, the company has hired a computer on lease basis to handle the production inventory. The management is highly pleased with the arrangement, for the inventory processing has improved terribly afterwards. But unfortunately, the production people have resisted the move strongly. Now, Mr. Prasad is in a tight corner. Strangely, he is entrusted with the responsibility of introducing the computer in his own section.

QUESTIONS

1. If you were the section head, entrusted with the responsibility of installing the computer, how would you go about informing your employees about the proposed change and make them accept it?

INDUSTRIAL ENGINEER

An industrial engineer was assigned to an electronic assembly department to make some methods improvements. In one assembly operation he soon recognised that a new fixture might reduce labour costs by about 30 per cent. He discussed the situation with the group leader and then the supervisor. The group leader was indifferent, but the supervisor was interested and offered additional suggestions.

Feeling that he had approval of the supervisor, the industrial engineer had the fixture made. With permission of the supervisor, he assigned a women assemble to try the fixture. She was cooperative and enthusiastic and on the first day exceeded the expected improvement of 30 per cent. When the group leader was shown the results at the end of the day, he claimed that this was one of the fastest girls in the department and that her results could not be generalized for the whole department.

The next day the industrial engineer asked the supervisor for another operator to help prove the fixture. At this point, the supervisor noted the fixture did not include his ideas fully. The industrial engineer explained that he had misunderstood but that he would include the other suggestions in the next fixture built. The supervisor, however, continued to be negative about the fixture.

When the industrial engineer attempted to instruct the second woman the way he had instructed the first one, her reaction was negative. In fact, when he stopped instructing her, it seemed that the woman deliberately stalled as she used the fixture. She also made some negative comments about the fixture and asked the industrial engineer if he felt he deserved his pay cheque for this kind of effort. At the end of the day this woman's production was 10 per cent below normal production by the old method.

QUESTIONS

1. Analyse the causes of this problem.
2. Recommend the course of action the industrial engineer should take.

MERGER AND HEARTBURNS

XYZ foundation runs a training cum production centre in Bangalore. Sometime back, management drew two separate structures, one for training centre and another for production centre. Subsequently, the management drew a single chart combining both training and production functions. Reorganization was implemented according to the combined structure–Management was aghast at the heartburns caused by the merger.

Required

1. Critically comment on the compulsions and consequences of the merger of training and production centres. Lay stress on behavioural implications of the merger.
2. Can you make the combined structure flatter? Try.

3. Can you make out a matrix structure from the three charts?

ADDITIONAL INFORMATION

1. Asst. Manager Stores, has to report to Asst. Manager Production, whereas earlier they were both reporting DGM (Prodn). This is not acceptable to the stores man who is senior in experience.
2. The Manager Accounts, and Asst. Manager Stores, were getting along very well and both are very senior people with direct links to MD. They are unhappy and are on to politics.
3. The Manager-SPM is a well qualified, foreign returned and experienced officer who was expecting to be designated as Principal when the G.M. resigned. Now he is very frustrated and has be come hostile towards the new Principal.
4. The Lady Warden is the wife of the Manager-Admn. Earlier she was also incharge as Library Officer for which she was drawing additional allowance. The new dispensation took away library and allowance from her. She is upset.

SCANDINAVIAN AIRLINES SYSTEM

The Scandinavian Airlines System (SAS) originated when the airlines of Sweden, Norway, and Denmark formed a consortium. During the 1970s competition became fierce and resulted in a loss of market share, deterioration of service, and reduced profitability. The external environment was marked by high fuel prices and rising costs, a decrease in demand for air service, and price wars.

To help SAS recover from this slump, Jan Carlzon, the CEO, undertook drastic decentralization in 1981. The use of top-down authority was replaced by open communication and by the transfer of greater decision power to personnel close to the customers. Furthermore, service quality standards were set at a high level. While the rest of the industry was stagnant, Carlzon turned the company around by "filling seats." Air Transport World elected SAS "Airline of the Year."

What, then, accounted for the airline's turnaround? Detailed rules and regulations inhibiting frontline personnel were reviewed and changed. Frontline people received 2 to 3 days' training so that they could respond better to customer's needs. Carlzon gave customer relations and services high priority. The previous top-down approach in communication inhibited creativity, initiative, and prompt action of frontline personnel. The new company philosophy emphasized that personnel in all divisions and at all levels have to support personnel close to the customers.

To make intelligent decisions, employees throughout the company need to be informed. Carlzon spends a great deal of time communicating the goals and strategies of SAS in a way that is understandable to all employees – managers as well as non-managers. For example, one of SAS's strategies is to become known as "the businessman's strategy" (with rather high fares), with upgraded service, on-time performance, good food, and comfort. Less emphasis is placed on the leisure traveler, with iower fares and reduced service.

To implement the strategy, management by objectives is used. The 1987 Annual Report states : "SAS's organization is based on management by objectives and decentralized profit responsibility." The role of the managers is not only to give direction but also to give responsibility for the means of achieving the ends to subordinates. The managers are supporters and advisers rather than autocratic bosses.

For the future, SAS has two important goals: (1) to become the most efficient airline in Europe by 1992 and (2) to be one of the five major airlines in Europe after 1995.

A keystone in SAS's global strategy is to form strategic alliances. In fact, SAS sought partners before such alliances became popular. The first attempts to forge alliances failed. The proposed 1986 merger with the Belgian World Airlines, Sabena, failed because of legal complexities. An attempt to take over British Caledonian Airway Ltd. was blocked by British Airways PLC. And the Peronist party of Argentina blocked the deal with Aerolineas Argentines.

Undeterred by early failures, Carlzon pursued his alliances strategy in order to make SAS competitive with larger European airlines such as Lufthansa (German), British Airways, and KLM

(Dutch). Carlzon realized that in the larger EC 1992 environment (Sweden is not a member of the European Community), when many of the trade barriers will fall, SAS will need alliances. One such arrangement was made with Thai Airways International (1987) to coordinate services in Bangkok, Copenhagen, and Stockholm. Similarly, the 1988 agreement with Texas Air, the parent company of Continental Airlines gives SAS access to the Newark, New Jersey, airport in the United States. In 1988, SAS also bought a stake in Airlines of Britain Holdings. An agreement to exchange equities with Swissair was reached in 1989. In the same year, alliances were made with All Nippon Airways (Japanese), Lan-Chile Canadian Airlines International, and Finnair to gain access to airline hubs in Tokyo, Latin America. Toronto, and Helsinki. But critics question whether SAS's strategy will work or whether SAS is wasting money on other airlines it cannot control.

QUESTIONS

1. In a geographically dispersed company such as SAS, how can you decentralize without losing control?
2. How would you set verifiable objectives in these areas: (1) on-time arrival, (2) customer satisfaction, and (3) company success ? Set objectives in other key result areas.
3. Are Carlzon's philosophy and the organizational culture conductive to a management by objectives program?
4. Are top-down and bottom-up managing incongruent?
5. Do you think that the strategic alliances with many different airlines will work?

AGRICULTURAL FERTILIZER DIVISION OF THE NORTHERN CORPORATION

At the end of a busy day, a group of middle-level managers of the Agricultural Fertilizer Division of the Northern Chemical Corporation gathered to reflect on their problems. The headquarters of Northern Chemical had recently set up a central data processing department in Houston, where all the corporation's data processing would be done for its various divisions located throughout the United States. At that time, the data processing equipment of every division had been taken away; each division headquarters office was given a terminal connected to Houston, and each division was required to get any report processing it needed from the Houston, and each division was required to get any report processing it needed from the Houston facility.

The headquarters of the Agricultural Fertilizer Division was located in Sacramento, California. This division had long concentrated on developing and selling fertilizers to the large agricultural growers in the West and on distributing its garden and house plant fertilizers to stores throughout the country. It had been very successful, with sales growing rapidly and profits even faster. But the line managers of the division were quite unhappy about not being able to have their own computer faculties to give them the analyses and reports they needed.

Bill Jacobs, production planning and control supervisor, was particularly disturbed about the change to centralized data processing. "There is no way" said Jacobs, "that I can plan our products, especially with our many products and customers and the demands of our large growers for good service, if Houston runs our programs. The people there do not always have the data needed in their data bank, and, by the time I get it worked out with them I have lost much valuable time."

Barry Hill, district sales manager for Northern California, was even unhappier. He pointed out that he often needed to run productivity and profitability studies for large growers and that he could not be so unless the division in Sacramento. "The growers will never understand why I cannot make these analyses for them quickly, nor will they understand why they must be made in Houston: they will soon tell me that there are other companies that can serve their needs," moaned Hill.

"You do have a problem," said Mona Fredericks, head of statistical analyses and reports in the division controller's office. "But yours is a small one compared with mine. I have to get many special and regular reports to headquarters, to the division managers, and to all people in sales, market research, product development, and production, You always want them right away and in the form you can use most easily. How can I do that for you now ?"

The frustration reached its peak when Joe Morey, cost control supervisor, startled the group by saying : "Did you know that all the departments in our division are being charged fees each month for Houston's services and that these are higher than the costs when we each had our little computer system?"

QUESTIONS

1. Do you agree that these people have a serious problem?
2. If you were one of them what would you do about it?
3. If you were to view this purely as an organization problem what conclusions would you draw and what suggestions would you make?

SIEMENS THE SLEEPING GIANT

Siemens, the over-140-year-old German giant, is loaded with cash. The company generates its revenues from energy and automation, nuclear power, PBX's (private branch exchanges) and computers, telecommunication and security systems, medical equipment, electrical and automotive products, and a variety of other sources. There is some concern that the proliferation of products may be detrimental.

The company's some 365.000 employees will face a different environment in the future through the EC 1992 program. Which eliminated trade barriers for the twelve member states of the European Community. In the past, Siemens benefited from. profitable state contracts. For example, the company sold cordless telephones to the state at a price eight times higher than the price of Japanese products.

The goal of the CEO, Karl-Heinz Kaske, is to transform the sleeping organization into an aggressive multinational corporation battling with companies such as AT&T in the field of telecommunications and with General Electric in factory automation. The key building block in the new strategy is microelectronics. Indeed, the company spent more on research and development than its competitors, yet it lags behind many of them in profit margins.

To prepare for the new competitive environment, the company started reorganization. In 1988 two layers of management were eliminated, and the following year the seven operating divisions were transformed into fifteen (later reduced to thirteen), organizational units with separate sales and marketing personnel. This should speed up, for example, the approval of new products. Unprofitable lines are being shut down, an approach very uncommon in German industries. Managers who expected lifetime employment are concerned – Telecommunications, which lost over $100 million a year, will be compared with the medical unit, which showed an annual growth rate of 17 percent.

In the past, the corporate culture placed high value on technology but de-emphasized marketing. This is changing, Siemens is re-educating its focus on market share not only within Europe but also in the United States and Japan – to very important markets.

The power of Central Research was reduced by giving more responsibility to the business units to do the application driven research. Central Research now focuses on basic research. Furthermore, business units not only have more responsibility for research but also are held more accountable for their costs. Actually, Siemens can look back at over 140 years of innovations. Here are some examples : The pointer telegraph was patented in 1847, the first electric railway in 1879, the world's first telex network in 1938, the world's first high-performance laser printer in 1977 and the first European – built 1-megabit chips in 1988. However, the organization structure that was appropriate in the past may not serve the future competitive, global market.

QUESTIONS

1. How can one demonstrate to the cash-rich organization that change is necessary?
2. What kind of organization structure would you recommend to Siemens to help it prepare for a future strongly influenced by the EC 1992 program and the competitive U.S. market?
3. How should research and development activities be organized?

REORGANIZATION AT GM

In the early 1920s, Alfred P. Sloan installed a novel organization structure at General Motors (GM) that eventually enabled it to become the largest industrial company in the world. Under Slan's plan, GM was divided into five independent car divisions, each operating in a different price segment of the industry. Chevrolet would produce inexpensive cars for the younger segment of the market. As these customers grew older and more affluent, they would upgrade their next purchase to Pontiac, then to Oldsmobile and Buick, and finally to Cadillac. Under the corporate umbrella the five divisions designed, manufactured, and marketed their own cars. They competed against each other for both customers and corporate resources.

The system worked so well that by the 1960s, GM was clearly the dominant company in the automobile industry. In fact, GM was so successful that it was vulnerable to antitrust action. During this period, GM modified its classic structure. All car bodies were now manufactured at the Flasher. Body Division, and final assembly was centralized at the newly formed GM Assembly Division. Although the ostensible reason for these changes was to cut costs, critics contend that making the firm more difficult to dismember was also an important factor in the decision.

In the mid-1970s, GM further centralized operations by assigning design and engineering functions to project centers. Under this system, for example, Buick specialized in brakes. Pontiac in rear suspension, and Fisher Body in the design and manufacture of car bodies. GM executives reasoned that these changes would save money and shorten the time between design and production. The results were not components, the distinction between went beyond began to blur. And the problems went beyond style. In 1977, some Oldsmobile ended up with Chevrolet engines. This disclosure triggered an avalanche of lawsuits from disgruntled Oldsmobile owners. Despite these problems, GM continued to expand the project center concept to reduce costs and save time.

By 1985, the look-alike phenomenon came to a head with Ford's successful advertising campaign that poked fun at Cadillac. And further, the similarities among the five divisions* models were more than just appearance. Each was producing a full-line of similar automobiles. Chevrolet made cars as large as the biggest Buicks, and Cadillac produced a subcompact. Thus, the GM divisions were competing directly with each other rather than in different market segments as Sloan had envisioned.

Still another problem was the lack of performance accountability. Engineering, manufacturing and marketing decisions were under the authority of different executives. Consequently, it was difficult to control costs and no single manager couid be held responsible for market performance. As one analyst put it: "Too many people had a say about the product, but nobody had responsibility."

In response to these problems, which GM executives believed contributed significantly to its declining market share and profitability, the company initiated a major reorganization in 1984.

Under this plan, operations were divided into a small-car group and a large-car group. Chevrolet and Pontiac were included in the small-car group, and Oldsmobile, Buick, and Cadillac in the large-car group. The divisions within the two groups would continue to share basic car body models, but greater efforts would be made to distinguish one line from another. For example, instead of three presses punching out the same fender for all models, each press would punch out a different fender. Further, the plan decreed that the two car groups would not make cars outside their size designations. Hence, Chevrolet's and Pontiac's larger models and Oldsmobile's, Buick's and Cadillac's smaller models were to be phased out.

The new structure provided for separate organizational units within the two car groups, for engineering and manufacturing. The idea was that if the individual car divisions concentrated strictly on marketing, they would become more consumer-oriented. Thus, Oldsmobile executives could focus their efforts on product planning, promotion, and distribution, and not have their attention diluted by having to make V- 8 and Diesel engines. However, to help further distinguish Cadillac 8n market, about a year later a separate engineering unit was assigned to the Cadillac division.

Another important feature of the reorganization was that the two group managers had total responsibility from design to sales. Thus, if sales drop or profits decline, they can be held accountable. The small-car group was headed by Lloyd Reuss, the former general manager of Buick and the former

Chevrolet general manager. The two executives were selected to lead car-groups that did not include their previous divisions to discourage favouritism.

Even after the reorganization, GM remained a highly bureaucratic organization with as many as 14 management layers (compared to 5 at Toyota). Some pundits feel this structure stifles initiative and innovation, thereby inhibiting GM's hope of automobile industry.

QUESTIONS

1. Explain how the organization at GM is expected to overcome the shortcomings of the previous structure.
2. Could the problems have been overcome without such a drastic reorganization? Explain.
3. Contrast GM's reorganization plan with Alfred Sloan's original plan.
4. What potential problems do you see with the new structure?
5. Given that GM unseated the reorganization even then come to a lead in 1985?
6. Do you think the high number of management layers at GM will inhibit its competitiveness? Explain.

HOME RADIO AND TELEVISION COMPANY

Mr. Mohan founded a small radio manufacturing plant in Banglore in the 1930s. From this small start came out one of the nation's largest radio, television, and allied product companies. By 1965 its sales approached Rs. 300 million annually, with 15,000 employees and ten manufacturing locations, throughout its growth the founder remained the active, imaginative, and driving force of the company. In earlier days every manager and worker knew him, and he was able to call most of them by their names, so even after the company grew fairly large, people felt that they know the founder and chief executives and this strong feeling of personal loyalty had much to do with the fact that the company was never unionized.

However, as the company prospered and grew, Mr. Mohan worried that it was losing its "small company" spirit. He also worried that communications were suffering, that his objectives and philosophy were not being understood in the company, that much wasteful duplication was occurring through poor knowledge of what others in the company were doing, and that new products developed and marketing were suffering as a result. Likewise, he was concerned that he had lost touch with the people.

To solve the communication problem, he hired and had report to him a director of communication. Between the two, they put into effect every communication device they found other companies using; bulletin boards in every office and plant throughout the country; a revitalized company newspaper carrying much company and personal news affecting the locations; "Company Facts" books for every employee, giving significant information about the company-sponsored courses to teach communication; monthly 1-day meetings at headquarters for the top 100 executives; annual 3-day meetings of 1200 managers of all levels at a resort area; and a large number of special committees to discuss company matters.

After much time, effort, and expense, Mr. Mohan was disappointed to find that his problems of communication and of the small-company feeling still existed and that the result of his programs did not seem to be significant.

QUESTIONS

1. Why do you think that Mr. Mohan was disappointed? Should he have been?
2. What do you see as the company's real communications problem?
3. What would you suggest to improve communication in the company?
4. Was Mr. Mohan right in believing that communication would solve his problem in maintaining the "small company" spirit?

DEVELOPING LEADERS AT THE SAHNI GROUP

NG too has a serious problem. He can't find enough of the right kind of managers.

NG is chief executive of the Sahni Group, a Singapore shipyard and construction company that he is trying to expand into a diversified multinational corporation. Like many other chief executives in Asia, he sees an abundance of business opportunities and has the financial resources to pursue them. Yet there is a shortage of managers in the region. Not just many managers, but flexible, creative professionals who are comfortable in any increasingly competitive and sophisticated market. Most managers that NG finds have skills that are no longer appropriate for the changing competition they face. As wages have risen, the region's traditionally low-tech companies have had to move into higher-value-added products whose success depends on expertise–overseas marketing sophistication and ability to direct highly skilled professionals for instance – that old-line managers often do not have.

To compound NG's problem, the pool of potential managers with the educational level he needs is small. In India, only six percent of workers are university educated. This compares with twenty-three percent in the United States and sixteen percent in Japan. And the competition among Asian companies for skilled and educated managers is fierce.

NG realizes that he must invest hi developing his company's future leaders. He could offer formal classes in management and leadership, and supplement this with on-the-job training. But he's not exactly sure what such a formal leadership program might look like. Or maybe, he should look to graduates of business schools outside of Asia.

QUESTIONS

1. What kind of leadership do you think is necessary to succeed in India?
2. Do you think hiring non-Asians with advanced business degrees could solve NG's problem? Discuss.
3. Should NG hire Asians from abroad? Discuss.
4. As a consultant hired by NG design a leadership program that would meet his needs.

L. ATTITUDE, VALUE, JOB SATISFACTION

CASE OF VELU

Foreman Velu never liked men of a particular stock. Years ago he had worked under one who was unfair very hard taskmaster. Velu always resented the way he had been treated and felt that all people of that origin were unfair and could not be trusted.

Velu has 20 years service with the company. Because of his excellent record, he was promoted six months ago to head a larger department. He knew the methods in his department, but he did not know many of the employees. He was upset to find that one of the best rated workers, Balu, was of that particular parentage. Velu was sure that the man had been overrated and was not that good. He decided to watch him closely and find out the truth.

Balu soon became aware of Velu's close supervision. He resented being singled out by the foreman, who checked up on every detail of his work and behaviour. At first, Balu tried to pass it off, but his irritation came out when he answered some of Velu's prying questions. One word led to another, and over period of time an obvious feud developed. One day Velu passed Balu's work place caught him apparently breaking a minor rule. Velu promptly accused him and called him a dirty slander. Balu knocked Velu down.

The following statements apply to particular case. Study each one carefully. If you agree with the statement, put a circle around T. If you do not agree, put a circle around F. If you are in doubt, circle'?'

1.	Since Velu disliked a particular section of people, he should be allowed to fire or transfer them out of his department.	T	?	F
2.	Balu was completely justified in hitting Velu.	T	?	F
3.	Velu's prejudice against the section of people disqualifies him as a foreman.	T	?	F
4.	Velu's boss should educate him to develop positive attitude towards the section.	T	?	F
5.	Velu's judgement in this case is so poor that he probably has many other prejudices, and he should be demoted.	T	?	F
6.	Balu should be transferred to another department.	T	?	F
7.	Velu's treatment of Balu lowered the morale of the department.	T	?	F
8.	Velu should have tried other means to get to know better about Balu as an individual.	T	?	F
9.	Many people have prejudices like Velu and can't even know that they have them or remember how they got them.	T	?	F
10.	Since Balu was guilty of breaking only a minor rule for the first time, the foreman should have overlooked it entirely.	T	?	F

QUESTIONS

1. How did Velu acquire his attitudes?
2 What action might management take if it wanted to change the attitude of Velu?
3. What are the implications to the morale and motivation of a group and the company as a whole if a person like Velu with strong biases were to occupy a responsible position?

EMPLOYEE GRIEVANCES

Personal Data

Name	:	Ganesh – Around 35 years – Married and has two children
Education	:	SSLC (failed)
Trade	:	Turner
Service in the company	:	Seven years
Previous experience	:	Centre Lathe Operator in a private firm for 6 1/2 years.

Case History

When Ganesh joined the company, he was placed in the training centre for two weeks and made to work on a centre lathe. He was then sent to the factory and made to operate a vertical turret lathe. At the outset, he was not happy about having to work on a vertical turret lathe as he was not familiar with that machine. After working for a period of two years on the lathe, he started complaining about pain in the eyes. He asked for a change of machine. His foreman, Shreyas, referred him to the doctor for a medical check up.

Although the doctor's report said that he was 'fit' for normal duties in the section, out of consideration for him Shreyas put him on the horizontal lathe for a period of six months. His health apparently improved.

Again he was put back on the vertical turret lathe with the instructions that he could take it easy. He continued on the lathe for 2 years without complaining. He got along well with his fellow workmen.

It so happened that this vertical turret lathe had to be transferred to another section. Ganesh was transferred along with it. This transfer upset him a great deal and he felt unhappy. After working for some months in the new section, he started complaining of pain in his chest.

He absented himself frequently, performance declined and was warned as a consequence. Finally, he asked for a change of machine, on medical grounds. It was made clear to him that there was no other lathe in the section but was referred to the doctor again. The doctor's report confirmed that he was 'fit' for normal duties in the section. Foreman and the manager asked Ganesh if he was willing for a transfer to another section. He refused and strongly pleaded that only a change of machine would solve his health problem. His bosses did not agree with him. They felt that Ganesh was adamant and his attitude towards his job should change.

Present Position

He is still working on the vertical turret lathe. He feels that his health is fast deteriorating and suffers from self pity. He has become a thoroughly disgruntled workman. He is indifferent to his work and defiant in his attitude. He has become a real problem to the supervisory staff.

QUESTIONS

1. "Working conditions that are compatible with an employee's physical comfort contribute to job satisfaction." Justify this statement through the case of Ganesh.
2. "While working conditions constitute a source of job satisfaction, they are a relatively minor source." But still the vertical turret lathe has rendered Ganesh a problem employee. Trace the factors that really contributed to this state of affairs.
3. Two of the supervisory actions recommended for maintaining job satisfaction are:
   (a) Change the perception of dissatisfied employees, and
   (b) Exhibit concern for employees.

   Suggest a plan of action for tackling Ganesh on the above lines.

EXECUTIVE'S TANTRUMS

Mr. Rao is an electronic engineer having worked for 20 years in Middle East and returned to home town. He is 51 years old.

Now he is the manager of product development laboratory in a well-known production cum training centre. Six engineers report to him. Right now the lab is developing some automatic test equipments for a leading auto electric equipment manufacturer. During previous financial year the lab achieved only 50% of the targeted production.

Mr. Rao is perceived as highly egoistic and egocentric personality. He thinks that all others are wrong and that only his department is the most competent and hard working unit.

When the previous G.M. resigned abruptly, Rao was expecting to be inducted into the slot. But due to Rao's unpredictable behaviour, he was not considered and retired Wg. Commander was appointed instead. Rao felt let down by the management.

Once Rao needed the services of a few trainees for his lab. He called the trainees directly without going through the proper channel. The concerned staff complained to the Wg. Commander who promptly ordered the trainees to be called back. This angered Mr. Rao, who came briskly and barged into the chambers of the ex-army-man, without even knocking on the door, and started shouting at the top of his voice. The people there pacified Rao and physically took him out of the room. Later they told the Wg. Commander that everybody had accepted these tantrums of Mr. Rao and nobody took them seriously.

QUESTIONS

1. "Through their actions and deeds senior executives establish norms that filter down." Discuss the implications of this statement vis-a-vis Mr. Rao's behaviour.
2. What type of culture gets established by a department head like Mr. Rao? What is the impact of the sub-culture of the development lab on the organizational culture?
3. Role play the critical incident of Mr. Rao barging into Wg. Commander's Chambers and discuss the outcomes and suggest alternative ways of tackling the situation.

MIXED CULTURE

X Watches is a joint company promoted by a leading business house and a state government. The plant was set-up 45 kms away from Bangalore.

The company is known for its professional work culture and very attractive remuneration packages.

When the plant was set-up five years ago, the management was able to attract many senior and middle level managers and operators from a reputed public sector company, also manufacturing watches.

For its room, X Watches poached on a well-known tool room and training centre and weaned away couple of managers and tool makers.

Key posts of the plant, however, were held by personnel drawn from other own group companies. The group had its plants in all parts of India, except in South. X Watches is the first to be established in South of Vindhyas.

X Watches, therefore, had a mixed group of personnel – hailing from public sector, tool room, (operating in South India) and group's top ranking executives (came to South India for the first time). Added to this were the workers who were all localities.

After six months, around disillusionment had set in and everyone was cursing himself or herself for quitting his or her previous job and joining X Watches.

QUESTIONS

1. List out the cross-cultural undercurrents in the above case-incident.
2. How do you bring about pervasiveness or homogeneity in the above situation?
3. Discuss the case incident under the following culture maintenance factors:
   (a) selection, (b) top management practices, and (c) socialization process.

M. CONTROL

BHARAT FABRICATION LTD.

Bharat Fabrication Ltd. has large plant in Kolkata. The job of each worker in the plant has been fixed scientifically. Accordingly each worker is entrusted with a certain amount of work. A time clock is installed in the company as a time recording and control device.

In a particular section, the workers selected on the basis of their skill were able to complete the work two hours earlier than the departure time. They had been following the practices of leaving the organization every day immediately after the job is over. They had come to an understanding among themselves that one of them, on rotation basis, would stay back to punch the time clock for the whole group.

This practice came to the notice of the plant manager one day. The next day he met all the workers and told them that all of them could be removed from service as per the company rules. However, he said that he was leaving them only with a warning and asked them not to repeat it again. To this, the group leader reacted and replied "we are doing our work. We are not leaving the organization without completing the job that is entrusted to us. Why don't you follow the basis of "finish your job and go home."

The plant manager said "I like your suggestion. But the problem is if I follow that basis, the senior workers may apply for your jobs as they have that right under the contract. Definitely, it happens because they prefer to go early. In fact, the senior workers are not as skilled as you are and, therefore, quality of production will be affected."

In the period that followed, the workers continued to work fast as usual. But, since they had to remain in the organization until the departure time, they started loitering around the plant distracting other workers.

QUESTIONS

1. If you are the plant manager how would you remove this problem of control?

PATEL MILLS

Patel Mills manufactures woolen clothes. Over the years, it has earned an envious reputation in the market. People associate Patel Mills with high quality woolen garments. Most of the existing employees have joined the company long back and are nearing retirement stage. The process of replacing these old employees with younger ones, drawn from the nearby areas, has already begun.

Recently, the quality of the garments has deteriorated considerably. Though the company employs the best material that is available, the workmanship has gone down. Consequently, the company has lost its customers in the surrounding areas to a great extent. The company stands, in the eyes of general public, depreciated and devalued. The production manager, in a frantic bid to recover lost ground, held several meetings with his staff but all in vain. The problem of course, is its roots in the production department itself. The young workers have started resisting the bureaucratic rules and regulations vehemently. The hatred against regimentation and tight control is total. The old workers, on the verge of retirement, say that conditions have changed considerably in recent years. In the days gone by, they say they were guided by a process of self-control in place of bureaucratic control. Each worker did his work diligently and honestly under the old set up. In an attempt to restructure the organizational set up, the managers who have been appointed afterwards brought about radical changes. Workers under the new contract, had very little freedom in the workplace. They are expected to bend their will to rules and regulations. Witnessing the difference between the two 'cultures' the young workers, naturally, began to oppose the regulatory mechanism devised by top management. The pent up feelings of frustration and resentment against management, like a gathering storm, have resulted in volcanic eruptions leading to violent arguments between young workers and foremen on the shop-floor. In the process production has suffered, both quantitatively and qualitatively. The production manager in an attempt to weather out the storm, is seriously thinking of bringing about a radical change in the control process that is prevailing now in the organization.

QUESTIONS

1. Analyse some of the problems leading to the deterioration in the quality of manufacture in the company.
2. What do you say about the finding that old supervisors complain and new workers, too, resist any type of control?
3. What type of control system would you suggest to the company to improve the production?

N. ORGANIZATIONAL CLIMATE

BUDGETS AND HUMAN PROBLEMS

Mr. Eswara Chandra worked hard right from his joining Hindustan Machineries and became the Assistant Plant Manger at an early age in the Srinager Unit. The Hyderabad plant was facing difficulty in meeting its budget and production quotas. Hence, he was promoted as Plant Manager and transferred to the Hyderabad unit. He was directed to set right the functioning of the unit.

Mr. Eswara Chandra was very ambitious and also little bit autocratic. He believed in the exercise of authority and control to carry out his decisions. He made a preliminary study of the plant and issued instructions to all departments to reduce their budgeted expenses by 5 per cent. A fortnight later, he also instructed the departments to increase production by 10 per cent. He required several new reports and watched the operations closely. At the end of second month, he dismissed two supervisors who had failed to meet the production quotas. Four other supervisors resigned. Eswara Chandra insisted that all rules and budgets should be followed scrupulously without any exception.

With his efforts, he succeeded in producing desired results. Productivity increased considerably and exceeded the standard set by 8 per cent. Within 6 months, the unit was very much within the budget. He thus showed outstanding performance in Hyderabad unit and was promoted to the Bangalore Office towards the end of second year. Shortly after he left, productivity in Hyderabad Plant dropped to 20 per cent below the standard and the budget was again in trouble.

QUESTIONS

1. Analyse the kind of organizational climate created by Eswara Chandra in Hyderabad plant.
2. Discuss why productivity dropped immediately after his departure.

THE MODI TEXTILE MILL

The Modi Textile Mill was established in 1946. It was a composite mill with spinning, weaving and processing departments, besides staff departments, such as personnel, safety, industrial health and industrial engineering. It had 70,000 spindles and 2,000 looms, and employed about 5,000 men. The annual turnover of the mill was approximately Rs. 4 crores, yielding a profit of Rs. 50 lakhs. Nearly 25 per cent of the products of the mill were exported. This earned foreign exchange worth about Rs. 80 lakhs per annum.

The day-to-day administration of the mill was entrusted to the Manager who was assisted in his work by four Assistant Managers, *viz.,* the Assistant Manager (Manufacturing), the Assistant Manager (Processing), the Assistant Manager (Personnel) and the Assistant Manager (Technical Services). Under the Assistant Manager (Technical Services) were the Chief Engineer, the Safety Engineer and the Industrial Engineer.

During the first quarter of 1980, the management decided to increase the volume of their exports. For this purpose, it was considered necessary to step up the output of quality fabrics at a reduced cost. To achieve this, it decided to install 500 automatic looms by scrapping 500 old non-automatic looms. As the efficient operation of the automatic looms required yarn of improved quality, it was decided to set up Quality Control Section.

Mr. Manchanda was selected to head the new section. For the last seven years he had worked as the Staff Assistant to the Spinning Master dealing with waste. During the same period, on his own initiative, he had taken a course in statistical quality control. On account of this promotion, Mr. Manchanda was placed in the next higher scale of pay.

When the Manager informed Mr. Manchanda of his selection for the new position, namely, the head of the Quality Control Section, he mentioned that Mr. Manchanda would be responsible for standardizing quality, and that for this purpose, he would receive instructions from the Industrial

Engineer. Mr. Manchanda maintained that the Quality Control Section should be an independent unit. The Manager told him that the Industrial Engineer was a good man and Mr. Manchanda would soon grow to like working with him. Subsequently, the Manager routed all his communications to Mr. Manchanda through the Industrial Engineer.

In February, 1980 Mr. Manchanda started collecting data in the Spinning Department with the help of two assistants. During the course of this work, some difficulties were experienced in the relations of Mr. Manchanda with the Industrial Engineer and the heads of other departments.

The first shipment of automatic looms was received and installed by December 1980. Shortly thereafter the Industrial Engineer asked Mr. Manchanda to discuss with details regarding processing of data, setting up standards, and future plans for quality control. Mr. Manchanda refused to discuss the matter, stating that he was not responsible to the Industrial Engineer.

QUESTIONS

1. As a student of Organizational Behaviour, explain where the thing went wrong?
2. As an Industrial Engineer, what would you do now? Would things have been different, if you had acted differently? If yes, how?
3. As a Manager, to whose attention the matter has been brought, how would you handle the situation?

SELF ASSUMED PROMOTION

"The Labour Officer is not just concerned with law; he has got to deal with people. He has to keep up workers' morale. He should be tactful and sometimes firm in his dealings," said Mr. Chand, the Labour Officer of Ramdass Mills, referring to a situation which he handled.

Ramdass Mills was a textile manufacturing concern employing over 1,200 workers. In the mechanical section of the mills, the supervisory staff consisted of a foreman, an assistant foreman and a reporter. The foreman, Mr. Singh, was incharge of the section. The assistant foreman, Mr. Chadda assisted Singh and officiated as foreman in the absence of Mr. Singh. The reporter Mr. Papiah did the writing and routine work of submitting reports, keeping records, etc. Chadda and Papiah were on probation for six months as per the company's orders in writing. Prior to this promotion, Chadda was reporter and Papiah was a senior workman. It was not an established practice in this company to confirm in writing transfers and promotions.

On 7 January 1960, Mr. Chadda left the company for better prospects elsewhere. Soon after this vacancy, Papiah started working as assistant foreman and Dhar, a senior workman assumed Papiah's position without any instructions from the management. Mr. Singh was not sure whether he should inform the management about these promotions or wait for instructions from the management. He preferred to keep quiet. On 19th January, the Production Manager came to know about these self-assumed promotions. Papiah and Dhar were therefore summoned before the Production Manager to explain why they "promoted themselves" without official orders. Papiah and Dhar confessed that they officiated in higher posts without consulting the management. They did so because they were not aware of any policy or procedure regarding promotions. Being the rightful claimants, they thought, the promotions would anyway be given to them. The Production Manager drew their attention to the written order given to Papian when he was promoted as reporter and said that self-assumption of power was against discipline and order in the company. He told them that when Chadda resigned, the management did not want to fill that post as they thought the post of assistant foreman was redundant. He asked them to go back to their original posts till further orders.

Papiah and Dhar, however, held on to their promotions. The matter was therefore referred to Mr. Chand, the Labour Officer of the Company. Mr. Chand invited Papiah and Dhar for a personal discussion over the matter. After patiently hearing their points of view, he tried to explain to them about the undesirability of self-assumed promotions and how such action on the part of some employees, besides causing injustice and unfairness to the deserving parties, would affect the morale of the entire organization. He advised them to go back to their original posts. Contrary to his instructions in writing, Papiah and Dhar continued to enjoy their assumed promotions.

Chand was, therefore, forced to issue show cause notice to them for their" misconduct and ordered them to present themselves for any enquiry before him on 29 January. At their request, the secretary of Union was allowed to be present at the inquiry. After some discussion, Chand had succeeded in arriving at the following amicable settlement:

(1) Dhar would go back to his original post of workman.

(2) Papiah would go back to his original post of reporter.

(3) The post of assistant foreman was considered redundant. Till the matter was finally decided by the management, Papiah would, however, hold the designation of "reporter-cum-assistant-foreman."

(4) Papiah and Dhar would not claim wages applicable to the higher posts for the period of their assumed promotions.

(5) They were promised that no disciplinary action would be taken against them.

Discuss the alternative courses of action open to the management of this company in solving the problem. They could also critically examine the terms of an amicable settlement arrived at by the Layout Welfare Officer with particular reference to the clause: Papiah and Dhar would not claim wages applicable to the higher posts for the period of their self-assumed promotions.

TEACHING TECHNOLOGIES INC.

Teaching Technologies Inc. had been organized to produce and distribute videotaped course lectures. However, market research experience and conversations with teachers at professional meetings convinced Mr. Piaget, President of the Company, that the demand for his product would not justify continued operations. A set of lectures for one course had been produced, but sales of it were disappointing. Students who viewed the tapes said they preferred a live teacher, even if he were not as highly technically qualified as the video lecturer.

Although Mr. Piaget had invested $ 20,000 for his personal funds and had spent one year working full time for the company, he reluctantly concluded that he would dissolve the company. He could not recover his $ 20,000, but he decided that further investments would be unwise.

QUESTIONS

It has been said that two conditions are necessary in biological and social systems for a viable innovation (new species, organism, or organization that survives). First, a mutation (new system).

Second, an environment supportive of the mutation. Describe the failure of the company in these ecological, biological-analogy terms.

Describe the resources Teaching Technologies Inc., has taken from its environment and how its outputs are valued by the environment. Where did this interaction break down, causing the failure of the company?

What steps might Mr. Piaget take to make his environment more supportive of his organization? Do you think he then could succeed? Why?

THREE MANAGERIAL DECISIONS

1. You are a manufacturing manager in a large electronics plant. At considerable expense, the company's management has recently installed new robotic assembly equipment, trimmed the work force, and put in a new simplified work system. To the surprise of everyone, yourself included, the expected increase in production has not materialized. In fact, production has begun to drop, overall quality has fallen off, and the number of voluntary employee separations has risen.

You do not believe there is anything wrong with the robots. Reports from other companies using them confirms this opinion, and representatives from the firm that built them have inspected the robots and reported they are working at peak efficiency. The robot made assemblies are of uniformly high quality.

You suspect that the new work system may be responsible for the fall-off in production. But this view is not shared by you immediate subordinates – four first line supervisors, each in change of a section – and your supply manager. They variously attribute the drop in production to poor retraining of the operators, lack of adequate financial incentives, and poor worker morale due to fear of increasing automation. Clearly, this is an issue about which there is considerable depth of feeling among workers and disagreement among your subordinates.

This morning you got a phone call from your division manager. She had just received your production figures for the last six months and was calling to express her concern. She indicated that the problem was yours to solve as you thought best, but that she would like to know within a week what steps you plan to take.

You share you division manager's concern over a falling productivity and know that your workers do too. The problem is to decide what steps to take to rectify the situation.

2. You are a general supervisor in charge of a construction team laying a coal slurry pipeline and have to estimate your rate of progress in order to schedule materials deliveries to the next field site.

You know the nature of the terrain you will be crossing and have the historical data you need to compute the mean and variance in the rate of speed over that type of terrain. Given these two variables, it is a simple matter to calculate and earliest and latest times at which materials and support facilities will be needed at the next site. It is important that your estimate be reasonably accurate, for an underestimate will result in idle supervisors and workers, and an overestimate will tie up materials unnecessarily for a period of time.

Progress has been good so far, and your five supervisors and other members of the team stand to receive substantial bonuses if the project is completed ahead of schedule.

3. You are supervising the work of 12 chemical engineers. This formal training and work experience are very similar, permitting you to use them inter-changeably on projects. Yesterday your manager informed you that a request had been received from a Middle Eastern affiliate for four engineers to go abroad on extended loan for a period of six to eight months. For a number of reasons, he argued – and you agreed – that this request should be met from your group.

All your engineers are capable of handling this assignment, and from the standpoint of present and future projects, there is no particular reason why anyone should be retained over any other. The problem is somewhat complicated by the fact that the overseas assignment is in what is generally regarded as an undesirable location.

Source: Adapted from "A New Look at Managerial Decision Making" by Victor 11. Vroom, Organizational Dynamics Summer 1793, pp. 72-73,1973 by American Management Association, New York.

QUESTIONS

After reading about the three situations, but before analyzing them, decide which of the decision-making styles alternatives (Al, All, Cl, CU, Gil) you would personally prefer to use in making each decision. Then answer the remaining questions.

1. Which is more important in the situation, quality or acceptance of the decision?
2. How critical is time in making a decision?
3. Does a manager have the information necessary to make the decision?
4. Is the decision-making situation highly structured?
5. Choose the best decision making style (Al, All, Cl, CÌl, Gil) and give the reason for your choice.
6. Did your choice of the "best" style in question 6 differ from the style you would personally have chosen in question 1? If so, why do you think it differed?

O. ORGANIZATIONAL DEVELOPMENT

MAX PHOTO FILM MANUFACTURING COMPANY

Recently Max Photo Film Manufacturing Company has done well. The marketing department has been receiving a flood of orders for its photo films from customers, scattered throughout the country. To meet the demand, the production department has expanded its operations considerably. The company has sufficient funds to meet every eventuality. Raw materials were available in abundance. Meanwhile, the personnel department kept itself busy in administering various kinds of tests before selecting people to man various positions in the organization.

It is all part of history now. Nowadays things have changed dramatically, affecting the performance of all branches in the organization seriously. Raw materials have disappeared from the market. Resource constraints have cropped up overnight. The company had to crumble under the weight of these scarcities. It had to cut down its sales inevitably. To add to its woes, Government had instructed all the companies to follow the reservation policy strictly while hiring new employee. As a result, the personnel department had to bury its programmes concerning selection tests in files.

The Chief Executive is in a fix. He wants to come out of this. The need for an effective programme of organizational development is acutely felt over. Uncertainties have perplexed employee brains for a painfully long time. They are now in a state of turmoil. Interdepartmental and inter-personal conflicts have soared. Cracks have appeared in every area of organizational performance. In order to cement the loopholes and improve its prospects, the company is seriously thinking of introducing an ambitious OD programme.

QUESTIONS

1. If you are entrusted with the responsibility of designing an organizational development programme, what kind of programme would you advocate?
2. What problems and prospects do you foresee in the implementation of such a programme?

CULTURE SHOCK

Warren Oats was a highly successful executive for American Auto Suppliers (AAS), a Chicago-based company that makes original-equipment specialty parts for Ford, GM, and Chrysler. Rather than retreat before the onslaught of Japanese automakers, AAS, decided to counterattack and use its reputation for quality and dependability to win over customers in Japan. Oats had started in the company as an engineer and worked his way to become one of handful of senior managers. He knew he needed to distinguish himself somehow, so when he was given a chance to lead the AAS attack on the Japanese market, he jumped at it.

Oats knew he did not have time to learn Japanese, but he had heard that many Japanese executives speak English, and the company would hire a translator anyway. The toughest part about leaving the United States was persuading his wife, Carol, to take an eighteen-month from her career as an attorney with a prestigious Chicago law firm finally persuaded herself that she did not want to miss an opportunity to learn a new culture. So, armed with all the information they could about Japan from their local library, the Oats headed for Tokyo. Known as energetic, aggressive salesperson, Warren Oats wasted no time getting started. As soon as his office had a telephone – and before all his files had arrived from the States – Oats made an appointment to meet with executives of one of Japan's leading automakers. Oat stoned that if he was going to overcome the famous Japanese resistant foreign companies, he should get started as soon as possible.

Oats felt very uncomfortable at that first meeting. He got the feeling that the Japanese executives were waiting for something. It seemed that everyone but he was in slow motion. The Japanese did speak English well and appeared grateful for the presence of the interpreter, but even the interpreter seemed to take her time in translating each phrase. Frustrated by this seeming lethargy and beginning to-the much-touted

Japanese efficiency, Oats got right to the point. He gave oral presentation of his proposal, waiting patiently for the translation of each sentence. Then he handed the leader of the Japanese delegate packet containing the specifics of his proposal, got up, and left, the labour trailed behind him as if wanting to drag out the process every time.

By the end of the- first week, both Oats and his wife were frustrated. Oats office phone had not rung once, which did not make him option about his meeting with another top company the following week. He could scarcely contain her irritation with what she had perceived Japanese way of life. She had been sure that a well-respected U.S.A. would have little trouble securing a job in a Japanese multinational corporation, but the executives she had met with seemed insulted as she was asking them for a job. And the way they treated their secret. After only a week in Japan, both Carol and Warren Oats were back home.

A month later, their perspective had changed drastically, and both back on those first meetings with embarrassment. Within that period they had learned a lot about the Japanese sense of protocol and view towards women. Warren Oats believed he was beginning to get the feeling of doing business with the Japanese in their manner: establishing relationship slowly, almost ritualistically, waiting through a number of things before bringing up the real business at hand, and then doing respectfully. It was difficult for Oats to slow his pace, and it made him nervous to be so indirect, but he was beginning to see some value sometimes humbling, learning process he was going through. He thought, he and Carol could become consultants for other executives needed to learn lessons he was beginning to understand.

QUESTIONS

1. What specific errors did Warren and Carol Oats make during their first week in Japan?
2. If you were talking to a non-U.S. business person making a first contact with an American Company, What advice would you give?

(*Source*: Adapted from *Organizational Behaviour* by Moorhead and Griffin, pp. 726-727.)

RESTRUCTURING AT KOREA'S DAEWOO

Daewoo was founded in 1967 by its hardworking relentlessly driven chairman, Kim (surname) Woo-Choong. After its initial success in exporting textiles, the company expanded into autos, machinery, consumer electronics, construction, heavy shipping computers, telephones and financial services, becoming Korea's fourth largest business group. The company became, for example, a example, supplier for Sears, Christian Dior, Calvin Klein and London Fog. Daewoo also engaged in a joint venture with General Motors to build the Le Mans car. However, labour and other problems limited the car shipments.

Chairman Kim's philosophy of hard work and the value placed in people were important factors in the firm's success. However, in the late 1980s and early 1990s the company faced several problems. For one, Kim was concerned that with the increasing prosperity of Koreans the work force might lose the spirit of hard work. Moreover, there was a growing discontent among the younger workers and a lessening of motivation.

Through Kim's hands-off approach to managing some of the companies in the Daewoo business group went out of control. For example, in the unprofitable heavy shipping industry, he noticed many unnecessary expenses. The elimination of company sponsored barbershops saved the company $8 million a year.

In general, Daewoo's work force is young and well-educated. In contrast to similar positions in many other Korean companies, top positions at Daewoo are occupied by managers with no family ties.

Although Daewoo is major company with its 91,000 employees, it is not dominant in any one industry. The strategy of being a supplier for major foreign companies, such as Caterpillar, General Motors, and Boeing may have led to bypassing opportunities for becoming a major marketer of its own brands. Now, in the 1990s, Kim is also looking at opportunities in Europe. For example, he formed a joint venture with a distribution company in France.

The massive restructuring has already had some positive effects. Kim sold some steel, financial and real estate units. The hands-off managerial style has been replaced by a hands-on style, resulting in recentralization. Managers were "retired" or otherwise let go. Thousands of positions were also eliminated.

Things were looking better in 1991. The company lost money in 1988 but made some profit in 1990 partly because of the sale of some major assets. The joint venture with GM registered a healthy growth. The company was also optimistic about the future of the new compact car Espero. Still in the early 1990s, Daewoo has had to cope with the strong Korean currency, its labour costs, Japanese competition and recessions in various countries in which it operates.

QUESTIONS

1. What are the advantages and disadvantages of a hands-off, decentralized management approach?
2. How can Daewoo stay competitive with the Japanese?
3. What are some of the controllable and uncontrollable factors in this case? How should Mr. Kim respond to those factors?
4. Is Mr. Kim's strategy of joint venture with U.S. Organization good for Company's future growth?

P. WORK STRESS

A CASE OF BURNOUT

When Mahesh joined XYZ Bank (private sector) in 1985, he had one clear goal – to prove his mettle. He did prove and has been promoted five times since his entry into the Bank. Compared to others, his progress has been the fastest. Currently, his job demands that Mahesh should work 10 hours a day with practically no holidays. At least two days in a week Mahesh is required to travel.

Peers and subordinates at the Bank have appreciation for Mahesh. They don't grudge ascension achieved by Mahesh, though there are some who wish they too had been promoted as well.

The post of General Manager fell vacant. One should work as GM for a couple of years if he were to climb up to the top of the ladder. Mahesh applied for the post along with others in the Bank. Chairman has assured Mahesh that the post would be his.

A sudden development took place which almost wrecked Mahesh's chances. The Bank has the practice of subjecting all its executives to medical check up once in a year. The medical reports go straight to the Chairman who would initiate remedial measures where necessary. Though Mahesh is only 35, he too was required to undergo the test.

Chairman of the Bank received a copy of Mahesh's physical examination results, along with a note from the doctor. The note explained that Mahesh was seriously overworked and recommended that he be given an immediate four week vacation. The doctor also recommended that Mahesh's work load must be reduced and he must take to physical exercises every day. The note warned that if Mahesh did not care for advice, he would be in for heart trouble in another six months.

After reading the doctor's note, the Chairman sat back in his chair, and started brooding over. Three issues were uppermost in his mind: (i) How would Mahesh take this news? (ii) How many others do have similar fitness problems? (iii) Since the environment in the Bank helps create the problem, what could he do to alleviate it? The idea of holding a stress management programme flashed his mind and suddenly he instructed his secretary to set up a meeting with the doctor and some key staff men at the earliest.

QUESTIONS

1. If the news is broken to Mahesh, how would he react?
2. If you were giving advice to the Chairman on this matter, what would you recommend?
3. What is burnout? What are its symptoms? What are its effects? Substantiate your answer illustrating the above case.